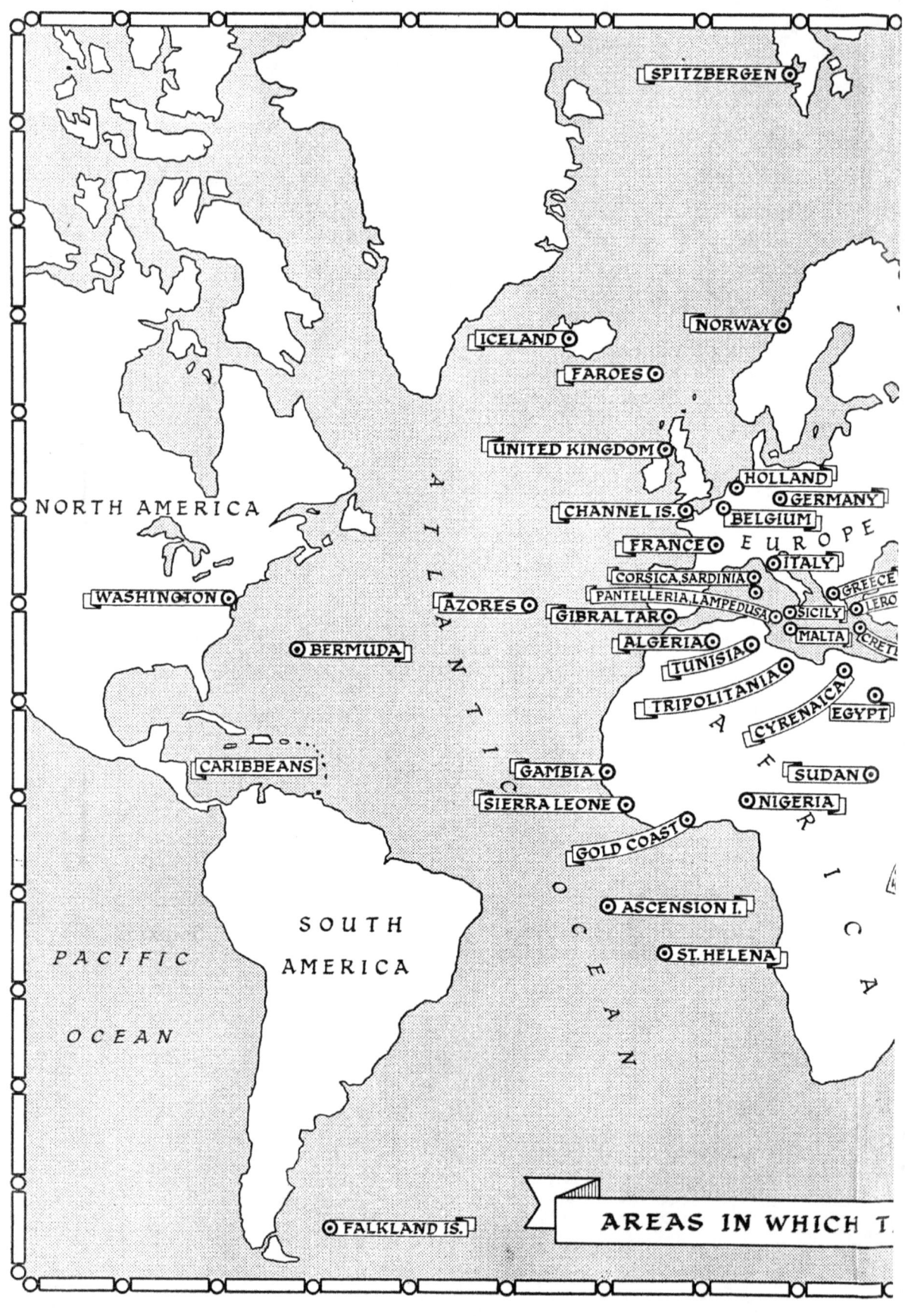

THE STORY OF THE
ROYAL ARMY SERVICE CORPS
1939–1945

THE STORY OF THE ROYAL ARMY SERVICE CORPS
1939–1945

The Naval & Military Press Ltd

Published by

The Naval & Military Press Ltd
Unit 5 Riverside, Brambleside
Bellbrook Industrial Estate
Uckfield, East Sussex
TN22 1QQ England

Tel: +44 (0)1825 749494

www.naval-military-press.com
www.nmarchive.com

In reprinting in facsimile from the original, any imperfections are inevitably reproduced and the quality may fall short of modern type and cartographic standards.

Dedicated

To the memory
of all Ranks of the

Royal Army Service Corps

who Laid down their Lives for their Country
During the World War of 1939-1945

YORK HOUSE,
ST. JAMES'S PALACE.

    The following pages are a record of the work done by The Royal Army Service Corps in the Second World War.

    The work of the Corps covered activities by land, sea and air, and its soldiers were to be found in every theatre of operation. They were often faced with difficulties and hazards, but rose to each occasion in the fulfilment of their diverse tasks.

    Although the role of the Corps is administrative, the awards for individual gallantry and the Roll of Honour, which records some 10,000 names, are an indication of its devotion to the forces it served so well.

    As Colonel-in-Chief I recommend this History to all past, present and future members of the Corps who will, I know, read it with interest and pride.

Henry.

Colonel-in-Chief.

PREFACE

THIS is a book of many authors, written for the most part by those who had first-hand knowledge of the actions and events which they describe. It is the story of the work of the Royal Army Service Corps from 1939 to 1945 and because it covers every theatre of war it is necessarily much condensed. In the space available it has not been possible to name more than a few of the many units concerned and to recount but a small part of their deeds.

In spite of this it is hoped that the story will suffice to illustrate the extraordinary diversity of the work of the Corps and the degree of high endeavour demanded of its officers and men.

To those readers who may look in vain for mention of their units in which they served, the R.A.S.C. History Committee (on whose shoulders lies the responsibility for producing this book) offer their apologies and regrets that limitations of space forbade a fuller treatment of the story.

The Committee was originally composed of Major-General Sir Cecil Smith, K.B.E., C.B., M.C. (Chairman), Major-General E. H. Fitzherbert, C.B.E., D.S.O., M.C., Major-General H. C. Goodfellow, C.B., C.B.E. and Lieut-Colonel P. M. Edgell, O.B.E., with Major-General H. M. Whitty, C.B., O.B.E., as Honorary Secretary. Major-General W. H. D. Ritchie, C.B., C.B.E., joined the Committee in 1954.

The preparation of the book has been rendered difficult by the lack of war diaries of some campaigns, and by the absence of suitable information on which to base an account in some of the diaries available. In these cases, the authors have had to build up their story from personal narratives collated with the general history of the operations concerned. Fortunately, instructions were sent to theatres during the war by the D.S.T. that they should collect records from which a history might eventually be compiled and this material was for the most part available.

The book may truly be described as a co-operative effort, shared in varying degree by a large number of people, mention of every one of whom would be impracticable. The share of some contributors has, however, been so great that the Committee feel that these names must be mentioned, but their gratitude to those whose names are omitted is no less sincere.

The Committee wish to pay tribute to those who have been mainly responsible for the preparation of the various chapters.

They use the word 'mainly' because they know that in some cases those who undertook the work sought assistance from sources of which the Committee is unaware. In such cases much research and hard work was necessary and in the hunt for information many Corps and ex-Corps officers with the required knowledge were run to earth in many lands. For these reasons, individual authors' names have not been linked with particular chapters.

The preparation of the subject matter has not, in the view of the Committee, been the most difficult task; they are quite certain that the most onerous task in the compilation of the story has fallen on their Honorary Secretary, Major-General H. M. Whitty. Not only has he had to discover those who could provide suitable material but he has had constantly to follow up his contacts and to send manuscripts to others who might be able to add to or elaborate the original contribution. In addition, the views of the senior officer in each theatre have been obtained wherever possible.

To find suitable contributors, to persuade them that they alone could perform the duty, to collect, distribute and re-collect manuscripts, to circulate them to Committee members for reading—all this has been a colossal task which few but General Whitty could have undertaken with such success.

The Committee were fortunate enough to obtain the assistance of Captain H. L. Brigstocke, who served in the Corps throughout the war, to carry out the duties of Sub-Editor, but before his work was completed he had to take up an appointment abroad. His place was taken by Captain F. A. Baughan who was an officer with the Royal Fusiliers in the Middle East. As both Captains Brigstocke and Baughan are journalists by profession their help has been invaluable.

Major-General Sir Bertram Rowcroft, K.B.E., C.B., has earned the special gratitude of the Committee for his assistance in the preparation of material and for his constant and willing help and advice on many problems.

Apart from authorship, editorial and secretarial work, there have been various other contributions of great value. Colonel D. W. Boileau did much original research. Lieutenant-Colonel P. M. Edgell has placed his wide experience of book production and illustration at the disposal of the Committee of which he was a member. Tribute must also be paid to the four artists who were responsible for the coloured plates, in particular Mr. Aubrey Sykes, R.I., who served in the R.I.A.S.C. in the war, and who also executed the drawing for the wrapper. The Committee are grateful to the Imperial War Museum for permission to use the photographs reproduced in the book, and to Mr. T. White for help in their selection. The choosing of the photographs was in itself a problem.

PREFACE

The Museum had many showing the Corps at war, but only a limited number suitable for reproduction, and it was not easy, with the limited space available, to make a selection that would include as many facets of Corps activities as possible.

For the compilation of the Roll of Honour and for the particulars of recipients of Awards the Committee are indebted to the staff of AG 8, The War Office, who consulted all relevant authorities. The Committee also received much help from the Director of Supplies and Transport and his staff, and from the R.A.S.C. Training Centre.

In deciding the nomenclature of units and forms of abbreviations to be used, the Committee have been guided less by standard military custom than by the desire to use terms which will be easily understood and which are in accord with the best publishing practice.

A common criticism of war histories is that the maps provided are inadequate. Large numbers of maps and sketches on various scales are ruled out for a work of this nature because of cost. The Committee hope that the course adopted of providing a limited number of sketches on a standard plan will serve as an adequate guide to the course of the various campaigns.

Throughout their labours the Committee have enjoyed the expert guidance and assistance of the publishers, Messrs. G. Bell & Sons Ltd. In particular, Colonel Hugh Bell, D.S.O., O.B.E., late Royal Engineers, placed his wide knowledge unreservedly at their disposal. His combined military and publishing experience has been of the greatest value. Indeed, he has gone far beyond what would normally be expected of a publisher in the great personal interest he has taken in every aspect of the book.

Apart from those whose outstanding contributions have been mentioned above, the Committee would like to acknowledge the help and assistance of the following:

Colonel S. Acheson, O.B.E., Brigadier W. J. J. Allen, O.B.E., Major G. L. W. K. Bird, Lieut-Colonel I. S. Bisset, Brigadier G. C. G. Blunt, D.S.O., O.B.E., Brigadier D. H. Bond, C.B.E., M.V.O., Major-General G. A. Bond, C.B.E., Major-General D. H. V. Buckle, C.B., C.B.E., Lieut-Colonel M. P. Buckley, Brigadier M. J. Cahill, O.B.E., Major-General W. d'A. Collings, C.B., C.B.E., Major E. Collins, M.B.E., Lieut-Colonel R. C. Collings, M.B.E., Brigadier R. T. Cooke, C.B.E., Brigadier C. E. Davis, C.B.E., Colonel W. B. S. Deverell, O.B.E., Lieut-Colonel A. J. Dewar, D.S.O., Colonel H. C. Dudman, O.B.E., T.D., Brigadier E. Dynes, O.B.E., Major-General W. J. F. Eassie, C.B., C.B.E., D.S.O., Major H. Edmondson, Brigadier A. F. J. Elmslie, C.B.E., Brigadier M. F. Farquharson-Roberts, C.B.E., Major L. Feeney, Major T. A. Gardner, M.B.E.,

Colonel H. T. Gilchrist, O.B.E., Brigadier J. K. Gillespie, O.B.E., Major-General C. le B. Goldney, C.B., C.B.E., M.C., Colonel E. R. Goode, C.B.E., Lieut-Colonel R. K. Gregory, Brevet-Colonel T. H. Hunter, O.B.E., T.D., Major C. Harston, Lieut-Colonel W. Horsfall, O.B.E., Colonel A. F. J. Kingsmill, Major H. F. L. Knockolds, Lieut-Colonel E. H. G. Lonsdale, M.B.E., Lieut-Colonel J. G. C. Low, Brigadier C. M. C. Luff, O.B.E., Brigadier R. W. Lymer, C.B.E., D.S.O., T.D., Lieut-Colonel G. W. Moncur, Brigadier J. A. Mullington, O.B.E., Lieut-Colonel J. B. Muriel, O.B.E., Lieut-Colonel F. Newmarch, Brigadier W. P. Pessell, O.B.E., Brigadier W. O. Philips, O.B.E., Colonel H. P. Raymond, O.B.E., R. A. Richardson, Esq, Colonel G. E. C. Rossall, Major N. Severwright, Brigadier W. S. Seymour, C.B.E., Major J. S. Southworth, Colonel J. C. B. Stephens, T.D., Colonel P. G. Turpin, O.B.E., Major J. D. Webb, Major L. Williams.

The thanks of the Committee are also due to *The Times* for permission to include the quotations which appear on page 100, and to Messrs. Cassell and Company Ltd. for the quotation on page 311 from *The Second World War* by Sir Winston Churchill.

CONTENTS

	Page
Dedication	v
Foreword	vii
Preface	ix
List of Photographs	xv
List of Maps	xvii
List of Coloured Illustrations	xvii
Honours and Awards	xix

Chapter		Page
I	Prelude (1919-1939)	1
	General Survey	1
	Transport	19
	Supplies	31
	Petroleum	40
II	The British Expeditionary Force, 1939/1940	48
III	Norway, 1940	88
IV	The Middle East I	101
V	The Middle East II	160
	Greece, 1941	160
	Crete	167
	The Sudan and Eritrea	169
	East Africa and Madagascar	177
	Iraq, Syria and Persia	192
	The Dodecanese	205
	Arabia: The Locust War	207
VI	The Western Mediterranean	209
	Malta, G.C.	209
	Gibraltar	218
	North Africa	221
VII	The Central Mediterranean	249
	Italy	249
	Greece, 1944	287

CONTENTS

Chapter		Page
VIII	South-East Asia	298
	Hong Kong	298
	Malaya	305
IX	Burma and Ceylon	338
	Burma	338
	Ceylon	360
X	The Invasion of North-West Europe	367
XI	Other Theatres	401
	West Africa	401
	Miscellaneous Overseas Stations	406
	British Army Staff, Washington	408
XII	The R.A.S.C. in the United Kingdom	411
	General Survey	411
	Transport	426
	Supplies	452
	Petroleum	476
	Manpower	490
	Barracks	501
XIII	Air Despatch	508
XIV	Airborne R.A.S.C.	524
XV	Animal Transport	542
XVI	The R.A.S.C. Fleet	563
XVII	Some Unit Narratives	590
	4 Company (Tank Transporter)	590
	534 Company (Tank Transporter)	592
	536 Company (General Transport—Dukws)	598
	486 Company (Tipper)	612
	146 Company (Motor Ambulance Convoy)	619
	A Divisional R.A.S.C.	623
	716 Company (Airborne Light)	629
	6 Base Petrol Storage Company	633
	88 Detail Issue Depot	639
	Embarkation Supply Depot	645
	Escape from Malaya	647
	Round Tour of Europe	648
	Roll of Honour	655
	General Index	713
	Index of Names	717

LIST OF PHOTOGRAPHS

These official photographs are reproduced with grateful acknowledgements to the Curator, Imperial War Museum, and, in the case of two taken at 'Hove Dump', to the Canadian Army.

	Facing page
Convoy on a Desert Road	16
Lorry dug in in the Desert	16
Men of the B.E.F.	17
At an O.C.T.U.	17
Supply Dropping	32
Diamond T in the Desert	33
In Workshops	64
Workshop Lorry	64
The Helmsman	65
Caique under Sail	65
Typical Group, 1940	80
Carrying Bridging Material	81
Inspecting the Batch	112
Supply Men under Training	112
Supplies and Petrol at Tobruk	113
'Flimsies' in the Desert	128
Desert Roadside Pump	128
Vehicle Assembly	129
R.A.S.C. Motor Vessel (M.V.)	176
Launch helping to place Pontoons	176
Field Ambulance Transport	177
At a Field Dressing Station	177
Weasel at Lake Comacchio	192
In the Arabian Desert	192
'Aid to Russia'	193
In the Chindwin Hills	193
Pack Transport at Hove Dump	224
Ammunition going forward	225
Ambulance Mules	225
In the North African Hills	240
On the Way to the Front	240
H.M. King George VI	241
Supply Dump at Anzio	256
Forage for the Mules	257
Army Supply Dump	257

LIST OF PHOTOGRAPHS

	Facing page
Hove Dump	272
Supply Point	272
Jerricans	273
Refuelling the Navy	273
Loading a Landing Craft	336
Carrying a Churchill	336
Mobile Bakery	337
Waiting to Load	352
Checking Air Freight	352
Carrying Landing Craft	353
Carrying Buffaloes	353
Dukw making for Shore	384
Dukw Loading	384
Dukw Casualty	385
About to Land	385
After Launching	400
Dukws in a flooded Street	400
Dukws waiting to Land	401
Dukws in the Far East	401
Her Majesty the Queen when Princess Elizabeth	432
Convoy on the Road	433
Field-Marshal Montgomery presenting the Military Medal to Dvr. G. E. Callaghan	448
H.R.H. The Duke of Gloucester, Colonel-in-Chief, R.A.S.C., presenting the Military Medal to Cpl. J. O. Sheed	448
A.T.S. Convoy—Halt for Lunch	449
Petrol Pipelines	480
Roadside Petrol Dump	481
Can Filling	481
Petrol Filling Point	496
Dukws in a Wood	497
On the Ground	512
'They're Away'	512
Air Mails	513
Air Dropping Containers	513
At Railhead	528
Crossing a Pontoon Bridge	528
Landing and Wading	529
Moving Forward	592
Carrying Captured 15-cm. Gun	593
Carrying Cruiser Tanks	593
At Tobruk	608
Scaling the Loaf	609
Double Deck Field Ovens	609

LIST OF MAPS

	Pages
The B.E.F. Main Lines of Communication	53
B.E.F.–Situation on May 20th and 26th, 1940	69
Norway	91
The Western Desert	119
Operations of the Eighth and First Armies in North Africa, November, 1942, to May, 1943	150–1
Greece and the Dodecanese	162–3
East Africa	184–5
Madagascar	191
Iraq, Syria and Persia	194–5
Southern Italy	251
Central Italy	269
Northern Italy	279
Athens	289
Hong Kong	301
Malaya, showing dispositions on December 8th, 1941	309
Singapore	327
Burma	343
North-West Europe, 1944/1945	372–3
Areas in which the Royal Army Service Corps served	*Endpaper*

LIST OF ILLUSTRATIONS IN COLOUR

	Facing page
Desert Convoy	144
Dukws at Work	304
In the Italian Mountains	544
Tank Transporter	624

HONOURS AND AWARDS RECEIVED BY ROYAL ARMY SERVICE CORPS OFFICERS AND MEN 1939-1945

To have published the complete list of Honours and Awards received by Officers and other ranks of the Royal Army Service Corps in all theatres would have taken more space than could be spared for the purpose.

It was therefore decided to give only the total numbers in each grade appointed to the Most Excellent Order of the Bath or to the Most Excellent Order of the British Empire, but to publish the names of those who were made members of the Distinguished Service Order or awarded the Military Cross, the George Medal, the Distinguished Conduct Medal, the Military Medal and the Distinguished Flying Medal.

THE MOST EXCELLENT ORDER OF THE BATH

Companion – 3

THE MOST EXCELLENT ORDER OF THE BRITISH EMPIRE

Knight – 1
Commanders – 25
Officers – 213
Members – 798
Medals – 554

DISTINGUISHED SERVICE ORDER

Name	Initials	Rank	Name	Initials	Rank	Name	Initials	Rank
Appleyard	J.G.	Maj	Gilman	H.J.	Lt-Col	Lymer	R.W.	Maj
Divers	S.T.	Lt-Col	Hackforth	C.A.P.	Lt	Nichol	W.M.	Lt
Eassie	W.J.F.	Col	Langdon	C.B.	Maj	Rea	J.W.	Maj
Geddes	H.H.E.	Lt-Col						

MILITARY CROSS

Name	Initials	Rank	Name	Initials	Rank	Name	Initials	Rank
Abraham	J.A.G.	Maj	Band	V.H.	Capt	Castle	K.G.	Capt
Aldridge	A.S.	Maj	Barker	E.N.	Maj	Childs	E.W.	Maj
Alpe	J.G.	Capt	Bennett	J.C.	Capt	Clark	H.D.	Capt
Appleyard	J.G.	Maj (and Bar)	Beverley	A.	Capt	Crane	C.P.R.	Maj
			Bland	F.J.	Lt	Cranmer-Byng	J.L.	Capt
Atkinson	J.G.P.	2/Lt (and Bar)	Boone	F.E.deB.	Maj	Crawford	J.M.	Capt
			Boorman	G.H.	Capt			
Baillie	C.	2/Lt	Butterworth	H.S.	Capt	Cuthbertson	J.R.	Maj

MILITARY CROSS—cont.

Name	Initials	Rank	Name	Initials	Rank	Name	Initials	Rank
Dugdale	J.F.	Capt	Johnson	J.E.	Capt	Reid	W.F.	Maj
Ferrey	C.W.	Maj	Kent	J.C.	Lt	Ricconimi	J.A.	Lt
Finney	D.M.	Capt	Knight	F.L.	Lt	Riddell	E.D.	Capt
Flemyng	B.A.	Capt	Lindon	B.W.M.	Capt	Roberts	W.H.B.	Capt
Forward	A.	Maj	Mackay	A.S.	Maj	Smith	I.C.D.	Lt
Fraser	A.D.	Lt	Mann	M.W.	2/Lt			(and Bar)
Gilmour	R.	Maj	Mansfield	J.K.	2/Lt	Smith	R.B.	Capt
Hayes	J.B.	Maj	Marks	L.A.G.	Capt	Stanley	I.G.	2/Lt
Henderson	P.J.W.	Lt	Medlicott-			Tocher	H.D.	WOI
Hickham	D.S.	Lt	Vereker	J.C.	Lt	Valentine	P.W.	2/Lt
Hickson	J.S.	Capt	Molyneux	E.V.	Maj	Wagstaff	L.A.	Lt
Hodgson	J.R.	Capt	O'Connor	T.M.	Capt	West	T.H.	Lt
Hunter	I.G.	Capt	Philo	G.C.G.	Lt	Wicks	R.S.	Capt
Jackson	S.A.	Capt	Prioleau	R.A.	Capt	Wigg	D.E.W.	Lt
Jeffries	T.H.	Maj	Reid	P.R.	Capt	Williams	R.J.	Capt
Jenkins	H.D.	Lt				Witchell	G.G.H.	2/Lt

GEORGE MEDAL

Name	Initials	Rank	Name	Initials	Rank	Name	Initials	Rank
Ellingham	R.	Cpl	Hill	J.	L/Cpl	Scott-		
Everett	J.	Dvr	Keddie	A.McR.W.	Cpl	Williams	H.	Sjt
Fisher	D.	Dvr	Kurn	W.H.	Dvr	Smith	A.E.	Sjt
Gibson	N.	Dvr	Lowe	A.	Dvr	Styles	W.H.	L/Cpl
Gurnham	E.O.	Dvr	Marshall	J.W.	Dvr	Wakeford	A.G.	Sjt
						Wisbey	A.G.	Cpl

DISTINGUISHED CONDUCT MEDAL

Name	Initials	Rank	Name	Initials	Rank	Name	Initials	Rank
Bach	C.W.	Dvr	Green	S.	Dvr	Massey	L.G.	Dvr
Cameron	D.I.	Cpl	Hausmann	F.S.	L/Cpl	Platten	C.H.	L/Cpl
Cunningham	J.	Dvr	Hogan	N.J.	Cpl	Rimmer	G.L.	L/Cpl
Easterbrook	R.H.	Pte	Lister	E.E.	Cpl	Rochberg	S.	L/Cpl
						Shaw	A.G.	Dvr

DISTINGUISHED FLYING MEDAL

Name	Initials	Rank	Name	Initials	Rank	Name	Initials	Rank
Bilton	K.	Cpl	Hutchinson	W.	Cpl	Whittaker	W.	Cpl
			Purvis	W.	Sjt			

MILITARY MEDAL

Name	Initials	Rank	Name	Initials	Rank	Name	Initials	Rank
Abbott	J.L.	Dvr	Bacon	R.	Dvr	Bott	C.F.V.	Dvr
Abercrombie	H.R.	Dvr	Baker	A.J.A.	Sjt	Bottley	G.J.	Dvr
Ackrill	G.H.	Sjt	Baker	B.R.	Dvr	Bowman	J.E.	Pte
Aggett	W.S.P.	Dvr	Baker	F.A.J.	Dvr	Bowyer	G.	L/Cpl
Ali Faik		L/Sjt	Baldry	R.E.	Dvr	Boydell	T.P.	L/Sjt
Allen	H.T.	Dvr	Baron	J.	Dvr	Bromley	W.B.	Dvr
Allen	J.M.	Dvr	Barratt	A.	Dvr	Brooker	F.E.	Dvr
Almond	S.	Dvr	Bifield	W.C.	Cpl	Broderick	J.	Cpl
Ambrose	N.	Dvr	Biggs	J.H.	Dvr	Buhayar	E.S.	Pte
Armstrong	R.W.	L/Cpl	Bingham	W.	Dvr	Burford	J.	Dvr
Ash	A.G.	Dvr	Blackburn	C.A.	Cpl	Burrows	E.C.P.	Pte
Askew	V.	Dvr	Blackmore	C.E.	Dvr	Burrows	J.H.	Dvr
			Bond	F.G.	L/Cpl	Burrows	N.	Dvr

MILITARY MEDAL—cont.

Name	Initials	Rank	Name	Initials	Rank	Name	Initials	Rank
Burt	T.	Sjt	Ellison	E.J.	Dvr	Holden	F.	Dvr
Butler	J.	L/Cpl	Fairchild	J.A.	L/Cpl	Holleron	E.	L/Sjt
Cahill	A.D.	Dvr	Farrell	F.	Dvr	Hook	L.H.	Cpl
Calderwood	L.W.	Sjt	Farrer	J.E.	L/Cpl	Horlock	J.	Cpl
Callaghan	G.E.	Dvr	Featherstone	W.	Cpl	Houghton	G.	Dvr
Carter	J.W.B.	Dvr				Howard	D.	Sjt
Carty	A.	Dvr	Field	B.E.	Dvr	Howle	D.G.	Dvr
Caudwell	E.	Dvr	Findley	F.G.	WOII	Hudson	V.F.G.	Dvr
Chad	E.J.	L/Cpl	Fisher	A.W.	Dvr	Hughes	C.W.	Dvr
Chamberlain	W.A.	Dvr	Ford	G.W.	Sjt	Hughes	E.	Dvr
			Fouracres	J.M.	Dvr	Hughes	E.J.	S/Sjt
Chappell	D.	Dvr	Francis	E.A.	Dvr	Hughes	J.W.	Dvr
Chilton	A.B.	Dvr	Francis	S.	Dvr	Hughes	L.G.	Dvr
Clapham	A.	Cpl	Fraser	W.	Cpl	Hughes	R.F.	Sjt
Clark	J.A.	S/Sjt	Freeman	A.B.	Sjt	Hughes	T.	Sjt
Clarke	B.V.	Sjt	Fry	C.	Dvr	Hyde	R.C.R.	Dvr
Clarke	J.	Cpl	Fulton	A.	Dvr	Icke	K.R.	Sjt
Clarke	J.P.L.	L/Cpl	Gage	C.G.	L/Cpl	Jenkins	G.	L/Sjt
Cockburn	R.S.	Dvr	Galloway	D.	L/Cpl (and Bar)	Johns	R.G.	Cpl
Cole	C.J.	Dvr				Johnson	J.S.	S/Sjt
Coleman	J.A.	Cpl	Gardner	G.W.	Cpl	Johnson	S.	Dvr
Cook	A.A.	Dvr	Garon	F.R.	L/Sjt	Johnson	W.	Pte
Cordner	I.	Dvr	Georgiou	T.	Dvr	Jones	F.G.	Dvr
Cowell	W.	L/Cpl	Gilbert	A.B.	Cpl	Jones	G.C.	Cpl
Cox	C.H.	Dvr	Good	J.J.	Sjt	Jones	J.G.	L/Cpl
Craven	K.	Sjt	Goodsell	F.	WOI	Jones	J.W.	Dvr
Creasey	F.E.A.	L/Cpl	Goulding	W.B.	Dvr	Jordan	W.	Sjt
Crichton	I.P.	Dvr	Govan	J.G.W.	Dvr	Jury	G.H.	Dvr
Crompton	S.	Dvr	Gracie	J.M.	Dvr	Keir	A.	Dvr
Cross	J.L.	Dvr	Grady	G.	Dvr	Kent	A.H.	Dvr
Crouchley	N.K.	Dvr	Gray	H.G.	WOII	Kerr	G.S.	Dvr
Cuddington	S.L.H.	Sjt	Greatorex	H.	Cpl	Killey	R.	Dvr
Cunningham	C.L.	Cpl	Green	A.	WOII	King	L.G.	Dvr
			Grierson	W.C.	Sjt	Knightley	L.T.C.	Cpl
Dalton	G.J.	Cpl	Groves	E.R.C.	L/Cpl	Lawrence	F.R.	Sjt
Davey	G.R.	Dvr	Groves	F.	L/Cpl	Lawton	A.A.	Dvr
Davies	H.A.	Dvr	Hale	W.R.	L/Cpl	Lee	D.	Sjt
Davies	J.	Dvr	Hall	J.	Dvr	Lee	J.G.	Dvr
Davis	A.T.	Sjt	Hall	W.H.	Dvr	Leese	R.	Dvr
Dickens	L.W.	Cpl	Hamlin	F.	Dvr	Lewis	E.	Dvr
Dixon	W.H.R.	Sjt	Hand	H.E.	Dvr	Lewis	S.E.	Dvr
Dollard	J.	Cpl	Harper	J.	Cpl	Lewis	W.D.	L/Cpl
Donnelly	R.	Cpl	Harris	C.H.	Dvr	Lilley	L.	Dvr
Dransfield	G.D.	Dvr	Harris	R.T.	Dvr	Lines	S.B.	L/Cpl
Drennan	J.W.	Dvr	Harris	W.B.	Cpl	Lister	S.	Dvr
Duckfield	E.E.	Sjt	Hart	F.	Cpl	Little	E.B.	L/Cpl
Dudgeon	D.	Dvr	Hartley	T.S.	Dvr	Lomax	R.	Dvr
Duke	J.A.	Dvr	Hawkins	G.	Pte	Lowe	J.C.	Dvr
Duncan	G.	Dvr	Hawthorne	R.C.	Dvr	Lynch	J.	Cpl
Dundas	R.	Dvr	Hay	A.J.	Cpl	Mack	T.S.	Dvr
Durkin	B.T.	Dvr	Headen	G.A.	Dvr	Mackenzie	W.A.	Dvr
Durrant	J.	Sjt	Hedley	R.N.	L/Cpl	Macklin	G.W.	Dvr
Dyer	D.R.	Sjt	Hemmings	F.	Dvr	Maiden	W.J.	Cpl
Edwards	A.J.	Dvr	Herrivale	P.L.	Cpl	Malloch	C.M.	Sjt
Eglon	E.	Cpl	Higgins	J.	Dvr	Mann	A.W.	Cpl
Ellis	F.	Sjt	Hobson	H.	Dvr	Mann	G.P.	Cpl

MILITARY MEDAL—cont.

Name	Initials	Rank	Name	Initials	Rank	Name	Initials	Rank
Mansell	N.L.	Cpl	Rasche	C.E.	Dvr	Tams	W.J.	Sjt
Maplethorpe	F.	Sjt	Ready	M.J.	L/Cpl	Taylor	P.C.	Dvr
			Redfearn	N.	Cpl	Taylor	T.J.	Dvr
Marland	L.	Sjt	Reynolds	E.J.	Sjt	Tebbutt	W.G.	Dvr
McCarthy	M.J.	Sjt	Rhodes	C.	Sjt	Thompson	S.	Cpl
McCloskey	S.	Dvr	Roberts	B.E.	Dvr	Tickle	E.W.	Dvr
McCloy	W.S.	Dvr	Robertson	H.	Dvr	Tinsley	W.T.	Dvr
McConnell	A.H.	Dvr	Ross	J.	Dvr	Tipper	B.A.	Dvr
McDonald	G.	Sjt	Rowe	G.R.	WOII	Tomkins	A.E.	Sjt
McFarlane	D.H.	Pte	Rushby	R.E.	Cpl	Tomlin	J.H.	L/Cpl
McGrath	T.	Cpl	Rust	J.S.	Dvr	Tomlinson	J.	Dvr
McGrath	W.C.	Dvr	Sankey	J.E.S.	Dvr	Toye	R.	Sjt
McLean	R.	Cpl	Sanson	A.N.	Dvr	Turnbull	J.P.	Sjt
McNally	P.	Dvr	Saunders	R.T.	Sjt	Turrell	W.C.	WOII
Meaden	B.G.	Cpl	Scott	R.E.	Cpl	Varney	J.A.	Cpl
Meese	A.A.	L/Cpl	Seed	J.O.	Cpl	Wade	J.B.	Dvr
Melville	K.	L/Cpl	Senior	W.	Dvr	Waghorn	R.P.	Dvr
Millar	J.	Dvr	Sharpe	G.H.	Cpl	Walker	E.	Dvr
Millea	R.C.	Dvr	Shaw	A.G.	Dvr	Walker	T.	Dvr
Miller	C.F.	Dvr	Shaw	H.	L/Cpl	Wallsworth	B.	Dvr
Miller	D.G.	Pte	Shearby	F.A.	Dvr	Warren	E.A.	Cpl
Moore	G.	Sjt	Shepherd	E.	L/Cpl	Watson	A.S.	Cpl
Muir	A.J.	Dvr	Sherwood	J.B.B.	Sjt	Watson	E.	Sjt
Murphy	P.	Dvr	Shillito	H.	Dvr	Webber	J.	Cpl
Murray	C.E.	Dvr	Sidney	G.S.	Dvr	Webster	W.A.A.	Dvr
Murray	H.	L/Cpl	Simpson	R.W.	S/Sjt	West	F.J.	Sjt
Murray	J.B.	Dvr	Slater	W.F.	Cpl	Westaway	A.H.	Sjt
Mustafa	I.S.	Cpl	Sloan	J.	Dvr	Westmoreland	W.	Dvr
Neill	J.H.	Cpl	Smith	A.E.	Sjt			
Neill	R.S.	Dvr	Smith	F.	Sjt	Whatsize	J.	Dvr
Noble	J.G.	Dvr	Smith	G.F.	Cpl	White	H.	Cpl
Norman	A.J.W.	Sjt	Smith	K.T.	L/Cpl	Whittaker	W.	Cpl
O'Brien	J.	Dvr	Smith	L.W.	Cpl	Wilcox	J.F.	Sjt
O'Donnell	J.	L/Cpl	Smith	W.T.	Sjt	Wills	W.	Dvr
Oliver	J.W.	Dvr	Solley	D.	Dvr	Willsher	R.	Dvr
Ord	A.	Dvr	Sonnino	W.	L/Cpl	Willshire	G.F.	Dvr
Orford	E.	Cpl	Spear	S.F.	Sjt	Wilson	P.F.	Dvr
Paine	B.	WOII	Spooner	C.R.	Cpl	Wilson	W.	Sjt
Paragreen	V.E.T.	Dvr	Sproston	C.B.	Cpl	Windsor	G.	L/Cpl
Perry	D.	Dvr	Stacey	E.C.	Cpl	Wood	E.	Dvr
Perry	D.C.	L/Cpl	Stangroome	L.A.V.	L/Cpl	Woodason	H.	Dvr
Philip	D.R.	Cpl	Stern	A.	Dvr	Wooding	G.A.	L/Sjt
Phillips	B.	Sjt	Stewart	R.	Dvr	Wragby	A.S.	L/Cpl
Philpot	R.H.	Dvr	Stewart	W.	Dvr	Wratten	F.J.	L/Cpl
Pitcher	D.V.	Dvr	Stokes	A.	Cpl	Wright	C.E.G.	Cpl
Pont	L.A.	L/Cpl	Stotter	W.A.	L/Cpl	Wright	E.C.	Dvr
Price	G.E.	Cpl	Straw	C.	Dvr	Wright	R.L.	Dvr
Prickett	W.	Dvr	Strong	A.T.	Dvr	Wyborn	E.A.	Cpl
Priest	J.W.	L/Cpl	Sutton	G.C.	Cpl	Young	R.	Dvr
Pye	R.F.A.	Dvr	Swales	A.	L/Cpl	Zoumberis	J.	L/Cpl

CHAPTER I

PRELUDE

GENERAL SURVEY

WHEN the Second World War broke out in 1939 the Royal Army Service Corps was still a young corps when compared with some other arms of the service but it traced its origin back some 145 years. It was given the prefix 'Royal' for the part it played during the war of 1914–18.

The Corps had been able to give tangible proof of the wisdom underlying its original charter, for if an army were to be successfully maintained with supplies and transport, the Corps responsible for those duties must be fully combatant, both officer and man being trained soldiers as well as masters of their particular administrative tasks. The charter implied that, even though the Corps was concerned principally with administrative duties, all ranks must be inculcated with a strong sense of the regimental spirit, or what is perhaps better referred to as *esprit de corps*. The second war was to give even further proof of the wisdom of its original founder.*
When the first history of the Corps came to be published it was thought appropriate to include some account of its forbears, even though many of them were short lived and met with varying degrees of success, to be disbanded and then resurrected in different guise when need arose. Hence this first history was given the title '*R.A.S.C.—A History of Transport and Supply in the British Army.*' It is thought that the now well-founded regimental character of the Corps can, in relating the record of its work in the Second World War, be best expressed in the simple title which has been chosen for this volume.

Days of Retrenchment

The end of the first war brought with it the natural reaction which follows any period of such national stress—the hope for a lasting peace. Peace seemed to be the object of all nations, and British defence policy was based on an assumption that no great war need be expected for a period of 10 years. The primary training objective of the army was defined as imperial policing.

---

* General Sir Redvers Buller, V.C., G.C.B., G.C.M.G.

The need for national retrenchment and the limited role of the Regular Army led to sweeping reductions in the strength of the forces to be maintained and in the sums voted by Parliament for their upkeep. The RASC had of course to take its share of this financial stringency, but in doing so it became a shadow of its former self, being left with barely enough officers and men to carry out minimum routine tasks. The military conscience was put at rest by the thought that if war did occur the Corps could be easily expanded again. Such a premise was based on the grounds that the general nature of RASC duties were considered comparable to those performed by equivalent civilian agencies.*

The 'no great war policy' was, at the end of the tenth year, to be again extended until the failure of the Disarmament Conference of 1931 made it quite evident that if there was to be 'peace in our time' it could only be at the cost of such a strong defence policy as would deter any potential enemy from aggression, not only against Imperial interests, but also on the continent of Europe. The nation, however, was not in the mood politically to accept heavy defence expenditure, nor indeed was it ready to recognize the growing menace of Nazi Germany. The first effective decision to rearm was not taken until 1934, but the prodigious cost of rearmament on the scale which was eventually proved to be necessary limited the steps which could be taken by the army to re-equip and orient its training. At that time policy tended to place protection of Middle East interests first and any Continental commitment second. The dual nature of these objectives was to cause immense complications in obtaining types of equipment and transport and in the location of strategic reserves.

The size and shape which the British Expeditionary Force was to take was not finally settled until after Munich. By that time it had also been driven home that with the growth of air power Great Britain would be vulnerable unless she could offer adequate military support in Europe so as to deny the use of the Low Countries and Northern France to a potential enemy.

With this general picture as a background a short description of the life and work of the Corps in the period between the wars will perhaps be more readily understandable.

Adverse effects of Retrenchment on the RASC

The nucleus of RASC officers and men left at home dealing with routine duties between the wars were robbed of much of their interest by the paucity of men at their command. However, they completed their daily tasks reasonably well but could not, for lack of time and numbers, manage the bigger task of

* The RASC were directly affected on questions of food, transport and petrol.

preparing themselves for future operations. Indeed, they were so few on the ground that, outside the purely training units, they could not muster sufficient numbers for ceremonial occasions. Nor was it possible to raise sufficient men for collective training. The lack of vehicles, too, was so acute that the smallest composite units allotted a part in such training that did occur, were almost invariably in a neutral role so as to husband resources. Even as late as 1937, with rearmament in full swing, it is on record that one divisional RASC, to carry out its own exercises on company training, was constrained to borrow vehicles and drivers from 11 other units of all arms to make *one* of its companies up to a semblance of its war establishment! The predecessors of this unit were even less fortunate, for there was for a long time a Treasury ban on the use of MT in training schemes if, as was inevitable, this meant hiring civilian vehicles in home stations.

The Corps had, too, to find the men for the administration of the barrack services at home and overseas. The responsibility of the RASC O i/c Barracks towards the buildings and their occupants was comparable to that of the landlord of an unfurnished house, but with the additional duty of supplying the tenant with fuel, light and water, plus a certain minimum of furniture. This was unexciting work, but it filled a need and was of great benefit to the Corps, because the barrack service offered scope for the employment in commissioned rank of the best of our senior warrant officers, particularly on the supply side. It proved a great incentive in the enlistment in the Corps as clerks of an excellent stamp of man (often the son of a Corps soldier) with ambition to make a career of the Army.

While the Corps was unavoidably stuck in a rut of routine and deprived of opportunities of training for war, it suffered also the almost total loss of its horses with which it had been closely associated since its beginning in 1794 in the guise of the Royal Waggoners. It is a curious paradox that the horse in the army is a strong humanizing element! The soldiers' regard for their mounts and their pride in appearance of their charges provide a strong bond of union between all ranks and, in war, provide perhaps a sense of man-animal comradeship which may be lacking in other units. The loss of their horses was thus a distinct blow to the mounted units of the army, and the Corps was one of the first to be affected, although none who witnessed the horses' sufferings during the First World War would wish to see them used, and expended (over 800,000 died in the British service alone), to the same extent again. At the same time an unfortunate decision on the eligibility of RASC officers for Corps pay and on its amount, coupled with an unwelcome block in promotion for officers, were further setbacks. There was also the situation which was common to the whole army, in which service overseas meant in many cases for the married soldier long periods of separation from his family.

All these factors combined to minimize the attractions of the Corps, particularly to officers, and at one time the maintenance of the officer intake was seriously threatened.

The horse had now gone and the promotion block, even up to the rank of major, remained obdurate until the introduction of time promotion in 1938. However, the status of the Corps and its chances of training improved gradually, especially after certain reforms had been propounded in the late nineteen twenties, and were a little later adopted. Eventually an improved intake was obtained, though never enough in numbers to meet all commitments in peace. This was achieved by retaining a call on the Royal Military College Sandhurst for a quota of cadets, by opening the door wider to University candidates, including those with engineering degrees, and by making transfer to the Corps more worth while to selected candidates from other arms.

Minor campaigns and Imperial policing

It was an onerous task that faced Major-Generals Sir Evan Carter, P. O. Hazelton and G. F. Davies who filled successively the appointment of Director of Supplies and Transport after the retirement of Major-General Sir Alban Crofton-Atkins at the end of the First World War. With resources which diminished with far greater rapidity than the military commitments with which they had to deal, the years from 1919 to 1927 were fraught with great difficulty and offered little opportunity for reorganization or for long term planning on a satisfactory basis.

A great deal was achieved during these difficult years. There were a whole series of minor campaigns in various parts of the world and each one required the services of the Corps in one form or another. British India, for instance, demanded and indeed obtained a constant flow of reinforcements for the companies and 'base units' which the RASC operated there.

During the Irish 'troubles' after the First World War, there was a special demand for supplies and transport because the British garrisons in Ireland were so scattered. The Corps suffered many fatal casualties during these troublesome months which led up to the establishment of the Irish Free State in 1921, yet in spite of all the difficulties that ensued the Corps met all demands made upon it.

Further east MT companies of the Corps in India were taking part in the Third Afghan War. This campaign proved valuable, for it showed up the serviceability of motor transport in mountain warfare in territory which was undeveloped. Indeed the lessons learned from the campaign were to have a vital bearing on the policy of keeping the peace in the North-West Frontier Province, particularly in Waziristan, for a good motor road was built to open up the interior. This road ran in the shape of a horse-shoe with one end at Bannu, in the north, and the other at Dera Ismail Khan in the south. RASC companies were stationed at all the intermediate garrisons on the road, and subsequently units of the Corps took part in operations in this area in 1923. By the time the next Frontier war took place the Corps had handed over its responsibilities in India to the RIASC. It may be said that in building up the MT organization in India, as well as in the services rendered there to the British Army, the RASC performed a task of which it may be justly proud.

Nearer home a tense situation arose when in 1922 the new Turkish leader, Mustapha Kemal, fresh from his victory over the Greek Army in Asia Minor, threatened to occupy the Gallipoli peninsula and to close the Dardanelles. To counter this situation a British force was despatched hurriedly to the scene with orders to occupy Chanak on the Asiatic shore of the Dardanelles. This force was fortunately not called upon to fight, statesmanship ultimately achieving its object without bloodshed. From the RASC point of view, the expedition was of special interest because of the use for the first time of the new pneumatic-tyred 30-cwt lorries.

After Chanak and the Indian Frontier war came the crisis in China in 1927 and 1928. It was caused initially by the rise of the Kuomintang party. Although it governed one of the Allied nations in later years, at its rise this party adopted a strongly nationalistic attitude and made things 'difficult' for foreign, especially for British, nationals and business interests in the Yangtse Valley. To safeguard these interests a special 'Imperial Police Force' was sent to Shanghai in 1927. Some RASC units went out from the United Kingdom to this force, and others joined it from India. The Shanghai Force, like the Chanak force, eventually achieved its object without open recourse to arms and was later withdrawn.

Meanwhile the RASC hand-over to the RIASC in India was taking place and was completed by early 1928. It involved *inter alia* the transfer of some 112 officers from the British to the Indian service, many of whom were men of a calibre which could ill be spared.

In Western Europe, the Saar plebiscite in 1934 necessitated the despatch of a small international force to this scene of Franco-German controversy in order to ensure free and orderly elections. The British contribution included 5 Company, RASC, and a supply detachment. This force was joined by an Italian and a

Belgian contingent. The political issue involved was whether the Saar should remain German or become French, and the plebiscite showed that the Saarlanders preferred to remain in the Reich.

Before 5 Company had time to settle down at home after its duties in the Saar, the Near East 'Emergency' resulting from Mussolini's invasion of Abyssinia in 1935 and his subsequent truculent attitude to France and Britain led to the hurried despatch of reinforcements of all arms to Egypt for deployment on the Libyan frontier. This move was to counter any possible Italian threat to the Suez Canal zone. This small desert force, which included five RASC companies, was centred on Mersa Matruh, near the frontier, and here the companies were able to learn invaluable lessons in desert operations, transport and maintenance under practically active service conditions. Some of these RASC units did not see England again for 11 or 12 years.

In 1936, while the British Forces in Egypt were maintaining their watch on Mussolini, the old Arab-Jewish troubles flared up in Palestine as they had done in 1929. During some of this time the British garrison was able to maintain vigorous police action against the Arabs by calling upon the services of the two infantry brigades and their RASC units which had been hastily sent from Egypt. However, as time passed and there was evidence of support for the Arab cause not only from the Arab States and the Grand Mufti himself, but also indirectly from German and Italian sources, it was found necessary to make a demonstration of the firmness of British intentions by the despatch of the 1st and 5th Divisions, under a force headquarters, to Palestine in September, 1936. The 5th Division was already largely there, and the 1st Division, less its gunner support, was sent hotfoot from England, leaving its own RASC companies at home, and picking up units already in Palestine. The disturbances were rapidly quelled but not without some fighting, and RASC units, operating under their CsRASC, had their first opportunity of proving their value on active service. Indeed, in the early stages of the revolt, when every convoy was a military operation, the Corps had ample opportunity to develop and to display its fighting qualities, being responsible for its own protection and in many cases providing escorts for the force and for divisional commanders. Troop carrying was one of the main duties of the Corps both in Palestine and in Libya, and this commitment has remained an important one ever since. Members of the Corps earned several awards for bravery in the field, which did much to enhance regimental prestige, and it may be said that in all these minor but nevertheless necessary expeditions the Corps never failed to gain the good opinion of the Army.

Domestic Events

From now onwards the shadow of coming events in Europe was spreading over the world. Rearmament was in progress, and the plans by which the Corps fitted itself for the coming ordeal were taking firm shape after the long period of retrenchment and improvisation, but before discussing this new turn of events it is necessary to turn for one moment to the period of the late nineteen twenties.

While spearheads of the Corps were earning fresh laurels in the lesser wars and campaigns, morale among units in other fields was also high. At home and in the stations overseas which were not immediately affected by these unending crises, officers and men settled down to the routine of garrison life. Units had been grievously cut and were largely operated on civilian establishments. Nevertheless the Corps was well represented in individual Army and inter-service sport, the RASC Training College winning the coveted Army Football Cup in the years 1923 and 1937, and the tug-of-war team of the Feltham depot, together with their very strong boxing team, winning several service and inter-service competitions. The Corps was also well to the front in international events, contributing representatives to football, hockey, lawn tennis and equestrian events. Even the almost complete disappearance of the horse failed to prevent them from taking part in mounted events, and they remained one of the diminishing number of regiments and corps to carry on the military coach tradition. Furthermore even the Chanak crisis furnished the opportunity for a team of six RASC officers to improve on classical history by swimming the Hellespont *en masse*.

Mention should be made here of the Royal Army Service Corps Regimental Association. Its predecessor, the ASC Old Comrades Association, was founded after the South African War, but it was not until 1927 that the association obtained its more impressive title, although in later years the word regimental was dropped. This organization has indeed played a great part in bringing together members and former members of the Corps. It looks after, where necessary, their families and dependents, and attends to the proper administration of funds subscribed by members of the association.

The Corps Band, raised on a voluntary basis in 1892 and supported entirely by the individual contributions of officers, was resuscitated in 1919 after its wartime quiescence. It continued on that basis until 1938 when, thanks to the support of the War Minister, Mr. Leslie Hore-Belisha, who had himself served as an RASC officer in the Territorial Army, a somewhat reluctant Treasury agreed to its recognition as an official band.

The RASC, Territorial Army and Supplementary Reserve

During these lean years between 1919 and 1927 the Territorial Army was hard hit but, with the unquenchable public spirit which has always marked its members, it contrived to keep its organization and traditions alive. The RASC Territorials were at this time in an even worse position than their brothers in the Regular Army. The establishment of officers and men was reduced to such proportions that it was only the spirit and vision of the faithful few that kept the almost nominal headquarters RASC and the skeleton three companies alive in each of the 14 divisional trains. These RASC Territorials were still on a HT basis, but had no horses! This policy of contraction seems inconsistent when the Territorial Army was at the same time recognized as the means of expanding forces in time of war.

In the case of the RASC as a whole, an attempt was made in about 1922 to combat the officer shortage, in the event of mobilization, by the enrolment of suitable candidates in the Supplementary Reserve. Many men came forward in response to this call, passed through a preliminary training of four weeks at the RASC Training College, and took their place in the cadres which were eventually called up in 1939. However, there was no corresponding Supplementary Reserve of other ranks.

Reorganization of the Divisional RASC

Such, then, was the general position in the nineteen twenties, but towards the end of this period events were to take place which exercised a profound effect on the whole structure and outlook of the Corps. The somewhat unsatisfactory position in which the Corps found itself at that time was not entirely due to the general policy of retrenchment. The Corps, though fully combatant and drawing its officers from the same sources and through the same channels as other combatant arms, had, nevertheless, remained outside the normal army framework for staff questions, training and manpower, i.e. the directorates covered by the General Staff and the Adjutant-General. The DST took his orders in these matters directly from the QMG.

Strangely enough it was the small 'policing expedition' to Shanghai that was the indirect cause of the great changes which were made in Corps organization, training and manning from 1930 onwards. Lieut-Colonel D. C. Cameron, who was made responsible for the organization of the small RASC component of this force, was so impressed by the difficulties inherent in organizing its few units that he worked out a more logical and operational basis for the organization and training of the Corps. This was adopted some years later when he was Commandant of the RASC Training Centre. Unconventional in his outward appearance, he possessed nevertheless a precise, determined and logical mind, so that those who worked with him said in later years that he never wasted a word and that every word was worthy of attention. He declared that unless the RASC could be fitted into the normal framework for training and manpower, and unless every fighting formation was furnished in peace with a nucleus of those Corps units which it would require in war (a policy sometimes dubbed 'divisionalization'), the Corps must remain virtually untrained. It was moreover impotent to fill its true role and liable to break down under the strain of modern war. Not destructive for destruction's sake, he at once proceeded to demonstrate at the RASC Training Centre how that centre, itself the key to his proposed reforms, should be reorganized, and at the same time he pressed for the adoption of his new system in its entirety.

He could not have formulated his ideas at a better time, for they coincided with those of the newly appointed Director of Supplies and Transport, Major-General Evan Gibb, himself an original thinker, a man of great drive and of considerable 'extra-RASC' experience. General Gibb was, moreover, under the orders of (and strongly supported by) a Quarter-Master-General, Lieutenant-General Sir Hastings Anderson, of like ideas, and these two men were to prove invaluable to the Corps in the campaign for self-improvement, for there were still the General Staff, the AG's Department and the Treasury to be convinced. Looking ahead a little, one may add that the Corps was fortunate also in the 'run' of DsST succeeding General Gibb at the War Office.

Happily for us the General Staff and the AG welcomed the proposed changes and the Director of Military Training quickly assumed responsibility for instructing the Corps, while the Director of Recruiting and Organization undertook the manning of it. The formation of RASC divisional troops and brigade companies for each regular division followed soon afterwards, and in due course a skeleton organization on similar lines was adopted for the TA.

The new status of the Corps acted as a strong inducement to its younger officers to study for the Staff College, while the new appointments open to Corps officers offered some reward to the number of far seeing and public spirited officers who had already passed through that establishment. It is hard to convey in these few paragraphs the widespread beneficial effect of the new policy. It infused new life and enthusiasm into the regimental officer and man, and it provided the opportunity for the RASC staff at the War Office to ventilate, directly or indirectly, the whole question of the requirements of the Corps and of the part it could, and should, play in a future war.

The reorganized RASC Training Centre prepared a series of war courses for senior officers. These gave officers of the Corps opportunities for examining every aspect of Corps work connected with higher planning and with the administrative background of imaginary but highly realistic campaigns. Nor was co-operation with other arms and with the General Staff overlooked. A GSO 2, usually an infantry or artillery officer, was included in the establishment of the headquarters of the RASC Training Centre and, as the courses were open to officers of other arms beside the RASC, a useful interchange of ideas and points of view took place.

The preparation of these courses was complicated in the early days by the lack of a firm governmental policy. There was little guidance on either the form of the next campaign or on the requirements of the mechanized formations which would undoubtedly play a part in it. Moreover the strategical and tactical effects of air forces on military operations were by no means predetermined, while the size and probable nature of the forces which could be equipped and put in the field was equally doubtful. All the more credit is therefore due to those on the staff of the Centre who, helped by the co-operation of the Staff College and War Office staffs (both G and Q), were able to forecast future administrative trends with considerable accuracy. While imparting valuable instruction to the students at the Centre, they provided material for working out the plans of many big projects vital to our war effort.

Higher direction of the Corps

The debt owed by the Corps to its two DsST from 1928 to 1936 should not be forgotten. General Gibb has already been mentioned, while his successor, General C. W. Macleod, after his four years as DST, returned voluntarily during the war as a deputy director, combining a rare degree of determination and single-mindedness with great personal charm and great readiness to help his staff.

Recognition of the need for reforms came just in time. In spite of the heavy cuts in the Army's vote which resulted from the financial crisis of 1931, no steps were taken to whittle away the small additions made recently to the Corps. A few years later, preparations for war began in earnest. The main responsibility for this, from the point of view of the Corps, rested, of course, on the DST at the War Office. For that reason the most important activities of his directorate are related later in this prelude under the specific headings of Transport, Supplies and POL. The DST's staff was small. He had no personal aides, and the Inspector of the RASC was not even one of his staff officers (the IRASC, for his part, had no personal staff either!). The DST's two branches each consisted of an ADST (colonel) with a DADST (major) and a staff captain, and dealt respectively with transport, QMG 3, and supplies and petrol, QMG 6. Barrack duties, though performed at the War Office to some extent by RASC officers, were the responsibility of another of the QMG's directors, the Director of Quartering. DST's former third branch, QMG 5, was transferred to the AG's Department as AG 8 when the reforms already described took place in General Gibb's time. Coupled with AG 8, the designation QMG 5 still remained, signifying the sub-branch which dealt with questions affecting civilians employed in RASC establishments. This simple and slender organization, by dint of the devotion and foresight of its members and the guidance given by its directors, was able to lay the foundations of a sound ST service in the field in a very short time. This was made evident when the testing time came in 1939.

The Divisional RASC takes shape

Cursory mention has been made of 'divisionalization'. This, and the integration of the Corps in peace with operational formations, must now be described in more detail. By 1932 the 1st and 2nd Divisional RASC, each of a headquarters and three companies, had already been established, and these were followed a year later by those for the 3rd and 4th Divisions. That for the 5th Division was to come later. The headquarters consisted of a CRASC and his clerks, and the companies were of uniform size, each having two officers, 50 men and 15 vehicles.

Although these units bore little relation to the form and size they would assume on mobilization, the adoption of small standardized units spread resources to the best advantage. They also assisted in producing a uniform method of training and provided a field, hitherto lacking, for training both officer and man in leadership and readiness to assume higher responsibilities on mobilization. The divisional RASC progressed from a mechanized model of the old HT divisional train to a headquarters and three companies designed on a 'commodity basis', i.e. a supply company, an ammunition company and a petrol company. The last named was also responsible for the carriage of blankets and baggage when required. At the same time the CRASC was made the divisional commander's adviser on transport matters and, in peace, had the duty of co-ordinating the availability and use of the transport of other arms in the division when not required for training. The resources of the divisional RASC companies could not, themselves, be set aside entirely for training purposes, and they took their part in performing the general transport duties of the station, except during company, divisional and collective training. Their identification with their formations and their appearance with the fighting arms on collective training provided a new opportunity for the staff to make a practical study of their operation and capabilities.

In the early part of the period under immediate review (1929 to 1937) there was still no armoured force of the nature foreseen some years before, and infantry transport was not yet mechanized. Mechanization of second line transport, however (which was the generic title for RASC transport of divisions), was shown to bestow a new degree of mobility and flexibility. This flexibility was well illustrated when occasions arose to divert RASC units to the tactical movement of troops, a definite technique being worked out for the purpose. This technique eventually led to the introduction of special companies for troop carrying as part of the armoured division and as a pool for general allocation as required. So important did this role become that, at a much later date, when the Corps was reorganized on a basis comparable to that of the infantry, the transport platoon, RASC, was designed, not only to equal the infantry platoon in numbers, but also, on a 3-tonner basis, to lift the 'foot sloggers' of an infantry battalion.

Divisionalization also helped to test the principles of training which had been laid down officially in 1933 in the first RASC training manuals to be published since some years before the First World War. Before 1933 the only available data upon which to base training had been of a semi-official nature, resulting from the studies at the RASC Training Centre and recorded in the *RASC Quarterly*. This was a professional magazine published by the Training Centre and financed entirely by the officers of the Corps. Indeed, even after the publication of the official manuals, limited by necessity to the declaration of basic principles, the *Quarterly* remained the medium for disseminating more detailed information, especially in connection with the handling of tactical situations by divisional and corps unit officers, and with the siting and operation of base and lines of communication units (which had no existence as such in peace). The latter information in particular proved of great value to many officers who suddenly found themselves responsible for their organization on mobilization.

Horse transport was not overlooked in this reorientation of ideas, but its use was not provided for as a normal course, and the one animal transport company, embodied in the Training Battalion, RASC, remained the potential core of whatever horsed units might be needed in the future. The training battalion itself was the outcome of the reforms and played a most important part in the preliminary military training of all ranks. It was also the unit responsible for the fitting out and posting of all Regular and certain Supplementary Reservists.

The Territorial Army again

While these reforms were in progress the RASC TA units were still organized in divisional trains, with a headquarters and four HT companies. Steps were now taken to bring them into line with the Regulars, and although an extremely slender establishment of 11 officers and 99 other ranks only was allotted, the units were reorganized on the basis of a headquarters and three companies. They now felt themselves 'not forgotten', and the mere act of reorganization acted as an incentive to fresh interest and endeavour. Arrangements were also made at this time by the Training Centre for a wider distribution of training data, to include TA units among the recipients, and by the organization at the Centre of special courses for TA officers and senior other ranks to keep them abreast of developments. The number of vehicles at the permanent call of TA units remained extremely small, but the enthusiasm of all ranks, the running of week-end exercises and TEWTs* and the additional vehicles made available to them during annual training camps served to build up an informed nucleus of officers and other ranks. This proved an invaluable foundation on which to build up efficient units on mobilization. The TA insurance, in fact, amply repaid the slender premium which was apparently all that the country could afford in peacetime.

No further change in the position of the Territorial Army took place until 1935, when the need for an air defence organization, which could be called out and deployed at short notice, unrestricted by the legislation involved in official mobilization, became so urgent that the Air Defence of Great Britain (ADGB) was brought into being. It was based on the formation of two anti-aircraft divisions, TA, raised for this purpose. The small cadre adopted for the RASC of TA infantry divisions was soon found to be inappropriate to these new AA divisions, and by 1938 it was established that the RASC of an AA division must not only be of sufficient strength to fulfil its role at a few hours' notice, but must also be completely self-contained. Also it has to be, in certain respects, independent of the existing general ST lay-out of the Army Command in which it might happen to be deployed. This new organization and system had a trial in consequence of 'Munich' and proved itself to be sound.

Planning for War

For reasons apart from Mussolini's threat to Egypt and the open rebellion of the Arabs in Palestine, 1936 and 1937 were busy years

* Tactical exercises without troops.

for the War Office staff, who were engaged increasingly in making concrete plans for the impending war. The brunt of this planning fell on Major-General M. S. Brander, who succeeded Major-General Macleod as DST in 1937, and whose place as Inspector of the RASC was taken by Major-General R. T. Snowden-Smith. The two branches dealing with RASC matters, QMG 3 under Colonel E. H. Fitzherbert and QMG 6 under Colonel H. M. Gale, strove manfully to perfect the plans for transport, supplies and fuel for an expeditionary force, the form and strength of which was becoming more well defined with the passing months. It was not until 1938, however, that the full requirements of the RASC on mobilization were finally settled and that the Training Battalion could be given firm data on which to build a mobilization scheme.

Outside the War Office, commands at home and overseas were also making plans and preparations for war. In each case the senior RASC officer in the command had his own local problems to solve. Those at home knew that they would probably be denuded of their resources in units and men, which would be required at once to mobilize for service with the field force. At the same time arrangements would have to be made to cope with the influx of TA divisions at full war strength, and to meet the needs of many new units which would be formed to swell the organization and to reinforce garrisons overseas. The task in overseas commands was no lighter, for few did not have a local defence problem. Their resources were meagre and their arrangements for augmenting them varied from place to place. Gibraltar and Malta were likely to face a siege, possibly of long duration, before they could be relieved. Both places supported a civil population and were wholly dependent on imports. Protected accommodation for essential stocks of food, fuel and ammunition was vital and would take time to provide. Hong Kong was faced with a similar problem, though possibly not of such urgency. The defences of Singapore were by no means complete. The Middle East was, of course, the nerve centre of our Imperial communications, and the future attitude of Italy, now in a greatly strengthened position in North and East Africa, was doubtful. Many territories came within the orbit of the two commands then responsible for the Middle East area, and vast frontiers had to be watched and defended by a British garrison which was pitifully weak. The main problems of the ADST at Cairo were how to deploy his limited transport resources to the best advantage and how to become, from a supply point of view, as self-supporting as possible.

The defence of certain colonies rested solely on colonial troops who were trained and equipped for little more than internal security or punitive measures. Their organization, based as far as the

RASC were concerned, on a tiny nucleus of officers and clerks with a somewhat heterogeneous collection of civilian subordinates drawn from the local populace, was quite inadequate to meet the conditions arising from a war against a well equipped enemy. The presence of Italian troops in Italian Somaliland and Abyssinia constituted a menace to British East Africa and British Somaliland, while the security of the West African littoral was essential for the safety of convoys passing to the south or east by the Cape route. All three territories (Somaliland, East Africa and West Africa) would have to be reinforced and their administrative organization, including their RASC, developed and augmented by local recruitment of both Europeans and Africans. Every colony needed improvements in its defence arrangements. Even the western possessions, such as Bermuda and the British West Indies, had to be prepared to deal with attack from the sea and the possible onslaught of raiding parties. When war finally broke out, the RASC in stations overseas did their best to reduce their demands for both men and material from Britain to a minimum, to expand their organization to meet all demands, and to inculcate the Corps spirit into the people of many diverse nations who were enlisted locally.

The year 1938 was critical. A general review of the military position and future commitments took place early in the year and was referred to as the 'New Conspectus'. The security of Britain and the safeguarding of Imperial interests still took first place over the question of any Continental expeditionary force. The necessity for increasing the strength of the ADGB and for additional expenditure on the new form of defence, Passive Air Defence later known as Air Raid Precautions (ARP), entailed a diversion of funds which might have been devoted to the improvement of the equipment of the TA and increasing the effectiveness of the field forces. While the AGDB was being raised from two to five AA divisions the Munich crisis occurred. The increased responsibilities of the headquarters ADGB and of the Anti-Aircraft Corps was recognized by the formation of a separate Anti-Aircraft Command, with its own command headquarters, on which the RASC were represented by an ADST and a small staff.

A few months before the Munich crisis deliveries of the new Albion six-wheeled lorry had begun, and first priority of issue had been given to the 1st AA Divisional RASC TA and had already gone a long way towards bringing this column to a high state of efficiency and readiness for war. At one stage immediately after the crisis there was a plan to send British troops to Czechoslovakia at short notice. This force, known as C Force, was in the nature of a parade, which would come under the critical eye of the Führer's troops. The preparation of the RASC contingent necessitated the withdrawal of all the new Albion lorries from the TA. In the end the force did not embark, but great credit is due to the column concerned for the manner in which they assembled the required number of vehicles during one weekend.

'Munich' led to accelerated military planning, so that early in 1939 a decision on the size and rate of despatch of the force for operations on the Continent was at last reached.

The search for Manpower

Throughout the years which had passed since the first decision to rearm, one major question had remained almost unsolved, namely, the need for more men. Ever since the first war there had been difficulty in maintaining the Army at the desired strength. Apart from public apathy, always a failing of the British people, and a natural reaction after the years of strife from 1914 to 1919, part of the fault lay with the British Government. Not until the early nineteen thirties was it recognized that many of the conditions of service were out-moded and that pay, of all ranks, was not comparable with the rates which could be earned for the same skill and effort in civil life. Various changes were made including improvements in feeding. The Army still had a bad press, however, for with few exceptions little heed was paid to military affairs, and one may search in vain for a single book or play produced during these years calculated to enhance the prestige of the Army or to further its interests, though many denigrated its qualities and its performance.

It was obvious that, if national service were to be introduced (and it seemed that this unpopular measure was the only solution in the absence of a large trained reserve) it would have to be launched on a better informed public. The introduction of a public relations department at the War Office and the personal efforts of the then Secretary of State for War went far towards improving the situation. The natural anxiety of many parents was allayed by the publicity given to the conditions under which their sons would be called upon to serve. The decision to introduce compulsory service (the new 'Militia') was not taken until the spring of 1939, when it was also decided to double the size of the Territorial Army. These two measures, welcome as they were, threw a heavy additional burden on our small Regular establishments, particularly on the Training Battalion which had to provide duplicates and the key men for them.

Apart from the lack of reservists which might, in time, be overcome partly by the training of the conscript Militia, the RASC were faced with another serious mobilization problem. This was the paucity of units on which to build, for a high proportion of the

Convoy on a Desert Road

Lorry dug in in the Desert

Men of the B.E.F.

At an O.C.T.U.

RASC units required in war had no counterparts in peace, and many of them were vital to the successful operation of the maintenance system for supplies, fuel and transport. By this time the staff outlook on Corps needs was sympathetic and appreciative, one of the benefits accruing from the reforms in Corps direction, training and operation. Even before the nature of the field force was definite, it was clear that the number of units in peace must be increased, and authority was now given for the formation of 14 new RASC companies. With this, a permanent increase in the peace establishment of the Corps was also sanctioned, but of course the new vacancies created by this increase had to be filled, and officers and men trained for the purpose.

As far as other ranks were concerned, when national service was introduced the Corps was given special priority in men who possessed the technical qualifications required by the RASC, mostly in respect of MT drivers. By the end of August, 1939, the first two intakes had been received, yielding some 2,000 men. Even so, soon after war was declared another 3,000 had to be transferred from other arms, mainly from the Royal Artillery, to try to make up outstanding requirements. A scarcity of men still remained, and this was made up by opening voluntary recruitment for drivers and artificers. In all, some 29,000 men passed through the depot and training battalions between September 3rd and November 15th, 1939, compared with a planned intake of 8,000 Regular reservists in the first fortnight and 1,600 recruits in October.

The Regular reservists were quite insufficient even though they were to be augmented by a small Supplementary Reserve of technically skilled but militarily untrained civilian tradesmen who, in return for a small annual bounty, undertook to answer the call on mobilization.

For a Corps of such varied activities the officer problem was even more serious. The only available reserves were the Regular Army Reserve of Officers, the Territorial Army Reserve of Officers, and the small Supplementary Reserve of Officers, whose highest admissible rank was that of lieutenant. Many of the officers in the first two categories had, of course, aged since they last saw active service and had received no refresher training. The number of Regular officers would barely permit of more than one or two being allotted to each unit, and there would also be calls for them to fill staff and ST appointments at various headquarters. In an attempt to make good the deficit on peace establishments, several expedients were resorted to in the months before the outbreak of war. Officers of the Regular Reserve (and some retired officers of the Indian Army) were invited to return on short term engagements, short service commissions were offered to likely young men, and temporary

Regular commissions were offered to officers of the TA and SR. Although some of these measures amounted to 'robbing Peter to pay Paul', on the whole they were successful as far as they went. The remaining deficiencies were, partly, made up by the creation, for the Army as a whole, of the Army Officers' Emergency Reserve (AOER), consisting mainly of former temporary officers of the First World War, who volunteered for service again. Although most of these volunteers had previous service, there were some difficulties over age and rank and even shape (three outraged members of the AOER were on one occasion ordered by their young Regular commanding officer to 'get rid of their stomachs in three weeks'!), and some of this intake was not quite up to standard. So in spite of all these measures the Corps had to start the war handicapped by serious deficiencies both in quality and quantity of its men.

Help from the Auxiliary Territorial Service

Here special mention must be made of the Auxiliary Territorial Service (now the Women's Royal Army Corps), which was to relieve the manpower problem of the Corps considerably by the provision of drivers and clerks and 'housekeeping personnel' in many static establishments. The RASC had a direct interest in the formation of the new corps as for many years past it had undertaken the technical training and general sponsoring of the First Aid Nursing Yeomanry (the 'FANYs'). This was an unofficial body possessing limitless enthusiasm which, although not recognized by the War Office, still managed to maintain their identity from South African War days to 1939, and to carry out annual training at their own expense in similar camps to those of the TA, with the loan of WD equipment. From the FANY were drawn most of the officers for the MT branch of the ATS. No doubt the history of the WRAC and of their forerunners in the ATS, will be written in due course, but this seems an appropriate occasion on which to record that the thanks of the RASC are due to all those officers and women of the ATS who helped them so admirably during, and after, the war.

Conclusion

If it is thought that too much emphasis has been placed on the difficulties of the Corps during the aftermath of the First World War and preparations for the second, let it be said that, when the call came in September, 1939, the Corps was duly and smoothly mobilized. The British Expeditionary Force crossed to France with its full complement of RASC units, the RASC organization at home expanded and met all the calls made on it, while reinforcements, supplies and material began to flow to all parts of the world. The machine was working.

TRANSPORT

A predominantly Mechanical Transport Corps

At the end of the First World War, the RASC, though largely composed of mechanical transport units, was still one of the mounted arms of the service. They owed full allegiance to the horse, and their general way of military life, even their dismounted drill (foot drill), followed the mounted tradition. In the years immediately after the war, their horse transport companies were reduced to one only, and that was the Animal Transport Company of the Training College. MT companies were reduced to a handful, being scattered over the main military stations. By 1925, some 2,000 vehicles (excluding those in India), were operated and maintained, compared with the 125,000 of the First World War. Yet the RASC remained the only Corps to have MT operating on a world-wide scale, and to have built up a complete supporting organization for vehicle maintenance. They were the pioneers of this branch of the Army (due credit being given to the Royal Engineers for their early and limited efforts of 1899–1903), and their activity embraced every phase of the life of the vehicle from the drawing-board to the scrap-heap.

The decline of horse transport and its gradual eclipse by the motor vehicle had a profound effect on the training and outlook of all ranks. All officers had to acquire the necessary knowledge of this 'science' to make them intelligent, economical and enterprising operators of motor transport, as well as competent horsemasters and supply officers, while the way was open to a small proportion (about one in 10) to qualify as fully trained mechanical engineers. The 'other ranks' joined as horse transport drivers, mechanical transport drivers, or artificers, but they all received the same basic military training (in company with their colleagues of the supply branch), followed by specialist training in their own particular lines, the HT drivers and artificers and the MT artificers at the Training College (later Training Centre) at Aldershot, and the MT drivers at the Driving School RASC (R Company) at Feltham, Middlesex.

The Training Centre, therefore, thus taught the principles of horse mastership, of the operation of MT units, and of hirings. On its more specialist side it taught artificers (including boy artificers) their trades, and gave many officers with a mechanical bent a good grounding in mechanical engineering, bringing them up to the standard required for associate membership of the Institution of Mechanical Engineers. Officers who took up this side of Corps duties spent some three years in advanced engineering studies, including two years of practical training at selected civilian vehicle manufacturing works.

The output of the Training Centre and Driving School went to fill the cadres of the transport units and transport offices at home and overseas. These consisted (apart from those in India) of a number of MT companies on a modest establishment at the larger military stations, backed up by a group of three maintenance units at Feltham, a vehicle reserve depot, a MT stores depot, and a heavy repair shop. Mention has already been made of the driving school there, which was more in the nature of an 'outpost' of the Training Centre than of a technical unit.

In India, the Corps was organized on much the same lines, substituting Indian other ranks for British, except for certain supervisory grades, artificers in particular. The location of the companies however, was on a tactical plan, and they were integrated more closely with the formations which they supported than was the case in Britain. From 1920 to 1927, India absorbed about half of the vehicles operated by the RASC.

As the horse began to disappear, infantry drill took the place of dismounted cavalry drill, and the tactical side of RASC training gradually assumed greater importance. This was especially important because of the growing menace of air power and the increasing adoption of tanks and armoured cars in Europe. With the reforms in RASC training and organization already referred to, the Corps took the shape in which it went to war in 1939. But much happened, particularly on the technical and the planning side, during the intervening years.

The RASC lead on the technical side

The Corps, in its short life as an operator of MT, had always been responsible for provision, inspection, maintenance and, except for a very short period before and after the start of the First World War, repair of its own vehicles. It relied on obtaining its requirements in vehicles from normal commercial production. In 1914, the 1,200 vehicles required for the original British Expeditionary Force were obtained partly by means of a subsidy scheme and partly by impressment, both of these activities being a Corps responsibility.

Technical research and development on a lesser scale had been vested in the ASC 'Inspection Branch, MT' before 1914. This branch functioned under the wing of the ASC Training Establishment, and by a natural sequence the same work fell to the MT School of Instruction, under the RASC Training Centre, after the First World War. The School of Instruction was fortunate in having at this time the services of a civilian professor of mechanical engineering, Colonel H. Niblett, who was an automobile engineer of wide experience in the heavy transport field and formerly a temporary officer of the Corps. What was achieved at almost negligible cost was without doubt due to Colonel Niblett and his band of enthusiasts, and it was this small group which had to develop the ideas of the 'MT Advisory Board'. This board was the successor of the pre-1914 'MT Committee', charged with the examination of the development and use of MT for military purposes. The new board, of which the DST was chairman, dealt with wheeled vehicles only, tracked vehicle development being the responsibility of another body.

The first task of the board after the war ended was to develop a 3-ton load carrying vehicle with improved performance over rough country. Our 1914–1918 vehicles, 3-ton and 30-cwt with solid tyres, while giving excellent service on hard ground, were instantly bogged down if driven over fields, sand, or anything except the smallest irregularities on the ground.

The use of pneumatic tyres for commercial vehicles was still in its infancy, and their practicability and cost were being considered with anxiety by the motor industry. The Corps took the plunge however, and by 1922 the force sent to Chanak was equipped with a number of 30-cwt pneumatic-tyred vehicles, which earned good reports. The question of a wider distribution of the driven axle load was still unsolved. The French firm of Renault made a big advance by producing a six-wheeled light load carrier with twin driven rear axles which demonstrated its power in a trans-Sahara expedition in the early nineteen twenties. The MT School of Instruction secured a sample of this type and greatly increased both its riding qualities and its tractive power by designing a torque reaction gear which forced both driven axles downwards with an even thrust, thus countering the tendency, in the original design, for the forward axle to lift at the precise moment when maximum power from both axles was required.

By 1925, designs for a heavy and a medium type six-wheeled vehicle with four-wheeled driven bogies at the rear were perfected and accepted as the standard for Army vehicles. These vehicles, with pneumatic tyres, gave a fair cross-country performance, and were calculated to cope with any of the duties expected of a primarily road operating machine. It was hoped that this design would also be adopted for general commercial use, fostered by the attractions of a free gift by the War Department of the various patents which it embodied and by the payment of a small subsidy in annual instalments to those who made use of such vehicles and kept them in fit condition for possible military use. This subsidy scheme, unfortunately, produced only meagre results, because of the comparatively high initial cost of the vehicles and of licensing difficulties. The main object had been attained, however, for the medium six-wheeler was still one of the standard types of Army vehicle which had the necessary performance when the Second World War broke out 14 years later.

The Training Centre also produced schemes for a four-wheel drive tractor, based on the best features of a large range of captured or ceded German equipment, besides many fresh ideas incorporated in the finished design. Other schemes included an adaptation of the Morris one-ton truck to convert it into a field gun towing machine, a three-wheeled motor cycle with an astonishing cross-country performance (which was not, however, adopted), and many developments in pneumatic tyres, culminating in the sand tyre of later years.

The Technical Position assailed

While these events were taking place, the use of MT by arms other than the RASC was increasing rapidly, and the whole question of unifying control and responsibility for what was then known as 'mechanization' came under serious consideration. The divergence between the avenues of development for wheeled and tracked vehicles was only one pointer in the rapidly developing situation. In passing, it might be noted that a healthy rivalry between the two schools of 'wheels' and 'tracks' may have contributed to the sense of urgency impelling both teams to extra effort. (This rivalry reached a moment of greatest drama when, at a trial of wheeled versus tracked machines, the tracks won over a particularly soft and treacherous bit of ground, and a French manufacturer, interested in the production of tracked vehicles, hurled his hat into the air, and subsequently into the bog, yelling at the top of his voice, 'C'est la mort de la roue'!) In the more practical field the RASC organization and its wheeled MT vehicles covered a great part of those in the hands of the Army as a whole, and represented also one of the simplest aspects of the much wider term, mechanization. This implied not only the replacement of horse transport by mechanical vehicles, but also the provision, operation and maintenance of a great variety of armoured, semi-armoured and special types of machines, both wheeled and tracked, to meet the present or future needs of the fighting arms.

A British compromise

The provision and maintenance of wheeled vehicles were familiar and relatively easy administrative tasks. Commercial production could be relied on for the production of the types of vehicle required, and for the necessary supply of spare parts for their maintenance.

The provision of armoured fighting vehicles and gun towing machines was a very different matter, and entailed the reorganization of many industries to meet the purely military demands made upon them. But before any such reorganization could profitably be undertaken or any solely military vehicle could be designed, the whole question of the size and composition of the mechanized armies of the future, and of their tactical and strategical uses, had to be determined. When these had been defined, their practical requirements could be translated into a series of General Staff specifications from which the technical specifications followed. Throughout there were always two vital factors affecting such decisions, one the question of mounting cost, and the other the progress of our potential enemies in mechanizing their forces.

The matter of design, provision and maintenance of such fighting equipment belonged to the province of the Master-General of the Ordnance at the War Office, and followed the precedent set up for similar services in the production of weapons. The General Staff laid down the tactical requirement, the Armament Inspection Department (under the Chief Inspector of Armaments, CIA) produced the technical specification, and the Design Department (or a selected manufacturer) produced the design to meet these specifications. The MGO branch concerned ordered production of the equipment, after which its receipt, storage, issue and maintenance were the responsibility of the Royal Army Ordnance Corps. In 1936, the mechanization requirements of the Army had become so widespread that the whole of the above chain of responsibilities, down to the receipt of the finished equipment or spare part, became the responsibility of a separate ministry, the Ministry of Supply, to which certain of the officers in the MGO's branches, and all those in the Design and Inspection Departments were seconded, while the MGO ceased to exist.

Before and after this happened there were thus two branches, the QMG's and the MGO's (later the Ministry of Supply) dealing, as far as transport vehicles were concerned, with the provision and maintenance of closely allied and sometimes even identical, articles. After the departure of the MGO the situation became even stranger, for two QMG departments, those of the DST and of the Director of Equipment and Ordnance Stores, were competing in the same field, and this form of duplicated endeavour continued for many excellent reasons until May, 1942. To understand these reasons and to grasp the delimitation of responsibilities between the RASC and the RAOC in vehicle matters, it is necessary to revert to the 1920's again.

The first great measure towards centralization was the passing of responsibility for all research and design, both for wheeled and for tracked machines, to the MGO and the creation of a new 'Mechanical Warfare Board', later styled the 'Mechanization Board', which absorbed the duties hitherto performed by the Mechanical Transport Advisory Board and the Tracked Vehicles Sub-Committee. To mark the importance of the new board, the MGO himself assumed the chairmanship. The RASC were represented on the board and also in the new Army experimental establishment, the Mechanical Warfare Experimental Establishment (MWEE), which was set up at Farnborough. This measure was welcomed on all sides, though not without a shade of regret on the part of the Corps, who thus lost their intimate responsibility for research, which they had borne with great enthusiasm and no little success since the end of the war. The Mechanization Board had its teething troubles but evolved into a most useful clearing house for investigation and research.

From this time, too, executive action within the War Office for the provision of wheeled vehicles was officially the task of an MGO branch, MGO 6, but in practice the QMG with the DST as his adviser, still remained responsible for deciding what vehicles he required, and the DST's QMG 3 branch still remained responsible for the receipt, custody and issue of RASC vehicles and for their repair. To discriminate between the QMG's responsibility and that of the MGO, the Army's vehicles were divided into three categories, A vehicles (purely fighting vehicles), B vehicles (first line transport vehicles for arms other than the RASC), and 'RASC' vehicles. A and B vehicles were the responsibility of the MGO, RASC vehicles that of the QMG.

To the outsider this organization was confusing, to put it mildly, yet the new scheme worked well until it became strained by war production programmes, with their implications in manpower, material and shipping priorities.

At a time when the very best use had to be made of the limited amount of public money available, the contract procedure for producing a complete vehicle was indeed a complicated one. No fewer than ten separate contracts had to be drawn up and tenders invited to cover the separate provision of the body, and the mounting of it, the driver's cab, and canvas for lorry covers, and there had to be another contract to make them into the complete canopy. Considerable patience was necessary in fitting in the delivery of all these components so as to be able to issue a complete vehicle to a unit. There were even two separate contracts, one for the spring draw-bar and another for the towing hook which was attached to it! The assembly and equipping of all vehicles was one of the many important features of the work in the heavy repair shop at Feltham.

The relations between the two branches, MGO 6 and QMG 3, were of the closest, partly because of the presence of several RASC officers who were posted to the new organization, including its Mechanization Board and its Inspection Department, as well as its War Office branch. Some of these officers transferred to the RAOC Engineering Branch, and of these Major J. S. Crawford was eventually to become Director of Mechanization and later Deputy Director General of Tank Supply in the Ministry of Supply. Of those who remained with the RASC, Major W. S. Tope, who went to MGO 6, later became the second Director of the new Corps of Royal Electrical and Mechanical Engineers formed later in the War. Lieut-Colonel M. S. Brander and Major E. B. Rowcroft, who became the first Director of REME, were successively Inspector of Tanks and Major C. C. Saunders-O'Mahoney was the first Inspector of Mechanized Vehicles (i.e., wheeled transport vehicles), and was succeeded by Lieut-Colonel J. C. Mackie.

The Corps had always placed special importance on their own system of inspection under which the mechanical and operating efficiency of every RASC company was known personally to the DST, from which he gauged the efficiency of the commanding officers and of the transport organization as a whole. Resolute action in meeting all shortcomings ensured that everything was kept at a high pitch of efficiency. The fact that the officers of the Inspectorate were regimental officers who took their turn at this, as well as other duties, ensured that they brought a practical as well as a reasonable mind to their task. This rearrangement did not, however, affect the Corps vitally, but it did have an unfortunate effect after the outbreak of war, for no plans were made to continue the CIA's inspections of unit equipment after mobilization. The DST had, therefore, from his already strained resources to set up again the RASC Inspectorate at home and in every main theatre of war.

At this stage, then, the division of responsibility between the MGO (or the RAOC) and the QMG was such that the former inspected ALL equipment for the Army and provided, stored, issued and maintained all equipment for all arms except the RASC. The QMG for his part, remained responsible for the vehicles and their operation in the RASC and in any such other arms or services for which the RASC provided drivers, for instance of ambulances, staff cars and military fire engines.

The RASC retains its MT Depots and Workshops

Now a different and more threatening question arose, when a strong body of opinion put forward the view that the RASC organization for provision of spares and the execution of repairs should pass to the MGO's organization. It was felt that it was uneconomic to have two parallel systems running concurrently, one for the Corps and one for the rest of the Army. This was no new proposal, and it may be mentioned that 19 out of some 20 enquiries or committees had rejected it before something on these lines was adopted later under the stress of total war. In theory there was much to be said for the proposal, even in these early days. A central organization seemed logical and calculated to save overheads as well as some duplication at lower levels. Economy in skilled manpower, a matter of supreme importance, could be expected, and the work of the MGO branches (later M of S) would be simplified. The senior officers of the Corps were against the proposal, as there was neither an organization of sufficient scope and experience to cope with the whole load, nor one which could be called into existence in a short time. The view of these officers was upheld. Later events proved this stand to have been justified, for the successors of the MGO's organization had to be drastically reformed in the early days of the war to cope with their own side of the work, and a wholly new maintenance and repair organization, the REME, had to be called into being before the full implementation of the proposed reforms could be tackled. Provision, storage, and issue of vehicles and spare parts then passed wholly into the hands of the RAOC. Even so, it was not until some years after the war that the forward repair of RASC vehicles was handed over to the REME and the Corps lost its workshop platoons.

Rearmament on the transport side

So much for the framework of the Corps. While these policies were taking shape, the rearmament programme kept the DST's QMG 3 branch busy in concrete preparations for war. The main task was the provision of the vast fleet of vehicles and motor cycles required by all arms on mobilization. Responsibility for the provision of new production rested now with the MGO, but the brunt of the task fell on the DST, who was responsible, under the QMG, for procuring the large balance of the Army's requirements from vehicles already in commercial use. He also had to make arrangements for the scheme of hiring vehicles for use in home commands, when the latter lost their service vehicles to the proposed British Expeditionary Force.

The question of provision in the early 1930's was vitally affected by the rising cost of re-equipping and modernizing the Army. Every penny that could be spared in the Army's annual vote was required for armaments. The purchase of new wheeled vehicles had naturally to take second place as long as there was a ready supply of vehicles in commercial use, which could be tapped if necessary. There could be no question of producing a standardized military vehicle in large numbers. The whole matter was investigated in 1934 by a War Office committee which laid down certain general principles of great assistance to the planners. They recognized the desirability of all load-carrying vehicles conforming to the six-wheeled design, but took into account the great improvement in the design and performance of four-wheeled vehicles in later years, especially when those four-wheelers were fitted with large low pressure pneumatic tyres. They concluded, therefore, that six-wheeled vehicles should only be provided where a high performance was required, while most of the load carriers should be four-wheeled.

To build up the number of six-wheelers required under this policy, it was decided that every RASC unit in peacetime should be equipped with this type, and that the further numbers required to complete mobilization tables should be ordered and kept in store on a care and maintenance basis. At the same time, as most of the 'high performance' vehicles were for technical purposes, arrangements were made to purchase the special bodies, storing these in the vehicle depots and fitting as many as possible to the stored mobilization stocks of six-wheelers. The balance would be fitted on mobilization to the six-wheeled load carriers operating in peace in RASC companies.

These activities necessitated a big expansion of the RASC Vehicle Reserve Depot's storage space, and this could not be achieved at Feltham. Therefore a new site was sought and found at Ashchurch, near Tewkesbury, and it was opened in 1940. While waiting for this to become available, arrangements were made to take over temporary accommodation in the Slough Trading Estate in hangars and standings originally planned by the RASC for a long term storage scheme as long ago as 1918!

In order to leave production available for armaments and fighting vehicles, only five firms in the United Kingdom were allotted to six-wheeler production for the RASC. They were Messrs. Albion, Austin, Karrier, Morris and Thornycroft. Output was of excellent quality, but small in quantity.

Then, in 1935, came a sudden call for vehicles for the Near East and Palestine emergencies. This was the first occasion when QMG 3 obtained vehicles from a firm which was not wholly British-financed. The General Motors Corporation controlled firm of Bedfords, of Luton, were able to furnish 300 Bedford lorries in a modified form within a comparatively few days, thus overcoming an emergency which could not have been met in any other way in the available time. The Munich crisis three years later further emphasized this inability of British manufacturers to meet, by themselves, an even greater emergency. The War Office discussed with the General Motors Corporation the serious situation likely to arise if 'Munich' really meant war, with the result that, with War Office approval, GMC representatives telephoned to every one of their agents throughout the world, instructing them to freeze the sale of all load-carrying vehicles and give the United Kingdom the first option of purchase. By the next day the Corporation had produced a written statement of the vast numbers and the locations of all the vehicles so held. However, the Munich crisis did not lead to war at once, and their offer was not followed up.

Very soon afterwards, however, it was decided to stockpile 500 load carriers in the Middle East and, as a mark of appreciation of the firm's services, and also because they could offer immediate deliveries, Treasury approval for the purchase of 500 GMC lorries was given. These were shipped in a 'completely knocked down' pack, and QMG 3 thus inaugurated a system of vehicle shipment for army purposes which was later to have a most important bearing on the economical use of shipping tonnage and to which the Prime Minister himself in the war years attached the very greatest importance. The degree to which vehicles were knocked down depended on the capacity of receiving theatres to erect them quickly and efficiently, and so the forerunners of the war-time vehicle and equipment assembly units were called into being. The Corps can feel a justifiable pride that they were the medium for the introduction of this principle into the Army's economy.

Another contribution to the successful mechanization of our forces in the Middle East was the introduction of the sand tyre, a super low pressure tyre with a special 'sand tread', which has already been mentioned. Low pressure tyres were first introduced for infantry 15-cwt trucks, and their use was soon extended to heavier vehicles. Fortunately, the sand tread was developed in time to be fitted to the 500 GMC vehicles ordered for stockpiling in the Middle East. These gave a performance of outstanding value in the Libyan Desert a short time later. It was certainly a feather in the cap of the British Army that they were the pioneers in the production of these tyres and that their lead was followed so wholeheartedly in America in later years. A spontaneous tribute to the efficiency of the sand tyre was actually paid in an order promulgated by General Rommel himself, stating that for a particular operation of the Afrika Korps only captured British vehicles would be used, as they were capable of superior desert performance. So, it seems, everybody was satisfied!

Vehicle impressment

To meet the responsibility of the Corps for impressment, a small nucleus of officers, styled the Inspectorate of Supplementary Transport, was set up under a Chief Inspector, with representatives in every area of Great Britain. The basis of the scheme was to conduct a first-hand inspection of civilian vehicles, suitable for military use, by makes and types, the necessary powers being given to inspectors by specially enacted legislation. The inspectors also were to maintain a record of such vehicles. No vehicle was listed unless it had at least three years' useful life before it. In the event of mobilization, orders would be issued to owners to drive their vehicles to selected vehicle collecting centres, which would be established for the purpose. Events proved that the scheme not only saved the day in September, 1939, but that it continued to be of inestimable use in re-equipping the Army after Dunkirk when every vehicle (with the exception of one staff car allotted to a staff officer who had no intention of being deprived of his vehicle at any cost), was left behind in France. The original plan called for the impressment of some 14,000 vehicles, but during the course of the war this figure rose to over 35,000. The scheme for hiring vehicles for use in home commands on mobilization yielded an initial 10,000 vehicles, and was arranged with admirable promptitude and efficiency.

The MTSD and the HRS prove their worth

The activities of the MT Stores Depot at Feltham also merits a brief description. By 1930 this had become the storing and issuing depot for the RASC only and it had reached a high degree of efficiency. The Corps realized the vital need for a steady and prompt flow of spare parts and assemblies to its heavy repair shops and its workshop sections, and were well experienced in forecasting needs and knowing how to translate formal rates of wastage and theoretical estimates into a practical provision plan. Some of the best and most experienced officers of the Corps had set up a similar establishment, the MT Stores Depot at Chaklala, in India, and had operated it with equal success, handing it over with the rest of the MT establishments and units in India to the RIASC in 1927. During the period immediately before the war, not only were stocks of spares increased against the expansion of the Corps, but they were also pre-packed in cases ready for despatch in such a way that the quantities in each batch comprised roughly two months' spares for each 50 vehicles of any one make. At the same time complete lots were packed in readiness to stock the base MT store depots which would form part of the field forces.

All the work of body changing, modifications, etc., which has been mentioned, was rendered possible by the existence of the Heavy Repair Shop RASC, Feltham, which was close to the MT Stores Depot. This repair unit, intended primarily for the complete overhaul of RASC vehicles in service, was also naturally used for a large number of varied engineering tasks connected with mobilization. One of the most important of these was the assembly of machine tools and equipment in workshop lorries destined for the workshop sections of RASC companies. This particular task might well have been seriously handicapped by the extremely limited machine tool capacity available in the United Kingdom for the needs of the Army. In the case of lathes, the key machine tool of the workshop section, only four or five firms could be induced to tender for supplies, and the best delivery offered was 10 months from date of order, and the delivery rate two lathes a month!

Once again the General Motors Corporation came to the rescue at the request of QMG 3. The parent corporation in the United States made 250 $7\frac{1}{2}$-inch lathes available at once, meeting all immediate requirements of the Corps. As a direct result, no RASC unit went overseas without having the workshop capacity to maintain its fleet of vehicles.

Welding together Men and Materials

All this planning and all these technical labours could be of no avail, however, if the people into whose hands the equipment and plant was put proved unworthy of the confidence placed in them. Mention has already been made of the recruitment, training and preparation for active service of officers and men of the Corps. As far as the transport side was concerned, it is no exaggeration to say that our successes in the field were due as much to the far-sighted policy initiated when the training of the Corps was put under the General Staff, and when Colonel Cameron's vision of an operational RASC in all formations in peacetime was realized, as to the devoted work of those who laid the plans for the provision of the material and for the framework of mechanical maintenance. It was the integration of these two aspects of planning, carried out by officers trained equally as regimental soldiers and as transport operators and maintainers, that built up the whole edifice of RASC transport. Individual training, company training, divisional training, manœuvres, technical courses and war courses, already referred to, all played a vital part. Nor must we lose sight of the horse transport side, which was kept in being by those with vision enough to foresee the problems of mountain and jungle warfare which might confront us and which might severely strain, if not completely overcome, the best of mechanized units. The growth of pack transport operated by both the RASC and the RIASC, was only accomplished by the retention against considerable opposition (mainly from the Treasury) of one animal transport company in the RASC Training Centre.

Allied to the transport branch, too, was the War Department Fleet, operated by civilian masters and crews under RASC control. The story of the War Department Fleet and of the RASC manned motor boat and water transport companies, as well as that of the pack transport companies, is told in greater detail in later chapters.

In this summary of RASC transport between the two world wars, enough, it is hoped, has been written to show that, for the Corps at least, the years 1919 to 1939 were not wasted ones. Those at that time who strove to overcome obstacles and difficulties in their endeavour to improve the body of the Corps had their reward when they saw in 1939 how smooth was the transition from a peace to a war footing, and how sound the organization was under active service conditions.

SUPPLIES

The Position after the First World War

When the First World War ended, the RASC had the satisfaction of knowing that the slogan of 'The best fed army in the world' was substantially true. To have supplied an army of several million men was a considerable achievement. But there was not the same acute shortage of food which existed between 1939 and 1945, and the rations which were provided in the first war, although consisting of simple fare were adequate. The armies of those days moved comparatively slowly, so that it was rarely that the daily ration for man or horse failed to arrive. When it did not arrive, the soldier was content to fall back on the unit's reserve of 'hard' fare, which he accepted without demur. The food provided was plentiful, perhaps too much so, so that stories of trenches being 'paved' with boxes of rations were not unfounded.

Of course there were 'grouses' and grumbles about too much plum and apple jam, and jokes made about the service biscuit by the divisional concert party were always sure to draw a ready laugh. But the general feeling of the Army was probably more faithfully expressed by *Punch* in a cartoon picturing two soldiers eating their ration under the caption *'Sinews of War'*—*'Private Atkins, "For what we have received and are going to receive, here's to the ASC".'*

The RASC organization which had been employed on supplies for maintaining the armies in the First World War was a small and simple one. Barely one tenth of the Corps were engaged on supply duties, and the field units consisted of a relatively small number of large depots at the base and on the lines of communication which held the main reserves. Train loads of food (pack trains) were forwarded from these depots daily to railheads which were situated in the rear of the battle zone. The supplies for each division were then collected by divisional supply columns, which were mechanized, and carried forward to refilling points, where the food was taken over for the last stage of its journey by the companies of the horsed divisional trains. The bigger and more technical task of procuring supplies and provisioning the theatres of war fell mainly on the War Office and the general headquarters overseas, although local resources were drawn upon as far as possible, especially for fresh vegetables and hay.

The effects of Retrenchment

The apparent ease with which the Army had been supplied had an unfortunate effect on the RASC after the war, as it was decided that it was unnecessary to maintain supply units in peacetime comparable to those used in war and, on the grounds of better management of messing and of economy, the Army at home was to procure most of its food by purchasing it from the new canteen (NACB, later renamed NAAFI) organization with a cash allowance provided for the purpose. Only a few staple items such as meat and bread were to continue to be provided by the RASC, and the Corps were left with only a few supply depots at home. At small stations these commodities were delivered direct to units' cookhouses by contractors. True the RASC were to continue to feed the army abroad, but as most of the forces were stationed in India, where supplies were an IASC responsibility, there was little opportunity for any practical training in supply work at overseas stations. The few supply officers and men allowed for in the peace establishments had little to do beyond acting as accountants—for a few commodities which they never saw or 'handled'. Thus in the 1920's the RASC were left with neither a nucleus of units on which to build if war came nor any physical stocks of food to meet an emergency. The lack of supply units for training and as a nucleus for an expeditionary force nearly caused disastrous effects in France in 1939. The best that could be done between the wars was to give special prominence to the theoretical examination of war supply organization in the war courses which were held at the RASC Training Centre from 1928 onwards.

But although the RASC were divested of practically all responsibility for supplying the Army at home in peacetime, the DST was still charged with responsibility for the inspection of messing and, theoretically, messing accounts, although the latter were in fact more the concern of the local auditor's department. In practice the good management of messing depended not on the DST, but on commanding officers and on the interest displayed by unit messing officers. The officers commanding units had to find cooks as best they could from within their own ranks. The 'cook' was, however, regarded as a trained soldier rather than a craftsman and had to be prepared to take his place in the ranks at any time. He was, therefore, not graded as a tradesman or paid as such, although the officer

Supply Dropping

Diamond T
in the
Desert

commanding the unit was allowed to compensate him with a small sum from any funds which accrued from the sale of cookhouse refuse. Usually the potential cook, often detailed for the task on the grounds, 'he's only fit for the cookhouse, sir', had to be trained in the unit. There was a small Army School of Cookery at home for which the DST was made responsible, but the number that could be trained there was limited, and it is noteworthy that units were expected to contribute to the cost of training. No cooks were officially allowed on the establishment for officers' or sergeants' messes, although courses for officers' cooks were held at the school.

Messing Reforms

The supply branch at the War Office, then called QMG 6, sensed that all was not well with either the systems of messing or the provision of trained cooks, but in the absence of any collective representation from the headquarters of commands, the branch was prevented from seeking their official opinion, as it was against financial policy to 'invite criticism'. It was a case of 'letting sleeping dogs lie'. QMG 6 were, however, not content with the situation and took the opportunity of sending their Inspector of Catering, who was the only one for the whole Army, on an extended tour of the principal home and Middle East stations. He was specially briefed to collect detailed information at first hand on specific points on which a case could be built to review both questions of messing and cooks. The Inspector, Captain R. G. Leggatt, was a retired officer of the RAMC re-employed at a small salary, which was indicative of the lack of importance attributed to his duties. He performed his task thoroughly, and his reports, which were supported by extensive statistics, revealed a sorry situation. There was ample evidence that many units were being forced to subsidize their messing from unit funds, and some from small sums paid in voluntarily by the men to maintain the desired standard. Even so the soldiers' last meal of the day, and a not very substantial one, was served at about five o'clock in the evening. Small units found it especially difficult to make both (messing) ends meet. Most of the 'cooks' employed were only partly trained. They had no incentive, and many worked for as much as 70 hours a week. The report included a host of other points which invited attention, and an analysis of the rates and conditions of the ration allowance issued to those living out of barracks showed that this question also required review.

The officers at QMG 6 who had to deal with the matter and were directly responsible for preparing the cases for the reforms which followed were Major R. T. Snowden-Smith (a future DST) and Major T. W. Richardson (a future IRASC), both of whom had, among other attributes, a special flair for anything which was likely to improve the soldier's lot. Their efforts were duly rewarded, as with the help of the new policy which was followed after 1930 to make army life more attractive, financial agreement was obtained, after protracted negotiations, to provide a fourth supper meal in the daily diet, to the grant of extra messing allowances to small units, and to a revision of the methods of assessing individuals' ration allowances. The introduction of a 'supper meal' was aptly recorded in *Punch* by the portrayal of the then Secretary of State (Mr. Duff Cooper) 'angling for his supper'.

The improvements which were made in the training and status of cooks and their pay and conditions of service followed gradually and are described separately at the end of this section.

War Preparations

When the Government decided in 1934 that the nation would have to begin to rearm, QMG 6, as the branch at the War Office which was responsible for both food and petrol supply, had to lay the foundations of their arrangements on what was almost virgin soil. The existing field service ration scale was out of date; the productive capacity of the food manufacturing industry to produce the large stocks which would be needed for a field force was untested, and there was little storage space available for holding reserves.

The usual practice of expanding the peace organization, to produce the units required for a field force, could not be followed, as the few supply units which existed at home were units in name only, and the reserve of trained officers and men which could be drawn on on mobilization was known to be quite inadequate.

The creation of a petroleum supply organization meant breaking completely fresh ground, as there was not even a peace nucleus on which to build or any settled policy regarding the requirements of the forces to be supplied or the methods which should be adopted for distribution in a theatre of war. Any petrol wanted by the Army in peacetime was provided by civil contract, and when the question of supply in the field had been considered a few years before the order to rearm, there was an open difference of opinion on whether distribution should be by special bulk tanker or by utilizing a small container.

Nearly all the preparatory measures to be taken to provide food and petrol if war came involved fairly heavy expenditure, and before any plan was accepted it was necessary to get the agreement of the financial departments in the War Office, and, when that was obtained, the projects had to receive Treasury sanction.

The latter process was hastened by the institution of a Treasury Inter-Service Committee, known as TISC, which allowed of each project being discussed 'round a table' and decisions given, or deferred, on the spot. But even when the Treasury agreed to a project, the executive action which had to follow was again subject to the scrutiny of the War Office financial branches. The procedure often resulted in the military branches having to devote what appeared to them to be an undue proportion of time and energy on matters of financial detail at a time when their staff was very small and rather overworked and when they had many other military responsibilities to perform. The general effect was, therefore, to increase the concern of the military branch that plans might not be completed in time, that supply to the field force might be jeopardized, and also, perhaps less important, that the good name of their service might be impugned.

The first step taken by QMG 6 in connection with food supply was to redesign the field service ration which, through being inoperative for so many years, was outmoded in relation to changes in social outlook and food manufacturing technique since the end of the first war. A new scale which was more in keeping with modern nutritional practices was prepared and it included a complete range of tinned or preserved foods to replace the old 'hard fare' which used to be issued when fresh food could not be distributed.

An opportunity to test the new scale came soon afterwards when it was agreed that the small force which was to take part in the Saar plebiscite should be provided with it. For once there were no financial demurs, as any additional costs incurred were not to fall on the Army Vote.

The test was so successful that the new ration was accepted as the basic active service scale of the future, but the difficulty of obtaining the components of the ration in a reasonable time made it clear that considerable stocks would have to be held in peacetime if the maintenance of a field force of any size were to be assured. But there was a general feeling at that time that food was abundant and that stocks for the forces which would have to take the field could be obtained easily when war came. Indeed, when the Committee of Imperial Defence began to examine national food defence measures, the emphasis was laid on price control and the avoidance of inflation rather than on stockpiling as, in the Admiralty's view, there would be no serious interference with our imports. The apparent abundance of food was reflected in its cheapness. Before the war the War Office could provide the best quality imported meat for $4\frac{1}{2}d.$ a lb, and the average price of bread was a $1d.$ a lb.

However, QMG 6 pressed their case with the General Staff, who recognized the importance of holding a reserve and, with their support, authority was received to spend £250,000 on purchasing a 30 days' reserve for 170,000 men. From a practical point of view, 30 days' reserve was insufficient for maintaining the force and for providing a reserve overseas, so that the money was devoted to buying approximately 120 days' supply of those commodities which took time to produce, reliance being placed on the ability to obtain foodstuffs in everyday use (such as flour and frozen meat) when war became imminent. The purchase of the reserve was to be spread over two years and was bound up with an intricate plan of turnover (i.e. eating down and replacing stocks when the commodities neared the end of their useful life). There were, however, many departmental delays, and the Munich crisis came before the first half of the programme could be speeded up to schedule.

The reliance which was to be placed on obtaining staple commodities at the last moment was influenced by the knowledge that the embryo Ministry of Food, the Food Defence Plans Department of the Board of Trade, had undertaken to meet demands at once and without the delays which seemed to be so inseparable from normal contract procedure.

This arrangement of relying on the future Ministry of Food to be the suppliers of provisions broke fresh ground for the Armed Forces. It resulted from a lead given by the War Office in the establishment of an Inter-Service Committee to work with the Defence Plans Department to co-ordinate the supply of military with civil requirements. The department for their part responded by asking that a Services Liaison Officer should be appointed to join them. The appointment was filled by Colonel J. H. Morris, late RASC, who remained as head of the Services Supplies Branch of the Ministry of Food throughout the war. There could have been no better choice, as he fulfilled his dual function of being a member of the Ministry and the mouthpiece of the services in an admirable fashion.

As the future Ministry of Food only planned to provide staple commodities, planning for the production of commodities which had to be specially manufactured to service specifications remained a direct War Office responsibility. But here again the Defence Plans Department assisted in the investigation of productive capacity and in undertaking to arrange for the supply of the staple raw food which would be needed for fulfilling service contracts. Dormant contracts (i.e. contracts which only became effective if war occurred) were then concluded by the Services with most of the principal industries of the food manufacturing trade.

By early 1939 the triple plans of purchasing of reserves, perfecting detailed plans for the supply of Ministry of Food commodities, and the conclusion of dormant contracts were well in hand. The arrangements were primarily intended to ensure the maintenance of the field force, but they also covered the supply of the few commodities which the RASC were at that time responsible for providing for the Home Army.

In QMG 6's view the standing arrangements for feeding the Army at home in war, which were laid down in *Mobilization Regulations*, were imperfect and quite unsuited to the conditions which might prevail at home. Put simply, the standing instruction was that 'the peace system of messing would continue'.

To QMG 6 it seemed evident that if these islands were subject to enemy air attack, as was generally expected, there was bound to be some dislocation of the normal civil organization for distribution which implied the need for reserves at the main military centres. They knew it was highly probable that rationing would have to be introduced, and that this implied the need for official control over units' purchases, and it was also common knowledge that to operate the peacetime cash system called for some skill even on the part of trained messing officers. Unless well trained messing officers could be provided for the hundreds of units to be embodied, there was every risk of units' messing accounts soon falling into debt. QMG 6 emphasized strongly that standard diets should be issued and charged up to units at a fixed sum per head, and that a chain of RASC supply depots and complementary NAAFI stores should be set up in each command. They also urged that specific reserves of all the principal commodities required for the standard diet(s) should be held in case of any dislocation of normal means of distribution.

The short experience gained from the partial mobilization of the Air Defence of Great Britain organization at the time of the Munich crisis proved that it was vital to all anti-aircraft formations to have their own RASC supply and transport organization which could undertake to 'draw' the commodities provided by the RASC and NAAFI on a standard basis. But even so, the proposal that a standard scale at a fixed sum per head should be issued to all units on mobilization was met with vigorous opposition. This was based solely on financial grounds and embraced many questions, varying from NAAFI's legal status and its charter to the matter of rebate, much of which accrued from purchases made for the official messing of a unit. It is therefore of interest to record that barely a year later all these 'arguments' proved, on the threat of invasion, to be illusory and were swept away, and that the new system of messing introduced after Dunkirk still persists to-day. Failure to adopt QMG 6's suggestions before the war resulted in hundreds of units getting into official messing debt—and such debts could never be unravelled. The plea for the creation of supply depots before war was declared was, however, met, and nearly 40 were set up in time. Authority was also granted to procure three days' reserves of food to be held in them—but only of the few commodities (meat, biscuits, tea, sugar and salt) which were a RASC responsibility at that time. However, it was a case of something being better than nothing, and there were firm arrangements with the embryo Ministry of Food that seven days' fresh meat, flour and sugar would be delivered in given quantities to each of the 40 depots on the word being given.

The plans for providing reserves for the field force went hand in hand with the provision of more storage room and facilities for making large scale shipments of food overseas.

In 1936 the War Office had only one large supply reserve depot—situated in an unwanted cattle market at Deptford, on the Thames. The site was highly vulnerable to air attack and fire risk, and space was so limited that it was impossible to expand the activities there. A project for a second depot was prepared with the agreement of the General Staff.

The site selected was at Barry docks which, apart from having good railway and supply facilities, was expected to be just outside the range of enemy aircraft as their potentialities were known then. The greatest care was taken that this depot should be a perfect one for its purpose, and it was so planned as to provide for a maximum dispersion of stocks and at the same time every facility for the quick handling of large tonnages. Although rearmament was in full swing, it was no mean feat on the part of Colonel R. T. Snowden-Smith, by that time the ADST, QMG 6, to steer through what was a million-pound project. No. 2 SRD remains a memorial to his foresight.

Although the depot was still being built at the time of the Munich crisis, the urgent need for evacuating a portion of the small reserves held at Deptford, which were then beginning to flow in from the food industry, led to a hasty decision to transfer part of the Deptford stock to Barry. It is an interesting sidelight on the financial outlook that within a few hours of the return of Mr Chamberlain and the (sic) end of the crisis, a demand was made that if any trains were being loaded at Deptford they must be unloaded at once, as the cost of transport to Wales was now unnecessary.

A further preparatory measure was taken by QMG 6 by the introduction of a new organization for controlling supply reserve depots, for undertaking the administration of contracts, and for arranging all the details for shipments overseas—work which had hitherto been done partly at the War Office and partly at No. 1 SRD. This new office was created with a modest staff of one colonel and one captain, and it was later named the Chief Provision Office (Food Supplies). It was a wise move, as later in the war there were 15 supply reserve depots, and it was essential to have a central organization for control.

When war came QMG's plans had matured well except for one feature, the provision of sufficient trained officers and men—but this unfortunately was beyond their control.

Development of Catering

The investigation made by Captain Leggatt into the Army's messing and catering arrangements was followed by an inquiry by QMG 6 into the general messing arrangements in the Royal Navy and the RAF. The inquiry showed that the arrangements in the other two Services were superior to those in the Army. The civil catering industry was also consulted about supervision, management and equipment, and it was evident that the Army's outlook on such matters fell far short of the standards required. Sufficient data had been collected by 1936 to prepare such a strong case for a review of the Army's catering arrangements that it was agreed that an official War Office committee should be appointed to examine the questions of the provision of cooks, their training, pay and conditions of service and certain other aspects of catering.

The verdict of the committee was that a drastic revision of the Army's outlook on messing and catering was urgently needed. They maintained that there was a pressing need for providing skilled advice on catering in each command, and for the early modernization of cooking equipment and arrangements for the service of meals. They advocated more comprehensive training and enlargement of the School of Cookery, and the abolition of the sums paid by units towards training expenses was advocated. They considered that the establishment of cooks in each unit should be increased in order to reduce the working hours, which were in some cases shown to be no less than 70 a week, and that the more menial tasks should be performed (in peace) by civilian dining hall orderlies. The length of initial training courses should be nearly doubled so as to bring them into line with those of the sister services, and trained cooks should be officially allowed for officers' and sergeants' messes, which had not been the case hitherto.

The recommendations for allowing better continuity of employment and improved prospects and pay and promotion did not go so far as QMG 6 had hoped. Unfortunately the majority opinion of the committee was that the formation of a special corps of cooks was not warranted on the ground of the lack of flexibility to meet the varying requirements of units, and of the sudden calls, difficulties in drafting and posting, and the technical overheads and charges which must accompany the establishment of a new corps. The committee were also unable to recommend that cooks should be even regarded as regimental tradesmen.

Better rates of additional pay were to be recommended, however, and for the first time, there was a framework for promotion which would allow a cook to reach a higher rank than sergeant and ultimately commissioned rank as a messing inspector. The report was, however, accompanied by a financial minority opinion aimed at reducing the scope of the recommendations made.

Naturally the findings of the committee required some study by the many authorities who would be concerned by their recommendations. It was not long before the question of improved catering became linked with the view, which was being strongly pressed home by the then Secretary of State, that the status of the Army and the soldier should be radically improved.

In 1938, therefore, Sir Isidore Salmon was invited to become Honorary Catering Adviser to the Army, and within a few days of his official acceptance he was hard at work exploring every aspect of the messing position of the Army. No better choice could have been made, for not only was Sir Isidore the titular head of the largest catering organization in the country, but he was well versed in the ways of public life and had given frequent service on many parliamentary committees.

By June, 1938, Sir Isidore Salmon had completed his first survey, which showed that although the recommendations of the committee of 1937 had gone some way towards the improvements required, the committee had failed to realize that a cook should be a highly skilled craftsman and that the Army was not in a position to provide the special type of training to produce catering advisers. He emphasized that the direct connection between the standards aimed at under peace conditions and the more difficult conditions of active service had been overlooked, and that the greater the skill of the cook in peacetime, the greater would be the general state of efficiency and well-being of the soldier in the field.

The general scope of Sir Isidore Salmon's recommendations was accepted. Although the Army Catering Corps was not formed until three years later, a great deal was done in the intervening period. Expert catering advisers were brought in from the civil catering industry, the first being Colonel R. A. Byford. Cooking equipment was modernized, and work on building a new School of Cookery, planned on the most modern lines, began in August, 1939. Courses of training at the existing school were expanded and reorganized, and a new interest was created in the whole of that important sphere—the soldiers' messing.

PETROLEUM

Provision of Fuel and Lubricants in the First World War

During the First World War the RASC had no special organization for petrol supply. Nor did wartime experiences indicate that one was required, as it was found that petrol, oils and lubricants, now commonly referred to in the Army as POL, could be easily handled and distributed through the normal food supply organization. POL supply had not been a big task. Only about 125,000 mechanical vehicles of all kinds had to be provided with fuel, and the consumption of aviation spirit, for which the Corps was also responsible, did not exceed $1\frac{1}{2}$ million gallons a month in the peak period in 1918.

Supplies of petrol were obtained either by contract or through the agency of the oil industry, which held the stocks in bulk and produced filled containers with their own commercial facilities or quasi-military organizations, which were established especially to meet war needs. After the war, POL remained, therefore, an administrative question of no particular significance and no special courses of training in either supply or petroleum technology were considered necessary.

Mechanization calls for New Methods

The gradual spread of mechanization in the Army in the early twenties began to change this outlook slowly. The visionaries of those days foresaw the replacement of the marching army by small forces composed entirely of armoured and unarmoured vehicles moving freely over great distances, maintained by an equally mobile administrative organization and dependent for their mobility on petrol. Early exercises which were held, on paper, to study the organization and potentialities of armoured forces indicated that vastly greater quantities of petrol would be required than anything which had been known in the First World War. It seemed that the replenishment of petrol might have to be effected at any time of day or night if momentum were to be maintained, and under certain conditions supplies might have to be delivered into vehicle tanks during short lulls in the heat of battle. These trends of thought began to throw doubts on the adequacy of the previously accepted means of refuelling by means of small cans. Even if cans still proved to be the best means of replenishment, the re-collection and refilling of the huge number which would be required also seemed to present new problems.

Probing the question

In 1928 exercises specially designed to examine petrol and lubricant supply were held for the first time at the RASC Training College. These exercises went far towards placing the many new problems which arose from mechanization in a better perspective. They showed that the question was not only a quantitative one, or one of methods of distribution and storing in bulk, but also was one of the means of providing and protecting the stocks which would have to be held in every potential theatre of war.

Although the policy of mechanization was one which was followed cautiously in the first decade between the wars, the need for rearmament brought about the decision to start mechanizing the whole of the transport of the Army. The Corps itself had already been placed on a fully mechanized basis in 1926. The decision to rearm was accompanied by fairly firm information on the pattern of the force which would be required for an expeditionary force overseas in the event of war. This field force, as it was known then, was to be composed of infantry divisions, apart from a single tank brigade. Preliminary calculations showed that the quantity of petrol required for its transport, which was to be wholly mechanized, would be extremely large, and, if the can continued to be used for distribution, would involve the provision of a prodigious number of containers.

This first positive requirement provided the supply branch at the War Office with firm data to open the question of a plan for supply and to seek a defined policy on methods of distribution. Here it should be mentioned that a War Office committee had been set up a few years before to examine petrol and lubricant supply in the field, but had not produced any effective solution.

Oil supply was, of course, a national problem, and a special sub-committee of the Committee of Imperial Defence, the Oil Board, was charged with the responsibility of ensuring that national defence requirements would be met in the event of war. They had to cover a wide field. Their deliberations embraced the whole question of supply and maintenance of strategic reserves and the general plans for meeting the requirements of the three services.

It was the duty of the service representatives to put forward their detailed requirements to the Board, and to indicate the means which they considered would have to be adopted to meet their needs.

The RASC have always accepted that administrative preparedness for war must be based on making the best use of existing commercial facilities. With this in mind, the DST had already instituted unofficial enquiries into the whole question of the existing and future trends of supply and distribution of oil in commercial life.

The range of petroleum products required by the Army was increasing. There was already a growing use of diesel oil which would undoubtedly increase as the diesel engine became perfected for use in small MT vehicles. A second, high octane, spirit was by this time required for certain fighting vehicles and even 'motor spirit', the type used for normal commercial vehicles, did not imply a single standard, particularly on the Continent where the low grade in general use was not thought to be suited to British built engines, under service conditions. This fact seemed to indicate that, if a war was to be fought on the Continent, all supplies required would have to be specially shipped from the United Kingdom in the initial phase.

The Plan takes shape—carriage in Bulk or in Cans?

The Director saw that it was essential to seek independent expert advice on an official basis and then to seek agreement within the War Office on the methods to be adopted for storage and distribution.

Time was pressing, as preparations were to be completed by 1939. It was then 1935, and the news that an invitation had been extended by the Quartermaster General, and accepted by Mr. William Fraser,* then deputy chairman of the Anglo-Iranian Oil Company, to act as honorary adviser to the War Office, was received with great relief by the Directorate of Supplies and Transport. From then plans were to materialize rapidly, and the liaison with the oil industry began to take shape. There were, of course, many important matters of policy to be settled, such as the location and protection of reserves, particularly as all commercial installations were highly vulnerable to air attack and usually situated at or close to highly populated or congested areas. But the first thing to be settled was the method to be employed for distribution.

There were at the time two schools of thought within the War Office, the 'can' school and those who considered that special bulk carrying road vehicles should be provided which could rapidly refill several vehicles at the same time. The use of bulk vehicles would mean the provision of a fleet of vehicles which were not in general commercial use. No doubt bulk tankers could be adapted for military needs, but their use implied the possibility of bringing bulk supplies for replenishing the tankers up to near the forward areas, which in turn hinged on the existence of rail tankers and generally restricted the system to the more developed countries of the world.

The War Office committee which had considered the general question some years before was resuscitated, and after considerable briefing and perhaps unofficial 'steering', the can school of thought won the day. Immediate steps were then taken to form a plan for supply and to relate other cognate questions to it.

Provision of Reserve Stocks and of Containers

The deliberations of the Oil Board on military requirements showed that, whereas the normal stocks held in the United Kingdom were sufficient to meet day to day civil needs, they were not enough to provide for the strategic reserves for the services, which ran into many hundreds of thousands of tons. It was decided that considerable additional bulk storage would have to be constructed for both the Army and RAF, the cost being borne by the two services votes. In the first place, this extra storage was to be built with adequate spacing to minimize the effect of air attack and with sufficient earth

* Sir William Fraser, C.B.E.

bunding to localize the effect of any spillage from tanks which might be damaged through enemy action. At a later stage fully protected storage room was to be constructed. To reduce the cost of overheads and the time required for new construction, it was agreed that this additional strategic storage should be sited at or near existing installations and, in Great Britain, should be at points close to ports or to the can filling plants. Requirements in the Middle East and other potential areas of operations were also considered and will be referred to later.

The provision of extra storage was, of course, mainly a matter of money, material and labour, but the production of containers and the means of filling them raised a very different question. Even if war did not occur, the extra storage provided would have some commercial value, but the provision of cans in the numbers required was a different matter, as the can was rapidly dying out of commercial use. In Europe and in the more populated centres of the East, the kerbside pump was the accepted means of distribution to the civilian customer, although in the Middle East the 4-gallon light metal tin (the 'flimsy') was still in general use, particularly for the large trade in kerosene—still the standard fuel in countries where wood and coal were scarce or expensive. An unofficial census for the War Office showed that the number of 2-gallon cans, the standard container in the United Kingdom, was only a fraction of the number needed, and productive capacity was limited. To make good the deficiency, a huge programme of stockpiling would have to be started. In any case the little 2-gallon can was costly, it was made only in the Midlands, and would have to be transported for storage to the main installations for filling before shipment overseas. In France the standard container was the *bidon*, which was thought to be difficult to handle and especially to store. The only other alternative commercial containers in existence were the heavy and costly 40-gallon barrels which were also much in demand for other purposes than the carrying of spirit.

The adoption of the 4-gallon 'flimsy'

It was decided that the standard container to be adopted for service would be the light ('flimsy') 4-gallon tin. It was hoped that risk of leakage by damage in shipment or by rough handling would be reduced by clothing the tins in wooden shooks, the tins being boxed two to a case. The plan only involved the provision of plant for tin-making, and filling, and securing supplies of tin-plate. The type of plant required was obtainable from the United States, and was already in use in the Middle and Far East. The plan avoided any question of stockpiling cans in peacetime, and the capital expenditure was small compared to the rather futile expenditure which would arise in the same period if the 2-gallon or other form of strong returnable container had been adopted.

The use of the 4-gallon tins also seemed to meet the difficulty of having to ship petrol in quantity to a field force and making the force independent of any local facilities which might be put out of action from the outset in consequence of enemy air attacks or sabotage.

Four plants were to be purchased and erected on an agency basis by the Shell and Anglo-Iranian Oil Companies. Two plants, to be located at Llandarcy and Avonmouth (considered to be safe areas at the time) were allocated to the Army and two, at Stanlow and Ardrossan, to the RAF, on the understanding that the capacity for production would be at the general disposal of both services if required. When the plant was ready, men were to be trained in the use of the plant for a short period each year, and the output was to be used during the normal Territorial Army training period in the summer. As soon as production started stoppages which are common to new plants occurred and it took some time to reach the full output, but the main objective of keeping the BEF supplied was attained.

As there must have been few items of equipment which were cursed so much as the 'flimsy', it is important that the reasons which led to the adoption of this form of container should be made clear. It was, of course, fully recognized that these tins were far from ideal, and even though they were packed in wooden boxes, they were inferior to the stout so-called returnable cans. However, it was the only practical method of producing and placing petrol in the quantity required at any point, so that it could be distributed easily and speedily in the circumstances which were foreseen at the time.

As will be seen later, the use of returnable cans was not entirely discounted, but even when the decision to adopt a returnable can as the normal means of distribution was made, it was recognized that the tin-making plants which were available both at home and later in Africa formed a useful reserve to make good any deficiencies in the number of returnables needed. Whether the decision to replace the flimsy by the newly found jerrican type was unduly deferred or not is a matter which perhaps can be judged by the reader from the information given in later chapters of this volume.

Reserve storage in the Middle East and Mediterranean

A survey of the position in the Middle East and other garrisons overseas showed that supply would have to be developed in various directions to meet war requirements. The situation in the Middle East, Malta and Gibraltar was examined at first hand by a party of representatives of the Army, RAF and the oil industry. Their recommendations led to the construction of new bulk storage installations in Egypt at Jebel Dave and Agrud and a new intake point on the Bitter Lake. By the end of the war, capacity in underground storage had been increased by no less than 175,000 tons. There is little doubt that the speedy action taken to put these recommendations into effect had a most important bearing on the subsequent operations which were to lead eventually to victory in that region.

Here it may be of interest to record that, at the request of the mobile force (the Mobile Division in Egypt), for some returnable cans which would withstand rough usage and could be easily refilled, a prototype was designed in the RASC Heavy Repair Shop at Feltham and 250,000 tins were despatched to the Middle East just before the war. The problems in Malta and Gibraltar were mainly ones of security of stocks from air attack. For reasons which are difficult to trace, action on recommendations for Malta seems to have been deferred, but in the case of Gibraltar recommendations were adopted, and well protected storage was duly provided.

A Reserve built in France

By early 1939, the ST Directorate at the War Office were able to look forward to the future of petrol supply with some confidence, as plans had been laid and made, and work on them was progressing as fast as possible. Although the requirements of the BEF were thought to be well insured, there was a possibility that the despatch of initial stocks might be interrupted temporarily by enemy submarine action in the English Channel.

As war appeared to be imminent, and in French military circles it was considered only a matter of time before the two armies would be fighting side by side, conversations took place with the French General Staff. It was agreed *inter alia* that a small stock of British motor spirit should be built up in France as soon as possible. This would have to be done without arousing the suspicions of potential enemy agents or exciting undue curiosity from local inhabitants. Any false step might have had serious consequences. British controlled oil interests in Paris were consulted in secrecy, and it was agreed that some 20,000 tons of spirit packed in 2-gallon cans, the only type available at the time, in unmarked but sealed cases would be 'imported' into France under the guise of a commercial transaction. They were to be stored at Donges in the area which was to be allotted to the British Army in the event of war. Details of the plan were carefully prepared and worked out by Mr. Norman Fuller,* assisted by Mr. A. K. Joseph,* of the Anglo-Iranian Oil Company.

* Both were to serve with the Corps: Col. A. K. Joseph, Col. N. B. Fuller.

The plan involved money, but it is of interest to record that the imminence of war led to financial sanction for the project being given in the time of 20 minutes. By August 1st the stock was safely housed in France, together with a complement of filling apparatus. The course of the war was fully to justify this last step.

The Planners

The onus of all planning and arrangements for supply fell on the same branch (QMG 6) at the War Office, which was staffed by three officers. Although the work connected with POL constituted a completely new and wide range of activity, no permanent increase in the numbers employed could be allowed. Permission was, however, given to employ one regimental officer, a captain (Captain D. H. Bond*), and later to obtain the loan of a Reserve officer from the oil industry to provide expert advice and liaison (Captain A. M. Macintosh†). Names are invidious perhaps, but it was these two officers who laid the foundation of the organization which developed upon a world wide scale before the war came to a close.

Thus when the war began the policy persisted that petrol should continue to be provided by the supply organization. There was not a single unit in the order of battle specifically allotted for petroleum supply, although each base supply depot had one section nominated for the storage of canned petrol, and each division and corps troops had transport companies allotted for the carriage of packed petroleum supplies. To QMG 6 it was only too evident that the complexities of supply were bound to lead to a separate organization for fuel and lubricants, and the nature of the units which would be required was already in their minds. But any attempt to advocate a separate organization would have been fruitless because of restrictions on manpower and the changes which would be needed in the administrative framework for maintenance. It only took a few weeks of war to show that such an organization would have to be set up, as speedily as possible, and a heavy call had to be made on the members of the oil industry to set it on its feet—a call to which there was a ready response.

* Brigadier D. H. Bond, C.B.E., M.V.O.
† Colonel A. M. Macintosh, O.B.E., M.C.

CHAPTER II

THE BRITISH EXPEDITIONARY FORCE, 1939/1940

THIS story of the RASC with the BEF is necessarily only a brief record of the work of the few Regular units which could be made available when war broke out, of the RASC of the first divisions of the Territorial Army to take the field, and of the many thousands of individuals, some of whom had no previous military experience, who joined the Corps as soon as war was declared.

It cannot be claimed that the campaign was a successful one in the accepted meaning of the term, or that the RASC's particular task of maintaining the Army with food, petroleum and ammunition went true to expectations. Administrative complications arose within the first few days of landing which nearly led to a breakdown in supply and, when the battle opened nearly nine months later, the essential functions of the Corps were almost negatived by the BEF being cut off from its main bases within 11 days. For the 14 days which followed until the final withdrawal from Dunkirk the RASC could only do its best.

Their record shows how difficulties, so inseparable from war, were surmounted as they arose and how the Corps lived up to their motto, *Nil Sine Labore*.

Pre-war Preparations

Although the need for rearmament was recognized some years before the war, the Government's policy, which had to be largely dictated by economic facts, was, so far as the Army was concerned, one of limited liability—a liability for ensuring home defence and the security of our overseas possessions. The national contribution to the defence of Europe was to rely on a strong navy and powerful air force. If a force had to be placed on the continent of Europe for direct assistance in the defence of France it would have to be a token one.

Administrative planning for the despatch of a field force to the Continent was limited to the requirements of a force of two divisions only. It was not until the end of April, 1939, that it was decided to increase the strength to two corps of four divisions* in all, a

* The 1st, 2nd, 3rd and 4th organized in two corps, I and II.

decision which was preceded by the announcement that the Territorial Army was to be doubled and national service introduced at once. These last minute decisions gave little time to provide the increased number of trained officers and men who would be wanted.

The Plan

The strategical plan which was agreed by the British and French Staffs was a defensive one; French territory was to be held inviolable while the Allies built up their military resources. It was the only feasible plan and seemed to have every chance of achieving its object, as the main frontier of France contiguous to Germany and Luxembourg was covered by the defences which were thought to be impregnable, the Maginot line. Westwards, from about Sedan to the sea, neutral Belgium lay between the French frontier and the potential enemy. The role allotted to the BEF was to take its place with the French armies which were to be disposed along the frontier with Belgium.

If the strategical role of the BEF was militarily simple the administrative plan was relatively complex. The nearest ports on the French coast and the shortest sea routes to the future battle zone were the Channel ports, but owing to the expected risks of air attack and the effects of air power, the choice of ports for landing the BEF and for establishing the bases fell upon those in Normandy and Brittany. Cherbourg and Brest were to serve as ports of entry for a northern base at Rennes, and St. Nazaire and Nantes were those selected for a southern base. Their choice meant that the everyday needs of the BEF would have to be carried forward by rail over a distance of up to 400 miles; but the apparent advantages of security from air attack outweighed every other consideration.

The administrative plan was a bold one, as it provided for nearly 170,000 men and their impedimenta, more than 20,000 vehicles and many thousands of tons of stores of all kinds being landed in France in a matter of three weeks.

Planning was a War Office responsibility which had to be done mostly by staff officers who had many other preoccupations. Few of these officers would see their plans put into effect, as they were destined either to remain at the War Office when war broke out, or to fill appointments not necessarily related to the work they had been doing as planners. The headquarters which would have to put the plan into effect, GHQ and the HQ of the L of C Area, did not exist in peacetime, but were to be 'formed on mobilization'.

RASC Preparations

The general war preparations of the RASC were well advanced when the decision was made to increase the size of the expeditionary force from two to four divisions. The 'impressment scheme', for procuring the vehicles wanted for the Army on mobilization, was ready to be brought into action, and detailed plans had been made for withdrawing all six-wheeled vehicles in service and refitting them for special purposes. The manufacture of reserves of spare parts and packing them ready for issue on mobilization was proceeding apace.

The arrangements for petrol supply were well in hand. Orders had been placed, in America, for four petrol tin-making and filling plants, and one factory was nearly ready for trial production. Considerable progress had likewise been made with amassing the large stocks of tinned and special foods which were required for the field service ration, and a second large (supply reserve) depot for storing reserves was nearing completion.

The one missing feature was the means of providing the additional number of trained officers and men who would be wanted, but this was not a problem peculiar to the RASC. It was the result of the policy followed since 1918 of 'no war for 10 years' which took no account of the fact that trained officers and men cannot be produced at short notice by merely increasing the official 'establishment' at the last moment.

The RASC for the BEF were to take the field for the first time as a completely mechanized Corps. Each division was to be provided with a CRASC headquarters and three transport companies, one for ammunition, one for petrol, spare blankets and anti-gas stores, and the third, which had two echelons of vehicles, for food. A similar organization was allowed for corps troops, and each corps was allotted two companies, designated by the old fashioned term 'park', for holding reserves of ammunition and petrol. Separate companies were provided for carrying the general needs of GHQ troops and non-divisional artillery, and five units were allotted for the carriage of casualties. Four companies were reserved for troop-carrying, and one for bridging material, and there were seven companies for general duties on the lines of communication. The standard equipment was the 3-ton lorry but two of the lines of communication companies were equipped with 6- and 10-ton vehicles. All the available six-wheeled vehicles held in peacetime were to be converted when war broke out into ambulances and workshop vehicles.

The 12 companies required for the four divisions were in existence when the war broke out, but only in cadre form; the remainder of the 50 companies on the order of battle had to be formed on mobilization from units which were normally engaged on routine station transport duties at home.

There were no counterparts in peacetime for the supply units required, so that all had to be formed anew on mobilization and manned with officers and men drawn from other types of RASC units. There was to be one base supply depot, field bakery and cold storage unit for each of the two bases. All the other supply units needed, such as small detail issue depots, railhead supply detachments and advanced depots, were to be found from a single supply personnel company. No special organization for storing or distributing petroleum was provided, as petrol, oils and lubricants were to be handled throughout by the (food) supply organization. It was an 'economy' organization designed to try and make good a lack of manpower and of properly trained men.

The greatest problem which had to be solved on mobilization was how to man the number of units required for the BEF and at the same time meet the calls for RASC officers for reinforcing overseas garrisons, for expanding the home training establishments and filling the numerous ST staff appointments which would be created when war came. There were not enough regulars to go around, and the experience of reserve officers who were liable to recall was one of the dim memories of war in 1918. The Territorial Army could not be drawn on as they were fully occupied by the sudden decision to double their number of divisions. The gaps had to be filled by officers who volunteered to join when war broke out and were registered under the Army Officers' Emergency Reserve Scheme. The result was that many 'square pegs' had to be fitted in, and a policy of posting the greater proportion of experienced officers to field units left the base and lines of communication at a considerable disadvantage. The shortage of officers and men who were trained in supply duties was even more acute owing to the lack of opportunity for practical training between the wars in the handling and issue of a ration in kind at home.

The Administrative Plan

The general arrangements for the move of the BEF to France were that most of the men of the force would embark at south coast ports and, after disembarking at Cherbourg, would go to an assembly area about 150 miles inland between Le Mans and Laval, which were about 50 miles apart. Transport vehicles and the mass of ammunition, food, petrol and other stores were to be directed to Brest, St. Nazaire and Nantes. Units' transport was to be collected from these ports by parties despatched for the purpose from the assembly area. Stores were to be sent on by rail to the sites which were selected for establishing the main base depots. When units had linked up with their transport, the two corps were to move forward some 300 miles to the north to concentrate in the region of Arras, their daily needs being sent forward by rail to convenient railheads in the proximity of the concentration area.

It was a plan which was dependent on the railway facilities in France being adequate, and on the labour available for handling and unloading the ships which were to arrive with clockwork regularity according to planned programmes. It also depended on the speed with which depot sites in France could be selected and organized to perform the dual act of taking in large stocks as they arrived from ports and at the same time issuing sufficient stocks to the smaller distribution depots which had to be set up on the long line of communication extending to the north.

The arrangements for providing food, in the initial period after landing, appeared to be well insured. All units had instructions to draw three days' landing rations from their place of mobilization for use while the supply service were landing their stocks and opening up detail issue depots. Special embarkation depots were established at each main home port to issue each unit with one day's emergency ration and to provide rations for the voyage if required, as ships were not equipped to feed the men while on board. In the event of any small parties finding themselves temporarily out of reach of a supply depot, authority was given to make agreements with local cafés for the supply of meals. Although men and stores were to be embarked in separate ships, the first ship destined for Cherbourg was to carry a small supply detachment and sufficient food for 200,000 men.

Bulk shipments of food, which were to follow, were to be matched with the numbers landed day by day plus an extra quantity in increasing proportions so as to build up the necessary reserves.

Somewhat similar arrangements were made for initial petrol supplies. As the tanks of all vehicles had to be emptied, because of Board of Trade regulations against fire risks, at the ports of embarkation in England, small amounts of petrol in tins were carried as deck cargo. The emptying and collection of petrol from tanks were among the duties of the embarkation supply depots.

Bulk shipment of filled tins followed in separate ships, the despatches being related to the number of vehicles which were shipped to France each day.

Mobilization

The order to mobilize was given on September 1st, two days before war was declared, and on September 4th Brigadier G. K. Archibald, the newly appointed DST for the BEF, left for France in company with the heads of other services and the first reconnaissance parties.

The business of mobilization went well on the whole, but in some cases commanding officers found that the mobilization schemes,

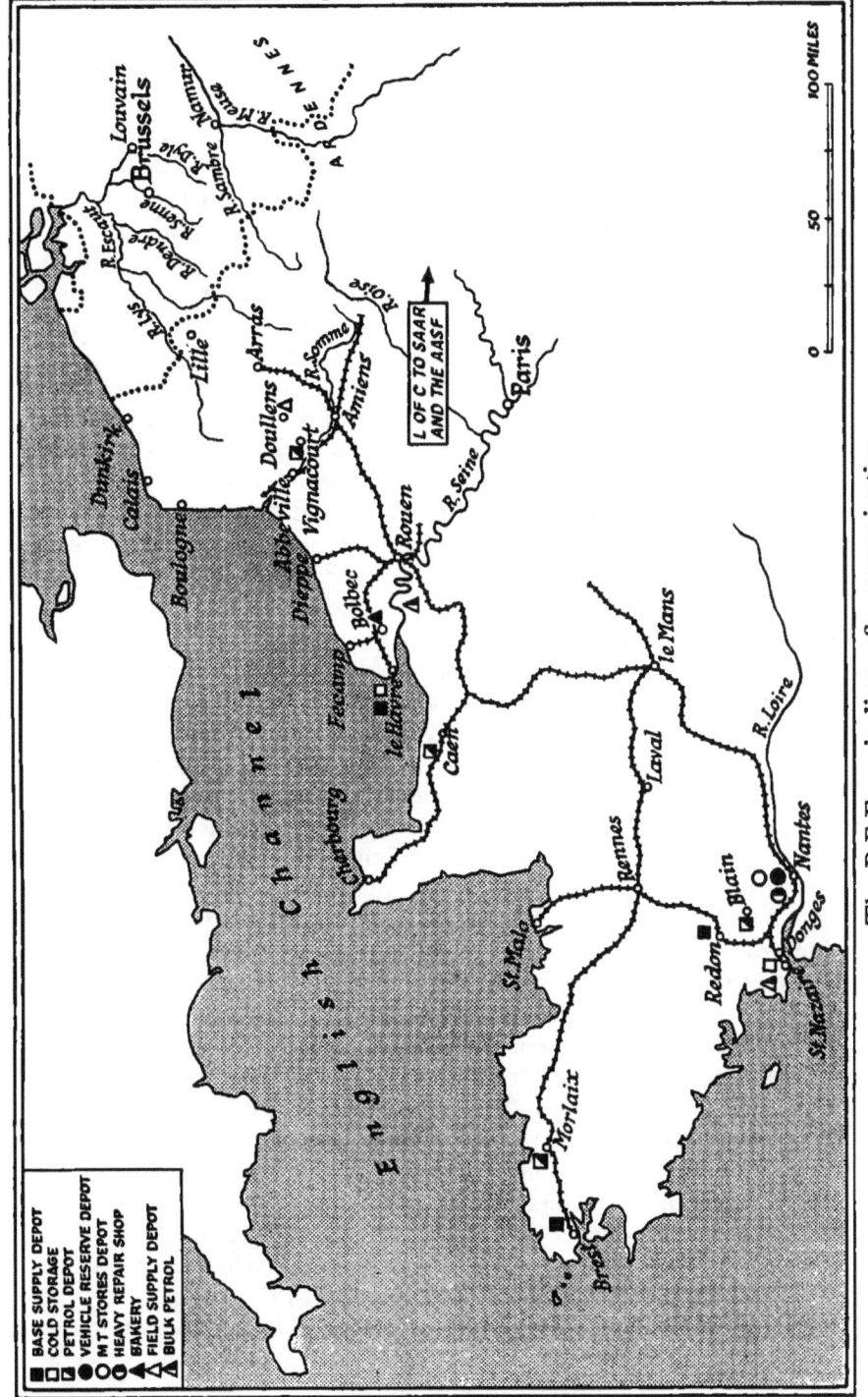

The B.E.F. main lines of communication

which had been prepared in peacetime, had to be scrapped and completely remodelled.

Officers, men and stores began to flow in to their appointed places and vehicles began to arrive from the four vehicle collecting centres which had been set up to receive, register, inspect, equip and repaint the thousands of vehicles which had been collected under the impressment scheme. These centres were key units, as much depended on the speed at which they worked. The vehicles were brought in to the centres by their civilian drivers, many of whom wished to take the opportunity of enlisting, thus creating an unexpected problem. All vehicles had to be passed fit for service and deficiencies in equipment made good, and the final act was to spray them with the standard service colour. The units worked at high pressure—so much so that an unwary visiting officer who left his private car while at lunch returned just in time to find it already repainted and about to be driven away with a departing convoy.

All units were ready to embark at the allotted times and all were in good heart, especially those which had the honour of receiving a short visit from his late Majesty King George VI before their departure.

The Landing in France

The first body of troops were due to arrive in France on September 10th, and the main flow to start on the 12th, so that the reconnaissance and advance parties were given little time to reconnoitre the tentative sites which had been selected for depots and other centres of activity in the administrative scheme. In many cases sites proved to be unsuitable or accommodation and transit facilities inadequate and the choice of alternative sites was found to be extremely limited. The headquarters of the L of C area, to which Colonel C. L. St. J. Tudor had been appointed as DDST, was established at Le Mans. From the outset the staff were handicapped by the wide dispersion of the base areas, imposed by the fear of air attack, and difficulty of communications. Distances to be covered were great, and transport was scarce. The French telephone system was unreliable, and its use restricted for security reasons. Countryside and language were unfamiliar to despatch riders. Unexpected conditions also arose at the ports. There was considerable difficulty in finding enough labour; and the port facilities provided by the French were, owing to some misunderstanding, inadequate, while the railway facilities also proved to fall below the expected standard. The immediate result was that delays began to occur in the turn-round of ships and there was considerable congestion at the docks.

The plans made at home for the shipment of balanced train loads of rations also went awry, as it transpired that consignments were considerably split up over different ships.

The arrangement whereby each unit was expected to be self sufficient for the first few days by bringing three days' landing rations with them was not fulfilled, as some units packed their rations in their transport, which they were not to see until some days after landing, and others ate part of them on the sea voyage on the grounds that the voyage ration was an 'untouchable' reserve. This combination of unfortunate circumstances nearly led to a crisis but no one starved, thanks to wholesale local purchases and the aid of the French Service d'Intendance, which provided food from their reserves; but this unfortunate miscarriage in plans caused considerable concern, and it took some weeks before the supply organization was working properly.

The War Office remained unaware of this situation until an urgent request was received from the Air Ministry for some rations to be flown at once to the Advanced Air Striking Force which, it was said, was living on the charity of the French. A hasty telephone call to the BEF confirmed that all was not well, and an ADST left the next day by air to investigate the position. He found that it was impossible to judge the real stock position or to relate the quantities which left the home depots with those which had actually arrived and been unloaded in France. Even where there was no physical lack of food, the inexperienced supply units found difficulty in handling the field service scale which, to provide variety, included a great choice of foods. There was no doubt that the force was living from hand to mouth.

Certain of these factors were or should have been within the control of the DST BEF, but many were not. Movement was not an RASC responsibility, and the organization for the control of movement had still to be built up into the efficient machine which it became later in the war.

The administrative plan as a whole was so shrouded in secrecy that, for example, the maintenance project for the force was not revealed to the DST at the War Office until after the disturbing news of the supply situation was received. When the project was examined it appeared from an ST aspect to be an unrealistic document. An equally striking example of the anxiety to preserve secrecy was the fact that the ST representatives who took part in a reconnaissance in France well before the war were not permitted to acquaint their own ST staff at the War Office of where they had been or what they had seen.

The arrangements for shipping RASC transport also seemed to be open to question and there were many delays before units could come into operation. In one instance the 220 vehicles of a company were split up by being loaded in 10 different ships. The first general transport company was not scheduled to land until several days after the force was arriving in some strength, and divisional ammunition and petrol companies were landed before supply companies. This led to the caustic comment by a very senior officer that 'he always liked his breakfast first before going out shooting'.

However these temporary setbacks did not prevent I and II Corps from moving forward from the assembly area and occupying their positions close to the Belgian frontier thus fulfilling our promise to the French that the BEF would be in position by October 12th.

It was evident, however, within the first few weeks after the BEF had landed in France that the original maintenance project would have to be completely revised. More administrative units were wanted to operate such extended lines of communication, and the number of administrative units provided for the maintenance of the Advanced Air Striking Force increased. Two new subsidiary lines of communication would have to be opened, one for the maintenance of a British brigade which was to be stationed in the French army sector of the Saar, and the other to Marseilles for the transit of men and material to the Mediterranean.

The general lack of storage and other accommodation would have to be made good by new construction, and the decision to start work on a new defence line along the frontier, on the sector held by the BEF, also meant that additional labour and vast quantities of materials would have to be provided. Extra transport would also be wanted for all these new commitments, for the carriage of material and for moving labourers from their camps to their place of work.

It had also to be remembered that the BEF would be reinforced from the end of the year by the arrival of Territorial divisions which were completing their training at home.

The original decision to maintain the force through the southern ports in Brittany and Normandy had also to be revised, as the Admiralty were emphatic that more ports should be opened to the north, to reduce the turn-round of ships plying between England and the base ports.

In consequence it was decided to open a new base in the area of Le Havre and Rouen and to take into use all the available ports as far north as Calais.

So far as the RASC were concerned, these decisions led to an immediate demand being made on the War Office for the extra supply and transport units which would be needed to keep pace with this considerable expansion of effort.

The Supply Organization

A request by the BEF for the temporary cessation of despatches of supplies from home ports in October gave the opportunity for a general 'stocktaking' of the position, and by the end of the month it was estimated that about 30 days' food for 250,000 men had been safely landed and stored, but the two base supply depots which had been sited at Redon and near Brest could barely keep pace with the inflow. A request for increased establishments and for a third depot, which was established at Le Havre, was met quickly, but few men in these new units had any practical knowledge or training for their task. All three sites which had been chosen for the base supply depots were really unsuited for the purpose, and it was decided to design and construct three new depots. Only one of these, near Abancourt, was partially completed when operations began in May the following year.

The original supply personnel company had been followed by a second company, but this also consisted almost entirely of untrained officers and men. A third field bakery was also asked for. Two bakeries were established north of the Seine at Bolbec, a third being split up over the L of C area. For reasons which are difficult to ascertain, the calculated output of the bakeries never seemed to be achieved, and as late as April, 1940, it was still necessary to have about 100,000 loaves a day baked in civil bakeries. It was planned to construct a new static bakery at Abancourt, with an output of 350,000 lb a day, and when operations began in May the machinery had arrived but had not been fully installed.

As the strength of the force increased it was found necessary to centralize arrangements for the procurement of fresh produce and coal which were required in considerable quantities, so as to prevent competitive buying and to co-ordinate arrangements with the French civil and military authorities. A Central Purchase Board was set up for the purpose. The headquarters of the board was established in Paris, with sections operating over the lines of communication which arranged for the collection and forwarding of vegetables to formations and the collection of coal in military transport direct from the mines.

Another central organization, the Supply Investigation Department, was introduced to assist in accounting for food and petrol and to devise methods of stock control. It did useful work in initiating methods of accounting and in helping the many inexperienced supply officers in their unaccustomed tasks.

Transport Organization

It is rare that an army in the field admits to having sufficient transport, but there is no doubt that the BEF were hard pressed to find enough to fulfil all the demands made on the RASC. Requests for more transport placed the War Office in the difficult position of having to rob Peter to pay Paul, as their resources were limited and their plans for raising more transport units were regulated by priorities laid down by the staff. They were also faced with the unexpected necessity of raising a number of companies for use at home. However, they met the urgent need for transport for carrying material for the new defence line by producing 'works companies' which later became the well known maid of all work, the tipper company, and answered the call for troop-carrying units for conveying labour to their daily place of work, by converting some Territorial load-carrying companies.

If the word 'phoney' could be used to describe the period between the landing of the BEF and the beginning of active operations the next year, it certainly did not apply to the task of the RASC transport in the force. All divisional and corps units when not under training were fully employed and the severe winter conditions and ice-bound roads made their task no easier.

The RASC had few new vehicles. Most of them had been obtained through the impressment scheme so that the RASC organization for maintenance was well tested. Although the original site selected for the Heavy Repair Shop, an old cattle cake factory, was by no means ideal, the unit was soon hard at work with its mobile equipment and it was not long in reaching a maximum output. An idea of the effort put out may be gained from the fact that the equipment provided was on a basis of 3 per cent wastage of 4,000 vehicles and that by early 1940 the number of vehicles to be maintained had risen to over 10,000. There were 21,000 vehicles in May, 1940, and as a temporary measure some of them which required overhaul were sent back to the newly introduced Ministry of Supply repair organization in England.

The unit which handled spare parts, the MT Stores Depot, was established about 15 miles from the Heavy Repair Shop, but as stores took as much as 10 days to reach the BEF, an advanced section was set up near Rouen. The MT Stores Depot kept pace with the 1,300 demands received each week which sometimes involved handling and packing some 4,000 different spare parts.

Replacements for vehicles which were beyond the repair capacity of MT companies were made by the Vehicle Reserve Depot, which spread its sub-parks between Amiens (Fleselles), the assembly area near Le Mans, and its permanent headquarters near Nantes.

By March, 1940, there were 104 RASC transport units in France, and it is to their credit that only 3.7 per cent of the RASC vehicles had to be evacuated to the base for repair and that two thirds of the heavy overhauls were effected in France.

The transport story of the so-called 'phoney' period would not be complete without some mention of the arrival of the RIASC animal transport companies, and later a British company drawn from that traditional source of muleteers, Cyprus. The arrival of the RIASC companies made history, as they were the first units of the Indian Army to take the field.

Petroleum

The plans made for providing the BEF with petrol in tins had worked, but it soon became obvious that a separate organization was required for handling petrol and other fuel oils and lubricants, and that more economical arrangements should be made by making use of existing bulk storage facilities in France—which, contrary to expectations, remained free from enemy air attack. For the first few weeks the main stocks for the force were stored in tins by the no. 5 sections of the two base supply depots which, covering a large area and having to be located well away from their parent headquarters, were practically separate units. As soon as the War Office agreed to separate petrol organization, speedy action was taken to acquire from the French sufficient bulk storage for about 70,000 tons at Le Havre, at Honfleur on the opposite bank of the Seine, at Rouen and other places, and a new unit, a bulk storage petroleum company, was provided for supervising their operation. The existing no. 5 sections of the base supply depots were converted into petrol depots for packed stocks. New units, base petrol filling centres, were introduced for filling cans and established at Rouen and later near Lille. Transport companies for carrying petrol in bulk were formed and manned by men enlisted from the United Kingdom Petroleum Board. All petrol units included a high proportion of officers and men who had been employed in peacetime by the large petroleum corporations.

Before the Storm

While the months passed by the BEF grew stronger. A 5th Division had been formed in France and, between January, 1940, and April, the 42nd, 44th, 48th, 50th (motorized) and 51st Divisions had arrived from home. A third corps (III Corps) was formed in April, so that just before the battle broke out the BEF had three corps with nine divisions on the main front and a tenth, the 51st, disposed with the French armies in the Maginot sector.

Three other divisions which had not completed their training, had also arrived—the 12th, 23rd and 46th—which were intended for labour and guard duties on the lines of communication. They lacked the usual complement of the ancillary fighting arms and had only a skeleton administrative organization.

The original deficiency in general transport and troop carrying companies had been made partly good by the arrival of more companies from England, and the supply organization had been again strengthened by a third supply personnel company and a fourth bakery and cold storage units. The increase in commitments and strength of the BEF in France had in the meantime led to splitting responsibility at GHQ for supplies and transport. Brigadier Archibald, the DST, remained responsible for transport and Brigadier G. C. G. Blunt was appointed Director of Supplies (and petrol) in December. This arrangement followed the precedent in France in the First World War, but it was not introduced in any of the later campaigns.

The Campaign opens

Soon after 5 o'clock on the morning of May 10th, 1940, the German armies began their invasion of France, Luxembourg, Belgium and the Netherlands. The first intimation that the officers and men of the BEF received that the war had begun was from widespread and heavy air attacks on the hitherto peaceful area which they occupied behind the line of the Franco-Belgian frontier from about Halluin to Maulde. The German challenge was met at once by orders being issued a few hours later for the French and British armies to put Plan D into action. This entailed the French Ninth and First Armies and the BEF executing a vast wheel to the right, to stem the enemy advance, along a line running from the River Meuse to the open country beyond Namur, and thence along the line of the River Dyle. The plan assumed that Belgium, which up to an hour or so before the German invasion began, had maintained a strictly neutral attitude, would join the Allies and the resistance of their frontier guards would give the Allied force time to get into its new position. The strategy of the plan rested on the assumption that the strength of the Maginot line and the difficult country presented by any enemy attempt to advance through the Ardennes would force the Germans to make their main thrust through the plains of Belgium.

For this reason the French had allotted their best equipped and trained army, the First, to the defence of the open country between Namur and Louvain and their Ninth Army and the Second on their right, which were not so well equipped and had a high proportion of reservists, to the defence of the Meuse and the Ardennes country. The French Seventh Army, which was of similar quality to the First, was given a role of moving forward in general support of the Allied left.

Plan D had been carefully prepared, and by 1 p.m. on May 10th the 12th Lancers, who were to cover the move forward of the BEF, crossed the Belgian frontier by nightfall and gained the line of the River Dyle, 60 miles ahead. That afternoon the four RASC troop-carrying companies, which had the distinction of being the first

RASC companies to be engaged, were hard on the heels of the 12th Lancers, carrying forward the leading brigades of the 1st, 2nd and 3rd Divisions, which were in their new positions the next day.

By May 14th the three divisions which held the main front on the Dyle, with the 4th and 48th divisions in support, were in contact with the enemy along the whole front. The remaining divisions of the BEF were disposed in depth behind them. But on the previous day news had been received that the enemy, advancing in unexpected strength against the French Ninth Army and part of the Second, had been able to reach the Meuse and had established small bridgeheads early that morning.

The Administrative Plan

The administrative instructions for Plan D provided for all formations moving forward with full echelons of petrol, ammunition and food and for railheads to be moved forward into Belgium in conformity with the advance. Stations for these new railheads had been selected in advance, but owing to the neutrality of Belgium it had not been possible to confirm their suitability by a reconnaissance.

Mobile reserves were to be provided on rail *en cas mobile*, and in the two RASC L of C railhead companies which normally carried reserves of anti-gas equipment and other stores. Three trains of food and three of petrol, holding supplies for two or three days, were to be loaded at the main depots on the Seine and ordered forward as required. The L of C companies were to dump their loads and pick up another two days' supply of food and petrol for the force. The only static reserve of food forward of the Seine was a field supply depot at Doullens, which held six days' preserved rations. Static reserves of petrol were held in the large petrol depot at Vignacourt, just north of the Somme, near Amiens, and other reserves were available in the newly established petrol filling centre at Lomme, near Lille.

All went well with the divisional and corps RASC as they moved forward to replenish their formations, although there were minor hindrances caused by some enemy air activity, by movement in a strange country heavily intersected with small bridges and level crossings, and by refugees appearing in some numbers on the three main routes of advance. Some of the sites selected for the new railheads had, however, to be changed at the last moment, as many were found to be in unduly congested areas and the alternative sites which had been selected at smaller stations had poor facilities which tended to cause delays in the work of clearing supply trains.

Demands for petrol and ammunition soon began to arrive. The first demand received in earnest for ammunition was one for 200 rounds a gun by the 3rd Divisional Ammunition Company for a dumping programme—a technique which had been well practised in peace. The programme was completed within the allotted 24 hours. The company thought itself well tried by the end of the day, only to find a little later that this effort was to be a commonplace. Some of the first demands for petrol seemed to indicate that formations must have had an unquenchable thirst; for instance, that made on one divisional petrol company which cleared the whole of their stock, of 20,000 gallons, at one fell swoop and was followed by urgent representations that unless more could be provided the formation would be immobile. But it was a case of crying wolf, as further supplies were already within sight at petrol points on the main route over the Escaut, and petrol trains had arrived at their new railheads.

It took a few days for our RASC units to settle down, but before they had the opportunity of getting fully used to the system of replenishment for supply during an advance, they were called upon to carry out a reverse procedure.

The Enemy cross the Meuse

By the evening of May 13th the enemy had established themselves firmly west of the river Meuse on either side of Dinant and Sedan, and they followed up their success the next day by pressing forward, with an overpowering weight of armoured formations, against the French Ninth and part of the Second Armies. It was the German preliminary to a thrust to the coast, and from then onwards the French were unable to make any concerted effort to restore the situation. The immediate effect of the advance was to threaten the security of the right flank of the First French Army and the BEF. Space does not permit of examining the causes of this sudden disaster, but it now seems to be confirmed that neither the French Ninth or Second Armies had reached or consolidated the positions allotted to them when the enemy made his unexpected and rapid advance through the Ardennes country.

On May 14th touch was lost between the French First and the Ninth Armies and there was a wide gap between the Allies in the north and the main forces which held the Maginot defences. Although the BEF held the line of the Dyle firmly on the 14th, the 2nd Division, which was on the right of the line, had to be withdrawn in the evening to the Lasne, a small tributary of the Dyle, to conform to the movement of the French First Army which had been heavily engaged and forced back.

The Germans continued their advance on the 15th, and by the evening were well to the west of the Meuse on a front of about 50 miles, when it became obvious that the original Allied plan for holding the enemy's advance on the Dyle was no longer feasible and a withdrawal was imperative. So serious was the position in the eyes of the French Prime Minister M. Reynaud that he declared 'We are beaten, we have lost the battle'.

More bad news came with the announcement by the Dutch High Command that they had capitulated to the enemy at 11 a.m. on the 15th. The struggle in the Netherlands had been a short but violent one. Little direct help could be given to them apart from some British naval support and answering an appeal for assistance to safeguard the departure of their Government from the Hague, which was threatened by the landing of enemy troops by sea and by air. The appeal was answered by the hasty formation and despatch of a composite battalion of the Guards who embarked at Dover and landed at the Hook of Holland at first light on the morning of May 13th with orders to move to the Hague to restore the situation there, and, in the event of the Government withdrawing, to re-embark for Britain. The only officer of the administrative services to accompany them was an RASC captain who, in the absence of any material supplies, was presented with a large bag of money and told to buy what he wanted to maintain the little force. The Queen of the Netherlands arrived soon after the Guards had landed and was embarked safely in one of His Majesty's ships. She was followed by members of the Diplomatic Corps, but their arrival coincided with the appearance of enemy aircraft which, with little regard for diplomatic immunity, showered bombs down on the village and its surroundings, and these attacks could only be met by the light automatic weapons of the Guards. Further air attacks took place the next morning and the battalion, having completed its task, arrived back in Dover, battle scarred but, as always with the Guards, in good order. A tired and dusty RASC officer reported back to the War Office the next day, to return his bag of money—intact.

The First Withdrawal

Orders for the BEF to withdraw to the River Escaut were issued on May 16th, the first stage, to the River Senne, to start that night, to be followed the next day by withdrawal to the Dendre and then to the Escaut which was to be reached on the 19th.

Action had already been taken, on May 15th, to select new railheads from 20 to 30 miles to the rear and to reconnoitre others as far back as behind the French frontier. The 15th also marked the first heavy attacks by low flying aircraft on the rear areas, as the enemy, no doubt heartened by the success of the blitz tactics which contributed to the sudden capitulation of the Dutch, made indiscriminate attacks on both military and civil traffic and the refugees who by this time were tending to paralyse all traffic on the lines of retirement. Many RASC columns suffered casualties and some vehicles were destroyed or burnt out. Companies' anti-aircraft teams were in action throughout the day and gave a good account of themselves. Many awards for gallantry were earned in the ensuing days, for example by L/Cpl J. H. Fairchild, who fought off 14 enemy aircraft, by Dvr W. H. Hall, of 50th Division, who carried on firing although seriously wounded, and by Dvrs B. Wallsworth and J. G. Lee, of 42nd Division, who were given immediate awards of the Military Medal.

As the withdrawal went on, some confusion arose from the various cross movements of formations, continued changes in the location of units, and alterations in the points used in the chain of replenishment, which caused temporary loss of touch between the RASC and formations. But in the absence of detailed information about future movements, petrol and supply points were established on the main routes for the withdrawal. CsRASC chief preoccupation was how to maintain communications with the ST staff at corps headquarters, with their own Q staff and with their own units. Telephone communication was usually impracticable, and motorcyclists were often crowded off the road or jammed in heavy traffic. An extensive use had to be made of liaison officers who set forth each day to get the latest information of the operational situation and to keep in touch with those they were supplying.

However, RASC motorcyclists played an important part during the campaign as did also car drivers. Many motorcyclists were awarded the Military Medal for their devotion to duty in acts such as those of Dvr E. Shepherd, HQ RASC 42nd Division, Dvr V. Askew, 44th Division, and Dvr J. W. Priest, 45 Company. But perhaps the most unique award was earned by a car driver who, running into direct enemy fire, put his car into reverse gear and drove backwards at 30 miles an hour, for over half a mile, thus saving the lives of his passengers.

Officers and men got little rest during the withdrawal. Many transport units had to give a hand, in addition to doing their own duties, in collecting up the stores and ammunition which had accumulated on the ground during the advance. Hundreds of lorries which had to dump their own loads were needed for this purpose and for moving semi-mobile units such as hospitals, railhead detachments and various headquarters to the rear.

Even when the day's work was done it was not uncommon for men who had been at the wheel all day to spend the night manning their unit's local defences. The situation in the rear areas was already being affected by the break which had occurred in the French lines to the south, and the need for guarding against sabotage

In Workshops

Workshop Lorry

The Helmsman

Caique under Sail

and fifth column activities had been learned. One instance of the uncertainty which existed is given in the following extract from the personal diary of the officer commanding an ammunition park.

'May 17th.

'I have been held up for hours on end on the way back from Headquarters to my unit. About 21.00 we received an urgent message to be prepared to repel enemy AFVs from any direction. This meant double blocking 14 roads and finding inlying picquets with double blocks of lorries from men who had been all day at the wheel and were dog tired. We mounted every AA and AT gun, 30 in all, and then spent the whole night trying to sort out who should and should not be allowed in from the mass of refugees and Belgian soldiers who wanted to pass through.'

Such instances were, however, accepted as being all in the day's work and helped to make all ranks believe that they were becoming seasoned veterans and ready to meet any new situation as it arose.

When the withdrawal from the Dyle began on the 17th it is probable that few of those who took part in it realized that their Commander-in-Chief, Lord Gort, was being faced on that day with having to make many decisions to counter the serious situation which had developed on his right flank and what appeared to be a direct threat to the security of his communications. Nor could they know that by the time they reached the Escaut the BEF would have been cut off from its bases.

The Threat to the BEF's Communications

From the first day that news was received that the French lines had been overrun on the Meuse, Lord Gort had received little positive information of the situation in the gap which was developing on the right of the French First Army, but it was obvious to him that the direction of the advance of the German forces in that area was a direct threat to his communications with his bases. His own rear headquarters at Arras stood right in the path of the German advance as also did the main railway link with his bases which ran through Amiens. All his divisions were already fully committed in the withdrawal on his main front, but he considered it vital to provide protection for his right flank although part of the area was nominally outside his jurisdiction. The only formed bodies of troops which were not engaged in the main battle were the three Territorial divisions, the 12th, 23rd and 46th, which were employed on the lines of communication on labour and guard duties.

A general alert had already been sounded on the British L of C, and defence schemes, to counter sabotage and the landing of parachute troops, had been put into action. In the days which followed every man who could handle a rifle and be spared from his normal task was formed into small bodies to take part in stemming the enemy's advance. It is gratifying to record that the part played by RASC men in these actions receive a special commendation in the official despatches.

The Commander-in-Chief's first steps were to give orders for the formation of an extemporary force, known as 'Macforce', based on a brigade of the 42nd Division, to safeguard the line of the Scarpe among other tasks; to establish a small garrison for the defence of Arras; and to order the three Territorial divisions to the threatened area.

Macforce was only the first of many temporary groupings which had to be made and from that time onwards it became increasingly necessary to detach brigades or other parts of divisions to meet each situation as it arose. All the extemporary 'forces' did magnificently, but most of them suffered from the handicap of having no administrative organization of their own. The RASC had no pool of officers to draw on, and the few general transport units were all heavily committed so that even if time had been available it was impossible to provide any temporary organization for them. Macforce was fortunate in having a brigade RASC supply officer whose total assets were a section of the 42nd Divisional Ammunition Company, a large dump of petrol, and four days' food 'to go on with'. Yet he was able to report that his force never went short. In other cases the forces had to fend for themselves by drawing food, ammunition and petrol as best they could with their own transport from other formations or local dumps or depots.

The frequency with which brigades and artillery units were detached from their parent formation showed up a weakness in the divisional RASC organization in that the companies were only organized to carry a specific commodity, and the detachment of a brigade involved drawing on three different companies to provide the requisite complement of RASC vehicles.

The three Territorial divisions were soon on the move to the north, the 46th being directed on Seclin, the 23rd to the defence of the Canal du Nord, and the 12th to protect Abbeville, Doullens and Amiens. Part of the 12th Division did not reach its objective but took part in the operations which were to follow later in the south.

The divisions only had sufficient RASC transport—one company each—for carrying a day's food and some petrol. For reasons which cannot be ascertained, two of the companies were retained for general duties on the line of communication and the third, for the 12th Division, was cut off south of the Somme but then reverted to maintaining the remains of the division until the final evacuation from Cherbourg in June.

On the evening of May 18th advanced units of the 1st German Armoured Division reached the Canal du Nord and occupied Peronne, about 20 miles to the west of Amiens. The next day enemy panzer divisions began to arrive in full force. The battle which ensued on May 19th was a hopelessly unequal struggle and left the Germans in possession of Amiens and Doullens and the last railway link to the south at Abbeville.

It may be said, therefore, that on the 20th the BEF was completely cut off from its bases, and the enemy was in a position to begin to strike against its rear. The immediate threat to the rear of the main front was met by the formation of another extemporary force, Polforce, which was ordered to protect the main crossings of the line of canals, from Gravelines to Béthune, supported by Macforce, and by the move of the 5th and 50th Divisions and First Army Tank Brigade to the region of Arras. Portions of these formations attacked the enemy with some success on the 21st, and the part played by RASC troop carrying companies in that operation and the subsequent withdrawal was the subject of special mention in the official despatches.

By May 21st the general situation was, however, such that a further withdrawal on the main front of the BEF was imperative in order to shorten the line and free troops for what was from then onwards to be a fight on two fronts.

Taking Stock

The operational situation was undoubtedly one for concern, but the administrative position was even more serious, as the only alternative line of supply from the United Kingdom was *via* the three Channel ports, Boulogne, Calais and Dunkirk. On the day before communications were cut, the Quarter-Master-General had asked the War Office to make immediate emergency despatches of vital requirements to all three ports and he also discussed the possibility of developing the three ports as a new line of supply. But the outlook was not very hopeful, as it was doubtful if the ports could be organized to handle the 2,000 tons of stores a day which the force required for its normal maintenance, and the railway system in the area was disorganized. If this alternative line of supply could not be organized, and organized quickly, the main question to be decided was how long the BEF could remain an effective fighting force with the few resources left to it.

When the break in communications occurred it is estimated that about 229,300 troops were in the BEF area north of the Somme and about 113,000 left south of the river, most of the latter being all those administrative units which constitute what is sometimes referred to as the military tail. There are no accurate statistics of the amount of food, petrol or ammunition which were available with the BEF on May 19th, although the food in their possession has been assessed as high as 12 days' rations. The personal experiences of CsRASC do not substantiate this estimate, as formations only managed to exist by having recourse to wide scale foraging. Most formations had two or three days' food in their unit and RASC transport, and some CsRASC admit to having acquired unofficial reserves quite irregularly at the beginning of the campaign, but, as it so turned out, most opportunely. Orders had been given on May 17th for all rail traffic from the base to be switched from through Amiens to *via* Abbeville, but it seems to be generally established that the last pack trains to be received were those which arrived on the 18th. The only static reserve of food held north of the Somme, at Doullens, had been disposed of just before the enemy captured the depot. Two of the reserve trains of food left the BSD at Le Havre on the 14th and 16th respectively, but it is doubtful if the third, which left on the 18th, ever reached its destination.

The petrol position was probably better, as stocks were available in some civil installations, so long as they could be decanted and distributed. Some stock was available in petrol trains and at the newly established filling centre near Lille. The large static depot at Vignacourt, north of the Somme, fell into enemy hands on the 19th, but most of the stock was reported as destroyed before it was captured. The available supplies of ammunition included unit reserves, some dumps and some stock which was on trains which had reached the area before the break occurred.

There was little that the Directors of Supplies and Transport could do to influence the situation, and their task was made no easier by the sudden decision to move the rear maintenance staff and heads of services at GHQ from their headquarters at Habarcq, a few miles from Arras, to Boulogne on the 18th and then to Wimereux. Any reserves available were already under corps control, and the three DDs ST at corps headquarters (Brigadiers L. G. Humphreys, C. le B. Goldney and V. O. Beuttler) could do little more than see that the resources left were fairly apportioned. Effective control by the DDs ST of RASC transport became almost impossible owing to continued changes in the responsibility of corps for formations, the numerous detachments which were made from one area to another, and the fact that many units or detachments which were in the vicinity of the Channel ports were evacuated without any warning.

Supply became a matter for the individual initiative of CsRASC and their officers, and the success with which they were able to maintain their formations largely depended on their personal

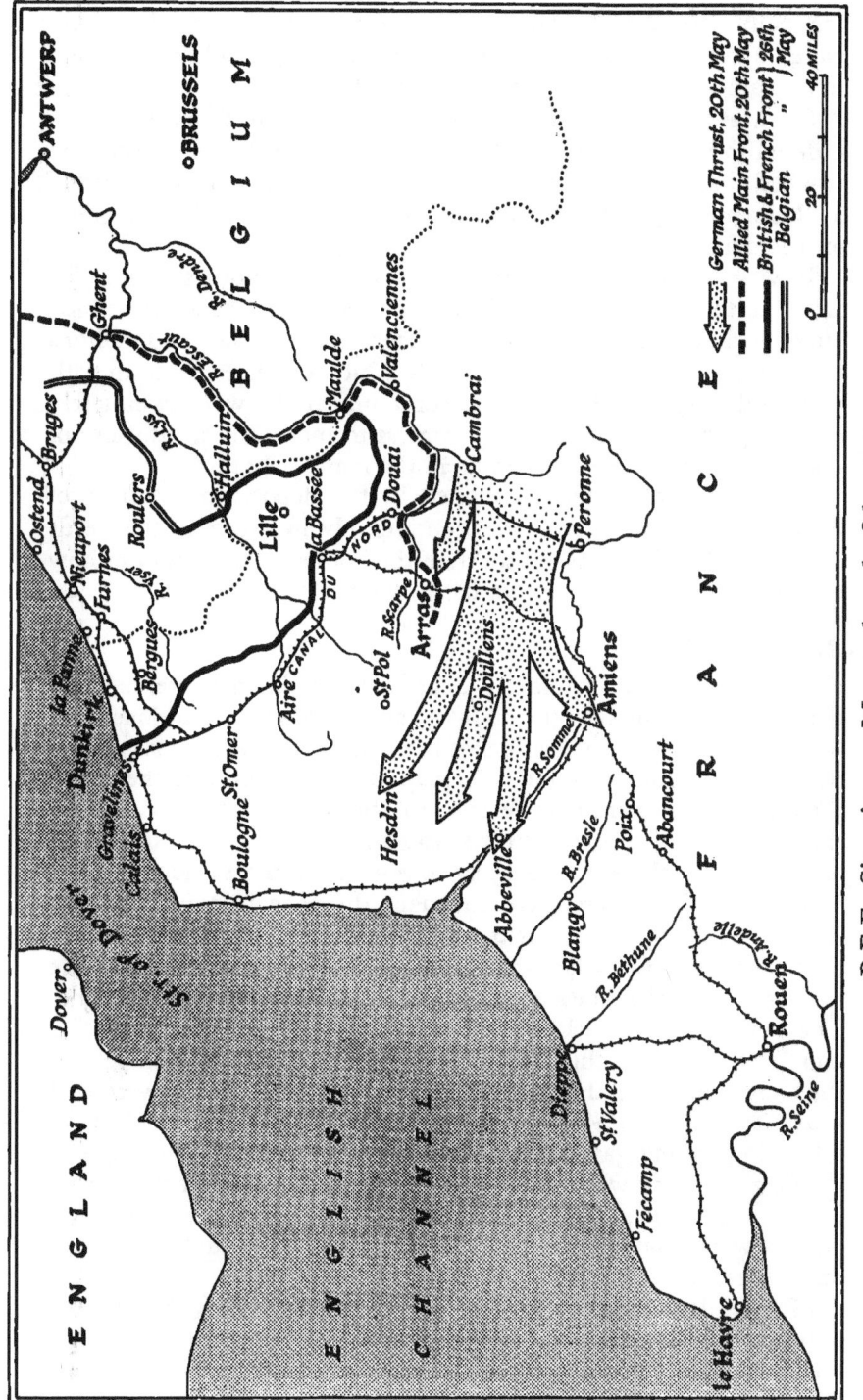

B.E.F.—Situation on May 20th and 26th, 1940

ingenuity. It was a strange position for the RASC, as they were called upon to do the very thing which the Corps had been created to obviate—the army 'living on the country'.

On May 21st the staff and services of GHQ at Wimereux were ordered to join the QMG at Dunkirk. Some of the ST directorate reached their new destination. But the appearance of enemy tanks at Boulogne cut off the remainder who were evacuated to England on the 23rd.

It was a humiliating position for both directors and for the DST at the War Office to have to accept that their combined efforts to amass the 60 days' food for nearly 400,000 men and millions of gallons of petrol and other fuel oils, which had been built up with such difficulty on the lines of communication, were completely stultified, and that they were powerless to make any fruitful use of the reserves which were available in the home depots.

The vast stocks which remained in the depots on the lines of communication were of course considerably in excess of the needs of the few British troops left south of the Somme. The story of how they were disposed of must be left to later in this chapter.

Boulogne and Calais

General Weygand replaced General Gamelin in supreme command of the Allied forces on May 20th. Many discussions then took place between the leaders of the three Governments regarding the course of future action. A plan that the Allies in the north should stage a counter offensive to the south and that a fresh regroupment of French troops should conduct a simultaneous offensive from the south, across the Somme, came to nought, as it was impossible to disengage sufficient divisions in time, and the practicability of the plan for the French offensive was problematical.

By the 23rd the BEF were back to the frontier defences, the original line which they occupied before the advance to the Dyle. The new front was held by the 42nd, 1st and 3rd Divisions, the 2nd, 48th and later the 44th, being directed to stem the enemy on the southern flank, the canals line. The 5th and 50th were still near Arras, but on May 25th they had to be hastily moved up to fill an impending gap on the left of the BEF, where the defence of the Belgian Army was rapidly crumbling. All hope of any counter offensive had gone, and the next day it was decided that the Allied Armies would have to withdraw to the coast. Evacuation was the only course left.

Meanwhile the War Office had lost no time in meeting the QMG's request for emergency shipments to be directed to the three Channel ports, as on the evening of the 21st they were able to inform GHQ that shipments of food, petrol and ammunition were already on their way across the Channel and that these were being followed by further consignments in ships, in the train ferry, and even in barges. GHQ then issued a simple instruction for developing the new hoped for line of supply, but made it clear to all formations that for the time being they would have to rely on their own resources. Here it is of interest to record that the supply and petrol branches at the War Office had many days before foreseen the possibility of emergency shipments being needed, and had assembled special emergency scales of food and stocks of petrol ready for despatch to any port on the south coast.

Swift action had also been taken to reinforce the garrisons at both Boulogne and Calais. The 20th Guards Brigade and some artillery left Dover for Boulogne on the 21st, and a tank regiment and brigade taken from the 1st Armoured Division were hastily despatched to Calais, but the enemy were at the very gates of both places.

Although both towns were gallantly defended and did not fall to the enemy until the 24th and 25th, they were unusable as ports of supply. The first ships which approached came under direct enemy gun fire and, after some had been sunk or damaged, all craft had to be diverted to Dunkirk or to home ports to await further orders.

By the 25th the CsRASC of most formations were already having a struggle to keep their formations supplied, a struggle which can be best illustrated by the short personal accounts which follow.

Corps Supply Column

'Once the Somme was cut, supply became a matter of individual effort. I sent out foraging parties under officers who were on the go continually, and covered a considerable area, but with good results. In one case, we found a local "Harrods", where we acquired everything which could be loaded on the vehicles available. We also discovered a pork factory full of sides of dressed pork, and other pig meats. By making a wide sweep we found parts of "ghost" trains with some trucks still full of food. No doubt some may have been intended for the French Army, but they were abandoned. If we came across any supply dumps and the guards had no orders, and as in any case they would have little future if they had remained at their post, we gathered up the men and swept the stocks into our larder.

'There were some wild goose chases too. We received orders to pick up an alleged dump of rations at the Merville airfield which were supposed to have been landed from aircraft, only to find on arrival that the enemy had got there first. On another occasion we were directed to search a large wood for food dumps which were reported there, only to find again that the area was already in the hands of the enemy. However, we did not do badly; our great difficulty was to keep sufficient lorries, as they were being constantly detached to artillery units, and many did not appear again. Eventually the situation became so precarious that we had to go almost as far as Dunkirk to salve abandoned lorries which we manned and had running again!'

The reference to supplies being landed at Merville refers to a War Office request to the Air Ministry to fly more than 80 tons of emergency rations and small arms ammunition. The appeal was promptly met. Lorry loads of preserved meat and biscuits were sent at once to Croydon airport, and 30 aircraft loads despatched, but further flights had to be cancelled because of casualties and the loss of the only airfield, Merville, available to the BEF.

The experience of the 3rd, 42nd and 2nd Divisional RASC was somewhat similar to that of the Corps Supply Column, as may be judged from the three personal narratives which follow.

3rd Divisional RASC

'During the withdrawal from the Dyle, everything went well, and I cannot recall any shortages. When communications over the Somme were cut we were fortunately fairly well stocked up with two or three days' supplies and another three days' stowed away in the supply column. We seemed to have pretty good stocks of petrol and ammunition as well. The only real grumble was the lack of bread, but we had a windfall in discovering a large stock of flour and an empty bakery. Our Q officer rose nobly to the occasion and at once screened the ranks of the Guards Brigade for guardsmen who had been bakers in civil life. Within a matter of hours a master baker and 20 bakers reported for duty, and we were able to provide for the whole division. All went well until we were back on the frontier, when things became more difficult, and in the withdrawal to the coast we lost the supply column—later to find that it had been ordered to re-embark for home on the 25th. But the division did not starve.'

42nd Divisional RASC

'Generally speaking, there was not too much difficulty in producing some sort of ration scale, as Lille was almost deserted by its inhabitants, leaving well stocked warehouses and shops behind them. The orthodox commodity was requisitioned as well as the unorthodox, so that delicacies such as tinned asparagus and tinned lobster were solemnly issued to units as equivalents for the missing, but plainer, items of normal army supply. One of our sources of supply was the well-known firm of Messrs. Felix Potin, so we called our ration the "Felix" ration. The last pack train from the Base Supply Depot at Le Havre which was due to arrive on the 19th at Comines, was reported missing, but after a search it was discovered some miles away at Choques, where it was duly cleared. Thereafter requisitioning was essential. Fresh meat was supplied with the aid of an improvised gang of butchers, who for their trouble were soundly bombed while at the work of dressing the meat, but remained undeterred, determined to finish their task. Bread was produced by persuading a civilian baker to collect a few local men. This gave the division sufficient supply until the 26th, and the discovery of a large stock of ready sacked potatoes kept them going until the 28th. Even on that day, the day on which the division began its final withdrawal, there were sufficient Felix rations to last up to the 31st.'

2nd Divisional RASC

'When railheads ceased to function and our third line transport units were diverted to other tasks, I realized that it was a question of the old adage "those who help themselves", and acted accordingly. It was a case of operation "scrounge", but we had a lien on several dumps which we had found some time before and had placed under guard. We also collected large quantities of both petrol and ammunition which constituted our main reserves for the rest of the campaign. Later, we found that the NAAFI at Lille, which was evacuated, was well stocked and could be drawn on. At the same time we roped in abandoned cattle and were able to keep up a fair supply of fresh meat. Many of the animals which had been abandoned were in a pitiful state, so when possible men with experience of milking were set to provide a welcome addition in fresh milk to the ration. Of course, there was no question of issuing any regular ration scale, but units realized our position and gladly accepted what we could give them.'

The reference to the clearance of the NAAFI abandoned stocks at Lille, which were also drawn by other divisions, had a sequel. Two years later a CRASC heavily engaged in the heat of the Western Desert operations received an important looking document addressed personally to him from the War Office, and in it was a bill—for several thousand pounds. He was asked to verify it and comment on the fact that his division had appropriated a stock of cigarettes which appeared to be 'in excess of normal entitlement.'

The Search for Petrol and Ammunition

There was also a general hunt for canned petrol, but the position up to the 26th was made easier by the existence of the large newly constructed filling centre at Lomme, near Lille, and the presence of detachments of bulk tank petrol companies which had been pushed forward from the lines of communication when operations began, and there were still small civil stocks in the area.

The depot at Lomme (No. 3 Base Petrol Filling Centre) faced no fewer than 70 air raid warnings in the first three days of the operations, but continued to work to its utmost capacity. On the 19th the officer commanding the depot was informed by the managers of the local civil installations on which the depot was dependent that French Army headquarters had given orders that they were to be destroyed. The officer adopted the well worn means of delaying the issue by politely telling the managers that he must refer the matter to his corps headquarters. On the 21st the situation had so deteriorated that it was planned to dismantle the permanent plant in the depot and resume operations elsewhere, with mobile filling apparatus, using road tankers to draw off supplies from such civil installations as remained in the neighbourhood. When the depot tanks were dry the unit moved out, only to be ordered back again to the site on the 24th. On that date they resumed work with their mobile plant and drew bulk supplies by RTWs. They also erected three of their filling machines and, working four shifts a day, carried on until the 26th, when once again they were ordered to evacuate the site.

The search for ammunition was also continuous. Royal Artillery units had to eke out the reserves they carried while the RASC tried to replenish their 'wagon' lines from the stock remaining in the divisional and corps troops companies. There also had to be a wide search for abandoned dumps, trains or trucks. The provision of ammunition was not, of course, an RASC responsibility, but it was their task to carry it forward and distribute it to units, and hence their task to find it. One notable case of the will to 'deliver the goods' is that of Captain R. S. Wicks who, finding a train on fire, detached the burning portion, collected a French engine driver and engine and set out for Hazebrouck. In spite of being badly bombed on the way, he brought the train safely to its destination. The Military Cross awarded to Wicks was only one of several awards made for devotion to duty in connection with ammunition supply. 2nd Lieutenant M. W. Mann, 56 Company, received a similar award, as did 2nd Lieutenant J. K. Mansfield, 522 Company, for keeping his ammunition point open under heavy fire. Cpl R. E. Rushby, 42 Company, was given a Military Medal for keeping his artillery unit supplied under continuous enemy fire.

The Transport situation

As the withdrawal to the coast went on, the rear area of the BEF became smaller, and uncertainty regarding the proximity of the enemy to the region where RASC transport was operating increased. The officers commanding companies had some difficulty in keeping their commands together, as empty vehicles returning to their unit were apt to be ordered here or there to do some immediate job, and detachments often found that their return route was reported to be held by the enemy. There were, consequently, many brushes with the enemy and some pitched battles. One of the two railhead companies had a series of encounters and, although they fought off enemy tanks with the aid of their few weapons, they eventually suffered severe casualties. Major C. B. Langdon was awarded the Distinguished Service Order for his part in one of these encounters. In another instance Dvr A. N. Sanson, a motorcyclist of 4 Company, was awarded the Military Medal for repeated reconnaissance and message carrying through the enemy lines. One troop-carrying company which landed in France after the battle had begun was on the road continuously and, owing to casualties, had lost most of its effective strength by the time it was called in for evacuation. In one case the survivors of an RASC unit about 100 strong held a position on the Nieuport canal for 48 hours. Forty per cent became casualties but the remainder made their way to La Panne where they at once volunteered to help to unload some ammunition which had arrived just off the beaches. Several other actions were fought, such as that of a section of 99 Company, when 2nd Lieutenant G. C. H. Witchell and a few drivers beat off five enemy tanks, Witchell being awarded the Military Cross.

There were also many cases of individual gallantry and determination like that of Cpl Merrivale of No. 7 Motor Ambulance Convoy, who, in charge of two ambulances, found all canal bridges on his route were destroyed. Nothing daunted, he found a small boat and ferried his patients across. After destroying his ambulances he returned to the other bank, then searched for two more vehicles and finally delivered his charges to a neighbouring hospital. Among other ambulance drivers who were decorated for their gallantry were Dvr L. Lilley, 150 Field Ambulance, and Dvr N. Burrows, 4th Division.

A Final Endeavour—at Dunkirk

The small band of officers of the ST directorate who managed to reach Dunkirk were under the leadership of Colonels A de B. Jenkins and A. F. St. C. Collins, who were assistant directors for supplies and transport respectively.

They were soon engaged in assisting the local staff in trying to produce order out of what appeared to be chaos against an increasing measure of uncertainty and destruction resulting from continuous enemy air attacks. Colonel Jenkins busied himself with the task of clearing supplies from the ships which had been able to make the port and, in face of many hazards, as much as from 200 to 400 tons were unloaded in a day. But as the days went on, the disinclination of local labour to face the continued raids and the final defection of skilled men wanted for operating the dockside cranes brought unloading almost to a standstill. At low tide ships' derricks could not be used owing to the damage to dock gates, and holds could only be emptied by hand—a laborious process. Major A. Forward, who was in charge of unloading supplies, was awarded a Military Cross for his devotion to duty, and Captain C. V. Ferrey was given a similar award for his work in clearing ammunition.

Some of the food unloaded was used for supplying a small detail issue depot which had been set up outside the town, and other consignments were sent forward to rendezvous which had been fixed for each corps. The detail issue depot was kept hard at work, as units and smaller bodies of men were by that time arriving in great numbers. Communal cookhouses were established for feeding the hundreds of men who had become detached from their parent units.

There was such a shortage of transport that Colonel Collins took over any sections of transport which came his way and manned abandoned vehicles to form makeshift columns. Work in the docks area was hazardous, and several awards were earned in those last days. 2nd Lieutenant C. Baillie, who had already distinguished himself in an encounter with enemy infantry at Ardres, was given a Military Cross, and Dvr J. E. S. Sankey, of the same unit (4 Company) won a Military Medal as did also Dvr J. C. W. Govan, 76 Company.

Colonel Jenkins was able to report that the last of the two supply ships had been unloaded by the evening of May 26th with the exception of a few tons of damaged packages. No other ships were in sight, and the days of Dunkirk as a supply port were at an end. In a report dated May 27th Colonel Jenkins records:—

'I spent the afternoon at the docks. Bombing increased considerably, and by 1700 hours it was impossible to get any of the few remaining lorries either in or out of the docks, which were blazing furiously. It was impossible to get any of the water away from the quayside out of the docks. The QMG arrived at the HQ at the Bastion at 1830 and told us that the BEF was to be evacuated. No further supplies should be sent forward, but if any lorries were under load they should be placed on the lines of withdrawal and formations would help themselves as they passed. There was nothing more to be done except to obey the orders we received to proceed to the beaches and await our turn for evacuation, as the telephone line to the UK had ceased to function from 1700.'

The water referred to was 200,000 cans of drinking water which had been sent from England for the use of the men on the beaches. It could not be moved because any transport available at that time had to be used for ammunition.

Because of fire and destruction all troops were ordered to clear the town that night, GHQ taking over control of the port as the outer mole was still usable. There was nothing more which the RASC at Dunkirk could do except to obey the order they received to await their turn for evacuation.

The Last Phase

There was great congestion in the area around the Dunkirk perimeter as units were directed to the beaches. Roads became almost jammed with a flow of French military and civil vehicles converging from all directions, and instructions that units should abandon their vehicles in selected places outside the bridgehead do not seem to have reached them, while there was also some uncertainty as to whether vehicles should be put out of action or how this was to be done.

A report by the CRASC 5th Divisional RASC at that time reads:—

'We had orders to destroy all surplus kit and office equipment on the 27th, so the end was obviously near. I was told that a dump of supplies had been found at Steenworde, but on arrival there found that the stock seemed to consist mostly of rum, and there appeared to be no one in charge. The congestion on the roads was terrific (the HQ of the Div. RASC were at the time at Ploegsteert) and drivers are almost whacked with long hours at the wheel and keep dozing off. Orders to withdraw to the coast were received on the 29th. The roads were almost impassable, with streams of traffic joining into our route from every possible direction. We eventually arrived at Adinkerke (close to Dunkirk), where we handed over our remaining stock of ammunition to 50th Division, but where we also found some abandoned trucks full of Belgian supplies. This chance find enabled us to open a supply point between the time we received orders to be prepared to move for embarkation, at 30 minutes' notice, and our actual departure later in the evening.'

But as this account by the officer commanding a corps ammunition park shows, not all of those embarked were to arrive unscathed in England:—

'When we eventually arrived at Dunkirk the town was ablaze and seemed to me to be completely destroyed. It was a depressing business, this departure, as although I got my unit of nearly 700 aboard ship, we had barely left port when we came under the fire of shore batteries, and could not escape by dodging about owing to the Channel being mined on either side. We were hit just above the water line and had barely got out of range when we were attacked by five Messerschmidts which came at us again and again, causing us heavy casualties in dead and wounded. It was a sad curtain to our short lived expedition.'

The fortunes of those awaiting their turns on the beaches were, of course, no different to the general experience of the many thousands who were to be taken off by the fleet of every conceivable type of small craft which had assembled for the purpose. But it must be recorded that at the same time RASC men took their share in many simple acts of heroism. Among these were Dvr R. Baldry (35 Company) who swam out under heavy fire to rescue a drowning man; Pte W. Johnstone, a 'volunteer' stretcher bearer, who carried on although badly wounded himself; CSM A. Jones, 9 Company, who, after embarking on one of his Majesty's ships, was instrumental in saving many lives by taking command when his officers were killed; Dvr A. Ord, 48th Division, for his work in embarking the wounded and Captain L. A. F. Gould Marks for his more prosaic deed of turning his ammunition section into a supply 'point' and feeding all who came his way from May 29th to June 2nd. Marks was awarded the Military Cross, CSM Jones a Distinguished Conduct Medal and the other men the Military Medal.

Although such acts seem to be a fitting note on which to end this brief story of the RASC with the BEF, before turning to an account of the operations which followed south of the Somme, mention must be made of the special part played by the WD Fleet (as it was then called). The vessels employed in the evacuation brought away nearly 2,000 men, although many of the craft were badly damaged. Four vessels returned as late as June 2nd to bring off French troops from Dunkirk. It is probable that the vessel *Marlborough* was the last to enter harbour, as it did not leave France until 2 a.m. on June 3rd and was towed home—less both its propellers.

South of the Somme

When the German forces reached Amiens and Abbeville on the Somme on May 19th, there were few British fighting troops left south of the river to protect the vast network of lines of communication which reached back from Le Havre and Rouen, on the Seine, to Cherbourg and to St. Nazaire and Nantes on the Loire. The only complete division, the 51st (Highland), was 300 miles away to the east holding a sector of the French front in the Saar area. Advanced elements of the 1st Armoured Division, which was being hurried over from England, had arrived a few days before, but the main body was only just beginning to land at Cherbourg with orders to concentrate at Pacy, south of the Seine.

Immediate protection depended on a few battalions, some of which had been raised from reinforcements in the base depots, under the command of Brigadier Beauman, who was responsible for the defence of the area around the Seine.

There were three important RASC base units in the threatened area—No. 3 BSD at Le Havre, the large central bakery at Bolbec, close by, and No. 1 Base Petrol Filling Centre at Rouen. All these units had been actively engaged in maintaining the BEF and supplying other small depots on the lines of communication, as far afield as Boulogne in the north and Metz in the east.

As mentioned earlier in this chapter, the first news of the break in the French defences along the Meuse had led to local defence schemes being put into action, but the first practical effects on the working of the depots were difficulty in obtaining civil labour and at times in procuring sufficient empty rail wagons to make up the pack trains which had to be despatched on fixed programmes to the BEF and elsewhere.

By May 14th the BSD was supplying a peak figure of nearly 180,000 rations a day and having to handle 2,000 tons a day, as ships with supplies from home were still being unloaded. The first serious news came on the 19th, when a message was received from the railway regulating station at Abancourt, through which all rail traffic was passed forward to the BEF, that there was such a congestion in the marshalling yards that some supplies would have to be unloaded and stored temporarily until the situation was clearer. A detachment was despatched at once to Abancourt to offload as many trucks as possible into the new but partly finished depot which was being built close by, but heavy bombing stopped all work. Later that evening the Movement staff declared that they could accept no further traffic for the BEF. All railway lines had been cut and were in enemy hands.

The appearance the next day of strong enemy patrols south of the Somme and the absence of any information regarding the situation of the BEF or the steps which were being planned by the Allied high command to restore the position, made an immediate withdrawal of the base units on the Seine seem imperative, and the next day orders were received by the BSD and bakery to cross to the opposite bank of the river. The night of the 20th brought a heavy air raid on the BSD, and that more damage was not caused was largely because of the action of Pte R. H. Abercrombie who, single handed, extinguished 18 incendiary bombs, an act which earned him the Military Medal.

On May 21st, detachments of the BSD and a bakery were despatched to the south bank with orders to set up small depots to maintain the units still in the area, and a small ship was loaded with supplies to provide initial stocks. As the situation became clearer, the orders were cancelled on the 22nd, and by the 24th the depot was again concentrated at Le Havre, but one of the two field bakeries was withdrawn to Rennes, where it came into operation again until finally evacuated in June.

In the meantime the 1st Armoured Division had begun to arrive from England, but it was not complete as part of the support group and a tank regiment had been taken for the defence of Calais. It was the first division of its kind to take the field, but it never had the opportunity of fulfilling its real role, or of operating as a complete formation, because it was employed piecemeal as it landed.

The RASC organization for the division was also a new one, as it was composed of seven companies in place of the three allowed for an infantry division. Each armoured brigade, the support group and the divisional troops were allotted one company for carrying their food, ammunition and petrol, and three companies were provided for carrying sufficient reserves to make the division self-contained for several days. Four of the companies were Territorial RASC, one of them being a true family affair, as it had been raised by a well known brewery firm. The division was one company short on landing, a deficiency made good by forming it in France with vehicles drawn from the lines of communication reserves.

The urgent necessity for trying to relieve the situation on the Somme then led to a series of abortive attacks by the 1st Armoured Division, or rather by units and sub-formations of it, as they arrived, between the 22nd and 25th, and by the end of that period they had suffered such heavy losses that the division had lost its potential power, as a formation. The divisional RASC had preceded the arrival of the brigades. Their sealed orders, 'only to be opened after embarkation', indicated that they were to concentrate near Brussels —by that time almost in enemy hands. They were just assembled in time, in the region of Pacy, to go straight into action, under all the circumstances which surround a losing battle. All movement and the work of clearing supplies from railheads had to be done by night, no lights being allowed, so that the first practical work of checking and sorting their loads had to be done with the aid of well dimmed hurricane lamps.

The division was badly mauled in its attacks on the Somme bridge-heads and, less part of the support group and a composite regiment which was detached to the 51st Division, had to be withdrawn to refit to the south of the Somme.

On May 20th the 51st Division received a warning order that they were to be relieved by French troops and were to concentrate at Etain, north of Metz, before moving to the west with the avowed object of rejoining the BEF. The move had to be conducted by

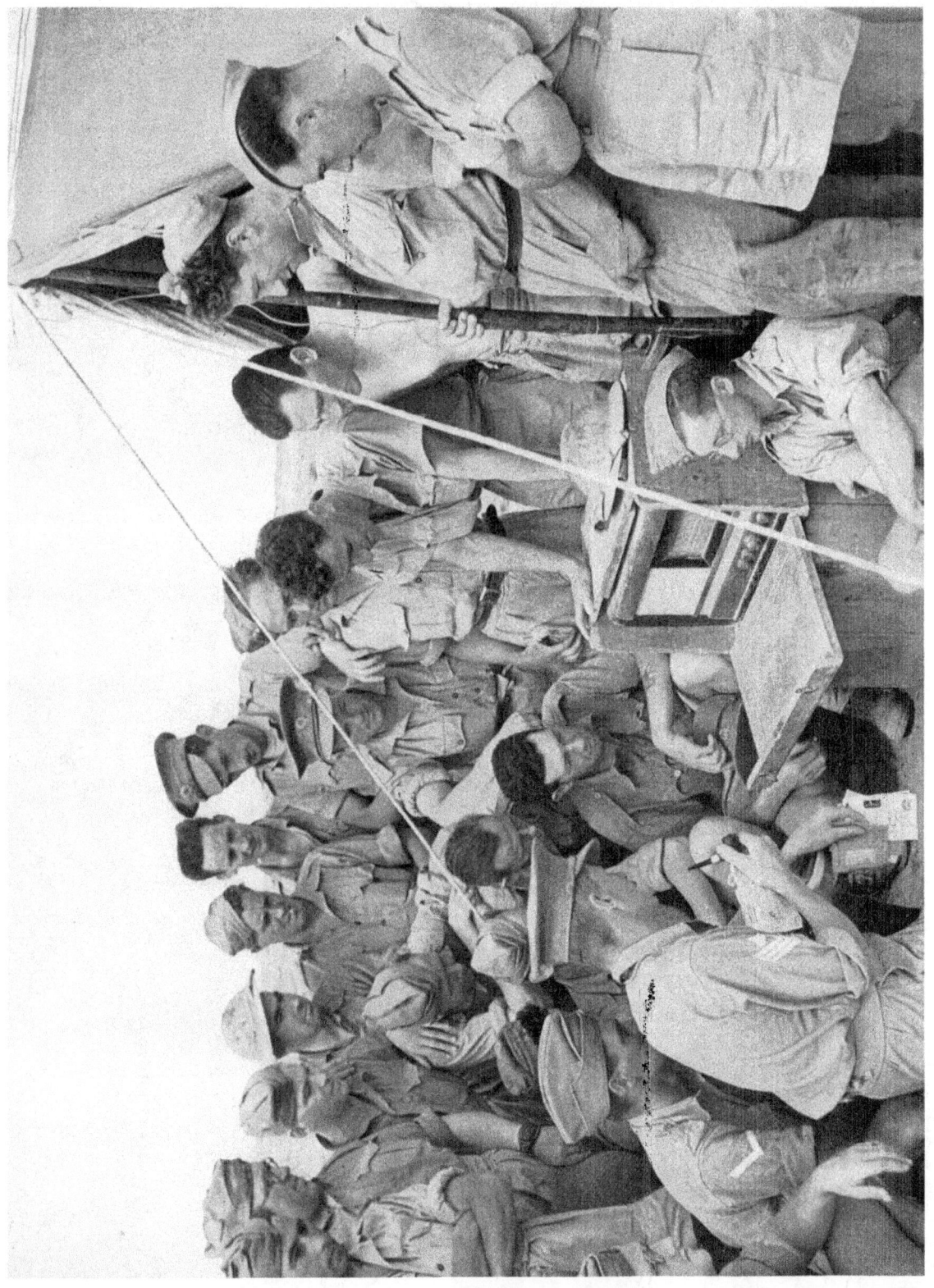

Typical Group, 1940

Carrying Bridging Material

rail and road as quickly as possible, and the CRASC had little time to make his arrangements for clearing the area and at the same time maintaining the force (the division had several corps troops units attached to it) while on its journey. More than 1,000 tons of ammunition had to be collected, but neither the section of a corps ammunition company left behind for the purpose nor the ammunition trains which were loaded were seen again. The supply company had to be divided to feed the road parties on a relay system and to maintain units as they arrived by rail at their new destination. At one period of the move the petrol company was spread over 300 miles. They had dumped their normal load of blankets and anti-gas equipment to make room for more petrol on the understanding that the loads they had dumped would be forwarded later by train.

By the time the division had taken up its new positions at the end of May, on the River Bresle south of the Somme, the divisional RASC had already had a gruelling test which makes their subsequent behaviour in the final days of St. Valéry all the more praiseworthy.

Situation at the end of May

By the end of May the situation was becoming clearer, although plans, or the future outlook, were by no means firm. In the area between the Somme and the Seine the French were deploying their divisions which later became the French Tenth Army. The British had the 51st Division, part of 1st Armoured Division and the miscellaneous units which by May 31st had been organized into three nominal brigades and designated the Beauman Division, so that the immediate security of the British base about Le Havre and Rouen was no longer in imminent peril. There was also the first inkling of the hope that it might be possible to reform a new BEF, when it could be equipped, and transfer it to France to fight again.

The administrative situation was, however, a peculiar one, as the base depots had to be prepared on the one hand to carry on, and on the other to reduce the risk of losing the valuable stocks which were held to a minimum. The more northerly depots were therefore ordered to run down their stocks as soon as possible, and in the depots to the south preliminary steps were taken to sort and prepare for the evacuation of the more valuable goods. Orders were given for all further despatch of maintenance stocks from home to cease, and in certain cases for material which was urgently required at home to build up the home defences, to be shipped back to England as soon as possible.

The manner in which the RASC was able to fulfil their two apparently contradictory roles of carrying on and at the same time being ready to 'go' will be described later. The only RASC shortage on the lines of communication was transport, as many of the units normally employed there had either been cut off with the BEF, or had incurred many vehicle casualties. The reserves in the Vehicle Reserve Depot were almost drained owing to the demand for replacements, and the Heavy Repair Shop, although working to capacity with an output of 30 vehicles a week, could not keep pace with the inflow of damaged vehicles. The demands for forming a company for the 1st Armoured Division, for replacing losses by the 51st Division and producing transport for the many mobile columns, and small forces (Beauman's force had to be provided with about 200 lorries) left Colonel Tudor with little transport at his disposal, but even so, when the 52nd Division arrived in June, ahead of their own RASC companies, they also were provided with a temporary complement of RASC transport.

51st Division—The Last Stand

On June 4th the 51st Division, with part of the 1st Armoured Division and French artillery and tanks under command, was committed to attack the enemy's bridgehead around Abbeville and St. Valéry-sur-Somme, but the attack did not achieve success, and the division suffered heavily. The next morning the enemy opened a full scale offensive against the thin Allied defences from the Somme to the Aisne, and by June 7th the 51st Division had been forced to withdraw to the River Bresle. The direction of the enemy attack made a gap in the French Tenth Army which soon isolated the French IX Corps, of which the 51st Division formed part, and by June 8th the British and French forces were being pressed back to the pocket formed by the coast and the wide estuary of the Seine. The 51st Division still held their positions on the Bresle on the 8th, but the remnants of the 1st Armoured Division and Beauman's force had been ordered to withdraw across the Seine that evening when they were closely followed by the enemy who reached Rouen the next morning.

In the withdrawal the RASC company for the support group of the Armoured Division was nearly cut off, just managing to get across the Seine before the bridges were blown, but losing their supply and petrol points to the enemy.

From June 6th no further pack trains reached the 51st Division, and supply columns sent to Le Havre found that, although the BSD had just been evacuated, there were still stocks of food at a local DID, which they cleared just before an order was given to destroy any remaining stocks. Part of the column was unable to rejoin the division, but the stock brought back by the remainder was enough to help the division eke out its few reserves to last them until their final stand.

There were continuous demands for ammunition throughout the operations which at one time entailed an almost continuous ferry service by the ammunition company—deliveries often being made direct to gun sites. Replenishment then became difficult, but a lucky find of a fully loaded ammunition train helped to maintain supplies until June 10th. On June 11th there were barely 500 gallons left in the petrol company when orders were received to destroy the remaining vehicles. Space does not allow of a description of the gallant stand of the division at St. Valéry, or the mishaps which prevented the survivors from being evacuated before they were forced to capitulate on the 12th, but during the operations the RASC had successfully maintained their division and had also met every demand for troop carrying. They had their share of casualties, especially when assembling on the beaches for the hoped for evacuation. Perhaps the best tribute is that of their divisional commander who when addressing all commanders after the surrender said: 'The RASC never let us down.'

The Final Phase

June 8th was a bad day for the Allies, as it looked as if the French armies were gradually becoming incapable of putting forward any concerted resistance. Paris was already threatened, and to the Allied commander, General Weygand, the only alternative seemed to be to seek an armistice. The hope that a BEF could be re-created in time to sway the issue was a faint one,* although the 52nd (Lowland) Division had begun to land at Cherbourg. The 51st Division was almost out of the battle, and the 1st Armoured Division and Beauman's force, through lack of equipment and casualties, were incapable of taking any effective part in the operations which ensued.

The RASC of the 52nd Division did not begin to land until the 12th, when 157th Brigade had already been sent forward to join the French III Corps, which was facing the enemy as he debouched over the Seine. During the few days which the 52nd RASC spent in France, they were primarily employed in troop-lifting, as by the 14th it had been decided that all British troops were to withdraw from France.

The 1st Armoured Divisional RASC, after it crossed the Seine, gradually fell back with its division. There was no lack of stocks to draw on, as they were withdrawing along the main line of supply, so that their main occupation was one of maintaining contact with the units they were still supplying. The main task of the RASC base units on the lines of communication then became one of

* As late as June 12th a party of officers was sent to La Rochelle to make a plan for establishing a new British base for the maintenance of a force of four divisions.

endeavouring to save as much of their stocks as possible from falling into enemy hands, in the limited time left to them before they were ordered to evacuate their sites.

The RASC base units on the Seine were not withdrawn until June 7th. The Base Petrol Filling Centre evacuated their site that evening, but managed to collect and take with them sufficient mobile equipment to operate again at Donges. The main site was subsequently destroyed by the East Kent Fortress Destruction Unit, which was to play a considerable part in denying the stocks in bulk installations to the enemy.

No. 3 BSD was ordered to cease all work at 1700 hours, but a rear party was left to complete the loading of a ship and despatch a last train before it withdrew to rejoin the main body the next day. Their departure was preceded by a severe air raid, but there was little left to destroy, as the unit had managed to evacuate more than 11,000 tons of food in the preceding days by rail, and ship, and by issues to the units remaining in the area. After some adventures the BSD and the bakery from Bolbec reached Cherbourg, and they left France on June 12th with the knowledge that they had fulfilled their task.

No. 1 Base Supply Depot at Redon had been working 24 hours a day at taking in supplies which had been evacuated from the depot at Le Havre when on the 15th it received orders that the unit was to be evacuated in 24 hours. There were still about 8,000 tons of supplies in the depot which they were instructed to hand over to the mayor of the town. The main body of the unit then left for embarkation in the ill-fated *Lancastria*.

The ship, with nearly 6,000 souls on board, was heavily dive-bombed after leaving port and sank in 15 minutes. There were many other units on board, but the BSD was the only one able to man its Bren guns. 2nd Lieutenant J. C. Medlicott kept his gun in action until the angle of the decks of the sinking vessel brought the water to his knees, and Sgt J. Clarke and Cpl J. Durrant, manning their guns on an upper deck, also kept firing to the last. Their gallantry earned them the awards of the Military Cross and Military Medal respectively.

No. 2 Base Supply Depot, at St. Tregonnec, near Brest, did not receive orders to evacuate until the 17th, and working up to the day before their last despatch, was to send 700 tons of supplies by road and rail to Brest for the troops and civilian refugees which were pouring into that port. Their remaining stocks, about 3,000 tons, were, under orders from the headquarters at Brest, handed over to the French sous-prefet at the neighbouring town of Morlaix.

The fate of the big petrol depots differed. Orders were received on June 14th by the large petrol depot at Moult d'Angence, near

Caen, to pack all equipment at once and be ready to move the next day. But as Beauman's force was still in the vicinity, a rear party was retained at the depot to be ready to issue supplies to the force if they required them. On the afternoon of the 15th a French unit arrived and asked if they could take over the remaining stocks on the understanding that they would destroy any balance if they were forced to withdraw. After reference to Sub-Area HQ, this was agreed to, but the French had barely signed a receipt for the contents of the depot when they reported that their higher headquarters would not allow them to take the depot over, and in the early hours of the 16th they announced their intention of retiring. By that time the enemy were getting closer, and orders were received from the staff of Beauman's force to fire the depot. Most of the stock was in tins and drums, but by 0500 hours the depot was successfully alight, some 1,049,000 gallons of petrol and 60,000 gallons of lubricating oil being destroyed, little being left intact to the enemy. The officer and small rear party then made their way to embark at Cherbourg.

No. 2 Petrol Depot at Morlaix was prepared for destruction preparatory to orders being received to evacuate, when it was ordered at the last moment that the contents of the depot, some 7,000 tons of petrol, were to be handed over intact to the French. The other depot, No. 1 Petroleum Depot at Blain, was heavily stocked, but with the aid of a special detachment of Royal Engineers, tins were punctured in each of the many stacks, and when the final order to destroy the depot was received it went up in good style, the quantity being approximately 10,000 tons of petrol and 660 tons of diesel. Had the war continued, the loss of these stocks, although serious, would not have been irreparable, as by that time the factories in Great Britain were producing more than 1,200 tons of packed petrol a day in the 'flimsy' tins. There had, however, been a loss of more than a million returnable containers, 300,000 being destroyed in a single night's bombing raid on Le Havre.

There were also considerable stocks held in bulk, in addition to the packed supplies in the various petrol depots. Most of the bulk stocks in ocean installations were held in French civilian storage tanks, and as they would have been a military prize of considerable value to the enemy, orders were given for their destruction. The work of destroying these bulk storage tanks at ports was not an RASC responsibility, but an RE one. But it may be recorded with the thanks of their sister Corps that the almost will-o'-the-wisp arrival of the RE Fortress Destruction Unit at port after port and depot after depot was almost inevitably followed by palls of smoke which nearly blotted out the sky.

On the whole the three main RASC MT base units, the HRS,

MTSD and VRD, were able to withdraw without leaving any large quantities of valuable equipment to the enemy.

The Heavy Repair Shop, while continuing to recondition as many vehicles as possible, at the same time began to set aside and pack all stores and movable plant not required for immediate use. But a good deal of the heavier and expensive machinery could not be moved without reducing the output of the depot. After the unit had been given 48 hours' notice on June 15th to move, 30 cases of the more valuable equipment such as generators, lathes and drilling machines were ready packed and put on a train, and it is of interest that 12 of the cases eventually reached home. As much heavy equipment as possible was buried and any vehicles awaiting repair were rendered useless. This unit also embarked in the *Lancastria* but, thanks to the perfect discipline which prevailed, many of the men of the unit survived the ordeal.

When plans for closing and evacuating the MT Stores Depot were considered it was thought that at least a week would be required to clear it, but within 36 hours of orders being received to evacuate the installation, the greater part of nine months' accumulation of engines and assemblies, machine and other tools were safely removed to the docks at Nantes. About 300 tons of stores could not be moved, and eleven railway trucks loaded with tyres had to be abandoned. The notice for departure given to the Vehicle Reserve Depot was, however, so short that, although the more useful vehicles were disabled, many had to be left before the work was completed.

No account of these days would be complete without some reference to the supply personnel companies. It most cases the RASC had to carry on until the very last moment with the issue of rations and petrol. When operations began, each of the three companies were divided among at least a dozen different places, the little detachments usually being the arbiters of their own fortunes. Some were operating small depots in the BEF area or manning supply and petrol railheads, others were engaged in the Field Supply Depot at Doullens and the remainder were operating detail issue depots on the L of C as far south as Marseilles. When pack trains failed to materialize, formations invariably began to look around for the nearest DID, which also often served as the official centre of information when detachments became separated from their parent unit. A DID was essentially a command for the self-reliant, the officer commanding having to be prepared to use his own judgement in meeting the many extraneous calls made on his resources.

The Climax

When the decision to evacuate the remaining troops in France was made on June 14th, the 157th Brigade, Beauman's Force, and the 3rd Armoured Brigade were still employed with the French Tenth Army. On the 16th events moved to a climax when the commander of that army ordered a withdrawal on the axis Alencon-Rennes, which, if they had conformed to it, would have taken the British troops (by that time the 157th Brigade) well off the line of their ultimate withdrawal to Cherbourg. Orders were therefore given by the British commander to disengage the brigade, an operation which was only carried out by the skill of the brigade commander in extricating them from a most difficult situation.

This seems to be a fitting juncture to wind up the story of the RASC south of the Somme, by recording that the final move of the brigade over the 200 miles which lay between them and Cherbourg was conducted by 226 Company RASC, which embussed the formation at midnight on the 16th, and covered the distance before them over roads encumbered with troops and refugees in 24 hours.

At 4 p.m. on June 18th, the last British troopship sailed from Cherbourg.

CHAPTER III

NORWAY, 1940

AS in the First World War, the Scandinavian countries strove to retain their neutrality at all costs. Their peoples were by no means universally in favour of the aims of either the Allies or the Nazi Powers. Their governments feared the latter, especially when allied to the Russians, but could not trust the Allies, who seemed too far off to give adequate defence; their commercial prosperity demanded free use of the seas and free exports of their resources; and their armed forces were in no condition to take an effective part in their own defence. They had, in fact, everything to gain, and nothing to lose, from continued neutrality. In retrospect, however, it is quite obvious that Norway at least could not remain neutral indefinitely. She was in several respects of far too great importance to both sides. From the Allied point of view, this importance related to three principal considerations.

A glance at the map shows that off the whole length of Norway's western coast, which is plentifully endowed with deep sheltered inlets, lies a continuous line of rocks and islets. The channel between them and the coast, known as 'the Leads', affords a safe passage in territorial waters from Stavanger to North Cape. Enemy shipping, which the Norwegians were powerless to halt, could by this means proceed from the Baltic to the Arctic Ocean, evading the British minefields and naval patrols in the North Sea. This very serious leak in our blockade could not be allowed to go on indefinitely; the Leads must sooner or later be closed by British mining, with or without the sanction of the Norwegians.

The second factor of great importance was the existence of high-grade iron ore in North Sweden. Germany had always been the biggest customer for this ore, and now that her other supplies were stopped by blockade, while her armaments industry was daily accelerating its output, the Swedish ore was of the most desperate importance to her. The ore is exported both from Lulea, in Sweden, on the Gulf of Bothnia, and from Narvik on the Norwegian coast, just within the Arctic circle; but whereas Lulea is frozen up for some months in the winter, Narvik remains ice-free, and handles the greater part of the exports. Adherence by Norway to the Allied cause would therefore deny great quantities of steel to the German armaments industry.

With the sudden and vicious attack upon Finland by Russia on November 30th, 1939, a third consideration was presented which made the co-operation of Norway of still greater importance to the Allies, who were able to supply the Finns with some material aid—aircraft for example—but could send no forces to fight with them, except through Norway. This particularly irritated the French, who held the opinion that the best way into Germany was from the north, and that the opening of a Finnish front provided the most certain way of winning a war which seemed elsewhere at stalemate. The Norwegians, however, obstinately continued to refuse all facilities to the passage of Allied troops, even in civilian guise. To them the British guarantee of defence, which had ignominiously failed to save Poland from disaster, seemed of small value. Nevertheless, the Allies pressed on with the preparation of a force for Finland, which in March was to land at Narvik, Trondhjem, Bergen, and Stavanger, as the forerunner of a much greater army of some 150,000 men. But Allied counsels were divided, and the excuse for action vanished when the Finns surrendered on February 12th. The forces were stood down.

Instead, it was decided to proceed with the operation (thought to be less objectionable to Norway) of mining the Leads. Simultaneously a force was to be prepared to occupy Narvik, Bergen, and Trondhjem, since it was feared—or perhaps hoped—that the mining might provoke Germany to invade Norway, which would give the force an excuse to land.

During the long period of Allied indecision, the Germans, who did not feel obliged to take any account of Norwegian feelings, and who moreover had been led by Vidkung Quisling to expect a hearty welcome from a large part of the people, prepared to the last detail a plan to invade Norway with six divisions and more than 1,000 aircraft. Their invasion was timed for March 20th, but was postponed because of persistence of the ice in some ports, until April 9th.

The British mine-laying expedition, fixed for April 5th, was postponed through last-minute Allied disagreements, until the 8th.

The German Invasion

The various naval evolutions which took place are of great interest, but their place is not in this volume: the official history deals fully with them. It is perhaps sufficient to say that the Germans, having every advantage, seized Oslo, Bergen, Trondhjem and Narvik on April 9th, and thus established themselves firmly before our land forces could reach the coast. In particular, they had obtained complete air superiority by occupation of the airfields. Strenuous naval and air force efforts to dislodge the enemy followed; but in spite of much gallantry, they were ineffective, and it was necessary to turn to counter-invasion instead.

By now, however, such action was not easy. News from Norway was scanty, confused and unreliable; there was some disagreement between the French and ourselves about the relative importance of different objectives; many of the troops who had been prepared to sail before the German coup had been disembarked; and in any case this force was equipped to land without resistance in friendly ports.

In the event, two regular and two newly-formed Territorial British brigades were available (though one never landed), while the French contributed a considerable mixed force, not all well-trained, which we need not detail here.

The objectives finally selected were:—Narvik, and the railway thence to Sweden; Namsos, on a fjord some 80 miles north of Trondhjem, and Andalsnes, similarly placed 110 miles south of Trondhjem. The two last named places were selected as suitable entries for the encirclement of Trondhjem, by now thought too strong for a frontal assault; while Andalsnes also afforded a means of preventing the movement of the Germans northwards from their main bases in southern Norway, to interfere with our operations.

A surprising number of code-names were employed to describe the various Norwegian operations and the forces engaged in them. For the present account, only a few need be known, and they are perhaps best simplified as follows: the operations at Narvik, at the time they actually began, were known by the code-name 'Avonmouth', and the force engaged was Avonforce. All other operations at about the same time, elsewhere in Norway, had the generic name of 'Rupert'. The two principal forces engaged in 'Rupert' were Mauriceforce at Namsos, north of Trondhjem, under Major-General Sir Adrian Carton de Wiart, and Sickleforce at Andalsnes, south of Trondhjem, under command of Major-General B. C. T. Paget. After the failure of operations at the two last named places, and the evacuation of Mauriceforce and Sickleforce, the troops at Narvik ceased to be called Avonforce, and succeeded instead to the name Rupertforce. From the RASC point of view, few details are available of the Namsos operation, but it was similar to that at Andalsnes. This account will therefore discuss Narvik first, and conclude with the forces based on Andalsnes.

Headquarters 49 (West Riding) Division, commanded by Major-General P. T. Mackesy, was modified to form HQ Avonforce, which was charged with the recapture of Narvik. Under command were the 24th Guards Infantry Brigade and administrative units, the RASC

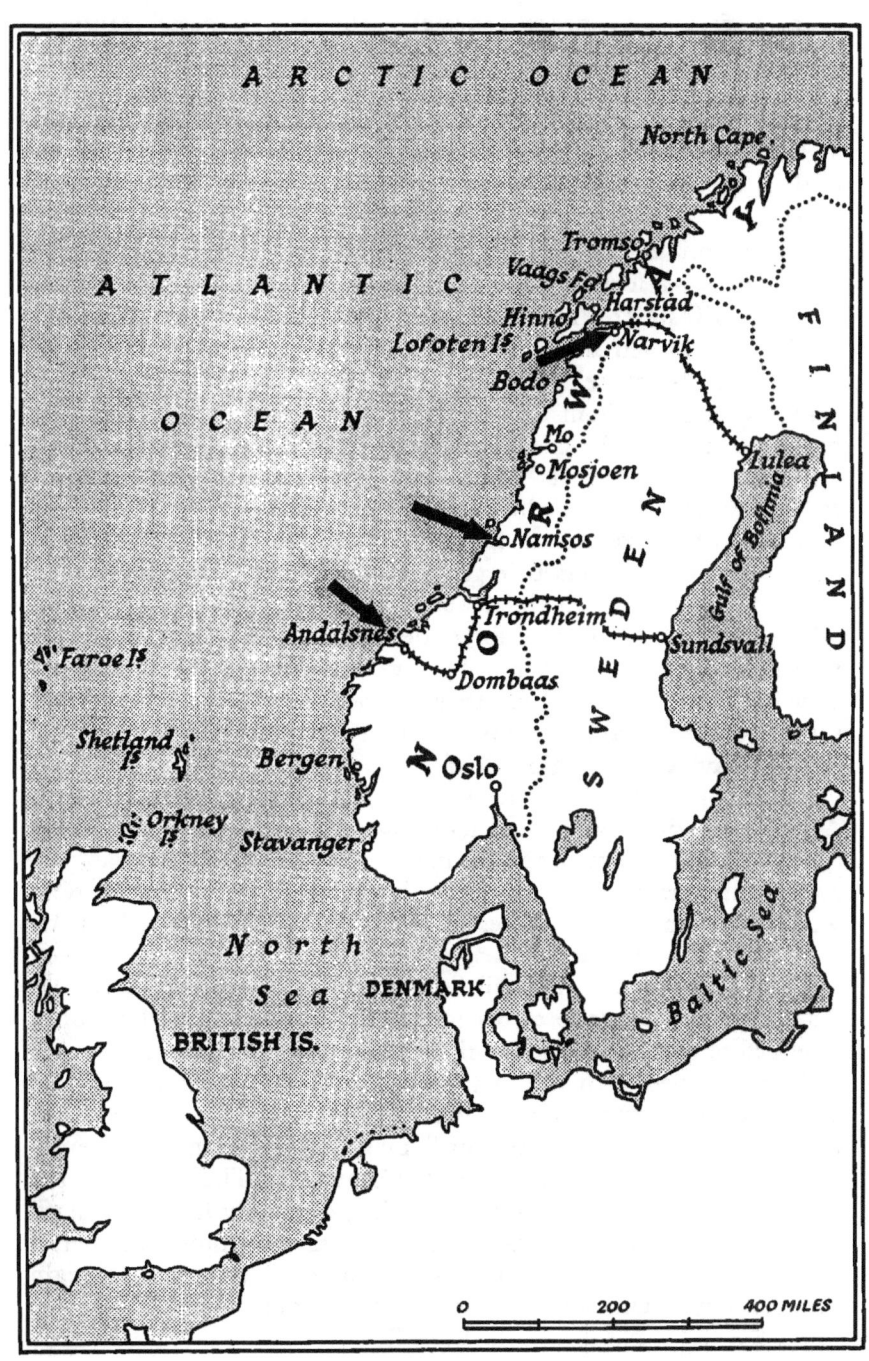

Norway

element of which comprised a special petrol depot, a special transport section, a field bakery section, a field butchery section, and 4 Supply Personnel Company with three sections. The transport was extremely limited, consisting only of a car for the GOC, six light ambulances, four Bedford Scammell tractors with 5-ton semi-trailers, and four Austin two-seater cars for the use of the Guards Brigade.

The intention was that all general transport needed should be hired locally—a forlorn hope based on over-optimistic information.

The RASC staff of Avonforce was not formed from 49th Divisional RASC, but posted in to fill a special establishment consisting of ADST (Lieut-Colonel H. M. Hinde), DADST, DADS, and two captains, one of whom was for local purchase duties. This little party, with their clerks and batmen, formed on February 22nd, 1940, was disbanded at Easter, only to be reconstituted on April 1st, before its individuals had time to disperse.

Avonforce embarked at the end of the first week in April at Clydeside, headquarters being in the Polish liner *Batory*, and sailed to Scapa, where it remained about 24 hours, waiting to join up off Cape Wrath with naval forces destined for Andalsnes. Officers were told on board that the objective was Narvik, but it was not until well on the way that they learned that the Germans had invaded Denmark and had forestalled their arrival at Narvik by a *coup de main*, having had a ship full of troops lying there for some weeks.

Sailing on north about the Lofoten Islands in a severe blizzard, Avonforce arrived on a clear morning on April 12th in the Vaags fjord. By good fortune the leading destroyer located and sank an enemy submarine which was sheltering in the fjord. After turning south, now escorted by scores of fishing boats nicknamed 'puffers' from the exhaust note of their single engined diesels, the convoy anchored off Harstad, a small fishing port on the island of Hinno. The decision was made to disembark the force there and set up a base before marching on Narvik some 50 miles to the south.

ADST landed with the first 'recce' party and the remainder of the ST headquarters an hour later. Contact was made early with the British Vice-Consul, Mr. Per Sanvig, a Norwegian and a representative of the Anglo-American Oil Company. The help rendered by this gentleman was of immense value, especially to the ST staff.

The immediate task was to locate suitable supply and petrol depots and organize transport, as unloading of stores was to begin the next day. Unloading of troops began immediately.

Lack of Transport

The transport picture was depressing. There was only one contractor, who was also owner of the main garage and workshops.

It was arranged that he should provide as many load carriers as possible as well as taxis and private cars for use as staff cars. The first night only four 30-cwt trucks could be raised. These were used to help clear kit from the quay, while a few private car owners helped by transporting staff officers about the town.

For the first night, headquarters, including services, were quartered in the Grand Hotel, but on the following morning ST Branch moved to a pension for quarters, and took an office backing on to the water-front. The supply depot and the bakery were located in and around a disused fish canning-factory on a promontory about half a mile from the centre of the town. The petrol depot was to be in a field about a mile out of Harstad on the Solaagen road. The only points at which stores could be landed were the town quay, which could berth two ships, the coal quay (one ship up to 5,000 tons), and the oil wharf, served by a very narrow road (one ship).

In view of the extreme scarcity of transport, hired vehicles were allocated according to three degrees of priority, the first operational as ordered by the G Staff (one or two only); the second priority being for dock clearance; and the third to meet individual demands. On an average daily hirings were 14 cars and 14 lorries, the peak being 21 lorries. Unfortunately these vehicles were somewhat unreliable, especially during air raids, when the drivers were apt to disappear with their vehicles into the hills as soon as the warning went and not to return for hours.

The RASC transport landed about three days after disembarkation began and did sterling work, especially the four tractors and trailers, which were put on to dock clearance and worked 24 hours a day with drivers in shifts. The same day heavy snow began to fall, developing into a blizzard which raged for three days without respite. The vehicles sent with the force had been supplied with snow chains, but these had been shipped separately from the vehicles and proved to be all of wrong sizes. Every available set of chains in Harstad was bought and adapted, and urgent signals were sent to the War Office demanding chains of the proper sizes for all vehicles.

Reinforcements which arrived about four days after the initial landing included a French Chasseurs Alpins demi-brigade, with four sections of a supply personnel company and a section of a motor ambulance convoy. After these troops had been landed and the blizzard, which had given some relief from German aerial attention, had died down, Harstad base began to achieve some sort of order. Preparations were then made to mount an attack on Narvik and, in support of this, to establish an advanced base at Skaanland (on a snow covered swamp) and an air strip at Soreise.

Both these points had to be supplied by sea from fishing boats, of which many were now on permanent hire working under the transportation branch. Detachments from the supply personnel company were sent to establish DIDs.

By this time the supply depot was firmly established, prodigious efforts having been made by the RASC supply men who, working with little sleep in foul weather, managed in one period of four days to unload 350 tons of supplies without outside help.

The field bakery had to clear three feet of frozen snow before it could erect its Aldershot ovens, but it came into action within three days and rapidly attained an output of 5,000 lb of bread a day, backed up by a further 3,000 lb daily from local resources. Fuel for the Aldershot ovens was a constant worry, wood being scarce and of poor quality.

The petrol depot had to abandon its first location after the blizzard as the site was unworkable while the land was under snow. It was moved to the Anglo-American Oil Company's jetty, on which a packed petrol and oil depot was opened when the first shipment of cased petrol (14,000 gallons), arrived on April 26th. This site was unsuitable in that it did not allow of any dispersion and, in consequence, late in May the packed stocks were destroyed during one of the air raids. Luckily local bulk stocks were untouched and proved to be adequate for all purposes.

Air raids occurred daily, and for some time the only anti-aircraft protection were the guns in his Majesty's ships lying in the fjord together with units' Bren guns.

Meanwhile in the south of Norway the British forces landed at Namsos and Andalsnes had been driven back by the Germans, and had re-embarked and returned home. This left NWEF alone in their assault against Narvik. To contain the Germans in the south it was decided to despatch the Irish Guards south to hold a defensive position in the region of Bodo, with its air-strip, and Mosjoon. A supply section was embarked with the battalion in the Polish liner *Chrobry*. This expedition was doomed to failure, as the liner was bombed two nights later while at anchor in the Solangen fjord. Casualties to officers were heavy, as the bomb went through the saloon. The troops were taken off the sinking ship by escorting destroyers and returned to Harstad. A second force, consisting of the 1st Battalion, Scots Guards, with supporting troops, was then embarked in HMS *Effingham*. Again disaster overtook the project as, on entering Bodo, the ship struck a rock and foundered. The troops were once again returned to Harstad by destroyer. At the third attempt the Scots Guards were landed, but they too eventually had to be taken off by sea and returned to the Narvik area.

Early in May further reinforcements arrived, including a Polish brigade which was landed on the mainland north of Narvik and passed straight on to join up with the Norwegian 5th Division which was advancing south on Narvik through the mountains. A heavy mobile anti-aircraft regiment and a mobile light anti-aircraft regiment arrived with their attached RASC sections. The former section was fully employed with its parent unit, but the latter was able to contribute daily to the transport pool and greatly eased the situation. A welcome addition was a reserve MT company, but by a staff decision only the men were landed, the MT ship being held at Tromsö until the roads were more free of snow, which did not help matters.

Lieutenant-General Auchinleck (Commander IV Corps) arrived early in May with a small staff drawn from IV Corps which included an AQMG Lieut-Colonel (now Major-General Sir) Reginald Kerr, and a DDST (Colonel W. Warren). General Auchinleck took over command of NWEF from General Mackesy, and the service elements of the original headquarters were transferred to the base sub-area.

Early in May a reconnaissance party comprising representatives of services was sent up by 'puffer' to Tromsö to plan the establishment of a medical and services base in that area in order to afford some relief to Harstad, which was highly congested.

Back at Harstad reorganization of the base was taking shape. Bombing was becoming more frequent with the lengthening days, but some relief was obtained with the arrival at Soreise of one Gladiator and one Hurricane squadron, which had been flown in from HMS *Glorious*. The supply depot was hit, but not put out of action, and a direct hit on the oil jetty destroyed almost all our packed petrol. With the expansion of the area of operation, for the most part supplied by sea, requests were made to the War Office for the provision of larger launches with military crews who would be more reliable than some of the local ones.

Towards the end of May Narvik was captured, but it became evident that with the turn of events in France, no further troops could be sent to Norway and that the maintenance of the forces already there would be an unwarrantable drain on our naval resources. Accordingly evacuation was planned. At Narvik the shore and coal handling installations were destroyed, and as part of the cover plan to deceive the many local spies, a small advance party from the base sub-area proceeded to Tromsö for the ostensible purpose of opening up the secondary base on the lines of the plan suggested by the original reconnaissance. This took the form of hiring, clearing and preparing warehouse accommodation. Local labour was hired, and a battery of heavy and light anti-aircraft guns was brought into position.

Aided by this cover-plan, a high degree of secrecy was secured, and all troops were successfully evacuated; those from Tromsö were taken off by HMS *Devonshire*, which also conveyed the King of Norway and Crown Prince Olaf, beside many other prominent Norwegians.

All ranks of the RASC acquitted themselves in accord with the highest tradition of the Corps. They evacuated such vehicles as they could, including a German petrol tanker, formerly a Luftwaffe refueller, which was found at Tromsö, and was used at Harstad to good effect after the destruction of the packed petrol and oil stocks. The tanker, the first captured enemy vehicle, was later tested by the Weapons and Vehicles Experimental Establishment and inspected by the Quarter-Master-General.

The Andalsnes Operations

We must now go back to the beginning for a short account of the operations based on Andalsnes.

The RASC destined for this port had spent several days swinging at anchor in the Clyde, dispersed among various liners, before returning to Glasgow to be hurriedly disembarked, transferred by rail to Rosyth, and re-embarked at once in cruisers which immediately left for Norway. The result of this haste was, of course, disorganization. The only transport unit embarked was 2 L of C Brigade Company (though there was no L of C brigade), and its vehicles were left in other ships still peacefully anchored in the Clyde. It did, however, enjoy first reinforcements in the shape of a corporal and about 20 men of another unit who, on their way as normal postings to Catterick, had been helplessly swept into the movements channel for Norway. Two ST headquarters, that of ADST* Sickle Force and that of ADST Base Sub-area, also landed, and dwelt somewhat uncomfortably together in the restricted base, though there was only work enough for one headquarters, since the base installations and units did not arrive at all.

The approach up the deep and lovely fjord, with its magnificent precipitous mountains towering straight from the still water to the blue of the evening sky, soon to be flickering with the delicate fringes of the Northern Lights, was no proper preparation for the turmoil which followed in the next few days.

Andalsnes itself proved to be a wooden village of great charm, but of no real value as a base, having only one small concrete quay, one much smaller wooden one, and one 5-ton crane. The land immediately behind the port, approachable from the quays only by two narrow roads through the village, opens out into a fairly wide plain, formed from the silt of the river which tumbles down the

* Lieut-Colonel C. J. Williams.

Romsdal; but at this season of the year it was marshy and quite unsuited for depot areas. Two or three miles up, the plain gives place suddenly to the mountains, among which it would be hard to find even half a level acre for a depot. From Andalsnes one road, broken by winter frosts and floating on a deep sea of greasy green mud, inter-wound its way with the single-line railway and, in places, the river, 60 miles to Dombas, beyond which to the south our troops were operating. The mountains on either side were snow-covered halfway down. Waterfalls, which flung down their sides in hundreds, froze to silence about tea-time.

After quick reconnaissance by night, the most likely places for supplies and petrol depots, though insecure and far from ideal, had been picked, and the transport company secured comfortable billets in the wooden hotels of the village. The DAD Transport, thanks to the willing help of Captain Starhem, the indefatigable Norwegian officer engaged in hunting and allocating local transport, obtained about 20 vehicles, mostly Ford 2-tonners, and well before daybreak the clearance of supplies, ordnance stores, and ammunition landed overnight by HM ships was begun. Turn-rounds were short, the depots being only three or four miles up the valley; however, only part of the stores could be cleared from the quay, since soon after 0800 hours on April 26th the flow of transport for loading thinned rapidly and then stopped altogether. It turned out that the first air raid of the day was (correctly) expected at 0830.

From that moment the Luftwaffe made life continuously and increasingly difficult with HE, incendiaries, and bullets. An hour without a raid was considered a long respite. Some further clearance of supplies took place later the first morning during a lull, when some 'compo' (of excellent quality and variety) left behind by units which had gone straight to Dombas was moved to swell the slender stocks in the supply depot. 2 L of C Company was ordered out of its billets at 1500 hours to find a safer location four miles inland. As the last man left, the buildings were hit and quickly joined the rest of the town in smoking oblivion.

An organized hunt for the missing Norwegian vehicles occupied most of the day, and as each was found in nooks and crannies of the hinterland, it was put in charge of a RASC driver, instructed never to let the Norwegian driver, or the ignition key, out of his sight. This hunt in fact never ceased during the remaining days of the campaign: as vehicles broke down beyond repair, it was necessary to discover and borrow fresh ones, and there were not many available in the district. During a lull, a supply train was assembled, loaded with ammunition and 2,500 composite rations and despatched to Dombas. Our troops who were operating up to 80 miles south of this place, and 130 or 140 from base at Andalsnes, had to fetch their supplies and ammunition from whatever point on the railway the train could reach. There was no second line transport available for them, and little transport of any kind. Throughout, supply forward was difficult and precarious. The one road and single rail track were frequently cratered by bombs, and since they were soft-bottomed, the road in particular being borne on slimy mud many feet deep, even a small bomb would blow a hole of great depth and 20 feet across, which had to be painfully plugged to its base with tree trunks before passage could be resumed. Travel by vehicles off the road was nowhere possible. Even without bombing, the weight of loaded vehicles was often sufficient to break through the crust of the road, releasing great gouts of the mud which squirted up under the pressure.

On April 27th, bombardment was again heavy all day. Food supplies began to cause anxiety, especially as 1,500 composite rations were burned at the quayside, time and transport still being insufficient to move them from the quay during brief lulls between attacks.

Local procurement was impossible: there was simply nothing there. A few eggs could be bought from a place named Henn, some miles away, and this was the limit of local purchase.

The staff had by now, however, begun to think of evacuation as a matter of urgency. It was thought, therefore, undesirable to press the War Office for a supply ship, and the occupation was completed on half-rations.

Late that night SS *Delius*, the only maintenance ship which ever arrived, docked by the remnants of the quay, which was too short to enable all holds to be worked. Unfortunately, one hatch was almost immediately put out of action by an accident with a gun. The ship was worked for five hours before the master was forced to sail to escape from the fjord before daylight. He had had vicious bombing on the way in. A good deal of anti-aircraft ammunition, some food and petrol, and nine load-carrying vehicles came off the ship, all very welcome, and were removed from the quay by devoted efforts before the first raid of the new day. The ammunition was particularly useful. Our few guns had been silent for a long time, and after the 30 RAF Gladiators had been quickly destroyed, there was nothing left with which to hit back at enemy aircraft. Unhindered, they bombed and machine-gunned at will. Casualties were surprisingly light, but morale sank lower and lower, soaring again immediately when two intrepid anti-aircraft sloops arrived about once a day off the port and blazed away into the sky. They took awful risks in those restricted waters, where they were sitting targets, and one, the *Black Swan*, was hit by a bomb which passed straight through the bottom without exploding; but the gain in morale which they brought was quite remarkable, and the soldiers have every cause for sincere gratitude to them.

Having a little anti-aircraft ammunition of our own now allowed us the satisfaction at least of firing our own guns, though rather slowly.

The railway was not working, but the 14 lorries now available carried 4,000 rations, some wire and other stores forward to Dombas. With them went an officer and six men of 1 Supply Personnel Section to try to set up a forward depot there to sustain the now retreating troops. This was rather a wasted effort, since the next day the actual withdrawal from Norway was in train, and 5,000 badly needed rations were abandoned at Dombas.

The tasks set to the ever-diminishing transport strained it to the utmost, but it succeeded in 'rescuing' wounded from various isolated sanatoria and private houses before they were overrun, and also distributed rations to retreating troops, and dumped 1,000 rations in each of the three base defence sectors. They supplemented the one remaining train as troop transport, and carried some sea-mines salvaged from a sunken destroyer up the valley to act as demolition charges for bridges.

On the night of April 29th, about 300 wounded and some surplus base sub-area personnel were evacuated in destroyers. This work was continued on the following two nights in face of determined enemy efforts to prevent it. Daily the Luftwaffe fired the surrounding woods to give them light enough to bomb the destroyers, which could not manœuvre in such narrow waters; but the enemy had no success. On April 30th, the remaining wounded, and as many others as possible were got away, including half of 2 L of C MT Company, the two supply sections, and some RASC clerks.

On May 1st, the few remaining vehicles moved up to ferry the last of the forward troops across a 17-mile gap between two craters on the railway, but they were not needed. Instead, they brought in wounded, Royal Marine outposts, demolition parties, and stragglers, and then stood by to bring in the troops, including the remaining half of 2 L of C Company, RASC, holding the port perimeter some three miles up the valley. In the end all were successfully evacuated after midnight, the last three to embark being Major Genders (major supplies, Force HQ), and Major Thompson and Lieutenant Norman (both of 2 L of C Company).

The general opinion of all who took part in this operation was that, from the RASC point of view, it was hopelessly impracticable from the start: at the same time many valuable lessons emerged and were recorded. It may be hoped that in some small way they helped to secure final victory.

The British campaign in Norway is one of which the official

history has already been published. In its review of the book *The Times* said that Allied action was 'flurried, ill-found, inadequate and essentially amateurish', and that 'contributory and less uncontrollable causes (for failure) included bad planning, worse intelligence, inadequate training, poor as well as sometimes unsuitable equipment, and the lack of an interservice outlook.'

With such a background it could not be expected that the part played by the RASC would be a very happy one, and we were perhaps fortunate not to have a sadder tale to tell.

So ended an unfortunate expedition—by no means the last in that category in which British forces were to be involved before the war was over. The fact that this was the first operational venture in which the commercial ports available were inadequate for disembarkation and maintenance was a contributory reason for failure. Apparently few steps had been taken to overcome the deficiency.

Perhaps it was all part of the inadequacy of our intelligence of which *The Times* complains, and little seems to have been known about the condition of roads or availability of vehicles. Other factors making the work of the RASC difficult were the lack of air cover and the fact that ships were not tactically loaded. It is comforting to learn that the compo ration stood up so well to its first real operational trial.

CHAPTER IV

THE MIDDLE EAST I

Situation on the Outbreak of War

NO unified Middle East Command existed before the outbreak of war; British troops in Egypt, with Cyprus and the Sudan, formed one command, and British troops in Palestine and Trans-Jordan formed another. Each of these commands had its own RASC organization on the usual peacetime lines. There was a general lack of RASC personnel, and the very low peace establishments had to be supplemented by the employment of local civilians.

There were a dozen MT companies in Egypt and Palestine, most of them having the standard establishment of 24 vehicles. The company (39), which was stationed at Abbassia (Cairo), with Repair Shop, Vehicle Reception and MT Stores components, served both Egypt and Palestine. On the supply side, there were four small depots in Egypt and two in Palestine, and each contained a reserve of two months' supplies. A few static field bakeries were in operation, manned largely by native civilians, and cold storage facilities existed at Port Said.

The peace-time rationing system was in force. As elsewhere petrol and oil were dealt with by the supply branch, RASC. A reserve of two months' fuel was held to meet initial requirements in the event of war. Civilian bulk storage for petrol existed at the Suez refinery, at Alexandria, and at Haifa, and plants for the manufacture of 4-gallon non-returnable containers were in operation at these places, and also at Port Sudan, whilst considerable additional tinning facilities existed at Abadan. The only method of distribution envisaged was by means of the 4-gallon tin.

The lack of reserve bulk storage for petrol had caused anxiety for some time before the war, but in January, 1939, a joint War Office and Air Ministry mission investigated the matter. It examined several schemes, and the one accepted was a joint Army and RAF undertaking, known as the Jebel Dave scheme. It entailed the construction of buried storage to hold six months' reserve should the Suez Refinery be put out of action. The storage was to be located in the Geneifa area, between Suez and Fayid, and pipe lines were to connect it with a new tanker berth in the Great Bitter Lake and with the Suez installations. Work on the Jebel Dave scheme began in 1939.

Formation of GHQ Middle East, and expansion of ST Directorate

GHQ Middle East was formed in Cairo on the outbreak of war, and assumed operational control of British troops in Egypt, Cyprus, the Sudan, Palestine and Trans-Jordan. Responsibility for British Somaliland was added in January, 1940. On the declaration of war by Italy in June, 1940, active operations began in the Western Desert, and this remained the main theatre in the Middle East, until, after many vicissitudes, victory was achieved in 1943. Formidable problems arose for the RASC from this new type of warfare. The areas over which operations took place were vast; railways and roads were inadequate or non-existent; water was scarce. Troops had to be maintained by transport following desert tracks or crossing open desert with few landmarks. This necessitated the special training of transport units in such matters as the use of compass bearings for desert navigation. A high standard of driving was required over desert terrain with its stretches of soft sand, and even higher standards of vehicle maintenance, of discipline and of initiative. Because of the need for the wide dispersion of transport by day, the difficulties of controlling units scattered over large areas were manifold.

Problems at GHQ were not only concerned with operations in the Western Desert. Operations in the Sudan and Eritrea began soon after the entry of Italy into the war, and responsibility for Aden was taken over from India in November, 1940. Early in 1941, the campaign in Greece took place, followed by the defence and evacuation of Crete. In March, 1941, Middle East also became responsible for the provisioning of Malta, and in the early summer of the same year operations had to be undertaken in Iraq and Syria. Finally, in January, 1942, the Tenth Army in Persia and Iraq passed from the control of India to Middle East Command. It was inevitable that there should be an ever-increasing expansion of the ST Directorate to cope with these diverse responsibilities.

The appointment of DST (brigadier during 1940) was raised to major-general's status, and was held by Major-General C. Le B. Goldney, from early in 1941 to June, 1944. Active operations had then ceased in this theatre, and DST reverted to a brigadier's appointment (Brigadier C. E. Browne).

When first formed, the directorate was composed of a skeleton staff, chiefly concerned with planning, the two pre-war commands continuing to carry out normal maintenance, until GHQ gradually assumed administrative control. At first the directorate consisted of two branches (supplies and transport) only, but in 1940 a POL branch was added, as the importance that petrol was to take in the course of operations soon became apparent. A local resources branch was also formed which, by exploiting various sources of supply within the countries of the Middle East, helped to save shipping, and to provide fresh supplies for the forces. It was found essential to have a planning branch to manage the organization, formation and disbandment of all types of RASC units, including questions of war establishments and the RASC manpower ceiling.

Numerous local units of non-British nationalities were formed with British cadres, and units for which no previous establishment existed had to be improvised to meet special needs, or for special operational roles. Because of the lapse of time between the demand for units and reinforcements and their actual arrival from Britain, units had to be broken up and reorganized with a disturbing frequency, to meet changed conditions. The closest liaison was maintained at all times between ST (Plans), G, Q and A branches, and the staff were kept constantly advised as to what was and what was not possible with the RASC resources available.

Other additions to the directorate were a branch of the MT Inspectorate, a catering branch controlling a school of cookery, an accounts and supply investigation section, bakery, meat and petrol inspectors, and an Indian branch. At first, there was a personnel branch under DST dealing with reinforcements, postings, promotions, etc., but towards the end of 1941 this branch became part of the A branch of the staff, as is the normal procedure.

Expansion of RASC Services

In June, 1940, the entry of Italy into the war, and the threat to our sea communications in the Mediterranean, made the holding of large stocks of essential commodities a matter of vital necessity. The creation of a large base involved not only the despatch of enormous quantities of RASC supplies and stores from the United Kingdom, but also the provision of members of the Corps to man the depots and units dealing with them. Furthermore, the construction of the depots and installations, the building of railways and roads to serve them, and the laying on of water in desert areas, presented serious problems to the Royal Engineers. All this took a considerable time, and the magnitude of the task was increased by the wide dispersion considered necessary to minimize losses from air attack. The provision of adequate transport for such RE services was difficult at a time when there was a great shortage of transport for operations in the field.

The arrival of men and stores was delayed when the Mediterranean was closed to merchant shipping, and convoys had to follow the long sea route round the Cape of Good Hope, a voyage of 10 weeks or more. Heavy losses of shipping added to the difficulties of the situation, and RASC units and stores ready for despatch in Britain were frequently delayed for long periods because of lack of shipping space. Efforts were made to offset the deficiencies in British manpower by the employment of other nationalities, and in this some success was achieved, particularly in the case of transport units. But the period from June, 1940, till the end of 1941 was one of great difficulty in the build-up of the base. The gradual growth in the strength of the RASC made it necessary to set up certain organizations in the base area.

An RASC training school was established in February, 1940, for the training of officers and other ranks, and courses were run with a comprehensive syllabus on supply, petrol and transport subjects. A surprising amount of hidden talent was discovered, and it was possible to re-muster many NCOs and men to trades in which there were shortages, such as clerks, MT artificers and petrol technicians. The school also trained officer cadets, drawn from units in the theatre, and large numbers of them were commissioned during the war. This reduced demands from Britain, and had the advantage of providing officers with experience of desert conditions.

An RASC base depot was formed at Geneifa in September, 1940, to receive and hold RASC reinforcements and men from hospital, and to train locally enlisted men. It hardened those coming out from hospital, and conducted the technical and military training of reinforcements, including trade testing, upgrading and re-mustering.

The large number and differing types of RASC units made their organization, equipping and training a complex business, and the continuous demand for units called for quick improvisation. To meet these needs, an RASC Mobilization Centre was formed at Tahag early in 1941, and all units newly arrived from Great Britain, those which had to be reorganized or reformed, and those raised locally were given such training at the centre as was possible to fit them for service in the field.

Supplies

Lack of men for base supply depots was the chief difficulty in the build-up of stocks. Many depots were needed for the holding of reserves, for issues to detail issue depots, and for the despatch of supplies by road, rail or ship to the various theatres of operations. Demands for supplies were made on the War Office on the principle of maintaining a reserve of 60 days for all troops in the Middle East, plus a working margin of 30 days. A supply holding of some 150,000 tons was eventually reached, representing a reserve for a force of 900,000 men. Base supply depots were located at all base ports at which supply ships were discharged, and the largest holding was at El Kirsh in the Canal area, where a group of depots was established. When two or more BSDs were located together, a base provision officer was appointed to command the depots and to co-ordinate stock returns: he assumed general responsibility for the technical efficiency of his charge.

The increasing volume of supplies coming into the ports made it necessary to provide special RASC staffs to clear and load at the docks. For this purpose port detachments RASC were set up at each port. They helped to ensure proper handling of supplies in the discharge of ships, and correct loading when supplies were despatched. They were the representatives of the ST Directorate in the port organization, and the technical advisers of movements and transportation on all matters affecting supplies. The broad principle of stock control was to hold balanced rations at every BSD and to connect the latter with theatres according to the type and grade of the rations held.

Concurrently with the formation of BSDs, large numbers of DIDs were needed to provide for the ever-increasing numbers of troops of diverse nationalities, many of which required special scales and different types of food. Ration scales became a serious problem, and although every effort was made to achieve as much standardization as possible, there were more than 30 different ration scales in force in the Middle East to meet particular needs. The British field service scale applied, with modifications, to, among others, Americans, Belgians, French, Ceylonese, Greeks, Jews, Maltese, Mauritians, Poles, Czechs and Yugoslavs, the Union Defence Force (European, Cape-coloured and Indian) Seychellois and the Trans-Jordan Frontier Force. Then there were scales for Indian troops (Hindu and Muslim), the Sudan Defence Force, troops from French and Belgian Africa, Ethiopians and so on. There were also special scales for women's services, operational air crews, for prisoners of war and internees, and for a variety of animals. This threw a great strain on DIDs, each of which, although designed to feed only 7,500 troops, was often obliged to serve 20,000 or more. The feeding of prisoners of war presented a problem in the very early days, as in the first battle of Libya the number of prisoners far exceeded expectations and caused some concern at a time when resources were limited.

Food for the civilian population in occupied areas also became a serious commitment at times. The civil administration was held responsible for this task, but the RASC depots had to handle the supplies at any rate in the initial stages, and to despatch them as required. The RASC also assumed responsibility for the provision of common user commodities for the Royal Navy in the Mediterranean, including many items obtained from local resources.

The exploitation of local resources, which began in quite a small way in 1940, gradually assumed large proportions, and it is estimated that in the year ending March, 1943, over a million tons of shipping were saved by this means. Perhaps the most important of these schemes was the growing, in Egypt and Syria, of potatoes, without which the British soldier does not consider himself properly fed. Other undertakings included the production of cooking oil, oil cake and soap from cotton seed and ground nuts, the administration of dairy farms, a fishery scheme in the Port Said area, fish curing establishments, the making of jam and marmalade, and the dehydration and canning of vegetables. Quantities of forage were grown under contract, and pig farms were formed, managed by the Veterinary and Remount services, the product being handed over to the RASC for slaughter and distribution. Live cattle were imported in large numbers from the Sudan, thus saving valuable refrigeration shipping.

There was insufficient cold storage at the beginning of the war to meet war-time needs, and a large cold storage project was carried through between 1940 and 1943. This met the requirements of the theatre. At no time did stocks of frozen meat run out at the base, and its issue to troops in the base area, supplemented by fresh meat from the Sudan, was the normal procedure. Supply to troops fighting in the Western Desert was a different matter, and the fluidity of the operations, the lack of rail communications and other factors, made the supply of all fresh food a tremendous problem. The aim was always to provide fresh food, particularly meat and bread, to as many troops as possible, as far forward as possible. The supply of both meat and bread required special equipment. Frozen meat needed cold storage at the advanced base, and special refrigeration facilities for movement by ship or rail, while field bakeries had to be located well forward. Naturally, much depended on the length of the lines of communication. After the withdrawal to the Alamein positions in 1942, the short distance from the base made the issue of a full fresh ration comparatively easy, whereas during the final advance in 1942/43 the difficulties increased as the troops moved beyond the range of the Western Desert railway. After the ports of Benghazi and Tripoli had been opened, a small quantity of cold storage was made available, but because of insufficient refrigeration shipping, only a few consignments of meat could be sent. Fresh fruit and potatoes were shipped successfully to these ports, but it was impossible to ship fresh vegetables without deterioration. However, there were some small local supplies at Benghazi and Tripoli.

During the siege of Tobruk in 1941, it was difficult to supply fresh food, which is more important than ever in siege conditions.

Bread was produced throughout by the existing bakery, and dehydrated vegetables were sent up. The normal ration was modified to meet the special conditions, and such items as chocolate and lime juice were introduced. The only vessel available for carrying frozen meat was unreliable, and could only accomplish one delivery. The lack of fresh meat was a great trial to Indian troops locked up in Tobruk, and it was difficult to provide a suitable substitute, but on two occasions live sheep for them were conveyed on the deck of a destroyer. When the ship reached the entrance of Tobruk harbour, the sheep were thrown overboard, and those that managed to swim ashore had their throats cut by the cheering Indians.

Malta convoys were sent at irregular intervals, and at moonless periods, when fast shipping became available. Each time elaborate cover plans were made in an attempt to disguise the destination of these vessels from enemy agents at the port. Supplies were restricted by the amount of space available in the convoy, and the most nourishing food was sent within the space allotted. Every ship was loaded 'balanced', so that ships which arrived safely carried a complete ration, however meagre in quantity. Until command of the Mediterranean was regained, no convoy ever reached Malta without serious losses.

The field service ration scale, as issued in the Middle East, proved adequate throughout the war, and when fresh items could not be issued tinned equivalents were provided. This ration had, however, the disadvantage of being bulky, and therefore uneconomical in the desert, where transport was always scarce. Accordingly, in 1941, a simplified form of ration was devised, known as the 'battle ration'. Consisting of fewer commodities, it provided a less varied diet, but the easier handling made it useful in actual fighting. During the final offensive in 1942/43, successful efforts were made to keep the rations up to the full Middle East field scale throughout the whole advance, with fresh food whenever possible. Naturally commanders in the forward area were equally anxious to have a fresh ration when possible. But there were many snags. Fresh meat could be despatched to railhead or by sea, but its onward despatch to the troops through several echelons of transport presented difficulties in warm weather. True, methods of keeping it fresh by the use of dry ice were devised, but its cooking presented another problem. Most of the troops in the desert were widely dispersed, and any form of central cooking was disliked both for the congestion it caused and the distances which had to be walked to get food. The method most popular, both for tactical reasons and with the troops themselves, was to cook on a 'vehicle' basis. This meant in, say, the case of a tank, the tank crew of three or four, but there was very great variety in the size of messes. For instance, an RASC platoon might run about five, varying in strength from half a dozen to a dozen—and so on throughout all arms. Cutting up fresh meat to provide for such conditions was not easy, nor was the meat particularly easy to cook.

A source of waste was the 'vehicle' ration. Under the prevalent conditions in the Middle East campaign a vehicle might easily be lost or stranded in the desert for several days. It was, therefore, necessary for every vehicle to carry three days' 'hard rations' and, of course, water for the number of men forming its crew. In the absence of any better method in those days this involved carrying a number of tins of 'bully', packets of biscuits, tea, sugar and milk in any available container, frequently a discarded flimsy petrol can. Their condition was not improved by weeks of bumping about the desert, and it was difficult to ensure the restriction of their consumption to legitimate occasions. However, they were necessary and proved their worth on many occasions.

'Composite rations' were never available for issue during operations in the Middle East, and, when shipping supplies to ports along the coast, the only method of ensuring the arrival of a 'balanced ration' was to load ships in balanced units of 100 tons. Unsatisfactory as this was from the shipping aspect, the need of a 'balanced ration' for immediate use outweighed the disadvantages.

In spite of tremendous losses at sea and on land, it can be said that there was never any real lack of food in the Middle East. Instances of losses are the abandonment and destruction of supplies in Greece in 1941, and at the fall of Tobruk in June, 1942, where more than a million rations were lost. Often a heavy strain was thrown on supply resources, and an example of this occurred after the capture of Tripoli in 1943, when the GHQ provision commitment was fourfold. In addition to Eighth Army loadings (the greater commitment), loading took place simultaneously for re-stocking Malta and for providing Benghazi and Tobruk by sea and rail. The locking up of such large stocks in transit caused a severe drain on reserves in Egypt and Palestine, and it became necessary to transfer stocks from Syria and the Sudan to meet demands. However, at no time was there any failure to send a full and balanced ration to meet the requirements of all troops in the command.

Petroleum

Throughout the war the provision and distribution of petroleum products raised greater problems in the Middle East than did any other forms of RASC supply. This had several causes. First, on the outbreak of war there was no separate RASC petrol organization, and no petrol units existed. Secondly, there had been little pre-war planning, and except for the Jebel Dave scheme, provision had not been made for a large scale organization for the storage, transportation and distribution of petroleum products. Thirdly, the light 4-gallon (non-returnable) can, designed as the sole means of distribution in the field, was not stout enough for use in war.

However, starting from zero, a large and efficient organization was built up, which never failed to despatch from the base the quantities required to meet the needs of the field forces. The occasions when petrol was scarce may all be attributed to the 4-gallon 'flimsy' can, from which the losses in transit were so great as sometimes to imperil operations. In the early days, the Army had to depend almost entirely on the civilian oil companies until it could build up its own organization, and it was the civilian employees of these companies who performed the task. Many of them were later commissioned in the RASC. The oil firms placed their technical skill, and advice, and material resources unreservedly at the disposal of the Army, and without their help there might well have been a failure to meet operational needs in 1940/41.

As in the case of supplies, lack of men at the outset was the main problem. No petrol units arrived from Britain until August, 1940, and later many units were excluded from convoys, giving place to fighting troops. But gradually an organization was built up, and by August, 1941, there were in operation more than a dozen petrol depots, two base filling centres, two storage companies, and some bulk transport companies. The storage companies were the most useful. They had a high ratio of officers, and were made up of self-contained sections, which could be employed on detached work. Among the duties they performed, generally in detachments of one or two sections, were dealing with bulk stocks at main installations, operating refuelling stations and petrol DIDs, construction and maintenance of bulk outfits, and filling containers.

The main source of supply of petrol was by tanker from Abadan. There was an initial lack of tankage for the reception of bulk stocks until the completion of the Jebel Dave scheme, but the tanks for holding MT spirit were installed and filled during 1940, and those for aviation spirit were ready by the middle of 1941. Additional tankage was constructed later as an extension of the Jebel Dave scheme, and thereafter the situation was reasonably satisfactory.

In the early stages of the war, reserves of packed spirit had to be built up, because of the initial shortage of tankage, but the accumulation of these reserves was limited by the lack of can factories, and a certain amount of canned petrol had to be imported from Abadan. Difficulties also arose over the lack of reserves, as in addition to its other shortcomings, the 4-gallon can showed poor resistance to Middle East climatic conditions (for which nevertheless it had been designed in peace), and many of the cans leaked, if stored in the open for any length of time. A great number of cans were saved by the early development of bulk distribution in base areas. At first, lack of equipment was the limiting factor, as the ordinary roadside filling stations, so common in Britain, were almost non-existent in the Middle East; hence much improvisation was called for. Use was made of tanks of all sizes, barrels, drums captured in large numbers from the Italians, and every sort of container that could be found. There were three forms of bulk distribution: first, main road refuelling points for filling up convoys; secondly, bulk outfits in camps and unit lines; and thirdly, semi-bulk, i.e., barrels and drums located with units, and filled from road tankers. By the end of 1941, refuelling points were established as far forward as Sidi Barrani, and later at Tobruk and Capuzzo, but they had to be abandoned or destroyed in the retreat of 1942. At a time when can factories were barely keeping pace with demands, these somewhat primitive makeshifts helped to save the situation. Later stocks of orthodox equipment started coming through from Britain, and eventually bulk distribution became the normal system of supply in all base areas, where well over nine-tenths of the petrol was issued by this means.

This did not, of course, solve the more important problem of distribution in the field, where the 'flimsy' remained the normal means. Its one merit was easy local production. While adequate for normal commercial purposes in peace-time, the 'flimsy', as mentioned above, was not strong enough to stand up to constant handling and rough usage under war conditions. Canned petrol had to be sent by rail and ship to advanced bases, and carried in lorries for long distances over rough tracks and open desert. Whether packed in fibre cartons or wooden crates, or transported 'naked', enormous losses occurred through leakage, the amount of loss depending on the number of handlings, the type of transport used, and the distance carried. Under the worst conditions, losses reached 30 per cent or even more. Also, 'flimsies' could only be moved by sea in ships specially adapted for the purpose, and even then a considerable fire risk had to be accepted. As consumption increased, many additional can-making plants became available from Abadan and elsewhere, but even so all plants had to be worked night and day in continuous shifts in order to meet demands. At the peak, the factories were producing at the rate of more than four million cans a month. Many difficulties arose in connection with the operation of these plants. Tin-plate was scarce, particularly after Japan entered the war, and the maintenance of adequate stocks was often a cause for anxiety. Some of the plants were old, and needed constant maintenance, or the quality of the container suffered. Native labour for the operation of the plants was unreliable, and comparatively small air raids resulted in an exodus, which seriously affected production, so tin factory operating companies had to be formed, with a nucleus of British personnel. It was at this time that petrol inspectors had to be appointed, one of their duties being to supervise the loading of ships and trains to see that canned petrol was properly dunnaged, and carefully handled. But in spite of every effort, the waste through leakage continued to be enormous, and the shortcomings of the 'flimsy' tin, only too apparent for all to see, became a great operational problem.

In 1941, when the German forces arrived in the Western Desert, they brought with them a petrol container superior to any other type, the existence of which was known in the United Kingdom before the war. This was the German 20-litre steel welded can, which became known universally as the 'jerrican'. Its superior qualities were immediately if belatedly recognized, and a captured jerrican was sent at once by air to the War Office, with an urgent request that it should be adopted for use in the Middle East. It was produced eventually on a world wide scale for the Allied Armies, but only after all operations in the Middle East were over.

Luckily, large numbers of jerricans fell into British hands from time to time, and were invaluable in supplementing our supplies of 'flimsies'. Other forms of strong container were manufactured in comparatively small quantities by the Director of Works, who assumed responsibility for the manufacture of returnable containers, while the RASC continued to operate the tin factories. The Director of Works produced the 'tucan', a 2-gallon welded container, and also numbers of 40/44-gallon drums made of steel plate, after drum plants had been obtained from America. The drums were used chiefly for the distribution of aviation petrol to airfields, thus minimizing loss of this valuable spirit through leakage. At a later date, a number of 'merricans', the rather inferior counterpart of the jerrican, were sent to Middle East from America, but there were never enough strong containers, and the 'flimsy' remained the principal method of distribution to the end.

At the beginning of the war and for some time afterwards, the engineers and staff of the Shell Oil Company were able to undertake much engineering work on behalf of the DST, but, as the war progressed, the company's resources diminished, and it could no longer provide engineers and material. Consequently, as DST did not command the technical resources necessary for such work, it was decided that the Director of Works should build and repair bulk tankage, lay pipelines, and maintain bulk installations, while the RASC continued to work the installations. This arrangement worked well, and the fullest co-operation in all petroleum projects could always be depended upon from the Works Directorate. Schemes were discussed for the laying of petrol pipelines in the Western Desert, but they were not considered practicable. A pipeline was, however, laid from the main installation in the Canal zone to Cairo, a scheme which had been rejected before the war as inessential on military grounds. Now it released numbers of tank lorries and rail tank wagons.

The high proportion of petrol and oil, compared with other maintenance commodities, required by modern Armies and Air Forces, is not always realized. By far the easiest and most economical method of moving petrol is in bulk, but this depends on bulk storage, and discharge and filling facilities at the delivery terminal. This was understood only too well by the enemy, who always did his best to demolish bulk petrol facilities before evacuating a port. By curtailing the use of bulk storage, he compelled us to maintain heavy tonnages of packed petrol. It was, therefore, most important that, in every British advance during the Western Desert campaigns, skilled technicians should be available to begin the repair of tankage immediately after the capture of a port; and this was always done. For example, on the capture of Tripoli in 1943, work was put in hand at once by the Royal Engineers to recommission some of the tanks, and the discharge and filling facilities, which had been put out of action by the enemy. Within a month, 10,000 tons of storage capacity was ready, and the first tanker was discharging; and to enable full advantage to be taken of this bulk supply, a tin factory moved to Tripoli and started work, while all serviceable returnable containers were retained for filling at the bulk installation. This at once relieved the pressure on the main base. The same principle was adopted after the capture of Tobruk and Benghazi, but in the former case, bulk supplies were sent by rail and not by sea. Mobile petrol filling centres proved invaluable for filling from bulk into small containers.

A mobile petrol laboratory was formed to follow our troops during the advance, in order to test stocks of captured fuels and lubricants. Those found suitable were issued to our own vehicles, thus effecting considerable economy in despatches from the base.

Transport

To say that lack of transport was the second greatest single factor adversely affecting operations in the Middle East is probably correct. But any quantity of transport would not have served to overcome our fighting inferiority in the Western Desert, which arose largely, tactical handling excepted, from the fact that the Germans were usually one step ahead of us in tank armament and anti-tank guns.

The question is frequently asked by those insufficiently informed

Inspecting the Batch

Supply Men under Training

Supplies and Petrol at Tobruk

why the unexpectedly successful advance in February, 1941, almost to the Cyrenaica-Tripolitania frontier, was not continued to Tripoli. Had this been done, they say, the subsequent troubles would never have occurred. However, even if we disregard the fact that Rommel and the Afrika Corps were even then on the way, and that the 7th Armoured and 6th Australian Divisions were almost exhausted, there were simply not the lorries or the men to drive them in order to maintain any appreciable force forward of the limits already reached. As will be found recounted later in this volume, lack of transport also affected operations in other parts of the Middle East, notably Iraq and Syria.

The chief difficulty was scarcity of trained men, and a big scheme of 'dilution' was put in hand to eke out the limited number of Britons. In the early days, local Cypriots and Maltese had been trained as drivers, and two MT companies were formed, with British officers and NCOs. One of these companies was employed in the desert in the first battle of Libya. But there were few such men, and other sources had to be tapped. Many companies were formed, composed of Palestinian Jews, and these did good work in an operational role. Later Palestinian Arabs were trained as drivers, and were formed into companies with British cadres for work at the base. The Sudan Defence Force provided many GT companies with Sudanese drivers, and two of these units took part in the final advance. Ceylon was found to be a good source of supply, and a RASC officer was sent there from Middle East to take charge of a training school. In consequence, several Singalese companies took their part in operations. A company was formed in Mauritius and later worked in the desert. East African, and later, West African transport companies were supplied. Dominion forces provided third line transport, and there were Australian and New Zealand companies, and also many RIASC companies. After the arrival of the South African division, third line units were made available, manned by the Cape Coloured Corps.

Horse transport companies were formed with civilian native drivers, and were usefully and economically employed for short hauls in base installations, on dock clearance, road and airfield construction, and on the building of the Haifa-Beirut railway. Eight of these companies were formed, and released a considerable amount of mechanical transport.

By all these means, transport resources were augmented, and, with additional companies coming from Britain, it was at last possible to visualize a campaign in the Western Desert with enough third line transport.

This rather more happy state of affairs occurred in spite of the losses in transport units when Tobruk fell and coincided with the period of preparation for a fresh offensive when the retreat in the summer of 1942 had been stopped on the Alamein line. By this time, many RASC units with the Army had sustained heavy losses of vehicles, and nearly all the remaining vehicles required overhaul or replacement after hard service in the desert. The problem was to provide the greatest amount of transport for the offensive in October, and the target agreed upon with the Eighth Army for third line transport was the equivalent of 36 3-ton GT companies, nine water tank companies, six tank transporter companies and one bulk petrol transport company. The refitting of existing companies, and the provision of new ones, was a heavy task, and required much ingenuity, but by October 23rd, when the battle began, the target had been reached, and seven other GT companies were also available in GHQ reserve. Later, as the advance progressed, yet another three and a half companies were made available from the Delta, by depleting base transport, and a Sudan Defence Force GT company was moved to the Army from the Sudan, via the oasis of Kufra. A further 10-ton company was produced from the members of a tank transporter company for which no transporters were available. This improvisation was only made possible by the arrival of more 10-tonners from overseas. Even so, it was necessary for Eighth Army to retain second line transport from divisions withdrawn from the battle, raising the number of third line companies to 58, which was just sufficient to maintain the Eighth Army to Tripoli, which was entered on January 23rd, 1943.

After the capture of Tripoli, the administrative organization changed. Hitherto RASC matters had been managed direct between ST, GHQ and Eighth Army, but with the Army 1,000 miles distant from Tobruk, the nearest railhead, maintenance by direct contact on a day-to-day basis was no longer possible. Moreover, the situation was eased when the port of Tripoli was opened to ocean-going ships. A complete Base and L of C Staff was formed at Tripoli, under the control of the Army, and demands were met through this headquarters. However, requests for transport continued to be received, and seven more platoons of 10-tonners were produced, bringing the transport provided to a total of the equivalent of 63 3-ton GT companies.

Middle East depended largely on the United States for its supply of vehicles, and as a rule transport units from Britain arrived with men and headquarters vehicles only, and were equipped with load carriers on arrival. In 1940, 4,000 Chevrolets (with an agreed proportion of spare parts) were shipped from the United States to the Middle East for the equipment of RASC and Dominion ASC transport units. Requirements of RASC vehicles for 1941 were estimated at 14,000 but deliveries did not reach this figure, and the deficiency was made worse by heavy losses in Greece. Up to May, 1941, vehicles were received assembled, and this was heavy on shipping space, but, on arrival of assembly plants, vehicles came in cased, and 'completely knocked down'.

The first assembly plant began to operate at Ataka, near Suez, in June, 1941, and was an RASC responsibility, being originally manned mainly by the members of 36 Company RASC. Later in the year, a South African workshop unit did the assembly work, while the company was responsible for the workshop and inspection sections, and did the ferrying to vehicle reception depots. There were considerable difficulties at first, and production was slow, because of lack of previous experience, but soon vehicles were coming fast off the line, and when REME took over in October, 1942, the total output under RASC control had been some 45,000 vehicles of many different types. Meanwhile, three other assembly plants had been installed (not operated by RASC), and the four plants had an average output of 180 vehicles a day in August, 1942. This big intake made possible the equipping of Eighth Army for the offensive in October, 1942.

It was at this time that responsibility for the provision of RASC vehicles passed to the RAOC, and vehicle repair depots ceased to be RASC units. This loss was felt acutely, as having complete control over the issue of RASC vehicles and their equipment had meant much to the Corps, and the VRDs had done splendidly in equipping RASC units and replacing vehicle casualties in the field. Now the RASC was only one of many regiments and corps competing for vehicles from the RAOC. But the new system had to be accepted loyally and made to work. The actual handing over was delayed for a few weeks, by local arrangement, until the equipping of the transport for Eighth Army had been completed.

As the amount of transport began to increase in Middle East, the small peace-time detachments forming 39 Company, RASC, at Abbassia when the war began, were soon found inadequate. Moreover, the type of warfare which developed in the Western Desert threw a great load on this one and only workshop and stores organization at the base. Therefore, in August, 1940, it was expanded to a full scale heavy repair shop, MT stores depot, and vehicle reception depot, and a short time later a similar group of installations came out from Britain, and was located at Tel-el-Kebir. In 1941, a third group arrived, and was installed at Alexandria. The constant movement of RASC units in the desert limited the extent to which repairs could be done in the field, and great delay occurred if vehicles were evacuated to the base whenever they needed extensive repairs. Therefore, it was realized that the best policy was replacement of complete assemblies from the base, defective ones being returned for repair. This was particularly necessary in the case of engines, which, because of desert conditions, needed overhaul after a comparatively small mileage. With three HRSs at work, it was possible to adopt this policy, and a regular flow of major assemblies was kept up, in addition to normal vehicle repair. A high standard of efficiency was reached by the MT stores depots in meeting the demands of the HRSs, and also in supplying the technical needs of RASC units, either working in the field or at the base, or mobilizing.

Elements from the HRSs, the MT stores depots, and the VRDs were formed into advanced MT depots, of which one was sent to Tobruk in 1941, and a second to Greece when operations began there. A third was located at Haifa, to serve units in Palestine and Syria. It was a cause of deep regret to the RASC that, in October, 1942, the base workshops were taken over by the REME, when this Corps was formed, and assumed responsibility for third line repairs. At the same time, the RAOC took over MT stores depots and VRDs. Almost all the members of the RASC at these installations were transferred to the other two corps.

The RASC second line workshops remained, and kept up their standard of technical efficiency. Credit must also be given to the Chief Inspector Mechanical Transport, and his staff, whose regular technical inspections and help were big factors in maintaining this standard.

In May, 1943, after the surrender of the Axis forces in North Africa, Middle East was no longer an important operational command, though it took part in the mounting of the operations for the invasion of Sicily. A large number of RASC MT companies from North Africa came back to the Delta for refitting, most of their vehicles badly needing overhaul. This was now a REME responsibility, but as their workshops were heavily engaged in the overhaul of fighting vehicles, the work was undertaken at the RASC Mobilization Centre, Tahag. The RASC companies' second line workshops were grouped, and carried out an overhaul programme, chiefly by assembly replacement, under the direction of an Inspector of MT RASC, with a REME liaison officer attached, to deal with the supply of assemblies. By this means, more than 5,000 vehicles were reconditioned in four months, and a valuable contribution was made to the mounting of the Sicily expedition.

Experience throughout the Middle East showed the advantages and elasticity of the organisation of the GT company, formed of standard platoons, which enabled units to be readily converted from one role to another. Although the main need was for normal load carrying companies, other specialized units had to be provided, such as tank transporter companies, bulk petrol transport companies, and water tank companies. For all these purposes the organization of the GT company was satisfactory, and the number of platoons could be varied as circumstances demanded.

A number of 10-ton GT companies were employed in the desert, chiefly on those stretches of the lines of communication where the mileage between terminals was greatest, and where the heaviest loads had to be lifted. The reduced number of men required in relation to the tonnage carried eased the manpower situation, and the 10-tonners did fine work; more could well have been used.

The wear and tear of desert warfare on transport called at all times for the highest standard of vehicle maintenance. Only the strict adherence to this standard, and the rigid application of the 'task system' of maintenance made it possible for success to be achieved.

The Western Desert

The Desert: something about the name is forbidding, bringing with it a picture of heat and hunger and thirst. Yet as a Corps we had had much desert experience. As well as in India, large numbers of Corps units had served in Mesopotamia and Palestine in the First World War and there, even with the solid-tyred, low-powered MT vehicles of the time, they overcame conditions of terrain almost as bad as, and conditions of climate probably worse than, exist in any other part of the world. Moreover, the Western Desert was not unfamiliar to a Corps which had operated there in 1914-18 and which had since had several opportunities to gain experience. For example, during the 'flap' of 1936, there was considerable RASC representation in Mersa Matruh for some time.

Such excursions as this apparently did not succeed in creating any general feeling of confidence: rather the contrary seems to have occurred, arising perhaps from the discovery of the short life of an internal combustion engine unequipped with a suitable air cleaner to remove the sand and dust which is otherwise drawn into the cylinders. Moreover, the driver of the vehicle, who has the greatest difficulties to overcome in the desert, and upon whom falls the burdens of the sheer physical strain of driving and bad going, of the glare of a seldom obscured sun in the summer, of the blast of the cold winds of the winter, of the blowing sand which prevails at both seasons and works its way into every opening in man and machine, and of the long hours of work, was replaced every few years and his experience was lost. Consequently, in 1938, there were comparatively few RASC men in Egypt with much desert experience.

September, 1938, brought another 'flap': this time, Munich. Once more there was a rush out to Mersa Matruh, the terminus of the desert railway. Little advantage was, however, taken by the

RASC of this opportunity to gain experience in the desert itself, and foul though the road as far as Fuka then was, it was not desert.

In the year before the outbreak of war, there was built up in Egypt an unestablished, under-strength, formation known as the 'Mobile Division (Egypt)' afterwards to become the famous 7th Armoured Division.

The planned RASC contribution to this formation was two companies of 24 vehicles (5 and 65 Companies) and the vehicles of two others (25 and 66 Companies). This vehicle strength affords an interesting comparison with that of the present-day armoured division. In fact, however, the division itself was proportionately weak in all arms and the 96 vehicles, though below requirements, proportionately were not really inadequate.

Towards the end of August, 1939, the usual rush out to Matruh took place, and as the war with Italy did not break out then, a unique opportunity for training presented itself. Full advantage of this was taken by all arms, including the RASC, and when the division went back to the Delta in December, there was probably no better trained divisional RASC, small though it was, in the British Army.

Transport Problems

Moreover, it had become apparent to the RASC and to the AA and QMG (Lieut-Colonel later Major-General C. M. Smith, RASC) that the system of refilling second line transport and subsequently transferring the loads to first line transport at ammunition, petrol and supply points, was impracticable in the desert. There were two important reasons for this. The first was that an expected, and later realized, Axis air superiority would find a sitting target in the collection of vehicles that inevitably occurs at refilling points. The second and even more important reason was the terrain in which the division was likely to operate. The only road in the Western Desert was that which followed the coast from Alexandria and Sidi Barrani. True, there were caravan routes, very ancient ones, running inland from the coast to Siwa, but only that from Matruh could be readily traced throughout its length, and for the most part they ran in the wrong direction for this particular war. Parallel to the coast there were no defined routes, and the going varied. There was lumpy lava which would never break up, but which could only be traversed at a few miles an hour, and had a disastrous effect on vehicles wheeled or tracked: there was sand of many kinds which could be crossed at varying speeds, and there were tracts of soft loose sand impassible for wheels and sometimes even for tracks.

The Trig el Abd which appears on so many desert maps as if it

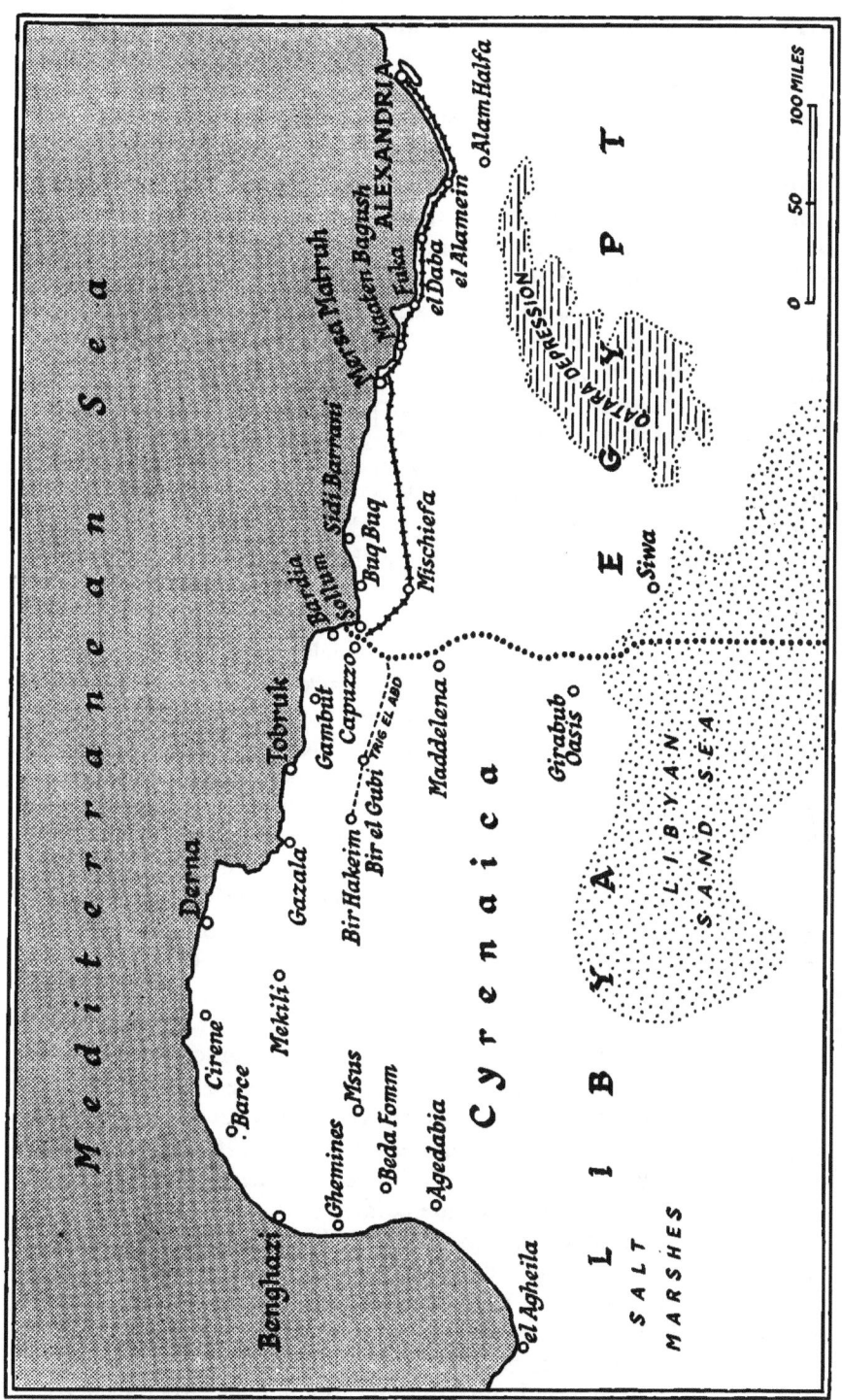

The Western Desert

were a well defined road was nothing of the sort. It was just a trail, and as time went on it was wiped off the face of the desert by the multiplication of wheel tracks which, as the years went on, began to make a spider's web of shallow troughs on the hitherto almost unblemished surface of the sand.

In such country it was not possible to establish supply, petrol and ammunition points. There were no means by which points would be identified on the ground, and individual drivers, even if equipped with compasses, could not be expected to find map references in a sandy waste. At a later date, formation axes were to be established. These were marked at suitable intervals by means of steel rods carrying the divisional or corps sign. Units could place their unit signs on the axes with suitable directions in the way of bearings and distance so that they might be located—when the sign had not been blown down. But in the early days it was visualized that war in the desert was going to be even more like war at sea than it eventually turned out to be, and it was considered undesirable to mark our 'wash' to allow it to be picked up by the enemy. Moreover, the necessary steel rods were hard to come by and wandering Arabs took all wooden posts for firewood.

What was required was some system which would include dispersion, as no other method of evading air attack was forthcoming, and yet would overcome the difficulty that all transport would be compelled to operate in sub-units, probably under an officer.

The transfer of second to first line was tackled first, as taking place nearer the enemy: anyway, there was no third line. It soon became clear that any idea of a 24-hour service would have to be abandoned, and that except perhaps in the case of 25-pounder ammunition, where the quantities were likely to be large, and it was impossible to estimate them in advance, the whole operation of replenishing first line transport would have to take place at the same time and once a day only.

A map spot in the desert, usually devoid of any landmark, was selected for each brigade. The first and second line transport of the brigade approached this point from west and east respectively, dispersed at least 100 yards between vehicles. All vehicles were marshalled by units, and by commodities within units, in such order that, when they were lined up facing each other, each first line vehicle was opposite its second line counterpart.

Needless to say, good navigation and discipline were required, but in due course all concerned became extremely expert. It was usual for the two bodies to halt some miles apart and for the leaders to meet and arrange for an orderly forming-up. During the transfer of commodities to first line, the second line vehicles dumped their loads and withdrew before the first line vehicle came forward.

When the enemy has air superiority, and there is inadequate anti-aircraft protection, and no cover, dispersion is the only answer.

It was truly a wondrous sight if one could find a high place from which to view it. High places were hard to find in the desert, but on the other hand 'high' had a relative value, and the spoil heap of a desert *bir* or water tank afforded a view for miles around. If replenishment took place near one of these, the vehicles could be seen approaching each other, halting, exchanging their wares and going off home again, almost as well as from the air. And the fact that an insignificant air target was afforded could be fully appreciated. Subsequently this system, or some variation of it, was adopted by all units operating in the desert, and not only rations, petrol and ammunition were transferred in this manner, but all the requirements of the fighting troops, including reinforcements. Return loads of prisoners and salvage were transferred at the same time. A similar system was, when applicable, followed in the case of transfer from third to second line, but, as will later be described, there was in most cases some reserve on the ground at this transfer point. Although, therefore, most second line transport was loaded simultaneously, third line vehicles were not tied to a definite timetable.

Because of heavy user demands, the above system could not always be applied to 25-pounder ammunition. It is the responsibility of the RASC, if required, to deliver ammunition to battery wagon lines, or even gun positions, in order to avoid unnecessary transfer of complete loads from one vehicle to another. The vehicles are guided forward from ammunition points. Obviously a system by which 25-pounder ammunition became available once every 24 hours only could not meet artillery requirements if expenditure exceeded the amount of one day's lift, which it frequently did, although there were corresponding slack periods. It was usual, therefore, for 25-pounder and any other type of ammunition for which there was a considerable demand, to short-circuit the daily transfer system. This could obviously be applied to any commodity for which there was an urgent or heavy demand, but it required careful arrangements and, above all, enough competent guides. Adequate dispersion was still necessary, and many more navigators had to be made available. RASC vehicles had to be retained in sub-units under their officers or NCOs, otherwise the vehicle and driver as well as the ammunition were likely to be retained by the customer.

After a winter of uneasy peace in Cairo, Italy finally staged her back-stabbing act, and the Mobile Division, now known as the 'Armoured Division (Egypt)', took the field still with its attenuated RASC resources. As time went on, the odd additional vehicle became available, but the conditions under which this RASC formation now found itself operating were severe.

The theoretical distance at which the division could operate from railhead at Mersa Matruh was 40 miles for second line plus perhaps another 15 to 20 miles for first line, which had been increased to give this additional range. The divisional armoured car regiment had a double first-line echelon, and could therefore operate further afield. But almost immediately the armoured cars were sent to Sollum, and the armoured brigade and the skeleton support group were pushed forward in their support. This left a gap of more than 80 miles in front of the railhead: two additional echelons. This gap was filled by using the RIASC of 4th Indian Division, newly arrived in the country, as third line operating in two echelons on alternate days. Fortunately they had the advantage of being able to use the metalled road from Matruh—refilling was done some miles east of Sidi Barrani. Later, RASC Reserve MT companies manned by Cypriots and by British subjects resident in Egypt augmented 4th Indian Division RIASC.

Meanwhile, second line was carrying out its regulation 80-mile turnround a day. Between the wars, the view was sometimes expressed that this distance was too short and should be increased. The Armoured Division's heavily loaded vehicles were soon to find it too long, particularly the vehicles supporting the armoured brigade, which was operating farthest from the coast and had to be maintained over some very bad going.

Eventually, the strain of about 14 hours at the wheel each day proved too much, and a temporary additional echelon to work on alternate days was provided for this brigade by vehicles from the 4th New Zealand Reserve MT Company. Thus began a close liaison between NZASC and RASC, which was to endure for the remainder of the war.

The useful load on the normal 3-ton vehicle in the desert did not exceed $2\frac{1}{2}$ tons. Any increase over this figure only resulted in the vehicle stalling in heavy going, or in broken springs. Broken springs were indeed a serious problem. Both assembled springs and spring steel were hard to come by throughout the campaign in the desert. The average speed varied according to the going. Across the occasional area of baked mud it was as high as on any good road. At the other extreme it might be less than 5 miles an hour over rocky ridges, and if many vehicles were stuck in the soft sand, the average speed of a convoy could become very low indeed.

Until the Italian advance in September, the work of the Corps, though strenuous, was only exciting in that the Italians had air superiority and bombed where they pleased. Dispersal reduced casualties to a low figure, and more vehicles were destroyed by the fires, which are inevitable when petrol is carried in flimsy tin-plate cans, than by enemy action. During this period we began to realize what a curse these cans were going to prove. Those who have never had to handle this receptacle under desert conditions may find it difficult to appreciate what an abomination it was as a carrier of petrol, although much in demand throughout the east as building material. Subjected to the jolting of lorries over the desert, large numbers sprang leaks and the loss of petrol increased according to the period before the can could be emptied into a vehicle's tank. Probably the adoption of this unsuitable container instead of a stout vessel like the jerrican which later became available was the greatest single equipment error made before the war. It caused many difficulties and dangers arising from lack of petrol.

The strenuous conditions of work soon eliminated the weaklings of all ranks, of whom there were few, and developed a body of officers, NCOs and men whose knowledge and experience of transport under desert conditions were to be invaluable in the more adventurous days to come. Splendid material was available. Many of those early desert rank and file were to be commissioned and many more were to achieve warrant and non-commissioned rank. As an example: two young lance-sergeants, who early became CSM and CQMS of one Company (65) into which at first the 96 vehicles of the Armoured Division were formed, were to become colonel and lieut-colonel respectively before the war was over and are now regular officers and Staff College graduates. Moreover, both were to command the 7th Armoured Division RASC itself: for one soldier serving in the ranks to rise to command his own unit is unusual: for two in the same unit to do so must be unique.

Water Supplies

At an early stage the problem of water carriage became acute. During peace training this had been met, in first line, by 150-gallon water tank vehicles augmented by a supply of $12\frac{1}{2}$-gallon camel tanks (the beautiful copper tanks which were carried one on each side of a baggage camel) and by the use of local *birs* or tanks. But the water tank vehicles were few in number and stood up poorly to desert conditions. The supply of $12\frac{1}{2}$-gallon tanks was also unequal to the demand, and it was feared that if the *birs* were used too extensively, the local Arabs would be deprived of water for themselves and their camels. It must be understood that these *birs*, which in many cases dated back to Roman times, had, with few exceptions, no underground sources of supply, but depended on the periodical rains which became progressively less towards the south. At one time they had existed in large numbers, but many had fallen into disrepair. In some cases the spoil from the original excavation, augmented by the accumulated sand of countless cleanings-out, had produced landmarks which were almost the sole physical features in many hundreds of square miles of desert. In this respect they were of great value, particularly as many were marked on the map with fair accuracy.

Now whereas it is a Royal Engineer responsibility to produce water from a well or from a pipe, it is the responsibility of the RASC to distribute it therefrom, but this was a matter to which the RASC had not recently given any great thought: some head scratching was now to take place.

For the purpose of bulk distribution in third line, 350-gallon water cistern lorries could be used, but they were not suitable for second line, because of the delay in decanting which would arise at the replenishing point.

There was nothing for it but that forward of the transfer point from third to second line, the bulk of water for all purposes had to be carried in the 2-gallon petrol can, which was in army, but not commercial use in the Middle East. This involved a heavy manufacturing load in the Delta and the provision of the necessary steel plate.

It will be remembered that the desert climate led to boiling of radiators, particularly in the case of vehicles of certain American makes, and to loss of water due to damage to radiators and connections. Water was also required not merely for drinking but for tea-making, cooking generally, washing up in cookhouses, and the washing of the person and clothes. Those unable to obtain a true picture of what it meant to do all these things with a ration of water which often did not exceed $\frac{3}{4}$ gallon a day for long periods and sometimes dropped to $\frac{1}{2}$ gallon, might select a nice warm summer day, put on shorts and a shirt, work all day in the garden and see how far 4 or even 6 pints will go towards quenching their thirst in tea or other beverages, cooking their meals and washing up, having a bath at the end of the day and washing the shirt and shorts. There will not be much left for the radiator.

To return to the system: as time went on the Royal Engineers, by magnificent work, brought water by pipe from Alexandria far into the desert beyond Matruh, but in 1940, except for a source being developed at Maaten Bagush, which was of use to rearward troops, the main source of supply was from the old Roman system at Mersa Matruh supplemented by distillation.

Thus the RASC carry began in third line. A limited number of 350-gallon water tankers was available through pre-war foresight in planning. Later 300-gallon tankers were improvised by bolting rectangular tanks on Chevrolet chassis. As a last resort

44-gallon drums carried in ordinary load carriers had to be used.

In the early days, during the summer of 1940, the tankers operated from Matruh to east of Sidi Barrani, where the 2-gallon containers were filled by the tedious and laborious method of a row of taps at the rear of the vehicle. Much thought and effort were spent on improving on this method as time went on, and eventually an 'octopus' was produced, but, generally speaking, throughout the campaign the somewhat elementary method of a gravity feed from a row of taps was used. Another method introduced was that known as a 'Sportapool'. This was a canvas tank, the sides of which were supported by the weight of its contents. It was similar to tanks used as children's pools in gardens. Although it had the advantage of providing static storage and thus released much needed vehicles to keep up the turn-round, it had many disadvantages. Vehicles had to discharge into it, and this was a slow process with danger of congestion. The water had then to be put into the containers by one means or another, most of them insanitary. It had to be kept covered with canvas to keep out sand, reduce evaporation, and minimize the risk of its being seen from the air. But the cover became soaked and sank, and the sand got in just the same. Where 'Sportapools' were used, it did not much matter what beverage was prepared from the water: tea, coffee, rum, lime juice, just plain— they were all the same colour and the taste did not vary much.

Forward of third line, as had already been stated, except for the occasional introduction of other containers to make up deficiencies, most water was delivered, until the advent much later of the water-carrying jerrican, in 2-gallon petrol cans. These vessels were, of course, returnable, but everyone knows the difficulty in enforcing return under operational conditions. They were fairly easily damaged, although nothing like so easily as the 4-gallon flimsy, and could, and invariably did, lose their caps. Moreover, several sets or echelons were required, as may be readily worked out. Taking a case where second line was operating in a two-day turn-round, which sometimes occurred as in the case of the armoured brigade mentioned above, then at least five complete sets were required, namely:—

> one being filled at water point,
> one in each second line echelon (2),
> one in first line, and
> one in the possession of troops.

The only method of ensuring return was a rigid one-for-one basis at the water point. Incidentally there was no surer way of infuriating the RASC in the field than to send up empty water containers from base where so much beautiful water was available.

As a transport load, water easily gave more worry and anxiety than any other, not excluding petrol. A simple calculation will show that to deliver even one gallon a man a day requires for a division, say, 18,000 strong, about 27 additional 3-ton vehicles. But as the 3-ton vehicle was seldom loaded to that amount in the desert, the equivalent of more than a platoon was required for each echelon. This was something that had never been taken into account when planning transport establishments.

Desert Navigation

The difficulties of finding one's way about the desert have been mentioned earlier. It cannot be pretended that desert navigation presents the difficulties of sea navigation. Wind has little effect on the direction pursued by a lorry, and there are fortunately no tides or currents. On the other hand, few sea going vessels operate with a normal crew of one, and where anyone is expected to navigate at sea he is usually provided with a compass.

Few compasses were available in the desert, and the ordinary army prismatic compass, excellent though it is, will vary many points according to the position it occupies in a vehicle. Many types of sun compass were produced, based on sundial principles, and very helpful they were. But they also were limited in number and even in the desert there are dull days periodically, there are frequent sandstorms and inevitably there are nights. Because of navigation difficulties, therefore, it was nearly always necessary to operate transport in sub-units. Indeed at one time the supply of prismatic compasses did not even go to one for each officer.

Fortunately, some people seemed to have, or to develop, an extraordinary sense of direction. On one occasion, in 1941, during an advance, when water was becoming scarce, a RASC sergeant arrived at an FMC with one water cistern lorry in which he, for lack of any other vehicle, was riding passenger. On being welcomed with open arms, he announced that he had nine more vehicles. 'Where?'—'Over there'. 'On what bearing?'—'I couldn't say, Sir, I haven't got a compass'. 'Good heavens, man, can you ever find them again—how far away are they?'—'Oh, about 10 miles—I'll fetch them along.' He departed amidst gloomy forebodings that he would never be seen again, but at any rate he was not likely to die of thirst. However, in an hour or so he was back with 3,500 gallons of precious water. He could not see anything difficult about it.

Plans for an Advance

The end of the first phase in the desert was marked by the advance of the Italians who reached Sidi Barrani in September; in consequence the third line lift was considerably shortened. Soon, however, plans were afoot for a possible advance by our troops, and the RASC had to support it with the limited transport likely to be available. 4th Indian Division was now forward, their RIASC thoroughly desert-worthy in consequence of exercises in the winter and of their gruelling experience acting as third line forward of Matruh. But, except for the Cypriot companies, there was little available in the way of third line. True, two British MT companies, 345 and 346, had been formed in Cairo from reinforcements, and others were beginning to appear from the United Kingdom, but so far these consisted of men only: vehicles were not yet available. It was clear that an advance of, say, two divisions could not be supported by normal transport echelons operating from railhead.

During the earlier stage when we held the frontier, there had been established here and there a number of reserve dumps of ammunition, food, water and petrol, from which troops could have been maintained for a short period in the event of the extended line of communication between Alexandria and the forward troops being cut by sea raids, parachute attacks, or other methods. The dumps, for lack of a better name, were called by the old 1914 war name, field supply depots—FSDs—although they held much more than supplies.

Someone had the bright idea of applying this system to an advance. Thus available transport would be used to establish FSDs well forward. When the advance took place, second line transport would switch to these FSDs and third line begin to build up further depots as far in advance as was operationally desirable.

The rapid advance in December of the Western Desert Force (later known as XIII Corps) from east of Sidi Barrani to the frontiers of Tripoli, where it arrived in about two months, put an enormous strain on the system. The attack went even better than had been expected, and 7th Armoured Division (by which title the Armoured Division (Egypt) was now known), made a rapid advance. On December 9th, 4th Armoured Brigade cut the coast road west of Sidi Barrani, and then went on to do the same west of Bardia. This strained administrative resources almost to breaking point; 5 Company drove night and day without stopping, collecting captured petrol from Sidi Barrani, and delivering it to the brigade.

Several RASC companies were working with 4th Indian Division, 61 as a water tank company, and 231 troop-carrying 16th Indian Brigade. The latter company was one of those locally raised, composed of Cypriots and Maltese, with British officers and NCOs. During the operations leading up to the capture of Sidi Barrani, it was very hard hit, coming under heavy shell and machine-gun fire and being dive-bombed and machine-gunned from the air. Its casualties were 15 other ranks killed and 14 wounded, while 14 vehicles were destroyed and 54 were damaged. The unit did well under fire and gave the infantry all the fire support it could. Two men were given the immediate award of the Military Medal in this action: L/Cpl J. Zoumberis, a Cypriot, for saving three men under fire, and L/Cpl W. Sonnino, a Maltese, for courage and coolness under artillery fire and bombing. After the attack on Sidi Barrani, 4th Indian Division was withdrawn, and its place was taken by 6th Australian Division. On the whole, the transport stood up to it magnificently, mainly because of the strenuous efforts and notable devotion to duty of the RASC drivers and artificers. Improvisation was essential, particularly in the FSDs. Although originally required to handle RASC commodities only, they soon became traffic centres through which passed all the requirements of the troops. Neither RASC nor RAOC personnel of the correct categories were available to man the FSDs fully, and on one occasion, for example, RASC butchers from a cold storage unit handled ammunition, while on another a FSD was manned by the borrowed QM staffs of a brigade. But the system worked, and with minor modifications had come to stay as that of the transfer of loads from third to second line under desert conditions. With little further change, its final development was to be employed in the battle for Europe.

Not the least of the problems arising was that presented by the unexpectedly large number of prisoners of war which fell into our hands. Enough supplies were captured with them to afford a meagre ration. The prisoners were taken to Egypt as quickly as possible in all the ships available, but even so, more than 2,000 were recaptured by the enemy when he advanced in April.

The arrival on the Cyrenaica/Tripoli frontier of 7th Armoured Division and 6th Australian Division, whose fine second line did a magnificent job in the advance, presented a third line transport problem of no ordinary magnitude. The farthest back that these divisions, and their eventual replacements, 2nd Armoured and 9th Australian Divisions, could reasonably be expected to send their second line, was 18 FSD near Ghemines. From there to Tobruk (the Navy finding Benghazi untenable in the face of enemy air superiority), was about 350 miles. To maintain the forward troops and establish reserves, two 3-ton companies and one 10-ton company were available. Any RASC officer can calculate the extent of the task presented. In the event the troops were maintained during February and March, but little impression was made on the reserve situation. The fact that it was only possible, by making use of all available transport, to maintain a very weak force on the frontier

'Flimsies' in the Desert

Desert Roadside Pump

Vehicle Assembly

is an effective answer to those critics who think that General Wavell missed a chance to press on to Tripoli.

What of the MT companies arriving from Britain? The men who could be made available were sent to the desert to equip themselves from the large number of vehicles left by the Italians. But there is a long step between seeing abandoned vehicles scattered in the desert and in parks in Bardia, Benghazi and Tobruk and getting them in running order. Many had been damaged by our air and ground action, and others by the careless driving of those who first captured them. Most were diesels of which the British had little experience; the parks were frequently casualty parks. In the event, no really efficient units were formed, although much of the port operation was effected by captured vehicles, and every credit must be given to those who achieved even that result.

Retreat

The problem of the maintenance of 18 FSD and the build up of reserves was solved, not by us, but by the action of the enemy. On March 31st, 1941, Rommel advanced from El Ageila, and the partially equipped elements of 2nd Armoured Division and 9th Australian Division, which had relieved the better equipped and very desert-worthy 7th Armoured and 6th Australian Divisions, were soon in full retreat, the former by the desert route to Mekili and the latter over the Jebel.

As always during a retreat rumours and scares were not lacking. Notable among the latter was an air reconnaissance over Msus which reported enemy armour in that place and thus considerably accelerated the withdrawal of Command HQ from Barce. In fact, the reported AFVs were only some rectangular tanked water trucks from a water tank company dumping water in bulk at Msus for use of 2nd Armoured Division.

The fate of the unfortunate 2nd Armoured Division has been related by many historians. The divisional RASC fared as badly as the other arms. It was long before formations from home began to realize that there was a vast difference between operating in the desert and operating in well-mapped Europe with its highly developed road system. At a later date, no unit went into the desert without some desert trained officers, NCOs and men allotted to it on arrival in the theatre, but 2nd Armoured Division RASC was not so provided. The lesson took a long time to learn, and formations continued to come from home full of the confidence born of ignorance, and convinced that their triumphs in some endurance exercise under winter conditions in Britain qualified them for immaculate performance in the practically trackless desert. Fortunately they were not in the majority. It would be absurd to maintain that desert warfare was something apart. It was not, but it had its little peculiarities of which notice had to be taken if you wished to continue in the business.

After this digression we must return to the 9th Australian Division withdrawing from position to position on the Jebel in conformation with the withdrawal of the remains of 2nd Armoured Division—little more than headquarters and administrative units—before the determined German advance. The division had no vehicles for its second line transport and few for its first line. Cyrenaica Command HQ, which had replaced XIII Corps at the end of our advance, placed supplies, ammunition and petrol within reach of its unit transport as it withdrew, and also provided troop-carrying transport. The only transport available came from third line companies on FSD maintenance, and as platoons of the third line companies came forward they were off-loaded in *ad hoc* FSDs and allotted to troop-carrying. At the same time attempts were made to establish dumps for the elements of 2nd Armoured Division to the south. Unfortunately, many 10-tonners loaded with petrol fell victim to enemy air superiority.

Eventually, the headquarters and remnants of units of 2nd Armoured Division surrendered at Mekili, and 9th Australian Division withdrew to Tobruk to begin its historic defence of that place. A few people withdrew much faster and went much farther. It is said that some were only finally brought to a halt by the Suez Canal.

In Tobruk, steps were taken to introduce a ration based on the unbalanced stocks available. It may be mentioned that such unbalanced stocks were caused by enemy action against shipping from the Delta and not by any ST failure. The 9th Australian Division ASC provided a headquarters, but owing to lack of vehicles, many of them were employed as infantry. As the fortress area was compact, units drew direct from FSD. For operational reasons British 3-ton companies had to provide troop-carrying elements at brigade disposal. It was found possible before the gate was shut to get back to Egypt many 10-tonners which had poor troop-carrying capacity and were urgently needed for the maintenance from railhead at Matruh of forces being formed to build up a new front on the Egyptian frontier. And so we may leave Tobruk for the moment. Throughout the siege, the RASC with some AASC assistance ran supplies, transport, petrol and ammunition, while many of the AASC of the 9th Australian Division did gallant service as infantrymen. RASC units included 9 BSD, 48 DID, 115 Petrol Depot, a section of 1 Bulk Petroleum Storage Company, a field bakery section, 25 Company (MAC), 61 Company, and 345 Company. At a later stage of the siege, 9th Australian Division was relieved by 70th Division, the RASC of which was composed of 61, 145 and 419 Companies. Needless to say, only the men and not the equipment and vehicles were subjected to the dangerous passage between Tobruk and Alexandria.

Cyrenaica Command HQ, leaving its transport behind, withdrew by sea to Maaten Bagush and became once more HQ Western Desert Force. With some difficulty fighting troops to man the frontier line and administrative troops to support them were found. Fortunately Rommel had outrun his administrative resources and both sides were for the moment incapable of any great activity.

This condition of stalemate continued throughout the summer with the exception of certain alarms and excursions in both directions, of which the most important was the abortive operation 'Battleaxe', of which much had been expected. An FSD, complete with stocks of rations, water, petrol and ammunition, was placed on wheels for this operation and was to have opened in the escarpment just south of Sollum, from which it was hoped to maintain it by sea. As the operation was unsuccessful the FSD never opened.

Mention has been made earlier of the presence in the desert of a 10-ton company—286—operating Mack and White vehicles. Real scope for them was found during this period in maintaining the FSDs from railhead at Matruh. 30 FSD was right by the side of the road and trailers could, therefore, be used although of course this was impracticable in the desert, but there the Macks and Whites had a very fair performance without trailers. As time went on these excellent vehicles suffered from lack of spares and of tyres. The latter was a particularly serious problem and was ingeniously alleviated by a system of repair involving cutting out burst or damaged portions and bolting a piece of another damaged tyre in place of it. This method worked and many vehicles were thus kept on the road, but it was expensive in manpower.

Consolidation

The six comparatively quiet months before the considerable operations which were to take place in November were of great value to the RASC in building up their strength and in training for desert work the third line companies which were now coming forward in satisfactory numbers.

Moreover, two most important events occurred which were to influence the operation of the Corps in all theatres for the rest of the war. These were (*a*) the formation of the Field Maintenance Centre, and (*b*) the provision of RASC column headquarters for command of third line transport.

The FMC grew out of the FSDs whose formation has been already outlined. What had become evident during the advance to the

Tripolitanean frontier became even clearer during the summer of 1941: the 'FSD' had become a focus of all maintenance and evacuation traffic behind division and had, therefore, come to stay as part of the administrative machine so far as the desert was concerned. No longer could the RASC captain commanding the DID control this centre and perform his own duties as well. An FSD was not merely an RASC organization, but a small formation dealing with every aspect of administration, including such diverse elements as NAAFI and prisoners of war. To meet the situation a small headquarters named a 'Field Maintenance Centre' was evolved. Although not an RASC responsibility, the first trial FMC was formed by HQ 30 Company RASC, all of whose platoons happened to be temporarily detached. It quickly became evident that the scheme would work, and when six FMCs were formed for the impending operations, they were schooled by 30 Company.

The column headquarters were something quite new both to the DDsST of the Corps who were to handle them, and to the lieut-colonels in command. For forthcoming operations, four column headquarters were allotted to XXX Corps and one to XIII Corps. It should be mentioned that in October, Desert Force Headquarters had been replaced by HQ Eighth Army and Force HQ had reverted once more to XIII Corps. The first DDST Eighth Army was Brigadier W. d'A. Collings. Brigadier F. S. Clover took over in November, 1941, and Brigadier H. A. Kelsall rather more than a year after that. A new Corps, XXX Corps, had been formed and was primarily intended to command armoured formations. The operations of XXX Corps involved a sweeping movement to the south across the desert to outflank the frontier defences and bring the enemy armour to battle on ground of our choosing. By that time the railway from Matruh and a water pipeline from Alexandria had been extended into the desert and had reached rail and pipe heads in the vicinity of Mischiefa, approximately 30 miles south of Buq Buq. On this XXX Corps and certain army troops would be based for the operation.

The DDST XXX Corps assembled his four column commanders and together they planned a method of operation. It must have been their lucky day because the method which they evolved formed the basis of all subsequent operations of large bodies of corps and army transport both in the desert and in the European theatre. The idea was that one column headquarters would remain at railhead to supervise the loading and despatch of daily convoys to FMCs. Another column headquarters would be established in the forward area to receive convoys and control them while at FMCs, ensuring their speedy return to railhead to maintain turn-round. A third column headquarters was stationed 'on the wire', that is, on the Egyptian-Libyan frontier in the area of which it was expected companies might bivouac on their way forward or back. In the event this last headquarters proved unnecessary and was sent back to railhead to assist in loading and despatching, and in the administration of companies' headquarters which remained in the railhead area.

The fourth column headquarters was given command of the water tank companies and certain 3-ton companies carrying drums for water. This proved to be a mistake. It was done because pipe head was initially some distance from railhead, but it would have been much better if the water companies had come from the beginning under the operational control of the forward and rearward columns controlling the remaining companies, the fourth column commander serving as an administrative commander only, to supervise loading at pipe head. As it was he could not be both forward and back, he had inadequate wireless sets, and so lost touch with his companies, and the all-important water supply was inclined to get out of step with other commodities.

If this story seems to concern XXX Corps to the exclusion of XIII Corps, it will be remembered that the latter, which was operating along the sea coast, had a limited transport problem in the initial stages and only one column headquarters. Never before in history had an operation precisely like that planned for XXX Corps on November 18th, 1941, been conducted and the operation was never to be repeated on quite such a scale so far as RASC transport was concerned. The Corps was to be assembled in a featureless desert, sweep forward more or less due west across that desert, swing to the north and engage the enemy. Allowing the second line of armoured formations to operate to their maximum range this involved FMCs being established some 100–120 miles from railhead—or three third line echelons at 80 miles for each echelon. There could be no establishment of FMCs in advance, and therefore all commodities for initial stocking had to go forward behind the advancing troops.

The Corps (XXX), which consisted of 7th Armoured Division, made up to three Armoured Brigades, and 1st South African Division (less one brigade) was 'formed up' on the desert. It was centred some 50 miles south of Buq Buq covering a large area. The method employed was to allot a number of map squares running north and south to the various echelons. Thus the armoured cars, which were to lead the advance, were allotted the most westerly squares, and in succession to the east were the fighting arms, first line transport, divisional RASC of 7th Armoured Division, and 'Q' Services of 1st South African Division and, finally, more than 20 companies of RASC third line (the water tank companies included) occupying a considerable depth and a front of about 10 miles to ensure adequate dispersion.

The advance proceeded by waves, as it were, the third line wave coming last. The senior column commander controlled the forward movement of third line companies, and it is unlikely that on any other occasion has a lieut-colonel of the RASC given the advance signal to a couple of thousand RASC vehicles on a 10-mile front. He had a 'point to march on', that being a certain kilometre post on the frontier track, north and south of which the necessary gaps in the wire would have been made by the armoured cars. It must have been an imposing sight from the air when that enormous mass of vehicles started moving. Of course the armoured cars had gone forward earlier, but most of the remainder were on the move throughout the daylight hours of November 18th.

A gap was allowed between echelons, but the commander of the third line had the dust of the very desert-worthy 7th Armoured Division RASC to guide him. However, as he had not been long in the desert, he was provided with a competent navigating officer. The two disagreed as to bearings throughout the advance, and the commanding officer still maintains that he was right. One would be more inclined to support him if his navigational record had always remained as immaculate as his otherwise spotless reputation.

Be that as it may, second line transport followed up and replenished its troops during the night, and early next morning gathered round the FMC like vultures. The plan was for 62 FMC to feed 7th Armoured Division; and 63 FMC the South Africans. At both FMCs anxious members of the corps Q and ST staff scanned the horizon to the south for the first sign of dust which would mark the arrival of the third line columns known to have spent the night on the Libyan side of the wire. Glasses swept the desert, and at last, at about 1000 hours, dust clouds like the steam from dozens of express trains began to come over the horizon. Navigation had been excellent, and at 62 FMC Captain A. J. Hillman (later to have both feet blown off by an anti-tank mine) arrived first, with four platoons of 10-tonners.

As the FMCs were three days' turn-round from railhead and the third line transport was barely sufficient to meet requirements, no vehicles could be held at FMCs under load, and commodities had either to be accepted or returned—and it took a strong-minded man to send a load back all that way. Scales and load tables had been carefully worked out, but inevitably there were over-estimates as well as under-estimates. Rations and water were simple. Petrol was in such demand that the infamous 4-gallon flimsies scarcely had time to leak. However, because of the large percentage of new or practically new vehicles in units, the normal 6 per cent lubricants against petrol proved much too generous. Again, some of the more exotic types of ammunition were not being discharged at field force ceiling rates. As convoys were loaded 48 hours in advance, the flow of these unwanted items could not be stopped, and there was an accumulation of goods for which there was no sale until scales were adjusted. At 62 FMC in particular there was an embarrassing surplus which never sold: it may be there still.

Rommel's Break-through

Life in the RASC stratum of this war, never at any time really dull, was much enlivened on November 24th. On that date Rommel made his famous break through from west to east. This resulted, so far as XXX Corps was concerned, in much first line transport being dispersed and second line driven off to the south. Admirable coolness was displayed by the company commanders of 7th Armoured Division in withdrawing their units under control. For instance, Major E. V. Molyneux was awarded a Military Cross when, attacked by enemy tanks, he withdrew his unit to the south completely under control, ignoring the considerable confusion prevailing at the time. In consequence, only three vehicles of his unit, 65 Company 7th Armoured Brigade, were lost, and replenishment of his formation was not interfered with.

Even those who actually took part in the widespread movements of units and individual vehicles which occurred at this time could hardly object to being described as slightly hurried. In daylight it was difficult, and after dark almost impossible to distinguish friend from foe. There is lacking, however, reliable confirmation of the tale that a certain irascible officer whose vehicle collided with another of similar appearance in a race for a gap in the frontier wire had his fluent comments replied to in equally fluent German.

DDST XXX Corps was fortunate in being out of camp when Rommel arrived. On the DDST's return journey, ominous 'brew-ups' marked the former site of rear headquarters, so he decided to withdraw to 62 FMC, which then operated as *ad hoc* rear corps headquarters for some days. The senior officer present in the vicinity of 62 FMC when trouble blew up was the second in command of 7th Armoured Division RASC. Although he had only been in his appointment, and indeed in the desert, for a few days, he unhesitatingly assumed command and, informed over his W/T of the turn things were taking, prepared the area for defence. On the arrival of DDST, this young RASC TA major, later to become a brigadier, had collected four fully-manned 25-pounders which had strayed from the main battle, and many other weapons, to form a nucleus defence.

Although enemy parties came very close to both 62 and 63 FMCs during the night, they remained unaware of the booty that lay so near them.

Meanwhile, there was much consternation back at main Eighth Army HQ 'on the wire' at Maddelena, and attempts were made by certain persons, only some of whom were well informed, to stop the forward move of third line transport to the FMCs. In the event such attempts were misguided, although in the light of available information at the time the action was perhaps excusable. Fortunately the RASC platoon commanders, most of them 2nd lieutenants, were not over-awed by unofficial, or indeed properly impressed by official, attempts to stop them and continued stubbornly on their way. Their action proved to be correct, and had not the FMCs, 62 FMC in particular, continued to receive convoys throughout November 24th and 25th, the maintenance of 7th Armoured Division might well have been compromised, with disastrous results.

Meanwhile, things were not quiet on XIII Corps RASC front, and at one time the commander of 51 FMC, together with his RASC DID, were driven off their dumps, while the enemy refilled. The FMC commander reported the progress of his battle by field telephone. On the 25th, XIII Corps were trying to pass a third line convoy to the NZ Division fighting outside of Tobruk. Under the command of Captain J. M. Crawford, it passed near 62 FMC. The Chief Engineer of XXX Corps, Colonel (now Brigadier) G. H. Clifford, a New Zealand Officer, who had spare time on his hands for lack of engineer tasks, was appointed to command this convoy and certain other elements and get them to their destination. This distinguished New Zealand officer still has a soft spot for the Corps with which, as he puts it, he won his first award of the Distinguished Service Order. Captain J. M. Crawford and Captain J. C. Kent, who accompanied him, were awarded Military Crosses, and Sergeant (now Major) W. C. Grierson the Military Medal.

When 9th Australian Division was relieved by 70th (formerly 6th) Division the divisional RASC of the latter consisted of 61, 145, and 'Z' (later 459) Company, on an *ad hoc* establishment which was a typical, if not exactly endearing custom in MEF. They had plenty to do, as the existing organization had grown rather than been set up and had many imperfections less apparent to those who had made it work during the months of siege than to the comparatively fresh 70th Division. There was the Polish ASC to train, and soon plans were being made for the break-out to assist the operations taking place in the desert outside. In these operations both 61 and 145 Companies were very actively engaged.

Around Tobruk there was confused fighting, and particularly good work was done by ambulance drivers. Captain W. H. B.

Roberts won his Military Cross by recovering many New Zealand wounded from enemy territory, and Dvr A. G. Shaw was awarded the Distinguished Conduct Medal for an excellent individual effort. He was later to win the Military Medal at Salerno.

The Advance continued

Rommel's incursion into our back areas proved to be only temporary, and after a few days' chaos, affairs were tidied up and he was compelled gradually to withdraw westwards. Tobruk was relieved. HQ XXX Corps was withdrawn from the battle in early December, and it fell to XIII Corps, with all available columns under command, to maintain the forces which pursued the enemy once again to the frontier of Tripoli.

The period was not without incident so far as the RASC was concerned. The rapid advance from Tobruk to the frontier and the subsequent rapid withdrawal when once again Rommel counter-attacked gave rise to much troop-carrying, and RASC vehicles were involved in many scattered fights. For instance, on a day in early December, 11th Indian Infantry Brigade was dismounted from its RASC transport to attack Bir el Gubi. The enemy attacked with tanks and the infantry had to make a hurried withdrawal. It is on record that the RASC drivers behaved with great steadiness, picking up their passengers within a few hundred yards of the advancing tanks and withdrawing in good order.

The weather and the condition of Benghazi placed out of question any material assistance from that port, so that maintenance was on a six days' turn-round across the desert from Tobruk to FMC at Msus, all available transport being concentrated on this task. The 20 or more GT companies employed on these runs worked with almost complete regularity, with a turn-round of up to 400 miles, and they never failed to deliver the daily quota of essential supplies of all sorts, proving once again that RASC transport could operate on the desert, running for continuous periods with reliable results, provided that the mileages were not above 60 a day. This allowed time for meals, rest, and maintenance, and could not be exceeded, except for brief periods, without risk of breakdown.

Over such distances, the problem of carrying the petrol, food and water for the convoys themselves was one of great importance. The daily despatches from Tobruk to Msus were sometimes as many as 200 lorries, and the petrol alone for these for the round trip came to about 16,000 gallons. When lubricants, rations and water were added, from 35 to 40 lorries were necessary for the domestic maintenance of the convoy. It was no use delivering 50,000 gallons of petrol, the average daily figure, at FMC, and then withdrawing 8,000 for the convoy's return journey. These facts had to be taken into consideration when the tonnage capacity of the third line transport was worked out.

During December, 1st Armoured Division had joined Eighth Army. Its RASC companies were 10 (22nd Armoured Brigade), 925 (2nd Armoured Brigade), 903 (Support Group), and 910 (Divisional Troops). The two third line companies, 911 and 918, became GT units. Early in January, the division was facing the Germans in their El Agheila position, much as the ill-fated 2nd Armoured Division had been nearly a year before. To make up for the absence of an FMC at Agedabia, an extra link had to be found from XIII Corps' slender transport resources, working forward 60 miles from that at Msus; then 10 Company took over, and delivered to the second line 25 miles farther on; and it was still 40 miles to delivery point.

This was not the only demand on the inadequate transport available for Eighth Army. Tobruk did not receive enough stores and petrol by sea to meet the army's demands, and a daily convoy had to be run from railhead, which was still back at Mischiefa, south of Sidi Barrani, to the El Adem area, south of Tobruk, a distance of 170 miles. This tied up GT companies urgently needed in the forward area. Another call on the transport pool was for the maintenance of XXX Corps, which was engaged in clearing the enemy from the Sollum-Halfaya-Bardia area. In this area 75 Company, second line transport for 1st Armoured Brigade, was employed.

Tank transporters were now at work in the forward area, though as yet only in small numbers. There was one company (144) and an independent section. As these vehicles were a novelty, there was a good deal of uncertainty as to the manner in which they should be employed. Some were attached to various Ordnance recovery units and to the tank reinforcement unit at Tobruk.

The company moved both 7th and 1st Armoured Divisions forward, and then delivered reinforcement tanks from Tobruk to Msus, and later to Antelat, 230 miles across the desert. On arrival at delivery point, the transporters would be used for operational moves, or be sent back to fetch up tanks from Mischiefa and or even from Mersa Matruh. On the return trips, the company always asked for loads of 'dead' tanks for evacuation; but at that time the organization for the recovery of tank casualties was not fully developed, and the unit had enough to do without going round the desert looking for them.

Rommel's New Offensive

When the enemy offensive began on January 21st, 1942, 201st Guards Brigade was beyond Agedabia, with 67, 903 and 910

Companies. Two days later, these units suffered severely at the hands of enemy columns; 67 Company had only 17 lorries left; 903 Company was split up and reported 80 of its vehicles and a large percentage of its men missing, though 30-odd lorries found their way back a few days later; and 910 Company lost all but three officers, 50 men, and 20 vehicles. The remnants continued to maintain the division, which was obliged to withdraw before the enemy thrust, and on February 10th it was reorganized to consist of 2nd Armoured Brigade, 1st Motor Brigade, and divisional troops. The companies remaining with the formation were 903, 910, and 925; 67 Company was withdrawn to join 10th Armoured Division, and 10 Company went to an L of C transport column.

Meanwhile, 4th Indian Division had counterattacked south from Benghazi, but had been cut in two, and 7th Indian Brigade was isolated in that place, together with several RASC companies, including 49, 241 and 278. Major R. Gilmour, officer commanding 49 Company, had won the Military Cross a little earlier, when taking a convoy of 132 lorries with petrol to Msus. On arrival, he found Msus in enemy hands, but succeeded in extricating the column and bringing it to safety through 600 miles of strange country under trying conditions. The same award went to Captain J. F. Dugdale, the workshop officer of the same company. When an enemy mobile column began to shell the company location, he got away many vehicles which were under repair and which would otherwise have had to be abandoned, together with the technical vehicles and valuable MT stores. Eventually the officer commanding ordered him to leave the location, which was by then being shelled from a range of 500 yards. The slow-moving breakdown lorry with a non-runner in tow soon got into difficulties, and Captain Dugdale went back to help. He also aided two officers of another company, one of them wounded, who had been forced to abandon their vehicle, and would otherwise have been captured.

In Benghazi, Sgt G. H. Ackrill, also of 49 Company, won the immediate award of the Military Medal, when there was a heavy air raid after the town was cut off. By his calm and resolute example he kept his men together and, though wounded, he brought a party out through the enemy positions under small arms fire.

The brigade in Benghazi formed itself into three columns and broke through to join the armour at Mekili, 70 miles eastward. In this operation, many members of the RASC took part, and several men distinguished themselves. For example, L/Cpl G. L. Rimmer, of 49 Company, was with a platoon carrying an Indian battalion when 19 two-wheel-drive lorries became bogged in soft sand. The rest of the column was disappearing, but although he might well have been lost or captured, Rimmer, who had a four-wheel drive lorry, turned aside, towed out 11 and sent them on. He then stayed until the others had been towed out by the battalion carriers. Nearly 300 men were thus saved from capture. This column got through with the loss of 31 vehicles in all, some of which had to be destroyed to save petrol. By the end of the march, lorries were each carrying 35 men. L/Cpl Rimmer was awarded the Distinguished Conduct Medal.

L/Cpl C. H. Platten, also of 49 Company, was cut off south of Benghazi, so, immobilizing his vehicle, he made his way towards our lines with the help of tribesmen, until he was picked up by a patrol on March 4th, having covered 250 miles in 36 days in most arduous conditions. On his way he had acquired valuable information about enemy dispositions, and volunteered to lead a patrol back and point them out. In consequence, our aircraft were guided on to important concentrations of enemy troops, which were successfully bombed. He too won the Distinguished Conduct Medal.

Cpl J. O. Seed, of 241 Company, which was also engaged in troop-carrying for 4th Indian Division, brought up transport to assist in the withdrawal of a company which was in position on an exposed ridge, with enemy tanks less than 1,200 yards away, shooting at our guns and lorries. The drivers drove round in circles picking up the men of the infantry company, who were dispersed on a 500-yard front, and did not move off until all who could be seen had been embussed. It was because of the initiative of the RASC men, who acted promptly and with complete disregard for their own safety under heavy shell fire, that the company was withdrawn with only a few casualties. Cpl Seed received the immediate award of the Military Medal.

Two other recipients of this award were ambulance drivers. Dvr V. F. G. Hudson, 25 Company, evaded enemy columns for two days and brought the patients in his ambulance into hospital. He was cut off on the return journey, so he collected casualties from a column he met, and brought them in as well. Dvr T. Walker, 1st Armoured Division, had a load of patients when his ambulance was bogged in sand; he took them out, put them under cover, and then walked for four hours to get help, being twice attacked from the air and in danger of capture. But he completed the evacuation of his patients in the end.

Lieutenant P. J. W. Henderson, of 31 Company, who was in charge of an ammunition point at Antelat, won the Military Cross when he got the ammunition away safely, in spite of heavy shelling and being harassed by enemy patrols.

While all honour must go to the gallant recipients of these awards, it must always be remembered that for every one individual whose timely fortitude brought him deservedly in the limelight, there were thousands of RASC men in all kinds of units from the lordly tank transporters to the humble water section who, day in and day out, carried on their essential duties conscientiously and well, in the trying conditions which prevail in the desert in winter. The essential work of the RASC, to maintain the forces in the field, must for the many represent solid hard work and little variety; only for the few does it mean action in contact with the enemy.

The Gazala Line

The withdrawal to the Gazala Line was most disappointing after the strenuous efforts before and after the relief of Tobruk. However, it did afford a breathing space. Railhead was pressed forward to Tobruk, and some opportunity was given to the hard worked third line to recover from its hammering during the winter. Meanwhile, there were newcomers among the divisions, and the RASC of 1st Armoured Division and 50th Divisions soon became as desert-worthy as the columns of 7th armoured, 4th Indian, and New Zealand Divisions. It is probable that 50th Division was unique in having its own properly organized and trained anti-tank platoon based on its pre-war band and armed with weapons acquired by means other than normal issue channels.

This comparatively easy spell in the Gazala Line was not to be of long duration. On May 26th a German attack developed, the enemy coming round the open desert flank south of Bir Hakeim in strength. The subsequent three weeks of fighting in the area between Tobruk and the Gazala Line eventually went in favour of the enemy and once more, on June 17th, 1942, Tobruk was surrounded. Few expected that the second siege would last but four days. The period of hard fighting in which, it must be admitted, the enemy got the better of us, is admirably described in *Crisis in the Desert*, compiled by the South African official historians. This volume examines all facets of the battle, including the administrative problems. Such was the confusion of the fighting which went on in the area around the Gazala Line and extending as far west as Tobruk–El Adem or even farther, that normal maintenance was rendered extremely difficult at the best and, at the worst, impossible. The problems arising and the manner of their solution are illustrated by some of the incidents recounted below. They could be multiplied. Great persistence and ingenuity were displayed by many members of the RASC of all ranks in performing their maintenance duties at that time.

Administrative elements of 50th Division had for safety and ease of handling been formed into a column ('Teecol') under command of the CRASC, Lieut-Colonel S. T. Divers. He withdrew his command in safety, and was awarded the Distinguished Service Order. Many of his officers and men were also decorated. When so many have behaved so gallantly, it is invidious to select any individual for special mention, but the circumstances under which Major J. W. Rea won the Distinguished Service Order were so illustrative of the problems that faced RASC convoy commanders in the desert that they justify summarizing. During the operations 150th Infantry Brigade of 50th Division was surrounded and cut off in its sector of the Gazala Line. It was eventually compelled to surrender. While it was still holding out, efforts were made to maintain it, and Major Rea tried to lead in a convoy of 40 lorries of his company (523), which were loaded with various commodities, by going round south of Bir Hakeim and coming in from the west. He failed in his effort, as 150th Brigade was completely encircled. On the morning of June 3rd, he left his convoy under protection of the French in Bir Hakeim and went off with his driver to reconnoitre a route to return to Teecol. By this time the area was infested with enemy elements, and he could not get through. It will surprise no one who knows what conditions were like at the time that he also could not find his convoy again. However, in the course of three days spent looking for it, he found many other British vehicles, including tanks captured and later abandoned by the enemy, and either destroyed them or recovered them as best he could. Altogether, 523 Company lost 5 officers and 90 men in three critical days.

The divisional RASC of 1st and 7th Armoured Divisions also had difficult problems. Fortunately, in anticipation of just such a 'soldiers' battle' as took place in the area, considerable reserves of essential items had been established in selected localities. The fact that their existence was unknown to the enemy made it unlikely that he would locate and capture them. This scheme proved successful, although it was, of course, uneconomical in stocks and resulted in heavy waste. The RASC were not therefore tied to a fixed daily delivery but brought forward urgently required items on demand.

The maintenance of 7th Motor Brigade, which was operating 'round the corner' of the Gazala Line west of Bir Hakeim between June 2nd and 11th, was done by 550 Company, with which the name of its commander, Major Duncan Riddell, will always be associated. Enemy columns were also operating in the area and, although 550 Company's convoys were frequently dispersed and vehicle losses were heavy, the maintenance of the brigade was secured. Major Riddell was awarded the Military Cross for his gallant leadership during this difficult operation.

L/Sgt E. Holleron, of 373 Company, was sent to recover some 6-pounder guns which had been left behind in the Bir Hakeim box.

They were difficult to handle, as they had been dug in and were dismantled, but this NCO worked on until he was obliged to retire by an enemy armoured car patrol which entered the box. He brought away six guns with the loss of only one trailer, and well deserved his Military Medal.

During the fighting many vehicles of both armoured divisions, either singly or in small numbers, became detached from their units and were destroyed or captured. One young officer reported, by wireless, the progress of the battle in which he was involved up to the point where, just before 'going off the air', he announced that he and his driver had eaten their codes. The Germans took advantage of the fact that they possessed many captured vehicles of British or American make to drive up to unsuspecting British vehicles and hail them in English. This ruse sometimes worked: it also worked both ways. That the maintenance of the brigades of both armoured divisions continued throughout this very 'fluid' period says much for the efficiency of the RASC units concerned.

Many RASC platoons were, as usual, employed in troop-carrying, and this gave scope for the display of initiative and leadership by the type of junior NCO with which fortunately we were well provided. Some examples of the task which they were required to perform can be deduced from the citations of their immediate awards.

On one occasion a battalion of the Highland Light Infantry was being carried in vehicles of 240 Company. The battalion had suffered heavy losses and was being forced to withdraw. Sgt Freeman was in command of vehicles under the control of battalion headquarters, which was in immediate danger of being overrun by enemy tanks. This NCO went forward from the regimental aid post under heavy fire, and attended to the wounded, running from one position to another. He saved many wounded from falling into the enemy's hands, and also, oddly enough, saved the battalion's secret files after the adjutant was wounded. He was awarded an immediate Military Medal, as was also Dvr J. Whatsize, who was twice wounded, and had three tyres punctured by shell bursts; he changed the wheels for some off derelict vehicles, and went on with the work of withdrawing the remnants of the battalion.

There had been a scheme (Freeborn) on the stocks for a withdrawal to 'the wire', but it was now evident that the enemy superiority in armour was not going to permit this position being occupied, and that we should have to retire to the Alamein Line of which the right flank was protected by the sea, and the left flank by the Qatara Depression. There was the added advantage that the enemy's lines of communication would be well stretched.

The 'gates' of Tobruk were shut on June 17th and by the 21st the fortress had fallen.

The Fall of Tobruk

The pros and cons of holding Tobruk a second time and the whys and wherefores of its fall have been discussed in many other volumes. We are only concerned with the disastrous results to the RASC. As many ancillary units as could be spared were evacuated before June 17th but, unfortunately as it turned out, it was decided that the garrison should be completely mobile. As 2nd South African Division was very short of transport, this meant a considerable RASC commitment. Moreover, the town was stocked for a siege in supplies and petrol. In consequence of the decision regarding mobility, not only were the second line units of 201st Guards Brigade and 32nd Army Tank Brigade, one RIASC company, and certain Q service units of 2nd South African Division incarcerated, but with them was an RASC column headquarters and 31, 49, 129, 278, 903 and 906 Companies, together with a BSD and sundry minor supply and petrol units. The total loss of troops in Tobruk was severe. To the RASC the loss was extremely heavy—more than 2,000 highly trained, desert-worthy officers, NCOs and men.

It was a sad blow. There were not lacking those who had the initiative, wits and good fortune to effect their escape, but they were very few. In the confused conditions which prevailed in the last hours of the place, some members of the RASC, including men of 906 Company, were still resisting after the official surrender, of which they had not been informed, but they eventually surrendered to enemy tanks. Destruction of vehicles, rations and petrol was only partially successful. Tinned food is difficult to destroy in bulk. The cases can be burnt off, but the contents of the cans remain edible. Cased petrol is easier to dispose of, but a lot was left for the enemy, and Rommel was very glad to get it.

The Retreat to the Alamein Line

While this was going on in Tobruk, the forces outside, which were intended to remain mobile and to act as a threat to the rear of the enemy should he turn aside to attack the town, were steadily pressed back on the frontier and had no relieving effect on the short-lived siege. When additional enemy forces were made available by the fall of the fortress the retreat was continued and, apart from certain rather unfortunate clashes in the area south of Matruh, was not stopped until the Alamein Line was reached. The disengagement from the battle around Mersa Matruh and the exit from the defences of that place of troops detailed for its defence was not achieved without difficulty and loss. As usual in such circumstances from the RASC point of view it was the transport on troop-carrying which drew most of the limelight.

Desert Convoy

In one incident, L/Cpl J. P. L. Clarke, 524 Company (50th Division) was concerned. He won the Military Medal when he drove his lorry, loaded with troops, many of whom were wounded, through a gap in the enemy defences which was under enemy machine-gun fire. A bullet shattered his right elbow, but he went on driving until they were clear of the enemy, when he collapsed.

Headquarters X Corps had a difficult passage, and two of the staff car drivers won Military Medals. Dvr V. E. T. Paragreen was driving the car which was leading the column of corps vehicles. The convoy was continuously under fire, and on one occasion was attacked by a 2-pounder anti-tank gun. Paragreen drove his car to within 15 yards of the enemy, and engaged them with his rifle, under cover of which fire the column was able to proceed. Dvr G. Duncan was driving the DA & QMG of the corps (an officer of the RIASC). The route was over unknown and difficult tracks, and his car was acting as leader to vehicles which had straggled from the main convoy. The driver's window was shot away, and a bullet went through the windscreen, but Duncan was unperturbed, although he had never been under fire before. It was his skill and devotion to duty that brought his officer and many vehicles to safety.

As a result of fighting during the withdrawal, many tanks were stranded, damaged in action or broken down, in the desert south west of Alamein, and the tank transporter companies were kept busy. Captain W. M. Nichol, of 144 Company, with 21 tank transporters, was ordered to recover as many as possible. In spite of much interference from enemy armoured fighting vehicles and artillery, he succeeded in recovering 12 tanks and their crews. For this action he was awarded the Distinguished Service Order.

The Alamein Line

The situation was stabilized with the Eighth Army holding the El Alamein position which had been partially prepared in the previous year, and from the beginning of August preparations went on for the offensive which was to be launched in October. Losses and wastage in men, equipment, and vehicles had to be made good, forward stocks built up, and the administrative machine conditioned to be able to maintain the momentum of the pursuit.

Some initial difficulty arose in establishing FMCs at the normal distance behind the front line, as in the general area in which they would naturally be established (it will be remembered that except for a few minor escarpments this was all featureless desert), there was a great deal of bad going including large patches of soft sand impassable to 10-tonners and difficult for 3-tonners. Until the staff and the RASC got to know the area better, the sight of fleets of 10-tonners, immobile and looking as if they had in some way 'run aground', was a common one. Three-tonners had to be used as tenders to unload them and allow them to make their way out when lightened. The effect and cure were indeed exactly as in the case of vessels run aground.

One undesirable result of these areas of soft going was that the whole rearward services of both corps tended to be thrust towards the sea as the area in rear of the left corps (XIII) was very soft indeed. The commander of XIII Corps directed that every effort should be made to find suitable routes further south with a view to the corps being maintained from the Cairo-Alexandria road should the congested road and railway from Alexandria through Amiriya westwards along the coast be out of action.

But although routes breaking off some distance south of Amiriya had been reconnoitred before the war and one (the 'Barrel' track) had actually been marked out, they were found impracticable for regular use by convoys. Small numbers of 8- and 15-cwt trucks or indeed 3-ton lorries in first class running order and with experienced drivers can, by keeping up a good rate of speed and picking their way, negotiate going which will prove quite impassable to large convoys of heavily laden 3-tonners driven by less experienced men. After several fiascos the attempt was abandoned, and XIII Corps was maintained exclusively from the coastal railheads. In any case a new régime—and reinforcements in troops and equipment—had arrived in the Eighth Army, and looking over the shoulder was officially discouraged. Two new divisions, 44th and 51st, were in the field, and soon the desert was to be covered with boards bearing the letters HD, many of which are probably there to this day. More armour was on its way. A new morale had replaced the universal depression which followed the retreat and the loss of Tobruk.

All thoughts were now directed towards preparations of a new offensive and a new swing of the pendulum in the right direction, from which it was hoped there would be no return swing.

Alamein and after

The period was a busy one for the RASC. Many companies in all echelons were in a battered condition after a long retreat and many months of previous campaigning in the desert. This called for re-equipping and reorganization. New formations and units including the 9th Australian Division once more in the Western Desert, required concentrated training in all aspects of campaigning in the desert; water discipline, control by wireless, dispersion, desert formations and the like. Transport was not alone in gaining new experience. Eighth Army was built up of a great variety of formations from all parts of the Empire and indeed outside it,—all on different ration scales,—Australians, New Zealanders, South Africans, Indian Army, Greeks, and Free French. Because of the commodities demanded even the 51st (Highland) Division were regarded by some as foreigners.

Not the least factor which heartened all branches of the RASC during this critical period was the give-and-take attitude and co-operation between all members of this mixed community. This process of reorganization and training was carried out with a general feeling of suppressed tension and expectation. That Rommel would attack everybody knew, but the Army Commander had prophesied the lines on which this attack would occur and how it would be met. His prophecy proved to be accurate. The battle of Alam Halfa was fought and won. Rommel had shot his bolt, and the second phase of El Alamein began by the building up for the attack. Camouflage took a high priority. For example, one new field maintenance centre was formed on the site of an old ruined desert castle and village. Stocks were built up on partially demolished walls and existing walls were demolished and rebuilt with stocks. All this was a very realistic disguise from the air, but quite a headache for the individuals running the FMC. There were many artillery reinforcements, and ammunition of all types had to be dumped in gun positions for the opening bombardment of the Alamein Line and the subsequent barrage. This bombardment was to be on a scale unheard of by Eighth Army, and most of the dumping had to be done at night. A further interesting undertaking was the siting of reserves for the armour to be drawn on after the break through had been accomplished. It was necessary that these reserves should be well forward so that the second line of the armoured divisions should not have long and difficult return journeys to the area behind the Alamein Line. The solution lay in the gradual distribution of a very large number of vehicles widely dispersed right forward immediately behind the forward defended localities. Over a considerable period the RASC went forward in small parties at night, together with the camouflage experts. Some of the vehicles previously mentioned would be removed and a dump of some commodity suitably disguised as a lorry substituted. This deception was amazingly successful. Even from the ground at a short distance away the dumps were taken for lorries by the uninitiated.

For the battle of Alamein, XXX Corps occupied the northern portion from the sea half way down the Alamein Line and XIII Corps the southern portion; behind, in reserve, was X Corps, now the Armoured Corps. The great evening arrived and never has the desert been so shaken as by the thunder of that concentration of guns; every pulse was beating a little quicker—even the most cold blooded—Eighth Army was 'off' again, and this time they were not swinging back. The drivers were straining at the leash, and strain they had to because it took approximately one long week to break open Rommel's Line and let the armour loose! It was a strenuous and in many cases a hazardous week for the ambulance drivers, six of whom were awarded the Military Medal:—Dvr B. A. Tipper, Dvr W. G. Tebutt, Dvr J. Tomlinson, of 10th Armoured Division; Dvr I. P. Creighton, of 51st Division; Dvr G. W. Machlin, and Dvr T. S. Hartley, of 1st Armoured Division.

This desert campaign was one of big 'jumps' either forward or backward. The bigger the backward jumps of the defence, the greater the strain placed on the attackers by their continually lengthening line of communication. The solution of this problem of course lay in the establishment, as far forward as possible along the coast, of supply by sea; hence the vital importance of the immediate opening up of any possible port once it was uncovered. It was unknown whether Rommel would attempt to hold Tobruk or not, and the immediate short term policy was the re-establishment of Mersa Matruh as an advanced base. Various units were put on what was known as the 'golden list', a priority of movement into this well-known desert village. The main road from Alexandria runs direct to the southern side of Matruh, but there is an alternative route by which it is possible to reach the barracks area without passing through the town. On the golden list was an RASC bakery commanded by a warrant officer, who, not long before, had been forced to evacuate his well established position in Matruh. This unit became detached from the main body of the golden list and the warrant officer, knowing his way, took the alternative route direct to his old bakery site. On arrival, however, he was met by a platoon of German infantry! But the warrant officer did not lose his head, although it took him a little time to convince the German infantry commander that he was surrounded and that his only alternative was to capitulate. This incident, no doubt, is the foundation of later stories of how the RASC recaptured Matruh.

Pursuit of Rommel

To return to the main operation. The armour had bad luck. For once, it rained in the desert, and this made going difficult and in places impossible. This enabled Rommel to withdraw in comparative safety and the idea that he would call a halt at Tobruk proved incorrect; it was occupied without opposition by X Corps. It was decided that XXX Corps should continue the pursuit while XIII Corps, much to their chagrin, were left behind at El Alamein. With them was left the 9th Australian Division. During the short period of their stay at El Alamein the 'Aussies' had won both the affection and admiration of their British comrades. Their divisional RASC, commanded by Lieut-Colonel (later Brigadier) J. A. Watson, adapted themselves to desert conditions with quite remarkable rapidity. On one occasion they earned the personal commendation of the Commander XXX Corps for their driving and desert discipline. But XXX Corps were not to be without Dominion representation; 2nd New Zealand Division remained with them, then and for many a long day.

It speaks highly for the training of the RASC MT units of all echelons that XXX Corps were able to advance with such rapidity and without any administrative hitch to the area of Mersa Brega, a distance of nearly 800 miles from El Alamein and 400 miles from Tobruk. This was all the more so since for some units, and indeed formations, it was their first experience of a 'desert gallop', while even the 7th Armoured Division found themselves breaking new ground. It was during this advance that Lieut-Colonel H. J. Gilman, CRASC 7th Armoured Division, gained an immediate award of the Distinguished Service Order. Tobruk was, of course, opened without delay, and a start was made at feverish speed to build up stocks. X Corps remained in the Tobruk area, presenting no maintenance problem, while XXX Corps in the Agheila area initially were maintained by road from Tobruk. However, a prerequisite to any future advance on Tripoli was the formation of an advanced base considerably further west than Tobruk. Benghazi was the obvious location. On our previous visits Benghazi had not been a workable proposition as a port, because of enemy action and weather. Now, with a great effort, the port and docks were gradually got into working order, and simultaneously with Tobruk the stocks in Benghazi began to mount steadily, coming in by both sea and land.

Luck was not with us, however, and by the middle of this build-up an unprecedented storm destroyed the harbour mole, and ships broke their anchorage and bounced about like corks in the harbour. To meet this disaster, the Army Commander ordered X Corps, which were in the Tobruk area, to be 'grounded'. Every unit, no matter how large or how small, was to unload all its vehicles and form them into transport units. Every possible vehicle was used and amazing results were achieved. General Brian Horrocks, commanding X Corps, offered weekly prizes to the unit covering the most mileage and carrying the greatest tonnage proportionate to their strength, and types of vehicle. The RASC were regular winners, but it was hardly a worthy contest, as the Corps were being taken on at their own job, and knew all the tricks of the trade. In the meantime, the second and third line transport of XXX Corps were busy building up their FMC for the coming attack on Agheila.

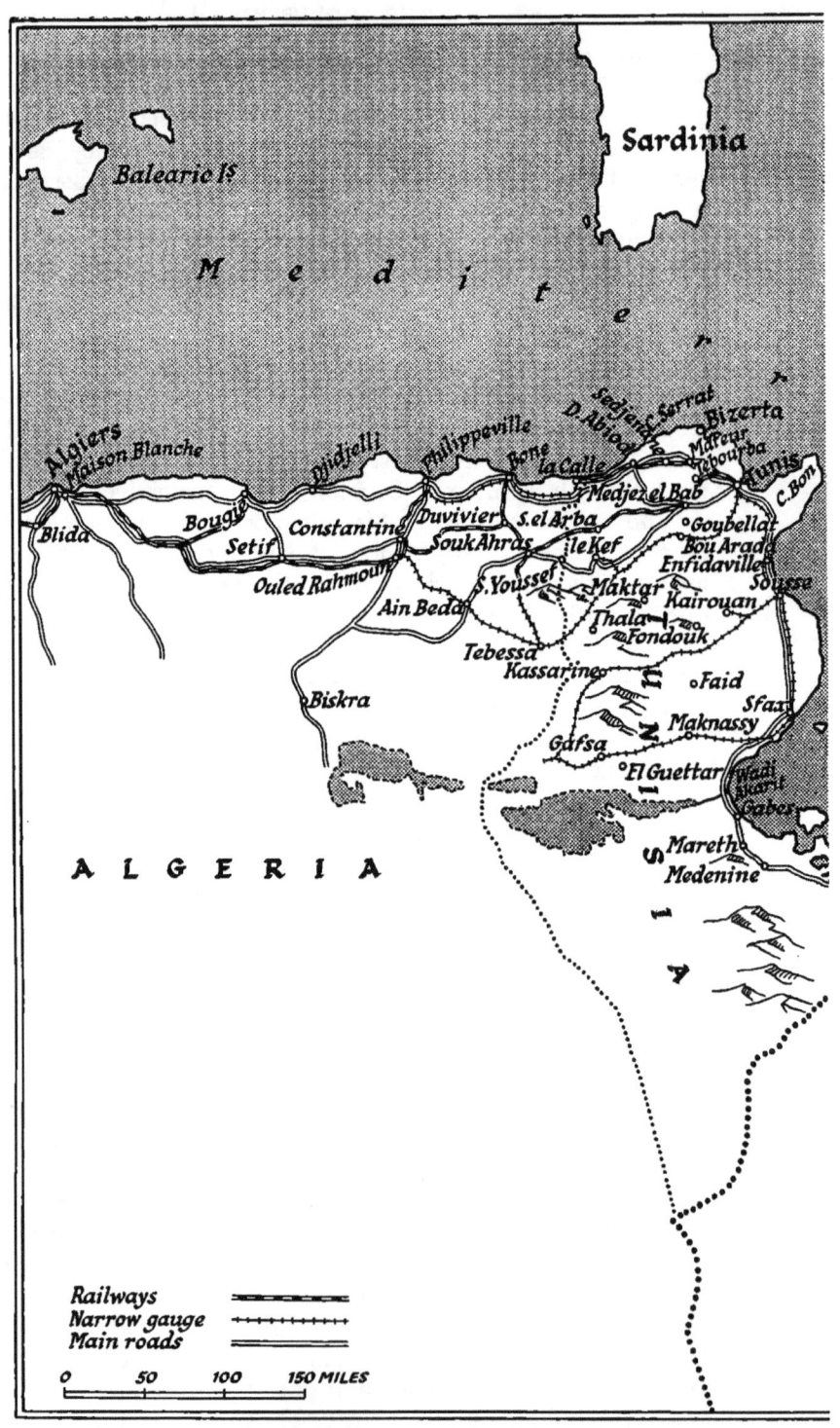

Operations of the Eighth and First Armies in

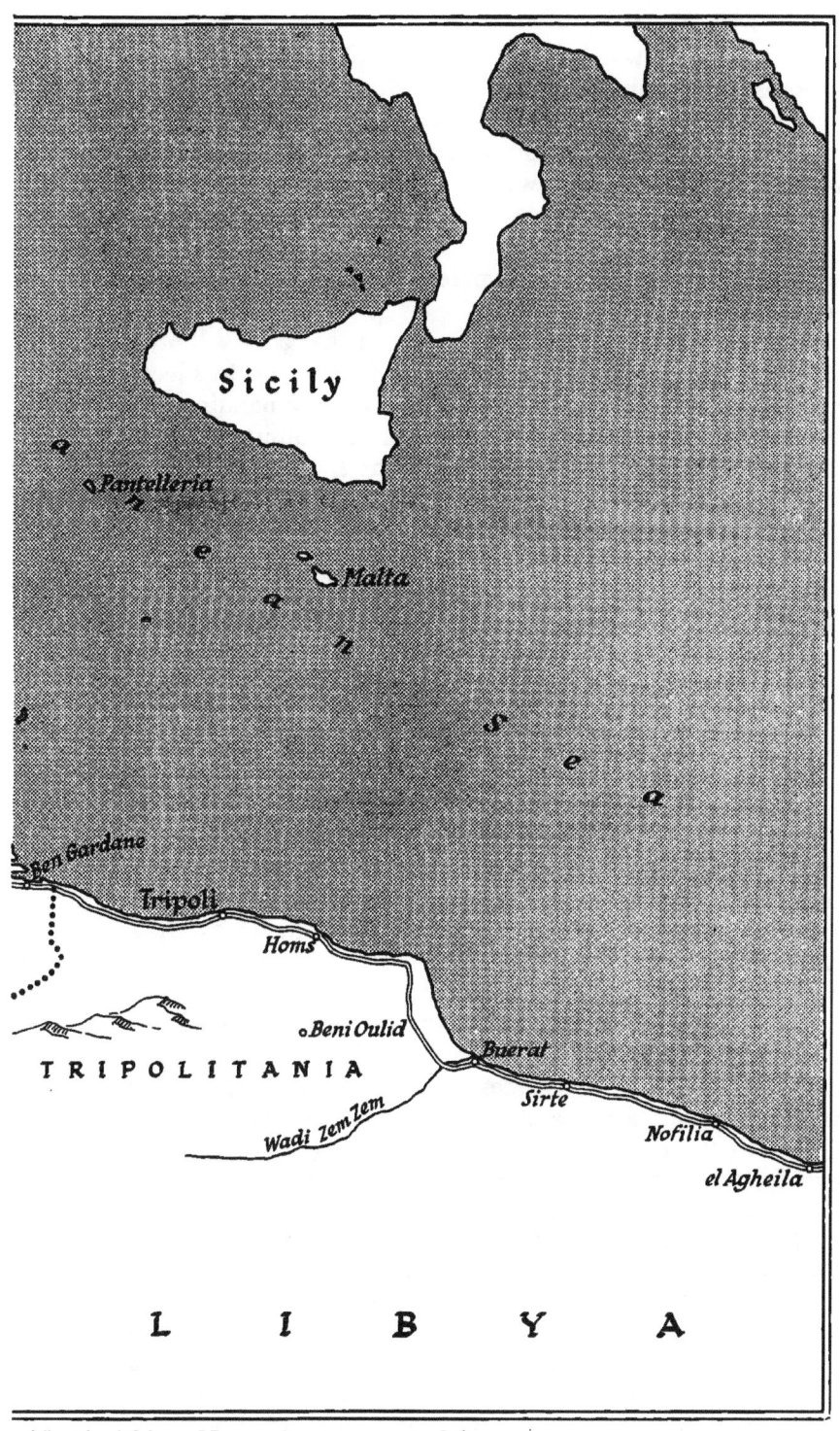

North Africa, November, 1942, to May, 1943

Even to the old desert warriors this was something new; they had never been as far as this before. To the New Zealanders it was something even newer, since to them fell the lot of doing the first 'left hook' in a wide and circling movement from the south through unknown desert. This division was not on a British establishment and was more generously provided with vehicles. The divisional second line included at least one authorized reserve MT company, and the quantities which could be carried by the divisional second line seemed unlimited.

It was during this pause in active operations that a new RASC 'baby' arrived, a mobile bakery, and the credit must go to Lieut-Colonel (subsequently Brigadier) S. H. Crump commanding the New Zealand Division Army Service Corps. It consisted of oil-fired Baker Perkins ovens mounted in 3-tonners, together with a variety of canvas in the form of tents and shelters to provide cover for the kneading and proving. The experiment was to be a great success. It was a very mobile unit and, apart from providing bread for its own division, it was able to supply some of the ration for the rest of XXX Corps.

The Air Arm

From the battle of El Alamein onwards one of the greatest contrasts to the previous periods of the campaign was the situation in the air. Superiority had gradually been wrested from the enemy, with obvious advantages to the RASC transport units. They were subject to occasional bombing and low level sneak raids, but that solitary ribbon road along the north coast was no longer a death trap, and with consequently decreased dispersion, the individual driver no longer had to walk anything from a quarter to half a mile to collect his cup of tea at halts.

During these latter stages of the campaign a high degree of co-operation was developed between the fighter wings and squadrons and the RASC. The Desert Air Force provided fighter squadrons operating far behind the enemy lines. To obtain the range it was necessary that these fighter squadrons should be based as far forward as possible. In the early stages all the RAF were maintained at army level, but immediately after an advance some RAF formations would suddenly appear on improvised landing grounds as far forward as the divisional areas. From the army point of view this meant unexpected and heavy demands on corps FMCs; from the RAF point of view the FMCs could never provide for all their wants. The solution lay in the maintenance of these squadrons being made a corps responsibility. A corps troops RASC liaison officer was attached to the RAF, and a firm friendship was formed between members of the two services. The RAF had a limited amount of transport of their own, and soon this transport was co-operating with the corps third line from which great mutual assistance developed.

El Agheila

When sufficient stocks had been built up, the attack on the Agheila position was launched with, as previously mentioned, the New Zealand Division doing their first wide left hook. It was eminently successful and once more the Afrika Corps was in retreat with the Eighth Army in full pursuit. The achievements of all transport units from the divisional second line back along the lines of communication towards the advance base are difficult to appreciate fully. At each pause they were called upon to redouble their efforts to build up the stocks in the minimum of time for the next advance, but such was the tempo of the campaign that the next attack was launched when the reserves had reached the bare minimum required, and all these transport units were being called upon for yet another effort to cover greater distances. This could not have been achieved without the determination of the individual driver not to be 'out of the hunt'. It was largely this urge in the individual which was responsible for the high standard of vehicle maintenance. Each driver 'nursed' his vehicle, and the development of individual improvisations was quite remarkable.

Wadi Zem Zem

The next pause came in the area of Buerat on the Wadi Zem Zem, now a distance of 300 miles from Benghazi and 950 miles from the far distant point of El Alamein. A big goal was in sight —Tripoli—and everybody knew it, including the RASC driver. But the terrain was changing. The coast line was more developed, and it was obvious from the map that units would be unable, as in the past, to leave the coast road at any moment for the wide open spaces of the desert. To the south of Tripoli lay foothills passable only by road and track. These new features called for careful study and planning by all RASC transport units and particularly by the divisional second line.

In the well-developed drill in the maintenance projects established between army and corps staffs, if the expected distance of the forward jump did not warrant a new army base, corps FMC stocks were maintained at a minimum and when the jump took place they were already eaten down, leaving no great transport problem. When a new army base was envisaged the FMC was built up as far as time permitted. On the corps going forward, taking with them their requirements, the FMC was handed over to the army. It was already stocked to a varying degree and the layout took this expansion into account. The army roadhead for the final attack on

Tripoli was located at Nofilia, 350 miles from Tripoli. From there reserves were drawn up for the final advance of this stage of the campaign.

In general, the plan was that 51st Division, having forced the crossing of the Wadi, was to advance on foot up the coast route, while 2nd New Zealand Division and 7th Armoured Division were to cross the Wadi or get round it on the left and approach Tripoli from the south. In reserve was 22nd Armoured Brigade under the personal control of the Army Commander. The distance between Wadi Zem Zem and Tripoli was 180 miles. The administrative plan was normal second line supply in the first place, together with the rapid establishment by third line of 112 FMC at Beni Oulid, south-east of Tripoli, from which the final assault on the town could be made. Things rarely go according to plan, and still less so when every formation, and indeed every unit commander, is determined that his troops will be the first into Tripoli. Everyone galloped, including 51st Division, and what devices they resorted to in order to cover the distance are still somewhat of a mystery. It was during this advance with 51st Division that Captain T. O'Connor, 25 Company RASC, won an immediate Military Cross. The speed of this advance could easily have resulted in an administrative crisis had not the third line units been equally determined to achieve the goal. The speed at which 112 FMC was established was one of the achievements of which XXX Corps Troops might well be proud, particularly in view of the difficulty of the intermediate terrain. But Tripoli had been captured—Tripoli, the dream for months and indeed years, of those veterans who so often before had advanced half way to their objective, only to be thrown back again to their starting point, if not farther. For their part in this victory the RASC drivers were commended by General Montgomery in his special Order of the Day: 'I would like to make a special mention of our RASC drivers; these men drive long distances by day and night for long periods; they always deliver the goods. The RASC has risen to great heights during the operations we have undertaken, and as a Corps it deserves the grateful thanks of every soldier in the Army'.

Tripoli and the build-up for the next phase

The capture of Tripoli ended another phase of the campaign. A light covering force with mobile long range patrols covered the western approaches in the direction of Mareth. The main tasks for the moment were the reorganizing and re-equipping of the Army, the opening up of Tripoli as a port, and the establishment of yet another army base. This re-equipping presented many a problem. The distance from the great Middle East base of the Delta was considerable. Maintenance by road was out of the question. Supply by sea was limited by the number of craft available and by the port facilities of the already heavily bombed Tripoli. The wear and tear of the RASC vehicles in all echelons in the advance from El Alamein was very great. Apart from the distances and mileage covered, sand was the great enemy. The speed of the advance had been such that any comprehensive engine changing programme had been out of the question; cylinder wear had raised oil consumption to a startling figure. It was approximately another 1,000 miles to Tunis. There was no possibility of replacement vehicles becoming available, but to Tunis the Army was going. It was decided to set up a repair organization at various civil factories in Tripoli to which all RASC workshops would contribute men. Through these establishments would pass every suspect vehicle to be 'doctored'. From the technical point of view, serious crimes were committed. Nevertheless all credit is due to the workshop platoons and to the Chief Inspector Mechanical Transports' representatives who were mainly responsible for the organization and supervision of the undertaking. Supplies of small parts were flown from the Delta and Tobruk, others were collected from garages in Tripoli. The proof of the pudding was in the eating. Most of those same vehicles eventually completed the African campaign. If rumour is correct, 51st (Highland) Division were so attached to these vehicles that some of them are reported to have been taken to Sicily and to have completed that campaign.

The base at Tripoli was a pleasant one, and it was good to see something green again. Tripoli harbour looked big and well developed even if it had been bombed. There was a real town, although there was precious little in it, and there was time to rest and think. A cheering item was the sudden unexpected arrival of and inspection by Mr. Winston Churchill.

It was during this phase of rest that an extraordinary incident occurred which illustrates the uncertainty of war. It entailed the death of an RASC staff captain of Eighth Army. Rear Army HQ was situated under bivouac conditions on the extreme outskirts of Tripoli—it was almost desert. As a protection against the icy winds at night some men had pitched their bivvies in a wadi. Like all wadis in the desert it was dry and dusty. But one night a cloudburst occurred many miles distant, the wadi was apparently one of the natural drains in this area, and by the time the water had reached Eighth Army location it was almost a raging torrent, but confined strictly to this one narrow little wadi. All the bivvies of the occupants of this wadi were washed away, and the unfortunate staff captain, unable to disentangle himself, was drowned in the middle of the desert.

Throughout this period, the work of the MT companies on the lines of communication was at high pressure. The initial stocking of the Tripoli base was from Benghazi by road. As the port opened and developed, this commitment was gradually reduced. But the greatest weekly tonnage to the port of Tripoli reached the figure of 36,000 tons. This was the average figure for five weeks, and all of it was moved by RASC transport. In addition to this, an army roadhead had to be established at Ben Gardane, 120 miles west of Tripoli, with the minimum delay to enable further operations to be undertaken. It was on this roadhead that the eventual attack on the Mareth Line was based. There was only one road from Tripoli to Ben Gardane. Much of it was in bad condition, and a part of it was on a narrow causeway constructed across the marshes. It was estimated that this road would have to sustain an average of at least 1,200 vehicles a day in each direction, and might have to accept as many as 3,000 vehicles a day in one direction during operational moves. The strictest control was instituted. Fixed block timings and traffic priorities were laid down; marshalling areas and control points were established. The slower traffic moved by night and staged by day. As an example, in one day 5,500 vehicles passed the control point at Ben Gardane. The operation was successful, but although the distances were considerably smaller when compared with previous experience, the strain and fatigue of the drivers were greater.

During this build-up of the roadhead, news was received that Rommel was pulling out of his attacks on the First Army, and there was the obvious possibility of a quick switch by him to attempt a destructive blow to the Eighth Army. Further, it was known that some at least of his armour was now equipped with the new and powerful Tiger tank. It will be recalled that most of the Eighth Army fighting troops were still in Tripoli. It was questionable whether they could be brought to Medenine to take up battle positions before Rommel could complete his switch. It was a vital race for which the honours went to the RASC tank transporter column under the command of Lieut-Colonel D. R. Hall. For three nights and four days those tank transporter units drove backwards and forwards on this difficult road between Tripoli and Medenine, loading and unloading, and snatching meals and sleep between turns at the wheel until the task was completed. Many were so tired, after unloading for the last time at Medenine that they crawled under their transporters where they stood and fell asleep. The CRASC received on return a complimentary message from the Army Commander, and the tank transporter companies received a special mention in an Order issued by Field-Marshal Alexander after the battle.

Although later than expected, the surmise about Rommel's possible action was correct. A few days later he debouched in two columns from the foothills only to receive, in spite of his Tiger tanks, an even bloodier nose than he had been given a few months previously at Alam Halfa, and to retire hurt behind the bastion of the Mareth Line.

Even the Donkeys helped

The build-up continued, and it was during this period that Eighth Army had their first, if somewhat unorthodox, experience of the controlling and handling of animal transport. High in the mountains to the south of the Medenine position was located a gun position from which occasionally the Germans would shell the rear areas including the advanced fighter airfield. The Commander decided that this irritation must cease and that the Gurkhas of 4th Indian Division must stop it. Promptly to the RASC came the call for donkeys. To those with desert experience such a demand would not appear to present difficulty as they were frequently to be seen, but when actually wanted they were extremely hard to find. CRASC XXX Corps Troops Column was ordered to produce 200. Officers, NCOs and drivers were despatched far and wide in 3-tonners, 15-cwts, and even cars in their search. In the meantime the MT column headquarters prepared a wire corral in a wadi and arranged water and forage supply. Some hours later delivery began. In some respects it was not unlike seeing the conjuror produce an unbelievable quantity of paper from his mouth. A small 15-cwt would arrive. The canvas flaps in rear would be unstrapped and out would be lifted one, two, three, four, five donkeys—but that was not all—following them would come their hooded, bearded, Bedouin owners.

It was unfortunate that this MT column headquarters had no previous training in animal management. Donkeys of all sizes, shapes and sexes were hustled into this 100-yard square corral. The combination of flying heels, noise and movement presented an unforgettable sight. The CRASC ordered the rapid construction of a second corral, on completion of which gallant RASC drivers hurled themselves into the *mêlée*, seized a jackass and, with the utmost danger and difficulty, conveyed him to the second corral. Little did they know that their companions were still arriving with yet more donkeys and quite innocently were adding fresh reinforcements to the battle from the far end of the original enclosure. And all this time sitting round the uppermost banks of the wadi huddled the numerous Bedouin owners, no doubt wondering at the form of amusement provided for the British soldier. Suffice it to say the Gurkhas got their donkeys, the gun positions were eliminated, and with only one casualty the donkeys were returned to their correct and rewarded owners.

The Mareth Line

But to return to the more serious operations and the attack on the Mareth Line. The attempt to pierce the line between the sea and the road on the northern flank failed in spite of the tremendous efforts of the gallant 50th Division. As at El Alamein, this attack on a strongly defended position provided the ambulance drivers with the opportunity to distinguish themselves. Drivers G. Houghton, S. Crompton and S. Francis all won the Military Medal. It once more fell to the lot of 2nd New Zealand Division to carry out another and possibly their most difficult 'left hook' in a wide sweep through the difficult mountainous terrain south of the main position. The division, supported by additional armour under the command of General Freyberg, moved south followed by 'Crump's Private Army', which was reinforced by additional RASC companies. They carried four days' maintenance for the force. And here a lesson might be learned. The operation was estimated to last three or four days. Stocks were carried for consumption during that period and during that time only wireless communication would be functioning continually. There was no question of 'mobile reserves on wheels just in case'—there was no over insurance. As the operation proceeded stocks were consumed, and the empty vehicles returned in convoy under escort. After much hard fighting they were in the rear of the Mareth Line, the Germans pulled out and the force once again resumed maintenance from the normal lines of communication along the north coast. If ever over insurance might have been justified, here was a case; but it was never advocated. If need be further stocks could have been demanded and despatched round the long circuitous southern route, but transport was conserved and the build-up of army roadhead for further advance was continued uninterrupted.

The widespread nets of First and Eighth Army were now closing in on the Afrika Corps. Included in this was General Le Clerc's Free French force which had struggled from West Africa northwards across the Sahara. At about the time of Medenine, news was received of the location of this force, and it was also reported that food, petrol, ammunition and other stores were scarce. The honour of being sent to the rescue was given to 385 Company. It is doubtful whether any company ever had such a mixed load. This small French force had in its travels collected a variety of armaments of all nationalities. The company had far greater difficulty finding its commodities than finding the consignees and delivering the goods.

The Final Stages

With the fall of the Mareth Line the back of the campaign was broken as far as the Eighth Army was concerned. The advance continued via Sfax and Sousse up to the mountains in the Enfidaville area. Once more the lines of communications grew longer and longer, and were now based on Tripoli. Once more the MT companies were strained to the limit, but the old and well used vehicles, most of which had started from Alamein, stood up to it and kept going. Some divisional RASC indeed accompanied their divisions in a southern sweep to join the First Army and to take part in the final break through to Tunisia. The greatest distance L of C units went to maintain these divisions was as far as el Krib on the road running south-west from Medjez el Bab.

It was during these final stages of the advance that 385 Company (MT), under command of Major K. Newton, was pulled out at Sfax to be re-equipped and trained as a dukw company in preparation for the invasion of Sicily. Invaluable help was given to the unit by Captain Spears, of the United States Army, in both the handling and technical peculiarities of this new, strange vehicle.

Thus ended a long, trying and finally victorious campaign throughout which the RASC driver had played a not only decisive but determined and at times gallant part.

The next act for which most of the veteran desert units were to plan was the invasion of Sicily. To one and all at the time it appeared a tremendous undertaking, and so in many ways it was. There were many advantages: all the Eighth Army MT units were trained and battle-worthy; divisions knew what they would want; staffs knew each other and everyone was full of confidence.

There were likewise disadvantages. The attacking force would embark from places as far distant as Alexandria, Sousse, Bone and Malta, while a Canadian division would embark in Britain and join the army for the first time off shore from Sicily. Dukw companies had to be trained; they were a completely new and exciting baby. Would the FMC of the desert work in mountainous Sicily? Many pundits denied its value. Did water-proofing vehicles really work? How would the desert driver compete with the mountain tracks of Sicily? Chapter VII provides the answer.

CHAPTER V

THE MIDDLE EAST II

GREECE, 1941

IT is not with very cheerful feelings that one sets out to try to describe the part played by the RASC in the brief campaign in Greece in early 1941. Whatever benefits may have been conferred upon the Allied cause, looked upon from the broadest aspect, by British intervention in Greece—and that is a matter on which there can be more than one opinion—there can be no doubt about its catastrophic effects on the unfortunate Dominion and British troops involved. In this the RASC and its allied Corps were no exception. It has been calculated, probably with reasonable accuracy, that of the 138 officers, 4,424 other ranks and some 2,700 vehicles of the RASC to land in Greece, 75 officers, 2,076 other ranks and not one vehicle returned eventually to Egypt. Losses in men, therefore, exceeded one half in the RASC alone and were presumably equally heavy in the AASC and NZASC.

The first British troops to be sent to Greece consisted of a small RAF detachment, and to maintain it a small supply depot was established near Athens. The despatch of further British forces began in early March. By April 6th the Germans had crossed the frontier and the Greeks had been rapidly overcome and driven back in spite of the assistance of British forces, which eventually amounted by early April to Force HQ, Australian Corps HQ, 2nd New Zealand Division, 6th Australian Division, 1st Armoured Brigade (from 2nd Armoured Division), and supporting and ancillary troops, amounting in all to about 58,000 men. Before the end of April, 43,000 had been driven out, many to be lost at sea or in Crete, and the remainder were dead or prisoners of war.

Such a short-lived campaign, full of incident though it was, gave little opportunity to any unit to settle down, to become battleworthy, and to do itself justice: only the Australians were seasoned troops.

The RASC order of battle consisted of the second line of the formations concerned, 1st Armoured Brigade being particularly well provided, its brigade company (211) and two other companies of similar strength, 308 and 312, being sufficient to provide third line as well. Other units were 1 and 2 Reserve MT Companies and

232 Company (Cypriot), on a reduced establishment; 2 Advance MT Depot; 31 Base Supply Depot, four field bakeries, seven detail issue depots, one field butchery and cold storage depot, one petrol depot, one base petrol filling centre, one bulk petrol storage company, and many minor units and miscellaneous detachments, including a detachment of 285 Company (L of C (RH)) of 10-ton lorries. The force was thus well provided with RASC units, few of which however got into their stride in their proper functions.

RASC detachments which accompanied the early RAF party included 232 Company and the detachment of 285 Company, as well as a few ambulances. DDST to the force arrived on March 3rd. Before his arrival a CRASC had been attached to the RAF HQ. Most of the remainder of the force headquarters arrived after the DDST, so that it was some time before a firm maintenance plan was available. However, it eventually became clear that the line which there might be some prospect of holding was what was known as the Aliakmon position, running from the Aegean Sea and Mount Olympus to Edhessa on the Yugoslav frontier. The problem of co-operation with the Greek equivalent of supplies and transport apparently did not arise: they had none worth speaking of. The base area was to be in the Athens area using the port of Piraeus.

It has been mentioned above that a small supply depot had been established at Athens to maintain the RAF: actually it was on the race-course. Supplies from Egypt for the maintenance of the whole force and for building up a reserve now began to arrive in early March in such quantities that this depot was overwhelmed and quite incapable of reducing the mass of stuff arriving into any sort of order. Matters were not helped by the high proportion of broken cases usually found in any consignment of supplies moved by sea in the Middle East. However, as it had been decided to establish an advanced base in the Larisa area, some relief was effected by consigning stores direct from the docks by rail to that place. Unfortunately the only RASC troops in Larisa were a detachment of 232 Company, hardly ideally suited by education or training to run a supply depot; but they did their best. Although the arrival of supply units continued to be behind that of stocks, the unfortunate outcome of the campaign rendered this of little eventual importance, but it was trying to tidy-minded ST staff officers at the actual time. However, when 31 Base Supply Depot came along the supply situation was soon in hand and work proceeded in the establishment and stocking of FSDs within second line reach of the troops, which was the system successfully employed in the Western Desert. Similarly No. 2 BPFC at the base and No. 1 Petrol Depot in the field got down to the distribution of petroleum products.

M RASC

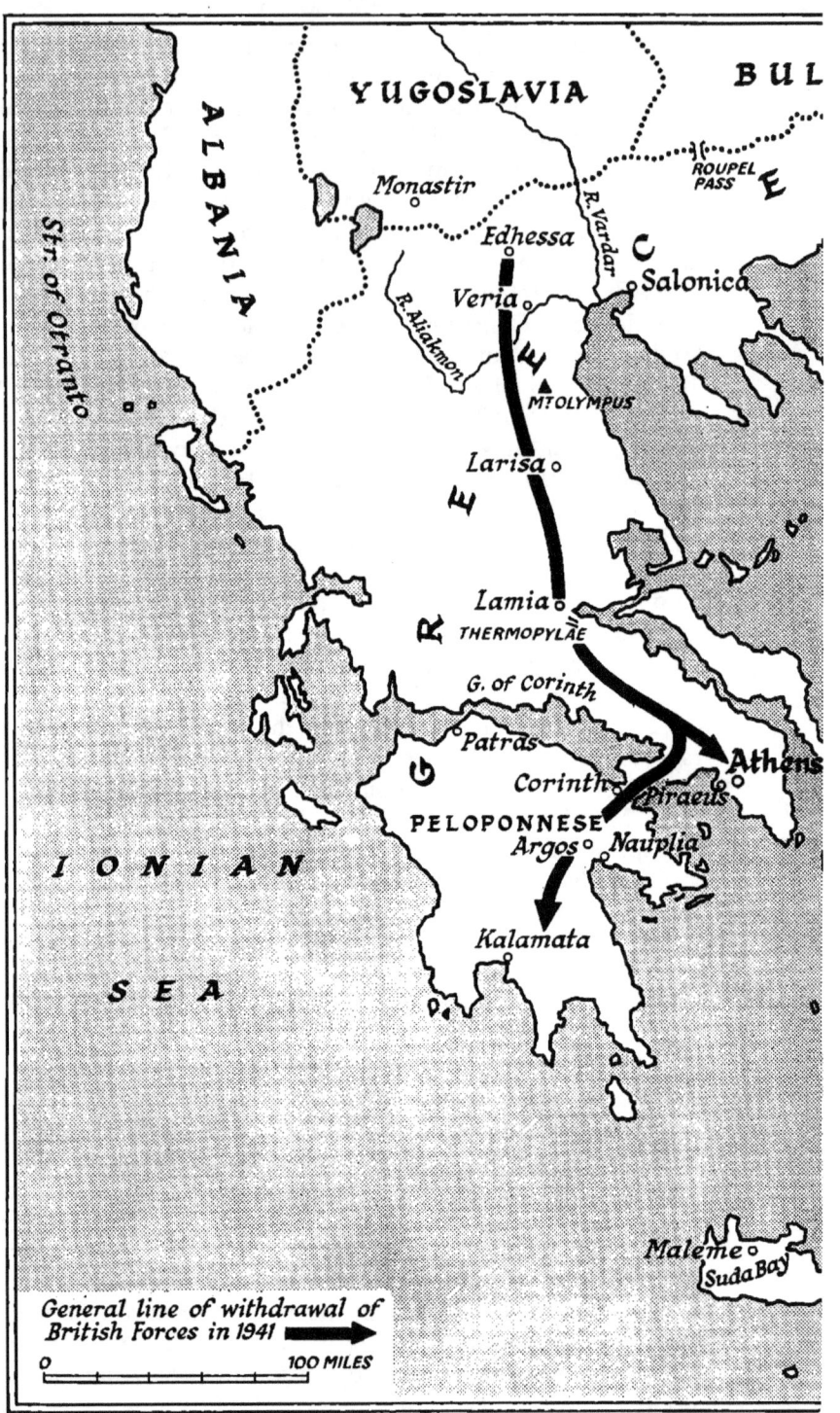

Greece and

the Dodecanese

Petrol plans and their initial execution were much assisted by the existence of some 100,000 tons in bulk storage belonging to the Shell Company with the necessary canning plant.

No. 2 Advance MT Depot, one of the three units of this type which are mentioned earlier as having been specially formed in the Middle East, arrived in an early flight and did useful work, but unfortunately suffered heavy officer casualties in a bombing raid.

By the end of March the bulk of the force was ashore and had deployed. Now 1 Armoured Brigade was on the Bulgarian frontier watching the Reupel Pass. The New Zealand Division and 6th Australian Division, the latter not yet completed, were under the command of Australian Corps HQ on the Aliakmon position. The L of C was becoming organized and a start had been made with establishing the Athens base.

Every day saw the force more firmly established and, given breathing space, it might have rendered a good account of itself, but on April 6th the Germans attacked southwards across the frontier. Events moved quickly, and within a few hours the situation was already looking serious. In particular the Greek Macedonian Army, with which the armoured brigade was associated, was in danger of being cut off, and the Greeks asked the British for several hundred lorries to assist in their withdrawal. Except for the second line of 1st Armoured Brigade, which was fully engaged, there were no vehicles within two days' march. Nevertheless 50 lorries, mainly from 211 Company, were placed at the disposal of the Greeks, but they never succeeded in getting through to their destination. The main German attack was launched on positions in advance of the Aliakmon line, held so far as the British were concerned by elements from the two infantry divisions, as well as so much of 1st Armoured Brigade as had succeeded in withdrawing from the Macedonian front, on April 10th. In consequence withdrawal to the Aliakmon line was forced upon us and was completed by April 13th. This was merely the prelude to a further withdrawal, under the difficult conditions of enemy air superiority to what was known as the Thermopylae line. This was completed by April 20th. While it was going on the possibility of evacuation rapidly became a probability, and eventually a certainty. Enemy air attack was rendering Piraeus practically unusable as a port. On the 21st the Greek Army capitulated, and the date of British evacuation already fixed for April 28th was advanced to April 24th/25th.

During this period, 1 Reserve MT Company was employed on troop carrying with the Australians. Maintenance of formations was conducted under the *ad hoc* arrangements inevitably connected with an involuntary withdrawal. The stocks in FSDs were either issued or transferred to new locations farther back. Dumps were maintained by road convoy from Larisa, until that place was overrun. The DIDs were established at railway stations along the axis of withdrawal, but, as trains loaded with stocks for them were mostly destroyed before reaching their destinations, replacements had to be sent by road convoys operating by day and night. These were subjected to continual air attack, and on the outward journey were driving against a stream of refugee traffic. The RASC drivers showed great courage and determination in carrying out this dangerous duty, and the DDST of the force, Brigadier W. d'A. Collings, placed it on record that no praise was too high for their steadiness and morale. There was apparently no failure to issue rations during the retreat.

The first embarkations were to take place at Nauplia near Argos in the Peloponnese Peninsula. For the RASC, this operation had two aspects: the rendering of the necessary supply and transport services to the last possible moment and the embarkation of RASC men. Plans were drawn up for the formation of beach supply dumps, and men were detailed to staff them. A DID was set up at Nauplia, well stocked with food and POL. The remaining supplies in the BSD were handed over to the Greeks, who were short of food for the civilian population, and large quantities of petrol were denied to the enemy by puncturing tins, as wholesale destruction by fire was forbidden. The DID at Nauplia was meeting demands up to the night of April 27th/28th, and water in tins was placed at various evacuation points. The transport units continued at work, moving stores and troops southwards. When they could no longer make use of their vehicles, they destroyed them.

RASC units coming in from the north were assembled in a corps concentration area near Athens, where they were given their orders for embarkation. The Corps was particularly unfortunate in the evacuation, as a large proportion of them went to Nauplia and Kalamata, and at these two points the operation was least successful. About 1,500 were at Nauplia on the night of the 24th, when embarkation was only partially achieved owing to one ship being disabled and another burnt out. Several thousand men were then moved from Nauplia to Kalamata, 50 miles away at the south-western extremity of the peninsula. Some went by train, and some by a road convoy composed largely of 232 Company, which did particularly well. The convoy arrived safely, after an adventurous journey over difficult roads, during which it was attacked from the air several times.

On the 27th, the New Zealand Division asked for transport to take 18,000 rations from Nauplia to Argos. A call for volunteers met with a total response, and the convoy went off inland led by the CNZASC. This party was evacuated with the New Zealand rearguard. A considerable number of RASC embarked in SS *Slammat* that day, but the ship was sunk on the way to Crete. Survivors were picked up by HM destroyers *Wryneck* and *Diamond*, but these too were both sunk before reaching Crete. It is believed that there was only one RASC survivor from all those who embarked in the *Slammat*.

At Kalamata on the 28th, Lieut-Colonel H. H. E. Geddes, when the enemy were trying to prevent the embarkation, organized a counterattack with 300 men of different regiments and corps, who were on their way to the pier, and directed operations which were successful in clearing the town and harbour. This led to the capture of 120 prisoners, two guns, and five machine guns, and enabled the embarkation of many troops, mostly wounded, to be completed. Colonel Geddes was awarded a Distinguished Service Order, and the immediate award of a Military Cross went to 2nd Lieutenant P. W. Valentine, of 285 Company, for his part in the action. He led a detachment of the unit down a street covered by a German machine gun and by troops in a house. He took the gun and captured the house. This was yet another example of the fact that RASC units, even those with a nominal line of communication role, have to be prepared for any eventuality. It cannot be assumed that they will not be involved in fighting. Incidentally, Valentine is said to have shot down a German aircraft a few days before, when it was flying low over the unit location, and he happened to be standing by the anti-aircraft gun.

Undoubtedly, the conduct of all ranks of the RASC throughout this disastrous campaign called for the highest praise. During the latter period, their work was ceaseless, they were continually driving under air attack and suffered many casualties. Even when they had destroyed their vehicles and were assembled near the beaches awaiting evacuation, there was an immediate response to any appeal for volunteers to take over other vehicles and drive inland again. Finally, when faced with the bitter disappointment of repeated unsuccessful attempts at evacuation, their morale and discipline remained good. It need hardly be added that the conduct of the AASC and NZASC was equally excellent.

Many of the troops evacuated from Greece went direct to Egypt, but others were taken across to Crete, to continue the fight there. For some months after the campaign, odd parties of officers and men escaped and made their way back by various 'underground' channels; and several who remained hidden eventually joined British special service missions and did good work. L/Cpl S. Rochberg, 285 Company, who helped with sabotage, and later escaped, was awarded the Distinguished Conduct Medal; and the Military Medal went to Private E. S. Buhayar, who helped two officers to attack a strongly held German airfield and to destroy three aircraft.

Perhaps this campaign would serve to illustrate a point which is often lost sight of. When we think and write of the RASC in the field we naturally think in terms of formed units, such as MT companies and supply depots. It is easy to forget that there are probably a greater number of RASC men detached in small numbers to units of other arms and services than is the case of any other corps except REME, the present duties of which corps were of course still being performed by the RAOC in Greece.

An examination of the order of battle in Greece reveals the fact that whereas there were about 30 RASC units or formed detachments of units, there were about the same number of units to which RASC men were attached in numbers varying from 66 with a light field ambulance, RAMC, to one with an advance depot of medical stores. Only very few of these attached men seem to have returned eventually to Egypt.

Of the RASC from all units who escaped, most were taken to Egypt but some were to go through a further series of adventures in Crete from which, in their turn, only a few escaped. ·

CRETE

British troops were sent to Crete in November, 1940, and by early 1941 the garrison consisted of a brigade whose commander was instructed to prepare a base for one division. During operations in Greece the island was of importance to the Navy, and a Mobile Naval Base Defence Organization (MNBDO) arrived to improve the defences of Suda Bay. The garrison was much increased by troops evacuated from Greece, but this reinforcement was, of course, not in accordance with any plan. The result was that with the exceptions of the units which were already in the garrison the force in occupation when the Germans attacked was unbalanced, ill-armed and ill-equipped for its task. There were many useless mouths, including a collection of unarmed and unorganized men, mainly belonging to the administrative corps, who were an embarrassment rather than an assistance to the defence. Unorganized bodies, which occupied four sectors (Iraklion, Retimo, Suda Bay and Maleme), consisted, in addition to the regional garrison, of the remains of 4th and 2nd New Zealand Brigades, a composite brigade formed from various New Zealand details, six Australian battalions, about 2,000 riflemen (British, Australian and some Royal Horse Artillery armed as infantry) and 14 Greek battalions of which two were in the improvised brigade. The strength was about 28,000: there were also 16,000 Italian prisoners of war. Reinforcement between sectors, except Suda Bay–Maleme, in any numbers was not practicable because of lack of roads and of transport.

The RASC element before the evacuation of Greece consisted of three detail issue depots and a petrol depot with various sections and detachments including the RASC portion of 189 Field Ambulance and a section of 231 Company, of which the majority of the personnel were British citizens locally enlisted in Egypt. The total was about 340 all ranks. Of these, considerably less than 50 per cent returned to Egypt, but they were accompanied by about 280 all ranks who had also been in Greece, so it may be concluded that about 1,000 members of the RASC were on the island in one capacity or another.

Transport was at a premium throughout the operations. The detachment of 231 Company possessed 36 3-ton lorries, and was later increased by 44 personnel who had been in Greece. They were double manned and worked continuously. All other RASC detachments were similarly reinforced so that a base supply depot and sufficient minor supply and petrol units to meet all requirements were made available. There was no lack of food or petrol, and reserves were held in all sectors, but once fighting commenced it became very difficult to keep them up to strength.

The main attack began on May 20th with the attempted air-landing of paratroops and glider-borne forces. In spite of heavy casualties inflicted, about 7,000 are reckoned to have landed, the majority at Maleme where there was an airfield. Landings continued from May 21st to 25th. Two reinforcing battalions arrived from Egypt, but by May 27th the enemy was estimated at 30–35,000 and he was in the ascendancy. Once more we had to evacuate, and some 14,600 only came away between May 28th and June 2nd. Had it been possible to continue the fight in the island, continued maintenance by sea would have probably been impossible as the enemy had command of the air and supply otherwise than by HM ships would have been impracticable. As it was, many dumps of supplies and petrol were destroyed by air attacks and the feeding of troops during evacuation was effected with difficulty.

There is little information about the action of any RASC who may have been included amongst the riflemen organized to assist in the defence, but undoubtedly a number took part in the fighting.

In addition, at one time 34 Detail Issue Depot, commanded by 2nd Lieutenant J. G. P. Atkinson, was ordered to occupy part of a defence perimeter, and did so for seven days under heavy air bombardment, and engaged a number of enemy gliders. This officer was taken prisoner, but escaped from Greece with a party he had collected, and brought back valuable information. He volunteered to return to Greece to arrange further escapes. For all these activities he received the immediate award of the Military Cross. Later he was awarded a bar to this decoration, having gone back yet again, obtained more information, and brought away 20 British soldiers.

THE SUDAN AND ERITREA
Refer to Map at p. 184.

Organization on the outbreak of War

The part taken by the Corps in the campaign in Eritrea and Ethiopia cannot be fully appreciated without a knowledge of the pre-war RASC organization in the Sudan. Until 1939 the Corps had only a detachment in Khartoum, commanded by a major, which ran a small supply depot and the barrack services for the two infantry battalions normally stationed in the Sudan. In addition, however, there was the Sudan Defence Force, which before its expansion in 1939 consisted of some 5,000 Sudanese officers and men and about 60 officers seconded from the British Army.

The Corps was represented in this small Sudan Army by some six officers, who formed the British element of a Sudan Service Corps. As the Sudanese soldier was not rationed, except on patrols, the supply duties were not heavy and transport was the main task of the RASC officers in the SDF. The DST, HQ SDF was responsible for purchasing and maintaining all the mechanical transport for the SDF and for the maintenance of civil government transport throughout the million square miles of the Sudan. It was on this small nucleus that was built the supply and transport organization which eventually supported two Indian infantry divisions, the SDF expanded to a strength of 25,000, an Ethiopian irregular force, various British and South African units, and a considerable RAF contingent in a campaign covering five fronts and many hundreds of miles of Sudan, Eritrean and Ethiopian desert and mountains.

At the outbreak of war with Germany in 1939, it was decided to amalgamate HQ British Troops Sudan and HQ Sudan Defence Force. Local differences in administrative methods made the fusion of the services a difficult and lengthy progress and, as far as ST were concerned, it was not until Lieut-Colonel J. K. Gillespie was appointed ADST HQ Troops Sudan in September, 1940, that a unified ST directorate was achieved. Even then the supply and transport services of the SDF proper, requiring specialized knowledge and experience was left largely in the hands of El Kaimakam E. R. Goode Bey, the senior RASC officer at that time still seconded to the SDF.

In June, 1940, when Italy entered the war and reinforcements began to arrive in the Sudan, there were no second or third line administrative units to deal with any large influx of troops. Spare storage space was non-existent, although depots to hold 150 days' reserve for about 30,000 troops were planned. Supplies, ammunition and other stores soon began to pour into the country. Improvisation became essential and, for the Corps, remained so throughout the campaign. RASC and RIASC reinforcements trickled in and such was the urgency that they were often formed into units on the platform at Khartoum station and hurriedly sent on to their unit locality, usually a virgin patch of sand or small village beside the single track Sudan Railway line.

The Italian Advance

By the end of June, 1940, the Italians had advanced from Eritrea to Kassala and Gallabat just inside the Sudan's eastern boundary. Here, for reasons known only to themselves, they halted although of considerable strength, immensely outnumbering the two British infantry battalions, the SDF, one squadron of Vincents, and an ancient gun (which fired one blank round at noon daily in the old fort at Khartoum) which constituted the Sudan garrison. However, the 5th Indian Division arrived before the Italians realized how meagre were our defences, immediately moved up to the eastern front and was concentrated there by the end of October.

Because of the complete absence of third line units, the division had now to undertake many of the administrative duties normally performed by Corps staffs and troops. The abnormally long line of communication, its vulnerability to air attack, and the lack of transport rendered it essential to hold large stocks of all commodities well forward. These dumps had to be formed and held by 5th Indian Division and this threw a heavy load on the divisional staff and services. The calls on the limited administrative resources available rapidly multiplied, and the burden on units and formations throughout the theatre became heavier and heavier.

The magnitude of the task confronting the small ST staff at HQ Troops Sudan and the pressure on the limited RASC and RIASC units committed to the battle at that time can be well appreciated since there were soon five separate fronts stretching from Equatorial Province in the southern Sudan to the Red Sea littoral, about 1,200 miles to the north. Also the total ration strength was now about 28,000 all ranks, and the MT resources available consisted only of two sections of an SDF reserve MT company, second line transport of 5th Indian Division, one MT company of the Sudan Defence Force; altogether totalling about 500 military vehicles, together with a limited number of hired civil lorries.

In December, 1940, it was decided further to reinforce in the Sudan so that defence could be turned to attack and the Italian forces in Eritrea destroyed. The reinforcements allotted were the 4th Indian Division together with a considerable number of non-divisional units including a squadron of I tanks and anti-aircraft units. The fighting formations arrived first, followed by a very inadequate administrative backing. Further considerable strain was therefore placed on staff and services already overworked in a trying climate. It soon became obvious, that with the large distances to be covered in the advance into Eritrea, the provision of extra transport was vital. After repeated requests four South African Cape Corps MT companies were allotted. They arrived by overland route from South Africa in the middle of January, 1941, and helped to relieve the anxious MT situation.

On January 18th, 1941, because of exaggerated and distorted intelligence of the strength of our forces, the enemy evacuated Kassala and withdrew eastwards to the safety of their own border. The order was given for the two Indian divisions and attached troops to pursue, and so swift was our advance that by January 25th, 4th Indian Division had reached Agordat, 120 miles from Kassala, and the 5th Indian Division had reached Barentu, 100 miles from railhead.

The lack of line of communication units was now most acutely felt. Recovery vehicles were non-existent, with the result that all removable parts were stripped from abandoned vehicles by the local natives until in most cases nothing but the chassis remained. The lack of supply units was particularly acute and both divisions had still to run their own railheads. Yet neither now nor later did the administrative staffs of divisions fail to get forward all essential requirements. Headquarters Troops Sudan could do little to help. Not even the men to form a corps headquarters were available.

Agordat fell on January 31st, Barentu was occupied on February 2nd, and the enemy fell back on to strong positions at Keren where they were able to halt the advance.

The campaign had been controlled from HQ at Khartoum until mid January when a small advanced HQ was established and moved forward in touch with the two divisional HQ. No ST officers could be spared permanently from Khartoum for this headquarters. The time of the ADST and his staff, already over full, had therefore to be divided between Khartoum and the advanced headquarters. The lack of aircraft for visits of staff officers to the forward area was a serious drawback, since it took three days by road and rail to cover the return trip even to Kassala.

While the main effort was concentrated in the Kassala-Keren

area, operations of considerable importance were taking place elsewhere, straining still further the limited administrative resources available. A force of four companies of the Equatorial Corps SDF were advancing over the Boma Plateau to occupy Maji and join up with an East African force advancing from Kenya. Lack of transport was the main difficulty here since the distance to Maji was about 450 miles over roads which were impassable from May to October because of rain. A Belgian infantry contingent, together with a force of Sudanese irregulars, were moved 200 miles eastwards from Malakal to occupy and hold the Akobo-Gambela-Daga line.

A force of Ethiopian patriots had been raised in Khartoum during 1940 with great secrecy, and at the end of the year was moved to the Roseires area with the object of containing large enemy forces, fanning the patriot revolt and eventually advancing into Ethiopia through Kurmuk, leading the way for the re-entry to his kingdom of Emperor Haile Selassie. This meant the dumping of huge tonnages of supplies and stores along the line of advance. The provision of sufficient transport was out of the question, and the task was eventually effected mainly by camel and mule transport, the feeding of which again added to the problem. At the peak there were 15,000 camels and 4,000 mules employed, most of which died for the cause, since it was quite impossible to maintain both the patriots and the animals.

When Keren was decided upon as the main front it became operationally necessary to make a large diversion along the Red Sea littoral. The force allotted to this task was about 6,000 all ranks, and again the motor transport available for their maintenance was totally inadequate. Supply by sea was the only solution, and all available native dhows were collected for the purpose. The force was maintained successfully by this method from Port Sudan by the use of small anchorages along the route, but the chief difficulty lay in providing the essential supply detachments.

Apart from these larger operations minor commitments were continually arising and adding to the administrative difficulties. For instance the French Tchad Battalion arrived at the Sudan frontier with French West Africa at only 48 hours' notice, being conveyed in vehicles under orders not to go farther than Fasher. This entailed chartering a civil aircraft to fly rations to the battalion and hiring civil vehicles at El Obeid to transport it the 375 miles from Fasher to the railhead at El Obeid.

Again in mid March it was learned that some 1,200 South Africans with 800 vehicles, which were urgently required in Egypt, were arriving at Juba in the southern Sudan and were to move by road through the Sudan to Wadi Halfa in the north. Staging arrangements over the 1,500 miles of rough track were made, and the last convoy successfully reached Wadi Halfa on May 15th.

The Main Advance

However, returning to the main area of operations, it had become clear by the beginning of February that the enemy intended to stand on the heights of Keren dominating the plain in which our forces were now deployed. The position was a formidable one with no way round. Its capture would need the full strength of both divisions. This required a comprehensive administrative plan.

Both divisions had, within 14 days, advanced some 180 miles mostly across country. Vehicles were badly in need of maintenance, spare parts and tyres were scarce, particularly for the Cape MT Companies. Altogether the MT situation was so acute that drastic measures were inevitable if the maintenance of the required force in the Keren area was to be assured. It soon became abundantly clear that both divisions could not be maintained so far forward of railhead and at the same time sufficient ammunition and other stores dumped for a major and intense action. It was decided therefore that 5th Indian Division, less one infantry brigade, should withdraw to the Tessenei area, whence it could maintain itself with first line transport from railhead at Kassala. On completion of this withdrawal HQ troops Sudan assumed control of the maintenance of 4th Indian Division and the dumping programme. The Cape MT companies, two of the three second line RIASC companies of 5th Indian Division, and one SDF MT company were pooled under a hastily improvised HQ L of C sub-area. This ill-staffed and ill-equipped headquarters arrived at Kassala railhead on February 15th and the dumping programme began on the next day.

It was planned to establish forward sufficient rations and petrol for both divisions for 14 days and enough ammunition for the battle. The tonnages were: petrol 1,340; supplies 840; ammunition 1,120; a total of 3,300 tons. There were also considerable quantities of other stores to be moved, and the normal daily requirements of 4th Indian Division and the brigade of 5th Indian Division, some 200 tons. The distance from railhead to the dumping area was 160 miles, the first 40 miles of which was over rough desert tracks and wadis. Two pack mule companies which had recently arrived from Egypt were used for the maintenance of troops in forward positions. Not only did they release vehicles, but they were of inestimable value in the rocky hills where it was impossible to use motor transport. To supplement the total lift available, hired camel convoys were used to move petrol forward. These convoys, although slow and uneconomical, were none the less of value.

By the end of February the units of 4th Indian Division were feeling the effects of continuous hard fighting on the hills, and it became evident that the division must either be relieved or the attack launched at an early date. March 21st had been fixed as the date for the final attack. To relieve the division would have meant the cessation of dumping and the postponement of the attack to a much later date—in all a vicious circle. The weather was becoming hotter, and the troops committed in this campaign were sorely needed in the Western Desert. It was therefore decided to quicken the dumping programme and attack on March 15th. This decision called for drastic measures. All possible 1st and 2nd line vehicles of both divisions were used. The move forward of 5th Division was delayed as late as possible to enable it to free its transport for dumping. The camel convoy was increased, and the turn round of vehicles between Kassala and the dumps was reduced from four days to three and the consequent lack of time for maintenance accepted. It was only by a hastily arranged delivery of springs by air from South Africa that the Cape vehicles were kept on the road.

By these measures a difficult administrative problem was solved, and by March 9th the dumping programme was completed, with the exception of 350 tons of petrol. By March 14th a 40-mile extension of the railway from Kassala had been completed. The relief afforded by this link was considerable, and the rapidity of its construction an outstanding feat of the Sudan Railways.

During this period special arrangements had been instituted for the delivery of fresh fruit and vegetables to forward troops. With the distances involved the normal system resulted in such food, an essential item of diet, rotting before it reached the troops. The provision of European type vegetables was itself a considerable problem in a country where previously only a handful of Europeans had lived. But this had been foreseen by the ADST HQ Troops Sudan. With the ever ready help of the Sudan Government many acres of the Gezira, the area between the White and Blue Niles south of Khartoum, had been planted during the 1939-40 winter with suitable vegetables under arrangements made by the Sudan Agricultural Department. Fruit and vegetables were therefore now available from the growing area and were despatched, packed in ice in special railway trucks, to arrive at railhead in the early morning. They were then immediately off-loaded into Cape Corps vehicles which ran direct to supply refilling points. The average number of lorries required for this task was five to six daily. The troops thus received the vitamins so badly needed in the climate in which they were fighting. Fresh meat—especially male goats for the Indians—was fortunately available in sufficient quantities in the area around Kassala and was provided by local purchase. Bread was baked by an Indian bakery unit in a former Italian civil bakery at Agordat.

Between March 1st and 28th some 16,000 tons of supplies, ammunition, petrol, etc., were moved forward by road, that is, 550 tons a day. The transport available consisted of 480 Cape Corps vehicles, of which at least one-third were always off the road for lack of springs and tyres, the second line vehicles of 4th and 5th Indian Divisions, and part of the SDF MT Company. There were no replacement vehicles. The men of a company known as S had arrived in February from Egypt, the intention being for it to be equipped with captured Italian vehicles. This was a failure for precisely the same reasons as a similar optimistic project failed in the Western Desert—most of the vehicles were casualties. Out of a 100 possibles only 14 were starters, and only one of these did not have to be towed to start. When this eventually broke down the company had no runners.

The Fall of Keren

The battle of Keren lasted 12 days, from March 15th to 27th. The battlefield was a tumbled mass of formidable hills swelteringly hot by day and miserably cold at night. The enemy was superior in numbers and fought well. The issue was long in doubt, but the British and Indian troops were not to be denied in spite of heavy casualties. On March 27th white flags appeared in all the enemy positions and the victory was complete. The fighting troops merited the highest praise; the administrative services could be proud of their achievement. While forward troops were denied luxuries, they at no time lacked essentials. The policy was 'guns not butter'.

With the fall of Keren the advance was immediately continued, now only by 5th Indian Division, as 4th Indian Division was to move back to Egypt, where it was badly needed. The administrative relief afforded by the withdrawal of one division was balanced to a large extent by the extended lines of communication and it was vital that the port of Massawa should be captured as soon as possible. After a short check at Ad Teclasan, between Keren and Asmara, the advance continued. The Italians sent a party forward to meet the leading troops of 5th Indian Division and declared Asmara an open town. The capital was occupied on April 1st, while the remnants of the Italian force retreated east to Massawa and south on two roads towards Gondar and Addis Ababa. The news was conveyed to Khartoum in a signal which read 'Asmara captured, this is NOT repeat NOT an April fool.'

Although the maintenance of active operations against Massawa was now the main administrative commitment, the feeding of the 40,000 Europeans and 40,000 natives of Asmara was a serious added burden. Fresh milk had to be flown in from the Sudan for the children, and it was only through the usual ready 'co-operation' after their defeat by the Italian authorities themselves in repairing the Eritrean railways that wholesale civilian starvation was averted.

Massawa, about 60 miles down a steep incline from Asmara, was captured on April 8th, but owing to the damage to the harbour it was not until the end of April that anything but small coaster ships could use the port, and the main line of communication was switched to the route from Port Sudan.

The intensity of the administrative activities during the month of April can be well imagined, and to add to them orders had been received for the Sudan to undertake the responsibility from May 1st for the maintenance of the Free French garrison at the oasis of Kufra, some 650 miles from Wadi Halfa, from which it was separated by trackless and waterless desert. To meet this commitment a platoon of the SDF MT Company which had been employed on the Tessenei-Asmara route was withdrawn. In the meantime the Italian forces which had retreated south from Asmara had still to be dealt with. They eventually stood for the last time under the personal command of the Governor and Commander in Chief of Eritrea, the Duke of Aosta, on the heights of Amba Alagi, a position of even greater natural strength than Keren. It soon became evident that nothing short of a set piece attack would dislodge the Italians, and the tedious task of dumping the essential reserves of ammunition, supplies and petrol had once more to be undertaken, the main difficulty again being lack of transport. However, just as before, by improvisation, sweat and administrative juggling the dumping programme was completed, and the final attack launched, which resulted in the capitulation of the enemy garrison at Amba Alagi.

Thus the campaign was ended. Immense administrative problems involving the services, especially supplies and transport, still remained in the evacuation of the forces now freed for service in Egypt, and in the organization of the maintenance of the forces left to occupy the former enemy territory. However, the operational urgency had gone and by now also the supply of Corps units and men, so much needed throughout the previous arduous months, had greatly improved. So the work of reorganization and tidying up generally filled the following months as gradually the Sudan assumed a position of minor importance as a transit centre for stores and aircraft on the route from Accra to Cairo. It was also the base for the control of Eritrea, and, as far as the Corps was concerned, for the continued expansion of the Sudan Service Corps, which was still, among other commitments, responsible for the maintenance of the Kufra Oasis, now occupied by British forces. This Corps, with RASC officers, reached a strength of 5,000 in 1943 and provided

R.A.S.C. Motor Vessel (M.V.) 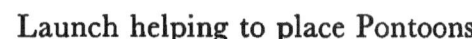 Launch helping to place Pontoons

Field Ambulance Transport

At a Field Dressing Station

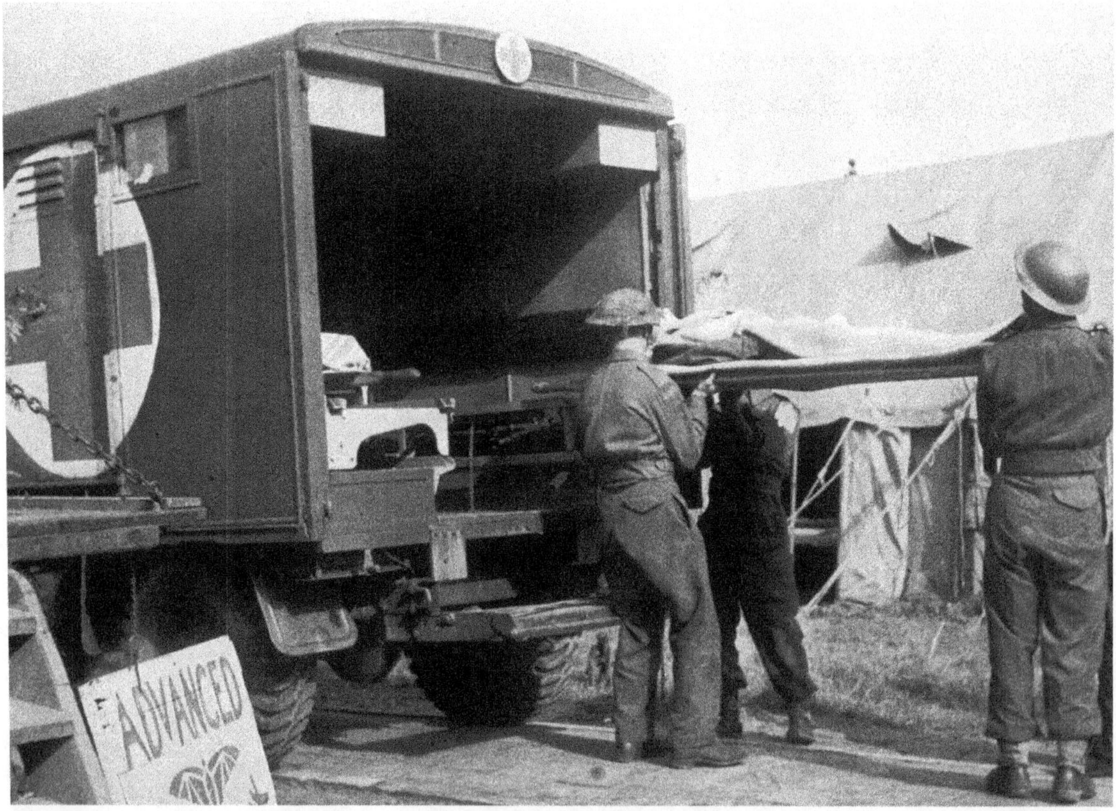

several MT companies for duty in the Western Desert, where they loyally and efficiently fulfilled their purpose.

No account of the Sudan-Eritrean campaign would be complete without a tribute to the Sudan Government and the Sudanese. Throughout the campaign the services of all the government departments were unstintingly placed at the disposal of the GOC, General Sir William Platt. Inestimable help, both material and administrative, was given by all these departments especially the railway, agriculture, survey and medical. Both Sudanese and British Government officials, many of whom took an active part in the operations, did their utmost in helping the fighting forces. The Sudanese soldiers, who in peacetime were recruited only for internal security duties, lived up to their highest traditions and proved themselves brave and efficient and fully able to fight beside their British and Indian comrades.

EAST AFRICA AND MADAGASCAR

Introduction

Before the war, British East Africa, in which were included Kenya Colony, the Uganda and Nyasaland Protectorates and the mandated territory of Tanganyika, was under Colonial Office administration and no British troops were stationed there. The garrison consisted of two brigades of the King's African Rifles. A small number of RASC officers and other ranks were seconded for duty with the Supply and Transport Corps, KAR, but there was no actual RASC organization for the operation of supply, transport and barrack services.

From this small beginning grew a command, which was to mount and support the invasion and capture of Italian Somaliland, Ethiopia, and Madagascar, and of which the feeding strength reached a peak of nearly a quarter of a million. In addition the 11th East African Division was sent to take part in the re-conquest of Burma.

From the outbreak of war until the summer of 1941, East Africa was under the Commander-in-Chief, Middle East, but it subsequently became an independent command under the direct control of War Office. At its zenith, besides the original territories, it included Northern Rhodesia, Madagascar, the Seychelles, Mauritius, Ethiopia, British Somaliland, and the former Italian Somaliland.

Although no RASC unit served on the mainland of East Africa during the war, there was not a single unit of the East Africa Army Service Corps from 1941 onwards that did not contain a high proportion of RASC officers and other ranks. Most of these had no previous experience of native troops, but they adapted and acclimatized themselves well and helped to establish the reputation of the EAASC in accordance with the traditions of the parent Corps.

There are four phases in the story of the war in this theatre: first, from September, 1939, to June, 1940, mobilization and adjustment to war conditions; second, from June, 1940, to February, 1941, preparation for offensive operations; third, from February, 1941, to December, 1941, active operations in Somalia and Ethiopia; and, fourth, occupation of those territories and the mounting of the invasion of Madagascar during the period to the middle of 1943.

Until 1938, the administration of supplies and transport services in British East Africa was the responsibility of the ST Corps of the King's African Rifles. Supplies were then divorced from transport on the grounds of economy, and became, with petrol, the responsibility of the brigade staff quartermaster, supplies being delivered to railhead under contract.

The transport part of the Corps continued as the Transport Corps, King's African Rifles, comprising in peacetime four officers, nine Asians, and 105 Africans, with 58 lorries. This strength must be compared with a mobilization requirement of about 3,000 all ranks and 1,900 vehicles.

The general East African mobilization scheme, which was drawn up in May, 1939, provided for the formation of an East African Army Service Corps, which would assume responsibility for both supply and transport services; this took effect on the outbreak of war. The general organization of the EAASC was based on the pre-war system designed to meet the operational needs of the KAR, the foundation of which was the 'group' intended to serve one battalion, and maintain it at a distance of 80 to 100 miles from railhead. The new Corps, therefore, comprised a headquarters, three operating groups and base units. Each group consisted of a headquarters and repair shop wing, a field supply depot, a bus company, two supply companies, two ammunition companies and a motor ambulance convoy. The bus companies were designed to carry one battalion, and were later re-designated reserve MT companies.

The existence of the Transport Corps naturally facilitated the introduction of the new system, but there was nothing on which to build a supply branch. However, accommodation for a main supply depot was obtained and, although nobody employed there had any previous experience of supply work, the depot was ready to operate by September 4th, 1939, when the staff quartermaster ceased to control the rationing of the forces.

The transport base installations included a vehicle reserve depot, to deal with the receipt, inspection, registration and allotment of impressed civilian vehicles; a heavy repair shop which was formed by taking over civilian workshops complete, until workshop machinery arrived; and a main MT technical stores (later MT stores depot), the existence of which was only made possible by a firm placing its entire accommodation and staff at the disposal of the Army.

The number of supply and transport units required by the battalion group system was found to be uneconomical when the force was concentrated and battalions were brigaded. A new ST organization for a brigade group was therefore designed, consisting of headquarters with a workshop wing, two transport companies for the carriage of supplies, two ammunition companies, two field supply depots and one reserve MT company. There had previously been no provision for divisional troops' second line, so this was now organized as a divisional troops group, consisting of a transport company, an ammunition company and a field supply depot.

The theory of operation of transport was the 'endless chain' system between rail and roadhead and delivery point. The brigade group had a range of about 80 miles, but the divisional troops group had a good deal less, and the gap was made up by reserve MT companies acting as third line transport. The function of the two FSDs in each group was that one should be located at railhead as a railhead supply detachment, and one at roadhead or intermediately, to break bulk, or hold a reserve stock in front of a possible break in the line of communication.

Reorganization

This organization was inflexible and uneconomical. The number of small units tended to an extravagant use of officers and British NCOs, while the small size of the units themselves led to an uneconomical allotment of workshop sections, which aggravated the already serious lack of maintenance facilities. Supplies and petrol were both carried by the transport companies, the former in detail over excessive distances. Finally the existing organization of the divisional troops made it difficult to detach the appropriate second line vehicles for units of divisional troops which had to operate over long distances in support of one brigade.

In June, 1940, the group system was abolished, and a new organization substituted. The basis of this was a brigade RASC company, divided into a supply section, a petrol section and an ammunition section, and a divisional troops company organized on similar lines. These companies were to carry one day's requirements of all commodities for the troops they served. The remaining transport was organized into three troop-carrying companies, each capable of transporting one battalion, the remainder to form reserve MT companies.

The second line companies were designed to operate a double echelon of 80 miles, and their workshop sections were intended to maintain the brigade group B vehicles as well as their own.

The four brigades now available (two East African and two West African) were at the same time organized into two divisions, and the allotment of the four brigade companies followed suit. The reorganization made men and vehicles available from which were formed 16 reserve MT companies, each able to carry four days' supplies in bulk for one brigade, from railhead to refilling points.

The supplies system was also reorganized, the field supply depots being changed into sections of a supply personnel company, which were allocated to divisional groups as required. Each section was able to maintain 7,500 men. Another supply personnel company was formed from existing supply units, and took over the railhead supply depots and detail issue depots on the line of communication.

The vehicle situation was far from satisfactory. Not only had the EAASC units to be equipped, but also first line transport had to be provided for West African troops coming into the Command. The vehicles required on mobilization had been obtained by hasty requisitioning without inspection, and large numbers that came into VRD were unsuitable. Many of those accepted had covered 30,000 to 40,000 miles and all had suffered from rough usage and poor maintenance; consequently a heavy strain was placed on the semi-trained workshop staffs in keeping the vehicles on the road. Another unfortunate result of the poor condition of these vehicles was that the first consignments of spare parts from abroad were exhausted soon after they were received, in meeting the continuous demands for replacements on impressed vehicles.

Small consignments of new vehicles came from South Africa, but in general neither the quality nor the quantity was sufficient for operations against the Italians, who were numerically superior and better equipped.

A contributory factor to the unsatisfactory situation was the inadequacy of workshop equipment. In June, 1940, with the exception of a few made locally, the EAASC had no mobile workshop sets.

It was represented to the War Office that 1,100 3-ton lorries must be provided to meet operational needs involving the maintenance of two brigade groups for 500 miles, one brigade group for 260 miles and one for 300 miles beyond railhead. The War Office agreed to this and planned to ship 250 lorries at once, with instructions to East Africa Command to report the stages at which the remainder could be accepted when trained men were available. There still remained a large deficiency of technical stores lorries, breakdown lorries and ambulances.

Besides a West African reinforcement of 600 trained drivers, the Mobile Field Force of the South African Union Defence Force began to arrive in May, 1940. The first ST elements included a base supply depot, which was set up at Mombasa, an advanced supply depot, and a detail issue depot. While the supply men of the Mobile Field Force came by sea, the MT came overland. Vehicles were railed as far as Broken Hill in Northern Rhodesia and thence driven 1,500 miles to Nairobi, along what was known as the Great North Road. In all, about 13,000 out of 15,500 vehicles passed along this route, and in spite of the difficulties of the road and the inexperience of many of the drivers, not a single vehicle was left derelict on the road. The South Africans brought their own mobile general workshops, so that they were self-contained in this respect.

The influx of all these troops placed a strain on the East African supply system which it had never been designed to carry. By the end of January, 1941, the feeding strength reached 122,000, comprising a heterogeneous collection of races, which required six main and numerous subsidiary ration scales. It was at first suggested that the South African troops should be maintained from the Union, but eventually it was decided that as much use as possible should be made of local resources.

Until May, 1940, petrol and its associated oils for the Army and RAF were obtained under Government contract direct from the oil companies. With the arrival of the Union army and air force units, it was estimated that monthly consumption of MT and aviation spirit would increase from 60,000 to three million gallons and from 40,000 to 500,000 gallons respectively.

A petrol section under an ADS (petrol) was therefore formed to undertake provisioning, supply and distribution of all MT and aviation spirits for the combined forces, and the oil companies agreed to increase and re-distribute their bulk storage to meet army requirements. MT spirit tankage was increased by 8,000 tons to 22,000 tons and aviation by 6,000 tons to 8,000 tons.

In July, 1940, the only container in use was the 4-gallon non-returnable tin. The plants for can-making in the Command belonged to the oil companies. Of these, two in Mombasa could produce 25,000 a day between them, while there was also a small plant in Zanzibar.

Preparation for the Offensive

Such then was the general situation of the EAASC in June, 1940, when Italy entered the war. It had not altered greatly by November that year when General Cunningham assumed command, and announced that his forces would be thoroughly prepared for offensive action by June, 1941. The principal problems confronting the EAASC were that the MTSD was exhausted, supply staff and storage were inadequate to contend with the ever-increasing feeding strengths, there was a serious lack of trained officers, British NCOs and artificers, and the HRS had no machinery. The vehicle situation was gradually improving, but transport was fully extended in meeting existing demands. Yet it was required to support two additional brigades which were being formed, and to maintain a line of communication which would lengthen if the advance were successful. Finally there were two separate supply and transport organizations, East African and South African, each operating independently and to some extent duplicating each other's work. These problems were further aggravated when the Commander advanced his plans by four months.

There were, however, some assets. The War Office had undertaken to reinforce the EAASC with drafts of RASC officers and other ranks. Shipment was promised of 5,000 3-ton lorries, including some of workshop, stores and breakdown vehicles, over a period of six months. About 3,000 lorries and many smaller vehicles were bought through local agents. These would make possible the formation of 15 new reserve MT companies and three more infantry brigade group companies. However, after the arrival of the first 1,500 lorries, Middle East claimed the remainder, and this loss caused a shortage throughout the campaign.

There was a chronic dearth of MT spares, because of the failure of the South African forces to make provision for an adequate reserve. Thousands of Fords came into the country with the Union forces, and provision for their maintenance was completely inadequate.

Important reforms were introduced early in 1941. It had all along been obvious that, to have two separate services, South African and East African, was not only wasteful, but would be fraught with difficulties if big operations took place. The entire supply and transport organization for the campaign was, therefore, consolidated under the DDST (Brigadier C. V. Bennett).

Until November, 1940, petrol was controlled by the staff, through ADS (petrol), which was unsatisfactory from the ST point of view, and arrangements were therefore made for this service to become the responsibility of DDST. In addition to the oil companies' bulk storage, a reserve stock of nearly eight million gallons of packed petrol was built up just before the advance. In the event of the source of supply from the Middle East, Persia and Iraq being cut off, nine million gallons were held in Durban, representing about three months' supply, of which one-third was packed ready for immediate despatch. Alternative routes by which petrol could enter East

Africa were planned, one from South Africa either through Broken Hill by road, or through Dar-es-Salaam or Tanga, and the other from Leopoldville in the Belgian Congo by road and river.

The northern part of Kenya adjoining the 900-mile-long frontier of the Italian possessions was a desert waste over which the roads were few and poor, often little more than camel tracks. All types of surface were encountered; belts of lava rock sometimes 40 miles wide consisting of sharp-edged rocks, which tore tyres to pieces and ruined springs and radiators; fine sand sometimes two feet deep; and treacherous black cotton soil, which became glutinous after the least rain. There was a great scarcity of water. Fine dust penetrated carburettors, radiators, clutches and dynamos. It was over the roads traversing this country that the transport units worked between June, 1940, and February, 1941, maintaining the forward troops, and building up large reserve dumps of food, petrol, ammunition and other war material.

The distance from our railheads to the frontier averaged about 300 miles. It was partly these bad conditions that deterred the Italians from advancing into Kenya, after they had driven back our advanced troops near the Sudan frontier in July, 1940. They preferred to adopt a containing policy as far as our forces in Kenya were concerned, and to make a more spectacular conquest of British Somaliland, from which our small force, hopelessly outnumbered, was forced to withdraw in August, 1940.

The main dump was at Garissa, about 200 miles east of Nairobi, and was based on the Thika railhead, 30 miles from that city. It might have appeared easier and more economical to supply Garissa by road direct from Mombasa, but the road connecting the two places was poor, liable to interruption by flood, and involved ferrying at two points, besides passing through the coastal malarial belt. It was therefore, more economical in time and labour to avoid splitting the stores arriving in bulk at Mombasa, and to send them by rail to the MSD in Nairobi. From there they were sent to railhead, where the reserve MT companies loaded and delivered to refilling points. South African reserve companies, with European drivers, were used for the carriage of water, as it was vital that there should be no failure of supply in this respect.

The Advance

In February, 1941, when the advance began, the chief problem from the supply and transport point of view was the physical endurance of the men, especially those of the transport units, who had been working without respite for nearly nine months in bringing up stores, and now had to face operational conditions without any opportunity for rest and refit. Simply to drive a lorry on the

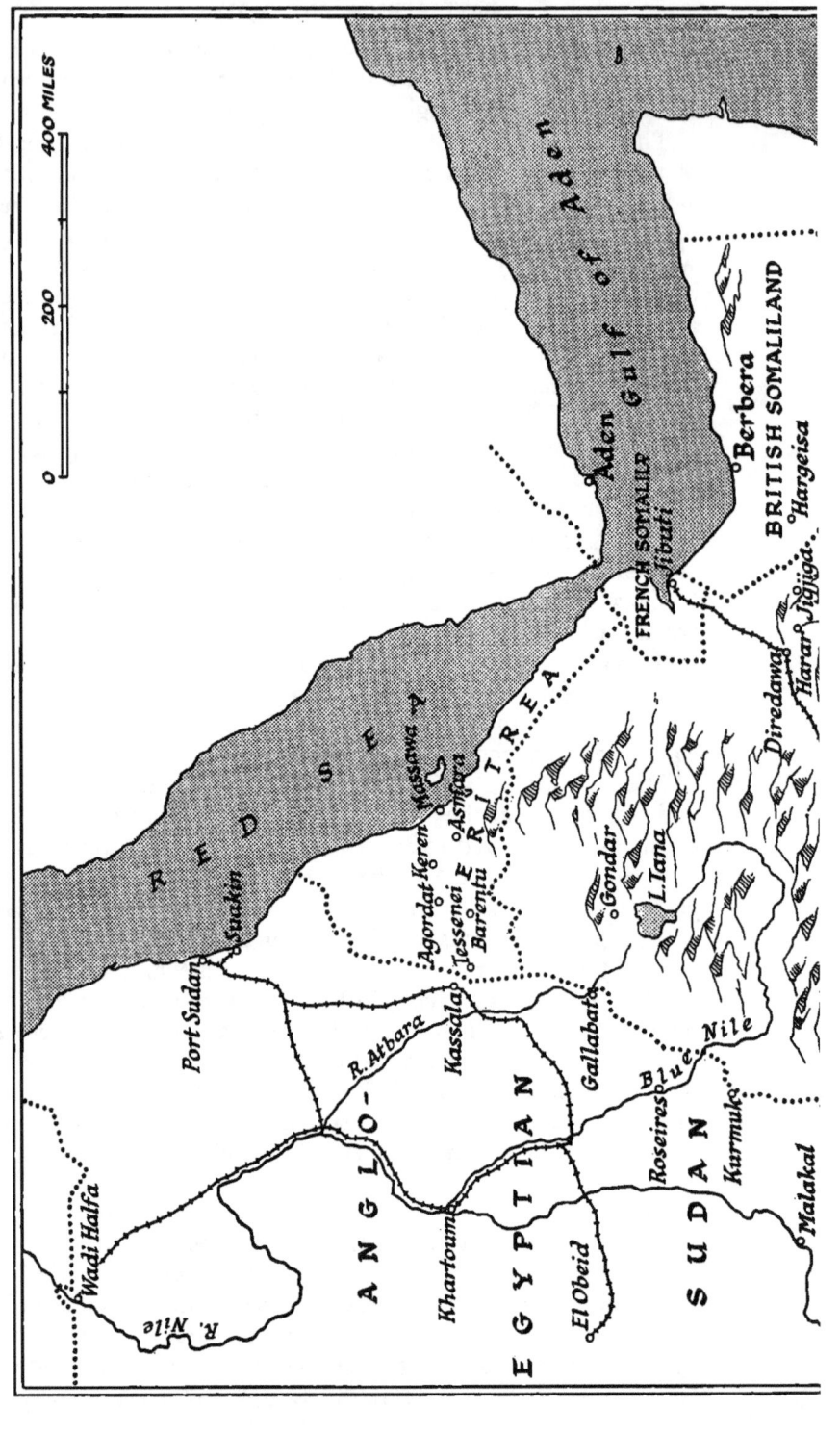

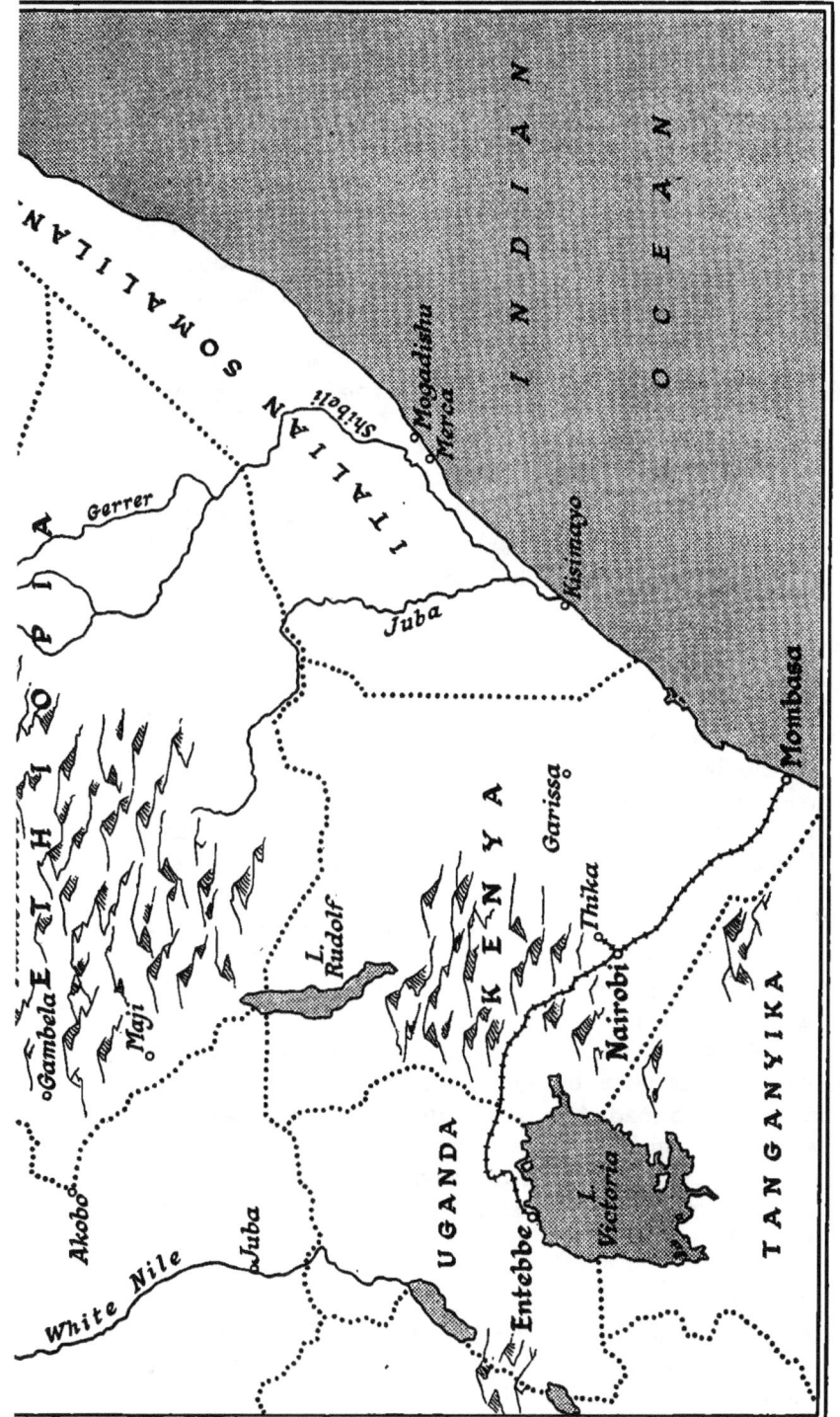

East Africa

deplorable roads was a test of stamina, and the heat was so intense that it was difficult to keep awake at the wheel.

The advance was extremely rapid, the Italians offering little resistance, and the port of Kisimayo, 200 miles from Garissa, was occupied after only four days. The unexpected rapidity with which the lines of communication lengthened, and the consequent heavy demands on third line transport for troop-carrying, petrol and water supply meant that second line transport had to go back to roadheads for supplies. They worked on a continuous shuttle system, collecting one week's supplies at a time, and in this way a regular and adequate stock of all commodities was made available to the fighting troops. Fortunately the demand for ammunition was small, as there was little real fighting.

Through scrub so thick that drivers had to hack their way, a brigade pushed on and crossed the Juba River where the enemy had hoped to make a stand. Three days later, on February 25th, the British entered Mogadishu, the capital of Somalia, and the first stage of the campaign was over. The transport had been operating for a fortnight, in an advance of over 600 miles in difficult country. While the fighting troops rested, transport men were occupied in re-fuelling, repairing, adjusting loads and re-grouping. Workshop men had had no rest, stocks of spares were diminishing, springs in particular had suffered and considerable improvisation was necessary to make good the damage.

A three weeks' rest for overhaul and refit was promised, and it was sorely needed. But the chance discovery of an Italian MT petrol dump at Mogadishu of half-a-million gallons, mostly in 40-gallon drums, made this unnecessary, which was in some ways unfortunate. However the advance could be, and was, set in motion again. Up to this point petrol had been carried in cased 4-gallon tins, which naturally did not stand up well to the road conditions, leakage being about one fifth of the total.

The port of Mogadishu had been mined by British aircraft, and was unusable, so ships were brought to Merca, about 80 miles away. They had been loaded in the greatest haste, and food and explosives were mixed in indescribable confusion. There were no proper port facilities, and although the whole work of supervising the off-loading fell on the supply section of an infantry brigade group company, the transport was loaded and despatched.

Advance into Ethiopia

The Italians were in full retreat with our forces following hot on their heels, reaching and capturing Jigjiga in Ethiopia, a fortnight later, 650 miles from Mogadishu. The first 230 miles of this had been easy going, along the tarmac surface of the Strada Imperiale.

Then the road degenerated into a flint-strewn track, followed by a stretch of jagged rocks, laid down as the first stage of metalling; then, after a sea of dust, the last 40 miles were over a grass plain. The enemy were again put to flight, and the GOC decided to pursue them relentlessly. This threw an enormous burden on those responsible for maintaining the force, as the line from Mogadishu was already stretched to its limit. If the force had advanced any farther it might have become impossible to maintain it.

However, at the critical moment, Berbera, the capital and port of British Somaliland, was recaptured from the Italians and the maintenance of the East African force was rapidly switched to that port, reducing the road line of communication to the comparatively short distance of 200 miles. On March 29th, Diredawa was captured, which allowed the railway to Addis Ababa to be put into operation as far as the Ausac gorge. Here the railway bridge was in ruins, and a ferry service operated by MT companies was conducted in difficult conditions for three months, until the bridge was rebuilt.

All available transport, including companies formed only three months before, was sent up from Kenya to keep open the line of communication from Berbera to Diredawa. The rains had broken and the roads were seas of mud. *Shifta* (bandits) and Italian stragglers made the road dangerous for supply convoys, which were profitable plunder. The rapid advance over such bad roads put many vehicles out of action, but the ingenuity of workshop men and drivers, in spite of great scarcity of spares, enabled repairs to be effected.

Petrol supply was a crucial factor. The 500,000 gallons taken in Mogadishu had lasted 12 days, and many corps troops units were stranded 400 miles from the port. Captured petrol dumps again helped. In the final stages of the campaign, in the drive for Addis Ababa, petrol was the only limiting factor.

On April 6th less than two months after the start of the campaign, East African troops entered Addis Ababa. A total of 1,687 miles had been covered at an average rate of 76 miles a day for each day of movement, and of 32 miles for each day of the campaign. The distance was equivalent to that from London to the Black Sea. Pursuit of the enemy was continued northwards from Addis Ababa, and the main Italian force finally surrendered on July 3rd. The campaign was at an end, except for the attack on the last Italian stronghold at Gondar, the operations for which lasted from October to December, 1941.

In the light of experience gained in the operations, a final reorganization of the infantry brigade group company was effected in December, 1941. Sections were now placed on a commodity basis. The supplies section worked a double echelon between road or railhead and delivery points on the standard RASC system.

Although a superficial glance at the East African Campaign may give the momentary impression of a 'text book' operation of exceptional brilliance, it is as well not to gloss over the facts that the luck ran largely on the British side and that at no time was the fighting calibre of the East African forces submitted to a real test.

So far as the supply and transport services were concerned, in spite of the difficulties encountered and the initial inexperience of most officers and British NCOs, their enthusiasm and loyalty were unbounded, and a solid tradition of unselfish work was steadily built up, which evoked the finest praise that can be given to any ST Corps, when Lieut-General Sir Alan Cunningham, on saying farewell to the East African Command, spoke these tense and significant words: 'You boast you are a service—and, by God, you are!'

With the Ethiopian campaign at an end our main forces were gradually withdrawn leaving garrisons at strategic points. The only further event of outstanding interest was the mounting of the expedition to Madagascar.

Madagascar

Madagascar is a large island lying off the east coast of Africa, from which it is divided by the Mozambique Channel. It is about 1,000 miles long and 360 miles wide, and has a mountainous central axis running up to more than 8,000 feet in a few places. In 1942 there was no through road system, and such roads as existed were frequently interrupted by mainly unfordable rivers and were little better than tracks. Communication was effected usually by air, so that movement was severely restricted. The island as a whole was under-developed. The only useful railway was single track and ran from Tamatave, the modern port on the east coast, up to Antananarivo, the capital in the centre of the island.

Madagascar is a French possession, and after the capitulation of France, was governed from Vichy. Its long coast line and many creeks and estuaries suitable for lying-up early attracted the Japanese, whose submarines began to take heavy toll of the Allied shipping routed round the Cape. In order to stop this interference with vital traffic, operation 'Ironclad' mounted from Britain saw Force 121 carry out an assault landing on May 5th, 1952, and continue to the capture of Diego Suarez. Diego Suarez lies at the head of a fine large harbour at the northern tip of the island. The Force comprised HQ Royal Marine Division (Major-General R. C. Sturges), 29th Independent Infantry Brigade Group, and 13th and 17th Infantry Brigades. CRASC was Lieut-Colonel R. A. E. Dunlop.

The 29th Brigade carried out the assault before first light on May 5th. Assisted by aircraft from HMS *Indomitable* and HMS *Illustrious* and supported by HMS *Ramillies*, cruisers and destroyers, they reached the outskirts of Diego the same night. A dawn attack by 29th Brigade on the town on May 6th failed; but a full scale attack was mounted that night by all available troops, supported by a party of Royal Marines. They landed in behind the enemy from HMS *Anthony* on the main quay of Diego itself and brought 'cease fire' in the early hours of May 7th.

This operation was only just in time to forestall a Japanese task force with a similar mission. The Japanese achieved some measure of revenge a few days later when one of their midget submarines severely damaged the *Ramillies* and sank an oil tanker. The midget submarine and its occupants were destroyed.

RASC support to Force 121 comprised 55 DID with a few additional bakers and butchers and a transport detachment of 20 15- and 30-cwt vehicles, and six ambulances. The 13th and 17th Brigades had their RASC companies, though initially no vehicles could be landed for them. During the operation and subsequently until all vehicles were landed, the available transport was at full stretch, but was able to meet requirements because of the short distances. Ammunition and petrol replenishment proved to be singularly free from trouble, as also in the first place was that of supplies. In the period of consolidation and reorganization for the advance south to the capital, some difficulty was experienced in getting satisfactory bread because of the deterioration of the yeast in the climatic conditions.

As the first instance of an amphibious assault mounted from a distance of 10,000 miles, 'Ironclad' provided success and justification of current methods of planning and training. Best of all, the preservation of surprise was achieved beyond highest hopes, although these were somewhat dashed when the leading troops of the Royal Welch Fusiliers landing on White Beach in Ambararata Bay in the darkness at 0430 hours on May 5th were welcomed by one old man clad only in a loin-cloth who, greeting them in good English, said: 'Good-morning, Gentlemen! We expected you last week!' It transpired that he was a Goanese who had been a steward in a British India steamer and had retired to this resort!

The impossibility of making a satisfactory rate of progress southward to the capital was realized when the force was only 100 miles south of Diego Suarez after much strenuous effort over several months. By this time, 22nd East Africa Brigade and 7th South Africa Brigade had arrived, and 13th and 17th Brigades had been moved on to India. Headquarters Royal Marine Division and 29th Brigade were therefore pulled out to Mombasa to refit and to plan another assault, farther south down the coast, and so to reach Antananarivo, the capital.

Operation 'Stream-Line-Jane-Esme' (a favourite expression of Force Commander, and qualified by the South African Brigade) was therefore mounted with 29th Brigade assaulting at Majunga nearly halfway down the west coast on September 10th. This was 'Stream'.

The 22nd East Africa Brigade followed up, and with four East Africa Army Service Corps reserve MT companies and small supply detachments additionally in support, struck out for Antananarivo. There had been negligible opposition to the assault, but the landing of the follow-up troops was much delayed by difficulties in working unfamiliar ships not wholly suitable for the purpose, and because contrary to intelligence the so-called harbour at Majunga dried out for 16 out of the 24 hours. In consequence the leading troops found the quarter-mile-long Kamoro bridge over the Betsiboka River, 120 miles inland, blown over its whole length, and the advance was much handicapped. This was 'Line'.

Majunga was developed as the base for operations until Tamatave and the railway line to Antananarivo had been cleared. A main supply depot, three DIDs and seven POL sections were supplied from East Africa and maintained their role under difficult conditions. In the meantime, 7th South Africa Brigade had resumed the attempt to advance south from Diego. This time the west coast route was tried in an effort to link up with 22nd East Africa Brigade through Majunga, and to back them up in their advance in the capital. This was 'Esme'.

Having seen 22nd Brigade started on their long trek to Antananarivo, 29th Brigade re-embarked and sailed for Tamatave on the east coast. Here they assaulted again on September 18th, and after a show of resistance the town fell without fighting. This was 'Jane'.

While the island of Dzaoud-zi in the Comores had already been captured in July, successful diversions were now also staged simultaneously at Morondava and Tulear.

For this operation, because of the preponderance of East Africa troops, Lieut-Colonel J. H. Hawtin was brought in from Nairobi as CRASC, Lieut-Colonel Dunlop remaining at Diego Suarez. No breakdown in the maintenance of RASC services was experienced, although necessarily at times there was nothing to spare. The issue of cash to officers of all arms to enable them to purchase requirements, with a minimum of reasonable accounting to be observed, proved of great value in helping to maintain the momentum of the advance. In one skirmish the opposition was bought over! The 22nd East Africa Brigade finally reached Antananarivo on September 23rd, beating elements of the 29th Brigade from Tamatave, by only a few hours. The 7th South Africa Brigade from Diego

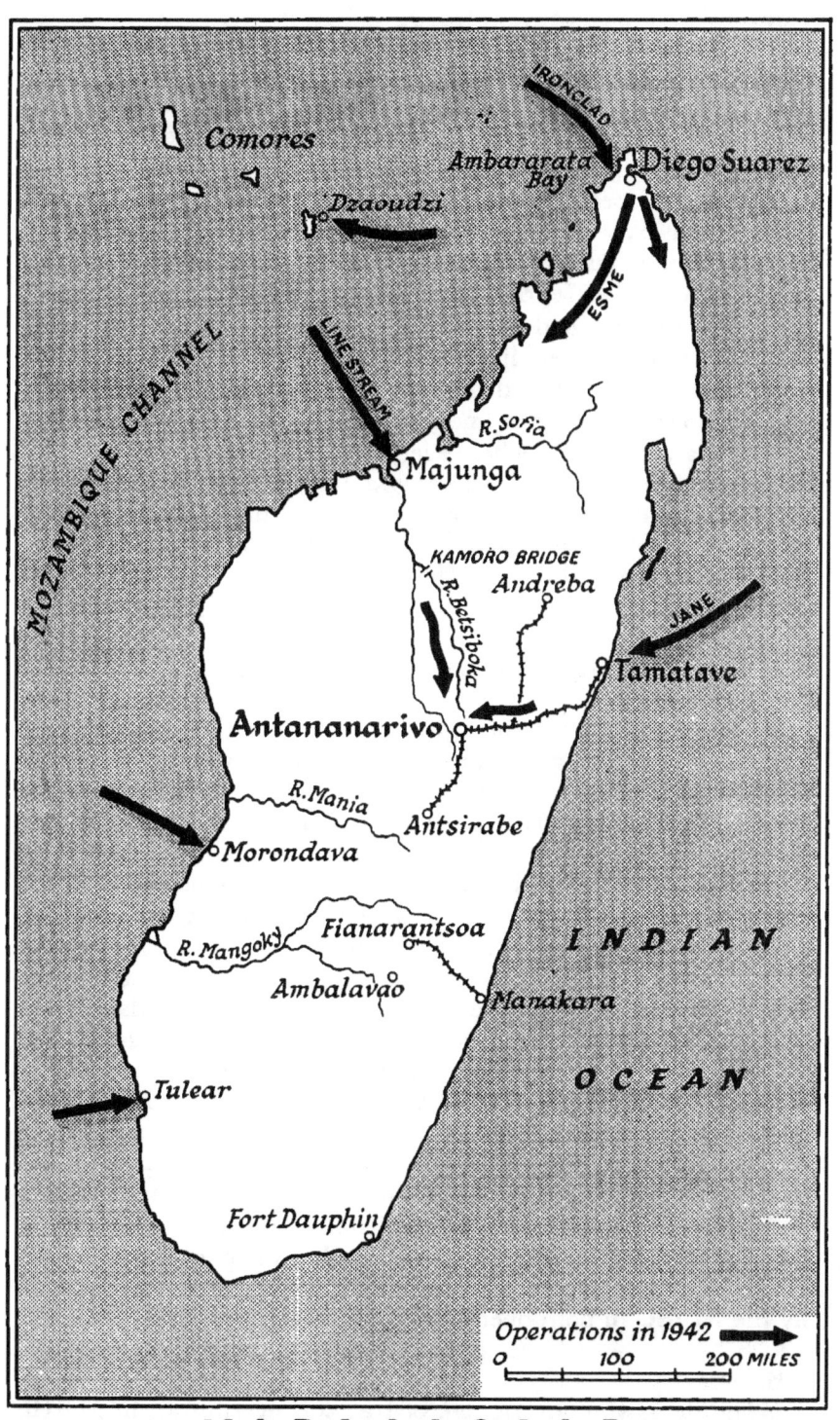

reached Majunga about the same time. The 29th Brigade were now withdrawn to India, but 22nd Brigade continued the operations southwards until an armistice was signed at Ambalavao on November 6th.

Seen in retrospect, except that the Majunga landing was so much slower than had been expected, the Madagascar assaults were carried through much as originally planned. This was only possible because HQ Royal Marine Division, 29th Brigade and supporting arms and services had planned and trained together for many months. Transport, equipment and stores of all kinds were necessarily drastically scaled down for the assaults, and assets were loyally pooled. Everyone knew everybody else and was prepared to co-operate in a party where every man did his best.

Constantly overworked, and always under pressure to do more, the RASC staff and units remained a cheerful and happy team throughout, and never failed to produce what was required. They were well supported from the United Kingdom.

IRAQ, SYRIA AND PERSIA

In the early months of 1941 General Wavell's Middle East Command was being strained to the limit. Rommel's counter offensive in Cyrenaica in April had driven our main forces in the Western Desert almost back to the Egyptian frontier. Three weeks' desperate fighting in Greece had ended in evacuation; the battle for Crete was impending; Ethiopia had still to be conquered and, at the end of April, rebellion in Iraq produced yet a further commitment. Every advance which the Germans made in their drive through the Balkans increased the potency of the air attacks they could make against us and if they were allowed to occupy Syria they could threaten the Canal Zone and the vital communications between Palestine and Iraq. The infiltration of German agents into Vichy-occupied Syria was increasing and the German Air Force were being granted landing facilities there.

The operations which followed at the end of April in Iraq and in Syria in May were shared by the British and Indian Armies, and although the short accounts which follow must be restricted so far as supply and transport are concerned to the part played by the RASC, the reader is asked to bear in mind the prominent part played by the RIASC in both operations.

Iraq, 1941

When the lawful government of Iraq was overthrown in March, 1941, by Rashid Ali and his caucus of adventurers and mutinous

Weasel at Lake Comacchio

In the Arabian Desert

Left:
'Aid to Russia'

Below:
In the Chindwin Hills

army officers, the only British forces in the country were the RAF at Shaiba, a few miles from Basra, and at Habbaniya. They were maintained from India via the Persian Gulf. Fostered by the Germans whose agents had been relentlessly spreading their propaganda against the Allies, the rebels soon showed their real intentions by despatching, at the end of April, a force of an infantry brigade with artillery and tanks to the plateau overlooking the RAF cantonment at Habbaniya.

Thanks to the prompt action of our Ambassador an Indian infantry brigade had already been diverted from its destination, Malaya, to Basra and a second brigade also from India was on its way. But the only reinforcement which could be sent at once to Habbaniya was about 350 men, of the King's Own Royal Regiment, who were hastily bundled into Valencia aircraft and deposited there on the last day of April. The Indian brigade was not equipped for desert operations, nor had it been loaded tactically and the 400 intervening miles to Habbaniya, owing to annual flooding, made the movement of armed forces by land to the north impossible.

Action had, however, also been taken to draw on the 1st Cavalry Division then in Palestine and to assemble a force which was to secure the communications across the desert to Habbaniya, relieve the beleaguered RAF station there and then strike at the rebels and restore the situation around Bagdad. Units which were horsed had to be quickly mechanized for the purpose, but by the evening of May 13th 'Kingcol', a column made up of the headquarters, 4th Cavalry Brigade, the Household Cavalry Regiment, a company of infantry, and some artillery, engineers and signals, with 51 and 552 Companies RASC, was assembled at H4 on the oil pipeline. The remainder of the force, which included the divisional headquarters and their CRASC headquarters and 543 Company, was to follow and to open up the new long line of communication which was to stretch from the Haifa base to Habbaniya. On the morning of the 14th 'Kingcol', with its 1,800 men and 500 vehicles, of which 300 were of the RASC, reached Rutba, which had been cleared of its rebel garrison the day before by the Arab Legion. From Rutba the force had then to leave the oil pipeline and negotiate a desert track until it joined the tarmac road about 30 kilometres from Ramadi. The road from Ramadi to Habbaniya was impassable because of floods so that the force had again to make its way over the desert and to skirt Lake Habbaniya. Some feeble attacks from the air and the attention of guerillas had to be brushed off on the day, and the move was one of considerable physical endurance.

As most of the drivers had no experience of desert work, and most vehicles had normal home service tyres, many lorries were soon stuck in soft sand. After much effort all were extricated in a

O RASC

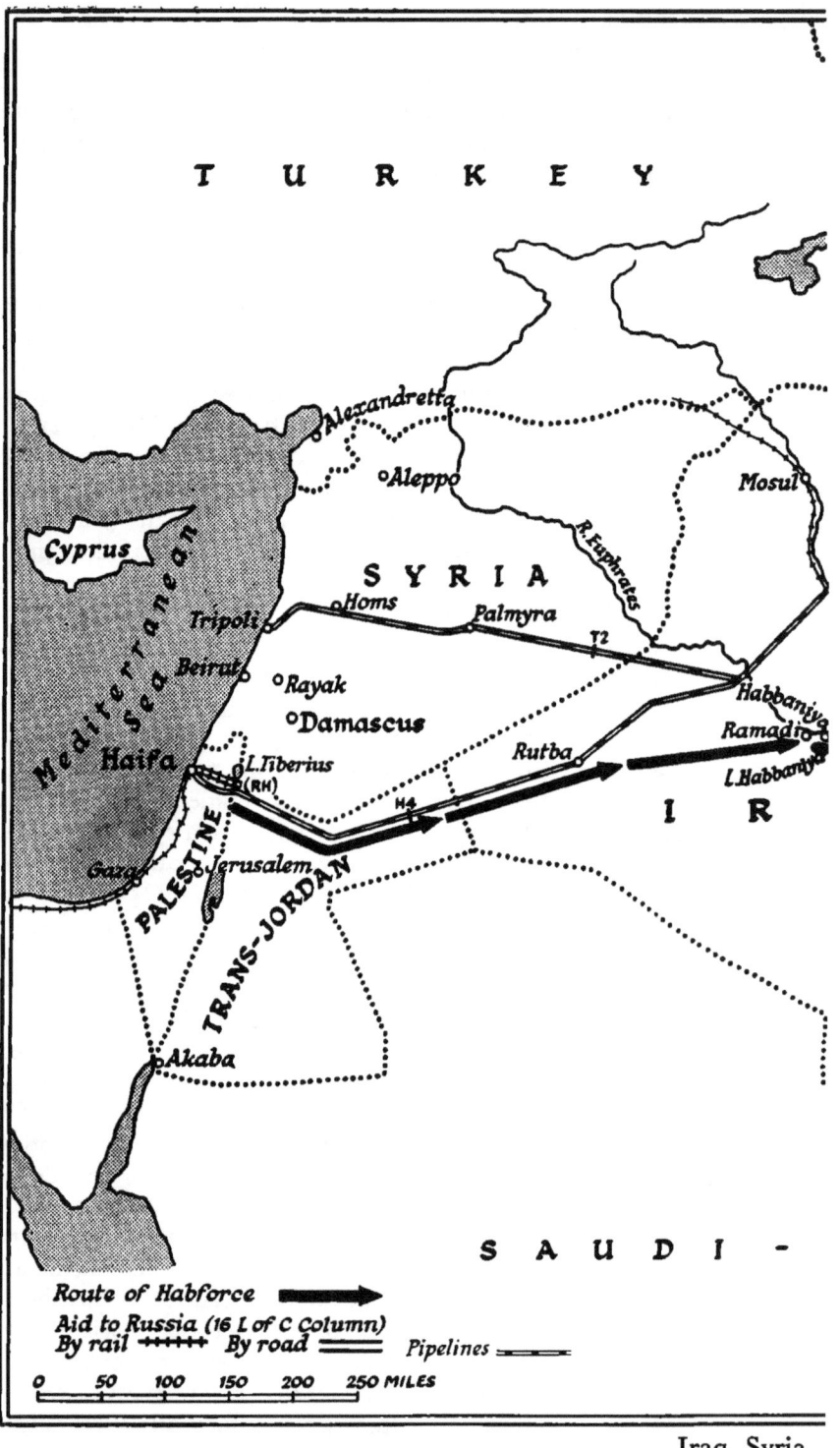

Iraq, Syria

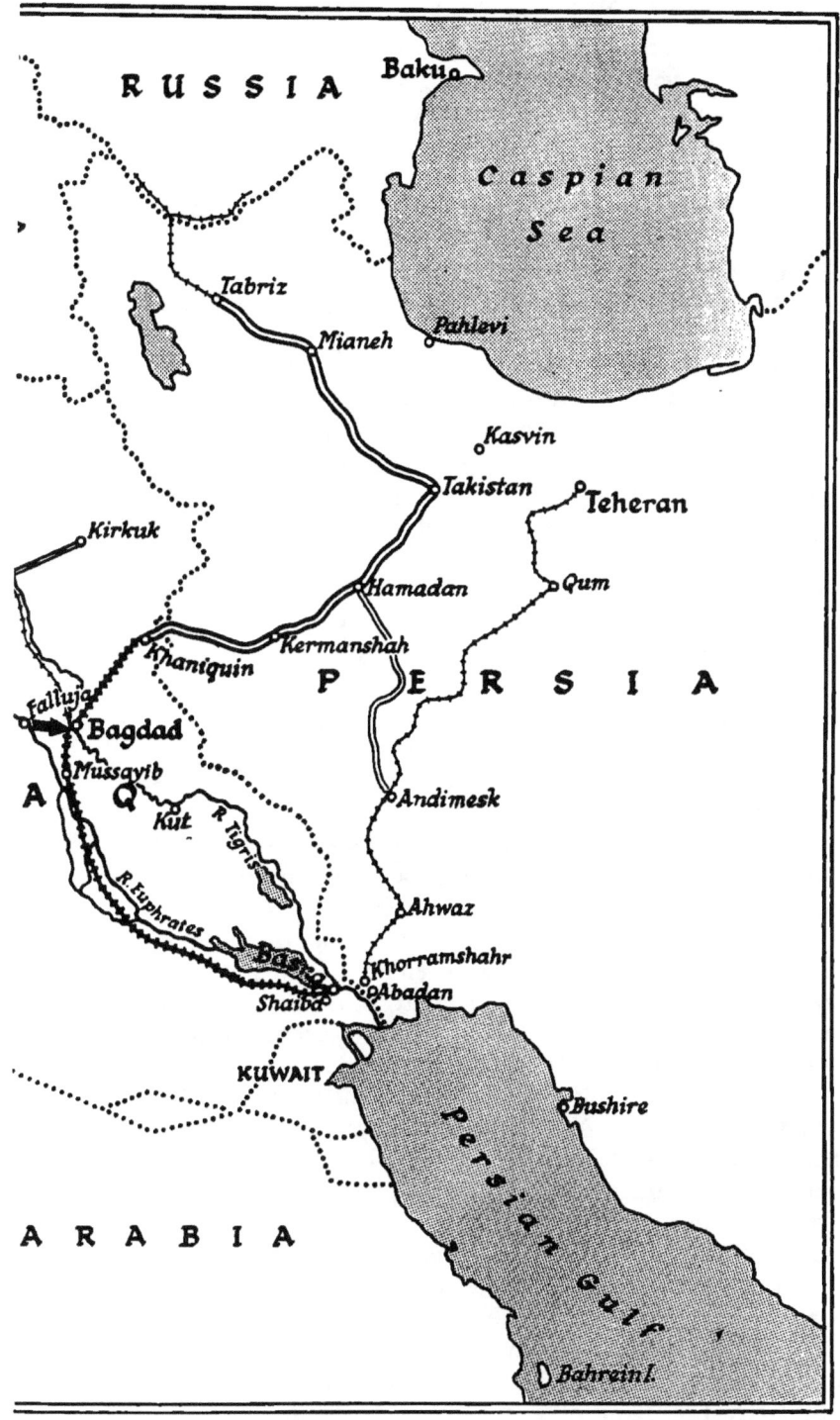
and Persia

temperature of 127 degrees in the shade—of which there was none—and withdrawn to laager. May 17th was spent in the reconnaissance of a better route, and this was eventually found by way of a number of *wadis* (dry water courses). On the 18th 'Kingcol' reached Habbaniya from Majara Bridge, the only way across the flooded area. The comparatively large number of vehicles apparently created a great impression among the local tribes, and from intelligence reports afterwards received it was clear that the Iraqis must have had exaggerated ideas of the number of British troops advancing against them. No doubt the early collapse of the rebels was partly due to this cause. The dust cloud created by such a column was undoubtedly impressive at this stage in the war.

The defence of Habbaniya by the RAF, by the companies of the King's Own Royal Regiment and by the loyal Arab levies was an excellent example of how determination, improvisation and the will to win brings success, but space does not allow of a description of it here.

Habbaniya being secured, Habforce was ordered to advance on Bagdad, while containing a small enemy force based on Ramadi. Many actions were fought towards the end of May, the heaviest being in Falluja. The rebels capitulated on May 31st when, however, Bagdad was threatened by two columns advancing from the west and north-west. 'Kingcol' then marched into Bagdad and the Regent Abdullahi, who had taken refuge at Habbaniya, once more became ruler of Iraq.

The new line of communication was soon firmly established and supply depots set up at H4, H3 and Rutba Wells, from which maintenance columns went forward to Habbaniya. Owing to enemy activity these were invariably escorted by fighting troops. The Arab Legion was employed, as it had been on the advance, as a cavalry screen. This force was also of great value in obtaining information about the enemy. The maintenance columns consisted of not less than two platoons ('sections' at this period). It was found that the round trip took seven days: the distance from H4 to Habbaniya was 400 miles. As a rule two convoys a week operated over the desert most of which was poor going. In this task 51 and 552 Companies were reinforced by 543 Company. Towards the end, the direct road through Ramadi was cleared of the enemy and secured against floods. This reduced the turn-round time by lessening the distance and reducing the element of fatigue.

Supplies and petrol received at Habbaniya from incoming convoys were taken over by a small supply depot which was a combined RASC and RAF unit. The RAF had run short of many commodities before the arrival of 'Kingcol' and had had to devise their own ration scale based entirely on what they had available. With the arrival of 'Kingcol' a normal balanced ration was restored. From this supply depot local units drew their rations, petrol and oil. Petrol was at that time issued in 4-gallon 'flimsies'.

The troops forward of Habbaniya were maintained by sections of transport loaded at the supply depot and taken by unit guides to various points notified by HQ Habforce. After the fall of Bagdad, fresh supplies were obtained by local purchase. Many self-contained columns of Habforce were at that time employed to establish control of vital points farther north such as the airfield and oil installation at Mosul and the pipeline station at Haditha.

Early in June Habforce was withdrawn for further work in Syria and Persia, as by that time the 10th Indian Division had been landed, the rebellion had fizzled out and the Regent of Iraq had been restored to his rightful position on June 1st.

In a special order of the day dated June 7th, 1941, Major-General J. Clarke, the GOC, 1st Cavalry Division, after congratulating all ranks on the successful outcome of the task, said: 'I would specially single out for mention the units of the RASC whose efforts in keeping the force supplied over a hot and arid desert have been beyond praise.'

Syria, 1941

The increasing infiltration of German aircraft into Syria has been mentioned at the beginning of this chapter. In May, 1941, the British Government decided that this threat to the Middle East must be eliminated although it involved the distasteful task of entering into armed conflict with our former ally, France.

The Free French forces available in Palestine were judged inadequate in strength and equipment to perform the task on their own and the barrel had to be scraped to find troops to assist them. Eventually Habforce, two Australian brigades and one Indian infantry brigade took part. Elements of 6th Division (afterwards to become 70th Division) arrived too late to take any part in operations.

The General Staff plan provided for the invasion of Syria with a force consisting, broadly, of 21st and 25th Australian Brigade Groups, the 5th Indian Infantry Brigade Group, with certain Free French forces in Palestine, and that part of the 1st Cavalry Division (Habforce) which had completed its task at Habbaniya and Bagdad. These columns were deployed from the coast to the desert in the order named. Habforce, having been withdrawn from Iraq to H3 and H4, pumping stations on the oil pipeline through Trans-jordan from Kirkuk to Haifa, was to operate on the right flank, with Palmyra as its first objective and Aleppo and Deraa as its second objective. Headquarters at Jerusalem were responsible for the maintenance of the whole force from the coast to H4. Habforce continued to be maintained from roadhead at H4, railhead being at Semakh.

The Australian brigades had their own second line, and 4 and 5 British Reserve MT Companies (50 and 97 Companies RASC) provided their troop carrying vehicles.

4 Reserve MT Company (50) was re-equipped with diesel engined buses and Ford V8 scout cars, which latter vehicles, with a Lewis gun mounting, were used as defence vehicles. Habforce had 552 Company (late Cavalry Divisional Supply Column), 3 Res MT Company (51) and 543 Company RASC.

The opening phase, which began on June 8th, involved the advance of the three left columns. All went well at first, but resistance stiffened on the second day, and thereafter until about June 22nd, fortunes varied. Habforce's advance had all but encircled Palmyra, when it was checked by heavy air attacks in the open desert. The employment of one squadron of aircraft in the vicinity of Palmyra was successful in countering the French air effort around that town which was eventually occupied with little resistance. By July 11th the southern half of the country was in our hands, and General Dentz, commander of the Vichy forces, asked for an armistice.

The maintenance system was similar to that adopted in the Western Desert and Greece. Field supply depots were stocked with all commodities as far forward as was safe from the operational point of view.

The narrow gauge railway from Haifa via Semakh to Damascus and farther north had a limited capacity. Its use beyond Damascus could not be relied on, as it was subject to interruption from demolition by hostile retreating forces.

Up to three days' rations and petrol were held in first line transport. Ammunition dumps seldom exceeded two first line refills. Water was limited to one gallon a head a day, and was, on the eastern flank, obtained from local wells.

Habforce remained based on H4 until some days after the fall of Palmyra, when maintenance was switched to Damascus. Convoys from H4 were sent forward every few days, guarded by the Arab Legion and by a few RAF armoured cars. A certain Fawzi Ackli who, with his armed guerillas had been responsible for a considerable force being tied up on line of communication protection ever since the advance on Habbaniya aerodrome in May, continued his operations, in consequence of which RASC convoys had several casualties in men and vehicles in Syria as they had already had when operating with Habforce.

The officer commanding 51 Company, whilst on personal reconnaissance in the vicinity of T2, a pumping station on the pipeline from Kirkuk to Tripoli, was captured. He got as far as Salonika, but on the surrender of General Dentz, was returned to Syria, having in the meantime travelled through southern Europe for embarkation at Marseilles (see page 648).

On another occasion a convoy of 552 Company returning from the outskirts of Palmyra, was attacked by a sortie of guerilla armoured cars from the pumping station at T3. About 12 drivers were taken prisoner, and some vehicles were captured, while others were destroyed. Subsequently, the bodies of four drivers were found, but the remainder were handed over to the French and returned after the armistice.

The mechanical condition of the requisitioned vehicles of 50 and 97 Companies was poor. The tyres were inferior and this fact, added to the inferior roads, reduced availability considerably. Operating the troop carrying vehicles allotted to the Free French under command of the 5th Indian Infantry Brigade presented a problem as they were buses normally employed on roads and our Allies quite justifiably took them into the most forward positions. At the conclusion of the campaign, the unit received a well-earned appreciation from the French, who had been well aware of the difficulties.

The great activity of the Vichy aircraft gave much practice to our anti-aircraft gunners, who achieved some success, as was proved by the award of Military Medals to L/Cpl A. S. Wragby and Dvr A. Barratt.

The insistence of the Free French here, as later at Bir Hakeim in the Western Desert, on taking the Hadfield-Spears Hospital into battle, introduced a 'Beau Geste' flavour into the affair, as many of the cars and ambulances of this unit were driven by women, some of them British. The vehicles were RASC maintained.

Rations throughout the campaign were mainly tinned. Variety was provided where possible by the issue of fresh vegetables and oranges. When these were available, supplies depended on whether there was any spare transport to collect them. The Free French were issued with red wine in large barrels, which was obtained from the French fleet in Alexandria. Forage was issued to the Trans-Jordan Frontier Force. Petrol was supplied in 'flimsies', and stocks in FSDs needed careful and frequent checking, because of the high percentage of leakage. Workshop platoons were seldom up to establishment in technical vehicles. Sections worked independently, usually being located at delivery and loading terminals. Communications were difficult. There were few wireless vehicles, and numbers did not permit of an issue to the RASC who had, therefore, to use the Q net.

On the eastern flank there were no roads, and all traffic was over the desert, which proved, on the whole, not difficult. As distances were not great, navigation did not present a problem. CRASC Habforce, from the beginning of the operations in Iraq in May, 1941, until the conclusion of the Syrian campaign, always worked with a forward and rear headquarters. The CRASC himself was usually located with AA & QMG at divisional headquarters, and his rear headquarters controlled loading and despatching of convoys between roadhead and FSDs. FSDs for Habforce were located at H3, Juffa and Qtannia, in that order.

Persia and Iraq, 1942—Aid to Russia

Up to September, 1942, Persia and Iraq had formed part of the wide flung responsibilities of GHQ Middle East in Cairo. The Persia and Iraq Command (PAIC) came into existence in September, 1942. The territory having been the scene of pro-Axis rebellions, which had been successfully quelled, was now garrisoned by a force mainly consisting of Indian Army units. For a period of six months it looked as if that zone might be destined to play a vital role in the war. The tide of war then turned and the command, which continued to exist as such until the end of the war for other purposes, ceased to be a potential theatre of active operations.

The importance of the area to the Allies was twofold: it contained important oilfields, including the huge refineries at Abadan, near Basra, on which the RAF relied for much of its aviation spirit; and it was one of the few routes through which supplies could reach South Russia from the outside world.

During the summer of 1942, the German advances in South Russia were meeting with alarming success, and had almost reached the Caucasus Mountains, which separate Russia from Persia. The great fortress of Stalingrad, on the north side of the Caucasus, was heavily besieged, and there were no very solid grounds for expecting that it would be able to withstand the hammer blows which were being rained upon it. The fall of Stalingrad would leave the road to Persia, the oilfields, and to India wide open; it would also create a dangerous exposed flank for the Middle East.

The role allotted to the Persia and Iraq Command was to prepare to prevent the German forces from sweeping into Persia and Iraq if the Russians failed to hold them, and to develop and maintain a line of communication from the Persian Gulf to Russia along which supplies and material could be sent to the Russians. This latter role was to be carried out with the aid of the United States Persian Gulf Service Command which was established some months later. The former role, that of preventing a victorious German army from invading Persia and Iraq and controlling the country so that the

United States Service Command (which had no combat troops at all) could operate, was left entirely to the British and Indian forces.

The Indian Army Force HQ, which had been established in Bagdad, was reorganized into HQ Tenth Army, and moved up to Persia, to be prepared to fight the battles that might lie ahead. General Sir H. Maitland Wilson, who had been appointed C-in-C PAIC, set about establishing a new GHQ in Bagdad. The new staff immediately settled down to planning. The comparatively narrow neck of land between the Black Sea and the Caspian, about 300 miles across and just south of the Caucasus, was selected as the line to be held, and plans were based on 11 divisions being available. Planning was necessarily on a somewhat broad pattern, for no one could answer such questions as where the divisions were coming from, whether they would be British or Indian, armoured or infantry, what weapons they would have, and many other facts necessary for detailed planning. One thing, however, was quite clear—that to maintain a force of 11 divisions in any kind of action 300 miles in front of a railhead, which itself was the end of a 600-mile single-track railway from the base, a great deal of development in the base and line of communication areas would have to be put in hand without a moment's delay.

When the Tenth Army moved up to Persia and began to expand into an operational headquarters, it took with it most of the maintenance units, which were soon replaced by British Army units; it was thus that many RASC units found themselves in Iraq or Persia during the autumn of 1942. Supply, petroleum and transport units of all sorts, mostly organized on new war establishments evolved as a result of experience gained in the Western Desert, began to pour in.

One of the divisions which came under command of Paiforce was the 5th British Division. Its entry into the theatre was the culmination of a long journey. It had been moved by road from Ranchi in Johore down to Bombay and thence up the Persian Gulf to Basra arriving there at the peak of hot season. From Basra it moved overland to Bagdad and thence by means of convoys to Qum, just south of Teheran. Its exit from the theatre was equally difficult since it moved in winter and by road from Qum to Bagdad and thence across Trans-Jordan to Damascus in Syria.

The RIASC was still organized largely as the RASC was before the war; each transport unit was tailor-made for the role it was designed to fill, and the broader organization of standard platoons had not got beyond the GT companies. In one respect the RIASC was in advance of the RASC; it had already lost its first line repair units, and each RIASC unit had attached to it a detachment of the

Indian Army Ordnance Corps of inadequate strength. There were similar discrepancies in the organization of supply and petroleum units; what was a DID in the British army was a DIS in the Indian; DISs were all detachments of a parent unit called a supply company, which was the central accounting and administration unit of eight or ten DISs strung out from one end of the country to the other, each probably in the area of a different local commander. It was decided that too many complications arose from having these different organizations side by side in the same formations, and that the RIASC in Paiforce must be reorganized on British war establishments. It was not without a struggle that this was achieved, for Army Headquarters in India viewed these innovations with considerable misgivings.

The port of entry into the command was Basra, a well equipped port which had been developed as a military base for the Mesopotamian campaign 25 years before. Basra is the base for two lines of communication, the one running through Iraq with a metre-gauge railway system, and the other through Persia with a standard gauge. The nature of the country is such that after these two lines diverge at Basra, there is no lateral communication between them till the Bagdad-Teheran road is reached 300 miles farther north. The base was split in two by the broad Shatt-el-Arab River, and it was necessary to divide the installations. What should be held on the Iraq side and what on the Persian side of the base became an absorbing and never ending calculation. As the base grew, installations were scattered over an ever widening area of desert, many of the RASC units being at Zubier, a desolate spot about 20 miles from Basra. Zubier has already had a mention in commissariat history, for it was there in 1914 that a mule transport company of the Indian ST Corps (afterwards the RIASC) arriving on the battlefield with a load of forage at the crucial moment, was mistaken by the Turks for a fresh cavalry regiment which induced their immediate surrender. It was here, in 1942, that an accidental fire in the petrol depot provided, for many, their first demonstration of the advances that had been made in fire-fighting technique.

A cold storage installation, petrol tin making plants, and assembly plants for vehicles were among the many developments at the Base during this period. Work was also begun on an advanced base area in the neighbourhood of Bagdad, which included among its units a combined RASC/RIASC Training and Reinforcement Depot at Mussayib, to which newly arrived units were sent to complete their equipping and acclimatize themselves, and where new locally raised units took shape.

The planning of a military campaign is necessarily done in secret, and only a limited number of people take an active part in it.

The units themselves are usually quite unaware of what is being planned for them, and they judge the value of their contribution to the war effort by what happens around them. Yet in PAIC—a command in which not a single shot was fired at the enemy—many officers and men of the RASC and RIASC took part in an operation whose direct connection with the war was obvious to the least observant. This was the 'aid to Russia' operation, which continued during the whole of the active life of PAIC.

When the command was formed in September, 1942, a considerable tonnage of supplies of all kinds was being transported to Russia both over the Trans-Iranian railway, which was being operated by the British, and by the United Kingdom Commercial Corporation, which had chartered a large number of Persian civilian lorries and had added to these many Lend-Lease vehicles which had been assembled at the UKCC plant at Bushire and were driven by Persians. Most of these lorries operated from Andimesk, at the foot of the mountain barrier, to the Russian railhead at Tabriz and to Pahlevi on the Caspian Sea.

In November, 1942, the Russians fighting in the Caucasus had urgent need of ammunition, and 203 and 204 GPT Companies, RIASC, were allotted specially for this task. As an increased lift of ammunition and other warlike stores was required, HQ 16 L of C Transport Column was formed in December. Two further companies were provided almost immediately, and early in 1943 the strength of the column was built up to eight companies.

In the spring of 1943 the United States Service Command began to operate at strength on the route from Andimesk to Kasvin. It was therefore decided to leave the main Persian line of communication route to the Americans and to concentrate PAIC resources on the Iraq line of communication. Supplies and materials were transported by river and railway to Khaniqin on the Persian border and thence by road through Persia to Tabriz.

This route was 700 miles in length and included four great mountain passes, the highest being 7,700 feet. Temperatures varied from 120 degrees or more in summer to minus 10 degrees or less in winter. Every kind of weather was met—dust-storms, rains, floods, snow, ice and blizzard—and it was not unknown for a convoy to start out in khaki drill and to finish up in battledress, sheepskin coats and gum boots.

The vehicles of 16 Transport Column were operated in platoon convoys, and the normal turn-round was 17 days, including loading and unloading, maintenance, repairs and time off. The platoons of one company, 51 (Mysore) GPT Company, which joined the column soon after it was formed, each completed 15 round trips (20,000 miles) before being withdrawn for rest.

These 'aid to Russia' convoys provided a wonderful training ground for junior officers and NCOs, who afterwards went to more active theatres. Staging, medical, repair and recovery facilities were in time provided throughout the route, but the job of getting the convoy through complete and to time, in spite of all the hazards, always remained with the platoon officer.

The method of convoy operation used by the column was that laid down in the British Army, with slight modifications to suit local conditions. At first these convoys came in for some criticism by the Americans and the Russians on the grounds that they were too slow. The Americans were using what became known as the 'red ball route' system, with each vehicle proceeding independently, and the Russians moved their vehicles in large numbers and at high speed without much regard to spacing. It is interesting to note that in quite a short time the British way had proved itself much more economical by preventing avoidable accidents and unnecessary wear to engines, transmissions and tyres, and in the end both our Allies were operating in accordance with our well-tried methods.

The refuelling of our convoys, which at the beginning was effected by means of pumps and non-returnable tins at the highly efficient stations of the Anglo-Iranian Oil Company, was later developed to something of a fine art by well laid out petrol points where 100 or more vehicles could be refuelled simultaneously.

In spite of our best efforts to supply our Allies, who were engaged so heavily with the common enemy, our relations with the Russians remained formal. It was only with difficulty that permission was obtained for our officers to visit their railhead at Tabriz, at which our convoys were delivering hundreds of tons a day. Minor irritations were frequently caused by the high-handed action of junior, and sometimes not so junior, Russian officers and officials, but it was soon apparent that the problem could be solved by an equally high-handed threat of immediate action at the highest level.

Altogether, the British and American 'aid to Russia' organizations, both military and civil, by road, rail, water and air delivered some five million tons to Russia—aircraft, tanks, guns, lorries, ammunition, food, petrol, clothing and raw materials of all kinds.

Another task of great importance which fell to PAIC was mobilizing and training a corps of Polish troops. These Poles had been prisoners in Russia, but from the Russian point of view their status had changed when Russia was attacked by Germany and thus became one of the Allies. They were released from Russia, and brought *via* Persia to Iraq; there they were formed up into units of British war establishments, and were finally moulded into the Polish Corps which, under General Anders, fought with such distinction in Italy and elsewhere. A British military mission, on which the RASC was strongly represented, supervised the formation and training of the Polish Corps. Three complete divisional columns, plus a number of supporting units including GT companies with women, were raised and trained under the guidance of the RASC members of the military mission. It was not long before these Polish ASC units were in operation, and they rapidly became absorbed into the general administrative organization of the command, so much so that the customary expression 'RASC/RIASC units' had to be expanded to 'RASC/RIASC/PASC'.

In addition to attending to its own affairs, PAIC found itself involved in the purchase and despatch to Syria and Palestine of large numbers of cattle on hoof. These were assembled at Mosul, from where they were taken by rail, through part of Turkey, to Aleppo, Beirut and Haifa. This involved quite a considerable organization of a type for which the RIASC was well equipped, and in which they had much experience. Units such as 'cattle conducting sections' and 'cattle collecting centres', manned by experts in this kind of traffic, were gradually produced.

The resounding Russian victory at Stalingrad in February, 1943, removed any serious threat to Persia and Iraq; but the territory continued to be one of the main lines of communication to Russia till the westward advance of the Russian armies opened up other routes. The British, Indian and Polish forces were urgently required elsewhere, and 1944 saw the run down of Paiforce, which gradually handed over its responsibilities for 'aid to Russia' to the United States Persian Gulf Command.

THE DODECANESE

Refer to Map at p. 162

Plans to deny the use of the naval and air bases in the Italian islands of the Dodecanese had long attracted the attention of the planning staff in the Middle East.

When the collapse of Italy appeared to be imminent in August, 1943, the project was revived, and a division and shipping were collected for the capture of Rhodes; but the plan had to be abandoned at the last moment when both troops and ships were needed elsewhere. It was only when the Italian armistice was announced in September that it was decided to make an attempt to stiffen the resistance of the Italian garrisons in the Dodecanese to their late allies, the Germans, by sending British troops to the islands of Castelrosso, Cos, Leros and Samos.

The operation was effected by an infantry brigade, and the

initial RASC contribution was small, consisting of one DID, some stocks of food and petrol, and later some assistance by water transport. Land transport was to be obtained locally from the Italian garrisons and from civil sources.

Towards the end a somewhat ambitious higher headquarters was formed in which it was intended to include the Italians. On this the Corps was represented by an ADST, but he had hardly time to begin functioning before the campaign was ended.

The plan for landing in Rhodes could not be carried out as the Italian commander was unwilling to co-operate and oppose the German garrison in the island.

In the event the limited operations were unsuccessful. Troops were disembarked as planned, but support from the Italians was negligible. The Germans attacked in superior numbers and overran Cos and Leros in succession. By that time there were insufficient troops left to put up any resistance at Samos, and those who had escaped from the other two islands were evacuated to Egypt, mainly through Turkey.

The original maintenance plan was that Cos, Leros and Castelrosso (which was used extensively as a distribution centre for the approach to the other islands) should be maintained by store ships from Middle East ports and Cyprus. Samos was to be provided for by transhipments by caique or LCT from Cos and Leros or from Kusadasi, in Turkey. Arrangements were also made to meet urgent demands by air. The plan worked fairly well from the first landings in the middle of September up to the fall of Cos on October 3rd, but after that it was impossible to get store ships through, and reliance had to be placed on various methods which included despatches by caique from Castelrosso and from Kusadasi, by submarine from Beirut and Haifa, by destroyer from Alexandria, and by air. It was often a question of hit or miss, and it became increasingly difficult to find local civilian caique crews to continue to face the risky nature of their task.

The sole RASC DID had to be split between Leros and Samos until an Indian DID arrived in Leros. The British DID was then concentrated in Samos. No one went hungry, as most warships which arrived brought some food, and although caique loads were often pilfered, it was always possible to issue a full ration and to supplement the stocks which came in by local fresh produce. There was enough petrol to keep going the limited amount of transport, as supply had been organized through Turkey to Samos and thence onwards to Leros. A floating petrol reserve was held in caiques at Castelrosso. Up to the end of October the organization of the fleet of small vessels employed was somewhat haphazard. To replace local fishermen, the RASC crews were raised by calling for volunteers from units in the Middle East, and they eventually manned, among other vessels, six caiques of 782 Motor Boat Company, which was also running some other small craft for the same purpose. Assisted by Greek civilians, who were well acquainted with the local waters, these vessels had many adventures. Their operations showed that there was a definite place for a military organization to perform tasks which were impossible by other normal means, and led to the formation of a further two companies which did useful work when the islands were re-occupied towards the end of the war.

The few RASC men on land also had their share of adventure. The OC RASC and a part of the DID on Leros managed to escape and reached Turkey, where, after a short internment, they were released and returned to Egypt. Part of the DID at Samos, which was evacuated with the headquarters of the force, were brought off from the blazing port of Vathi and, running the gauntlet past Leros, arrived in Turkish waters at dawn. Their subsequent movements through the occupied islands were followed by many narrow squeaks, but they eventually landed in Cyprus a week after leaving Samos.

Small and unsuccessful operations of this nature put a disproportionate strain on those responsible for their maintenance, in particular the Royal Navy. It was only because of the devotion of the Senior Service that the RASC was able to accomplish its limited task.

ARABIA: THE LOCUST WAR

'All we want is 50 lorries—here.' So spoke the charming and scholarly member of the Middle East Supply Centre, and 'here' was in the middle of Arabia!

So great was the danger to the economy of the Middle East likely to arise from the locust threat, and so heavy would be the resultant demand on shipping for the importation of grain to replace that devoured by these insects, that it was considered worth while to divert military effort to their destruction, although the time was the winter 1943/44 and transport was badly needed in Italy. On the Middle East Supply Centre fell the responsibility for planning and organization. The MESC planner, with his civilian outlook, probably genuinely thought that the 50 lorries which he at first demanded to distribute poison for the destruction of the insects at the hopper stage (before they take flight), represented the limit of his demands on military resources. How they were to be made available in the Arabian desert, driven, maintained, provided with poison, petrol and food, had just not occurred to him. Eventually 300 vehicles, some 400 British other ranks and 360 Palestinian other ranks, mainly RASC, were involved in this operation which, unwarlike though it was, would, had it been conducted in peacetime, have been in the headlines of the world's press.

The force employed in Arabia consisted of two parties. One, 38 Company RASC (GT) moved in from the east and the other, the larger, consisting of 446 GT Company (Palestinian Arabs), two platoons from 175 (Tank Transporter) Company equipped with 10-tonners, and signal and medical details moved in through Aqaba.

The force included men with desert experience, which was fortunate, as the Arab drivers had had no experience in desert driving and the conditions which they were to meet were in some cases more exacting than those to be found in the Western Desert and in the campaigns in Iraq, Syria and the Italian colonies. The route from Aqaba to Yenbo on the Red Sea where a base was to be established, was unknown to the column, but guides were provided by King Ibn Saud. Unfortunately the guides started with little knowledge of the capabilities of MT vehicles and presented the column with some pretty obstacles to negotiate in the way of soft going, sand dunes, and hill country. Oddly enough, at one point assistance was afforded by the formation of the derelict Hedjaz railway built by the Germans for the Turks before the 1914–18 War, which featured so largely in Lawrence's campaigns. One of Ibn Saud's guides claimed to have been with Lawrence. That the column eventually got through to Yenbo was most creditable to all concerned and particularly to its commander.

Of him a medical officer wrote 'Never have I served under such a man. When a vehicle is bogged in the sand, his shoulder is the first behind it.' There was so much soft going that he must certainly have had a sore shoulder before reaching his destination. But reach the end of their journey both columns did and accomplished great destruction amongst the hoppers, finally concentrating in the triangle Hail-Hanakiya-Rumahiya. The whole operation had taken nearly six months, but its success justified the diversion of transport and men.

CHAPTER VI

THE WESTERN MEDITERRANEAN

MALTA, G.C.

Peacetime Conditions

THE epic of Malta, G.C., lends a special interest to the part played by the RASC in that island during the long period of the siege before it was finally relieved by the advance of the Eighth and First Armies in North Africa. Before the war, Malta was regarded as an attractive station. Its climate, reasonable cost of living, nearness to home, and facilities for recreation made those stationed there count themselves fortunate. Military life in the garrison was not too strenuous. There were exercises for seaborne and air defence of the little colony, but there was little opportunity for training on a large scale because of lack of space.

The pre-war organization of the RASC in the island was not unlike that in Gibraltar. A small transport company of about 40 vehicles and a few War Department vessels for military harbour duties and target towing were adequate for meeting the needs of the garrison of some 3,000 troops. Food was provided through a small supply depot and bakery located at Sa Maison, Valetta, and a cold storage depot which was at Marsa. Petrol was obtained by contract, and no special military reserves had to be held.

It may perhaps seem to be unnecessary to remind the reader of the conditions which existed in the island during the two years of siege. Situated only 60 miles from Sicily, the inhabitants and the garrison had to withstand a constant assault from the air day after day and the attacks reached their peak in the spring of 1942. Many were short of food and petrol and at times of water and means of lighting, and little could be done to relieve their plight as each successive attempt to run a convoy from either east or west met with heavier attacks and casualties in both ships of the Royal and Merchant Navies and their ships' complements. Throughout the period there was also the continued threat of an enemy assault by sea and the possibility of full scale airborne landings. In the background was the knowledge that the island was the only stepping stone in the Mediterranean for the flow of reinforcing aircraft for the Middle East and the only harbouring place for our submarines over the 2,000 miles which separated Gibraltar from Alexandria in Egypt.

War Plans

Pre-war planning took into account that the island might have to depend on its own resources, but the period before which it could be relieved if it were invested was determined as being six months, and all plans for laying in stocks of essential war material were based on that premise. War planning had to be a joint service and civil affair as the civil population of about 250,000 were largely dependent on imports for their existence.

When plans were being considered before the war, each service made its claims for the provision of the stores and accommodation which would be needed for the maintenance of the garrison, but as will be seen later in this account not all these claims could be fulfilled and the unexpected fall of France and entry of Italy into the war found many preparations far from being complete. In some instances final approval for projects was not obtained until the siege was nearly over, but nevertheless the RASC carried on and were able to fulfil their role successfully.

The principal RASC defence commitment was to build up sufficient food for six months for the garrison, which was to be reinforced when war came, but no one could have foreseen that the estimated strength of about 6,000 would eventually reach a peak figure of nearly 40,000, or that the DDST, Colonel H. P. Raymond, who relieved Colonel H. A. C. Gardiner two days before the island was first invested, would be placed in the contradictory position of trying to supply an ever increasing garrison with continually diminishing stocks, as convoys became less frequent, as sinkings increased and losses through enemy action and pilferage became greater.

Mobilizing the Transport

Mobilization arrangements differed from those at home inasmuch as no additional men (reservists) units or vehicles were to be sent from England. A request, made a year before the war, for an additional company was refused on the grounds that vehicles and civilian drivers could be obtained locally. The refusal was no doubt due to the limited resources which would be available in the United Kingdom and to the knowledge that distances in Malta were short and no well organized mobile transport units would be needed. Expansion was, therefore, dependent on a scheme whereby about 1,000 civilian vehicles were assigned by the RASC, with the help of the civil police, to provide for the extra transport which would be needed by the garrison to bring their first line transport up to a war strength, and to produce the additional vehicles which would be wanted by the RASC Transport Company. It was estimated that about 600 of these vehicles would only be wanted as a temporary measure for conveying units and their equipment to their war stations. In fact only some of the vehicles assigned were requisitioned. There were plenty of civilian cars, lorries and small buses, but a dearth of ambulances had to be made good by converting small vehicles.

The drivers of the vehicles which were required for permanent duty were not enlisted but were enrolled for the duration of the war as members of the Malta Auxiliary Corps.

Although subject to military law these men retained their civilian status and received no military training. They continued to wear plain clothes but for distinguishing purposes were given a cap, an armband and a greatcoat. Proposals to enlist Maltese into the RASC were considered in 1941 but, because of training and accommodation difficulties, were not proceeded with, but in the following year a Malta section of the RASC was formed, known later as the Army Service Corps, Malta Territorial Force. A special tribute must be paid not only to the civilian drivers and men of the MTF but also to those Maltese civilian employees who were permanently employed by the RASC before and during the war. Men in all categories gave loyal service and many of them still remain with the Corps in one capacity or another.

As the siege went on there was no lack of transport, so long as the petrol stocks lasted; the main concern of the DDST was how to keep the vehicles in running order. In some cases the owners of impressed vehicles were made responsible for keeping their vehicles on the road, but in others maintenance and repairs had to be conducted by the RASC Company Workshops which, like all other units, had to do their work under continuous bombardment from the air.

Authority had been given in February, 1939, for preparing a stock of six months' spares for military vehicles, but there was no special plan for providing reserves for the large number of civilian vehicles which would have to be taken over. No protected storage could be provided for the main stock of army spares which had to be dispersed over five garages. Two of these garages were destroyed by enemy bombing, but the net loss of stocks only amounted to about one twentieth of the holding. In August, 1941, instructions were received that the reserves of spares were to be built up to last 300 days, but by that time shipping was scarce and, in response to a demand placed on the Middle East for 640 items, two small packages only were received; the rest had been shut out to make room for more vital stores. A few priority goods, however, were brought in by submarine.

As spare parts became fewer the greatest ingenuity was displayed in endeavouring to keep both military and civilian vehicles on the road. It was with pride that the RASC company workshops fitted a Morris truck with a Ford back axle and then, when the gear box gave out, replaced that assembly by adapting one taken from an old Austin. Although many of the vehicles were on their last legs there were always enough of them, especially when lack of petrol caused an almost total stoppage of all but essential traffic.

For the first three years of the war the single RASC company had to carry the whole of the transport load of the island. In 1941 two transport sections, each of 44 vehicles, had to be formed for field ambulances, and by June, 1942, the vehicle strength of the company, exclusive of these sections, had risen to 280 vehicles. It was only then that an appeal to the War Office for a second MT company was met, and the opportunity was also taken of giving to the existing and new companies the newly adopted RASC platoon organization.

Petrol Supply

A growing problem was how to make the best use of the small amount of petrol that could be spared for the Army. Every pint used mattered, so that every possible means of saving the precious spirit had to be adopted. Strict control was of course exercised over the use of both civil and military transport. A five-day week forbade the use of civil transport on Saturdays and Sundays, and no public vehicle was allowed on the road on those days without a special permit which was sparingly granted. In November, 1942, barely 11 days' petrol remained in the island, and the Army's allotment was cut to 6,000 gallons a week.

In 1941 it was decided to make use of the large number of mule carts in the island, and at one time no fewer than 500 of them were in use—at a cost of £5 a week each. They carried only a small load, but usually got there—in their own time. Had the siege continued it might have become a question of whether to use the mules as transport or as food.

Petrol was one of the commodities which were accepted as a common requirement, and was demanded centrally by a co-ordinating committee set up by the Malta Government; looking back, it now seems regrettable that planning for provision and storage could not have been centralized before the war. In January, 1939, the Army was given authority to hold a reserve of six months' supplies. Up to that time there was no military petroleum installation in the island, and reserves were ensured by the petroleum contractors guaranteeing that their normal stocks were adequate to meet certain additional requirements if the occasion arose. The main civil installation was owned by the Shell Company, at Kallafrana, and the army needs were met by the refilling of kerbside tanks or delivery in cans. The best that could be done to follow the War Office instructions was to draw up 30,000 gallons, the estimated requirement for six months, in cans and to disperse the stock over various points in the island. Authority for the construction of 300 tons of bulk storage in protected accommodation was given in March, 1939, and six tanks holding about 240 tons between them were landed in April, 1940. Sites were selected for their installation at Naxar and Falka, and the tanks were set up and ready for filling by April, 1941, but they were only partly below ground level although protected by blast walls. A small military filling plant was also provided from home and was installed at St. Patrick's, a few miles away from the new bulk tanks. In the meantime, the Navy were asked to construct 22 500-gallon tanks, which were installed in disused quarries at Pembroke, each tank being enclosed separately by splinter walls.

Lack of Petrol

The general lack of petrol began to be felt in early 1941, and continued to be acute, so that the Army's holding began to fall until it was eventually reduced to 'a last ditch' reserve. There was also a lack of other sorts of liquid and solid fuels which were vital for the operation of plant for anti-aircraft defences and essential services. The island's water supply was entirely dependent on pumping apparatus, and when the power station failed, candles had to be used for lighting. Little or no fuel wood was available locally, and efforts to burn sump oil which had been drained from the sump pits of vehicles were stultified by the reduced number of MT vehicles on the roads. Towards the end of the siege the old RASC fire engine had to be diverted from its proper use and, after the wheels had been removed, it was taken into use at a pumping station. Whether the heart of the War Office was touched by this incident is not recorded, but a demand for its replacement brought two new Merryweather engines in its place.

Food Supplies

Undoubtedly the greatest achievement of the RASC was the continued maintenance of a daily ration of food even though for some time during the siege it had to be reduced to what is known in military language as a siege scale.

As comparatively little food was grown in the island, food supply was a problem common to civilians and servicemen. Following the usual practice, the Army was responsible for supplying the RAF and the Navy maintained their own victualling organization. The need for co-ordinating requirements in essential materials and foodstuffs was accepted by the civil government and the services early in 1940, and a committee for the co-ordination of supplies was set up under the chairmanship of the Lieutenant Governor in August of that year. The main aims of the committee were to ensure that there should be a common supplies policy so that the fortress's reserves were evenly maintained and the effect of losses through sinkings could be evenly spread. It was fully recognized how vital it was to reduce the sea freight required, and arrangements were made to co-ordinate demands for essentials such as flour and sugar and for fuels such as petrol and coal. The committee, referred to as COSUP, put forward bulk demands on home on behalf of the services and civil population, each service keeping its own department acquainted with the nature of the demands it had made on COSUP and with the extent of its own stocks.

A co-ordinating committee at home also did their best to make certain that the despatches made in response to the island's demands were in the most economical space saving form and of the greatest food value for the space they occupied. But even these measures could not solve the problem of safeguarding convoys through the Mediterranean or prevent the heavy losses which were experienced both in merchant ships and his Majesty's ships which were escorting them.

Once the stores were landed safely, fortune seemed to favour the supply service, bearing in mind that no special deep underground storage accommodation had been provided even for the stocks which were to be built up for the original war garrison. A request was made in August, 1939, for the construction of a new supply depot, which was to be above ground, but although the project could not be agreed to, permission was given to put up six large huts, which when built seemed to be singled out for attack by the enemy air forces which demolished all six. In April, 1941, plans for an underground depot, to be located at St. Michael's bastion at Valetta, were prepared. War Office sanction for the project was not received until April, 1942, when work on the pilot tunnels began, but the tunnelling company employed on the work had to be withdrawn to work on the more urgent project of an underground hospital.

In October, 1942, the Navy appeared in the field as a rival claimant for the site and, as it was thought that the tunnels required for the approach to the supply depot would weaken the structure of the adjoining naval project, the plan was dropped. Perhaps it was a question of 'an ill wind', as the Malta rock tunnels are damp, and the storage of anything but tinned supplies might well have been the cause of even more concern for the harassed supply officer than the method adopted which was the dispersal of reserves in little dumps all over the island to spread the risk of damage from bombing.

Dispersal of Stocks

Just before the war, the garrison's food stock was held at one point only, the permanent supply depot; in 1940 the reserves were divided between three storage places, and in 1941 the stocks were spread out over the island in no fewer than 100 different places. It was not an ideal arrangement, as it was difficult to safeguard the many points from pilferage when food was scarce; but it worked and, although 21 of the dumps were damaged by enemy action, the total losses did not amount to more than about 160 tons of food.

Fortune also seemed to favour the Army's cold storage arrangements. The original peacetime store, which held about 1,000 tons, had been constructed above ground, but happily the actual storage chambers had been made by digging out holes of suitable size in the ground. The installation bore a charmed life until 1942, when a bomb put part of the plant out of action and reduced the capacity of the plant for maintaining the required temperatures by about 300 tons. By this time, however, there was little or no meat to store. The provision of a fully protected underground installation had been considered in 1936, and a site selected, but the subsequent action, or rather deferred action, is indicative of the old principle that if one waits long enough the need may not arise. The store was to hold joint stocks for the Navy and the Army but, when the cost—£32,000—became known, the Admiralty and War Office could not sanction the project. The Inspector, RASC, who visited the island in February, 1939, recommended an immediate review of the project, and approval was given to it in May, but by that time the proposed site at Weid Kebir was considered by the naval authorities to be too far from the Grand Harbour. In August, 1940, it was deemed that an alternative site selected would be too near the adjacent coal yards, and the Navy suggested an alternative site. This in turn was considered by the Army to be too near some ancient sewers which could not be properly sealed off. By this time it was July, 1941, and more urgent projects made it impossible to do anything about the matter for at least two years.

The production of bread was also beset by various problems. Both wheat and flour were imported as not enough was grown in the island. The Navy possessed a little mill installed about 50 years before, the successor of an original stone mill dating from the occupation of Malta by the Navy a century before. There were also several civilian mills but, because of the increasing damage by enemy action, it was thought at one time that recourse would have to be made to the old biblical method of grinding the wheat, by hand, between two stones.

Various expedients had to be adopted to make the available flour supply go round. Fortunately, in one year of the siege there was a glut of potatoes and it was found possible to make a passable loaf out of flour consisting of three quarters wheat and one quarter potato. In the following year the potato crop was entirely ruined by bad weather. Even biscuits had then to be carefully rationed. When one of the ships which contained a cargo of flour was sunk it was found that even after three weeks at the bottom of the sea, the salved stock could be used. The outer caking caused by its immersion had provided a protective layer for the inner contents of the sacks and, after a little 'sorting', good bread was made from the remainder.

So long as flour was available everything possible was done to continue a supply of bread. Some yeast was brought in as a special priority requirement both by submarine and by air, but for some time baking had to be done with potato balm, and the skill of the bakers was well tried. The question of providing an underground bakery does not seem to have arisen and in view of the conditions it was a creditable performance that the army bakers produced some nine million lb of bread in the year when the siege was at its height. The main bakery was not unscathed; in 1942 it received a direct hit. The ovens, which were protected by an intervening wall, were untouched, but the damage by blast was considerable and for some time afterwards the bakers had to work without a roof.

Throughout the siege there was usually some fresh local produce available after meeting the needs of the civil population, but the supply was irregular and the price was high. At the height of the siege the Government Gazette showed the controlled price of potatoes to be £90 a ton, and eggs, of which there was a small supply for hospitals, were 3s. 6d. each. Every means of conserving and utilizing the produce available was adopted, and at one period the civil loaf of bread was being made of any type of corn that could be grown, the yeast being replaced by potato balm.

Rations reduced

From 1940 onwards the ration scale had to be constantly adjusted according to the stocks available, but matters became really critical in early 1942. Between January and April it was only possible to make two issues of frozen meat, and the ration of tinned meat was drastically reduced. In May, 1942, the whole ration scale had to be cut, and life was made no easier by the heavy and continuous air raids which were being made on the island and seemed to be the forerunner of a full scale combined offensive by air and sea. It had to be decided whether the defenders could be expected to hold out without further relief, and consequently whether one more attempt should be made to get a convoy through. It was a most serious decision to make, as even if any ships could be got safely through, and the hours of darkness were getting less as the summer drew near, there was every chance of their being sunk in harbour as had happened in March, when one of the two ships was sunk before they could be offloaded and only about a quarter of the cargo could be salved. Relief was needed not only by the garrison, but also by the large civil population whose ration was at this time so meagre that there was a danger of famine, their main means of sustenance being one meal a day provided through communal kitchens.

It was decided that another convoy must be sent, but it was to be the 'last'. It is now a matter of history that only five of the 14 merchant ships survived the heavy attacks made on the convoy, and the naval escorting vessels suffered grievous losses. Three of the five ships made harbour on August 13th, another arrived the next day, and the remaining vessel, the tanker *Ohio* limped in under tow on the 15th. These ships may have been few in number, but their arrival saved the day, as it was again possible to refuel submarines and to eke out the remaining stocks of food until relief finally came in December.

The most meagre ration issued during the siege was in the fortnight before these ships arrived, after which it was possible to make small token increases in such items as bread, bacon, milk, and cigarettes. Even then all troubles were not over, as in October and November it was again necessary to make other reductions in the ration scale which persisted until the advance of the Eighth Army to Benghazi made it possible to run a convoy from the east, which reached Malta on December 7th, 1942.

Water Transport

No account of the RASC in Malta would be complete without some mention of the water transport detachment even though a reference is made to its deeds in the chapter on water transport. There were only a few vessels, and there were many long periods when they could not be used for their legitimate tasks, but they earned their keep in other ways by helping in the laying of underwater obstacles, by air-sea rescue, and by undertaking various hazardous tasks. When their crews were immobilized they did yeoman service in helping to unload army cargoes from submarines and in giving a general hand in anything they were put to. When the final enemy effort began on March 20th, the opening of a period in which 7,000 tons of bombs were dropped on the island, many of the vessels were damaged. The largest, the *Lord Plumer*, came off with minor damage to rigging, the *Rundle* had her engine room roof stove in, the *Pike*, awaiting repair in the dockyard, was crushed by heavy stones from the roof of a boat house, the *Trout* was sunk by part of the bridge of a neighbouring ship being blown on to her, and an attack on the *Clive* by Messerschmidts only resulted in broken windows. The remaining ship, the *Snipe*, escaped damage, but after repairs most of the vessels were soon made shipshape and were ready for work again.

End of the Siege

When the island was relieved at the end of 1942, there was still much to be done. The first need was to give some change to the many of those who had served for six and even seven years continuously in the garrison and to give some respite to those who had borne the brunt of the siege. The RASC were kept busily at work in transporting the stocks of essentials which began to arrive in quantity and in supplying the everyday needs which the garrison had to forego during the siege. There was no time to be lost so that Malta, G.C., could play its next part as one of the launching places for the landings in Sicily and for the return of the British Army to the offensive in Europe.

GIBRALTAR

The Second World War was to add once again to the rich fund of historical military associations of Gibraltar. Living in the shadow of investment, the peninsula remained the one bastion on the route to beleaguered Malta and to Africa and the Middle East. Its garrison had not only to face an almost continuous threat of siege, but also had to minister in one way and another to the many thousands of men, aircraft and ships which made use of the Rock.

Although the peninsula seemed impregnable, plans for defence had to be made to meet a possible three-sided attack. Weapons and defensive sites needed modernization. Both serviceman and civilian were living tightly compressed in the little town at the north end of the Rock, and the houses were so situated that they could all be swept by enemy fire from both land and sea. The Naval Dockyard, public utilities and storehouses were equally vulnerable, and the military and civilian populations were entirely dependent on imports for their daily needs. Much of the labour employed in the dockyard had to be drawn from Spanish workers who daily crossed the border from Spain and returned each evening at nightfall.

There was no airfield, and the only means of providing one was to utilize the small strip of land contiguous to the border and to extend it by building an extension into the sea. Water supply was solely dependent on catchments, the rainfall being collected into huge cisterns dug out of the heart of the Rock.

Given labour and equipment, it was not difficult technically to provide protected accommodation by tunnelling at suitable points in the Rock, but the work would take time—millions of cubic feet of rock would have to be blasted and removed before all needs were met. There were many projects to be fulfilled which were to concern the small RASC establishment, which at the outbreak of war consisted of a motor transport company of 34 vehicles, a supply depot, and a bakery located in the heart of the town. A cold storage depot was situated in a gully which afforded protection from everything but a direct hit and, being the only one of any size, it also held the main requirements of the civil population. There were four WD vessels for harbour work and the usual transport and barrack offices and stores. The whole was commanded by an OC RASC.

Pre-war plans included the reinforcement of the garrison. At the time of Italy's entry into the war, the strength had grown from 3,000 to 10,000, and in 1943 it was to reach a peak figure of 20,000. Among the main administrative defence problems were the storage of enough food to enable the garrison to withstand a siege of many months, protection of the food from damage by enemy action, and keeping it in good condition. Nothing could be grown on the Rock, and no livestock could be maintained. Apart from a few horses the only animals were the famous apes on which the fortunes of the fortress were supposedly so dependent. In normal times there was a plentiful supply of fresh produce of all kinds from Spain and Africa, but even if the colony were not invested an embargo might be placed on this daily flow. The civil population would be equally affected, although their needs and food habits were perhaps simpler than those of the garrison.

Stocks of all types of tinned and preserved foods were gradually amassed, special care being taken to select those which, thanks to the advance in food science, had good anti-scorbutic properties. Unfortunately, protected storage room could not be provided at the rate at which the stocks were being built up.

This nearly led to a minor disaster. A sudden scare that the fortress might be besieged, one of several during the war, led to a hasty decision to remove the more important stocks to a place of safety, and to use one of the main water cisterns, which had been emptied. When the last case of the precious reserves were safely stowed, the key was turned in the doors of the cavern with a feeling of relief that all was well.

A few weeks later it was reported by a passer-by that curious odours were emanating from the cavern, and when the stores were examined it was found that rust was causing their deterioration. It was obvious that the risk of the stock being destroyed by enemy fire was considerably less than that of leaving it in its temporary storage place, and the whole of the stores again had to be hastily moved.

The huge consignment had to be picked over case by case, sorted and dried out, and the process was watched with some anxiety until the full extent of damage could be ascertained.

The high rate and virulence of rusting could not have been foreseen, but it was evident that special arrangements would have to be made to provide some form of damp-proof and rust-proof containers. The War Office took immediate action by unpacking all stores destined for the fortress and placing them in strong 4-gallon petrol tins which were impervious to damp and rust. However, it was found impossible to dry out the sawdust used for preventing internal damage to tins, while the natural moisture content of other foods such as flour still caused some deterioration. Both difficulties were eventually overcome, but the whole incident showed again that even the seasoned supply officer may always have something to learn.

As events turned out, it was possible throughout the war to maintain a fair supply of fresh produce, although the existence of such large stocks of 'siege' foods meant that the garrison had to take a share of them. A second bakery was opened, and later two bakeries were installed in protected places in the Rock. Bread on the Rock assumed a special importance, for in Spain it was both scarce and dear, and it was thus highly prized by the Spanish worker in Gibraltar. Arrangements were made permitting each worker to purchase a specific ration which he bore back with him, to the delight of his family and the envy of his friends. Eggs, however, were always scarce and the situation was only relieved by the arrival in North Africa of the First Army, who arranged to fly over supplies as a regular service. It was whispered that a form of mutual aid was instituted by small return parcels of sherry, which always seemed to be plentiful in Gibraltar.

The growing strength of the garrison and the variety of material to be moved soon led to increasing demands for transport, and every vehicle which could be made available not only from the Corps but from other arms was kept busy. There was a special demand for small vehicles capable of negotiating the hairpin bends and steep inclines on the roads leading to new positions on the Rock. Strong heads and skill were needed for much of the work—a miscalculation might mean a fatal accident or the loss of a vehicle. The small MT company was gradually reinforced by locally enlisted men, by a loan of infantry drivers and later by two independent platoons from the United Kingdom. Speed of turn-round became the order of the day. Tunnelling for cover for batteries, ammunition, stores, workshops and supplies went on by day and night. It entailed a constant race to remove the spoil blasted out inside the rock, as any delay was looked upon askance by the tunnelling teams, many of whom had spent their lives at similar tasks in various parts of the world. The extension of the air-strip was also a continuous task. Chains of lorries drew up at the north face to load the rock which had been blasted and then made for the airstrip as fast as they could to dump their load, returning at once to repeat the process in a never ending stream. As the strip grew foot by foot so did the competitive spirit of all those engaged on the work, who eagerly awaited the results, published daily, of tonnage moved. The heavy nature of the loads carried and the rough conditions of work led to a good deal of damage to vehicles which kept the workshops of the company fully occupied.

The RASC transport used in these projects was, of course, only complementary to the main task, which was an RE responsibility, but the strong liaison which grew up between the two Corps made the RASC driver feel that as much depended on him as on his more skilled comrade in the Royal Engineers.

There were certain parts of the Rock to which even a single track road could not be successfully driven, but which were vital to defence. This led to the formation of a small pack transport company of about 50 animals. The company did not see any active service during its life in the fortress, but gave a good account of itself later in North Africa and Italy.

The little fleet of RASC vessels also played its part. Extra vessels had to be requisitioned to keep pace with demands for the various duties to be performed. Craft had to be provided for inshore anti-sabotage patrols for watching those parts of the coast that were inaccessible from the land or difficult to keep under observation. Other vessels took a share in air-sea rescue work, and the constant coming and going of convoys led to many requests for ship to shore services. Later in the war, the volume of work grew to such an extent that a water transport company had to be formed (No. 726), reinforcements being sent out from the United Kingdom for the purpose.

The supply of petrol and oils did not present any difficulty at any time, thanks to the arrangements which had been advocated and put into effect before the war.

Although the war receded from the western Mediterranean, RASC duties on the Rock did not diminish, as it still remained the first port of call on British soil on the route to the east.

NORTH AFRICA

Operation 'Torch'

The agreement made in the summer of 1942, between the British and the United States Governments, to invade French North Africa, was one of the most far reaching decisions of the war. If the assault were successful and the immediate objective, the seizure of the enemy's airfields in Tunisia, could be fully exploited, there was a good hope that the enemy could be driven out of Africa, that the Mediterranean sea routes would be freed, and that firm bases could be established for the invasion of Sicily and Italy.

It was a serious decision because French reactions to an incursion into their territories were unpredictable and so much depended on whether the move of our forces could be conducted over many thousands of miles by sea without the enemy learning our intentions.

The outline plan for the operation, which was finally confirmed in September, was that three separate task forces, the western, central and eastern, would land at Casablanca, Oran and Algiers respectively, the eastern force being predominantly British. The British force and the 34th United States Division were to be mounted in Britain, and the western and central forces in America. The specific role of the British force, after landing and capturing Algiers, was to strike at once for Tunis which lay over 500 miles to the east.

The decision to implement operation 'Torch', which was the code name for the plan, was a momentous one for our forces which had been training so assiduously at home for a return to the offensive. Perhaps it was a happy coincidence that the orders to begin planning and training for 'Torch' were received by the nucleus of the future expeditionary force, formerly known as Force 110, while they were engaged in 'Dryshod', the most elaborate amphibious exercise that had been staged up to that time.

Each task force was to be responsible for planning its own share of the operation, their joint efforts being co-ordinated by a new Allied Force Headquarters. General Eisenhower was appointed as Allied Commander, and Major-General H. M. Gale became his chief administrative officer.

The headquarters, which began planning on August 8th at Norfolk House, London, was the first of its kind in that British and American officers worked together. It was not possible to integrate all the service sections because of differences in equipment and organization, but plans were made for exercising unified control of supply over items which were common to both armies, such as petrol. But although there were separate supplies and transport, and quartermaster branches, both services maintained a close liaison throughout the campaign and wherever necessary undertook to give mutual aid.

Two imponderables faced the planners for 'Torch': the probable attitude of the French forces in North Africa, and the speed at which the enemy might be able to reinforce his garrisons in Tunis when news came to him of our landings. Two plans had therefore to be made, one on the assumption that the French would oppose the invasion, and the other on the supposition that little or no resistance would be offered and that the French commanders might even be disposed to co-operate actively against the Axis forces.

But whichever plan turned out to be the correct one the forces to be used for the initial landings had to be trained and equipped for an opposed landing and provided with the special craft required for an amphibious operation.

The amount of shipping and special craft that could be provided was limited, and the number of fighting troops that could be landed for the initial assault had to be carefully balanced against the administrative units which would be needed to maintain the striking force in the first drive on Tunis. To have staked everything on a striking force which could not be adequately maintained would have been to court disaster. This resulted in a high proportion of the available freight being taken up by administrative units, with a consequent diminution of the number of fighting troops that could be employed in the first months of the campaign.

The British force was to land at Algiers only. There were other ports nearer Tunis, notably Bougie, Philippeville, Bone and Bizerta, but they were closer to the enemy's airfields in Sicily, and the Royal Navy had not enough escort ships to guarantee the passage of convoys with safety. The best that could be done was to provide for a floating reserve, to land at Bougie, if all went well at Algiers.

The British task force was named the First Army and placed under the command of Lieut-General Kenneth Anderson. It was to consist of two corps, V and IX Corps, with the 1st, 46th and 78th Infantry Divisions, the 4th (Mixed) Division and the 6th Armoured Division and 25th Tank Brigade. The American element in the force consisted of two combat teams.

The strength of the British force was estimated as 200,000 men and 35,000 vehicles, but several months elapsed before the whole of the force could be landed, the last division, the 4th, arriving four and a half months after the date of the first assault.

For those who are unacquainted with this campaign it is important to bear in mind that in practice the British force which fought the first campaign in North Africa was an army in name only, as for the first weeks of the operations there were only two divisions, the British 78th and American 34th, and a regimental armoured group, and that for some weeks the army was little more than the strength of a weak corps.

Even then the divisions had to be landed short of their own unit transport which was not due to arrive until the second main convoy. Thus the 'army' which made the first thrust to Tunis was in fact only a small striking force and not completely equipped at that.

It was recognized that a little time would have to elapse before the Allied headquarters could assume effective command and administrative control over the three task forces. HQ First Army were to be responsible for the initial build-up of the line of communication, and were to have the assistance of a small increment of officers from AFHQ for the purpose.

Brigadier Hinde, who was appointed DDST of the army, had many new problems to consider in planning the RASC organization required for this expeditionary force, which was the first to leave these shores since 1940. The supply organization had been re-modelled since the days of the BEF. The RASC petroleum organization was also a post-1939 development. Water transport units would be wanted for work along the North African coastline, and provision had to be made for a pack transport organization which could be expanded at short notice by using local animals and locally enrolled muleteers. The system for effecting heavy repairs to RASC vehicles and for providing replacement vehicles and spare parts had been radically altered and had still to be tested in the field.

The ultimate order of battle which was settled included 70 transport units of various kinds in addition to the usual complement of companies which formed part of formations. There were about 30 supply units and about the same number of petroleum units, which included sufficient units for four separate bases, as it was hoped that all three ports east of Algiers—Bone, Bougie and Philippeville—could be used for that purpose as soon as the striking force had cleared Algiers and air superiority in Algeria and Tunisia had been achieved.

Few of the units had seen active service before, but what they may have lacked for that reason they made up for by their keenness and sound training. Many of the officers of the force had been trained by Brigadier Hinde when he was commandant of the RASC Officer Cadet Training Unit. They were first rate material. So were the men, most of whom had been enlisted during the war.

The Plan

The role of the eastern force was to land on the beaches on either side of Algiers whereupon the 11th Brigade (78th Division) was to seize the airfield at Blida, south of Algiers, and cut the main road leading to the south. The 39th Combat Team and some rangers were to make for Maison Blanche airfield, a few miles to the east of Algiers, and then march on the city; while the 168th Combat Team was to attack Algiers from the west. Parties of commandos and rangers had the task of seizing Algiers harbour to prevent sabotage.

The 36th Brigade was to form a floating reserve, in ships which were to lie off during the assault over the beaches. If the landings

Pack Transport at Hove Dump

Ammunition going forward

Ambulance Mules

were strongly opposed the brigade was to be drawn on to assist in the struggle but if not required for that purpose the ships were to sail for Bougie where a force was to be landed to seize the airfield at Djidjelli, 40 miles farther down the coast from Bougie.

As immediate land based fighter cover was vital to the plan, five squadrons of the RAF were to fly from Gibraltar to Maison Blanche a few hours after the assault began, and one squadron of Spitfires was then to fly on to Djidjelli. Such was the confidence of the RAF that when the day came the first fighters took off from the airstrip at Gibraltar before news of the seizure of the airfield was signalled to them.

Once Algiers was in our hands a striking force of the 78th Division, less a brigade, the 17/21st Lancers Armoured Regimental Group ('Bladeforce'), and two battalions of paratroops were to be employed in the dash for Tunis. The chance of capturing Tunis was of course largely dependent on whether the paratroops could reach their objectives and with, it was hoped, the aid of local French anti-aircraft gunners, hold the airfields and deny their use to enemy airborne reinforcements.

The remainder of the force was to follow from home in a series of convoys. After the first four, convoys were to arrive at regular fortnightly intervals, but the number of men and quantity of stores and equipment to be landed meant that the full strength of the force would not be built up for many weeks after the original landings.

The administrative plan for the initial period was largely based on the hope that the striking force could be maintained through the three ports which lay to the east of Algiers, thereby obviating the need for transport for the long carry from Algiers over the main inland road and rail systems, which led over the hills and mountains through Setif and Constantine to Tunis.

There was little reliable information regarding the state of the railway system which linked Algiers and Tunis and the intermediary ports but it was expected that they would be in a poor state of repair and there was known to be an acute scarcity of coal. It was estimated that at least 45 days would elapse before the railway could be taken into effective use, but even so shipping limited the amount of transport which could be landed to a bare minimum officially referred to as assault or light scales.

The RASC contribution to the assault force was detachments of second line transport for the 11th and 36th Brigades, a DID, a small petrol depot, a transport platoon for each of two beach maintenance groups, and six other transport platoons, which included tippers, ambulances and one platoon for Bailey bridging. A DID, petrol depot and one platoon of transport was also included in the floating reserve for the development of the port at Bougie.

The second convoy, which was due to arrive on the fourth day (D plus 4), was to carry a transport detachment for the striking force (for Bladeforce), a troop carrying company, a tank transporter company, four other platoons of various kinds, and five platoons of general transport.

The rest of the second line transport for the 78th and 6th Armoured Divisions and their third line companies was not due until the third convoy, which was scheduled to arrive from D plus 14 to D plus 18.

All troops in the force were to be provided with a 48-hour mess tin ration and thereafter with the new 14-man composite ration until base supply depots could be established and the normal field service ration taken into use. Petroleum was to be provided in packed form, although it was hoped that the existing bulk storage facilities could be developed within a short time to allow of can filling being done on the spot and distribution in bulk where possible.

Before describing the course of the campaign it may assist the reader to know that it can be viewed conveniently in four phases:— the original landing; the advance of the small striking force, which arrived within a few miles of Tunis only to be delayed by the enemy and weather; the winter period, when the army was forced into the defensive; and the final period, when by the combined efforts of the First and Eighth Armies the enemy was finally driven out of Africa.

The Landing

The first slow convoy, carrying vehicles and heavy equipment, left the home ports on the night of October 22nd, the time of its departure almost coinciding with the secret landing, from a submarine near Algiers, of the American general, General Mark Clark, who was to negotiate with pro-Allied French generals and officials to pave the way, it was hoped, for an amicable reception of the Allied project. The first of the fast convoys, which carried the units for the assault, sailed from home a few days later and, after it had joined up with the slow convoy, the combined armada passed through the Straits of Gibraltar on the night of November 5th. The destination of the force was then announced for the first time by the convoy commander to the troops on board. Their objective had been a well kept secret.

At daylight the next day the convoy, which was ostensibly heading for Malta, was attacked by JU 88s but received little damage, and at one o'clock on the morning of November 8th our troops began to land on the beaches around Algiers in the face of negligible opposition. The commandos and rangers, who were to seize the docks, met with fierce opposition, but succeeded in their purpose. Progress inland was rapid and decisive, some resistance offered by French tanks and artillery being quickly overcome. Later in the day Admiral Darlan was persuaded to surrender the city of Algiers without further bloodshed. Three days later he broadcast a 'cease fire' throughout all French territory in North Africa.

This swift success allowed the ships which were standing off the beaches to enter the harbour at Algiers for unloading, although some difficulty was experienced in berthing and beginning the work of discharge as labour was scarce and the sea, which had remained calm during the first landings over the beaches, became rough. It was a race against time to clear the ships before the second convoy, which was due in four days' time, arrived. The first task for the RASC was to get supplies of petrol to the airfield at Maison Blanche and the airfield at Djidjelli, as it was vital to refuel the fighters which were arriving from Gibraltar. One platoon of tippers, specially loaded with 100 octane spirit, was put ashore in landing craft over the beaches, and made straight for Maison Blanche with an escort which cleared up some minor opposition. Later in the day one of the two petrol depots which had been landed with the beach maintenance parties was able to begin passing more supplies up to the airfield.

The successful landing at Algiers allowed the floating reserve to be directed on Bougie, on November 10th, the plan being to land one battalion and stocks of petrol at Djidjelli. Because of rough weather a landing was impossible, and the ships had to turn back to Bougie, where a landing had been effected without opposition, but the port was soon the target for heavy enemy air attacks. On the 12th the battalion made its way by road to the airfield at Djidjelli in a column of charcoal burning lorries gathered together at Bougie, and the petrol stocks were sent on by landing craft the same day. As an added precaution it was decided to send more petrol up from Algiers by road. A detachment of an RASC 6-ton platoon drove over 210 miles of hilly twisting roads to arrive just in time to back straight up to the waiting aircraft which were refuelling on the spot. The RASC detachment drove without a pause. It was a good omen for the future.

The first few days at Algiers were hectic ones for the few transport platoons and the companies which began to land on the fourth day. No vehicle was ever at rest, as there were sufficient men to provide a double shift, but even so it was difficult to keep pace with the rate at which stores were being emptied on to the quays. The workshops platoon of a troop carrying company manned the winches of the MT ships which carried their and other units' vehicles and worked for two days and three nights without a stop to disembark the vehicles, much to the surprise of the docks operating company, which arrived to find that their first task had already been done for them.

Twelve hours after landing the DIDs were in operation, issuing composite rations and water, and reconnaissance parties were at work on the sites which had been selected for the base depots due to arrive on the second and third convoys. Complete information was obtained about the petroleum facilities in the country thanks to the help of the local Shell Company headquarters, and tentative arrangements were made to take over 60,000 tons of bulk storage and to plan for their cleaning and rehabilitation before bulk supplies arrived.

As soon as the two DIDs at Algiers could be relieved one was sent forward to Bone. Its convoy was heavily attacked on the way, but it was in action again issuing supplies on D plus 7. The other reached Philippeville on D plus 12 but it also had an adventuresome journey owing to accidents on the mountain roads. The DID and petrol depot landed at Bougie were also in action by the same date.

The Advance of the Striking Force

With Algiers in Allied hands the striking force left lost no time in moving eastwards and, encouraged by the active help of the French, General Eisenhower gave orders for the transfer from Oran to Tunisia of various American combat teams, tanks and air force units and for the rest of II Corps to follow as soon as possible.

The advance began with the 36th Brigade moving by road, rail and sea for Bone on November 13th (D plus 5) and by D plus 7 the pattern of the campaign began to take shape. On that day part of the Brigade pushed on to Tabarka which was only 60 miles from Tunis. They were carried forward in the charcoal burning buses which had been collected together for the purpose. Meanwhile the Column of the 11th Brigade was rushed up by road close to Beja. Bladeforce left Algiers by road on November 15th and on the 16th French patrols made their first contact with enemy troops near Beja and some French troops drove back small parties of the enemy near Mateur. The action of these French forces marked the beginning of military co-operation with the French troops which were stationed in Tunisia. On the following day British troops made contact with the enemy, the 36th Brigade at Jebel Abiod and the 1st Parachute Battalion in the vicinity of Beja.

It was already evident that the Axis forces in Tunisia could not be lightly brushed aside, so orders were given for the 78th Division to concentrate the troops under command for an attack on Tunis with the immediate objective of the line Mateur–Tebourba. Before the concentration was complete, the enemy struck heavily at the 36th Brigade, near Jebel Abiod, and the French, near Medjez el

Bab. The Germans were only driven back towards Medjez with the aid of a detachment from Bladeforce and an American field battery.

By November 24th all was ready for a combined assault against the enemy positions, and for three days the attacks prospered. The 36th Brigade got within 10 miles of Mateur; Bladeforce reached a point midway between Mateur and Tebourba and pressed on to within 16 miles of Tunis. The 11th Brigade took Tebourba. The prospects looked bright, but a combination of adverse circumstances brought all three attacks to a standstill.

The Axis forces were being heavily reinforced from Sicily and Sardinia, more than 50 troop-carrying aircraft arriving daily. Our small force of fighters had the almost impossible task of covering the forward area and communications which stretched back towards Algiers for over 400 miles. The Germans' main bases in Sicily were only half an hour's flying time distant. The spearheads of our advance were over 100 miles ahead of the nearest railhead, and second line transport and the few additional platoons of load carriers were still on light scales. To complete the list of adverse factors heavy and continuous rain began to fall, turning the roads into mud covered slippery tracks with boggy verges.

An uneasy pause followed during which each side strove desperately to accumulate sufficient strength for a crowning punch. The enemy struck first and nearly isolated the 11th Brigade at Tebourba and as the 78th Division had already suffered severe casualties it was decided to withdraw from the more forward position at Medjez el Bab. The withdrawal was however not at all easy as rain had turned the forward area into a veritable quagmire from which a large number of tanks of Combat Team B were never recovered.

Medjez el Bab was held by the 1st Guards Brigade, the third Brigade of the 78th Division which on its arrival in North Africa was immediately carried forward by a GT company to occupy that keypoint. In the meantime a Franco-American force had seized the important pass Faid on the Kasserine-Sfax road. It was at Tebourba that L/Cpl G. Bowyer, of 463 Company, won the Military Medal for gallant work when in charge of a section of water-tank lorries. He organized the defence of his section and supplied units under heavy fire. It was about this time that Sgt B. Philips, who was one of the RASC clerks at 36th Brigade headquarters, was awarded a Military Medal for his gallantry in helping to remove a blazing ammunition lorry and extricating a wounded man from an adjoining burning building.

General Eisenhower hoped to make one last attempt to reach his goal, but as the result of a personal inspection of the situation on the ground it was obvious to him that General 'Winter' had won the day, as movement off the roads was practically impossible, airfields were becoming unusable, and the enemy had been able to mass about 40,000 men to oppose him. On December 24th, after two postponements, he reluctantly had to call off the operation.

Transport in the First Advance

For the RASC this first phase of the campaign, was something of an unequal struggle in trying to maintain the striking force so far from its bases and at the same time endeavouring to keep pace with the rate at which thousands of tons of stores of all kinds were being dumped on to the quays at Algiers and at Bougie, Philippeville and Bone as those ports were gradually opened up.

Providentially, the state of the railways was better than had been expected. Although rolling stock and locomotives were worn and old, it was found possible to use the branch lines which led from Philippeville and later Bone to the main line from Algiers and to forward supplies by rail in two directions, eastwards to Souk Arhas and Souk el Arba and to Tebessa in the south. The railhead at Souk el Arba station received considerable attention from the enemy and in one raid Sgt L. Marland of 350 Company was awarded the Military Medal when, in company with Lieutenant Broach of 58 DID, he emptied a lorry filled with hand grenades which had been set on fire by an exploding bomb.

The narrow gauge line from Bone to La Calle was also taken into use for maintaining the troops in the north. But the capacity of the system was quite insufficient and had to be supplemented by road transport when the advanced portions of the striking force had reached points as much as 80 to 100 miles from the nearest railhead.

For the first few weeks the only transport available for the force was the second line companies which at their assault scale amounted to little more than a platoon each although they were gradually brought up to strength as further convoys arrived. The third line company for the 78th Division did not arrive until December and that for the 6th Armoured Division until the winter battle was over. Transport at the bases for docks clearance was equally scarce yet some had to be diverted to help with the maintenance of the forward troops. In spite of the precarious general transport position, last minute decisions to postpone the despatch of some companies, including some much needed 10-ton lorry units due to arrive in the third convoy, and to defer them to later convoys, left the DDST short of more than 400 vehicles at this critical period. Unfortunately many of the heavy lorries which had been received were a mixture of various makes and types of vehicles which had been requisitioned from the Liverpool docks. They presented an almost impossible spare parts problem.

At one time two brigade companies, designed to maintain 9,000 men, were working to support 20,000. Even if the programmes for embarking transport units at home had not been altered the situation would have been difficult, as in addition to the arrival of American units without their maintenance transport, assistance had also to be provided for the ill-equipped French forces and a large number of RAF units which began to arrive in the eastern zone.

The only redeeming feature was the discovery that the intelligence reports on the availability of local transport were over-cautious, and although many civil vehicles had been converted to producer gas burners, some vehicles were hired for work at the base in Algiers, and more would have been obtainable if the French Army had not had to depend on requisitioned vehicles for mobilizing their units.

The absence of the third line companies in the forward area during the first few weeks was keenly felt, but the second line companies and the various platoons of other companies which were sent up to help did splendid work. No. 328 Company, the brigade company for the 36th Brigade, lost some of its effective strength through being badly bombed at Tabarka, and the company of the 11th Brigade also had losses when its ammunition point was overrun by enemy tanks. Much of the work had to be carried out by night. No. 328 Company was a versatile unit; it undertook to test the railway from Tabarka to Sedjenane by running an engine and couple of trucks 'to make certain that the track was not mined', and at Christmas collected pigs, poultry, fruit and eggs in such quantity that all units enjoyed the usual seasonable fare.

In the four base sub-areas there were so many demands for transport for various purposes, in addition to the main task of dock clearance, that special organizations had to be set up to decide on priorities and relate the matters of labour, transport and turn-round so that every vehicle could be used to the best advantage. Our transport companies had much to contend with. Some ports were subject to heavy bombing raids, and as the winter became more severe, road surfaces began to deteriorate through use and rain and mud, and in some parts of the forward area whole sections of vehicles became bogged. The weather was appalling, and at one time communications with the forward troops were almost severed, a factor which is well brought out in the official despatches as one of the reasons why success was not achieved earlier.

Weather, work, and losses by enemy action threw a heavy load on the companies' artificers and as the organization for providing vehicle replacements or spare parts had not been built up, every form of ingenuity had to be used to keep vehicles on the road. The position was made no easier because units' technical (workshop) vehicles had in many cases to be shipped in later convoys, so that

Brigadier Hinde's foresight in ordering each unit to fit up an 'unofficial' 15-cwt 'first aid' vehicle and the provision of 'picnic baskets' (sets of spare parts) saved the day.

Supplies in the First Phase

The dominant factor in the advance of the striking force to Tunis was the tendency of the forward troops to outrun their sources of supply because of their speed of advance, the unexpected arrival of American units, and the expansion of the air forces in central and southern Tunisia.

Supplies were sent to Philippeville and Bone, where base depots were established, and then forwarded by rail and road. Every column of lorries moving to the east also carried forward a load of supplies.

Four supply railheads were established for the forward troops and two for lines of communication troops, at Setif and Constantine, and three railheads were brought into use for the American air force. Stocks of supplies had also to be provided at five staging points on the lines of communication.

There were insufficient DIDs to go round, and officers and men had to be taken from other supply units to man these numerous points. Many of the detachments were still without their 'G 1098' equipment, and only the fact that the composite ration was so easy to check and issue enabled them to cope with the situation. Labour had to be found in most cases from local Arabs, indifferent workers who, as the weather became worse, had to be persuaded with some difficulty to carry on.

In the bases everything had to be sacrificed to a quick turn-round of ships, which in turn necessitated a rapid turn-round of the vehicles employed in clearing the docks. The result was that supplies were discharged pell-mell and the whole problem of sorting assumed such proportions that special re-sorting centres had to be organized. The rough handling to which supplies were subjected led to hundreds and later thousands of cases being broken, and there was also considerable loss by pilferage. This was a perpetual bugbear and was almost impossible to stop owing to the confused conditions. Thousands of cases of composite rations were broken open to remove the cigarettes and chocolate, an easy process as cases had to be made of fibre-board because of a lack of timber at home. In Algiers 120 arrests were made for pilferage in three days, and an order declaring that pilferage would be regarded as looting seemed to have little deterrent effect.

The general conditions at the bases made it difficult to take stock at first of the supplies which were available in the country, but by the beginning of December the fog had lifted sufficiently to disclose that about 20 days' food had been accumulated although it was not sited to the best advantage. By December 21st the stock had grown to 29 days for 170,000 men. As it was becoming clear that the original estimated strength of the force would be considerably exceeded, an urgent demand was made on the War Office for extra supply units to be sent out as soon as possible. During this early period a large number of American troops had to subsist on British rations, and the British supply organization had to give a helping hand as the Americans were not at first able to provide their own supply depots.

For the first six weeks of the campaign the Army was fed entirely on composite rations. The arrival from home of the normal field service ration commodities coincided with the first issues of fresh bread, although only one of the mobile bakeries which had been landed at that time was accompanied by its equipment, a deficiency made good by taking over French bakeries. The hope that fresh meat could be obtained locally was not fulfilled, as contrary to intelligence reports the supposed vast sheep population of North Africa proved to be illusory, and this led to some delay before plans could be made to import frozen produce. Cold storage was available at Algiers, but elsewhere accommodation was limited, and the refrigerating plant was in need of repair.

The initial Petroleum Organization

During the initial drive to Tunis by the striking force the amount of petrol and oils required was relatively small and supply was at first maintained in the form of packed stocks forwarded by road and rail and by sea from Algiers and the other base ports. On the other hand the supplies which were in four-gallon tins were already showing the effect of much handling and it was not uncommon to see lorries leaving for the front with petrol streaming from them. The principal task of the petroleum organization was to build up and develop supply in bulk so that the amount of road and rail transport required for packed stocks could be reduced.

As sections of the bulk storage companies began to arrive, existing civil storage for about eight million gallons was taken over at Algiers and six million at Bone. There was a great deal to be done before the tanks could be filled, but with the aid of the civil oil companies who collaborated in the work in every possible way and of the French authorities, tanks and pipes were cleaned and put into order and the installations made ready for use. At the same time active steps were taken to develop the system for distribution in bulk.

At Bone work was often interrupted by air raids, which necessitated further inspections to make certain that the repairs which had been effected had not again been damaged.

It was found that about 300 rail tank cars were available, but not all could be used for petrol and orders were placed for further cars to be shipped to Africa as soon as possible. Many of the cars were very dirty internally, some of them having a thick coating of a tenth of an inch of oxidized oil, and a strong body of pioneers had to be employed in cleaning them out. The next stage in organizing supply was to take over and provide additional tanks at airfields and other centres of activities, and pumping arrangements for intake from rail or road cars. A large number of barrels were taken over from the French for the use of small units and for carrying supplies to kerb-side pumps, which were also requisitioned or re-installed in large numbers.

The first bulk supplies to be handled into the main installations came by rail from Oran in the American sector and in cars which had been filled by a short sea line fitted up from a torpedoed and beached ship. The first ocean tanker to discharge its cargo arrived on the 22nd day after the first landing and small coastal tankers were obtained for carrying supplies to Bone. Intake into the installations at Algiers did not present any special problems, but the position at Bone was fraught with many hazards. Because of the layout of the harbour tankers had to be berthed stern on. In some cases their cargo had to be discharged through some 300 to 400 feet of 6-inch and 8-inch pipeline which was built up on pontoons to connect the ships' discharge points with the intake pipes on land. In some cases the ships' pumps were not sufficiently powerful to withstand the back pressure from the partly filled storage tanks on land, which involved considerable delays as the connecting lines had then to be transferred to other empty tanks.

Although the bulk stocks available at the end of December were adequate, largely because of the transfer of American stocks from Oran and a loan of French reserves, there was a serious and unforeseen loss through leakage of the non-returnable containers which had been shipped from home. Special arrangements had to be made for decanting all leaking tins as they were discharged and for despatching the contents to the nearest installation for testing and redistribution.

Many ships arrived with cans stacked so high that in some instances the holds of the ships were swimming with spirit to a depth of a foot or so.

The Second Phase—On the Defensive

When rain and mud brought operations to a standstill at the end of the year it was inevitable that each opponent would seek to extend his lines to guard against surprise flank attacks. The

Allied line extended from Cap Serrat in the north to Gafsa in the south. The British V Corps held the sector from the north down to the Goubellat-Bou Arada plain; the French XIX Corps held the central positions along the natural barrier of the eastern Dorsale, which included the important gap at Fondouk connecting Ousseltia and Kairouan; and the United States II Corps continued the line to the south.

Headquarters First Army moved to Constantine at the end of December, as Allied Force HQ had arrived and assumed executive command of the whole theatre.

As there were still few formations in the theatre—there were only the 78th and 34th Divisions, until the 6th Armoured was brought up to strength—the presence of so many superior headquarters excited the remark that 'never have so few been commanded by so many'. The chain of command consisted of AFHQ, HQ First Army and V Corps, besides the main administrative headquarters on the lines of communication.

It was a critical period in the campaign because the Axis forces had, generally speaking, the initiative, and their future position in Africa would largely depend on their efforts to counter the hold which the Allies had gained on their flank, in North Africa. They knew that it was only a matter of time before the Allies could develop their full power when communications could be developed and our air power increased.

When General Eisenhower reviewed the situation at the end of the year he decided to attempt to regain the initiative by thrusting through the Dorsale in the south to the coast at Sfax, and so threaten the communications of the Axis forces facing Eighth Army. The attack (operation 'Satin') was to be carried out by the American II Corps, but as it was learned later that General Montgomery did not expect to be in a position to attack the Mareth Line before mid-February, the plan was cancelled.

The build-up of the reserves for this operation threw a heavy load on the transport of the First Army, which undertook to lift 2,000 tons of American stores from the Souk Ahras area to Tebessa. In addition to this task a 6-ton GT Company and a 3-ton Company had to be provided to operate a shuttle service to supplement the railway to Tebessa. While the work of building reserves went on, the opportunity was taken to use the lorries returning empty to carry grain from the Ain Beda area for the civil population at Constantine, where there was a food shortage. The decision to cancel operation 'Satin' was therefore received with some relief by the DDST of the army and the ADSTs at the base ports, who had to provide the GT companies from their already impoverished resources.

Meanwhile the 46th Division had arrived from home. The

divisional RASC consisted of 519, 520, 521 and 570 Companies. Of these the first three had originally belonged to the 49th Division. The first company to go forward was 520 Company, which remained in the Sedjenane area until April. Two of its men soon earned immediate awards of the Military Medal: L/Cpl R. Butler for continuing to issue ammunition until the site of his dump became untenable after being machine-gunned and bombed, and Dvr P. Murphy, who delivered supplies to an isolated unit, although his route was under direct fire from snipers and his lorry was hit three times.

The other units of 46th Divisional RASC came forward in February to about Beja. It was there that Dvr A. A. Lawton, a motorcyclist attached to 128th Brigade HQ, earned a Military Medal for reconnoitring the enemy's movements and that Dvr W. J. Hughes, of 183 Field Ambulance, was also awarded the Military Medal for collecting casualties under heavy fire.

The first part of the defensive period was marked by both sides carrying on sparring activity in the central sector. In early January the 6th Armoured Division made a successful probing attack and encountered little opposition. The Germans, after a preliminary thrust at Fondouk, attacked the junction of the French and British sectors. The French, who were ill-equipped, gave way, and it was only after a week of severe fighting when British and American troops had to come to their assistance that the situation was stabilized on a line a little to the rear of the original front held. The enemy, having gained the initiative, was determined not to lose it. Well aware of the small strength of the Allies who opposed him and the difficult terrain on their long lines of communication, he planned to strike hard at the southern flank with the object of capturing Tebessa. This would jeopardize the position of the British in the north and would be the signal for Von Arnim to attack our forces in that area.

By the end of January the continued need for strengthening the line at each point of enemy attack from the comparatively small resources available to the Allies had left the army in a somewhat unsatisfactory position. General Eisenhower was fully aware of this and had given orders for the 34th (US) Division to complete its concentration by February 15th, and for the 9th (US) Division to move up from Oran. The 25th Tank Brigade was also due to arrive in the same month.

The storm broke on February 14th, when the enemy struck in force against the widely dispersed United States 1st Armoured Division, inflicting heavy losses in men, tanks and equipment on the Americans as they withdrew. By nightfall of February 17th the enemy had captured Kasserine and Gafsa and was infiltrating through the Kasserine pass. Then, breaking through the pass, he directed two armoured columns on Tebessa and Thala, and for some days the situation was critical. It was at Thala that 4 Company, RASC was ordered to stand by to fight as infantry in support of The Leicestershire Regiment. Allied reinforcements were already on their way, but the situation became so serious that regiments and even companies had to be committed to the battle as they arrived. These reinforcements were, however, able to turn the tide, and a week later the enemy had withdrawn to almost his original starting line while the attacks made on the British in the north gained little success, although the fate of Beja at one time was in the balance. When the enemy's break-through was assuming dangerous proportions, the RASC men in a reinforcement unit were organized into a temporary company of infantry and went into action.

The defensive period ended with two further attacks by the enemy at the end of February, one in the Bou Arada area and the other against the Eighth Army at Medenine. Although both these enemy thrusts were a failure the Axis had been able to keep open the land routes between his two commands (Von Arnim in the north and the Italian General Messe, who replaced General Rommel, in the south). When the fighting died down, the Allied forces in Tunisia were in a confused pattern as British, American and French troops had become intermingled and dispersed with little regard to the position of their parent units or formation.

While the enemy was making his last efforts it was decided that the two converging Allied armies, the Eighth Army and the First Army, with Americans and French, should operate under the unified command of headquarters 18 Army Group, with General Alexander at its head. The army group had two clear cut tasks: to reorganize the First Army into British, American and French formations to simplify administration, and to build up reserves for the future combined efforts of the unified command.

At about this time there were some changes in the senior ST appointments. Brigadier Hinde relieved Brigadier White as DST, AFHQ, and Brigadier J. K. Gillespie became DDST of the Army.

The 1st Division did not arrive in North Africa until March. Three of its RASC Companies—7, 40 and 42—were those which went to France in 1939, and the fourth company was 295 Company. All the companies had undergone battle training when at home, and it was put to good purpose when each company was ordered to provide one platoon of an 'infantry' company to hold a sector and guard a minefield in a likely line of approach for enemy tanks.

The 4th Division arrived later in March with two of its original 'BEF' companies, 21 and 44. The other two were 107 and 473.

All 44 Company's vehicles were lost on the voyage from home, but a party of the workshop men of the unit assisted in assembling a reserve of lorries which were being uncrated, and the company was re-equipped within a week.

Thus the strength of the army was being gradually built up with both British and American formations. But the early period of the year had been a critical one, and the strength of the enemy opposing us had been clearly demonstrated by the determination and vigour of his attacks, especially at Kasserine.

Transport in the defensive period

Although the number of RASC transport units increased during the winter defensive period, the tasks to be performed were far heavier than had been foreseen, and many units were short of vehicles owing to lack of replacements and to the deferred arrival, for various reasons, of their equipment. But the ruling factor which affected British road transport during this defensive phase—and indeed throughout the campaign—was the low carrying capacity of the railways. This necessitated the organization of supplementary road lifts as a permanent measure, which meant that AFHQ had to skin the base transport maintenance units to the bone to provide a pool for the First Army.

The administrative situation in the forward area had become extremely confused owing to the intermingling of the forces of the three nations which had resulted from the constant need for reinforcing threatened areas with such troops as were available at the time. On February 1st the French Corps d'Afrique and 139th Brigade Group were being maintained from La Calle; Souk el Arba was used to supply most of V Corps, an American combat team and six French battalions. The French XIX Corps was maintained from le Kef, and the 1st American Division and British Army troops from Ebba K'Sour. Tebessa was the main railhead for the American II Corps and another French division.

This confused pattern was reflected in the transport organization; for example, at one time the CRASC 6th Armoured Divisional RASC had none of his own units under command. Each situation had to be met as it arose without thought for the niceties of text-book organization. Assistance had to be given to the French and American forces, as the former had little transport of their own and some American formations were short of special types of vehicles such as ambulances and tank transporters. The transport with the French led an eventful life in keeping pace with Gallic *élan*, in clearing up enemy minefields and in building up dumps in the more lonely desert-like country in the south.

Almost all types of units took a share in carrying out special tasks.

One GT company detailed to convey an American combat team from Biskra to the battle position at Thala covered 497 miles of difficult terrain in 41 hours. Tank transporters performed some quite spectacular deeds, such as the ferrying forward of the Churchill tanks of 25th Tank Brigade, when drivers had little or no rest for several weeks. Their work is instanced by the award of the British Empire Medal to Dvr R. Roberts who drove his 70-ton load for 14 days with never more than a few hours' rest. On some of the mountain passes the speed of these vehicles was reduced to about four miles an hour, and the general road conditions were so bad and the expenditure in tyres so high that replacement stocks became depleted. There were some losses too. For example, during the approach to the Kasserine battle, one company lost 16 transporters through enemy air attack and many of the other vehicles had an epidemic of burnt-out clutch plates.

The roads from Philippeville and Bone leading to the forward area were narrow and hilly but men and vehicles emerged from these tests with complete success. The general dearth of ambulance car units and water tank companies meant that the only ambulance car unit available had to operate over a huge area and perform tasks which normally fall to the vehicles with field ambulances and ambulance car companies. The individual gallantry of many members of the ambulance units was recognized by various awards. CSM Rowe of 16 Para Field Ambulance received a Military Medal for a series of acts of gallantry which included his maintaining a supply of water to an advance dressing station, the rescue of a badly damaged ambulance and repairing another vehicle under heavy fire. Dvr R. Willshire was awarded a Military Medal for driving under fire over a road which was known to be heavily mined, and Dvr A. Stern of 88 Company was also given a similar award, for gallantry in bringing wounded (he was an ambulance driver) to safety.

The lack of water-tank lorries was due to the mishap which befell the second company to arrive in the theatre, which lost most of its vehicles and unhappily some of its men when the ship carrying them was sunk on the voyage out. A tipper company, too, had many adventures before it was finally concentrated in Africa, as its men were spread over no fewer than nine different ships and its vehicles over eight ships. A ship carrying one platoon was torpedoed and another platoon was caught in a heavy air raid as it was disembarking. An MT ship which contained some of the unit's vehicles was torpedoed, but made port with holds flooded, and all vehicles had to be stripped after landing and reassembled before they could be used. Another of the ships was sunk off Oran, but without any loss of life.

Building up the Supply Organization

While steady progress was made during the defensive period in building up the supply organization, the First Army continued to be handicapped by having to maintain so many American land and air force units. There was also a rise in the strength to be fed in the theatre as a whole which was accompanied by a decision to increase the reserves to be held. By the end of January the strength was nearly 250,000, which included 45,000 Americans. Even so only about 87,000 were in the army area forward of the railheads, the remainder, about 160,000, being engaged at the bases or on the lines of communication, although of course that figure included a large number of air force units. The French formations in the army area were fairly well self-contained for supplies and indeed came to our rescue by producing large quantities of barley and straw for the newly formed British pack transport units.

Although the general stock position often lagged behind the official levels, reserves and working stocks were generally adequate by the end of February. The chief problem which exercised the ADSTs and base provision officers (now called CsRASC supplies) was how to provide sufficient units and accommodation to handle the stocks which were pouring into the theatre. Supply had outrun the pace at which supply units were being sent from England, so that any type of unit which could be spared, such as field butcheries and the composite platoons for anti-aircraft artillery regiments, had to be diverted to operate DIDs.

Everything possible was done to provide fresh rations. Fresh vegetables and fruit were sent forward to Tunisia, where the soil was less favourable for cultivation than in Algeria. Bread production had been handicapped by the belated arrival of units' bakery equipment, much of which was in ships which did not arrive until a month after the units had landed. The first two mobile bakeries were producing 20,000 lb a day each by the New Year, and in February three mobile bakeries were in operation in the army area, so that a full ration of bread, 12 oz, was available for all. Plans for providing meat were not so successful. The cold storage available was limited and refrigeration wagons were few, and inquiries about the local sheep 'harvest', which before the war allowed the export of 800,000 head to France, indicated that the annual movement of the scattered flocks to the sea would not begin before March and that local consumption, because of lack of other foods, had greatly increased. There was enough storage accommodation to accept some fresh bacon and cheese, and supplies began to arrive in February.

In the North African Hills

On the Way to the Front

H.M. King George VI with Lieut.-General Sir Humfrey Gale

Developing the Petroleum Organization

The gradual transfer of American troops from the central and western to the eastern forces considerably increased the rate of petrol consumption in the First Army area until, in February, about 1,000 tons a day were being used. The intermingling of so many British and American formations made it imperative to co-ordinate supply, and a petroleum section was set up at AFHQ for the purpose with the rather wide charter of 'controlling and co-ordinating all problems of petroleum products brought to and stored in and distributed to naval, military, air force and civil agencies'. Each service prepared its own claims for its requirements which were co-ordinated by what became known as the Oil Slate Committee, and this in turn placed a consolidated demand on the two bodies in London and Washington which were jointly responsible for supplies to all Allied countries. Although each army was to preserve its responsibility for the intake and storage of its supplies, the planning and development of all main pipelines became an integrated responsibility of the new petroleum section.

In the meantime RASC units in the forward areas carried the main burden of filling and distribution, but they had the help of an American gasoline company and 100 men lent by the French. It fell to a petrol unit to make the first contact with Eighth Army when supplies were sent down to the oasis at Toggourt for the Long Range Desert Group at the end of long sorties which it had made behind the enemy's lines.

By January the reserves to be held were assessed at 220,000 tons, of which about half would have to be stored in bulk and about half in packed form. The development of bulk storage arrangements proceeded steadily but involved a great deal of ingenuity and was accompanied by various problems which had to be overcome as they arose. Ocean-going tankers began to arrive at Algiers and the RASC men responsible for discharging them soon became experts at the task. But even then their 'drill' was not yet foolproof, for it was once discovered that part of a cargo of aviation spirit was by some mischance being pumped hard for nearly half an hour, not into the storage place but into the harbour. Every possible step was taken to reduce the consequent fire risk, and providentially an enemy air raid that evening missed what would have been an ideal opportunity of producing a general conflagration in the harbour.

There was a general lack of equipment which had to be made good by improvisation, a small civil foundry and workshop being taken for the production of moulded and machine-cut special spare parts.

The greatest difficulty was in keeping up the required flow in bulk to Bone, which was the nearest port to the forward area, until coastal tankers arrived, as ocean tankers could not be employed on the task. Bone was continually bombed, and the sea lines were set on fire twice and a tanker holed in 36 places by near misses. Other losses were sustained at Bougie. Although tankers arrived fairly regularly many losses were sustained on the high seas, as in the case of one convoy when two ships were sunk, four were damaged by enemy action but managed to make Algiers and one, also damaged, limped back to its home port. To make matters worse, three ships containing petrol cargoes were shut out altogether from the same convoy.

Rehabilitation of plant and equipment went on steadily but took time. Tanks and pipelines which had been previously used for alcohol had to be classed as being irremediably contaminated, while installations which had not been in use for some time were difficult to clean satisfactorily before the RASC petroleum chemists were satisfied that motor or aviation spirit could be stored in them without any risk to vehicle or aircraft engines.

Preparation for the Final Phase

The first task of 18 Army Group was, so far as the First Army was concerned, to sort out the position of American, British and French formations which had become intermingled as the result of the enemy's attacks around Kasserine. This was achieved by the allotment of distinct sectors to each of the three corps (V British, XIX French and II American) and the gradual concentration of their troops within the new boundaries. By early March the army group was disposed into First Army (V and French XIX Corps) in Northern Tunisia, the American II Corps in Central Tunisia and the Eighth Army facing the enemy in Southern Tunisia. IX Corps Headquarters which had arrived from home was placed in reserve with the 6th Armoured Division and the American 34th Division under command.

Even so it was not possible to make a complete regroupment. For example I AGRA had to be left with the French corps, and an RASC artillery company allotted for its maintenance, and a pool of general transport had also to be provided for the French in the form of a headquarters of a transport column with general transport, troop carrying and ambulance units. Similarly a British transport column had to be provided to supplement the railway from Philippeville to Constantine, where both British and American advanced bases were being established, the column also controlling the American convoys which were working on the same route. An average of 700 tons of American stores was lifted by the British column daily.

Intensive efforts had to be made to build up the reserves of food wanted at the new advanced base at Constantine and in the army area at a time when the strength of the force was increasing rapidly. Conditions at the base depots had greatly improved with better weather, the arrival of more supply units from home and the provision of some hutted accommodation. But the two problems of preventing pilferage and of how to deal with the never-ending flow of broken packages remained a constant bugbear.

The flow of broken cases became so great that the organizations which had been set up to repair and recase the hundreds of tons which arrived damaged could not keep pace, and loose tins had to be sent forward to DIDs in any form of basket or sack which could be obtained locally.

The 2,000-ton food reserve for the advanced base was completed by March 25th, and smaller reserves were also in position at or close to all railheads in the army area by the same time.

The First Army was to be supplied through railheads at La Calle, Souk el Arba, Souk Ahras and Le Kef. Supply to La Calle was by narrow gauge railway from Bone, supplemented by small coasters and landing craft. Souk el Arba and Souk Ahras depended on the broad gauge railway and road transport from Bone. The maintenance of Le Kef was by narrow gauge and road *via* Tebessa. Six DIDs and some artillery composite platoons were provided to look after reserves and act as railhead supply detachments, and four and a half bakeries were provided to make the army self-contained for bread.

By the end of April the feeding strength had risen to 360,000, most of whom were British troops, as by that time the Americans had taken over the maintenance of most of their own troops.

The French had their own *zone d'étapes*, and the American II Corps relied on their advanced base at Constantine which was supplied from Philippeville, forward supply being by narrow gauge to Tebessa and onwards by road.

All railheads were to be moved forward as soon as the situation allowed, the V Corps railhead to Oued Zarga, IX Corps to Medjez el Bab, and XIX Corps to Bou Arada. Two DIDs were held ready to operate in Tunis and Bizerta when those towns were captured.

The period leading up to the final offensive was also a busy one for the British and American petroleum organizations in achieving their object of having over 180,000 tons of spirit in place before the battle began. About half the quantity was to be held at the bases and half divided over an advanced base and the forward area. The first step was to stock an advanced depot at El Guerrah about 18 miles south of Constantine. The depot was staffed by a base petrol filling centre early in March, and stocks were built up at a rate of about 800 tons a week brought forward in the main from Philippeville by road.

The build-up in the army area was completed by April 20th, much of it in the form of barrelled stocks which were distributed over the axis La Calle–Souk el Arba–Le Kef and at Souk Ahras. Although the work of building up these stocks went on unmolested from the air, a small dump of 1,000 tons which was put down for the use of the Eighth Army received much attention from the Luftwaffe in the form of hundreds of flares dropped at night, but a combination of scrim nets and olive groves defeated the German efforts to locate the stacks.

The petroleum units in the army area worked with a will, MPFCs filling 21,000 gallons a day for days on end, and at one 'B' type depot barrels were emptied faster than they could be cleared away. As there was no room to stack the barrels in the depot they were placed 10 deep along an adjacent railway line, eventually stretching along it for over three miles.

There was no lack of petrol during the battle although anxious moments were caused by intensive air operations, so much so that when a special trainload of 100 octane petrol reached Souk el Arba the station was besieged by queues of RAF and USAAF lorries which had come from all over Tunisia.

The building up of the organization on the lines of communication had made rapid strides, and work was done at great speed once the order to go was given; ocean tanker storage was installed at Philippeville, by an American unit, in the form of 13 bolted tanks of 1,000 tons capacity each, in a matter of six weeks, while the 'stringing' together of two 4-inch pipelines and the setting down of pumping stations went on simultaneously. The line which led to the American advanced base at Ouled Rahmoun, where four 1,000-ton tanks had also been built, had to traverse 55 miles of mountainous country rising to a peak of 2,000 feet above sea level. The first ship discharged its contents into the tanks at Philippeville between April 16th and 19th, and the first supply took 33 hours to go through the line to Ouled Rahmoun. As there had been no time to test the line with water, about $8\frac{1}{2}$ per cent of spirit was lost.

The same American unit then left for Bone, where it erected four 500-ton tanks for the British base and at the same time completed a line 69 miles long to the British pipehead at Souk el Arba. This work was finished in a month, after which the line was handed over in working order to the British engineer unit detailed to maintain it.

The engineers and the staff of the CsRASC petroleum installations had full scope for displaying their ingenuity at many places, such as at Bone, where special arrangements for intake from ocean tankers were made and a refuelling organization was set up to provide a 24-hour service for small naval craft. They also took a hand at pipe laying at Algiers by running a nine-mile line to Maison Blanche airfield which, helped by half a section of pioneers, they completed in nine days.

Transit of petroleum by road and rail was also developed with the aid of 8,000-gallon railcars imported from America and additional rolling stock obtained from Morocco, and British road tank companies and American quartermaster companies maintained shuttle services of bulk supplies for refilling barrels and small inland installations.

The pool of road transport which could be provided for the Army was not great, the two corps being left with only one third line company each, as the remainder of the third line companies had to be drawn into the general pool. The First Army was undoubtedly very short of transport, a fact brought home when the Brigadier A/Q of a corps found that his opposite number in the Eighth Army had many more companies at his disposal. The First Army had only the equivalent of 10 general transport companies, and many of these had to be employed in operating a shuttle service from Bone to try to relieve the railway bottleneck at Duvivier. There were three tank transporter companies and four troop-carrying companies, but each corps could be given one bridging platoon and some sections of tippers. Of the three MACs available one had to be lent to the French.

During the advance, supplies were usually drawn direct from the railhead, but ammunition and petrol were obtained from a series of FMCs. But owing to the heavy expenditure in 25-pounder and 105-mm ammunition, the ammunition companies had to return to the more rearward FMCs and even to the Ordnance Depot at Tebousek to keep up supply—journeys which involved a turn-round of 120 to 180 miles.

The Final Battles

Space does not allow of anything more than a brief chronological description of the operations which followed the opening battle, when the American II Corps attacked with vigour on March 17th to draw off troops from the Mareth position and six days later occupied Gafsa, El Guettar and Maknassy, after which bad weather brought the movement of armour to a standstill. However, the operation pinned down a considerable Axis force and allowed the establishment of a dump of ammunition and petrol for the use of the Eighth Army when it approached Sfax. This project was surrounded by such great secrecy as to warrant a code name 'Sahara'. Four GT companies, taken from the First Army pool, were employed on the task and were made self-contained with food and petrol for a week. Convoys left at intervals, the first convoy setting off before the town had been captured. Throughout the business of discharging the loads, fighting was never far away, and sometimes the RASC drivers had a 'grandstand' view of the battle around them.

On March 20/21st the Eighth Army began its famous onslaught on the Mareth line which forced the enemy under the Italian Marshal Messe to fall back to the Wadi Akarit. The month closed with the 46th Division and French troops of the Corps d'Afrique pushing back the enemy in the north to beyond Jebel Abiod.

The surrounding hills in the Sedjenane area were impassable to motor transport and consequently the whole operation had to be supported by pack transport. The mules, advancing with the infantry, carried up ammunition, rations, water and even OPs, as well as weapons and tools. The two RASC companies engaged had casualties both in men and animals, but acquitted themselves with distinction.

The Axis forces were given no time to rest. In the south the Eighth Army forced the passage of the Wadi Akarit on April 6th, and on the same day forward patrols of the American II Corps made contact with men of the Eighth Army.

A second attack was made by IX Corps, which had been brought up from reserve, to force the Fondouk Gap, and on April 9th contact was made with the Eighth Army near Sfax.

There were no rail communications in the IX Corps area of operations, and a road line of communication of over 100 miles had to be organized. The roads were little more than tracks and soon deteriorated to rock protruding through a thick carpet of dust, and the going was so rough that an alternative line *via* Maktar was taken into use; but before long this route also was almost impassable. The surface was too rough for the passage of tank transporters and the tanks which had been employed in the operation had to return on their own tracks.

In the meantime V Corps launched an attack in the Medjez el Bab sector and, after a fortnight's continuous fighting, advanced some 20 miles, a first step towards clearing the entrance to the Tunis plain. It was also a period of great air activity, for operation 'Flax' accounted for a bag of more than 400 enemy aircraft, a blow from which the Axis forces never recovered.

This last of the lesser operations which were preparatory to the final offensives was marked by a tremendous expenditure of 25-pounder ammunition which could only be met by keeping the second line transport continuously on the road with relays of drivers, fitters, butchers and cooks—anyone who could drive being impressed for the purpose. At one period 20,000 rounds were lifted forward by 30 lorries in 24 hours.

The enemy had by this time withdrawn into his predetermined stronghold behind the hills running north from Enfidaville to Bizerta and had reduced his frontage to about 100 miles, so a redistribution of our forces became necessary. The American II Corps was switched to the north, and the First Army was joined by the 1st Armoured Division from the Eighth Army. Railheads were moved forward, and forward reserves were replenished in preparation for the first onslaught against the enemy's new positions, which took place on the night of April 19th/20th, when the Eighth Army attacked and captured Enfidaville. On the 21st, V Corps, with the 1st and 78th Divisions and 4th (Mixed Division) under command, stormed the enemy's strong positions of Longstop Hill and the hills to the north, and the 78th Division made history by finally capturing the hill in their third gallant attempt. Fighting was bitter and progress was slow. Meanwhile IX Corps, with the 1st and 6th Armoured Divisions and 46th Division, made progress over the hills eastwards from the road Bou Arada–Goubellat, and the American II Corps and French troops in the north had advanced to within 15 miles of Mateur.

General Alexander then decided on April 27th to change his plan for the capture of Tunis by concentrating all his strength in a mighty drive from the Medjez-el-Bab sector direct for Tunis and to cleave the enemy forces in two.

The final great offensive began on May 5th with V Corps gaining the hills which dominated the Tunis plain and IX Corps advancing in bright starlight on the morning of May 6th. By the afternoon their infantry had gained their objective, and the 6th and 7th Armoured Divisions (the latter from the Eighth Army), swept forward and entered Tunis on May 7th. On the same day the American II Corps and Corps d'Afrique gained Bizerta. The enemy had not been finally defeated, but his two armies had been cut in two at last.

By May 9th the Axis forces in the northern pocket had been completely mopped up, while the divisions of the First Army then turned to assist in the encirclement of the southern force, which they achieved between May 11th and 13th.

The strategy designed in London less than a year before had been developed according to plan. The Axis forces had been cast out of Africa, and the Mediterranean was free to our ships. The way was clear for the final phase in the invasion of Europe from the south.

The Aftermath

Although the battle was over, the surge forward of the First and

Eighth Armies into the north eastern corner of Tunisia, the capture of about 257,000 prisoners of war, and the need for bringing relief measures to the civil population created an administrative situation which necessitated drastic action. The influx of Allied troops was dealt with by dispersing them—the Eighth Army beginning to retrace its footsteps southwards to Tripoli a few days after the Axis surrender. The First Army formations could not be withdrawn so rapidly, but by the end of May only one British and one American division were left as a garrison in Tunis. The emergency relief of the civil population had been carefully planned by the North African Economic Board, and the first train with food and much needed coal was on its way to Tunis on the day of the final surrender.

The maintenance of such large numbers of prisoners of war was another matter, as the Intelligence forecast had been that only 157,000 would have to be evacuated to the west. The capture of a million German and Italian rations helped to tide over the immediate problem, and the transfer of prisoners to the 'cages' prepared for their reception was assisted by their obliging habit of organizing their own convoys and arriving in good order at the appointed place. The feeding and clothing of the prisoners according to international agreement earned the praise of the officials of the International Red Cross who supervised their general well-being.

The RASC could look back on the seven months' campaign with some satisfaction. The British North Africa force had been well fed and had enjoyed a high standard of health, a fact which was conceded to be largely due to the excellent and plentiful rations on which it subsisted. The 6,000-odd RASC 'task' vehicles had covered 35 million miles between them. Some units did not arrive until the campaign was nearly over, but the vehicles of one bulk petrol company averaged over 15,000 miles and one vehicle held a record of 30,000 miles. The record of the companies' workshop sections was one to be proud of, as during the whole campaign only 418 task vehicles had to be evacuated, and it is perhaps significant that replacements were received for only 298 in return. The young petroleum organization had shown what well-planned organization and the use of modern equipment could achieve. Pack transport had established its reputation which was to be excelled later in Italy. RASC casualties were 103 officers and men killed and 146 wounded.

CHAPTER VII

THE CENTRAL MEDITERRANEAN

ITALY

Decision to Invade Italy

THE campaign in Italy, which was preceded by the capture of the small islands of Lampedusa and Pantelleria and the invasion of Sicily, was one in which the RASC had to develop each of its activities to the fullest extent, as, in addition to an extensive supply and transport organization, both animal and water transport were used on a large scale, and the campaigns provided the RASC with their first opportunity of demonstrating the value of their new form of transport—the amphibious vehicle.

Plans for the invasion of Sicily were well advanced before the final defeat of the Axis forces in North Africa had been accomplished, but the decision to invade Italy was the subject of much discussion because it was thought that the effort which would have to be devoted to such an enterprise might detract from the main Allied objective, the invasion of North-West Europe in the coming year.

Pantelleria and Lampedusa fell with surprising swiftness, in two days, in June, 1943. The first airborne landings were made in Sicily on the night of July 9th/10th, and by August 17th the whole of Sicily was in our hands.

In the event the decision to follow the invasion of Sicily by an invasion of the mainland proved to be a correct one, as it achieved the original limited objectives of knocking the Italian Army out of the war and gaining possession of the airfields at Foggia for use as bases for operations against the southern and eastern areas of Germany. Moreover the campaign tied down 20 Axis divisions which might otherwise have been employed against the Russians or against our own forces in the main battle in Europe.

For convenience the forces employed in Italy will be referred to as the CMF (Central Mediterranean Force) although, as will be seen later, this name was only given to the headquarters for a short time. But before describing the work of the RASC with the CMF, there follows a short account of the part they played in the two preliminary operations.

Preliminaries to Invasion—Capture of Pantelleria and Lampedusa

The capture of Pantelleria and Lampedusa was an essential preliminary to the invasion of Sicily. Although the offensive value of the islands had been largely destroyed by the capture of Tunisia, the Italians had set up advanced listening posts there from which they could get early warning of our intentions. Moreover the airfield on Pantelleria could hold some 80 fighters. This airfield in enemy hands, could be a great nuisance; in our own it would be an important asset, as it would increase the fighter support available for the assault on Sicily.

Considerable opposition was possible from the island garrisons, which were estimated to number 10,000 on Pantelleria and 4,000 on Lampedusa. The plan involved the use of some 12,000 men, the task being allotted to the 1st Infantry Division. The assault, which was mounted from Sousse, was preceded by an extremely heavy air bombardment. On the morning of June 11th, 1943, soon after the first wave of assaulting troops got ashore, the garrison of Pantelleria surrendered. Lampedusa followed suit the next day.

The RASC was represented by more than 100 men, including one transport platoon. It had been expected that there would be a lack of water, and provision had been made to import enough to meet all requirements. However many wells and cisterns were found to be undamaged, and sufficient water was available on the islands.

There was nearly a crisis in the supply situation when stocks fell to only two days owing to the manner in which the stores LCTs and a coaster from Algiers had been loaded. Ammunition, which, in the event, was not required, had been loaded on top of the supplies, and even if it had been agreed to unload the unwanted ammunition, the difficulty of getting the coaster into the port would have delayed the off-loading of the supplies for several days.

After the capture of Pantelleria the enemy made repeated air attacks on the port, and it was during the withdrawal of that part of the invasion force which was not to remain on the island that the few casualties were incurred. The RASC had six men killed and nine wounded out of a total of 113 who took part in the operation.

The Course of Operations in Sicily

The final plan for the invasion of Sicily was based on a series of simultaneous seaborne assaults, assisted by airborne landings, on the south-eastern corner of the island. The plan was to seize the ports of Syracuse and Licata and the airfields within striking distance of the coastline between these two ports, in order to establish a firm base for operations against the Augusta, Catania and Gerbini

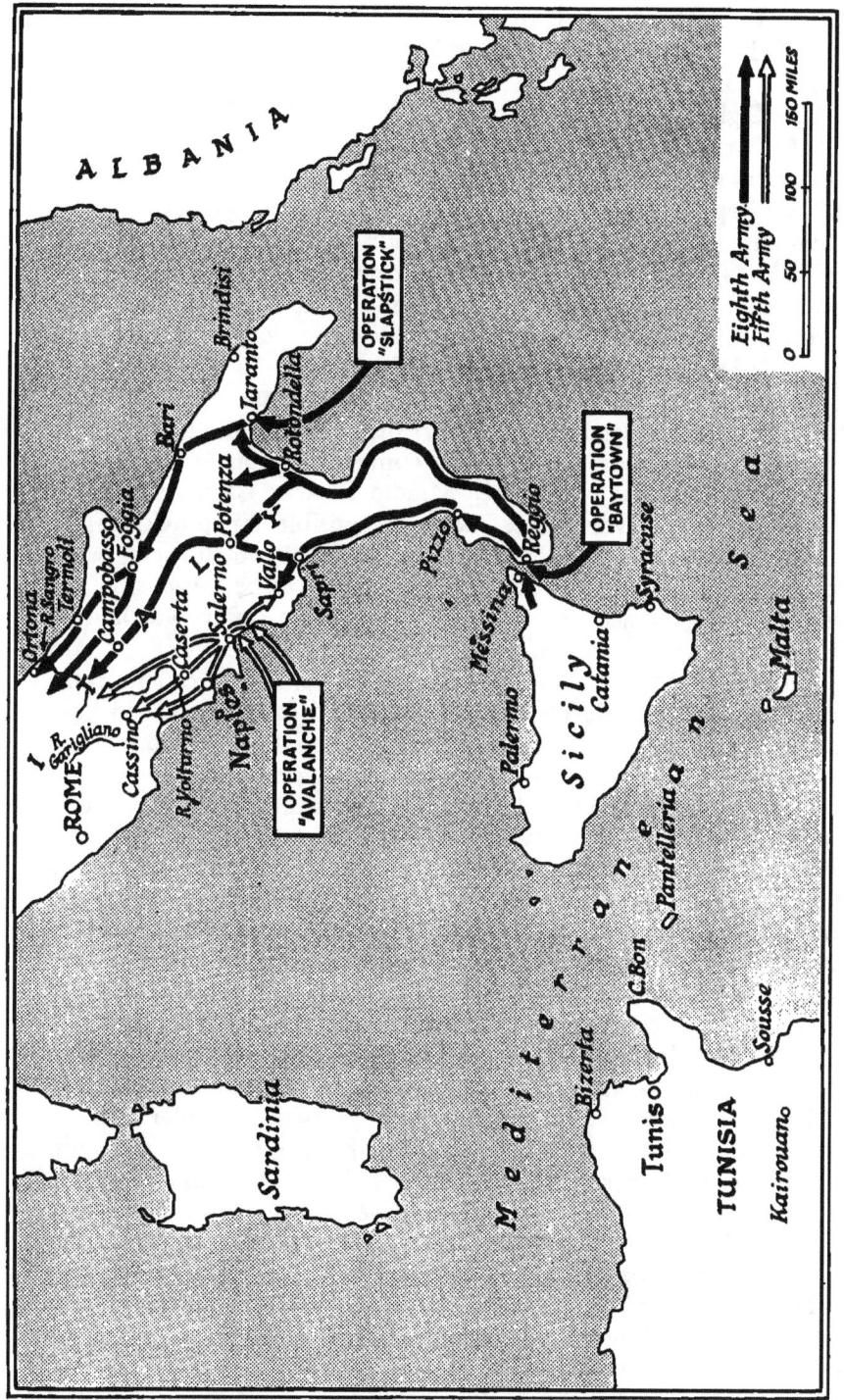

Southern Italy

airfields. The Eighth Army was allotted the eastern sector which included Syracuse, while the American Seventh Army were on their western flank.

The Eighth Army consisted of the XIII and XXX Corps and the 1st Airborne Division. The XIII Corps had the 5th and 50th Divisions and the 4th Armoured Brigade under command. The XXX Corps was made up of the 1st Canadian and 51st (Highland) Divisions, the 23rd Armoured Brigade, and the 231st Infantry Brigade Group, which had been formed from units which had garrisoned Malta. The 78th Division and the 1st Canadian Army Tank Brigade were to be available as a follow-up reserve, and the 46th Division could be called on if required.

Planning and mounting was made difficult because the formations and their headquarters were spread over the Middle East and in North Africa and some were in the United Kingdom. Each of the mounting headquarters—GHQ Middle East at Cairo, AFHQ at Algiers, and the War Office—were responsible for providing the initial maintenance requirements of the forces which were being mounted in their area. GHQ ME was then to be responsible for regular maintenance convoys until D plus 42, after which date fortnightly convoys were to arrive direct from home.

Because of Malta's dominating position and its excellent communications it was decided to use the island as an advanced base and a staging post in the early stages. Eighth Army Headquarters was set up there and a ferry control organization was formed to control the ferrying of build-up units and stores from Malta and Sousse in LSTs. Units awaiting embarkation in the Sousse area were placed in a forecast order of priority, which could be altered to meet the current operational situation in Sicily. Similarly, estimates of probable requirements of stores were worked out to cover the first fortnight and these were to be shipped automatically unless instructions were received from Sicily to alter the order of priority.

One of the chief points of interest for the RASC in the preparations for this operation was the arrival at Djidjelli and Sousse of the first dukws. Of these amphibious vehicles 230, with a smaller number of amphibious jeeps, were allotted to the Eighth Army for the main purpose of getting urgent stores and anti-tank guns ashore in the early stages, before it was possible for vehicles to be driven ashore from LSTs. Three platoons of dukws were also to accompany the 1st Canadian Division.

Most of the dukws were not due to arrive from America until just before the date of the invasion, but a few were provided for training purposes at the end of May, and for six weeks 385 General Transport Company was busily engaged on a sandy beach near

Sousse, training as many men as possible to drive and navigate this novel form of transport.

Because of the lack of port capacity in the American sector, it was planned that the Seventh Army would share the port of Syracuse after D plus 14. In order to meet conflicting claims and settle priorities a special headquarters was planned, known as Fortbase, to control the operation of Sicilian ports and to make allocations between the Allies. As it happened, the great success of the dukws in increasing beach maintenance capacities and the rapidity with which the Americans captured Palermo (D plus 12) made it unnecessary for Fortbase to adopt this role, and it became the British L of C Headquarters in Sicily.

By July 4th all training exercises had been completed and the final stages of water-proofing vehicles were rapidly undertaken. All was ready for the first step in the liberation of Europe.

The airborne landings were timed to take place before midnight July 9th/10th. For many reasons these landings did not go according to plan. Nevertheless a vital bridge south of Syracuse was captured and saved intact by the gallant action of men of the 1st Airborne Division, and a small detachment of American paratroops succeeded in holding valuable high ground at Gela and preventing enemy reinforcements from reaching the beach defences.

The seaborne landings everywhere met with success. Owing to the rough sea the attack completely surprised the enemy. The initial objectives were soon in Allied hands, and the business of beach clearance went rapidly ahead. The dukws immediately proved their worth and, in spite of the bad weather, ensured that the build-up of beach maintenance areas was up to schedule. In less than two days 80,000 men, 7,000 vehicles, 300 tanks and 900 guns were ashore. Both Licata and Syracuse were captured on D Day, and on D plus 3 ships were discharging in the latter port, as well as at Augusta, which had been captured by the 17th Infantry Brigade of the 5th Division.

After early counterattacks against the American sector, the enemy gradually withdrew to strong positions defending the Catanian plain and the western approaches to Etna. With the pressure thus eased on their sector, the American Seventh Army rapidly overran the western half of the island and on July 22nd occupied Palermo without opposition.

Things had gone so well in the first days and the stock position was looking so healthy that it was decided to ferry across the 78th Division from Sousse in LSTs at the expense of a more rapid build-up of stores and supplies. Their arrival was well-timed, as the frontal attack against Catania was meeting with little success, after the initial achievement of the capture of Prima Sole bridge over the

Simeto by a parachute brigade of the 1st Airborne Division and leading elements of the 50th Division.

General Montgomery decided that he would try to turn the enemy's position by a left hook executed by the 1st Canadian Division, which had already reached the important road centre of Enna, and the 78th Division, which he directed on Centuripe. This manœuvre, in combination with an attack by the 51st Division on the Sferro hills, was designed to cut the enemy's communications between the Catanian plain and the road round the western slopes of Mount Etna. At the same time the Americans were making a wider sweep and were advancing along the coastal road from Palermo towards Messina.

On August 2nd Centuripe fell; on the 5th Catania was captured by the 50th Division, and on the 6th the Americans, by capturing Troina, once more linked up with the left flank of the 1st Canadian Division.

The enemy was now mainly concerned with extricating his forces from Sicily and imposing the greatest possible delay on the Allied advance. Aided by a number of small-scale amphibious operations, the 50th Division along the east coast road and the 3rd United States Infantry Division along the north coast made steady progress. On August 17th, after 38 days, the Sicilian campaign came to an end, as patrols of the 3rd United States Infantry Division, closely followed by the 50th Division, entered Messina to find it deserted by the enemy.

The Coming of Dukws

Without doubt, the most important aspect of this campaign for the RASC was the coming of the dukw. It is no exaggeration to say that this wheeled amphibious vehicle revolutionized the business of beach maintenance. By being able to unload direct from LSTs into dukws, which could deliver their loads to beach maintenance dumps without any intermediate handling, we were able to speed up enormously the rate of discharge of stores over beaches. We became less dependent on the weather and calm seas and were not so restricted in our use of beaches. It was easy to divert dukws from an unfavourable beach to a better one without the necessity of moving landing ships and craft and without causing congestion at the beach exits. Owing to the reduced handling there was also a great saving in labour.

Beach maintenance was undertaken by beach groups in the case of formations mounted from the United Kingdom or from North Africa and by beach 'bricks' in the case of formations mounted from the Middle East. These beach 'bricks' consisted of an infantry battalion with the necessary service units and depots attached. In the case of the RASC these consisted of two platoons of a general transport company, a small petrol depot and a detail issue depot. They had been rapidly formed and trained in the Middle East and carried out their beach maintenance functions admirably.

In the planning of an amphibious operation there is always great competition for the available transport capacity in the assault and follow-up phases. In some cases in this operation the maintenance of formations was made more difficult by the failure to include sufficient second line transport in the early stages of the build-up.

Another problem faced by the RASC was that of rapidly collecting the transport of the divisional column in the beach-head. In the case of the 5th Division the RASC was dispersed over 46 different ships.

There was no real problem in connection with supplies. All troops landed in Sicily with a 48-hour mess-tin ration. 'Compo' rations were issued until D plus 18 (July 28th) after which normal bulk rations were issued. Fresh bread was supplied from D plus 13. To begin with, this was baked in Malta and despatched daily by LCT. Later two field bakeries were set up in Sicily, and contracts were made with civil bakeries in Syracuse and Catania.

Although plans had been made for the supply of petrol in bulk to airfields in Sicily, it proved impossible to develop bulk supply until the campaign was over. Good bulk storage existed at Syracuse and Catania, but this was extensively sabotaged by the Germans and took several weeks to put in order. There was no movement of petrol in bulk by road tank wagons during the campaign, as it had not been possible to give a sufficiently high priority to bulk petrol transport companies.

In the maintenance planning large tonnages had been set aside for drinking-water, a great deal of it in 44-gallon drums. In the event, none of it was required and considerable delay in unloading other urgently required commodities was caused by the necessity of unloading the water first.

It had been foreseen that there would be a need for pack transport in the mountainous areas in central Sicily, and six pack transport companies had been included in the order of battle. However these were very low on the priority list, and there was hardly a hope of their arriving until the end of the campaign. Plans were also made to make use of local Sicilian mules and saddlery. The 1st Canadian Division brought 250 sets of pack saddlery with its reserves of equipment, and every infantry battalion, field regiment and field company in the Eighth Army was equipped with 30 pairs of mule pack ropes each. A small veterinary detachment was attached to each corps headquarters. As it turned out these arrangements proved most valuable, but the improvisation that was necessary in order to raise local pack transport placed a heavy burden on all those involved, and it would clearly have been much better if a properly trained unit had been shipped across in the early days of the invasion. Two troops of a RASC pack transport unit did actually take part in the final stages of the advance on Messina.

As soon as infantry brigades found themselves in hilly country, they made sudden demands for pack transport. Apart from the 78th Division, which had operated with pack transport in Tunisia, the only formations which had received any mountain warfare training at all were part of the 5th Division and 51st Division, which had a few men who had been through the mountain warfare wing of the Combined Training Centre in North Africa. These men were lent to the 1st Canadian Division, which had the greatest need for pack transport, but even so they were quite inadequate to meet the situation. For instance, in the carriage of one batch of 115 mules to the forward area in 3-ton lorries, no fewer than 36 mules became casualties; 15 jumped out of the lorries, two arrived with broken legs, and 19 others were unfit for work for one reason or another. Most of the work of requisitioning mules fell on CsRASC, who already had their hands full. The animals obtained varied from donkeys, yearling half-breeds, brood mares (in season) and jack mules to first class mountain pack mules. This requisitioning was not popular, and Sicilian owners engaged to assist in looking after the animals frequently disappeared with their beasts. In all 600 mules were used, and 150 of these were later taken over by the RASC Pack Transport Group. There was no difficulty in obtaining all the forage that was wanted in Sicily.

One other point on RASC supply is worth mentioning: in the final stages of the 50th Division's advance on Messina the leading troops could not be reached by road owing to the extensive demolitions along the Corniche road. These troops were maintained by embarking six loaded lorries in a LCT which plied between Riposto and Scaletta, a distance of over 20 miles.

The Sicilian campaign taught us many lessons, which we were able to put to good use in subsequent amphibious assaults. Perhaps the lesson which struck home most forcibly was that many of the expected difficulties and problems which had been a great source of worry during the planning stages, in practice never materialized at all. After the successful invasion of Sicily, all those who had taken part were supremely confident of the next step—the invasion of the mainland of Italy itself.

The Invasion of Italy

Owing to the promise of an early surrender by the Italians, after their loss of Sicily, there was little time to plan for the assault on

Forage for the Mules

Army Supply Dump

Supply Dump at Anzio

the mainland, and some of the formations due to take part in it, such as the 5th Division and 1st Canadian Division, were still awaiting the balance of their transport and equipment, which was not due to arrive until some weeks after the assault was to take place.

The plan for the assault involved three operations: 'Baytown', an assault across the straits of Messina on September 3rd, which was to be effected by XIII Corps with 5th British and the 1st Canadian Divisions; 'Avalanche', the assault on Salerno on September 9th, which was to be undertaken by the American Fifth Army, which included X British Corps, with 46th and 56th Divisions and the 7th Armoured Division under command; and 'Slapstick', which was to be directed against Taranto on the evening of September 9th by V Corps, which was allotted the 1st Airborne Division, the 78th Division, and the 8th Indian Division for the purpose.

Other formations, which were to be available if required, were the 1st Division, 2nd New Zealand Division and the 25th Tank Brigade.

The general direction of the campaign was the responsibility of the Supreme Allied Commander, at that time General Eisenhower whose headquarters, Allied Force Headquarters, was located at Algiers. General Alexander, whose headquarters was the HQ 15 Army Group, was responsible for the conduct of operations, his two armies the Eighth (British) and Fifth (American) being commanded by General Montgomery and General Mark Clark respectively.

Initially HQ 15 Army Group was relieved of responsibility for administration and maintenance, a special headquarters, an advanced administrative echelon of the AFHQ, called Flambo, being provided for the purpose. The provision of the requirements of the force was undertaken by the main Allied headquarters which remained at Algiers until May, 1944, when it was moved to the Royal Palace at Caserta, near Naples.

Some time after the armies were established on the mainland, HQ 15 Army Group was renamed HQ Allied Central Mediterranean Forces, and the Flambo organization was incorporated into it, thus reverting to the normal organization whereby operations and administration are controlled by the same headquarters. A little later the name of the headquarters was changed again, to HQ Allied Armies in Italy.

As AFHQ did not move to Italy until May, 1944, the brunt of the task of building up the RASC organization in Italy fell on Brigadier Hinde who as DDST at Flambo and its successors was the senior RASC officer in the theatre. When AFHQ took over direct responsibility for the administration of the force the HQ AAI

S RASC

reverted to the original name of HQ 15 Army Group and became an operational headquarters only. The DST (Major-General Whitty) then dealt direct on ST matters with the DDSTs of the two armies and the DDSTs of the districts into which the rear areas were divided. Both the DDSTs of the two armies were officers of the Territorial Army, Brigadiers H. J. Gilman and S. T. Divers, and each in turn held the appointment of DDST of both armies.

There were several changes in the high command during the campaign. When General Eisenhower was withdrawn to take command of the forces in Europe his place was taken by General Wilson. When he left at the end of 1944 to take up another appointment in the United States, General Alexander became the Supreme Allied Commander, his place at Army Group being filled by General Mark Clark.

The Landings in Italy; Operation 'Baytown'

During the early stages of the assault across the Straits of Messina and the subsequent advance, the 5th British and 1st Canadian Divisions were maintained by four amphibious companies, RASC, plying backwards and forwards across the Straits from dumps in the neighbourhood of Messina to the beaches just north of Reggio. The dukws of 385 Company were off-loading on the beaches within one and a half hours of H hour. Because of the early withdrawal of the enemy, there had been little expenditure of ammunition, and the beach maintenance areas were rapidly stocked up. The dukws presented a considerable traffic problem in the narrow walled roads just north of Reggio, and, until traffic circuits had been made and roads widened, the congestion presented a vulnerable target to the enemy air force.

Two troops of mules accompanied one of the leading brigades of the 5th Division which advanced direct into the hills behind Reggio. They crossed the straits in LCTs. Considerable difficulty was experienced in embarking the mules, which took a great dislike to the ribbed decks of the landing craft. These mules accompanied the 5th Division as far as the River Garigliano, where they had to be left behind when the division went to Anzio; they covered the whole distance on foot and although they often marched well behind the rest of the division, they managed to keep up with the average rate of advance of the division over a period of five months.

The advance up the coast road on either side of the toe of Italy was hampered by frequent obstructions, and the rate of advance was only maintained by the use of dukws and landing craft, which were used both for ferrying troops forward and for the carriage of maintenance stores.

A landing by the 231st Infantry Brigade (the Malta Brigade) at

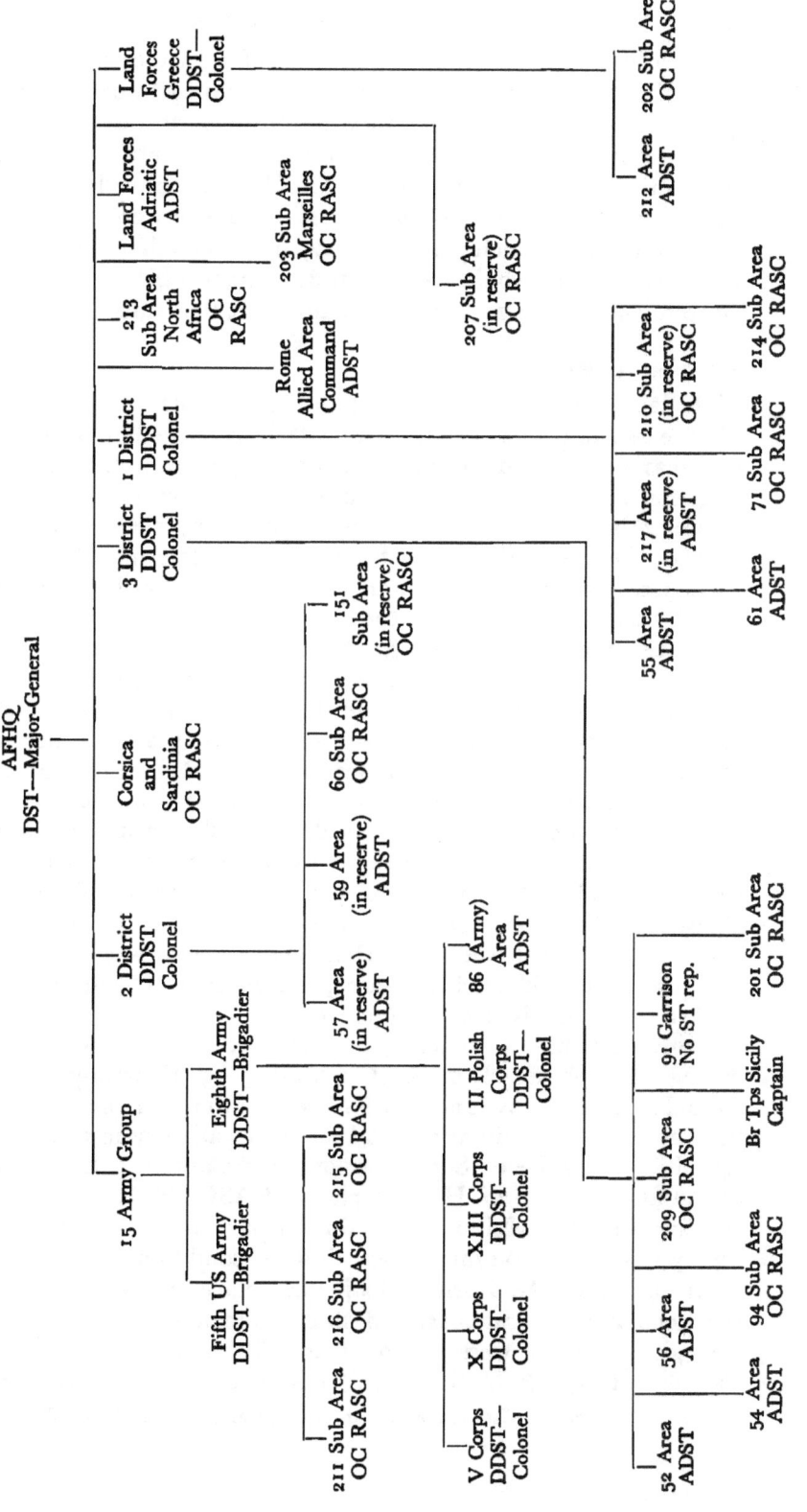

Pizzo early on the morning of September 8th in the enemy's rear materially assisted the advance and the continued threat of similar operations hastened the German withdrawal northwards.

It was seldom possible for XIII Corps to establish a FMC* sufficiently far forward, and so CsRASC were compelled to hold and carry larger reserves than is normal. These were moved forward by ferrying, which placed a heavy burden on divisional second line transport and would have been quite impossible if the column had not consisted of 10 transport platoons at that time.

Operation 'Avalanche'

The landings at Salerno were planned to take place on September 9th, the morning after the armistice with Italy, signed on September 3rd, was to be made public. It was hoped that the resulting confusion would enable the assaulting troops to get well established ashore without having to overcome strongly organized opposition. Instead, they met on the beaches strong and determined German resistance. Anticipating such an assault, the enemy had strengthened his defences, and at the time a German division was engaged on an exercise in Salerno Bay. Instead of being demoralized by the defection of the Italians, the Germans redoubled their efforts and fought fiercely to annihilate the assaulting forces, to give themselves time to reorganize themselves in Italy and to meet the possible threat to their communications from their turn-coat ally.

For a week Fifth Army's position at Salerno was precarious. During this period the RASC played their full part in keeping the forces in the beach-head supplied. By the evening of D Day, 519 Company and a detachment of 521 Company, part of the 46th Divisional Transport Column, were ashore and maintained the division for the first week. 58 Detail Issue Depot was also ashore on D Day in the 56th Divisional area, and the dukws of 239 Company worked continuously from ship to shore.

Many immediate awards for gallantry were earned by RASC men during this phase. Dvr R. G. Millea, 25 Company (Motor Ambulance Company) and Dvr R. Leese, of the 56th Division, were both awarded the Military Medal for their gallantry in evacuating casualties under fire on September 9th, and Captain J. E. Johnson, ammunition officer of Headquarters CRASC, X Corps Troops, was awarded the Military Cross for his part in ensuring the vital supply of ammunition under most difficult conditions. During the following days RASC drivers took their place in the line to help repel enemy counterattacks, and three more ambulance drivers of the 56th Division were awarded the Military Medal: Dvr E. Caudwell, Dvr C. F. V. Bott and Dvr K. E. Shaw (who had already

* Field Maintenance Centre, now known as Corps Maintenance Area (CMA).

won the Distinguished Conduct Medal in the Western Desert). The same award was also earned by Dvr F. Shearsby, Headquarters, 94 Sub-Area.

By September 16th, when patrols from the 5th Division advancing through Calabria linked up with a patrol of the Fifth Army at Vallo, the beach-head was at last secure and the Germans began to withdraw.

The Capture of Naples

The infantry divisions of X Corps opened the way for the 7th Armoured Division to pass through. This formation now consisted of the 22nd Armoured and 131st Lorried Infantry Brigades, and with it were 58, 67, 287 and 507 Companies, RASC. The Lorried Infantry Brigade fought its way into the plain of Naples against the stubborn resistance of the German rearguards. In this fighting Dvr H. Woodason, of 287 Company, won an immediate award of the Military Medal.

Naples was captured on October 1st; X Corps, with the 7th Armoured and 56th Infantry Divisions, pushed on rapidly to the River Volturno.

The docks area of Naples had been heavily damaged by Allied bombing and German demolitions. Nevertheless by the full use of beaches and small ports the capacity soon reached 9,000 tons a day. Base supply depots were rapidly established, and field bakeries were soon in operation; fresh bread was already being issued to forward troops by the end of September.

Landings at Taranto

It had been appreciated from the beginning that, owing to the lack of communications across the Apennines, an advance up the Italian peninsula could not be maintained entirely from the west coast ports in the Bay of Naples and that any forces following the east coast would require maintenance ports in the heel of Italy. It was not expected that the maintenance routes through Calabria would be able to support XIII Corps's advance much beyond Potenza; even before the advance had reached as far as this, it was necessary to develop Sapri as a sea-head, in order to cut out the long road haul from Reggio. With a view to capturing the ports of Taranto, Brindisi and Bari, operation 'Slapstick' was planned, on the assumption that with the surrender of the Italian Navy there would be no opposition at Taranto. Elements of the 1st Airborne Division were embarked in ships of the Royal Navy and on the evening of September 9th captured the port and its neighbouring airfields. Among the first troops of the Airborne Division to land were 136 all ranks of the divisional RASC. No army vehicles accompanied the landing, and so the maintenance of the division depended on the greatest use of requisitioned transport and of the railway, whenever possible. Brindisi was occupied on September 11th and Bari on the 13th, and while the 78th Infantry Division were beginning to arrive at Taranto, patrols linked up with the 1st Canadian Division advancing from the south-west near Rotondella on September 16th, the same day that the junction between the 5th Division and the Fifth Army took place. By September 25th the Allied line ran roughly Bari–Potenza–Auletta–Salerno, and the two armies were poised for their advance to Naples and Foggia.

The Administrative Situation

While the Fifth Army went on to capture Naples, it was now necessary for the Eighth Army to make a short pause in order to allow certain administrative adjustments to be made. For several days the Eighth Army formations had been pushed on as fast as possible in order to ease the pressure at Salerno, and this had stretched the maintenance resources to their limit. The lines of communication had now to be switched from the toe to the heel of Italy. At the same time V Corps was in process of landing at Taranto, and XIII Corps was being side-stepped across from Potenza to the Foggia plain. Not until October 1st was the advance resumed. This did not, however, prevent the 4th Armoured Brigade, which was still maintained by 5 Company, RASC, from making a sudden thrust forward and capturing the important group of airfields around Foggia on September 27th.

This was a time of great strain for the transport, stretched as it was along winding coastal roads from Reggio to Sapri, with innumerable diversions and one-way stretches. It was a common experience for drivers to be at the wheel for 36 hours at a stretch with only occasional snatches of sleep. The 5th Divisional Transport Column had to maintain the division for 10 days from Sapri to its location in the Foggia plain and at the same time meet troop carrying commitments. The use of dukws was invaluable, and without them it would not have been possible to maintain the speed of advance.

The supply problem presented no unusual aspects during this period, except the need to hold larger reserves than normal within divisions.

The supply programme for the forces assaulting at Salerno was:—

D Day to D plus 1: 48-hour mess-tin ration supplemented by one tin of preserved meat and a packet of biscuits.
D plus 2 to D plus 18: Compo rations.

D plus 19 onwards: Half compo and half field service scale gradually changing to 100 per cent field service scale.

By the end of September (D plus 21) the issue of 'compo' rations had ceased and fresh bread was being issued to forward troops.

The scale of petrol landed at Salerno was based on vehicles travelling 25 miles a day from D Day to D plus 6 and 50 miles a day from D plus 7 onwards. An allowance of 30 per cent was originally made for waste, leakages, losses by enemy action and other causes, but this was later cut to 10 per cent.

The main problem in the supply of petroleum was to keep the rapid advance up the east coast supplied. This advance had outrun its stocks and, until a ship could be unloaded at Taranto, convoys consisting of whatever transport could be made available (including dukws), were run across from the west coast from Salerno and Sapri.

Bulk storage tanks at Naples, Taranto and Bari, many of them damaged, were soon repaired, and two bulk petroleum storage companies were set to work in order to introduce bulk supply as soon as possible.

For the RASC the keynote of this phase of the campaign was improvisation. Divisional RASC maintained units of their divisions without any transport; field butcheries acted as port detachments; field bakeries operated as base supply depots; a mobile petroleum laboratory supervised the manufacture of a substitute for hydraulic brake fluid from captured castor oil and industrial alcohol. Planning yardsticks and establishment capacities went by the board. Somehow, by one means or another, the results were achieved and the armies were successfully supplied, until gradually a normal state of affairs was restored.

The Italian Theatre

At this stage in the narrative we may suitably pause to examine some of the general features which were to affect the operations which ensued and the administrative problems which arose. The forces which could be made available for the campaign had to be subordinated to the claims of 'Overlord', the operation for the invasion of north-west Europe, which began on June 6th, just two days after the forces in Italy had taken Rome.

Italy was therefore always low on the priority list, particularly where American resources were concerned. This resulted in the withdrawal of experienced formations and units from Italy for service in North-West Europe, while at the same time the army in Italy was being gradually increased by formations drawn from elsewhere. Thus the order of battle was rarely static and from an

ST point of view the business of forecasting the strengths and nationalities to be fed became something of an art.

As the campaign progressed the army began to assume an almost international appearance as in addition to American, French, Brazilian and British formations there were divisions from the Canadian, New Zealand and Indian Armies and a Polish Corps, and there were also single brigades of Palestine Jews and from the Royal Greek Army. When the Italian Army was reformed, a number of 'gruppi' joined the armies.

The RASC, whose strength rose to almost the same as the total strength of the pre-war Regular Army at home, had an even greater diversity of nations in its ranks, with companies manned by Ceylonese, Cypriots, Mauritians, Basutos, and Arabs from both Arabia and North Africa. They also had a large number of units manned by Italian co-operators, former prisoners of war who volunteered to serve with us, and later more companies were found by the Italian army. It was a process of what was known as 'dilution', the replacement of British ranks by others, the British then being used as cadres to raise more units, as all units had a cadre of British officers, senior NCOs and technical tradesmen. Towards the end of the campaign the Corps had to give up many men to other arms and in turn to take in men of lower medical categories who were surplus to the requirements of their own arm. In the last stages several RA anti-aircraft units were converted into GT companies.

Many changes also had to be made in the role of units, such as the conversion of surplus artillery companies into GT companies. The RASC Training Depot which had to be formed in Italy was an interesting experiment, as instruction had to be given to eight different nationalities and 42 different courses arranged for giving instruction to the various categories of RASC men which were required. The formation of new units and reorganization of others were done by a RASC mobilization centre which was also formed in Italy for the purpose.

The geographical features of the Italian peninsula had a considerable effect on both the operational and administrative plans, the country being divided by mountain ranges running from just south of the northern plains to the 'toe' and 'heel' of Italy. There were few good lateral communications between the Adriatic coast and the coastline along the Tyrrhenian sea. In the initial advance the Fifth Army made its way up the western coast and the Eighth Army on the eastern. There had to be a common system of communications for both armies, as during the ensuing operations the weight of one army was transferred from one coast to the other. The factors which were common to both road and rail communications were the almost complete destruction of every bridge, of which there were hundreds, by the enemy as he withdrew to the north, and vast damage to culverts, tunnels and road passes. Docks also were in many cases badly damaged, and the general result was to create a never ceasing demand for road transport, for the repair of roads, for carrying forward bridging material, and for dock clearance. The Italian campaign was administratively an engineer and a transport battle.

The first principal administrative task was to repair the port facilities which had been damaged and then to develop them to keep pace with the desired rate of intake of the thousands of tons of stores of all kinds which were wanted for the armies and for the civil population, as the division of Italy by the opposing forces had left the peoples in the south bereft of their main sources of supply of manufactured goods and grain.

The main base ports were at Naples on the west coast and Bari, Brindisi, and, to a lesser extent, Taranto on the east. Port clearance had to take first priority, and special organizations were set up to co-ordinate the activity of the American and British transport allotted for the task.

Owing to the extensive damage to the railways and damage to road bridges and road works, the early capture of other ports, and getting them into working order, as the army advanced to the north were vital. Even so, when Leghorn on the west coast, and Ancona on the east, were taken, supply to the two armies still remained partly dependent on the main bases in the south. As the armies moved up to the north, movement by rail was only possible in the British sector from Naples as far as Arezzo, which lay to the west of the great mountain range which divided the country, as it was found impossible to repair the main line which ran from Bari on the east coast to keep pace with the rate of advance.

Consequently, in the later stages of the campaign, the armies had to be maintained by three methods: by direct shipments, for example, from home to advanced base ports and then by road or rail to army roadheads; by coastal shipping (many RASC vessels being employed on this task) from the main base ports to the advanced bases; and by rail, where it was possible, from Naples and Bari.

Although every means of raising new transport companies was employed, when the final advance to the Po was being planned, the number of divisions which could be employed had to be restricted, as there was insufficient road transport to keep all available divisions supplied.

To some extent the lack of internal communications was made good by water transport, and eventually four RASC water transport companies were operating 131 vessels, most of which were chartered.

These vessels carried nearly 200,000 tons in 12 months, and not only plied along the coast, but went farther afield to Corsica, Sardinia, Sicily, Malta, and to the island of Vis, which served as a base for assistance to the partisans in Yugoslavia. They were a valuable contribution towards the general transport problem, and it is pleasing to record that the RASC ensign was usually the first to be seen at each coastal port as soon as the 'all clear' to enter had been given by the Navy.

Another main contribution, which the RASC were able to provide, was pack transport, although it only had a limited use under conditions when other forms of transport could not be used. But by the end of the campaign nearly 40,000 mules and horses were being employed, and unquestionably the campaign could not have been fought without them.

The methods adopted for supplying petroleum also helped considerably to reduce the load on rail and road. Pipelines were laid wherever practicable, and supply in bulk was used to the greatest possible extent. The speed with which bulk supply could be arranged depended on how soon the existing civil installations, both coastal and inland, could be taken into use and large scale filling points and filling centres set up in the forward areas. As the army advanced reconnaissance parties from the HQ CRASC petroleum installations were among the first to arrive as each main town or port was taken, when they made an immediate survey of the means of intake and storage facilities available and assessed the labour and material wanted for any repair or rehabilitation. By this means no time was lost, and the work of repair was put in hand at once. Considerable ingenuity was displayed in the provision of filling points and extemporary filling places. Although the constructional work was nominally an engineer responsibility, many of the points were set up by the petroleum unit's own men, who vied with one another in attaining that 'oil man's' objective, the right bend in the pipe.

The main pipeline which was used in support of the armies in their advance from Cassino to Rome started at Naples and was then built up as the army advanced. It followed the line of advance approximately along the main national road, Route 6. When Ancona was captured main lines were laid from there *via* Senegalia to Forli and as far north as Ferrara on the eastern coast. On the west coast lines were laid from Leghorn up to Bologna.

Another comprehensive system of pipelines was provided for supplying the many airfields in the Foggia Plains, bulk supplies being drawn from Taranto and Manfredonia.

An account of the other special features which marked the work of the RASC in Italy can be more appropriately reserved until the end of the general narrative which follows of the work of the Corps in the advance to Rome and after.

Preparations for the Capture of Rome

After the capture of Naples and Foggia and the evacuation, at the end of September, of Corsica by the Germans, it appeared that the German intention was to withdraw gradually to the north of Italy, delaying our advance as much as possible on a succession of natural defensive positions. But by the end of the first week of October it was clear that the enemy was determined to defend the capital. Considerable reinforcement of German troops south of Rome became apparent, and it was clear that with the assistance of the winter rains and by making full use of the natural obstacles in the way of an Allied advance, the Germans could make the capture of Rome a hard and difficult task. And so it turned out. The Allies had hoped to be in Rome before Christmas, 1943, but it was nearly six months before the first European capital was liberated on June 4th, 1944.

The series of positions on which the Germans based their defence was known as the Winter Line, which included both the notorious Gustav and Hitler Lines and the key position of Monte Cassino.

This part of the campaign falls into two distinct phases; the advance of the Allied armies to the Winter Line, and the series of battles for Cassino, culminating in the capture of Rome.

The first phase in the battle for Rome consisted of hard and bitter fighting in steadily worsening weather as the Fifth and Eighth Armies slowly drove in the outposts of the Winter Line and prepared for the assault on the strongly defended main German positions.

The Fifth Army, after crossing the River Volturno in the face of stubborn resistance, found on their western flank a level plain intersected with irrigation canals and overlooked by the formidable Monte Massico, and on their eastern flank a series of strong mountains which had to be stormed in turn before the advance could continue. At the end of October the assault on Monte Massico was launched by the 7th Armoured Division, and by November 2nd patrols of the 7th Armoured and the 46th Divisions reached the River Garigliano. Meanwhile, to the north-east, the 56th Division and the 201st Guards Brigade were pushing ahead through the mountains. On November 5th the mountain mass of Camino, La Difensa and Monte Maggiore, dominating the road to Rome through Cassino, was attacked by X Corps while the United States VI Corps attempted to force its way through the Mignano Gap. A fortnight's bitter fighting just failed to secure these objectives, and on November 15th the advance was halted.

After a period of regrouping (the 7th Armoured Division had

been withdrawn from the Fifth Army in order to take part in the assault on North-West Europe), the attack was resumed with X Corps (46th and 56th Divisions and 201st Guards Brigade) and the United States II Corps. By December 9th Camino was taken and, with the capture of Monte Trocchio by the Americans on January 15th, the stage was set for the great battles for Cassino.

Meanwhile the Eighth Army made steady progress on the east coast. A spirited seaborne attack by the 78th Division secured Termoli, and soon afterwards the River Trigno was crossed. XIII Corps, with the 5th Division and the 1st Canadian Division, captured Campobasso and Isernia and fought their way through the mountains to the higher reaches of the River Sangro. At the end of November V Corps, with the 78th Division, the 8th Indian Division, the 2nd New Zealand Division and the 4th Armoured Brigade, crossed the River Sangro, only to come up against increasing German resistance. In order to increase the weight of the attack, the 78th Division relieved the 5th Division and 1st Canadian Division in the comparatively quiet central sector, and four divisions—the 1st Canadian, the 8th Indian, the 5th British and the 2nd New Zealand—were packed into the bridgehead across the Sangro. For the whole of December the enemy's defences were hammered, but it became clear by the end of the year that further attempts to break through in this sector would be unprofitable and that a completely new plan would be required to defeat the enemy's Winter Line.

This phase of the campaign introduced or foreshadowed most of the difficulties of supply which the RASC was going to experience during the rest of the Italian campaign: the extensive use of jeep and mule tracks, of porterage and air supply, the delivery of great quantities of gun ammunition to most awkwardly sited gun positions, and the carriage forward of many tons of bridging material.

The United States Fifth Army was well equipped with jeeps (or 'bantams' as they were then called in British formations) and 10-cwt trailers. It was not long before X Corps was able to get some of these for the British divisions in the Fifth Army. The 46th and 56th Divisions, and later the 5th Division, all had a jeep and trailer platoon as part of the divisional column. These platoons, which had a carrying capacity of about 30 tons, were invaluable. With four-wheel drive, double reduction gear and chains, they could go almost anywhere where a tracked vehicle could go. They could go around most obstacles and across the lightest bridge. They were mainly used for delivering artillery ammunition to gun sites and for extending the MT link beyond the point where 3-tonners could go. Without them a great deal more mule transport than was ever likely to be available would have been required, and many

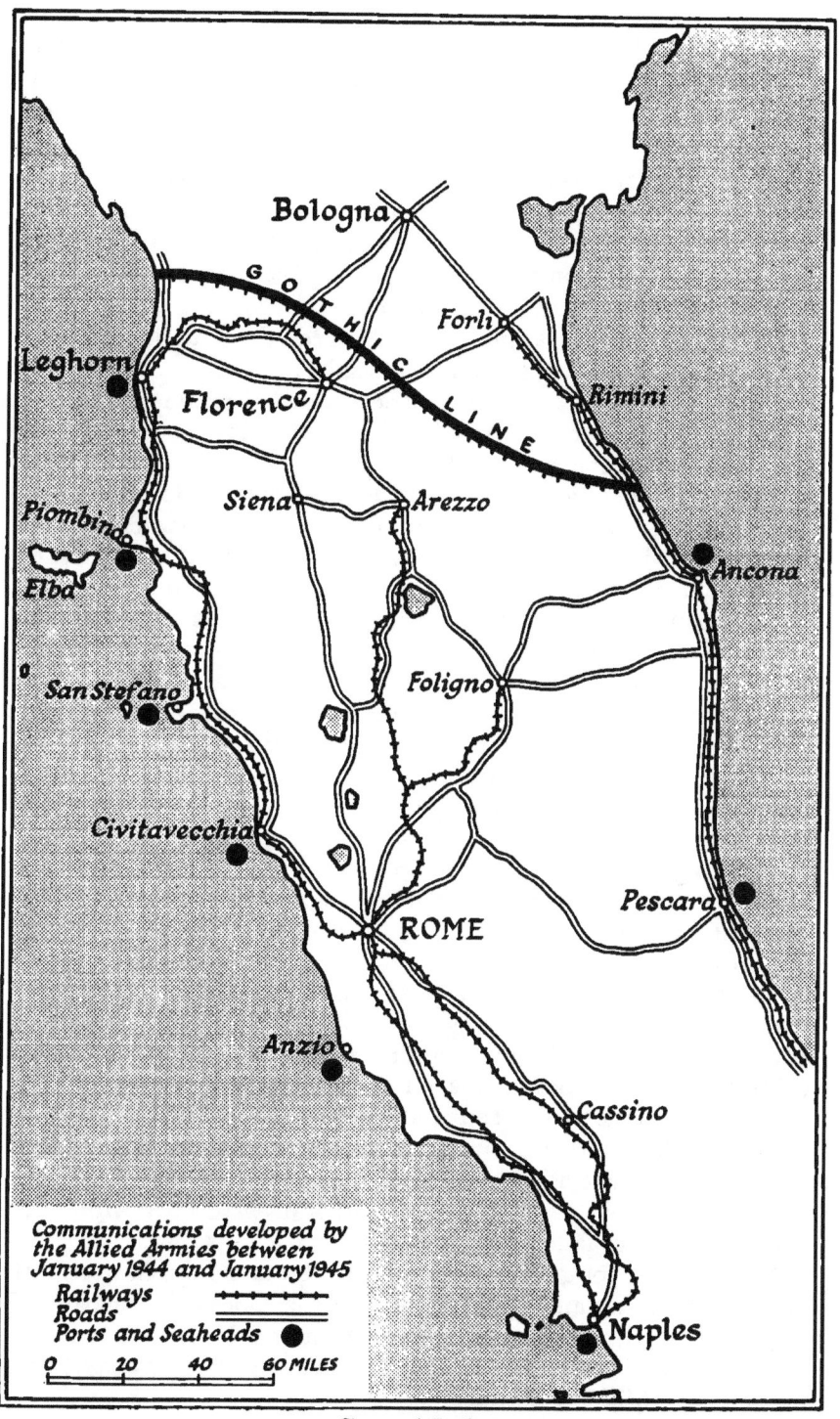

Central Italy

operations would have been quite impossible to undertake. An example of their use can be taken from an operation of a battalion in the 5th Division to take the small town of Alfedena. This operation involved an advance of some 12 miles over very difficult country. The route was inaccessible to ordinary motor transport owing to the narrowness of some of the tracks and the destruction of many small bridges, one of them over a rapidly flowing stream. Two companies of mules were barely sufficient to meet the requirements of the battalion over six miles. By using jeeps and trailers a 'jeep-head' was established four miles beyond the point where MT could go, and it was just possible to keep the battalion supplied long enough for the capture of its objective.

During this phase two North African mule companies—573 and 574 Pack Transport Companies, which were formed into a pack transport group commanded by Lieut-Colonel J. Dudgeon—were constantly in operation; there were never enough mules to meet all the commitments, and these two companies were switched from division to division in the Eighth Army as each formation established its claim for their assistance. In the type of operation undertaken, two companies were just about enough to meet the first line requirements of an infantry brigade, so that operations over country restricted to mule tracks were limited in their range of action to about 8 to 10 miles from a road-head or 'jeep-head'.

In X Corps improvised pack transport units were formed from Italian army mules, and these proved invaluable in the mountain areas in which the corps was operating.

The pack transport companies throughout, in spite of being heavily over-worked and of the unpleasant conditions and the many casualties which they suffered, kept up a high morale, as the following extract from a letter by the Officer Commanding 4 Pack Transport Group shows:—

'We had rather an interesting incident a few days ago. A party with 50 mules were returning to roadhead early in the morning and came across a German fighting patrol of one officer and 17 other ranks. Our party took all the Germans prisoner. Really rather remarkable as you can well imagine the gigantic superiority of German fire-power! It appears to have been a foggy morning, and the Germans evidently came to the conclusion that they were faced by a big party. Our British corporals were busy with their Tommy guns but failed to score a hit!'

Many awards for gallantry were earned by men in pack transport units at this time; among them were Farrier Cpl G. H. Sharpe, of 574 Pack Transport Company, who won the Military Medal at Jelsi, and Cpl E. Orford, of 573 Pack Transport Company, who also won the Military Medal.

X Corps found that it was necessary in the mountainous country in which they were operating to rely on porters in addition to mules in order to get supplies forward. At a later stage these duties were performed by auxiliary military pioneer companies, but during this period, when such companies were not available, infantry battalions were used in this role, and during the autumn of 1943, when they were badly needed in the firing line, as many as three whole battalions had to be used for carrying supplies.

Numerous attempts were made to drop supplies to forward positions, mainly in the Fifth Army sector, but few of these sorties were successful owing to the small target areas and the very difficult flying conditions in the mountains. In the central sector, after a particularly heavy fall of snow, a number of units of the 5th Infantry Division amounting to almost a brigade group, were cut off for over a week near Agnone and were maintained entirely by air supply, the RASC having to collect the widely dispersed loads on skis.

Some idea of the quantities of artillery ammunition fired in these battles can be given by the following example: in a 24-hour period on December 2nd and 3rd, 1943, the artillery of the United States II Corps fired 64,000 rounds (about 1,500 tons) of ammunition, and the X Corps artillery fired 89,883 rounds, of which nearly 76,000 was 25-pounder ammunition. Later in the campaign even heavier barrages were fired. This all placed a heavy burden on RASC transport, owing to the inaccessible positions in which the gunners often managed to site their guns. Here the jeep platoons proved invaluable.

Most of the Royal Engineers' effort at this time was devoted to the re-building of bridges and the repair of the heavily damaged roads. This involved the carriage forward of great quantities of bridging materials and of army track.

In the operations on the Volturno, 236 Bridge Company took part in the building of six bridges over the river in the X Corps sector: and for the 390-foot-long Bailey bridge which was built over the River Trigno in the Eighth Army sector, 71 3-ton and two 10-ton lorries were required as well as six tippers. Great quantities of army track were also carried forward. Most of these operations had to be conducted either by day under enemy machine-gun and artillery fire or by night. For his part in a bridging operation in the 78th Division's area, Cpl G. P. Mann, of 142 General Transport Company, was awarded the Military Medal.

The bridge over the River Sangro was 1,000 feet long, and tank transporter tractors were used to winch Bailey bridging across the gaps. Owing to their length these bridges were only single-track and caused severe bottlenecks on the maintenance routes, and traffic blocks of up to 15 miles were quite normal.

Because of the delay in building bridges under enemy fire, it became a common practice to maintain the troops in a bridgehead round the mouth of the river which had just been crossed. This was done on the Volturno, where 519 Company maintained units of the 46th Division from a dump established on the south bank of the river, using its dukws to carry supplies and ammunition down stream and round the mouth of the river to the beaches just north of it, where an advanced dump was established. LCTs were also used for the same purpose.

Similarly 385 Amphibious Company ferried stores in its dukws across the mouth of the Sangro (an hour's journey by sea) after the river had risen seven feet and washed away the temporary bridges, isolating the troops on the far shore. This method of maintenance continued for five days (mostly at night and in mist) until the bridges were rebuilt. Casualties and prisoners were brought back in the returning craft.

During this period many RASC men won awards for gallantry, among them Cpl L. W. Dickens, of 276 Company (V Corps Transport) and Dvrs G. H. Jury and D. V. Pitcher, of the 5th Division, Dvr F. A. J. Baker of the 46th Division, and Dvr A. Keir, all of whom were awarded the Military Medal.

It was quite clear, by the middle of December, that all hope of breaking through the German positions by frontal attack was gone. Early in November a plan had been made for a sea-borne flank attack in the Anzio area, in order to turn the enemy's position and hasten the capture of Rome, but the main attacks had failed to make sufficient progress in time. Now the landing craft were to be withdrawn for the projected assault on North-West Europe. However, it happened that the Prime Minister was recuperating from a serious illness in North Africa, and on Christmas Day, 1943, he held a conference at which most of the commanders-in-chief in the Mediterranean were present.

It was decided that the early capture of Rome was essential both for political and other reasons; that the best chance of accomplishing this lay in reviving the Anzio plan and staging the sea-borne attack in conjunction with a new assault on the main German positions; and that sufficient landing craft would be retained in the theatre to meet the needs of the assaulting formations.

The plan involved the strengthening of the Fifth Army by the move of the 5th Infantry Division from the Eighth Army to X Corps and the formation of an Allied assault corps—the American VI Corps, consisting of the American 3rd Division and the British 1st Division—for the attack at Anzio.

This first battle for Cassino began with the Fifth Army's attack on the Gustav Line on January 17th, followed five days later on

Hove Dump

Supply Point

Jerricans

Refuelling the Navy

January 22nd by the landings at Anzio. At first everything went reasonably well. Strong German resistance was met on the Garigliano and the Rapido, but this only showed that the German reserves were committed. The sea-borne attack took the enemy completely by surprise and for 48 hours was almost unopposed. Thereafter, however, the German reaction was swift, and enemy formations and units hurried piecemeal from all over Italy soon succeeded in containing our beachhead before we could break through the Gustav Line. X Corps had succeeded in making a substantial bridgehead over the River Garigliano, but had insufficient reserves to effect a break-through, while further east the American II Corps had broken through the Gustav Line only to be defeated by formidable German positions at Cassino.

During February and March, 1944, two more attempts were made to capture Cassino, this time by the New Zealand Corps, consisting of the 2nd New Zealand Division, the 4th Indian Division and the 78th British Division. But still the enemy resisted stubbornly, in spite of the stunning effect of probably the heaviest aerial and artillery bombardment that any troops endured during the war. General Alexander now decided on a wholesale regrouping of his armies in order to achieve sufficient local superiority to make a final successful assault on the Gustav Line.

Meanwhile at Anzio the unfulfilled promise of the early stages of the assault had been succeeded by a critical situation as the Germans attempted desperately to drive our troops back to the sea. The assaulting divisions were reinforced by the American 1st Armoured Division and the 45th Division, and soon afterwards by the 56th Division from X Corps in the middle of February. The 56th Division was in turn relieved by the 5th Division during the first week of March, and the 1st and 5th Divisions continued to be the British component of the American VI Corps until the breakout from the beach-head at the end of May.

Owing to the congested area of the beach-head, only a portion of the administrative units of the divisions were required. In the case of the RASC, five transport platoons were sufficient to meet all the commitments of a division. The rest of the divisional column remained in a rear area south of Naples. Vehicles and dumps of stores were dispersed as widely as possible and all vehicles were dug in, to avoid damage from shelling.

The maintenance arrangements for the beach-head were of a novel character. LSTs sailed nightly from Pozzuoli, a small port north of Naples, to Anzio, each carrying 50 loaded 3-ton lorries. They arrived at Anzio in the early morning; the loaded lorries drove ashore and were replaced by an equal number of empty lorries which had been landed the day before. An LCI sailed daily with a supply of fresh produce. The allotment of tonnage between the American divisions and the British divisions was made at Headquarters VI Corps, where there was a small British increment to look after the requirements of the British formations.

On several occasions in Anzio the RASC provided platoons to act as infantry. After the German attempts to wipe out the beach-head had failed, the morale of all units in the beach-head remained very high and many diversions were improvised. Highly organized race meetings were arranged, at which local Anzio beetles competed.* On one occasion three bookmakers clubbed together to buy one over-successful beetle for the extravagant sum of £40. A first-class concert party staged by the 5th Divisional Column RASC provided excellent entertainment for most of the units of the division, and was much appreciated by all those who had an opportunity of seeing the show.

The Capture of Rome

General Alexander's final offensive against the Gustav Line opened on May 11th, 1944. The regrouping of formations in the Fifth and the Eighth Armies, which had been effected with the utmost secrecy, gave us a large local superiority in the critical area of Cassino and the Liri valley, and the enemy was completely surprised. After several days of strenuous fighting, a break-through by the French Expeditionary Corps in the Fifth Army sector was the prelude to victory. Cassino at last fell to the Polish Corps on May 18th, and the pursuit to Rome and the north began. On May 23rd the break-out from the Anzio beach-head at last took place and threatened to cut the Germans' line of retreat. Finally, on the evening of June 4th, the leading troops of the Fifth Army entered Rome, hot on the heels of the last Germans hurriedly withdrawing to the north without waiting to demolish the bridges over the Tiber.

This great success was not achieved without the great efforts of the administrative services. Frequent regrouping of formations entailed an enormous amount of organization. For the final battle of Cassino, almost every division was moved to a different corps. In many cases this involved moves across the winding mountain roads of the snow covered Apennines, with all the maintenance difficulties that such moves bring about.

Because of the need for secrecy, stores dumps in maintenance

---

* The beetle races took place in circular arenas constructed like cockpits. A number of concentric circles were painted in the arena and the beetles, which carried the colours of their owners, were placed in the centre under glass jars. Races of different lengths were included in the programme by selecting different circles as the winning line. Units vied with one another in trying to make their own arena the smartest in the beach-head and their meetings as well organized and 'professional' as possible.

areas had to be carefully camouflaged, and in many cases the movement of vehicles building up these dumps had to be restricted to the hours of darkness.

Up to the capture of Rome the armies were based for their maintenance on the port of Naples for formations operating on the west side of the Apennines, and on the ports of Taranto, Brindisi and Bari for those operating on the east coast. From the ports the greatest possible use was made of the railways following the coastal plains on the east and west coasts and of the arterial roads, Highways 6 and 7, which converge on Rome.

Corps maintenance areas were established as far forward as possible, and during the period of static warfare on the Gustav Line were only a few miles behind the forward positions, with an army roadhead (or maintenance area) not far in rear. The stocks in these maintenance areas proved invaluable once the pursuit began, while the reserves laboriously built up in the Anzio beach-head, which were located some 80 miles nearer Rome, helped to sustain the rapid advance beyond Rome, without the inevitable delay usually involved in moving stocks forward. Petroleum pipelines were constructed for the first time as far forward as corps maintenance areas, and mobile petrol filling centres were set up under corps control.

Right up to the fall of Cassino great reliance was placed on supply by jeeps, mules and porters, and the French Expeditionary Force showed how even the apparently most inaccessible mountains can be crossed by troops who are sufficiently flexible in their system of supply.

The crossing of the Garigliano by the 5th Division gave a good example of the alternative methods of supply which can be planned when there is a possibility of considerable forces being cut off from their usual system of supply. In this operation it had been estimated that it would take the Royal Engineers 48 hours to build bridges over the river to take maintenance traffic. All assaulting units were therefore made self-contained for this period, and arrangements were made to pass a maintenance convoy consisting either of trucks or jeeps and trailers over the river, as soon as the bridges were complete. However, the Germans were likely to retain control of the upper reaches of the river for some time and would be in a position to flood the lower Garigliano and perhaps to carry away the bridges. The bridges would also be within artillery range of the German guns and under observation from observation posts in the mountains beyond the river. An alternative system for maintaining the troops in the bridgehead was therefore arranged by using the dukws of a detachment of 53 (US) Quartermaster Battalion and LCTs to ferry stores by sea from Mondragone to an advanced dump short of Minturno beyond the mouth of the river, a distance of 12 miles by sea. Finally an emergency plan was made to supply the bridgehead, in which four brigades and half the divisional artillery were concentrated, by air. In practice, all these alternative methods of supply were used in the operation except supply by air.

Jeeps and trailers proved once again their value in delivering ammunition to gun positions, and between January 17th and February 9th 10,000 to 12,000 rounds of 25-pounder were delivered across the Garigliano each day by 28 jeeps and trailers of the 5th Divisional Column RASC, which operated only in the hours of darkness.

In the Cassino area, a platoon of 40 jeeps manned by drivers of the 78th Divisional Column were continuously engaged in maintaining units of the division in most inaccessible positions and a jeep platoon of 563 Company RASC, XIII Corps Troops Company, was employed for six weeks with the Royal Engineers in building a vital road to forward positions within 800 yards of the enemy.

The dukws of the amphibious companies continued to do invaluable work. Fifty of these were used as infantry assault craft and for landing anti-tank guns in the 5th Division's attack on the Garigliano. At Anzio 239 Company distinguished itself by being awarded the Fifth Army plaque, which carried the following commendation from General Mark Clark:—

> 'From Headquarters, Fifth Army.
> Commendation to whom it may concern.
> 239 General Transportation Company (Dukw) is hereby commended for outstanding performance of duty.'

Other RASC units which bore the brunt of early difficulties at Anzio were 295 Company, which served the 24th Guards Brigade, 7, 40 and 42 Companies, which completed the 1st Divisional Column RASC, 548 Company, and a section of 348 Tipper Company. Later they were joined by the RASC companies of the 56th Division —513, 514, 515 and 49 Companies—which, in their turn, were relieved by the divisional column of the 5th Division (2, 69, 80 and 434 Companies).

In March, 1944, it was at last found possible to start a system of relief for those divisions which had been continuously engaged in operations since the assaults on the Italian mainland, and whose value as fighting formations was beginning to suffer. The first divisions to be relieved were the 46th and 56th, which handed over all their vehicles and heavy equipment and were sent to Palestine and Egypt to refit and recuperate. The 56th Division's positions at Anzio were taken over intact, complete with vehicles, weapons and equipment, by the corresponding units of the 5th Division, the relief being done by a brigade at a time and taking from four to five days. The 5th Division's turn for relief came after the fall of Rome, and the divisional RASC once more found themselves taking over the transport of the 56th Divisional Column—this time in Egypt.

The Build-up for the Final Offensive at Cassino

The two and a half months available for the build-up for the final offensive at Cassino was a busy time for the many RASC depots involved. The three base supply depots at Naples, none of which was rail served, handled an average daily turnover of 4,000 tons. During March, the record figure of 32,000 tons was cleared from the Naples docks in one day, and it is a matter for pride that 25,000 tons of this total were cleared in RASC transport.

Between January and June, 1944, the following awards for gallantry were made to RASC officers and men: two Military Crosses, 20 Military Medals, two George Medals, two Memberships of the Order of the British Empire, three British Empire Medals and two Distinguished Flying Medals.

The Pursuit North of Rome—Capture of Florence

The capture of Rome gave no respite to the Allied armies. It was imperative to continue the pursuit of the beaten enemy as far as our advancing columns could go without having to pause for administrative reasons. The enemy's powers of recuperation were sufficiently well known. If he were given a chance of regaining his breath he was quite capable of reorganizing his forces on another strong defensive position and compelling us to deploy our full strength to break through his defences again.

We have already seen how the reserves accumulated at Anzio assisted the advance. The quick capture of Civitavecchia on June 6th helped to shorten the lines of communication still further.

The first real check to the Allied pursuit came at the historic Lake Trasimene. Here the Germans succeeded in checking our advance for nearly 10 days at the end of June, thereby gaining an invaluable breathing-space in order to begin organizing their next serious line of defence.

The immediate task of the Allies was expressed as: to destroy all German forces south of the Pisa-Rimini line. This was greatly hampered by the withdrawal of substantial forces from Italy to support the projected landings on the French Riviera. The whole of the American VI Corps was withdrawn between June 14th and 27th, and the French Expeditionary Corps followed soon afterwards. Not only did this interrupt the impetus of the pursuit, but later on it was to have a serious effect on the campaign as a whole, as it took away from Italy the very formations which were most valuable in mountain fighting, of which there was to be so much in the battles on the Gothic Line. Their place was taken by the 92nd United States Infantry Division and the Brazilian Infantry Division, which did not, however, arrive in Italy until September and October, 1944.

Nevertheless, the advance went relentlessly on. By the middle of July the River Arno was reached, Pisa, Ancona and Leghorn were captured, and the most important administrative centre of Arezzo was in our hands. All this involved heavy fighting; during the first 10 days of July the 34th United States Division fired an average of 117 rounds a gun a day, and in one day fired 715 tons of ammunition.

Arezzo was rapidly developed as a railhead, and a system of pack trains was introduced. Although this system, no doubt, effected considerable economies in transport, it caused great difficulties in front of railhead, mainly because of the irregularity in the arrival of trains and the frequent discrepancies in the contents of the various packs. It made the establishment of railhead depots absolutely essential, with the additional handling that this involved. As one DDST put it: 'Pack trains are the bugbear of any forward planning. Transport is kept hanging about near railhead for hours and then probably arrives at the FMC just when issues are in full swing.' With the capture of Florence in the first week of August resistance south of the River Arno came to an end and the Allied armies found themselves coming up against what was to prove the last great German defensive position in Italy—the Gothic Line which extends from north of Pesaro on the east coast, through the Futa Pass on the crest of the Apennines, to south of Spezia on the west coast.

The Autumn and Winter Battles of 1944

Throughout the autumn and winter the battles went on, the Eighth Army, with its British, Canadian, New Zealand, Indian, South African and Polish formations, slowly working their way forward on the Adriatic sector, while the Fifth Army, with its American and Brazilian divisions, and later, once more, with many British troops, gradually overcame opposition in the mountainous western half of the front. The weather was indescribably bad, and shortage of ammunition and of reinforcements reduced a great deal of the front to inactivity during the worst of the winter months. The engineer commitment can be well appreciated from the figures of stores handled by the Engineer Stores Depot at Ancona, which amounted to an average of 600 to 800 tons a day of bridging material and 400 tons a day of other engineer stores.

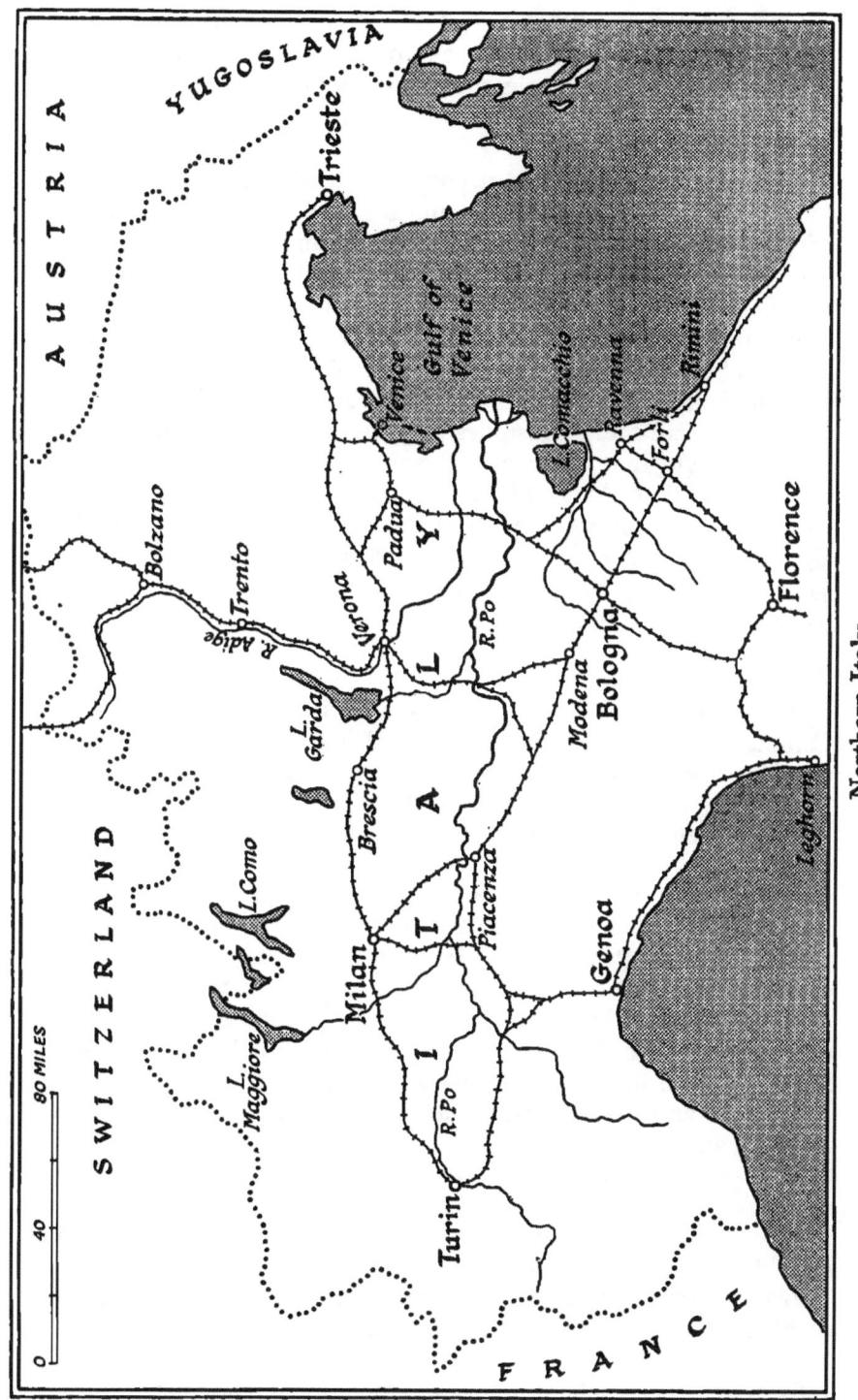
Northern Italy

During October, difficulties of supply resulted in ammunition expenditure being rationed to 25 rounds a gun a day for field artillery, and 15 rounds a gun a day for medium and heavy artillery. Later, in January, 1945, an 'all time low' of five rounds a gun a day was reached.

A further drain on Allied strength was imposed by the necessity to withdraw the Greek Mountain Brigade and the 4th Indian Division to Greece at the end of October, and a still further blow fell on the preparations for the spring offensive, when it was announced in February that the North-West Europe campaign would require the 1st Canadian Corps and 200 American fighter-bombers from Italy, and the 1st, 5th and 46th Divisions from Greece and the Middle East instead of their returning to Italy.

In spite of all these difficulties the Allied armies were buoyed up by the thought that they were advancing the whole time, however slowly, and that their ultimate victory was assured. The only serious German threat came at Christmas, 1944, when a sudden German attack down the Serchio valley took the United States 92nd Division by surprise and was only held after determined resistance and counterattacks by the formations on the flanks.

The Final Offensive

In December, Field-Marshal Alexander became Supreme Allied Commander in the Mediterranean and handed over command of the Allied armies in Italy (henceforth to be known once more as 15 Army Group) to General Mark Clark.

All our efforts were now concentrated on making adequate preparations for the final spring offensive. Stocks of ammunition were built up; bridging material for crossing the countless rivers and canals, including the Po, was amassed; equipment and spare parts were brought up to scale; reinforcements were absorbed; communications were improved and railheads pushed as far forward as possible. At the same time certain formations were given special training in the use of a new tracked amphibian, which had already proved its value in north-west Europe and in the Pacific—the LVT (landing vehicles tracked)—known in Italy by its code name, 'Fantail'.

The spring offensive opened with an attack by the Eighth Army in the Adriatic sector, making use of the 'Fantails' to overcome the flooded areas around Lake Comacchio, on April 9th, 1945. This was followed by the attack of the Fifth Army on April 12th.

From the start everything went well. Bologna was captured on April 21st, followed swiftly by Genoa on the 26th, Padua and Venice on the 29th, and Milan on the 30th. The Germans in Italy were finally defeated, and on May 2nd, 1945, the German

Army Group in Italy surrendered unconditionally, and the war in this theatre was at an end.

The battle casualties sustained by the RASC during the campaign in Italy amounted to five officers and 156 other ranks killed, 34 officers and 679 other ranks wounded, and two officers and 48 other ranks missing.

During these last 11 months of the campaign in Italy the pattern of RASC work did not change much; the same problems of supply under difficult mountainous terrain and in appalling weather were met with and solved by the same methods that had been learned in the earlier stages of the campaign. The use of mules and jeep and trailer platoons became as much a part of the normal maintenance systems as the 3-tonner. The efficient operation of transport over the limited and winding roads demanded a high standard of traffic control and discipline. The regular supply of many formations of many different nationalities became a commonplace RASC experience. Perhaps the outstanding achievement of this campaign from an RASC point of view was the way divisional columns of many nations unfailingly and successfully followed the same methods and systems that had been studied and learned by the RASC.

In the later stages of the campaign men of the RASC continued to earn their share of awards for gallantry. Space alone precludes a recital of their many achievements.

The foregoing account of the RASC in Italy has necessarily to be a short one, but before closing the chapter a brief note is given on some of the other aspects of the work of the Corps, both usual and unusual.

Amphibious Transport

We have already seen what an important part the dukw companies played in the invasion of Italy, in the assault at Anzio and in many of the great river crossings. They were invaluable too in assisting in the early development of captured ports, and in the final stages of the campaign they helped to run a ferry service across the Po.

One of the greatest contributions which the RASC made to the success of operations in northern Italy was the provision of a regiment of LVTs. These lightly armoured tracked amphibious vehicles were equipped with heavy machine guns and could be used for transporting infantry or 25-pounder guns across rivers and swamps or over flooded areas.

This regiment of tracked amphibians was formed in February, 1945, to enable the Eighth Army to turn the enemy's left flank which was securely protected by Lake Comacchio and a large area of flooded country. The regiment proved a conspicuous success, and its equipment contributed materially to the advance of the

Eighth Army across the Po valley, which with its many swamps and waterways presented a considerable obstacle to a normal advance.

In six weeks 55 officers and 1,200 other ranks were trained for their new roles in this regiment, most of the men coming from HQ RASC, 15 Army Transport Column, 385 Company (GT), and 931 Company (GT). Training took place on Lake Trasimene and the River Tiber and was conducted in great secrecy, as was also the move to the concentration area south of Lake Comacchio. The regiment, which consisted of five squadrons, was capable of carrying an infantry brigade headquarters, three infantry battalions, 16 25-pounder guns and crews, a RE assault squadron and recovery equipment.

After a sticky start on April 1st, the regiment soon proved its worth and, after a visit by the Supreme Allied Commander, Field-Marshal Alexander, on April 6th, achieved its first big success on April 11th when two battalions of the Queen's Royal Regiment completely surprised the enemy and captured the Menate Gap. From then until the end of April the regiment was continuously employed with great success and earned its share of awards for gallantry.

The RASC were involved in one other type of amphibious operation on Lake Comacchio and the River Po: the manning of storm-boats, which were shallow draught, unarmoured craft, about 20 feet long and were driven by an outboard motor. They could carry 18 fully equipped men and their speed, when laden, was about seven knots. Sixty of these craft were operated by 237 Anti-Tank Battery, RA, reinforced by 60 dukw drivers of 239 Company, RASC. They were used either as assault craft, mainly by commandos, or as maintenance craft for small isolated parties on islands or the shores of Lake Comacchio. On May 4th after the German capitulation the RASC dukw drivers left to rejoin their company, with a few more landings to add to their already imposing record.

Local Resources

The Italian campaign provided ample scope for that important RASC activity, 'the use of local resources', which resulted in an average monthly saving of 37,000 tons of shipping space and involved a monthly expenditure of about £1,394,000. The organization was directed from AFHQ with local resources officers stationed at the principal headquarters and at centres of production. More than 100 different commodities were procured, varying from articles in daily use to more exceptional ones such as tobacco seed, live rabbits (for RAMC in connection with anti-rabies serum), and garlic.

Arrangements were made for the collection, inspection and

grading of millions of eggs. Special forage depots were set up for the collection, storage and distribution of large quantities of animal feeding stuffs, the main depot being situated just outside Foggia in the great central plain. At the peak period this depot supplied forage for about 32,000 mules and 8,000 horses.

Meat on the hoof was another of the main activities of the organization. In one year 125,000 sheep were obtained for the use of Indian troops, and supplies had to be drawn from as far afield as the Sudan and North Africa. Things did not always go smoothly, as is instanced by the failure of arrangements made to draw on Sardinia, where everything seemed to combine to bring the plans made to nought owing to foot and mouth disease and other causes.

Poultry and fish for hospitals were purchased in large quantities. In the Eighth Army a regular supply of fresh fish was arranged from San Benedetto and forwarded in refrigeration vehicles for issue to the troops.

Fresh fruit and vegetables were obtained in vast quantities to meet the demands of an army which in numbers had topped the million mark. Fruits such as peaches and grapes, which are regarded as delicacies at home, were in daily issue during the season, and tomatoes and celery, asparagus and sea kale often formed part of the ordinary fresh vegetable ration.

Providing supplies of potatoes was one of the most difficult problems. They were comparatively scarce, and to avoid demands on the United Kingdom a combined plan between the British, the Americans and the Italian Government was made to organize production to grow, it was hoped, 20,000 tons from local seed. The crop was to be grown on an old extinct volcanic basin known as Lake Fucino, in Avezzano, where 2,500 acres were to be planted. But the scheme turned out to come under the old adage, 'the best laid plans', as with the restoration of self-government to the Italians and the lifting of control, little of the produce was returned for sale back to the forces.

Many manufactured foods were also obtained through the local resources organization, such as spaghetti (over 700 tons a month was wanted for feeding the Italian co-operators), and jams and marmalade, the sugar and pectin being provided by the organization. Vinegar, coffee, pepper and fruit juices and ice cream for hospitals were also made to order. Many other items had to be obtained such as alcohol, pigeon corn, capers, and even rat poison.

Although bread production does not strictly speaking come within the scope of local resources, it may be mentioned that 40 per cent of the bread produced in Italy was baked in civil bakeries from the Army's ingredients by Italian bakers working under British supervision.

Other Activities

As already mentioned the campaign, largely because of the geography and climate of the Italian peninsula, involved RASC units in a greater diversity of roles than probably any other theatre. We have already seen how motor transport units were compelled to convert themselves overnight into extempore pack transport units in Sicily; how, in deep snow, a composite platoon was forced to take to skis to collect supplies dropped from the air on a scarcely defined dropping zone; and how at Anzio, the RASC took their place with infantry in the defence of the beach-head perimeter. On many other occasions RASC units found themselves employed in unusual roles.

One dukw company, after playing a considerable part in the battle of the Sangro, took part in air-sea rescue work, saving pilots and salvaging aircraft, and also collaborated with a field security section in picking up escaped prisoners of war, refugees and enemy agents moving down the coast from behind the enemy lines.

Early in April, 1944, when the 1st Guards Brigade of the 6th Armoured Division took over a sector in front of Cassino, 477 Company was made responsible for providing a continuous smoke-screen for nearly a fortnight to prevent enemy observation on the approaches to Cassino. This involved about 150 men remaining in slit trenches all day within 1,000 yards of the enemy and crawling out intermittently to light the smoke canisters. At night the replenishment of the pits with 1,600 canisters under enemy harassing action involved the use of eight 3-ton lorries, seven jeeps and trailers, and 50 porters.

No. 352 General Transport Company was selected for training in air despatch, and in March, 1944, a detachment from this company was attached for duty with an organization called SOMTO (Special Operations Mediterranean Theatre of Operations). This detachment made many operational flights over Italy and Yugoslavia, dropping supplies to Allied prisoners of war, helping to maintain partisans in Yugoslavia, and supervising the dropping of liaison officers and agents behind the enemy lines.

Between October 11th and 17th, 1944, this company took part in the air supply of the 2nd Independent Parachute Brigade Group, which landed in the Athens area as the spearhead of the British occupational force in Greece.

During the winter of 1944/45, when the armies were still delayed in the Apennines short of Bologna, a detachment of the same company succeeded in dropping an average of over 300 tons a month of arms and equipment to partisans in Northern Italy. Full advantage was taken of good flying weather, and on one day as many as 40 sorties were flown. Because of the difficulty of finding the concealed dropping zones, all such sorties were flown in daylight. The work of this detachment continued to the end of the campaign.

No. 514 Company, which had been one of the divisional transport companies of the 56th Division, was given the interesting task of supporting the Yugoslav forces in their resistance to the German Mountain Corps. The company left Bari in November, 1944, and landed at Gruz in Yugoslavia. Consisting of two platoons, it performed various tasks, including dock clearance, normal maintenance of supplies, petrol and ammunition, and troop and mule carrying. The company was based on Dubrovnik and worked as far as Cetinje, 140 miles away, on a double echelon system.

An artillery platoon RASC, complete with A section of a composite platoon, found itself employed as a forage depot in the Foggia plain. Its task was to exploit this valuable source of forage to the full (in conjunction with the Allied Military Government), to arrange for the loading of pack trains to the army areas and to western Italy, and to maintain a reserve in its own depot.

Two ambulance units (Nos. 485 and 567 Car Companies) were manned by the American Field Service, a volunteer organisation of United States citizens. We owe them a debt of gratitude for providing these units. Although a para military body they had a self-imposed condition of service—that they should be employed as close to the battle front as possible, a condition they fulfilled nobly with the army in the desert campaign and with the Eighth Army in Italy.

Finally it should be placed on record that many RASC men volunteered and were accepted for service with 'Popski's Private Army', the organization built up and trained by Lieut-Colonel Peniakoff to carry out demolitions and create havoc deep behind the enemy's lines. Three of them, Cpl D. Galloway and Dvrs E. G. Burrows and A. D. Cahill, were awarded the Military Medal for the parts which they played in these adventurous exploits.

Because of the nature of the campaign, many RASC units were constantly engaged on work with the Royal Engineers. Their main tasks were the carriage of bridging materials and assistance in road repair and construction. As early as December, 1943, the Chief Engineer of the Eighth Army had under his control four general transport companies, two tipper companies and five bridge platoons. By the end of the campaign these had been increased in number to seven tipper companies and two bridge companies. The command of these units and any general transport companies allotted to the Royal Engineers was given to the CRASC of a transport column, who came under the operational command of the Chief Engineer.

In many instances, when the Royal Engineers had not sufficient men for their tasks, RASC units came to their assistance in the repair of roads, the construction of minor bridges and the erection of petroleum storage tanks. Throughout this campaign the co-operation between the two Corps was complete and harmonious.

Another instance of the RASC coming to the aid of the army occurred soon after AFHQ had moved to Caserta, when for the first time almost all the officers in that huge headquarters were gathered under the one roof (the Palace at Caserta is reputed to have 1,000 rooms) and the arrangements for their messing broke down badly. It was a novel problem for the DST, who was asked to find a solution and act as a super PMC. With the expert aid of the catering officers on his staff, he formed a special mess unit with a staff which was the replica of the 'ranks' and 'trades' employed in a large hotel. Men who were leading chefs and head waiters and barmen of many well-known hotels were brought in to man the new unit, and before long 900 officers were being messed at a good hotel standard in the main ballroom of the palace, and two other messes for about 100 each were set up in huts adjoining the main building. The only difficulty experienced by the officer commanding the mess unit was, eventually, how to keep down the profits.

While the campaign in Italy was in progress, AFHQ, in its capacity as the headquarters of the Supreme Allied Commander for the Mediterranean area, had other preoccupations than the operations in Italy. At the end of 1944 a force was despatched to Greece, and a fuller account of the operations in which it was unwittingly involved will be found at the end of this chapter. There were still troops in North Africa, although by the end of the campaign in Italy most of the vast stocks which had been accumulated there for the original operations in Tunisia had been exhausted and all units which could be had been transferred to Italy; but the running down was a slow process. There were small detachments to be administered in Corsica and Sardinia. British forces had been represented in the Allied invasion force which landed in southern France as part of the main 'Overlord' plan.

Conclusion

In this short account of the activities of the RASC in the Italian campaign we have tried to show the diversity of roles which military operations under difficult conditions of terrain and climate impose on our Corps and the necessity for improvisation which is constantly before us. The course of this campaign showed that the RASC organization, by virtue of its simplicity and flexibility, was admirably suited to such conditions. Perhaps the best tribute to our organization was the successful way in which so many nationalities and races

GREECE, 1944

The Return to Greece

After the British troops had been forced to withdraw from Greece in 1941 a continuous and relentless war was carried on by Greek guerillas against the German occupying forces. During the years that followed, the Allies continued to plan for an eventual return to the country and close touch was kept with the Greek Government, which was exiled in Egypt, so that when the opportunity arose we would be ready to assist in re-establishing law and order and to provide the relief that would be so sorely needed by the stricken Greek people.

Early in 1944 there was good hope that the combined efforts of the guerillas and the gradual encirclement of the Axis Powers would cause the Germans to withdraw. Plans for a return to Greece were then perfected and by the Caserta agreement of September, 1944, the GOC designate of the British force which was to be landed was nominated as Supreme Allied Commander, on the understanding reached with the Greek Government that all the guerilla forces would place themselves under his command. The object of providing a British force was to help the re-establishment of the exiled government and to assist in the preservation of law and order. A separate organization for supply and relief had been set up in Egypt under the name of the Headquarters Military Liaison Greece, which was to assist in the rehabilitation of the civil economy.

The force placed at the disposal of the GOC, Lieut-General Sir Ronald Scobie, was small, and consisted of the 3rd Armoured Brigade, the 4th Indian Division, the 2nd Independent Parachute Brigade, and ancillary services.

The situation moved quickly, and on October 14th British troops re-entered Athens amid scenes of the wildest enthusiasm and rejoicing by the civil population. Public opinion saw in their arrival the end of all want and the possibility of the extension of Greek frontiers, a hope so close to the heart of the Greek irredentist. But internal politics soon changed the situation as the strong left wing element of the guerillas, who were numerically superior to other factions, saw the opportunity of seizing political power. Open attempts by the left wing political party known as EAM, who controlled the Communist dominated guerillas referred to as ELAS, to undermine the newly returned Government led to growing tension in November, and the first shots of what developed into a civil war were fired on

December 3rd. On the same day the 139th Infantry Brigade (46th Division), began to arrive in Athens by air to reinforce General Scobie's command.

The Beginning of Civil War

Armed columns of the ELAS began to converge on the city that night, and there were many attacks on the police, gendarmerie stations and barracks on December 4th, followed by the first clashes with our own troops, whose duty it was to maintain law and order. General Scobie, in his position as Supreme Commander, issued an ultimatum that all ELAS forces should withdraw from Athens by midnight of December 6th/7th. But the situation began to deteriorate so rapidly that on the 5th he was compelled to issue orders for offensive action against the rebels where necessary. Civil war had broken out in earnest.

Our small forces were placed in a dangerous predicament as they barely amounted to the equivalent of a weak division with a small armoured element, but with little artillery, and they were scattered over the built-up areas of the city. There was no clear line of demarcation between them and the enemy. Their lines of supply were threatened everywhere, as all their sources of supply were surrounded by hostile detachments. The headquarters of the force which was formed from HQ III Corps (afterwards designated Headquarters Land Forces Greece) was situated in the heart of the city, with offices in the since renowned Metokhikon/Tamion building, most of the staff officers being billeted in the adjacent Grand Bretagne Hotel.

Brigadier Arkwright, who had been placed in command of the available troops, disposed his own formation, 23rd Armoured Brigade, in the centre of the city. He allotted the northern area to the parachute brigade, and entrusted the defence of the Piraeus and Faliron areas to 139th Infantry Brigade. The Greek Mountain Brigade, which had been brought over to Greece from Italy, was allotted to the south-eastern quarter of Athens. The 4th Indian Division was responsible for Salonika and Patras.

A glance at the sketch map of Athens will show that the units of the RASC were very scattered, as indeed were those of other services. Their original dispositions after landing had been entirely influenced by the understanding that the occupation was a friendly one, and their location had been wholly conditioned by the desire to cause the least inconvenience to the civil population. In most cases the sites occupied were ones which had previously been occupied by the Germans and were suitable in every way, except for defence.

RASC units had been allotted to the force on the basis that civil

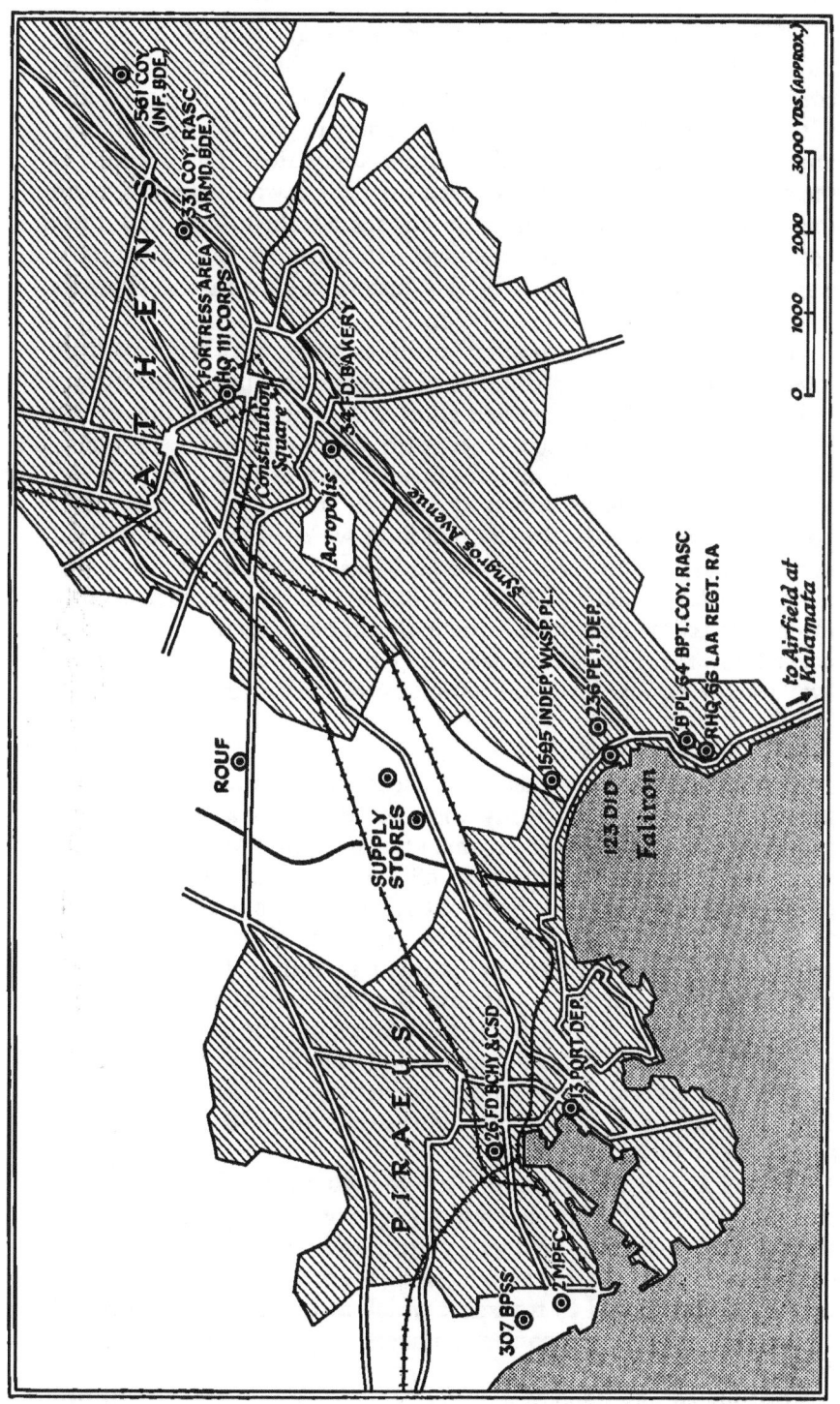

Athens

transport for general purposes would be obtained locally, and that the supply and petrol organization need only be sufficient for static conditions. It was considered that the RASC brigade companies with each of the brigades and a small supply depot, bakery, butchery and static petrol units would be quite adequate. The account of their actions does not rest so much on their lawful activities as on their conduct when called upon to defend their lives and their positions. Hence a more detailed reference to specific units is warranted than the length of this history allows in the chapters concerned with the main campaigns.

For the first day or two after hostilities broke out there was little interference with the distribution of supplies and petrol apart from some sniping, and no concerted effort was made against the several buildings which were being occupied as storehouses. This may have been because of the military inexperience of ELAS, or possibly, a desire to avoid direct action against our troops, and it was found possible to remove a large stock of food which was stored at Rouf and to transfer it to more secure positions. But this situation was not to last long, and by December 8th 'Arkforce' was split up into three semi-isolated groups in which almost every available man was needed for manning the defensive perimeters, any local reserves available being employed on patrolling the main supply routes.

Attacks on the 'Fortress'

ELAS, heartened by their first success and being in numerical superiority began to intensify their efforts, especially against the centre sector. This sector became known as the Fortress Area, and also contained the headquarters of the force. Its defended area covered about 3,000 yards by about 1,000 or 2,000 yards from north to south. The DDST, Colonel M. J. Cahill, had only just been transferred from a similar appointment in Italy. His appearance seemed to bear out his reputation that his arrival was inevitably followed by some sort of blitz, as before long the enemy brought mortar fire against the headquarters building, began to open attacks against the several RASC units scattered over Athens and the Piraeus, and almost cut off the centre sector from its only source of supply—at Faliron.

Colonel Cahill quickly appraised the situation. He saw that it was vital to establish at once an emergency maintenance centre in the middle of the city for food, petrol, and water, to have central control over an organized system of night convoys, suitably escorted by AFVs, and to add to transport which at the time only consisted of the two brigade companies, numbers 331 and 561 and a small corps car company.

The only supply depot operating as such was 123 DID, with two sections at Faliron. The third section, with a detachment of 22 Indian DID, was holding bulk stocks on the Athens–Piraeus road, and was completely isolated. Stocks of canned petrol were held in the small 236 Petrol Depot, also at Faliron. The bulk petrol storage section and mobile petrol filling centre had been located at the main civil installations in the Piraeus and were soon cut off by land, although it was possible to gain access by water. Both 123 DID and 236 PD were within easy range of any type of weapon possessed by the enemy, and were subject to desultory fire. The detachment of 26 Field Butchery, which controlled the only stock of frozen meat held in a civil cold store, was also isolated in the heart of enemy territory and could do little more than guard their position with the help of a small party of Royal Engineers. The field bakery was also isolated until it was extricated by the 2nd Parachute Brigade.

The long straight road, the Syngros Avenue, which linked Faliron with the heart of the city was under fire from various enemy posts and detachments, and the roads joining the centre of the city with the Piraeus ran through territory occupied by strong ELAS forces.

The first step taken by the DDST was to organize an escorted convoy which was successful in bringing in 100,000 composite rations into the fortress area, where a small extemporary DID was formed with the aid of a borrowed major and his clerk, and a few men, also borrowed, from the composite platoon of a brigade company. A petrol point was established in the well known Constitution Square, the meeting place for all good Athenians in normal times, and a detachment of 64 Bulk Petrol Company was drawn in to form a mobile reserve. Static water tanks were built up by the Royal Engineers in the streets around corps headquarters and were supplemented by a platoon of water tankers which made nightly runs to Faliron, eight vehicles being retained full each night as a mobile reserve.

To overcome the lack of transport the DDST arranged for the withdrawal of about 250 vehicles, originally landed for the Greek Government, as an organized night operation from the ordnance depot. He then formed a new company with the aid of loyal Greek adherents. At the same time agreement was given to the employment of the transport of 66 Light Anti-Aircraft Regiment RA as a temporary transport company.

After the visit of F-M Alexander, the Supreme Allied Commander in Italy, on December 12th, orders were given for hastening the despatch of reinforcements, the 4th British Division and the King's Dragoon Guards (an armoured regiment) and for the establishment of a temporary base at Faliron and a firm line of supply with a view to the resumption of the offensive. The use of the deep water harbours of the Piraeus had been denied for some days past and ships awaiting unloading had been withdrawn to the mouth of the bay. But there were two 'hards' suitable for unloading very light craft at Faliron. Fortunately Faliron adjoined the all-weather airstrip of Hasani at Kalamaki, and the area was still in our hands, although it could only be lightly defended until reinforcements were landed, and could not be used by night.

An improvised headquarters for the new base 'Greenbase' was in position by the morning of the 13th and set to work at once to organize the intake of stores over the beaches and to receive the reinforcements from the 4th Division which were beginning to arrive on the adjacent airfield. Their landing was often greeted by intermittent small arms fire from the insurgents in the hills nearby.

Transport offices were set up for the control of transport at the beach-head and airfield; a new site was taken over for building up stocks of canned petrol and another site for forming a temporary depot for bulk stocks of food. The DID, which also housed a part of the garrison, was cleared of all men except those needed for its defence, and within a few days the little base was in working order. Troops in the locality drew their needs direct from the supply and petrol depot. 'Arkforce' and the central sector were supplied by nightly escorted convoys run along the Syngros Avenue where various enemy posts were being cleared up, and supply to 139th Brigade and 5th Indian Brigade (which had arrived as a welcome reinforcement) was arranged by sea to the Piraeus. With the arrival of the first infantry brigade of the 4th Division, Major-General Dudley Ward, the divisional commander, assumed command of that brigade and those defending the Piraeus. His first object was to re-establish communications by road between the two parts of his command.

The first element of the 4th Divisional RASC arrived by ship and set to at once to assist in ferrying troops ashore in assault boats. The 4th Divisional Composite Company, which was landed by mid-December, was equipped with 50 vehicles borrowed from the ordnance depot and other units, and was soon busy maintaining its division.

RASC Units in Defence

The first and most serious attack against our forces took place early on December 13th against the collection of units in the infantry barracks, which included 331 Company, RASC. Throughout the night of December 12th/13th there was heavy firing around the barracks, which proved to be attacks on the Greek Mountain Brigade who were expected to reinforce the garrison of the barracks if they were attacked. In the first confusion which resulted in the pitch dark night, when the ELAS blew a hole in the barracks wall, it was difficult to distinguish between friend and foe until blazing petrol and burning huts lit up the scene. It is estimated that nearly 700 ELAS troops were able to gain an entry before the situation could be taken in hand, but not before there had been many casualties. The men in the stronger buildings held out, but intense heat and fire gave the platoons in the flimsier billets little chance. There were many acts of individual gallantry on the part of the garrison, such as that of Dvr W. Prickett who performed one hazardous task after the other until badly burned, but even then refused to give up until the enemy had been cleared. Captain V. H. Band, in spite of enemy fire, organized the clearance of petrol stocks to a safer point and later went in search of wounded under enemy fire until, wounded himself, he was rescued under heavy fire by Dvrs J. W. E. Carter and H. Hobson. Captain Band and the three drivers were given immediate awards of the Military Cross and the Military Medal respectively.

Three days after the attack on the infantry barracks the small detachment of 26th Field Butchery who were operating the FIX cold stores were overrun after ELAS troops had blasted their way into the rear of the installation. This little detachment in company with a few sappers had been surrounded in enemy held territory since December 9th, but were, up to the 18th, able to repel the various attempts to force an entry and refused to give in to several calls to surrender. No. 13 Port Detachment were more fortunate as, also surrounded in their location in the Piraeus, they were extricated and evacuated by sea on December 17th, and were then employed at Faliron on their normal duties and in helping to develop the temporary base supply depot. During this period, the original site, on the Athens/Piraeus road, selected for holding bulk stocks which was manned by a section of 123 DID, continued to be surrounded. Protected by a detachment of infantry and the small depot staff, they held out, although one of the three sheds in the depot was captured, until the enemy were cleared from the area at the end of December when the unit came into operation again.

The other two transport companies, 561 and 690 Corps Car Company, although they were not subjected to concerted attacks, also had their share of the fighting. No. 561 Company was affiliated to the Greek Mountain Brigade, against whom ELAS seemed to make a concentrated effort. The location of the company was under continuous fire and a good deal of damage was caused to their vehicles, although their casualties were relatively light with one sergeant killed and eight wounded. Throughout the period from December 4th to about the last week of the month the unit fulfilled its normal task of maintaining petrol and supply points for the brigade and at the same time defending its location. Some indication of the conditions experienced by the unit may be gained from such entries in its daily diary as—Monday, December 4th: Vehicles called out to carry two battalions to Constitution Square and fired on repeatedly. December 5th: Company location subject to furious sniping. December 6th: Location heavily mortared and three Bren guns despatched to answer enemy fire. December 8th: Vehicle maintenance impossible as barrack area swept by SAA fire.

The corps car company, although principally used for defence, also performed numerous transport duties in collecting vehicles from the ordnance depot and running night convoys to Faliron.

The fortress area where the car company was located was, of course, the hub of the British forces and also housed a large number of the leading Greek pro-Government officials. Although the area was as far as possible wired in, an attempt to blow up the Grand Bretagne Hotel was only spotted in time by an observant sentry. Noticing that the wire around a manhole near his post appeared to have been tampered with, he reported the matter, and it transpired that ELAS had worked their way through a sewer and placed a handcart full of explosives timed to go off at 7 a.m. when the staff would be sitting down to their breakfast. It is related that for days afterwards one staff officer found difficulty in sitting down to any meal.

While the 4th Division were arriving and the enemy were being gradually cleared from the Piraeus area, the work of building up stocks went on steadily at Faliron. By December 21st it is recorded that all depots were on the telephone and lighting was installed in the temporary BSD. Strenuous efforts had been made to provide some bread in place of biscuit. The 2nd Parachute Brigade were able to extricate men of the field bakery who were set to work in civil bakeries, and a lack of fuel wood in the fortress area was made good by the corps car company, who improvised 'trombone' burners which burned derv oil. The larger formations which could not be provided with supplies of bread in kind were given the materials and started their own temporary bakeries. The feeding strength had been increased considerably as the large number of Greek police and gendarmerie and units of the newly formed Greek National Guard had no means of subsistence and had to be taken on the British ration strength. By the end of December the original figure of 16,000 to be fed had risen to more than 70,000.

During the first three weeks of hostilities the bulk petrol storage section and No. 2 Mobile Petrol Filling Centre, which were located at the Shell, Socony and Secombel plants, had remained at their posts. All the civilian employees who worked the plant had left when a general strike was declared on December 3rd, and all civil power lighting and telephone facilities had ceased.

Although the units were cut off by land it had been possible to reinforce them with the 64th Light Anti-Aircraft Regiment by water, and counter measures were taken as the enemy gradually encroached on the adjoining areas. No direct attack took place until the raising of the alarm by a RASC sentry 'at 0158 hours' on the morning of December 21st, which was immediately followed by heavy fire from automatic weapons and rifles on the front of the installations. The small garrison of about 90 under the command of Major A. S. Mackay, RASC, returned the fire with every available weapon, and the enemy fire died down to sporadic bursts from well selected machine gun posts. After the first 10 or 15 minutes of the attack, considerable help was given by a RAF aircraft which dropped parachute flares and later this illumination was supplemented by star shells fired from warships. One of the main storage tanks which held about 45,000 gallons of aviation spirit was holed, and as it was impossible to plug the leak, fitters broke the feed line at a flange so that the main loss took place within the bund wall at a point farthest from where the action was taking place. The enemy reopened his attacks at about 4 a.m., this time using incendiary flares against the storage tanks, but in the interval between the attacks the small band of defenders had resited many of their weapons in the light of the enemy's location, and were again able to beat down the enemy fire. Small arms fire of varying volume continued until daylight when the enemy withdrew. In the second attack a second, kerosene, tank was holed, but the puncture was successfully plugged. The next evening was without incident, but on December 23rd and 24th the installations came under fire from enemy 75 mm guns. The only effective damage was one 10-inch pipe completely fractured. Major Mackay received an immediate award of the Military Cross for his spirited defence and his personal efforts in plugging the leaking tanks.

As the British strength developed, the systematic process of clearing up the Piraeus and communications from Faliron to the centre of the city continued over the Christmas period, which was marked by a visit from the Prime Minister. It was announced that the usual official Christmas festivities must be postponed, but it was with some pride that the supply officer to Arkforce records that a special ration was issued for that day. It so happened that the F type of composite ration included a fruit pudding, and an extra tin of 'variety' (e.g. steak and kidney pudding) meat, a double issue of dried fruit, a fresh orange and a 'full issue of bread' provided the day's fare. At Faliron the brigade supply officer of the 28th Brigade, with official connivance, organized a children's party for about 150 Greek children, many of whom were on the verge of starvation. Requisitioning a large café for the evening, he enlisted the aid of his men to act as waiters and his young friends then sat down to a big meal. Tinned meat and vegetable ration, a tin of peaches and as many army biscuits as they could eat constituted the fare, and it is said that one small boy of about six broke all M and V records by consuming no fewer than six platefuls before his hunger was satisfied.

The Civil War Dies Down

By early in January the city was gradually being cleared of the remaining insurgents, and ships could be unloaded again at the Piraeus, but the tragic war did not come to an end until February 12th. The Army was then faced with the new problem of helping to repair the ill effects of this unfortunate chapter in Greek history. Many of the inhabitants were near starvation, and thousands had been dispersed from their homes, and the civil economy was hopelessly disorganized. Bread was the first need. There was little flour left in the civilian mills and bakeries, most of which had been in insurgent hands, and there was no fuel or power. Bread was so scarce that a two-pound loaf commanded the equivalent of £2 to £3 in the black market. A committee under the presidency of the DDST was set up, and mill-owners, the Greek Ministry of Supply, the Red Cross and other authorities were gathered together to make a plan for immediate relief. With the help of the Navy a grain ship was unloaded, supplies of oil and petrol were provided by the Army and, as soon as the mills were in action again, bread was put on the market at a reasonable controlled price.

All available transport was also set to work to help in carrying relief stores and supplies, and the 4th Divisional RASC spent a large part of their time in carrying forward essential stocks into the outlying districts, where roads were roads in name only, and in helping refugees, of whom there were thousands, and ex-combatants to return to their homes and to more peaceful avocations.

The whole venture had been a strenuous test for the training and teaching of the RASC, although they had suffered severe casualties for their strength. In killed, wounded and missing they represented one sixth of the total casualties of the force. Their work merited the appreciation of their commander, Major-General Arkwright, and for that reason it is quoted in full below.

'Now that the Athens/Faliron road has been cleared of the enemy, I wish to express my profound admiration for all ranks of the RASC companies operating in this area, who night after night have run the gauntlet of enemy fire in order to maintain vital supplies to the centre of Athens.

'I fully appreciate the risk run by drivers, many of them with loads of explosives, and I consider the accomplishment of their tasks, almost without accident, to be a feat of the highest courage and skill.

'I also wish to say how much I regret the losses incurred by 66 LAA Regiment and 331 Company RASC when the enemy attacked the infantry barracks, and to thank them for the gallant show which their officers and men put up on that occasion.

'The supply services have borne far more than their usual share of danger and fighting during these operations, and I cannot pay high enough tribute to the bravery and cool efficiency which has made success possible.'

In turn the RASC owed a debt to their comrades of the Royal Artillery who operated a transport company on their behalf, and who helped so much in the defence of the several installations. The mutual feeling of the Royal Regiment was recorded at the time by Lieutenant-Colonel W. Powell, RA, in the words: 'I shall miss them (the RASC of No. 2 MPFC) very much on their departure —they have set a fine example of first class co-operation and fought with great courage and determination.'

CHAPTER VIII

SOUTH-EAST ASIA

HONG KONG

The China Command

AT the outbreak of war, the China Command consisted of the forces stationed at Hong Kong, and small garrisons for the protection of British interests at the former treaty ports of Shanghai and Tientsin. The regiment at Tientsin provided the guard for the British Embassy in Peking.

The attitude of Japan was unfriendly, but over two years were to elapse before she sided openly with the Axis powers by declaring war on December 8th, 1941. In the event of a war with Japan the small garrisons at Shanghai and Tientsin would be completely isolated. They were, therefore, withdrawn in the preceding August. However, it was part of our general strategic policy to deny the use of the harbour and other facilities at Hong Kong to an enemy.

Undoubtedly, the island was not easy to defend. Even if it were possible to keep the enemy at bay on the leased territory on the mainland, which formed part of the Colony, the necessary air power could not be provided because of the lack of aircraft and adequate airfields. Victoria, the main centre of population, with its harbour, was overlooked by the mainland, barely a quarter of a mile away. There were numerous bays and inlets open to sea-borne landings, and there was a difficult problem of civil defence because of the presence of nearly a million Chinese who were permanent inhabitants of the Colony.

There were only 207 men from the Corps in the garrison who provided the small MT Company (No. 12), a supply depot and a bakery, and the usual barrack and transport office. There were a few WD vessels, most of their crews being locally enrolled Chinese, and there was also one Indian Army unit, the Hong Kong Mule Corps, equipped with small (AT) carts and pack equipment.

In spite of this small number, and the short lived nature of the campaign, the Corps were to give good account of themselves, but in doing so they sustained 25 per cent casualties.

Up to November, 1941, it was considered that with the forces available it was not possible to defend the Colony from the mainland. However, with the arrival of two Canadian battalions to reinforce the two British and two Indian Army battalions, the Commander decided to defend the mainland from the general line known as the Gindrinkers Line which had been reconnoitred and partly prepared before the war. In making this decision, he considered that there was a good chance of achieving his purpose, and that even if he had to meet a powerful and sustained enemy offensive there would be time to destroy the many facilities at Kowloon before being compelled to retire to the island. These hopes were not to be fulfilled, as after 17 days the little garrison had been fought to a standstill, and with starvation in sight and the only water supply in the hands of the enemy, the Colony was forced to capitulate on Christmas Day.

War Preparations

All the RASC installations were located in the town of Victoria, on the north side of the island. A scheme prepared some years before the war for providing new barracks and buildings for the RASC had come to nothing because of lack of money, and the Corps were consequently working under the most primitive conditions. When war became imminent, however, plans were made for the dispersal of supplies held in the supply depot, and for their storage in buildings to be erected in various parts of the island. This was not done until September, 1939. Other preparatory measures had been taken, however, such as the establishment of a breeding farm for goats to supply fresh meat for the Indian troops and the importation of a shipload of firewood from Malaya for the bakery. There was a scheme for the impressment of vehicles, and an arrangement whereby 12 Company would be augmented in the event of war by the ASC Company of the Hong Kong Volunteer Defence Corps, comprising about 30 Europeans, as well as Chinese civilian drivers and impressed vehicles.

During the first six months of the war, the new storehouses were built and the supplies were moved into them, but otherwise the RASC, like the rest of the garrison, remained on a peace footing. Reserves of supplies were only enough for two months and did not include provision for the Indian troops or local forces, or forage for the animals, while petrol was held by contractors. The transport scheme for mobilization called for drivers for 600 vehicles. There were insufficient RASC and local European drivers and Chinese had to be hired by the day. This was obviously an unsatisfactory solution as they might be liable to disappear if things became dangerous, and this, in fact, happened. A few months before hostilities broke out, the raising of a Chinese transport corps on Territorial Army lines was approved, but the unit was not ready in time to be of use.

A scare in July, 1940, when all women and children were evacuated, led to the adoption of many RASC ideas on the arrangements for the supply and transport services. The RASC took over all food stocks from NAAFI, a full war-time ration was introduced, reserves were bought for the local forces, and stocks of petrol were amassed. Supply stores, petrol dumps, goat stables, a flour mill, a bakery, and other installations, were built or improvised in the country on the east, west and south sides of the island, away from the vulnerable north. The headquarters and workshops of 12 Company were also to be located in the south of the island in case of emergency. By the middle of 1941, four and a half months' reserve of supplies was in hand, nearly all the new storehouses had been erected, the stocks were dispersed, 3,000 goats were in their stables, and the mill was working.

In the fortnight preceding the Japanese declaration of war, tension mounted. The situation deteriorated to such an extent in the first days of December that, by the evening of the 7th, our troops were ready in their battle positions, and when the opening attack came, there only remained the mobilization of the local volunteer forces and final moves of rear parties to their war stations.

The Japanese Attack

The Japanese attack on the mainland began on December 8th, 1941, and soon forced the forward defended localities. On December 9th the enemy began probing attacks on 'Gindrinkers Line', the main defensive position. On the night of December 10th the key position, Shing Mun redoubt, fell into Japanese hands, and the evacuation of the mainland was ordered on the following day. During this period, RASC water transport had been operating at full scale to evacuate the military hospital from Kowloon and move NAAFI stores from their mainland godowns to the island. On the night of December 10th the artillery garrison of Stonecutters Island was evacuated, and the next afternoon the WD vessel *Oudenarde*, under continuous shellfire, delivered a lighter load of mules to the RASC camber. These were unloaded under heavy shellfire by RASC, HKMC and Chinese, the only casualties being two mules and Lieutenant Keeler, RIASC, who was slightly wounded. As the RASC camber then became untenable, it was evacuated.

Withdrawal from the Mainland

The main evacuation of the mainland proceeded throughout December 11th under the direction of the Royal Navy, and vessels were supplied by the Royal Navy, the RASC and the civilian ferry

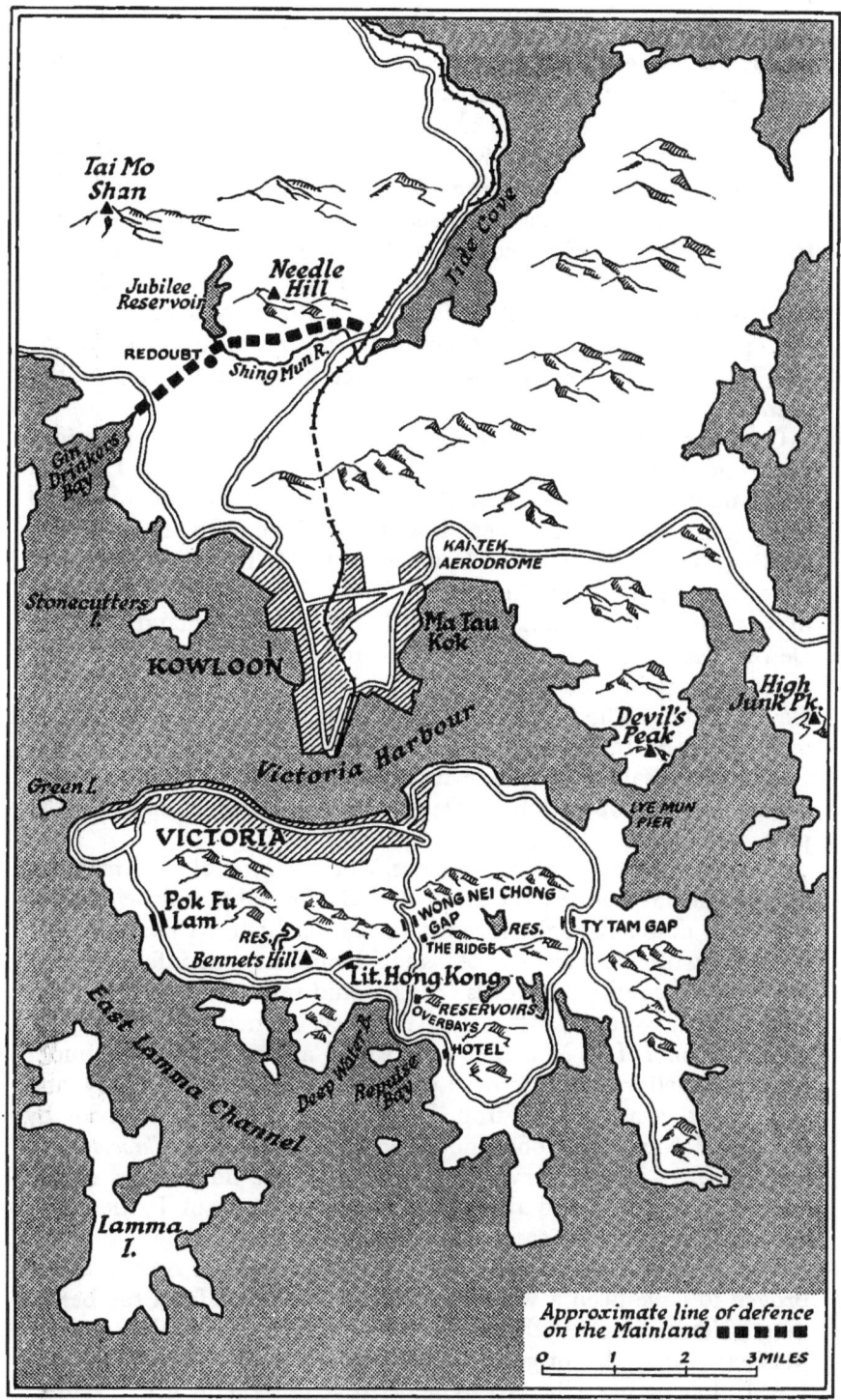

Hong Kong

companies. The task was rendered difficult by the desertion of Chinese crews, even though they were covered by rifles.

On the night of December 11th, supplies and forage for 10 days were put ashore at Devil's Peak, a mainland position which was to be held to the last, and men who had missed their normal evacuation timings were brought back from Ma Tau Kok, Kai Tek and Devil's Peak. These operations were successfully conducted with water transport which worked continuously for 24 hours. In addition, the WD vessel *French*, a target tower of MTB type, went outside the harbour to High Junk to take off a Royal Artillery observation party. The *French* was commanded by its civilian master, Mr. Holden, who was later killed in action in the fighting on the island.

On the night of December 12th three water transport operations were undertaken. One, directed by the Royal Navy, and with a vessel manned by Europeans of the Harbour Department, was to bring explosives from Green Island to Victoria to assist in fire fighting; a second controlled by Captain C. G. Turner, RASC, was to tow the mule lighter from the RASC camber to Devil's Peak to move mules to the island. The third, under the command of Major Dewar, was to evacuate remnants of units which had missed their evacuation points on December 11th and were known to be at Devil's Peak. The first vessel was, unfortunately, fired on by our own troops on its return journey and blew up with all hands, the second was disabled by our own fire, and launch and lighter abandoned, but the operation at Devil's Peak proceeded according to plan.

Operating initially with two vessels, the WD vessel *Victoria* and a hired launch, Major A. J. Dewar, RASC, effected the move of some 300 men, despatched the hired launch to a sheltered position, and stood by with the *Victoria*. At 2300 hours, he was informed that the final evacuation of Devils' Peak would take place and that the Royal Navy would assist. The task was carried out during the night although Lye Mun Pier, the island arrival point, was under constant shellfire, and some 1,200 men, with pack artillery and equipment, were cleared from Devil's Peak. Help was given by the Royal Navy after 0630 hours with the destroyer *Thracian* and four MTBs. Major Dewar was assisted in the final stages of this operation, which ended about 0800 hours, by Captain Turner, who had made his way by car to Lye Mun pier.

The precaution of moving the RASC installations on the island proved to have been a wise one. Within 24 hours from the beginning of hostilities everything had been evacuated from the crowded northern area, the original buildings, occupied formerly by the RASC, having been the first to be destroyed by enemy fire. Within a few days that part of the island was in complete ruins, and had the installations remained there, they would soon have been out of action. As it was, supply was maintained, though in the face of many difficulties. The CRASC (Lieut-Colonel K. T. Andrewes Levinge), had to cope with broken communications, constant changes in orders and in the location of units, desertion of Chinese drivers with their lorries, and the employment of his few technical and supply men on operational duties.

The MT workshops had one of the most difficult tasks of any unit in the garrison, and it was largely due to Mechanist Staff-Sergeant Keast that the transport services were maintained until the end, in spite of almost insurmountable difficulties. Damaged and abandoned vehicles were recovered at all hours of the day and night, often under heavy fire, and put in service again and the RASC workshops even produced improvised armoured cars. Credit was also due to Lieutenant M. H. Howell, who was in charge of transport and workshops.

The final withdrawal from the mainland on the night of December 12th was at once followed by a peremptory Japanese demand for the surrender of the Colony. This was categorically refused. The island was now open to direct fire from all directions, and the volume, intensity and accuracy of both artillery fire and bombing increased, causing considerable destruction, fires and interruption of communications. There were many signs of movement indicating preparations for attempted landings on the island, but it was not until the night of the 18th that the enemy gained the first foothold. To appreciate the subsequent situation would entail a detailed description of the operations which developed, so that this account must be restricted to mentioning that by the 19th troops had been in action for 11 days without respite, but the small garrison, although hopelessly outnumbered, continued the struggle for six days more.

Soon after midday on the 19th, a force of about 70 RASC men was collected in the Pok Fu Lam area and moved up to Bennet's Hill to take up an emergency defensive position in case further exploitation by the enemy was attempted. They were then to move up to support the Winnipeg Grenadiers at the neighbouring Wong Nei Chong gap. Later in the evening, a second party of RASC from the transport details at Repulse Bay were ordered to hold on and defend their transport area and not to withdraw. Meanwhile the small force on Bennet's Hill had been reinforced, but as they were unable to reach the gap they joined up with a party of RAOC at the Ridge.

Early the next day, the enemy had surrounded the hotel at Repulse Bay in which there were many women and children. The area around the hotel was cleared in the afternoon, but in the meantime

Lieutenant Tresidder, RASC, took over as second-in-command of the small detachment of bluejackets and men of the Middlesex Regiment who were defending the hotel. On the same day, Major Dewar was one of a party which was ambushed, but he collected some stragglers, and engaged the enemy patrols which he came across and got away across country. He then collected a party of 20 naval ratings and organized a defensive position at Little Hong Kong to prevent the enemy from reaching the ammunition magazine which was so vital to the garrison. Ammunition continued to be supplied through a narrow corridor which was at times cut by the Japanese, but final deliveries were made up to the night of December 24th, although the Japanese were within 150 yards of the loading point.

The Last Stand

On the evening of the 21st, the small party of RASC and RAOC, now about 100 strong, still held out on the Ridge, but after gallant fighting it was decided to evacuate the position. The party was intended to withdraw to the south, but was cut off by heavy enemy machine gun fire, so made its way to Deep Water Bay, where it sheltered for the night. In contact with the enemy for the whole of the next day, they set out in the evening to try to join the small garrison at Repulse Bay. Most of them succeeded in getting past the enemy.

Major Dewar and his small party continued to hold out to the last, the action being best described in the words of the official despatch: 'This island of defence resisted all attacks from the 20th to the afternoon of the 25th of December, and fought very gallantly.' For his bravery on this and other occasions throughout the defence Major Dewar was made a member of the Distinguished Service Order.

One of the last steps taken to try to stem the enemy tide was on December 24th, when about 30 of the headquarters clerks and others were sent under command of the DAAG to the help of a small party of the Middlesex Regiment, who held on gallantly at Morrison Hill until the afternoon of the 25th.

By Christmas Eve there was little hope of continuing the defence. All units had suffered severe casualties and every man who could bear a rifle had been called into the fray. The Japanese were in possession of the main reservoirs and the city of Victoria, with its teeming Chinese population, was the scene of innumerable fires and destruction. On Christmas Day it had to be accepted that no further useful military resistance was possible, and capitulation of the Colony followed.

Dukws at Work

MALAYA

Introduction

The campaign in Malaya opened almost simultaneously with the Japanese attacks on Pearl Harbour and Hong Kong on December 8th, 1941. In Malaya there was no question of a surprise as there was in the case of Pearl Harbour. It was only a matter of where the enemy would make his attempted landings and the strength he could bring to bear against our relatively weak forces which had to be disposed throughout the length of the Malayan Peninsula and in the island of Singapore. It is well known that what is so often mistakenly referred to as the 'defence of Singapore' has been the subject of criticism and controversy. But although such matters are not germane to this account, it is necessary to give a brief outline of the main events and conditions before hostilities broke out, as they were to have a considerable influence on the initial dispositions for defence and consequently on the accompanying administrative arrangements.

The decision to establish a naval base at Singapore was taken as far back as 1921. Subsequent defence policy was based on the premise that if war broke out in Europe the fleet would sail for Singapore and that its arrival within 70 days would automatically put an end to any serious threat of attempt at invasion. Thus the role of the garrison, which before the war was about an infantry brigade, was accepted as being one of the defence of the island base and the adjoining waters.

In the years that followed, the building up of the defences in Singapore and its adjacent islands moved slowly. It took time and money to strengthen the anti-aircraft and coast artillery defences, and to provide more airfields, some of which were located in Malaya. Plans were also made, which never fully materialized, for fortifying the island of Penang, which lay some 300 miles to the north off the west coast of Malaya. But the general conception of defence remained as being one of protecting the naval base.

When the international situation began to deteriorate in the late thirties, the defence of Singapore was only one of the many questions which had to be considered by the Government and their service advisers, and with the expected resources which would be available in the event of war, it was impossible to be strong everywhere. In common with the defence requirements of many other vital areas this plan for defending Singapore was becoming rapidly outmoded. In an appreciation of 1938, the then GOC of the command put forward the view that the danger to Singapore lay not in a direct attack against the island but from an invasion from the north through Malaya. He considered that it was unlikely that the Fleet would be allowed to leave home waters as originally planned and concluded that the potential enemy, the Japanese, would have time to mount a more deliberate attack than had been previously supposed. The appreciation foresaw Japanese infringement of Siam's neutrality and an attack down the west coast supported by landings in the east.

These views were not accepted officially until war was imminent, although agreement had been given to the construction of a defence line on the mainland in the state of Johore at Khota Tinghi on the Johore River, in addition to the defences which had already been constructed at Mersing on the east coast.

Thus before the war the RASC had a distinctly limited liability—a liability restricted to maintaining the small garrison in Singapore, an Indian battalion stationed at Taiping (in Perak) and a small body of troops which garrisoned the island of Penang.

In the early summer of 1939 there was a critical change in defence policy by the acceptance of the view that it might not be possible to relieve the garrison within 70 days, and the period was extended to 180 days, but the general defence task still remained one of guarding against attacks on Singapore. This decision, coinciding with the imminence of war, led to the immediate despatch of the 12th Infantry Brigade Group of the Indian Army which, arriving in August, 1939, brought the strength of the garrison up to about 10,000.

Looking back at the position of the RASC in the command just before the war, it is difficult to realize that the transport available to the Officer Commanding RASC was 52 MT Company and a small water transport detachment, the only British members of the company being one officer and 12 other ranks. The 25 lorries and 10 ambulances in the unit were manned by Malay civilians. The water detachment also had Malay crews, but was supervised by a British master mariner. There was a plan for providing civil road transport in the event of war, but not for the RASC. A total of 500 civil vehicles were to be impressed to bring units' first line transport up to their higher scale, but the movement of their stores and equipment to their places of deployment was to be effected by hired civilian vehicles. This plan was no doubt actuated by the current War Office policy that commands overseas should draw as far as possible for expansion on the peoples of the colonies. It was a sound policy so long as suitable material and facilities for training could be provided, but it was one which was often accompanied by sharp difference of opinion between those on the spot and the legislators of Whitehall on such matters as pay and conditions of service. It will be seen later that the RASC was forced to rely entirely for the additional MT companies required on locally raised companies backed by small cadres of British officers and NCOs.

Political considerations debarred the use of the vast Chinese population of the Peninsula, so the field of recruiting was confined to Malays and local Indians. The bar was not lifted until just before the outbreak of hostilities, but the first Perak Chinese MT company which was formed gave a good account of itself, as did the several locally enlisted RASC Malay and Indian units.

There was a potential RASC reserve of personnel in the form of the small element of ASC in the Singapore Volunteer Corps. This old established corps included Europeans, Eurasians and Malays. Most of the ASC were Europeans and excellent material, but they had had little training and seemed to have no specific war role. There were no ASC echelons in the other volunteer forces in the Malay States, although four infantry battalions of the Federated Malay States volunteers had the equivalent of a transport platoon for performing both first and second line transport duties.

The Officer Commanding RASC was more favoured in his supply arrangements, as a new supply depot, modern bakery and small cold storage had just been completed at Alexandra in Singapore, the bakery being a model of its kind. But, as is usually the way in peace time, financial stringency restricted the site acquired to one which was only sufficient for the day, and left no spare ground for the inevitable expansion needed in war. The supplies commitment was mainly a British one, as a large part of the food eaten by the few Indian troops and the Malay Regiment was indigenous to the country and was procured from contractors who were also nominally responsible for holding reserves. Contractors also provided all fresh vegetables and fruit, most of which had to be imported from Australia or Palestine, as the local supply was confined to the small areas of the highlands at Frasers Hill and the Cameron Highlands, the 'hill' stations of Malaya which were soon overrun when the Japanese invaded the country. There were plenty of local types of vegetables grown in quantity but although possessing such delicate names as Ladies' Fingers, Chinese Radish, etc., they were not acceptable to European tastes.

There were no special military reserves of petrol because units normally refuelled their vehicles from kerb-side pumps installed in their barracks, which were kept refilled under contract by the civil oil companies.

Preparations for War

When war was declared in September, 1939, the command at once took certain preparatory steps in connection with the defensive plans, but distance from Europe and from the territories of the potential enemy, and a seeming lack of any immediate concern in what the future might hold in the Far East, tended to produce an atmosphere of 'business as usual' in the life of Malaya. This outlook is perhaps understandable. The BEF, although landed in France, was not engaged with the enemy, and the threatened air offensive against Britain which most thinking people felt would be the enemy's first move had not materialized. The volunteer forces in Malaya and the island were still plying their normal civilian professions or trades. The nearest territories were neutral Siam, and the Netherlands East Indies and Indo-China which were occupied by friendly nations.

It also even seemed as if the seriousness of the impending position was imperfectly understood at home as, for example, the financial powers on defence works of the GOC were limited to £500, and any project involving more than that sum required reference to the War Office. No new unit could be raised locally or establishment increased without a similar reference, and the business of obtaining authority for action seemed to be hedged about with endless queries and frustrating delays, factors which had an intimate effect on the RASC, which had to rely on raising local units to create the required transport reserve.

The story of the RASC in Malaya after the outbreak of war should perhaps be more properly called the story of the Imperial ASC, were it permissible to coin such a term, as almost all the reinforcements to join the command were drawn from India and from Australia, their formations having their own respective complements of Royal Indian Army Service Corps and Australian Army Service Corps (later made Royal). But as the primary responsibility for the supply and transport services in the command remained an RASC one, this short account is told from that angle.

The first reinforcement, the 12th Indian Infantry Brigade Group, was a welcome addition to the garrison. Designed to act independently, it was self-contained and included RIASC base and line of communication supply units. Army HQ in India had appointed a DADST to administer the ST services for the force, which was known as Force Emu, on the understanding that he would demand direct on India for requirements. The RIASC units in the force differed in name and nature if not in purpose from the British Army pattern. There was a supply issue section for the detailed issue of rations, a cattle stock section for providing and handling meat on hoof acceptable to the various religions of the Indian troops, and two supply depot sections for the storage of reserves and making issue in bulk at the base and on the line of communication. A further difference arose from the fact that the Indian formation was to be given an active service scale of food in kind while the normal garrison of the command continued to follow the peace system of messing on a cash accounting basis.

Malaya, showing dispositions on December 8th, 1941

There was clearly no point in superimposing a separate supply system on that of the command, especially as some Indian troops were already being successfully supplied by the normal command organization and, after an exchange of signals with Army HQ in India, which at first demurred, it was agreed that supply arrangements should be merged. The two supply depot sections and cattle stock section, although continuing to cater for their own formation, were incorporated with the British rearward organization, and the issue section remained with its brigade, the officer commanding the section being appointed brigade supply officer. Demands for Indian foods were included in the command's general requirements. The two different systems of accounting were maintained without undue trouble.

Thus the arrival of the Indian brigade brought home the differences that can exist within the Commonwealth, differences to be repeated to some extent with the arrival of the Australian Imperial Force. Later, when an Indian corps was formed, the DDST took into his staff two DADs ST (RIASC) to advise on Indian matters, to maintain liaison with the DST India, and to ensure permanent liaison with the Indian formations in the command.

Mobilization

On the outbreak of war in Europe the GOC took the opportunity of testing the plan for the mobilization of impressed and hired transport. On the appointed day the Registrar of Vehicles (an official of the Government of Singapore), with the aid of the civil police, diverted some 500 civil vehicles which were returning home —it was a Saturday afternoon—to a parking place close to 52 MT company's lines. There the drivers were told that they must stay and await further instructions. The drivers, a mixture of Malays, Indians and Chinese, had visions of being 'shanghaied' and shipped off immediately to Europe to the war without even an opportunity of taking leave of their families, and they began forcibly to demonstrate their displeasure. The RASC subaltern in charge sought the aid of an adjoining British battalion which quickly turned out a company to surround the 'rioters'. After a good meal hastily provided by the MT company, the test was completed, and when the real day came the lessons had been learned, and the drivers were content to sit and wait and gamble, only leaving their vehicles to take their turn at the cookhouse door. What pleased them particularly was the thoughtful plan, a security one, of providing a ring of lights around their camp to enable them, as they thought, to continue their gaming throughout the night.

The outbreak of war also gave the first opportunity for pressing for the need for systematic training and the allotment of a definite war role to the ASC element of the SVC. RASC instructors were provided, and drill nights and weekend exercises on the lines of territorial training at home were arranged.

The DDST's long term plan was that the FMSVF transport element should be used to form a reserve MT company when mobilization was ordered. The plan was furthered when in early 1940 all volunteers were called up for two months' training, the MT men being concentrated in Singapore and given an intensive period of instruction. The company which was formed eventually from the FMSVF was designated No. 45 (FMSVF) Reserve MT Company.

A further review of the military situation made in the early part of 1940 showed that if the island base were to be denied to an enemy, it would be vital to prevent him from making any large scale incursion into the Malayan Peninsula which would allow him to set up a base for operations against Singapore and to establish airfields on the mainland. There was a clear case for the protection of the whole of the Malayan Peninsula, and it was obvious that considerable land, air and sea reinforcements would be required for the purpose, with a special emphasis on the air. Unfortunately the estimate of the air strength required could not be accepted because of the time it would take to build up the requisite organization, and the best that could be offered was an increase in the number of ground troops to be provided. These decisions had barely been made when the defeat of France and the occupation by the Japanese of pro-Vichy Indo-China followed, thus opening the way to an immediate occupation of neighbouring Siam if the enemy decided on such a course. This produced a fresh need for more air power, but once again the resources were not available. By this time there was no question of the seriousness of the position being unrecognized, but, as is so aptly described by Sir Winston Churchill, 'the Japanese menace lay in a sinister twilight compared with other needs'. Thus within a matter of months the whole complexion of defence arrangements was to alter, and military reinforcements began to arrive in considerable strength. The first to land, in August, 1940, were two British battalions which had been withdrawn from Shanghai (see the section on Hong Kong) and, with a battalion of the locally raised Malay Regiment, were formed into a second Malaya Brigade. Between October, 1940, and May, 1941, the 9th and 11th Indian Divisions, each of two brigade groups, arrived. The Australian Imperial Force also joined the command, the second of the two brigades of the 8th Australian Infantry Division completing the Dominion contingent when this arrived in August, 1941. A brigade of Ghurkas—the 28th Brigade—came from India in September, and individual field regiments, an anti-tank regiment and a reconnaissance regiment arrived from India and the United Kingdom in November and December.

By September, 1941, the DDST had become responsible for supplying, in round figures, 55,000 Indian, 21,000 British, 15,000 Dominion troops, 3,400 Malayan enlistments and 1,400 Chinese, each of which had their different ration scales.

The growing strength of the command and increased transport commitments entailed new plans being made to build up reserves of food and petrol and the setting up of a supply organization to cover the whole of the Malayan Peninsula and the expansion of the arrangements for providing transport.

The Malayan Peninsula covered an area approximately equal to that of England and Wales. Served by a railway and main road roughly running parallel to the west coast, there were few lateral communications with the east, because of the extensive mountain ranges that divided the western and eastern territories. A branch railway line ran to the north and east, but did not join the east coast until some 400 miles from Singapore, when it reached Kota Bharu. Unfortunately the last stretch of 30 miles of railway from Kuala Kry to Kota Bahru could not be used when operations began owing to the presence of two viaducts which could be shelled from the sea and were vulnerable from air attack, and there was no road between the two towns although the gap in the supply line had to be filled by road transport. The terrain of the country was mostly thick jungle or vegetation except where the land was cultivated, most of the cultivated areas being rubber plantations or paddy fields.

Early in 1941, there was to be further development in defence policy that tended to increase the transport commitment even further by the acceptance in principle of the plan known as 'Matador'. Put broadly, the plan was one of taking a leaf out of the enemy's book by invading Siam and getting there first to deny its use as a base to the enemy. It was a logical plan, but was accompanied by some military risk. As it involved the infringement of the neutrality of Siam, it was not to be put into effect without the authority of the Cabinet. But arrangements had to be made to put it into action if required. It was on this general background that the RASC had to develop its defence organization.

Amassing Stocks

The decision made to raise the command's reserves from 70 to 180 days and the stream of reinforcements which began to arrive in 1940 presented a great supply problem. Given time it was mainly a matter of amassing stocks of tinned and preserved foods acceptable to British tastes, but many of the staple commodities required for the growing number of non-European ration scales had no equivalents in canned or preserved form. At the same time it was vital to provide a high proportion of reserves in fresh form if health and well being were to be maintained in the hot and humid climate of Malaya. It was also necessary to try to reduce the calls for food on the United Kingdom to a minimum and to save every ton of shipping freight which was possible. Australia was the obvious source to be explored, but that country was still primarily an exporter of fresh or frozen agricultural and dairy produce. It was developing its industry for the production of manufactured (e.g. tinned) commodities in the variety required for field service rations.

The provision and storage of each main commodity offered a different problem, and many of the main items such as meat and flour (wheat) were required in different form by the European and non-European. Atta was the largest single commodity needed for the Indian and native troops but, although obtainable from India, it could not be stored with any safety for more than three months unless air conditioned storage, which was out of the question, could be constructed for the purpose. There were wheat mills in both Singapore and in the FMS, so it was decided to import wheat from Australia and then mill it as required. But what is generally referred to as infestation had not been reckoned with, and the pest *Calandra granaria*—better known as the weevil—soon made his appearance. The need for shipping wheat that was 'clean, sound and new season' was represented to Australia and produced better shipments, the difference being markedly noticeable on arrival, but this did not stop the insects breeding, although the sprinkling of slaked lime between bags stopped the carrying of infestation to some extent. Storage of this wheat in the main supply storage places was also accompanied by the risk of infestation of other commodities, so that it was decided to construct simple silos made of wood and lined with corrugated sheeting. Twelve of these silos were made in the supply depot in Singapore (Bukit Timah). Before the grain was fed into them it was passed through a cleaning machine to remove the extraneous matter and various impurities that are always to be found. When required for milling, the wheat was again cleaned before being milled.

The provision of reserves of meat presented what were really two separate problems because of racial differences. Fresh or frozen beef was wanted for the British troops, and it was, of course, known that the expected arrival of the AIF would considerably increase the amount to be provided, as meat was regarded as being one of the most important parts of their ration—they even ate steaks for breakfast. Sheep or goat on hoof was required by the units of the Indian Army and by most other non-European troops. The relative proximity of Australia meant that supplies of frozen beef and mutton could be easily procured, but cold storage was not available for the large tonnage which would have to be stored, and the inroads which could be made on civil storage were limited because of the large European civil population.

There were few cattle in Malaya. There was an experimental herd in Malacca, but it was insufficient to meet the Army's needs even if the climate and local conditions had been suitable for distributing fresh meat; so any question of maintaining a reserve on the hoof could not enter the DDST's plans. Taking into account the amount of extra storage that could be hired, additional space for 1,000 tons of cold storage was required, and plans were made accordingly. After months of delay and disappointments due to lack of local experience in cold storage construction, and the non-arrival of certain essential plants, the project was not completed when operations began in December, 1941.*

The short-lived campaign meant that the full reserve was not to be needed, and in the operational period distribution of frozen produce was successfully arranged by means of special small containers, each holding 250 rations, and several 3-ton lorries each of which, after being fitted out on the spot with insulating material, could carry two tons of meat.

Although the meat ration required by the Indian and other troops was small, the influx of about 50,000 men of the Indian Army meant that their aggregated needs could not be met from local resources. There was no lack of meat in Malaya suited to the taste of the Indian troops, as there was a large goat population, but as they were owned in ones or twos by the local inhabitants, and were the principal providers of fresh milk, they could not be purchased in sufficient quantity for meeting the needs of the Indian formation.

India was first drawn upon and a large goat farm established at Blakang Mati, but the removal of the animals from their local pastures to new fields and the sea journeys involved led to heavy losses. Although some fine and healthy animals were received from Afghanistan, most of them were soon found to be suffering from one complaint or another, and, in spite of segregation and the efforts of the civil Veterinary Department, were dying daily in large numbers, and the civil government had to prohibit any further imports. It was a discouraging start. Later this ban was removed, and supplies were obtained partly from India under contract, partly from the Netherlands East Indies, and the rest in the form of live sheep from Australia. These new arrangements were not long in force when once again disaster overtook the goats from India, which were found to be arriving with rinderpest. All

* It is of interest to know that the store was finally completed 10 years later.

further imports had again to be banned while the problem was re-examined. On this occasion the veterinary authorities in India were asked to arrange for special inspection and quarantine before despatch and for veterinary supervision on the voyage and inspection again before issue. Quarantine stations were set up in Singapore and at Butterworth on the mainland opposite Penang, but in the meantime the Dutch islands had to be drawn upon and limited purchases made through state veterinary officers. In practice the problem of supply was never overcome, and a plan to provide tinned curried chicken so prepared that it would meet the various religious requirements came to nought at the last moment because of the fear of future doubts which might lead to a political issue in India.

Many other difficulties which arose in the endeavour to provide fresh produce such as vegetables and fruit were overcome in due course, but as it was evident that an outbreak of hostilities would interfere with certain sources of supply, considerable stocks of tinned and dehydrated produce had to be built up in case of need.

The storage space in the existing supply depot at Alexandra was insufficient for the many thousands of tons of food that were required as reserves, and further accommodation had to be sought for both food and petrol. The choice rested on a large rubber factory at Bukit Timah and the adjoining area where stacks could be well dispersed as protection against air attack. Advanced base supply and petrol depots were established at Kuala Lumpur and smaller depots at other suitable places. The siting of all these various types of depots and the stocks held in them was a matter of some importance, as it had to be carefully related both to the nature of the operations that were expected when hostilities broke out and to the efficient distribution of stocks.

The supply of bread did not offer any special problems. The modern bakery in Singapore was adequate to meet the needs of the troops in the island. In Malaya, units were supplied from military bakeries at Kuala Lumpur, from civilian bakeries, and by sections of the RIASC with their simple but effective 'beehive' ovens. These ovens, fired with fuel wood, produced excellent bread and had the great advantage that they could be easily moved and quickly set up again.

Men and Transport

There had been no particular difficulty in providing the number of supply units required, as India was a fruitful source. The main problem was the provision of transport units. India could not spare any apart from those which formed an integral part of the formations she was providing, and could not produce any transport units for corps troops. It will be appreciated that there were many calls on India from the Middle East and elsewhere. The AIF, on the other hand, were complete with corps troops and their Government came to the rescue by despatching two reserve MT companies to be at the disposal of the RASC. They were magnificent companies manned by veterans of the First World War, and they gave invaluable service.

As already mentioned, the only means of providing the number of companies which were required was by raising MT companies locally. When the question of the establishment of locally enlisted companies was considered, the War Office were naturally anxious to conserve their resources in British officers and NCOs, and urged strongly that all NCOs should be locally enlisted Malays. But the command were adamant in their view that it was impossible to produce efficient NCOs above the rank of corporal because of lack of experience and education. As the need for expansion became pressing, the GOC gave authority for raising three companies, but in doing so he had to set aside the local demurs that War Office authority would have to be obtained first. The companies were soon recruited, but only a few of the Malays could drive or had any mechanical experience, and the number of British officers and other ranks for providing the requisite cadres was limited. When the local transport organizations were built up, the officer reinforcements proved to be first class material and excellently trained. It was not long before they showed themselves well fitted for promotion to captain and later for commanding companies. Some direct commissions were also given to local residents who brought with them their knowledge of the country, its inhabitants and languages.

Until vehicles could be supplied by the War Office, units were equipped with lorries which were purchased locally, as there was a fairly good supply of both Ford and Chevrolet trucks to be obtained in Singapore. As soon as the first two companies—28 and 35—had been raised, they were allocated to act as second line transport for Force Emu and the Malaya Brigades, and a third company, 42, was completed soon afterwards.

To provide for the number of ambulances which would be wanted, plans of the standard Flint stretcher gear were obtained from Britain and, with certain modifications, this equipment was manufactured locally so as to equip vehicles improvised for the purpose. In 1941 two motor ambulance convoys were raised locally. While the RASC were exploiting local resources in manpower to the utmost and had successfully raised three MT companies, it was impossible to get enough skilled MT artificers, and with the growth of the MT organization it was imperative to provide the equivalent of the three main maintenance units which were an essential part of the RASC MT organization—a heavy repair shop, an MT stores depot and a vehicle reserve depot. A call had therefore to be made on home resources, which was eventually met by a composite British unit, 28 Combined MT Depot, to fill all three functions. The depot arrived just in time to assist with the uncrating and assembly of Canadian vehicles (4 x 4 Marmon Herringtons) which were arriving in large numbers. On arrival the depot was temporarily established in a large exhibition hall known as the MAHA Stadium at Kuala Lumpur. It was augmented by drivers of one of the Australian Reserve MT companies, many of whom had been employed in peacetime in the Ford works at Sydney, and part of the work had also to be let out to civilian garages in Singapore. The War Office had also begun to send other vehicles from Britain, principally cars, motorcycles and technical vehicles, and these, with the vehicles which had been purchased locally, enabled all the locally raised units to be well equipped before hostilities began. There were many vehicles still remaining to be uncrated and assembled when the first Japanese landings took place, and the work had to be continued on the dockside, the second Australian Reserve MT Company undertaking the task.

But towards the end, the supply of suitable men for enlistment and training as drivers began to fail, and it was decided to extend recruiting to the Federated Malay States. In 1941, a Malay Company, No. 43, was recruited at Kuala Lumpur and was being followed by a second when hostilities broke out. But a few weeks before, it had been possible to break fresh ground when an approach was made to the influential Chinese in Perak with a view to raising the first Chinese company. After a conference lasting three hours in the Chinese Secretariat at Ipoh, the plan was agreed to on the understanding that the unit should be known as a Perak Chinese company. It was raised in a very short time, as about three quarters of those enlisted were fully trained drivers, many of them having had experience on the Burma Road. This unit, 47 (Perak Chinese) Reserve MT Company, did excellent work when the time came to operate a few weeks later, and a special mention must be made of the loyalty and courage of the two Chinese officers who, although there was no known form of legal commission which could be given to them, upheld the tradition of the uniform they wore.

The mobilization plan for impressing and hiring transport was also expanded and perfected. Fortunately the RASC had a close liaison with the central authority for the control of civil transport in Malaya, the FMS Transport Board. The head of this board was Mr. A. L. Stallworthy, and his technical adviser, a former Corps officer, was Lieut-Colonel Mervyn Cox. Many lorries and cars were requisitioned, and on mobilization all vehicles reported to 43 Reserve MT Company, who arranged the delivery of impressed vehicles to those units which were some distance away, while units in the vicinity came and collected the vehicles that had been allotted to them. The scheme worked well in practice, although disobedience of orders and indiscriminate impressment by one formation nearly wrecked the carefully made plans for the use of the transport in the district. One Indian officer, in a moment of exuberance, stopped a car at pistol point and demanded that it should be taken over at once. The owner was the chairman of the board and the sequel can be imagined.

While there was adequate bulk petrol freely available in the hands of the oil companies, special steps had to be taken to make certain that the military reserve, which represented about a year's supply at peacetime consumption rates, did not deteriorate, as normal motor spirit (cracked spirit) tended to 'gum up' after some months' storage. Most of the reserve had, therefore, to be obtained in the form of 'straight run spirit' which could be stored safely for periods of over a year.

Distribution was a matter of getting enough containers, and although the 4-gallon tin was in use for kerosene in the commercial market, a large supply of 44- and 60-gallon drums were manufactured locally from sheet steel, of which there was fortunately enough, while as much use as possible was made of the normal kerb-side pump fed from underground 1,000-gallon tanks. A chain of petrol depots was also established, on the line of communication and in the forward northern areas close to the complementary depots of the food supply organization. In many places the proximity of plantations or forest offered a serious fire risk, but all depots were provided with protection from blast, and dumps so bunded as to prevent a fire from spreading. As no tarpaulins were available for covering stacks to reduce the effect of the sun's rays and tropical rainstorms, each dump was protected by an 'attap'* shelter.

Decanting from the 44- and 60-gallon drums was a problem, as no decanting apparatus could be obtained from Britain. The RIASC POL sections were equipped with a hand operated decanting apparatus and can cleaning and testing plant, but the output was small although rotary, and even stirrup, pumps were introduced to speed the flow. In consequence it was a common sight to see a military vehicle with its own reservoir of a 60-gallon barrel on its tail-board, which was decanted by the driver into his own tins. The Australian reserve MT companies went one better by decanting direct from barrel to tank by means of rubber hoses taken off stirrup pumps, the flow of fuel being started by the simple process of what is known in the Royal Navy as 'sucking the monkey'.

* 'Attap' = The branch of the palm tree which was used extensively in building huts.

There was, of course, wastage, but it was less than would have been incurred by an extensive use of the flimsy can.

An increasing demand for water transport was met by the formation of a water transport company from the original peacetime detachment, some British officers and NCOs being provided from Britain for the purpose. Additional vessels were obtained locally by purchase and new construction. The locally purchased vessels were of the Tongkon variety fitted with a Ford V8 engine. Some were mounted with small guns, but their performance was somewhat hazardous as the boats were apt to sink when the guns were fired! High speed target towers were under construction when hostilities broke out, but as the engines had not been fitted they had to be abandoned as hulks. The new company was located at Pulau Brani with a large detachment at Changi to serve the many islands where coast defences had been developed.

Meanwhile the period of preparation was gradually drawing to a close as the months of 1941 passed by and tension increased. In the autumn many Japanese nationals who were resident in Malaya received orders from their Government to leave. There were clear indications that the Japanese were preparing to establish themselves in southern Siam, and their reconnaissance aircraft were already flying over Malaya and Sarawak.

On December 1st a state of emergency was declared, and the volunteer forces were mobilized. Six days later Japanese convoys of warships and transports were reported to be steaming westward, and on December 8th the enemy began to land strong forces at Singora and Patani in southern Siam and at Kota Bahru.

Inadequate Defences

The opening moves of the enemy on December 8th bore out in only too realistic a fashion the accuracy of the several military appreciations of his probable course of action. Gaining a strong foothold almost immediately, the Japanese forces began to press over to the west coast and down the centre of northern Malaya and consolidated their possession of Kota Bahru and its important airfield.

To meet this threat III Indian Corps was so disposed as to be responsible for all that part of Malaya which lies north of Johore and Malacca, the 11th Indian Infantry Division being in the west, and the 9th Indian Infantry Division in the south centre and watching Kota Bahru and Kuantan in the east. The Australian Imperial Force was responsible for the defence of Johore and Malacca, and the protection of Singapore was the task of the two Malaya infantry brigades. The 12th Indian Infantry Brigade in GHQ Reserve was located in Singapore.

It was a case of trying to watch everywhere and being strong nowhere, as the land forces at the disposal of the Commander-in-Chief were undoubtedly insufficient for the purpose. Many of the fighting units were still militarily immature, and few had the opportunity of receiving any specialized training in the type of warfare to which they were to be committed. From the start of the campaign the forces were hopelessly handicapped by lack of air-power, many of the aircraft were out of date, and there was a lack of fully trained air crews. The power of the naval forces available, although reinforced a few days before by the arrival of the powerful battleship *Prince of Wales* and the battle cruiser *Repulse*, was unbalanced, as the force lacked any aircraft carriers or heavy cruisers. The arrangements for civil defence were far from being fully developed.

It was truly not an inspiring situation. All the forces were imbued with the will to do their best, but the campaign resulted in our troops being hopelessly outnumbered and outfought. Within a few days the enemy was able to establish complete air superiority, and the sinking of the *Prince of Wales* and *Repulse* left the Japanese in undisputed command of the Far Eastern waters.

So far as the RASC were concerned, preparations for the supply and transport services were fairly complete when hostilities broke out. On the west coast stocks of food and petrol for the 11th Indian Division were held as far north as Alor Star, backed by 20 days at Sungei Patani, while a month's supply had been built up at Bukit Mertajam, to be drawn on if plan Matador was put into effect. The 9th Division were also well provided, for 20 days' stocks had been laid down at Kuala Krai for replenishing Kota Bharu, and 20 days at Jerantut for replenishing the small garrison at Kuantan on the east. To enable the garrison at Penang to hold out if by-passed by an enemy advance, six months' supplies had been laid down there. Various other stocks were held at other centres such as Ipoh and Seramban on the main Western Railway, the main forward reserves being stored in the advanced base supply and petrol depots at Kuala Lumpur.

In principle the replenishment of the northern depot was to be done from Kuala Lumpur, and the depots to the east and south were to be re-stocked by rail from Singapore, but in the event of any break in the eastern railway line there were alternative arrangements for supplying both Kuala Krai and Jerantut from Kuala Lumpur by road.

Food Supplies

So long as the various forces on the north could hold their ground there seemed to be little danger of their lacking food or motive power even if they were temporarily cut off from their normal line of supply, and approximately 120 days' stocks were held in the base depots in Singapore to make good any losses and maintain supply for several months.

The available general transport was also so disposed that it could be used to the best advantage as the course of the operations became revealed. Formations (i.e. the Indian and Australian divisions) were self-contained with sufficient transport to draw their daily requirements from the nearest depot or dumps. Two companies, 47 (Perak Chinese) RASC and 2/1 Reserve Company, AASC, were located at Ipoh. Nos 45 (FMSVF) and 43 Companies RASC were stationed at Kuala Lumpur, two platoons of the latter company being disposed at Kuala Krai and Jerantut. An independent platoon was provided for Penang. The remainder of the companies were held in Singapore, and formed temporarily into a transport column under a CRASC.

The enemy was quick to follow up his success at Kota Bahru and, finding it impossible to dislodge him, the Indian brigade, weakened after heavy fighting, was withdrawn to avoid the risk of its being completely isolated in the event of further landings on the east. The brigade was then redeployed about Temerloh to watch the road approaches from the east and to protect the rear of the 11th Indian Division fighting in the north. All stocks from Kuala Krai were successfully back-loaded to Singapore by rail, and the evacuation of the brigade afforded the first opportunity for the RASC (Malay) Transport to prove its worth. If there were any doubts about these untried men, they were soon dispelled as the platoon of 43 Company, which was the last to leave, earned the commendation of the divisional commander for its work.

The strength of the enemy's main forces employed in his drive to the west soon began to tell, and the 11th Division, after losing heavily at Jitra, were forced to begin to withdraw to the south. Alor Star and the adjoining airfield were lost and Sungei Patani overrun, but not before most of the stock of petrol and food had been evacuated. The advanced depots at Bukit Mertajam proved to be an embarrassment as, stocked up for the proposed Matador plan to advance into Siam, the stores were untouched and could not be removed in time, although valiant efforts were made to destroy them. The island of Penang was soon left uncovered from the mainland, and as heavy air attacks had completely disorganized the civil services, it was decided to evacuate the garrison by sea to Singapore. Efforts were made to destroy the stocks of food and petrol, and the MT Platoon, after its arrival at Singapore, was sent forward to join 43 Company at Kuala Lumpur.

The losses sustained by the 11th Division in its continued marching and fighting were so severe that by the time it reached the Krian

River two brigades had to be amalgamated into one before the formation was pressed back again to the relatively strong positions which were taken up behind the Perak River about Kampar. By December 23rd this gallant division had been driven back no less than 160 miles, and the 12th Indian Brigade which had been brought up from GHQ reserve to reinforce the division, had already been engaged for 14 days and was called upon to make yet a further stand against ever increasing odds. Fresh threats then developed from seaborne landings at the mouth of the Perak River and to the south, and orders were given to break off contact for a further withdrawal to the next natural obstacle, the Slim River.

During the withdrawal the stocks at Taiping had to be abandoned, although partially destroyed, but the supply depot at Ipoh was successfully evacuated, two days' rations being left to be collected by the 11th Division on its way to the south. The two MT companies at Ipoh were withdrawn to Kuala Lumpur. They were a useful reinforcement, as there was a great deal to be done in the way of forming dumps behind the Perak and the Slim Rivers (many of which had to be retrieved soon after), carrying RE demolition parties and collecting and backloading of stores of all kinds as part of the scorched earth policy, on which directions had been received from the home Government in mid-December. This policy, which involved the denial of anything in the wake of the withdrawing army that might be useful to an enemy, had been successfully applied by the Axis powers in Europe, but obviously required some modification in a withdrawal in a friendly country where the inhabitants left behind were so reliant on local produce and facilities for their livelihood. The scorched earth scheme was obviously one which required careful co-ordination between the civil Government and the military, but there was neither time nor the organization for carrying it out. The attempts to put it into force reacted most adversely on the arrangements for backloading essential military stores, caused a great waste of transport, and led to such dispersion that many RASC detachments were not seen again for long periods. The general transport situation was serious enough, as before long railways became congested with some military stores being sent back, and others, more urgent and essential ones, being sent forward; and the sudden additional load of civil material made for a hopeless traffic jam. It is credibly reported that in one instance the urgent civil stores that had to be carried by RASC transport turned out to be the private furniture of a civil official.

Kuala Lumpur evacuated

After the reverse of the Perak River and the withdrawal to the Slim River position, the evacuation of Kuala Lumpur which was the main advance base, became imperative. No. 28 Combined MT Depot, which fulfilled the triple function of MT repairs, stockholding MT spares and maintaining a reserve of vehicles, was evacuated to Singapore, the new vehicles which the unit was engaged in erecting being used to backload the more attractive and less plentiful supplies from the advanced base supply depot. A daily allotment of railway trucks enabled the supply depot to be cleared of all but 200 tons of wheat before the advanced base was finally evacuated, but a stock of 800 tons of frozen meat had to be destroyed through lack of refrigerator transport.

Petrol was less easy to dispose of, as the heavy 60-gallon barrels proved to be too cumbersome to be handled at any speed by the locally employed labour. About half of the stock had to be left, and attempts by the Royal Engineers to destroy them were not very successful. Three days' stocks of rations were left for the oncoming troops, and when the last train left the party on board saw the railway tunnel blown up behind them.

In the east, although the enemy did not effect any landings at Kuantan until the end of December, heavy air attacks on the airfield had put it out of action, and Japanese columns which started to infiltrate through the jungle from Kota Bahru began on December 20th to come into contact with the small garrison found by the 22nd Indian Infantry Brigade. After various engagements and the loss of the airfield, the garrison was withdrawn from this remote area, the MT platoons engaged in the operation playing a staunch part. One of them was heavily ambushed, but drove straight on and gained its objective after suffering some casualties.

So far the RASC had been able to keep pace with their task. The plan of distributing stocks at strategical points had on the whole worked well, although some losses had been sustained, especially through constant demands as the situation altered to form fresh dumps of about seven days' food here and there. In many cases it was found impossible to move the food, as units' vehicles were already fully loaded. Had the technique of air supply been then developed, the situation might have been easier, but even if it had been there seems to be no doubt that aircraft could not be found for the purpose. One or two attempts were made to carry out free dropping, but in consequence of lack of skill and organization the supplies were never retrieved.

The locally enlisted transport units had also done well and, although operations had parted many of the men from their homes or smallholdings, there were a negligible number of desertions. For example when the 45 (FMSVF) Reserve MT Company had to withdraw from the State in which they were raised and were given the option of returning to their homes, 85 per cent agreed to remain with the unit. When hostilities began none of the Malays were armed because of the difficulty of weapon training and lack of weapons. Yet it is recounted that at least some platoons acquired rifles and tommy-guns from abandoned stocks and soon trained themselves by using them in earnest, to such good purpose that they were allowed to retain them. Because of the lack of artificers, many civilians had to be employed in the units' workshops and they too remained with their units, perhaps because of the ready agreement to the request that their families should accompany them under the wing of the unit.

Withdrawal to Singapore

By the time our forces in the west had been redeployed on the Slim River positions, they were in no fit state to continue to oppose the strong enemy columns which were being reinforced continually. Weeks of fighting and marching had already taken their toll. The situation was extremely serious, as it was considered vital to continue to hold the enemy on the mainland until the arrival of promised reinforcements which, with the entry of the United States into the war, were to be on a scale that had not been possible before. Information had already been received in December that the 18th British Infantry Division, with anti-aircraft and anti-tank units, and some 50 Hurricane aircraft and crews, were on the high seas and other immediate reinforcements were on their way from India. The only course was to withdraw to a shorter line. The two Indian divisions broke off contact with the enemy and a new line of defence, Segemat-Muar, was selected about 150 miles to the rear. It was held by the Australian Division and 45th Indian Infantry Brigade. The III Indian Corps was brought back into Johore to reorganize and, it was hoped, to refit.

During the evacuation from central Malaya, the MT companies were moved back towards Singapore by stages, 43 and 47 being placed at the disposal of the Officer Commanding, RASC, who had been appointed to the Administrative headquarters of Johore and Malacca, a few miles from Johore Bahru. The supply depot at Seremban was successfully evacuated under heavy air bombardment, and the remaining depot on the mainland at Segamat was reorganized to supply the increased numbers of troops in that area. By the middle of January, arrangements were made to send forward all formation requirements from the base depots at Bukit Timah on Singapore Island to various roadheads where they were then collected by formations' own transport. As our forces were pressed back after the sanguinary fighting which took place in the battle of Muar, the depot at Segamat had also to be given up, and from then onwards all troops were supplied from depots on the mainland or from dumps established near Johore Bahru, distribution being effected by 43 and 47 Companies, assisted by three Indian brigade transport companies, to three roadheads in the areas of Yong Peng, Kluang and Labis (See Fin Estate). A new depot established at Rengem had a very short life and had to be evacuated on January 25th. The work of endeavouring to save as many stores and material as possible went on apace there; then 140 vehicles a day had to be found to move ammunition from Johore Bahru to island sites, and some 50 vehicles were used for removing the equipment of the British and Australian General Hospitals. Other transport had to be found for clearing the Engineer Stores Depot, and this work was combined with the forward move of defence stores such as concrete blocks which were urgently wanted in the Johore area for anti-tank defences.

Heavy attacks on the new line of defence and further landings by strong enemy forces on both the east and west coasts demonstrated that there seemed to be little hope of continuing the struggle on the mainland and that a withdrawal into Singapore was inevitable. Reinforcements were arriving, but the first to land on January 3rd was the 45th Indian Infantry Brigade, consisting of untried troops. Being soon committed to battle, it suffered grievously in the battle of Segamat. The first elements of the 18th British Division, the 53rd Infantry Brigade, also arrived in the middle of January, and they also sustained heavy losses for the same reason.

The landing of the division, which was only completed at the end of January, marked the arrival of the first British divisional RASC in the command. Originally destined for service in the Persian Gulf, the RASC had, in common with the rest of this division, been embarked in Britain in October, 1941. The formation went first to Canada, where it was re-embarked in American ships and set sail *via* Trinidad for the Cape, where its destination was altered to the Middle East. While on its way to the Middle East, there was a further change in destination, the convoys being split, two of the RASC companies being directed to Burma and two to Malaya, but a further change then brought all four companies to Singapore. By the time the CRASC had landed, two companies had already arrived, the remaining two following about 10 days later, their convoy being heavily bombed as it passed through the approaches to Singapore.

Units were equipped with borrowed vehicles until their own transport could be landed, and all four companies came into operation immediately after landing, but they were never to function as a divisional RASC, as only one company carried out its normal role, the others being used for troop carrying, for carrying bridging material, and for forming an extemporary infantry unit which took its place in the firing line and held it until the final capitulation.

The progress of operations in the last week of January made a withdrawal into the confines of the island inevitable. On the 25th, responsibility for the evacuation of all the remaining RASC depots and dumps was handed over to the Officer Commanding RASC, Johore, who describes the task somewhat lightly as a 'tedious' one, mainly because of traffic congestion and the continued panicking of the native labour on which he was forced to rely. But by January 30th, 1942, most of the stocks and all MT had been cleared, to such good account that when he withdrew at 0530 hours on 30th he was able to report that the stores remaining were:— Geram Choh SD, about 200 tons of rice; Galang Patah SD, small quantity of rice; Senai SD, small quantities of food; 113 SPS, nil; 76 Petrol Depot, nil; 9 SPS (AIF), 100,000 rations.

The Battle of Singapore

The withdrawal of the British forces from the mainland to the island of Singapore was completed by the morning of January 31st, 1942, when a gap was then blown in the only road link—the causeway—with Johore. The future battle ground was not, as popularly supposed, a fortress; it was only a large area of land and water with permanent defences designed to meet seaborne attacks and with reasonably good anti-aircraft defences. The total area in which our forces were concentrated only measured about 37 miles by 15, but even so there were insufficient troops to man the perimeter in any strength, and there were no tanks to support them. There was a huge Asiatic population, and even if the facilities had been available, there was an almost insuperable civil defence problem to be overcome.

On the completion of the withdrawal formations were so disposed that the western coast was defended by the 44th Indian Brigade and the 22nd Australian Brigade, but the former consisted of untried troops who had no practical battle training for the conditions they were to face. Northwards and to the east the perimeter was defended by the 27th Australian Brigade and the III Corps, which consisted of the reformed 11th Indian Division and the 18th British Division. The Malaya brigades were disposed to defend the southern coast lines.

A lull in land operations followed the withdrawal, but the enemy lost no time in bringing the full weight of his air power and long range artillery against the many targets which presented themselves, and there was little respite or rest which was so badly needed by the battle scarred and weary formations. When the enemy resumed the offensive on January 8th, the battle developed so quickly that

Singapore

plans for dispersing reserves of material and strengthening the landward defences were not completed, and a week later the forces were compelled to capitulate.

Since it has been asserted that among contributory causes for capitulation was a lack of food and petrol it is pertinent to outline the position when the battle opened. In fact the supplies and transport situation was not unfavourable. The enemy's rapid advance through Malaya had, of course, led to losses in both the stocks of food and petrol held there north of Kuala Lumpur, but it had been possible to back load most of the contents of dumps and depots south of that town. Some of this stock was, because of a lack of labour, still on rail and part of it had to be dumped off the rail trucks at any convenient point.

When the question of the division of the command reserves between Singapore and the mainland was first considered, the DDST had urged that not more than 30 days of the 180 days' supplies to be held should be kept on the mainland. But because of the expected vulnerability of communications and the possibility of an advance into Siam (plan 'Matador'), it was decided that a higher proportion had to be held in the mainland depots. However, there were still substantial stocks available in Singapore when the withdrawal to the island took place. Main stocks were held at the base supply depot at Bukit Timah, where there was also some cold storage, a field bakery and the atta mills for supplying Indian troops. The principal cold storage depot and static bakery were at Alexandra, and there were several subsidiary stores at the Turf Club, in a factory, in a cinema and in various godowns. There was a plan for putting down a number of other small dumps so as to disperse the main reserves and to reduce the distance to be covered by units' transport; and it was also ordered that all units were to draw up nine days' preserved rations, but because of the speed of events these arrangements were not completed.

Petrol supplies did not give the new DDST* any real cause for concern, as the canned and bulk reserves held in Singapore were backed by the large civil stocks held in the civil oil installations at Pulau Bukum and Pulau Sambue. When the campaign opened there were six million gallons stored in Malaya and further despatches of about 100,000 gallons a week had been sent forward from Singapore, but some of these had not been unloaded and were returned intact. A good deal of petrol had been lost on the mainland in spite of energetic attempts to back load stocks at outlying depots and dumps. But because of the distance from the railway,

---

* Brigadier C. E. Davis had been withdrawn to take up a similar appointment with the new HQ South-West Pacific Command and replaced by Lieut-Colonel C. W. Richards, who had been commanding the RASC general transport units in Singapore.

and the large quantities involved, these attempts were not always successful.

It is known that when the final withdrawal to the island took place a million gallons were held in the main depot at Bukit Timah and a reserve of another million close by; one and a half million gallons were held in bulk at a civil depot, taken over by the army, at Woodland road, and there were also smaller reserves of about 100,000 gallons each held at other points.

There was no lack of transport, as all the locally raised companies which were operating in Malaya had been withdrawn and were in good order and the RASC resources had just been reinforced by the arrival of the four companies of the 18th Division. In fact there was so much transport on the roads in the relatively restricted area that an embargo had to be placed on all but essential civil transport and as distances were short there was no need for making use of second and third line transport. If there was a transport difficulty, it was caused by the time taken to carry out a given task as communications became more congested and temporarily interrupted in consequence of the enemy's bombing raids. These raids caused some losses, and the first serious loss was the destruction of garrisons' mobile reserve of ammunition, which had been held under load in an RASC platoon.

When the campaign first began the only RASC workshops for repairing RASC MT vehicles were at Kuala Lumpur and at Alexandra. The former, the heavy repair wing of 28 Combined MT Depot, was well accommodated but was never put into full use, as the unit was the only large British unit at Kuala Lumpur and, soon after its arrival was required for defence duties. The workshop at Alexandra was small and was a development of the permanent peace workshops belonging to 52 Company. The siting of the main repair unit at Kuala Lumpur was governed by the fact that the fullest possible use was made of local civil repair facilities in Singapore.

Although it was possible to evacuate the Combined Depot to Singapore and a good site in a reinforced concrete garage was found for it there was no time to reinstal the machinery. The men of the unit were used to assist the various company workshops and later to find crews for the WD vessels which had been deserted by their civilian complements.

It can be safely affirmed that the general resources behind the RASC when the offensive against the island began were more than adequate. But the fighting strength of all formations had been sadly depleted. Orders were given about January 7th to the 18th Divisional RASC, the only RASC organization with a full strength of British ranks, to form two companies for an infantry role. The order was carried out quickly by drawing on about three-fifths of the available strength of 54 and 55 Companies and men from two field ambulances and within 24 hours the two RASC 'infantry' companies were on their way to take their place in the future battle zone. These two units did well and took their full share of the fighting that followed and, although they suffered many casualties, they came out of the fight with high morale—a morale which they maintained during three and a half long years as prisoners of war, in spite of being separated from their officers.

The Japanese Advance

The respite from land attack was short. On January 8th there was much enemy activity on the opposite shores and late that evening the enemy made a determined attack, with the aid of armoured landing craft, across the straits of Johore against the positions held by the 22nd Australian Brigade. After gaining a foothold on the Island the Japanese pressed forward towards the important positions of the Tengah airfield and Bukit Timah. The next day the airfield was captured, and new attacks were opened on the 27th Australian Brigade, who were driven back by vastly superior numbers, and reinforcements from III Corps were unable to restore the situation. The continued pressure of the enemy towards Bukit Timah directly menaced the main reserves of both food and petrol which were held in that area. On the 10th a large quantity of petrol was destroyed, on the 11th the main petrol depot fell into enemy hands, and the same evening the base supply depot was captured.

The staff of the base supply depot at Bukit Timah had been withdrawn on February 10th and ordered to take over dumps on the racecourse, but were forced to withdraw from there to Farrer Park on the 11th, and their final move thence, to No. 55 godown in the harbour area on the 12th. These moves did not take place until the infantry were forced to concede the ground, so that the RASC supply and petrol units were constantly in what might be described as the front line, and transport units ordered forward to clear a given dump often found it was already occupied by the enemy.

The siting and the loss of the main reserves at Bukit Timah have been criticized, but any first-hand knowledge of the restricted area around the confines of Singapore city itself amply confirms that no suitable alternative sites were available and, even if they could have been found in the city, they would have been an obvious target from the air. If there is a case for criticism it should be directed to the lack of organized labour which prevented stocks from being dispersed when the final withdrawal to the island took place, and to the lack of adequate guards for preventing pilferage and sabotage by the increasing number of lawless natives. Yet it must be recorded that the permanent Asiatic employees who had served with the RASC for many years stuck loyally to their posts, and in such establishments as the barracks stores went on working to the last, knowing well that all hope of further resistance was getting less day by day.

The enemy extended his offensive in the north on February 11th by attacking in strength with a Japanese Guards Division against the front held by III Corps. By this time the causeway, being no longer under our direct fire, had been repaired, and he had no difficulty in following up his initial success. On the next day, III Corps were ordered to withdraw to a general line from Bukit Timah road to Paya Lebar and thence to Kallang. The 22nd Australian Brigade were still holding their ground south of Bukit Timah but, being in danger of isolation, were also ordered back to link up with the 44th Indian Brigade to their left. On the same day it was decided that all shipping should leave and make for ports of safety, and that as it was impossible to defend the main oil installations at Pulau Bakum they should be destroyed so as to deny them to the enemy.

Although the enemy made little headway on the 13th, the situation was already desperate. It was decided that certain technical personnel and others with special qualifications should be evacuated by sea on the grounds that they were already surplus to the immediate needs of the garrison and that they would be of more use elsewhere. As history relates, few of the ships of the military and civilians who left Singapore reached their destinations, and they were either captured or lost.

The city of Singapore was at that time in the range of field artillery fire and the conditions due to constant bombing were such that pestilence might break out at any time. Water was already running short and all normal distribution of food and other essentials was completely disrupted. Our forces were almost fought to a standstill and were in such a position that further resistance could only lead to unnecessary suffering.

The depth of the enemy's advance into the island had led to the loss of all our main reserves of food and petrol, and of the many subsidiary stocks at various points which were already in enemy hands. As late as the 10th the DDST, who had been in constant touch with the Civil Food Controller, was able to confirm that supply ships were still being unloaded by improvised labour, as most of the regular civilian labour had deserted their tasks, but it was impossible to tally what was landed because of constant air attack and the need for pushing any stocks landed at once into the nearest godown. There was still a large quantity of meat in the Government cold storage at Orchard Road and there were sufficient other commodities to have provided a modified form of ration if the general conditions had allowed. It is also recorded that there was some petrol remaining at a dump at Balestier Road formed from stock which had been backloaded from more forward dumps and from supplies obtained by draining the tanks of unwanted vehicles which had been directed there for the purpose. Because of a shortage of water transport, it had been almost impossible to maintain a supply of petrol from Pulau Bukum. One lighter load had been brought over to Keppel Harbour, but it was bombed while being unloaded and only a little was saved. No doubt there were also stocks of petrol in the many civilian pumps which might have been drawn on.

On February 15th the Commander-in-Chief had no option but to order the cease fire. Capitulation followed and our officers and men passed into captivity. The RASC were required, as prisoners of war, to perform some of their duties and a short account of the period is given at the end of this chapter. It was prepared by an officer who was a prisoner in Changi camp.

There are few official records of the last days in Singapore but it is thought that the following first hand account of an RASC company employed on general duties may be of interest to supplement the short general description of the last battle.

Narrative of an Officer of 28 L of C Brigade Company

Two days before the initial attack by the Japanese, 28 L of C Brigade Company RASC located within Singapore Fortress, moved from Ulu Pandau camp to Adam Camp, Adam Road.

The unit, though formed to operate with 1st Malaya Infantry Brigade, remained under command of the officer commanding RASC Singapore Fortress. I, as the company commander, was also appointed OC Troops of Adam Camp, in which was located 29 CMTD, 36 Field Company RE and an Indian supply section.

The administration of the camp placed a heavy load on the unit organization, although later, when the officer commanding 29 CMTD became OC Troops, the company was relieved of some administrative duties. Nevertheless, 28 L of C Brigade Company provided guards for the water transport company at Pulau Brani and the command petrol dump at Buller Camp, which was subsequently bombed and destroyed by Japanese aircraft.

In addition to these duties the company was responsible for passive air defence within the Adam Camp/Samawah Camp area and also the operation of the fortress reserve petrol dump, including a petrol point.

Within the organization of 28 Company a training section had been formed and apart from normal driver and DR training I was required to recruit, equip and train Malays to form fire brigades for five different areas in Singapore.

On December 10th, 1941, a Chinese transport section was formed and placed under my command. It consisted of 60 vehicles of all types, and drivers were supplied by the contractors or owners of the vehicles. The drivers were local Chinese who were given a daily ration allowance of 40 cents, their wages being included in the cost of hiring the vehicles. The maintenance of these lorries was undertaken by the company workshop section.

The workshop section was heavily committed and worked well throughout the operations. When regular maintenance and inspection became impracticable the VOR rate was kept to the minimum. Apart from the normal repair commitments of the company, the workshops maintained the vehicles of 85 Anti-Tank Regiment RA, 1 Malaya Field Ambulance and a hygiene section, in all some 277 vehicle units.

At that time the unit was dispersed throughout Singapore with detachments at Changi, the Botanical Gardens, Raffles College, Caldicott Estate and Lake House, at which the fortress ammunition reserve was located.

During this period 28 L of C Brigade Company was called upon to give assistance to newly arrived units, which included 4th Australian Reserve MT Company, 44th Brigade Transport Company, and 18 Divisional RASC Companies.

Our supply section, later to become 151 SPS, was detailed and operated as a SIS under the control of the fortress supply officer.

The Chinese section was located at Watten Estate, where it remained until the area was so badly shelled that it became impossible to operate from it. The Chinese drivers behaved well throughout the operations and were later allowed to return to their homes.

In the course of the Japanese offensive it became likely that food supplies left at the naval base would fall into enemy hands. From February 3rd, 1942, up to and including the morning of February 9th, 28 L of C Brigade Company was engaged in the removal of these supplies. As the base was under enemy observation it was necessary to effect this operation under cover of darkness.

The approaches to the naval base were often under shell fire, but the base itself was almost completely deserted. The Japanese had captured the entire mainland of Malaya, and they were preparing for the final assault on Singapore Island.

On the first and second nights of the company's operations within the naval base the docks were a circle of fire from end to end. Oil tanks blazed continuously during the whole period and towards the end we came directly under shell fire. Ammunition explosions occurred regularly and added to the hazards of our tasks.

I cannot speak too highly of our Malay drivers and British other ranks; their behaviour was beyond praise. They made several journeys each night to and from the base, and it was often difficult to get the drivers and loaders to take cover when the occasion demanded. Malays make excellent drivers and quickly develop what seems to be a natural road sense. Their behaviour under fire was good considering their limited military training. Towards the end it was inevitable that all Malay units would have some deserters, chiefly because of our reverses and because it was so easy for them to return to civil life without fear of detection either in the FMS or in Singapore.

During the seven nights the company moved 2,000 tons of supplies and 18 tons of sail cloth. All but a few tons of supplies stored in the outer base were cleared to Singapore. There were no casualties to men or vehicles, and throughout the operation almost perfect speed and distance were maintained by the drivers under the most appalling traffic conditions which existed on the main road.

Early in the morning of Monday February 9th, 1942, heavy fire in the vicinity of our rear indicated an enemy landing on the island. As conditions deteriorated further operations became impossible.

Much credit is due to Captain Gibbs who accompanied me throughout our tasks in the naval base. He showed considerable courage, and his energy and drive was of the greatest help.

On February 11th heavy shelling of Adam Camp necessitated the withdrawal of the company to Government House grounds. During two days at this new location our duties were mainly confined to troop carrying. We were continuously under fire from both the ground and air, and we suffered five casualties and the loss of many vehicles.

This location became untenable on Friday February 13th, and the unit moved to River Valley Road. The ammunition section was dispersed to the docks and Teang Bahru Road where the vehicles were hit in an air raid and all destroyed.

The unit remained at River Valley Road until the capitulation. Before marching out to Changi prison, where the company ceased to exist, the balance of the Malay drivers, who had not already left, were paraded and ordered to return to civil life.

Narrative of an Officer in Changi POW Camp

On the surrender, we were all ordered to move to Changi, at the extreme end of the island. Units were given a small amount of transport to enable them to move, and with this some took food, and some personal comforts. The DDST was authorized to take

10 days' rations for the 50,000 in the camp, but no lorries were forthcoming to move this. The food brought by units was collected in supply depots and issued from there. Thus, from the very beginning, normal army principles were in force. From the Royal Army Service Corps point of view, that meant that the supply and transport services were controlled by the DDST, and under him Commanders RASC, AASC or RIASC, in each of the areas into which the camp was divided. Although the normal duties ceased for those prisoners of war who belonged to units of fighting arms, yet the troops had still to be fed, and so for some of the RASC the work of the Corps went on even in captivity.

The first drawing of rations under Japanese arrangements did not take place for a week after the surrender. The scale laid down was most inadequate, and it was brought to the notice of the Japanese authorities that it did not compare in any respect with the field service scale for British troops; but they refused to consider any increase, their attitude being that prisoners of war had no right to anything but bare rations, and they were adamant against what they called luxuries coming into the camp.

The original daily ration scale they laid down consisted of:— rice, about $17\frac{1}{2}$ oz; fresh or tinned meat, $1\frac{1}{4}$ oz; flour, $1\frac{1}{2}$ oz; fresh or tinned vegetables, $3\frac{1}{2}$ oz; milk, $\frac{1}{2}$ oz; sugar, $\frac{3}{4}$ oz; and salt, tea and oil, $\frac{1}{8}$ oz; with 40 cigarettes and 7 oz of poor quality soap a month. No fresh meat was issued until March, and there were no fresh vegetables until May.

In such circumstances, it is not surprising that a black market sprang up, especially in tinned goods. The Japanese punished many officers and men for taking part in this activity, but after a time canteens were permitted, and local purchase officers, working under the DDST, did good work, which resulted in breaking the black market. The quantities which could be bought were small, however, and at first were only sufficient to produce fresh vegetables, fish and eggs for the hospital. When fresh meat appeared at sporadic intervals it was in the form of very poor quality cattle. Frozen mutton was issued until the end of 1942, and after that very poor quality fish took its place, including shark. When beri-beri appeared in consequence of vitamin deficiency, rice polishings and palm oil were allowed to be purchased.

Later even this limited ration was cut, and at one time the rice ration was down to 8 oz. Four small consignments of Red Cross parcels helped to supplement the ration, but on the other hand numbers of other prisoners of war were brought in, and they had to share the slender food resources. Fuel control was vested in the DDST, and considerable credit is due to the RASC officers in charge of this work who ensured in spite of great difficulties that a ration of 3 lb a day was maintained, and a reserve built up.

From August, 1942, ST were directly responsible for the control of supplies, the central canteen, wood supply, gardens and the central piggery. Help was also given to units in their messing arrangements, and a Changi cookery book was produced.

The 18th Divisional RASC, which remained as a unit throughout, maintained a high standard of discipline and so of morale. In May, 1943, a reorganization of the camp by the Japanese resulted in most of the Corps units being split up, and their men distributed among those of other units. But one thing survived which had already been instrumental in helping RASC men to endure the conditions and keep their self-respect, and that was what they called 'Corps spirit'. In face of adversity it proved its reality, not least in the following way.

To enable the officers to keep in touch with their men, and to help the sick in hospital, an RASC welfare club was formed. A president and a welfare officer were appointed, and representatives of the various groups of other ranks were elected. Fortnightly meetings were held for informal talks and coffee. Voluntary subscriptions met the cost of these, and enabled tobacco and cigarettes to be sent to Corps men in hospital, where other ranks only received a nominal rate of pay. Sometimes the business of delivering these amenities to the patients was difficult and dangerous, being contrary to orders, but men were never lacking to undertake the work. The welfare officer advised men on family and personal affairs. Corps Sunday was celebrated with a church parade and a march past. Later it was only possible to provide tobacco and cheroots for the men in hospital; then these became so costly that members of the club were asked to give one day's pay a month, from which 'insurance money' of 5 to 7 cents a day was paid to hospital patients. When numbers fell too low, the officers increased their subscriptions, and the insurance was kept up.

Of the other ranks employed in the ration and fuel service, 19 were from the RASC, with eight from the AASC and one local man. The majority of men were so employed from the time of the capitulation. The hours of work were long, and the work was extremely strenuous on a prisoner of war diet. In spite of this, it is on record that it would be impossible to find a more loyal, competent, trustworthy, and hard-working staff.

By 1945, the ration situation became more and more complex, and a constant watch had to be kept on stocks and scales. The Japanese insisted that the practice should stop of pooling the different classes of rations (heavy duty, light duty and no duty) for the benefit of the worst off, and that each class should receive the appropriate ration; this, in the case of the staple item, rice,

Loading a Landing Craft

Carrying a Churchill

Mobile Bakery

was 17½ oz, 10½ oz, and 8¾ oz respectively. However, the manipulation of employment returns, etc., gave a margin to play with, and so the men in hospital, classed as 'no duty', could be brought up to the light duty scale. By March, 1945, the rice even for heavy duty had been cut to about 9 oz, and sometimes was as low as 8 oz.

All the prisoners of war had to undergo humiliations and ill treatment, such as being made to stand motionless on the parade ground for hours at a stretch, and being slapped on the face and having to take it without protest. But even this was not the worst.

In the latter part of 1942, 50,000 prisoners of war were sent up to build the notorious Siam railway from Bangkok to Moulmein, a distance in a direct line of 240 miles. It was said that every sleeper in it cost a man's life. In April, 1943, another party, called F Force, 7,000 strong, and in May, 1943, H Force, 3,000 all ranks, including an officers' party of 350, left Changi. They were told that they were going to a place where there would be better food and less work. They were taken by train from Singapore to a point 50 miles from Bangkok. From there, F Force began to march. No transport was provided, the food was bad, and the staging camps were just open fields. Most of the men marched in this way about 190 miles to the Burma border, and on arrival were driven to work by Japanese engineers. Cholera caused many casualties. In spite of strong representations, there was no slackening in the work, and when the party returned to Changi in December, 1943, no fewer than 2,500 had died. H Force was slightly luckier, as transport was provided part of the way, but the officers suffered the indignity of having to work as coolies. This party lost about 800 of its strength, and the RASC casualties in the two forces amounted to more than 300.

After the war Lieutenant W. S. Mitchell was made a Member of the Order of the British Empire, Cpl C. E. Johnson, Dvr J. H. Clegg, Dvr J. Greenberg, and Pte J. F. Higgins received the British Empire Medal. Lieut-Colonel G. E. C. Rossall, Majors Jenson and Marsh, Capt E. F. Moisson, and SSMs Wier and Carey all received mentions in despatches in recognition of their services whilst prisoners in Japanese hands. In this same list was included the name of Major R. S. Sykes who, after being wounded on February 14th, 1942, was killed in an Allied raid on Siam in 1944.

CHAPTER IX

BURMA AND CEYLON

BURMA

Between the Wars

IN the campaign against the Japanese on the eastern frontiers of India, and in Burma, the RASC were the subsidiary partners in the supply and transport services, as the theatre was the responsibility of GHQ, India, which had its own Directorate of ST services, performed by the Royal Indian Army Service Corps.

Although this Corps was originally modelled on the RASC it differed in some respects for two reasons. First, Indian racial characteristics and abilities influenced organization and establishments. Secondly, the Army in India which it served had long been organized for the purposes of internal security and defence of the North-West Frontier rather than for warfare with an external enemy equipped with modern weapons.

Before the war, there were few links and little liaison between the two Corps. From 1916 to 1928 the RASC provided British officers, warrant officers and non-commissioned officers to command the motor transport organization of the Army in India and give it technical assistance. After a proposal to merge the Indian MT units with the RASC had been rejected, India set up its own MT organization within the Indian Army Service Corps,* and the RASC left India, though many of its members transferred in order to remain in that country.

The following Indian Army Order, by General (afterwards Field-Marshal Lord) Birdwood, was published on that occasion:—

'On its departure from India, H.E. the Commander-in-Chief in India wishes to place on record the deep obligation of the Army in India to the Royal Army Service Corps. The members of the Corps who came to India have worked with such loyalty that they have brought into being a service which the Indian Army Service Corps will be proud to maintain. In doing this, they have carried out the traditions of their Corps at the cost of nine officers and 163 other ranks who have died in this country. In saying farewell to the RASC, H.E. takes the opportunity to welcome those members of the RASC transferring to the IASC. They are coming into a Corps

---

* The Indian Army Service Corps became 'Royal' in 1935.

which is embued with the same traditions as that which they have just left. Those traditions are "service for others", whatever the risks that may be entailed.'

The transfer involved more than 100 officers and 800 other ranks (about one-fifth of the strength of the RASC at that time) to fill up the enlarged establishments of the IASC. The influence of the RASC was thereby retained, until, in 1939, there came a new development when the workshops of that Corps were handed over to the Indian Army Ordnance Corps. This had a most depressing effect on the RIASC since most of the former RASC officers and men who were still serving went with the workshops to the IAOC. During the war these men were absorbed by the Indian Corps of Electrical and Mechanical Engineers on its formation, and they held most of the key appointments connected with the new corps. Whatever might be the feelings of individuals about the new organization of the services for the repair of mechanical transport, the RASC in India and South-East Asia Command during the war found themselves working with officers, many of whom had been trained in the same school and shared the same basic ideas on transport.

The RIASC and the BEF

When war broke out in 1939, India was not at once directly affected, and so was able to respond to calls for help from the RASC. A hundred RIASC officers were sent home to reinforce the Regular element in the vastly expanding British Corps; and a contingent of four animal transport companies of the RIASC were sent to join the BEF in France to meet a requirement for pack transport in the forward areas. They were the sole representatives of the Indian Army in the BEF and were very proud of the fact. One company was captured by the enemy; the others reached the United Kingdom and remained there until they were repatriated in 1944 when India urgently needed men experienced in animal transport. These original animal transport companies had given a good account of themselves during their short time in France and Belgium, and, moreover, after their evacuation in 1940 to the United Kingdom, the three surviving companies set an excellent example in discipline, in the recovery of smartness in turn-out, and in the speed at which they became rehabilitated. Long before then, the expansion of the RIASC had made necessary the recall to India of the officers it had lent.

The Corps in India

Indeed, the pendulum had now swung the other way, and it was the turn of the RASC to help out the RIASC. Large numbers of officers were needed for the many motor transport companies being raised in India, and the resources of that country in respect of officer material were inadequate. Many junior officers of the Royal Armoured Corps and infantry sent out as reinforcements for those arms and surplus to their requirements, were attached to the RIASC, but the arrangement was unsatisfactory, and did not meet the need for properly trained MT officers. So 'middle-piece' RASC officers, majors and captains, and other ranks suitable for commissions, were sent out to give balance to the RIASC. They did this effectively, and their influence on the standards of vehicle maintenance and road discipline was marked.

Apart from these, there was no great number of RASC in India and SEAC during the war. The largest bodies were the divisional RASC of 2nd Division and 70th Division. There was also the RASC component of HQ IV Corps: the ST staff, the staff clerks, and the staff car and other drivers. This formation had originally been sent to Persia, but it eventually arrived in India, and in May, 1942, it took over in Assam the organization of the reception of the retreating Burma Army, and the defence of that frontier. Gradually, the RASC officers in it were replaced by those of the Indian Army, and were absorbed into the general pool of RASC/RIASC officers; but the Corps HQ, still retaining its RASC other ranks, was to see the campaign through to the end.

Some of the RASC companies intended for the Persian lines of communication also found their way to India, as did others which were too late for the campaign in Malaya. A motor ambulance convoy (No. 928) worked for over three years in East Bengal on casualty clearing duties far behind the line, but it was specially valuable for work in connection with the evacuation of patients by air. A higher standard of driving was required for the specialized work with aircraft than could generally be found at this stage among the Indian drivers, most of the experienced ones being in the Middle East. At the end of 1942, two artillery companies, 92 (Northern Ireland) and 169, and 102 GT Company, were used to form four mixed tank transporter companies, 553, 554, 589 and 590 Companies, RASC—mixed, because the headquarters and workshops were British, half the drivers British and half Indian. This worked well. Three of these units were to do excellent work with Fourteenth Army, while the fourth, 554, did equally valuable service, though of a more humdrum nature, on heavy goods lifts in the docks of Bombay and Calcutta, its workshops maintaining far more than its own vehicles.

A small but important RASC contingent was the cadre of some 20 all ranks sent out from the Amphibian Training Centre in England to organize the Indian Amphibian School at Cocanada on the east coast of India. There, several Indian transport companies learnt to handle dukws and tracked amphibians, and one of these units successfully effected the ship-to-shore transfer of supplies as XV Indian Corps worked its way down the coast of Arakan.

The Corps in Burma, 1942

Operations began in the area when the Japanese invaded Burma in the extreme south in January, 1942, and were opposed by 17th Indian Division and the Burma Division. Burma had become independent of India in 1937, when its small army was organized only for internal security. In the autumn of 1941 the Army in Burma, although larger, was gravely deficient in ancillary troops and services, the Burma Army Service Corps being still in its infancy. Our forces were driven back, in spite of the arrival of reinforcements. Among these was 7th Armoured Brigade, accompanied by 65 Company RASC. This was the only RASC unit engaged in the campaign; but there were some RASC officers in the RIASC units.

The brigade arrived at Rangoon on February 21st. There was no labour or dock staff working at the port, and the fact that 2nd Royal Tank Regiment was able to take part in the operations in the Pegu area was due in no small degree to the efforts of four sergeants of 65 Company, who operated winches, etc., while the drivers whose lorries had not been disembarked worked as stevedores until the off-loading had been completed. About 1,500 vehicles were discharged, with only one casualty.

Maintenance of the brigade could only be done under armed escort, and even so the company sustained losses in an ambush. Orders on maintenance arrangements failed to come through, and the company carried on without. It loaded up all the 25-pounder and tank-gun ammunition it could carry, even at the expense of other items, and up to six or seven tons was carried in a 3-ton lorry. What could not be lifted was destroyed.

The retreat from Rangoon began on March 7th, and it soon became the practice for units to find their own rations, while 65 Company concentrated on the supply of ammunition and fuel to the brigade. It also helped out 17th Division on more than one occasion.

After the Irrawaddy had been crossed, a platoon of the company went back to Mandalay to try and collect high octane fuel for the tanks; but the dump had been set on fire 10 minutes before the lorries arrived, and it was then a race against time to cross the river again before the Ava bridge was blown. The last vehicle over was one of 65 Company's.

Meanwhile an RASC officer in charge of the BSD at Mandalay,

had managed to move a large part of the stocks across the river, and so ensured the supply of rations during the final withdrawal. This began with a race for the Chindwin crossing at Kalewa, 7th Armoured Brigade covering the retreat. The RASC convoys were often ambushed, fortunately without loss, and the company took part in a sharp action against an enemy force trying to cut off the rearguard. On arrival at the Chindwin, the order was given to destroy vehicles and equipment, as there was no means of ferrying them over. All the second line lorries were still under load, some carrying as much as five tons of petrol and oil. The company had kept the brigade supplied with its requirements throughout.

The last place in the order of march was given to 65 Company, which therefore had to act as a rearguard, with some untrained Gurkhas attached; but when night came, contact with the enemy was lost. The last of Burma Army crossed into India early in May, 1942, where HQ IV Corps was doing the best it could to help with limited resources and in very difficult conditions.

Problems on the Lines of Communication

The chief trouble was the lack of proper communications. From the railway at Dimapur, or Manipur Road, to Imphal, the capital of Manipur State, a distance of 135 miles, there was a motor road only wide enough for one-way traffic. It was a typical Indian mountain road, winding along the jungle-covered hillside with innumerable corners and hairpin bends, a steep slope up on one side, and a precipitous fall on the other. In the first 46 miles, from Dimapur to Kohima, it climbed 4,000 feet, reaching its peak of 5,500 feet at Mao, 20 miles farther on. It then dropped 3,000 feet in 40 miles to the Imphal Plain, and the last stretch to Imphal was comparatively flat. From Imphal to the frontier at Tamu, 65 miles, there had been only a bridle-track, but this had been improved into an unmetalled fairweather motor road in time to help the passage of Burma Army. Cross-country movement for wheeled traffic was impossible almost everywhere.

The difficulties of the route were increased by the monsoon rains. These normally break in the middle of May, and the heavy tropical downpour goes on almost continuously until September, making the movement of wheeled transport impossible except on the few all-weather roads. The monsoon broke on time that year, and this made the Manipur road even more hazardous. Thousands of labourers were working to convert it into a two-way road, the method being to cut into the bank on the inner side, carry the earth across the road, and drop it over the 'khad', or lower slope. Some of the soil fell on the road, and became in the rain a greasy menace on the tarred surface, causing vehicles to skid, often with disastrous

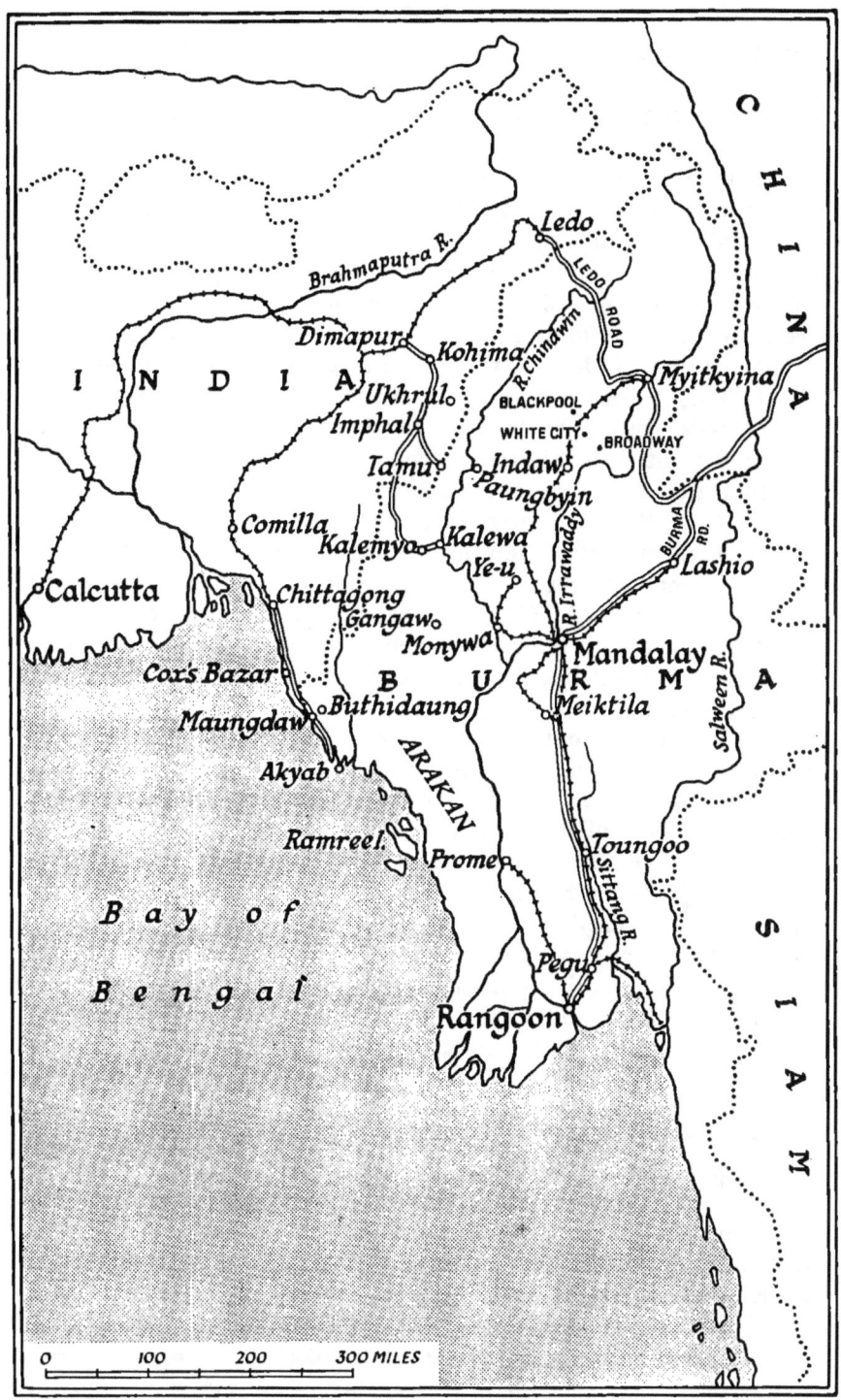

Burma

results, for there was nothing to stop them going over the edge.

Even these conditions would not have been so bad if the drivers, who were responsible for carrying forward the requirements of some 40,000 men, had been experienced; but they were not. India was still in the early days of expanding her army, and the only motor transport companies she could make available to send up to this front were some which had been raised a few months before. The men had no experience of driving before they joined the army, and even then had only been driving for a few weeks, when they were called upon to work on this difficult and dangerous road. Somehow they did it, though many crawled in low gear all the way up the hill; if a lorry stopped, it could not pull off the road to let others pass, and the resulting block often stretched for miles. There were at first only six of these companies, each with a total of 120 lorries, and many of these were off the road in need of repair. At that time, RIASC companies had no workshops, but only a light aid detachment with a few mechanics and electricians, and they had to depend for repairs of a more serious nature on the static workshops of the IAOC, which were hopelessly overloaded and unable to cope with the mass of vehicles requiring repair. Burma Army had brought out no transport, and its men were exhausted, so there was no help from them.

This was not the only anxiety of the ST staff of IV Corps. The supply situation was desperate, and the stocks in the advanced base supply depot at Dimapur constantly showed less than a day's supplies of some of the most vital commodities: rice, atta, barley, sugar, milk, and even tea in a tea-growing area. Often lorries had to be loaded direct from trucks discovered just in time in the trains which reached Dimapur.

The railway system, never intended for heavy traffic, had become almost completely disorganized, largely because of the defection of the railway staff, and trains were simply left standing after the Japanese bombed Imphal. Farther back, every wagon had to be ferried across the Brahmaputra, and still farther back there was a break of gauge where all loads had to be transhipped, but unfortunately the opportunity was not taken there to ensure that the supplies sent forward first were those most needed.

Local purchase was almost impossible, especially of meat, as the Manipuris objected on religious grounds to the slaughter of cattle, and drove them away out of reach. Those that were caught were generally diseased and unfit for food. Somehow or other, in spite of all those difficulties, enough food was got forward, and small reserves were built up, before landslides blocked the road. Fortunately the enemy remained inactive during the monsoon, and the situation gradually improved.

Supply by Air

The ensuing two years on this Assam-Manipur front were a mainly defensive period, while the lines of communication were improved, as part of the process of preparation for an ultimate offensive, and India expanded her army. The principal operations were the great defensive battles around Imphal and at Kohima in 1944, to be mentioned later, and the actions of Wingate's long range penetration troops, famous under the name of 'Chindits', which in 1943 and 1944 infiltrated far behind the enemy lines in Burma, creating confusion and damaging enemy communications. During their inroads they were maintained entirely by air supply; and it was in this connection that the RASC were again in operation on this front.

The British components of Special Force, a development late in 1943 on Wingate's original Long Range Penetration Group, were drawn from 70th British Division, and it was decided that, although an RIASC air despatch organization was in existence, the British Chindits must be served in this respect by their own RASC. So 61 Company was reorganized as an air despatch company, and continued with this task until the Chindits withdrew. Its duties included the establishment of air bases in the advanced strongholds of the Chindits such as 'Broadway' and 'White City', deep in Japanese occupied territory. After this special task, the company continued to be employed as part of the great Army–Air Transport Organization, on which Fourteenth Army depended to an ever-increasing extent for its maintenance as it drove south through Burma.

The land L of C eventually stretched so far that it could not provide for the Army's needs, and supply by air became the normal method. By April, 1945, nine-tenths of the supplies of all sorts for the army in Burma were being delivered by air: air-landed when airstrips were available on which aircraft could come down, air-dropped when landing was impossible. In this process, 61 Company played its part, helping to maintain the forces which were pursuing the retreating enemy, down to the Chindwin, on to the Irrawaddy, and beyond to Meiktila and Mandalay. In February and March, 1945, this company sent almost 10,000 tons of supplies to the two corps engaged. When mechanized forces made their dash for Meiktila, 61 Company supplied them with over 250,000 gallons of petrol. Then the advance of IV Corps towards Rangoon was maintained, until Toungoo was reached in April, by which time air supply from East Bengal became uneconomic, and the task was switched to the airfields in Arakan. When the company had done its air despatch work, many of its members had 100 flying hours to their credit. They would have had more if the skill of the trained RASC men had not been needed for packing at the air base, so that the task of ejecting supplies from aircraft was mainly assumed by men of the infantry unfit to go with the Chindits.

Another air despatch company, 799, took part in the later stages of the maintenance of Fourteenth Army. Having supplied the French resistance forces, our troops in Normandy and at Arnhem, and the Americans in the Ardennes, it was sent out East, and began operations with the United States Army Air Force in May, 1945. Hitherto, the unit's work had been for emergencies only, but in Burma operations were a daily routine, and the climate made conditions different. After a month there, the unit was withdrawn to take part in the invasion of Malaya, and later went to work in Java.

Although the RASC and RIASC performed the air despatch duties in SEAC, control was not an ST responsibility, as in the United Kingdom and other theatres, but that of the staff. This was because of local difficulties which often required decisions on the spot. These difficulties included bad communications; long distances, especially from depots; limitations of airfields in numbers and availability—many were fair-weather only; a chronic shortage of aircraft; and the fact that, to a far greater extent than in other theatres, reinforcements, units, and even formations, were air-transported. Strict staff control of rear airfields was consequently considered essential, and the ST responsibility was for the executive duties. These consisted of holding supplies and petrol, packing stores for dropping, loading aircraft, providing men for ejection duties in aircraft, receiving and distributing stores at the forward airfields and dropping zones, and all the business connected with supply dropping equipment.

The 'odd-job' units

When 70th Division arrived in India from the Middle East early in 1942, it brought with it some small RASC supply and petrol units as its quota for employment on the lines of communication. These included several DIDs, a field bakery, a field butchery, and 102 and 106 Petrol Depots. One DID, 78, had quite an active career, and so did the petrol depots, but the other units remained in India and Ceylon on routine tasks. In May, 1942, an urgent request reached IV Corps from the manager of the oil wells at Tinsukia in the extreme eastern corner of India, for a British unit, trained in handling petroleum products, to be sent up there to stand by and, if necessary, take over the installations if the local staff decamped for fear of the Japanese, which they were likely to do.

India could not have produced a suitable unit from her own resources, for the RIASC organization for handling petrol and oil had not gone beyond the stage of using ordinary supply issue sections for issuing petrol in containers. The DDST IV Corps knew that those two depots were idle in India, and that they exactly suited the bill. It was soon arranged for one of them to go up to Tinsukia, but then the request was cancelled. Later, when the pipeline from Chittagong reached Dimapur, this depot organized and operated the bulk installation there; and, when Akyab on the Arakan coast was captured early in 1945, the depot was put in charge of the bulk installation there too, which it helped to erect. It operated both the main depot and the pipelines running from it, took in its first delivery from an ocean tanker in April, and at once began pumping to airfield tankage; and so it continued the task of keeping Fourteenth Army moving. The other depot, which had been working at Chittagong, was brought down to operate the bulk installations at Kyaukpyu on Ramree Island, performing a role similar to that at Akyab.

The 2nd Division in waiting

In April, 1942, 2nd Divisional RASC arrived in India. The division had formed part of the BEF in 1939-40, and after the evacuation was for about two years in Yorkshire. When it left for India, its RASC, commanded by Lieut-Colonel C. M. G. Luff, consisted of 8, 24, and 29 Brigade Companies, and 387 Divisional Troops Company. For nearly two years, the division as a whole remained in Western India, and the RASC was engaged in jungle training at Belgaum, amphibious training near Bombay, and famine relief work at Bijapur. In order to take part in projected amphibious operations in Arakan, 387 Company became a dukw company. However, its only real job there turned out to be a rush troop-carrying one, by land from Cox's Bazar and over the difficult Ngakyedauk Pass. The project for an attack on Akyab was cancelled, so none of the divisional RASC saw active service during 1943-44, except for a small detachment which went with 6th Brigade to Arakan early in 1943, where it worked with 78 DID.

Towards the end of that year a new chapter in the story of the war in this theatre began, when SEAC was formed and took over from India the control of operations. The Supreme Allied Commander was Admiral Lord Louis Mountbatten, who initiated a new policy for the war against the Japanese. Hitherto, when the enemy employed his favourite tactics of cutting our communications, our troops had fallen back to restore them; and the process was then often repeated. Also, both sides had been more or less inactive during the monsoon. Now all that was changed. Troops were to fight on, march on, and fly on, throughout the monsoon; and if they were cut off they were to stay where they were, and would be maintained by air.

When, after waiting and training, 2nd Division was told that the ships which had been going to take it to Arakan were required to transport the armies for the invasion of Europe, there was naturally great disappointment, and the men wished that they could have gone home in the ships. But in the end the division was in the fight two months before D Day in Europe.

The Japanese March on Delhi

The Japanese attacked in Arakan, and were defeated by the new policy of 'staying put' and being maintained by air. The enemy force was completely shattered, but in spite of that they used the same tactics when they attacked in Assam in March, 1944. They cut the Tiddim Road, but not the Tamu Road. They severed the Imphal–Kohima Road early in April, so isolating IV Corps in the Imphal area, and they attacked Kohima as a preliminary to the capture of Dimapur. The two forward divisions were withdrawn to the Imphal Plain, 17th Indian Division being involved in hard fighting. In this, Captain I. G. Hunter, RASC, Staff Captain, 48th Indian Infantry Brigade, distinguished himself, earning the immediate award of the Military Cross. In the battle of Sahaung Hill, he carried out a masterly administrative plan which made the next phase of the operations possible. It involved supervising the delivery by pack transport of all the troops' requirements when not 200 yards from the enemy and under constant fire from mortars and snipers.

The 2nd Division in Action

At Imphal and Kohima our forces stood firm and were supplied by air. Everywhere the administrative troops took their share of the fighting. At Kohima this was particularly severe, and the siege, which lasted 16 days, has justly become famous. It was here that 2nd Division entered the battle. Dimapur had to be protected and the road to Imphal reopened. The fighting troops of the division were flown in, and with them went the CRASC and his staff and details of the composite platoons. The transport companies parted regretfully from the Bedfords and Fords which they had brought from the United Kingdom, and which were still going strong in spite of an enormous mileage, and obtained other makes to take their place. Then they set out by road for Calcutta, a distance of over 1,500 miles, and from there went on by rail and road. When at last they rejoined the division, it was fully engaged in the fighting to relieve Kohima. This was more than the infantry could do unaided, and while two transport companies carried on with the maintenance of the division, the other two were turned into defence companies to make good the lack of fighting troops; 24 Company took over the defence of FSD Ridge after its capture, and 387 Company a part of Aradura Spur. Then casualties in the infantry made necessary the attachment of 300 men of the divisional RASC to battalions to fill the gaps in their ranks. They earned the commendations of the infantry commanders for their good work.

Without these men the transport situation became increasingly difficult, and the two remaining companies were hard pressed and had to be helped by the RIASC. Dumps were opened close behind the line; deliveries to units were made by RIASC pack-mules, and even by man-pack. Lorries carrying supplies to the dump at Jail Hill got through at irregular intervals without too much interference, though the road was closed to troops on account of enemy sniping and machine-gun fire. The work was not done without casualties.

At last the Japanese began to withdraw, and the division pursued them hotly up the road. Troop-carrying and maintenance made the greatest demands on all transport. Guns and all materials had to be ferried forward, and this involved a double mileage. Dumps were carried forward a few miles, but were no sooner unloaded than the battle moved forward, and the loads had to be lifted again. Every available man in the transport companies was continually loading and unloading vehicles, and drivers were often driving for 24 hours at a stretch over the tortuous mountain road to complete one delivery. By the time the road to Imphal was opened on June 22nd, the divisional RASC was showing signs of the strain of the previous three months, culminating in the day and night effort to keep the troops supplied during the last three weeks. It had certainly earned the long rest which the division enjoyed when the operations were over. All ranks had the satisfaction of knowing that the tide had turned, and that the enemy had been soundly beaten and was falling back.

The divisional commander expressed his appreciation of the work of the divisional RASC during these operations in the following terms: 'I want to send all ranks of the Divisional RASC a personal message of thanks for the splendid service which it has rendered to the division during my long period of command, and more especially during the past three months when the resources of the RASC have been stretched to the utmost, but have never failed. The work of the Divisional RASC has not always been spectacular, but it is an essential part of the efficient working of the divisional organization, and I go so far as to say that with a less efficient RASC the division could not have carried out its rapid advance from Dimapur for the relief of Kohima, and subsequently for the opening of the Imphal Road.'

Meanwhile, IV Corps had been maintained by air for over two months. The main problem had not been that of transporting sufficient supplies to keep the troops alive—they never fell below a two-thirds ration—but rather of maintaining an even flow of the stores required for battle. Air supply in the monsoon was difficult; the clouds were sometimes 30,000 feet thick, and very dangerous for aircraft. Weather prevented flying for days on end, and operations had to be concentrated in the fair periods. This involved additional strain on the air despatch men both at the base airfields and at the receiving end.

While 2nd Division was resting, its RASC underwent reorganization on to what was known as the 'standard' basis. This meant that the four transport companies, each of two platoons, became two companies each of four platoons, which were equipped half with lorries and half with jeeps or 15-cwt trucks. In the process, 24 Company ceased to exist, and 387 Company went back to its amphibious role, being equipped with 40 dukws organized in two platoons.

The East Africans

In this capacity, 387 Company was kept busy. Its first job was to provide 12 dukws as a water link for 11th East African Division, which was now a few miles within Burma, on the River Yu, all bridges on the road having been swept away by the floods. The river was only just navigable, with a current of four to five knots, and the trip downstream took four hours for 30-odd miles, but going back took 16 to 19 hours. The heavy logs and other debris floating down river continually damaged propellers and shafts. Dukws that had broken down could only be brought ashore at a few places, and so the expedient was adopted of fitting out a dukw as a machinery lorry. This proved invaluable later, when detachments of the company were widely separated, and the absence of roads prevented communication by land with company headquarters and the workshops.

Mention of the East African Division makes it necessary to recall that the British element of the East African ASC was drawn entirely from the Corps. The division joined XXXIII Indian Corps in July, 1944, and took over the advance from 23rd Indian Division (after that formation had captured Tamu on August 4th) and began with the task of clearing the road to Kalewa. The route down to the track to Sittaung was passable for four-wheeled drive lorries only as far as the Yu river, 10 miles from Tamu; after that jeeps could go for another six miles, and then pack or porter transport had to be used. The road southwards from Tamu down the Kabaw valley was a road only in name, being in fact a sea of mud. Corduroy tracks were laid, down which jeeps and 30-cwt six-wheeled lorries bumped their way. Because of these difficult communications the division was maintained very largely by air during its slow advance, but it eventually took Kalewa on December 2nd.

More maintenance problems

The rest of XXXIII Indian Corps, of which Colonel Luff was now DDST, was meanwhile concentrating in the Yazagyo area. It consisted of 2nd Division, 20th Indian Division, and 254th Indian Tank Brigade, with 589 Tank Transporter Company. It was claimed by XXXIII Indian Corps, not without justification, that never before had a corps been committed over 170 miles of such bad roads with such inadequate resources. The air lift tonnage allotted to the formation was insufficient to maintain the troops and at the same time enable reserves to be built up against the crossing of the Chindwin. The air lift was supplemented by the corps transport working from Moreh and Imphal, while 2nd Division and the tank brigade drew their own petrol from Moreh. All the L of C transport that could be spared, only 100 tons a day, was allotted to help. Then 50 Dakotas were withdrawn from the air lift to go to China, and finally Yazagyo airstrip was put out of commission by rain. In such circumstances, it said much for the services that there was no real breakdown, though the troops were on half rations and had no cigarettes. Matters improved when the Supreme Allied Commander arranged for the air lift to be restored.

Some idea of the polyglot nature of the ST set-up in this theatre may be gained from the following facts. The field maintenance area at Khongkhang was manned by 78 DID RASC. This moved up the road to relieve a composite platoon of the EAASC, when a new FMA had been opened at Moreh by sections of the Burma Supply Company. Near the FMA, an East African bakery produced its bread under the supervision of RASC bakers.

The West Africans

Farther west, yet another offshoot of the RASC was working, the West African ASC of 81st West African Division, which in October had crossed the hills from Arakan into the Kaladan valley. It had begun its advance, down the river, which continued until the division was withdrawn in March, 1945, when 82nd West African Division relieved it. The officers and British other ranks of the WAASC were also all drawn from the RASC, and so were many of the British personnel of the West African Auxiliary Groups. These units were composed of enlisted African porters, trained as soldiers, each able to carry 40 lb on his head. The West African divisions depended largely on them for their transport, as wheeled transport of any kind could not be used in the Kaladan valley. Major E. W. Childs was successively adjutant, company commander and second-in-command of 5th Auxiliary Group during the campaign. He won the Military Cross during an enemy attack, when his commanding officer and the second-in-command were mortally wounded, and he stood in the open under heavy fire to apply dressings to their wounds.

The West African divisions also used river boats and a pack bullock company was also tried; but it was not satisfactory, as the animals were slow movers, and needed much time for rumination and grazing. It was also found difficult to produce a suitable pack saddle for them. The two divisions were supplied by air throughout the campaign.

These two colonial ASCs or their representatives in SEAC rendered the same excellent service as their parent Corps. Enough has been written of the adventures of their RASC partners to indicate what they were up against, and they were no less resourceful or successful in attaining their objects. The West African ASC units with their divisions relieved one another in the fighting area. The one 'out' resting and refitting in Assam or in Eastern Bengal had the difficult 'chaung' country to negotiate, where their route was continuously interrupted by deep crossings over fresh, or more often estuarine, waters with forested banks. These necessitated detours, ferries or transhipment of loads. The East African ASC was, as already stated, employed under IV Corps in the Fourteenth Army, which moved initially against the grain of the country in the difficult area between Tamu and Kalewa.

Excellent relations existed between the British, Asian and African members of these units. This was once demonstrated, somewhat to the embarrassment of the officer addressed, when an askari, seeing off his commanding officer to the United Kingdom by aircraft, remarked loudly (fortunately in Swahili): 'It will be nice for you seeing all your wives again.'

Beyond the Chindwin

The East African Division crossed the Chindwin in December, 1944, and established a bridgehead opposite Kalewa. The plan was for 2nd Division to go through the bridgehead and make for Shwebo, but the road on the far side of the river was broken down for several miles, and only passable for light vehicles. One of the dukw platoons was called in and, towing pontoons, moved all the troops, tanks, guns and transport of the division some eight miles downstream to Shwegyin, where the road could be picked up again.

Waiting to Load

Checking Air Freight

Carrying Landing Craft

Carrying Buffaloes

The same platoon towed into position the sections of the 1,000-foot Bailey bridge built to span the river at Kalewa; and it also stocked the bridgehead with thousands of tons of stores.

On December 21st, 2nd Division broke out of the bridgehead and covered 130 miles in 20 days to reach its objective at Shwebo on January 8th, 1945. It had started with 150 miles of petrol for each vehicle, besides the reserve carried by the RASC, and three days' reserve rations. In spite of this, the shortages in the air supply drop, on which the division depended for its day-to-day maintenance, were such that the division arrived in Shwebo with empty fuel tanks, and was on half rations for three days. Then an airstrip was opened, and supplies and petrol came in fast; but ammunition had to be fetched from the dump 125 miles back, and it took the RASC lorries eight days for the round trip to make one replenishment.

It was at this time that the Kabo weir, controlling the irrigation of the whole Shwebo plain, was saved. It was feared that the enemy would destroy it and the problem was to get the troops there in time to prevent this. RASC lorries were emptied of their loads of ammunition, and by driving through the night, two companies of infantry were conveyed to the weir just in time, for they were hardly dug in before the tardy appearance of the enemy.

The Dukws earn their keep

Meanwhile the other dukw platoon was supporting 20th Division in its advance down the river to Monywa, providing a river L of C in conjunction with the outboard vessels and rafts of the Inland Water Transport branch of the Royal Engineers, which in this theatre controlled the water transport. On this run, the trip of 60 miles to Maukkadaw took three days because of the uncharted sandbanks. In February, this division crossed the Irrawaddy at Myinmu, using dukws for towing rafts which carried vehicles over. A few of the dukws also assisted in the crossing of IV Corps near Pakokku.

As well as the perils of the waterways, the dukws engaged in these operations had to suffer the attentions of the enemy. Thus, when Japanese aircraft came over to bomb the bridge at Kalewa, and were put off by barrage balloons, they shot at anything else nearby, and a dukw loaded with petrol was hit and caught fire. The crew swam ashore, to be greeted by their friends with the comment: 'Perhaps that will teach you not to smoke with a load of petrol.' Then, when one platoon was working with 19th Indian Division at its crossing of the Irrawaddy, serving as second line transport one way and evacuating casualties the other, the unit itself received some casualties from a Japanese '75' that always opened up on the dukws as they entered and left the stream by the only practicable route.

By February, 1945, these vehicles were becoming rather the worse for wear, as nearly all of them had been in use continuously for several months. The situation was not improved by there being no spare parts throughout the period. Another trouble was that the intensive employment in three detachments required extra men—there were only five officers and 160 other ranks in the company—but manpower was short.

It was at this point that the company brought off its crowning achievement of the campaign, at the crossing of the Irrawaddy by 2nd Division at Ngazun, 25 miles west of Mandalay. Here the river is from 1,000 to 1,500 yards wide, and the current about two and a half knots. The stream contains many large sandbanks and shifting shoals, and so the channel to be followed was one and a half miles long, on a diagonal course, which lengthened the time that the boats were exposed to the view of the enemy.

Across the Irawaddy

The plan for the assault was to land on three beaches at once, the troops being carried in assault boats. Beaches A and B lay some two miles and one mile respectively west of Ngazun village, and C Beach on a large island north of the village which it was necessary to secure since it enfiladed the other crossings and was patrolled by the enemy. To add to the other difficulties, the moon was nearly full. Zero hour was 10 p.m.

The first assault wave on C Beach was fired on, but one company reached the shore and charged through the enemy positions. The next wave failed to land, and enemy fire prevented the return of the first wave's boats to fetch more troops. The assault on A beach met heavy fire from artillery, mortars, and infantry, many boats were sunk and the assault had to be abandoned. The situation was serious, and it looked as if the crossing might fail; but there remained B beach. There the assaulting battalion, which had the longest crossing to make, had got ashore, and by 3 a.m. had established a bridgehead with two companies; but again no boats returned.

What followed is described by the C-in-C ALFSEA in his despatch as an outstanding feat of control, staff work, and discipline. It was obviously essential to reinforce with infantry the bridgehead on B beach, but to do so entailed a complete change of plan. The possibility of partial failure had been foreseen, and an alternative plan had been prepared; but the fact that it was rapidly and successfully executed in darkness (the moon having set), in spite of the inevitable confusion of the initial failures and the lack of equipment, reflected, stated the despatch, great credit on all concerned.

That includes the dukws, for they now entered the fray. Apart from four loaded with RE stores for the assault, their original role had been to stand by to ferry over, on rafts, loaded vehicles and ammunition and food for the build-up in the bridgehead. Now they were called on to perform a much more active and exacting role, that of carrying troops to the beaches. Every crossing came under fire, and dawn found five of the dukws out of action through grounding on sandbanks or enemy action. Captain H. D. Clark, officer commanding 387 Company, undertook to sound a way round the banks, and accomplished his task under fire, so earning the immediate award of the Military Cross.

In the next few hours, the drivers took over an average of seven loads each of troops to strengthen the bridgehead, and every trip meant coming under machine-gun fire as they rounded the sandbank; casualties were inevitably incurred. Cpl E. Eglon, L/Cpls S. B. Lines and A. A. Meese, and Dvrs J. Hall and J. O'Brien, received the immediate award of the Military Medal for gallant conduct. They continued at the work for 16 to 18 hours. By nightfall the leading brigade was over and the situation was saved. During the next 72 hours, rafts towed by the dukws moved the rest of the division, 6,000 men and 200 vehicles, including tanks and guns, and supplies as well.

The rafts represented a more prosaic, but none the less valuable contribution by the divisional RASC to the river crossing. Everyone was called on to help make good the lack of equipment, and the workshops of 8 and 29 Companies had to build rafts. These were made from salved Japanese pontoons, the holes in which were patched and welded. Three rafts each of five pontoons were constructed, and three pontoons were made self-propelling by the installation of Chevrolet engines, everything else but the propellers being made from scrap. A raft carried a 30-cwt lorry or the equivalent. With these, 325 vehicles, 600 tons of supplies, and several hundred infantry, were ferried across.

With the bridgehead secure, the dukws turned to the task of carrying over the division's reserves of ammunition, supplies, and petrol. They did this for another month as a vital link in the maintenance of XXXIII Indian Corps, which by then was reducing Mandalay. Another RASC unit employed on the water link was 884 Motor Boat Company, which arrived in March.

The share of the RASC in the crossing of the Irrawaddy had been no small one, and it is fair to quote once more from General Leese's despatch: 'I would like to emphasize here the magnitude of Fourteenth Army's achievement in crossing this great river obstacle, in the face of a brave and determined enemy and with a minimum of modern equipment. It is worth considering that the Irrawaddy is four times as wide as the Rhine, while the Japanese soldier in well-prepared positions is no less formidable than the German. It is the greatest tribute to the Commander, officers and men, of Fourteenth Army that such a hazardous and exacting operation was crowned with success.'

Meiktila fell to 17th Indian Division on March 5th, 1945, and Mandalay to 19th Indian Division on March 20th, after stubborn resistance. The Japanese suffered a crushing defeat in this area, and began to withdraw. The 2nd Division took part in the clearing-up operation until it was withdrawn in April in order to prepare to take part in the campaign for the reoccupation of Malaya.

Tank Transporters

The RASC interest in this theatre now turns to the tank transporter companies, three of which were with Fourteenth Army. One of them, 553, was engaged in an unspectacular but necessary role on the L of C. The conveyance of replacement tanks over the very long line, 300–400 miles, with the limited number of rather worn out transporters available, was a great problem, which called for herculean efforts from the company, which were on the whole successful. The unit had also to cope with other heavy loads, such as six 21-ton locomotives, and large craft for use by IWT. The movement of these awkward loads over the difficult roads of the already congested L of C presented many problems.

It had been doubted at first whether loaded transporters could negotiate the tremendous hills and sharp corners of the Manipur road. So, in 1943, a transporter of 589 Company went up on a trial trip, which proved that the route was passable, though with great difficulty. The last six miles into Kohima took a transporter with a 28-ton tank on the trailer over two hours to traverse. The tractors slowly ground their way up the gradients with engines running at 1,500 rpm, in second gear on the main box, and the auxiliary gear in direct or under-drive.

In January, 1944, a squadron of tanks had to be moved to Tamu. The 45 miles of mountain road to that place from Palel were appreciably more severe and difficult than any part of the Manipur road, and it was by no means certain that loaded transporters would be able to climb the hills. For security reasons, it was imperative that the tanks should not be off-loaded, as was the invariable practice on the steepest climbs in later days, and the squadron had to be carried through in the time allowed. On the second day out, the climbing began with the long pull up to the saddle at Shenam, 10 miles up a steep winding mountain road, only just wide enough for transporters. The first five miles took 22, 19, 15, 14 and 12 minutes respectively. The next section of three miles took three and a half hours. Then came the descent from the saddle to Khongkhang down the staircase, a fearsome zigzagging drop of some hundreds of feet. Next day's task included the climb from Lokchau to Sibong, in which an extremely sharp rising corner gave great difficulty, reversing being necessary in most cases. Then the surface went to pieces, and the transporters could not get up with their 40-ton loads, so double-heading had to be resorted to. Half the tractors were coupled to the other half, two tractors taking up each trailer. The whole convoy covered five miles that day.

After Sibong, the route was mainly downhill, but short steep rises gave much trouble because of slipping, and it was only by 'boosting' that these sections could be negotiated without off-loading. The transporters were closed up so that each one was pushed so far by the one immediately behind, and the final stretch was overcome by a third transporter, giving the required boost to the two in front. The breakdown lorry pushed at the end of the column. The journey was completed in four and a half days instead of the scheduled three.

When the Japanese invaded Assam in March, 1944, 589 Company joined 254th Indian Tank Brigade in a 'box' or defended area, on the Imphal Plain, and went on ferrying tanks and stores and bridging material. Then, when the enemy was retreating again, it moved tanks to Nanhanwe, a round trip of 300 miles. It reached the Chindwin at Kalewa on January 12th, 1945, and while some transporters crossed by the bridge, others were towed on pontoons by dukws to Shwegyin. Thence the unit went forward, by way of Shwebo, to Myittha, and eventually by way of Taungtha to Prome; this was virtually the end of the company's active role.

The other transporter company, 590, served 255th Indian Tank Brigade, and probably had the hardest task of them all. In order to effect a surprise crossing of the Irrawaddy at Pakokku, and from there make a dash for Meiktila, IV Corps, which included this tank brigade, was switched from the left flank of Fourteenth Army to the right, and sent down by way of the Kabaw and Gangaw valleys. The route was difficult; it was 400 miles long, of which 110 through the Kabaw valley were over a fair-weather road, already the main L of C of XXXIII Indian Corps, and deep in dust. After that, there was only an indifferent fair-weather road, which required re-making throughout its length to enable it to take transporters. In one section of it, the dust was three feet deep, and proved a barrier even to jeeps. The difficulties encountered by 590 Company in moving the tank brigade over the last 200 miles, without using too much track mileage, were immense. The whole move took eight weeks to complete, because of the arduous nature of the route and the lack of transport. Throughout this period the company worked extremely hard in terrible conditions.

A transporter shuttle service in five stages was the method employed. In one stretch of 20 miles, south of Gangaw, the tanks had to be off-loaded 17 times and in some places they had to tow the empty transporters. The company had little opportunity and no facilities for maintenance; but it finally accomplished a task which the brigade described as well-nigh impossible, and IV Corps duly effected its surprise.

On to Rangoon

Across the Irrawaddy, the country was quite different. Instead of in the jungle-clad mountains north of the Chindwin, Fourteenth Army was now fighting in level country, sparsely wooded, with all-weather main roads. Mechanized forces could operate here with advantage, and IV Corps, which was highly mechanized, was consequently given a suitable task, that of driving all out for Rangoon, which it was to try and capture at all costs before the monsoon broke. If that plan were not achieved, it would be impossible to maintain Fourteenth Army in Burma during the rains, which would make movement on much of the land L of C impossible, and would prevent or at least severely restrict supply by air. It might be necessary for the army to go right back behind the Chindwin.

IV Corps started on its 350-mile journey down the Toungoo road on April 5th, and 590 Company went with it. The formation was maintained entirely by air throughout. It reached Pegu on May 1st; two days later, its spearhead, 17th Division, delayed by mines, demolitions and mud, was still 30 miles from its goal, which fell that day to XV Indian Corps, which had been brought round by sea from Arakan. The rains started a fortnight earlier than usual and on the day that Toungoo was captured.

Strong Japanese detachments still held out in the Pegu Yoma mountain tracts; in July they tried to break out, and were severely handled, but not before they had caused considerable trouble to the maintenance arrangements by cutting the road between Toungoo and Pegu. A platoon of 590 Company was attached to IV Corps for these operations.

The war with the Japanese in this theatre ended with the surrender of their forces on August 15th, 1945. In recognition of the valuable work accomplished by the RASC during the Burma campaign, the commander of the Twelfth Army (which controlled the final operations in Burma) presented Brigadier Luff with a sword which formerly belonged to the Commander, Japanese field supply depots, Burma Area Army, and this is now in the RASC Museum at Aldershot.

Some reflections on India

In assessing the maintenance difficulties of the Army in Burma it must be remembered that, during the initial stages of its advance into Burma, Fourteenth Army's railhead at Manipur Road was about as far from its base at Calcutta as London is from Glasgow, and that the forward echelons were anything up to 200 miles farther ahead. Paucity of communications made it impossible to build up and carry forward any appreciable reserves from the advanced base to the forward area. All available transport was used, on the return journeys, for carrying sick and wounded and men who were returning for one reason or another to the base. Whenever possible the returning vehicles were also used for bringing back damaged equipment for repair at the base workshops. On the forward journeys priority was given to the L of C transport column and, ammunition, stores, and men were given priority in that order. The work carried out by this column was regarded as being so important that HQ ALFSEA dealt direct with the column commander. Arrangements were made that the column had priority over all other units for such MT spares as were available. Each of the companies of the column were given spare vehicles to make certain that they would have a 100 per cent carrying capacity and they were also allotted strong IEME second echelon workshops.

The facilities which were given to the column were perhaps a little extravagant in certain respects, and some other units and formations cast envious eyes on its wealth of vehicles, its ample workshop cover, and its priorities; but it literally delivered the goods, when no other agency could have done so, overcoming enormous difficulties on the way.

During the later part of the war in Burma, a growing flow of RASC units and individuals arrived in India and SEAC, mainly because of the build-up in preparation for the intensive war against Japan which was planned to follow on the defeat of the Germans in Europe; but also partly because of the increasing tendency on the part of the ST Directorate in India to look to that at the War Office for assistance, and partly because SEAC, while an independent command, was responsible to, and supported by, the War Office and not India.

There was no ST representation on the staff of SACSEA, but on that of 11 Army Group, later to be known as ALFSEA, there was a DST with all the usual staff. At first that officer was drawn from the RIASC, and had as his deputy an RASC DDST. Later, the position was reversed, and the DST was an RASC officer (Brigadier P. A. Arden), whose staff was partly from one corps and partly from the other. Gradually, more and more RASC officers arrived in the theatre, and the RIASC was more and more closely associated with the RASC. There was a much closer liaison between the two directorates in London and Delhi, marked by the exchange of senior liaison officers. A RASC officer was DDT at GHQ, India, during 1943-44, and after him another became DDS (POL).

A RASC officer was sent out from ST 1, War Office, to the Indian Directorate, to help in organizing the growing water transport service of the RIASC. A CRASC water transport unit, with a boat stores depot, and a harbour launch company, went out as what would have been the advance guard of a considerable body of water transport units for employment with SEAC which was being prepared in the United Kingdom. This included units of an entirely new type, such as an ambulance launch company, and a floating workshop company for the repair of craft and amphibians; but the sudden end of the war in the Far East prevented the despatch of these units.

The RIASC at length, after a delay of more than two years, adopted the standard component organization of supply and transport units which had been introduced into the British, Dominion, and colonial Army Service Corps in 1941, and had proved so successful. It was equally so in the Indian Corps.

Headquarters transport columns, for the command of groups of half a dozen of the many Indian transport companies working on the roads between Dimapur and Mandalay, began to arrive in the theatre in the early part of 1945. The flow of RASC supply units to ALFSEA and India began in January, 1945, and some 30 supply platoons and other units had left the United Kingdom by the middle of the year; but not many were actually employed in the theatre before the end of the war with Japan. The POL units began to go out earlier, and at the end of the war there were three companies, a dozen platoons, and some technical units serving in SEAC, besides those previously mentioned.

As a footnote to this story of the work of the RASC in a theatre predominantly the sphere of the RIASC, it may be observed that, after India was granted her independence in 1947, a considerable number of British officers of the RIASC was absorbed into the RASC; and so it may be said that union of the two Corps was eventually achieved, but it had been to a great extent effective throughout the war wherever they had worked together.

CEYLON

Ceylon at Peace

Before the war, the Ceylon garrison consisted of an artillery regiment, with ancillary troops. The regiment had batteries at Colombo, Dyatalawa and Trincomalee. Apart from these three stations there were no troops of any sort except that, during the hot season in Colombo, Headquarters Ceylon Garrison moved from Colombo to Nuwara Eliya, a hill station. The military command of the island was vested in a brigadier.

The RASC representation was two officers (a major and captain), seven other ranks, and a few civilian employees. The major, in addition to his Corps duties, usually functioned as DAQMG, while the captain, in addition to ST & B normal duties, acted as adjutant to the Ceylon Army Service Corps. The CASC were part of the Ceylon Defence Force, which was more or less of Territorial Army status, that is, it carried Regular British Army instructors and periodically attended drills and summer camps. The Ceylon Defence Force was a composite force equivalent to approximately a British brigade.

On the outbreak of hostilities, the Defence Force was mobilized, but as Ceylon at that time was unaffected by the war, partial demobilization took place soon afterwards. Several officers of the CASC remained embodied, however, and two of them (a major and captain) took over the duties of the two RASC regular officers who were ordered to the United Kingdom. These two officers (one located at Colombo and one at Trincomalee), with the assistance of three Regular warrant officers and non-commissioned officers of the RASC, carried on the whole of the Corps duties in the island until May, 1940, when a Regular quartermaster, RASC, arrived from Singapore. This posting was to implement an increase in the Ceylon establishment which had been asked for just before the war. The officer was intended as Officer in charge of Barracks, Ceylon. In fact he had, in addition, to assume the duties of officer in charge of transport, and embarkation staff officer. Embarkation duties at that time were still the responsibility of the Corps in overseas stations, and, with a war in progress, the port of Colombo was a hive of activity and the duties were fairly onerous. Supplies for the island were demanded direct from the War Office and shipped to Colombo. Transport was mostly hired, and extensive hiring was essential at Trincomalee in connection with the extension of the naval base there. Barrack duties were continued as in peacetime, the same system of accounting being maintained. Early in 1941, consequent upon a decision to use Trincomalee as a transhipment port for Australian forces on their way to the Middle East, it was found necessary to form a movements branch for Ceylon. The only officer in the island with any experience of movements was the RASC quartermaster who had been with the pre-war embarkation establishment at Southampton. He was entrusted with the task of forming Movement Control, Ceylon, and became the first staff captain (movements) Ceylon, in February,

1941. The formation of 'movements' relieved the RASC of all embarkation and disembarkation duties, but also took away the only Regular RASC officer then in the island!

Ceylon is Transformed

The entry of Japan into the war at the end of 1941 put a completely different complexion on activities in Ceylon. Reinforcements poured into the island. First came 34th Indian Division (of two brigades) at the end of 1941, followed by 23rd East African Brigade and 16th British Infantry Brigade early in 1942. Both these brigades came under command of 34th Indian Division which thus became unique with one British, one East African and two Indian brigades. 16th Brigade was closely followed by two brigades of 6th Australian Division which had originally been destined for Australia after service in Middle East. The two Australian brigades were ultimately replaced by 20th Indian Division later in 1942. Headquarters, Ceylon Army Command was set up in March, 1942, and was located at the Colombo Museum. The commander was Lieut-General Pownall; and Brigadier C. E. Davis, who had been DDST Malaya, became DDST Ceylon. The staff hailed mainly from Singapore and the Dutch East Indies.

Such a rapid expansion obviously put a great strain on the existing Corps establishment until such time as the CASC and reinforcement units got really under way. The Ceylon Army Service Corps units consisted of two transport companies, a base supply depot and a detail issue depot. The Indian division had general transport companies and had provided an advanced base supply depot at Kurunegala. The British, Australian and East African Brigades brought their own ST units, the RASC being represented by 61 Company which later pioneered air despatch in India and Burma.

The supply situation was complicated at the outset. There were several types of ration scales to cope with—British, Indian, African, Ceylonese, to quote the main ones. The responsibility for supply was transferred from the War Office to GHQ (India) in November, 1942, and it took some time before the system worked smoothly. The supply of meat presented difficulties. Most of it was carried by the Royal Navy, and it included goats which had to be imported from India for Indian troops. Fresh vegetables were also a problem. The resources of Ceylon were inadequate to meet the increased demand, and an organization was set up to import from southern India direct to a vegetable reception depot in Colombo. This importation of vast quantities of vegetables took place every day once the organization got going, and was most successful.

A point worth mentioning in connection with the fresh vegetable supply is the fact that it was necessary to supply Trincomalee by road from Kandy. The vegetables were supplied under local contract, and road transport was the only satisfactory method of despatch to Trincomalee, rail facilities being poor. On one occasion the vegetable convoy was delayed by a rogue elephant on the jungle road. One lorry was overturned, and the vegetables were promptly devoured by the animal.

Eggs were also supplied under local contract, and were routed by road from southern India to the same depot in Colombo for redistribution throughout the island. Local contracts were made wherever possible to supplement the vegetable supply, and in 1943 a project was started by the DDST with a view to increasing the local supply. Labour was specially imported from Cochin State. About 40 acres of jungle near Nuwara Eliya were cleared and terraced, and a really first class vegetable garden was quickly established. The products of this garden were first used to meet the needs of hospitals, the rest going to the general vegetable pool.

The supply of fresh meat on hoof for Indian troops, to which reference has been made, was another difficult problem. The goats were shipped from Cochin to Colombo in batches of approximately 500. Voyage casualties were high, and reception facilities in Colombo poor. To overcome these difficulties a goat farm manned by Indians was established at Kurunegala. All goats arriving in the island were sent to this farm and conditioned before issue. Breeding was carried on, together with attendant clinical facilities. In this way the main difficulties were resolved. Another venture, which was not as successful, was the establishment of a cattle farm near Colombo. Live oxen were imported from southern India and kept at this farm, but their quality was poor, disease incidence high, and the climatic conditions far from ideal. The experiment was eventually abandoned, together with a similar one of importing cattle from Australia and grazing them in the hill country. The climate did not appear to suit these animals, and they were quickly prone to disease. In 1944, in a further effort to increase the fresh meat supply for hospitals and convalescent depots up-country, a War Department stock farm was started in the hills. This was run by members of RASC and the CASC, under the guidance of an officer of the CASC who was a former planter. Pigs, poultry and rabbits were bred, and a cowherd maintained to provide milk for hospitals. This was a most successful venture, although lack of refrigerator rolling stock limited issues to up-country stations.

The supply organization consisted of a CRASC Supply Units in Colombo, with base supply depots at Colombo, Kurunegala and Trincomalee, manned by the RASC, and a base depot in Colombo manned by the CASC. The Kurunegala depot was the advanced depot. The Colombo depot, RASC manned, functioned as a reconditioning unit; such a unit was essential because of the bad state in which supplies were arriving in the country from India. All supplies were thoroughly examined and reconditioned where necessary. To assist in this work, a War Department chemist was carried on the establishment of CRASC Supply Units. This reconditioning unit, which was much overworked, undoubtedly effected substantial financial savings.

In December, 1943, Brigadier C. E. Davis was relieved by Brigadier J. T. Reckitt as DDST, and in 1944 Brigadier M. F. Farquharson-Roberts arrived from ALFSEA to take over from Brigadier Reckitt.

From the time of the fall of Singapore in February, 1942, the situation in Colombo docks had become increasingly chaotic. The docks are small, and no ship can go alongside. Civilian lighter fleets were limited to the normal requirements of peace, and labour was scarce. Thousands of tons of stores were pouring in for the rapid expansion of the defences of the island and for the maintenance of the increased numbers in all three services. In comparison the clearance rate was negligible. Ships were delayed, and transit sheds filled to capacity. By the end of 1943 organized clearance was practically at a standstill, although an Indian docks operating company had arrived and was assisting in the actual handling of cargoes from ship to shore. In an effort to solve this problem, the Commander-in-Chief called a meeting with Admiralty and naval officials, Army and RAF representatives, and members of the Colombo Civil Council. At this meeting, the RASC offered to take on the task of clearing the docks. The offer was quickly accepted. A CRASC transport column was flown out from Britain, and within five months the docks had been cleared and restored to normal. The method was the establishment of dumps, one for each of the three services and one for civilians, located some distance from the port. Clearance to these dumps was then effected by the RASC transport column.

Ceylon's Contribution

In 1941, at the request of Middle East, an effort was started to recruit Ceylonese into the RASC for clerical duties, primarily in the Middle East, although enlistment was for service in any part of the world. The response was gratifying (pay and marriage allowance at British rates was attractive to the average Ceylonese), and recruits of a high standard were sent to the Middle East after being trained in Corps clerical duties. This training had to be undertaken personally by the three RASC officers and three Regular RASC warrant officers and non-commissioned officers, in addition to their normal day's duty. Later, Ceylon Command were asked if they would set up a training school for RASC drivers, to be recruited locally. This task was accepted, and Middle East provided the officers and NCOs to run the school, while Ceylon provided recruits in abundance. These men, unlike the clerks, were not required to speak English, so the field of recruitment was enlarged, and the difficulties of the instructors correspondingly enhanced. The success of the whole venture, however, can be gauged from the fact that nearly 7,000 were recruited, of whom some 4,500 saw service in the Middle East. Ceylonese were also recruited for labour duties at base supply depots and petroleum installations. This labour was controlled by the CASC.

The supply of petrol for the island did not present any great problem, as initially it was effected from the Shell Company's installations in Colombo and elsewhere. Later, however, petrol depots were formed with RASC fire-fighting sections.

In 1944 Ceylon Army Command were made responsible for the launching of a combined operation in the Cocos Islands in the Indian ocean about 1,500 miles from Ceylon. The islands were difficult to approach, as they are surrounded by a coral reef, and mooring alongside was impossible.

The task consisted in the setting up of an RAF airstrip where bombers could touch down and refuel before launching an attack on the Japanese positions on the mainland of Malaya, then in Japanese hands. Surprise was of paramount importance. Had the Japanese become aware of the venture before the island defences were erected, the whole enterprise would have been doomed to failure, since the Royal Navy had insufficient forces to give much protection.

The maintenance of the force responsible for the protection and operation of this base was difficult. It was decided that the main requirements for maintenance were to be shipped from Calcutta. The time and space problem controlled from Ceylon was therefore complicated. Petroleum tanks had to be conveyed to the islands, transhipped to the mainland and finally erected.

The first requirement was the clearance of jungle to make way for the air strip. A reconnaissance party was flown to the islands, and on its return a plan was carefully prepared. One of the main problems was water supply, and it was decided that water for the force would have to be shipped to the islands until such time as the Royal Engineers could arrange normal supply. The water was ultimately shipped from Calcutta in cans, and this was a RASC responsibility.

Fresh vegetables were obtained from Ceylon, but great care had to be exercised in the absence of refrigeration space in ships. A large percentage of waste had therefore to be allowed for.

For the Indian troops forming part of the garrison, a consignment of live goats was collected from the goat farm and duly embarked on a small vessel with a Scotsman as master. A certain amount of fodder was placed on board which it was calculated would be sufficient. Unfortunately the ship was somewhat delayed on its journey, with startling results. The goats broke out of their pens and roamed all over the ship. According to the master they ate everything except the crew, and anything made of metal. Only one quarter of the goats reached their destination, and the captain on his return, swore that whatever happened he would never take goats to sea again.

The whole enterprise of setting up this staging post was a great success, and a perfect example of combined operations. The strip was made, the petrol tanks erected and the bombers actually landed, but the war against Japan came to an end before they could be used.

CHAPTER X

THE INVASION OF NORTH-WEST EUROPE

Introduction

ON Monday, November 26th, 1945, the Commander-in-Chief, Field-Marshal Sir Bernard Montgomery, visited the Headquarters of the RASC Training Brigade, BAOR, at Lippstadt, Westphalia, to inspect 1,500 men and 50 vehicles, representing a cross section of RASC units which had maintained the armies in the field during the North-West Europe campaign. The Commander-in-Chief was accompanied by the DST, Major-General W. d'A. Collings, and the parade was commanded by Colonel W. J. F. Eassie, who entered the theatre as DDST of XXX Corps, and was soon afterwards appointed as DDST Second Army. After he had taken the parade and decorated those who had won awards for gallantry in the campaign, the Field-Marshal addressed all those present, and he paid tribute to the Corps in the following words: 'I consider the work done by the RASC has been quite magnificent. I know well that without your exertions behind—and often in front—we should never have been able to advance as we did. No corps in the Army has a higher sense of duty than you. You have delivered supplies in all weathers and over all roads; you have driven your vehicles in mud, rain, snow and ice, and you have never once let us down. Without your supplies, our battles could never have been won. It is a fine record, and I am glad to be able to be here publicly to pay the RASC the tribute it deserves.'

The operations of the British Liberation Army in North-West Europe in 1944 and 1945 were conducted on a scale and over an area which prohibit detailed accounts of units' operations. In each phase of the campaign, therefore, episodes have been selected from the histories of units of varying types and roles, with the idea of giving a general but vivid picture of the work of the Corps in that particular phase. Throughout, the object has been to create a picture and not to compile a historic record.

Ever since the British armies left North-West Europe in the summer of 1940, the main object in the minds of the planners had been the re-entry into that part of the Continent, the liberation of our conquered Allies, and the final subjection of the German armed forces. All other campaigns had been subordinated to this primary object, and, when the time came when re-entry became practicable, the resources of all kinds which were concentrated and employed exceeded anything which had been seen before. These remarks apply to the manpower and equipment of the RASC as much as to any other arm or branch of any of the three services.

For the purpose of this story, the campaign can be divided into the long planning and preparation period, stretching from early 1942 until D Day, the amphibious assault and operations in the beach-head, the advance to the Rhine, and finally the Rhine assault and the sweep across the North German plain.

Planning and Preparation

Serious planning for the re-entry into North-West Europe, the original code name for which was 'Round Up', began at the beginning of 1942, when a special army planning staff was set up within the framework of GHQ Home Forces. C-in-C Home Forces was also appointed as one of the three 'combined commanders' for these projected operations. The MGA Home Forces was Major-General H. M. Gale. He was responsible for the initial administrative planning, including the build-up and preparation of the administrative units which were to form part of the order of battle. The executive work in this connection was done by the War Office and other Ministries concerned, and General Gale co-ordinated their planning efforts through the medium of a series of inter-service and inter-ministerial committees known as the Round Up administrative planning staff. The efforts of this staff were delayed by the decision to launch the North African Expeditionary Force, to the headquarters of which General Gale went as Chief Administrative Officer.

Early in 1942, a new planning headquarters was formed, known as 'Cossac' (Chief of Staff to Supreme Allied Commander Designate). This staff examined the west coast of Europe from North Cape to the Pyrenees to find the most suitable area, and devised an outline plan for the initial assault and build-up which was tentatively accepted by the Combined Chiefs of Staff. By the end of 1943, General Eisenhower had been appointed Supreme Commander, and General Montgomery had also returned to England to command 21 Army Group. Early in 1944 a revised plan was produced by 21 Army Group and approved by SHAEF, the Combined Chiefs of Staff of the two Governments (see diagram on p. 369).

On May 15th, 1943, Major-General H. R. Kerr had assumed the appointment of DST at the War Office, and the work of building up the ST order of battle for 21 Army Group and the RASC units in the United Kingdom to support the expedition began in earnest.

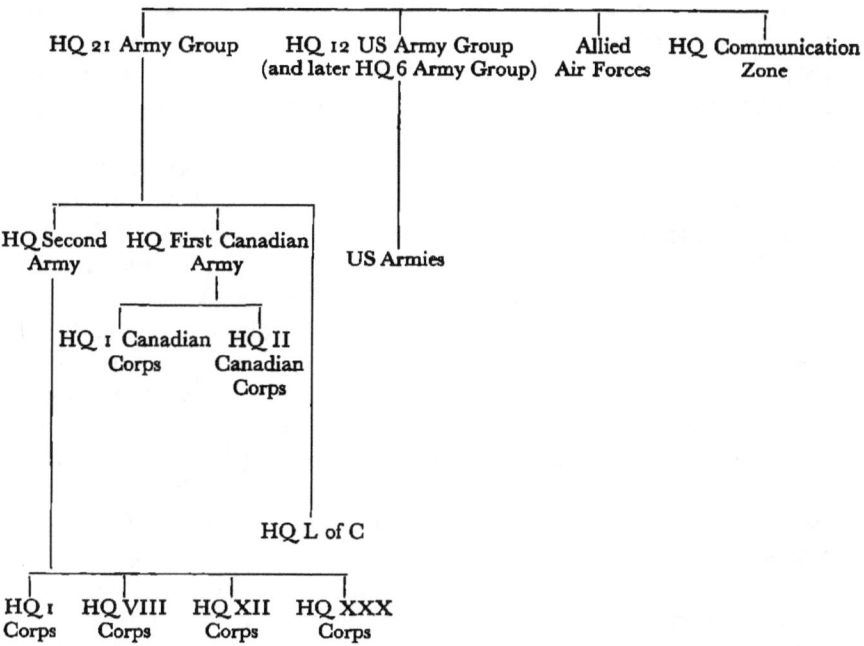

Note: Corps are shown under their National Headquarters. But HQ 1 Corps served under HQ First Canadian Army for the greater part of the campaign and XXX Corps served under HQ First Canadian Army for operation 'Veritable' (Reichwald).

That period provided many examples of the Corps' ability to improvise and of the adaptability of RASC units and individuals. For example, an artillery platoon was successfully converted into the original Dukw Training Unit, and a GT company located on Belfast racecourse was hastily summoned to England to perform air despatch duties. In neither of these cases were any of the personnel changed and in both cases the speed of conversion was remarkable.

It would be difficult to exaggerate the volume and variety of the work done by the ST branches in the War Office in preparation for the mounting of operation 'Overlord', as it had now been named. A few general examples only can be given here. A new 24-hour pack ration was devised and produced at short notice and proved itself light, compact and highly nutritious. A reserve of 75 million bulk rations and 60 million special pack rations had to be built up in spite of a world scarcity of foodstuffs and shipping. The great transport problem was the formation of some 200 companies in the face of the inevitable manpower difficulties and a lack of certain types of equipment. Perhaps the most spectacular achievement of the petroleum planners was the provision and training of the units required to operate the terminal installations of the submarine petroleum pipeline known by the code name 'Pluto'. Men were specially picked and were trained for their task on a submarine pipeline running from Swansea to Ilfracombe. During 1943 more than 17 million jerricans and three million returnable containers of other kinds were produced in the United Kingdom.

In QMG House at the War Office was a room in which, by early 1944, all information regarding supply and maintenance by air could be found. It contained, among other statistics, the availability and locations of road transport and stocks of various kinds, and from it all RASC air despatch activity was co-ordinated. The RAF Air Freight Control Centre was in the Swindon area, and around it the airfields used for air supply and maintenance were grouped. The headquarters of the RASC Air Despatch Organization, commanded by Colonel S. W. Walsh, was located with this centre and received orders direct from ST 3 at the War Office. Colonel Walsh's command consisted of three air despatch companies, comprising 12 air-dropping platoons, each of 15 air-dropping crews of four men. These 180 crews had an approximate capacity of 360 tons a sortie. Two sorties could be flown daily in an emergency, but not for any length of time. A pool of six general transport companies under CRASC War Office Transport Column divided its services between the Air Despatch Organization and DDST Airborne Forces. All RASC units in this organization were trained with the RAF for emergency supply (in case of severed sea communications), for schedule supply (a daily service in which about 25 tons of urgent ordnance stores, blood plasma, mail and newspapers were carried), and for temporary maintenance of ground formations. Air supply was affected by air landings and air maintenance by parachute dropping of pre-packed panniers.

The complex organization for mounting operation 'Overlord' had been planned in great detail by the Directorate of Movements in the War Office for more than two years in close co-operation with the two commands primarily involved, Southern and South-Eastern. The War Office (in conjunction with HQ 21 Army Group) allotted extra resources to these commands as circumstances demanded.

The two DDsST mainly concerned in the basic part of the operations were Brigadier P. A. Arden (Southern Command) and Brigadier A. de B. Jenkins (South-Eastern Command). The rationing of our own troops passing through the mounting machine and of certain elements of the other two fighting services probably provided the greatest problems with which they had to contend.

Troops stationed in the United Kingdom received a messing cash allowance and were supplied in part by the NAAFI. As soon as they entered the concentration area, they came on to the home field service ration scale. But in marshalling and embarkation areas all troops fed on a 'hotel basis', organized by the Army Catering Corps. In the marshalling areas every soldier also received two 24-hour landing rations, a tommy-cooker and a bag ration, containing biscuits, chocolate and chewing gum. Special RASC staffs were required in the embarkation areas to load rations in certain landing craft and ships. Men of the RAF travelling by sea, and air-sea rescue launch crews had to be rationed, and ambulance trains, as well as one large camp for the receipt of refugees from the invasion area, had to be stocked.

Troop-carrying from the concentration to the embarkation areas, ammunition-lifting from depot to ports, tank-transporting, and the secret road delivery and collection of prefabricated mock landing craft for the cover plan were some of the big transport commitments. The War Office kept a pool of specialized and general transport companies under their own control during this period, and the Road Haulage Organization helped in these tasks. The refuelling of many of the minor landing craft and the conveyance of water to ships in the South Coast ports were other important and extraneous commitments.

By the end of May, 1944, the Corps was ready to play its part in the greatest amphibious operation in history.

The Amphibious Assault

The plan was to assault, simultaneously, beaches on the Normandy coast immediately north of the Carentan estuary and between the Carentan estuary and the river Orne, with the object of securing a lodgement area as a base for further operations. This area was to include airfield sites and the port of Cherbourg. The left or eastern flank of the lodgement area was to include the road centre of Caen. The beaches were selected because they offered a better shelter for shipping and were less heavily defended than other possible areas along the Channel coast. They also satisfied the minimum requirements of the Air Forces, regarding distances from home bases, for the provision of air cover. The absence of big ports was partially overcome by the construction of two artificial ports in the United Kingdom, which were towed across the Channel in sections and erected, one in the American sector and one in the British.

The plan provided for simultaneous landings by eight equivalent brigades, of which three were British, two were Canadian, and three were American combat teams. Commandos and Rangers also took part. The Americans assaulted on the right because they

North-West Europe,

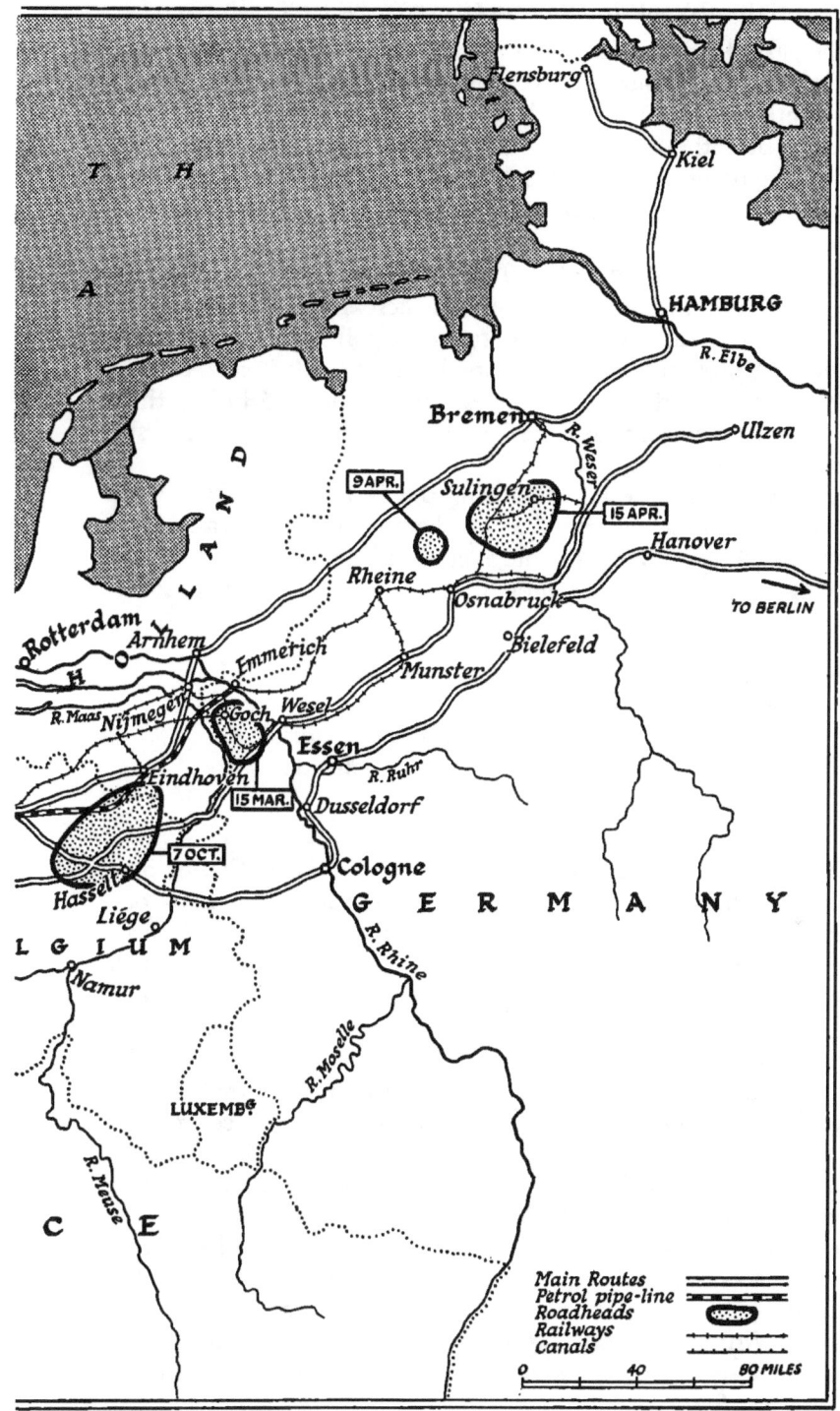

1944/1945

were to be partially maintained and supported direct from the United States through Cherbourg. Airborne forces were used on both flanks; the 6th British Airborne Division was given the task of seizing the crossings over the Caen Canal and operated on the British left. General Montgomery commanded all the land forces for the assault, for which task he had an American increment attached to his headquarters.

The administrative plan entailed the shipment of a community the size of the population of Birmingham across the Channel and over beaches, and the wherewithal to support it in a great static battle with the prospect of an early break-out and advance. More than 287,000 men and 37,000 vehicles were pre-loaded before the assault, and 1,100,000 troops were landed in Normandy in the first 30 days of operations.

The part played by the RASC during the assault and within the bridgehead can best be presented as a coherent story by breaking it down into headings related to the operations, and giving suitable examples of Corps units under those headings selected, which are:—

>   The airborne assault
>   The seaborne assault
>   Beach maintenance
>   The British 'Mulberry' and the 'great storm'
>   General conditions within the bridgehead

The Airborne Assault

The honour of being the first RASC unit to land in France on D Day, June 6th, 1944, belongs to the light composite company of 6th Airborne Division (716 Company). Two platoons of this company parachuted down among the earliest, some hours before the beach landings. The company's task was to organize themselves for the supply of the division and to collect the containers which had been jettisoned by the aircraft from which the men had jumped. By 6 a.m. a dump had been formed in a quarry north of Ranville, from which units were drawing direct. The company commander was wounded soon after landing, leaving Lieutenant F. J. Bland in command for that day. The jettison drop had fallen over a wide area occupied by the enemy, but in spite of this difficulty, which entailed working under fire most of the time, with very slender resources, Bland kept the fighting troops supplied with ammunition. He was awarded the Military Cross and Sgt Wilson received the Military Medal for collecting mines and delivering them to the Royal Engineers in a captured lorry while under constant mortar fire.

The men of the 224 Para Field Ambulance were widely dispersed after the drop. Lieutenant G. C. G. Phile, the unit transport officer, rallied them and led them through enemy occupied territory. That same night the main dressing station at Le Mesnil was crowded with wounded, and there was no transport available. Lieutenant Phile, with four men, forced 63 Germans to surrender, and captured their five vehicles and a motorcycle. This transport made possible the rapid collection of wounded all over the brigade area and saved many lives. Lieutenant Phile also received the immediate award of the Military Cross.

The Seaborne Assault

On the extreme left of the British assault was 3rd Division (I Corps) supported by an armoured brigade. The RASC of these formations had the additional task of maintaining 6th Airborne Division for the first 10 days of the operations. The bridges leading to the Ranville dumps were bottlenecks and naturally received attention from enemy aircraft as well as intermittent shell, mortar and small arms fire. Major J. R. Cuthbertson, commanding 27th Armoured Brigade Company (90 Company), was responsible for the task of maintaining the division and was awarded the Military Cross for his part in its successful accomplishment. The first RASC units ashore in this sector were two assault platoons of 172 Company, with one platoon of 90 Company attached. The story of 3rd Division's part in the invasion says of these early days: 'These were days of effort and danger, in which none could fail to feel proud of his job; there was glory in driving a lorry load of ammunition or petrol down to the Pegasus bridge at Benouville and over to the ground held by the airborne division'. The platoons of 172 Company made a good landing, and ammunition points were established in the brigade assembly areas. When two battalions were almost isolated near Cambes, all available ammunition was dumped in forward positions. B Platoon of 90 Company carried out an urgent troop-carrying detail on June 7th by lifting the 2nd Battalion the Lincolnshire Regiment to St Aubin d'Arquenay. For the first three days, both divisions had to be supplied from beach sector dumps because the ground intended for the beach maintenance area was still partly in enemy hands. Throughout the operations described above men of the RASC were often in action and under fire.

In the right sector of the British area XXX Corps assaulted on a one divisional front. The 50th Division was supported by 8th Armoured Brigade, and was followed up immediately by 7th Armoured Division. No. 522 Company was the first of the 50th Division RASC to land with detachments of 346 and 552 Companies. The latter company served 8th Armoured Brigade. One of the first tasks of 522 Company was the maintenance of 47th Commando at Port-en-Bessin, which was destined to be the 'Pluto' port and which was still well inside enemy territory. Delivery of vital requirements to this commando was continually effected in the face of small arms fire and shelling from enemy tanks. Captain B. W. M. Linden and Sgts T. Burt and W. J. Tams received immediate awards of the Military Cross and the Military Medal respectively for their part in these operations. Two hours after the first landing 39 GT Company came ashore. Their first task was to deliver antitank guns required for the defence of the beach maintenance area. Delivery was effected under mortar and small arms fire, and three awards of the Military Medal were made to members of the company. A platoon of 127 Company, which had been with XXX Corps since 1941, and detachments of XXX Corps HQ Car Company were also ashore on D Day.

The performance, in general, of divisional second line transport in the period immediately after the landings was most creditable. Although distances were small, demands for petrol and ammunition were heavy and urgent. These units were only skeleton, and they worked like tigers to maintain their divisions.

Beach Maintenance

There were two beach groups with each of the assaulting divisions, and each group included, as beach maintenance area units, a detail issue depot and a petrol depot. Maintenance areas for 50th and 3rd Canadian Divisions were established without much incident and within three days of landing. DDST XXX Corps landed at about H plus 6 on D Day and found a DID and a petrol depot with stock on the ground and actually making issues—a truly remarkable achievement and undoubtedly a factor in our success. Opposition in the 3rd Division's sector prevented the maintenance area from functioning until D plus 10. Nevertheless, the average stores tonnages brought ashore were not below that of the other two sectors. Supplies began to arrive at 5 DID on June 8. Units' vehicles began drawing the same day, and the DID worked continuously on receipts and issues for 14 days. After a few days, 5 DID and 2 DID, belonging to the other beach group, combined their resources, receiving and issuing on alternate days. Men worked round the clock in eight-hour shifts, achieving an average handling in or out of 112,000 compo packs, in addition to large numbers of jerricans, drinking water, hospital supplies and coal. The petrol depots were delayed by bad weather in the Channel, but were nevertheless all in operation by June 7th. Petrol demands were less than expected, which compensated for the heavy expenditure of ammunition. In 3rd Division's sector a stick of bombs set alight dumps containing the whole reserve of petrol and half the ammunition reserve. The area quickly became a blazing inferno of bursting petrol cans and exploding ammunition. An officer, a sergeant and a 19-year-old soldier of 96 DID with only a month's service received immediate awards for driving loaded vehicles out of the blaze. In spite of their efforts 100,000 gallons of fuel and 400 tons of ammunition were lost.

The dukws were a big feature in the success of the assault and build-up. There were 11 companies of them altogether, employed in ferrying stores from coasters and other craft to shore, and in evacuating casualties from the beaches to LSTs lying off.

Individual training of the drivers had been thorough, but there had not been enough time to complete collective and inter-service training. Most of the dukws were carried across the Channel, stowed in the LSTs, but some were slung from davits, and a few were carried in Rhino ferries, which were towed by LSTs. The crossing was rough. Major M. J. B. Hornsby writes of the landing of the dukws on XXX Corps sector: 'The dukws were launched in an angry sea and headed for the shore. Visibility at the time was poor. The wind was blowing from west to north at about 15 knots, which made the beaches a lee shore and raised a considerable sea. However, enemy interference from the air was practically non-existent, and that from the shore batteries was ineffective. Beach obstacles were numerous but, with one or two exceptions, were avoided by the drivers' skilful handling. It was extremely difficult to handle an amphibian in the sea without having to negotiate such obstacles, and these hazards, added to a rising tide, tested the drivers' ability to the utmost. On one beach the first wave of amphibians was held up for some time by mortar and machine-gun fire and had to take cover, such as it was, among the sand dunes. Eventually, the enemy strong point which had been offering this resistance was silenced by the assault infantry. Altogether on the first tide, 104 dukws were landed. These mostly contained ammunition, RE stores for beach roadways, medical stores and unit G 1098 equipment. Casualties to both men and vehicles were extremely light.'

Until sufficient GT companies had been landed, the dukws had to carry their loads through to the dumps, but as soon as possible, transhipment areas were established in the vicinity of the beaches where the dukws dropped their loads and returned through a control point to the sea. During the 24 hours ending 1800 hours June 11th, dukws carried 10,850 tons of stores over the beaches. On June 12th one dukw brought Mr. Winston Churchill and General Eisenhower ashore and, on June 14th, another, known thereafter as the 'royal dukw', had the honour of carrying King George VI. Two dukw drivers who were wounded while attached to an American

Ranger battalion were awarded the Military Medal on the recommendation of the United States Army authorities. The work of 624 (fast launch) Company in shepherding the dukws deserves a mention, and 626 (harbour launch) Company performed every kind of task in and about the 'Mulberry', including fire-boat duty with the petrol and ammunition ships and carriage of barrage balloons for the RAF.

The British 'Mulberry' and the Great Storm

The great storm which destroyed the American prefabricated harbour, and caused severe damage to the British 'Mulberry', began on June 19th, and blew for three days and nights. Men of the motorboat companies distinguished themselves in rescue efforts. In one case, 160 anti-aircraft gunners were marooned on isolated rocks, swept by huge seas, and the emplacements were breaking up. The Navy was busy trying to save its own small craft, and the RASC was asked to do what it could to bring the men off. Sgt R. J. Yeabsley and a crew of four of a motor fishing-vessel at once volunteered, and fought their way into the teeth of the gale. It was unsafe to bring the vessel alongside, and the coxswain approached bow on. As the craft neared the rock, Cpl K. Popperwell accomplished the difficult and dangerous feat of jumping across the gap with a line to make fast. Half the men scrambled on board the first time, and the rest on a second trip. Sgt Yeabsley was handling his craft for five hours in the most difficult conditions of wind and sea, and brought off the rescue only just in time. He was awarded the British Empire Medal for gallantry.

Even without a storm, conditions in and around the 'Mulberry' were none too good. The Rear Admiral who was naval officer in charge wrote: 'We at Arromanches had one object only, to maintain the discharge of stores at the maximum rate. The whole time shipping lying in a dense mass off the Normandy coast was being attacked in one way or another. You had your share of V weapons in London, but I do not suppose you ever saw a human torpedo going up in Piccadilly, or a one-man submarine in the Round Pond. All the time we had those waspish weapons, including E-boats, explosive motorboats and circling torpedoes, making a nuisance of themselves. Every night about 30 to 40 aircraft dropped either mines or torpedoes.' The Admiral went on to relate how one night a mine came down in a narrow bottleneck, through which nearly all the traffic had to pass, and a buoy was put to mark the place until the mine disposal men could get to work. A RASC boat made fast to the buoy, and the crew began to have lunch; they were told forcefully to move on. Next morning there was an explosion and at the site of the buoy there was the plume of a mine, a mound of water some 200 feet high, on the side of which was a dukw. But that was not the end of the dukw. It slid off, and came ashore under its own steam. The Admiral sent a signal to CRASC: 'I am aware of the many and varied duties which your dukws so efficiently perform, but until this morning I did not realize that minesweeping was one of them. If the crew of the dukw report at Navy House, they will receive the customary award the Admiralty makes to anyone who sweeps a mine.' Whether customary or not, the reward which the drivers received was a bottle of Scotch. The inevitable result was that dukws tended to meander in search of mines.

General Conditions within the Bridgehead

By June 7th, 50th Division had captured Bayeux. Caen fell after fierce resistance, on July 9th, and there followed the crossing of the Orne by the three armoured divisions of VIII Corps. The Americans broke out of the beach-head in the Cherbourg Peninsula on July 25th, and the fighting in the Falaise pocket lasted until August 22nd, when the next phase of the campaign may be said to have begun. During that period, the build-up of formation transport and of GHQ and line of communication corps units proceeded steadily, the maintenance system gradually developed and settled down, and divisional units inevitably became closely involved in the bitter fighting within the bridgehead in the course of their arduous routine tasks. But the incidents are too numerous to quote here and too repetitive to interest the general reader.

The transport driver casting his memory back to those days in the beach-head must have a picture of long hours, including much night work, over hard, narrow sunken roads, and his fair share of shelling, mortar and small arms fire. The tipper driver will recall, in particular, his work with the divisional engineers on the bridges and tank crossings over the Orne and the Odon. Many of the ambulance drivers have proud memories of gallant work in collecting wounded under forward battle conditions and of driving them back through sniper fire and shelled bottlenecks. The delivery of mines at night to the forward positions in front of Caen must form part of the dream repertoire of many a Corps reservist who served with the 3rd Division. Again the voracity of the guns of 7th Armoured Division, when delayed south of Caen, has probably made a lasting impression on all ranks then concerned in the delivery to that formation of an average of 62 lorry-loads a day.

Finally, a few significant entries into the theatre during the period should be recorded. Two weeks after D Day, bread with special keeping properties was flown in for consumption in hospitals, and RASC bakeries were established and in production by early July.

British beer made its first appearance in the beach-head in July. The first bulk petrol transport company (252 Company of 37 Transport Column) landed on June 23rd, and on June 30th the first cargo of bulk petrol was discharged from a coastal tanker to prefabricated storage in Port-en-Bessin. It was during the final phase of the Falaise fighting on August 20th that the Air Despatch Group in England made its first appearance over Normandy, when they dropped 60 tons of ammunition to a Polish armoured brigade. By late August, the RASC content of the rear maintenance area was eight BSDs, eight DIDs, 13 field bakeries, two field butcheries, 14 petrol depots, and six mobile filling centres.

The Advance to the Rhine: Outline of Operations

The Seine was crossed by the Third United States Army, while the battle of the Falaise pocket was still in progress, and this initial American success was swiftly exploited by First Canadian Army. The immediate tasks for 21 Army Group after crossing the Seine were:—

(*a*) The destruction of the enemy in North-East France;
(*b*) the clearance of the Pas de Calais and the elimination of V bomb sites;
(*c*) the capture of airfields in Belgium; and
(*d*) the capture of Antwerp.

The axis of Second Army advance was north-east, that is towards central Belgium. The First Canadian Army was given the task of advancing up the Channel coast with its series of heavily fortified ports. XXX Corps was the spearhead of the Second Army's advance. Amiens was entered on August 31st, Brussels on September 3rd, and Antwerp the following day.

On September 6th the Commander-in-Chief 21 Army Group ordered the resumption of the advance of Second Army towards the Rhine, and by September 17th a bridgehead over the Meuse–Escaut Canal had been secured. The plan for the Battle of Arnhem, which began on September 11th, was to secure with airborne troops and hold for a limited period the road through Eindhoven–Uden–Grave–Nijmegen and Arnhem, which runs across the waterways from the Meuse–Escaut Canal to the Neder Rijn. XXX Corps was to advance along this 'airborne carpet', as the Commander-in-Chief termed it, and establish itself north of the Neder Rijn with bridgeheads over the Ijssel, facing east. The plan failed because of rapid enemy concentration to oppose these moves and because of bad weather, which prevented the build-up of adequate forces in the vital area. On September 26th, the gallant Arnhem bridgehead forces were withdrawn.

The task of clearing the Scheldt Estuary was a hard one, and these operations by the First Canadian Army lasted from early October to the end of the first week in November. While these operations were in progress, C-in-C 21 Army Group began to regroup his forces and, when this had been done, First Canadian Army assumed responsibility for the Nijmegen bridgehead. By early December, Second Army was lined up along the Meuse, its right in touch with the Ninth United States Army at Marseyck. Plans for the battle of the Rhineland were well advanced by that time, but their implementation was postponed by the unexpected German counter-offensive in the Ardennes.

The British part in the Anglo-American pincer movement which constituted the battle of the Rhineland began on February 8th, 1945, when XXX Corps, under command of First Canadian Army, launched its attack into the Reichwald Forest and the northern extension of the West Wall on a front of five divisions, supported by more than 1,000 guns and strong air forces. German opposition was fanatical, and the weather was terrible. On the northern flank, the Reichwald operations were conducted mainly in the various types of amphibious vehicles in deep mud and slush, and through heavily wooded roadless country. On March 3rd, however, the British and American pincer movements had linked up, and 21 Army Group was lined up on the western banks of the Rhine as far south as Düsseldorf.

The Transport Units

This brief account of operations from Falaise to the Rhineland is sufficient to accentuate to any military reader the transport problem which they created. During this phase, every artifice had to be employed to make the limited resources keep pace with the advance; the range of all echelons was extended to the limit. In emergencies, first line transport drew from FMAs, and second line from army roadheads. VIII Corps and two independent brigades were grounded, and their transport thrown into the general pool ferrying between RMA and roadheads. Fortunately the capture of many bridges intact allowed the bridge companies to be released for general transport purposes, and anti-aircraft and tank transporter units were also made available for similar work. Later on, the War Office, which still controlled the main base and kept in closest touch with the administrative plans of HQ 21 Army Group by constant liaison visits, improvised a total of 18 transport units from Anti-Aircraft Command and Driver Training Brigade sources and despatched them to France to fill gaps in the ever lengthening lines of communication. In fact, plans for this improvisation had been made by the DST War Office long before the need for it arose, or it could never have been effected in time to meet the crisis.

The first stages of the advance from the bridgehead were slow, and Second Army was being maintained from No. 2 ARH* (Army Roadhead) in the area of Bayeux. Plans were in hand to establish the next ARH (No. 4) between Glos la Ferrière and Rugles by expanding the area occupied by XXX Corps FMC. Since the distance then being covered by the Corps in stocking their FMCs were not too great, Army transport was available and was held in readiness to stock this ARH. While the necessary transport was still available, it was decided to lift forward stocks of ammunition, petrol and supplies as far as Falaise, and hold them there ready to move forward to the new RHs. As soon as this was done the move forward to the Seine and on into Belgium began, and was so rapid that issues were made from the stocks held at Falaise, while stocking of No. 4 ARH was done from Bayeux. The next ARH to be established was No. 6 at Hal, south of Brussels. This was followed by No. 8 ARH, centring around Bourg-Leopold.

This system of lifting forward and establishing dumps of goods which were then rapidly consumed was adopted as standard practice during the advance to the Meuse. In retrospect, the system seems undesirable; it places an unnecessary strain on depot staffs. But it did maintain a long and rapid advance and kept transport in centrally controlled pools.

The method of operation of Army transport was to establish a CRASC (Control) at the delivery end of the transport chain, that is to say at the roadhead in use. This CRASC had no transport under command, but he and his headquarters received convoys as they arrived, co-ordinated their unloading arrangements and despatched them back to RMA, with the least delay. A similar headquarters was established at the loading end in the RMA, whose task was to regulate arrival of transport at the various loading depots, ensure provision of labour and do everything possible to lessen the time of the turn-round. Most of the transport companies were located at the loading end of the route, where they could most effectively be rested, maintained and allocated to tasks. But some were located along the route, where companies were grouped under CsRASC (Operational) who were also responsible for organizing staging camps. Really good wireless communications were essential to the success of this organization and ST Second Army operated a rear link with RMA when distances became great, and also intercepted all wireless signals between report centres. DDST Second Army was thus in possession of the current position of all convoys and the probable state of his forward stocks at any date in the near future, for which plans were being made.

* ARH stands for Army roadhead or railhead.

By September 10th, 1944, the railway lines from Bayeux to the Seine had been repaired and rail was introduced in the L of C as far as the Seine. Second Army set up an organization on the Seine for the clearance of railheads on the south of the river and for movement of stocks by road transport to railheads on the north of the river. A ST rear link formed part of this organization, and was later supplemented by representatives from Q and Q (Movements). It continued to control the transfer of stores across the Seine until such time as No. 6 ARH was established, when HQ 21 Army Group set up a special control at Amiens. 'Trance', as it was called, took over from Second Army rear link and controlled all movement on the L of C behind the army rear boundary.

No. 8 ARH was stocked by road and rail. Ten different railway stations were used as railheads, and these circumstances forced Second Army to create a special organization for the stocking of this roadhead. The railheads were divided into two groups, with a CRASC Transport Column HQ allotted for the clearance of railheads in each group. The two CsRASC set up a combined headquarters at which were representatives of Q (Movements) and Labour, Second Army. When rear Second Army moved from the area of the roadhead, a rear link was left behind to co-ordinate activities there. This organization worked well in conjunction with the following arrangements which were made for obtaining accurate information on the arrival of trains, in order that the most economic use could be made of limited transport at the disposal of the CsRASC. In order to overcome the effects of a civil railway system which had not recovered from the destruction caused by Allied bombing and enemy sabotage, ST Second Army formed a railway check point with a Q (Movements) representative on the main 'up' route. This check point informed the CsRASC direct by wireless of estimated times of arrival of trains at each railhead.

The control of transport links forward of Army was often on a similar basis. ST corps established their rear and forward control points at ARH and FMA respectively. These were formed by CRASC corps troops and an additional MT column headquarters allotted by army. On the few occasions when the latter could not be spared, CRASC corps troops split his headquarters to meet the emergency. The ST wireless net linked the DDST corps and both control points, providing the means for full control over transport. As the advance continued, the distance between ARH and FMAs fluctuated. The establishment forward of a new ARH would result in corps transport being required to cover only a small mileage. As corps established new FMAs this mileage would increase until the advance justified the establishment of a new roadhead by army. Corps' demand for transport varied with the distances involved, and so army transport companies were continually being allotted to corps and subsequently withdrawn. Corps basic transport was, of course, used to the full, and on the few occasions when a division was in reserve on a non-operational role the assistance of portions of the divisional second line transport for corps duties was sought and given. According to normal standards, all transport was overworked and none could be spared for rest. High standards of morale and training enabled our transport units to maintain the high pressure and swift improvisation demanded of them.

The administrative lessons of the campaign compiled by XII Corps give a clear picture of how their links in the transport chain worked. During the advance from the beach-head to the Dutch frontier, a distance of some 500 miles, nine FMAs were established, and a further six were used during the winter campaign in the Netherlands. The distance from army roadhead to FMAs varied from 30 to 150 miles. Corps basic transport was mainly engaged in lifting from army roadhead to FMA, and, for 'third line' tasks. Corps was often dependent upon second line transport withdrawn from divisions. Assistance by army was confined to the allotment, for a limited period, of a varying number of companies or the positioning of 'packs' of ammunition, petrol and supplies to help the Corps in specially difficult circumstances. Under these conditions, CRASC corps troops obviously had to control the maintenance and traffic between army roadhead and FMA. Two transport lying-up areas were established, one just forward of the army roadhead and the other just behind FMA. The CRASC corps troops with a small staff was stationed at one, and his second-in-command at the other. DDST corps had two RT sets, one forming a direct line to ST army, the other working on the corps ST net to CsRASC. The daily volume of traffic in the corps area was large, and much of the maintenance transport had to be filtered forward in small blocks. Section commanders, shepherding their six vehicles, were largely responsible for getting the vital loads through, and a high standard of training and resource was demanded of them.

For the RASC transport columns and their companies operating between the RMA and FMAs, it was a long period of sheer hard work. Except that they knew the Germans were on the run, there were no thrills to maintain morale. In the words of the drivers themselves, it was just a continuous 'hard flog', and how well they did it! On one occasion, for example, a convoy from 17 Company arrived back in the RMA from the Netherlands and was immediately detailed for a further trip to Brussels. Off they went, without rest, and completed the run in 26 hours. On another occasion, a column from 905 Company did the same trip in 22 hours.

Dukw making for Shore

Dukw Loading

Dukw Casualty

About to Land

The bridging companies were stretched from divisional areas right back along the line of communication, assisting in the building of bridges, from the 'Baileys' in the forward areas, to the heavy railway bridge across the Seine. The first operational move of the tank transporters was to move 4th Armoured Brigade from Le Beny Bocage to Evrecy. But these units were delivering and evacuating tanks steadily, and 372 Tank Transporter Company carried heavy equipment for the Royal Engineers throughout this phase of the campaign.

There are two stories of special transport operations during this phase of the operations which are worth recounting. The first story concerns two British transport units working in II Canadian Corps during the operations for clearing the approaches to Antwerp. There were three 'islands' to be cleared: the Braehems area south of the Scheldt, South Beveland and Walcheren to the north of it. Large tracts of the countryside were flooded and vehicles could only move on the dyke roads. The country offered almost no cover, and the land above water level had been heavily mined. No. 147 Bridge Company had a strenuous time in support of the Canadians. After building up dumps of bridging equipment, four platoons of the company were located on South Beveland for the assault on Walcheren. The causeway connecting these two islands was, throughout the assault, under enemy artillery, mortar and small arms fire. This bridge company delivered, salvaged, repaired and re-delivered large numbers of assault and storm boats under continuous and heavy fire. Sgt R. F. Hughes remained at a bridge site under constant observed shell fire for 15 hours, and was awarded an immediate Military Medal. A platoon of 'weasels' (tracked amphibian vehicles) formed part of 529 Company of 52nd Division. The platoon maintained units which could not be supplied by normal first line transport. It maintained a succession of battalions which were relieved at regular intervals and evacuated their casualties. The 'weasels' route lay across extensive minefields and under heavy spasmodic small arms fire. Cpl J. Lynch of the platoon won a Military Medal for completing his task in these conditions while suffering from severe wounds.

The second story concerns the only two dukw companies which had been retained in the order of battle at the time of the Battle of the Rhineland (operation 'Veritable') and were used for second line maintenance and evacuation of casualties in the flooded areas between the rivers. The operations in the Cleve area could not have been supported without them. Strengthened by the drivers of two platoons from other companies, these dukws worked 24 hours a day for five consecutive days. The water on the main road was three feet deep and only passable for amphibians. Many were put out of action by mines and under-water obstacles, and one convoy narrowly escaped capture when they stopped to ask some sodden soldiers the way, and discovered that they were Germans. The surprise must have been mutual because the convoy was able to turn about on a mined road and escape with only one casualty which was 'ditched'.

The Airborne and Air Despatch Units

The RASC of 1st Airborne Division shared to the full the experiences of the devoted band in the Arnhem bridgehead. They went in among the first to land, and for the first day or two carried on with normal activities. A maintenance area was formed, the supplies landed by glider were cleared under spasmodic enemy fire, and a fair proportion of the earlier drops were collected. Soon the dumps came under heavy attention from mortars, small arms and machine-gun fire, so that issues became difficult and dangerous. The dumps were moved, but were still subjected to increasing and accurate mortar and shell fire, especially after a supply drop. In spite of this, collection and issue of the meagre supplies which did arrive were carried on without interruption. The roads became impassable even to jeeps, and the dump area was a mass of debris; but tireless, and seemingly fearless, drivers went on with their task until they were hit, or their jeeps were knocked out under them. Many under the Red Cross were continually engaged in carrying casualties to the enemy occupied hospital, or fetching water from an enemy controlled well. One driver so engaged met a German tank, but was allowed to proceed after being asked to give an undertaking not to disclose its position. The losses to the transport became crippling; only two jeeps remained serviceable, and nearly all the trailers were holed. Before the withdrawal, on the night of September 25th, there had been no rations to issue for several days, but ammunition was issued until that evening.

By the fifth day, the gaps in the perimeter had become wide and dangerous, and a RASC party, 70 strong, was ordered to take over a sector. This they held in face of considerable attacks by infantry, tanks, guns, mortars, etc., and withdrew in good order when required to do so. The officer commanding the party, Captain J. L. Cranmer-Byng, 250 Light Company, was awarded an immediate Military Cross. Many acts of heroism were performed by the RASC in the Arnhem battle. One officer ran into an ambush while collecting supplies, and sacrificed himself by advancing in the open under machine-gun fire, to give covering fire with a Bren while his men withdrew. A driver took a captured enemy lorry into Arnhem with a load of ammunition for the isolated parachute battalion there; several times he came under fire, but he hid for the night in a side street, delivered his load, and came back for more, his vehicle riddled with shot holes.

Of the 10 officers and 243 other ranks of the RASC who took part in the airborne operations, five officers and 83 men came back, 30 were left in hospital wounded; the number of fatal casualties cannot be established, but the rest were mainly prisoners, including a whole platoon which went down in the first lift and made straight for the town to take over supply installations there.

All three airborne divisions employed in the Battle of Arnhem (1st British, and 82nd and 101st American) were supplied by air in daylight on the four days after zero. A total of 596 sorties were flown on this task, and the stores were ejected from Stirling bombers by RASC crews, drawn from the air despatch and airborne divisional companies. Air supply was only partially successful. The weather was bad and the area into which supplies had to be dropped was extremely restricted. Furthermore, German anti-aircraft fire was intense. The bombers were obliged to fly in very low to make sure of dropping the loads on our own troops, and an observer in the Guards Division speaks of the unforgettable sight of the Stirlings flying low under a heavy cloud bank, searching for their exact bearings before making the final run in to drop the supplies on the pocket-handkerchief which was 1st Airborne Division. He describes the big bombers, which formed an easy target for enemy fire, swinging in unflinchingly to perform their desperate mission from which many did not return.

Not only the RAF, but also the RASC engaged in these missions, did all they could to deliver the goods, and of the 900 RASC men who flew on the missions 264 were shot down and 116 were killed or missing. Several were decorated. The Distinguished Flying Medal was awarded to L/Cpl W. Whittaker, NCO commanding a despatch crew. As the aircraft approached the dropping zone, one of his crew was badly wounded, and he had to decide quickly that he must leave him, rally the rest of the crew, and despatch the load. The drill went through without a hitch, and all the panniers went down in one run in. Later the aircraft crash-landed; Whittaker had been given the chance to bale out, but stayed to tend the wounded men. Rejoining his company, he volunteered for another sortie, but this was not allowed as he was suffering from shock. Cpl W. Hutchinson won the Distinguished Flying Medal, when his Stirling was hit in many places, and he was wounded in the legs and back. He still succeeded in despatching the load while the aircraft was over the dropping zone. Cpl C. B. Sproston was awarded the Military Medal. His aircraft was hit and caught fire, and he was ordered to despatch the load, which consisted of high explosive. He got it away at the right moment, although the rear gunner's ammunition was exploding inside the fuselage. The pilot was thus enabled to crash-land in our lines without loss of life. On the way back to the airfield in the TCV convoy, the party from the aircraft was attacked by four German tanks, and a number of vehicles were knocked out. Some soldiers, including Sproston, took up a position in a house, and Sproston directed the fire of a Bofors gun with great effect, although under heavy fire.

Air freight, which had not in the earlier stages exceeded 200 tons a week, was used much more after the Seine had been crossed. In September, 32 despatch crews were provided by 223 Company for special air service missions, with food and stores for resistance movements. These involved such large quantities that at one time 300 lorries were at work, moving them in the United Kingdom. Emergency supply by air continued on a growing scale. After the fall of Paris, 500 tons of food a day for a fortnight were supplied by air for the civil population. Incidentally, the first British soldiers to enter the city at that time were the RASC drivers of the cars carrying the French Military Governor and his staff, and they were closely followed by a transport company with more food. Early in September, 432 tons of compo were lifted by air to Douai. All told, 18,000 tons were lifted by air freight in five weeks at that period, even though there were two or three non-flying days a week.

Supply Units

The supply units in the 'long flog' from Normandy to the Rhine were constantly on the move as army roadheads and corps field maintenance areas leapfrogged each other on the move forward. Each army roadhead was allotted a CRASC supply units, who had under command two BSDs, four DIDs and six mobile field bakeries. Each corps was allotted two DIDs and a composite platoon for holding and issuing supplies in their operating FMA, and making the supply arrangements for establishing another one further forward. The DIDs were employed flexibly throughout the campaign. Sometimes they operated as small BSDs, at others as coal depots or railhead detachments; 58 BSD, one of the army roadhead units, handled an average of 1,400 tons a day for a fortnight. This represents one 3-ton lorry load every three minutes, night and day.

With the opening of the port of Antwerp in the third week of November, it was no longer necessary to depend on the RMA round Bayeux as the source of maintenance for the forward troops. The stocks there were used to supply the troops south of the Seine, and were shipped up to Antwerp or backloaded to the United Kingdom. As a precaution against heavy air and sea attacks on Antwerp, the advanced base supply depots were established in three groups around the cities of Antwerp, Brussels and Ghent.

There were 12 BSDs initially between the three groups, holding 35 million rations.

The calls on the smaller supply units were varied and often far in excess of their nominal capacities. No. 5 DID performed its normal function in Brussels, but was for some months feeding between 50,000 and 85,000 a day with innumerable 'splits'. No. 538 Composite Platoon was given the job of serving all the leave hotels in Brussels. A field butchery and cold storage depot which had been working with portable cold storage plants in RMA, was sent up to Brussels to take over large quantities of German supplies in cold storage there. It also collected and slaughtered 4,000 German pigs for issue to forward troops, and its sausage factory produced 100 tons a week.

POL Units

A roadhead had two B type and three C type depots, which held a stock of about 26,000 tons of packed petrol. Where the roadhead was within reasonable distance of pipehead, it also had three filling centres. Bulk petrol was brought forward by pipeline, or by road tank lorry, but bulk supply could not be much used during the advance, because there were not enough road or rail tankers to carry the quantities forward without undue waste of time on the return journey. The road tankers of 37 Transport Column at first delivered bulk fuel mainly to filling centres. After the breakout, they also delivered from pipeline and rail tankers to further storage, airfields and consumer units. With an extended line of communication, an increasing number of more or less static units took bulk supply, which they held in barrels, tanks and civilian petrol pumps. This released jerricans for the use of formations. The petrol units allotted to corps for FMA work were one petrol depot and a composite platoon.

In the main, this period of the campaign was a petrol battle for the armoured formations. As General Patton said of the American armour: 'My men can eat their belts, but I must have gas.' The actual distance covered by the Guards Armoured Division was 495 miles. During this advance, in the 18 days between August 28th and September 12th, the petrol company of the divisional column issued 692,000 gallons (more than 1,000 lorry loads) of high grade motor spirit. In one night it issued 130 loads.

The consumption of the petrol had doubled during the second half of August, and stood at 4,000 tons a day. During the early stages of the advance, packed petrol was carried forward from Bayeux. Some 450 additional road tankers were issued to the bulk petrol transport companies, about one-fifth above establishment. By September 18th, the pipeline had reached Rouen, and filling centres there dealt with large accumulations of jerricans. 'Pluto' was then working to Cherbourg. Ostend came into operation for bulk petrol supply on September 20th, when the first ocean tankers discharged. CRASC 8 Petrol Installations took up the task of opening up bulk installations, first at Ghent, Brussels and Antwerp, of laying down resources of 130,000 tons, and of establishing a filling centre near Brussels.

Petrol and oil depots in the advanced base were grouped geographically in the same three areas as the supply groups. In Antwerp, seven V bombs fell within one depot area, and the bulk installations themselves received three direct hits. One of these started seven separate fires and there were many casualties, but only 3,500 tons were destroyed. Captain J. B. Hesber climbed on top of threatened tanks and flame-proofed all the vents. He also entered tanks and opened valves. He was made a member of the Order of the British Empire for gallantry.

The second phase of 'Pluto' (pipeline from Dungeness to Boulogne), was completed in October and the overland pipeline system was steadily developed. The pipehead was at Eindhoven and it was fed from Antwerp. Thence petrol was carried forward by the road tankers of 37 Transport Column at a rate of 1,000 tons a day. The use of bulk petrol on the lines of communication was expanded by the setting up of petrol stations along the routes, staffed from the composite platoons of the bulk petrol transport companies. The convoy-lane method of refilling by this means was employed, and many vehicles could be refuelled at one time. Petrol points were also established for bulk issues to large units.

From the Rhine to the Baltic

While the Battle of Rhineland was being fought, the Rhine crossing was being planned. Administrative preparations for it had begun as early as December, before the German counter-offensive in the Ardennes. Roads and railways had been repaired and developed, and Second Army depots had been stocked with some 130,000 tons of stores. In consequence of all this forethought, 21 Army Group was able to launch the operation for crossing the Rhine a fortnight after the completion of the Rhineland battle.

The attack began on the night of March 23rd, and by the next morning all the assaulting divisions (two British and two American) and the British Commando Brigade had accomplished their initial crossings between Rheineburg and Rees. The key to the crossings was the important communication centre of Wesel, which was captured by the Commando brigade after an intense air attack by Bomber Command. On the morning of March 24th, XVIII United States Airborne Corps, with the 6th British Airborne

Division and one American airborne division, dropped on the east bank of the Rhine, within supporting distance of our guns on the west bank. These drops were successful and the British and American bridgeheads were quickly joined. The Royal Navy played a considerable part in ferrying across the river with craft which had been carried by road across Belgium, the southern Netherlands and the Rhineland.

Within four days the bridgehead over the Rhine had been established, and on March 28th the advance to the Elbe began. Second Army advanced with its left flank directed on Hamburg. On the extreme left, II Canadian Corps, after crossing the Second Army bridgehead, swung north along the Rhine to outflank Arnhem and open up routes leading northwards from the Arnhem area. Later I Canadian Corps assaulted across the river at Arnhem and turned into the western Netherlands, where they established a protective flank between the Rhine and the Zuider Zee.

The subsequent operations of 21 Army Group were similar to those in the drive across North-West France. The German communications from east to west towards the coast were progressively cut, and a series of right hooks were delivered to round up the enemy. The formation on the left flank advanced towards the coast to complete the enemy's defeat. VIII Corps of Second Army crossed the Weser near Minden on April 5th, and was followed a few days later farther north by XII Corps. The latter corps then worked its way along the east bank in an advance which brought it to the outskirts of Hamburg. Bremen fell at the end of April after a further 'hook' on that city from the east. By mid-April, the Canadian Army had liberated most of the northern Netherlands, had safeguarded 21 Army Group's flank in the western Netherlands, and isolated the large enemy garrison there.

The main drive to the Elbe continued towards Lüneburg, which was reached on April 18th, when the British forces began to line up on the southern bank of the river to mask the city of Hamburg. The Elbe was crossed on April 29th, and spearheads made straight for Lübeck in order to seal off Schleswig-Holstein peninsula. Across the Elbe there was hardly any opposition and on May 2nd a German party came out from Hamburg to negotiate its surrender. The countryside was crowded with masses of German soldiers and refugees fleeing, in opposite directions, from 21 Army Group and from the Russians with whom contact was established on May 2nd.

The negotiations which began in Hamburg led on May 3rd to the despatch by Admiral Doenitz of envoys to Field-Marshal Montgomery's tactical headquarters on Lüneburg Heath. On the evening of May 4th, General-Admiral Friedeburg, Commander-in-Chief of the German Navy, signed the instrument of unconditional surrender of all German naval, land and air forces opposite 21 Army Group. The cease fire was ordered on 21 Army Group front as from 0800 hours on May 5th.

Reference has already been made to the intense period of administrative preparation between December, 1944, and March, 1945, which enabled the Rhine crossing to be made only a fortnight after the end of the Battle of the Rhineland. Since road transport played a great part in that preparation, this seems a suitable place to record some of the tasks on which our transport was engaged during the period, certain reorganization which took place and, in broad terms, the transport which was available to 21 Army Group during the period immediately preceding the assault across the Rhine.

Once the advanced base had been established in Belgium, the main task of the GHQ transport pool became dock clearance at Antwerp and the Channel ports. But there were many other and varying jobs to be done, from bridge building and airfield construction all over the BLA area, which involved general transport as well as the ubiquitous 'tipper', to civil affairs tasks. Examples of these were bringing pit-props from the Ardennes for the French and Belgian mines and moving civil patients from the uninhabitable hospitals in the damaged area to other accommodation, or evacuating lunatics from enemy-held territory under special truce arrangements. As always, the calls for transport exceeded the availability, and the strain was increased in February by operation 'Goldflake'. A road line of communication was organized between Italy and BLA, for which the Corps provided a headquarters RASC. Along this line of communication, I Canadian Corps and 5th British Division were transferred from Italy to 21 Army Group. They brought their own formation transport, but not their quota of GT companies. In order to relieve this strain, a large number of Belgian and Dutch companies were formed and trained by the Corps. Captured German and civil horse transport was also brought into use, and played quite a large part in short dock clearance hauls in Antwerp. A further strain on the transport organization was the 'pruning' which took place at the end of 1944 to provide more fit officers and other ranks for the infantry. One divisional RASC had to find 11 captains and subalterns for transfer, while a group of four GT companies produced 140 other ranks.

In early March, 1945, there were the equivalent of 80 3-ton companies working on the lines of communication, whilst First Canadian Army had nine and Second Army had eight from GHQ pool. In the GHQ pool itself there remained only about 20 equivalent 3-ton companies, all of which were committed on permanent tasks, such as timber haulage and construction work.

In the period before the Rhine assault, as much as possible was moved by rail right up to within three miles of the front line. But the tonnages to be lifted by road were still formidable. For example, the tonnage off-loaded into road transport at Canadian Army railhead in February amounted to 343,000. As the build-up progressed, the lift with the armies was increased to 10 companies with the Canadian Army and 22 with the Second Army. The main task confronting Second Army was the formation of 10 Army Roadhead immediately west of the Rhine. The work could not begin until the Rhineland battle was over and the country between the Maas and the Rhine cleared of the enemy, and there were only three two-way bridges over the Maas, so that maintenance traffic was not allowed to use the bridges at night. In addition to the stocking of 10 Army Roadhead, large quantities of ammunition had to be dumped for division and corps. Stocks were drawn from the accumulation already built up in No. 8 Army Roadhead Depot west of the Maas, direct from 10 different army railheads in the same area, and also in certain cases all the way from advance base. Thanks to close co-ordination of all transport echelons and the sustained efforts of commanders and drivers, 152,000 tons were moved in 16 days. The tank transporters effected 4,000 operational moves in the Second Army area during the week preceding the opening of the battle, while the bridging and tipper companies were fully engaged and in many cases working under heavy fire.

On March 26th, Brigadier Eassie, DDST, Second Army, issued the following letter to CsRASC concerned:

'In response to the call given in my letter dated February 15th, 1945, the results have been even beyond my personal expectations. You reached a target which was considered almost impossible three, four and five days ahead of D Day and schedule. This was a really grand achievement and at a time when weariness and war fatigue might well have been a sound excuse. Yet the build-up was a record build-up, and the time in which it was completed another record. Such a success is not the result of a "flash in the pan". It is achieved only by solid and speedy thinking and hard manual work. It was done by ranks in all trades, well and truly aided by the Pioneer Corps. My staff prepared the plot, the officers and men of the units carried it out. Everyone was on it from colonels to cooks. Drivers, artificers, clerks and issuers all played their part and played it well. You can all be justly proud of your share in the crossing of the Rhine.

'What lies ahead? There is little doubt it will be to your liking. Possibly a real "flog" and, not impossibly, a fast one. It may be that some units will be allotted to support the advancing corps. Whatever it is, I have no doubt whatsoever, it will be a success.

'May I remind you, possibly for the last time, of the necessity of three things:—

Speed in turn-round. This means speed in loading and unloading, speed in thinking, speed in repairing, quick off the mark. But not necessarily speed in driving—go like Hell, but *not* when you're driving.

Good road discipline. Don't double bank or cut in. Get *right* off the road if halting. Watch behind you and use your signals. Look out for the b——y fool driver, but don't imitate him.

Good maintenance. Keep those wheels turning at all costs. Tyres, loose nuts, that bit of grease, in and out of shops like lightning, improvisation.

'You are coming to the last lap. Let it go, good luck and good going.'

Two units of the Corps deserve special mention for their part in the actual assault. The light company of 6th Airborne Divisional RASC landed by parachute and glider and met heavy opposition, suffering, before and after landing, a total of 36 casualties out of a strength of 90. The company commander, Major C. P. R. Crane, was landed wide of his objective, but he collected his party and fought his way through to it. In spite of his heavy losses in men and equipment, and the difficulties of working under intermittent heavy fire, he organized and inspired his company, so that the work was satisfactorily performed. Major Crane was awarded the Military Cross, and Cpl L. T. C. Knightly, of the same company, received the immediate award of the Military Medal, for devotion to duty when severely wounded. The other unit selected for special mention is 536 (dukws) Company. The preparations for the airborne assault included the formation of a dump on the west bank of the rivers, which had to be ferried across to the airborne divisional RASC as soon as the bridgehead had been established. The dukws conducted this ferrying successfully under heavy fire on March 24th. Their casualties were considerable, and two drivers were awarded the Military Medal.

It took Second Army four weeks to get from the Rhine to the Elbe, and although this advance was not so rapid as the one across France and Belgium, the strain on transport was as great. Large commitments, apart from those connected with the advance of our own troops, arose. The backloading of German prisoners of war as well as our own, whom we continually uncovered, the clearance of refugees and inmates of concentration camps, including the notorious Belsen, and relief to the starving population of the Netherlands, were all added to the battle tasks of troop-carrying, dumping, bridging, and normal maintenance. Two examples from divisional transport diaries are worth quoting. On one day all the companies of the RASC of a division moved with their normal loads, then lifted three brigades and finally dumped a large amount of ammunition. Another divisional RASC never spent more than one night in a location throughout the four weeks' advance. By the end of the advance GHQ had given Second Army a total lift of 31,000 tons, excluding basic corps and divisional transport and bridge companies.

At the beginning of the advance from the Rhine, No. 10 Army Roadhead lay west of that river, and in the first stages of the move of the three corps (VIII, XII and XXX), eastwards, bridges were again a limiting factor, and the railways in Germany were not working. No. 12 Army Roadhead was established near Rheine, a distance of about 110 miles from No. 10. CRASC 22 Transport Column co-ordinated and controlled most of Second Army transport located in the area of 10 Army Roadhead, CRASC 45 Transport Column, received convoys at 12 Army Roadhead. A second army roadhead was soon required further east, but it was impossible to eliminate 12 Army Roadhead because of the wide area to the north in which Second Army was also operating. CRASC 46 Transport Column controlled the transport arriving at 14 Army Roadhead in the area of Sulingen, some 45 miles from No. 12 Roadhead, and about 150 miles from No. 10. In the main, both 12 and 14 Army Roadheads were stocked from 10 Army Roadhead, which later was taken over by I Corps, but all transport returning from 14 Army Roadhead was routed *via* 12, so that an urgent demand could be met immediately and stocks could be kept balanced in the interests of economy. As soon as it became obvious that Second Army would not proceed beyond the Elbe and that no further established roadhead would be necessary, 65 FMC, established by XXX Corps in the Lüneburg area, was stocked under control of Second Army and maintained the most forward troops.

Although some mention has already been made of the work done by the tipper companies, no adequate picture has been given of the range and scope of their operations. This can be more effectively described now against the general background of the campaign than in relation to any one phase. A large number of tipper companies in 21 Army Group, were organized into one transport column. Their headquarters started in Normandy and finished the campaign in Germany. But the location of their headquarters and the whereabouts of their CRASC bore no relation to one another. He might appear anywhere from Hamburg to northern France in the later period of the campaign, or from Bailleul to Brussels in the earlier days. His units, sub-units and individual vehicles were to be found working for the sappers on airfield construction, or bridging, road making and repairing, and a thousand and one hard, dirty and vital jobs, sometimes under fire and close to the enemy, but more often far from the areas which attracted publicity. There was certainly no more essential element of the transport service than the ubiquitous tipper.

Naturally, supply units were hard worked like everyone else in this phase, and the unexpected calls on their resources and initiative for prisoners, refugees and starving populations were many. Perhaps the only aspect of special interest was the 'drill' which was evolved for GHQ to take over successive roadhead stocks with their units from Second Army, thus relieving army of unwanted responsibilities for behind their operational area. DDST Supplies at 21 Army Group kept close touch with ST at Second Army by air, and arrangements were made during these visits regarding the details of location, stocks, men, and the timing of the take-over. The arrangement worked to the benefit of both headquarters and the troops. It is also interesting to note that by the time of the surrender in May, GHQ controlled supply units and installations stretched from Hamburg to Antwerp, and that the total feeding strength of the theatre eventually reached two million.

All the movement used up a lot of petrol, and at the end of the campaign 7,500 tons of petrol a day were being issued in the British area alone. But the supply of fuel never caused any anxiety. By March 15th, the pipehead was the source of bulk petrol for both armies, and this was coming into the theatre at the rate of 15,000 tons a day. The total quantity of petrol and oil imported for 21 Army Group during the campaign in bulk shipments alone amounted to nearly 1,200 million gallons, and at the end the RASC was operating 300,000 tons of bulk storage. In addition, 2,500,000 jerricans and over 4,500,000 4-gallon tins were sent over.

No account of the Corps' activities in the campaign would be complete without some mention of the contribution it made to the staffs of formations. Lieut-General Gale was the Chief Administrative Officer of SHAEF. The Brigadier in charge of Q plans at the planning headquarters for 'Overlord' was Brigadier Buckle. Brigadier Lymer, who was a staunch member of the 42nd Divisional RASC TA, was Brigadier Q Maintenance at HQ 21 Army Group and the Brigadier A/Q at HQ L of C for the first part of the campaign was Brigadier R. T. Cooke. There were many other RASC officers on the staff of HQ 21 Army Group and at other formation headquarters. There was also the usual complement of RASC clerks at the headquarters of all formations, men who are sometimes forgotten, but who share all the physical stress of the officers whom they serve and, in lower formations, the same hazards.

After the breakout from the Normandy bridgehead, 3rd Infantry

Division was taken out of the line and grounded in the neighbourhood of Les Andelys on the Seine. The division's second line transport was taken away to assist VIII Corps in moving petrol from the maintenance area at Bayeux to No 3 Army 'Cushion' at Arras. The headquarters of the divisional RASC and the four companies were therefore left on the Seine with no men other than clerks and issuers. On September 8th, the division was suddenly ordered to prepare to move on two days later, passing round Brussels and right across Belgium to assault over the Escaut Canal. This order caused a considerable crisis, since, on account of the great scarcity of petrol, the divisional RASC held no more than 7,000 gallons on the ground in the location of the petrol company, and there was no hope of the first and second line transport platoons being returned to divisional command until the evening before the move.

It was therefore necessary to mobilize an extraordinary transport column consisting of stripped-down office lorries, quartermaster stores vehicles, workshops trucks, and a wide variety of captured German vehicles and trailers. Some 50 load carriers were collected in the space of three or four hours, but it was only possible to find 20 men who were normally employed as drivers. The remaining vehicles were manned by clerks and a few issuers. The chief clerk at HQ RASC acted as platoon sergeant, and other sergeant and corporal clerks as section NCOs. This column was mobilized and despatched, within some six hours of the warning order having been received, from the Seine back to Bayeux with orders to return as quickly as possible with as much petrol as could be loaded on the vehicles. The distance from Les Andelys to Bayeux is pretty considerable, and it was a remarkable achievement that the whole of this column got back as an organized unit, with no stragglers, within 24 hours, and in possession of 40,000 gallons of petrol, without a single incident. After the successful conclusion of this foray, many clerks applied to be re-mustered as drivers. It was perhaps fortunate that while training in England before the invasion of Normandy, it was ordered that every man in the company, no matter what his employment, must be trained as a driver.

On September 5th, the headquarters of the Guards Armoured Division reached Brussels and established itself in the Royal Park immediately in front of the Palace. A rumour circulated that the Germans had capitulated, joyful crowds flocked into the streets and around the park—deliriously happy and keen to see the headquarters of 'les Anglais'. However, just after lunch the order to continue to advance came through, and the GOC's conference was timed for 9 p.m. Barely a half hour before it was due to begin, a paraffin lamp in the 'ops room', a tent joining both ACV 1 and ACV 3, spluttered and set fire to the talc covering the huge operations map. Within minutes, both ACVs were blazing furiously; the preparatory work and the orders for the conference were destroyed. The conference was held punctually elsewhere, orders and instructions were prepared again, maps were collected and re-marked and at first light, as planned, the division moved out. The 'team' including its valued clerks had risen to the occasion. A newspaper report of this episode, some days later, read: 'As darkness fell, the sky was lit by a huge bonfire that the local population had lit in the public gardens to celebrate their liberation!'

Mention has been made of the transport task involved in 'uncovering' our prisoners of war. Here is the story told by a Corps officer, Major F. G. Ruff, of his experiences as an 'uncovered' prisoner of war during this final phase of the war in Europe.

'In March, 1945, I was in a camp south-east of Kassel. At the end of the month, when the Allied advance into Germany had gathered momentum, the camp was closed, and the 400 officer prisoners were marched away eastwards to an undisclosed, and probably undecided, destination. We played the Germans up in a manner we were now experts at; for each fall-in half of us would have lost our boots in the dark, blisters were exaggerated into the most painful hobbling. After marching for five nights, and sleeping during the day in barns and village schools, we had covered a distance of 30 miles and had reached the village of Leganfeld on the east of the river Werra. Here further movement became impossible, as the armoured units of the American Third Army were already well to the east of us.

'A SS division occupied the village also, but early one morning withdrew their FDLs about half a mile further east, leaving us between them and the advancing American motorized infantry. That evening we were discovered by the Americans, after calling them up on the village telephone. The following morning, the Germans counter-attacked strongly and we had an uncomfortable few hours until a truck company managed to reach us just before the Americans were forced to draw back temporarily.

'We were then taken, through the astonishing lines of modern mechanized units waiting to cross the river Werra, to an airfield at Eschwege. Here we were welcomed as potential infantry and at once issued with arms. I and two other RASC majors spent our first night of freedom standing in the rain guarding German prisoners. Others guarded vital points on the perimeter of the airfield against German units which were still active. Four days later the first Dakotas to use the airfield took us back to Le Havre as a return load. From there, the RAF lifted us to the amazingly efficient machine in Buckinghamshire through which released POWs were processed. Seven days after seeing the first American soldier, I was in my own home with 42 days' leave ahead of me.'

Aftermath

Major-General Collings, DST 21 Army Group, issued the following message to all ranks of the Royal Army Service Corps and Royal Canadian Army Service Corps on Victory in Europe Day, May 8th, 1945:

'The achievement of victory in Europe provides an opportunity to review the work of our Corps in this campaign, upon which we entered determined to enhance the high traditions earned in many others.

'Throughout the campaign, from the beaches of Normandy over many rivers to the banks of the Elbe, the Corps has been working almost continuously at the highest pressure. It has endured almost every form of enemy attack, from small arms fire to V 2s, and every condition of weather. It has been called on with almost monotonous regularity to make "that extra all-out effort" whenever vital operations were in preparation or in progress, and it has never failed.

'This has been the greatest military operation ever conducted by the British Army and, in some of its phases, the fastest moving. These are the conditions which throw the greatest strain on the RASC and it is safe to say that not only did it never fail, but it never appeared in any danger of being unequal to the strain. This magnificent result is the reward of good training, good leadership, good discipline and comradeship, and above all a determination to live up to our traditions. This applies equally to the Royal Army Service Corps and the Royal Canadian Army Service Corps. As Director of Supply and Transport in 21 Army Group, the ultimate responsibility for all that you have done falls upon me, and I wish to place on record that I have never once during the campaign been called upon to answer criticisms on the work of the Corps. I send you my congratulations, grateful thanks, and best wishes for the future.'

The rounding up and dispersal of the remnants of the German armies in Schleswig-Holstein, the 'cleansing' of concentration camps, repatriation of prisoners of war and staging, direction and transport of displaced persons became the pressing military commitments immediately the surrender had been signed, and the Corps was probably more deeply committed in most of these tasks than any other arm or service. Then, as it gradually became possible to hand over these commitments to military government, the fighting machine had to be converted to the post-campaign problems of demobilization, training of leaders and harnessing local civil manpower and resources in support of the occupation forces.

The Second Army was disbanded very early, and the DDST found himself starting up the RASC Training Centre BAOR, while a transport column headquarters was selected to organize a RASC demobilization centre close to HQ 21 Army Group, soon to become HQ BAOR.

Those who knew they had to stay and see things through had to exercise a tight hold on themselves to maintain their enthusiasm, self-control, sense of humour and sense of proportion in the face of an inevitable and almost overpowering reaction caused by the end of hostilities and the expectation of release. As the release machinery got properly into its rhythm, endless celebrations marked each batch of departures, and the end of one overlapped the beginning of the next. The term 'release happy' became an accepted and understandable 'write-off' of three-quarters of those who had been given their date. Here once again, the pre-war Regular Corps officer and NCO came into their own and showed their mettle.

Armies and corps were replaced by divisional districts. The barracks services came back, and German ex-soldier transport companies, with small cadres of Corps officers, warrant officers and NCOs, made their appearance. The policy was to garrison the British Zone with the minimum military expenditure, thus setting free our much reduced forces for service at first in the Far East, and later in all the places overseas where immediate post-war crises arose.

Almost immediately the trouble with our Russian Allies began, and the endless battle over the Berlin autobahn traffic had been joined long before the end of 1945. It is no exaggeration to say that the war in Germany never did end. It slid imperceptibly from battle conditions into police control of our past enemies, combined with a clearance of the horrors and muddle of war and growing tension with our Allies in the east. In 1948 came the isolation of Berlin, and the renowned 'Berlin airlift', in which the RASOs and FASO earned further laurels for the Corps.

Now, in 1955, the direct successors of 21 Army Group in BAOR comprise what is almost certainly the most highly trained field army that Great Britain has ever possessed in peace time. The four divisions in Germany are all imbued with the traditions of 21 Army Group and of the campaign for the liberation of Europe, whose continued freedom they are defending by their presence and efficiency. This is the 'nursery' in which most young officers in the Corps now hold their first position of responsibility in command of troops. It is a fitting and inspiring background for their initiation.

After launching

Dukws in a flooded Street

Dukws waiting to Land

Dukws in the Far East

CHAPTER XI

OTHER THEATRES

WEST AFRICA

ALTHOUGH West Africa was never an operational theatre, it became for some time a heavy RASC commitment.

The frontiers of the four colonies, the Gambia, Sierra Leone, the Gold Coast and Nigeria, march almost entirely with French colonial territory and so long as France was our ally no external defence problem existed, and the Royal West African Frontier Force could concentrate its efforts on raising and training forces for use in other theatres—a use to which indeed they were eventually put. Suddenly, at a few days' notice, all that was changed, and in the middle of 1940 the colonies found themselves surrounded by a neutral nation in possession of considerable armed forces the continuance of whose neutrality was doubtful. This condition of affairs prevailed to some extent until the beginning of the North African campaign in the autumn of 1942, after which the potential danger disappeared. Thereafter garrisons were reduced, and the training reinforcements of West African troops for duty overseas became the main commitment.

Apart from a small detachment at Sierra Leone, the RASC was not represented in West Africa in peacetime, the Royal West African Frontier Force managing its own affairs in regard to supplies and transport, which were administered by the colonies themselves. This state of affairs continued until September, 1940, when the War Office took over the administration of all ground forces in West Africa.

The four colonies, which together made up what is now West Africa Command, had certain special features which need to be remembered in relation to the supply and transport services. Widely separated, each a distinct entity with its own problems, they had no rail communication between them, and little road connection. The only practicable means of getting from one to the other was by sea or by air. The length of the coastline from the Gambia to the Niger is about 2,000 miles.

In late 1940 the RASC was faced with the task of forming and building up the West African Army Service Corps. This would have been easier if the RASC had worked with West African troops in peacetime, even on a limited scale. If there had been small peacetime cadres, the standard of training to make units ready for an operational role could then have been reached much sooner. Another difficulty was that the routine supply and transport duties had to be performed at the same time as, and in conjunction with, the training of the men of the WAASC.

The first RASC supply units arrived in the command in September, 1940, as cadres for West African units; a BSD each for Nigeria, the Gold Coast, and Sierra Leone, detail issue sections, and field bakery and butchery detachments. But many in these cadres had themselves but a scanty knowledge of supply duties, and European supply men were so scarce that quite often driver sergeants, and even fitters, had to be used for supply work. And the troops had to be maintained, so the Africans had to learn as they went along, by repetition of the same type of work. Close and constant supervision had to be exercised by British soldiers, to prevent defalcations.

On the provision side there were many difficulties. For instance the pride of the Fulani and the tribes of Mauretania in the possession of cattle was such that they were loth to part with them for money. In due course they were persuaded to trade cattle for lengths of blue savannah cloth, but the nature of a contract never became clear to them.

Cold storage for meat only existed in the larger towns and was insufficient to meet the Army needs. The 'bush cow', though not up to the standards of European cattle, nevertheless provided reasonably good meat. The problem was how to bring it to the slaughter-house in fair condition. The cattle-rearing areas were up to 1,000 miles from the consumption areas, and except in Nigeria, there was no railway. In the Gold Coast for example the cattle had to trek from water hole to water hole. Much time and money would have been saved had there been in the West African colonies a peacetime nucleus, however small, of an ST organization, but then West Africa had never really seemed a likely theatre of war, as France was our close ally.

As time passed and experience grew, useful experiments in the production of local resources were made. A vegetable farm of 1,000 acres was set up at Media, in the Gold Coast, which in due course supplied all the fresh vegetables requirements. A jam factory was also set up. Schools of cookery were organized for the Africans, staffed by 'mammies', and were completely successful. On the other hand a fish-curing industry was a total failure, defeated, it is said, by local juju!

Another difficulty on the supply side was lack of storage accommodation in every colony, which led to a high rate of pilferage and loss. There was a lack of lateral communications, which meant that reserves built up in up-country areas to meet specific threats could not be rapidly transferred to other colonies as the troop dispositions altered, and could not be turned over correctly or eaten down according to programme. There were thus considerable losses through waste.

Petroleum (which was handled by supply units) was purchased from the civilian installations in each colony. These oil firms packed the spirit into 4-gallon non-returnable containers for the Army. The history of petroleum in West Africa is one, therefore, with that of other theatres: a tale of leakage and loss.

The first RASC mechanical transport men reached West Africa in August, 1940, and until the middle of 1941, the story of transport there was one of a constant struggle against odds. The main troubles were the lack of equipment, of accommodation, of military vehicles, and perhaps most important of all, of sufficient British soldiers.

Africans were available to be trained as drivers and artificers, but the necessary vehicles and tools were not present. Each company had a few impressed vehicles, but these could not all be used for training, as there were routine transport duties to be performed, and the WAASC had also to assist other arms in driver and other training. Training was not a simple process. The raw African had no idea of the necessity for lubrication, tyre inflation, and so on, and the whole business of driving had to be explained to him in ways which he could understand. He was quite without fear, and drove accordingly, which resulted in an alarming accident rate.

Because of the almost complete deficiency of military vehicles until 1941, all transport had to be requisitioned. It consisted largely of trucks which had already been driven by African civilians and were not in good condition. Even when the flow of new vehicles from overseas began, large numbers of them were lost on the way through submarine activity. The working life of the vehicles which did arrive was restricted because of acute shortage of MT spare parts, due again to sinkings. Besides this, West Africa was on a low priority for its requirements in the earlier days, compared with the urgent needs of other theatres.

In the face of heavy repair commitments, caused mainly by accidents, the WAASC workshop organization operated under difficulties. Workshops were set up in clearings in the bush under matting shelters, with improvised benches, inspection pits dug in the ground, and no tools except those borrowed from civil garages. A section of an HRS was eventually established in each colony (except the Gambia) but they could do no more than help with second line repairs, because of lack of equipment.

On top of its normal commitments, the WAASC workshop

organization was called upon to shoulder the maintenance of the first line transport of other arms. This was because in August, 1940, the Royal Army Ordnance Corps had been doubtful of their ability to meet this commitment, and the RASC had undertaken to maintain all MT in West Africa. Exceptionally, in Sierra Leone where there were already Ordnance workshops, it was arranged that Ordnance should maintain the base units, and the WAASC the transport of forward troops. This proved unworkable, and in October, 1941, the WAASC took over the maintenance of all army vehicles in the colony, including those hitherto looked after by Ordnance. The arrangement continued until October, 1942, and is one of the few instances of first line transport being maintained by the RASC on such a large scale. In October, 1942, the third line workshops went over en bloc to REME; but the amount of repair work which had accumulated made it necessary for the WAASC workshops to help REME as the latter were just as much handicapped by lack of men and stores, etc., as the WAASC had been.

The work of the MT stores depots was a long uphill fight. Besides the sinking of spares and equipment, lorries arrived without tool kits, workshop and stores lorries without essential stores and equipment, and the deficiencies had to be made good out of stock. In October, 1941, it was decided that all MT spares held by Ordnance were to come under WAASC control in the MTSDs which had been established in each colony.

In late 1940 relations with the French worsened because of our abortive attempt on Dakar, and had there been an attack on British West Africa from the French territories, it is questionable whether it would not have been possible to offer effective opposition. A rough and ready force was hastily produced, but there was a serious shortage of transport. Thus, in Nigeria, there were only sufficient vehicles to equip the three brigades available with one general transport company each. When this threat receded, two West African divisions, the 81st and 82nd, were formed to take part in the campaign in Burma. The officers and British warrant officers and NCOs of the WAASC companies were all RASC.

The needs of jungle warfare had made clear the need for another kind of transport—to work in advance of jeep or muleheads—porters. The WAASC therefore raised a number of units named auxiliary groups, each about 1,000 strong, commanded by a lieutenant-colonel with a cadre of British NCOs. These porters were trained to carry a 50-lb load on their heads, and also in bush-clearance. Their usefulness was proved in the Burmese jungle, where, though they were redesignated infantry, they still retained many of their original RASC officers and NCOs.

There was no WD fleet in West Africa before the war. Then vessels gradually came into use at the main ports, and it became necessary to send out a motorboat company in April, 1940, to take them over. The RASC who went out included officers, coxswains, and administrative and workshop personnel only, the deck crews and engineers being recruited locally into the WAASC. The unit took out a number of craft and made up the balance of its requirements by local acquisition.

The company, which later became a water transport company, had a difficult career, partly because of the lack of appreciation in the command of the principles of administration of water transport, and partly because of the lack of proper slipways for the maintenance necessary to counteract the ravages of the teredo worm. In this branch, too, the lack of British personnel made itself felt. This deficiency, and lack of craft, led to the service falling into a bad state, but this was eventually rectified by an increase in the British strength, and in the number of vessels employed, while workshop and slipway facilities were provided. The commander of the company had to administer a unit stretched over 2,000 miles of coastline. Added to this difficulty, there were the lack of rail and telephone facilities, and the effects of continuous tropical rainfall, humid heat, rust and mildew—all to be contended with.

Many of the above problems were at that period of the war common to all theatres. Possibly, however, West Africa's most difficult problem lay in the raising and training of the native soldiers, a problem which also existed in East Africa.

The Hausa from Northern Nigeria made fine soldiers, but were slow to learn the RASC trades, and most WAASC men were found from 'coast boys', mainly of the Ibo and Yoruba tribes. The Fulani, also northerners, and accustomed to cattle, were enlisted for RASC cattle and butchery tasks. The language difficulty in such circumstances was almost insurmountable, and finally the old system whereby British officers learned the language of their troops was abandoned, and pidgin English was taught to all native soldiers.

The battles were won, in the Middle East, in Europe, in the Far East. The war ended. The West African divisions returned and were disbanded. Transport training centres ran down, and supply officers pored anxiously over their remaining surpluses. The end had come without a shot having been fired in West African territory, but the WAASC had made a useful contribution to victory.

Their success is a tribute not only to the skill and pertinacity of the relatively small body of RASC officers and warrant officers and NCOs who created the WAASC out of nothing, but also to the courage, cheerfulness and hard work of the Africans who filled in the ranks and who, in two short years, learned and mastered techniques completely foreign to their tribal history and experience and did their work satisfactorily as WAASC soldiers.

MISCELLANEOUS OVERSEAS STATIONS

In the chapters of this volume the reader will find set out the achievements of the Royal Army Service Corps in the bigger theatres of war. While these events were taking place, here and there in remote corners of the world small RASC detachments did their duty unheralded and unsung. Many of these detachments found themselves in pleasant places climatically and otherwise. Others laboured amid snow and ice and in conditions of acute discomfort. Some knew that enemy action in their neighbourhood, though possible, was unlikely, while a few knew not what excitements the next day might bring forth.

The most important in size of these detachments was that stationed in Iceland. When that wintry island was occupied as a precautionary measure in 1940 by the 49th Division, the divisional RASC did not accompany it. Corps duties were performed in difficult terrain and climate, by a base supply depot, a field bakery, four detail issue depots, four petrol depots, a field butchery, 275 (Reserve MT) Company, a detachment of 70 (WT) Company, and a section of 246 (motorboat) Company. These units had a total strength of about 60 officers and 1,400 other ranks. The work was arduous, especially for the road transport in the building and maintenance of airfields. In 1942 the force was relieved by American troops, but a small RASC detachment remained for some time to look after naval and RAF units, the officer commanding RASC also doing the duties of Officer Commanding, British Troops, Iceland.

Even more arduous climatic conditions were faced by the small RASC parties in the Faroe Islands, where water transport detachments served with distinction in maintaining the forces which were sent there to forestall any enemy attempt to seize them. This does not complete the list of our Arctic commitments. Small RASC detachments were sent to Archangel and Murmansk to maintain the convoy bases at those ports. Here to the Arctic weather were added the restrictions imposed by our suspicious allies, the Russians. These produced difficulties of an unusual kind which must have been most frustrating. However, they were overcome. Finally there was the RASC participation in the raid on Spitzbergen, where we provided launches. A section of a motor boat company was carried as deck cargo on the ships of the expedition.

In the Antarctic the augmentation by a battalion group of the local forces in the Falkland Islands called into action an RASC detachment of about 100 all ranks. The climate was nothing like so severe as that endured by their comrades in the far northern regions—the islands being about the same distance from the equator as Great Britain—and the occupation was uneventful.

In between these two terrestrial extremes were the isolated islands of St. Helena and Ascension. The reason for garrisoning these small places was to deny their possible use to the enemy as submarine refuelling and victualling points. No attempts to do so were evidently made, so the RASC detachments, which totalled under 30, of which only two were in Ascension, had an uneventful time.

There was one other RASC station in the Atlantic. The force which occupied the Azores was mainly RAF, but the Army provided certain services, including RASC. This gave rise to some difficulties in planning and in the early stages of occupation. Things settled down, and the RASC contingent, which eventually amounted to three officers and some 50 other ranks, functioned satisfactorily.

Better known, because of popular peacetime garrisons in Bermuda and Jamaica, were the Corps stations on the former island and in the Caribbean. Except for the introduction of a few motor vehicles Bermuda underwent little change from peacetime conditions. In the West Indies, however, many of the islands had small volunteer forces, which were mobilized and augmented. The area was divided into North and South Caribbean with officers commanding RASC in Jamaica and Trinidad respectively. The theatre proved to be uneventful and there was no great difficulty in performing RASC duties, including maintenance of the islands by sea.

Half way round the world from the West Indies was the peacetime garrison of Mauritius, with one officer and four other ranks of the RASC. It is of interest that on the outbreak of war the officer commanding RASC (Major—later Brigadier—A. J. W. Bavin) was also Officer Commanding Troops, and on him fell the responsibility for all mobilization arrangements. As the war went on, Mauritius, from being a quiet backwater in the Indian Ocean, found itself facing a new enemy, Japan, whose submarines sank shipping in sight of the island. Defence against any determined attack would have been of doubtful success with the small forces available, but the danger was removed with the British occupation of Madagascar and the establishment of a naval base in that large island. During the course of the war Mauritius became an important reservoir of manpower for the recruitment of pioneer corps companies, and the RASC commitment was thereby considerably increased.

In November, 1942, the island became a sub-area in East Africa Command, and the direct communication with the War Office, which had lasted some 40 years, came to an end. Responsibilities were much increased as the Mauritian local forces, which had hitherto been fed under colonial government arrangements, were now to be rationed in the normal manner, the change over taking a little time. This and other increased responsibilities involved the enlistment of Mauritian other ranks. There was nothing new about this, as a Mauritian MT Coy (163) had already been raised for service in the Middle East. A water transport section was formed to operate half-a-dozen motorboats requisitioned locally. The total RASC strength, including those locally enlisted, amounted at its height to two or three officers and about 100 other ranks.

The Seychelles Islands, off the east coast of Africa, had only a small volunteer force in peacetime and never became a heavy RASC commitment, but one or two RASC officers and a few other ranks were there from time to time.

The last remaining RASC commitment in the Indian Ocean was the Cocos or Keeling Islands. The object of the presence of troops here was to establish airfields for operations in South East Asia, and they did not arrive until early 1945. The senior ST officer was an RASC major and the small units were of the RIASC except for 353 Petroleum Platoon, RASC, and a platoon of 898 GT Coy (Ceylonese) RASC. The conditions were relatively pleasant.

Before the war there was no RASC detachment in Aden, where the garrison was maintained by the RAF. During the war the operations in British Somaliland and in the Sudan resulted in a detachment from No. 7 Petrol Depot being stationed there. All other ST duties were performed by the RIASC.

BRITISH ARMY STAFF, WASHINGTON

At the beginning of the war, the Ministry of Supply was responsible for the purchasing, management, and despatch of fuel, food, lubricants, vehicles and spare parts in and from the United States and Canada. After September, 1939, the Ministry set up a purchasing organization for trade with the two countries. When the United States in March, 1941, passed the Lease-Lend Act, under which they would supply Britain with many of her needs in exchange for the use of bases in British territory, and other services, this arrangement still held good as long as the supplies and material were shipped from North America to the United Kingdom.

Soon afterwards, however, it was decided that stores should be sent direct from North America to theatres of war overseas, in order to save shipping space. As the maintenance of theatres of war was one of the responsibilities of the Quarter-Master-General, a suitable military staff was established in North America to take over the material procured in Canada and the United States and to be responsible for despatching it to the required destinations. Later on the staff established depots in the United States for holding reserves. The staff was amalgamated, with other British military missions to the United States into a new headquarters which bore the title of 'British Army Staff, Washington'. The DQMG at this headquarters was Major-General (then Brigadier) H. R. Kerr and a DDST headed the RASC staff at the headquarters.

The functions of the ST branch of BAS, were to supervise the business of obtaining vehicles, spare parts, food, and petrol, the maintenance of reserves in North America, and the shipping of these goods to the United Kingdom and various theatres of war. They also had to effect liaison between the War Office, the British Food Mission in North America, and the United States Service departments; to ensure the co-ordinated action of the various Ministries and other bodies concerned in provision and shipping; to place War Office demands; and, as a sideline, to look after the RASC maintenance of the Caribbean areas and Bermuda.

Before the establishment of ST branch, BAS, vehicles and spares had been bought in Canada against orders placed by the Ministry of Supply and, in the United States, on a cash basis by the British Purchasing Commission. These arrangements made any control over the progress of supply difficult, and for several months the transport section of ST branch was engaged in compiling an up-to-date record of all vehicles supplied, and of orders outstanding and not yet placed. Next the complicated method of arranging shipments was simplified, and ST BAS eventually assumed greater responsibility for the distribution and shipment of vehicles and spares. Another difficulty was that the United States Army vehicles in their own country were serviced almost entirely by the manufacturers. This gave the United States Army authorities false ideas about the scale of spares required in operational conditions, and consequently the provision of spares was inadequate. After protracted efforts, ST succeeded in getting larger supplies of spare parts, and also persuaded the authorities of the necessity for their being shipped with the vehicles, and not many months afterwards. Soon afterwards the transport section of ST BAS was transferred to Ordnance in accordance with the reorganization of vehicle provision and maintenance, and the RASC then ceased to be directly concerned with the business of provision.

By August, 1942, a supply section had been set up in ST branch. Until 1941, all foodstuffs acquired from the United States on War Office account had been shipped to the United Kingdom, and then sent on to overseas theatres. Then the War Office began to ask for small quantities to be despatched direct to these theatres, but this caused a disproportionate amount of difficulty, since the Americans were not interested in the shipment of such small quantities. Therefore, a depot in the United States was established, to act as a buffer for small consignments.

With the entry of Japan into the war, and the consequent threat to the supply lines from the southern dominions to India and the Middle East, it became necessary to increase considerably the quantities of foodstuffs bought in the United States. A reserve was also accumulated against the requirements of an expeditionary force operating in Europe, amounting to 70,000 tons. The larger orders were of more interest to the Americans, and business went forward much more smoothly. A RASC officer was sent out to the United States to supervise the collection, packaging, and storage of these supplies.

During the latter part of 1942, and the early months of 1943, the shipping position deteriorated so much that foodstuffs could not be shipped, and a 'backlog' accumulated which could not be made up. This proved awkward for those depending on shipments from America, especially in the Middle East. The difficulty was partially overcome by giving priority of shipment to the items most urgently needed.

On the petrol side, ST branch was concerned mainly with the provision of lubricants, and not with bulk supply of liquid fuel, and much good was done by standardizing types of lubricants.

With the end of hostilities, the activities of the ST portion of the British Army staff were reduced to the dispersal of stocks already held, and to the maintenance of liaison with their American counterparts at the Pentagon. In a short time even this ceased, and the ST branch closed down. So ended an interesting and important field of RASC endeavour which did much towards maintaining the war effort in overseas theatres, saved much shipping space and, as a side issue, introduced many appreciative officers and men to the American way of life and (perhaps with less appreciation) to the vagaries of the Washington climate.

CHAPTER XII

THE R.A.S.C. IN THE UNITED KINGDOM

GENERAL SURVEY

THE outbreak of war found the RASC fully alert and alive to the tasks which lay ahead of them, but their resources were limited. Scarcity of money and material had restricted the preparations which could be made before the war to the immediate requirements in the days after mobilization. The main task of building the foundations on which to expand had to await the declaration of war.

Expansion of the organization for the day to day maintenance of the Army in the home commands of the United Kingdom had to go hand in hand with the development of the organization for procuring the vastly increased quantities of transport, food and petroleum products which would be needed, and all these activities depended on the rate at which the thousands of additional officers and men required could be enrolled, trained and organized.

As the United Kingdom is the strategic and economic centre of the Commonwealth, the expansion of the Corps and the development of its several activities were essentially home responsibilities, and although later in the war they were decentralized to overseas commands to some extent, they remained the primary responsibility of the DST at the War Office.

In the War Office in peacetime, branches of the different QMG directorates had all borne titles prefixed with 'QMG'. Not long after the outbreak of war however new titles were adopted with the prefix of the particular director under whom the branches served. This system facilitated expansion and rapid multiplication of branches. Old numbers were adhered to where possible, and the titles of those under DST were ST 1 (Water Transport), ST 2 (Petroleum, Oils and Lubricants), ST 3 (Transport and Air Despatch), ST 4 (Catering), ST 6 (Supplies), and ST 7 (Barracks). It was not until well after the war that minor changes were made in these nomenclatures.

The three main responsibilities of maintenance, procurement and training were from time to time to be directly affected by the general but changing situation at home resulting from the unexpected course of the war. It is therefore convenient to open this account of the effort of the RASC in the United Kingdom with a brief description of those conditions, with special reference to the tasks which fell on the home commands.

At the outbreak of war the United Kingdom was divided into five home commands, Northern Ireland being classed as a separate district, and all of these areas had to be denuded of their experienced men to provide for the field force and for reinforcements for our garrisons overseas. It was left to the senior RASC officer in each command headquarters, the ADST (later upgraded to DDST), to carry on to fill the gaps in his ranks and at the same time to cater for his increased commitments. However, the gaps were filled and the first rush was tided over. It was intended that commands should rely initially on extensive hirings of civilian vehicles and drivers to replace those transport companies which had disappeared almost overnight to join the field force, but this temporary arrangement was found to be both unsatisfactory and costly. Before long new companies had to be raised on an equal priority with the requirements of the field force. These companies were named 'station transport companies'. Six had to be provided before the end of 1939, and a further 17 by April, 1940. To economize in man power they were not provided with the usual company workshops sections, but separate arrangements for repairs and inspection were made by forming, at the same time, 'station maintenance companies' which took care of all RASC units in their area except those belonging to field formations.

As the months went by ATS transport companies took their place beside the RASC units, and, later still, members of both corps were merged into 'mixed transport companies' with great success. To the station transport companies and ATS companies were added various specialist companies, such as motorcoach companies, water transport or motorboat companies, GT companies allotted to ammunition carrying, a company for work with the Royal Navy on the disposal of mines, and a host of other units. Most of these will be mentioned later.

The pre-war plan for providing each command with a small number of supply depots and complementary NAAFI stores in peace and for opening further new depots on mobilization succeeded in coping with the greatly increased numbers in the Army and the Royal Air Force when mobilized, but lack of staff and some delay in opening stores as the NAAFI had been denuded of many of their experienced men who were army reservists, meant that for some weeks a large number of units, particularly those of the Territorial Army, had to rely on making civil meal contracts or on similar arrangements for their sustenance. This eventuality had been foreseen, and rates of monetary allowances had been settled for the purpose before the war. The experience of the first few weeks of the war gave, however, satisfactory proof that the pre-war arrangements for supply, through RASC supply depots, by the triple agencies of the Army, the NAAFI and the new Ministry of Food, were generally sound.

The small ST staffs in commands had also many other preoccupations, with the barracks and transport services, and with the supervising and assisting of units which were mobilizing, for at the beginning of the war responsibility for the successful mobilization of RASC units in a command was that of the ADST. It was, of course, only natural that the people left in the home commands had to take second place in reflected glory to those who were to take the field, so this is, perhaps, a fitting place to record what credit is due to the many older officers and NCOs and former civilian employees of the RASC who rallied to the flag in the time of need.

The supply and transport organizations in home commands were static, as indeed was the whole structure of the home organization. Evolved over a period of many years, the home organization was solely related to administrative considerations, such as the availability of accommodation and training areas, and its structure had no bearing at all on defence requirements. The only exception was the newly formed anti-aircraft organization, later raised to the status of a command, which, having to cover the whole country, contained mobile units for deployment as occasion demanded, each anti-aircraft division being provided with an RASC transport organization of its own. The AA Command relied, however, on the home commands for its food and for any transport which could not be found from its own resources.

Defence Policy

The whole question of the defence of the United Kingdom had been carefully examined before the war, but the risks from enemy action were assessed as being primarily from air attack, and to a lesser extent from naval aggression. The probability of enemy troops being able to land in any numbers was regarded as remote. There was a broad plan providing, in the event of invasion, for the command of the military forces for defence to be vested in a C-in-C, Home Forces, with a GHQ Home Forces, and a small nucleus headquarters was formed on the outbreak of war.

The first duty of this headquarters was to co-ordinate the planning for the military defence of the country, but it was not until the actual threat of invasion arose that the headquarters had any tangible premises on which to work. Even if invasion became a reality, the forces engaged were to be maintained by the home command's supply and transport organization, so that the task of the senior RASC officer at GHQ Home Forces was primarily one of maintaining a close liaison with the ST representatives at command headquarters and at the War Office.

The newly created Civil Defence organization was already in being, and all military units were responsible for what was then known as their 'passive air defence'. The direct interest of the RASC in, and their partial dependence on, civil transport meant that they were intimately concerned with the regional transport organization and, on questions of food and petrol, with the Ministry of Food and the Petroleum Board's emergency organization respectively. There were general exchanges of views with these three bodies, and certain broad plans for mutual aid in the event of emergency were agreed upon and made known to home commands. Relations with our civilian opposite numbers were always cordial.

But the lull of the so-called 'phoney period' of the war tended to divert interest from home defence to the more immediate problems of the day, and to shelve the problems which might arise with an attempted invasion, a risk which appeared to be receding. It was not until April, 1940, that the forceful demonstrations of the power bestowed by the use of airborne troops in the enemy's attacks on Norway and, a few weeks later, in the Low Countries, showed that these shores might be by no means inviolable. The alarm had been sounded, and 'invasion' became a matter of moment. A new impetus was given to the settlement of the arrangements which had to be concluded between the civil and military authorities for defence, and immediate action was taken to place the country in a state of defence against large scale land attack. GHQ, Home Forces, from being a small planning nucleus, at once became an active headquarters, and all the home commands were suddenly faced with new and considerable operational responsibilities. There were few trained troops in the country at that time, as the divisions available were still in various stages of training and equipment, and the remaining units were either depots or training or administrative units, engaged upon their own specific tasks. A few weeks later the BEF was fighting for its very existence in northern France.

The overwhelming response to the call for volunteers for the newly created Local Defence Volunteer force could only go a limited way towards meeting the deficiency, and there were many physical preparations to be made, which varied from the re-disposal of the available divisions to form a central reserve to the re-distribution of vital stocks in the more threatened areas which had at all costs to be denied to a potential enemy.

Administratively, the creation of the LDV (later the Home Guard) did not at first have any particular effect on the work of the Corps, as the volunteers were not to be provided with any permanent transport organization and were to rely for their food on the civil economy, although later arrangements had to be made to provide special reserves of food and to provide the staffs for training and organizing Home Guard transport columns.

From the outset the lesson that an airborne enemy is dependent to a considerable extent on the amount of petrol, food and other essentials that he can seize after landing had been taken to heart. Immediate decisions had to be made to ensure that a happy medium was struck between complete disruption of the food and petroleum distributing agencies and the farming industry and making certain that the forces and the inhabitants in threatened areas would not be starved.

The general policy concerning food stocks was to remove large stocks from threatened to less vulnerable areas and to disperse other stocks which might be required for the civilian population. But the measures taken to safeguard petrol supplies had to be more drastic. Many proposals were made for the use of easily applied contaminants which would render the stocks useless, but none of these proved to be wholly effective. In certain danger areas stocks were reduced to a minimum even in roadside pumps, and installations and pumps in those areas were so prepared that they could be quickly 'sabotaged'. When the danger was at its greatest all pumps were rendered inoperative nightly by the removal of working parts. The same was done to motor vehicles. Other stores which might be vital to the enemy were also removed or dispersed, and military depots which it was not essential to retain in coastal areas were withdrawn inland.

Even before the return of the BEF to these shores the country was rapidly being converted into an armed camp. There was a heavy call on transport and the period provided a good test of the elasticity of the RASC transport organization. They were strenuous days, and as the invasion fever increased demands for transport for mobile columns became more frequent. On May 17th, 1940, there was a particular scare, and the transport branch at the War Office were told at noon to organize a column by taking over 2,000 taxicabs for the conveyance of a small party of anti-parachute troops. With the help of the trade unions concerned, and of the Ministry of Transport, a considerable number of cabs had been assembled by evening in London, and within 48 hours all preparations had been completed.

Operation 'Dynamo'

Within a few weeks there were other urgent calls on both the supply and the transport organizations in commands for the priority operation known as 'Dynamo', the withdrawal of the BEF from France. The main function of this operation at home was to remove inland the thousands of men who were being landed at the south coast ports. This had to be done as rapidly as possible for, apart from the need to reform the many shattered units at once, it was vital to avoid delay, as it was feared that the enemy might try to follow up his success by heavy bombing attacks on the south coast ports and on the railways leading from them.

Not only was transport needed for carrying the fit and the unfit to entraining points and from detraining points to reception centres, but also considerable reserves of transport had to be assembled to continue movements which might be interrupted by enemy action against the main railway arteries. An instance of the adaptability shown by all units was the temporary 'mobilizing' of a fleet of about 2,000 civil motorcoaches and buses by the MT Stores Depot, RASC, a unit which was normally concerned with the holding and issuing of stocks and not with the operation of transport.

The unexpected return of some 300,000 additional mouths to be fed was taken in its stride by the supply organization, but operation 'Dynamo' was to be an excellent test of the newly formed catering organization which by this time had grown sufficiently to be represented at the War Office by a branch of its own under the DST. There were few men who did not arrive both hungry and thirsty, but as speed in moving the men inland was essential, the general plan was based on providing each man as he arrived with a snack meal and something to drink and then of providing more solid fare at halting places, outside the immediate coastal evacuation zone, on the way to the reception areas.

There were 14 of these halting places, and the people to staff them were gathered from Army schools, depots, etc., and elsewhere, while an appeal, most generously met, had been made to the various voluntary organizations, such as the WVS and YMCA, to lend a hand in providing hot drinks and cutting sandwiches, each main point being in charge of a catering adviser. At one point alone no fewer than 24,000 men were fed in 24 hours and, as the organization got into its stride, the meals provided were supplemented with hard boiled eggs and a ration of cigarettes and matches. NAAFI rose to the occasion and among other things produced 120,000 bags of fruit and chocolate.

The arrival of unexpectedly large numbers of French troops meant a hasty whip round to produce a ration suitable to their taste. The provision of the food required was soon arranged but finding the daily quota of red wine which every good French soldier expects was a different matter. However, an immediate appeal by the War Office Wine Adviser* to the wine trade produced casks of the desired 'vintage', although the suppliers knew well that the stocks would be irreplaceable.

Although, apart from the hard work and additional effort required, the return of the BEF was easily dealt with by the supply organization, the possibility of the United Kingdom becoming an area of active operations clearly indicated the need for adjusting the existing system of messing to one suited to active service conditions, and for expanding the policy of making commands more self contained for supplies in the event of any given area being isolated in consequence of the landing of large numbers of enemy airborne troops on a large scale. To the supply branch at the War Office it was a case of 'an ill wind', as they had before the war pressed strongly for the replacement of the peacetime 'cash' system of messing by one more practically related to war conditions. Reserves in commands were immediately increased and then backed up by the establishment of nine large new depots, sited strategically throughout the country. These, thanks to the efforts of the two supply reserve depots and of the Ministry of Food, were stocked with 11 million rations by July.

Possibly at no time in our history has the country been faced with such imminent danger as during the months which followed the reverse in France. There was no time to be lost in reforming and re-equipping the Army. The returning RASC men were first directed to the newly formed RASC mobilization centres which were specially designed to raise, equip and organize RASC units. These centres, which were unique in Army organization, immediately set about re-forming units and, when these were sufficiently organized, passing them back to the care of the division or other formation from which they originally came.

The most serious aspect of the return of the BEF was the loss of equipment, particularly of weapons. So heavy was this loss that a special branch of the War Office General Staff had to be formed to control supply and priority of issue. Fortunately the re-equipment of RASC units with their particular need, the vehicle, although by no means an easy task, had been helped by plans for new production and by the continuance of the impressment scheme (as an example, 16,000 vehicles and 7,000 motorcycles were procured and issued between August 6th and 16th, 1940).

By the end of June five divisions were deemed to be sufficiently

* By custom a member of the wine trade acts as honorary adviser to DST, War Office, on the provision of spirits and wines.

D1 RASC

equipped to take an active part in defence, and the remainder were ready by the end of July, although all formations lacked much of the weapons and equipment they needed most.

The advent of this new field army in the United Kingdom tended to complicate command and administrative control, but generally speaking, as soon as the divisional RASC had been re-formed and become effective, they drew their food and petrol from command resources and undertook their detailed distribution to their own formations. These active divisions were supplemented by specially formed static 'county' divisions, independent brigades and home defence battalions, so that the mobile formations could be directed to any threatened area if required. The RASC establishment provided for the county divisions was, in view of their limited role, one composite company, RASC.

Almost without exception, in the early days every RASC unit in the vulnerable areas was given an operational role. One such unit which had assumed a part time infantry role was assigned to guarding the beaches of Harlech, in Wales, together with certain vulnerable points in the area. The unit spent a few weeks in section training and getting to know the ground over which they were to operate. When their training was completed, they were required to furnish night patrols in the hills with the particular task of stopping any signalling to enemy aircraft. On one occasion a scout from one of the patrols reported a flashing light some distance away. The need for a silent but swift approach was impressed upon the patrol, and they advanced towards the light. In that part of the world the fields are divided by walls of loose stone. On nearing the light a wall was met and the patrol began to clamber over with great care, one by one. Suddenly the silence was broken by the noise of collapsing stones, the thud of a falling body, the clatter of a rifle, and an outburst of oaths; the light was doused and seen no more. In spite of failure to make a capture, it was clear that their task was a real one, for there was no more signalling from this area.

Another most important role fulfilled by the Corps was the provision of 'mobility' for the re-formed infantry divisions. It was essential that the divisions guarding our coasts, and even more so the general reserve, should be able to move rapidly from one sector to another. To this end 32 RASC units were re-formed into motor-coach companies. They were corps troops allotted to divisions and placed under command of CsRASC. There were no troop-carrying vehicles available, and 2,500 civil motorcoaches had to be requisitioned. By this time the RASC impressment scheme, admirably suited for this sort of transaction, was coming to a halt, and demands for civilian owned vehicles were met by the Ministry of Supply in collaboration with the Ministry of Transport. Suitable vehicles were difficult to find, and it was decided that the best readily available type was the 30-seater coach. Unfortunately these had to be obtained and issued within a few days, and the RASC had to accept what the Ministries offered, and were unable to carry out searching inspection before acceptance. To get these vehicles quickly and at the same time not to dislocate the public transport service, the Ministries decided to take over the coaches held by civil organizations as a reserve to meet sudden demands for transport. These were delivered to our vehicle reserve depots and quickly issued to units.

Then the trouble began. Issues were made to units so that each had to operate as few as possible of different makes and types. No stocks of maintenance spares were available, and units had to overcome this difficulty by approaching manufacturers or agents direct in order to meet their needs.

Later, coaches were redistributed to give units vehicles of similar performance in convoy, and all vehicles were modified as time permitted to facilitate the carriage of fully accoutred troops (a very different sort of load to the tourists for whom they were designed). In a short time, therefore, the technical drawbacks were overcome and the technique of troop-carrying was perfected. In the former task the RASC Vehicle Census Branch gave valuable help. This branch was a small team of 'backroom boys' whose efforts are little known or appreciated, who not only kept the record of RASC vehicles up to date but also collated much valuable information on their technical history.

These motorcoach companies played a valuable part while our Army was in its defensive role. Never before, one imagines, was a whole 'service' of troop-carrying companies, 32 in number, formed, equipped and operative in a fortnight.

Reorganization at Home

While the Army was being rapidly re-formed, decisions on many important measures of defence and of organizational policy were being made and put into effect, and the gradual conception of preparing for the immediate danger and at the same time looking forward to the day when it might be possible to challenge the enemy on his own ground began to crystallize.

The superimposing of what was really a mobile field army on the static organization of the home commands gave rise to many problems which required settlement before the home organization could be regarded as a satisfactory working entity, capable of meeting the conditions which might arise should invasion come.

The situation which had resulted from the presence of the Air

Defence of Great Britain, which was superimposed over the whole of the country, of the divisions of the normal organization which were grouped under corps headquarters, and of the specially formed county divisions, apart from the mass of training and administrative units outside these categories, is too complex to relate here, nor indeed is it necessary to do so. But it was obviously important to examine the situation to ensure that there was unity of operational control and that duplication of administrative effort was avoided.

Our readers will be interested to know that the responsibility for sorting out 'by examining the respective administrative responsibilities of field formations, ADGB, areas and sub-areas (into which commands were divided) in the United Kingdom, having special regard to administrative requirements in connection with possible operations' was entrusted to an RASC officer, Major-General H. M. Gale, who was appointed chairman of the committee which bore his name. The resultant recommendations went a long way to rationalize organization and stood the test of that critical period of the war.

To perfect the general organization at home, a standing committee was set up in 1940 to consider the whole question of the administrative organization of the War Office and of home commands, with a view to simplification of effort. Among the important measures which resulted from its deliberations was the institution of an executive committee of the Army Council, which did much to hasten administrative decisions, and the decentralization of financial responsibility to the general officers commanding in chief home commands by the appointment of a member of the civil controlling bodies at the War Office, as command secretary to each command. Both measures were a welcome step to an administrative corps such as the RASC, to whom speed of decision was vital when important measures had to be put in hand.

As the months of 1941 passed the Army grew stronger and stronger, and although the risk of invasion was little more remote, the outcome of any large scale attack by the enemy was anticipated with confidence. By autumn there were 27 divisions, eight county divisions and five armoured divisions under arms, together with various brigaded and unbrigaded troops, all ready to take their part in the overthrow of the invader. The setback at Dunkirk had produced a new outlook and determination in the Army, and the emphasis in training had already changed from defence to offence. New methods were being tried, and the operational experience of units in the Middle East was carefully studied, large scale exercises being held to test the efficiency of the newly formed Army.

The first general plans, including the preparation of many divisions, were being made with the ultimate object of a return to the Continent in force and the defeat of the enemy on his own ground. In October, 1941, instructions were given to start the preparation of one armoured and two infantry divisions for engagement in an amphibious operation. This plan, 'Gymnast', was exactly a year later to bear fruit under the renamed and more ambitious operation 'Torch', when the first convoys of some 650 ships left these shores for the landing in North Africa.

The adoption of new methods and techniques of warfare was also to enlarge the scope of the Corps' activities and to increase the number of specialist units required. In this direction air supply, amphibian operations and specialized petrol units and installations come to mind.

Following six months after Hitler's initially successful invasion of Russia, the formal entry of the United States into the war after the Japanese attack on Pearl Harbour in December, 1941, was of course the most important event of the year, although it coincided with, and was to be followed by, many grievous blows, by the capitulation of Singapore and Hong Kong, the loss of the Dutch East Indies, the invasion of Burma, and the setback at Tobruk. The entry of the Americans, however, gave a fresh impetus to the whole of future planning, and the first big reaction from the home organization was the inception of the plan, known as 'Bolero', for the reception, accommodation, and maintenance of all those forces of the United States which were eventually to take part in operation 'Overlord', the final operation of the war in the west. But before describing the direct effects of 'Bolero' on the RASC in the United Kingdom, it is necessary to digress and refer to the growth and development of the home transport organization.

While the re-equipment of field units with their RASC transport went on apace, the home organization was also being developed. To meet the requirements of GHQ Home Forces for improvised troop carrying in an emergency, 12 home service companies had to be raised, and plans were made, in case of actual invasion, to form 63 emergency MT companies of 100 lorries each from assets to be found from three driver training brigades, the three mobilization centres, and the Officer Cadet Training Unit.

As previously mentioned no provision had been made for transport for the Home Guard but, as this body was obviously a source from which to supplement the transport which would be wanted for active operations in the United Kingdom, it was agreed that the nucleus of 26 columns, consisting of 133 companies, should be organized, RASC officers of home service category being posted to assist with training, and a regular adjutant and two permanent instructors being allowed for each column. More than 12,000 vehicles were reserved from civil sources for the purpose on an understanding that the owner or driver would drive his own lorry when called out for active service. About 17,000 men were enrolled out of the 20,000 wanted for these columns.

This Home Guard organization was, however, solely an 'invasion' reserve and was destined never to be embodied. It did not, therefore, ease the general transport situation in the country, which was one of increasing requirements accompanied by demands for economy in effort and savings in manpower.

To meet the many different circumstances which had arisen the general growth of the body of military transport for performing the duties proper to the Corps had of necessity been on rather haphazard lines. Thus there were a large number of vehicles for which the RASC were responsible but over which they had not complete control. Notable cases in point were the ATS companies and a large ambulance pool, manned partly by the ATS and partly by the Corps. By custom the RASC were charged with offering technical assistance and advice to ATS units, and this was readily accepted.

In 1942 a War Office committee, appointed to examine the home transport organization, recommended that all RASC vehicles (i.e. those maintained by the RASC) should form part of an RASC unit and that the officer commanding the RASC unit should be responsible for all aspects of operation, administration and maintenance of the vehicles, and for administration of the drivers. The effect of these recommendations was that the separate ATS companies and the groups into which they were formed were abolished, and the pools and various vehicles attached to other units such as headquarters of commands and districts were drawn into RASC units.

At the same time the opportunity was taken to rationalize the transport organization by the formation of command mixed transport companies to replace the existing ATS transport and RASC station transport companies. These new units were commanded by an RASC officer with ATS officers to assist him, and were made up of separate RASC and ATS platoons in proportions suited to local conditions. Initially these companies numbered 51, and the immediate effect was a considerable saving in RASC manpower. By the end of 1942 the proportion of RASC to ATS platoons was 128 to 102, as there were few normal duties which could not be satisfactorily performed by the ATS driver. On the whole the system of mixed companies worked well and, where minor differences of opinion arose between the senior ATS officer and the officer commanding, they could usually be smoothed out by the DDsST of commands through their 'DADsST ATS', who were specially selected ladies and appeared to combine the art of diplomacy with that intangible feminine intuition which produces the right answer.

No attempt can be made here to give a detailed account of the work which fell on the RASC transport units during the years of endurance and preparation between 1940 and 1944 beyond recording that, when both civilian and soldier were sharing equally the hazards of the enemy's heavy and continuous air attacks on this country, army transport took its full share of special duties. Apart from help in connection with air raids, there were many calls for assistance by military transport, so much so that all requests had to be referred to the regional transport commissioners and the War Office. RASC transport had to be freely used for carrying troops to work on the farms, to carry munition and factory workers during transport strikes, and to assist in dock clearance during dock strikes. During the London bus strike of the war years they ran an extempore bus service, and at Christmas they helped the GPO in the delivery of Christmas mails.

To revert somewhat in dates, in the later months of 1940 several units were permanently employed in assisting the Civil Defence service in the clearance of debris, carrying casualties, and distributing water, and in 1941 a special company (known as the 'Land Incident Company, RASC') was formed to work for the Admiralty on land mine disposal work. Many of the men of this unit shared in the hazardous duty of mine disposal. Among them were Dvrs A. I. Evans, J. S. Coates, H. Kaye and C. S. Ridge, who were awarded the British Empire Medal, Evans later being awarded a bar to his medal. There were many other awards to RASC men who were engaged in other rescue work. The first George Medal to be won by an RASC man was that awarded to Dvr E. O. Gurnham who, in company with an RAF sergeant, rescued a pilot from a burning aircraft. Another George Medal was awarded to Cpl A. M. W. Keddie for an action which was perhaps more in the traditional role of the Corps, that is driving away a blazing lorry loaded with ammunition and petrol, thereby saving a lorry park and its occupants from disaster.

As the number and type of RASC road transport units was increased in the early years, there had to be a corresponding development in the three main types of RASC MT maintenance units on which the transport companies were so dependent for the replacement of vehicles and spares, the provision of stores, and for the execution of repairs beyond the resources of unit workshops. The three units concerned were the Vehicle Reserve Depot, the MT Stores Depot and the Heavy Repair Shop, all sited before the war at Feltham, Middlesex. By October, 1939, two new VRDs and an MTSD had been opened in accommodation taken over in the Slough Trading Estate. The completion in 1940 of a new permanent depot at Ashchurch, Glos., which had been planned before the war, provided room for another VRD and MTSD, while other units were also established in the north and in Northern Ireland. More heavy repair shops were also opened, but this expansion had only just been completed when there was to be a profound change in the allocation of responsibility for the maintenance of MT. This caused the RASC to hand over complete responsibility for heavy repairs to a new corps, the Royal Electrical and Mechanical Engineers, and that for the supply of vehicles and spare parts to the Royal Army Ordnance Corps. This change is discussed in more detail later.

The main impact of operation 'Torch' on the home organization was the work of fitting out and mobilizing the many RASC units which were to accompany the force and are referred to in more detail in the relevant chapter of this book. To provide the transport needed, 21 companies had to be withdrawn from the home establishment, but the various measures already described helped to overcome the fact that they could not be replaced. Unlike the planning of the BEF, it was found possible to preserve adequate secrecy without impairing the administrative preparations required, and past lessons were taken to heart when it came to the allotment of RASC units for the force and the priority of their landing. The accumulation of the tonnage of food required was mainly a matter of stepping up production, but the expedition was the first occasion on which the newly designed 'composite pack' was to be provided in considerable quantities. As this form of pack and its provision was to play such an important part in the war effort, it is discussed in more detail elsewhere in this volume.

Arrival of the Americans

Meanwhile the plan ('Bolero') to bring over the United States forces which would ultimately be engaged in the final return to the offensive on the Continent was being rapidly perfected. This project for receiving, housing and providing all the ancillary services and accommodation needed by 1,500,000 men, and superimposing this vast army on the already strained resources of the United Kingdom, was probably one of the greatest administrative achievements of the war. It involved not only the provision of new camps, hospitals, airfields and training grounds, but also a redistribution of the accommodation in use by our own forces, particularly in the Southern and Western Commands.

'Bolero' also marked the first opportunity afforded to the British Army to get to know and to understand their 'cousins'. Before long the RASC officer began to realize that the 'quartermaster' was not that well known character, the CQMS or RQM, but was a highly placed general, that food was 'subsistence', that the Q Staff were 'G4', and so on.

The main impact of the plan fell on the RASC supplies organization as, working on the well accepted relation of host and guest, the two model and main depots (SRDs) which they prized so much had to be cleared and handed over to the American forces just at a time when extra accommodation for housing the reserves being built up for operation 'Torch' was being sought. However, with the co-operation of the Board of Trade's department of storage and factory control, alternative depots were found, and the work is described in more detail in the section dealing with supplies which follows later in this chapter.

The years 1941 and 1942 saw great developments in transport techniques on land, in the air and in amphibious operations. The years 1943 and onwards were more marked for the growth in petrol installations and petrol handling plants. This, based on the experience gained in Africa, went ahead with much quickened tempo until the very complete fuel replenishment organization which served 21 Army Group in North-West Europe came to full fruition.

The year 1941 saw, too, the reorganization of RASC units, beginning with transport units, into platoons, companies and columns, following closely the infantry pattern and simplifying war establishments, equipment tables and, where necessary, the switch of Corps units to an infantry role.

As the tempo of operations overseas, particularly in Europe, quickened and as victory came in sight, so the scope and size of training units at home decreased until, during operation 'Overlord', whole training brigades were disbanded, and their assets in men and vehicles were built up into GT companies for immediate service on the Continent. In somewhat similar style the dukw and Terrapin amphibious companies gradually 'lost their webbed feet' and reverted to their alternative role as GT companies.

This run-down of the effort at home was becoming increasingly evident from late 1943 onwards, and explains why the greater part of this chapter appears to deal with the early struggles of a beleaguered Britain. It was the early years which saw the more striking improvisations and special efforts.

In 1944 and 1945 history repeated itself when the Corps was called upon to transfer to the infantry a number of officers and men, thus fulfilling what has become its traditional role when the manpower resources of Britain dwindled, this time happily not solely through battle casualties, but partly through the increased calls of the Royal Navy and Royal Air Force.

While these later events were taking place, operation 'Bolero' ceased, most of the United States forces having moved across the

English Channel. Its place was taken by operation 'Orelob', a reversal involving the handing over of establishments by the United States army to the British. There were still certain establishments retained for depot use by our Allies, England being used not only as an air base but also as a staging point in the reinforcement of American formations on the Continent and as a base for the reception of American sick and wounded from Europe.

But a steady return of camps and depots of all sorts was in progress from the last months of 1944 onwards. Several 'legacies' came to the British Army in the way of former American hospitals and camps of semi-permanent construction and of more lavish lay-out than our own. These formed welcome additions to the Army's post-war accommodation.

Finally, with the overthrow of the last of our enemies, Japan, and the setting up of occupation forces in Germany, Austria, Venezia Giulia and Japan, the RASC establishments were everywhere severely cut and, in Germany, transport companies administered by the RASC but manned almost wholly by our late enemies (albeit reduced to the status of civilians) and supply and petrol depots similarly 'civilianized' came into being. The wheel had come full circle, but this time, thanks to our occupation forces and to our overseas commitments, and thanks to the need to be on our guard against Communist aggression, the Corps was not crippled by such drastic cuts as in 1919.

TRANSPORT

Planning for War

Between the Munich crisis and the outbreak of war, the ordering of vehicles and equipment from civil industry for the RASC formed a large part of the work of the transport branch at the War Office, ST 3. The 12 months' grace proved to be barely enough to obtain all the material wanted, but it was sufficient to equip the RASC units of the field force adequately.

War was imminent at the end of August, and it was only a question of receiving the code word for mobilization to use, at a moment's notice, the assets available, and to set the mobilization machinery into motion. The code word for general mobilization, which was to be despatched to all commands at home and abroad, was 'Haig'. At that time there was a staff officer called Captain Haig in the Quartering Directorate, and an amusing situation (on the day before mobilization), which might well have been a serious one, was created, when ST 3, on being asked by Captain Haig's director 'Has Haig gone out?' replied, 'Yes, about 10 minutes ago'!

The ambiguity of this reply was luckily detected in time to prevent the British Army from going to war too early.

When the order was issued, the success of the venture depended largely on the ability of the War Office to provide units with their vehicles, particularly their technical ones. The load carrying vehicles were to be obtained by impressing civil vehicles. Technical vehicles such as workshops and stores lorries and ambulances were a different problem because they had to be found from the 3-ton and 30-cwt. load carrying six-wheeled vehicles operated by RASC companies in peace and converted for such purposes when war came.

All units' holdings had to be despatched to the Heavy Repair Shop at Feltham, where normal overhaul programmes were swept aside and the whole of the shop was devoted to this great task. Most of the 3-ton six-wheeled vehicles had to be fitted with workshop machinery, breakdown lorry equipment, or MT stores bins from the stock which had been built up and held in the MT Stores Depot. There were many other specialist vehicles, such as hygiene and bacteriological laboratories and bridging vehicles, which necessitated the removal of the load-carrying body and its complete replacement by a technical body. The layout of the HRS resembled an organized production line, and it was important that when vehicles had been converted the flow should be maintained through the Vehicle Reserve Depot to the field units being mobilized. Similar activities were required in respect of the 30-cwt six-wheelers which had to be refitted with ambulance bodies, stored in peace by the VRD.

The whole of this task was performed precisely as planned, every divisional unit receiving a quota of technical vehicles, and there were only a few other units which had to embark with one workshop lorry instead of two. About this time it was decided that there would be no objection to units having one set of workshop and store lorries mounted on four-wheeled chassis and, as events proved later, these vehicles were as effective as their six-wheeled counterparts.

The number of ambulances required was far in excess of the number of 30-cwt six-wheeled vehicles in use in the United Kingdom. To meet this requirement many hundreds of ambulance bodies had been purchased in peacetime, so designed that they could be readily fitted to impressed four-wheeled chassis. The conversion programme, therefore, was a gigantic task for the HRS in the space available, but the unit stood up to the task extremely well, as did the other main depots at Feltham.

Gifts from the Nation

In every national emergency the generosity of the nation comes to the fore and, as in the First World War, so on September 4th,

1939, the War Office quadrangle was filled with a large number of civilians who had brought their private cars for presentation to the War Office. This was an embarrassment at a time when the three officers in ST 3 who were in charge of the arrangements for provision and issue of vehicles and MT stores for the whole of the RASC had other things on their minds. Remembering the experiences of the First World War, one of these officers originated a system, at a moment's notice, which was to prove its value throughout the whole war. Every potential donor was asked to leave his name, address and particulars of the vehicle he wished to give, and it was explained to him that all gifts would have to be 'outright' and that there would be no question of attempting to return the vehicle to the donor when the war ended, or of giving any form of compensation. A letter of thanks was then sent to each one of them, but only vehicles of makes and types operated by the Army were accepted. All donors were listed in a special 'record of presentations', which covers some 14,000 vehicles and is still held by ST 3, War Office.

Mobilization: the CIST and Ministry of Supply

The mobilization plans worked smoothly and well, though of necessity throwing great burdens on the few people on whom most executive responsibility had to rest. The first and heaviest loads fell on the provision branch of ST 3 and on the Chief Inspector of Supplementary Transport (CIST). The latter found the civil vehicles to swell the number of Army vehicles and 'new production' vehicles available, and the former was particularly concerned with the production of technical vehicles. Some idea of the activities of both these organizations is given in the Prelude to this history but more notice is due to the CIST's work without which, even with the help from the Ministry of Supply, it would have been impossible to equip the Army to war scales in anything like sufficient time.

Once mobilization had been ordered, all eyes in the RASC transport world were focussed on the ability of the CIST to impress from civil life the vehicles on which the RASC depended. The success of the impressment scheme was undoubtedly due, in the first instance, to the excellent plan drawn up during the four or five years before the war. One of the most important features of the plan was the setting up of the peacetime inspectorate who visited civilian owners of vehicles and to decide whether or not the vehicles were of desirable types and mechanically sound. The list of potential vehicles included none over two years old, and the inspectorate were selective in choosing only those makes and types of vehicle which were considered to be of use. The procedure for impressment was a legal one, and the owners were given one of four centres to which they had to deliver their vehicles when war came. It was quite surprising to find out how few of these vehicles failed to arrive at their proper destinations in time. The four vehicle collecting centres soon became scenes of great activity and it was not many days before units were receiving their establishments of vehicles at incredible speed. The impressment machinery stood up to its task and the officers and men who had been pre-posted to the organization functioned with marked efficiency. Although some may have had qualms beforehand about the suitability of these civil vehicles for field force units, it was found that there were very few indeed which were not sufficiently roadworthy to take their place in the newly mobilized units.

The Ministry of Supply provision of wheeled vehicles was managed at the start by a retired RASC officer, Brigadier K. M. F. Hedges, who had left the Corps 'between the wars' but had retained a clear memory of the problems which had faced us in 1914, and who linked his own capacity and foresight with the productive capacity of the motor manufacturers (the benefit of their recent improvements in this respect being offset to a large extent by the increased demands of our mechanized Army on them) to produce an immediate flow of new vehicles. These were, it is true, of 'civilian' types and of an inconveniently large variety of models. but the Army got the desired numbers and carrying capacity. A certain amount of criticism has been levelled at the Ministry of Supply for the multiplicity of types introduced into the service which led to an almost insoluble spare parts problem; but this was inevitable because of the large number demanded and the many different types in use.

New Commitments

Nevertheless, certain measures of self-help were still required of the War Office. The plan which had been compiled in peacetime only covered the provision of transport for the field force units. But the war had not been in progress many days before there were claims for additional transport. Such tasks as the equipping of the Territorial Army and the expansion of maintenance work in the United Kingdom, which had of necessity been left for solution until after mobilization day, brought a heavy and sudden demand on our resources. Furthermore, demands were soon received from the newly established Expeditionary Force in France for units over and above their original order of battle, and of these demands some related to works MT companies equipped with tippers, and also additional troop-carrying companies. At that time the Ministry of Supply had only recently been formed, and much of its time was occupied in building up the big machine and in getting vehicle production under way. The formation of new units in addition to those in the planned order of battle could, therefore, only be done by continuing the impressment scheme for much longer than was originally intended. Impressment was also used to get new vehicles which were on the production line and could not have been purchased quickly by normal Ministry of Supply contract procedure.

Works companies were a new type of unit to operate with the Royal Engineers on airfield and road construction. These units had come to stay, and under their later designation tipper companies were found to be indispensable in most theatres of war.

The formation of four troop-carrying companies was a typical example of the rapidity with which a unit could be prepared for service overseas. It was only a matter of weeks after war had been declared that the formation of these new units became an urgent necessity. It was decided to provide men from two Territorial formations, namely, the Mobile Divisional RASC and the 55th (West Lancashire) Divisional RASC, which at that time had reached an advanced state of embodiment. For the vehicles it was clearly impossible to upset the smooth operation (already under way) of equipping units of the field force, particularly as the vehicles of the new units had to be modified for troop-carrying. It was fortuitous that the production line at Messrs. Austin Motors had just completed a batch of 300 civilian type 3-ton lorries. These were impressed and despatched immediately to units. There was not time to enter into contract procedure, nor were facilities available to modify these vehicles in Regular Army units. The sides of the lorries had to be heightened, folding seats had to be fitted, and some form of canopy protection devised. The work was left entirely to the Territorial Army commanding officers, who were able to complete it in a matter of days by direct contact with the large number of small and medium body builders and garages spread over most of north Wales and Cheshire. Resort was also had to the impressment of new machines coming off production lines when the influx of recruits called for an immense increase in the number of vehicles required for driver training. About 500 Austin taxi chassis were impressed and fitted with dual controls and small van type bodies, and 100 of these were issued to each of five driver training battalions in a few days.

Standardization

Later, the supply of vehicles and tanks was merged in the Ministry of Supply under a 'Director of Mechanical Equipment' (Sir Geoffrey Burton), whose deputy on the vehicle side was Major-General M. S. Brander, after the age limit had removed him from the Army, and on the tank side Major-General J. S. Crawford, who has already been mentioned in the Prelude as an early transfer from the RASC to the RAOC. A greater degree of standardization was eventually reached and the spare parts problem was brought more under control. But, under any form of government except a military dictatorship, it is not practical politics to standardize transport equipment absolutely. The inroads on civilian design and consequently on the export market will not permit of it, nor do the high clearance and relatively large engine power of the military vehicle commend themselves to the civilian user at home.

Nevertheless, from time to time people have been very critical of the British Army because so many different types of vehicle were operated, with the consequent multiplicity of different spare parts required. The subject had received close attention before the war, but on the demise of the subsidy scheme standardization of the British Army vehicle would have been much too expensive. Once war had broken out, the Ministry of Supply had to produce vehicles very quickly, and any vehicle at that time was better than no vehicle at all. British manufacturers could not be allowed to delay production while new patterns and jigs were provided to enable one standard vehicle to be produced by all of them, and the problem was accentuated by the complete loss of the vehicles of the BEF in Europe. In contrast with the United States of America, Great Britain was in distress, and the Americans were fortunate in that they had time to build up, in organized stages, an immense output of standardized transport. They were not embarrassed by having to limit the increase in production to the availability of newly made jigs and patterns. It is also worth mentioning that the task of the British manufacturers was made extremely difficult by the lack of particular metals and of materials. At one time aircraft manufacture had priority over all other work, and aluminium and substitute alloys had to be devised at short notice for road transport components. At another time nickel was diverted in large quantities to other production, an event which was to prove of far reaching importance when the eventual adoption of leaded petrol meant the replacement of a prodigious number of engine valves which had been constructed, without nickel content, merely to stand up to low octane fuels.

The question of standardizing vehicles became one of such moment that, in 1943, the Quarter-Master-General called for a paper on the subject so that the lessons learned in this war might anyhow be taken into account—in the next war. The paper included a scheme whereby the Army adopted an ideal specification for its vehicles operated in peace, and held in store a liberal reserve of foundry patterns, jigs and plant. The last named would then be available in emergency for many different manufacturers to switch over without delay in producing the standard military design.

In our war establishments there were no 'reserve parks', those useful horse-drawn maids of all work of the First World War which, basically rolling magazines, formed an invaluable reserve of horse transport for short hauls. Now, their place was taken by two L of C railhead MT Companies RASC, equipped with 10-ton lorries, each with a carrying capacity equal to 14 days' hard rations for a corps, and actually with these supplies in their possession. During the quiescent period from September 3rd, 1939, to May, 1940, they provided a useful reserve of transport, and one of them was to earn laurels for its tactical prowess during the subsequent withdrawal to Dunkirk. The experience gained with these companies led to the adoption of the 10-tonner, initially as a possible transport link between Iraq and Palestine and later for general transport purposes in the Western Desert and on other fronts.

The Vehicle Reserve Depots

On the provision side, the flow of vehicles from the Ministry of Supply contracts was not long in getting under way. The British load-carrying vehicles were nearly all of the single driven axle type during the first year of the war, but as time went on many manufacturers built four-wheel drive lorries, and to the ranks of these came the Bedford lorry firm (General Motors) and the great numbers made by this firm were of inestimable value. It was soon evident that the one vehicle reserve depot at Feltham could not cope with the influx of vehicles, and an offshoot was started first of all at Olympia, as a temporary measure until the large depot at Slough could be established. Even then the capacity of Slough was inadequate, and an overflow was placed in Burnham Beeches. There were several occasions when the Slough depot attracted the attention of the public, particularly of passengers on the then Great Western Railway system, which passed beside the depot. Habitual passengers jumped to the conclusion that the vehicles they saw there each day were exactly the same as they had seen the previous day. It was not long, moreover, before this came to the notice of the Prime Minister, who issued a peremptory order from 10, Downing Street urging the removal of this vast quantity of transport. Some 24 hours later it was difficult to find a single vehicle in the Slough depot, and this clearance was rendered possible by the fact that the new depot at Ashchurch, which had been planned in 1938–39, was at that time just ready to function. This episode is mentioned in Volume II of Sir Winston Churchill's *The Second World War, Their Finest Hour*, on page 519, which reprints the actual instruction verbatim. Burnham Beeches was retained for a long time after this because of the excellent concealment afforded in that location.

The Ashchurch depot had been designed originally to hold

5,000 six-wheeled vehicles with a liberal allowance of open concreted space for marshalling areas. It also included an MT stores depot twice as big as that at Feltham, and the total area was sufficient to allow for considerable expansion as both a vehicle and a stores depot. It was ideally situated in relation to the southern and western ports and was safe in that it was not adjacent to any large city. The plan of this depot may be said to have been ideal, and it was erected in its entirety except that the incidence of war forced us to accept hutted accommodation for officers and men instead of the originally planned brick barracks. This depot was handed over to the RAOC in April, 1942, when certain responsibilities, details of which will be given later, were handed over to that corps.

Although vehicles provided by the Ministry of Supply were provided with equipment such as tools, the RASC had to fit each one of them with three 2-gallon petrol cans for carrying spare petrol, oil and water. The cans were procured by contract by the sister petroleum branch at the War Office (ST 2), and large stocks were held on their behalf in the MT Stores Depot at Slough, so much so that they took up accommodation wanted badly for other things. Quite by chance, during the Dunkirk evacuation, the duty officer of ST 3 received an urgent telephone call from a worried movement control officer at Dover to the effect that the troops on the beaches at Dunkirk were in desperate need of drinking water. The ST 3 officer thought and acted quickly. Within a few hours two MT companies were loaded with 60,000 of the new cans, held at Slough, and were on their way to Dover. At the coast they were filled with drinking water and shipped to the Dunkirk beaches in time to save the situation.

The ATS

During these opening months of the war new units were formed for home service and some of them were 'manned' by the ATS. Already, on mobilization, companies of this corps had been placed in certain static establishments, such as training centres, to relieve men of clerical, cookhouse and store-keeping duties, and had won golden opinions. Now, under the inspiration and leadership of many former members of the First Aid Nursing Yeomanry and of the Women's Legion, complete transport companies were formed, initially for driving staff cars and ambulances only but later extending their scope to load carrying vehicles as well, and these units provided a service which could otherwise only have been met by inroads on our already hard pressed manpower resources. The ATS, too, provided large numbers of administrative personnel and convoy drivers for our vehicle depots. With the lengthening of the war and the ever growing demands on our male population, they took over more and more of the home transport units and were merged finally into the mixed transport companies which did all the hack work in home commands.

The ATS girls in their transport units kept an extremely high standard of vehicle maintenance, accounted for partly by the unparalleled keenness of their first cadre of officers, partly by the happy fact that they were not interested in games or football pools so that for lack of off-duty relaxation they put extra time into 'petting' their precious vehicles, and partly no doubt because of a wholesome determination to show the men that they 'could do better'. So important did the work of the ATS for the Corps become on the transport side, that from 1941 onwards ATS officers were drafted into ST 3 (the first staff captain was inevitably known as 'Scats') and proved as good there as in their units. The very fine services rendered by the ATS on the gun sites of Anti-Aircraft Command is now history, but their work in our field of 'ST' has not received acknowledgement to the same degree.

The Anti-Aircraft Command

When the Anti-Aircraft Command was formed it was hoped to keep the establishments small and to dovetail the duties of army command transport units with the more specialized duties, such as ammunition carriage, of the AA Command units. It was soon evident, however, that the load on army command units was all they could support and, moreover, the enormous dispersion and the inaccessibility of many of the anti-aircraft sites called for an entirely separate organization of their own. The 'Command' grew from one Regular and two Territorial brigades to no fewer than 13 divisions organized in eight groups. The delivery of ammunition, fuel and food to these divisions became the sole responsibility of the AA divisional RASCs, the work of the whole being directed and co-ordinated by a DDST with a small staff at AA Command headquarters.

The system of ammunition supply differed slightly from that adopted for the field armies, and may be described briefly. The ammunition was initially stored in RAOC central ammunition depots and was distributed by them, usually by means of home command transport, to intermediate ammunition depots. From these it was carried by RASC transport to emergency ammunition magazines. The anti-aircraft divisional RASC normally carried it from the emergency ammunition magazines to the gun sites, and the Corps responsibility was for keeping both EAMs and gun sites up to strength in ammunition. The magnitude of the task may be appreciated when it is realized that a brisk night's firing in the London area alone put some 600 tons of metal into the sky. Where it all fell goodness only knows, but at least one 3·7-inch shell fell, in the first daylight raid on London, almost on top of two RASC lorries at the south-west corner of the War Office. The lorries were wrecked and the drivers wounded, while the blast seemed to take a malignant delight in shattering the windows of the financial 'high ups' in the War Office.

This business of anti-aircraft ammunition supply, complicated as it was by the multiplicity of types required (40 mm Bofors, 3-inch, 3·7-inch, 4·5-inch, 5·25-inch and rockets) caused some anxiety at first, until it was tried, in miniature, in the first raid on the Shetland Islands. Everything worked according to plan and, except for the increased mileages and expenditures of ammunition called for during the deployment of AA Command units four years later to meet the V1 attacks, little difference in organization or operation was found necessary throughout the war.

Animal and Water Transport

To economize in our use of mechanical vehicles and skilled drivers, horse-drawn wagons were requisitioned, with the necessary animals and hired civilian drivers, in 1940 and 1941. They did useful service in our larger cities and garrisons and in rural areas they were accompanied by pack transport companies, awaiting absorption in some war theatre. The two RIASC pack transport companies evacuated from the BEF were soon on their feet again and formed an interesting 'Indian enclave', under Colonel R. W. W. Hills, RIASC, in the British organization at home, with their own reinforcement 'depot' and hospital arrangements. They settled finally in the Scottish Highlands, near Grantown-on-Spey, and were returned to India in 1943.

During the First World War considerable tactical use had been made of motorboat companies, ASC, on Lake Doiran in Macedonia on the Sea of Galilee, and on certain of the lakes in East Africa. It is not surprising therefore, that at an early stage of the second war the use of RASC operated boats for supplying outlying forts, inaccessible except by sea, round our coasts and, later, for supply and inter-communication purposes in certain threatened areas, particularly on the south-east coast of Britain, led to the formation of motor boat companies, RASC, which were equipped mainly with requisitioned launches. Eventually two motorboat training units were raised, and one of them was located at Salcombe, in Devon, and the other at St. Austell, in Cornwall. These were manned chiefly by temporary RASC officers with a knowledge of small craft and of coastwise navigation, with as many other ranks of sailing experience as could be found. In time they found themselves assisting the Royal Navy in the examination service on the east coast, patrolling estuaries in search of magnetic and acoustic mines, supplying the Maunsell forts in the Thames estuary and other island forts round our coasts, and building up a valuable reserve to skilled men and serviceable craft for use in various theatres, both as 'staff cars' in harbours and as tactical and administrative transport. One such unit early found itself sent to patrol the Gt. Scarcies River on the western border of Sierra Leone at a time when a sore and angry French colonial army, greatly outnumbering the troops in Sierra Leone, lay in French territory just across the border.

With the development of amphibious warfare the motorboat companies came into their own. At the same time (that is soon after the outbreak of war) the WD Fleet became a greatly expanded, and expanding, 'RASC Fleet' and a War Office branch, ST 1, was expressly created to take over from ST 3 the administration of the motorboat companies. The RASC Fleet remained essentially a sea-going service with ships, steam and diesel engined, varying from 100 to 2,000 tons burthen, while the motorboat companies consisted for the most part of launches or passenger *cum* cargo ships ranging from quite small craft to vessels capable of transporting a platoon of infantry with their equipment. The Fleet was manned by civilian masters and crews, the companies being wholly military. For technical maintenance the vessels of the Fleet were looked after by various dockyards while the motorboats had their 'first and second echelon maintenance' done by their own artificers and only had recourse to dockyards for extensive refit and repairs. A special motorboat section of the MTSD was formed at Molesey and in one guise or another remained in the hands of the Corps until the end of the war.

Preparations for Norway

The transport commitment in this plan was comparatively small, the force proceeding with skeleton scales of transport. For the most part 30-cwt and 15-cwt vehicles were used, and great care was taken in the preparation of the RASC contingent to provide light lubricating oils, heavy density electrolyte to avoid the freezing of batteries, and non-skid chains. The campaign was dogged by ill luck, in addition to a good deal of faulty planning, but the 'arcticizing' of the transport was a useful lesson, applied again when we sent formation transport and a section of a GT company to Iceland later. In no other theatres were these precautions found to be necessary.

The CIMT

The rapid expansion of the RASC at home and overseas led soon to a certain falling off in the standards of vehicle maintenance, inevitable with new drivers, unfamiliar vehicles and long hours of work. Before the war the Corps had adopted the 'sixteen task system', which was calculated to enable drivers to carry out, with little supervision, all the essential daily or weekly maintenance tasks on their vehicles. This proved a great help, but there was still a basic need for inspection and reports to the War Office on the vehicle state. These duties had been performed in peacetime by the Inspection Department under the Chief Inspector of Armaments. On mobilization, unfortunately, the CIA's officers were all required for full time work under the Ministry of Supply, and the inspection of unit equipment was left to the RASC (and RAOC, for other arms).

Early in 1940 therefore the DST (Major-General R. T. Snowden-Smith), on realizing that the CIA's branch could no longer carry out any inspections of RASC units, directed the formation of a special 'Chief Inspector of Mechanical Transport' branch for the RASC. A charter was drawn up at once by ST 3, which was to be their guide until they were eventually re-modelled in 1942. So important did the DST consider their work that he perused all their reports in the early stages, and was thus able to raise the efficiency of RASC units throughout the country.

The Corps was lucky to find ready to hand a Chief Inspector in the person of Colonel J. C. Mackie, who had been until the previous year the Inspector of Mechanized Vehicles under CIA. An enthusiast at his job, Colonel Mackie quickly secured a good team of inspectors, and before the end of the year there were routine inspections of RASC units. In France, too, a similar inspectorate was set up with the result that the RASC transport alone emerged intact and roadworthy from the very severe winter of 1939–1940.

As the forces in other theatres of war grew, so the system was extended to them also, and by 1942 a state of '84 per cent efficiency' was recorded throughout the Corps. At that time, without a similar organization for other arms, the comparable figure outside the Corps was 40 per cent. The institution of an inspectorate for them in 1942, again under the indefatigable Colonel Mackie, raised this by June, 1944, to 65 per cent. This 'state of efficiency' figure did not refer solely to mechanical availability of the transport, but also to such essentials as correct maintenance of fuel and lubricant stores, cleanliness of vehicles, correct maintenance of records, reasonable mileage per gallon of fuel, and so on. The savings in premature repair and evacuation of vehicles and the maintenance of units at full establishment achieved by these means paid a handsome dividend on the cost of the inspectorates.

In May and June, 1940, little could be done to help the BEF with transport. Many relief drivers and vehicles were sent to the nearer French Channel ports, but they could accomplish little and the

War Office was, in fact, requested to stop sending reinforcements which promised only to become an embarrassment. Finally, Rear GHQ went off the air altogether. Later they established telephone contact (with ST 3, War Office) from La Panne at midday on May 30th, asking again for no more men or ammunition, but for water for the troops at Dunkirk.

Operation 'Dynamo' for the evacuation of the BEF and its allies from Dunkirk was not primarily a transport commitment for the Corps, but there was a call for the carriage of foodstuffs, water and stores to the ports of disembarkation, and for the provision of reserves of troop-carrying transport (in this case hired motor coaches) at certain centres. In the event, most of the returning troops were moved by rail and the transport service was not stretched.

The Corps could then take stock of its losses. In men these were grievous enough but not, all things considered, unduly high. In vehicles, however, nearly the whole of the Army's equipment had been left behind, most of it having been immobilized or destroyed first. Similarly, all mobile and heavy workshop equipment was lost.

The Threat of Invasion

The next and most pressing tasks were to equip the troops deployed along our coasts to repel the now expected invasion, particularly in the south and south-east, and to render mobile such fighting formations of the former BEF as could be equipped.

The first task called for the employment of every available armed man and of the few guns left in this country. As far as the Corps was concerned, the newly formed mobilization centres and the training brigades and Officer Producing Unit assumed an operational role in their localities, the most important of which were in the Isle of Thanet, at Bournemouth and in the possible paratroop dropping areas of Aldershot and Salisbury Plain. The troops were eager and willing, and they were reasonably well supplied with small arms, including light automatics, but ammunition was scarce throughout the country.

Similarly, in the case of artillery, ST 3 equipped a number of Royal Marine detachments with 6-ton lorries hurriedly adapted for the carriage of 12-pounder guns. They also helped Western Command in its task of defending some 250 miles of coastline by giving them lorries adapted for the drawing of their seven field guns.

But more practical measures were taking shape. The defence plan was based on a thin screen holding the coast line, with a mobile and fairly hard hitting reserve held at strategical points, ready to rush to any threatened spot. These reserves were composed of the less disorganized and depleted divisions from the BEF, who were given high priority in the replacement of equipment. Re-equipment was by no means complete, especially in artillery, but some sort of fighting force was scraped together.

The fiat then went forth, from the Prime Minister himself, that a sufficient lift in motor transport for some 70,000 infantrymen must be forthcoming in a fortnight from about June 10th. This led to the impressment of coaches, already referred to in the General survey. There were several interesting features in this hurried operation. First, the order came on a Friday, when the War Office 'Financial Authority' concerned was enjoying a long week-end off. Nobody could be found to agree to the expenditure of the necessary money, and the 'Financial Authority' was duly shocked on the following Monday to learn that he would have to foot a bill of £2,500,000 odd. But he played up nobly. So, too, did the Ministry of Transport and, even more so, the teams of inspectors and impressment officers. The War Establishment Committee passed a special establishment for a 'Motor Coach Company, RASC', with a headquarters and three sections, each of 30 32-seater coaches, providing a lift, per section, of the marching personnel for an infantry battalion. A 10 per cent reserve of coaches was provided in each company and instead of a workshop section there was a small complement of fitters with hand tools.

Although many coaches of dubious age and fitness were to be found in the total complement (there is more than a suspicion that large numbers of first class up-to-date machines were withheld from inspection), the establishments were passed, the vehicles were collected, the companies were formed and in their locations, and the reserve force was mobile in 11 days—a striking effort sometimes overlooked by those who had to sit in, or, worse still, operate the coaches.

Meanwhile the overworked CIST and his staff were also impressing vehicles for the re-equipment of the rest of the Army, and the Ministry of Supply was striving to step up new production for the same purpose. This new production came from factories both in the United Kingdom and, in increasing numbers, in Canada and the United States. North America sent a quota direct to the Middle East, and the large vehicle assembly plant at Ataka, near Suez, came into being. At first vehicles were shipped singly, 'knocked down' in crates. Later, as the need to conserve tonnage grew and the skill of the assembly gangs increased, multiple unit packs were used, components for four complete vehicles being in many cases shipped in a group of crates with a great saving in shipping space.

While the anti-invasion measures were being completed on the ground as far as resources permitted, the threat of attack from the air, which would precede any landing of ground troops, had to be met. The Anti-Aircraft Command organization was by now complete though not at the full strength to which it later attained. But there was another commitment for the Corps. The use by the Luftwaffe of parachuted mines led to the formation of the Land Incident Company, which worked under Admiralty control, and whose exploits have been mentioned already.

The Battle of Britain

The Battle of Britain and the subsequent night bombing offensive against London gave much emergency work to RASC transport companies. They removed débris, delivered water to areas whose supply had been cut off, removed the homeless, and made themselves generally useful. Usually re-mobilized formation transport was made available for these duties.

August 24th, 1940, saw the first night bombing of London. Nobody, it may be supposed, enjoys being bombed, though familiarity may breed contempt. But the effect of enemy raids on movement generally was considerable, and there were indeed times when the safe arrival at one's place of duty could be counted an achievement. For a spell the raids were a daily occurrence both by day and by night, and provided a handicap to work which may by now be nearly forgotten. Apart from the extra work thrown on headquarters of commands, formations, etc., road transport was necessarily inflicted with very severe lighting restrictions so that, while movement by night was still possible, it could only be done at a slow pace and at the cost of much fatigue to the driver.

ST 3 could congratulate themselves, for their old offices received a direct hit a few days after they had been moved, protesting strongly, from the War Office building to QMG House nearby. This was only one of many hits on the War Office which displayed unexpected powers of absorption of high explosive. Although the adjoining 'Queen Anne' building in Whitehall Place was totally wrecked, QMG House escaped all but minor damage.

ST 3 was concerned in certain emergency plans for the evacuation of the War Office from London in the event of invasion forces overrunning or directly threatening the city, or of the bombing becoming impossibly severe. These plans luckily never had to be put to the test.

The growth of the RASC led to increasing demands on the vehicle reserve depots, the MT store depots and the heavy repair shops. The first two types of unit were increased to three of each (at Feltham, Slough, and Ashchurch). The HRS was not so easy to duplicate or triplicate owing to its requirements in machinery and skilled workers, but a site at Ashford, near Feltham, which had been acquired for an extension of the VRD, Feltham, was converted into a new HRS, while an entirely new shop was set up, on a smaller scale, in requisitioned premises at High Wycombe. These three shops, with a further one which had been opened in Northern Ireland, coped with the load at home, with the help of the Ministry of Supply 'Army Auxiliary Workshops', which were civil workshops run under Ministry of Supply control for the repair of B and RASC vehicles at home. These AAWs grew out of the hundreds of works, large and small, which were harnessed by the Ministry in 1940 to the rapid overhaul of vehicles for the unequipped BEF after its return from the Continent. They were a great help, receiving repairable vehicles and engines direct from the Army and returning the overhauled ones, in the case of the RASC, to VRDs and MTSDs. (A heavy repair shop, RASC, it may be noted, was calculated basically to provide an overhaul service for a fleet of 4,000 vehicles, but it had a flexible organization capable of great expansion by the addition of one or more increments of men and tools.)

The MTSDs did not each have a provision office, submitting separate demands on the Ministry of Supply. To save overheads a Central Provision Office was set up, at Molesey, which co-ordinated the demands from all MTSDs, adjusting stocks where desirable in the case of home MTSDs. This was a great economy, introduced at the suggestion of Colonel E. Watts Allen, a stores expert who gave his services as a voluntary and unpaid stores adviser to the QMG in both world wars. Colonel Allen also introduced an extremely simplified accounting system into the MTSDs which, by using one copy of a unit's demand as an issue voucher in due course, saved thousands of man-hours in clerical effort and, literally, reams of paper. His system of maintaining a check on stocks and of automatic warning when fresh ordering was due, and of follow up action on uncompleted demands were all of enormous assistance in keeping the MTSD's service to home and overseas theatres a model of efficiency and quickness.

Reorganization of RASC Transport Units

The importance of these technical units in the RASC organization may be realized from a glance at the numbers of vehicles in the service. In the First World War the Corps operated about 90,000 load carriers and 35,000 light vehicles and motorcycles. At the end of the Second World War the number of B and RASC vehicles in depots and units was nearly 1,500,000, and of those with units roughly 40 per cent were in the hands of the RASC.

This immense fleet owed much of its existence to the Canadian and the United States motor industries. As the war progressed an ever growing proportion of our vehicles was of North American origin, and we, as a corps, were dependent for our life-blood, our vehicles, largely on the operation of the lend-lease scheme.

The growth of the Corps in numbers and types of units tended to a somewhat chaotic collection of 'companies', 'sections' and 'sub-sections' of varying strengths, particularly in the case of sub-units. War establishments were 'tailor made' to suit each individual unit, and standardization was a secondary consideration. In 1941 a start was made on a complete reorganization of the transport units of the Corps, adopting as sub-units the platoon and section, almost exactly comparable in size to the infantry platoon and section, thus producing a unit whose size was immediately appreciated by officers (especially staff officers) of other arms, and one, moreover, which could be switched readily to an infantry role when required.

The section was composed of seven vehicles, with a section commander mounted normally on a motorcycle. The platoon consisted of a headquarters which included a platoon officer, a platoon sergeant and a fitter and four sections. The total strength of the platoon was 30 vehicles. This platoon was not only the exact counterpart of the infantry platoon but also, if equipped with 3-ton lorries, it could carry in one lift the marching portion of an infantry battalion. This made troop carrying a simple matter to plan and execute.

If a second driver was required on each vehicle, the platoon remained unaltered but was given a 'relief driver increment'. As the advantages of the system made themselves apparent, platoons of supply and petrol men were formed, or, for commodity companies such as supply companies and petrol companies of formation RASCs, 'composite' platoons were adopted which included men of various trades. But the platoon remained of its calculated size, or very nearly so. Mobile workshops were similarly organized on a platoon basis.

The company consisted of a headquarters, one or more workshop platoons, and as many transport platoons and composite platoons as were necessary for it to fulfil its role. Where, as in a division, armoured division, army corps, lines of communication or base area, a number of RASC companies were required to perform the RASC duties for a formation or area, these companies were grouped into a 'column' under a CRASC, the column being the equivalent of a battalion in the infantry. The term 'column' was a timely revival of the early nomenclature for grouped ASC companies.

This new organization, which remained in being after the war, received a warm welcome not only from the RASC but particularly from the Staff Duties branch of the War Office and from the War Establishments Committee, whose labours were considerably simplified thereby.

The course of the war in 1941 was not favourable to the Allies. The German attack on Russia led to an additional load on the British producers of tanks and vehicles, while the Japanese assault on Pearl Harbour in December of that year meant (as did the American entry into the First World War in 1917) a partial cessation of the supplies of American vehicles.

Reorganization of the MT Maintenance System

The operations in the Middle East, with their waxing and waning success, constituted a serious drain on the Army's resources in men and material, in which the RASC was heavily involved, and much anxious thought was given to the maintenance of the flow of vehicles from North America to the Middle East. All this was initiated and co-ordinated by the transport branch at the War Office.

Towards the end of the year difficulties arose over the supply of technical manpower to the three fighting services. Industry, under constant urge to increase output, became alarmed at the drain on their human resources as the increasing complexity and amount of technical equipment in the hands of the three services led to ever increasing demands for the call up of skilled men to maintain this equipment. A feeling was evident that some waste of this skilled manpower was occurring. Eventually a committee was set up under the chairmanship of Sir William (later Lord) Beveridge, on which sat representatives of the Ministry of Labour and National Service and of the trade unions. Their duties were to examine the numbers of skilled workers in each of the three services, to ascertain if there was any overlap in their duties and, if so, to make recommendations for their more economical use.

As far as the Army was concerned, senior officers of the RE, RASC and RAOC branches at the War Office were examined, and the committee paid visits to the technical establishments of all three corps. They also took note of the numbers of skilled men serving in all arms, including the RAC, RA and R Sigs, as well as in the main technical corps concerned.

It may fairly be claimed that the RASC emerged well from this examination in the matter of skilled men required for, say, every 100 'lorry units', except for the number of driver-mechanics carried on the war establishment of transport units. Rightly or wrongly, the Corps had always regarded its driver-mechanics as very much drivers first and mechanics, generally, only on occasion. They were mainly used on first echelon maintenance, in the sub-unit, and had little part in the workshop platoons or the heavy repair shops, being as their name implied, essentially drivers.

But the committee, with their great urge for economies in technicians, did not see things in this light. Even had they done so, the time had come when separate RASC and RAOC (and to a lesser extent RE) workshops doing much work of a similar nature on three separate systems could no longer be tolerated (the RE with two echelons of repair, the unit and workshop, the RASC with three, the sub-unit, the company workshop and the heavy repair shop, and the RAOC with four, the unit, divisional workshop, the third echelon shop and the base workshop). The Beveridge Committee, while leaving the Royal Navy and the Royal Air Force comparatively free from criticism, were strong in recommending the rationalization of the Army's system, to bring provision and maintenance of spares stocks and repair under one head.

The Army Council lost little time in appointing a strong committee to make detailed proposals for the implementation of the Beveridge Committee's plans. The members of the committee were Lieut-General Sir Ronald Weeks, a Territorial officer who had been DQMG(AE) at the War Office before advancement to the post of Deputy Chief of the Imperial General Staff, Sir Robert Sinclair, a high executive and later chairman of the Imperial Tobacco Company, who had been lent to the War Office to be Director General of Army Requirements, and Mr. A. W. Dunkley, a director of the Anglo-Iranian Oil Company and a member of the Petroleum Board. They produced a scheme whereby the RE workshops were to confine themselves to processes connected with their civil engineering role, the repair and maintenance of electrical and mechanical equipment leaving their hands, the RASC were to give up the provision, storage and issue of their own vehicles and spare parts, and the heavy repair (outside their workshops platoons which they were to retain) of their vehicles, and the RAOC, while acquiring full responsibility for vehicle and spare part provision, storage and issue, were to give up the whole of their engineering side and to cease to be responsible for the repair of their own or other arms' equipment, from guns to bicycles. To bear this immense combined inspection and repair load for all arms, a new corps was to be formed, combining the technical elements of the RE, RASC and RAOC. This was to be called the Corps of Royal Electrical and Mechanical Engineers. For the present, the RAC, RA, RE and R Sigs would retain their technical men engaged on maintenance within their units, and the RASC would retain the men in their transport and workshop platoons. As a second phase, when opportunity offered, the whole of the remaining technicians and their functions would pass to the new corps.

Naturally, the Corps were dismayed. They had provided, maintained and repaired their own fleet of vehicles almost without a break from the earliest days of motor transport 40 years before, and had built up a sound, well tried organization which had never failed. They had seen failure or partial failure in other organizations, and now they were to be called upon to break up this organization, intimately interwoven in the fabric of the Corps, and to depend on other corps for the provision and repair of their primary 'weapon', the vehicle. (That other arms had been so dependent for years was very little consolation.) They would lose a considerable, though not a preponderant, part of their organization, and the future seemed black.

The Army Council adopted the report *in toto*, and ordered its immediate implementation, in essence as from May, 1942, and in fact from October 1st, 1942, when the new repairing corps would officially come into being.

By this decision the RE lost a handful of technicians, the RASC lost the 'provision' sub-branch of ST 3, all its VRDs and its MTSDs to the RAOC and all its HRSs to the REME, altogether perhaps about one tenth of its strength. The RAOC lost the whole of its engineering branch, some 60 per cent of its strength, to the REME, whose initial make-up was about 1 per cent ex-RE, 4 per cent ex-RASC and 95 per cent ex-RAOC.

To form and direct the new corps, Brigadier E. B. Rowcroft, DDST in charge of ST 3, was promoted major-general and ordered to assume his new duties in a week's time. He took with him from ST 3 such staff as were employed on heavy repair or workshop matters. The remainder of the technical portion of ST 3 were transferred to the Directorate of Warlike Stores, where Colonel H. C. Goodfellow became the head of WS 6 branch. He took with him about 12 officers and 30 other ranks and, with those of the RAOC already on the job, became responsible for the vehicle and MT stores activities relating to the whole Army. It is interesting to recall that the reliefs for both General Rowcroft, as DME, and for Colonel Goodfellow, as DDWS in WS 6, were also RASC officers.

Outside the War Office, all VRDs, MTSDs and HRSs throughout the world were handed over, together with their men, to the RAOC for vehicle and stores work or to the REME for repair work. The number of officers and men who had to change their cap badges may not have appeared great, but there was a great change in the RASC outlook, and it is a matter of great credit to those who took part that the transfer was effected smoothly and loyally.

Contrary to the expectations of the more gloomy, the new division of responsibilities amongst the RE, RASC, RAOC and REME did not spell disaster. All the older corps were co-operative in their attitude to the newcomer, and with this co-operation came vigorous growth for the REME. But the RASC suffered nevertheless, because in its original form it had enjoyed what was, in effect, a favoured position among the users of motor transport by reason of its store of experience, its perfected methods of stocking and distributing vehicles and spares, and the intense 'unit pride' of its workshops. Justification for the change may be found in the fact that the benefits of this 'most favoured' situation were now spread more evenly over the whole service, with loss of efficiency in vehicle administration (for lack of a better term) in the Corps and a corresponding gain in other arms. This was poor consolation.

Plans for return to the Offensive

Operationally, the first half of 1942 was still disastrous overseas, with the retreat of the Eighth Army to the Alamein line, the loss of Hong Kong, Singapore and Malaya, and the overrunning of Burma, but at home preparations were in hand for launching two offensive enterprises, both entailing amphibious assaults. These were the minor operation for the snatching of Madagascar from Vichy French control, and the much larger and more ambitious plan for the invasion of North Africa, operation 'Torch'.

The Corps were closely concerned with the waterproofing of vehicles for both these operations. The question of amphibious operations had been studied at the Combined Operations training centres in Scotland and, later, at a Combined Operations experimental establishment (COXE) which was set up at Westward Ho! in Devon. These were 'all arms' establishments, with strong RASC representation.

Methods of waterproofing were considered initially by manufacturers working with the Ministry of Supply, and practicable schemes were prepared in time for application in both these early operations. In general, military teams or individuals were instructed at firms' works in the schemes applicable to each maker's products and, on return to their units, these men were responsible for instructing their fellows. The results proved that they performed their duties satisfactorily and that the schemes were suitable for somewhat limited application under favourable conditions.

But time showed that these methods, with their great variation in regard to different makes of vehicle, and with the types of materials then available, had two great drawbacks. One was the difficulty of application of the various methods, including difficulty of manipulation of some of the plastic materials used. The other was the deterioration of the waterproof qualities of the materials during any appreciable time of storage.

In 1943 the responsibility for the preparation of waterproofing schemes for all vehicles and armaments, including those of the RASC, passed to the REME, and standardized or near-standardized methods were adopted. Their application remained the duty of the user units, except in the case of other arms destined for the assault force for operation 'Overlord' itself. At a later date these principles were extended to the South-East Asia Command, which had a number of amphibious projects in view. The record of the waterproofing and of the landing of RASC units in Normandy, under most unfavourable conditions, both in respect of weather and of enemy opposition, is a tribute to the good work done by vehicle crews and workshops beforehand.

The amphibian duties of the RASC grew from the early days of combined operations until the Corps operated dukws and Terrapins, in the wheeled category, and Buffaloes and Weasels in the tracked. In 1943 an Amphibious Training Centre was set up at Towyn in North Wales, where all ranks received instruction. The amphibious companies were based on GT company war establishments, and could revert to a GT role when not required for special operations. The exploits of these companies are mentioned in the chapters dealing with each campaign and in the chapter on RASC activities. It must suffice here to mention that the dukw was a converted United States General Motors standard six-wheeled drive $2\frac{1}{2}$-ton truck, with an astonishing degree of sea-worthiness and of reliability, though naturally much time had to be given to maintenance. It was both wheel and propeller driven. An amphibious jeep was also produced on somewhat similar lines and was used in limited numbers. The other wheeled amphibian, the Terrapin, was a British product, sponsored by the Ministry of Supply and built by Messrs. J. I. Thornycroft. It had the same capacity as the dukw, was an 8-wheeler with four wheels normally in contact with the ground, and had, like the dukw, propeller drive. An interesting feature was that the Terrapin had two engines, one driving each 'side', and steering was effected by a combined throttle which reduced speed on one set of wheels, and increased speed on the other. This was a reversion to the steering system in the 'Whippet' tank of the First World War! The Terrapin had not come into full production before the end of the war, and almost all of the wheeled amphibian work of the Corps was done by dukws.

Of the tracked carriers, the Buffalo was a large capacity lightly armoured machine built on tank hull lines, with a track of light construction and a propeller drive for sea work. It had a good performance in water and on mud, and a fairly high freeboard. It could carry three tons of stores or 24 infantrymen in full fighting equipment. It was particularly valuable in the Pacific and would have been so in SEAC had opportunity offered. The Weasel was a small tracked machine of very light construction, with very little freeboard. It was thus handicapped in a sea-way, but had an amazing performance in mud, marshes or still water. It was used in Europe, and would have been excellent on the mud of estuaries and in mangrove swamps in the Far East.

The period 1941–1943 saw the increasing use of the ATS companies to run transport units and VRD convoys at home, and the emergence of the mixed station transport companies to which reference has already been made earlier in this chapter.

Airborne operations now promised to assume important proportions, and the setting up of centres for RASC airborne and air despatch units' training was undertaken in 1941 and 1942, the tempo being stepped up in 1943. The work of the air despatch and airborne units is discussed in the chapter devoted to them and in the narratives of the campaigns in which they operated.

During this period, too, the strength of the Corps in tank transporter companies increased steadily to match our growing strength in armour. Most of these units were equipped with United States 'Diamond T' tractors and Rogers or Crane multi-wheeled trailers. The purchase of these tractors and of a quota of the trailers built in America was fortunately put through before the big switch of American production to meet the needs of the American army was fully felt. The companies did excellent service, first in the Middle East and in North Africa, where they not only carried live tanks into battle but also met an urgent need for tank recovery vehicles at a time when few others were available. Later, in North-West Europe, they assumed for a time the role of super-heavy transport vehicles to move stores and supplies forward in bulk from Normandy to the Low Countries.

A new spirit was now in the air. The year 1942, which had opened with apparent disaster everywhere for the Allies, ended on a rising note of victory—in the Middle East, at Stalingrad and in North Africa. Great Britain, too, had long respites from appreciable air attack, though there was to be a sharp recrudescence of Luftwaffe activity in the early months of 1943. This year (1943) continued the tale of victory in North Africa, with the Middle East freed from threat and Malta relieved, Sicily occupied by us, Italy successfully invaded, and with active preparations afoot for the assumption of the offensive in North-West Europe and in South-East Asia.

Aid to Russia assumed large proportions from 1942 onwards, not only by direct shipments to Archangel and Murmansk from British ports but also through the Persian lines of communication to the Russians in the Caspian Sea area. The operation of the latter route was, of course, the responsibility of the Middle East or of Paiforce, but the former threw a considerable load on ST 3 and on the home VRDs. Though, indeed, hard pressed at this time to provide our own forces with their vehicles, Aid to Russia was

Her Majesty the Queen when Princess Elizabeth

Convoy on the Road

Right:
Field-Marshal Montgomery presenting the Military Medal to Dvr. G. E. Callaghan

Below:
H.R.H. The Duke of Gloucester, Colonel-in-Chief, R.A.S.C., presenting the Military Medal to Cpl. J. O. Sheed

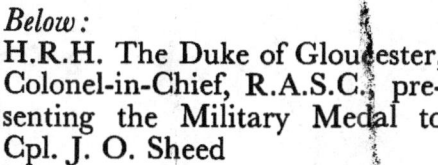

A.T.S. Convoy—Halt for Lunch

given a very high priority. It was felt in the War Office that many things could be done to the vehicles before despatch, calculated to help the Russians to operate them more easily on arrival at the North Russian ports, where temperatures were far below anything in the experience of British manufacturers or of the British Army. ST 2 devised special oils of very low viscosity which were also used for our vehicles in Norway earlier. Frantic efforts were made to ascertain what form of anti-freeze, if any, would be of use, and consideration was given to providing batteries of higher voltage than normal to facilitate easy starting, though this last proposal never reached fruition.

After some months ST 3 were anxious to find out how these lorries, which were of Bedford make, were behaving, and a questionnaire was sent to our Russian allies. One question naturally referred to their ability to start their engines in temperatures of minus 30 degrees Fahrenheit, and mild surprise was registered when the Russian reply told us that they had no difficulty whatever in starting and warming up their engines because they always lit a fire underneath them beforehand!

The latter part of 1943 and the early months of 1944 were periods of intense preparation of formations and units for participation in the coming invasion of Normandy. The vehicles of all the assault formations and of the follow-up formations had to be put into first class mechanical condition and then to be waterproofed. The operating crews had to be taught the technique of waterproofing and of driving through deep water. As a 'target' they and their vehicles had to be prepared for at least six minutes' immersion in salt water 5 feet deep, with a 'wave height' of 18 inches, and they had, moreover, after landing, to know how to de-waterproof their vehicles immediately and to carry on with their transport tasks without a break. All this kept our training centres and our formation transport companies fully stretched while, superimposed on their normal full time programme, the home transport companies were given the heavy task of moving and delivering the numerous articles of equipment required by units preparing for the invasion and by the concentration and embarkation areas which were being prepared in southern England.

While all this was in train, the threat of the V weapons had to be met. It was known that a pilotless aircraft and a heavy rocket had both been nearly perfected by the enemy, but the speed of approach and the range of these weapons were not accurately known, nor, although their 'breeding ground' at Peenemunde had been heavily raided and damaged, could the date of their launch to the attack be exactly foretold. The intensity of the attack was known to be designed to wipe out, in a few weeks, the area of London from which the government of the country and the direction of the war was conducted, and elaborate transport plans had therefore been drawn up for the orderly evacuation of all those engaged on this work (save for a few who could be given adequate shelter). The strict secrecy in which these things were very sensibly veiled did nothing to ease the task of the planners, but, long before the threat came to a head on June 13th, 1944, all plans had been perfected.

Happily, the defensive measures taken, the destruction of launching sites and of the facilities for the transportation of the weapons thereto, the fighter and AA defences, and the alertness of the fire fighting and rescue organizations, reduced the attack to manageable proportions and, once again, ST 3 could, with a sigh of relief (echoed by many others), file away their emergency plan unused.

Exactly a week before the first V 1 fell in Sussex ('I saw the bastard fall, his tail was properly afire!', a Sussex publican was heard to exclaim triumphantly), the landings in Normandy took place, and the months of preparatory work came to fruition. The task in the United Kingdom, for the transport side of the RASC, became one of moving the stores required for transit to Normandy, of raising additional transport units for the reinforcement of BLA in its almost rail-less lines of communication, of raising further transport units for service with the Air Despatch Group, and of organizing the direction of this Group from the War Office. On top of these commitments came a little later the inevitable call for transfer of officers and men to the infantry.

On the credit side, however, the commitments in trained drivers could be forecast on a diminishing scale and to meet them and these additional loads, resort was had to the training brigades and mobilization centres, which were becoming in part redundant. So, with the help of the ATS and of our hired civilian drivers, our heads were kept above water.

From October, 1944, until the end of the war there was little change in the transport position at home. The training brigades continued to run down and to be disbanded, the transport companies in commands were able, without the aid of the departed formations' transport, to meet the requirements of the depleted commands, the V weapon counter measures were no longer actively operating and AA Command enjoyed a welcome freedom from its continuous labours of the preceding five years. (It is not generally realized that, during the whole period from September, 1939, until May, 1945, the defences of Great Britain were, somewhere, in almost ceaseless action. If it was not attack from the air it was attack from the sea or from the heavy coastal batteries in the Channel.)

The obvious approach of the end on the Continent, however, spelt no relaxation for our fighting formations because of the continued resistance of the Japanese. Elaborate plans were laid for the re-deployment of formations from the Middle East, Italy and North-West Europe to carry out what promised to be a series of coast hopping operations from Malaya to Hong Kong. The sudden collapse of Japan on August 15th, 1945, hastened by but not wholly attributable to the dropping of the first two atomic bombs to be employed in warfare, stopped the execution of these plans, to the general relief, and so the tale of the RASC effort in respect of transport at home comes to its end.

Looking back on this effort one is conscious of the great debt owed to the planners of pre-war days—the small team of officers in ST 3 which was led by Colonel Fitzherbert (later Major-General E. H. Fitzherbert, Inspector RASC). Their sound appreciation of what would be required, and for their well directed efforts, at a time of financial stringency which only eased (for the fighting services) in the last few months before the war, to put the system of procurement of new, and utilization of existing, resources on the best possible lines.

The standard of vehicle maintenance in the Corps, too, stands out as an important factor in the sustained mobility of our forces, backed up as it was in the initial years by a provision and maintenance system second to none.

It will have been noted that, since the days of 'divisionalization' increasing attention had been paid to the military training of the RASC officer and soldier. This paid handsome dividends, for the increased use of armoured forces, the disappearance of the old 'front line' of trench warfare, the liability of rearward areas to airborne and seaborne attacks as well as to aerial bombardment, the employment on our part of independent raiding forces such as the Long Range Penetration Group in the Middle East and the Chindits in Burma, the place of the Corps in amphibious assaults and airborne operations and, finally, the temporary adoption in all theatres of war and at home of an infantry role by many units of the Corps all depended for their success on the qualities of the RASC officer and man (particularly in transport units) as soldiers first and foremost.

The future is obscure, the shape of formations and, particularly the proportions between 'teeth' and 'tail', will doubtless be profoundly affected by the advent of atomic weapons, the development of airborne forces, developments in pilotless aircraft and guided missiles, but if the Corps' traditions of preparedness and service remain at the same high level as during the war years the transport services of the Army will not be found wanting.

SUPPLIES

The System of Supply

The preparations which were made by QMG 6 before the war were necessarily limited in their scope. The reserves of food which had been acquired were only sufficient for filling the supply pipeline to the BEF and for part of the additional reserves required by the principal commands overseas. The organization in the commands at home for supplying the Army and RAF after mobilization was only a nucleus, and additional accommodation for holding War Office reserves was still under construction when war broke out.

The maintenance of the Army at home and abroad once war was declared was therefore largely dependent on how quickly pre-war plans for supply would be effective. These plans were based on the Army being able to procure most of the staple commodities wanted from the Ministry of Food which was to be created if war came and on dormant contracts, made by the War Office contracts departments, with selected firms in the food industry for other foodstuffs required.

Thanks to the work of the Food Defence Plans Department the system of supply, distribution and accounting for the staple foods which the Government intended to supply had been settled in detail. The department had arranged that certain commodities would be provided by special agencies which were appointed before the war to look after the Services' needs and in other cases supply was to be through trade organizations acting on behalf of the future Ministry of Food. The arrangements made worked so well when the time came that they made normal methods of procurement by contract unduly cumbrous.

There is no doubt that the success with which ST 6 were able to feed the peak strength of nearly eight million mouths at the height of the war was largely due to the help and assistance of the Ministry in meeting every demand made on them so efficiently and expeditiously.

The home commands had prepared detailed plans for expanding their organization by setting up new depots and complementary NAAFI stores. Some of these depots were to be established in the anti-aircraft mobilization stores, which held the equipment for the ADGB in peace, and which were to be cleared on mobilization. They were ideal for the purpose. Other sites had to be acquired or requisitioned after war broke out. But this took time, and there was some delay before NAAFI were able to man and stock their new depots as many of their men were reservists and were withdrawn from them when war was declared. This eventuality had, however, been foreseen and units which could not be supplied in kind were given a special rate of cash allowance to purchase their food from civil shops.

As soon as war was declared, the partly finished depot for holding War Office reserves (No. 2 SRD at Barry, in Wales) was taken into use and construction work hastened, as although the existing depot at Deptford was adequate for immediate needs, its location was thought to be so vulnerable that it was to be cleared and shut down as soon as possible. Plans for a third SRD, located at Taunton, were also hastened, and work on construction began at once.

The first important war measure was taken by ST 6 two days before war was declared, when authority was sought for their first order, for 30,000 tons of food, to be put into production. It seemed to be a large quantity, but it had soon to be followed by two further orders, and by early 1940 the total demand had risen to 100,000 tons, exclusive of the everyday needs of the Army at home which were being supplied by the Ministry of Food and NAAFI. It soon became clear that the Army's requirements would have to be forecast for over a year or more ahead, so as to give the food industry the necessary opportunities for advance planning and developing their productive capacity. This resulted in the placing of long term orders for as much as twelve months' supply at a time.

Although calculating the amount of food which would be required was theoretically a matter of multiplying so many men by given scales of food, in practice the business of forecasting depended on various factors, few of which were necessarily firm, and some only conjectures, as the course of the war changed so considerably. Forecasting was an art and not a science and was one of the most important duties which had to be performed by the supply service both at the War Office and at the headquarters of all the theatres of war. Inaccurate or unintelligent forecasting could only lead to a crisis—a crisis of not having enough or of having too much—to waste of shipping, and to all the attendant evils of over-provision.

Even if there had been only one ration scale for the whole of the Army, it would have been a difficult matter, but account had to be taken of many basic scales, as it was no uncommon thing for a single command overseas to have to design and administer up to as many as 50 different scales to cater for the needs of the many nations which formed part of the British Army. There was, however, no known case of loss occurring through inaccurate forecasting, although there were some near shaves caused by unexpected changes in operational plans.

Sources of Supply

Although the first war demands made by the services were fulfilled smoothly, the outbreak of war was followed by a violent dislocation of world shipping routes and many normal sources of supply dried up almost immediately. Some neutral countries were cut off owing to their proximity to enemy territory, others adopted an unfriendly attitude through fear or leaning towards the future Axis, and the unexpected need for conserving certain currency barred other countries which were a fruitful source of supply. At the same time strong pressure was brought to divert exports from neutral countries which were normally drawn upon by the enemy.

Source of supply was primarily a national question, but the Army had to play its part by helping in exploiting sources which had hitherto been untapped because of economic or other reasons, particularly in connection with the maintenance of the Middle East and Far East.

The southern Dominions, with their vast resources in agricultural and dairy produce, had, of course, always been drawn on for such commodities as meat and grain, but their capacity for producing manufactured foods, and especially the types of packing needed for service use, was limited. India, with its huge population, had its own problems and could contribute little more than the special foods which were required for the Indian formations which had begun to land in the Middle East and Malaya. The first call on South Africa was to be the maintenance of the army which was to be employed in East Africa. Canada could not be drawn upon to any extent owing to its geographical position and currency. The resources of the Middle East countries, although extensive, were limited to certain foods, and industrial capacity was low.

All commands abroad were fully aware of the need for developing their own local resources and reducing the demands on home to a minimum. But time was required before the situation could be fully explored and countries encouraged to acquire the requisite skill and plant needed, and the necessary arrangements made to switch imports to countries which had productive capacity but which lacked the raw materials required. Thus the United Kingdom remained the main source of supply of certain commodities for the Middle and Far East and was the main base for supplying most of the requirements for North Africa, Italy and North-West Europe.

The food industry at home had developed considerably since the First World War, but even at the outbreak of the Second World War it was in some respects a young industry when compared, for example, with that of the United States. No doubt it was the outcome of the notable British preference for 'fresh' food, so that the Services' huge demands for manufactured foods placed a considerable strain on productive capacity and on the industries which provided the cans and packages required. Thanks to the foresight of the largest firm of tin box makers, extra plant had been installed for can production before the war, but still was scarce and with the fall of Malaya tin plate had to be replaced by untinned ('black plate') for anything which could be safely packed in that type of can. The capacity for producing outer packages, mostly wood, was great, but supplies of seasoned timber became scarce. Eventually timber cases had to be replaced by fibre for which materials were also 'short'. The adoption of fibre package considerably increased because of the high rate of breakage which occurred as the result of shipping and handling under war conditions. Even nails at one time were scarce, and there were few materials which were not subject to complicated systems of determining priorities and allocating supplies accordingly. It was often a question of having to replace one material by another only to find that the alternative also came into 'short supply'.

The development of the food manufacturing industry abroad was also naturally accompanied by similar difficulties to those at home.

The extent to which commands could develop resources in their immediate vicinity varied greatly. Stations such as Hong Kong, Gibraltar and Malta were almost entirely dependent on imports and were denied any resources which were available in neighbouring countries. Gibraltar was able to obtain some fresh produce but little else, and at one period in the war all supplies sent from home had to be packed in special damp-proof packing to withstand the humid conditions of the storage places in the Rock. There was little surplus over the needs of the civil population in Malta, and when the siege was intensified supplies from home had to be sent in such a form that they occupied the smallest amount of freight consonant with a high food value. Malaya, owing to its relative proximity to Australia and the presence of Australian troops in the country, was able to obtain a high proportion of its requirements from Australia until Singapore fell in February, 1942.

The Middle East had the greatest problem, as it covered so many countries and had the biggest feeding strength. The DST (General Goldney) made every effort to make the command nearly self-supporting. It was a big task, as the strength at the beginning of the war was only about 35,000 and rose to over a million. Long term contracts were made to encourage the local production of foods grown in the Nile Delta and adjoining countries for 12-monthly periods. The War Office arranged for other goods such as meat, flour and tinned fruits to be shipped from Australia and tea from Ceylon. The creation of the organization known as the Middle

East Supply Centre in Cairo, which was set up to meet the needs of local consumers and to exploit the export of surplus foods, allowed wider fields to be tapped and enabled the Army to obtain such foods as dried fruits, sugar, cereals and coffee in quantity. The large number of colonial troops of one nation and another which were employed in the command involved the importation or local procurement of all sorts of food which were peculiar to their tastes so that supply depots became veritable emporia. With the advent of Lease-Lend shipments of other foods were made from America, but even with these various sources of supply it was still necessary to draw on home resources to some extent.

The high proportion of West Africans in the forces in West Africa eased the supply position, as the greater part of their rations could be obtained on the spot, but the requirements of the British troops had to be imported from home, and the supply organization also had to cater for the Free French forces in the Chad and Cameroons areas. St. Helena was victualled from Royal Naval sources at Simonstown in South Africa, but the maintenance of such places as the Faroes, Iceland, the Falklands and many other small stations too numerous to mention had to rely on the United Kingdom for most of their needs.

With a return to the offensive and the planning of the main operations of the war, which were to be conducted in North Africa, Italy and North-West Europe, ST 6 became engaged in planning on an unprecedented scale. Where possible these plans took into account the feasability of arranging large shipments of supplies in bulk from other sources, but for the first period of the campaign all supplies had to be shipped from home, as the type of rations required (a mess tin ration and composite rations) had to be specially assembled and packed and shipped in accordance with tactical requirements. Reference is made in more detail later in this chapter to the effort involved in the designing and production of these special rations, but also vast quantities of commodities for the field ration required for the subsequent maintenance of the forces had to be built up. Thus over half a million tons of food were eventually shipped to North Africa, and the quantity handled and despatched for the operations which followed operation 'Overlord' amounted to 1,100,000 tons.

The Supply Reserve Depots

The physical effort of collecting, storing and despatching these large quantities of food rested largely on the War Office controlled depots, the SRDs, which were grouped under the CPO. It has already been stated that the original depot at Deptford on the Thames was scheduled for evacuation when the war broke out, but because of lack of accommodation elsewhere it had to be kept in being until September, 1940, when it was repeatedly bombed. There was little actual loss of stock by fire and destruction, for although the old site (a former cattle market) was congested it seemed to bear a charmed life. By this time a third depot had been completed at Taunton and a fourth depot, adapted from some existing accommodation at Swindon, had been opened. A new site was found at Glasgow, and the loyal civilian staff of Deptford volunteered to serve there.

The four big depots were sufficient for their purpose until 1941, when there was a complete upheaval caused by having to hand over the two specially designed depots at Barry and Taunton to the Americans under plan 'Bolero', and having to find alternative accommodation for the new reserves which were to be laid in for operations 'Torch' and 'Overlord'. This entailed a complete survey of all possible sites in the country, which was conducted with the aid of the storage and factory control department of the Board of Trade which, among other duties, was responsible for the concentration of non-essential industries to free accommodation for the war effort. One site after another was found, but it was a race against time, and at one stage it looked as if the production which was flowing from the food factories would outpace the rate at which storage accommodation was being made ready, as in many cases plant and machinery of the industrial sites which were being taken over had to be stripped and moved and various other alterations made before the sites could be occupied.

New depots were opened at Lancaster, Leeds, Purfleet and Osterley, and in some cases subsidiary accommodation was taken over for use as sub-depots in the vicinity. Another large depot was constructed at Steventon, and in 1944 the last to be opened was at Barby in the Midlands. It was a considerable achievement, as by the end of the war accommodation was provided for 360,000 tons.

Other Activities

The maintenance of North Africa and later Italy and North-West Europe went on the whole very smoothly, as by that time the technique of demand and supply between ST 6 at the War Office and their opposite numbers at the headquarters of the theatres of war had been highly developed and mutually understood. Supply for the operations contemplated by the South-East Asia Command was to be the responsibility of GHQ India, but in October, 1943, the DST India arrived home with a request for the provision of half a million '24-hour' rations in December and a quarter of a million monthly from January onwards. As the standard pack for this ration was not considered suitable for use in the Far East, a special 'jungle' ration was evolved, and the first deliveries of this new ration to India began in early 1944. The ration was subsequently modified, and a new series of Pacific packs was introduced which included some specially designed for Indian troops, the whole of the supply being arranged from home. The War Office had also to undertake the provision of supplies which could not be procured in India, and demands were then made direct by the headquarters of the Pacific Command on the War Office.

ST 6 had many other duties apart from procurement and the wide field of work connected with rations and rationing. One of the first questions which had to be explored was the reorganization of the supply system in the theatres of war. The experience of the BEF showed that the base supply depots were too big and inflexible, and the arrangements for providing all other types of depots required, such as DIDs, railhead supply detachments and other field supply depots, from a single unit were quite unworkable. The internal organization of BSDs was altered in such a way that they could be used singly or in groups. They were provided with their own transport specially designed for depot work and labour-saving equipment which could be used under field conditions. The supply personnel company was abolished and eventually replaced by a system of standard sized supply platoons, each self-contained and of such a size that they were easily adaptable for the various supply duties which they would have to perform. These platoons could, where necessary, be grouped together to form larger field depots, and suitable headquarters for both groups of BSDs and groups of DIDs were also provided for.

The arrangements for producing bread in the field were considerably improved by the introduction of mobile bakeries which were completely self-contained for transport, power and plant, could move quickly from place to place and come into action within a few hours of arrival at their site. The design and production were largely due to the willing co-operation of Messrs. Baker Perkins, and they were such a success that the same design was adopted by the American Army. The organization for providing frozen meat in the field underwent little change and perhaps lagged behind progress made in other directions. The supply of frozen meat for large numbers under field conditions and particularly in hot climates, was beset with certain drawbacks, as it involved the installation of large stores at bases, and the provision of rail or road refrigerator trucks, and the provision of some form of cool storage at every railhead or DID. Full use was made wherever possible of existing facilities in theatres of war, but it was rare to find that the requisite facilities for all three stages of distribution were available. Mobile, or rather movable, cold stores were designed which could be erected in the field, but their size was limited, and for various reasons there was often some delay before the whole of the parts and plant were shipped and could be erected.

Experiments had been conducted with providing refrigerator road vehicles, but these were not adopted as standard equipment, as the number of vehicles which would have been required was prohibitive, and as they were one-purpose vehicles only, it would have been an uneconomic proposition.

There were few dull moments in the life of the supply branches at the War Office and at the headquarters of the theatres of war overseas. As stated above they had to keep a continuous watch on the expected future strengths to be supplied, on the existing stock situation, and on the demands which had to be placed so many months ahead. At the same time they had to be prepared to meet any new commitment which might arise. Later in the war they had frequently to come to the rescue of the organizations for civil relief. In one theatre they had to 'lend' a matter of a million pounds of flour for the purpose. As the war turned in our favour they were frequently confronted with being asked whether they could feed some indeterminate number of expected prisoners of war. They had to produce new ration scales one after the other to provide for practically every nationality under the sun. They were also called upon for 'ration scales' for a variety of animals, other than horses and mules. They included dogs, pigeons and even guinea pigs. When the occasion demanded they supplied all and sundry whether the latter was some merchant ship which had temporarily run out of food or some new 'secret mission' which was to be set up in neutral territory.

Perhaps one of the strangest demands made in a certain theatre of war was a request to produce some French champagne and 'real' brandy for a very very important person who was expected on a visit. It was a request which was gladly met.

The Soldier's Ration

Pre-war Planning

The general plans made by the Food Defence Plans Department of the Board of Trade for ensuring the nation's food in war had to be based on the premise that as early war measures, the Government would assume control of all essential staple foods and introduce rationing if required. Consequently the arrangements for applying rationing to the Services had been discussed and agreed in some detail well before the war broke out. The view that a serviceman, by nature of his calling, required a higher scale of rations than the civilian was generally accepted, and it was agreed that rationing could only apply to the forces stationed in the United Kingdom. There was broad agreement that the service scales in force when war broke out would not be altered until rationing had to be introduced for the civil population.

It was not considered possible to discriminate between actively employed and sedentary troops because of the service system of communal messing and the difficulty of determining a dividing line between the two classes. The serviceman who lived out of barracks was to be permitted to purchase a scale of rations comparable to what he would receive if living in barracks.

The Services undertook to be responsible for the control of rationing arrangements within their own spheres. The forms of ration cards to be provided for those living out and on leave were approved and supplies of ration cards were already printed by the time war came.

It seemed to the War Office that rationing was a subject which had been satisfactorily planned, but later events proved it to be the most uncertain question that had to be dealt with.

The Food Policy Committee

Contrary to expectations, no steps were taken by the Government to introduce rationing in the first few weeks of the war. No doubt the unnatural lull in operations during 1939 had something to do with this, and it was not until the newly appointed Minister of Food urged upon the Government the necessity for taking immediate steps to ration meat that the subject received any prominence. National food policy was the responsibility of a special sub-committee of the Cabinet. Although the plea of the Minister of Food was rejected, the Services were invited by the Food Policy Committee to examine how they could reduce their demands on what were represented as dwindling national meat stocks. This request was the beginning of what the supply branch at the War Office later referred to as 'the Battle for the Soldier's Ration'. From September, 1939 until 1941, and indeed after the war was over, the question devolved into a triangular but unequal contest, with the Services on the one side endeavouring to maintain the standards which they considered essential and, on the other, the Government, who urged that ration scales should be reduced, and especially the Treasury, who sought to reduce the mounting cost of feeding the forces.

The serviceman's ration was a matter of considerable importance to all three services. It was the direct concern of the three chief administrative officers, the Fourth Sea Lord, the Quarter-Master-General and the Air Member for Supply and Organization, to make certain that their men were as well fed and contented as possible and that morale was maintained at the highest level.

The brunt of the detailed work which arose from rationing and ration scales fell naturally on the supply branch at the War Office, who had to provide for the largest body and also provided the food required by the Royal Air Force. The supply branch acted as the co-ordinating branch from a service angle. As will be seen later the means of co-ordination was considerably strengthened by the institution of a special Service/MOF committee to deal with all matters of service food policy.

The War Office were seriously handicapped from the outset of the discussions by being unable to offer any complete basic scale of rations as a bargaining point on which to support a case, and they were also unable to put forward any acceptable scientific opinion on the nutritional requirements of a service man, under the conditions which then prevailed in the United Kingdom—conditions which altered radically as the war continued. When the war broke out there was no fixed home ration scale. The soldiers' messing was arranged on a cash basis, that is to say, units were free to purchase what they required so long as the total amount expended was within the value of a daily messing cash allowance. This allowance was assessed by costing a scale of a limited number of staple foods, which bore little relation to actual usage, and then adding a further sum which could not be directly identified with any given quantities of food, but was nominally varied with the Ministry of Labour cost of living food index figure. The partial scale of rations used for assessing the messing allowance, although shown in Allowance Regulations as a 'standard ration', was obviously a relic of the days when a substantial quantity of meat and bread formed the basic diet of a soldier. For example, it included 12 oz of meat and 16 oz of bread, but only $1\frac{1}{2}$ oz of sugar.

There was good reason to believe that the average unit did not purchase these quantities of meat or bread; on the other hand they probably purchased considerably more sugar. It was difficult to convince a busy Cabinet Minister that, although there was a service scale of rations, it was both obsolete and incomplete, and yet at the same time to explain that any alteration in the scale was bound to have a direct effect on the purchasing power and consequently on the nutritional value of the food which could be obtained with the daily messing allowance.

The additional absence of firm scientific data to support the Services' claims led ultimately to the whole question of nutrition being reviewed, but even when there was agreement on nutritional requirements, there was still ample scope for differences of opinion about how those requirements could be best translated into a scale of food which would be acceptable to the service man. Various studies of the nutritional requirements of the service man had been made in the past, but like so many other studies they were not necessarily conclusive and opinion tended to change with the years.

As the war years went on, the situation became such that even though a given scale of food was considered desirable, and indeed necessary, the stocks to provide it were no longer available.

National Rationing of staple foods

When the question of rationing meat was first raised in October, 1939, the fact that a service unit could purchase up to 12 oz a head daily, and more if they wished, caused some perturbation and had the effect of bringing the whole question of service rations into prominence. The Food Policy Committee directed the War Office to set up a committee to consider (a) whether the military ration should differ from the scales that might have to be enforced for the civil population if national food rationing had to be introduced, and (b) if national rationing were not adopted, what the military scale should be, and (c) whether some discrimination should be made in the scales provided for active and sedentary service men.

The War Office Committee reported that they did not agree that the service man's requirements were necessarily the same as those of the average civilian, nor did they consider it administratively possible to provide different messing arrangements for those actively and for those less actively employed. They did agree, however, that the guide scales of meat and bacon could be reduced and recommended that the sugar scale should be increased. But they declared that any reductions or restrictions in the pre-war guide scale should be made good by a compensatory cash allowance. The cost of this compensatory sum was assessed at £1,500,000 a year, for the three services.

The proposal that reductions in staple commodities should be made good by such additional cash met with strong opposition from the Treasury. Their view was that as the value of the ration had been increased, by the addition of a supper cash element in 1937, 'solely as a recruiting measure', there should be no difficulty in returning to the pre-1937 standard; by that time service in the forces had been made compulsory. The Treasury felt that if compensation had to be given for reductions it should be in the form of foods cheaper than those reduced in scale, and they advanced the opinion that substitutes should be purchased at wholesale rather than retail prices from NAAFI so as to avoid the possibility of the accumulation of excessive NAAFI profits. Suggestions for economy even went so far as advocating that cocoa should be used in place of meat and dates in place of sugar!

It was clear to the War Office that the future path was going to be a thorny one and that if the war lasted very long, further attempts would be made to impose reductions in the standard of the forces' rations. The strong differences of opinion that arose between the War Office and the Treasury led to the Cabinet Food Policy Committee directing that a special committee be set up under Ministry of Health aegis to examine why the Services' rations should not be similar to those of the civil population; and if they should differ what scale should be provided for the forces, and whether a lesser scale should be given to troops employed on sedentary duties.

The committee was a strong one, and it met in February, 1940; it included some of the foremost nutritional experts in the country, with Professor E. P. Cathcart* as chairman, and Sir John Boyd Orr* and Professor Jack Drummond among its earlier members. Professor Cathcart had, with Sir John Boyd Orr, conducted the earlier studies connected with nutrition of the services in the 1914–18 war period, while Professor Drummond (later Sir Jack Drummond) had recently been transferred from his appointment as professor of biochemistry at University College, London, to be Chief Scientific Food Adviser to the Ministry of Food.

The committee came to the conclusion that the service meat ration could be reduced so long as the total service ration was maintained at 4,000 calories (gross). They recommended a greater use of certain other foods (cheese, sausages, etc.) and decided that, because of service catering arrangements, it was not possible to discriminate between the active and sedentary service man from a ration aspect. They also recommended certain reductions in the scale of meat and bacon for women. (At that time service women were receiving four-fifths of the soldiers' scale.) Their recommendations were referred to the Food Policy Committee at the end of February, 1940. By that time the Government had already accepted the need for rationing the civil population; bacon, ham, butter and sugar were rationed for the first time in January, 1940, and meat was rationed in March, 1940.

The Food Policy Committee accepted the recommendations in respect of the women's ration but considered that the total money value of the women's scale should remain the same. Before accepting the experts' conclusions on the men's ration, the committee directed that the Army should take a census of actual usage of staple foods in service messes. While these investigations were in progress the War Office invited units to adopt a scheme of voluntary underdrawals of meat, especially by large units, and it was agreed

* Professor E. P. Cathcart, F.R.S., was at that time Regius Professor of Physiology at the University of Glasgow, and Sir John, now Lord Boyd Orr, was Director of the Rowatt Research Institute.

to reduce the quantity of meat obtainable by service ration card holders. As a result of the analysis of consumption of staple foods, the War Office recommended to the Food Policy Committee that the service guide scales of commodities might be restricted to meat 10 oz, bacon 1⅚ oz, and bread 12 oz a head daily. They also recommended an increase in the guide scale of sugar from 1½ oz to 2½ oz.

The Home Service Ration Scale

The recommendations mentioned above coincided with the possibility of a German invasion. The unsuitable cash system of messing was, therefore, abolished and replaced by a complete fixed scale of rations which was issued in kind. It was called the Home Service Ration Scale (officers and men). Members of the women's services received four-fifths of this scale. The introduction of this scale was an important step in the history of feeding the army at home. The need for abolishing the cash messing system in the event of war had been constantly urged by DST, War Office; all such proposals were, however, countered by various arguments to show that they were impractical.

The new ration scale was so designed as to incorporate the proposed reduced scales of meat, etc., and to include all the components sufficient to provide a good breakfast, midday dinner, and substantial tea meal, which, if required, could be split into a light tea and supper. Valuable information regarding the average requirements and tastes of units was provided by the NAAFI and by an analysis of units' pre-war messing accounts that had already been made. With the agreement of the medical and financial branches, the Home Service Ration Scale was promulgated in June, 1940, and all commands were asked to report on its suitability at the end of July. The new scale was generally voted to be a great success; when command reports were received, it was only necessary to make some minor adjustments to the scale. Trial of the new scale also proved that the arrangement whereby members of the women's services received four-fifths of the men's rations was unsatisfactory. Furthermore certain items in the men's scale had proved unpopular with the women. A separate ration scale for the women's services was therefore introduced.

By arranging that all goods supplied by the NAAFI were provided at approximately wholesale prices, it had been possible to provide better fare within the previous cash messing allowance, a large part of which had to be expended by units at retail prices. War conditions, the increased strengths of units, and recognition of the need for providing central welfare facilities went far to compensate for any reduction in the income of units from rebate under the former messing system, which was the main source for providing welfare amenities in units.

The supply branch at the War Office had good reason to be satisfied with the speedy manner in which the new messing system had been introduced, and the home supply organization was fortified to meet the conditions which might arise if an invasion took place.

As soon as it became clear that the new messing system had proved to be a success, a further improvement was made by removing a few less popular commodities, e.g. meat and fish pastes and condiments, from the fixed scale and replacing them by a small cash allowance of 1½d a man a day. This allowance was paid from a unit's imprest account, and no special messing account had to be maintained for the purpose. The cash entitlement of a unit was determined by a simple certificate of the commanding officer showing the numbers fed. This arrangement obviated the previous meticulous post-checks by paymasters and the keeping of the pre-war complex messing account. To meet public suggestions that the forces in areas which had been evacuated of their civilian population should utilize surplus local fresh produce, units were permitted to buy fresh vegetables, fruit, etc., from sources other than NAAFI.

But even so the soldiers' ration remained one of the main preoccupations of the supply branch as the national food situation began to deteriorate and the first effects of Great Britain being virtually a beleaguered country were felt, particularly as the battle of the Atlantic became more severe.

In July, 1940, rationing for the population had to be imposed on tea and cooking fats, and margarine was rationed in September. (Jam and eggs were not rationed until 1941 and 1942 respectively.)

The Ration Situation, Autumn, 1940

In the autumn of 1940 there was growing evidence that the service ration was to come under close scrutiny again. The Government were faced with the continued and heavy sinkings by U-boats and surface raiders. These losses were reducing imports to a serious degree; furthermore, the continued bombing of London and other towns had created a situation where the hazards to life of the civilian seemed little different from those which the soldier at home might be called on to undergo. The fact that a soldier living out of barracks could obtain more highly prized food, such as meat, than the civilian living in the same house, caused resentment, and to many people there seemed to be little difference between the energy expended by the factory worker engaged in long hours on war work and that expended by the soldier under active training. These opinions were not necessarily well founded, as they failed to take into account the various differences in conditions of pay, living and other factors of the soldier compared with the civilian; however the criticism could not be ignored.

In November, 1940, the Ministry of Food represented that the amount of food purchased by the serviceman in his canteens, combined with his ration, exceeded his rightful share of national resources. This was followed by a demand for a cut of one quarter in the Services' meat ration, which was then 10 oz a day. This reduction was accepted, but the War Office again requested that the loss of meat should be compensated for by an addition to the cash allowance, by 1d for men and ½d for women. This proposal once again brought the Treasury into the field. That department maintained that to issue cash in place of meat in kind could only aggravate the national food situation, that the general situation called for some reduction in the service ration, and that the possibility of discriminating between actively employed and sedentary personnel should be reconsidered.

The War Office achieved its aim of offsetting reductions in rationed foods by additional cash to purchase non-rationed items. The revised scale of meat and increased ration cash allowance were promulgated in December, 1940.

Food Consumption in Canteens

The allegations then being made that the serviceman could obtain unlimited supplies of food through the many service canteens brought the supply branch into a field which was normally a Q staff responsibility. It was obvious that in the existing food position there must be some co-ordination between the quantities of food provided in the soldier's official ration and his private purchases in canteens. The Ministry of Food maintained that there were too many official service and voluntary canteens and that there appeared to be little or no control over the number of canteens or of the amount of food which was sold in them. An immediate investigation was initiated, and commands were asked to review the number, type and facilities provided in the various canteens, bearing in mind the national food situation. The reports were not received until some months later, but in the meantime the NAAFI undertook to provide the MOF with estimates and a note of the purposes of their requirements for canteen trade.

The inquiry instituted by the War Office resulted in a more stringent control being exercised over the number of canteens operating and the fare they could offer. The inquiry showed that many unofficial canteens had been started by civilians who, while having the serviceman's welfare at heart, did not subscribe to the organization (the Council of Voluntary War Workers) which had been accepted as the one to operate the various voluntary canteens under service control. There was a general pruning of all canteens, and arrangements were made to classify them for food allocations on similar lines to those established for the civil industrial canteens. Thus only certain canteens in a given military area were permitted to serve substantial refreshments; others were permitted to serve light refreshments only. Much of the work of control fell on the NAAFI, which by this time came to be regarded as the organizing body for the control of canteen food allocations and for maintaining the necessary records required by the Ministry of Food from corresponding civil organizations.

Ration Situation, Spring, 1941

Although the next great changes were not made in the ration scale until March, 1941, scarcity of various items involved continuous adjustments being made to the soldier's ration. The basic scale of bread was reduced to 10 oz with the option of drawing a further 2 oz if required. This arrangement was in deference to those who maintained that waste was occurring. Dried fruit had to be reduced temporarily, and no substitutes could be offered in its place. To accord with an appeal to the public to reduce consumption of milk, units were requested to exercise economy in that direction.

In February, 1941, when the national food situation had deteriorated appreciably and the outlook for the future appeared to grow worse, a further request was received from the Ministry of Food that the service ration scale should be reduced forthwith to the level then prevailing for the civil population. To support this case the Ministry of Food produced figures of the combined off-take of food through the official ration and canteens in 1940 to show that the Services were in an exceptionally favoured position. As the Services had recently reduced the meat ration obtainable on service ration cards, made reductions in the women's scales, and tightened up the supply of foodstuffs through the canteen supply organization, this new proposal from the Ministry of Food was regarded as something of a bombshell.

When the question was discussed between the principal administrative officers of the three Services (their standing committee was the instrument for considering service food policy) and the Ministry of Food, it transpired that even if the service and civilian scales were not aligned, heavy reductions were being demanded in practically every staple commodity. After some compromises the Services had to accept several reductions, principally in meat, which could only be made good by including less acceptable foods in the ration, within the limits of the financial saving arising from the cuts in rationed foods.

The result of these adjustments was that although the service scale had not yet been brought down to the level of the civil ration it was very near it. While the numerous alterations in the ration were being made, the need for maintaining the scale at a reasonable nutritional level had been kept in mind, but it was becoming increasingly difficult to do so and at the same time to provide for an acceptable ration. There was a limit to the amount of starchy foods, such as potatoes and bread, still in fairly ample supply, which could be absorbed. The growing national shortage of food in 1941 had brought with it the introduction of the points rationing scheme, and by the end of 1942 there were few commodities in general demand which were not subject to this form of rationing.

As the reductions made in March, 1941, were the last great cuts in the service ration it will be of historical interest to record the quantity of principal commodities, which were:—

	Men oz daily	Women oz daily
Meat (Bone in)	6	$5\frac{3}{4}$
Bacon	$1\frac{2}{7}$	$1\frac{1}{7}$
Offal or Sausages	$1\frac{5}{7}$	$1\frac{1}{7}$ (sausages only)
Bread	10	7
Flour	2	2
Butter and Margarine	$1\frac{1}{2}$	$1\frac{1}{2}$
Cheese	$\frac{4}{7}$	$\frac{4}{7}$
Milk, Tinned	3	$3\frac{1}{4}$
Sugar	2	2
Potatoes	13	12
Fresh Vegetables	$5\frac{5}{7}$	8
Tea	$\frac{2}{7}$	$\frac{2}{7}$

There were, of course, many other changes made before the war ended, but generally speaking it can be said that the ration was maintained at a level of about 3,800 calories gross for the rest of the war, which included the food value obtainable with the small cash allowance of $2\frac{1}{2}d.$ which accompanied the articles issued in kind. The soldier's ration both at home and abroad continued to be one of constant preoccupation, as although no attempt had been made to ration those on active service, overseas scales had to be adjusted from time to time in accordance with the general food situation.

At the end of 1942 a long felt want was filled by the setting up of a Services' ration scales committee under the chairmanship of a deputy secretary of the MOF, which allowed of the Services being kept in close touch with the national food outlook and provided a ready instrument for examining and presenting a co-ordinated view on matters of service food policy.

Before concluding this condensed account of the work connected with the service ration tribute must be paid to parts played by the Ministry of Food and the NAAFI. The Ministry had the difficult role of combining the duty of poacher and gamekeeper. When they had to poach on service preserves, it was as gamekeeper for the national good. At the same time they took good care that the serviceman received his due share of the national larder and that he received perhaps just that little bit extra of the few luxuries which were popularly known as 'being in short supply'.

The NAAFI were faced with a double task of acting as the agents of the Government for supplying a considerable portion of the ration for all three Services at home and at the same time of endeavouring to satisfy the demands of the serviceman in their canteens throughout the world. They also undertook the whole of the responsibility, on behalf of the Ministry and the Services, for the administration of the rationing procedure for canteens, for the control of sweets rationing, and for instituting unofficial 'rationing' for such much sought after articles as cigarettes. They had a great deal to contend with throughout the war.

The Composite Ration

The introduction of the composite ration was probably the greatest acquisition provided for the Army by the supply branch, because it ensured that there would be few occasions when either officer or soldier would have to put up with the hard fare, which, in the past, he was expected to exist on in times of stress. The idea of packing a complete day's ration for so many men into one box can hardly be regarded as an invention, but it was certainly an innovation in the British Army and one which was adopted by almost all our Allies.

The original ration, although a comparatively plain affair, was used for the first time in 1940 during the operations in Norway, and it was voted as an immediate success. The plan was then so developed that special ration packs were produced to meet many types of operational conditions, and by the end of the war no fewer than 40,000,000 packs were manufactured in different varieties.

The packs were not intended to replace the normal field service ration, with its variety of fresh produce. The object was to ensure that the man would be no less well provided for, until the normal ration could be issued to him.

The proposal originated from the experience gained by the BEF in 1939, when it was found that the administrative organization required for the landing of supplies in balanced form, for setting up supply depots, and for movement and distribution, could not keep pace with the rate at which the troops were being landed. This led to a suggestion that the RASC should provide the initial requirements for a force in such a form that each box or case would contain an equal amount of food for so many men for one day, and packed in such a manner that the cases could be easily recognized, handled, distributed and accounted for without the aid of skilled supply men.

Plans for aid to Finland were already being made when this suggestion was made, and no time was lost in putting it into effect. There was already a fairly comprehensive range of tinned foods in the normal field scale for issue when fresh food was unobtainable. The size of these tins was, however, regulated by commercial practice, and the contents did not generally relate to any particular ration scale of food. There was no time to undertake packing into tins of special size, as any departure from the standard sizes in use would have considerably reduced the output of can manufacturers, who were fully engaged in meeting demands for containers required for the normal ration. Other goods of a non-perishable nature were also packed in bulk in standard commercial packs (i.e. sacks, bags, wooden cases and cartons). Repacking into smaller sizes would have involved many technical difficulties which were not overcome until later in the war.

It was decided, therefore, to provide a ration for 50 men that could be assembled in three different cases. The ration, a simple one for packing, consisted of a case of corned beef, holding 48 12 oz cans, a case of biscuits, containing two 27 lb tins, and a case filled with other available tinned foods. Tea and sugar, however, were repacked by hand into separate tins provided for the purpose. The ration was by no means a really balanced one, but it provided rather more of the staple foods than in a normal scale.

In addition to the normal supply identification signs, the three cases were marked respectively with blue, yellow, and white circles. Provided that those responsible for handling consignments ensured that the same number of each colour was included, a complete ration was provided. This arrangement was, of course, rough and ready and far from ideal, but it was a start. The first consignments were packed at the SRD at Deptford for the "Aid to Finland" project. They were never taken into use but owing to continued changes in operational plans they had many travels. When they were finally returned to Deptford to be broken down they were so covered with force code and shipping marks that their coloured circles were barely recognizable.

From the limited experience gained from the 'three case compo', the supply branch then pursued the production of a complete ration in a single case, resulting in the '12-men ration pack'. This also was a fairly rough and ready ration, as the number of commodities to be specially packed into tins had to be kept down to a minimum, and tins of standard size had to be used as far as possible. The tins varied a good deal in size and shape, and this made it difficult to pack them into cases, but with the aid of packing material the ration stood up well to the rough handling which is inevitable under active service conditions. Two different varieties of pack were provided to allow for two separate diets. All the work of assembly and packing these rations was done by an improvised organization at No. 1 SRD, Deptford, and the experience gained in the type of organization required for this work proved to be of value later in the war when huge packing contracts were fulfilled commercially. The small section at the SRD reached a peak output of 500 cases a day, and before the pack was finally replaced by the 14-men ration they had completed more than 100,000 cases.

The first practical test of this new ration was during early 1940, when the several expeditions hastily despatched to Norway found it to be an instant success. One of the first supply signals received from Narvik was to the effect that the ration was an absolute boon and to 'please send as many more as possible'. The withdrawal of all our forces from Europe in 1940 brought a temporary halt to the demand for the new pack.

At the end of 1940, to meet the threat of invasion, there was an urgent demand for a ration for the Home Guard which could be hidden in 'caches' as a last resource. It was to be impervious to the effects of earth and damp. The ration had to be a simple one, and to consist of goods which were fairly plentiful and could be spared from the nation's larder at the time. To avoid the special packing of any of the perishable commodities, such as biscuits, and at the same time to provide complete protection from all weathers, the ration, sufficient for 10 men, was packed in a 4-gallon tin of the same type used for petrol. The sugar in this ration was provided for the first time in the form of solid plaquettes. About 350,000 of these packs were produced by No. 4 SRD at Swindon between February and April, 1941, and were eventually distributed to various commands in the United Kingdom. As soon as the Home Guard commitment had been met, the Supply branch turned its attention from the work of reorganizing and fortifying the home supply organization to meet the threat of invasion to that of examining the whole question of the types of packs that would be required to meet operational conditions in the future, and after extensive study by the Staff and planning branches, production proceeded as described below.

The One-Man Pack

The first requirement was for a ration for one man to meet the many occasions when the soldier had to be made self-supporting for the day. Hitherto each man was given some hard fare, usually in the form of a tin of meat, a packet of biscuits and a portion of cheese, or other food which could be carried loose in the haversack. The aim was to produce a ration which would not only provide enough for a full day, but was also light in weight, readily acceptable under conditions of stress, and completely unaffected by handling and weather. It was also required to have a specific food value and to be equally useful to the new commando parties for large scale amphibious operations when there was a general return to the offensive. The first problem was to explode the theory that a full day's diet could be produced in the form of a few tablets or the like, and to remember that however nutritious some patent foods may be, their acceptability to the soldier must be the ruling factor. This was an important principle, for it was reported that later in the war, when the British soldier was provided with an Allied ration of high nutritional value which was not to his liking, he preferred to go hungry.

It was necessary to convince the enthusiast that there was a limit to the extent to which a normal food can be compressed and at the same time retain its food value. The staff agreed that the new ration should be restricted to the size of the mess tin, which was made in two halves of oblong shape. It was obvious that several foods would have to be specially canned or packed for the purpose, and an appeal to the can box makers met with a ready response. There were many technical problems to be overcome. For example, it was found that a certain type of flat tin used for tobacco could be adapted for packing the newly introduced tea, sugar and milk powder, and that what appeared to be an outsize sardine tin (used for packing semi-perishable items, such as biscuit, sweets and chocolate), just fitted neatly into one half of the mess tin. The other foods, such as cheese, were packed in small tins and carried in the other half of the mess tin. The ration produced was sufficient for one man for two days, hence its official name, the 48-hour ration pack.

A practical trial of this new ration by an airborne unit confirmed that it was generally suitable for its purpose. The report recommended certain modifications in the contents, and the inclusion of matches. The ration was then improved by the replacement of the less acceptable items in it, and an improved lighter type of 'tommy' cooker, which was issued separately with the ration, was introduced. It was also recommended that some cigarettes should be provided in such a form that the contents of the packet would not get wet if it were opened in the rain. Once again the can box industry produced what was wanted: a tin, not normally used in this country, which held a packet of 20 cigarettes with the opening at one end. When emptied of its original contents, this little tin could be used as a cigarette case.

The improved 48-hour pack was introduced just in time to supply the 250,000 packs required for the North African campaign, but in the meantime, the whole question of reducing the weight of the rations by eliminating the use of tins was being investigated. At the beginning of the war, the tin container was the only satisfactory means of preserving food for any length of time and protecting it from damage. The use of plastic coverings was then in its infancy. After many experiments it was found possible to eliminate the use of all tins by using compressed meat, oatmeal, and tea and sugar blocks, and protecting biscuits, chocolate and sweets with an improved type of covering. By this means it was possible to provide a ration of about 4,000 calories weighing only 2 lb 3 oz including a small weatherproof carton in which each ration was packed. Some new items were included in the pack in the form of chewing gum, as an aid to the saliva, salt tablets to counter the effects of excessive sweating, and sugar tablets for those who liked a sweeter 'brew' than that provided in the 'tea and sugar' blocks. The ration was for 24 hours, and after it was accepted, as meeting staff requirements, some 7,500,000 packs were produced.

In April, 1941, a request was made for rations designed for the crews of armoured fighting vehicles, and the work of providing special packs for the needs of these crews ran concurrently with the production of the 48-hour ration. The packs were designed to provide a full day's diet for crews of two, three and five men respectively. The weight of the ration was not of particular importance, and it was possible to use the normal components of the field service ration specially packed into small tins—the whole being enclosed in a weatherproof fibreboard carton, and finally in a specially made tin with a shaped handle for easy carriage. Four million of these packs were produced, and later in the war an improved type of pack was issued.

The production of a special pack for use in the Arctic was in progress at the time the experiments for the provision of the 48-hour 'one-man' ration were being held. It was also a 48-hour ration, but all commodities were packed in a circular shaped tin. The constituents had to be specially selected from those acceptable under extreme cold and had to provide for a high food value of a little over 5,000 calories (approximately 1,000 more than were required for temperate climates). Pemmican had to be specially made to replace the normal form of meat, and the ration contained an anti-scorbutic in the form of ascorbic acid tablets. The ordinary type of match was replaced by flare matches which could be handled easily and would remain alight in a wind. The tin also contained special fuel starters for lighting oil pressure stoves, which were the accepted form of means of heating to be used under Arctic conditions. During September, 1941, and December, 1942, 2,800,000 of these packs were produced.

The greatest achievement in the provision of the special packs was undoubtedly the 14-men pack, of which 10 million were produced between 1942 and 1945. It was the successor of the simple 12-man pack, and was so generally used by all ranks in most parts of the world that some details of its development and production may be of historical interest. The requirements for this new pack were laid down by the War Office and executed by CPO(FS). The objective was to provide a good breakfast, a dinner, a substantial evening meal, and to include some items which could be used as snacks on the march or during short halts. So far as possible, the contents were required to be in such a form that they could be eaten cold, if no means of heating were available. Tommy cookers, however, were usually issued with the packs.

At least six varieties of this type of pack were required to be produced, so that troops could exist on it for several weeks without the risk of monotonous diet. There was no time to be lost in the designing of the ration and organizing the production, because at least one million cases (later increased to two million), were required for an impending operation—later revealed as operation 'Torch'.

Seven varieties of the pack were finally provided and stood up to the test. The only radical change which had to be made before the end of hostilities was the result of experience gained in North Africa, where it was found that biscuits tended to be wasted or not used at all when it became known that bakeries were in operation. Biscuits were then packed separately for use when circumstances demanded.

Several new commodities were included in the packs, one of them being canned puddings. The most popular variety was, strangely enough, rice pudding, mixed fruit pudding being a second favourite. Every effort was made to provide more varied meat dishes and the co-operation of the meat canning industry was sought accordingly. They rose well to the occasion, some of the firms even engaging chefs to prepare samples of every conceivable variety of tinned meat dish. While many new commodities were introduced, care had to be taken to include, in some of the packs, the standard popular items such as red salmon and tinned fruit. An ample ration of cigarettes, matches and soap was also provided.

Designing the ration, once the food to be included was selected, was not unlike solving a jig-saw puzzle, but it was the least part of the task compared to the organization required for production.

The production of the various components was spread as far as possible over the whole of the United Kingdom, and packing centres were established at suitable places in each main geographical production area. Lieut-Colonel G. R. Appleton, who controlled the organization, had more than 150 firms working on producing the commodities required, of which 60 were engaged in the production of biscuits and meats. To obtain the number of puddings needed, 20 manufacturers were employed. The organization had to be highly balanced to control the production and flow of as many as 30 commodities into 11 packing centres, and the scene in the control room of the headquarters of CPO(FS) was reminiscent of a busy 'exchange', as the reports arrived of production movement and packing progress. The numerous problems arising from the supply of material, etc., were dealt with as they came in.

No sooner was the organization for production and packing working smoothly, when an acute storage problem arose from the fact that the two largest SRDs being used for storing the completed packs had to be handed over to the American forces. Alternative accommodation was found, much of which had still to be cleared of its existing plant, etc., before it could be taken into use as storage space.

As the production increased, a dozen officers were specially appointed to live in the factory areas to watch and assist in production where possible. Their task was to remove any local difficulties which arose and to act as a link between industry and the central organization at CPO(FS).

Even after the finished products had been safely stored in the SRDs awaiting the day of shipment, some anxiety was caused by the discovery that several large consignments began to show signs of rust a few weeks after receipt. Although outwardly the wooden cases appeared to be perfect, expert examination revealed that the timber was not properly seasoned. The general scarcity of timber and especially seasoned timber, forced upon us (at the expense of pilferage and other damage due to rough handling), the adoption of fibreboard cases, strengthened with wooden battens.

As the enemy in Europe was being gradually encircled by the Allies and the future course of the war turned from the West to East, the production of packs specially designed for use in tropical and jungle conditions became a matter of first importance. Seven varieties were produced of a 6-man pack for one day containing a variation of some 39 foods. The pack, a sectionalized wooden case, protected each tin from damage and weather. Both the case and the tins were fully camouflaged with a dark drab colour.

A Pacific 24-hour ration was provided in the form of three hermetically sealed aluminium containers, one for breakfast, another for a midday snack, and one for supper. The ration consisted of 24 items, spread over three meals and varying from ham and egg, fruit bars and oatmeal block to cigarettes and salt tablets.

An emergency ration pack was also provided in a single aluminium container similar to that used for the 24-hour ration. It included biscuits, oatmeal block, chocolate, meat bar, salt tablets and sweets, and was purely for use as its name implies. Altogether some 15 million packs for the Pacific were produced from November, 1944, to October, 1945.

Before concluding it is desired to pay a special tribute to the co-operation of the various members of the food industry who assisted in designing and producing the Army's special packs. Both the management and operatives in all the firms which were engaged on production seemed to enter into the spirit of the day and often worked long hours to make certain that their contracts would be completed in good time in the knowledge that so much depended upon them.

PETROLEUM

Introduction

Although this chapter is intended to be devoted to a description of the work of the RASC in the United Kingdom, it includes some detailed references to the growth of the petroleum organization overseas.

This is because the development of the organization in the larger commands abroad was directly influenced by the gradual evolution of the petroleum organization and supply and distribution policy which originated at the War Office. The supply of spirit, other liquid fuels, and lubricants was a War Office responsibility throughout the war, as was providing the means of producing containers and the supply of plant and material required for the growth of the organizations overseas. Thus the petroleum branches at the ST Directorates at overseas commands had to rely more closely on the activity of the War Office than did the Transport and Supply branches.

Space does not allow the full story of the growth of the petroleum organization in the war being told in these pages, but it was a great achievement. No particulars are available of the total quantity of petroleum products that were used. It can only be said that they were enormous.

The ST Directorates at home and abroad could not, however, have achieved their purpose without the co-operation of the Oil Industry. Many members of the industry served with the Corps. But those who did not also made their contribution in many parts of the world.

New Organization

QMG 6's immediate concern, when war broke out, was for the arrangements for supplying the BEF because they depended almost solely on the production of new tin-making and filling plants, which had still to be fully tested when war was declared. When planning to meet the estimated requirements for the future BEF, for the first months of the war, QMG 6 had only reckoned on obtaining a 50 per cent output from the factories to start with. They had provided a small cover against any possible failure by placing 5,000 tons of spirit in France just before war was declared. But it only took a few weeks' working to show that even the predicted output from the factories was not being attained because of unexpected mechanical troubles. Shipping placed at Avonmouth and Swansea to load supplies was soon lying idle and GHQ BEF began to express some apprehension about their petrol stock situation.

Fortunately the consumption of MT spirit in France did not reach the expected level and the movement of the forces was not impaired for lack of petrol, but the passing shortage and preliminary adverse reports on the utility of the 4-gallon tin both served to precipitate the development of a new petrol supply organization.

From a War Office point of view the supply arrangements made for other potential operational areas were satisfactory. The civil bulk plants and tin-filling factories in Egypt and Palestine were running concerns and work on providing military protected bulk storage and filling apparatus in Egypt was already proceeding. Singapore had adequate bulk supplies and tin-making plant and the supply situation in Hong Kong was also satisfactory. Work was in hand at Gibraltar to provide protected storage accommodation for service liquid fuels and although similar plans for Malta had hung fire increased packed reserves and a small filling plant had been established there.

The plan for keeping the BEF supplied, by using 4-gallon ('flimsy') tins, was an expedient for the reasons which are explained in Chapter I. The arrangement was, however, only to hold good 'anyhow until permanent bases were established and the military situation permitted of any form of bulk installation being utilized'.

The standing committee which had recommended the adoption of the tin, '*The Standing Committee on the Method of Delivery and Distribution of Petrol in Front of Railhead*', had made it clear that although supply by tins filled at home would have to be the sole means of distribution in the first phase, they foresaw a second phase when supply would be partly in tins and partly in bulk—particularly for aviation spirit. A third phase would follow when all supply would be in bulk and tin-making and filling plants would be established in the theatre of war.

It was obvious to QMG 6 before the war that a new organization, separated from food supply, would be needed to develop supply in the second and third phases and that all other theatres of war would eventually have to be provided with a similar organization. But lack of time, manpower and money prevented any action from being taken to that end in peacetime. The most that QMG 6 could do was to plan the type of petroleum units which would probably be wanted.

However, it only took a few weeks of war before simultaneous action was taken to initiate the second phase of supply and to obtain agreement to the addition of 'petroleum' as a separate branch of the Corps' many activities.

The first requisite was to form a petroleum branch at the War Office. It was staffed by the three officers of QMG 6 who dealt with petrol, and was named QMG 17 until it was redesignated as ST 2 later in the war. A small staff headed by Mr Fuller of the AIOC, who was hastily commissioned for the purpose, was provided for the BEF. By the combined efforts of these two new branches an appreciation of the petrol situation in France and recommendations for development of the petroleum supply system was prepared in October, 1939.

The plan advocated that civil bulk storage should be taken over at Honfleur and Le Havre, a port which had been excluded from the original maintenance plan owing to possible risks from enemy air attack. Details of the methods of reducing fire risks were included in the appreciation. It was suggested that the civil installation at Donges should be developed for the distribution of supplies in bulk to units on the L of C which could accept petrol in that form, and that new filling centres should be established further forward on the L of C, for supplying filled returnable containers to the operational area. The proposal to take returnable containers into use was supported by a statement that 'it is hoped a petrol filling centre capable of filling 100,000 cans could be established in November (1939)'.

Although the advantages of a returnable container system were clearly seen at the time the main obstacle was the enormous number of cans which would be required, and the principle of bringing petrol in bulk to mobile filling points close behind the forward troops had still to be accepted. A total of 1,290,000 returnable cans were, however, shipped to France between January and May, 1940, from orders placed in 1939, for 1,800,000, on three firms who normally specialized on making motorcar bodies. Even so the BEF had to continue to make extensive use of the 4-gallon tin to maintain supplies.

There was no delay in settling the organization (establishments) of the new petroleum units required and the first unit, a bulk petrol storage company, was in France by December, 1939, and followed shortly after by another. Two base petrol filling centres were formed and were in France by early 1940. They were static units and were equipped with heavy plant which necessitated a good deal of preliminary engineering work before it could be installed. Mobile petrol filling centres were introduced later in the war. Petrol depots, formed from the No. 5 Section of base supply depots, were organized for holding packed reserves of spirit and other fuels and lubricants.

All these units required a high proportion of officers and men skilled in executive and technical petroleum duties who could only be drawn from the oil industry. An appeal for the manpower needed was met at once, and it did not take long before those who had been commercial rivals a few weeks before were presenting a complete unity of spirit and endeavour.

All the petroleum units required a good deal of technical equipment, some of which had to be specially designed and made at a time when the demands on the resources of the Ministry of Supply were many. Later on, the business of providing spare parts and technical stores grew to such an extent that special depots, petroleum technical stores depots, had to be introduced at home and overseas for replacing worn out equipment and fitting out new units.

The technical problems arising from handling bulk petrol were at first met by the inclusion of petroleum chemists in the bulk storage companies but the questions of quality control and analagous duties so increased in importance that this work was concentrated in petroleum laboratory units which were specially equipped for the purpose.

It can be said that the new petroleum organization was fairly safely launched so far as the BEF was concerned when operations opened in May, although it had been by no means perfected. But general progress in developing the organization was then brought to a temporary halt with the unexpected reverse in France, as ST 2 had to divert their attention to the more pressing question of denying the civil and military stocks remaining in France to the enemy and recasting their arrangements for supply at Home to the needs of home defence.

In the meantime the effort involved in supplying our expeditions to Norway was not a great one as the amount of MT spirit was small and little aviation fuel was used. MT spirit had to be specially provided in the form of 68 octane to suit the local climatic conditions and initial shipments were supplied in the standard 4-gallon tin. This spirit had a short 'life' of about four months after which it tended to gum (i.e. to lose its volatility). Some small bulk tanks and filling plant were taken over at Harstaad by No. 4 Petrol Depot and full use was made of them for filling drums and barrels. A new German tank lorry, taken from the SS *Alster*, was also found to be of great value and regarded as such a prize that it was shipped to England when the force finally evacuated the area.

The Home Front

By the time that the BEF was cut off from its bases in May, 1940, ST 2 had already made arrangements for opening a new line of supply. They earmarked stocks to be placed at each of the ports at home which might be used for shipments to the Channel ports and they arranged for a mobile reserve loaded into No. 104 MT Company to be held at War Office disposal.

Their next task, when withdrawal from France seemed inevitable, was to assist in organizing the wholesale destruction of the main civil installations in France before they were overrun by the enemy. The question of denying such important military objectives to an enemy was not a new one as it had been examined at the beginning of the war in consultation with the Admiralty, with special reference to installations in Holland and Belgium, and engineers had been specially trained in petroleum destruction technique. ST 2 collected much of the information and photographs and plans of installations were acquired by various lawful and, in some cases, unlawful means.

When the immediate problem in France was raised GS (Plans), the War Office branch responsible for the project, formed a small inter-service committee as Naval and Air Force activity was also affected. The small parties, known as 'XD parties' which were employed to carry out the demolition plans were on the whole successful in their efforts and it is estimated that over 1,200,000 tons of petroleum products were destroyed before the final withdrawal in June.

The threat of enemy invasion of Britain then made ST 2 turn to home defence. Up to that time the Army at home relied very largely for its petrol supplies on the civil system of distribution. The first need was to provide reserves of canned petrol for each command for

Petrol Pipelines

Roadside Petrol Dump

Can Filling

use in the event of the normal systems of distribution being dislocated. The tin filling factories were ordered into full production, and arrangements made to open petrol depots at each of the eight strategic points which had been selected for siting similar strategic reserves of food, in main supply depots. A separate supply scheme was already in being for the Air Defence of Great Britain (afterwards the Anti-Aircraft Command) as reserves of MT spirit and derv were held in tanks specially constructed in 1939 and 1940 in selected civil sub-depots.

As the denial of resources to enemy airborne troops was vital, elaborate schemes were prepared for joint civil and military action to reduce the risk of supplies being captured. Detailed instructions were issued and equipment provided for the destruction, if the occasion arose, of bulk stocks in the coastal belt and inland areas which the enemy might make his objective. Stringent instructions on safeguarding small bulk and canned stocks were widely publicized and the general co-operation of the motoring public was also sought.

As soon as the preliminary measures for defence were in train ST 2 began to extend the arrangements for bulk storage, can filling and packed reserves in such a way that they would not only serve to support large scale defensive operations in these islands but would also serve to support the launching of future expeditions against the enemy overseas when the Army was in a position again to take to the offensive.

These plans were gradually developed in 1940 and 1941 until the first offensive (operation 'Torch') in 1942 and continued into 1943, when they were linked up with the preparations for the final offensive in North-West Europe. But before describing the expansion of the United Kingdom organization we must touch on the development of the petroleum organization in the Middle East and other overseas theatres of war.

The Middle East

By the end of the first phase of the operations in the Western Desert, in September, 1940, it was evident that the petrol supply arrangements would have to be greatly expadned. The pre-war scheme of providing exclusively military tankage of 15,000 tons in the foothills of Suez and on the border of the Great Bitter Lake was just completed. The scheme was a sound one as the two separate tank farms were connected by pipeline and the intake of petrol, from ocean tankers, could be effected either at Suez or at Fanara. But the tankage was only sufficient for holding about 50 days' supply for a small force of about three divisions. The scheme also provided for two plants for filling returnable containers but the principal means of distribution was the 4-gallon tin and the capacity of the tin-making and filling plants, at Suez and Alexandria, was only about 15,000 cans a day.

When the future situation was appraised in September, 1940, it was estimated that an additional 155,000 tons of tankage would be required, to provide for a 60-day reserve for 21 divisions, and that extra filling plant would be needed for 76,000 tins a day.

The calculation for the extra filling plant was made on the assumption that only about 20 per cent of the petrol wanted would be distributed in bulk or in returnable containers. The decision to continue to rely on the 4-gallon flimsy tin may now seem to have been faulty in the light of subsequent pressure to adopt a returnable can. It seems probable that it was influenced by the resources available at that time. The deficiencies of the 4-gallon tin were well known but expansion was a matter of urgency. It has since been estimated that on a 20-day turn-round over 3,000,000 returnable cans would have been wanted as well as a supply of about 15,000 cans a day to make good wastage by loss or damage. The British 4-gallon returnable drum in use at the time was not regarded with particular favour. Even if it had been adopted the provision and shipping of such vast numbers would have taken a much longer time than would the provision of the eight extra tin-making and filling plants which were subsequently authorized. A further factor which had to be considered was that unless bulk supply could be carried forward and filling plant brought up to keep pace with the Army's advance, the number of returnable cans wanted would become greater as the distance between the bases and the forward troops increased.

The general scheme for the 155,000 tons of tankage and filling plant was called the 'Reserve Storage Egypt' scheme. It was authorized by the Treasury in October and work began on the new filling plants and expanding the existing bulk storage installations at the end of the year.

Expansion in the Middle East made heavy demands on ST 2 in arranging for the plant and stores required and providing petroleum units, at a time when technical men were beginning to be scarce. During the period that new units were being raised and trained at home the Middle East had been forced to run their petrol organization with men from their own meagre resources and although 18 units were earmarked for despatch to the command early in 1941 they were delayed by shipping difficulties. Shipping was disappointingly slow. Of 13 units 'offered' for shipment in July, 1941, only one was included in the last convoy. Before the final operations in 1943 the establishment in the command had, however, been increased by 40 petroleum units.

Supplies for the forces in the Western Desert and the Nile Delta was of course only one of the Middle East petroleum problems as the command had also to cater for operations in East Africa, Iraq, Palestine and Syria, and for the maintenance of garrisons in Cyprus and on the Red Sea littoral. Each territory presented a different supply problem.

Petroleum distribution and the Jerrican

Ample supplies of refined petroleum were of course available in the Middle East area. The whole of their territory was supplied from the output of crude oil in Iraq, central and southern Persia and to some extent from the Egyptian oilfields. The refineries at Haifa, Suez, and Abadan provided petrol and derv. Aviation spirit was produced at the Abadan refinery. Early in 1942 the output from Abadan was 200,000 tons of 100 octane and 100,000 tons of 90 octane. It was doubled by the end of 1942 and a target of 800,000 tons had been set for a later date. The principal problem was storage and distribution in each of the widely separated areas where our forces operated. There was usually some bulk storage at the bigger towns in each territory but the distribution of civil supplies was mainly in 4-gallon tins which were in common use in these eastern regions.

Full use was made of existing civil tin-filling plants but military requirements often exceeded their output and large shipments of ready filled tins had to be made from Abadan. There was a heavy demand in 1941 for 45,000 tons of reserves for Port Sudan, Massawa and Aden which could only be met by drawing on Abadan, but because of further unexpected demands from the forces in Iraq, packed supplies had to be obtained from as far afield as India and the Dutch East Indies. More petrol carrier ships had to be obtained at a time when shipping was at a premium. Heavy losses from leakage and from damaged cases were inevitable but the position had to be accepted.

At the end of 1941 there was a serious shortage of tinplate in the Middle East owing to the increasing demand and the non-arrival of shipments expected from America. An emergency demand, for 10,000 tons of plate, followed by a second demand for a similar quantity, had to be made by the War Office on the Ministry of Supply whose stocks were low. There were, at that time, some 20 tin-making plants operating in the Middle East. Some were civil plants, some had been obtained from the USA, a few were ex-enemy ones and others had been purchased 'second hand' from India. More plants were on order from India, Australia and the USA. The combined output of all the plants in operation was in the region of 3,000,000 tins a month. A year later it rose to 4,300,000.

With the loss of our resources of tin in Malaya, in February, 1942, it became imperative to find substitute materials for the petrol container. After some experiments it was found that a 'black' or terne plate could be used for the purpose, but the main effect of the shortage of tinplate was to turn attention to the use of steel returnable cans.

The Middle East Command had some months before recommended to the War Office that the German jerrican should be adopted as a standard container but a considerable interval of time elapsed before the pattern was accepted and put into full scale production, a matter which has been much criticized. Whether the reproaches directed at the War Office are well founded or not cannot be examined here beyond mentioning that any reversal of policy in war, which demands the employment of more labour, plant and shipping is a decision which cannot be lightly undertaken and must be subjected to exhaustive technical and high level examination.

The jerrican was a novelty and required novel methods of production. Special presses were required for stamping out its steel sides and parts and mass production welding plant was needed for welding the parts together. Hitherto the commercial method of producing durable containers was either to roll steel plates into drum shape and seam the sides and ends, or cut the plates to size and link them together, also by seaming.

Some time was lost by the first decision taken to produce a can somewhat similar in shape and appearance to the jerrican, and to order 1,000,000 of them from America (hence the reference to merricans). The new can lacked, however, one of the predominantly useful features of the German prototype—the aperture specially designed for pouring and the closure which combined ease of opening with a non-leak seal. The first shipments to the Middle East began in March, 1942. As an interim measure a circular 4-gallon drum was designed which could be easily manufactured and which could be produced at various points in the Middle East; can supply was also supplemented, from the available production in England, of 4-gallon square cans. Over a million of the latter and 800,000 of the former were shipped to the command up to April, 1943, and 800,000 merricans, allowing for the losses at sea, sent from America in the same period. The production of jerricans started in 1942 and 1,000,000 had been despatched to Africa by the end of the campaign in 1943.

These figures are given in detail not because they have any intrinsic value, but to show that in spite of the growing can population[1] of returnable cans provided between 1942 and 1943, and the

---

[1] Term used in the War.

capture of about 1,500,000 enemy cans, it was still necessary to use 4-gallon tins, to the tune of over 4,000,000 a month, to keep the forces maintained.

During the time when ST 2 were engaged on the development of returnable containers, operation 'Torch' had been put into action by the invasion of North Africa in November, 1942. The early maintenance of the force presented a considerable problem as 8,000,000 gallons of petrol had to be accumulated in the home depots for the purpose and, for example, the shipments for the assault convoys took 126 train loads of petrol for loading over 106 different ships. Initial supplies had to be in packed form as, although the expedition was the first to have a complete petroleum organization with it, no reliance could be placed on utilizing bulk supply until local facilities had been reconnoitred, rehabilitated and supplemented.

Operation 'Torch' was the first joint Anglo-American large scale expedition and as petrol was a common user commodity, ST 2's responsibility for supply eventually passed to an Allied organization set up by AFHQ when they were established in their new operational zone.

Oil Supply

Oil supply was only to a small extent a military responsibility. The Army, which was only one, and that not the biggest, of the claimants on resources, undertook the executive task of moving its own supplies forward from the ports in overseas theatres; but in this country the oil companies, grouped in a special organization known as the Petroleum Board, were responsible for distributing all supplies, both civil and service. Moreover the whole task of procuring supplies from their sources and shipping them to the various theatres, including the United Kingdom, was performed by the oil industry, which, however, worked under supervisory Government committees on which the Army was represented. Ultimate responsibility for all oil questions rested with a sub-committee of the Cabinet, the Oil Control Board, of which the Quarter-Master-General was a member.

The resources of petroleum which could be drawn upon were world wide. Before the war, Britain drew about 43 per cent of its supplies from the Caribbean area (Venezuela, Colombia and Trinidad), about 24 per cent from Persia and about 18 per cent from the United States. Fortunately, all these remained available to the Allies throughout the war. The maintenance of war supplies was thus primarily a matter of protecting the sea lanes and maintaining sufficient tanker tonnage, in the face of continued and often heavy losses by enemy action. There were several critical periods of tanker shortage, and throughout the greater part of the war the allocation of sources to supply the various areas was governed by the need to keep tanker journeys as short as possible. Thus with the closing of the short route through the Mediterranean Persia ceased to be drawn upon for home supplies and greater quantities had to be obtained from the United States.

The fields in Persia and Iraq, however, continued to be useful for supplying the Middle East where demands for local use within PAIC and other countries and for aid to Russia were mounting rapidly. By February 1st, 1944, it was estimated that the total annual production from the Persian fields, at Abadan and Kermanshah, and the fields in Iraq at Khanakin and Kirkuk, had risen to about 12 million tons. To deal with storage and transport problems special petroleum committees were set up in Cairo and Baghdad. Their chairmen were members of the home Ministry of Fuel and Power and the members consisted of representatives of the Services, the oil companies and other bodies interested in supply and transportation.

In the initial stages of the campaigns in North Africa and in North-West Europe supplies were drawn from Britain and depended on the security of the vast stocks which had to be held in bulk storage in this country. These, on the whole, sustained little damage from enemy air attack. The United Kingdom refineries were also almost unscathed although their loss would have been less important as the bulk of our national requirements were imported in refined form.

When America came into the war arrangements were made to zone responsibility for supply between Britain and the United States.

Before America declared war her resources were also drawn upon for lubricants. Up to 1941 the basic oils for manufacturing lubricants were shipped from the United States to Britain in bulk and blended and packed at home. Contracts were then made in America to supply the finished products and shipments were made direct to the Middle East. It was a satisfactory arrangement although losses by sinkings averaged 5,000 tons a month.

The entry of America into the war made it necessary to standardize the range of spirit and lubricants used by both armies. New vehicle designs and improved engine performance had brought with them demands for different grades of spirit and lubricants. After some give and take on the part of each country it was possible to obtain a fair degree of co-ordination by unification and simplification, particularly of automotive lubricants and greases.

A reduction in grades of spirit required was beset by many technical difficulties. A standard MT spirit, MT 80, was introduced for all general purpose vehicles. It was also used for AFV's, which had formerly required two different grades, MT 87 and MT 85, after suitable engine modifications were made. The elimination of other grades in use, MT 68, 70 (Middle East) and 75, was not so easily achieved until British and American automobile engineers got together and helped to produce engine modifications which eliminated the valve burning troubles attributed to the alternative spirit.

The Final 'Phase—Overlord'

Long term planning for the final phase of the war may be said to have begun over 1941 and 1942 when the War Office decided to increase the bulk reserves in England, to create six petrol reserve depots for packed stocks, to build satellite tin making plants and to install two large filling plants for returnable containers.

To save further construction of military owned tankage it was arranged that the additional military bulk reserves would be held in civil installations and would be administered by the Petroleum Board on the Army's behalf. By this means the military holdings in early 1941, of 227,000 tons of bulk tankage, was raised to nearly 1,000,000 tons by the end of the war. The six War Office controlled petrol depots were designed to hold 50,000 liquid tons of packed petroleum products. The plans to provide more filling facilities were changed as the strategic situation turned from defence to offence and the use of tins changed to that of cans. Two can-filling units, which were partly staffed by ATS, were built in the north in what were considered to be non-vulnerable areas. They fulfilled a useful purpose during the invasion period but were closed in 1943 when the threat of invasion had lifted. There was some delay in executing the plan for the satellite tin factories. They were intended to be an insurance against the two main factories at Llandarcy and Avonmouth being put out of action, and to provide a cover for extra output. The plan was only partly implemented, but the factories which were built made a big contribution to the supplies wanted in the final phases of the war. Two of the plants were later dismantled and crated for shipment to North-West Europe as reserve plant.

All these early measures taken by ST 2 were a valuable asset when the time came to review resources and to balance them against the 21 Army Group's future requirements which were gradually evolved by the Cossac planning staff in the summer of 1943 and by their successors, SHAEF, in December, 1943.

By the time that active planning for 'Overlord' began a great deal of experience had been gained in the Middle East, North Africa and Italy and in the Far East. The original conception of the functions of the various types of British petroleum units proved to be quite sound although various changes were made in their organization as experience was gained. One feature which was common to all was their ingenuity and their constant readiness to taken on tasks which were outside their normal function. Another feature was their ability to extemporize whether the task was a large scale one, such as the rehabilitation of a shattered installation, or the everyday one of erecting a roadside filling point. The dividing line between the responsibility of the Royal Engineers who were responsible for engineering work and that of the more technical petroleum units was small, which greatly assisted the co-operation between the two Corps. The speed with which new tankage could be erected and pipelines laid over both short and long distances had been amply demonstrated as had the rate at which bulk distribution could be introduced on lines of communication.

The plans for supply for 'Overlord' differed in many respects from those made for previous expeditions inasmuch as initial supplies were to be in returnable cans (jerricans) and bulk supply for refilling cans was to be developed immediately after the first landings and not deferred as had been formerly done, until civil installations were captured and rehabilitated. Portable and prefabricated tankage was to be landed quickly and supplied from floating tank barges and bulk petrol lorries used to carry forward supplies to mobile filling centres. The supply of bulk spirits from England was to be maintained by a fleet of small shallow draft petrol carriers and by a submarine pipeline which rejoiced in the code name of 'Pluto'.

The whole scheme was a gigantic one which involved the co-operation of the Navy, the Royal Engineers and the Oil Industry, and the production of huge quantities of material.

Although bulk supply was to be developed soon after the first landings many millions of cans were required to build up the can population. The reception and filling of the numbers wanted preparatory to the launching of the offensive entailed the construction of six more War Office petrol reserve depots. (There were six in existence before planning began.) Five of the depots were each equipped for filling 100,000 cans in a week. Three of the new depots were located adjacent to existing bulk storage installations, but the other three had to be placed at inland sites and fed by rail tank cars.

The production of jerricans was already proceeding apace. It had taken some time to work up production, as some of the presses required had to be ordered in America, but by 1943 four of the big steel manufacturers were fully engaged in mass producing the new pattern. Six plants had also been sent out to the Middle East and others had been provided for India and for Australia. It was planned that 30,000,000 cans would be manufactured by the summer of 1943. But even so the can supply had to be supplemented by the use of 4-gallon tins and 4,500,000 tins were actually shipped to the Continent in 1944.

The provision of marine craft portable tankage and pipelines was not a direct ST 2 responsibility although they were concerned with their ultimate use. Some idea of the overall effort involved will be of interest. The equipments on order in July, 1943, included 1,400 miles of pipelines, 900 rail tank wagons, 130,000 tons of 'quickly erected' tankage, 200 prefabricated 1,000-ton tanks, 200 barges, and a programme for 30 dual purpose carrier vessels for the carriage of petrol in bulk or in cans.

There were 121 contractors employed in producing the equipment which had to be provided by ST 2 alone. The items on order ranged from 155,000,000 clips, for identifying the contents of jerricans, to 55 mobile filling plants.

Raising and training the 85 RASC petroleum units which appeared in the order of battle was also a big task. It was greatly assisted by the existence of a Petroleum Technical Training Centre where courses were arranged for both technical and general duty men. A special headquarters (a HQ CRASC) was set up at No. 4 Mobilization Centre, where units were prepared for handing over to 21 Army Group. This HQ arranged for realistic training and rehearsals of units' future tasks in France and Germany. Another special unit was formed, the Petrol Supply Demonstration Unit, to instruct both RASC and other arms in the technique of the handling and use of petroleum products. Supervision and control from a War Office angle of the training arrangements was simplified by the addition of a training branch to DST's staff, ST 8.

The provision of the two high pressure submarine pipelines, 'Pluto', was the responsibility of the Petroleum Warfare Board, ST 2 being concerned with the control and pumping and operation of the land terminals. The two land terminals were named 'Bambi' and 'Dumbo' respectively, with the addition of the word 'Far' for the Continental ends of the lines. As the technique of control over pumping required a high degree of technical skill, units were specially trained beforehand.

The home commands played an important part in the preparations for concentrating and marshalling the forces. Additional petroleum units and equipment were given to them where necessary for refuelling vehicles and for other duties, which included the provision of fuel and lubricants for loading in the mass of ferry craft which were to carry a small deck cargo of 'POL' on each of their journeys.

Other special arrangements had to be made by ST 2 for emergency air supply of petrol and supply to the airborne forces. As in all the other plans made, no detail was omitted.

MANPOWER

Reference has already been made to the difficulties of the Army in general and the RASC in particular in the matters connected with manpower during the years leading up to the war. While establishments always lagged behind actual or potential commitments, recruiting always lagged behind establishments. Some of the measures taken to alleviate these evils have already been listed. This specialized section of the story deals with the months immediately preceding the outbreak of war and with the war years themselves.

AG 8/ST 5 (referred to in future, for the sake of brevity, as AG 8) was the War Office branch responsible, under the Adjutant-General, for the manning of the RASC. Like its counterparts under the DST's control, AG 8 was of modest proportions while, unlike the QMG 3 and QMG 6 branches, it had the difficult task of serving two masters, the Director of Recruiting and Organization (later the Director of Organization) under the AG, and the Director of Supplies and Transport under the QMG. Apart from the Civil Service element common to all War Office branches, it was staffed exclusively from the RASC. In 1938, even after Munich, when things were already warming up, it consisted only of an AAG (colonel), a staff captain, a supervising officer, a quartermaster, and eight clerks, of whom two were military. Its duties of 'manning' included the administration of all members of the RASC and all civilians paid out of 'Vote 6', that part of the annual Army Estimates which covered supplies and transport.

This organization was barely adequate to deal with normal peace routine and had little or no capacity to spare for considering in any detail the many problems bound to arise on and after mobilization. As an instance of its consequent divorce from real forward planning may be cited the fact that only three months before mobilization four of the military members of AG 8 were fully occupied for a month in preparing the normal programme of reliefs for the trooping season 1939–40 and the raising, from existing resources, of the RASC men required for the autumn manoeuvres.

On the eve of mobilization, however, approval was obtained for a marked increase in the branch, which thereafter consisted of an AAG and eight officers, of whom three were DAAGs, with a corresponding increase in other ranks and civilians. AG 8 was then organized into three sections—planning, officers and other ranks—and this general distribution of duties remained throughout the war, the numbers of subordinate staff required to deal with the increasing load being suitably raised from time to time. Those who held the key positions in AG 8 were Colonels P. L. Spafford, J. E. Witt, C. E. Browne, W. J. J. Allen, R. C. Atwill, H. N. Gallagher, W. N. Craig McFeely and deep is the debt of the Corps to all of them.

The first fence which AG 8 had to negotiate was mobilization on September 3rd, 1939, for which detailed plans had been made after the release by the War Office of the 'New Conspectus 1938' only in November of that year. Broadly speaking, this document provided for the mobilization of two army corps, with four divisions, and their supporting troops, to be built up of one third Regulars, one third Regular reservists, and one third Supplementary reservists. The follow up was to be the Territorial Army, the mobilization of which was to be spread over, following a priority dependent on the strength and state of training of its divisions in peacetime.

Some 51 cadres of MT companies existed in peacetime, 49 of which were intended for the field force against a requirement of 53, and two for home against a requirement of seven. The missing field force cadres were to be provided by two TA divisional RASCs of lowest priority, while it was hoped that recourse to hiring would meet home requirements until new post-mobilization companies could be raised.

To meet the mobilization commitments of the striking force there were available at home, 677 Regular officers, 320 Supplementary Reserve officers and 346 officers of various other reserve categories. The comparable figures for men were about 8,600 Regular serving soldiers and 15,000 reservists of all kinds. On paper the call for one third Regulars could be met for the two army corps, but in practice this was not so. Many Regular officers and men were reserved for staff, extra regimental employment and training units and, as mobilization drew nearer, still greater demands on the Corps for officers were made. These led to the appearance of some square pegs in round holes, the most notable being a highly qualified engineer commanding a field bakery. There was also a Ford distributor who was undoubtedly a capable executive in the motorcar world but, because of his bad handwriting, found himself a food distributor in a supply depot for some weeks. The principal shortages among other ranks were clerks, bakers and loaders. It was hoped, and the hope was justified, that the two first trades could be filled by post-mobilization enlistments. The loaders were provided by the Royal Artillery, who had some 2,000 unwanted reservists. Most of these RA reservists were eventually trained as drivers.

It was early apparent, however, that the Corps would require far greater numbers of drivers, and indeed of all tradesmen, to meet the needs of new units not covered by the existing Regular and TA framework, as well as for building established units to their proper strength. The agreement of the Ministry of Labour and National Service was therefore obtained to the voluntary enlistment of the necessary numbers, including a quota of such key men (in civil life) as heavy goods vehicle drivers, petrol installation workers, and certain classes of engineering tradesmen.

Mobilization proceeded smoothly according to plan. It was controlled by commands who managed to solve most of the manpower problems locally. The RASC Record Office beat the pistol in posting call-up notices to reservists. They were informed by AG 8 that the signal was ready and would be issued in about one hour. Notices could therefore be posted in an hour's time without waiting for the signal. This timing proved to be dead right.

What was not covered by long established planning was the fact that within 12 hours of mobilization being ordered volunteers from recruiting offices poured into No. 1 Training Battalion, RASC, at Aldershot by every train. Luckily there was a commanding officer (Bt Colonel E. B. Rowcroft) who could take this sort of thing in his stride. Barrack blocks were doubled up, drill sheds, mobilization store buildings, miniature ranges, gymnasia, and even stables emptied of their horses, were converted into dormitories, and finally Rushmoor Arena was taken over. By good fortune the weather was perfect, and no steps were taken by the enemy to bomb this loose knit concentration of men.

It was clear that Aldershot could not stand this indigestion for long, and there was also the problem of keeping the volunteers employed and out of mischief. Batches of up to 800 at a time were sent to those TA divisions which could find room for them. When the TA could take no more, the men were posted to home commands to fill the gaps left by mobilized units. This, however, was a policy of expediency; the men still had to be trained, a task completely beyond both the TA and the emaciated home units.

Movement to the embarkation ports of the mobilized units went according to timetable except for some third-line units which were delayed by shipping difficulties. One sub-park of an ammunition park was ordered to harbour at Eastbourne pending a call forward. The police at this early stage of the war were still very peaceminded and raised strong objections to vehicles being parked in the streets. The unit commander promptly appropriated the Sussex county cricket ground, a proceeding which was not too well received in ST 3, of which Brigadier E. H. Fitzherbert, a Corps cricket enthusiast, was in control!

At first the cadres were thus filled on the officer side by the all **too thin** spread of Regulars, by officers of the Regular Army Reserve, by short service officers who had been enrolled during the few months before the war, by a number of ex-Indian Army officers, by Supplementary Reserve officers and, for the balance immediately required, by men of previous officer experience who offered themselves for the Army Emergency Officers' Reserve. Although this catalogue may give the impression of haphazard selection, this was not the case. Every potential officer was interviewed by the DST's senior representatives in commands, and the records of all were 'vetted' in person by the Inspector of the RASC, who also interviewed large numbers of the applicants. The resulting intake was of great value to the Corps, whose wartime intake of officers (particularly in the early stages) compared favourably with that in any other arm of the service, and rendered excellent service throughout the world.

The reserve of other ranks was supplemented by some 2,000 national servicemen from the first two intakes of the newly formed 'Militia', by 3,000 similar men from the Royal Artillery not immediately required by that arm, and by the volunteers of all trades already mentioned. Of these, the Regulars, including reservists, and national servicemen, had had some military training (of varying degrees of completeness), but the RA militiamen had no trade training, and the Supplementary reservists and the volunteers had their civilian aptitudes and trades, but no military training. Much therefore remained to be done within units and formations before this hotchpotch of manpower could be regarded as fit to take the field. How was it to be accomplished?

In the very early stages the RASC Training Centre continued to function as the officer training unit for the Corps, and the existing training battalions, augmented by newly formed battalions which were later formed into three training brigades, gave both military and technical training to the men. Later, as the call-up became properly canalized and as the time available for basic military training became shorter, this part of the man's training was done by general service training units, which turned out the militarily finished product for all arms in a set period of six weeks, after which refresher training was left to the man's unit. The training brigades, however, remained in existence in modified form for the rest of the war, for continued military training and for trade training, and were an essential part of the RASC men-producing machine.

To revert to the officer question, it soon became apparent that the RASC Training Centre, like the training centres of other arms, would be inadequate by itself to produce and train the requisite number of officers for our expanding army. In mid-1940, therefore, an officer producing unit was planned and formed by the Training Centre and located initially at Bournemouth, later moving to Clifton College and thence to Southend. There volunteer and reserve officers with little training were given a thorough, if rapid, course of Corps duties, technical and military, and later, officer cadet training units of the pattern familiar to all arms were set up, to which promising potential officers were sent from the ranks of the training battalions and of all units which had such men to recommend. The RASC OCTU soon established a name for itself, and great credit is due to the initial propounder of the scheme, Colonel H. R. Kerr (later Major-General Sir Reginald Kerr who was DST at the end of the war), the Commandant, RASC Training Centre, and to the early commanders of the Officer Producing Unit and the OCTU: Colonels H. M. Hinde, E. S. Unwin, C. E. Browne, J. E. Witt, R. H. Elliot, C. E. Bowden, and M. S. Farquharson-Roberts. These officers set a standard which gave the Corps an excellent intake of officers at a time when all other sources of training had ceased to function.

But there was still something lacking. The Director of Organization could find the men, the training brigades could lick them into shape, the OPU could furnish a capable officer cadre, but the DDsST of home commands who were initially held responsible for the preparation of complete units for war service were manifestly in no position to do this indefinitely, with depleted staffs and increased commitments in every direction. The DST (Major-General M. S. Brander) and the Inspector of the RASC (Major-General R. T. Snowden-Smith) remembered the 'ASC Mobilization and Training Centre' located at Bulford during the First World War, where a picked headquarters and staff 'processed' forming units by allotting accommodation, arranging all Q services, issuing them with training equipment and, later, full mobilization equipment, and generally fathering them until they were fit to stand on their own feet and eventually to proceed to a theatre of war. There was little known precedent on which to build, but AG 8 knew what was required and produced a scheme and a draft establishment, authority being sought to set up one Mobilization Control Centre, RASC. The scheme was 'new ground' to the War Establishments Committee, who took much persuading to convince them of its necessity. Eventually a reduced establishment of four officers and 10 other ranks was agreed upon and No. 1 Mobilization Control Centre, RASC, was ordered to form at Ramsgate on November 30th, 1939, under the command of Colonel E. C. Pinder.

The plan was for AG 8 to post small but experienced cadres of officers and men for a maximum of 20 units. These units would gradually be completed to war establishment by postings from the output of the training battalions. The part of the Commandant, Mobilization Centre, was to arrange for units' reception and accommodation, to help them over their teething troubles and, when mobilization was ordered, to ensure that they received all their equipment and were fit to take their part in the field force. These tasks, simple though they sound, concealed a potential morass of problems, great and small, for every unit and, multiplied 20 times to cover all units on hand at any one time, proved far too much for the small centre staff permitted.

The first difficulty was that all the important cadres had, for lack of any other source, to be provided in the main from TA units low in the order of priority. The officers and NCOs, willing and hard working though they were, just had not the experience to raise successfully a unit *ab initio*. In particular the CQMSs were completely at sea. The Commandant and his one DADST valiantly tackled the task but it must be freely admitted that AG 8 had no conception of what was involved until the AAG went down to see for himself. On return his first instructions were for a new Commandant and a new DADST to be ready 'in case the present incumbents went mad'.

Indeed, bitter experience showed that the original establishment, even before pruning, was barely adequate, so that when the War Establishments Committee was approached for increases, these were granted almost without argument.

Demands from the BEF and the Middle East Command now became so great that another mobilization control centre became a necessity. Later, the output from training units matured before there were units in which to put them, so it was decided to raise units in anticipation. In all, three more centres were formed, No. 2 at Burford (Colonel T. W. Richardson), No. 3 at Guildford (Colonel H. A. Tapp), and No. 4 at Barry (Lieut-Colonel C. E. Custance). The last named centre was for supply and petrol units. This locality was selected because excellent unit training facilities existed at the Supply Reserve Depot, Barry, at Llandarcy oil refinery, and at the oil berths in Swansea Harbour.

Mention has already been made of the difficulty of providing experienced cadres for new units. It was therefore suggested to and agreed by the DST BEF (Brigadier G. K. Archibald) that the force should supply from their trained resources a number of capable officers and men and should accept in replacement private soldier reinforcements from the United Kingdom. This worked well, except for the obdurate scarcity of trained CQMSs. The only solution was to run special courses to train many of these.

When the evacuation from Dunkirk began, mobilization control centres were filled with men of all arms, most being separated from their own commanders and officers. These in time returned to their own units, when located, and were replaced by RASC men.

Some of the major problems of the mobilization centres are set out in the succeeding paragraphs. It may be said here that the quickest in solution took three months to sort out, and the most obstinate took just over a year.

From the start transport was practically unobtainable. Many mobilized units, particularly those destined for the Middle East, did not receive their transport until they arrived in their theatre of operations. How were units to draw rations, ordnance stores and the hundred and one daily requirements? What was to be done about continuation training of drivers straight from training units? In the end a pool of transport and a workshop element were authorized for each centre. This pool was sub-allotted to units and retained by them until they left the centre or were issued with mobilization transport. The pool permitted of the allotment of about 10 vehicles to each unit. After taking daily standing details into account, about five vehicles were available for training. It is not surprising, then, that overseas theatres complained that units on arrival had far too many semi-trained drivers.

It was soon found that the small staff of the headquarters of a mobilization centre was inadequate effectively to control and supervise the training and interior economy of the many units forming. Administrative guidance was particularly necessary because of the almost complete lack of experienced men. The only people available not only did not know the answers, but were not in possession of the books, regulations, etc., where the answers might have been found. Two increments were therefore added to the headquarters, one to supervise training and the other administration. The latter increment began its job by collecting a supply of manuals, pamphlets, army forms, and such things, most of them virgin copies of some antiquity with numerous amendments in separate parcels. Many units conveniently mislaid the amendments and were, like the Jackdaw of Rheims, not one penny the worse thereby.

Another worry was the crop of absences, sickness and compassionate cases which invariably arose on the eve of embarkation. These deficiencies were at first made good by taking men from other units in the centre. This was not very satisfactory as these men had often not had their embarkation leave or their inoculations. The unsettling effect on the robbed units was also not conducive to efficiency. Each centre was therefore provided with a sub unit, or 'holding unit' of officers and men of all ranks and qualifications, fully prepared in all respects for overseas, to meet last minute casualties.

Unfortunately not one of these holding units functioned as intended. Very soon the men held were a collection of sick, physically unfit, those awaiting trial by court-martial and the

Petrol Filling Point

Dukws in a Wood

occasional malingerer. In one mobilization centre the holding company at one time held 40 officers and nearly 1,000 men, only about five per cent of whom were immediately available.

The expansion of the Army as a whole was so rapid that army and command schools were unable to turn out instructors and specialists fast enough to meet the demand. To provide for RASC requirements the necessary courses of instruction were arranged in mobilization centres, no fewer than 12 different types running concurrently. Trained cooks for units were provided by establishing a cookery instruction unit near each centre. This system worked well but it absorbed, at its peak, 120 officers and 1,800 other ranks in the whole four mobilization centres.

The mobilization of units now went on with reasonable smoothness. As soon as a cadre arrived in a centre the senior officer was handed a brochure which, if it did not answer all his possible questions, did tell him where the answers were to be found. Among other things the brochure contained the war establishment and the mobilization store table of the unit, details of accommodation, an outline training programme, outline unit standing orders, training pamphlets and necessary books of regulations, a map of the locality showing neighbouring units, supply and ordnance depots, local police and fire services, and so on—altogether a company commander's *vade mecum*.

About a month before a unit was due to complete mobilization it was inspected by the Assistant Inspector of the RASC, Brigadier E. S. Hacker, who reported on its fitness for its war role. Backward units were given intensive training to bring them to the required pitch of efficiency. In spite of this some units did embark when only partially trained, in order that shipping space should not be wasted. When this occurred overseas theatres were warned and they arranged completion of training after the unit's arrival.

The story of the mobilization centres must be left here. That they met a definite want was manifest, and there is little question that a future emergency of the same proportions would call for some similar organization. The points to watch are that the permanent cadre is adequate and capable, that the medical category of this cadre is the lowest compatible with efficiency under home service conditions, and that the overlap between the functions of mobilization centres, training units and army schools is kept to negligible proportions.

It is time now to turn to the development, in war, of the training organization of the Corps. That existing in peace was split between Aldershot and Feltham. Briefly, the Training Centre at Aldershot dealt with the *ab initio* training of officers, and their advanced training in all spheres of Corps work. It dealt with the military training of all ranks and with the specialist training of clerks, storemen, animal transport men, and cooks for all arms. At that time the Army Catering Corps was not yet in being. Potential cooks were selected by commanding officers of units of all arms. On completion of training at the Army School of Cookery, Aldershot, they were returned to their units for employment as cooks.

At Feltham drivers and MT artificers were given their specialist training at the Driving School, RASC, and the Heavy Repair Shop, RASC, respectively. The whole organization was just adequate to deal with the flow of voluntary enlistments in peace, and consequently the advent of the Militia necessitated the provision of further training facilities, and a Militia Training Battalion was formed at Boyce Barracks, Crookham, near Aldershot.

The plan on mobilization was to expand each training company of No. 1 Training Battalion, RASC, Aldershot, into a battalion and to expand the depot company of that battalion into a depot battalion, RASC. Further, the RASC Training Centre at Aldershot was to form a company to train selected cadets to become officers.

Within a week of mobilization being ordered, it became abundantly clear that even the expanded training organization was totally inadequate to cope with the tremendous influx of recruits. Plans were therefore made to form another 12 training battalions as soon as suitable locations could be found for them. The main problem, however, was where were the officers, instructors and administrative staffs to be found? As has already been pointed out, the greatest difficulty was being experienced in finding even the small cadres wanted for the many new units in process of formation.

The Director of Recruiting and Organization called a conference at the War Office to discuss ways and means. It was agreed that, on the administrative and military training side, men of any arm would be quite suitable, but that specialists were essential for the driver, clerical and artificer training, and that none were available in the Corps at home.

The assets available were many elderly retired officers of the British and Indian service, greater numbers of officers and men of infantry training groups, which now had little or no training to do, in addition to any specialists we could get from civil life. The provision of these last did not prove an insuperable difficulty. Mr. Frank Pick, Vice-Chairman of the London Passenger Transport Board, agreed to encourage the voluntary enlistment of his experienced drivers, while the editor of the *Motor Cycle* gave an assurance that he could produce all the motorcycle instructors we wanted.

Clerical instructors were found by enlisting the aid of Pitman's

Commercial College and various other secretarial training colleges throughout the country. Artificer instructors presented a harder problem, in view of the variety of trades in the Corps and of the operation of the Schedule of Reserved Occupations. Luckily, two of our senior retired officers (one of whom was nominated to command the Artificer Training Battalion) were directors of large engineering undertakings, and they guaranteed to produce our requirements if given a free hand. They succeeded, but some of their methods would hardly have recommended themselves to the Ministry of Labour.

With this miscellaneous collection, the new battalions were formed and scattered far and wide over England. For convenience of administration they were grouped into three brigades, No. 1 at Aldershot, No. 2 at Bulford (later Carlisle) and No. 3 at Mansfield. There were teething troubles, but the battalions soon settled down to do a first class job of work. Most of the credit for this must go to those elderly officers in command, almost none of whom had any RASC experience but who all had a sound regimental and administrative background, based on many years of service. Man management was good, and the units were happy and hard working.

In the early days of the war many of the recruits who came into the Corps had varying degrees of proficiency at their military trades, and in consequence the output of training units varied from week to week. Later, as the young national servicemen provided most of the intake, this state of affairs ceased and a standard regular output was achieved. There were, however, occasions when tradesmen with previous civilian experience were required at short notice. A special demand on the Ministry of Labour, with which the War Office liaison was exceptionally good, usually produced requirements. The results were at times amusing, for instance on one occasion the Artificer Training Battalion found itself with 20 coal trimmers for conversion into coach trimmers, while a field force unit workshop found itself embarrassed with a corset fitter, who had, moreover, by some mysterious means risen to the rank of sergeant.

With the passage of time and the introduction of new equipments and techniques, further specialist training units became essential. Thus, in August, 1940, the War Office decided that global war demanded the provision of water transport units. Accordingly, a motor boat company was formed in Devon and another in Cornwall. Sections were detached to the Royal Navy and the Royal Air Force for training. Two years later the units, now combined, were moved to Mersea in Essex and renamed the Waterborne Training Wing, which, together with the Amphibian Training Wing, formed the Waterborne Training Centre. As larger craft came into service, a deep water anchorage became essential, and this was found at Rothesay, to which place the wings moved. In early 1943 the Americans developed the now well known 'dukw'. A considerable number of these admirable vehicles were provided for the British Army, and American instructors trained RASC men in their operation for the Sicily landings. After the invasion of Sicily, a nucleus of trained RASC men with experience of operating dukws on active service formed the Amphibian Training Wing at Towyn, where training for the Normandy landings was done. Some 11 amphibian companies, in addition to reinforcements to replace wastage, were trained there.

Again, it became clear at the end of 1942 that the maintenance of airborne forces once committed to the assault was a task beyond the capacity of their second line formation RASC. An air training centre was then formed with the object of training members of GT companies and DIDs of 21 Army Group in the packing of loads, loading into aircraft and their final ejection from these to troops on the ground. By March, 1944, this training had been completed, and a start was made in training air despatch companies, RASC. This training was conducted in very close co-operation with the Royal Air Force, and was most successful.

The manpower story from its provision and training aspect thus pursued a moderately even way after the early struggles to cope with the first sudden influx of volunteers and the early call-up were over, and after the teething troubles of the mobilization centres were past. There were always, however, a mass of administrative questions and special considerations, such as compassionate postings, the adjustment of medical categories (as the manpower situation became increasingly tighter) and, later, the matter of compulsory transfers to the newly formed Corps of Royal Electrical and Mechanical Engineers to keep AG 8 thinking hard. The casualty rate varied, too, from time to time. Altogether, it was heavier (in proportion to the casualties of other arms) than in the First World War, largely because of the more fluid nature of the fighting, the increased range of artillery, and the incidence of bombing on our lines of communication. At times, in the Middle East, the Corps had the melancholy honour of 'leading' the casualty lists for all arms. But whatever the wastage was the steps taken by AG 8 and their opposite numbers in the ST branches of the War Office kept the ranks filled with trained men, with the one incalculable exception of Arnhem. Here, however, the operations came to an end before the lack of surviving air despatch crews could be felt.

One final word on men should be stated in fairness to our sister corps, the Royal Indian Army Service Corps. There was considerable integration of the two Corps in South-East Asia Command, with the RIASC as the predominant partner, but what is not so generally recognized is the help, limited it is true, but of vital importance to us at the time, of the RIASC supply men who were lent to us by the 4th Indian Division in the Western Desert in 1940–41. Because of the lack of RASC supply men, for the 7th Armoured Division in particular, whose RASC companies were allotted locally from transport assets in the theatre (there were no assets anywhere else at this time), we should have been badly stuck without the small supply staffs readily lent by the RIASC for General Sir Richard O'Connor's operations. Nor was this the first help received from this Corps, for in the transport section of the Prelude is recorded the work of the RIASC pack transport companies in the BEF, and earlier in this chapter mention is made of the help received from retired officers of the Indian service lent to us at home during the early days of critical shortages.

BARRACKS

The branch of the RASC that is concerned with barrack services is commonly referred to as the Barrack Department. The title dates from 1794, when the first large scale construction of barracks was undertaken and soldiers ceased to be lodged in inns and alehouses. The Barrack Department has therefore, in fact, had a continuous existence for some 160 years.

Barrack services is an organization that is found only in the British Army. In other armies its services are generally performed either by Q staffs, or are divided between the equivalents of Q (quarters) RAOC (furnishings), RE (lighting, sanitary, window cleaning, chimney sweeping), and RASC (fuel). It has been advocated from time to time that the functions of the Barrack Department should be taken over under some similar arrangement, and such a proposal was, in fact, made by the Controller General of Economy at the War Office during the war, in 1943. But then, as on the other occasions, the advantages of the co-ordinated day to day service in meeting domestic requirements, which the Barrack Department can give, affecting directly, as it does, the welfare and consequently the morale of the troops, has turned the outcome of the controversy in favour of the retention of the department. In the early stages of a war this co-ordinated service that the Barrack Department can give may be of particular value, for if the arrangements for men to be housed, to have beds and bedding, and to be provided with heating, lighting and cooking facilities are not adequate, at a time when men have just left comfortable homes, morale can be adversely affected right at the outset. Before the war, however, a deficiency existed in this element of co-ordination, and this was in the War Office itself, where five different branches were dealing with the various matters affecting barrack services. In 1938 a review had been made by a War Office committee, which had recommended the appointment to the War Office of a senior and experienced barrack officer to advise the various branches on matters of policy, and to effect some co-ordination. The actual responsibilities, however, were still to be left divided among the same five branches.

The organization beneath the War Office level at that time provided no direct departmental channel for the functional control of the barrack services. The only officer directly related to the Barrack Department, above the level of the officers in charge of barracks, was a retired officer of the rank of lieutenant-colonel at each command headquarters, who was called a command barrack officer. He was neither a staff officer nor the head of a service and could issue no directions or instructions except through the medium of the Q staff.

The first wartime change in the organization occurred in 1942, when an area barrack officer of the rank of major was added to the establishment of each RASC district or area. At the same time it was decided that, because of the large increase in the number of troops located at home, and the consequent expansion of the RASC establishments for the administration of supply, transport and barrack services, it had become impracticable for the Inspector RASC to give the barrack services the full and detailed attention that they required, and the appointment of an Inspector of Barrack Services at the War Office was approved. Lieut-Colonel H. M. Wright assumed this appointment on January 12th, 1942. After his early inspection visits, and his review and examination of the barrack services in the United Kingdom, he made recommendations that eventually resulted in a further reorganization being approved, and this came into effect in the following year. Under this reorganization the responsibilities within the War Office were centralized in a new branch of the Directorate of Supplies and Transport, which was designated ST 7. The branch comprised three sections: ST 7(a), which dealt with all services except fuel and light, ST 7(b) which was concerned with fuel and light; and ST 7(c), which formed the inspectorate under the Inspector of Barrack Services. At the same time, at command level, the command barrack officer and his assistant became ADST (barracks) and DADST (barracks) respectively, and in areas and districts the area barrack officers were incorporated in the establishment of the ADST or OC RASC concerned under the title of Major (barracks). Thus, for the first time, a complete chain of representation of the Barrack Department at all levels, within the RASC organization, came into being.

The rapid formation of ADGB units in 1939, followed by the large expansion in the United Kingdom on general mobilization, made heavy demands on the barrack services. The initial equipping of accommodation entails the most work, and in this respect the greatest demand came at a time when the Barrack Department was losing many of its most experienced officers, who were needed to fill quartermaster appointments in field force units. Moreover, the clerical staffs of the barrack offices, which were half military and half civilian, lost many of the military clerks, mostly warrant officers and NCOs, who were withdrawn for field force duties. New barrack charges, as the areas administered by officers in charge of barracks are termed, had to be formed, and the number of officers in charge of barracks rose quickly from 40 to more than 100 by 1941. For the newly formed barrack charges, and for the expansion of the staffs of the existing charges, the manpower needs were difficult to meet. Accountants were particularly scarce. These barrack accountants, or barrack wardens as they were at that time called, are key men in the barrack services, for they handle all the indenting, issuing and accounting in connection with all forms of furnishings, table-ware, bedding and linen, and with fuel and light. They are normally appointed from among pensioned warrant officers and NCOs, who have invaluable knowledge and experience of the ins and outs of army ways, and have the sense of responsibility and quality of resourcefulness that go with such experience. It is typical of most of these accountants that they take considerable pride in the arrangement and lay-out of the stores which they hold as maintenance stocks. In the early days of the war a unit out in the wilds was found by a visiting barrack officer to be in a most unhappy state with regard to its accommodation, and to be relying on its mobilization equipment scale of two blankets to each man in the severe weather of that first winter. In the barrack stores the officer found a good reserve of white hospital blankets of high quality, which had been held for some time for a hospital commitment that had not materialized. They were beautifully arranged in the store, immaculately folded and with moth balls symmetrically arranged, the joy and pride of the accountant. It almost broke his heart to part with them.

The demand for more accountants quickly absorbed the remaining candidates for the posts who had their names on the waiting lists kept by commands, and recourse had to be made to the labour exchanges. These, however, had been more or less drained of any manpower of value by the widened demands in other fields of civilian employment. Among the miscellaneous assortment that was produced, including a number of very elderly gentlemen, there were not many who could be of service, and the process of training recruits in the accounting work took time. But in spite of the lack of trained men the Barrack Department coped efficiently with its ever increasing load. There had to be a good deal of improvisation, which needed much resourcefulness. An instance of this is the experience of the chief clerk of one barrack office, Staff-Sergeant (now Major) H. H. Brodie. In the period of the pre-war preparations the officer in charge was posted away and could not be replaced, so it was arranged that the officer from a neighbouring barrack charge would divide his time between the two offices. Unavoidably much of the work in preparing for the imminent mobilization fell on Brodie. He had never previously even seen the mobilization scheme, but he promptly set to work to get the necessary information about new units that were to form in the district, and he obtained the necessary stores, which he assembled in separate lots for each unit, and drew up a programme for their issue. Brodie was posted away to a mobilization appointment before these detailed arrangements had to be put into effect, but he learned afterwards from the officer who later took over the charge that the programme had worked without a hitch. Warrant officers and NCOs must, of course, be ready in war to step into positions of higher responsibility when occasion requires, in the administrative sphere as much as in the front line.

The pressure of work, the lack of staff, and the paramount necessity for getting on with the job without waiting for instructions from above led to a good deal of variation in procedure and in accounting practices. Some early simplifications in accounting were made, but it was not until the Inspector of Barrack Services was appointed that general measures for standardization and simplification began to be introduced. As the unified chain of responsibility for barrack services came into operation, new and simplified procedures for dealing with both accommodation stores and with fuel supplies were worked out and brought into use. Accommodation stores held by units ceased to be entered in the ledgers of the barrack store accountant, who became responsible only for the maintenance stocks held in barrack stores, and the officer in charge of barracks was no longer required to keep distribution records showing the number of articles in each room of every barracks within his charge. Instead, the stores held by units were transferred to inventory books, separate books being used for each unit. These books were maintained by a barrack inventory accountant, in duplicate, one copy being held by the accountant and the other by the unit, and they consisted, in effect, of a running total number of each different article held by the unit. The distribution of the stores within each unit's accommodation was thereafter left, within certain limits, to the commanding officer. It is worth mentioning that the introduction of barrack inventory accountants under the new system turned out to have a particular value during the war. Sudden moves of field force units would occur, sometimes overnight without warning; they would disappear without leaving any rear party. Often the barrack inventory accountant was able to secure the safety of the stores in the vacated accommodation, and not only the barrack stores but other public property as well. These accountants certainly more than proved their worth.

On the fuel accounting side the complex system of individual fuel scales for each class of accommodation was discontinued, as was the carrying forward of credits and debits from month to month. The new system substituted a bulk tonnage 'target' of fuel according to the total strength of the unit, which was to be a guide to consumption, and the new fuel account consisted of a simple monthly statement of receipts, issues and stocks.

It will have been noted that, in forming the new War Office branch to manage barrack services, a separate section, ST 7(b), was created to take over from ST 6 the work of supplying fuel and light, and this is an indication of the size and importance of this particular service. Possibly the biggest single job of the barrack services during the war was the provision of coal and coke for the forces in the United Kingdom and in operational theatres overseas. At home, as the war went on, the supply of solid fuel grew less and the demand increased. Supply diminished through falling output and lack of transport, due to bombing, non-repair of wagons, lack of staffs, and rail priority for troop movements and operational equipment. Demand was increased by the swelling production of armaments and, on the military side, by the needs of the growing British army at home and the large influx of American troops. By May, 1944, three and a half million troops, including well over a million Americans, were being supplied with fuel in the United Kingdom, requiring a yearly total of two and a half million tons. It was inevitable in the circumstances that at times reserves fell to low levels, and rigid economy measures had to be applied. The United States forces recognized the need for the economy campaign and co-operated in it, making a genuine contribution by bringing down the higher standards to which they had been accustomed to the level of our own. There was always excellent co-operation from the Ministry of Fuel and Power, and equally from the War Office side there was a ready appreciation of the constant difficulties that faced the Ministry, so much so that on several occasions it was possible for the War Department to help the Ministry in overcoming crises in civil supplies.

The provision of solid fuel from the United Kingdom to theatres overseas covered a wide area. Iceland was supplied, both for

British and American requirements, from 1940 to 1945. Supply was made to the garrison in the Azores, and a small amount was sent for Force Burglar in the Faroe Islands. The Falkland Islands were supplied at first from home, and later by shipments from South Africa. A supply was even sent to Persia under the 'Aid to Russia' scheme, when 10,000 tons of coal were included in the cargoes of ships carrying 46 coal burning locomotives. To meet the first requirements of the Channel Islands, when their relief could be effected, arrangements were made for 1,000 tons of coal to be put in bags and held in readiness at Southampton.

Requirements of coal in the Middle East were at first obtained from the Egyptian State Railways, but in 1940 the source of supply was switched to India. Because of constant increases in the demand, it never became possible to build up any substantial stocks, and by May, 1942, the holdings were down to a dangerously low level. Arrangements were made to ship 75,000 tons from the United Kingdom and 25,000 tons from the United States. From then until the end of the war supply was made from South Africa, the coal being shipped by civilian agents from Lourenço Marques or Durban to Suez.

During the early stages of operation 'Overlord' it was necessary to manhandle coal over the beaches. About 18,000 tons was bagged in 80 lb sacks, a sack being the equivalent of a one-man load, and for this purpose 250,000 rot-proofed sacks were obtained under Ministry of Supply arrangements. A buffer stock of 5,000 tons in bulk was laid down at Swansea, and was subsequently shipped. The War Office was responsible for all further supplies of solid fuel both for the British and the American forces from then until May, 1945, after which part of the coal required came from the United States. Demands were passed by SHAEF to ST 7 and these rose from 60,000 tons in September, 1944, at which time bulk shipments began, to 250,000 tons monthly in the early part of 1945. Some 140,000 tons of pitch were also sent in the first four months of 1945. During the period from D Day to the end of July, 1945, a total of over two million tons of solid fuel and pitch was supplied from the United Kingdom against SHAEF demands.

In reviewing barrack services during the war it is apparent that ample proof was given of the value of the system of co-ordinating the domestic services for static accommodation within one department. Possibly the greatest deficiency was that caused in the earlier part of the war by the lack of experienced staff; but this, of course, was a factor that affected more than only the barrack services. The larger measure of 'civilianization' of barrack staffs introduced since the war will, however, help to combat this in future, but as far as possible mobilization plans should make provision for the selection in advance of qualified warrant officers for immediate promotion to quartermaster rank to take over barrack charges from those officers who are required for field force duties. Finally, it may be confidently said that the organization for barrack services that emerged under wartime conditions, providing unified control within the War Office and a proper chain of responsibility throughout the lower levels, undoubtedly resulted in a considerable increase in efficiency, and is a feature that has come to stay.

CHAPTER XIII

AIR DESPATCH

General

SUPPLY by air was a new function for the Corps and was brought into being by the improvement in the reliability and capacity of aircraft, together with the increasing difficulty in many theatres of maintaining lengthy lines of communication. These lines were so extended that not only did their organization absorb an inordinate proportion of the 'ration strength' in the theatre, but also it became impracticable to protect them from being cut by the enemy.

Air despatch, in its broad sense, means the maintenance by air of a force not easily reached by ground maintenance organizations, and the term covers both landing supplies in the desired area by aircraft (which required the preparation and protection of forward landing fields or strips) and the actual dropping of supplies over a dropping zone, or DZ, from aircraft in flight. The latter entails using crews who are expert in the rapid and rather tricky business of completing the drops. Dropping may be by parachute loads which are required for all delicate loads (e.g. men, mules, guns, vehicles and stores, or supplies in containers liable to burst) or by 'free dropping', where articles are either of such a robust nature that they can be despatched in their own containers, or, if not so robust, can be packed in special containers. One example of the last named type is the double bag in which it was intended to drop petrol. The petrol was filled into the inner bag while the outer bag burst on impact with the ground. This container was quite successful on trials, but was impracticable for large scale use because it could not be stored filled, and the extreme difficulty of filling large numbers at short notice made its use prohibitive. Several other forms of shock reducing devices were tried with varying degrees of success. This free dropping, eliminating as it does the capacity of loads to 'float' for long distances in unpredictable directions with their supporting parachutes, simplifies the organization of the DZ, and reduces its proportions. These advantages are considerably offset, however, by the limitations on the types of load to be dropped, by the damage done to many of the loads when dropped, and by the danger to ground staff of the loads falling on them.

The Work of the Air Despatch Group

Technically, the tasks of the Air Despatch Group were divided into two types of maintenance by air: first, the air maintenance and re-supply, which meant the maintenance (normally by dropping) of ground or airborne troops as a routine task, after they had established themselves in an operational area, and secondly, supply by air. The latter means the loading of aircraft with stores and supplies straight from dumps without special packing, and landing the complete aircraft and load at the destination. The term 'air despatch' covers, too, the organizational bodies which exercise co-ordination and control at each end of the journey, the composite executive units required to fulfil the requirements of these bodies, and the aircraft placed at their disposal. Higher control was a staff matter on account of conflicting priorities, distances and the need for a communications 'net'; and the RASC provided most of the staff officers required. In the United Kingdom the executive portion was at first under a CRASC Air Despatch. Later, as the task grew, an Air Despatch Group was formed. This consisted of a Headquarters Air Despatch Group RASC, three HQs RASC, air despatch companies, and airborne divisional companies (attached from 1st and 6th Airborne Divisions). There were also general transport companies for collecting from supply and ordnance depots the stores for despatch, small RASC and RAOC depots for holding 'cushions' of commodities at ready availability, and an air maintenance company, RAOC, for holding and packing specialized and delicate RAOC stores. There was also a detachment RAOC for operating the 'cushion' ammunition depot, and a pioneer company for labour. The aircraft for the carriage of the stores were not, of course, part of the Air Despatch Group but were controlled and operated by the Royal Air Force. In SEAC, where there were no civilian or well established military communications, a signal regiment was also part of the organization.

Supply by Air before 1942

The idea of carrying supplies by air had been thought of long before the Second World War, but the scarcity of aircraft and their limitations of range and of size held out little promise of achievement until the latter part of the war. As long ago as 1916 attempts had been made to sustain the British force besieged by the Turks at Kut-el-Amara in Iraq by nine aircraft which flew 140 sorties in six days. The amount dropped, however, was insufficient to avert the disaster of capitulation. In 1918 a certain amount of ammunition was dropped to British troops on the western front who, in their victorious advance, had out-distanced their lines of communication. Small air drops were also made to British troops in action in minor operations in Somaliland and on the North-West Frontier of India in 1919.

It was not until 1936 that large-scale exercises in the dropping of men, equipment and supplies were conducted in Russia. These were shown, in part, in the cinema newsreels of the time, but apart from indication being given of the large scale of the operations, care was taken to release very little useful information, and fuller details were never made available outside the Soviet Union.

At the outset of the Second World War, an attempt was made, as an emergency measure, to supply the BEF at Dunkirk in 1940, using converted civilian airliners. It was not until 1942, however, that air supply on a large and organized scale was really begun. The initiative came from Burma, where the main supply line, the Irrawaddy River, had fallen under Japanese control, and the force there of two weak Indian divisions, the newly formed Burma Division and the British 7th Armoured Brigade had no land lines of communication worth the name. They managed to live largely on stocks in the country, but about 3,000 tons of supplies were dropped by air to the refugees struggling out of the country with hardly any means of subsistence. However, the question of subsistence by air as a routine matter was not seriously tackled until, with our last foothold in Burma lost, the eccentric but gifted guerilla organizer and leader, Major-General Orde Wingate, conceived the idea of raiding deep and long into Japanese held territory. He left columns of his long range penetration groups, the now famous Chindits, to range the country behind the Japanese lines, spreading disorganization and alarm among the enemy and encouraging loyal elements in the population to help the British and await the return of the Imperial forces. When confronted with the difficulties of carrying enough supplies with his groups to render them independent of any lines of communication, he advocated, in his own words 'bringing them down the chimney like Santa Claus!' And so the beginnings of organized air despatch took place. Later, profiting by the successful lessons in maintaining Chindits, and realizing that surrender was the only alternative to air supply (in the case of several beleaguered forces), this whole theatre of war passed over almost entirely to air supply. A complete and very efficacious Army Air Transport Organization (AATO) grew up mainly under the executive control of the Royal Indian Army Service Corps.

Air Despatch in North-West Europe

The problems to be faced in North-West Europe, however, differed from those in the Far East in several respects. With the exception of airborne operations, supply and maintenance by air were planned as emergency measures rather than as a normal system. For this reason the Air Despatch Group was only used spasmodically and was never stretched to its full capacity except for short periods. The enemy opposition from air and ground was very much heavier in North-West Europe and this had considerable influence on the technique for dropping, which was designed to eject the whole load in one run over the dropping zone.

The airfields used for supply operations, although spread over eight counties, were fairly concentrated, were served by excellent roads, had good rail facilities, and were connected by a first-class system of telephone and teleprinter communications. This made the central control of RASC transport and air despatch personnel reasonably simple, and enabled transport, stores and men to be switched rapidly from airfield to airfield in order to meet the frequent changes of aircraft and airfield availability brought about at short notice by casualties and bad weather.

Composition of the Group

In the United Kingdom the War Office assumed responsibility for all army functions connected with the supply and maintenance by air of ground formations and airborne forces from this country, including the Special Air Service Brigade. These duties were discharged by means of the Air Despatch Group, RASC, which included air despatch units, transport units, petrol and ordnance depots, and pioneers. The Air Despatch Group was nearly 5,000 strong (including those attached) with 1,500 vehicles. The main tasks of the group were, first, the maintenance and re-supply by air of ground and airborne troops. This was normally effected by packing stores in special containers and pushing them out of aircraft on parachutes. The group were able to find sufficient air despatch crews to man 205 Dakotas (four-man crews) or 410 Stirlings (two-man crews) on one mission. The reason for the smallness of the air despatch crew in the Stirling was that half the load was carried in the bomb bay and was released by the RAF crew.

The group's other task was supply by air, when aircraft were loaded with stores straight from depots and dumps without any special packing (except in certain difficult cases) and were landed at their destinations. In this case the group had to collect the stores from railheads or depots and dumps near the airfield, make them up into aircraft loads, load them, and lash them correctly for flight. The loading and lashing of stores, a most important task, were done by men who were specially trained for this job in addition to their duties as air despatchers.

The Work of Packers and Air Despatch Crews

The packers had to have a knowledge of the stresses to which the packages would be put, and had to make up loads which would conform to certain ruling dimensions. For instance, the completed package must be able to pass freely down the runway to the exit door of the aircraft, it must be of a size to pass easily through the door, and it must be of such a weight as to fall safely with the parachute 'lift' available to it. The load must be securely and immovably fastened to the bottom board of the container (in the case of 'pannier' containers), as any looseness in the lashings will upset the trim of the parachuted load, cause it to foul other containers in the aircraft, or even allow it to disintegrate and do an unrehearsed 'free drop'. The lashings of containers themselves to the aircraft must be done with meticulous care, and regard must be paid to the fact that the craft, by its acceleration or deceleration, or falling into and out of air pockets, may endow the object carried with a force of five times its true weight. (In mathematical jargon the value of gravity (g) may in effect become 5g).

Added to these considerations were the precautions to be taken when loading and dropping certain kinds of ammunition. This was where the expert knowledge and advice of members of the RAOC attached to the Air Despatch Group came in. Some kinds of bomb, for example, can arm themselves under the effect of sudden shock.

The drill for unloading the aircraft in one run over the target area entailed dropping 16 containers in eight to 12 seconds. Instant obedience to the orders of the captain of the aircraft (given by bell signal) was vital, and therefore constant training was required to keep air despatch crews up to the mark. Quickness and deftness were essential, as also was an instinctive habit of keeping the men's parachute harness clear of entanglement with the load. In the case of Stirling aircraft, when the supplies were dropped out of the parachutists' hatch in the floor, great dexterity was required to place the supplies correctly and despatch them rapidly without inadvertently despatching oneself. Loss of crew members through 'self-despatch', due to entanglement with loads, failure to secure life-lines and so on, did unfortunately sometimes occur.

Finally, as all air despatch crews were composed of MT drivers, crews had to be kept up to their normal standard of driving against the time when they might revert to such duties. For all these reasons training formed a large part of the company's programme of work.

Requirements of 21 Army Group

Early in 1944, 21 Army Group stated a firm requirement for

Right:
On the Ground

Below:
'They're Away'

Air Mails

Air Dropping Containers

supply and maintenance by air. The maintenance tonnage was so great that the formation of a large organization to carry out this operation under War Office control was considered necessary. War establishments were drawn up for HQ CRASC, Air Despatch, air despatch company headquarters, air loading platoon, and air dropping platoon. In March, 1944, Headquarters, 36 L of C Transport Column and 223 Troop Carrying Company RASC were temporarily released by 21 Army Group for conversion to these war establishments. They moved into the area of 46 Group RAF airfields at the end of April, and from that date the organization really began to grow.

In figures, their task was set at 170 tons a day for maintenance by air, and 700 tons a day for supply by air. These figures were later stepped up to 350 and 3,000 tons a day respectively. This increase entailed a great expansion in the air despatch organization, which was brought up to three companies with a total of 12 dropping platoons, each of 74 all ranks. The two additional companies got their men from a driver training battalion, which was disbanded for the purpose in May. As the whole organization had to be ready to operate by June 1st, 1944, a lot of hard work had to be done in less than one month, including the formation of dumps, and packing of a reserve of stores amounting to seven days' supply for an infantry or armoured division and five days for a brigade group. Moreover men had to be trained, and methods of control and procedure had to be studied, all of which was new. The airborne divisional companies RASC, which had been in existence for some time already, were of great assistance in providing technical information, but even they had had little practical experience.

How the Requirements were Met

To meet the requirements of maintenance by air, store dumps, as explained above, were sited near airfields. The supplies in these dumps were packed partly in panniers and partly in containers. To meet the needs of supply by air, 3,000 tons of ammunition of various 'common' types and 3,000 tons of petrol were dumped within easy distance of the airfields most likely to be used. The object was for these dumps to act as a 'cushion', subsequent replacements being made from railhead. They proved most successful although the airfields which were eventually used were some distance away. Later, the ammunition reserve was further increased by 1,000 tons of 25-pounder.

A petrol depot (Type C) was placed under command of CRASC Air Despatch, and an RAOC detachment looked after the ammunition dump, which was under the War Office and not under CRASC. As the group was near a supply depot at Swindon, it was not found necessary to form a supply dump. However, there was still the question of ground transport to bring all the 'bits and pieces' of the organization together. For this purpose a pool of general transport companies, under a CRASC, was made available in the area of the airfields. This pool grew to six companies of four platoons each.

The whole of this organization was controlled by DST War Office, through ST 3, where a control room was set up in which the latest position in stocks and transport availability was constantly maintained. Here all information regarding supply and maintenance by air was available and all supply and transport activities connected with them were co-ordinated.

There was also a small movement control organization set up by the RAF at the Air Freight Control Centre, for dealing with their own supply by air, and what was known as 'Schedule Supply by Air', a limited regular service with which the RASC had little to do.

While the air despatch organization was being built up, there also existed in the vicinity of the same airfields an organization for the maintenance by air of airborne troops. This consisted of two air composite companies, RASC (one from each airborne division) controlled directly by DDST Airborne Troops, with an extremely limited staff. These airborne companies were not organized on a special establishment as were the air despatch companies, but were each composed of a headquarters, three transport platoons, two relief driver increments, a composite platoon, and a workshops platoon. The drivers in the transport platoons and relief driver increments were intended to drive to the airfields with their lorries loaded with stores, to load aircraft, accompany the stores in flight, despatch them from the air, and then return to their airfields and their lorries and drive the latter 'home'. This was a heavy day's work, but even if it could be accomplished, the strength of the companies was insufficient to produce more than a maximum of 50 four-man crews. The daily maintenance for one division amounted to 270 tons, requiring at least 135 aircraft, and so it was obvious that these companies, by themselves, would be insufficient for any big airborne operation. Consequently, at the end of June, 1944, DDST Airborne Troops asked DST for help from the air despatch organization. The first result of this was the creation of a second CRASC Air Despatch to exercise, under DDST Airborne Troops, direct control over the two airborne companies, each of which had a large five-day dump of packed stores. The second result was that the two organizations, which were performing almost identical functions, were pooled, and placed under a local commander (colonel), known as 'Commander, Air Despatch Group RASC'. The War Office then undertook responsibility for the maintenance by air of all formations, ground and airborne, including Special Air Service.

The new group consisted of 48 Air Despatch (the original organization set up for ground troops), 49 Air Despatch (the headquarters originally given to DDST Airborne Troops, to look after the two airborne companies), and 53 War Office Transport Column (the transport mentioned as necessary to carry ammunition, supplies and stores from depots to air despatch's own 'cushion dumps' and from these to aircraft). The Commander was also made administratively responsible for 17 Ordnance Beach Detachment, and had under command 389 Company Pioneer Corps. This was the final shape of the organization which came into being on August 18th, 1944. It will be seen, therefore, that it did not take many weeks for the whole arrangement to be thought out, tried and given its final form.

The Story of Air Despatch in Europe

From the day it started, air despatch never had a dull moment. There were emergency calls for supplies for liberated French territories, special deliveries of fuel to the Americans, air maintenance of forces in the operations in the Falaise Gap and on Walcheren island, and stand-by jobs for the British and the Americans on the German frontier. Finally, supplies were delivered by air to the hard-pressed population of northern Holland when the Canadian Army turned quickly north-west again to drive out the invaders (this operation was cut short by the final surrender, but it still left the need for air supply for hungry people). All these tasks, superimposed on the daily programme for 21 Army Group, the continuance of the air drops to the Special Air Service Brigade and the French resistance troops, and the short, tragic but glorious affair of Arnhem, kept all concerned with air despatch constantly alert.

Towards the end of August, 1944, as the campaign in France developed, the demand for emergency supply grew very rapidly. After the fall of Paris, a daily lift of 500 tons of flour and other food was in operation for 14 days in order to feed the civil population. The Transport Column was also called upon for provision of up to 300 vehicles at a time, at very short notice, to transport specially packed supplies to airfields for delivery by air to the French Forces of the Interior and other patriot forces. This was no new service. For a long time air supply had been used for providing the resistance groups with material, just as it had been used for parachuting the men of the Special Air Service Brigade. The main items of supply were arms and ammunition. One or two air despatch crews were in the air every night on this duty. Theirs was an exciting task, and strangely enough the casualties involved were lighter than in any other air supply operations, mainly because the work was done over a very wide area by single aircraft, for the most part, and detection by enemy fighters and ground forces was thus rendered more difficult.

Considerable transport aid was also given to the United States forces in connection with the supply by air of petrol to General Patton's forces during his impetuous advance. As is now common knowledge, the advance of his Third Army (US 4th and 6th Armoured Divisions) took place simultaneously with the advance of our own Guards and 11th Armoured Divisions, the Americans covering 210 miles and the British 250 in the first 14 days. After this Patton went ahead faster. Priority of maintenance went to the American Third Army on the Allied right, but in spite of this both forces, after sensational advances and the capture of prisoners many times greater than their own numbers, were forced to halt for service and maintenance at a moment when German resistance was near to crumbling. It is possible that a more ambitious and pre-organized air supply plan might have sustained the momentum of the advance and have continued to keep the enemy off balance. As things were, this pause gave the enemy also the respite he so desperately needed, and from then on, with the toughness which we have come to expect of the German, he put up a strong resistance for many months. The subject is an interesting study in the influence of the services (in this case the ST service) in maintaining the power of an offensive, an influence which the student of war can trace and assess in most of our operations during this Second World War. This is no criticism of the Air Despatch Group for failure to deliver the petrol required by the United States Third Army. They were not asked to do more.

As the armies moved rapidly across France, the call for supply by air was intensified, and 1,000 tons a day were required. In this operation, ammunition, petrol, and composite rations were the main loads. Later, they became more varied and included large quantities of steel planking and of United States ordnance stores of all sizes and shapes. These had to be sorted into aircraft loads at railhead, a matter requiring a good deal of calculation, measurement and thought.

As regards maintenance by air, there were only a few small operations for ground troops, notably those connected with the Falaise Gap and with Walcheren Island. These were limited operations, and, important though they were, they did not present any unusual features. The number of sorties made in these and in other operations of the Air Despatch Group are given in a table at the end of this chapter.

Two other large scale operations were planned and effected almost to the point of take-off, when they were cancelled. One was the operation to be conducted in conjunction with the United States Army Air Force to drop supplies to American troops in danger of being isolated by the German advance through the Ardennes from December 16th, 1944, until the end of the year. The other was the operation in support of the Rhine crossing in early 1945.

In the first of these a detachment of the Air Despatch Group was pushed down to airfields in the south of England to prepare to drop about 100 aircraft loads. These were required for the 101st US Airborne Division, which made a stand at Bastogne that proved decisive in preventing the crumbling away of the right flank of the Allies' broken lines. The Germans, for their part, failed to reach the line of the Meuse or to overrun the maintenance and supply centres which were their main objectives, and the air drop was found to be unnecessary.

In the second operation, which promised to be second only in magnitude to the Arnhem supply operation, some 250 aircraft were loaded, despatchers prepared, briefed and standing by to maintain the British Army for 24 hours or more after crossing the Rhine. The crossing and advance were, however, performed so successfully that normal methods of supply were able to function and the air support was cancelled at the last moment, except for a few USAAF bombers dropping bomb cell containers.

Arnhem

The operation which gave the Air Despatch Group its biggest job of all, and its most costly and difficult one, was the attack of the 1st British Airborne Division at Arnhem. The chapter on operations in North-West Europe gives the outline story of the plan. The division, maintained by its RASC and by the whole of the Air Despatch Group, was to be landed, mainly by gliders, at Arnhem to seize the bridge over the Lower Rhine there, and to open the way for a left hook into North-West Germany. This might have cut out the costly fighting on the German frontier farther south and the big river crossing there. It was intended that the force, which landed purposely on the north bank of the river, should be relieved after 48 hours by ground troops passed up the main axis running through Eindhoven, Graves and Nijmegen from bridgeheads in Belgium over the Canal de l'Escaut which were already securely in British hands. The three towns named were to be seized by the American 82nd and 101st Airborne Divisions. The 'axis' would of necessity have little depth until the road and the surrounding country for some miles on either side of it were firmly held, for there were powerful German forces to the west and, of course, the main German force to the east.

The landings at Eindhoven and at Graves were successful, and at Nijmegen partially so, but at Arnhem most of the British 1st Airborne Division found itself at Oosterbeek, some six miles west of the bridge. A small body did seize the buildings commanding the northern exit from the bridge, but it was isolated and eventually destroyed after a heroic struggle of small arms against continuous assault by infantry, supported by artillery, and then by tanks. The force at Oosterbeek could not gain ground very much to the east as its dropping zone was restricted and under intense enemy fire. The weather let us down as it so often does, and, instead of a 48-hour operation culminating in relief by the ground forces, the division had to fight for its existence in a diminishing perimeter for nine days before its remnants, some 2,000 strong, were withdrawn by boat across the river under cover of darkness.

As the perimeter contracted, maintenance by air became more difficult every day, and much of the heroic work of the air despatchers and the RAF crews was rendered abortive. The DZ fell early into German hands and only 7·4 per cent of supplies and ammunition dropped reached 1st Airborne Division. Nevertheless, as long as a chance remained of giving aid to the men of the ground, the maintenance by air was kept up. Had the operation continued for only three more days, the last trained RASC crews would have been used up, for of a total of some 900 trained officers and men in the air despatch crews, 264 were shot down in four days of air supply operations. In these operations 600 sorties were flown involving the employment of 450 despatchers in the air daily for several days. Most of the 900 flying officers and men of the group did two sorties and some three.

The exploits of these air despatch crews are apt to be overlooked in most narratives of the Arnhem operation, owing to the more moving story of the struggle on land. However, they were appreciated by the Army and, as narrated later, in addition to the awards to individuals for valour, the Air Despatch Group itself were allowed to wear a distinguishing emblem in recognition of their part in the operation.

Finally, the Air Despatch Group played a large part in the feeding of Holland just before the German withdrawal from that country whose unfortunate people were faced with starvation even as liberation approached. Many tons of food a day were loaded into British bombers and free dropped.

A Sign is given

The formation sign of the Air Despatch Group was a yellow Dakota aircraft on a blue ground. The sign was designed by HQ RASC 48 Air Despatch in the first days of its existence and, although it could not then be worn, it was used on all notice boards, direction signs, etc. When the Air Despatch Group was formed, application was made for a sign to be granted as an official formation sign under the appropriate Army Council Instruction. This was eventually granted, in the words of the War Office minute, 'for the good work done by the Air Despatch Group over Arnhem'. It is believed that this was the first formation sign granted officially to an operational RASC formation, and for this reason, and because of the circumstances in which it was granted, it was a matter of great pride to all ranks.

Air Despatch in SEAC

Turning now to South-East Asia Command, when operations there came to an end in August, 1945, the RIASC organization for air supply had reached a state, both in size and in efficiency, unequalled in any other theatre. Air supply had become the most important form of supply in the whole theatre and without it many of the operations would not have been successful or even possible. No less than 96 per cent of the stores and supplies delivered to the Fourteenth Army in its advance in 1945 were airborne.

The development of the organization started in a small way. In 1941 at a time when the British war record in most theatres was one of defeat, retreat, and, in many cases evacuation, an Air Landing School was, with great vision, established at Delhi. Its charter was the study of airborne operations and tactical air supply, and it was from this school that the Airborne Training Establishment, the Army Air Transport Development Centre, and the Air Despatch Centre were developed. These three training units were all located at Chaklala (that old 'stamping ground' of the RASC in India), and 1 Company RIASC became the first company to be trained in air supply duties.

The first large scale air supply operation took place in 1942, when 1 Company RIASC was sent to Assam to help with the dropping of 3,000 tons of foodstuffs to refugees in Burma.

One of the most important lessons from the withdrawal from Burma was that air supply on a large scale would be required for the support of future operations, and Wingate, as has been mentioned, was quick to drive this home. Training at Chaklala was intensified, and during the years from 1942 to 1945 a total of 10,000 officers and men of the RIASC were trained in air supply duties. The development of air supply equipment and of the technique for dropping awkward loads reached a high degree of perfection, and even the problem of dropping mules by parachute was quickly overcome. And the mules did not seem to mind!

The Task and how the RIASC rose to it

During the operations in Burma, air supply varied from the support of an advanced patrol to the support of a complete army, necessitating the deployment of nine RIASC air despatch companies and one RASC air despatch company in the theatre. The first real advantage of having a sound organization for air supply was evident during the very heavy fighting in Arakan in early 1944. The 7th Indian Division, after being surrounded by the Japanese, was supplied by air to such good effect that it was able to stand firm against all attacks and, with the aid of the relieving 5th and 29th Indian Divisions, to force the enemy to withdraw. Soon after this, some hundreds of miles to the north, powerful Japanese forces attacked and surrounded IV Corps. Air supply enabled the Corps to hold the positions at Imphal and Kohima until relieving formations were able to defeat the enemy and reopen the road lines of communication.

Air supply had established itself, and it continued on all fronts, while the Japanese forces, having negligible air support and no organization for air supply, were never able again to launch a great offensive. In March, 1945, more than 60,000 tons of stores and 48,000 reinforcements were flown into Burma and 11,000 casualties were flown out. Serious casualties had priority on all returning aircraft, and it was not unusual for 'normal' passengers, of the rank of colonel or above, to be left on the air-strip while a stretcher case, of any rank, race or colour, took up five normal 'seats' in the plane. This did a lot to maintain the excellent relations between officers and men which distinguished this army of many races.

The Part played by the RASC

Although the RIASC played the greatest part in the provision of air despatch companies, that played by the RASC must not be forgotten. 61 Company RASC was trained in air supply duties at Chaklala and, after taking part in the support of formations and units of 70th (British) Division employed in the Wingate operations, it was made available for general air supply duties in the theatre. When working for 70th Division its duties included the establishment of air bases deep in Japanese held territory, notably at 'Broadway' and 'White City'—bases whose homely names were classic examples of British understatement.

Early in 1945 two further RASC air despatch companies and two headquarters air despatch arrived from the United Kingdom and, although too late for operations in Burma, one company and one headquarters air despatch were made solely responsible for air supply in support of operations in Java. One of these companies, 799 Company RASC, had an inter-allied existence. After serving with the British Air Despatch Group in support of the Special Air Service Brigade in Normandy and of 1st Airborne Division at Arnhem, it was placed in support of the USAAF in Burma, and finished up at the end of the war by helping the Dutch survivors and their Indian Army liberators in Indonesia.

The Final Organization

The organization evolved in SEAC for air supply is of interest as it became the pattern for the present organization for air supply. An Army Air Transport Organization (AATO) was set up, consisting of HQ AATO and a number of rear air maintenance organizations (RAMOs) and forward air maintenance organizations (FAMOs), and an AATO signal regiment.

The functions of the HQ AATO were to implement the overall air supply plan laid down by the Supreme Commander, SEAC, to control all RAMOs working under it, to receive demands from consumer formations and to allot priorities, and to correlate these demands with available air transport capacity. It also had to apportion accepted demands to RAMOs and to give them air lift forecasts, broken down into commodities, specifying landing or supply dropping, in time for the RAMO concerned to work out its own details, to ensure that adequate stocks were held by or were immediately available to RAMOs, and to act as a central authority in all matters connected with army organization for air supply. It was a staff headquarters, and consisted of a commander of brigadier's rank and a small staff, which included ST and other services representatives.

The RAMO was the executive despatching agency for both air-landed and air-dropped supplies. Its detailed duties were almost identical with those of the CRASC Air Despatch, already fully described in the paragraphs on the British organization. In its case it was a staff 'unit', although the commanders were often RASC/RIASC officers.

The FAMO was located forward and was the receiving agency for air landed supplies delivered by RAMOs. They were allotted on a scale of one for each corps, but were not put down where supply dropping was the planned method of supply. Their duties were to supervise the unloading of air landed supplies and to record receipts, to supervise the collection by the receiving formation of the air landed supplies, and to supervise the backloading of returned stores and of casualties (if no RAF organization existed to do so, they had to load the casualties into the aircraft). When stores were dropped on a forward air strip temporarily unable to accept air landed stores, they were responsible for the organization of the dropping zone in conjunction with the formation RASC/RIASC. The FAMO was under the command of the formation being supplied, and acted as a staff increment to assist and advise on the matters enumerated above. Transport and labour were provided for the FAMO by the formation.

The Work of the Men in the AATO

This short statement of the RASC/RIASC air effort in SEAC can scarcely do justice to the work of thousands of officers and men, British and Indian, who worked without respite to perfect and to operate this splendid service. As in Europe, the highest levels were staff controlled. The actual air despatch crews were in many cases 'unskilled' infantry soldiers (mainly Gurkhas) attached to the air despatch companies, for so great was the extent of the service that almost all the 10,000 trained RIASC men were required for the expert jobs of packing and stowing the airborne loads. Full recognition should be given to the sterling work of these 'infantry attached'.

The landing of supplies in the case of supply by air was fraught with great difficulties because of the rugged nature of the terrain and the limitation in the size of air strips and their approaches. Their troubles were not over when they had unloaded. It was often a question of whether the aircraft could get off the ground and make sufficient height for manoeuvre before coming up against the mountain mass which usually bounded the strip. Many were the breathless moments for the watchers (still more breathless for the crews!) as the craft laboured up and up—and always seemed to gain its height in the nick of time. Monsoon conditions, too, imposed added difficulties and dangers, with low cloud, unpredictable winds funnelling down narrow valleys, and with sodden airstrips. Had the Japanese had the material for and the skill in anti-aircraft defence of the Germans, the tale of losses would have been a heavy one indeed.

Air Despatch in SWPA

Finally, it is appropriate that the efforts of the Royal Australian Air Force and the Royal Australian Army Service Corps in air supply in New Guinea should be mentioned. That country is almost entirely devoid of communications apart from coast-wise shipping, the partly navigable Fly River and certain pack trails. Apart from coral roads made at our various large shore positions such as Lae, Milne Bay and Aitape, there was only one 'jeepable' track, the so-called 'Wau-Bulolo Trail' which connected these two places, the former boasting one of the worst air-strips in the world on a steep slope terminating in a mountain-side. The whole trail covered 110 miles. When the Japanese were driving for Port Moresby from the north side of the island, the defenders of the pass over the Owen Stanley Mountains (the Kokoda Trail) were supplied by air in 1942, and from then onwards the Australian ground forces were frequently moved and supplied by air.

Conclusion

The conclusion of the war was by no means the end of the endeavours of the Corps in the air, and with the further development of load and passenger-carrying aircraft and of armoured ground forces, whose mobility cannot often be fully exploited without air supply, this latest facet of Corps activities has a great future before it.

APPENDIX

Summary of Activities, Air Despatch Group, United Kingdom September 1st to December 31st, 1944, inclusive

(a) Emergency Supply (Freight)

Number of Aircraft	Type of Aircraft	Tonnage
10,575	C47	23,270·15

(b) Maintenance by Air (Airborne and Ground Forces)

Number of Aircraft	Type of Aircraft	Number of Aircraft lost	Tons loaded	Tons dropped
236	C47	29	1,561·14	1,347·23
366	Stirling	46		

(c) Air Landed (Airborne Forces)

Number of Aircraft	Type of Aircraft	Tonnage
104	C47	224.68

(d) S.A.S. Missions (Air)

Number of Crews operated for dropping missions	Number of Aircraft loaded for freight missions
60 2-man crews	54 C47s
2 1-man crews	3 Ansons

CHAPTER XIV

AIRBORNE R.A.S.C.

A New Problem

FROM almost every chapter of this book it emerges that the Corps was constantly faced, in the latest and greatest of all wars, with the need to solve new and unforeseen problems by adapting old and well tried principles. In few cases was adaptability stretched to such limits as in meeting the needs of the completely new airborne arm.

Before the war, airborne forces had never been seriously thought of as a part of the British Army. Any suggestion that the technique of maintenance of several airborne divisions should be worked out or studied would have been considered eccentric. Yet when the need came to launch a whole corps of troops by glider and parachute deep into enemy territory, a complete, efficient, highly-trained RASC organization was ready to deliver its daily load from base depots in England to the man fighting on the ground.

It was not until the middle of 1940 that the first few seeds of the airborne army were sown. In June of that year a handful of officers and men assembled at Ringway in Cheshire to offer themselves as experimental material for parachute development. Up to then, parachutists were regarded as highly paid stunt heroes of the 'Flying Circus', while mass descents of soldiers arranged by the Soviet Army were considered a rather feeble means of trying to frighten other nations with a turnip-bogey. German parachutists in the Netherlands in 1940 had, however, shocked the British out of such an attitude. The airborne arm was seen suddenly to be not only practicable, but powerful: indeed, for a nation isolated on an island, it now seemed to the more perceptive to be a really essential factor in any plan for resuming the attack on the enemy's territory. At the same time, it was about the only type of force of which we were completely ignorant, and for which we had not one ounce or stitch of equipment, not one man with the most elementary training.

So the small band of volunteers assembled, and they jumped or were 'pulled-off', wearing relatively untried parachutes of various kinds, from unsuitable aircraft flown by inexperienced pilots. They had no guidance on how to fall or land. There were, of course, casualties, and the first of these was Dvr R. Evans, RASC, of No. 2 Commando, who was killed when his parachute failed to open, on July 25th, 1940.

This is not the place to describe the steady development of airborne forces as a whole from such small beginnings. Suffice it to say that by early 1941, parachute battalions were being formed. They were soon to develop into brigades, which came together to form the nucleus of the 1st Airborne Division in April, 1942. Soon after this the RASC of the division began to take shape, but what shape was by no means certain.

The armoured and infantry divisional columns had clearly defined and strictly limited roles: to draw in bulk their divisions' daily requirements from a railhead, roadhead, or refilling point, to break down part of them into unit bulk somewhere on the road forward, and to establish nightly points at which to refill first line vehicles. The airborne divisional column, however, had to be designed somehow to draw its daily loads from the airborne base, whose position was necessarily decided by the locations of base airfields (of which there had to be several, to cope with the traffic). They had to take the loads to the airfields, fly with them often hundreds of miles, parachute them to a dropping zone near the formation and within enemy territory, collect and sort them, and then effect final delivery to APs, PPs and SPs. If this was not a sufficient task, the numerous special problems of detail made it so. For instance, the RASC had to do its own packing of all kinds of stores to a strict weight limit into containers which could be conveniently handled. These special containers had been developed after a series of trials. The parachutes had to be attached to the aircraft strong-points. The aircraft had to be loaded most carefully to preserve correct balance and trim, while each container, if inside, had to be settled on its plywood base in the correct position on the runways and made fast. Other types of containers had to be hoisted outside the aircraft into bomb-bays.

The impossibility of securing early demands for replenishment in detail from troops isolated by the enemy made it necessary to hold large stocks of prepacked panniers and other containers available to make up exact loads immediately demands did come in; in the meantime, predetermined average loads were flown.

The problem of getting the airborne element of the column on to the ground in the divisional area, together with vehicles and equipment to collect, sort, handle, and distribute the stores arriving by parachute, was itself a big one. The earliest arrivals had to be the parachute element of the column, who jumped with the earlier flights of the division, selected and made ready the supply dropping zone, reconnoitred dump positions and routes to divisional units, selected delivery points, and collected ready for issue any stores despatched by 'jettison drop' from aircraft of the early flights. They would barely have time for all this before the main part of their unit arrived in gliders which contained also their jeeps or armoured carriers and trailers, and often also a good weight of ammunition, supplies, or other stores to start the airborne dumps: and hardly would these be organized before the first supply drop would begin, from which moment work—usually under fire—would be continuous and heavy.

The term 'jettison drop' needs explaining. Many of the aircraft carrying parachutists or towing gliders were also capable of carrying a useful supply load in bomb-bays. In order not to waste this capacity, they were loaded with an assortment of stores which they dropped immediately after releasing their load of men, even though no organization existed then on the ground to collect it. Although some was inevitably lost, the rest was a useful insurance against delay or failure of subsequent supply missions.

After many trials, a fairly firm organization emerged which endured for most of the war. Under the control of headquarters CRASC (of whom the first was Lieut-Colonel T. H. Jefferies) were two so-called heavy companies (airborne divisional composite companies) and one light company. The former were equipped with 3-ton vehicles, and were expected to do all the packing of stores into panniers, movement to and loading of aircraft, and the provision of air-despatch crews. All this was done at the United Kingdom or base end of the lines of communication. The light company was provided with jeeps, each having two trailers, and had also a parachute platoon: its role was as already described, to collect and distribute the stores from the dropping zone, on to which they had been parachuted by the despatch crews of the heavy companies; and they themselves reached their stations either by parachute or glider.

For a long time this seemed an adequate organization. At any rate, it was the best that could be done without making the tail of the division too heavy. While actual operations seemed likely to be at long intervals, there was plenty of leisure in which to build up pre-packed dumps; the hectic periods of actual operation would certainly stretch every individual to the limit, but the duration would be quite brief. A series of exercises, however, together with the experience already gained by early operations based on North Africa, showed that these ideas were over-optimistic. Airborne formations were not in fact withdrawn immediately after action, but found themselves fighting on for long periods in a ground role, needing all their second line transport, which therefore could not be left to repack and pre-pack in the Airborne Base: and the dumps themselves were growing so fast as to be beyond the capacity of the divisional column to hold.

The Air Despatch Group

A completely separate organization was seen to be necessary, and the Air Despatch Group, whose story is told in another chapter, began to develop. The heavy companies of the 1st Airborne Division were the predecessors of the Air Despatch Group, to whom they handed over a complete technique, painfully worked out, for packing, holding, loading, and despatching stores not only to airborne formations, but to any others requiring emergency supply. The Airborne Column did not entirely relinquish its base work. There was always a heavy company of one of the divisions working with the Despatch Group, concerned more particularly towards the end of the war with the delivery of stores by night to Special Air Service units operating on secret missions in France, the Netherlands and Belgium, to individual agents, and to the underground organizations of those countries. Besides this, the heavy companies of the divisional columns retained the duty of mounting airborne operations —that is, of moving their divisions to sealed camps adjacent to the base airfields, and thence to their aircraft for emplaning, before themselves travelling by sea to join up later in a normal second line role. From these companies also came the steady flow of parachute volunteers who replaced the casualties in the light companies of their own columns.

In raising and training the 1st Airborne Divisional Column from scratch, and simultaneously working out practicable operating methods, there was plenty to do, and there was none too much time before the column left England by sea in May, 1943, for its first taste of active service in North Africa, where the 1st Parachute Brigade, which had been operating there since the previous October, was being joined by the rest of the division, namely the 2nd and 4th Parachute Brigades and the 1st Air Landing Brigade. The North African campaign was over by the time the column was established there, and about two months were spent in the completion of training, under somewhat difficult conditions.

There was little use for re-supply by air in the Sicily campaign, in which, of the division, only the 1st Parachute Brigade and some glider-borne troops were involved; and in the subsequent Italian operations, to which they moved from North Africa by sea, the division was employed in an infantry role. This, while it gave most valuable experience to the column, produced no problems special to airborne forces which might further its education in its proper functions.

While the 1st Division was away, the formation of a second division which would be necessary to form the spearhead of an invasion of Europe was begun. Early in 1943 the units from which the division was to form began to assemble in the Salisbury Plain area. Among these was 398 Company RASC, which had been detached from the Royal Marine Division, then undergoing reorganization. For some months this was the only unit to represent the RASC column, and it found itself employed almost exclusively on daily transport chores for the rest of the formation so that apart from building up its strength of parachutists it was able to do little in the way of training for war. In September, however, it was decided to complete the column and 716 and 63 Companies arrived for conversion. A CRASC headquarters was formed at the same time.

Planning for D Day

With the experience of the 1st Airborne Division now available and with the competitive spirit induced by the presence hard by of the 101st United States Airborne Division, the column, spurred also by the knowledge that D Day could not be far ahead, rapidly gained in efficiency and within a matter of weeks was fit for war. Many exercises on an unprecedented scale could now be undertaken. All the resources both of Transport Command RAF and of the United States Army Air Force were available for a complete divisional exercise, and the RASC column also took part in several American exercises, gaining valuable experience of operating technique.

The arrival of the 82nd United States Airborne Division in the United Kingdom led to the formation of an American Airborne Corps headquarters under General Matthew Ridgway. About the same time the return of the 1st Airborne Division to the United Kingdom was the signal for the formation of headquarters 1st British Airborne Corps. This had long existed, but in a much reduced form under the title of HQ Airborne Forces. As a fullblown Corps HQ it now received a DDST in the person of Colonel T. H. Jefferies, who was promoted from the 1st Airborne Division in which he was succeeded as CRASC by Lieut-Colonel M. St. J. Packe, who had been the first airborne company commander, RASC. There is no need to describe the intensive preparations which took place in the early months of 1944 since they had a parallel in every division of the British Army. The 6th Airborne Division had been selected as the one to play an essential part in the earliest phases of the assault upon the enemy stronghold.

The parachute brigades were to drop in the early hours of D Day (June 6th, 1944), before the seaborne assault approached the beaches, to seize the vital bridges over the Orne and the Caen-Ouistreham Canal, and secure the left flank of the intended beachhead. Reinforced later in the day by the air landing brigade in gliders, they were to extend the territory held and destroy bridges

At Railhead

Crossing a Pontoon Bridge

Landing and Wading

over the river Dives to prevent the approach of enemy reinforcements.

The CRASC's plan was to send two parachute platoons and three jeep-trailer platoons by air on D Day, the remainder of the light company travelling by sea. One heavy company would be engaged solely in air despatch duties, while the other, loaded with second-line holdings, was to go by sea with the assault force. So great was the competition for shipping space that the workshop vehicles of this unit were 'frozen out'. However, the artificers, determined to get there, went on foot, carrying their tools. Airborne supplies were to consist of a jettison drop, followed by a normal supply drop the same evening. It was expected that the assault forces from the beaches would join up with the division within a day or two, bringing further supplies, but since there would be a general scarcity in the beach-head in the early stages, three further supply drops to the division were arranged for the first week.

In spite of the various contretemps which seem inseparable from airborne operations, this plan was highly successful, and by 0600 hours on D Day a dump had been set up in the orchard of the Ferme d'Ecarde near Ranville and stocked with the produce of the jettison drop. Although this had been very scattered, enough was recovered to keep the division going until the link-up, the only shortage being of 75 mm howitzer ammunition, of which 15,000 rounds was expended the first day, 13,000 the next, and 2,500 on June 8th, when the first pre-loaded vehicles managed to get through by land.

Collection and distribution were complicated by the fact that several of the RASC men were 'dropped wide', and had to make their way some miles through unfamiliar enemy country to a location they had never seen. Among them was the senior supply officer, who encountered a German patrol, which he routed, killing some, but was himself seriously wounded, and had to be evacuated when he at last rejoined the column. The CRASC did not arrive until D plus 1, the tow-rope having parted on his glider, which landed at Worthing. In spite of these setbacks, by the morning of D plus 1 the DMA was in full working order, and the men, although very tired, were doing their job with great enthusiasm. For some time afterwards, all were overworked, for from D plus 1 onwards 1st and 44th Special Service Brigades (Commandos) came under command. They had no RASC units of their own, and in consequence one attentuated company was supplying the needs of five brigades.

During the afternoon of D plus 2, the enemy counterattacked in some strength across the glider landing zone, and many RASC men were in action. The attack was successfully repelled.

At first, the 8-gun 75 mm howitzer battery was located round the perimeter of the dump, and the peculiar situation existed whereby ammunition was issued direct from stacks to guns. Hardly less strangely, a little later the battery was withdrawn to the line of the River Orne, and the ammunition was issued to the rear. Both these situations caused some misgivings, since in the former counter-fire was directed straight on to the DMA, and in the latter case the dumps received the enemy's 'shorts'. Mortaring was constant, although the enemy did not seem to have discovered the dump; but it was revealed a week or two later when a shell set a vehicle in the ammunition depot on fire, and the resulting blaze attracted concentrated bombardment. The stacks were hit and began to explode. The first was promptly extinguished by the composite platoon, but another direct hit on the howitzer ammunition started a blaze which could not be controlled. The platoon did its best, but after two men had been killed, it was withdrawn, and the dump went on burning and exploding for 12 hours. It was subsequently found that the total loss was only about a quarter of the stocks. The method of stacking had been such that the remainder were 'balanced', and there was consequently no serious shortage.

By the sixth day, all vehicles of the heavy company had joined, and replenishment could be done direct from beach depots.

The airborne phase gradually lessened, the division becoming practically an infantry formation for the ensuing operations. A Belgian and a Netherlands brigade came under command, presenting certain ration problems, which were solved, but bringing some second-line transport with them which was a great help, particularly when, without warning, the RASC was called on to provide troop-carrying transport for the first break-out from the beach-head.

By off-loading everything and working 24 hours without a stop, they did it, and set off for Troarn, Pont l'Évêque, and Pont Audemer. This move was like that of any other column advancing from the beach-head: the RASC captured some Germans and killed others, and liberated various villages as a sideline to its more normal functions.

The column's casualties during the early phases had been two officers and 20 other ranks killed, three officers and 41 other ranks wounded, and 14 missing. The heavy company which had remained in England to carry out the air despatch suffered no losses, as far as is known: they performed the same duties later, however, on behalf of the 1st Airborne Division at Arnhem, where their casualties numbered 44.

The 1st Airborne Division had during all this time been chafing in England at the delay in finding them a suitable operation. The break-out from the bridgehead in Normandy seemed at last to promise one; indeed, it promised more, for in the 15 weeks after the initial landings, 17 operations were planned, only to be abandoned in succession as the objectives were taken by ground forces. The effect on morale of all these cancellations, some not notified until after the division was already emplaned, began to be felt: but at last came operation 'Market Garden'.

The Allies' Task

In brief, the task given to the First Allied Airborne Army, which now comprised two British and three United States divisions, was to seize the bridges over the Maas, the canal at Graves, the Waal, and the Neder Rijn, all of which were big obstacles, and hold them until XXX Corps could cross them all and debouch into the Eastern Netherlands and the North German plain. The seizure of the Neder Rijn bridge at Arnhem, which was the northernmost, and some 60 miles in advance of the forward troops of XXX Corps, was allotted to 1st Airborne Division, the other bridges being the responsibility of 82nd and 101st United States Airborne Divisions.

The CRASC's plan was for one parachute platoon to fly in with each of the three brigades of the first air-lift, collect the large quantities of ammunition which were to go in simultaneously in gliders and, after delivering it to their brigades, return to the pre-selected supply dropping point which would by that time have been captured. This they were to lay out and prepare, at the same time seizing any German and Netherlands transport which they could lay hands on. In the second lift on the following day, CRASC's headquarters and the remainder of the light company would arrive, their jeeps and trailers fully loaded, and begin ferrying supplies from the abandoned gliders and from containers of the jettison-drop to the divisional maintenance area, which would be completely under RASC control. On the third day would come the first supply drop, followed by further daily missions to maintain the force until XXX Corps reached them. From then onwards, the two heavy companies (one of which had been on the Continent, loaded, for a considerable time, awaiting any operation which might occur) would carry on normal surface maintenance.

The plan miscarried. Not being able to bring his whole force in a single air-lift, General Urquhart, the divisional commander, found himself compelled to engage an unexpectedly large enemy force piecemeal. In spite of this, the bridge was held for longer than was planned, but XXX Corps was unable to reach it and it had to be given up.

The RASC contingents landed as planned, but one of the parachute platoons was cut off with its brigade at the Arnhem bridge, could not return to the SDP, and all its men became casualties. The SDP itself was never captured. Signals sent to divert the supply drop on D plus 2 failed to get through, and in consequence the armada of Stirling and Dakota aircraft sailed through murderous fire right over the now restricted divisional perimeter and dropped their cargoes to the enemy. A second parachute platoon which made a fighting sortie to recover some of the supplies fell into an ambush and half of them were lost, only the personal gallantry of their officer, Captain D. T. Kavanagh, who lost his life charging a machine-gun post single-handed with a Bren gun, enabling the remnants to escape.

During the next few days, the rest of the RASC did what little could be done. Under continual mortaring and sniping, jeeps chased about recovering panniers and containers dropped both inside and outside the perimeter. A new DMA was formed and a new SDP marked out with improvised panels. For a brief period a fairly normal supply of ammunition could be maintained, but what little food arrived was reserved for the hospital. On some days the weather was foggy and no supply drop could be made. On others the drop took place, in face of an ever-increasing intensity of anti-aircraft fire and in spite of attacks by German fighter aircraft. There were many acts of great heroism on the part of the RASC air despatch crews and their RAF colleagues. Of scores of accounts, one only, written by an infantry officer, need be quoted as example:

'It was with excited hopefulness and an almost painful admiration that those on the ground watched these aircraft day by day, flying in to drop their loads. Through a continuous curtain of fire they flew on unwaveringly and very slowly—and so low that it seemed wonderful that more of them were not destroyed—to drop their loads which floated down mostly behind the enemy lines. Many were hit and set on fire, but continued to despatch their panniers until they fell from view; one unknown aircraft was already on fire when it arrived over the target, but dropped half its load, circled again, losing height the while, and dropped the remainder on the second run until it went down in a sheet of flame. There were many acts of great gallantry in the air, and there were fairly heavy casualties among the RASC despatchers. But it is consoling to know that the small proportion of the many hundreds of tons dropped which did reach our lines enabled hungry men to have some sort of a meal on the fifth day, and also provided sufficient ammunition of all kinds to keep weapons firing and to keep the RASC dump "in issue" right up to the withdrawal.'

Of all aircraft taking part in the supply operations 7 per cent were lost. Many of their RAF and RASC crews could have abandoned their mission and saved their lives. It was not all in vain: although only $7\frac{1}{2}$ per cent of the total drops could be collected, it was just enough to keep the attenuated division in action, and may have been decisive in enabling the final withdrawal to take place, instead of a total surrender.

On the ground, the situation steadily became worse, and the defended area progressively smaller. Mortaring and shelling, always continuous, increased to tremendous intensity after each supply drop. The ammunition dump caught fire, and the fire was put out several times with great difficulty. CRASC had a personal interest in this, as his headquarters, a slit trench, was between the 3-inch mortar stack and the small arms fire. The jeeps were knocked out one by one. By the end, there were no supplies of any sort, nor a single vehicle left.

On the sixth day, the remnants of the last parachute platoon, now without a job, were organized into a force some 70 strong, and sent to hold a sector of the perimeter, which they defended successfully to the end. Then, with the other survivors, they retired across the swift-flowing Rhine in the pouring rain, some in boats and some by swimming. Ten RASC officers and 243 other ranks had flown in to Arnhem. Five officers and 83 other ranks came out. Of those who did not, two officers and 36 other ranks were killed, and many more were wounded.

Some 10 miles south of Arnhem lies Nijmegen, the location of Airborne Corps HQ all this time. Although cut off for varying lengths of time on several occasions, Corps HQ had managed to secure fairly adequate supplies by setting up an improvised airfield at Grave, where one considerable Dakota lift, together with a jeep company, was landed. Stocks of excellent German food and less excellent petrol were discovered from time to time, the principal source being a huge depot 12 miles away in enemy territory at Oss, from which for a time Corps HQ drew by day and the Germans by night. This enabled the headquarters and several hospitals to be supplied, while the rations of 82nd United States Airborne Division near by could be supplemented, and a significant contribution was made to the resources of the beleaguered town.

It was not long before the road to Nijmegen was consolidated by XXX Corps, which established a front running through Elst, halfway to Arnhem. The remnants of the tattered 'First Airborne', having been received, fed, clothed and comforted at Nijmegen, were sent off back to England to reorganize and reconstitute themselves, followed not long after by Corps headquarters.

Assault on the Rhine

The failure of operation 'Market Garden' to secure a bridgehead across the Rhine through which the main forces could enter Germany meant that a full-scale assault of the river would have to be mounted, and the project was deferred until the spring. In the intervening months most of the territory west of the high ground which flanks the river was cleared up, an extensive series of muddy operations took place in the flooded Northern Netherlands, and the Germans staged their last great counterattack through the Ardennes, into Luxembourg and Belgium, cutting off the 101st United States Airborne Division in Bastogne. The 6th Airborne Division, in a ground role, was sent to help restore the position, and when this was done, was withdrawn again to England to prepare for the assault of the Rhine in the vicinity Xanten-Wesel, a joint Anglo-American, land, air, and partly amphibious operation known by the code word 'Varsity-Plunder'.

Hitherto, airborne forces had been employed as the spearhead of assault, to make the fullest use of the factor of surprise inherent in their rapid approach. On this occasion however, surprise was impossible—our intention to cross was only too obvious to the Germans watching from the other bank. So it was decided, by a really heavy artillery bombardment, to drive them as far back as possible. This would allow a night assault in boats and amphibian vehicles by ground forces. However, on the German side excellent cover was available in dense woods a mile or two from the river, and the bridgehead would be precarious if the German counterattack forces were allowed to build up. So the 6th Airborne Division was to be dropped some four miles on the German side in the general area of Hamminkeln after the assault phase had been completed to cover the consolidation of the bridgehead and the initial advances from it. American plans in the adjoining sector to the south were similar.

This was a short-range operation, and the CRASC's plans for maintaining the 6th Division were simple, although their actual execution demanded very careful co-ordination between the seaborne and airborne elements of the column, and between the former and the ground forces with which they were located.

The light company less two transport platoons (i.e. three parachute platoons and one transport platoon) equipped with 12 carriers and trailers instead of jeeps, were to fly in with the division, the transport being in Hamilcar gliders which also stowed as many pannier loads of stores as could be got within the weight limit. The company's first duty on landing was to select a divisional maintenance area and begin stocking it, the initial stores comprising the panniers from the Hamilcars, two boxes of composite rations from nearly all other gliders used in the operation, and whatever could be recovered from the jettison drop. Fast work was needed, since the first full day's supply drop was due three hours after the landing, and it was desirable to begin collecting it as soon as it came, so as to clear the SDZ for the next drop due at dawn the following morning and consisting of two days' requirements. In the event this latter drop was not needed, and was cancelled because the land maintenance route had been established before it was due.

Since the requirements of an airborne division are of somewhat different nature from those of more normal formations, it was thought necessary to have ready an immediate supply to bring forward when the ground forces linked up with the division; XII Corps CMA would not normally hold the required stocks. Accordingly, well before the operation, a depot area known as Nutcracker dump was established near Sonsbeck, about six miles south-west of the Rhine bend at Xanten.

At Xanten also there were assembled the land elements of the division, including HQ RASC and the two heavy companies. To them were attached 69 dukws, all of which were preloaded, ready to cross the river as soon as it was open, and, to begin to establish a second depot area, to be known as Pegasus dump, on the east side within reach of the battle. The adjutant, with provost and pioneer assistance, was to reconnoitre a suitable position for Pegasus dump as soon as he could get across, and, having guided the leading vehicles to it, would make contact with the officer commanding light company and let him know that maintenance was assured.

When the operation started CRASC's plan worked well, in spite of unforeseen difficulties. The airborne party, of seven officers and 91 other ranks, with 10 public relations men under their wing, met with formidable opposition when they landed at about 10.45 a.m. on March 24th, 1945. Visibility was bad, the whole ground being blanketed by a fog of smoke and dust set up by the intensive artillery bombardment. To show the risks of this kind of operation, a brief account of the fate of each RASC glider is given:—

No. 267—A good landing, but shelled and set on fire as the carrier was got out. The carrier crew went to assist in getting a wounded man from another glider, which was itself hit, and burned out. Casualties, one officer, six ORs RASC wounded, glider pilot killed.

No. 268—Crashed in England after take-off. All occupants badly injured.

No. 269—Missing.

No. 270—A good landing in the midst of a battle. Tail hit by anti-aircraft fire, but nobody injured.

No. 271—Shot down, breaking up badly, but nobody hurt. Carrier shed a track, but was repaired by unit fitter.

No. 272—Hit by flak, managed a fair landing, losing a wheel and crashing through a fence. No casualties.

No. 273—Subsequently found outside the divisional perimeter, with both pilots dead, but no sign of RASC crew or load.

No. 274—Right wing damaged by flak and torn off on landing. Carrier intact, and no injuries.

No. 275—Badly hit by flak, crashed in the Wesel area (United States sector) and broke up. Carrier and load much damaged, one officer, one OR wounded. The remainder fought with the Americans for two days until the way was open to return to their unit.

No. 276—Set on fire by flak, but made a fair landing and the carrier was extracted before the glider burned out. Two ORs wounded. The glider was quickly surrounded by a large enemy party and all were captured.

No. 277—Hit by flak, crashed and broke up, on a railway line. One or two war correspondents wounded.

No. 278—A good landing. Carrier struck by small arms fire on leaving the glider, but little damage resulted.

There can be small wonder that after one operational flight, most glider-borne troops wished they had elected to become parachutists.

Dumps established

In spite of these mishaps, the DMA was quickly reconnoitred and stores dumps began to be established, transport consisting only of three carriers, one trailer, and a captured lorry. At 1300 hours the first supply drop took place, and it was a bad one. Not only was it widely dispersed, but much of it was dropped from too low a height, giving the parachutes insufficient time to open, so that a great many containers burst open. This was not wholly a disadvantage, since it was decided to open all containers *in situ*, to save transport, instead of carrying them complete to the DMA.

The process was of course slow, and by 1600 hours the division was running out of ammunition, the situation being described for a while as 'tense'. However, by sheer desperate hard work, ammunition supply was maintained, and things became easier by 1800 hours, when three more carriers and two more trailers were at work. The officer commanding the light company badly needed help, but the CRASC's representative at divisional headquarters had been badly wounded, and the AA&QMG had not arrived. However, the officer commanding went himself and found a DAQMG, who promised the aid of 40 jeeps and trailers from the air landing brigade to get the dropping zone cleared during the night. Only 10 turned up, and those not until dawn, when they did good work.

Clearance continued through the night, in spite of parties of enemy infiltrating through the woods and crossing the dropping zone. One party of about 200 captured an RASC officer and four men, and also unfortunately the German lorry, thus cutting down the remaining lift quite seriously. However, later in the night, they yielded to the officer's threats, reversed their roles, and were duly delivered to the cage, when the lorry again became available for clearance of the SDZ.

In the meantime, progress from the far side of the river had been satisfactory. The first crossings had been made about 10 hours before the airborne landings, and CRASC's adjutant, arriving about 0945 with HQ RASC of the 15th (Scottish) Division, set out on his reconnaissance, although fired on several times, and selected and marked a site for the Pegasus dump. That day 18 dukws crossed, and by the evening of the next, 84 dukw-loads had been delivered at the Pegasus dump. At this point, amphibious transport was stopped, through fear that a breakdown might cause a dukw to be swept by the swift current against the newly-built pontoon bridge a little below the crossing point. Thereafter, all supplies crossed the bridge in the vehicles of the heavy companies, which were given bridge priority. Soon after this, normal supply to 6th Airborne Division from the Pegasus dump began, and the division became to all intents an infantry formation for the rest of the operation.

With the crossing of the Rhine, the last airborne operation was complete, and no more actually took place (though others were planned), during the remainder of the war, if the occupation of Copenhagen and other Scandinavian cities by 1st Airborne Division is excepted: these moves were peaceful ones, the forces being comfortably landed on airfields.

But the airborne arm had not finished its work; indeed, from then on to the final submission of the enemy, the 6th Division carried on its longest campaign, in the role of an infantry formation. For that purpose it was not at first ideally organized or equipped, and its RASC in particular were greatly handicapped by having only three companies, one equipped with jeeps. The new role of the division was, in conjunction with 11th Armoured Division, to lead the advance of VIII Corps in pursuit of an enemy whose capacity and will to hit back were so far unknown, and the intention was that the pursuit should be as rapid as possible—a chase in which the Germans were to be given no chance to stand and reorganize, or to prepare defensive positions. Clearly the column's transport was inadequate for this work, especially as it was called upon to 'motorize' two-thirds of the division at a time in the interests of speed.

Accordingly, during the first few days after the Rhine crossing, the column withdrew to the Pegasus area, and in a few days, allocations of five transport platoons, including two of 5-tonners, had been obtained from outside resources. A column transport office was set up to allocate vehicles rapidly to whatever function—troop-carrying, ammunition, petroleum, or supply duties—and to whichever company seemed to need it most. Rapid changes of requirement had to be foreseen, according to whether the enemy fought or fled, and according to the distances covered from day to day. In the meantime, replenishment continued to be drawn from the Pegasus dumps until VIII Corps CMA was established east of the river.

Not knowing exactly the scope of his task, the CRASC wisely adapted the 'jettison drop' system normal to an airborne division, and equipped every troop-carrying vehicle with 10 compo packs and 36 jerricans of petrol. This could sustain the whole division for two days and 150 miles, while each unit also carried a day's food and petroleum reserve; thus, however far the formation outstripped its normal second line system, the column would have three days (which it never in fact needed) to catch up, and could safely turn to its main preoccupation, ammunition supply. This was a real, though imponderable problem. So fast did the division move that it was almost nightly necessary to put out ammunition points in places far ahead which could not be reconnoitred, and which were often in enemy possession almost up to the moment of opening. The same thing applied to supply and POL points, since the division daily moved into areas beyond its planned objective, and could not be called right back to prearranged points for replenishment.

The RASC had to think and move rapidly, keeping well up to the forefront of the advance; on at least one occasion, near Lengerich, an ammunition point reconnaissance party was urged loudly by a platoon commander of a leading infantry battalion to get out of the way, as they were obstructing the line of fire.

Naturally, the location of points established at such short notice could not always be notified to all units; consequently, direct delivery of commodities to battalion lines from the points was often resorted to, which called for a good deal of intelligent work on the part of drivers in tracing the different units. It is often overlooked that in circumstances like these, the whole replenishment system in the end depends upon the stamina, endurance, and intelligence of the ordinary lorry driver, who is frequently 36 hours or more at the wheel, often quite on his own, before returning to his company location. Too often, too, the company moves to an unknown destination while the driver is away, and he then has to set off up the divisional axis with his eye on the unit signs, to find his own home.

To avoid failure through excessive fatigue (and there was in fact no recorded case of such failure) deliveries to units were kept to a minimum. The necessity was before long eliminated by selecting 12 hours in advance a point on the intended axis, well ahead, but certain to be captured during the day, at which CRASC set up an information centre. The position of this point was notified to all brigades and units early in the day, and to it they sent representatives in the evening, by which time AP, Sup P, and PP locations had been selected and notified to the information centre.

It was no easy matter for CRASC to keep control, especially as he was himself constantly on the move with his headquarters. Starting at Bislich on March 27th, he occupied 14 different locations by April 24th, and of these eight were used for only one night, and four for two nights. From the Rhine to the well-known Steinhudermeer, near Hanover, he moved in 12 days, occupying nine different nightly locations on the way; and of course the column moved in the same manner. Successful maintenance in these conditions is a measure of the high degree of training and physical and mental flexibility of this airborne divisional column, which was never intended or indeed formally trained for any such purpose. To add to the difficulties, the bad roads were often blocked by endless streams of prisoners and refugees (which the column was sometimes called on to clear); transport help had to be given in moving the corps maintenance area forward; drivers ran the continual hazard of snipers, with which the plentiful woods abounded; and the composition of the division as well as its location changed daily, no fewer than 35 additional units being attached for varying periods during the advance. Later, this number was still further increased by the responsibility for maintaining four huge prisoner of war camps and two German hospitals.

To combat the sniper risk some armoured jeeps were obtained for use instead of motorcyclists for intercommunication; of these 716 Airborne (Light) Company provided three for CRASC HQ and for each company, and also three for each of the brigade headquarters (3rd Parachute Brigade, 5th Parachute Brigade, and 6th Air Landing Brigade).

In spite of all difficulties every unit was supplied.

The next great obstacle was the River Elbe, and at first it was considered that this could best be crossed by airborne assault; but operation 'Audacious', planned to this end, was replaced by a commando operation, Enterprise, in the exploitation of which two brigades of the 6th Division were engaged, the third being held in case a drop was still found necessary.

Most careful planning was involved, the main RASC problems being, firstly, to establish a divisional dump area west of the river; secondly, to transfer it across the one class 9 bridge available and establish forward points as soon as the division was across (and as the bridge traffic was one-way for two days, the total quantity to be carried in a single lift was three days' consumption); thirdly, to maintain part of the division still on the west bank after the crossing had begun; fourthly, to replenish divisional stocks by drawing from VIII Corps CMA at Lüneburg; and fifthly the attachment of MT sections to other arms to supplement their light establishments. A sixth task, not usual for RASC, was the phasing of all units of all arms across the bridge, which was conducted with notable smoothness.

The assault took place on April 29th, 1945, and by May 1st the bridgehead was secure. The column had been strained to the uttermost, but there was no rest for it, since on May 2nd the rush for the Baltic began.

Now under command of XVIII United States Airborne Corps, the 6th Division was inspired in its dash over the next and last lap of 80 miles by three objects—to reach the Baltic coast before any of their American companions, to capture Wismar before the Russians could get there, and to be the first British troops to link up with the Russian forces.

No reliable information existed about the enemy; there was no indication of whether he would fight or yield, and consequently no chance to decide whether ammunition or petrol would be the more important load. The CRASC had to provide plenty of both, and in this he had perhaps the hardest task of the campaign, since, in addition to supplying the division along three separate brigade routes, covered at high speed, his transport resources were overstrained by the necessity of carrying two of the brigades (in 120 3-ton lorries). The third brigade hoped to move by rail in a German train they had discovered—if they could get it to go. It is worth mentioning too that the division had under command two field regiments and an anti-tank battery RA, and the Royal Scots Greys, the last named having one squadron with each brigade, which made the RASC task no easier.

CRASC decided that the second-line movement could only be on the central route, following up 3rd Parachute Brigade. On this, all supply, petrol and ammunition points would be established, and the brigades on the other two axes would have to draw from these by cross-country route. A 'signing squad' from 716 Company followed the RASC vehicles up the road, hammering in Pegasus signs so that no matter where unit vehicles joined the route, they would be automatically directed to the points.

To reduce the call on points as much as possible, in case anything went wrong, every one of the troop-carrying RASC lorries carried 51 filled jerricans of petrol, and each brigade headquarters had two 10-tonners of ammunition permanently attached. The food problem was less urgent, as all units carried reserves as well as their normal day's maintenance at the beginning of the move.

It might all have been necessary, but in the event, the advance began in a mad rush at 0800 hours on May 2nd, 1945, and 3rd Parachute Brigade reached Wismar on the Baltic at 1430 hours, later reporting that its total ammunition expenditure en route was one single round of .303 which was directed at a sniper. By midnight the same day, the whole division was in, and the three objects had been achieved in a few hours.

The RASC drivers of the troop-carrying vehicles had the privilege of seeing the complete collapse of the German armies north-east of the Elbe.

The activities of the column thereafter, though busy and interesting, need not concern us.

On May 19th the air party took off from Lüneburg for the United Kingdom; on the 20th the land party began its long journey to Ostend. The airborne divisional columns RASC had completed their task in the world's greatest war.

CHAPTER XV

ANIMAL TRANSPORT

This Chapter incorporates some personal narratives which give such a vivid impression of the operations of pack units that they have been included here rather than in Chapter XVII.

Introduction

IN the years between the wars, the horse lost its military importance, and was finally retained only for ceremonial occasions. Its passing from the army was undoubtedly watched with regret by both old and young. Pre-war plans for placing a force in France in the event of attack by Germany did not include a single animal in the vast quantity of transport which would accompany it.

Nevertheless, although it was hoped that mechanization and modern weapons would confine operations to country where their power could be developed to the full, it was obvious that the machine in mountains and jungle would often be useless.

The RASC, as the transport corps of the army, were therefore charged with keeping alive the technique of pack transport by maintaining a small training nucleus, which, considering its small number of animals, 25 only, was given the somewhat grandiose title of Animal (Training) Transport Company. Few people at this stage would have guessed that once again that sturdy, strong, rather lovable yet surly animal of uncertain mood, the mule, was to provide the backbone of the pack transport units, which were to make it possible for the army to advance in the steaming jungles of Burma and on the snow-clad hills of Italy.

The training company had a wide charter as the term 'pack technique' included not only the skills of using pack saddlery and making up pack loads but such matters as the organization of pack units and methods of instructing units in the use and management of small pack detachments. The normal practice in the British Army was to form pack units in theatres of war by using cadres of British officers and NCOs and filling the ranks from locally enlisted men. Animals also were normally drawn from those available locally in overseas commands. This practice involved the ability to train and equip a diversity of men and animals when the occasion arose.

The first indications that the animal was to return to his own came shortly after the war broke out with a call for animal transport companies for the BEF and with a decision that a mounted division was to be formed and despatched at once to Palestine for training. As the Indian Army still possessed animal (horse, mule and camel) transport companies, the Indian Government agreed to fill the wants of the BEF. Thus the honour of being the first Indian Army units to take their place in an active theatre of war fell to our sister Corps the RIASC. Their story is already well told in *Eastern Defence* but it is of special interest to record that the commander of the companies was Lieut-Colonel R. W. W. Hills, who had received his early training when serving with the Corps, before he transferred to the RIASC.

The divisional RASC for the mounted division was mechanized but the provision of the forage required for the mounted regiments produced a fresh problem for the supply branch at the War Office, as, having been assured a few months before that there would not be 'a horse in the force', they had disposed of their forage reserves just before the war. The new Ministry of Food, which had taken over the control of grain imports, responded to the occasion and made arrangements to produce what was wanted at home for the voyage to Palestine and to cover the transitional period after landing overseas before animals could be acclimatized to eat the grains which could be obtained locally. The division had a short life in its mounted role after arrival overseas, and many of its animals were then used to equip four pack companies which were needed in the Middle East and formed by cadres sent out from Home for the purpose. Not long after Dunkirk orders were given to form a pack transport company in the United Kingdom. Reorientation of strategy after the fall of France included the possibility of at least one division being required for operations in mountainous country generally assumed to be Norway. Later, in 1941, a second company was formed; both were composed of British officers and men. The disbandment of the Cavalry Training Regiment provided a source of trained horsemen who proved willing volunteers for the two new companies. North Wales was their training ground and, after a period of general toughening up, both units moved to Scotland for practical exercises with the 52nd Division which was being specially trained in mountain warfare, although, ironically enough, to the public it was famous as the 52nd (Lowland) Division. Perhaps the most unexpected demand for pack transport came from Gibraltar where a small company was formed in 1942 from the officers' chargers which were available in the station. The officer commanding the unit combined his official duties with being the honorary treasurer, honorary secretary and kennel huntsman of the famous Calpe Hunt until he took the company to North Africa a year later.

In 1943 pack transport (a cadre) figured for the first time in the initial order of battle for an expeditionary force—for North Africa; but it was not until the opening of the campaign in Italy that it was required on a really extensive scale. The Italian battleground was, until the armies finally reached the plains in the north, one of mountains and rivers and although bull-dozers, power tools and Bailey bridge tracks were used to the fullest advantage in making the impassable into the passable, there was usually a gap which could only be filled by the pack animal in the first instance. Thus the pack units in Italy were very much front line troops. Towards the end of the campaign no fewer than 30,000 animals were being employed by the Allied armies. All the pack units employed by our own army were led by British officers and NCOs but for convenience were designated by the nationality of the men in the unit. Thus references will be seen later in this account to Cypriot, North African (mostly Algerians and Tunisians) and Italian groups or companies. The RIASC units consisted of the usual proportions of British and Indian officers and other ranks.

The accounts which follow have been selected from the campaign in Italy because they are typical of the work of pack units and because they illustrate well the qualities which are needed by these units on active service.

The mention of names in a regimental history always calls for judicious care, but those of four pack group commanders in Italy cannot be omitted. They were Lieut-Colonels J. Hume Dudgeon, the Royal Scots Greys, R. B. Adderley, R. Fleming and C. T. Berridge. As Colonel Dudgeon was the first non-RASC officer to volunteer to raise a pack company in the United Kingdom and eventually came to be regarded as paternal adviser to the less experienced units, the Corps owe him a special debt of gratitude which can be most aptly expressed by saying that his reputation as a leader of pack transport rivalled his reputation in the international jumping world.

No account of pack transport would be complete without mention of the close liaison between the Corps and the officers and men of the Royal Army Veterinary Corps who tend and care for animal casualties. A special tribute is paid also to those officers and men from other corps of the armed forces who, when the need for expansion arrived, willingly joined the ranks of the Corps and played such a large part in the success of pack transport.

Nursery Slopes

Thanks to some far-sighted planner who sat in Norfolk House,

In the Italian Mountains

where the North African invasion was planned, a small body of 12 officers and 36 other ranks drawn from the pack companies training in Scotland, landed in Algiers in November, 1942. From this nucleus grew the many groups of companies of many nations which were to take the field in strength in Italy.

The reception of the two cadres represented by this handful of men was hardly enthusiastic, and some of them were immediately consigned to other work on the grounds that 'we shall not want any animals in this war'. Before long, however, when two British divisions (78th and 46th) became engaged in the mountainous country stretching from Souk El Arba to the sea, the cry changed to 'send us some pack transport at once'.

It did not take the cadres long to prove the value of their training days, as two companies each of four troops (75 animals in a troop) were now put in the field. These were made up with Arab recruits and animals hastily procured locally from the French. These Arabs with which the companies were filled had, of course, no military training being recruited straight from the fields. Not one spoke a word of English. They met the immediate need; but it soon became obvious that the training of both men and animals was inadequate. Furthermore, their task was made no easier by the ignorance of the use and capabilities of pack transport among the units they were supporting.

The companies could not be withdrawn for training until after the defeat of the Germans in North Africa.

Meanwhile an appeal to the United Kingdom brought reinforcements for the British cadres, and the French agreed to provide a number of officers and NCOs. The French, with their experience in dealing with the Arabs, were a great help, though their training methods often seemed rather rough and ready to the British. It was not long, however, before the strange mixture of British, French and Arabs was welded into a whole, and if there was no common language there was very soon a unity of purpose and of spirit among them.

During training the group were joined by the pack company from Gibraltar, which had been released by the C-in-C there now that the threat to the Rock had passed. They arrived complete with their former hunters and ponies and the best of English saddlery.

As it was essential that the two North African companies should complete their own training as soon as possible, and as the newly arrived Gibraltar company was ready trained and well toughened up after its tasks on the Rock, it was decided that half the unit should go at once to the battle school at Boufarik and half to the combined training centre at Djidjelli on the coast. To selected officers and men from many regiments, they gave 10-day courses in the art of making up pack loads and tying them, and in the technique of moving laden mules over mountainous country. It was soon evident at Boufarik that the hardy British HT drivers from Gibraltar could out-march their infantry comrades, but it was not long before both showed equal ability to master a 20-mile trek in blazing July weather over the most difficult country. At Djidjelli this ability could not be proved, as the animals hired from local civilians were unfit to stand up to any such trials.

At last the invasion of Sicily brought all training to an end. The Gibraltar company was transferred to Tunis, and the two North African companies left Tunis and went to Sicily, where it was intended that they should be re-formed and re-equipped with animals which it was hoped would be available locally.

On arrival in Tunis the Gibraltar company took over the 700 animals left behind by the North African companies. To bring the unit up to the desired strength a number of Tunisians were drafted in. These, though perhaps slower and quieter than the Algerians, were tough and were later to prove their worth in Italy. Helped also by a French cadre, the work of expansion was soon finished, and the unit was then allotted to support the 1st British Division which was then training hard for operations in mountainous country.

In the event the North African companies were not actively employed in Sicily. As recounted in Chapter VII, there was difficulty in getting mules and the small number obtained did not permit of any being allotted to the companies.

So ended the trials on the 'nursery slopes' of Africa. They proved that a small, well trained British cadre, given good material, animals and a little time to train local muleteers, could give a first-class account of themselves.

Thus when the campaign in Italy opened there were three pack companies prepared to join in the fray and share the fortunes of the RIASC and Cypriot groups from the Middle East and later the Italian groups of pack units.

'SS *Mont Everest*'

The title of this story does not mean that the newly formed Pack Group in North Africa was destined to operate on the highest mountain in the world. To those who moved to Italy from Tunis, however, the name will always remain in their memory as the ship which carried 450 officers and men and 700 animals to their new sphere of operations in the CMF.

The movement of animals by sea is never an easy matter, and it was with some misgivings that the old hands watched the arrival of the good ship *Mont Everest* flying the Panamanian flag and apparently completely devoid of any means of embarking an animal load. However, the ship's captain, the officer commanding and 'Jackie' Phrayre, the French pack officer, went into conference and decided to lift the animals on board by rope net.

The *Mont Everest* was a ship of about 8,000 tons which was said to have been originally a meat ship. She had been fitted on all decks with a series of bays so made that animals faced inboard and were secured in front, waist high, with bars. Thus the mules could hang their heads out as if from a stable door. No provision had been made for the accommodation of officers or men, or for carrying extra drinking water. The ship's crew were of all nationalities, and the captain was French.

When embarkation began 'Old Job', one of the few survivors of the former Gibraltar company and a great character who had a crafty habit of nipping unsuspecting people in a most vulnerable spot, and who worried about nothing except the next feeding time, was invited to have first go. He waddled, full of trust, on to the net spread out on the ground, with an NCO at each corner. The corners were immediately whipped up to the hook of the derrick cable; the NCO in charge gave the signal to the donkey man; and before Old Job could get his ears back he was swinging in mid-air. It must be said that the old boy was not the least upset, and he surveyed the animals below with a proud and disdainful expression, to the huge delight of the Arabs. This then was the way to do it, and towards the end of the day the animals were going on board at the rate of one every two minutes. The mules gave no trouble, although some of them went on board upside down in the net, some sitting up like cats, and some with their legs sticking through the netting.

No sooner had the ship put to sea than every Arab was sick. The wretched men, unable to understand what had happened, prayed to Allah and then went into a coma for three days. This meant that about 70 British soldiers of all ranks had to water and feed more than 700 animals—a 24-hour-a-day job.

The ship's performance in no way belied her appearance. Full speed ahead was four knots, and every now and then a terrific vibration started up. The engineer would at once fly down to the bowels of the ship, where he performed magic rites, after which the vibration would die down—but never for long; soon off it would go again.

After two days the ship anchored in the bay outside Augusta, Sicily, and there she stayed for five days, lying in the middle of a large convoy. On the second night the convoy was bombed, and some 60 ships opened up with their anti-aircraft weapons, causing mild panic among the animals. On the fifth day the officer commanding ordered a general 'muck out', and the consequent refuse floated inshore, much to the fury of the Royal Navy. Whether or not in consequence of this, orders were received for the *Mont Everest* to leave the convoy and sail alone. In the early daylight of the seventh day she rounded the heel of Italy with Albania well in view on the starboard side. No sooner had she reached the entrance to the Adriatic than one of His Majesty's destroyers approached and signalled 'You cannot come through here in daylight'. In vain did the captain point out that in fact he had already done so. He was ordered to turn about, go back through the danger zone and wait till dusk. The next night the destroyer picked her up and escorted her through the straits.

Adventures were still ahead, for, on entering the Adriatic, a furious storm blew up. The old ship plunged and creaked, rolled and pitched in the most alarming manner and, as the wind was from the north, her speed was reduced to about minus one knot as she drifted slowly towards the mined enemy coast. The mules on the top deck were drenched by the high seas, and one colossal wave, which broke over the bows, lifted three out of their pens and deposited them amid the NCOs shivering under their tarpaulins.

At last, on the fourteenth day, the ship reached an Italian harbour, but, on asking leave to enter, she was told to remain outside because of new wrecks from a bomb raid which would prevent any ships from entering for several days. This was too much for the officer commanding, who signalled, 'Ship loaded with mules urgently wanted in campaign, no water or food left, hold you responsible for any delay'. Back came the reply, 'Proceed at own risk'. This did not worry the French skipper. He slowly and carefully circumvented the hazards and brought his battered and now thoroughly odoriferous ship safely to the quayside. So ended that voyage of the *Mont Everest*.

In Full Cry, crossing the River Garigliano

Within a few hours of disembarking from the *Mont Everest*, the company was on its way by train to Naples. Then followed a two-day march of 60 miles, and three days after landing, the company assumed its active role with the 5th Division—later changed to the support of the British 46th and 56th Divisions preparatory to the crossing of the river Garigliano. No time had been lost in putting the company to work, and the next two years were to be a real test of their worth, as the country provided those extremes of climate and differences in terrain which called for their utmost skill. Heat and snow, mountain and hill, valley and ravine, stony rock and hillside path, river and stream, broken bridges, smashed viaducts and embankments and a thousand other obstacles followed one after another to slow up the pace of the armies. There were at this time—the end of 1943—in addition to Colonel Dudgeon's group of three Arab companies and one Italian, eight Indian companies of the RIASC (A & B Groups), four companies of No. 1 (Cypriot) Group, and five Italian companies formed by Italian landowners, cavalry officers, and Alpini.

Infantry and armour were now creeping slowly forward after the Eighth Army, which had crossed the Straits of Messina from Sicily and had linked up with the Fifth Army which had landed at Salerno. In the west the Allied armies had crossed the Volturno at Capua and were preparing for the crossing of the Garigliano just north of Sessa; in the centre the line was roughly from Monte Cassino to north of Isernia, extending in the east over the Foggia plain to the River Sangro.

The Garigliano flows through a flat little valley overlooked from the north by the mountains where enemy OPs had a wonderful view—and made full use of it. The approaches to the river were sown with thousands of mines, orange trees were laden with booby traps, and in fact all the devices had been employed which an enemy hopes will delay an advance.

The opening attack was made late in the evening. The first call on the company came in the early hours next morning for 12 ambulance mules, which soon set off under a British sergeant down to the river through the white taped lanes laid down by the sappers. The little band crossed by ferry, joined the advanced dressing station, and at once began evacuating wounded to the river ferry before daylight came. The detachment then dug slit trenches and prepared lines for the animals hidden from the enemy behind a wall. A second call came for a complete troop to try to cross by a footbridge farther up the river. The bridge proved too narrow, and the first pair of mules fell into the river. The resourceful troop leader had, however, noticed a recovery vehicle further back. This he fetched, rescued his two mules, and, by means of a winch fixed on the opposite bank, carried his whole troop across. Hurrying on, he then rejoined the infantry, who had by now crossed the plain and were climbing the mountain.

The time had now come for the company to push forward. The company commander located the AA & QMG of the division in a small cottage at the foot of the mountain, which was still under small arms fire. He was told to reconnoitre sites at the foot of the mountains for at least four pack companies; after which he was to go forward up the mountain and reconnoitre tracks and a dumping site within easy reach of the infantry.

The nearest mountain rose up in a series of vine terraces which would make excellent standings for animals, and a goat track, steep but firm, wound up its side. Over the top the track dropped into a little valley which would do well for a halting place or could even be used as a forward company site. The area was not overlooked, and from this valley the track rose steeply again up another mountain. Near the top of this was another little valley, just the place for a dumping site for the forward troops who were over the top facing the enemy not the length of a football pitch away. The 'carry', subject to the strict maintenance of silence, proper spacing and careful timing, could be performed in daylight.

That night the main body of the group—five companies—moved forward to mule-head. This term 'mule-head' was especially apt for the new location which the company commander had selected, as the lines consisted of tier upon tier of mules facing outward from the hill so that anyone looking up the mountain-side saw nothing but row upon row of mules' faces. Mule-head was called 'Skipton', and from there the lift was to a dump in the first valley known as 'Harrogate'. Here loads were re-sorted according to various needs. Gunners, sappers and signals all gave a willing hand before the next lift to the final destination, which was a small valley just out of sight of the enemy, but within easy reach of the forward troops facing the enemy on the top of the adjoining hill. This most forward spot was referred to as 'Cheshire'. As it was a dangerous spot, mules were only brought to it in small groups to have their loads shed and be sent back immediately. Here the RASC supply officer made his headquarters and, in the interval of manning his Bren gun, checked the loads as they came in.

Although the tracks used were not in the enemy's view, effective mortar fire was occasionally brought to bear on them. This always seemed to occur when there was a relief between companies. This was noticed throughout the campaign, and many attributed it to fifth columnists, but the truth is that however carefully a newly arrived unit is briefed, it does not possess the sixth sense about the enemy's characteristics and intentions that develops in an experienced unit. Little things such as a sudden shout, smoke from a fire which should not have been lit, or careless exposure, can attract the undesirable attention of a suspicious and active enemy. There were many examples of the effects of this lack of a sixth sense. At one time, as casualties grew and rest was needed, the group commander moved up a fresh relief company. Within an hour of the change a heavy barrage of both shell and mortar came down, causing the loss of one officer, 17 men and 30 animals.

Lack of experience was also the cause of many gaps in the ranks of the units, and unfortunately experience could only be gained in the hard way. On one occasion a newly joined young officer,*

---

* The late Lieutenant Maurice Irving, who lies buried in Minturno military cemetery.

keen to lead his troops into action for the first time, was detailed to carry up a load of mortar bombs to a commando with express instructions to hand over his load and return before sunrise. Delayed by the change-over of an infantry battalion, he was still determined to fulfil his task; but dawn found the troops still climbing. When the commando was reached, he was told to get back at once, but by then it was too late. He was killed in trying to extricate his troop.

Although life at 'Skipton' was rough, and accommodation consisted of two-men bivouacs and slit trenches, the early training in North Africa was shown to have been worthwhile. It was rare to see a man without his chin strap brightly polished, and that essential sign of cleanliness in pack transport—saddlery kept well soaped and supple—was in evidence throughout. This innate cleanliness meant that when a formal occasion arose the units were able to show themselves to the best advantage. This fact was recognized by the corps commander (who in peacetime was a well-known international polo player) when he arranged to inspect a unit which had only been relieved the day before. He found that breast lines and baggage ropes had been scrubbed, and those essential ancillaries, the saddlers, and farriers 'shops' and veterinary lines, had already been neatly laid out as if the unit had been in resting occupation of the site for weeks. The obvious pleasure of the commander was, it is believed, further heightened when, after accepting an invitation to lunch, he found that his meal had been prepared by a well-known chef whom the French element had taken good care to 'conscript' when the unit was first formed in North Africa.

Soon rumours arrived that the division and the pack group were to be relieved. So far as the division went, the rumour proved to be true, but the group had to stay on to help the relieving French division until its own pack units arrived. How these French units scared one—they seemed to do everything that might attract the enemy's attention, leaving lights blazing, blowing up rocks, and being quite oblivious of the effect of noise! Perhaps the Boche thought they must be 'hearing things', for not a shell dropped for days. Truly a quiet ending to the first adventure of the group in Italy.

Cassino

So many other writers have described the country round Cassino and the battle there, that little more need be said than that it provided the sort of conditions where pack transport could be used to the best advantage. The narrow gorge with precipitous mountains on either side, the monastery, which was a perfect observation point looming over the gorge and menacing the winding valley route to Rome, and the effective natural barriers formed by the Liri and Rapido rivers, provided the group with many opportunities to show their worth.

After weeks of intensive fighting and several abortive attempts to take the position, 24th Guards Brigade held half the town of Cassino, and the enemy the other half at the foot of Monastery Hill. To their right the 78th British Division hung on precariously halfway up the mountainside, and further still to the right, towards the top of Monte Cairo, the 2nd New Zealand Division almost looked down on the monastery. The first supply dump was located a few miles south of the village of Acquafondata and called 'Brighton'. From there all requirements were brought up to Acquafondata by motor transport in daylight. From Acquafondata to Portella, a hamlet almost facing the monastery, ran a small river winding its way between steep banks until, near Portella, it broadened out into a basin just hidden from the enemy. The sappers dammed this river and converted it into a usable track by laying wire netting on the river bed. The basin before Portella was converted into the forward supply dump called 'Hove'. Very little traffic was allowed on this track (called 'Inferno') in daylight, as much of it was in view of the enemy, and a pass was issued to those who had to use it.

'Hove' was a hive of activity. Round it were grouped Indian, Cypriot, Arab and Italian mule companies. A long water trough of canvas had been erected, filled by a little stream. All requirements for the infantry were brought to 'Hove' by motor transport at night, sorted into mule loads by day and taken forward by mule the next night. The 24th Guards Brigade and 78th Division were supplied direct across the short valley, but the carry to the New Zealanders half way up Monte Cairo proved too long to get there and back in darkness. This meant placing mules across the valley at the foot of the mountains and supplying them by jeep and trailer, and it is this operation which is now described.

The first to try to carry it out was an Italian pack company, but they suffered such severe casualties through faulty siting of their locations that they had to be relieved at once. The officer commanding the relieving company, after a thorough reconnaissance, decided to make Portella his advanced headquarters and to site B Troop one third of the way up Monte Cairo. All grey mules of this troop had to be dyed with permanganate of potash to blend with the landscape; A Troop on the right was in a disused paper factory at St. Elia; C Troop in the village of Vallerotonda was located on a small hill surrounded by large ones with the enemy on the highest looking down on them, and D Troop was back at Acquafondata to look after some South Africans who were on the right of the 2nd New Zealand Division. It was estimated that it would be dark enough for C and D Troops to march from 'Brighton' direct to their sites in one night, and this was proved right. C Troop stabled their mules in the empty houses on the south side of the deserted village, and D Troop found good, well hidden standings at Acquafondata. They had a long but fairly safe carry, but A and B Troops had to make two nights of it. Marching the first night to Portella, they then had to lie up all day. This in itself was a nerve racking ordeal for the men, who knew that, should the enemy suspect any new movement, a 'stonk' would come down which could not fail to do damage. Nothing, however, happened and the two troops safely reached their locations on the second night and carried out their lift forward that same night.

The sorting and tying of the jeep loads at 'Hove' was a most important factor in this operation, as too was the timing of the jeep convoys. Specified loads for specified units were sent off together, and the drivers were well briefed as to their contents. On arrival at mule-head, halfway up Monte Cairo or outside the St Elia paper factory, they were met by the pack troop leader. On learning the contents of the loads and intended recipients, he sent for the exact number of mules, the load was transferred from jeep to mule, the next jeep pulled in, and the process was repeated. Absolute silence was essential, and not a man or mule would linger in that danger spot for a second longer than necessary. Nevertheless, B troop suffered heavy casualties. At the end of three weeks only 16 of the original troop of 75 mules were left. The men too had a rough time. They lived in holes dug in the side of the mountain and could not move in daylight.

A Troop in their paper factory could also move only at night. They were shelled nearly every day, but fortunately the factory was well built and the shells exploded harmlessly on the walls and roof. The Boche, however, was not to be frustrated and started sending over unfused shells which crashed through the roof, killing mules the bodies of which could not be disposed of. Quick-lime was sent up, but those rotting mules did not add to the amenities of the area.

C Troop was well organized. Horses and mules were well bedded in the houses, and each man managed to borrow a bed from the evacuated village. The only trouble was drinking water, as the only village well was in view of the enemy, but the resourceful troop leader rounded up some stray donkeys, saddled them with water barrels, and sent the little herd with two muleteers to the well daily. Not once did the enemy interfere.

At Portella the officer commanding and the veterinary officer lived in an extraordinary house built up the side of a bank. The top floor was entered by the front door, which faced the monastery.

They used to leave their jeep in the basin or bowl, as it was called, at 'Hove', creep round to the front door and then dive in. By descending the stairs they reached the living room on ground floor level. This backed into the bank, looking away from the dreaded monastery, and here they felt and were as safe as could be. Once a week the CQMS would arrive with NAAFI stores. This must have been one of his most dreaded days, as the visit to the troops was rather an ordeal. The tracks were steep and narrow and frequently shelled or mortared. Other jeeps would suddenly appear from nowhere. All was inky darkness, and there was always the danger of new shell holes to drive into.

Sometimes the officer commanding would visit his troops on foot by daylight. Only one troop could be reached in a day, as it meant a round walk of some six miles. The trek to B troop on Monte Cairo was full of hazards. The valley, which in peacetime is one of the prettiest in southern Italy, was pitted with shell and bomb holes filled with dirty, green water. The little roads were also feet deep in water in consequence of damage to the river banks. The shattered olive groves were littered with knocked-out tanks, in some cases with the dead crews still inside them. Except for the occasional whine of a shell, there was a deathly silence. It was a world apart, as only those who lived in it can possibly visualize. The track to the paper factory led past the dead mules of the Italian company lying with their heads pulled up to the breast lines to which they were still tied. On approaching the factory the track topped a hill. The enemy was most sensitive about visitors to St. Elia and would shell even a single caller, to the ill-concealed amusement of the troop.

To reach C Troop the officer commanding drove to Acquafondata and then walked past our gun sites to reach a point where large notices proclaimed 'YOU CAN NOW BE SEEN'. Having climbed a brick wall, he descended into the enormous bowl, two miles wide, with the enemy on the far side. At the foot of the bowl he crossed a small river, and then climbed up the miniature mountain in the hollow of the bowl, on the top of which was Vallerotonda. After his tenth visit he said he was so conscious of being watched that he could hardly keep his eyes forward as he came down the mountainside.

After about three weeks of this work rumours of changes and relief started, and advance units of the Polish Corps began to arrive. The officer commanding was worried about B Troop on Monte Cairo, where lack of sleep and of hot food was beginning to tell, and he decided that D Troop should relieve them. It was decided not to relieve the mules, and some 15-cwt trucks were borrowed for the change-over. This operation had to be timed carefully in order not to clash with any movement on the tracks, which had not before been regularly used. The convoy formed up at Acquafondata in the afternoon and the officer commanding went down 'Inferno' to make final arrangements. Unfortunately, just before he reached 'Hove', the enemy lobbed a shell into the ravine and set a bale of tibbin on fire. At once, the shells poured in, and in no time the whole dump was ablaze, ·303 going off in all directions and all transport, including a dozen water trucks used for ferrying water over to the forward mule-heads, blazing furiously.

Within an hour all had been destroyed. However, D Troop got away and the change-over was effected smartly, the tired, haggard men of B Troop arriving safely back just as dawn was breaking. As they were watering and feeding D Troop's mules before turning in for their first good sleep for three weeks, they were considerably cheered by a few encouraging words of thanks by the DDST Corps, Colonel (now Brigadier) F. A. Shaw, who had made a special and difficult journey to welcome them. Lieutenant White and his acting troop sergeant, Farrier Sergeant Bone, were both mentioned in despatches for the gallant way they handled a most awkward operation on Monte Cairo. So too was Dvr Warrington of the company headquarters, who that night made four trips to Monte Cairo with his water truck to make up for the loss of the water trucks destroyed by shell fire. This meant filling his truck from the River Rapido at a spot which, even at night, was subject to constant and accurate shell fire, and then driving up three miles of hairpin bends on a narrow track without protection on the outside edge—all in darkness.

At last the final battle broke. When the pall of smoke finally floated from the valley and they spied the British and Polish flags fluttering from the now ruined monastery, the pack group knew that their immediate task was over. So ended their second main phase of operations. This was followed by a short rest near Rome —a rest which allowed at last some uninterrupted sleep and the opportunity to make and mend.

With the 4th Indian Division

It was not long before the group were once again following hard on the heels of the advancing army. For three consecutive days the daily marches were no less than 32, 36 and 42 miles. After a short respite on the upper reaches of the Tiber, the group were assigned to the support of the 4th Indian Division, which was already engaged in the hills north of the little medieval town of Perugia.

The division did not call for mule support until the fall of Umbertide. The line of advance marked by the usual dried up river and dusty 'road' winding to the north lay through a series of mountains which ran from west to east across the axis of advance, and the enemy had the advantage of holding the mountain sides overlooking the valleys. The only way to dislodge them was the usual tedious process of winkling them out, mountain by mountain. Two brigades were detailed for the task.

When a brigade is fighting a moving battle in mountains, it normally needs at least three pack companies to support it, but in this operation, with the main road being cleared by half a mile or so daily, motor transport was able to follow up to within gun distance and then fan out up the lateral lanes. As the enemy vacated a hill top, the advancing brigades would move down to the preceding valley and take up their positions just short of the lately vacated hill top. The sappers quickly constructed tracks over these hills which enabled the jeeps to deliver the division's needs to the last river bed, from which the mules took them up the mountain to the infantry. It was a short carry, but the companies suffered many casualties.

During this operation two sections under the command of a British corporal, with an infantry escort in attendance, had a skirmish with a German patrol. The escort, who were ahead of the party, were fired on as they rounded a bend in the track and in the subsequent scuffle all were killed or taken prisoner. The RASC Cpl, Copland, shouted to his Arab NCO to turn about and get the sections back while he covered the top of the track. The muleteers leapt on to their mules, and, led by Cpl Ali Ben Ali, charged down the hill to safety. Copland was wounded, but he wormed his way through the scrub and so rejoined his mules.

There was no respite for the division or its mules as the tedious process continued of prising the enemy off the hill tops. This operation, which after three weeks of hard fighting, gained about two miles of territory, was marked by the alleged prevalence of fifth columnists. Wherever the units halted they were frequently and accurately shelled, and on two occasions civilians were said to have been caught operating WT sets in contact with the enemy. One pack company commander, whose jeep had just been painted with the letters HQ over the crossed horse-shoes on the front of his vehicle, was within a few hours shelled out of a small villa which he and his veterinary officer were using as a billet. As a precaution he had 'HQ' painted out!

Although by this time the operations of the pack units were running fairly well to routine form, a foray behind the enemy's lines provided a fresh experience. An infantry company, made up of machine-gun and mortar platoons, was to make an incursion through and behind the enemy's lines with the aid of Italian partisan guides to carry out what was described, for want of a better term, as a patrol. Their immediate needs were to be carried by one of the pack troops and they were to 'live' on the country.

As dusk was falling the party, with 40 loaded mules and two spares, moved off and disappeared into the hills. The mules were split up into four parties of 10, each with a British corporal in charge, the rear being brought up by an infantry platoon. The head of the column was conducted by Italian partisan guides and a mule loaded with a walkie-talkie set was led with them. Unfortunately the guides lost their way after traversing only one mountain and a halt had to be made. The mules were dispersed for cover while a scouting party was sent forward. It was not until dawn that this party returned and led the main body over rocky tracks and dried river beds to a tiny village, where they lay up for the day. The following night they sent a section of mules back to bring up rations and extra horses for reconnaissance. On the following day the area was mortared, but there were no casualties. The next night they again moved forward to another village well behind the enemy lines and lay up. This village overlooked a small town occupied in some strength by the enemy; this was the patrol's objective. Moving towards it the next night, they halted as dawn was breaking, and dispersed in the neighbouring trees and bushes. An officer and two sections of infantry now crept toward the silent village and disappeared from the view of the excited pack men. Suddenly there was a terrific crash of fire; then again dead silence. After some time the pack men decided to investigate. Creeping forward in single file, hugging the walls, they suddenly emerged in the village square to find their infantry friends in complete control with the enemy force in their hands as prisoners of war. The loaded mules were brought up and quickly tucked away, but not quite soon enough, for the enemy reacted quickly and started to shell the village killing nine mules with the first shell.

Mules were sent back to fetch up another infantry company. This they accomplished without loss, bringing more rations and some fresh mules. The following night the whole party moved on to the next village, which offered little opposition after a machine-gun nest had been cleared up. A small town on a main road was next on the list. Patrols were sent out and occupied parts of this town, the patrols being gradually built up until the entire force occupied the town, allowing the road to be opened up for motor transport. The main forces then moved up and the operation was complete.

The troop leader ended his report thus: 'We were sorry the expedition was over because it had gone extremely smoothly and our casualties in men had been nil, although we did lose nine good mules. After the first two days our forage problem solved itself, as hay was plentiful and we found abundant grain in deserted farmhouses.'

The advance of the 4th Indian Division soon reached the vicinity of the Gothic Line, which was the great natural barrier to any further advance to the open, fertile plains of the River Po. The division's task was to break through the high hills north of Urbino. Tracks were few and all demolished. The rocky, bleak country was burned brown by the mid-summer Italian sun, as hot as in North Africa; the river reduced to a mere trickle. The division was allotted a pack company to each battalion, and it was over this wild territory that some 4,000 mules and their attendants were to march fully laden in support of the infantry. The real purpose of the animals was not maintenance in the usual sense, but to relieve the infantry soldier of his equipment so that he could march lightly and arrive fit for battle when the fortifications were reached. Feeding the mules was as far as possible to be on the country, and where an owner of a haystack could be found he was to be given a receipt for his hay at an agreed price to be settled later. This worked extremely well, and few complaints were received afterwards. The grain ration and rations for the men followed in jeeps on rough tracks opened up one after another by the sappers and pioneers.

The division concentrated at Sigillo which was a good five days' march from the Gothic Line. Each pack company then came under direct orders of the commander of the battalion to which it was attached. As the division approached Urbino that terrifying menace, the mine, began to be more and more frequently encountered. Corn stacks were heavily booby trapped, and many men and mules were killed by a mule grabbing at the stacks as it passed, thereby pulling the trip wire. Cpl Ali Ben Ali was blown to pieces in this way, to the great regret of all his company.

The country in front of the enemy positions had been completely cleared of cover, trees and hedges cut down and all buildings demolished. The infantry therefore halted before surmounting the last hill and the weary and battered mules were unloaded and given their first rest. The men crept into various little nooks and crannies overlooking the positions and had a first rate view of dive bombing by Hurricanes, then a terrific artillery barrage, and finally the assault by the infantry.

Usually a final and successful assault by the infantry meant that pack transport could be withdrawn to rest, as the enemy retired, and road communications were reopened. On this occasion it was not to be. Certain armoured units got into difficulties and the infantry division had to be passed through them to maintain the momentum of the advance. This operation was of particular interest as it entailed leaving Italy and entering the smallest of the world's republics—San Marino.

In spite of this theoretical violation of a neutral country, the advance soon brought the division down to the River Marrechia, when nature proceeded to alter the course of human plans as the trickle of water named Marrechia suddenly developed into a roaring torrent, carrying down shrubs, trees and boulders and smashing and sweeping away everything in its path. The little adjacent tracks broke down completely under the mass of transport on them, but fortunately some pack transport was already across the river; so once again the faithful pack animal was there on both sides of the river to tide over the period before the rains ceased and the river receded.

'*Nina*'

With mid-December came the snow, and some 12 to 15 degrees of frost were registered on the high hills, but as the ground hardened man and animal began to move freely again. Nature played its part by providing the mule with his thick woolly coat, and though tails were often a solid mass of ice, and icicles hung from the mules' noses, they kept fit and well. The right flank company was supporting the 1st Guards Brigade which took the company into their own lines. They soon developed a strong corps of pack 'supporters', who in all sorts of small ways helped to make the life of their newly adopted friends tolerable. The interest of the supporters was to be repaid in one unexpected instance, by the remarkable feat of Nina. Nina was an ambulance mule—a type specially selected for reliability, strength and tractability. Docile by nature, she had sufficient animal sense to extract the much prized soldiers' chocolate ration from her many admirers and, as the result of many other extra animal tit-bits, she waxed fat and smug.

An attack was to be made by men of the 61st Brigade which formed part of this force, and with them were to go the ambulance mules of 4 Pack Transport Company, including Nina. The attack went in on Christmas Eve and was successful. The enemy was pushed out of Borgo Tossignano, but reacted extremely quickly and some of our men and mules were cut off. A day or so later the men of the ADS were roused by a banging on the door, and there was Nina with two unconscious soldiers lying on the litters each side of her.

How it happened no one ever really knew, as the two men were too ill to remember anything. They had obviously been loaded on the mule by the enemy and then turned loose, probably to save them the trouble of evacuating wounded prisoners of war.

It was, however, an amazing effort on the part of Nina to get safely home. The first part of the trip would be new ground to her, and the journey of about two miles was over a winding mountain track a few feet wide and of course in darkness. Normally two stretcher cases would entail the use of three men, one to lead the mule and two to steady the litters, but this animal brought them back alone and unaided.

Finale: Winter in the Apennines

It seems fitting that the last account of the adventures of our pack units in Italy should not only describe the most arduous and protracted period of the whole campaign, but should also recount the work of a group composed of Italian companies strengthened by a single company of one of the well tried units of the RASC. There were two kinds of Italian companies, those composed of 'co-operators', and those of members of the Italian Army. Co-operators were those who volunteered to throw in their lot with us as individuals before the remnants of the Italian Army on the Allied side of the lines could be officially recognized as Allies and reorganized as an Italian army. The co-operators were in fact mercenaries accepting the British military system in all its aspects, while the officers and men of the re-formed Italian Army were a part of the Italian Army in all respects. Theoretically the Italians of the Italian Army were *inter alia* clothed and fed by the Italian administration, although they were working for us, but in practice the Italian Army administration was hard put to it to do this. Thus came the extraordinary situation of the co-operator enjoying all the advantages of well-made British uniform, relatively good rates of pay, and a substantial ration, and the Italian Army man doing his best with such clothing and standard of food as could be provided by the Italian Government from its meagre resources. The group concerned in this last phase had five companies formed between late 1943 and early 1944 and were drawn from Alpini, Italian cavalry, a mountain regiment, and other Italian units.

Whatever opinions may be held about the part played by the Italian Army in some phases of the Second World War, there is no doubt that the men of the pack units led by their British cadres displayed the greatest gallantry, night after night, under the most appalling conditions. The operations north of Florence before the final breakout to the River Po were most protracted and trying, starting as they did in the autumn of 1944 and lasting for 22 weeks.

This was to be the last drawn-out stand by the enemy, who craftily encouraged the advancing American formations and the 1st and 78th Infantry and 6th Armoured Divisions to pursue him along the difficult Route 65 and then contrived to force them, still in pursuit, to two axes—one the road leading to the Futa pass and the other the track which led to Castel del Rio. Rain and traffic were both heavy. Roads disappeared in a sea of mud so deep that a jeep's bumper pushed the mud along like a snow-plough. Moreover, these roads wound up in a series of hairpin bends to a height of about 3,000 feet. All the bends and parts of the mountain sides had been blown up by the retreating enemy, and although they were patched up by our sappers they were prone to disappear in a long slide whenever too weighty a load traversed them. The divisions, with their mules, had floundered on over the top and down to the valley until just after Castel del Rio, where they came up against solid enemy resistance on the last range of hills before the Po valley. This was exactly what the enemy wanted. He had about two miles of supply lines, whereas we had 35 over desolate, wild, mountainous country crossed by only one track. Motor transport managed to supply to divisions as far as just north of Castel del Rio, but from there on everything had to be carried by mule. This last range of hills, where the infantry were to stay for some 22 weeks, was one of the bleakest spots in the Apennines and—except for a rare farmhouse—offered no shelter at all.

The conditions for pack transport were miserable. It was a grotesque sight to see the columns lurching, splashing and floundering up steep muddy tracks, the mules sweating and grunting, and the men with the mud over their rubber knee boots hanging on to the odd strap to keep up and going. Over it all shone the ghostly light of the moon.

In the early stages of this operation an act of great courage was performed by Major 'Tommy' Arnott, one of the company commanders. In the darkness and heavy rain a troop leader missed the swept track and led his troop into the mines. He himself was the first casualty. Lying there, with a leg blown off, he ordered his men to stay where they were until the rear section, not in the minefield, could fetch a mine-sweeper. His shout was heard by Major Arnott, the commanding officer, who hurried back and without a thought for his own safety ran to the wounded troop leader,* picked him up and carried him to safety. After getting some tape, he then returned to the rest of the troop and, using himself as a human mine detector, led the whole troop back on the track, taping a lane as he went.

The End of the Campaign

The last phase came when the weather improved as the Eighth Army entered Bologna and the Americans reached it from the mountains. The units which the pack companies were supporting, having at last reached the plains, disappeared in clouds of dust, the pack troops struggling to keep up with them, and some even

* Lieutenant J. Niven; he died of wounds and was buried in the British Cemetery at Florence.

crossing the River Po. The end was at hand. On May 2nd the war in Italy was ended. The group commanders collected their scattered companies and marched them back over those hard fought mountains to the Florence area. There, one by one, they were disbanded and the men returned to their equitation establishments, training stables, farms, saddler's shops, blacksmith's shops, and all the other rural trades from which they had been drawn.

CHAPTER XVI

THE R.A.S.C. FLEET

TO the world at large—indeed, to many who served in the Corps—the activities of the RASC Fleet remain almost unknown. Here then is the story of that specialized organization which, starting with a modest 70 vessels at the outbreak of war, numbered more than 1,400 by 1945.

In 1939, before war broke out, the War Department Fleet, as it was then known, consisted of coastal and harbour craft, target towing vessels and a few specially built Governor's barges at such stations as Jamaica, Gibraltar, Malta and Singapore. Most of these vessels were used in home waters for routine peacetime tasks. The coasters carried military cargoes between the main ports and moved gun equipments to shipbuilding yards and emplacements. The harbour craft ferried men and carried fresh water to various sea forts, while the steam tugs and high speed launches towed targets off shore for coast artillery practices. There were also fast range launches to ensure the safety of other craft during shoots. All were manned by civilians.

The Fleet had its own distinguishing ensign—to quote Queen's Regulations, 'a blue ensign with crossed swords'—and was controlled centrally by the Assistant Director of Military Transport, Woolwich. His establishment included a technical staff to supervise overhauls and maintenance. (Local control was exercised by RASC officers in charge of transport.)

With the impact of war, the meagre resources of the Fleet became heavily strained, and additional craft, mostly of the launch and cabin cruiser type, were quickly requisitioned. Rapid expansion demanded a greater decentralization of control, and in January, 1940, the first 'water transport companies, RASC' were formed at Woolwich, Barry Docks, Leith, Portsmouth and Singapore under the command of selected RASC officers. These soon became well established in spite of the occasional false impression that they operated water-carrying vehicles.

About this time, too, the far-seeing decision was made to form RASC waterborne units with craft manned entirely by military crews. They were to be called 'motorboat companies, RASC'. Their job was to provide essential RASC water transport services in future field force formations and their role, broadly speaking, was to be analogous to that of general transport companies. Making up the crews was the problem. A call was made to all arms of the service for volunteers with experience as deep sea sailors, fishermen, longshoremen and yachtsmen. As was expected, this met with good response. Nos. 1 and 2 Motor Boat Companies, RASC, were formed in August, 1940, and located at Salcombe and Falmouth, providing for the operation of 40 launches, in four sections each of 10 craft. Thus, within one year from the outbreak of war, the two sister formations of the RASC Fleet, the old and the new, were in being.

Dunkirk

The first big operation in which the RASC Fleet took part was the evacuation of the British Expeditionary Force from Dunkirk in June, 1940. Eight of the fastest launches in the water transport companies—the 45 ft range launches *Grouse*, *Kestrel*, *Pigeon*, *Swallow*, and *Vulture*, the RASC high speed launch *Wolfe*, and the 57 ft target towing launches *Haig* and *Marlborough*—were diverted to the task and did valiant work, as the following letter* from General Sir Walter Venning, then Quarter-Master-General to the Forces, to each of the masters records:—

'I wish to thank you, your engineer and crew for the very fine part which you played in the recent evacuation of the BEF.

'In particular I wish to convey my admiration for the way in which the personnel of the WD vessels participating volunteered to perform a dangerous task quite outside their normal duties.

'To have been successful in saving the lives of over 1,300 British and Allied soldiers is a feat of which all of you concerned may well feel proud. The damage done to so many of the craft engaged is a testimony to the dangers which you and those serving under you faced with cheerfulness and gallantry.

'I am proud to think that, as Quarter-Master-General to the Forces, the War Department Fleet comes within my sphere.'

The RASC coasting vessel *Sir Evelyn Wood* evacuated many more from the beaches of St. Valéry. In the process, she 'salved' the beach-master and his party after their small craft had been damaged by shell-fire from a German tank, an incident recalled several years later in correspondence published in the nautical journal *Sea Breezes*.

These tasks were not completed without cost, for considerable damage was sustained by the craft. A typical example is that of the *Swallow*, which remained continuously in service for 24 hours after she had been badly damaged, working on only one of her three propellers, ferrying men from the beaches to the transports. The skipper, Mr. W. R. Clark, although fortunate on that occasion,

---

* Extract from Special Fleet Order No. 1 dated June 8, 1940.

was later to lose his life in the sister launch *Falcon* when she was destroyed by an enemy bomb while lying alongside Harwich Pier in April, 1941.

The Disbandment of Assistant Director of Military Transport

In July, 1940, there was a break with the past. The office of the ADMT, with his 'home port' at Woolwich, was disbanded, and a separate War Office branch known as STI was formed within the Directorate of Supplies and Transport. It took over not only the ADMT's responsibilities for RASC craft and civilians but also became the War Office co-ordinating branch for all Army demands for Admiralty controlled craft. Departmental liaison was also established with the Ministry of Shipping, later to be embodied in the Ministry of War Transport. In effect, STI became a miniature Admiralty for the RASC Fleet, complete with its own team of naval constructors and overseers under the Superintending Engineer and Constructor of Shipping.

The Expansion of the RASC Fleet and its work in Home and Northern Waters

Applications from volunteers for duty with the motorboat companies continued to flow in and selection and training afloat went on apace. Unfortunately standard RASC craft were not then available for these two first operational units, and they were provided with requisitioned launches. A strong spirit of pride in their unit developed, and it was most noticeable to all how every subsequent unit became imbued with it.

The evacuation of the BEF and the threat of German invasion brought in their train many problems for the RASC Fleet. Intensified defence measures on the east, south-east and south coasts created additional transport and ferry commitments for our units and gave birth to a host of launch patrols on estuaries, rivers and any stretches of water suitable for seaplane landings. The patrol craft—a most motley array of cabin cruisers and launches of all types and condition—were operated by sundry units, both of the Regular Army and of the Home Guard. In several cases, they had been 'requisitioned' locally by their operators. Naturally, as one would expect, claims for compensation, use of craft and so on began to filter back to the War Office in increasing volume. It soon became evident that STI and the RASC water transport organization alone had the facilities to investigate these. And so it was that the inspection of many non-RASC craft, and investigation into their use, fell to the lot of the STI technical overseers and the officers and staff of water transport companies.

The activities of the RASC Fleet in this direction, however, were by no means limited only to such administrative assistance. No. 2

Motor Boat Company was moved to the West Mersea area on the East Anglian coast and in October, 1941, took over from the Royal Navy the security patrols in the Rivers Stour, Deben, Blackwater and Crouch. Their job was to spot enemy aircraft on mine dropping forays, to keep a look out for mines, and to check and examine all craft entering the special defence zones. This operational role, although at variance with the original conception of the duties for which the motor boat companies were formed, was necessitated by the lack of naval manpower. The unit was administered through Headquarters, Eastern Command, but the chain of command was unusual in that the company was under the operational control of the Commander-in-Chief, the Nore, through the Flag Officer-in-Charge, Harwich. It is interesting to note, too, that in the water transport companies at this time, craft were being provided for the security control officers at all the big ports.

New defence commitments involving the provision of RASC water transport arose continuously. Notable among these was the decision to fortify the islands of Flatholm and Steepholm in the Bristol Channel. Thousands of tons of material and stores had to be ferried from Barry Docks and 12 cargo carrying barges and lighters were provided. The difficulties of maintaining this service in all seasons and weathers with such craft will be appreciated only too readily by those who know the vagaries of wind and water in the Bristol Channel. To the natural hazards was added the danger from mines, for the Bristol Channel was a favourite dropping zone.

In April, 1941, the third motorboat company was formed to operate off the West African coast, the cadre being provided from Nos. 1 and 2 Motor Boat Companies, but more will be told of this unit anon.

The next call for an operational unit came in August, 1941, when one section of an RASC motorboat company was included in Force 111 for operations in Spitzbergen. This was provided from No. 1 Motor Boat Company RASC and equipped with four launches requisitioned in Scottish waters. On arrival in Spitzbergen, the section found several Russian launches of various shapes and sizes and endeavoured to make them seaworthy. Starting them in cold weather, however, is reported to have caused not a little bad language. During their short stay there, our craft were employed continuously on ferrying men and stores between the transport *Empress of Canada* and the jetty at Barentsburg—a 12-mile turn round. The keenness of the crews and the way in which they improvised, impressed and earned the praise of many in the force.

By the end of 1941 the number of craft had more than doubled.

True, they were a heterogeneous lot, but they filled the gap until our own craft came off the stocks. The Superintending Engineer and Constructor of Shipping and his naval architects had prepared and approved designs for standard RASC launches for operational duties and also for bigger and faster craft for coast artillery practices. These were to simulate with the use of targets the fastest vessels the enemy were likely to use in a coastal attack. Construction had been arranged in conjunction with the Admiralty, and work pressed on, although it was not until late in 1942 that the first of the new craft was commissioned. Arrangements had also been made for the provision from naval construction of large numbers of 36 ft Admiralty harbour launches, 45 ft pinnaces, and motor fishing vessels varying from 45 ft to 90 ft in length. All these in the later years of the war more than proved their worth in all parts of the world. Likewise, the provision of boat stores and marine engine spares had become a great problem. Large contracts were placed by the War Office itself and through the Admiralty. The small WD Fleet Store which existed at Woolwich in September, 1939, was expanded first into F Group at No. 3 MT Stores Depot, RASC, Ashchurch, and then, early in 1942, when nearly all boat and vessel stores were transferred from RAOC to RASC supply, into the Boat Stores Group, RASC. Later it became a separate entity, the Boat Stores Depot, RASC, and was moved to Woolwich Dockyard. There it held all the marine stores, equipment, paint and the like required for the Service at home and overseas. At its peak, its stores holdings were valued at some four million pounds. It also provided the cadres for the RASC boat stores depots subsequently formed for overseas service, and played a big part in their mobilization and despatch.

In home waters, the demands on the RASC Fleet had become so heavy that more water transport companies had to be formed, and these came into being in 1942 at Plymouth, Sandbank (in the Clyde), Grimsby, and Sheerness. The beginning of 1942 also saw the despatch of the 400-ton steam target towing vessel *Sir Walter Campbell* to Iceland. She operated around that difficult coast for about six months on artillery practices seawards, and the value of her work can be judged from the following extract from a letter written by the DDST, Iceland:—

'The Gunners were loud in their praises of her, and without doubt she did an excellent job of work under extremely arduous conditions.'

The Fleet had the usual growing pains during those mid-war years, and a special Inspectorate of Water Transport Services was set up in 1943 to help advise home and overseas commands with their problems. The Fleet was fortunate, too, to have the wise counsel of Mr. H. Emory Chubb, a keen sailor and motorboat company commander of the First World War who, from 1940 until 1945, was honorary adviser to the Army Council on the WD Fleet. For his valuable services he was made a Commander of the Order of the British Empire.

New types of jobs constantly came along. Cargo carrying to the Faroes Islands Force on which the 500-ton *Malplaquet* was employed for some time, servicing the Maunsell anti-aircraft towers located at Liverpool and in the Thames Estuary, the provision and maintenance of the radio controlled *Queen Gulls* (self-propelled targets used for seaward artillery practices) and, in 1945, the operation of LCTs for ammunition dumping at sea were but a few. And common to them all were the dangers faced at sea. The range patrol launch *Falcon* was bombed and destroyed off Harwich Pier in April, 1941, two of her crew being killed. For some time the 450-ton *Sir Evelyn Wood* carried cargoes of bombs to Northern Ireland, and once a serious fire broke out in one of the holds while loading was in progress. The master, chief engineer and crew immediately entered the hold and fought the blaze, and their courage and initiative in so doing averted a serious explosion and loss of life. Incidentally, in 1944, this ship again narrowly escaped destruction when carrying a cargo of explosives and rockets for the Normandy beach-head. A V1 just missed her mainmast! Also in that year Able Seaman-in-Charge R. E. Davey, of the RASC launch *Pauletta*, was awarded the British Empire Medal (Civil Division) and the Lloyds Medal for Bravery at Sea. Davey saw an incendiary bomb pierce the engine room roof of the vessel lying alongside which had a large quantity of high octane petrol on board. He immediately clambered down into its engine room, seized the bomb which had severed the petrol connections and threw it overboard. These were typical incidents in the story of the Fleet in home waters.

With that rapid survey of its organization and vast expansion, let us retrace our steps a little and review the history of those RASC units provided for the field forces—the motorboat companies. Early in 1942 we had three: No. 1 employed in a training role, No. 3 operating in West Africa, and No. 2 engaged on patrols in the east coast estuaries and rivers. By the late summer, the planning of the invasion of North Africa—operation 'Torch'—was well under way and the order of battle for the force included one motorboat company, RASC. No. 2 Company was nominated, and the Admiralty were informed that the unit could no longer be spared for patrol duties. The naval authorities, however, made strong representations to retain its services, and this in itself was a tribute to the efficient and happy way in which the unit had done its job. But it had to go to North Africa nevertheless.

North Africa

In November, 1942, the unit, by then renumbered 247 Motor Boat Company RASC (No. 1 having become No. 246), landed on the North African coast with the 'Torch' expeditionary force. Ten vessels were shipped in the convoys from the United Kingdom, and as soon as a base had been established at Algiers steps were taken to acquire further craft locally. Some were requisitioned, and some were 'prize' vessels. These varied from 40–50 ft launches to 400-ton schooners and coastal craft. The wide variety of engines—diesel, petrol and even steam—gave the workshop officer many a sleepless night, and it says much for the spirit and training of the men, both deck and engine room staff, that they could take on the operation of these craft. In addition to the usual duties which its small launches performed in all the harbours from Algiers to Tunis, the coastal cargo carrying vessels of the company did valuable work. DST, Allied Force Headquarters frequently emphasized the great weight taken off the overworked general transport companies and the single railway line by their excellent efforts.

Further craft, too, were sent from home. In this connection it is worth digressing a little to tell the story of an unusual voyage, indicative of the close way in which the water transport and motor-boat companies of the RASC Fleet worked together. Additional craft were urgently required by 247 Company at Algiers and two drifters, the 100 ft *Ocean Breeze* and the 92 ft *Boy Phillip*, were refitted in this country for despatch. To give them a sufficient steaming range for the voyage it was necessary to fill their fish holds with coal. When required, the coal had to be loaded by the crew into baskets, dragged along the deck and shot down into the bunkers—a most difficult and risky business in bad weather, for there was always the danger of flooding the hold or the bunkers. Manned by civilian crews of the RASC Fleet under the Inspector of Shipping, Mr. G. Sparshatt (later made a Member of the Order of the British Empire for his distinguished services) they joined a convoy of some 40 ships sailing from Milford Haven on December 4th, 1943. They reached Gibraltar on the 13th, meeting heavy seas and strong head winds for the four last days of the voyage. After a few days' stay, they sailed for Oran, where they assisted in the rescue of an 8,000-ton Greek ship which had broken her moorings in a heavy gale. For this they received a signal of appreciation from the commander of the United States Naval Forces at that port. A British hospital ship arrived while they were there, and on hearing that there was a lack of cigarettes aboard, the RASC Fleet civilian crews sent them a case. Much to their surprise and delight, our men received not only the thanks of the wounded but also a large turkey and Christmas cake from the OC Troops. These they enjoyed at sea on the Christmas Day, while bound for Algiers in a full gale. The two vessels were delivered safely to the motorboat company the next day. Two more trawlers, the *Lucien Gougy* and *Elizabeth Therese*, were delivered in like manner by runner crews soon afterwards, and the 500-ton RASC vessel *Malplaquet*, with its civilian crew, was also diverted from the United Kingdom for duty in the Mediterranean.

With the opening of the offensive against Sicily and Italy, the company moved forward with 15 Army Group.

Work with the Central Mediterranean Forces

The shape of the Italian peninsula, of Yugoslavia, Albania, Greece, Corsica, Sardinia, Malta and the North African coastlines, with their many small ports, coupled with the limitations placed upon road and rail transport—both by the difficulties of terrain and by the destruction of war—made the Central Mediterranean an ideal theatre for the employment of RASC water transport. For years the Italians had made extensive use of coasting schooners, and consequently there were many suitable vessels available on the spot. No. 247 Company soon had far more commitments than it could properly handle, and from it three water transport companies (Nos. 797, 798 and 801) of special establishment were formed in October, 1943, and April and June, 1944. The motorboat company was then restored to strength with enthusiastic volunteers from all arms. As in the earlier days of 1940 these varied from professional seamen, through boat builders, barge hands and yachtsmen to mere land-lubbers.

The headquarters of 247 Company had been established at Torre del Greco, south of Naples, and operated around Sicily and on the North African coast, while the two first water transport companies, based on Bari and Torre del Greco, were responsible for RASC craft operating on the east and west coasts of Italy respectively. The waters of the east coast included the islands occupied by the Yugoslavs off the Dalmation coast, Albania and Greece, and those of the west coast included Sardinia and Corsica. As the Allied armies advanced, a reorganization of unit waters became necessary, and in the autumn of 1944 247 Company assumed responsibility for those around Southern Italy, Sicily and Malta, 797 for the Northern Adriatic from Ancona, 798 for the Northern Tyrrhenian Sea from Naples, and 801 for the Southern Adriatic, Yugoslavia, Albania and Greece. However, the activities of vessels were not confined to their own waters.

Some of the schooners were manned entirely by military crews, especially in the early days when shipments to Yugoslavia first began, for the Yugoslavs firmly refused to allow an Italian manned vessel to call at their ports. Those trips to Yugoslavia were very much of the 'sail-by-night' type, because of the attention of enemy aircraft in the Adriatic. Vessels were loaded in Bari and then sailed to Manfredonia, where they anchored until darkness fell. Then they would surreptitiously make the passage to the island of Vis with their cargo of ammunition or stores for the British forces and the partisans. Another route used was that to the Yugoslav port of Split, and trips were made even down to Kalamata in Greece. In addition to the hazards of war, there were always the forces of nature to reckon with on this passage. The *bora*, a very strong wind, often blew up without warning and caused many an anxious time. One vessel was blown so far off her course that when daylight came the master found himself uncomfortably near the shore of an enemy occupied island.

Other schooners were chartered, complete with Italian crews, and carried RASC 'escorts' of one NCO and one private waterman. The *Laura* of some 500 tons, was one. She was in the first flight of those which followed close in the wake of the liberating forces. Laden with food supplies for the starving Greeks, she received a warm welcome. The NCO escort (Sgt Jackson, RASC) sent this letter to his company commander:

'Sir—Please accept this 10-million drachma note as a souvenir from Greece. Our trip was most successful and very interesting.

'Our arrival at Pylos and Kyparissa was the signal for general festivity. We were entertained by the civil chiefs and officers of the Free Greek Army in a most lavish manner. We were the first British troops to return to this port after nearly four years and at both places dinners were given in our honour.

'Representing the RASC (water transport) in this historical episode gave me very great pleasure.'

The summer of 1944 was also enlivened by many incidents arising from the assembly of the force which was being prepared to land in the south of France. As an instance, one junior RASC officer's truthfulness was strongly suspected when he reported on his return from a training cruise in the Bay of Naples that he had seen a large and noisy canvas boat proceeding at three knots which, on investigation, was found to have a tank suspended in the bottom of it! This subsequently proved to be the Fleet's first acquaintance in the Mediterranean with the Sherman DD tank. Again, security measures were so secure that at least one of our units was not notified of them. This gave rise to several days of inexplicable silence from all the RASC schooners which were supplying the American Air Force and French Expeditionary Force in Corsica and Sardinia. The company became worried about the apparent loss without trace of all these vessels, until repeated enquiries brought forth the guarded answer that no vessels were allowed to return to the mainland until after the invasion had been launched. It therefore became questionable whether the invasion would be launched before the unit had run out of schooners.

Thousands of tons of stores of all kinds were carried by these vessels by many and devious routes. Supplies were ferried to special forces operating in Yugoslavia, Albania and Greece, including the islands off those coasts, coastwise shipments relieved the pressure on road and rail traffic in Italy itself, forces in Corsica and Sardinia were maintained, while smaller craft ran the more usual harbour services at the big ports. So vast and complex was the work that a special RASC water transport office was established at Allied Force Headquarters to co-ordinate it. The operational pattern gradually evolved until at its peak the RASC Fleet with the Central Mediterranean Forces operated 114 schooners of which one was a refrigerated meat ship, as well as a variety of launches, drifters, trawlers and MFVs over routes which covered most of the Adriatic, the west coast of Italy, Malta and the North African coastline. Naturally, the boat maintenance load was heavy. Two RASC boat stores depots were provided, No. 4 for North Africa and No. 5 for Italy, and for some time repairs were done in requisitioned shipyards, the locally employed Italian craftsmen being supervised by the company workshops' staff. The largest of these shipyards was at Molfetta. There up to 17 vessels of various types could be slipped at one time and the yard had its own foundry, machine shops, saw mill and carpentry sheds, a sail loft and rigging shop. Slipping the schooners was particularly exacting, since the method used was identical with that used in the last century and involved drawing the ships on to dry land while delicately balanced on their keels in a cradle which was rarely more than six feet wide. A sudden gust of wind while the vessel was actually in movement up or down the slip could easily lead to disaster. On one occasion, a particularly land-based officer inspecting the shipyard failed to appreciate the significance of the mass of cordage required to secure the slipped vessels and ordered the company commander to have the ropes put away and the place properly tidied up immediately. Later the control of these shipyards reverted to their Italian owners, although the work was still done under the supervision of the unit workshops officer.

The fall of Venice with its many waterways brought new problems, and it was decided that 797 Company should dispose of its schooners and operate the many small craft plying there. All motor launches, powered barges, steam ferries and so on were chartered on a 'bareboat' basis, and even the local 'Black Maria' was taken up for the Military Police. The only boats left to the Venetians were gondolas and electrically operated launches which were not considered suitable for military operation because of maintenance difficulties.

And so we have come to 1945. The RASC Fleet had played its full part throughout the operations and fortunately its casualties were light.

The RASC Fleet with the Middle East Forces

Farther to the east, yet other RASC Fleet units had come into being. In November, 1943, 782 Company (motorboat) was formed at Alexandria to take over all small craft operated by the military forces in the Middle East. Military crews were trained from local volunteers with the help of the RAF air/sea rescue instructional centres. Four 68 ft and one 57 ft high speed target towing launches were quickly manned and operated at Alexandria, Port Said and Haifa. Within a short time of its formation, the unit itself was training soldiers in handling the local sailing vessels known as caiques. These vessels, built at Tyre and Sidon since biblical days, still conform to the original schooner-like design. Fortunately two NCOs were found who had been in sea-going sailing ships, and a caique was purchased and based on Port Said and Alexandria for training purposes.

As crews became available, they manned caiques allotted by the Sea Transport Officer, GHQ Middle East, for duty in the Eastern Mediterranean, sailing between Alexandria, Port Said, Haifa, Cyprus, Beirut and northwards. They were affectionately known by their crews as 'apple barrels' and proved a valuable link in the supply chain. Moreover they did not attract undue enemy attention, and so were able to work almost under the very noses of the Germans, who held the islands of Rhodes, Cos, Leros and the rest. They ferried high-octane aviation fuel to forward bases on Castelloriso ahead of the RAF, ferried urgently required supplies from Famagusta to the recently occupied Dodecanese, carried Italian prisoners of war and enemy agents, and a hundred-and-one other cargoes. Some of the runs were fraught with danger and many with anxious moments.

The Fleet's high speed craft also had other duties more exciting than target towing. With the capture of some of the islands in the Dodecanese group, the General Staff decided to establish a fast launch service from the island of Simi, about 350 miles north of Alexandria, to carry mail, fresh meat and vegetables to them. Delivery of the mail by air had originally been considered but was ruled out because of the long turn-round and the difficulty of collecting containers in those heavily mined areas. The only vessels available were our fast target towing launches, all of which were diverted to this service. Two craft operated at a time on the run and they were replaced every two months. They left Alexandria at about 1700 hours, maintained a cruising speed of some 20 knots, passing Rhodes—still occupied by the enemy—early the next morning and arriving at their destination just before noon.

By 1944, the small craft commitments covered the whole coastal area from Tripolitania to Palestine and stretched as far south as Aden, much too large a parish for the one company. Consequently 782 Company was disbanded and two new units were formed—697 Company RASC (water transport) based on Port Said, covering the Mediterranean coast and eventually reaching as far north as Piraeus, and 698 Company RASC (water transport), based at Port Suez, covering the Suez Canal and the Red Sea ports.

Serving these companies was No. 3 Boat Stores Depot RASC, formed towards the end of 1943 and originally located at Tahag, near Tel-el-Kebir. Its staff consisted of one British officer and some Ceylonese who soon adapted themselves to this specialized job and also became quite skilled in making fenders, splicing cordage and the like. Incidentally, this unit was responsible for the design and construction of the successful 'Howard' spray target, which replaced the heavier Hong Kong target in those waters. In 1944 the depot was moved to Alexandria, where it remained until the end of hostilities, when it moved to Port Said.

Prelude to Operation 'Overlord'

At home, new motorboat companies (Nos. 467, 571, 624, 625 and 626) had been raised for the invasion of Europe, operation 'Overlord'. The first—No. 467 Company—was located in the April of 1943 at Rothesay. This, by the way, was the first RASC unit to receive the standard Admiralty 36 ft open harbour launches which were then becoming available for issue to the RASC Fleet. They were sturdy, seagoing little craft which gave yeoman service in every theatre, and rapidly became the 'maids of all work'. They would carry a platoon in full battle kit on an up-river or coastal fighting patrol or a good three tons of cargo, and perhaps more. In due course, the four other units moved to the areas of Inveraray, Irvine and Rothesay. To further their training and to overcome the lack of naval manpower, they took over from the Royal Navy the manning and operation of assault landing craft used at the Combined Training Centres (CTCs) in Scotland. For this task they were placed under the command of CRASC, CTCs. It was work which really suited them, and soon they were handling LCTs, LCMs, LCAs and the like with confidence and skill.

Early in 1944 these units, with the exception of 467 Company, were required to re-equip and reform for operation 'Overlord'. The assault landing craft were handed back to the Royal Navy and the companies were gradually concentrated in the West Mersea area, to which the central training unit, 246 Motor Boat Company, had already been moved. Such was the high esteem in which these motorboat companies were held by Headquarters, Combined Operations, that the Chief of Combined Operations wrote a personal letter to the CRASC expressing his appreciation and thanks for the way in which the military crews had carried out their duties.

The remaining unit, 467 Company, remained in Scotland and acted as a continuation training unit under War Office control.

Re-forming and re-equipment for 'Overlord'

Nos. 571, 624, 625 and 626 Motor Boat Companies, RASC, were then formed into 42 Water Transport Column.* Nos. 571 and 625 Companies were equipped with what were known as military oil barges—MOBs for short. They were, in effect, old iron Thames dumb barges into which had been fitted large tanks capable of carrying some 80 tons of bulk petrol. They were powered by two Chrysler Royal petrol engines, and were perhaps some of the most unwieldy craft that ever had to sail under their own power. To say the least, their seagoing qualities were limited, and the crews' quarters indifferent. Yet, in spite of these shortcomings, they gave valuable service. No. 624 Company manned 48 ft fast launches previously used for target towing and 40 ft launches of an RAF air/sea rescue type. Both were twin-screw and powered with Perkins S6M diesels. No. 626 Company was equipped with standard Admiralty 36 ft harbour launches. Each company also had its own unit vessels for headquarter and workshop duties.

Attached to the formation were many 45 ft motor fishing vessels, equipped for fire fighting. They were manned by the RASC, and Army Fire Service teams controlled the fire fighting equipment. Later these vessels were augmented by a number of converted LCVs.

Move to the Concentration Areas

The move of the column to the concentration area before D Day caused the CRASC 42 Water Transport Units much anxiety. For example, he received movement orders ordering two of the units to concentration areas on the Sussex downs. Eventually this was put right, and 624 and 626 Companies concentrated at Yarmouth in the Isle of Wight. This meant that the craft had to run the gauntlet of the Straits of Dover but all arrived safely by May 25th, 1944. The two MOB companies did not take part in this initial move and at the time, only three of the fire boats were equipped.

The briefing of crews for the operation created its problems too.

* Groups of water transport companies were later designated, 'No. . . . Water Transport Units'.

Unlike normal formations, the RASC Fleet craft were to operate off all beaches, and thus the whole plan had to be disclosed—a ticklish problem in security. This caused some anxiety when D Day was postponed, for the crews of the open launches could not be confined to their boats indefinitely. But all was well.

After the arrival of the craft at Yarmouth, the companies passed entirely under the control of the Royal Naval Headquarters at Portsmouth, and it should be recorded that no written orders or instructions were issued for the move to Normandy from start to finish. The arrangements for the move were made entirely by personal liaison, and this worked very satisfactorily.

The Crossing to Normandy

The first motorboat company craft to leave were three harbour launches of 626 Company which were to carry Sappers for erecting the Mulberry Harbour. They left in the convoy of D minus 1 day. The main body of the harbour launch company arrived off the beaches on June 9th and 11th (D plus 3 and D plus 5 days), the latter after a passage lasting some 42 hours, for they were placed in a slow convoy. In fact, there was some doubt whether the launches would have sufficient petrol to complete the passage at such a speed; so launches towed each other alternatively. The advanced HQ CRASC, 30 fast motorboats and six motor fishing vessels of 624 Company crossed on D Day, June 6th, 1944. Thereafter small parties of craft from both units left each day.

One of the most outstanding feats of the crossing was that of a section of eight harbour launches of 626 Company, which sailed under the command of an officer on D plus 11. They were struck by the violent storm which created such havoc on the beaches, and it is greatly to the credit of the party that seven out of the eight arrived safely. The eighth had engine trouble and was taken in tow by a minesweeper whose captain was much impressed by the crew refusing to abandon their launch. Of the two companies despatched, this was the only craft that failed to arrive under its own power.

Work on the Beach-head

Until the port of Mulberry had been constructed, it was not possible for craft to get nearer than one mile off shore, and so all crews had to live on their launches and MFVs. This was most arduous, especially for the harbour launch crews in their open boats. Eventually, however, they were accommodated in the unsubmerged portion of one of the sunken block ships around Mulberry.

With the exception of certain smaller vessels which were able to enter Mulberry, shipping lay some three miles off shore. The fast launch company was used in the control of this and to maintain contact between the dukw companies and the ships to be unloaded. Certain of the 48 ft launches were allotted permanently to the Port Commander and other senior officers, but perhaps the most important was the fast launch *Barham*. She was allotted for the personal use of Admiral Sir Rivett Carnac, Flag Officer, British Naval Assault Forces.

It is of interest to recall that when he inspected the craft at Westminster Steps before D Day the Admiral was much impressed, but he cast an eye of some disapproval at the blue ensign with crossed swords. Not unnaturally, he wanted the white ensign to be flown. However, his request was gently but firmly refused, and thus it was that the Admiral's FMB went to sea flying the ensign of the RASC Fleet! This craft was for a time under constant fire off Courseilles and often taken out in conditions that would normally be considered quite unsuitable for launches of this type. After the operation, Admiral Carnac paid us the compliment of borrowing the RASC crew to instruct his naval crew in FMB handling.

Casualties to propellers and steering gear were heavy, because of the considerable flotsam off the beaches. Without slipways or cradles, repairs to underwater gear had to be done at sea. Here much ingenuity was shown. On several occasions use was made of the derricks of merchant ships to lift a launch clear of the water and repairs to the props and rudders were then effected from a dinghy. But this was a hazardous and risky business even in calm waters.

The harbour launches had an extremely busy time ferrying men to and from Phoenixes and ships, towing barrage balloons in the Mulberry port area, carrying CMP water patrols, serving as tenders to IWT barges, and being engaged on many other tasks.

Although it may be invidious to give examples of the exploits of these RASC crews, mention must be made of two or three at least. It was the crew of MFV 610, skippered by Sgt R. J. Yeabsley, RASC, with Cpl K. Popperwell, RASC, as second coxswain, who earned renown on June 19th, 1944, when they battled for five hours in an appalling gale to rescue 160 gunners marooned on an isolated caisson. The newly-fashioned emplacement, swept by enormous waves, was in constant danger of breaking up.

Harbour Launch No. 278, with Sgt A. E. Smith, RASC, as coxswain, distinguished herself on June 10th and 11th, 1944, in gallant work before being wrecked in a third valiant rescue attempt 10 days later. On the first occasion, a motor launch blew up on a mine while engaged on the demolition of a wreck. The coxswain of HL 278 immediately went to the rescue and, in spite of the warnings of further explosions, succeeded in saving three lives.

The next day another motor launch blew up one and a half miles off shore. The same coxswain, although the crew were in the midst of doing gearbox repairs, quickly improvised a gear lever by using a Stillson wrench and hurried to the scene of the explosion. They saved six of the crew. On the 21st, HL 278 was ordered to the assistance of the destroyer *Fury*, which had struck a mine, caught fire and been blown on the rocks. HL 278 made many attempts to take a line from the destroyer to one of the tugs which could not get alongside because of the enormous seas. It was during these heroic efforts that the harbour launch herself was flung on the rocks and completely wrecked. Fortunately, her gallant crew were saved.

Another proud occasion for the Corps was on July 22nd, 1944, when 626 Company, RASC (motorboat) was called on at three minutes' notice to convey the Prime Minister, Mr. Winston Churchill, from the small boat pier to his ship. The following signal was received by the unit from the Naval Officer-in-Charge, Mulberry B:

'The Prime Minister was grateful for the use of your boat this evening. He remarked upon its smart appearance and its good handling.'

In addition to the FMBs and MFVs; a total of 48 harbour launches were finally employed off the beaches, while four were despatched up the canal to work under the Port Commandant at Caen. Also by September, 1944, there were approximately 14 army fire boats (10 MFVs and 4 LCVs) operating on the Normandy coast, and a further detachment was sent in the October to Dieppe. Marine spare parts for the theatre were provided by No. 2 Boat Stores Depot.

In all 10 of our men were decorated for gallantry in the Normandy operations.

Much to their disappointment, the two MOB companies were retained in the United Kingdom and employed at the request of the Admiralty to replenish shipping in the South Coast ports with water. All the craft were sailed to their various destinations under their own power—and this was no mean feat in itself. Although their role was unspectacular, it was arduous, and they performed a most useful task, freeing larger tankers for carrying petrol to Normandy.

The Return from Normandy

Towards the end of the August, it became apparent that the work of the RASC motorboat companies off the beaches was drawing to a close. The Allied armies were over the River Seine, and it was known that the weather by the middle of September was unlikely to be suitable for small craft operating from open beaches. Moreover, if they were to return to Britain under their own power, they must leave before the end of September.

As channels had not been swept, movement up the French coast was out of the question. The intention, therefore, was to return 624 Company and half of 626 Company to West Mersea to refit and then to despatch them to Antwerp as soon afterwards as possible. It was also proposed to employ the MOB companies, augmented by civilian barges, on petrol distribution along the waterways of Belgium, thus relieving the strain on the General Transport Companies. On September 9th, 1944, a detachment of HQ CRASC, 42 Water Transport Units, moved by road to Antwerp and there took over accommodation for the HQ CRASC and two companies. Many civilian barges were also obtained and, after many difficulties, began to move considerable quantities of petrol and oil in bulk from Ostend to Ghent and Bruges. With the exception of one section of harbour launches and two MFVs of 626 Company which returned early in the December, the move of the RASC vessels from Normandy could not be completed until October 23rd, and so the small craft had to be returned to England as deck cargo.

Although the MOB companies had been withdrawn from their water-carrying duties and kept for some weeks at 48 hours' notice to move, they could not be sent over to the Continent because of delay in the opening of the Ghent canal at Ostend. By the time the Scheldt was open, the number of civilian barges was adequate to meet our requirements. In fact, as they had a far greater capacity than the MOBs and were more suited to the job, it was decided (by December 10th) that the MOBs would not be required. The number of RASC craft required for operation in Belgium and the Netherlands was also reviewed and eventually, in mid-January, 1945, only 624 Company was sent to Antwerp, and that with a modified establishment of 10 fast launches or FMBs, 20 harbour launches and two MFVs. All these craft were sent as deck cargo. A few weeks later some of these FMBs were employed in the Rhine crossing.

Finally, the running of the civilian barges was handed over to IWT and the detachment of HQ CRASC was withdrawn to England by January 21st, 1945, for re-equipping with other RASC Fleet units for service in the Far East.

Provision of RASC Fleet Units for the Far East

Such are the stories of the RASC Fleet in the Mediterranean and European theatres. What of its activities in the Far East? Here again the motorboat companies demonstrated that same spirit and adaptability to take on anything and everything that came their way.

With the invasion of Hong Kong and Singapore we lost all our craft, including the very fine cargo carrying-cum-target towing vessel, *Sir Hastings Anderson*, which had been specially built for the fleet by Messrs. Harland & Wolff at Belfast in 1934. As the war against the Japanese progressed, plans were evolved for the recapture of Rangoon, Malaya, Singapore, Hong Kong and the other Far Eastern territories. In these plans provision was made for a large number of RASC Fleet units of all types, including such new companies as floating workshop companies, coaster companies, and ambulance launch companies.

In September, 1944, the HQ, CRASC, 56 Water Transport Units, was formed at Stranraer, quickly followed by Nos. 856 and 884 Companies RASC (motorboat), as they had then come to be called. Cadres of trained and battle experienced men were provided from 42 Water Transport Units, and the units were built up to strength from the output of 467 Company, at that time engaged on continuation training at Stranraer. The demand from Headquarters, Allied Land Forces, South-East Asia (ALFSEA) for these companies was urgent. In January, 1945, the CRASC and one officer from headquarters left by air for the Far East, the headquarters following by sea. By January, 1945, 856 Company was also on its way and soon afterwards 884 Company embarked. Their craft—the ubiquitous 36 ft harbour launches—were to be shipped as soon as cargo space became available.

RASC Motor Boat Companies in Burma

Arriving in India in February, 1945, as the Arakan campaign was drawing to its close, 856 Company was sent urgently to Akyab to assist IWT. As its own craft had not arrived, eight D-type tugs were taken over, together with the most unpromising camp site—Ezekiel's former rice mill on Satyogya Creek, a name that will conjure up to all those who knew it visions of dilapidated buildings, overgrown clearings, and a skeleton of what was once a jetty on the *chaung* edge. The company did work there that they had surely not been taught at Rothesay or West Mersea: how to assist in mooring a 10,000-ton freighter in a six-knot tide, or to tow one, possibly two, heavy barges laden with men and supplies through treacherous waterways without charts.

In April, 1945, the company was withdrawn to Calcutta and re-equipped with it own 36 ft harbour launches, which by then were arriving from Britain in large numbers. While in Calcutta, the unit was based at Dhoppa Lock, another name that will be remembered with anything but affection by all mariners of 56 Water Transport Units! Soon they embarked with the assault forces for Rangoon. There they took over what had once been a prosperous iron foundry on the muddy banks of the Rangoon River. It had its own jetty at the foot of the Sulei Pagoda road and operated various harbour services. Boarding and mooring craft were provided, but perhaps the most interesting, and frequently exciting detail was the weekly despatch boat which ran from Rangoon to Bassein to supply the garrison there.

In the meantime, 884 Company had arrived at Chittagong in March, 1945. Again, pending the arrival of its craft by freighter, this unit also were diverted temporarily to assist IWT, this time in the traffic down the River Chindwin from Kalewa to Myngynan. Headquarters and part of the unit were flown to Indangyi, from where they made their way to Kalewa through the famous gorge in a convoy—not of boats but of jeeps. At Kalewa, they took over many tugs which had been assembled on the banks of the river. Now the operation of craft on a swiftly flowing river is not quite the same thing as sailing in harbours and the open sea which, after all, the men had been trained to do. On the Chindwin particularly, situations arose which were not even hinted at in such publications as *Jottings for Young Sailors*! However, much experience was gained—the hard way.

The coxswain, on reporting for his sailing orders, would probably be told 'You will tow these four barges down river to ——. All you have to do is to follow the river, and the channel is marked by bamboo poles—starboard hand painted red—port hand painted white with a black tip.' (Note that even the markings were unusual.) Of the barges, three would probably be more or less normal, but the fourth might well be a curious and monstrous craft some 50 ft long by 20 ft beam, loaded with about 30 tons of steel girders, and perched on top of all would be Indian troops.

Where the river was fairly narrow, there was not much doubt about where the channel was, but buoys were often missing, and in the wider reaches sandbanks were numerous. Often a choice had to be made between three apparently similar channels. Running aground was by no means uncommon, in spite of cautious sounding with a bamboo pole. But how could one navigate with caution when so many unwieldy tons were being propelled on a three-knot current? The 'monstrosities' presented a problem in such circumstances, and bitter experience soon showed that the best way of getting them afloat again was to persuade the Indian troops to go overboard and push. The danger of running aground was less likely on the return trip, but then progress was desperately slow. Often it was only just possible to move, and this was by using the back eddies close to the banks. The round trip took about 10 days, and usually there was just time to collect the mail—and possibly the beer ration—before the crew were off again on another run.

Return to Malaya and other Far Eastern Territories

After some three months of this type of work, the men of 884 Company were withdrawn to Calcutta, where they joined up again with their workshops and the rest of the unit. These had been receiving their own craft from the United Kingdom and checking them over in readiness for operational service in the attack upon Malaya. Although the Japanese surrendered before this assault could be made, 884 Company went into Malaya as planned in September, 1945, with the initial landing forces at Port Swettenham and formed the basis for the RASC water transport services subsequently provided in that command.

The remaining unit of 56 Water Transport Units was 626 Company RASC (motorboat). As we have seen, this company had reverted to War Office control after service off the Normandy beaches. It was reformed and despatched to the Far East as the third harbour launch company of the formation, arriving in Calcutta in June, 1945. Events were moving rapidly at that time, and it became necessary to revise the plans for the company's deployment. One section, with attached workshop men and operating 10 harbour launches, went to Java with the occupying Allied forces, another similar section went to Hong Kong, and the remainder of the unit, equipped with both fast motorboats and harbour launches, entered Singapore with the HQ CRASC 56 Water Transport Units. There the pre-war RASC Fleet base at Pulau Brani was re-established, much to the joy of the local inhabitants, who gave them a special *ronggeng* as a warm and sincere 'home-coming'. Maintaining these units was No. 6 Boat Stores Depot RASC which, after being uprooted first from Chittagong and then Rangoon, finally became established at Singapore, also on Pulau Brani.

Meanwhile yet another group of big operational waterborne units was being formed in the United Kingdom to assist in the Far Eastern campaign when VJ Day (August 15th, 1945) was declared. Plans for its despatch were therefore cancelled, but before it was dispersed the formation was reviewed off Hurst Castle by the Director of Supplies and Transport. Its strength at that time was approximately 200 officers and 1,400 other ranks, and in all some 200 craft were in line astern. Had these units completed mobilization they would have opened a new era in the history of the RASC Fleet, for they were to consist of a floating workshop company, coaster companies and ambulance launch companies, and would have had to make the trip under their own power. In fact, the Ambulance Launch Company (No. 935) was mobilized and due to sail in its 112 ft converted motor launches seven days after VJ Day. This was a severe disappointment, as the unit had proved itself well up to the task, and the opportunity of making RASC history by undertaking the Army's first long-distance formation voyage was the ambition of all ranks. The vessels themselves are worthy of special comment. They were fitted out to carry 20 lying or 40 sitting patients, with the necessary medical staff. The crew of 12 was commanded by a captain, with a subaltern as first officer and a warrant officer in charge of the engine room. The main machinery consisted of two Hall Scot 660 hp petrol engines giving a maximum speed of 18 knots. The cruising speed was 10 to 12 knots, and the maximum range was 1,500 miles, enabling the voyage to the Far East to be accomplished easily in various 'legs'. Although these craft did not make the trip, it must be recorded that one of the large RASC 90 ft fire boats sailed to Singapore under her own power in 1946.

Let us conclude the chapter with incidents from one or two of the other overseas stations at which our vessels served.

Malta, G.C.

RASC water transport services had long been provided in Malta, the vessels in pre-war days carrying out the normal administrative and target towing details. Civilian officers of the Fleet were sent out from home on special agreements; a few officers and all ratings were engaged locally. The craft were controlled and administered by the local RASC officer-in-charge transport, Valetta being the main station, and it was not until July, 1945, that a water transport company was established there.

The difficulties and dangers under which the vessels operated during the years of siege need little emphasis. By 1943, of the six craft there, one had been lost, one sunk (but subsequently salved and recommissioned), and the remaining four had suffered damage of one sort or another, all from enemy air attacks.

One day in July, 1941, while standing by for air/sea rescue duty, the 57 ft high speed target towing launch *Clive* was called out to pick up a British pilot shot down some 25 miles north of the St Elmo lighthouse during an E-boat attack. Unarmed except for a single Lewis gun mounted aft (but with no gunner on board), the *Clive* proceeded to the area and found, not the pilot, but the crew of an E-boat clinging to the wreckage of their craft. They had been badly shot up and were taken on board the launch where their wounds were dressed. Search for the pilot was resumed, and another well armed E-boat was located in a seemingly undamaged condition. A rather active looking individual was hopping about on board waving the Italian flag, and as the rescued Italians were beginning to sit up and take notice they were secured below decks. The E-boat was circled warily, but as the *Clive* was almost unarmed and only carried a crew of five, permission was requested to return to base, land the prisoners, get an armed party and return to secure the E-boat. This was given, but in the meantime HMS *Jade* had put out to take the E-boat in tow. The active gentleman waving the flag turned out to be the missing British pilot! The crew sorely regretted this missed opportunity of towing in a prize. Not long after returning to base and resuming her air/sea rescue duties, the *Clive* received another urgent call to proceed about 36 miles to the north and take possession of another E-boat believed to be in that vicinity. The search, conducted without escort or air cover, took her to a position off Cape Passarro. Although unsuccessful in her primary task, she sighted and closed to investigate, first, an Italian schooner carrying German troops, and a little later, an Italian hospital ship coming at high speed out of the Straits of Messina.

'Cloak-and-dagger' tasks also fell to the Fleet's lot. Later in the summer of the same year, for instance, the *Clive* was detailed to land French agents at Hammamet in Tunisia, involving a run of about 200 miles each way. Unfortunately various troubles prevented this detail from being completed, and instead of landing hale and well in North Africa, a very seasick party of Frenchmen returned to Malta.

The older Fleet vessels played their part too. On one memorable occasion in January, 1942, the steam target tower *Lord Plumer* was returning from the north-west of the island with a load of sand for airfield runways when she was attacked by a Messerschmitt off Tigne Point. The machine gunner was killed and the chief engineer (Mr. C. Long) mortally wounded. The vessel, however, made port, and for his gallant part in this action with the enemy the master (Mr. E. W. Elson) was made a Member of the Order of the British Empire. Later the RASCV *Lord Plumer* proceeded with a military crew to North Africa, where she remained until the end of the war.

It was in Malta that official commendation was earned from the Lords Commissioners of the Admiralty—in most unexpected fashion. The *Clive*—she always seemed to be in the thick of it—was target towing off Maddalena in April, 1943, and to avoid delay, the master decided to steam round the targets at the end of each run instead of stopping, winding in and streaming the targets. All went well when making starboard turns, for the towing wire remained visible on the surface. However, when making port turns, the lay of the wire caused it to sink to the bottom—and it acted as a mine sweep. Mines began to bob up astern and it soon became apparent that the launch was operating in a newly-laid and undiscovered enemy minefield. Several mines were located in this way, and many more were subsequently destroyed by the Port Mine Sweeping Officer who quickly came on the scene. The work of the RASC Fleet's one and only (unofficial) mine-sweeper is laconically recorded thus in an Admiralty letter to the War Office:

'Their Lordships note with interest this occasion of a War Department vessel co-operating in mine-clearance operations.'

If only space were available, many more such stories could be told of the RASC vessels in Malta. Suffice it to say that to them also fell the unique distinction of target towing for the Royal Navy and for the American, Free French, Greek, and Yugoslav navies before the invasion of Southern France.

West Africa

As we have seen, it was in 1941 that No. 3 Motor Boat Company RASC was sent to West Africa in cadre form to meet the heavy demands arising in the Gambia, Sierre Leone, the Gold Coast and Nigeria, for RASC water transport. It had a most difficult task. Although its headquarters were established at White Man's Bay, Freetown, it was widely dispersed. There were no slipways and hardly any local maintenance facilities in any of the four colonies. The waters were infested with teredo worm, and those who have served in the tropics know how rapid and devastating the damage it inflicts can be. The unit also had to compete with the inexperience of the locally recruited crews, particularly of engineers. Teething troubles were many and serious, and yet, as an example of the way in which the unit tackled the job, some 12,000 men were carried in seven of its launches in one month alone.

On the operational side, a series of reconnaissances of the Sierra Leone rivers were effected by day and by night. Early in 1942 an attack upon British West African territory by Vichy French forces was regarded as a dangerous possibility, and the question of sending reasonably large numbers of troops and quantities of stores by river became of particular importance in Sierra Leone. The twin diesel engined ex-German vessel, the *Waja*, of 120 ft length and 25 ft beam, was obtained from Lagos, and the unit commander was given the task of taking her on a trial trip up the Scarcies rivers to see whether or not such means of transport was practicable. Popular opinion was that it was not, and inquiries among the native chiefs confirmed the fact that not within living memory had a vessel, even half the *Waja's* size, been seen up river.

However, on February 2nd, 1942, the *Waja* sailed from White Man's Bay and made the trip to within reach of the French Guinea frontier—incidentally carrying a cargo for the Sappers of 24 poles, each 55 ft long—thus proving that such an up-river trip was possible.

A similar reconnaissance was successfully completed on the Lesser or Little Scarcies.

Lack of Europeans and the very real maintenance difficulties increasingly took their toll as the months went on, and in 1943 the whole of the water transport requirements were reviewed. In consequence 793 Water Transport Company, WAASC, was formed to replace the existing services. It had its headquarters at Freetown and a section in each of the four colonies. As there are no docking facilities for large ships at Bathurst in the Gambia, four launches were stationed there and used for embarkation and for ferrying men across the River Gambia. They were also used for the transport of cattle from the interior, and even target towing.

As Freetown is another port where large ships cannot berth, the importance of our craft for embarkation and disembarkation needs no emphasis. That task therefore continued, and similar work was done at Takoradi in the Gold Coast.

The Nigerian section of the Water Transport Company operated in Lagos Harbour and lagoon, which extends parallel to the coast for some 50 miles. The section ran a ferry service from Lagos proper (which is an island) to Apapa on the mainland opposite, where the main supply depot was situated. It also ran a service and ferried drinking water to the Fire Service command battery at Tarquah, and later was engaged for some time on the dumping of ammunition in the sea.

East Africa

The RASC Fleet in East Africa Command has no epic tales to tell, but rather a record of steady achievement and tremendously hard training and work. No RASC craft were stationed there before the war, and although after the war began a few local craft were operated by various formations and units to ferry men, it was not until May, 1943, that the service really got going. Some 15 vessels were then transferred to RASC charge, most of them in poor condition. Many boats were requisitioned both for training and for service until delivery could be effected of motor fishing vessels from South Africa and fast launches and harbour craft from England. A training cadre was sent out from the United Kingdom to train the natives, and by 1944 510 Company, EAASC (water transport) was well established. Its parish was large, covering three main areas—the islands embracing the Seychelles, Mauritius, Diego Suarez and Tulear (Madagascar); Mombasa, Tanga and Mauza, Dar-es-Salaam and Zanzibar in the centre; and in the north, Mogadishu and Berbera.

Choosing and training African crews presented a problem at first. Men with good records in the East African Army Service

Corps were drafted to the unit and tried out. Training was rapid and intensive. Some of the initial trainees proved unsuitable and had to be replaced with special recruits from the coast and lake districts of East Africa. Yet the askaris soon became enthusiastic, and their greatest ambition was to win the sailor's cap issued to each man when he passed his proficiency tests. This was a real triumph for the Luo native from the lake district of Kenya. One of the greatest difficulties was the teaching of the tides, another was the language problem; for all commands were given in English. Workshop personnel were also trained, and so successful was the instruction, both in workshops and on the water, that many big African business concerns, as well as Government harbour departments, arranged to employ the EAASC water transport askaris on their discharge from the Army.

One of the company's best efforts was the voyage, unescorted, of four 46-ton motor fishing vessels from Mombasa right the way through to Alexandria, where they were needed for urgent transport work—a distance of 3,000 miles. Their route was via Mogadishu, Dante, round Cape Guardafui, Aden, Port Sudan, Port Suez, and thence to Alexandria. The voyage took 24 days, and enough food, water and fuel was taken on board at Mombasa for the whole trip.

'*Nil sine labore*' was indeed a reality to this unit. It achieved much in a very short time, not only afloat but on shore. How justly proud they must have felt when the *Mombasa Times* selected it as providing the best troops for general smartness on the VJ Day parade.

The Caribbean

Throughout the war, RASC vessels operated in both the North and South Caribbean. For most of the period, they were controlled by the officers commanding RASC, but in July, 1944, No. 899 Company, RASC (water transport) was raised to operate all Fleet craft in the northern waters.

Based on Jamaica, it had for its near neighbours the Naval, Air Force and Royal Artillery establishments at Kingston harbour. Its most interesting task was the long distance passenger and cargo run between Kingston and Belize, a distance of some 650 miles. For this service a 250-ton American Fleet auxiliary, re-named the RASCV *Catania*, was obtained under the lease-lend agreement. A RASC Fleet civilian crew took delivery of her at Boston and sailed her to Jamaica. She also made several voyages between her home port of Kingston and British Honduras, Nassau in the Bahamas and Turks Island. On one occasion, in the middle of the Caribbean Sea, the cook went mad (perhaps because of the heat of the galley) and jumped overboard. An English corporal, travelling as a passenger, dived after him without hesitation, although the waters were shark-infested, and saved his life. The NCO was decorated for his courage.

Although the war was far from the West Indies, strict measures were taken to guard Kingston harbour, which was a forming-up point for convoys, and its coastal defences were extensive. In addition to a heavy programme of target towing—effected by the small and somewhat antiquated RASCV *Abercorn*—the RASC Fleet provided craft for the examination service in the harbour approaches. An amusing story is told of a visit to the *Abercorn* by a very senior officer. The captain, a Jamaican who took an enormous pride in his vessel, was asked, 'How old is she?' 'About 45 years old, sir', was the answer. The VIP then remarked, 'She is about the same age as I am', to which the proud captain replied, 'Yes, but she is good for at least another 10 years' work!' Alas, this was not to be, for the *Abercorn*, although no longer in War Department service, went to her final rest in the hurricane of August 17th, 1951.

The third but not least of the company's commitments was the maintenance of water-borne communications across the harbour between Fort Clarence, Port Royal, Palisadoes, Fort Nugent and Kingston. Most of the crews were and are recruited from Port Royalists, whose families for generations have lived by and on the sea.

In the South, the water transport company did not come into being until after the end of the war, when, strange as it may seem, its commitments increased rather than decreased, largely because of the discontinuation of lease-lend and a new system of supply from the United Kingdom. However, even during the war, its water transport commitments were many. A second American Fleet auxiliary, named the RASCV *El Alamein*, was allotted for long distance passages throughout the area, embracing as it did British Guiana, Barbados, the Windwards, and the Leeward Islands. Port of Spain, Trinidad, was the main base, and a service was operated from the mainland there to the island of Gasper Grande near by, but one or two craft were also stationed in the Leeward and Windward Islands for local services.

It is fitting that units of the RASC Fleet, whose early history may be traced back to the days of sailing ships, should have operated from two such historical spots as Port Royal and Port of Spain, and sail again the romantic Caribbean seas.

Conclusion

In one short chapter it is impossible to record in full the diverse, world-wide activities of the fleet. Bermuda, Gibraltar, India and the Faroes too—RASC vessels served them all and each has its own story.

Thus from small beginnings developed this vast war-time fleet which at its peak consisted of more than 50 units—water transport companies, motorboat companies, boat stores depots and training school—their crews and shore staff, military and civilian, drawn from almost every Commonwealth nation.

CHAPTER XVII

SOME UNIT NARRATIVES

4 COMPANY (TANK TRANSPORTER)

'I Drove a Desert Dinosaur',

by

R. A. Richardson

(With acknowledgments to the *Evening News*)

As far as I know nobody has ever written a saga about the Eighth Army's tank transporter companies. Yet who in that army can have failed to see them at one time or other, trundling along the desert tracks, or have refrained from cursing them for slowing up traffic on the coast road?

Nor have I seen any eulogies of the little men—the army seemed to believe in the principle, 'the larger the vehicle the smaller the driver'—who manned those dinosaurs of the desert. Permit me, then, to say a word or two on behalf of the tank transporter units.

That tanks won't travel too far on their own tracks was discovered early in the desert campaign where distances were vast and horizons far. Tanks had to be taken almost into battle and, if damaged, to be taken out. And who better to do this than the RASC (this was before the REME really got going on recovery)?

Now this should have called for men with some knowledge of tanks, an appreciation of the problems involved in the loading and off-loading of tanks and vehicles specially designed for the purpose. But did this happy state of events obtain?

Take me, for instance. When I was posted to No. 4 Tank Transporter Company at Qassasin in mid-June, 1942, I had never been within 100 yards of a tank or Bren-carrier, and my driving experience was limited to one or two training runs in a 3-ton lorry.

'Drive that transporter down to the petrol dump and fill up,' said the sergeant. I climbed into the cab of the already war-worn converted civilian truck and, faced with an array of gear and winch levers and brakes and a dashboard with enough dials to do credit to an aeroplane, my panic was excusable. I started off in top, however, and gradually made my way down the gearbox until I got the giant rolling. Perhaps I was fortunate in not being in the heavy section with the new multi-wheeled trailer units.

4 COMPANY (TANK TRANSPORTER)

Experience of tank work came when we went to collect tanks from the dockside at Suez, where we learned that tanks had brakes and ought not to be secured to the truck with ropes. And how to load: Stand on the platform, guide the RAC driver up the 30-degree ramps with hand signals, and then jump clear as the tracks crashed down just where you had been standing.

Then to the desert, where the army stretched in retreat from Alamein to Alexandria, to wait until they had all gone by and then proceed up the empty coast road to recover what we could of damaged AFVs and whatever else was lying about; and, having loaded them, to find someone who would accept delivery. In those days the workshops of one corps were decidedly chary of accepting tanks not belonging to one of their own units.

With the line stabilized, we spent most of the time in the area just behind the line Alamein–Qatara. There, with maps and six-figure references but with few compasses, we would collect damaged tanks and deliver replacements. From Burg-el-Arab past Hammam and its flies we would jolt along the 'T' and 'Diamond' tracks, using the wrecked Lysander as a signpost before launching out on the mass of dusty trails which came into being, died and were born again at the whim of each successive convoy's commander.

I remember the burned-out tank—with the dead driver still in his seat—that we had with us for three days; the experience of being shelled by a newly arrived unit rather anxious about the sight of our laden truck skylined on an escarpment; and at night the Bostons of the RAF going over to disturb Axis dreams.

About this time I made the acquaintance of the 4th County of London Yeomanry, whom I am prepared to swear had the heaviest Crusader in the British Army. My vehicle carried this particular tank with its crew on several occasions during the campaign and each time had trouble owing to tyre bursts. The sequence of events would be: 'bang' from the tyre or tyres, followed at once by the rattle of the cooking tins of the tank crew and, almost before the transporter came to a stop, the CLYs were preparing a meal. I still wonder if there was any truth in my co-driver's firm belief that the Tankies used to shoot down at our tyres whenever they felt hungry.

There was no room for us at the front when the big show started, but it was not long before we were following in the wake of the advance; climbing Sollum Pass by night, loaded with reserve tanks, without lights and fearful of our brakes, seeing Bardia like a jewel in the first light of dawn, and then Tobruk, no longer the key to the gates of Egypt.

From there until we reached Tunis, we shuttled backwards and forwards, driving sometimes for 24 hours at a stretch, leaving the bones of worn-out transporters in 'returned vehicle parks' along the way. We carried New Zealanders, French colonial troops, the Foreign Legion, Indians, not to mention the British, noteworthy among whom were the Rifle Brigade, known to us for some reason as the Hackney Gurkhas. We met them all.

Perhaps you may have had a desert trip on a transporter, with its hoisted ramps rattling behind you, and the tracks of your tank rolling backwards and forwards ever so slightly but loaded with menace, so that the truck drivers were always conscious of 20 tons or so a few inches from the backs of their necks.

You may perhaps remember a transporter with a golfer calling 'fore' painted on the cab doors, with a worried-looking, usually unshaven, overalled corporal forever helping an equally dishevelled driver to change tyres, almost always 100 miles or so behind the convoy and short of rations, water and petrol. That was me, and I've never got over it.

534 COMPANY (TANK TRANSPORTER)

This company began its career as the ammunition company of the 54th Divisional RASC. The division did not go overseas and reverted to a beach role in 1941, with heavily cut transport resources. The divisional supply company became the divisional composite company, the petrol company became the Guards Armoured Divisional Troops Company, and the ammunition company was eventually converted into one of the earliest tank transporter companies with a headquarters, workshops and three platoons equipped with Diamond T tractors and Rogers trailers, for the carriage of Churchill tanks. This glad news arrived in April, 1942, together with an announcement that 66 of the new tractors and trailers were awaiting collection at Feltham.

No one could tell us anything about them—no one seemed to know, but someone must have driven them from the docks to Feltham. We found it was the civvy fitters at Feltham. So we sent 20 men a week to Feltham to drive them around, get the feel of them, and probe into them. Then we drew 15 vehicles, and it was denims for everyone. We crawled over and under them, and cursed because no maker's handbook was available to help us.

Then followed seemingly endless exercises, practising tank loading with 36th Tank Brigade, when we hauled them to ranges, later hauling 34th Tank Brigade and then 25th Tank Brigade.

We were the only Diamond T company, so we got odd jobs all over England. We reached a peak with our headquarters in Norfolk and jobs in hand in Luton, Doncaster, Scotland, Somerset

Moving Forward

Carrying Captured 15-cm. Gun

Carrying Cruiser Tanks

and the Isle of Wight. Coming back from the Isle of Wight, one of the transporters tried to swim ashore from a landing craft. Workshops had a happy time getting the salt water out.

In due course, when deemed fit for service, we were warned for North Africa. Before the end of January, 1943, embarkation leave was over and vehicles had had their baptism of snow on the mountains en route for the ports.

We duly embarked and on February 1st had our first glimpse of Africa—Algiers looking white and attractive in the sunlight. When we arrived at Philippeville, 25th Tank Brigade commander came on board to see us. It was not just a visit to the commanding officer's cabin, but a real unit visit including talks to the men in mess deck. It was but a little gesture, but it meant a lot when those same men were keeping going, brushing the sleep from their eyes, some weeks later. After disembarkation we marched through the night out to Sidi Moussa, our feet soft from weeks on board ship, and our language correspondingly lurid.

Some of us embarked early on a reconnaissance of the course we were to come to know so well: Philippeville—Bone—Laverdure—Souk Ahras—Ghardimaou—Le Kef. Meanwhile most of us were busy off-loading the transporters at Philippeville. There was some excitement when a sling broke and seven tons of ballast blocks spewed on to the quayside. Who said Arabs cannot move!

There followed arrangements for the night's work, tank regiment and transporter company commanders walking up and down the quayside in the rain. 'How many transporters can you get ashore by 0400?'—'Plenty—how many tanks will you have?'—'Oh, a dozen and a half.' Well, we had only six transporters ashore and only eight hours to go, but we would make it.

Later the company commander scrambled down a gang plank at midnight, all bluffs called. How many tanks? Twelve; thank God, we had got 14 transporters ashore, more than a mount for every tank, by 0400. The crews were briefed and warned of the mountains, the treacherous verges. Not a tractor or a trailer wheel must leave the metalling. Above all, we must keep moving.

Punctually at 0400 the first convoy moved out on the first long pull up from Philippeville to Bone. We were over the crest with a flat road now to Bone, harbouring at Mondovi, the first North African mountain conquered. Now the rest could be brought on.

Our first party went back to Philippeville with the dawn. In 24 hours the next bunch pulled out, and again, and three convoys were on the road. No, not three platoons, but groups, just as the vehicles came off the ships, so we called them the Cheltenham Flier, the Cornish Riviera, and the Flying Scot respectively. It took a long time to get out of the habit of calling platoon officers 'guards'.

P1 RASC

The first snag was a message that the Cheltenham Flier had taken 24 hours to take the 1,000 yards of the Medjez Sfa diversion. We were too early, and too heavy. The roads had not settled down, but the RE got Somerfelt track down, and the situation was saved.

Up and down we went, from Bone to Le Kef, Le Kef to Bone, grinding up through Laverdure at 4 mph. Messages arrived that the Cornish Riviera was two hours ahead of schedule, that the Flying Scot had slipped a coach on the Souk Ahras mountain. We dropped one off the Cheltenham Flier, as she came round next, to pick up the tank.

The tempo quickened with the deterioration of the situation round Kasserine. 'Speed up the schedule' was the cry. They wanted the tanks. We were already reckoning to drive 16 hours a day. Well, we would have to boost it to 20. We had to deliver our bulky and precious 'goods'.

We quickly developed a respect for, and appreciation of 'Movements', with their motorcycle patrol into Souk Ahras each day, bringing back all the positions of convoys relayed from Philippeville and Bone, and notifications of breakdowns. Movements—no we could not do without them.

The situation worsened. The Hun might come up to Le Kef. Did they want us as infantry? No, just keep delivering the tanks. Company headquarters and workshops stood by as a mobile reserve for the defence of Le Kef, but the non-arrival of the enemy frustrated their bloodthirsty preparations.

Aircraft were happily not too interfering. There was a bit of blasphemy when one came low at Le Kef and put a 20 mm incendiary plumb through the radiator, and a few tracer bullets through the fuel tanks. The fuel tanks did not blow up; bless the man who gave us a diesel engine. The workshops officer had to have the radiator news broken to him gently, as radiators were not possible to get, but in 48 hours she was under way with a combined Thornycroft-cum-Leyland radiator, which did till we could get a replacement.

Another enemy aircraft popped off 17 tyres on one vehicle once. The language of the corporal who had taken shelter under the trailer was unfortunately never recorded. Next we heard that another radiator had gone. A tank ran amok on the Souk Ahras–Ghardimaou junction after its transporter got a wheel spin and had to off-load the tank. This particular tank had faulty brakes and fluffed its gears on a bend.

The result on a wet mountain road with a gradient of 1 in 12 might have been shocking. The tank careered backwards for 30 yards, all 40 tons of it, but before it could disappear into space the next transporter heaved round the corner, and, rather involuntarily, 'collected' the runaway. The thought that one tank had been saved at the expense of one radiator was no consolation to workshops.

Then came a call from Sedjenane—Would we deliver half a dozen reinforcement Churchills to the squadron of the North Irish Horse up there? We ran them up from Beja by night, and what a night, with rain in torrents and six off-loads in 30 miles! The news that Hun patrols often crossed that road at night was no comfort. We remember an NCO mending his motorcycle by the roadside in the dark that night; for months afterwards it was the best maintained one in the unit.

Our contacts with various regiments, both armoured and infantry, made us many friends, especially the North Irish Horse, to whom we normally delivered tanks at Beja. Many were the kindnesses we received there. Infantry units, too, issued complete sets of clothing to our drivers when they pulled in.

In striking contrast to the kindness of our fellow soldiers was the cruelty of nature as evidenced to the south by the dreadful mockeries of road around El Aroussa, Gafour and down through Maktar.

But we were nearing the end; we were on the last lap. But still the cry was, faster! It was a fortnight now since anyone had had more than four hours' sleep a night, but it was the last lap and they wanted the tanks faster. We accepted the challenge and went flat out for a 60 hours' unbroken stretch.

We had promised the whole 180 tanks of the brigade by the night of March 2nd. Barring breakdowns, we would make it. Anxiously we counted our chickens later that evening. Were they all in? No, there was one with an injector pump gone at Ghardimaou. The transporter crew were determined to get it rolling; there were still six hours to go. She was moving, she was in, her tank was delivered. It was five minutes to midnight! We were through; there was not a tank left at the ports, and 185 had been safely delivered.

Now the transporters limped home off the last convoy. The last convoy was coming in. I stopped the leader and opened the cab door. The driver fell out. 'O.K. son, take it easy, you've only 800 yards to go, and then you're not going out for 48 hours.' A weary driver opened his eyes and grinned; 'I shan't speed, sir, I can only get 900 revs out of my engine.'

Sleep, blessed sleep, for 12 of our 48 hours, and then the other 36 to get the vehicles fit for the next jobs, and then off we went to re-equip 6th Armoured Division with Shermans. Ten tons less seemed to make it a rest cure. We had to carry Shermans for the division, Shermans as reserves, nearly 300 in all, but the pace was steadier. It was no longer a wild rush like that of 25th Tank Brigade.

Then 21st Tank Brigade, Churchills again, but the weather was drying, and we had only to haul them to Ghardimaou. The brigade were going forward for the battle, and we were ordered to haul them from Ghardimaou to Testour.

The telephone rang; BRAC asking for a squadron to go up to Gafour straight away. 'It's 1500 now,' said brigade. 'How soon can a squadron get to the loading base three miles away?' They suggested arrival by 1600, which meant that we would have to move fast. 1600 hours brought the sight that never palls—a quick load in village streets. Transporters wheeled in from their hide to the south, and the Churchills thundered in from the north, and RASC section NCOs were at the junction leading in the two troops they will carry. There was the noise of Churchill engines, and there was the smell of derv and petrol engines then, suddenly, there was peace, the village was deserted, and the convoy was moving steadily down the road to Souk el Arba. And the time—1620.

Later another ambition was achieved, to take a whole regiment forward at once instead of in penny numbers. Sixty-four transporters rolled out with 63 tanks on board: not only a regiment, but bits of brigade headquarters as well. Then there was the thrill of a 'pull' to Seven Dials and meeting our fellow craftsmen from the Eighth Army. There was, too, an almost romantic delivery in the moonlight at Testour, when all went like clockwork. As daylight came we suddenly noticed that the detector paint on the car had gone red. Gas at last? But no, that was another lesson learnt—never to open a tin of sardines on the bonnet in the dark and splash the oil on the detector paint. If you do, it may worry you at dawn.

April, 1943, saw us on the same old run: Souk-Ahras—Bone—Souk el Arba—Seven Dials—Testour, with reinforcement Churchills for our brigades. Frequently we had to tour our 'customers'' locations to make sure we knew their exact locations in case of a quick move. Once occasion arose to go from Bou Arada to Medjez. The direct road seemed suspicious, so we asked a lance-corporal (not a Corps man) nearby. He replied, 'O.K.'. Down the road we rocked, over a strand of barbed wire. There was a loud noise. We got out and discovered that the hub covers had been blown off, the rear light had vanished, and the boot had been blown off. We had driven into an anti-personnel minefield.

After creeping the car back slowly through it, we found we had previously driven through 10 rows of anti-tank mines. We crept even more slowly through that. Returning hastily to Bou Arada, we learned that German RHQ was in Goubellat, and it was just as well we did not lunch there as we had intended. We inspected the damage and replaced the boot of the car. But we were almost grateful to that mine when the layers of paint it removed exposed the old original 54th Divisional sign.

When we knew that Tunis had fallen, it meant a lot to us. There was a standstill order on tank movements, and for a blessed week nothing moved. It was the first time the vehicles had stopped since those 48 hours on March 3rd and 4th. But there was no time to idle. We vetted them, checked them and 'minor repaired' them, for there was more work coming. All the tanks we had hauled forward would have to come back, so we upped stakes and moved to Soliman. It was easier this time, for 228 Company had Diamond Ts as well now. We embarked on some really big convoys, with 90 vehicles in each. They were horribly unwieldy, particularly as we were moving at 10 mph, and someone had routed 1,000 AGRA vehicles at 15 mph, an hour behind us on the same route.

Soon Cap Bon was clear of tanks. There were a few odd last minute jobs for stuff going to Sicily, and then we were off to Algiers, picking up 47 'dead' Churchills to take to Bone as a pay load, these same Churchills we had hauled forward in February.

Then followed a series of long hauls—Algiers–Oran–Bone–Algiers, 1,500 miles as the transporter does not fly. Workshops were anxiously watching them as they came in after a fortnight on the road, and counting the number of tractors being carried on trailers.

It was now eight months since we unshipped those 65 Diamond Ts, and we had only evacuated two of them, a tribute to the grim unflagging determination of workshops to have them fit when wanted. Defects they had: cracked cylinder blocks (we had had 11), broken rocker bearings causing four trailer wheels to fall off (that happened 10 times), and fuel injector oil shafts always choosing the most awkward spot to break. But ask a driver to swap, suggest to an artificer he should lead a quiet life somewhere else. It would be a brave man who would suggest it.

Since the vehicles were landed in North Africa, they had averaged 9,850 miles each, and the aggregate mileages of the transporters had been 618,464. The tanks carried had been mainly Churchills and Shermans, but we also carried SP Guns, Scorpions, German Mark III's and IV's. Sometimes, when First Army could fit them in the programme, we had done rush jobs for the United States Army. The total of tanks and guns carried had been 1,666, and each of them had been carried an average of 165 miles—165 miles of African road, so called, struggling through fords a foot deep one day and nearly four feet deep the next.

We will never forget the punctures, with 34 wheels a vehicle; how we loved loose granite chippings on a hot road! Every puncture or blow out meant taking the tank off and jacking up either 11 tons of trailer or 19 tons of tractor. In the words of a Birmingham bus driver who had been on the same vehicle since June, 1942: 'Perhaps it's just as well we lost the asterisk Burma road; it's the only one that could be worse than these.'

536 GENERAL TRANSPORT COMPANY (DUKWS)

On January 26th, 1944, 536 Company took over its first dukws, having previously been trained in them at the Amphibious School at Towyn. From that day until May 26th, 1944, at Hursley Camp, when we were 'sealed' and briefed, we did training and exercises with the dukws until we were absolutely familiar with them and knew just what we, as a company, could do. These exercises of course were always done in conjunction with No. 9 Beach Group of which we were part, and consequently we came to know all the other people in the beach group and began to appreciate their problems and work as well as our own. Naturally also, these exercises were on the kind of work we would do from D Day onwards and on the actual landing itself, so that when the time came we knew what we had to do.

We were given key plans and maps a short while before D Day, showing us exactly where everything was to be—transhipment area, initial dumps, dukw exits, etc., and also how everything was phased in. We also had a scale model of King Beach and the surrounding countryside. Everything was planned in the greatest detail.

On May 30th, the company, which had been split up into various serials, went to the different ports and began marshalling and embarking. The next five days were spent in embarking and sailing.

Then before 0900 hours on D Day (i.e. H plus 90 minutes) Major Hurman, with an advance party, landed on King Beach and set up a headquarters at a prearranged spot near La Rivière. At 0900 hours Lieutenant Day, with 23 dukws of A Platoon, came in on the same beach. These dukws were loaded with ammunition and went to HQ 69th Brigade, near Crepon, where they were unloaded. Then they returned to the beach, where they parked while Lieutenant Day went to report to company headquarters. The times of arrival of all parties were some 30 minutes late because of the poor weather, a smoke screen laid by the Navy and the number of other craft milling around in the water.

Later in the day, all the rest of the serials due in on D Day arrived, and only three dukws were damaged by mines or underwater obstacles. Actually, the whole unit, with a few unimportant exceptions, had arrived by D plus 3. On arrival, it was found that the place reserved for a vehicle park was still occupied by the enemy, so we parked in the initial dump area. There were many Jerry snipers running about the whole area, and they were not completely cleared up until June 10th. Apart from the delivery of the loads on the dukws, the only work we did on D Day was the evacuation of casualties from the beaches to the various craft. The rest of the time was spent in some very necessary digging in and settling down. That night we were bombed fairly thoroughly by Jerry; but were fortunate to have only one casualty.

On D plus 1 the first coasters arrived, and we immediately began to unload them into the initial dump area. We soon found that King Beach was practically unusable, because of the amount of clay in the sand. Dukws were getting bogged everywhere; so we moved over a little just into Love Beach. During this day a dukw ran over a mine, killing Sgt Skinner, of A Platoon, and injuring Major Hurman, our commanding officer, who were standing nearby. The drivers were not hurt. This particular incident was one of many similar ones, and we proved time and time again that anyone inside a dukw when it hits a mine will not get hurt, whereas anyone standing near is pretty certain to catch a packet. That night was fairly peaceful compared with the previous one.

During the next few days, Dukw Control and a properly functioning transhipment area were set up at the beach exit. For several days, the dukws had to take the loads right through to the dumps, because there was not sufficient ordinary transport. This was the first time that it was realized that the dukws could be used as normal GT, as originally it had been planned that the dukws should operate purely in the sea and be scrapped at the end of 90 days, when it was estimated that the need for them would have passed.

For one or two days the dukws also had to unload from beached LCTs, again because of the lack of 3-ton transport. At this time, also, we were given some pioneers to act as spare drivers, and thus to provide some slight relief for the drivers who had been working flat out for 24 hours a day. Things were slowed up a bit by poor traffic circuits and by the distance of the coasters from the shore.

On June 10th two more platoons were attached to us, one from 633 Company and the other from 705 Company. This was also the day on which things were greatly improved and a definite pattern established, to which we were going to work for the next two and a half months. In other words, the traffic circuit was improved, the coasters were brought opposite Dukw Control, and we were given some RASC motor launches to use for control at sea. Off-loading of the coasters was stopped between 2300 hours and 0500 hours because vital maintenance was not being done, the drivers were not getting enough rest, and it was decidedly difficult to find the coasters at night through a thick smoke screen. When another 49 dukws were attached the next day, this, together with the other factors already mentioned, caused off-loading of stores to be much quicker.

All days from June 11th onwards, as far as the dukw work was concerned, were similar and can be represented by this description of a typical day's work.

The previous night, the officer in charge of Dukw Control, one Captain Leith, attended a conference and was informed by the MLO what coasters were expected in the next day, their ETA, their load, and how many holds or hatches they had. Consequently he was able to judge how many dukws could be used in each ship.

At 0445 hours, the dukws of the first platoon out this morning lined up in the road to the beach entrance and the Dukw Control. The driver of the first dukw was told the number of the coaster to which he was to go, and if that coaster had only just arrived, he would be told its approximate whereabouts, and so he pushed off to sea to this coaster. In the meantime, on a large board in Dukw Control a tag with his dukw number on it was placed opposite the ship's number. This process went on until sufficient dukws had been allocated to each coaster—that morning there were six coasters in. The officer in command of Dukw Control is able to foretell how many dukws will be needed to keep a coaster going; this depends on the number of hatches it has, its distance from the shore (which might be anything up to three miles), and its cargo (ammunition can be unloaded more quickly than ordnance stores, for example).

By the time all the necessary dukws had been sent out, the first loaded ones were returning and a man stationed by the dukw exit took the number of each loaded dukw; he then gave this number to Dukw Control, where that dukw's tag was carefully removed from a ship's number and placed in a space marked 'transhipment'. The dukw in question, having had its number taken, proceeded about 200 yards to the transhipment area, where it was unloaded, usually rather slowly. Each dukw is equipped with three cargo nets, and when a ship's derrick unloads a net on board the dukw, the driver gives the ship one of his empty ones in exchange.

When the dukw had unloaded, it went back round the circuit to the Dukw Control and was sent out again to a coaster, not necessarily, in fact probably not, the same one. On the way round it passed the cookhouse and, if he wanted to, the driver could jump out and get a cup of tea and a snack. This business went on all day until 2230 hours, when the last dukws were sent out. It might be an hour or more, however, before they returned. In the early afternoon the drivers were relieved, and another driver took over the dukw, this being done under platoon arrangements. There was a spare dukw standing by the Dukw Control all day for rescue purposes; and the driver kept a close look-out for the distress signal—a hat on the end of the boathook, waved about, or a Very light—from any dukw at sea.

During the day, one of the platoon officers was on duty, chugging about the harbour in a motor launch, checking on various things such as the ropes holding the dukws to the coasters, whether there were too many dukws to a coaster, and seeing that time was not wasted by the drivers.

So it is seen that the work of the dukws unloading on the beaches was hard and monotonous.

There were also occasions when we carried famous people on shore or for a trip round the Mulberry. For example, on June 12th, B 9 brought ashore Mr. Churchill, General Eisenhower and General Montgomery. The Mulberry, incidentally, although much praised and publicized, did not at any time unload more than a third of the total tonnage carried by the 11 dukw companies working on the British sector of the beach-head.

The one period that the dukws could not work was the time of the storm, that is between 0700 hours, June 19th and 1700 hours, June 22nd. The seas at this time were mountainous, and the devastation caused on the beach was remarkable.

On certain stretches of the beaches just after the storm, there was not room to get a dukw into the water, because of the wreckage of landing craft, rafts, etc., thrown up by the sea. The scene was one of utter desolation. Then on June 22nd, when we started operating again, the seas were so rough that two dukws were holed by being battered against the side of the coaster to which they were tied, in spite of fenders. These two were, fortunately, recovered. The only advantage of this storm from our point of view, was that we were able to put in some much needed maintenance on the dukws.

All the rest of the time we were operating from Gold, Item and Jig beaches. Towards the end of June the monotony of the job began to be felt; this, however, in no way impaired the running efficiency of the company.

It had been estimated that 90 days would be required by No. 9 Beach Group to unload on to the beaches their quota of stores. This was actually accomplished in 45 days. At the end of that time we moved to Buchot and operated inside the Mulberry, which of course was much easier from the drivers' point of view.

During the period on the beaches, the company kept up a good average of tonnage unloaded. The record figure was 2,800 tons on June 25th by 120 dukws working for 18 hours. It must be remembered that the factors controlling the daily tonnage were the labour available for unloading in the transhipment area, the number of lorries available in that area, the number of coasters to be unloaded, and the distance of the coasters from the beach.

On August 26th we received orders to pull in all the dukws from Arromanches and to stand by ready to move. At 2300 hours we moved by platoons to Liverot, a small town just south of Lisieux. As this was the first long move by road that we had done for four months, and as the visibility from a dukw at night is none too good, it was, to be honest, rather a shambles as moves go. Inevitably we had a lot of punctures on the way because the dukw tyre is not designed for long road trips.

At that time the company came under command of II Canadian Corps. Two pleasant days were spent at Liverot loading up ammunition, supplies and petrol, and waiting for instructions to take them to a forward dump on the other side of the Seine. Liverot itself had only just been liberated, and all the inhabitants were pleased to see us. In fact it was the first of many real welcomes that we received.

On the night of August 28th we moved up to Fouqueville, about three kilometres west of Elbeuf on the Seine, where we sat for a day waiting for disposal instructions for our loads. During the rest of the day (the 29th) Dvr Waters, of C Platoon, distinguished himself by finding a German paratroop officer and five other ranks in a loft. He got a small party together with Brens and Stens, and they fired a burst into the loft. The Germans surrendered immediately.

On the 30th we delivered the loads on the dukws to a forward dump on the other side of the Seine near Elbeuf, and then returned and loaded up again and again, and went over. We did quite a few lifts at this crossing, carrying about 2,000 tons a day with 76 dukws. This was the first time we had done much river work, and we found that because of the current (about two and a half knots) it was necessary to cross the river in a crabwise fashion. This, of course, put a big strain on the rudder cable, and the shearpin holding the cable to the steering column often broke. That the shearpin should go and not the cable was intended by the designers; every dukw is equipped with many spare shearpins, and the job of replacing one only takes about three minutes. Otherwise the crossing was uneventful, apart from the dead horses and other things that were constantly floating down the river.

We worked at Elbeuf for three days and then we were sent to Caudebec farther down the Seine, where stores had to be lifted from a temporary dump near the crossing to an FMC at Yvetot, fairly near Le Havre. The Seine at that place was remarkable for a rather vicious 'bore' or tidal wave. That happened, of course, twice a day, and the crossing, which was a motor ferry crossing, could not be used for an hour before the wave came up, because the level of the water fell below the edge of the ferry ramps. Similarly the crossing could not be used for an hour after the wave because of the fierce currents and eddies it caused. The result was that for four hours every day we were unable to use the crossing. During these days it rained. Another bad thing from the men's point of view was the number of dead horses lying in lines in the fields, where they had been shot by the Germans, and remained stinking to high heaven. There were platoons of several other dukw companies working on the same job; but we were the only ones to work the crossing at night, rather a risky business because of the underwater obstacles. Once again at this place the dukws lifted sufficient stuff to ensure the success of the operation.

Information had been received that the next move was to be to Dieppe, and we had heard that it was pretty badly knocked about. Everybody was feeling very pleased indeed about this move, when word came through that we were to move to Brussels. This was done on September 8th and 9th, the night of the 8th being spent on the road near Arras. On the 9th we reached Anderlecht, on the outskirts of Brussels, having loaded up with petrol and lubricants at Hal and delivered it at a forward FMC. Altogether, this move, although not so long (about 240 miles), was made remarkably well, with no mishaps. The company now came under command of XXX (British) Corps.

We received a wildly enthusiastic welcome from the civilians round our location at Zuen, and we could easily have billeted out all the 400-odd bodies in the company. People were clamouring to have soldiers stay in their houses. The next three days were spent on an intensive maintenance programme which was somewhat hampered by the hordes of small Belgian children who swarmed round and over the dukws, to say nothing of their parents, who seemed to take a pride in bringing all their friends and relatives to view the phenomenon.

On September 13th all three platoons were loaded with petrol at 160 FMC and took it to 161 FMC at Bourg Leopold. On the way we were halted by the roadside near Diest, as there was still some enemy resistance between Beringen and Bourg Leopold. Anyway, we delivered the petrol the following morning, once again being the first transport to arrive at a FMC and therefore more or less founding the thing. On the 15th we repeated this performance except that we did not halt the night on the road. On the 16th the company came under the command of 43rd (Wessex) Division and moved to Tessenderloo, where we loaded with ammunition, etc. On the next day, 22 dukws from each platoon were attached to 130th Brigade and thence to battalions, A Platoon to the 7th Battalion, the Hampshire Regiment, B Platoon to the 4th Battalion, the Dorset Regiment, and C Platoon to the 5th Battalion, the Dorset Regiment.

For the next 10 days the company was to be split into three groups consisting of 66 dukws from ABC Platoons, a new D Platoon hastily formed from the remnants of the others, and company headquarters and workshops with platoon administrative personnel. Returning to A Group as it were, i.e., the 66 dukws with 130th Brigade, these left the Tessenderloo area on the 17th and went to the Hechtel area, where they sat for two days waiting for the Guards Armoured Division to clear Eindhoven and the road to Nijmegen. When this was done, the brigade moved up to Nijmegen, taking two days in the process. During this move the dukws were used as TCVs. On arrival at Nijmegen one battalion went in to clear up the town. The dukws were then attached for some 24 hours to the 101st American Airborne Division and were used for conveying troops from the famous bridge of Nijmegen to a wood to the south east of the town. It was proposed that the dukws should remain the night in the wood; but when it was discovered quite by chance that there were still plenty of 'Krauts' in the woods, the officer commanding this party decided to move the dukws from a spot which might prove unhealthy. He was quite correct in his assumption, as some shells began to fall just where the dukws had been, as the last one pulled out.

This party buzzed around a bit more for the Americans and then was very pleased to be re-attached to 130th Brigade. The next day (the 24th) the brigade moved up slowly to the Driel-Valburg area, clearing the roads as they went. It was a novelty to see the vehicles at the head of the column stop, some infantry jump out of a dukw, double across a field, proceed to mop up a small pocket of resistance, then double back to the dukw and clamber on board once more.

That night six dukws stood by in case they were needed, when some troops of the Polish Airborne Brigade crossed the river—fortunately they were not needed. The next night was the night of the attempt of the 4th Dorsets to get across the river and to relieve the 1st Airborne Division. Six dukws of C Platoon were to carry urgently needed supplies across the river three hours after the assault had gone in. Various things happened, and only three actually got in the water under intense fire; these three got stuck in the mud on the other side, and the drivers had no alternative but to swim back. For this episode two men of C Platoon were awarded the Military Medal.

The following citation won Cpl J. A. Varney the Military Medal:

'On September 24th this NCO was in charge of dukws crossing the River Lek, carrying supplies to the airborne troops on the north bank. His dukw reached the opposite bank, but then became stuck in the mud, and attempts to release it attracted enemy fire, and they had to take cover. At last the dukw was freed and headed downstream to where the other two dukws were fast in the mud. Under harassing fire from the enemy, one dukw was completely unloaded and another partly unloaded. By this time, first light was approaching, and an officer from the Dorset Regiment instructed RASC men to endeavour to free the unloaded dukw and transport back wounded and notify brigade of the urgency for medical supplies. All efforts to free the dukws were of no avail.

'Cpl Varney and one driver thereupon decided to swim for help. This they did, and eventually landed on the opposite bank several hundred yards downstream. A patrol from a battalion of the Dorset Regiment was contacted, and Cpl Varney and the man who had swum with him went to the battalion's headquarters to report and thence to their platoon location. This NCO carried out a difficult task with great coolness and was an example to the drivers in his charge.'

The citation in Dvr Chilton's case was of a similar nature—he also received the Military Medal.

The following night the dukws carried the airborne troops back from the river bank to the FDS at Valburg and then to Nijmegen. This was an unpleasant job, because of the bad weather and the state of the roads, which were narrow and muddy with deep ditches on each side.

The dukws sat at battalion locations for a further two days before going back to company location, which by then had been set up at Nijmegen. C Platoon had had the worst time of it, as they were subjected to shelling by 88 mm mortars and to a twice daily dose of machine gunning by aircraft. During the five days on the island between Nijmegen and Arnhem this detachment lost one driver killed and five wounded, and lost five dukws.

Group B was a conglomeration of the dukws left out of Group A. It was under command of Captain Leith and was called D Platoon. This group did much the same as Group A in the push up to Nijmegen, attached to 129th Infantry Brigade. They stayed at Nijmegen until rejoining the company on September 27th, subjected to the odd spot of bombing and shelling by which they lost one dukw.

Group C, or company headquarters and workshops, stayed in the Tessenderloo–Hechtel area until the 24th, when they moved to Nijmegen. On their journey up the road was being shelled between Uden and Zeeland, and near Veghel the tail of the column was cut off by the enemy. One breakdown vehicle and a captured 3-ton vehicle with a total of nine men were missing. The vehicles were afterwards found burned out, and the men, all from the workshops except one, were heard to be prisoners of war. One man, Dvr G. Ferguson, of C Platoon, escaped, having spent an exciting few days. This man, while acting as a despatch rider with the convoy, was shot off his motorcycle. He got away and spent three days in the loft of a house in which the enemy set up a headquarters, and he and an NCO from another company were able to hide themselves by burrowing into a pile of wheat sacks.

One night German soldiers slept next to Dvr Ferguson in the loft, but the latter was not discovered. After three days, American airborne troops surrounded the house, and Ferguson and the NCO with him assisted in mopping up the enemy with a Bren. During the three days they had no food or drink.

From September 28th we stood by in our locations between Grave and Nijmegen in case either of the bridges across the Waal was destroyed. A reconnaissance had been made of a crossing just north of the road bridge at Nijmegen. On September 29th the bridge was damaged, and we had to take stuff across the Waal. This was not a good crossing, chiefly because of the steepness of the ramp on the south bank, and also because of the extremely strong current. We only had to work this crossing for one day, as by the following day the bridge was repaired.

The next small job we did was to carry 129th and 214th Infantry Brigades across the Waal from the north side about one and a half miles downstream from Nijmegen. Because of the softness of the banks, it was not possible for the dukws to get ashore to pick up or to land troops. This difficulty was overcome by the use of two extra dukws anchored to the bank, one each side of the river, and jutting out from the bank, thus forming a sort of quay against which ferrying dukws were able to berth and take on or land troops. In this way, six dukws of A Platoon were able to ferry about 1,300 troops across the river during one night.

Another job we did at this time was to have some dukws patrolling the river between the road bridge and the broken railway bridge with headlamps on at night. The job of these dukws was to ensure that no more enemy swam downstream with explosives, as they had done previously when they blew up the railway bridge. Apart from this, we were used only occasionally for ordinary GT work, our value lying in our potential capacity should the Germans blow the dykes and flood the island.

One of the more unusual of these GT jobs was when all three platoons collected the civilians from certain areas on the island and evacuated them to Grave and Nistelrode. The amount of furniture, etc., brought along by the civilians was amazing, and they quite hopefully tried to put beds and even wardrobes on the dukws. The dukws positively bristled with bicycles as they went along the road. This job occupied the whole of one day; but worse was to follow. For political reasons we had to return the whole lot the next day: 'Go along to the two refugee camps at Grave and Nistelrode, pick up the same people and take them where possible to their own houses.' Curiously enough, they were overjoyed to be returning to their homes. One would have thought that, with all the shells and the fighting that went on on the island, they would have been only too pleased to get to some safe place, but no, they just sat stolidly in their houses and took no notice of what went on.

We also carried some American airborne troops to the island to take over from the British troops there.

For the next few weeks we just sat in our location doing masses of maintenance and even a little training. We all saw plenty of films and one or two ENSA shows. Enjoyment was added to these shows by the thought that a bomb or shell was liable to fall on one at any time. On one occasion a woman mind reader was doing an act at Nijmegen when a bomb fell nearby. About half the audience immediately remarked that although she was able to forecast people's domestic affairs, she had not forecast the bomb.

The next event from our point of view was an inspection by Lieutenant-General Horrocks, GOC XXX Corps. He inspected A and C Platoons and then spoke to us. He praised our turnout and the work we had been doing, and made everyone feel rather important and useful. This was on November 3rd.

On November 4th we moved to Vucht, just north of Maastricht, the platoons backloading some empty jerricans on the way, and taking petrol and ammunition from army roadhead to 163 FMC at Eisden. At Vucht we were all put in civilian billets, a rather necessary move on account of the weather.

From November 6th onwards we were used as ordinary transport on road journeys between the Second Army roadhead at Hechtel and 163 FMC at Eisden, or else 164 FMC at Sittard. There were some bad floods a few weeks later, and the river Maas rose considerably, so much so that the bridges across, with the exception of one American one, were put out of action. The current was so strong (about five or six knots) that the dukws could not possibly be used on the river, although some experiments were conducted with dukws attached to cables. The whole idea, however, was unsatisfactory as even if the cable did hold, while the dukw got across, only one could cross at a time, and this method would have been so slow as to be ludicrous.

The whole of November and December passed by in this way, the company doing transport details nearly every day with only a few days for maintenance. Needless to say, we worked right through the Christmas period, and, also needless to say, the dukws were in a pretty poor state and in great need of some concentrated maintenance. The great point about this seven weeks' work was that although everybody worked hard at a necessary job, we all had comfortable billets and plenty of good food.

On January 4th, 1945, we moved to Bourg Leopold and there put all the dukws off the road for overhaul and refit. The plan was for six weeks of intensive maintenance and refitting, because otherwise the dukws could not have kept going. Workshops also drew 20 new engines here. As some new or reconditioned dukws and new engines had been drawn at Vucht, by this time the company's vehicles had undergone about 60 per cent turnover. On the 7th and afterwards we took over a total of 99 3-tonners to work as ordinary road transport on local army details. We put one driver on each vehicle and found that each platoon could also put a maintenance squad of approximately 20 men on the dukws which had been put in a pool before going through workshops. For the next four weeks we continued doing daily details and a few detachments with 3-tonners, which, incidentally, were in a pretty bad state when we got them. On January 24th, 1945, experiments were conducted with two dukws in freezing water to find out whether any damage was caused to the vehicle by the temperature. It was discovered that there was no damage.

The roads during the end of December and the beginning of January were very bad indeed, covered with a layer of ice. We found that, curiously enough, the dukws held the road better than other vehicles under these conditions because the tyres have a smoother surface and are run at comparatively low pressure (only 40 lb), therefore a bigger area is presented to the road than in the case of a normal tyre. At this stage it was also found that the dukw drivers were getting miraculously rapid at changing wheels.

Between January 29th and February 5th, all the 3-tonners were transferred to other units and the platoons took over complete charge of the dukws once more. On February 9th the three platoons moved off at 1800 hours, at only half an hour's notice, to 166 FMC at Veghel, where they loaded ammunition and petrol. On the following day they went to Nijmegen, where they spent the day waiting for orders to take loads up to an emergency dump at Nutterden, near Cleve. They eventually moved off at about 2000 hours, without lights of course. It was found that 'Monty's Moonlight' was a great help when night driving. The dump at Nutterden was not much more than 1,000 yards from the edge of

At Tobruk

Scaling the Loaf

Double Deck Field Ovens

the Reichwald in which, at the time, there were still pockets of enemy resistance. Many dukws missed the turning and went nearly into Cleve before realizing their mistake. They stopped and asked some German soldiers where they were. The surprise was mutual. However, all the dukws, except one which was ditched, turned round in a mined road in the least possible time and came back to the dump without a shot being fired, a fortunate escape. Anyway, all the dukws, there being now some 120 as we had a platoon of 297 Company attached, reached the dump, with the one exception, and there unloaded and stayed the night.

In the meantime, company headquarters and part of workshops had moved *via* Eindhoven, where they spent a day, to Nijmegen— in the town itself this time. By the next day the River Maas had not only overflowed its banks, assisted by the Germans, who had done some demolitions, but had reached the main road between Nijmegen and Cleve. The water on this road rose steadily until in places it was three feet deep, and only amphibious vehicles could move along it.

During the next few days, a transhipment area with a report centre, labour, both army and civilian, and a cookhouse with a sort of running buffet were organized. The dukws worked 24 hours a day for five days and, to enable a system of relief drivers to operate, one platoon of 633 Company and one platoon of Terrapin drivers were attached to act as reliefs. We once again proved our operational necessity, as without the supplies carried forward by the dukws, the operations in the Cleve area would have been delayed until the floods had subsided. In addition, a panzer concentration was broken up by 5·5-inch guns firing ammunition brought up by our dukws. Had this not happened, the situation would have become most awkward, to put it mildly. We also evacuated all the casualties from the Cleve area to a FDS in Nijmegen.

As tyre troubles were assuming large proportions, the company commander ordered that tyre pressures should be raised to 50 lb. This improved matters a little. The difficulty in this job was that the drivers could not see the surface of the road underneath the water and were, therefore, frequently hitting underwater obstacles. There were admittedly trees lining the edge of the road, but there were also some deep potholes and also floating tree trunks and other things. Consequently it was essential that two drivers should be on each dukw. On the 17th some 10-tonners were waterproofed and were thus able to get through the floods.

Captain L. Dashwood, workshops officer, did some experiments with two dukws, loading an armoured jeep into one by means of an A frame attached to the other. These experiments were satisfactory.

Between March 19th and 23rd we supplied only a few dukws for carriage of casualties, as 297 Company took over the run to the FMC. On the 23rd we moved as a whole to Boxmeer. A natural ferrying crossing on the Maas was found and the sappers were summoned to clear mines from the approaches.

There were many mines in this area and, as later events proved, the sappers did not by any means completely clear the ground. Between March 1st and 16th we worked spasmodically between the petrol depot at Haps or ammunition depot at Veghel and 168 FMC at Goch, crossing the Maas by water every time, thus relieving to a certain extent congestion on the bridges at Gennep. On March 5th two dukws of B Platoon were blown up by Teller mines on the east side of the Maas at Boxmeer. Once again no one was hurt as all men in the vicinity were sitting inside dukws. Of course the dukws concerned were written off. The mines had been buried about three feet down, because at least 300 dukws must have passed over them before they went off.

Between the 16th and 20th we were joined by one and a half platoons from 297 Company and half a platoon from 50 Company, both lots with their dukws, and also collected 32 dukws to form a D Platoon. An officer and 30 other ranks arrived from the Terrapin Platoon to man these dukws. So we now had nearly 200 dukws under command. This was of course for the Rhine crossing named operation 'Turnscrew'.

On March 22nd we moved to Till near the west bank of the Rhine. We found things very noisy on the next day, because we were surrounded by batteries of 25-pounders and 5·5's, to say nothing of the odd 7·2 inch. During the day we set up a dukw transhipment area, complete with a composite platoon, RASC, pioneer labour, and a corps ST report centre. Petrol, ammunition and supplies were brought into this area by corps and army transport. The enemy lobbed over a few shells in our direction, and four dukws were damaged by shrapnel. These were repaired overnight by workshops. H hour was 2130 hours that night. This was preceded by four hours of the most terrific barrage ever; we were practically deafened by the noise.

The sappers were supposed to have some ramps ready for us by midday on the 24th. For several reasons, one of which was the high casualties suffered by the engineers on the west bank, caused by mortar fire from that part of Rees still held by the German paratroops, the ramps were not ready. For this operation some dukws had previously been attached to various formations and units within the corps, and two of these, attached to 51st Divisional RE for rescue work, entered the water early on the 24th. These were both B Platoon dukws. The driver of one of these was killed, and his co-driver wounded by a German sniper firing from Rees; the wounded co-driver managed to get the dukw back on land again. On the morning of the following day the ramp was finally ready and the first dukws swam across. When the first dukw did cross the river it was discovered that because of continued resistance of enemy paratroops in Rees, the originally planned location of the FMC could not be used, so the stores had to be dumped in a temporary place by the river. Another driver of C Platoon was wounded by a sniper, and three dukws were sunk by enemy action, fortunately with no loss of life. During the 25th and 26th we continued to ferry vital ammunition, petrol and supplies across the Rhine. We found that the actual crossing was a comparatively easy one. The current was not as strong as at Nijmegen or Arnhem, because of the greater width of the river. The ramps made for us were not very good, being too steep, and some of the more inexperienced drivers who were attached from the Terrapin platoon had difficulty in climbing the ramp on the west bank, having to make several attempts. The usual dukw evacuation post for casualties was established on the east bank of the river, and eight dukws were kept solely for this purpose. On the night of the 26th a third bridge was completed right on top of our crossing, making it unusable. We had previously made a reconnaissance farther downstream for an alternative crossing, but had found nothing suitable. Consequently, on the 27th, we found ourselves with loaded dukws, a transhipment area with 1,200 loads in—and no river crossing. So we took the stuff over the bridge. After four days' intensive work the transhipment area was finally cleared, and the FMC at Rees pretty well stocked.

On the 31st the platoons from 297 and 50 companies returned to their companies. On April 2nd the company left XXX Corps and moved to Wijchen under I Canadian Corps. We were all sorry about this, as we had been looking forward to following XXX Corps up to the Hamburg area. As it turned out, the Rhine crossing was the last real job the company was to do. From Wijchen we discovered a suitable crossing of the Rhine at Millingen and proceeded to establish a dump at Pannerden on the east bank of the river, bringing petrol from Nijmegen and ammunition from Oss.

On the 8th we had been warned to take part in the assault on Arnhem from the south, the Drill area, by 49th Division. After we had been nearly snowed under with orders, instructions, and counter instructions from the division, it was reported by Dutch civilians from Arnhem that the Germans were expecting us, so the exercise was called off. It was later discovered that the Dutch were correct and that Jerry had a considerable number of 88s lined up covering where the assault was to have been effected.

The plan for this operation was then changed so that the assault would be made from the east side of Arnhem across the river Ijssel and from the Duiven direction. This new assault actually took place on the 12th. The amount of amphibious equipment was remarkable, and of course very little of it was used. There was some idea of using the dukws to swim downstream from Millingen down the Nederijn to the Ijssel to Arnhem and then land. These dukws would be carrying small arms ammunition. With this end in view, a reconnaissance was made of the part of Arnhem on the Nederijn for a suitable landing place. The officer who did this reconnaissance quite inadvertently found himself acting as an advance reconnaissance patrol for the troops who were street fighting. He later arrived back in a somewhat shaken state and demanded a drink. He did, incidentally, find a suitable crossing place which was, however, immediately snapped up by the sappers as being just the site for a bridge. So, in effect, we did nothing in this operation.

On April 15th we moved into Bemmel on the 'island' and stayed there until the war with Germany was over.

One event of interest that occurred there was when we entered a team for the Tabloid sports run by Canadian corps troops. Although we were the only British team out of eight teams, we won the sports fairly decisively, thus confounding the Canucks who had received our rather small team with a certain amount of amusement.

Taken all round, 536 Company from D Day to V Day enjoyed the campaign. While there were periods when we did no work, there were short periods when we worked very hard and, furthermore, were nearer the actual fighting than the normal RASC company usually gets. Yes—it was a good campaign!

486 COMPANY (TIPPER)

The company was formed and mobilized in No. 1 Mobilization Centre, going through all those long months of preparation and training. Quietly and unobtrusively, in November, 1943, the company assumed its first operational duty in the United Kingdom. Winter passed on into spring, while the company had established itself, preparing for the great day which all knew was coming. One platoon was operating in Scotland, one at Portsmouth, one at Ipswich and the other at Brentwood. This point is mentioned to bring out how great is, and can be, the dispersal of a tipper company. Then came the long-awaited information; platoons were concentrated, pre-loaded and marshalled, waiting, keyed up for the signal which would throw them into action from D Day to VE Day.

A Platoon, loaded and waterproofed, were on board LCTs landing on the invasion beaches on the second tide of D Day, to be followed in rapid succession of days by the remaining platoons, company headquarters and workshops. By D plus 10 the whole company was fully established on the beach-head and had taken up its place in the highly complicated machine of a modern army.

The main function of the tipper platoons was on road construction working with the Royal Engineers and the Pioneer Corps. From the time the first vehicle waded ashore it was almost a 24-hour day and a seven-day week. Officers, NCOs and men quickly settled down to their new life under active service conditions. Workshops arranged a system of LADs, one being attached to each platoon headquarters, the technical vehicles remaining at company headquarters, the arrangements being that the inspections and emergency repairs should be done in company headquarters' location.

The first vehicle casualty occurred when an A Platoon vehicle working on 'Love' Beach struck a mine. The company was under command of CRASC, Second Army Troops, and, as army troops, was made available for various RE formations. Platoons were working under RE GHQ Troops, Second Army RE, corps and divisional RE. There were many hectic days in the area of Bayeux, Tilly and Caen, names now famous in the days of the beach-head fighting. Wherever one went along the British Second Army front, the tippers of 486 Company were to be seen.

Caen was a great stumbling block to the armies' advance; it was a strongly fortified and defended town, but it was an obstacle to be overcome. At very short notice on July 18th, 1944, B Platoon were notified to take up a location at Benouville, working under 8 GHQ Troops with 70 Company RE. As soon as the RAF had completed a bombing raid, the RE and the tippers went in to bridge the Caen canal and the River Orne. These RE and tippers were at that time ahead of the infantry and armour. This was a typical situation: roads had to be repaired, even remade, bridges had to be built, before the attack could go in. It was a hard and tough experience for unseasoned troops like the drivers of the company.

At the same time, C Platoon were in location at Bronay, some eight miles west of Caen. Guns of all calibres were shelling the town, the naval guns in the bay were also adding extra fire power, and the RAF were contributing extra weight by aerial bombardment. Throughout all this, the platoons carried on with their vital task of road construction.

The operations in the beach-head were beginning to expand, and the expansion meant that tippers were detached by sections from platoon headquarters, and in many cases single vehicles were detached from sections. Life for a platoon officer became very harassing; sections moved from one RE company to another very quickly, so that he had a very difficult task in keeping touch with his section corporals and vehicles.

The attack swung southwards to Tilly and Villers Bocage. On this thrust one vehicle of D Platoon was working in advance of the infantry on a RE detail. The sappers and tipper were ambushed by a German patrol, and in a matter of moments the vehicle was under fire and left abandoned. Several days later the vehicle was recovered and towed into company headquarters' location, the whole vehicle being complete riddled with rifle and small arms fire. By the time the drivers had become accustomed to working under shell and mortar fire, there was hardly a tipper vehicle in the company that did not have some battle scars.

As battleships have destroyer and cruiser escort, so tanks must have an escort. The escort did not provide extra fire power for attack, but they were tippers loaded with rubble so that when the tanks met the obstruction of shell and mine craters, the rubble was tipped and so hastened the advance. A typical example was when one section of A Platoon were operating on the Villiers–Caen road. A small bridge had been blown, and tanks of the 7th Armoured Division were delayed. This section was immediately moved up and the stream was filled with rubble, thus allowing the armour to pass on again into the attack on Caen.

And so the tippers worked and worried throughout the whole of the beach-head campaign. Then came Falaise, the enemy was routed, and the company began the long journey from Falaise to Nijmegen. The company worked unceasingly. Problems of repairs were not so acute, owing to the job done by the workshops LAD teams in platoon headquarters. In company headquarters big repairs were effected under more static conditions. Platoons became scattered, and it was the policy of the company commander to place his headquarters as centrally as possible.

The Seine was bridged and crossed, all platoons taking part in assisting the RE in their magnificent work of bridging. A and D Platoons were left behind at Beauvais, and headquarters leap-frogged them to Songeons while B and C Platoons were still pushing towards Belgium. But even then, platoon officers had problems. D Platoon officer, although his headquarters was at Beauvais, had one section, in charge of his platoon sergeant, who were pushing on with the Guards Armoured Division. He lost his section for many weeks and finally caught up with it at Grave. B Platoon pushed on to the Belgian border and into Tournai, C Platoon, also hard on their heels, overtook them, and were in Brussels immediately after the city was liberated, and to this platoon fell the honour of having driven the first soft vehicle into the Netherlands. Again the tippers were escorting tanks of the Guards Armoured Division, the order of march being tank, tipper, tank, tipper, and so on. This continued up to Nijmegen, where the long flog came to a halt.

At this period of the operation, the Royal Engineers decided, now that the advance was approaching the Low Countries, that stone was essential. Overnight, A, B and C Platoons were ordered to take up location at Quenast Quarry, between Enghien and Hal, some 5,000 tons of stone having to be dumped at the stone dump, at Bourg Leopold. D Platoon headquarters moved up from Beauvais to follow up the rapid advance of XXX Corps.

The stone dump completed, A, B, and C Platoons returned to their normal role of roadmaking. C Platoon pushed up to Nijmegen, half the platoon going over the Maas to work with the airborne divisional RE, A and B Platoons operating at Bourg Leopold and Son, north of Eindhoven. Company headquarters moved into Eindhoven which subsequently turned out to be the company headquarters location throughout the winter. The move was made on October 10th, and it was in March, 1945, that it pulled out again to continue in the Battle of the Rhine.

B Platoon made a move from Son to Veghel farther north up the corridor between Eindhoven and Nijmegen—a mile from the actual line. Enemy patrols passed through the location, but, discretion being the better part of valour, these patrols were left entirely alone. But again we have evidence of how close the tipper platoons worked to the front line. Sections of C Platoon had a similar experience while they were operating with VIII Corps at Deurne. One particular section operating with the 15th (Scottish) Division were only 1,000 yards from the front line, and they also had the experience of enemy patrols passing through the location.

Between October, 1944, and March, 1945, static winter warfare set in, but that did not mean that the company had any periods of rest. Throughout the whole of the winter months the tippers were working all daylight hours on road maintenance. Platoons were moved with great rapidity to work with the RE in an area from Nijmegen in the north to Maastricht in the south, with the Maas making the eastern flank. These were hard months for the vehicles; owing to the pressure of work and climatic conditions it was difficult to carry out good maintenance, but every effort was made and the officer commanding the company started a big drive, realizing that only by harsh methods could he hope to keep his maintenance at a fairly high standard.

Then came the bombshell of Von Rundstedt's thrust to the Ardennes. The American Army was retreating, and the position on that sector of the front was becoming serious. Field Marshal

Montgomery pushed in XXX Corps and, with the corps, went A Platoon to Namur. Wherever the British Second Army were making a drive, the tippers of 486 Company were always to be seen in the forward sectors.

Throughout the remaining winter months, the company continued to carry on with road maintenance. There was no glamour in the job, but it was of the utmost importance to keep open the vital supply routes. During the hard frost, tippers were used for spreading sand over the roads, a difficult and dangerous job. Many drivers had hair-raising experiences with their vehicles. Then came the thaw of February. Roads began to collapse, and the tippers were operating night and day; a most unfortunate time for the company, as we were due for a visit by the MT Inspectorate. But everyone worked hard and conscientiously, and the company earned a good technical report.

Preparations were made at this period for the crossing of the Maas. C Platoon were moved north to a small village named Beugen, south-west of Gennep. The enemy had only been pushed out of this sector a short time before, the whole location was bristling with field artillery. Sleep was impossible, but the platoons worked cheerfully under these difficult conditions on the bridge at Gennep. The bridge was a magnificent feat of engineering both in its construction and in the time taken to erect it.

And now the armies were ready to make preparatory attacks. The static warfare of winter was over, and all formations were in their allotted places ready to drive over the Maas. The crossing was effected, and the platoons—A, B, C and D—took up locations between the Maas and the Rhine. From that period until the Rhine crossing was effected, information was difficult to get. The whole operation was shrouded in secrecy, but once again 486 Company operated on another D Day—D Day of the Rhine.

A and B Platoons were operating at Xanten, and C and D Platoons at Rees. A and B Platoons came under command XII Corps, and C and D Platoons came under command XXX Corps. A Platoon reverted to VIII Corps and were left behind on the long glorious push across the plains of Germany.

B Platoon continued to operate under command XII Corps, working with the 7th Armoured Division, 15th (Scottish) Division, and 53rd (Welsh) Division. Their drive was towards Hamburg, and as the platoon pushed onwards dispersals again became a big factor. It is interesting to note that on April 22nd/23rd, 1945, No. 6 Section of B Platoon transported 171 loads of rubble, weighing some 500 tons. This gives some idea of how badly roads were damaged, mostly by enemy mines. Drivers were working day in and day out. No. 9 Section of B Platoon, between April 25th/28th,

1945, carried on for 72 hours without rest. No. 10 Section detached three vehicles under command of a RE officer. Their small party was ambushed by SS troops, and their officer was killed, but the three drivers evaded the enemy and continued work. From April 28th the whole of B Platoon were concentrated and were engaged on the bridging of the Elbe, and on the 30th the platoon was 'strafed' by enemy aircraft, but without damage or casualties.

Meanwhile C and D Platoons, operating under command XXX Corps, were working for 43rd (Wessex) Division, Guards Armoured Division and 51st (Highland) Division, their objective being Bremen. It was a month of action and a few casualties for these platoons. On April 13th, 1945, C Platoon had one vehicle blown up on a heavy road mine, and Dvr Barton was killed, the first fatal casualty of the company throughout its many months of hard campaigning. The vehicle immediately behind was blown off the road by the force of the explosion, but continued to work later. D Platoon experienced mined roads; two tippers were blown up, and three drivers wounded. On the 24th, two D Platoon tippers were damaged by shell fire, but there were no casualties, and throughout it was move, change of location and move again. The advance was going on rapidly. A Platoon still remained behind, now being transferred to I Corps for maintenance of roads in the rear area.

At the beginning of May B Platoon, working as a whole platoon, were still operating under the command XII Corps and were engaged on the Mote Bridge. This bridge, 1,040 ft in length, was constructed in 29 hours. During this time the platoon were subjected to strafing and dive bombing. Just before the official cease fire, the platoon moved into Hamburg area for work on the approaches to Hamburg.

C and D Platoons were now striking north to Bremen, Zevan, Bremervorde, and Bremerhaven, and then came that long-awaited signal to cease fire.

During the last long flog from the Rhine to the time 'cease fire' was given, company headquarters and workshops had endeavoured to keep as near geographically central to the platoons as was possible. For one period, A Platoon were left a long way in the rear, and it was decided to leave with them a small LAD to do workshops inspections and repairs. In fact at this period A Platoon location was Xanten, west of the Rhine, and B Platoon were located at Nienburg, some 200 miles away, east of the Rhine. Once again it may be noted how widely scattered are the platoons of a tipper company.

Recommendations for honours and awards were passed on to company headquarters from platoon officers and other unit and formation officers. The first came through from B Platoon with a strong recommendation from CRE, 8 GHQ Troops. On July 18th, 1944, this platoon took part in the crossing of the Caen Canal and the River Orne. Cpl Harris, a section corporal of this platoon, was recommended for the Commander-in-Chief's certificate for devotion to duty, disregard of personal safety, and setting a fine example of leadership to his men. Lieutenant De Neuville was also recommended by the CRE for his leadership and his complete disregard of personal safety. Cpl Hinton of A Platoon, who was the first man of the company to set foot ashore, was also awarded the C-in-C's Certificate. He began work as soon as he landed, taking command of other vehicles as they waded ashore and continued to do so until his officer disembarked some hours later. L/Cpl L. Fry, Workshops Platoon, was recommended for devotion to duty. As NCO in charge of B Platoon's LAD, he disembarked on D plus 2 and, through his enthusiastic and untiring efforts, the vehicles of B Platoon were kept constantly on the road. This NCO was also awarded the C-in-C's certificate. The company chief clerk was awarded the C-in-C's certificate for his devotion to duty and the cheerful manner in which he performed the many and difficult tasks of chief clerk.

The crossing of the Rhine was in preparation, and Cpl L. Smith, of A Platoon, was strongly recommended by the company commander for the Military Medal, which was granted. Working with his section attached to 503 Company, RE, who were building the bridge at Xanten, before the crossing of the Rhine, and subjected to heavy fire from shells and mortars, he displayed great devotion to duty, driving a tipper himself throughout the night, and encouraging the other drivers by his leadership and example. During the same period Cpl Gardner, section corporal of D Platoon, was awarded the Military Medal on the recommendation of his platoon officer. His section were working on a bridge approach. Apart from being under constant shell and mortar fire, they had to traverse a cutting in the flood bank which meant that vehicles were silhouetted against the sky. This cutting was under fire by enemy Spandau guns on the opposite bank. Ignoring cover and casualties among the sappers and pioneers, Cpl Gardner stood in the cutting, directing and supervising his section. When one of the drivers faltered, he took over his truck and kept the vital supply of road-making materials flowing smoothly.

To sum up the history of this company from D Day to VE Day, it will be seen that it called for initiative and responsibility from platoon officers and section corporals in particular. Platoons had at all times been detached from this company headquarters, sections had been detached for considerable periods from platoon headquarters, and section corporals had to hold their own with RE officers. These sections worked under arduous and dangerous conditions, being assault troops operating with assault RE. There was little or no convoy work, each vehicle quickly tipping its load and returning for further loads. Company administration was often a slow and difficult task, the channels of communication between company headquarters and platoons being long and extremely elastic, and the workshops platoon had at all times been worked to its fullest capacity, but by close co-operation with RAOC and REME services they had been able to fulfil their commitments. An officer commanding a tipper company must at all times think, not in terms of a compact company area, but in terms of wide dispersal, which throughout this campaign has often meant thinking in terms of the whole of the British Army second front. And now that VE Day has come and gone, the tippers continue to give of their best towards the repair and maintenance of supply routes.

146 COMPANY (MOTOR AMBULANCE CONVOY)

This unit left Liverpool on November 9th, 1941, for Bombay, where it arrived in January, 1942. Its officers and men were then re-embarked on a refloated hulk, HMT *Nevasa*, more popularly known as 'the Hellship' or 'the Altmark's Sister', and sailed to Ma'Gil, disembarking there to join the MEF on January 17th, 1942. Camp was set up at Zubair nearby, vehicles and equipment being drawn from Shaiba. The establishment of the unit was 75 ambulance cars (all of the excellent Austin 2-ton type) and 18 other vehicles. Later four load carrying vehicles were added.

Thus equipped, the unit left MEF for India, leaving behind C Section of 25 ambulance cars. It embarked at Ma'Gil on March 8th, 1942, in a Free French ship, the *Cap St. Jacques*, to land at Bombay once again on March 15th. It went thence to Ahmednagar, where the RASC did further training and the RAMC complement were attached to a hospital.

Leaving Ahmednagar on April 30th, 1942, the company moved by road to Bangalore, where it was pleasantly located in the grounds of the Residency. Training continued, some evacuation of sick to hospital trains was done and, during disturbances instigated by Gandhi's supporters, many of the vehicles were stoned.

On September 19th, 1942, the unit was sent by train to Bombay for transfer back to the MEF, the larger vehicles having to be partly dismantled for the journey to meet the requirements of the loading gauge. The journey took four days, and was so slow that tea was frequently brewed beside the line during the passing of the length of the train.

On October 10th, part of the unit embarked in its old nightmare, the *Nevasa*, reaching Aden on October 17th and Port Taufiq on October 25th, while the remainder travelled by another ship.

C Section, meanwhile, left on its own since March, 1942, had gone from Zubair to Baghdad, where it remained for six months evacuating casualties from 24 and 25 CGH to the metre gauge RH there. In September, 1942, it moved into Persia via Khanikin and the Pa'i'Taq pass to settle at Kermanshah, evacuating casualties from 5th British Division, which was resting there after the Madagascar show, and watching with relief the end of the Germans' progress in their direction through the Caucasus. In that period the unit came under command of the newly formed Persia and Iraq Force (Paiforce), which moved it in October, 1942, deeper into Persia to Qum, the 'city of unbelievable virgins'.

From October to December, 1942, the section evacuated casualties of the occupying troops of Tenth Army northwards to Teheran. In December, 1942, however, it returned by the Pa'i'Taq and Khanikin to Baghdad, whither the rest of the unit had come the previous month by way of Palestine, Trans-Jordan and the half-completed H pipeline road to Rutbah.

The unit was now reunited and moved to Al'Musaiyib, 20 miles south of Baghdad. There was another period of waiting here, marked by redesignation of the unit as 146 MAC, RASC (it had begun its life as 15 MAC, RAMC). In spite of its changed designation it still had an RAMC commanding officer; assisted by an RASC transport officer. During this period the officer cadre of the company underwent a complete change.

On March 19th, 1943, a move was made to Middle East once more to the RASC Mobilization Centre at Tahag via Rutbah, H 4, Mafrak, Beersheba and Ismailia. An RASC commanding officer was now appointed, further refitting was carried out and, to the general excitement and satisfaction, waterproofing of vehicles got under way, while all ranks went under day-long instruction in swimming in the Bitter Lake and the Red Sea.

On the invasion of Europe, an operation known as 'Bigot Husky' to capture Sicily, the unit embarked piecemeal between mid-June and July 1st, 1943, at Beirut, Haifa, Alexandria and Port Taufiq, the main body going aboard HMT *Almanzora* at the last named port on July 1st.

The unit sailed westwards from Alexandria on July 9th, 1943, to land at Syracuse on the 13th. This port had been captured two days earlier and was the centre of an expanding beach-head. The unit was immediately and violently busy with the evacuation of battle casualties of XIII and XXX Corps, these being put on board returning LSTs for Malta until hospital installations could be set up in Sicily.

A period of command by Eighth Army began here, which continued with minor breaks until the end of the war in Europe, and was a source of pride to all ranks. Sections of the unit worked for XIII and XXX Corps, and a fortnight of daily and nightly air attention on Syracuse, the enemy still having the use of Catania, resulted in the loss of four of the unit's ambulance cars by the sinking of HMT *Fishpool* in harbour, while a great many more, together with their crews, had the escape of their lives off one of the beaches when a liberty ship, moored alongside them, exploded after a direct hit. Other ambulances were damaged by driving into bomb craters in the forward area at night.

On July 30th, 1943, the unit moved to Villasmundo for the Catania battle, and on August 12th into Catania, after which it was withdrawn from operations for a short period to prepare for the invasion of the mainland. Between September 3rd and September 10th it was ferried across the Straits of Messina to Reggio di Calabria and worked for the next six months under command XIII Corps. After the initial confusion of the battle, caused by the conflict of military and political strategy on the surrender of the Italian forces, the unit worked up the Tyrrhenean coast to Sapri, evacuating casualties sustained in Eighth Army's push to pull Fifth Army out of the 'Salerno mixture', and then on September 25th moved across to the Gulf of Taranto and up the Adriatic coast with a week's stop at Altamura, while the enemy around Potenza were being cleared up, and thence to Foggia.

From Foggia, so wrecked by bombing that locations had to be cleared laboriously of wreckage and bodies, the unit employed detachments on the evacuation of casualties from the German counterattack at Termoli, and then from the drawn out fighting for the Trigno and Sangro river crossings. On November 16th, with commitments in ambulance cars in the central Apennines round Campobasso as well as on the coastal sector, the unit moved to Larino and, on December 27th, 1943, to Cupello for refitting after the slowing up of the battle to a halt at Ortona.

Small detachments were operated in very severe weather, with the roads at times snowed up, but by that time the change over to Northern Campania for the spring offensive had begun, and the time of waiting was used for training, first under XIII Corps and then, temporarily, under V Corps.

On April 13th, 1944, the unit rejoined Eighth Army at Alife and, when the offensive opened, moved up Route 6, working very hard indeed as the communications lengthened. Company headquarters had short stays at San Vittore, Aquino, and Caprano, and moved to Rome on June 14th, when for three weeks it worked under 86 Area on both road and air evacuations, XIII Corps having meanwhile sheered off up the Tiber valley.

After Rome, by a jump to Chirisi on July 6th, the unit came back under XIII Corps, and, on the link up of forces engaged round Lake Trasimeno, moved to Cortona on July 12th, evacuating battle casualties from the strong German resistance before Arezzo, after the fall of which the unit moved to Rapolano on July 22nd and north, on the axis of the South African push on Florence, to Grevi on August 5th.

At this point, A Section of 25 cars was detached from command of XIII Corps to work directly under 6th South African Armoured Division with which it remained throughout the autumn and spring campaigns, including the spectacular South African advance of April, 1945, to Bologna, Finali, Padova and Milan. When the South Africans left Italy for home, this section rejoined the unit at Portogruaro.

In the meantime, the rest of the unit, under XIII Corps, moved to Montevarchi on August 24th, to Leccio on September 5th, and on September 18th to Florence, where it remained for the fight for the Gothic Line which ended the year's campaign.

With the movement of Eighth Army back to the Adriatic coast, the unit came indirectly under command Fifth Army, but still under XIII Corps.

On October 4th it moved to San Lorenzo and on November 29th to Vecchio where it was fortunate to secure reasonable winter quarters in a very overcrowded district. Operations were principally concerned with evacuating casualties from the desultory fighting, mainly artillery exchanges, in the mountainous upper valleys of the Lamoro and Santimo rivers. A good deal of refitting was done, and motorcyclists were trained for the coming summer by means of an ambitious riding trial. Four-wheel drive ambulances were taken into use by the unit for the first time, and were allocated to A Section with the South Africans.

The first participation in the final offensive began with the detachment of B Section to the Adriatic coast in the Rimini district, when it worked under 86 Area as soon as the battle started, and moved to Forli, Mirabello and to Gaiba, across the Po, on May 1st, 1945. Unit headquarters, now maintaining a virtually coast to coast service, stayed at Scarperia from March 30th, 1945, and carried the last of XIII Corps' battle casualties of the Italian campaign, while located at Mirabello and (on May 1st, 1945) at Ficarolo, on the north bank of the Po.

After the final surrender in Italy, the unit moved to Portogruaro, where it evacuated German wounded from their own hospitals in

Yugoslav disputed territory, and put a section into Cerugnano and a detachment into Trieste during the period of uncertainty of tenure that followed.

Suitable VE Day festivities were organized when the day came at Portogruaro, with illuminations, dancing and the operation of a 'wine point' which became quite famous, and the men of the unit were thanked personally by Brigadier Cheyne for their past work and enthusiasm.

From the first day of serving with the Eighth Army in a battle area, the men's spirits went up and up and the work of the unit was soon commended by the heads of services under whom it worked. The unit sign, a 'Donald Duck' with two fingers raised in the familiar type of soldiers' salute, soon became known far and wide and men falling sick in the unit and being left behind showed extraordinary, if officially improper, diligence in hitch-hiking sometimes hundreds of miles to rejoin it.

The unit carried for Eighth Army some 100,000 casualties, the highest weekly total being 10,000 during the battle of Cassino, and the courage and resource of NCOs and drivers in action have several times been the subject of comment by formations for whom they have worked.

A DIVISIONAL RASC
Narrative by the CRASC 4th Division

This narrative relates the experiences of CRASC, 4th British (Mixed) Division in North Africa on the eve of the break through to Tunis and Bizerta. This particular operation, in which an enemy thrust in considerable strength preceded our own attack (and the tale concerns the effects of this thrust on the operations of the divisional RASC) was distinct from the break through to Tunis, which took place some weeks later. The narrative is as follows:

The battle now started to warm up. Beja and Medjez el Bab are two towns 25 miles apart linked by an excellent road running from north-east to south-west. This road had been in Allied hands since the beginning of the campaign but the enemy, by occupying high ground to the north, denied us the use of it. To get from Beja to Medjez one had to make a wide detour to the rear through Thiba and Teboursouk. The first part of the operation in which the division was now engaged had been to clear the enemy from this high ground. This had now been completed, the direct road was ours to use, and the way was clear to start the push for Tunis.

On April 16th, 1943, I attended a conference at corps headquarters at which the Q side of the projected operation was fully explained, but information on the G side was not forthcoming, an omission which did not make the way easy for quick decisions and intelligent anticipation during later events.

On April 18th the division moved from Beja to the Medjez el Bab area, and the divisional RASC moved to Teboursouk, rather far in rear of the division. We had a certain amount of excitement before we moved, because a German fighter, which had obviously been hit in a dogfight with one of ours, suddenly flew very low over 21 Company's location. The company opened up on it with nine Brens and probably gave it the *coup de grâce*, for it crashed in a field a few miles away.

On going to look at it I found it surrounded by a ravening crowd of American soldiers, all armed with clasp knives, intent on getting themselves souvenirs. They were being kept at bay by a small light-infantryman with a broad Yorkshire accent, whose language cannot be described. The Americans had to be content with taking snapshots of one another standing on the wings.

I then made for Teboursouk, turning off from the Medjez road down a by-pass 'Whitehouse Lane'. At the entrance to the lane stood a military policeman with an oil lantern. He asked us to keep well to the middle of the road as the verges were mined. I replied that we should not mind keeping to the middle of the road, for which he politely thanked us. Feeling that the boot should be on the other foot, we drove on and immediately met a very large lorry. The care with which we both slowed up and edged past each other was unusual and rather funny.

I had taken Edge, a motorcyclist, with us, to follow behind the car. We had driven in silence for some way when suddenly my driver, Woolnough, let out a howl of laughter. I asked him what the hell he was laughing at, and he replied: 'I was just thinking that if we did go up on one of the bloody things, I bet old Jacky Edge would turn round and go home in a hell of a hurry.' But we got to Teboursouk safely and had a night's rest.

On April 19th, we started a heavy ammunition dumping programme which went on over the 20th, some 21,000 rounds of 25-pounder being involved. At the end of this detail we had some excitement.

We were dumping at night to the divisional artillery area about two miles away to the south of Grenadier Hill. The lorries, Peter Milford in command, arrived on time, and dumping started. The area chosen was in a basin with steep approaches down rough tracks. It would have been difficult in daylight, and the way in which those drivers handled the Bedfords by night, with no lights, surprised even me and made me feel extremely proud.

There were no gunner guides or loaders, which surprised us

Tank Transporter

until we heard that an enemy patrol had broken through and was somewhere in the hills on our left, and that the gunners had gone off with their rifles to drive them out. We started to unload the lorries ourselves, hoping the gunners would return soon.

The patrol, it transpired, was not at this time a threat to us, but the enemy were on the move against us. I once saw a clever sketch called 'The horse who blew first', depicting a man trying to give a horse a pill through a blowpipe, but the horse blew first. That is exactly what happened in our case. The enemy got wind of an attack and put in his own first, in an attempt to delay us.

I was at the bottom of the basin, unloading, when we received the first indication that something was wrong, for a certain amount of firing broke out on our left and tracer kept flying across our front.

We were working about 100 lorries that night and Peter Milford was at the top of the basin checking them in and out, so I did not know the exact situation myself, as all the wagons split up into small parties, dumping their ammunition in different parts of the area, according to the battery locations. However, I saw all the lorries eventually gathered together into one convoy and checked them out of the area. I then began to walk back to my own car. I had just reached some crossroads near a farm when another 20 laden lorries drove into the basin and vanished down a track to my left, in the direction from which the tracer was coming. I thought there was nothing to worry about and went on to my car, about 150 yards from the farm.

There I found Woolnough and Moulton lying in a most martial manner on a bank, rifle in hand and tin hat on head. They told me that a gunner officer had told them the patrol, a strong one, had broken right through and that they must help to defend the location. They had a 'last man, last round' atmosphere about them, but gave the impression that they had hoped I might be coming home at any minute now.

At this point a lot more tracer came over from the direction of my wretched 20 lorries, so I started off down the track again after them, getting a pillion lift from a gunner subaltern on a motorcycle. He took me straight to them, and we found the last half dozen still unloading, not the least concerned at the cross fire but very much concerned at the lack of loaders. I gave a hand in the unloading, and never had 25-pounder ammunition seemed heavier. I then rejoined Woolnough and Moulton, who seemed pleased to see me return, and we moved off after the empty convoy.

Once out on the road the convoy did not take its proper route. Instead of turning left down a track called 'Red Cap Alley', it kept straight on over the cross roads towards Medjez el Bab. Eventually I overtook it, halted with its head in an avenue of trees just short of

Medjez and its tail at the top of a winding hill near Grenadier Hill. Peter Milford was in front talking to the APM who said that the enemy had broken through in considerable force, captured Grenadier Hill and had crossed into Red Cap Alley, about a mile and a half behind our tail. I went back and sat in a sand-bagged observation post with Jimmy Boyd, watching some vehicles burning in the basin we had just left. I then returned to the head of the convoy, which had closed up and was told by the APM that we could not move yet as the main road in front was full of the transport of a gunner regiment moving up.

At this point a certain amount of firing broke out at the rear of the column. I got a lift back in a car. There was a lot of dust and smoke in the air and I found an infuriated Boyd lying in a ditch with the company sergeant major of 107 Company. He stood up and saluted when I arrived and reported, in a most official manner, that the enemy was bracketing the road with mortars.

We woke the drivers up and closed the vehicles up further so that the tail of the convoy avoided the danger area, and then Jimmy Boyd remembered his course at the battle school and came all over infantry.

It was now one o'clock, and the APM threw the road open to us. The convoy went down the hill towards Medjez, met the main road and swung hard left, almost back on its own tracks. The last lorry contained the rejoicing Jimmy, who said that Boche infantry had crossed the road 150 yards behind the lorry as they moved off.

Feeling that we were well out of it, I followed on and gradually overtook the convoy which had again halted near a track to the right called 'Dryshod Drive' which led away until it joined another track called 'Auchinleck Avenue', eventually coming out in the main Medjez-Teboursouk road.

The rumour was that the enemy had cut the road in front of us so, feeling rather jittery, I went up to the front and had a conversation with Peter. He, remembering his days in the East Lancashire Regiment, wanted to leave the lorries and wade into battle. To me, however, never having been in anything but the RASC, lorries were rather sacred, so I said: 'No, we will get these bloody trucks home somehow.'

I went forward in my car to find out what was happening and almost immediately found two moaning men in a pool of blood. They had run into a tank in a light car. I gave them two blankets and got some RAMC men from a field ambulance which had been overrun to attend to them. I then met a signaller who told me, quite untruthfully, that divisional headquarters had moved, and then a lot of Scorpion tanks, but I met no enemy although there was a fire in a farm on my left where the field ambulances had been. The road home seemed clear, so I returned to Peter.

Somebody was firing across the rear of the convoy, so I sent Peter with the front half down the road I had just reconnoitred, which turned away to the right down Auchinleck Avenue, while I took the rear half down Dryshod Drive.

The run was uneventful except for meeting a number of our tanks coming up, and eventually we ran into Auchinleck Avenue and joined up with the front half convoy as if on a march table. The whole convoy then turned left and made for Teboursouk with fire-eating Jimmy Boyd bringing up the rear, while I stayed behind, seated on a rock, thinking out my next move. The most important thing was to find divisional headquarters, so I started back again along Auchinleck Avenue until stopped a quarter of a mile on by a military policeman who said I could not get through that way. He did not know whether divisional headquarters had moved, but thought it likely.

I turned back and followed the main road to Testour, where I knew there was a REME company, which I hoped might be in touch with division by wireless. They were most hospitable, gave me a cup of tea and got hold of CREME by wireless. He lived at divisional headquarters and stated quite definitely that they had not moved. I went back to the car where I found Woolnough and Moulton eating spam and drinking tea. When they had had their breakfast we moved off again.

This time we took a more circuitous route past a cross roads called Tally-ho Corner. There was intermittent firing in the hills to our left, but otherwise things seemed peaceful and it was really a beautiful morning.

When we were getting near our goal our chaplain, Leslie Mitchell (who was temporarily attached to the Black Watch), suddenly appeared. He said it would be quite impossible to get through, as the Black Watch were just going to mount an attack. The Black Watch, however, seemed more intent on having their breakfast, so I decided to push on.

We had only gone a short distance when a terrific crash, as if someone were firing straight across our bows, sent Woolnough, Moulton and me into the long grass with incredible speed. It was only our own artillery firing across the road, so, feeling rather sheepish, we emerged from the long grass and resumed our journey.

The policeman at Handley Cross was at his normal place, quite unperturbed and wearing his white traffic sleeves. He said everything was quiet, so we just went straight on to divisional headquarters and into AQ's office, arriving just in time for his morning conference, after which I went back to Teboursouk and had a wash and a shave.

We learned later that the 'patrol' had been two German infantry battalions supported by tanks. The brigade major of our tank brigade had a lucky escape. He was taken prisoner with the others, and the 'gentlemen' put them all against a wall and shot them with a Tommy gun. He was not hit but fell and pretended to be dead. The Huns searched his 'body' and went away, leaving him to walk home.

That night I took my bedding to divisional headquarters, intending to sleep there, but had to go off to find more ammunition instead, finishing at four o'clock the next morning.

By April 22nd the enemy had been driven back to his starting line, but we had fired all the ammunition we had been so busy dumping for our own attack. So that night we had to dump another 19,000 rounds of 25-pounder, and I got back to my night's rest at six o'clock on the morning of the 23rd. I must have been rather irritable after my third night out for, when Harvey Jones came to see me later in the morning and asked Woolnough where I was, the answer was, 'He's over there; don't go near him, he's in a bloody awful temper. If he don't get some sleep soon I'm going to pack in this —— job when we get to Tunis.'

On this same day, which was Good Friday, we moved to an indifferent location at Testour, where we stayed over Easter. On Easter Sunday afternoon, after a grand church parade in an olive grove in the morning, I was starting for corps headquarters, after a small amount of aerial bombing, when I noticed a small fire burning some distance away. I told Bill Beeston to go over and see if it was near any of our companies, and went on my way.

When we were about half way to corps, Woolnough looked in his driving mirror and said, 'There's the very devil of a fire burning behind us,' and so there was. The whole sky was red and explosions repeatedly lit up the country round. I immediately guessed it was ammunition burning and thought of my companies. Arrived at corps, I reported myself and immediately asked for, and got, permission to return and investigate the fire.

At Testour bridge we were told that our location had been hit, but that most of the lorries had been got away. At the company location I found a terrific blaze in 21 Company's area. Only two bombs had been dropped, one a direct hit on an ammunition lorry and the other between two other lorries. The fire had been burning for at least one and a half hours when I got there and was as strong as ever. By great good fortune, there were only three vehicle casualties, all the rest of 21 Company's vehicles, as well as those of the other companies, having been driven away to safety.

There was no possibility of salving the burning lorries and as ammunition was going off all over the place, I gave orders for all the men to get clear. There was a small amount of ammunition on the ground very near the fire and, as I arrived, Charles Sharp was organizing a band of volunteers to go in and try to move it out. One of the 'volunteers', on hearing my orders to clear the area, remarked in a loud voice, 'Thank God the Colonel has come!'

On reflection, I am glad I gave that order. I felt at the time it looked like taking the line of least resistance but I argued to myself that ammunition could easily be replaced, that there was not much involved, and that it was not worth risking men's lives to save a few rounds. In fact, the fire never reached the stacks on the ground.

While these thoughts were passing through my mind, there was a loud explosion and Charles Sharp yelled 'Duck', so we both fell flat on our faces. A great lump of metal flew through the air and landed near us, but nothing else happened, so I got up again saying, 'Come on, it's all over', but a voice at my feet said, 'I can't get up'. I thought, 'Gosh, he's been hit', but it transpired that he had slipped the cartilage in his knee. I yelled for the doctor, who came and forced it back by the light of the fire. It must have hurt like hell.

After putting Charles to bed and seeing the fit vehicles collected, I returned in my car to the fire. We were approaching it up a narrow lane when a motorcyclist came hurtling down towards us, bouncing off the front of my car into a cactus hedge. Getting out we found 'Yorky' Smith, lying in the prickly cactus and using the most horrible language. The motorcycle was not damaged and he was not seriously hurt. When we had stopped laughing we pulled him out. This set him off again. He was as full of prickles as a hedgehog, and his language was magnificent.

By the time I left the company location the fire was nearly out, so we left a picket to watch it and went to bed. Next day, we moved again.

716 COMPANY (AIRBORNE LIGHT)

in the crossing of the Rhine

The air operational party consisted of six officers and 77 other ranks of the RASC with one officer and nine other ranks of 22 Independent Parachute Company, three other ranks of the REME, two other ranks of the RAOC, and a party of 10 from 'Public Relations'. The party was equipped with carriers and trailers, preloaded. The plan was for the force to fly in 12 Hamilcar gliders (Nos. 267 to 278).

On landing east of the Rhine the crews of gliders 267 and 269, with carriers and all available fire power, were to proceed at once under command of Captain S. Sutherland-Waite to reconnoitre the area of the forest clearing which was their destination. This was in enemy hands.

The remaining glider crews were to rendezvous at a certain hedge junction with carriers and trailers and to await the signal from the reconnaissance party that all was clear to proceed. The trailers would then be offloaded and the work of clearing packed panniers from the gliders would proceed. While this was in train, Lieutenant Campbell and the nine other ranks of 22 Independent Parachute Company, together with six spotters and as many RASC men as could be spared for defence, would go to the pre-selected supply dropping point, ready for marking it out and observing the supply drop planned for P plus 3.

All available transport from the gliders (with the help of 40 jeeps and trailers from air landing units which would be available at P plus 6) would then clear the dropped supplies. On the arrival of the air landing transport, Lieutenant Roberts, RASC, with six carriers and trailers, would be detached to clear the compo packs from gliders in the surrounding landing zones so that compo rations would be ready for issue by 1000 hours on D plus 1.

Finally, when all other tasks had been completed, the company would set about the collection of any supplies and ammunition left over from the jettison drop planned to take place over the dropping zones of 3rd and 5th Parachute Brigades.

This was an ambitious task for such a small force, and nobody expected any rest for at least 48 hours, but all were full of confidence and morale was high when they emplaned at Woodbridge, Suffolk, early on March 24th, 1945. Take-off was at 0730 hours, and all went apparently well until the Rhine was reached, when the air became bumpy and considerable flak was encountered. Visibility, hitherto excellent, suddenly closed down owing to smoke and dust from the artillery barrage, and the ground at the landing zone was only visible from a height of some 200 feet. This made the task of the glider pilots more hazardous than usual, and it is not surprising that the landings were made on widely dispersed points and not on the landing zone covered by the briefing.

Landings took place between 1040 and 1055 hours, and in all cases flak of varying intensity was encountered. Once on the ground, gliders came under small arms and mortar fire, which caused damage to loads and casualties to troops.

As there is a detailed account of the fate of the individual gliders given in the Chapter on Airborne RASC (page 535), it must suffice here to say that one crashed before crossing the English coast with serious injury to all its occupants, that three crashed well outside the landing zone with the loss (killed, wounded or missing) of their crews, while eight landed with more or less success, but with the loss of one glider pilot killed and two officers and 11 other ranks wounded. Three carriers out of the eight landed were put out of action almost immediately, mainly by enemy mortar and small arms fire.

One crew, under Sgt Whittall, landed very near the appointed rendezvous and were on the scene by 1100 hours, where they were alone until Captain Lewenhaupt and his crew, with their carrier and trailer, arrived. The captain went at once to reconnoitre the area, as he realized that the reconnaissance party which had been briefed for the job had not arrived. Soon afterwards the crews of three other gliders arrived. Captain S. Sutherland-Waite, though wounded in the arm, pluckily carried on in the absence of the company commander, and soon things began to take shape.

There were now available for work three carriers and one trailer! The party, however, captured a German 3-ton lorry, loaded with ammunition, which was quickly unloaded and pressed into service after minor repairs by the fitter. The result of all this was that when the supply drop was effected at 1300 hours, there was no transport available to clear the supply dropping point. The drop itself was extremely scattered and conducted from so low an altitude that most parachutes failed to open fully, and much damage was done to containers and contents.

When the exiguous transport already referred to became available, containers were emtied where they lay, to save space in the vehicles, and this was in hand when the company commander, Major C. P. R. Crane, arrived.

At 1600 hours the situation was tense for the RASC. Both 5th and 6th Air-landing Brigades were waiting for ammunition, and there was little available. There was no storeman present, and issues were made direct from the containers as demands came in. The position, however, gradually improved, and by 1800 hours there were six carriers and three trailers, plus the German lorry at work, while a dump had been set up containing most kinds of ammunition.

No contact had been made with Captain Turff, CRASC's representative, so at 1830 hours the company commander went direct to A/Q 6th Airborne Division to advise him of the position. He then learned that Captain Turff had been severely wounded and evacuated, and that A/Q, too, had not arrived. He arranged with the DAQMG that as many air-landing jeeps and trailers as were available should report to the landing zone and that, if opposition were not too intense, clearance of the zone should continue all night by moonlight. In hard fact, of the 40 jeeps and trailers which were supposed to report for this work, only 10 arrived, and these came so late that they were of little use till first light on D plus 1.

The job of clearing the supply dropping point was continued after darkness had fallen, but at about 2330 hours the enemy infiltrated into the woods and were crossing the dropping point itself. Clearance operations were therefore suspended, and all ranks stood to, ready for any eventuality. It was a very eerie experience, but all ranks behaved splendidly and complete silence was maintained while the stand to was in progress. At 0200 hours on D plus 1 half of the company stood down and snatched a few hours' sleep. There was spasmodic fire across the dump area and a certain amount of enemy movement could be heard. But there was no organized attack, and at first light, after the morning stand to, roll-call was held and the work of collection resumed.

The roll-call revealed that Lieutenant Roberts and four other ranks were missing. Of these, three other ranks had been sent with the German lorry to evacuate wounded from divisional headquarters to the main dressing station and had not been seen since, while Lieutenant Roberts and one other rank had not returned from 6th Air-landing Brigade HQ, which they were known to have left after delivering an urgent supply of ammunition.

The three men with the German vehicle had been surrounded by the enemy and taken prisoner just outside the dump area. They had been put in charge of a party of wounded Germans and had moved off with about 200 of the enemy across the supply dropping point towards Hamaenkeln. Lieutenant Roberts and his companion were returning in their jeep when this party opened fire on them, damaged the jeep, and took them both prisoner.

Then followed a long walk round the inside of the divisional perimeter during which the party disintegrated and was eventually reduced to some 50 or 60 men, mostly wounded. They were fired on periodically by our troops and the morale of the Germans was clearly weakening. Lieutenant Roberts, seeing this state of affairs, began talking to the Germans and persuaded them finally that their position was quite hopeless, for they could certainly be shot at first light, but if they gave themselves up to him at once he would guarantee a safe conduct to a prisoner of war cage. After a little persuasion, the whole party laid down their arms and he marched them off to Hamaenkeln, where they were handed over to the cage. Lieutenant Roberts and his four doughty men then returned to duty.

The strength of the company on the morning of D plus 1 was four officers (including one wounded and waiting evacuation) and 44 other ranks, including three wounded. This left a total of two officers and 33 other ranks missing, known killed, or wounded and evacuated.

Lieutenant Roberts, with two carriers, then went to the Airlanding Brigade's landing zones to clear compo rations, and the remaining vehicles were employed in collecting the ammunition from the first supply drop till 1200 hours. The supply drop fixed for 1300 hours was cancelled, and at 1400 hours CRASC arrived, having made the journey from the Rhine by road.

At 1800 hours, Captain Ballard and the platoon left in BLA arrived to reinforce the company, but they were immediately detached for other duty, and so the clearance of the dropping point had still to be done by the weary survivors of the first landing. This work continued till darkness fell, when all ranks of the airborne party turned in, under the protection of guards furnished by the land element which had just arrived.

On D plus 2 the work of salving containers, parachutes and other equipment was begun and the collection of outlying containers and their contents continued. At 1900 hours on that day, the remainder of 716 Company, RASC, under Captain H. E. Cubley, came into location, workshops were established in some farm buildings, and the remaining vehicles of HQ and C platoons were parked under trees for the night.

On D plus 3 all vehicles were put on to the collection of salvage, the Company losing one other rank killed and one officer and one other rank wounded when a jeep struck a mine. On D plus 4 and D plus 5 all cased ammunition and all ammunition left in Pegasus dump was cleared to the FMC and an urgent petrol detail was executed. Ammunition clearance went on throughout D plus 6, and on D plus 7 (March 31st) the company moved forward to Coesfeld, rejoining the rest of the divisional RASC and resuming its normal 'land' functions.

6 BASE PETROL STORAGE COMPANY

The company was raised in Yorkshire and, after training at the National Oil Refineries, Llandarcy, soon found itself at Alexandria amid the preparations for the invasion of Sicily.

In due course the company arrived at Syracuse with the official object of taking over the Italian installations in that town and those at Catania, Messina and Augusta, and putting them into working order to await the arrival of the first tankers, which were said to be already on their way. Each installation was of different design and each presented its own problems, but that at Catania is perhaps the most interesting as being an admirable first test of the ingenuity of the two sections employed there.

There was storage at Catania for spirit, kerosene, fuel oil and, it was believed, aviation spirit. Before Jerry pulled out, he mixed all the remaining stocks of these commodities thoroughly together in all the tanks, and intended to blow the place up. The Italians interfered with the charges so that their assets should not be destroyed.

Summing up, we had four very dirty tanks to be prepared for 100 octane, and without the following essential equipment and any idea where to get it: breathing apparatus, brooms, steam, water, pumps, and flameproof lamps. A true army inspection, or 'scrounge', was made of the bombed-out oil depots and sidings at Catania, and about six small forges were found. The hand blowers from these were mounted on benches and connected to long lengths of water hose from ordnance, and on the other end was fitted a standard gas mask facepiece, without, of course, the container, and here we had our breathing apparatus. Brooms were found, but no steam could we get. The workshop cleverly adapted a Bedford distributor for an Italian pumping unit, and we had a continuous supply of water, which was later supplemented by our fire section.

From the damaged oil depots enough parts were collected to enable a semblance of a Worthington pump to be virtually welded together, and we had our bottoming pump. Workshops applied rubber and adhesive tape to their portable floodlights to make them gas proof.

Work went ahead nearly 24 hours a day; the tanks being cleaned by sheer hard water brushing followed by a spirit wash; but the first tank was ready at the scheduled time, and soon afterward the tanker *British Endeavour* started pumping. Spirit was then sent to the Gerbini airfields, from where aircraft were soon taking off to give the Germans a taste of what they had been giving us. This was a most satisfying sight to the officers and men who had worked on this project, for at that time a large number were down with enteritis from having been exposed to petroleum fumes for so long.

It was not long before the company moved to fresh fields on the mainland of Italy and to spread its sections again to take over installations, one after the other, as they were freed by the advancing army.

The next story concerns the Il Fronte installation at Taranto in southern Italy, a large establishment formerly belonging to the Italian Air Force. The tale begins at Monopoli, about 60 miles from Taranto, the site of headquarters of 6 BPS Company, RASC, and of more large installations. One evening after dinner the company commander, captain (distribution), and captain (engineering), together with the administration officer, were sitting round the bar, as was their wont, playing ludo, when the telephone bell rang: it was for captain (eng). The captain of the section at

Taranto was away, and a worried subaltern wanted to know what to do, for the Navy said that 100 octane was running through his drains into the Mare Piccolo at about 1,000 gallons an hour. The underground tunnel system was full of gas and they could not get down, and a rushing sound could be heard. He was told to take any action he thought sensible and appropriate, warn all concerned to stand by, and that the captain (eng) would break all records to Taranto.

When the captain (eng) arrived at Taranto he was greeted by a young sapper subaltern armed with two large wooden plugs, repeatedly asking what he should do; fortunately at that moment the section commander returned. It was decided to descend into the tunnel system with Siebe Gorman breathing outfits and waders. It will be appreciated that all this time the level was rising, there were 5,000 tons in the defective tanks, and minutes were precious if the installation were not to go out of operation, which would cause the supplies to the airfields by pipeline to be cut off in a few hours.

After a hasty consultation, it was decided that lifelines were just out of the question, and in view of the unknown situation below, the captain (eng), the section commander and his second-in-command decided to make the investigation jointly. Having donned waders, SG breathing suits, and carrying a selection of tools, the party descended into the tunnels with the 100 octane swirling past their legs like a deep green sea. The electric lights were on, and dressed as they were, they must have presented eerie sights to each other.

All tanks were found to be in order except the last one, which was the farthest from the entrance and had no way of approach other than along the full length of the tunnel. The three officers would admit readily that they often cocked an anxious eye on the oxygen gauges upon their suits. They entered the valve chamber of the tank and were met by a vast swirling fountain lashing about in changing directions.

Here a tragedy nearly occurred, for one of the officers, in attempting to approach the main valve on the tank, was struck full in the face by the jet and his goggles were displaced so that the spirit must have got in his eyes. The pain must have been intense, for it seemed that he was about to remove the mouthpiece of the breathing apparatus, and he had to be escorted to the surface and receive attention. The other two then returned and the section commander made a rush, managed to get to the main valve and close it. It was found that a blank on the end of the line had collapsed, but the leakage was now controlled, although the whole tunnel system was now waist deep in petrol.

The next step was to clear the tunnel system. Upon inquiry it seemed that there was not in the whole of Italy a suitable pump capable of lifting the necessary 25 feet. Obviously we had once more to find our own salvation, and although fire trailer pumps were considered, it was thought inadvisable to risk cooling the engines by 100 octane, a point that could not be avoided because of the construction of the units.

At last an Italian fire tender was found with the pump driven by a shaft from the engine. Certain modifications and precautions were rapidly effected, special connectors made up, and a 4-inch Victaulic line laid to a battery of 30 ft by 9 ft tanks which were available. Pumping started, closely watched by the attending fire section, but apart from a certain initial difficulty in picking up suction from that depth the operation went smoothly and without a hitch. We now had the tunnels empty, but the concrete had absorbed so much of the 100 octane that it was impossible to go below without a breathing suit.

It was obvious that an entry had to be made into the cupola of the defective tank, in the first place so that we had full control of men working on the repairs, where also lifelines could be used, and, secondly, to make an air inlet to assist in freeing the tunnels of gas.

The captain (eng) made a careful reconnaissance, for there were no plans available of these tanks, and a squad began to dig, at last revealing the solid concrete wall which it was hoped adjoined the cupola and was not the top of the tank. The sappers were called in to supply a pneumatic drill, and the tricky nature of the task was explained to them, for with the amount of gas about a few sparks from the drill might easily have caused much discomfort. A red-haired Palestinian volunteered for the job and stood beside the captain (eng) who directed operations, and began to drill. At the back of them was the fire section playing 'fog' over them on to the concrete to damp it down and prevent sparking. This was a trying time for all concerned, and when at last the drill made a complete penetration into a cavity, all stood back and waited.

'No gas', said captain (eng), and instructed the driller to enlarge the hole. When it was about 2 ft square, it was possible to see that a cavity wall had been pierced, and ahead, over a 2 ft dark chasm, was the next wall. Drilling now went ahead again but at a much slower pace, and with frequent inspections and examinations of the concrete thrown out by the drill. At last once again the drill penetrated and the driller backed out over the plank upon which he was standing. The captain (eng) had a look and announced, 'We're there!'

The entry was 12 ft above the floor of the cupola, which was actually part of the roof of the tank, and the iron ladder, going down to the base of the tank where the burst was, could be clearly seen. The hole was carefully enlarged and a ship's windsail erected which sent a strong current of fresh air down below. On the morning after the inspection it was found possible to get a fitter with lifeline and smoke helmet down below to get measurements for a new blank. This was prepared and fitted, and all that now remained was to get rid of the gas. It was thought that this would be a long task, and it was to be undertaken by the fitting and fire sections using high pressure water which was the only means available. So effective was their work, however, that after about a week it was possible to go through the tunnels without any breathing apparatus at all.

Thus ended a period when not a few people passed many sleepless nights. The Taranto section stated that this incident completely eclipsed the fun and games to which they were regularly accustomed, with their floating pipeline at the discharge berth; and this had always had a remarkable name for going wrong, leaking, breaking up, or becoming unanchored in the night.

Some of our exploits of course were in the lighter vein such as the time we were called upon to go to Italian heavy oil storage on the Grande Mare, Taranto. They had a large quantity of MFO sludge which we were to get out, barrel at the rate of some 400 a day, load into rail trucks, and send to the north, where it was to be used in the making of air strips. As only a temporary machine was required, it was decided to use an electric rotary pump with a spring-loaded by-pass valve pumping direct through a 4-inch Victaulic line to a filling header containing some six 2-inch hoses with 2-inch trigger nozzles. This all worked well, but when the first nozzle went on, or the last one went off, the header and the hose in question were liable to jump about a bit.

Italian male labour was being used for the filling, and as it was a novel job they were jumping about and laughing, as was their wont. It should be explained that the trigger nozzles could be locked in the 'on' position. By some chance, only two barrels at one particular moment were being filled, and as one barrel was filled, the Italian shut off his nozzle rather sharply, which caused the header to jump. The remaining hose being used for filling also jumped—right out of the hand of the man holding it, and locked in the 'on' position. The scene can well be visualized: one moment, a chattering gang of happy Italian labourers, and the next, with a threshing hose squirting foul black sludge in all directions, we had a crowd of wildly gesticulating, madly cursing black labourers. The sight was really too much for the British soldiers who could not help roaring with laughter until the pump was turned off.

The fire in the filling area at Falconara was a day that few will forget. Apparently it was found out afterwards that an Italian labourer smuggled a lighter into the area to fill it, and then he thought he would see if it would light. Well, he will never need a lighter again where he has gone.

But to begin at the beginning, some of the workshop men were at Ancona building a new petrol point when a column of smoke was seen over Falconara about seven miles away. This was not unusual, for the oil fired locomotives often threw up a smoke screen, but this looked bigger and blacker than usual. The captain (eng) telephoned the headquarters to check and was told that 'Falconara was alight'. We jumped into a jeep with the mechanist staff sergeant and as many bodies as could hang on, and broke all speed records for the journey, in which we were joined by the AFS tenders that had been turned out *en masse*.

When we arrived on the scene, things were pretty grim. They had managed to get the female labour away, but barrels of spirit all alight were exploding and flying high in the air like balls of fire. The fire sections were fighting hard to save the front of the installation and offices, which had already been set alight in many places. Suddenly there was a near tragedy; the wind changed direction and the flames played right on to the front of the building. Rapid evacuation had to be made, for the heat was intense; two fire tenders had to be abandoned and were burned out. Water was pumped from the sea, and the flames were fought from the installation compound itself, and the struggle continued.

During this time, however, an officer with a party of men saved some 14 rail cars by keeping on the windward side and actually pushed them through the flames to safety. Then by good fortune the wind again changed, and steady progress was made until the fire was controlled. Now what did we see? A large area of smoke blackened, twisted metal, still sizzling with the heat, wrecked headers, burned out pumps, and twisted conveyors.

Then came an immediate conference to decide how soon the filling area could be put back into working order. There could be no question of leaving everything untouched until the inevitable court of inquiry had viewed the 'remains'.

The captain (eng) thought that, with 80 lorries and 200 prisoners of war available the next day, the site could be cleared in two days.

Every petroleum fitter available in the area, as well as those in the Petrol Technical Stores Depot, sweated blood from morning to night; they did not need to be told about the stocks on the ground steadily decreasing day by day; they could see them! Had the RASC ever let the front line boys down? And so on the tenth day it came to pass that the new facilities were erected, the labour returned, the valves were turned on, and once more the barrels and cans began their journeys along the conveyor to go forward and replenish those dwindling stocks on the ground.

There was a funny side to this story. The commanding officer, a real 'oilyboy' of the old school, not afraid of any man, had, just before the fire, broken a bone in his ankle and had been fitted up with a plaster cast, from the bottom of which protruded a piece of iron. When he left the hospital, the matron had warned him that whatever he did he was not to get it wet. Of course during the fire everyone got pretty well soaked, that is with water, and of course one could hardly tell the commanding officer that he could not come to the fire, but afterwards that plaster cast was just the funniest shape that a cast could be; even funnier was the expression on the commanding officer's face at the thought of taking it back to the matron to have it done again. He was not, as it has been said, afraid of any *man*, but——

88 DETAIL ISSUE DEPOT

The unit arrived at Algiers on November 12th, 1942, and, after disembarking, proceeded in full marching order by a circuitous route to the transit camp at Jardin d'Essai. On Monday, November 16th, the unit entrained for Souk Ahras. B Section, commanded by Lieutenant I. Treleaven, detrained at Setif on the 17th, and A and C Sections continued the journey to Souk Ahras, arriving on the evening of the 18th.

On Friday the 20th C Section, commanded by 2nd Lieutenant R. C. Roberts, entrained once again for Tebessa.

B Section arrived at Setif at about 1600 hrs on November 17th, 1942, and procured billets and office accommodation on the ground floor of a block of flats at the entrance to the station. Stocks of petrol and compo rations arrived during the night and were stacked in the station yard. The function of the section was to supply all road convoys moving up from Algiers with petrol and rations and also to feed troops passing through on the trains.

As all the convoys refuelled at night the detachment was split into two. Two sections of pioneers, supervised by two or three RASC men, unloaded trains during the day and the remaining RASC men and one section of pioneers worked at night. Every night from about 2000 hours until 0300 hours the next morning there was a steady stream of vehicles, many of them American, passing through the depot, and the average daily issues were 14,000 rations and 30,000 gallons of petrol.

On November 23rd, 1942, a French troop train was derailed four stations down the line and the wounded were brought up by train to Setif. Many were in a bad way, not having had any medical attention, and all ranks of the section helped the French to get the injured to hospital. No ambulances were available, and any car or cart that could be obtained was used to transport the injured. As far as could be ascertained, the casualties were 22 killed and 77 injured.

On November 29th a section of 95 DID arrived to take over and all stocks were duly handed over to them. The same evening the section entrained for Tebessa to join C section. A and C sections arrived at Souk Ahras at about 2300 hours on November 18th and at dawn next morning took over all stocks of petrol and rations at railhead.

They requisitioned the local cattle market for the depot and the local school for billets. There was no transport to clear stocks from the railhead to the depot, so use had to be made of local resources, which consisted of Arab carts. The price of hiring one of these carts was one packet of biscuits a load, and at this rate many carts were obtained and the transport problem overcome. The only money available was BMA, which the Arabs refused to accept.

On the 20th C Section entrained for Tebessa. Three days later A Section handed over stocks to 57 DID and 204 Petrol Depot and entrained for Constantine. There they opened a depot at the railway station, warehouses being used for stores. This was excellent accommodation for the purpose, as trains could be shunted right into the store-sheds. A petrol depot was also opened at the stadium.

Once again, the transport problem was acute, and Arab transport had to be hired. By this time, however, some francs were available, and the transport was paid for in cash.

Early in December, A Section handed over to two sections of 95 DID and moved to Canrobert. On arrival there they found that the RAF had dumped all their supplies and equipment at Ain Beda, 18 kilometres away. Transport attached to the unit from 239 GT Company, RASC, was used to transfer all these supplies to Canrobert.

On December 6th A Section moved to Tebessa and were replaced at Canrobert by B Section. The section was well billeted in the local Salle des Fêtes, and the rations were stacked in the yard of the local school. A small petrol dump was opened in the school grounds. The job of the section was to supply the RAF aerodrome here with all their requirements of rations, MT petrol, aviation petrol, and bombs..

The average daily consumption of 100 octane petrol was 7,000 gallons, and when the section moved out they had kept the RAF continually supplied and built up a reserve for them of over 100,000 gallons.

The airfield at Canrobert was paid spasmodic visits by German aircraft which, however, did not do much damage. On one occasion when three German aircraft gave their attention to the airfield the unit Bren gunner could not restrain his enthusiasm and opened fire with his gun, although the Germans were flying too high for LMG fire to reach them. Immediately every other Bren gunner in the vicinity joined in, and for several minutes there was a fireworks display worthy of the Crystal Palace. Although this may seem a needless waste of ammunition, the effect on the morale of the Bren gunners was remarkable. They felt that they had been 'in action' for the first time, and were as keen as mustard ever after that day.

Christmas Day was a great success, as we were able to purchase (at exorbitant prices) some excellent turkeys which were cooked in the ovens at the local bakery. The highlight of the festivities was a conjuring show given by a famous French illusionist called Minar who was a refugee from Bone.

At the beginning of the New Year, bulk rations took the place of compo, and new and larger stores were obtained. The change-over entailed a great deal more clerical work, but things went very smoothly, thanks to excellent work by the supply sergeant, Sgt W. J. C. Leese.

On the night of January 18th, 1943, the RASC men and attached pioneers went out to attempt to salve a trainload of supplies, petrol and ammunition which had been sabotaged at a point 15 miles away and was burning fiercely. Trucks not yet alight were uncoupled and pushed out of danger, and then the trucks already alight were attended to. Pte P. Jones, of this unit, and Sgt Elrick, RAOC, mounted a blazing truck of bombs and rolled them off on to the ground. For this exploit Pte Jones has been mentioned in despatches. Meanwhile, Lieutenant S. A. Green, of the Pioneer Corps, and some men had cleared another blazing truck of compo rations. For this work, Lieutenant Green was later awarded the George Medal. All salved stocks were placed under guard and later transferred to the depot. Apart from the people mentioned by name, all RASC and pioneers worked magnificently and, thanks to their efforts, many valuable supplies were saved.

On January 26th, 1943, B Section rejoined the remainder of the unit at Tebessa.

Two days after arriving at Tebessa on November 21st, 2nd Lieutenant Roberts was admitted to the French Military hospital suffering from dysentery. Command of C Section was assumed by Sgt C. H. Jones, after the consent of the officer commanding had been obtained by telephone.

Some French Army huts were taken over as stores, and the school was used for billeting. A petrol dump was established on a piece of adjoining waste ground. Among units on the feeding strength from this point on was the Tunisian Task Force commanded by Colonel Raff, referred to in newspaper write-ups as that 'stick of human dynamite from New York City' and 'the saviour of Tunisia'. Rations for this unit were later delivered by vehicles of 239 GT Company RASC, attached to this unit. Deliveries, including those of 87 octane petrol for half-tracks and ammunition, were sent forward each night to Feriana and Gafsa, necessitating a journey over a mountain range where the road was usually covered in cloud. On these runs and on many other occasions during the campaign when vehicles of this company were attached to us, the drivers deserved the highest praise for the excellent services they rendered.

Early in January, the unit changed over to bulk rations and moved their stores to the local theatre which made an excellent depot. At that time the unit were issuing between 70,000 and 80,000 rations and between 30,000 and 40,000 gallons of petrol a day. The American aerodrome at Youx-les-Bains was supplied direct from the railhead there, having a daily consumption of 20,000 gallons of 100 octane aviation spirit.

When we eventually handed over the depot to an American supply unit, an American sergeant produced a wonderful electric calculating machine which he set up in the office. He explained that this machine calculated the ration entitlement to two places of decimals. The first item they calculated was milk, and the ration calculated was 49.67 lb, for which the issuer immediately issued two cases (96 lb). On having his attention drawn to the fact that this was not correct, he replied: 'Sure it's not, but we only issue to the nearest case anyway.'

During the time the unit was operating at Tebessa they received large quantities of American rations, and the mixture of rations was such that a daily menu had to be worked out amalgamating the British and American ration scales and available stocks.

This worked well on the whole except that several American units thought that they should have been provided with the full American scale of rations. This was impossible owing to the vast difference in the scale of beverages. The British troops, who were very much in the minority, were satisfied, as such items as tomato juice, grapefruit juice, chile con carne, apple butter, golden corn, etc., made very welcome changes in the diet.

On January 26th, 1943, B Section rejoined the unit from Canrobert and on February 1st the complete unit moved to Ebba Ksour, where a depot was opened for the issue of compo rations to American forward troops and bulk rations to static troops. We were here during the Kasserine action and one night found that our trade had diminished alarmingly. On orders received from corps headquarters preparations were made for the destruction of all stocks to prevent them from falling into enemy hands. Defensive positions were manned for about 48 hours by this unit and five sections of pioneers from 119 Company.

On March 27th, 1943, the unit moved to Zafrane near Le Kef, transferring all remaining stocks to the new site.

While the unit was operating at Ebba Ksour, C Section was detached to Le Sers for a few days to start a petrol depot. After building up stocks of about 2,000 tons, the depot was handed over to 10 MPFC.

At Zafrane the unit had its first experience of a depot entirely under canvas. The depot consisted of eight store tents, heavily camouflaged. Additional stacking ground was levelled off beside the railway track and camouflaged by the erection of nets between the trees. At this depot the feeding strength rose to what is claimed to be a record for DIDs, namely 140,000 daily. This large feeding strength obviously necessitated considerable physical and mental effort by all ranks, and it is especially worthy of note that never before or since has the morale of the unit been so high. All felt that they were doing an important job and gave of their best. In the words of our sergeant clerk (with apologies to Sir Winston Churchill): 'Never before in the field of human conflict have so few worked so hard to feed so many.'

At Zafrane the unit fed the Eighth Army for the second time, the first having been at Tebessa early in January, when a special delivery of rations was made for a flying column of the Eighth Army Desert Group.

On May 9th, 1943, the two sections which had been helping 99 DID by loading the pack trains for them moved to Manouba, near Tunis. The site chosen for the depot was the barracks of the 62nd Artillery Regiment of the French Army, and was a former palace of the Bey of Tunis. During the occupation the Germans had used it as a tank repair shop. They had effected extensive demolitions before leaving, and had left behind them many booby traps which had to be rendered safe before work could be begun. The depot was cleared up and large stocks were received. In this location rations were issued to 218 units daily, which is claimed to be a record for two sections of a DID.

All enemy supply dumps in the area were taken over, and supplies were collected and brought into the depot. Here they were examined by Major Savage, RASC, the analyst who was making a report on all captured supplies. Captured German supplies included such items as Danish butter, tinned strawberries, and tinned hams. There were also large stocks of eau de Cologne, which was apparently used in the German Army instead of anti-mosquito cream.

After only a fortnight at this depot, during which a great deal of hard work was put in to put it in order, the unit was relieved by a BSD straight out from England. A and C Sections then moved to Sousse to join up with B Section.

On April 23rd, 1943, B Section moved from Zafrane to Sidi Ayed to operate as a railhead supply detachment. Issues were made daily from the pack train and two days' reserve of rations was held at the railhead reserve store, and the feeding strength was about 64,000, which included IX Corps, 1st British Armoured Division, 6th Armoured Division, and 46th Division.

On one occasion, during the battle, about 370 German prisoners were brought in by 1st British Armoured Division when coming to the railhead for rations, and these were left for the detachment to manage. Arrangements were therefore made for the guarding, feeding and entraining of these prisoners.

On May 8th the section moved again and opened another railhead at Bou Arada, for feeding 1st Armoured Division, 1st Infantry Division, and 46th Division. The area round Bou Arada was heavily mined, and great care had to be taken to avoid minefields all around the station sidings. Many dead cows lying around served as a warning of the danger.

At this point the train services, which had been operating quite well up till then, seemed to collapse, and the pack trains, instead of arriving early in the morning, used to turn up at four o'clock in the afternoon. This meant that a large number of vehicles had to be dispersed and hidden around the railhead for most of the day. On May 22nd, 1943, the railhead finally closed, and men and stocks from the reserve store were lifted by transport of 1st Division to Sousse.

B Section arrived at Sousse on May 23rd and opened a supply depot at the local olive oil factory. A week later A and C Sections moved down from Tunis and the DID was complete again. Under the title of 88 DID Bulk Section, a depot was started in addition to the ordinary detail issue depot, and this was eventually handed over to 50 BSD. After only two days' issuing, the depot was again handed over to 57 DID, and 88 DID moved to the holy city of Kairouan on June 10th.

The depot at Kairouan was started to meet the needs of the large number of RAF personnel operating from the aerodromes round about. Throughout the summer, the DID operated here under extremely trying conditions which included oppressive heat and large numbers of flies, mosquitoes and scorpions. Morale at this point was at its lowest. Two corporals reverted at their own request, and five other ranks applied for transfer to the Airborne Division.

The unit provided a detachment to represent the British Army at the parade held in the city on July 14th in honour of the fall of the Bastille. For their smartness of turnout and drill they were commended by the Area Commander, Brigadier A. E. Matthews, and by the ADST, as well as by the French Commander.

At the end of August, the unit handed over to the Supply Platoon of 221 Composite Company, and returned once again to Sousse.

EMBARKATION SUPPLY DEPOT

At the beginning of the war, the office of OIC Supplies Devonport, had a triple role, embracing the duties of OC Supplies South-western Area, OIC Supplies Devonport and Embarkation Supply Officer, Plymouth, but excepting a few vehicle ships in the early months of 1939, the ESD did not function again until May, 1940, when the port was again used for embarkation. I remember particularly a Canadian formation which had to be refuelled or embarked, only to return two or three days later, having been turned back at Brest or Cherbourg. They were a most disgruntled body of men.

One afternoon, at the end of May or early June, 1940, a conference was called by the AA & QMG, SWA, at which we were told we could expect 10,000 French troops before the evening, that these had to be accommodated for the night, fed and embarked the following day, and that a similar number would be passing through daily for some time. The supply of rations presented no particular difficulty, except that preserved meat had to be issued, as there was insufficient time to cook frozen meat this first day. The issue of biscuits was rendered unnecessary by a contractor undertaking to produce 5,000 lb of bread by midnight and a similar quantity by six o'clock the next morning. As this contractor was not holding the army contract at that time, his ready co-operation was much appreciated. By way of special rations, I received from SRD five 40-gallon barrels of French wine, presumably as a token issue. The whole operation proceeded very smoothly, haversack rations being put up for the 'guests' by the 'host' units, and at the end of the week all concerned were congratulated by the GOC SWA, and we were informed that in the seven days, a total 69,300 French troops had been passed through the port without preparation and the most significant fact was that not one single written instruction had been issued.

Soon after this, our own troops began to arrive in very large numbers, from the more western parts of France, and the feeding of these in transit and the rationing of ships for the return trips became a very big undertaking for the supply depot.

Up to this time I had been, and for the next week or so remained, without an assistant, and my surprise, not to say consternation, can be imagined when the first intimation that the embarkation side of my depot was to function to any great extent came in the shape of a bundle of Army Forms G 980, advising me that 62 truck loads of supplies containing a quarter of a million rations had arrived.

The storage space at the mobilization store at Fort Agaton being quite inadequate and too remote for immediate demands for the rationing of ships, I realized that storage with rail and road facilities was essential, especially as I had to be prepared to receive and issue supplies at the same time. Having spent many hours that I could ill afford interviewing civilian officials all over Plymouth, at 2000 hours on Sunday night, I think it was, I at last found a most helpful person who said I might use the bottom floor of two granaries at West Wharf, Plymouth, but only on the understanding that I vacated them in two weeks' time.

From this time on, for about six weeks, it was a matter of going all out. The telephone was abandoned as it was useless to try to make contact with Movement Control or the Naval Embarkation Officer by this means, routine calls for instructions being the only possible method. My final call to MC was at approximately 2000 hours, when it was not uncommon to receive instructions to ration another two vessels before midnight.

Whenever possible, troops were entrained immediately, a buffet being run on the quay under direct control of HQ SWA, where men received a much needed snack and a cup of tea. Train rations were put on the trains. Similar arrangements were doubtless made at all ports.

Another side to the Embarkation Supply Officer's duties was the rationing of troops on ships in the Sound who could not be disembarked owing to the bottle-neck in the railway system. This looked like being an almost insurmountable problem, but fortunately I received an assistant. His first job was to go out in the Sound in a small open boat with two issuers, scales, etc., and a stock of paper bags to ration all the small boats containing a variety of nationalities. His first day he brought back a list of some 36 boats rationed with quantities supplied to each, which miraculously balanced with his 'remains', a very creditable achievement.

In addition to our own troops there was a polyglot assortment of Poles, Czechs, Belgians, free and otherwise, who had to be fed and the rations accounted for separately, and charged to various governments. Additional fun was provided by a company of the RIASC, which necessitated the purchase of live sheep and substitutes for their normal rations until a supply of atta, ghi, turmeric, chillies, etc., could be received from SRD.

After the first influx until numerous mushroom camps were instituted for the housing of all and sundry until units were reorganized, names such as Pennygillam and Scarne Cross Camps at Launceston came into being. Unfortunately for the OC Supplies, the Camp Commandant had invariably been replaced by another when it came to obtaining a signature for rations and fuel supplies. At that time, fuel for camps was the responsibility of OIC Supplies.

After a time, all these duties shook down more or less into a matter of routine, but the difficulties were not lessened by the fact that units, at this stage of the war, were quite unaccustomed to home accounting and it is perhaps understandable that, after it was all over, the Financial Adviser and Army Auditor had to bless our efforts with a flood of observations. The sheepskin war was waged for quite six months. The point at issue was as to who could claim the value of the skins and 'plucks' of the sheep supplied to the Indian troops. In the end, the forces of the King Emperor prevailed.

Throughout the whole period my small staff, both in the office and outside, worked magnificently for extremely long hours, most willingly, with not a murmur of a grouse and maintained a surprising degree of accuracy in checking loads, etc., most of which work had of necessity to be delegated to junior NCOs. I think the peak was reached when 150,000 rations were issued in one day.

ESCAPE FROM MALAYA

This is a story of 'general' RASC endurance. It is one of the few fortunate stories from South-East Asia at the time of its being overrun by the Japanese. All branches of the Corps were represented in this little band of 'escapees'.

Many officers and men with technical qualifications were ordered to make their escape from Singapore on February 13th, 1942, and did so in the military vessels manned by the RASC men of the MT depot. The adventures of one of the parties of fitters, electricians, clerks, and so on, are worth recording. Sheer good luck attended them throughout their wanderings. They went off in a launch, making for Java, 500 miles away to the south-east. A blazing freighter bore down on them, missing them by a few feet, and then the Japanese spotted them and shelled them. Next morning they found to their dismay that they had gone north instead of south in the darkness, and had to return past Singapore. Enemy aircraft apparently decided that they were a native boat, and left them alone.

After rescuing some RAF men, whose boat had been sunk, they reached Sumatra, only to find that the Dutch were evacuating that island. But they were given some old lorries, in which they reached the west coast, where they linked up with 400 other refugees from Singapore. A cruiser took them to Java to continue the fight, but resistance was diminishing there, and the whole party got across to the west coast, where they were lucky enough to find an incredible contraption of a vessel, called the *Wuh-Chang*, an old Yangtse River boat which had been washed up there with 200 RAF bombs on board. She was quite unseaworthy and falling to bits, but she was a chance, and the 400 officers and men took it. They left on March 1st for a 3,500 mile trip across the Indian Ocean to Ceylon. The weather remained fairly calm, but the ship rolled about 25 degrees.

When she was about 1,500 miles from Ceylon, a Japanese submarine saw her and fired three torpedoes. Thanks to her flat bottom and shallow draught, only 6-8 feet, they passed beneath her, doing no damage. As the bombs were still on board, the effect if the torpedoes had hit would have been, to say the least, spectacular. The submarine surfaced 150 yards away, but for some reason, possibly because of a dummy gun mounted in the *Wuh-Chang's* stern, did not shell her, but submerged again and stalked the ship to try and fire another torpedo. The old boat had considerable manoeuvrability, and succeeded in taking evasive action, thanks to the frantic efforts of her crew, and the submarine at last made off. The *Wuh-Chang* reached Colombo about a week later and was taken over by the Royal Navy as an auxiliary submarine depot ship and stationed at Trincomalee. Considering the rough conditions of their trip, the men on board were all remarkably fit, and a few days later had already started their normal work again.

ROUND TOUR OF EUROPE

This is an account of an RASC officer's period of captivity in the hands of the Vichy French authorities, ending happily under the terms of the Wilson/Dentz armistice, thanks to our victory over the Vichy French authorities in Syria. It is a good indication of the spirit and resource of an RASC individual in the face of discouragement and, for him, disaster. The story is given in his own words. He was part of the force moving along the land L of C from Iraq on Syria at the time of our operations against the Vichy forces there.

My company was operating with Rabforce, the vehicles being loaded with ammunition, supplies and petrol and parked at H3 while the fighting troops were advancing on Palmyra. The code word for my convoy was 'Rabbits January', later convoys being designated 'Rabbits February', 'Rabbits March', and so on. When this code word was received by signal, I was to understand that Palmyra had fallen and that I was to proceed there immediately with my convoy.

After waiting at H3 for some days the code word came through by telephone and, immediately afterwards, an officer of the Arab Legion, Scott by name, reported himself as having been sent by General Clark (1st Cavalry Division) to escort my unit to Palmyra. We moved out forthwith and travelled for the remainder of the day. When dusk fell it became apparent that our guides had lost their way and we had to make a wide detour to get back on our course. Towards midnight we were still in some doubt about our exact location, as the night was very dark. As I naturally wanted to avoid falling into an ambush, I halted the company and sent a signal from my wireless PU to divisional headquarters, giving my approximate position and asking them whether I should continue or leaguer for the night. I received a reply to leaguer, which we did.

Daybreak found us again on the move and, on a pre-arranged signal the vehicles fanned out as soon as it was full light, as we had learned that certain troops of 1st Cavalry Division had been heavily bombed the previous day. We were then traversing a flat, open plain which was the area in which, I surmised, this attack had occurred. Right enough a number of Vichy aircraft swooped down on us but disappeared without attacking after circling round several times. Shortly afterwards I heard the noise of firing and, judging from some smoke billowing up behind a high sand dune, I concluded that mortars were in use.

I decided to halt my convoy and carry out a personal reconnaissance because, so far, we were in the lee of the sand dune, but would come into full view of any hostile elements if we proceeded farther. I arranged with Scott for two Arab legionaries to crawl up the rear slope of the sand dune to have a 'look-see', while Scott and I followed them as closely as possible in the car. The Arabs reported that there was a fort on the far side of the dune and that some English troops were firing at it from entrenched positions. A few minutes later they reported that the fort had apparently surrendered, as they saw the English troops entering it. In point of fact, as will be seen later, their appreciation of the situation was at fault. I then withdrew the Arab scouts and drove round the dune at speed. I noticed some British corpses being plundered by Arabs. Hardly had I drawn Scott's attention to this when an armoured car drove up alongside and a French officer in the turret called to us to surrender. He was a really villainous looking individual with a row of discoloured teeth leering behind a black beard matted with sand and dust.

My first impulse was to step on the gas and give him a run for his money, but on second thoughts I realized that if I were pursued (which was most likely) my action would give away the whole convoy. I decided instead to play for time so that my second-in-command would realize that I had 'bumped' something and could get busy extricating the vehicles before their existence was discovered. I was delighted to learn, three months later, that not a single vehicle had in fact been captured.

My captor was joined shortly afterwards by a number of satellites in armoured cars and I wasted time by pretending not to understand a word of French (which I speak fluently). However, after some 20 minutes' argument, Scott was taken off in one direction, while I was made to drive my car under Senegalese escort to the fort. On arrival I was met by a French cavalry colonel who ordered me to dismount for interrogation. At this moment I noticed a wounded British soldier lying in a pool of blood on the floor of a British 3-tonner. I asked the colonel if any medical assistance was available and he told me there was a dispenser in the fort, giving me permission to take the lorry inside under escort. While the guard was explaining to the *infirmier* about the wounded man, I took the opportunity of dropping my maps and orders down a nearby well. On returning to my car I found that the Senegalese had ransacked my valise, helping themselves to my personal belongings.

Shortly afterwards a convoy was formed up and my escort and I were allotted a position behind a troop-carrying lorry. This was possibly the most uncomfortable journey of my life. I was in considerable pain from a rectal abscess and I suffered from intense thirst. The Senegalese guard threatened my throat with a knife whenever I attempted to stop the car to get at my waterbottle. Finally I ran out of petrol and, when the car came to a standstill, one of the escort (thinking presumably that I was contemplating escape) made several passes at my head with the butt of his rifle. Eventually I was permitted to fill my tank from a 4-gallon container. While I was doing so one of the Senegalese improved the shining hour by unfastening my wristwatch which, needless to say, I have not seen since.

We then continued to travel until we arrived at a ruined building, where I was interrogated by the colonel I had met earlier in the day. I refused to give any information and eventually pointed to his medal ribbons and my own, suggesting that at one period we had fought on the same side. He merely shrugged his shoulders and apparently decided that I was wasting his time. I was accordingly marched back to my car and ordered to drive on.

Eventually we reached Deir-ez-Zor on the banks of the Euphrates, where I was taken to the officers' mess of the Camel Corps. Presently my black-bearded friend of earlier in the day appeared and I was able to conclude from his conversation that my own convoy had not been stopped, since he described his day's adventures, but made no reference to my command other than to my own unexpected arrival. Later on, Scott came in accompanied by a Yeomanry officer whose troops had been compelled to surrender owing to casualties and shortage of ammunition. It was these troops my Arab scouts had seen that same morning, but their appreciation of the situation had been considerably at fault.

Soon afterwards, Scott, myself, the Yeomanry subaltern and my two Arab legionaries were bundled into a bus with an escort, and we started out for Aleppo. During the journey we discussed several plans for escape by overpowering the escort and seizing the bus. However, we rejected them because we were not sure of the petrol situation and, in any case, we were closely followed by another vehicle carrying an armed escort. We arrived in Aleppo late that night, very tired after our 350-mile journey. We passed the night in an unsavoury cell in a French barracks, sleeping on straw palliasses which had obviously not been de-bugged for many months.

The following day we were transferred to a place called Idlib, where I greatly irritated a pompous French major by complaining about the conditions of the latrines, remarking that his race was notoriously lax towards this aspect of domestic economy. For the next few weeks we lived in ramshackle huts surrounded by a barbed wire perimeter and covered by four machine guns mounted in a tower. Time hung heavily on our hands, and we relieved the monotony by playing cards and by reading books kindly provided by the American consul at Beirut. Just as four of us, after lengthy reconnaissance, had perfected a plan for escape we were bundled into a bus and taken to an airfield at Aleppo. My fellow prisoners and myself (about 50, all told) were put into four aircraft, each with a gendarme escort. On taking off we bumped a bomb crater which had not been filled in and had to land again with a broken wheel.

We were then transferred to a comfortable Air France aircraft and set off again. My mind was not made any easier by the fact that I could not swim and our captors had neglected to provide us with any Mae Wests. However, we safely reached Eleusis aerodrome in Greece, where after a long wait we were transferred to some ancient French military aircraft and taken to Salonika, where we were incarcerated in a loft over a warehouse. We were strictly ordered not to smoke, this injunction being followed by a warning that if the building did catch fire our guards had instructions to lock the doors and leave us to it. While in this place we saw pitiful scenes through the window of our garret: children scrambling for the crusts of bread we threw them, old women dropping in the street and unable to rise again owing to disease and starvation, and horses which should have been shot long before they reached their present wasted condition. We also noticed large numbers of British captured lorries being driven by the Hun.

Eventually we were embarked in a Messageries Maritime liner of some 13,000 tons, the *Théophile Gautier*. We were locked up in the fo'c'sle (though all the passenger accommodation was empty) and only allowed on deck for two half-hour periods daily. The ship's captain adopted a very hostile attitude, and, when we asked for better accommodation, he spat on the deck and said, 'Don't talk to me about lack of comfort. How have you treated members of the French Navy at Aintree after Dunkirk, and what about Dakar and Oran?' Eventually he retracted a little and moved us to the third class accommodation, but how far he was influenced by the news of the British capture of Palmyra we did not know. Not long afterwards we heard that General Dentz had sued for an armistice.

We eventually disembarked and took a very interesting journey by train through Yugoslavia, Austria and Germany to France. We were very cold as, of course, we only had khaki drill shirts and shorts and some thin overcoats issued to us before entraining. The German escort went out of their way to point out places of interest such as Berchtesgaden. We saw large numbers of British and Empire prisoners of war working on the new autobahn roads under construction in Austria and Germany. They were very surprised as our train passed slowly by and they recognized British prisoners of war wearing French overcoats. We threw them Greek cigarettes and it was pleasing to see them so cheerful. One man in a glengarry started to sing, 'There'll always be an England'.

We passed through Munich, where German Red Cross nurses gave us chocolate and some ersatz coffee. The frontier into France was crossed at Besançon, and at Dijon we were allowed to detrain and to walk up and down the platform. Our next halt was at Lyons, where we were given a meal in a station restaurant. Here I got into conversation with a French general who told me he was a fervent admirer of our customs, as he had lived in England for some time. All the same he added that he could not forgive

England for having abandoned France after Dunkirk. His outlook was completely defeatist; he said we were only prolonging the agony for France, he had no confidence in Russia, and asserted that the German armies were unbeatable, as had been proved in France, Greece and the Western Desert.

From Lyons we went to Marseilles and thence to a fort at Toulon. The French sailors were very hostile and doubtless bore us a grudge over Oran and Dakar. A short time afterwards we were re-embarked in the SS *Champollion* and put to sea, passing large ships of the French fleet in the roads. This time we were given first class accommodation, but the ship's officers were taciturn and refused to acknowledge our salutes in the morning. We were bound for Beirut and were accompanied by two other ships which were going to Syria to evacuate those soldiers and civilians who had elected to return to France after the armistice. The names of the ships were painted in large letters, which were illuminated at night.

At the approach to the Straits of Messina we were picked up by an Italian warship and escorted through the mined channels. A British naval officer prisoner in our party improved the occasion by taking bearings of the minefields with a prismatic compass, guessing the speed of the ship. This information, together with any other data we had collected, was duly passed on to the Intelligence people on our arrival at Beirut.

We docked early one morning and came ashore shortly afterwards, to be greeted by a battery of cinema cameras. We were welcomed by Brigadier C. I. Chrystal, together with a representative of General Dentz. (The latter was unable to be present in person as he was under 'protective custody' pending our safe return.) Our adventures finally terminated with a lengthy interview with the Intelligence authorities. And so back to duty with the Corps.

With this the series of unit stories must be brought to a close. Many types of unit have not been included for reasons of space and not, be it understood, on account of any lack of comparitive importance. All corps units, transport, supply and POL, contributed in equal degree to the successful whole of the RASC's effort everywhere.

The Roll of Honour

'Lest we forget'

ROLL OF HONOUR

Aaron	M. L.	Dvr	Aitken	W. B.	Dvr	Allport	A. E.	Maj
Abbott	A. E.	Dvr	Akiah	T.	Pte		M.B.E.	
Abbott	A. W.	Pte	Akins	S.	Dvr	Allsop	C. M.	Dvr
Abbott	H.	L/Cpl	Alber	C.	Cpl	Allsop	J. H.	Dvr
Abbott	L. H.	Dvr	Alberts	A.	Dvr	Allwood	A. W.	Dvr
Abbott	R.	Dvr	Albery	V. G.	Cpl	Allwood	W. E.	Dvr
	2571263		Albu	F. G.	Cpl	Allwood	W. W.	Dvr
Abbott	R.	Dvr	Alcock	A.	Dvr	Allwright	F. K.	Dvr
	14438865		Alderton	J. L.	Cpl	Almy	A. F.	Dvr
Abbott	R. N.	Pte	Aldrich	J. R.	Sjt	Alton	A.	Sjt
Abbs	R.	Dvr	Aldridge	H. V. A.	Pte	Ames	C.	L/Cpl
Ablewhite	D. L.	Pte	Aldridge	W. F. J.	Pte	Amos	C. A.	Dvr
Abraham	T.	Pte	Alecock	F. D.	Dvr	Amos	C. S.	Dvr
Abramson	A.	Pte	Alee	T. J.	Dvr	Amos	G. E.	Dvr
Ackland	A. T.	WO I	Alexander	D. G.	Dvr	Amos	L. R.	Pte
Ackroyd	E. D.	Dvr	Alexander	H. W. G.	Dvr	Amsden	C. R.	Pte
Ackroyd	J. B.	Pte	Alexander	L. D.	L/Cpl	Anderson	A.	Sjt
Adair	L.	Cpl	Alexander	R.	Dvr	Anderson	A.	Dvr
Adam	H. V.	Cpl	Alexander	W. D.	Dvr		79003	
Adams	A. E.	Dvr	Alexander	W. G.	Dvr	Anderson	A.	Dvr
Adams	A. E. L.	Cpl	Alford	J. E.	Cpl		1037809	
Adams	A. R.	Dvr	Alimonda	L. A.	Pte	Anderson	C.	Dvr
Adams	C. F.	Dvr	Allan	A.	Dvr	Anderson	D.	Pte
Adams	D.	Cpl	Allan	J. D. S.	Pte	Anderson	E. M.	L/Cpl
Adams	F.	Cpl	Allan	J.	Dvr	Anderson	H.	Dvr
Adams	F. P.	Pte	Allan	J. W.	L/Cpl	Anderson	J.	Dvr
Adams	J. A.	Pte	Allan	S.	Cpl		165564	
Adams	J. D. L.	WO II	Allan	W.	Dvr	Anderson	J.	Dvr
Adams	N. P.	Dvr	Allan	W. C.	Pte		112585	
Adams	R. A.	L/Cpl	Allardice	D. S.	Cpl	Anderson	J.	Dvr
Adams	R. A.	Cpl	Allaway	R. G. D.	Capt		10661846	
Adams	R. F.	Dvr	Allcock	A. G.	Dvr	Anderson	J. B.	Dvr
Adams	R. T.	Dvr	Allday	D.	Dvr	Anderson	J. G.	Dvr
Adams	T. G.	Pte	Allen	A. E.	Dvr	Anderson	P.	Dvr
Adams	T. V.	Dvr	Allen	A. G.	Sjt	Anderson	P. S.	Sjt
Adams	W.	Dvr	Allen	C.	Cpl	Anderson	R. B.	Dvr
Adamson	D.	Pte	Allen	D. A.	Dvr	Anderson	R. J.	Dvr
Adamson	J.	L/Cpl	Allen	E. J.	Pte	Anderson	W.	Sjt
Adamson	S. L.	Maj	Allen	F.	Pte	Anderton	F. G.	Dvr
	D.C.M.		Allen	F. J.	Dvr	Anderton	J.	Dvr
Adamson	W.	Dvr	Allen	G.	Sjt	Andow	K. H.	Dvr
Adcock	J. F.	L/Sjt	Allen	G. C. E.	Dvr	Andrew	F. E.	Dvr
Addington	A.	Dvr	Allen	G. W.	Dvr	Andrew	G.	Sjt
Addison	A.	Pte	Allen	H.	Pte	Andrewartha,	D. J.	L/Cpl
Adey	J.	Pte	Allen	J. D.	Pte	Andrews	A. J.	Maj
Adnitt	K.	Pte	Allen	J. T.	Maj	Andrews	C. W. E.	L/Cpl
Affleck	S.	Dvr		M.B.E.		Andrews	J. C.	Dvr
Agass	S. J.	Dvr	Allen	L. C.	Pte	Andrews	J. J.	Dvr
Ager	C. E.	Dvr	Allen	M. J.	Pte	Andrews	J. T.	Dvr
Aiken	D. F.	Dvr	Allen	P. S. A.	L/Cpl	Andrews	J. W. F.	Dvr
Ainge	E. A.	Dvr	Allen	R.	Dvr	Andrews	T. B.	Cpl
Ainsley	H.	Dvr	Allen	S.	Cpl	Andrews	W. H. C.	Dvr
Ainsworth	W. R.	L/Cpl	Allen	S. G.	Pte	Andrews	W. L.	Pte
Airey	D. H.	Lt	Allen	W. H. J.	Lt	Angell	A. E.	Dvr
Aish	W. E.	Pte	Allen	W. M.	Sjt	Angove	V.	Pte
Aitken	C. E.	WO II	Allhouse	B. F.	Dvr	Anken	W. A. P.	L/Cpl
Aitken	I.	Dvr	Allison	J.	Dvr	Anness	G.	Dvr
Aitken	N.	Dvr	Allott	F.	Pte	Annetts	F. E.	Cpl

ROLL OF HONOUR

Anning	A. G.	Dvr	Ashley	R. J.	Sjt	Aylott	W.	Dvr
Ansell	E.	Pte	Ashmore	W. H.	Dvr	Ayre	B. W.	Dvr
Ansell	E. C.	Pte	Ashton	J.	Pte	Ayres	A.	Dvr
Ansell	L. D.	Dvr	Ashton	J. W.	Dvr	Azevedo	G.	Dvr
Anslow	D. H.	Dvr	Ashton	R. E.	Dvr			
Anthony	A. S.	Dvr	Ashton	R. G.	Dvr	Back	E. G.	Dvr
Anthony	R. C.	Pte	Ashurst	C.	Dvr	Backhouse	E. J.	Dvr
Apperley	W. W.	Dvr	Ashurst	T.	Dvr	Backhouse	W. L.	Pte
Appleby	F. H.	Dvr	Ashurst	G. A.	Dvr	Backman	F. J.	Pte
Appleton	A.	Dvr	Ashworth	J. R.	Dvr	Bacon	A.	L/Cpl
Appleton	R. J.	Dvr	Askew	D. C.	Dvr	Bacon	F. J. C.	Dvr
Appleton	W.	Dvr	Askew	H.	Cpl	Bacon	J. A.	Dvr
Appleyard	J.	Dvr	Askham	N.	L/Cpl	Bagge	S. J. A.	Pte
Appleyard	J. G.	Maj	Aspinall	T. H.	Dvr	Bagshaw	A.	Dvr
	D.S.O., M.C., Bar		Asquith	A. T.	Dvr	Bagshaw	E.	Pte
Apps	D. L.	L/Cpl	Aston	A. R.	Cpl	Bailey	A. H.	Dvr
Apps	S. W.	Pte	Aston	R.	Pte	Bailey	C. W.	Dvr
Archer	A.	Sjt	Atherton	E. L.	Dvr	Bailey	D. H.	Dvr
Archer	J.	Dvr	Atherton	J.	Pte	Bailey	E. W.	Dvr
Archer	P. A.	Dvr	Atkinson	A.	Dvr	Bailey	F.	Pte
Archer	S. G.	Cpl	Atkinson	C. J.	Dvr	Bailey	F. G.	L/Cpl
Archer	T. J. F.	Pte	Atkinson	C. W.	Dvr	Bailey	H. R.	Dvr
Archer	W.	Dvr	Atkinson	E.	Pte	Bailey	J.	WO I
Arden	M. V.	Dvr	Atkinson	E.	Dvr	Bailey	R. A.	Pte
Arends	R.	Sjt	Atkinson	J.	Dvr	Bailey	T.	Dvr
Arkwright	F.	Dvr	Atkinson	J. G. P.	Lt	Bailey	T. H.	Dvr
Armand	S.	Dvr		M.C.		Bailey	T. H.	Dvr
Armes	C. S. G.	Dvr	Atkinson	L.	Dvr	Bailey	W.	Pte
Armitage	G. D. V.	Dvr	Atkinson	W.	Dvr	Bailey	W. H.	Dvr
Armitage	R. P.	Capt	Atkinson	W. A.	Dvr	Bailey	W. P. A.	Pte
Armstrong	D.	L/Sjt	Atkiss	J.	Pte	Baillie	H.	Dvr
Armstrong	J.	Dvr	Attenborough, A. A.		Dvr	Bain	A. A.	Dvr
Armstrong	J. D.	2/Lt	Atto	C. H.	Maj	Baines	T. M.	Cpl
Armstrong	N. T.	Dvr	Attwood	C. L.	L/Cpl	Baird	H. T.	Dvr
Armstrong	R. J.	Pte	Attwood	T. J.	Cpl	Baitup	T. W.	Dvr
Armstrong	T. S.	Pte	Auger	G. L.	Sjt	Baker	A. E.	Dvr
Arnold	E.	Dvr	Aughton	R. J.	Dvr	Baker	C.	Dvr
Arnold	E. E.	Pte	Ault	J. T.	Pte	Baker	C. H. J.	Dvr
Arnold	F.	Dvr	Aumayer	F. J.	Dvr	Baker	D.	Sjt
Arnold	H. V. B.	Dvr	Austin	A. W.	Dvr	Baker	F. E.	Dvr
Arnold	J.	L/Cpl	Austin	F.	Sjt	Baker	F. R. C.	Dvr
Arnold	J. G.	Maj	Austin	F. C.	Dvr	Baker	H.	Dvr
Arnott	C. E.	Sjt	Austin	H. A.	Cpl		10693703	
Arnott	F. J.	Cpl	Austin	J. T.	Sjt	Baker	H.	Dvr
Arnott	G.	L/Cpl	Austin	S.	Dvr		14665070	
Arnott	H.	Dvr	Austwick	J. E.	Dvr	Baker	H.	Dvr
Arrandale	R.	Cpl	Auty	L.	Pte		4978605	
Arrol	J.	Sjt	Aves	H.	Dvr	Baker	H. A. E.	Dvr
Ash	E. P.	Pte	Aveyard	E.	Dvr	Baker	J. A.	Dvr
Ash	F. S.	Sjt	Avis	B.	Cpl	Baker	J. E.	Dvr
Ash	H. R.	L/Cpl	Avison	T. H.	WO II	Baker	J. F.	Dvr
Ashburnham, A. F.		Maj	Axe	H. W.	Dvr	Baker	J. W.	Dvr
Ashby	D. A.	Cpl	Axon	F. W.	CQMS	Baker	R. E. E.	Dvr
Ashby	G. G.	Sjt	Axtell	D. F.	L/Cpl	Baker	R. T. W.	WO II
Ashby	R. J.	Cpl	Ayers	M. T.	Dvr	Baker	S. W.	Dvr
Ashcroft	J.	Dvr	Aylett	C. H.	Pte	Baker	T. A.	Dvr
Ashe	J.	Sjt	Ayliffe	G. H.	Dvr	Baker	T. H.	L/Cpl
Ashford	V. W. G.	Pte	Ayling	A. W.	Dvr	Baker	T. H.	Dvr

658

ROLL OF HONOUR

Baker	T. S.	Cpl	Barker	E. J.	Cpl	Barrett	F. A.	2/Lt
Baker	W. J.	Dvr	Barker	F.	Sjt	Barrett	F. J. H.	Cpl
Baker	W. L.	Pte	Barker	F. H.	Pte	Barrett	H. J.	Sjt
Baldwin	A. A.	Cpl	Barker	S.	Pte	Barrett	J.	Dvr
Baldwin	F. A.	Dvr	Barker	T. H.	L/Cpl	Barrett	J. F.	CQMS
Baldwin	F. J.	WO II	Barker	W. R.	Dvr	Barrett	L.	Sjt
Baldwin	G. B.	Dvr	Barkley	E. T. Y.	Capt	Barrett	L. S.	Cpl
Baldwin	J.	Dvr	Barlow	C. F.	Dvr	Barrett	R. H.	Dvr
Bale	F. W. H.	S/Sjt	Barlow	C. W.	Dvr	Barrett	R. M.	Dvr
Balkwill	A. G.	Dvr	Barlow	D. A.	Lt	Barritt	W. E.	Pte
Ball	A. P.	L/Cpl	Barlow	G.	Cpl	Barrow	A. T.	Dvr
Ball	A. R.	Pte	Barlow	H.	Dvr	Barrow	F. C.	Dvr
Ball	G. H.	Dvr	Barlow	J.	L/Cpl	Barrow	T.	Dvr
Ball	G. T.	Cpl	Barlow	J.	Sjt	Barrow	W.	Dvr
Ball	H. J. F.	Dvr	Barlow	J. E.	Dvr	Barry	J.	Dvr
Ball	L.	Dvr	Barlow	S.	Cpl	Barry	R. E.	Pte
Ball	L. W.	L/Cpl	Barnaby	T. L.	Dvr	Barter	J.	Lt
Ball	R. W.	Dvr	Barnard	J. R.	Sjt	Bartle	J.	Pte
Ball	T.	Capt	Barnard	L. W.	Dvr	Bartlett	F. C.	Capt
Ball	T. L.	Pte	Barnard	V. W.	Pte	Bartlett	H. C.	Dvr
Ball	W.	Dvr	Barnard	W. K.	Dvr	Bartlett	J. R. G.	Dvr
Ball	W. D.	Dvr	Barnes	A. J.	Dvr	Bartlett	L. M. F.	Dvr
Ball	W. G.	Cpl	Barnes	C. H.	L/Cpl	Bartlett	R.	Dvr
Ballard	C. A.	Cpl	Barnes	E.	Pte	Bartlett	W. J.	L/Cpl
Ballard	J.	Dvr	Barnes	E. W.	Dvr	Barton	F.	Dvr
Ballinger	C. C.	Dvr	Barnes	F. M.	Dvr	Barton	J.	Dvr
Bamber	P. K.	2/Lt	Barnes	F. S.	L/Cpl	Barton	W.	S/Sjt
Bamberry	A. J.	Cpl	Barnes	G. E.	Dvr	Bartrom	R. J.	Dvr
Bamford	J. R.	Sjt	Barnes	G. P.	Cpl	Bartrum	E.	Dvr
Bamford	O. C.	Lt	Barnes	H.	Pte	Bascombe	D. E.	Cpl
Banks	A. E.	Dvr	Barnes	J.	L/Cpl	Bashford	C.	S/Sjt
Banks	C.	Dvr	Barnes	R.	Dvr	Bastable	R. W.	Dvr
Banks	E. J.	Sjt	Barnes	R. A. G.	Dvr	Basten	F. A.	Dvr
Banks	E. J.	Dvr	Barnes	S.	Dvr	Baston	G. W.	Dvr
Banks	M. F.	Cpl	Barnes	S. D.	Dvr	Batchlor	R. K.	Maj
Banks	P. F.	WO II	Barnes	T.	Dvr	Batchlor	R. V.	Dvr
Banks	V. W.	Dvr	Barnes	V. W.	L/Cpl	Bate	E.	S/Sjt
Banks	W. A.	Dvr	Barnes	W.	Dvr	Bate	J.	Dvr
Bannister	A. B.	Lt	Barnes	W. E.	Dvr	Bateman	F. A.	Dvr
Bannister	T.	Cpl	Barnes	W. H.	Dvr	Bates	E. G.	Dvr
Barber	G. D.	Cpl	Barnet	N. C.	Pte	Bates	F.	Dvr
Barber	G. R.	Dvr	Barnett	A. S.	Pte	Bates	F. R.	Sjt
Barber	H. D.	Dvr	Barnett	B.	Pte	Bates	J. J. A.	Dvr
Barber	H. G.	Pte	Barnett	C. J.	Pte	Bates	N.	L/Cpl
Barber	J.	Dvr	Barnett	C. W.	Sjt	Bates	W. H.	Dvr
Barber	R. F.	Sjt	Barnett	D. R.	Pte	Bates	W. J.	Dvr
Barber	S. E.	Dvr	Barnett	H. W.	Pte	Batey	N. T.	Dvr
Barber-Lomax, E. A.		Capt	Barnett	N. J.	L/Cpl	Bath	F. C.	L/Cpl
Barclay	J. 10674312	Dvr	Barnett	V.	Dvr	Bathew	G. A.	Dvr
			Barnsley	L.	Pte	Batten	S. G.	Dvr
Barclay	J. 87730	Dvr	Barr	P.	CQMS	Battersby	H. W.	S/Sjt
			Barraclough	F.	Dvr	Battiscombe	P.	Cpl
Barclay	J. F. S.	2/Lt	Barratt	A. E.	Dvr	Batts	E. R.	Pte
Bardsley	H.	Dvr	Barratt	W.	Dvr	Baulch	W. E.	Dvr
Barfoot	C. H.	Cpl	Barrell	R. T.	Pte	Baxter	A.	Sjt
Barke	R. C.	Dvr	Barrett	A. B.	Sjt	Baxter	E.	Dvr
Barker	A. E.	Cpl	Barrett	C. R.	Dvr	Baxter	J.	Dvr
Barker	C. E.	Cpl	Barrett	C. T.	Dvr	Baxter	R. N.	Dvr

ROLL OF HONOUR

Baxter	T. H.	Cpl	Behrman	G.	Dvr	Bentinck	G. J.	Pte
Baxter	W. J.	Cpl	Beighton	S.	Dvr	Bentley	C. W.	Pte
Bayfield	W. G.	Dvr	Belcher	A.	Pte	Bentley	G. W.	Dvr
Bayley	E. W. H.	Dvr	Belcher	A. J. J.	L/Cpl	Bentley	H.	Dvr
Bayley	P. T. G.	Dvr	Belcher	J. S.	Dvr	Bentley	L.	Sjt
Bayliss	R.	Pte	Belcher	L. F.	Pte	Bentley	R.	Dvr
Bayliss	R. R.	Dvr	Belfield	A.	Dvr	Benyon	J. W.	Dvr
Bayne	R.	Dvr	Belk	C. H.	L/Cpl	Beresford	J.	L/Cpl
Beach	N. J.	Dvr	Bell	A.	Dvr	Beresford	J. T. P.	Capt
Beacham	L. J.	Dvr	Bell	A. C.	Maj	Bernardes	J. E.	Dvr
Beadleson	C. B.	Dvr	Bell	A. H.	Dvr	Berrington	A. H.	S/Sjt
Beadnell	J. F.	Dvr	Bell	F.	Dvr	Berry	A.	Dvr
Beal	F. T.	L/Cpl	Bell	G. W.	S/Sjt		180569	
Beal	J. W.	Dvr	Bell	H. V.	Sjt	Berry	A.	Dvr
Beale	L. H.	Cpl	Bell	J. H.	Dvr		91067	
Beale	W. L. H.	Dvr	Bell	J. J.	Dvr	Berry	F.	Dvr
Bealer	C. W.	L/Cpl	Bell	J. T.	Dvr	Berry	F. R.	Dvr
Beamish	J. G.	Cpl	Bell	J. W.	Sjt	Berry	G. G.	Capt
Bean	F.	Dvr	Bell	K. J.	Dvr	Berry	H.	Dvr
Beange	P. M.	Sjt	Bell	R.	Capt	Berry	J. E.	Dvr
Beard	J. W.	Dvr	Bell	R. F.	L/Cpl	Berry	J. H.	Pte
Beard	R. G.	Dvr	Bell	S.	Dvr	Berry	J. S.	Sjt
Beard	W. E.	Pte	Bell	S. D.	Pte	Berry	S. P.	Cpl
Beardsley	F. W.	Dvr	Bell	T. F.	Dvr	Berryman	B.	Dvr
Beardsley	H.	Dvr	Bell	T. W. H.	Sjt	Berwick	R. J.	Dvr
Beare	D. H.	Sjt	Bell	W.	Dvr	Best	E.	Pte
Bearman	S. C.	Dvr	Bell	W. E.	Pte	Best	G. H.	Dvr
Beasley	B.	Dvr	Bell	W. S.	Dvr	Bethell	L. N.	2/Lt
Beasley	W. T.	L/Cpl	Bellander	S. C.	Lt	Bethune	A.	Cpl
Beaton	F. W. S.	L/Cpl	Bellenger	F.	Dvr	Betteridge	A. J.	Dvr
Beaton	J.	Dvr	Bellenger	W.	Cpl	Betts	D. G.	Pte
Beattie	S.	Dvr	Bellingham	E. A.	Cpl	Betts	S. B.	Sjt
Beattie	W.	L/Cpl	Bellows	W. G.	Dvr	Betts	W. J.	Pte
Beaumont	C. W. F.	L/Cpl	Bellringer	F. A. H.	Cpl	Bevan	C.	Sjt
Beaumont	E.	Pte	Bending	J.	Dvr	Bevan	C. H.	Dvr
Beaumont	S.	Dvr	Benelisha	S.	Cpl	Bevan	D. W.	Pte
Beaver	A. E. F.	2/Lt	Benford	L. A.	WO I	Beveridge	C. R.	Pte
Beck	A.	Dvr	Benham	B.	S/Sjt	Bewick	S.	Pte
Beck	G. E.	Sjt	Benison	E. W. A.	Lt	Bexley	G. R.	Dvr
Beck	T. E.	Dvr	Bennett	A. B.	Dvr	Bibb	A. G.	Pte
Beckerleg	L. C.	Capt	Bennett	A. F.	Sjt	Bibby	G.	Dvr
Beckett	J.	Dvr	Bennett	A. T.	Sjt	Bibby	R. H.	WO II
	68431		Bennett	C. C.	Dvr	Bibby	S.	Dvr
Beckett	J.	Dvr	Bennett	E.	Dvr	Bibby	T.	Dvr
	103774		Bennett	G.	Dvr	Bickard	C. H.	L/Cpl
Beckingham	G. F.	L/Cpl	Bennett	H. R.	Dvr	Bicker	C. T.	Dvr
Beddow	W. J.	L/Cpl	Bennett	J.	Dvr	Bickford	W. A.	Dvr
Beddows	C. F.	Dvr		935089		Bicknell	T. A.	Dvr
Bedford	J.	Dvr	Bennett	J.	Dvr	Biddlecombe, F. A.		Dvr
Bedford	W. H.	Capt		160562		Bidwell	T.	Dvr
Beech	P.	Dvr	Bennett	L. J.	Dvr	Bielby	E.	Dvr
Beecroft	D.	Dvr	Bennett	R. A.	L/Cpl	Biggs	P. C.	Dvr
Beecroft	R. G.	Dvr	Bennett	W.	Dvr	Biggs	R. M.	Dvr
Beesley	T.	Dvr	Benns	N. W.	Dvr	Bilclough	F.	Dvr
Beeson	C.	Dvr	Benny	J.	Sjt	Biles	W. E.	L/Cpl
Beeton	G. J.	L/Cpl	Benson	B. G.	Dvr	Billings	E. A.	Dvr
Beevers	L.	Cpl	Benstead	W. G.	Dvr	Binding	C. J.	Cpl
Begley	L. G.	WO II	Bent	C.	Capt	Bindley	G. J.	Dvr

ROLL OF HONOUR

Bingham	O. R.	Maj	Bloomfield	E. A.	Dvr	Boon	G. E.	Dvr
Binney	P. W.	Dvr	Bloomfield	L. A. T.	L/Cpl	Boon	T. F.	Dvr
Binney	W. M.	S/Sjt	Bloomfield	W. G.	Dvr	Boorer	G. H. W.	Dvr
Binnion	A.	Dvr	Bloomfield	W. T.	L/Cpl	Booth	A.	
Binstead	J. G.	Dvr	Blore	T. H.	Dvr		4348890	
Birch	E. N. W.	Lt-Col	Blowers	A.	Dvr	Booth	A.	Dvr
	O.B.E.		Bloxham	S. J.	Sjt		282787	
Birch	F. M.	Dvr	Bluett	H. F.	Cpl	Booth	E. W.	Dvr
Birch	G.	L/Cpl	Blundell	A.	Dvr	Booth	F. R.	Dvr
Birch	P. C.	L/Cpl	Blundell	D.	Dvr	Booth	L. G.	Dvr
Bird	C. W. J.	Dvr	Blundell	R.	Dvr	Booth	P. D.	S/Sjt
Bird	F.	Dvr	Blundell	T. H.	Dvr	Boothby	D. A.	Dvr
Bird	F. A.	WO II	Blunt	D.	Dvr	Boreham	A. E.	Pte
Bird	J. R.	Cpl	Blunt	F. A. J.	Dvr	Borer	W. L.	Dvr
Bird	K.	L/Cpl	Blyde	R. W.	Dvr	Bosi	J.	Dvr
Bird	W. C. S.	Dvr	Blyth	P. G.	Pte	Boslam	W.	L/Cpl
Birmingham, R. T.		WO II	Blythe	A.	Pte	Bosomworth, E. D. F.		Sjt
Birtwhistle	H.	Cpl	Blythe	G. E.	Pte	Bosworth	A. W.	Dvr
Birtwisle	D. I. P.	Lt.	Blyther	F. H. M.	Pte	Bosworth	C. R.	Dvr
Biscoe	B. L. S.	Sjt	Boak	C. B.	Maj	Bosworth	V. G.	Dvr
Biscoe-vincent, H.		L/Cpl	Boakes	C. G.	Dvr	Bott	A. W.	Cpl
Bishop	A.	Dvr	Boam	W. A.	Dvr	Bottell	L.	Pte
Bishop	A. J.	Dvr	Boardman	E.	Dvr	Botten	W. L.	Dvr
Bishop	E.	Dvr	Boardman	H.	Dvr	Botting	C. H.	Dvr
Bishop	F.	Dvr	Boardman	R. J.	Cpl	Bottom	E. V.	Cpl
Bishop	F. W.	Pte	Boath	R.	Dvr	Bottom	J. H.	Dvr
Bishop	J.	Dvr	Bocking	G. W.	L/Cpl	Bottomley	J. S.	Dvr
Bishop	R.	Dvr	Boddy	V. G.	Dvr	Bottoms	L.	Dvr
Bishop	W. F.	Sjt	Bodimead	E. A.	Dvr	Bottoms	W. G. H.	Dvr
Bissett	A. T.	Cpl	Bodimeade	G. A.	Dvr	Boud	J.	Dvr
Bissett	W.	Dvr	Bolam	J. W.	Dvr	Boulton	J. L.	Dvr
Black	H.	L/Cpl	Bolderson	N.	Sjt	Boundford	S. A. L.	Cpl
Black	J. G.	Maj	Boles	J.	Dvr	Bourgaize	E. E.	Dvr
Black	M.	Pte	Boles	P.	Dvr	Bourne	F. G.	Capt
Blackburn	C.	Cpl	Bolger	J.	Dvr	Bourne	G.	Cpl
Blackburn	F. W.	Cpl	Bolton	A.	Pte	Bourne	S. G.	Pte
Blackburn	G.	Capt	Bolton	F. C.	L/Cpl	Bourne	T. F.	Dvr
Blackburn	J. W.	Dvr	Bolton	G. S.	L/Cpl	Bourne	W.	L/Cpl
Blackey	G. A.	Cpl	Bolton	H.	Dvr	Bowater, Sir R. V.	*Bt.*,	Cpl
Blackman	A. A.	Pte	Bolton	J.	Sjt	Bowden	A. E.	Dvr
Blair	J. D.	Dvr	Bolton	J. P.	Dvr	Bowden	G. E.	Dvr
Blair	J. L.	Dvr	Bolton	T. G.	Dvr	Bowden	J. R.	Dvr
Blair	W.	Dvr	Bolton	W. A.	Dvr	Bowden	R.	L/Cpl
Blake	F. R.	Cpl	Bona	P. J.	Lt	Bowell	S. G.	Dvr
Blaker	H. G.	Dvr	Bond	C. R. W.	Sjt	Bowen	A.	Dvr
Blanchard	S. J.	Dvr	Bond	D. A. H.	Dvr	Bowen	A. G.	Sjt
Blanchard	S. J. W.	Dvr	Bond	R. G. R.	Cpl	Bowen	E. J. H.	Dvr
Bland	D. R.	Sjt	Bond	T.	Dvr	Bowen	G.	Pte
Bland	F. J.	Capt	Bond	W. T.	Pte	Bowen	G. T.	Pte
Blandford	F. A.	Dvr	Bondy	R. C.	Dvr	Bowen	T.	Dvr
Blanshard	R.	L/Sjt	Bone	W. J.	Maj	Bowerman	B. E.	Dvr
Bleasdale	J.	Dvr	Bonetto	E. G.	Dvr	Bowerman	E. T.	Dvr
Blencowe	R. W.	Dvr	Boniface	F. G.	Dvr	Bowers	F. R.	Dvr
Blenkinsop	T. R.	Dvr	Bonner	G. E.	Dvr	Bowers	G.	Dvr
Bliss	H. J.	Dvr	Bonnier	H.	Pte	Bowers	J.	Dvr
Blissett	D.	Dvr	Boocock	A.	Pte	Bowes	R. T.	Dvr
Bloch	M.	Sjt	Booker	W. E.	Dvr	Bowker	F.	Dvr
Bloomer	B.	Dvr	Boon	F.	Dvr	Bowles	J. W.	Dvr

ROLL OF HONOUR

Bowling	J.	Dvr	Brant	P. H.	Sjt	Brine	T. H. J.	Dvr
Bowman	C. S.	Dvr	Branwhite	H. E.	Pte	Brinsden	F. W.	Dvr
Bowman	F. H.	Dvr	Brassington	D.	Dvr	Briscoe	A. H.	Cpl
Bowman	G. R.	Dvr	Bratt	E.	Pte	Briscoe	H. R.	L/Cpl
Bowman	H.	Dvr	Bratt	J. A.	Dvr	Bristow	R. N.	Dvr
Bowman	J. H.	Dvr	Bray	A. G. D.	Pte	Brittain	S.	Sjt
Bown	C. C.	Sjt	Bray	G.	Cpl	Britton	R. C.	Pte
Bowsher	F. R.	Dvr	Bray	L. P.	Dvr	Broadhead	E.	L/Cpl
Bowsher	H. E.	Dvr	Braybrook	J. H.	Dvr	Broadhead	H.	Dvr
Bowtle	E. H.	Cpl	Braybrooke	A. C. G.	Dvr	Broadhurst	H.	Dvr
Bowtle	L. J.	Pte	Brazier	A. E.	L/Cpl	Brock	A. G.	Dvr
Bowyer	G. H.	Dvr	Breading	D.	Dvr	Brock	B. J.	L/Cpl
Box	J.	Dvr	Breakwell	H. M.	Sjt	Brockes	P. A.	WO II
Boxall	S. L.	L/Cpl	Breame	S. J.	Pte	Brockett	R. H.	Dvr
Boyd	G.	L/Cpl	Breeze	T.	Dvr	Brocklehurst, A.		Dvr
Boyd	G.	Dvr	Breeze	W. R.	Dvr	Brodhurst	F. J.	Maj
Boyd	H. J.	Pte	Brendon, C. R. McL.		Cpl	Brodie	D.	Dvr
Boyd	J.	Dvr	Brennan	J. P.	Dvr	Brodie	I. H.	Dvr
Boyd	S.	Dvr	Brennan	P.	Dvr	Brodie	R.	Dvr
Boyd	T.	L/Cpl	Brennan	T.	Dvr	Brodrick	C. B.	Dvr
Boyers	C.	Dvr	Brereton	F.	Dvr	Brogan	E.	Dvr
Boyle	A. M.	Cpl	Brereton	T.	Dvr	Brogan	J.	Pte
Boyle	W.	Cpl	Bretherick	T.	Dvr	Brogan	T.	Pte
Boyles	L. W. A.	Dvr	Brett	E. G.	Dvr	Bromby	L.	Dvr
Bracken	F.	Dvr	Brett	H. T.	Dvr	Bromfield	J. R.	Dvr
Bracken	P.	Dvr	Brettell	H.	Sjt	Bromberg	W.	Dvr
Brackenbury	W.	Dvr	Brew	E. J.	Sjt	Brook	H.	Dvr
Bradburn	R. A.	Dvr	Brew	L. C.	Dvr	Brook	J.	Dvr
Bradbury	G.	Dvr	Breward	W. H.	Dvr	Brook	R.	Dvr
Bradley	A.	Dvr	Brewer	C. E.	Pte	Brook	R. J.	Sjt
Bradley	J.	Dvr	Brewer	H.	Dvr	Brooke	A. W.	Lt
Bradley	J. A.	Dvr	Brewer	J.	Dvr	Brooke	W. H.	Sjt
Bradley	J. C. K.	Dvr		275173		Brookes	A. H.	Dvr
Bradley	J. R.	L/Cpl	Brewer	J.	Dvr	Brookes	A. W.	Dvr
Bradley	L. R. H.	S/Sjt		197725		Brookes	R.	Dvr
Bradley	R.	Dvr	Brewer	J. T.	Pte	Brookhouse	F. J.	Cpl
Bradley	T.	Dvr	Brewer	W. E.	Dvr	Brooks	F. H.	Cpl
Bradnam	F.	Dvr	Brewis	F. A.	Cpl	Brooks	J.	Cpl
Bradshaw	E.	Dvr	Brewster	J. E.	L/Cpl	Brooks	J. G.	Dvr
Bradshaw	G.	Dvr	Brewster	N. J.	Sjt	Brooks	R. A.	Dvr
Bradshaw	R. H.	Dvr	Briant	H. F.	Dvr	Brooks	S.	Cpl
Bragg	J. M.	Cpl	Brice	E. G.	Dvr	Brooks	T. R.	Cpl
Bragg	L. F.	Pte	Brickley	S.	Dvr	Brooks	T. W.	Dvr
Braggs	C. J. H.	Dvr	Bridge	R. J.	L/Cpl	Broom	J. H.	L/Cpl
Braidley	A.	Dvr	Bridgen	A. J.	Dvr	Broome	J. W.	Dvr
Braidwood	F. A.	Cpl	Bridges	C. J.	Capt	Broomhall	K. J.	Dvr
Bramley	E. D.	Cpl	Bridges	J. T.	Dvr	Brothwell	J. W.	Dvr
Bramley	F. J. A.	Pte	Bridges	R. E.	Dvr	Brough	A.	L/Cpl
Bramley	R. V. T.	Dvr	Bridgman	H. H.	Dvr	Broughton	E. C.	Pte
Bramwell	F. J.	Cpl	Bridle	F. J.	Pte	Broughton	S. J.	Dvr
Brand	A.	Dvr	Brierley	C. H.	Maj	Brown	A.	Sjt
Brand	H.	WO II	Brigg	G. T. W.	Capt	Brown	A. 67451	Dvr
Branigan	T. F.	Pte	Briggs	B. A.	Capt			
Brann	J. W.	Sjt	Briggs	E.	Sjt	Brown	A. 291071	Dvr
Brannan	G. L.	Dvr	Briggs	H.	Dvr			
Brannigan	T.	Dvr	Briggs	P. R.	Dvr	Brown	A. G.	L/Cpl
Brannon	L. J.	Dvr	Brightwell	B. J.	Pte	Brown	A. A.	Dvr
Branson	E.	Cpl	Brind	R. H.	Dvr	Brown	A. D.	Dvr

ROLL OF HONOUR

Brown	A. F.	Dvr	Brown	T. N.	Dvr	Budge	H. J.	Dvr
Brown	A. L.	Pte	Brown	W.	Dvr	Budge	W. C.	Dvr
Brown	C.	Dvr	Brown	W. A.	Pte	Budgen	G. N.	Capt
Brown	C. G. G.	Lt	Brown	W. C.	Pte	Budler	J. F. C.	Dvr
Brown	C. H.	L/Cpl	Brown	W. E.	Pte	Buggey	E. A.	Sjt
Brown	D. A.	Pte	Brown	W. I.	Cpl	Bull	E.	Dvr
Brown	D. E.	Cpl	Brown	W. J.	S/Sjt	Bull	G. J.	Dvr
Brown	D. V. E.	S/Sjt	Browne	H. C.	Dvr	Bull	P. A.	Sjt
Brown	E.	Dvr	Browne	M. E.	Pte	Bull	W. E.	Dvr
Brown	E. R.	Dvr	Browning	G. R. H.	Dvr	Bullen	C. E.	Dvr
Brown	F.	Dvr	Brownlie	G. A.	S/Sjt	Bullivant	H. E.	Dvr
Brown	F. G.	Dvr	Bruce	D.	S/Sjt	Bullman	E. F.	Pte
Brown	F. G.	L/Cpl	Bruce	W.	Cpl	Bullock	F. J.	L/Cpl
Brown	F. W.	Pte	Bruce	W. F.	Pte	Bullock	G.	Dvr
Brown	G.	Dvr	Bruckman	E. R.	Dvr	Bullock	G. M.	Pte
Brown	H.	Dvr	Bruines	F.	Dvr	Bullock	H.	Dvr
Brown	H. A.	Dvr	Brumby	A.	WO I	Bullock	H. P.	Dvr
Brown	H. F.	Dvr	Brummitt	L.	Dvr	Bullock	H. T.	L/Cpl
Brown	H. G.	Dvr	Brunskill	J. W.	Pte	Bulmer	D.	Sjt
Brown	H. J.	Dvr	Brunton	G. R.	Dvr	Bulmer	L. H.	WO II
Brown	H. L.	Dvr	Bryan	H. B.	Pte	Bulmer	R. O.	Pte
Brown	J.	Dvr	Bryan	W. R. H.	Dvr	Bumpus	R.	Dvr
Brown	J. 10665376		Bryant	A. G.	Lt	Bundy	H.	Dvr
Brown	J. 127668	Pte	Bryant	A. V.	Dvr	Bungay	F. R.	Dvr
			Bryant	E.	Pte	Bunn	F.	Pte
Brown	J. 163003	Pte	Bryant	J.	Pte	Bunn	F. A.	Dvr
			Bryant	J. H.	Pte	Bunster	F. R.	Dvr
Brown	J. 141788	Dvr	Bryant	R. C.	L/Cpl	Bunt	R. A.	L/Cpl
			Bryant	T. B.	Cpl	Buntin	T. J.	Dvr
Brown	J. E.	Pte	Bryant	T. J.	Pte	Bunting	W. H.	Dvr
Brown	J. H.	Dvr	Bryar	T. H.	Dvr	Burbridge	J. W.	Dvr
Brown	J. H.	Cpl	Bryce	W. F.	Pte	Burchell	F. T. G.	Dvr
Brown	J. R.	Dvr	Bryde	R.	Pte	Burchell	H. J.	Pte
Brown	J. R. P.	Dvr	Brydson	W.	Dvr	Burden	R. E.	Dvr
Brown	J. W.	Dvr	Bryson	J.	Dvr	Burdett	F. W.	Dvr
Brown	J. W.	Sjt	Bryson	S. G.	Pte	Burdett	W. G.	Capt
Brown	L. 267504	Dvr	Bryson	W.	S/Sjt	Burdon	J. H.	Cpl
			Bubb	S. T.	Sjt	Burfoot	F. J.	Pte
Brown	L. 10665933	Dvr	Buchanan	A. H.	Cpl	Burgess	S. H.	Dvr
			Buchanan	A. P.	Pte	Burgess	W. J.	Cpl
Brown	L. W.	Pte	Buchanan	J. K.	L/Cpl	Burgoyne	E.	Dvr
Brown	P.	Pte	Buchanan	J. MacG.	Maj	Burke	B. L.	Pte
Brown	P.	Dvr	Buchanan	T.	Pte	Burke	D. A.	Cpl
Brown	P. F.	Pte	Buck	G. T.	Dvr	Burke	J.	Dvr
Brown	R.	Pte	Buck	W. E.	Dvr	Burke	L. J.	WO I
Brown	R. A. 191004	Dvr	Buckell	C. E.	L/Cpl	Burke	M.	Pte
			Buckett	W. H.	Dvr	Burn	M. A.	Dvr
Brown	R. A. 14262710	Dvr	Buckingham, R. J.		Dvr	Burnet	W.	L/Cpl
			Buckingham, W. A.		L/Cpl	Burnett	A. G. R.	L/Cpl
Brown	R. D.	Cpl	Buckle	F. E.	S/Sjt	Burnett	E. C.	Dvr
Brown	R. F.	Pte	Buckle	W. H.	Capt	Burnett	H.	Pte
Brown	R. H.	L/Cpl	Buckley	A. H.	Dvr	Burnett	J. D.	Capt
Brown	R. J.	Cpl	Buckley	G.	Dvr	Burnett	T.	Pte
Brown	S. J.	L/Cpl	Buckley	H.	Dvr	Burnham	J. H.	Dvr
Brown	T. 3659864	Dvr	Buckley	J.	Dvr	Burnip	H.	Pte
			Buckley	W. J.	Dvr	Burns	A. W.	Dvr
Brown	T. 10669994	Dvr	Buckthorpe	T.	Dvr	Burns	B.	Dvr
			Budd	A. H.	Cpl	Burns	G. E.	Dvr

ROLL OF HONOUR

Burns	H. J.	Pte	Butterworth	P. E.	Dvr	Campbell	J.	Pte
Burns	J. D.	Dvr	Butterworth	S.	Dvr	Campbell	J.	Dvr
Burns	R.	Dvr	Butterworth	W.	Dvr		104895	
Burns	T.	Dvr	Button	G.	Dvr	Campbell	J.	Dvr
Burns	W.	L/Cpl	Buxton	J.	Cpl		91023	
Burnside	W.	Dvr	Byass	R. H.	Dvr	Campbell	J. B.	Pte
Burr	G. A.	Dvr	Bye	H.	Dvr	Campbell	J. B.	Cadet
Burr	L. G.	Cpl	Bye	R. R.	Pte	Campbell	P.	Dvr
Burrell	N.	Dvr	Byng	W.	Dvr	Campbell, R. M. St. C.		Pte
Burridge	E. T.	Dvr	Byrne	T. P.	Dvr	Campbell	T. F. E.	Dvr
Burridge	H. F.	Lt	Bysouth	R. J.	Sjt	Campbell	W. W.	Dvr
Burrough	J. S.	L/Cpl				Campion	H.	Dvr
Burrows	G. F. T.	Sjt				Canavan	L.	Cpl
Burrows	K.	Cpl	Cable	A. J.	Dvr	Candlin	W. J.	Pte
Burrows	L. T.	CQMS	Cabrelli	J. A.	L/Cpl	Cane	L. T.	Dvr
Burrows	W. J.	Dvr	Cadden	G. M.	Dvr	Cane	W. T.	S/Sjt
Burt	E. P.	Dvr	Caddy	A. S. D.	Dvr	Canham	H.	Dvr
Burt	F. J.	L/Sjt	Cadle	G. C.	Pte	Cann	J. A.	Dvr
Burt	V. L. P.	L/Cpl	Cadwallader, D.		Dvr	Canning	W.	Dvr
Burt	W. A.	Dvr	Cady	T. T.	Dvr	Cannon	D.	L/Cpl
Burtoft	J. T.	Dvr	Caffrey	F.	Dvr	Cannon	J.	Dvr
Burton	A. F.	Dvr	Cage	D. H.	Dvr	Cannon	R. W. G.	Dvr
Burton	F.	Pte	Cahill	T.	Dvr	Cannon	T. A.	Dvr
Burton	G. R.	Dvr	Cail	A. J.	Cpl	Cannon	T. F.	Dvr
Burton	J. L.	Dvr	Cain	J.	Dvr	Cannon	W. E.	Dvr
Burton	R. B.	Pte	Caine	F.	Dvr	Cant	H. H.	Pte
Burton	R. W.	Dvr	Caird	I. F.	Pte	Cantrill	D. N.	Dvr
Busby	E. J.	Dvr	Cairns	D. K.	Dvr	Capell	V. G.	Sjt
Bush	A. A.	L/Sjt	Cairns	J. I.	L/Cpl	Capes	A. E.	Dvr
Bush	K. A.	Dvr	Cairns	N.	L/Cpl	Capes	A. W.	Cpl
Bush	R.	Pte	Caisley	J. W.	Pte	Capps	D. R.	Dvr
Bush	T. H.	Dvr	Calcott	N. H.	Capt	Capstick	R.	Cpl
Bushby	H. T.	Dvr	Caldecott	L. H.	L/Cpl	Cardownie	A.	Sjt
Bushell	D. W.	Cpl	Calder	F.	Dvr	Carey	J.	Dvr
Bushen	R. J.	Dvr	Calder	J.	L/Cpl	Carey	T.	Pte
Buss	H. E.	Dvr	Calder	J. A.	Dvr	Cariss	R.	Dvr
Bussell	A. H.	Dvr	Calder	K. D.	Dvr	Carley	H. S.	Pte
Butcher	A.	L/Cpl	Calderwood	J. W.	Pte	Carley	L. C.	Dvr
Butcher	F. W.	Pte	Caldwell	J.	Sjt	Carlisle	E.	Cpl
Butcher	H. S.	Dvr	Callaghan	J.	Dvr	Carlisle	W. T.	Dvr
Butcher	L. S. D.	Dvr	Callander	J. McA.	Cpl	Carlo	K. F.	Pte
Butler	A.	Dvr	Callander	W. D.	Dvr	Carmichael	J.	WO II
Butler	C.	Pte	Callen	E. R.	Dvr	Carnegie	A.	Dvr
Butler	D. W.	Dvr	Callender	T.	Pte	Carpenter	C. E.	Pte
Butler	F. L.	Dvr	Callow	C. C.	Dvr	Carpenter	J.	Dvr
Butler	H.	Dvr	Calman	A.	Pte	Carpenter	W. C.	Dvr
Butler	J.	Dvr	Calveley	G.	Dvr	Carpenter	W. T.	Sjt
Butler	J. T.	Dvr	Calvert	G. W.	Pte	Carr	A. S.	WO I
Butler	W.	Dvr	Cameron	C. McF.	Dvr	Carr	E. H.	Cpl
Butley	T. A.	Cpl	Cameron	C. F.	L/Cpl	Carr	J. W.	Pte
Butlin	M. C.	Sjt	Cameron	J. R.	Sjt	Carr	R. H.	Capt
Butt	G. E.	Dvr	Cameron	W. A. E.	L/Cpl	Carr	R. R.	Pte
Butt	T. E.	Dvr	Cameron	D. H.	L/Cpl	Carr	W.	Dvr
Butten	J. S.	Dvr	Campbell	A. S.	Dvr	Carr	W. F.	Dvr
Butterfield	L.	L/Cpl	Campbell	B.	Capt	Carrick	R. J.	Dvr
Butterworth	A. G.	L/Cpl	Campbell	D.	Lt	Carrie	G. B.	Dvr
Butterworth	H.	Dvr	Campbell	D.	Pte	Carrington	D. J.	Dvr
Butterworth	J.	Dvr	Campbell	D. T.	Dvr	Carrol	D.	Dvr

ROLL OF HONOUR

Carrol	J. M.	Capt	Chadwick	W.	L/Sjt	Checketts	E. G.	Cpl
Carroll	J.	Pte	Chadwick	W.	Cpl	Cheeseman	D. H.	Dvr
Carruthers	J. P.	Lt	Chaffers	R.	L/Cpl	Cheeseman	E. L.	Pte
Carscadden	D.	Dvr	Chalcroft	G. J. A.	Dvr	Cheeseman	F. W.	L/Cpl
Carson	A. E.	Dvr	Chalk	F. G.	Dvr	Cheeseman	J. E. G.	Dvr
Carson	D.	Dvr	Chalk	G. W.	Pte	Cheeseman	M.	Dvr
Carson	J. G.	Sjt	Chalk	T. E.	Pte	Cheesman	A.	Dvr
Carter	A.	Dvr	Chalkley	J.	Dvr	Cheetham	J.	L/Cpl
Carter	H. 87547	Dvr	Chalmers	A. K.	Lt	Cheevers	T. J.	Pte
			Chalmers	D.	Dvr	Chell	R.	Cpl
Carter	H. 4977270	Dvr	Chalmers	T.	Dvr	Chelley	C. H.	Dvr
			Chalmers	W.	Dvr	Chellingworth, W.		Dvr
Carter	H. 235571	Dvr	Chamberlain, F. L.		Dvr	Chellumbrun, J. N.		Dvr
			Chamberlain, R.		Dvr	Chemery	L. G.	Pte
Carter	L. J.	Cpl	Chamberlain, R. J.		Dvr	Chenoweth	W. A.	Cpl
Carter	R. J.	Dvr	Chambers	A. W.	Dvr	Cherrett	A. E.	Dvr
Carter	R. R.	2/Lt	Chambers	G. J.	Pte	Cheslin	A. E.	Pte
Carter	R. S.	Dvr	Chambers	G. W.	Dvr	Chessar	J.	Dvr
Carter	T. R.	Dvr	Chambers	S.	Dvr	Chester	E.	Dvr
Carter	W.	Dvr	Chambers	W. A.	Dvr	Chettleburgh, H. J.		L/Cpl
Carter	W. C.	Dvr	Chammings	W. E.	Dvr	Chick	E. J. D.	Dvr
Carter	W. E.	L/Cpl	Chandler	E. W. F.	Cpl	Chilcott	F.	Dvr
Cartman	G.	Dvr	Chandler	F.	Dvr	Child	A. D. H.	Maj
Cartwright	A.	L/Cpl	Chandler	P. W.	Pte	Childs	A. E.	S/Sjt
Cartwright	G. E.	WO II	Channon	H.	Pte	Childs	I. J.	Dvr
Cartwright	H.	Dvr	Chaplin	W. J.	Dvr	Childs	S. J.	Dvr
Carver	A.	Pte	Chapman	A. E.	Dvr	Chilmaid	C. W.	Dvr
Carver	R. J.	Dvr	Chapman	A. G.	L/Cpl	Chilton	B.	Dvr
Case	S.	Pte	Chapman	A. J.	Dvr	Chilton	J.	Cpl
Case	T. L.	Dvr	Chapman	D. F.	Cpl	Chinnery	G. W.	Dvr
Casey	A. G.	WO II	Chapman	F. L.	Dvr	Chipchase	J.	Sjt
Cash	R. F.	Sjt	Chapman	F. W.	Dvr	Chipperfield, E. L.		Lt
Cass	V.	Dvr	Chapman	G. H.	Dvr	Chisholm	J. J.	Dvr
Castle	D. L.	Pte	Chapman	H.	Dvr	Chisholm	R.	Dvr
Castle	J. H.	L/Cpl	Chapman	H. F.	Dvr	Chisholm	W. H.	Dvr
Caswell	A. W. G.	L/Cpl	Chapman	L.	Dvr	Chisholme	G.	L/Cpl
Caswell	B. F.	Capt	Chapman	R.	Dvr	Chitty	A. R.	Dvr
Caswell	R. H.	Dvr	Chapman	R. H. D.	Dvr	Choat	A. E.	Dvr
Caswell	R. M.	L/Cpl	Chapman	S. R.	Dvr	Cholmondeley, H. A.		Cpl
Catchpole	F.	Dvr	Chapman	T. B.	Dvr	Chopping	G. N.	Lt
Cater	F. J.	Dvr	Chapman	W. E. C.	Sjt	Chrismas	C. W.	Dvr
Catt	H. J.	Sjt	Chapman	W. H.	Dvr	Christian	W. L.	Dvr
Cattell	A. J.	Dvr	Chapman	W. J.	Pte	Christie	J. C.	2/Lt
Cattell	C. A.	Dvr	Chapple	J. H.	Pte	Christison	J. E.	Cpl
Cattlin	C.	L/Cpl	Chard	A. T.	Lt	Christon	A.	Cpl
Caulfeild	W. H.	Maj	Charles	A. E.	Pte	Christopher	E. C.	Cpl
Caunt	F. A.	2/Lt	Charles	W.	Dvr	Christopher	V.	Dvr
Cause	L. E.	Dvr	Charlesworth, E. H.		Dvr	Chubb	K.	Dvr
Cavanagh	A.	Dvr	Charlesworth, F.		Cpl	Church	F. J.	Dvr
Cavanagh	S.	Dvr	Charlton	K. H.	Dvr	Church	G.	L/Cpl
Cave	A. F.	Sjt	Charlwood	H. S.	Sjt	Church	R.	Dvr
Cavens	J. W.	Dvr	Charman	A. J.	Dvr	Churcher	E. W.	S/Sjt
Caygill	B. J.	L/Cpl	Charnaud	K. A. W.	Maj	Churchill	R.	Pte
Cayless	E. F.	Dvr	Charnock	J. R.	Dvr	Churchyard, S. L.		Dvr
Cayton	J.	Dvr	Chase	W.	WO I	Chute	P.	Pte
Center	G. L. A. H.	Cpl	Chatburn	J. J.	Dvr	Civelli	J.	Dvr
Chadwick	G. W.	Dvr	Chaters	B.	Dvr	Clamp	R. E.	Dvr
Chadwick	J.	Dvr	Chatterton	A. J.	Pte	Clancy	F.	Cpl

ROLL OF HONOUR

Clancy	G. P.	Cpl	Clarke	T. F.	Pte	Cock	H.	Dvr
Clapham	C.	Dvr	Clarke	W. A.	Dvr	Cock	M. J.	Dvr
Clapperton	A. E.	Sjt	Clarkin	P. J.	WO II	Cockburn	A. L.	Maj
Clappison	D.	Dvr	Clarkson	A.	Pte	Cockburn	C.	Pte
Claridge	F.	Pte	Clarkson	H.	Dvr	Cockle	A. K.	Dvr
Claridge	R.	Dvr	Clatworthy	S. W.	Pte	Cockle	E. W. G.	Dvr
Clark	A.	Pte	Claxton	R. J.	Dvr	Cockles	F. W.	Pte
Clark	A.	Dvr	Clay	G. J. H.	Dvr	Cockling	J. W.	Dvr
Clark	B. G.	Lt	Clay	J. E.	Dvr	Cocks	C. H.	Dvr
Clark	D.	Pte	Clay	J. F.	Pte	Cocks	E.	Sjt
Clark	E.	Dvr	Clay	W.	Dvr	Cocorullo	A.	Dvr
Clark	E.	L/Cpl	Clay	W. R.	Dvr	Codd	L. W.	Dvr
Clark	E. R.	Dvr	Claydon	A. J.	Dvr	Codman	T. W.	L/Cpl
Clark	E. S.	Dvr	Cleary	A. W.	Pte	Codrington	H. S.	Dvr
Clark	G. W.	Dvr	Cleaver	J. P. F.	Dvr	Coe	W. E.	L/Cpl
Clark	H.	Pte	Cleaver	R. A.	Dvr	Coffey	C. M.	Sjt
Clark	H. J.	Cpl	Clegg	A.	Sjt	Coffey	G. P.	Cpl
Clark	H. M.	Dvr	Clegg	J. H.	Dvr	Coffey	P.	Dvr
Clark	H. W.	Dvr	Clegg	L.	Sjt	Coggin	A. W.	Dvr
Clark	J.	Cpl	Clement	D.	Cpl	Cohen	A.	S/Sjt
Clark	J. M.	Pte	Clements	L. H.	Dvr	Cohen	E.	Dvr
Clark	J. S.	Dvr	Clements	R. N.	L/Cpl	Cohen	J.	Pte
Clark	L. J.	Cpl	Clements	W. B.	Dvr	Coker	C. H.	Dvr
Clark	N. H. J.	Dvr	Clemett	L. G.	L/Cpl	Coker	J. R. W.	Dvr
Clark	N. M.	Dvr	Clemow	A. J.	Dvr	Colby	G.	Dvr
Clark	O. E.	Dvr	Clewlow	G. L.	L/Cpl	Coldrick	S. J.	Dvr
Clark	P.	Sjt	Clews	B. H.	Pte	Cole	A. J.	Dvr
Clark	P. R.	Dvr	Clews	J.	Dvr	Cole	C. F.	Pte
Clark	R. M.	Sjt	Clews	K.	Cpl	Cole	C. J.	Dvr
Clark	S. B.	Dvr	Cliffe	J.	Dvr		M.M.	
Clark	W. 64958	Dvr	Cliffe	L.	Dvr	Cole	F. G.	Dvr
			Clifford	R. F.	Dvr	Cole	F. J. 10668296	Dvr
Clark	W. 246344	Dvr	Clift	E.	WO I			
			Clifton	W.	Cpl	Cole	F. J. 3970953	Dvr
Clark	W. C.	Dvr	Clist	H. J.	Pte			
Clark	W. G.	Dvr	Clockart	D.	Capt	Cole	G. W.	Dvr
Clark	W. P.	Dvr	Cloke	N.	Lt	Cole	J. F.	WO I
Clarke	A.	Dvr	Close	H. C.	WO II	Cole	J. O.	Sjt
Clarke	A. G.	Sjt	Clough	E. R.	Lt	Cole	P.	Dvr
Clarke	A. R.	Pte	Clough	G. H.	Dvr	Cole	R. P.	Dvr
Clarke	C. J.	Dvr	Clouston	R. H. S.	Cpl	Coleman	D. H.	Dvr
Clarke	D.	Dvr	Clover	J.	Pte	Coleman	J.	Sjt
Clarke	E.	Dvr	Clow	J. R.	L/Cpl	Coleman	L. E. S.	Lt
Clarke	E. A.	Dvr	Coakley	W. J.	Dvr	Coleman	S.	Dvr
Clarke	E. C.	Capt	Coalflax	J. W.	Dvr	Coles	C. P.	Dvr
Clarke	F.	Dvr	Coates	A. F.	Sjt	Coles	E.	Dvr
Clarke	F.	Sjt	Coates	C. E.	Dvr	Coles	F. J. L.	Cpl
Clarke	G.	Pte	Coates	D. 131774	Pte	Coles	V. S.	Dvr
Clarke	G.	Cpl				Coley	C. F.	Dvr
Clarke	G. E.	Pte	Coates	D. 132832	Pte	Colgate	G. B.	Cpl
Clarke	H.	Dvr				Colkin	E. B.	Dvr
Clarke	J.	Dvr	Coates	D. W. S.	Dvr	Collard	S. J.	Dvr
Clarke	J.	L/Cpl	Coates	J. G.	Dvr	Colledge	E. H.	Cpl
Clarke	J. C.	Dvr	Cobbett	D. W.	Dvr	Colledge	H. W.	Dvr
Clarke	J. L.	Dvr	Cobbett	E. J. H.	Pte	Collett	F. B.	Dvr
Clarke	J. P.	Pte	Cobby	C. P.	Dvr	Collett	F. C.	Capt
Clarke	R. H.	Cpl	Cochrane	D.	Maj	Collett	T. W.	Sjt
Clarke	S.	Dvr	Cochrane, J. J. McM.		Pte	Collett	W. F.	Dvr

ROLL OF HONOUR

Collier	B.	Pte	Constable	F. H.	Pte	Cope	W.	Dvr
Collier	F. A. C.	Dvr	Constable	L. J.	Dvr	Copeland	E. C.	Dvr
Collier	H. J.	Cpl	Conway	A.	Dvr	Copley	C. E.	Dvr
Collier	J.	Dvr	Conway	D. S.	Dvr	Copley	W. J.	S/Sjt
Colligan	F.	Sjt	Conway	F. H. J.	Cpl	Coppick	S.	Dvr
Collin	J. M.	Cpl	Conway	G.	Dvr	Coppin	J. J.	Pte
Collinge	W. R.	Dvr	Conway	P. F.	WO II	Coppins	W. E.	Dvr
Collins	B.	Dvr	Cook	A. L.	Dvr	Copson	H.	S/Sjt
Collins	C. J.	Dvr	Cook	C. F.	Dvr	Cordell	F. A.	Dvr
Collins	J.	L/Cpl	Cook	C. J.	Cpl	Cordiner	G. S.	L/Cpl
Collins	J.	Dvr	Cook	D.	Dvr	Coreless	R. H.	Dvr
Collins	J. K.	Cpl	Cook	D. B.	Dvr	Corker	G.	Cpl
Collins	L. J. F.	Lt	Cook	E. G. B.	Dvr	Corker	M. L.	Dvr
Collins	M. J.	Dvr	Cook	G.	Dvr	Corlett	J. A.	Cpl
Collins	P. B.	Pte	Cook	G.	Capt	Corley	W.	Dvr
Collins	R. N.	Dvr	Cook	H. C. J.	Lt	Cornaby	F. A.	Dvr
Collins	S. F.	Dvr	Cook	J.	Dvr	Cornell	F.	Cpl
Collins	T. H.	Dvr		6030301		Corner	T.	Dvr
Collins	T. S.	Dvr	Cook	J.	Dvr	Cornes	H.	Dvr
Collins	W.	Dvr		200031		Corney	W.	Pte
Collins	W. R.	Dvr	Cook	J. R. N.	Dvr	Cornish	F. J.	Pte
Collinson	E.	Dvr	Cook	K.	Pte	Cornish	J.	Pte
Collis	C. T.	Pte	Cook	M. W.	Dvr	Cornish	W. H.	Dvr
Collomosse	J.	Pte	Cook	R. B. A.	Pte	Cornwell	S. W.	Cpl
Collyer	J. H.	Dvr	Cook	R. F.	Dvr	Corrick	P. A.	Dvr
Colman	R. A.	Pte	Cook	S.	Dvr	Corry	S. J. T.	S/Sjt
Colmer	T. L.	Cpl	Cook	T. H.	Dvr	Cort	W.	Dvr
Coltman	N. B.	Dvr	Cook	V. D.	Dvr	Cossins	L.	L/Cpl
Colwill	L. C.	Pte	Cooke	F. R.	Dvr	Cosson	R. I.	Sjt
Colyer	F.M.C.H.	Lt	Cooke	J.	Pte	Costa	M.	Sjt
Comber	K.	Dvr	Cooke	J. E.	Lt	Costall	F.	Dvr
Comber	L. C.	Pte	Cooke	R. C.	Pte	Costigan	J. L.	Cpl
Comfort	P. R.	Cpl	Coomber	S. H.	Dvr	Cottam	R. D.	Pte
Comino	D.	Pte	Coombes	C. W.	Dvr	Cottam	H.	Dvr
Comley	E. J.	Pte	Coombes	R. A. G.	Dvr	Cottell	C. A.	Dvr
Comley	W. J.	S/Sgt	Coombs	E. B.	Dvr	Cotter	W. J.	Pte
Commander	D. R.	Dvr	Coombs	E. S.	Pte	Cotterill	R. L.	Pte
Comrie	P.	Dvr	Coombs	W. T.	Pte	Cottingham	W. H.	Dvr
Conboy	J.	Dvr	Cooney	M.	Dvr	Cottle	W.	Sjt
Coney	E. A.	Dvr	Cooper	A. L.	Cpl	Cotton	P. A.	Dvr
Conn	J.	Dvr	Cooper	C. J.	Pte	Cottrell	B. D.	Pte
Connell	F. W.	Maj	Cooper	C. L.	Dvr	Cottrell	T.	Cpl
Connell	R.	Dvr	Cooper	E. R.	Pte	Couchman	W. T. J.	Dvr
Connell	T.	Dvr	Cooper	F. A.	Dvr	Coulter	G. B.	Pte
Connelly	A. W.	Pte	Cooper	F. J. E.	L/Cpl	Coulthard	I.	Pte
Connelly	C. E.	Dvr	Cooper	H. H.	L/Cpl	Coulthard	W. J.	Dvr
Connelly	W. McD.	Pte	Cooper	J.	Dvr	Coulton	G. J.	Pte
Conner	J.	Dvr	Cooper	J. L.	Dvr	Counsell	A. S.	WO II
Connolly	E. F. G.	Dvr	Cooper	J. W.	Pte	Couper	R. H.	Dvr
Connolly	J. E.	Dvr	Cooper	L.	Dvr	Coupland	T.	Dvr
Connolly	J. J.	Dvr	Cooper	L. H.	Cpl	Court	H.	Dvr
Connolly	T.	Dvr	Cooper	M. W.	Dvr	Court	L. C.	Cpl
Connor	A.	Sjt	Cooper	R. A.	Cpl	Courtier	W. T.	Dvr
Connor	B. H.	Dvr	Cooper	R. F.	Cpl	Courtney	J.	Pte
Connor	J.	Dvr	Cooper	S.	Dvr	Cousins	J. K.	Dvr
Connor	S. J.	Dvr	Coote	H. A. W.	L/Cpl	Cousins	J. W. C.	Capt
Connor	T.	Dvr	Cooze	A. J.	Dvr	Coussens	R. C.	Dvr
Connor	T. C.	Dvr	Cope	C.	Dvr	Coutts	J.	Dvr

ROLL OF HONOUR

Coutts	K. G. S.	2/Lt	Crawshaw	G. C. B.	Dvr	Crute	A. E.	Sjt
Coutts	R. B.	Dvr	Crawshaw	H.	Dvr	Cubbin	H.	Dvr
Couzens	R. T. A.	Capt	Creagh	J. F.	Cpl	Cule	R. T.	Pte
Cove	C. H.	Cpl	Crealock	E. J.	Dvr	Cullen	E.	Dvr
Coventry	N. C.	L/Cpl	Creed	C.	Dvr	Cullen	E. J.	Dvr
Coventry	R. B.	Sjt	Creed	E. W.	Dvr	Cullen	W. J.	Dvr
Cowan	A.	Dvr	Creer	H.	Pte	Culley	J.	Pte
Cowan	R.	Dvr	Creevy	D. W.	Dvr	Cullinane	J.	Cpl
Coward	C. G.	Dvr	Cressey	E. D.	Pte	Cullum	G. E.	Lt
Coward	C. H.	Sjt	Cresswell	H. H.	Dvr	Culyer	G. T.	Dvr
Coward	T. L.	Pte	Cresswell	S.	Dvr	Cumming	R. McM.	Pte
Cowburn	C.	Dvr	Cresswell	W.	Dvr	Cummings	W. B.	Dvr
Cowell	H. W.	Pte	Crewe	W. L.	Cpl	Cundall	F. G.	WO II
Cowell	J.	Dvr	Crickett	G. F.	Dvr	Cundy	H. J.	Pte
Cowell	R.	Cpl	Crisp	A.	Dvr	Cunliffe	J. H.	Dvr
Cowey	G.	Dvr	Crispin	W.	Pte	Cunnew	A. E. A.	Dvr
Cowland	D. J.	Dvr	Critchley	E.	Dvr	Cunningham, C.		Dvr
Cowley	H. E.	Pte	Croad	G.	Dvr	Cunningham, G.		L/Sjt
Cowley	J.	Dvr	Crocker	T. H.	Pte	Cunningham, J.		Pte
Cowling	E. J.	Pte	Crockett	D. G.	Sjt	Cunningham, J. A.		Dvr
Cowling	S.	Dvr	Crockett	F. A. W.	Lt	Cunningham, S.		Pte
Cowtan	J. V.	Dvr	Cronin	H.	Dvr	Curnow	T. E.	Lt
Cox	B. L.	Dvr	Crook	W. E.	Dvr	Currey	R. F. R.	Capt
Cox	C. H.	S/Sjt	Crooks	B. D.	Dvr	Currie	D.	Dvr
Cox	E. R.	Dvr	Crooks	J. C.	Cpl	Currie	H.	Sjt
Cox	F. R.	Sjt	Crooks	R. W.	Dvr	Currie	T. A.	Pte
Cox	J.	Dvr	Crooks	W.	S/Sjt	Currow	F. R.	Dvr
Cox	J. W.	Dvr	Crosby	A.	Dvr	Curry	J. E.	Pte
Cox	R.	Dvr	Crosby	R. H.	Capt	Curry	R. F.	Pte
Cox	R. G.	Dvr	Cross	A.	Pte	Curson	B. G.	Dvr
Cox	S.	Sjt	Cross	A. G. J.	Dvr	Curtis	F. J. W.	Dvr
Cox	S. J.	Dvr	Cross	W. C.	Dvr	Curtis	G. L.	L/Cpl
Cox	W. C.	Maj	Cross	W. D.	Dvr	Curtis	J. A.	Pte
Coyle	J. H.	Pte	Cross	W. H.	Dvr	Curtis	J. J.	Dvr
Coyle	W.	Dvr	Crossland	A. O.	Pte	Curtis	R.	Dvr
Coyne	W.	WO I	Crossley	E.	Dvr	Curtis	S.	Dvr
Crabb	A. E.	Sjt	Crossley	G.	Dvr	Cushion	R.	Dvr
Crabb	W. T.	Dvr	Crossley	P.	L/Cpl	Cuthbert	C. E.	Dvr
Crabbe	D. H.	Dvr	Crossley	R.	Dvr	Cutting	S.	Dvr
Crabtree	F.	WO I	Crossley	W. T.	Dvr	Cuzner	N. J.	Pte
Crabtree	J. F. L.	Dvr	Crouch	S.	Dvr	Cyples	L.	Sjt
Cracknell	H. A. C.	Dvr	Croucher	L. G.	Pte			
Cracknell	W. H.	Cpl	Croudy	H.	Dvr			
Cragg	T.	Cpl	Crow	R. G.	Dvr	Dack	E. H.	Pte
Craig	E.	Cpl	Crowder	T. E.	Dvr	Dackombe	R.	Dvr
Craig	W. L.	Cpl	Crowe	G. A. M.	Dvr	Daddy	J. W.	Dvr
Craigs	G. W.	L/Cpl	Crowe	H. W.	Sjt	Dadswell	D.	L/Cpl
Crankshaw	J. J.	L/Cpl	Crowther	A.	Dvr	Dagley	H.	Sjt
Crapnell	H. L. J.	Dvr	Crowther	D.	L/Cpl	Dagnell	R. J.	Pte
Craven	C. H.	Dvr	Crowther	S.	Dvr	Dalby	J. A.	Dvr
Craven	G.	Cpl	Crudgington, R.		Dvr	Dale	A.	Dvr
Craven	P.	Dvr	Cruickshank A.		Pte	Dale	C. A.	Dvr
Crawford	F. J.	Cpl	Cruickshank C.		L/Cpl	Dale	E. H.	Dvr
Crawford	H.	Pte	Cruickshank J.		Pte	Dalgarno	W.	Dvr
Crawford	J.	Dvr	Cruikshank J. B.		Dvr	Dalgarno	W. J.	Pte
Crawford	R. M.	Dvr	Crump	J.	Dvr	Dally	R. A.	Pte
Crawley	F. J. A.	L/Cpl	Crump	L. G.	Dvr	Dalton	C. W.	Pte
Crawley	R. A.	Dvr	Cruse	H. L.	Sjt	Dalton	E.	Dvr

ROLL OF HONOUR

Dalton	J. C.	Dvr	Davies	J. B.	Pte	Dawson	A.	Dvr
Daly	R. O.	2/Lt	Davies	J. E. H.	Dvr		185422	
Damms	H.	L/Cpl	Davies	J. H.	Pte	Dawson	A. G.	Cpl
Danby	A. G. G.	2/Lt	Davies	J. T.	Dvr	Dawson	E.	Dvr
Dance	A. H.	Dvr		190063		Dawson	G. E.	Cpl
Dance	A. W. D.	Dvr	Davies	J. T.	Dvr	Dawson	J.	Lt
Dance	R.	Dvr		50157		Dawson	N.	Pte
Dangerfield	J.	Sjt	Davies	L.	L/Cpl	Dawson	P.	Dvr
Dangerfield	W. J.	Pte	Davies	L.	Pte	Dawson	R.	Dvr
Daniel	F. K.	Dvr	Davies	N. H.	Pte	Dawson	S.	Dvr
Daniel	J. H.	Capt	Davies	P. J. G.	Dvr	Dawson	T. H. S.	Dvr
Daniel	M. C. C.	Capt	Davies	R.	Dvr	Dawson	W.	Dvr
Daniels	C. W.	2/Lt	Davies	R.	L/Cpl	Dawson	W. A.	Dvr
Daniels	H. B.	Dvr	Davies	R. J. H.	Dvr	Day	A. E. J.	Dvr
Daniels	H. G.	Dvr	Davies	R. W.	Dvr	Day	A. N.	Sjt
Daniels	H. W.	Cpl	Davies	S.	Dvr	Day	C. P.	Dvr
Danks	E. J.	Cpl	Davies	T.	Sjt	Day	D. A.	Pte
Danter	R. W.	Maj	Davies	T. E.	Dvr	Day	G.	Dvr
Darbin	R. E.	Dvr	Davies	T. S.	Dvr	Day	K. I.	Pte
Darby	D. W.	Dvr	Davies	W. C.	Capt	Day	P. R.	Dvr
Darby	K. R.	Dvr	Davies	W. I.	Dvr	Day	V. J.	Dvr
Darcy	P.	WO I	Davies	W. T. G.	Dvr	Day	W. A.	Pte
Darcy	R. C.	Dvr	Davis	A.	L/Cpl	Day	W. E.	Dvr
Dare	E. W.	Sjt	Davis	A.	Dvr	Day	W. W.	Dvr
Dare	F. C.	Sjt	Davis	A.	Pte	Daykin	A. G.	Dvr
Darke	A. G.	L/Cpl	Davis	A. C.	Pte	DeLa Haye	M. P.	Dvr
Darnell	S. A. J.	Pte	Davis	E. A.	Dvr	Deacon	H. L.	2/Lt
Darrington	H.	Cpl	Davis	F.	Dvr	Deadman	T.	Dvr
Darvell	A. C.	Dvr	Davis	F. D.	Dvr	Deamer	S.	Dvr
Dasson	C.	Dvr	Davis	G.	Dvr	Dean	A. G.	L/Cpl
Davenport	A. G.	Dvr	Davis	H.	Pte	Dean	E. F.	Dvr
Davey	A. E.	Pte	Davis	H.	Dvr	Dean	G.	Dvr
Davey	V.	Dvr	Davis	H.	Dvr	Dean	H.	Dvr
Davey	W. A.	L/Cpl		95773		Dean	P.	WO II
Davey	W. L.	Pte	Davis	H.	Dvr	Dean	R.	Dvr
Davidge	G.	Pte		14703038		Dean	W.	Dvr
Davidson	A.	Dvr	Davis	H. C.	Cpl	Dean	W. J.	Pte
Davidson	A. F.	Pte	Davis	H. C.	Dvr	Deans	T. S.	Sjt
Davidson	K. J.	Dvr	Davis	H. W.	Dvr	Deans	W.	Dvr
Davidson	R.	Dvr	Davis	J.	Dvr	Dearden	F.	Dvr
Davidson	W.	L/Cpl	Davis	L.	Dvr	Dearsley	B. A.	Capt
Davies	A.	Pte	Davis	M. J.	Dvr	Death	A. C.	Dvr
Davies	B. N.	Dvr	Davis	O.	Dvr	Debenham	N. E.	WO II
Davies	C. O.	Dvr	Davis	R.	Cpl	Deck	W.	Dvr
Davies	C. R.	Pte	Davis	S.	Cpl	Dedman	F. C. F.	Dvr
Davies	D. M.	Dvr	Davis	W. H.	Cpl	Deeley	J.	L/Sjt
Davies	E.	Sjt	Davis	W. J.	Pte	Deer	J. R.	Cpl
	50120		Davis	W. R.	Pte	Deighton	C.	Cpl
Davies	E.	Dvr	Davison	E.	Dvr	Delaney	C.	Pte
Davies	E.	Sjt	Davison	J. T.	L/Cpl	Delaney	J.	Dvr
	3647812		Davison	W. S.	Dvr	Dell	R. G. W.	Dvr
Davies	E. P.	L/Cpl	Davitt	C.	Dvr	Dellanzo	G.	Cpl
Davies	G. E.	Cpl	Dawes	C. R.	Dvr	Dempsey	T.	Dvr
Davies	H.	Pte	Dawkins	T. J.	Dvr	Denby	L.	Dvr
Davies	H. C.	L/Cpl	Dawks	H. H. G.	Dvr	Denford	W. H.	Dvr
Davies	H. G.	Sjt	Dawney	A. J.	Dvr	Denison	F. C.	Dvr
Davies	H. G.	Cpl	Dawson	A.	Dvr	Dennett	B. N.	Sjt
Davies	J.	Dvr		114779		Dennis	A. G.	Pte

ROLL OF HONOUR

Dennis	D. E.	Dvr	Dingley	J. C.	Dvr	Doughty	H. J.	Dvr
Dennis	J.	Dvr	Dingwall	C.	Dvr	Douglas	H. K.	Pte
Dennis	J. E.	Pte	Dingwall	H.	Dvr	Douglas	T. L.	Dvr
Dennis	J. H.	Dvr	Dipnall	J. D.	Dvr	Dove	B. S.	Capt
Dennis	R. E. A.	Pte	Disdel	A. O.	Dvr	Dover	W. E.	Dvr
Dennis	R. W.	Dvr	Disley	L. R.	Dvr	Dow	R.	Dvr
Dennison	L. T.	Dvr	Ditch	L. G.	L/Cpl	Dowding	K. B.	Cpl
Denton	B. C. B.	Dvr	Dixey	E. C.	Dvr	Dowland	A. E.	Dvr
Denton	C. A.	Dvr	Dixon	A. L.	Pte	Dowle	V. A.	Cpl
Denton	D. E.	Dvr	Dixon	C. J.	Dvr	Dowley	T. H.	Dvr
Denyer	D.	Dvr	Dixon	G. A.	Pte	Dowling	A. E. K.	Dvr
Denyer	V. G.	Sjt	Dixon	N.	Dvr	Downie	H. H.	Dvr
Depledge	F. R.	2/Lt	Dixon	R. J.	Sjt	Downie	J. W.	Dvr
Depper	J.	L/Cpl	Dixon	W.	Dvr	Downing	R. G.	Dvr
Deprose	D.	Dvr	Dobbins	A.	Dvr	Downes	C. C. M.	Pte
Derbyshire	W. W. C.	Pte	Dobbs	K. W.	Dvr	Downs	R.	Dvr
Derham	L. G.	Pte	Dobbs	W.	Dvr	Dowse	S.	Dvr
Derwas	T.	Dvr	Dobinson	W.	Dvr	Dowsett	D. A. L.	Pte
Deslandes	W. E.	Dvr	Doble	A. J.	Pte	Dowsing	W.	Dvr
Devenish	E. T.	Dvr	Dobney	J. G.	S/Sjt	Dowson	J.	Dvr
Deverell	S. E.	Sjt	Dobson	E.	Dvr	Dowthwaite	J. H.	L/Cpl
Deveson	R. G.	Sjt	Dobson	P. E.	Dvr	Doxford	E. M.	Capt
Devine	J.	Dvr	Dobson	R. A.	Dvr	Doyle	B. F.	Pte
Devine	J. H.	Dvr	Dobson	W.	Dvr	Doyle	C.	Pte
Devine	P. H.	Pte	Docherty	A. F.	L/Cpl	Doyle	C. A.	L/Cpl
Devlin	J. B.	L/Cpl	Docherty	B.	Dvr	Doyle	F.	Cpl
Devonshire	W. G.	Pte	Docherty	C.	Dvr	Doyle	P. E.	Dvr
Dewar	D. A.	L/Cpl	Docherty	D.	Dvr	Doyle	P. J. B.	Pte
Dewey	G. R.	Pte	Docherty	F.	Pte	Drake	F. R.	L/Cpl
Dexter	P.	Pte	Docherty	W.	Dvr	Drake	H. J. F.	Dvr
Diamond	P.	Pte	Dodd	E. L.	Dvr	Drane	G. W.	Dvr
Dibben	A.	Pte	Dodd	G.	Pte	Draper	G. P.	L/Cpl
Dibble	H. G.	Dvr	Dodd	J. H.	Lt	Draper	O. G.	Dvr
Dick	A. F.	Pte	Dodge	W. E.	L/Cpl	Draper	R. J.	Dvr
Dick	S. W.	Dvr	Dodson	G. T.	Dvr	Draper	T. M.	Lt
Dickie	A.	Dvr	Doe	C.	Pte	Draper	W. A.	Dvr
Dickie	W.	Sjt	Doel	A. E.	Dvr	Dray	H.	Pte
Dickinson	D.	Pte	Doherty	J. W.	Dvr	Drew	F. M.	Dvr
Dickinson	J. F.	Dvr	Dolan	J.	Pte	Drew	R. L. H.	2/Lt
Dickinson	R. G.	Dvr	Dolphin	R. D.	Pte	Drewett	A. C. W.	L/Cpl
Dickinson	S. 183399	Dvr	Donald	D. T.	Pte	Drinkwater	W. C. E.	Pte
Dickinson	S. 53657	Dvr	Donald	F.	Sjt	Driscoll	G. P.	Dvr
Dickinson	W.	Dvr	Donald	H. J.	Dvr	Drongoole	T.	Dvr
Dickman	S. E.	Sjt	Donaldson	J. J.	Dvr	Drower	F. W.	Dvr
Dickson	J.	Cpl	Donaldson	J. M.	Dvr	Drummond	A.	Dvr
Dickson	J. J.	S/Sjt	Donne	C. E.	Sjt	Drummond	V.	Pte
Didcock	J. F.	Dvr	Donnell	L. H.	Cpl	Drury	J.	Dvr
Digby	J. F.	Dvr	Donnelly	D.	Dvr	Drury	V.	Dvr
Diggle	R.	Sjt	Donovan	C. P. M.	2/Lt	Dryden	J. W.	Pte
Diggles	W.	Dvr	Dooley	J. J.	Dvr	Dryden	W. E.	Cpl
Dight	W. A. R.	2/Lt	Dooley	R. J.	Pte	Dryer	E. C. C.	L/Cpl
Dillon	R. J.	Cpl	Doonan	J.	Dvr	Drysdale	J.	Sjt
Dimmick	D. R.	Sjt	Dooner	E.	Cpl	Duck	L.	L/Cpl
Dimond	F. M.	Capt	Doorey	W. C.	Cpl	Ducker	J.	S/Sjt
Dimond	H. W.	Sjt	Dorkes	T. S.	Dvr	Duckett	A. G. F.	2/Lt
Dingley	E. R.	Pte	Dorris	C.	Sjt	Duckett	C. W.	Pte
			Doubleday	R.	Cpl	Duckett	W. E.	Dvr
			Dougan	W. M.	Dvr	Duddle	S.	Dvr

ROLL OF HONOUR

Duddridge	C.	Dvr	Dwyer	B. C.	Cpl	Edmunds	D. G.	Pte
Dudson	R.	L/Cpl	Dwyer	E. G.	Pte	Edmunds	H. J.	Dvr
Duerdon	R. L.	Dvr	Dyas	L. W.	Sjt	Edmunds	T.	Sjt
Duff	B. G.	S/Sjt	Dye	E.	Pte	Edmunds	T.	Dvr
Duff	W. W.	Pte	Dye	L. W.	Dvr	Edwards	A.	Dvr
Duffy	J. F.	Dvr	Dye	W. H.	Pte	Edwards	A.	L/Cpl
Duffy	P.	Pte	Dyer	D.	Dvr	Edwards	A. H.	Dvr
Dugait	J. M.	Dvr	Dyer	H.	Pte	Edwards	B.	Dvr
Duggan	A.	Dvr	Dyer	H.	Dvr	Edwards	B. C.	Dvr
Dukes	C. V.	Dvr	Dyke	H.	Dvr	Edwards	C.	Dvr
Dumas	G. J.	Cpl	Dyke	R. E.	Cpl	Edwards	C. A.	Dvr
Dumbleton	J.	Pte	Dykins	O. K.	Dvr	Edwards	D. M.	Pte
Duncan	D. M.	Dvr	Dyson	F.	Dvr	Edwards	E. A.	Pte
Duncan	H.	Dvr				Edwards	E. C.	L/Cpl
Duncan	J. C.	Dvr				Edwards	E. G.	Sjt
Duncan	R. C.	Dvr	Eade	G. W. E.	Sjt	Edwards	F. A.	Dvr
Duncan	S. R.	Dvr	Eade	H. H.	Dvr	Edwards	G.	Dvr
Duncan	W. H.	Cpl	Eadie	G.	Pte	Edwards	G. J.	Pte
Dunford	W. L.	Dvr	Eager	W. S.	Cpl	Edwards	G. J. C.	S/Sjt
Dunlop	A.	Dvr	Eagle	B.	Pte	Edwards	H.	Pte
Dunlop	J.	Dvr	Eagle	S. G.	Dvr	Edwards	H. A.	Lt
Dunlop	M. R.	Capt	Eagleston	J. N.	Dvr	Edwards	J.	Dvr
Dunn	A.	Dvr	Eales	L.	Dvr	Edwards	J. J.	Dvr
Dunn	F. 69617	Dvr	Eamer	G. T.	Cpl	Edwards	J. O.	Sjt
			Earey	C. W.	Cpl	Edwards	K. J.	Dvr
Dunn	F. 130124	Dvr	Earl	R. J.	WO I	Edwards	R. G.	Dvr
			Early	F. J.	Pte	Edwards	R. H. A.	Cpl
Dunn	H. E.	Pte	Earnshaw	J. R.	Dvr	Edwards	R. J.	Pte
Dunn	J. 14742913	Dvr	Earp	E.	Pte	Edwards	S. A.	Pte
			Earthy	A. S.	Pte	Edwards	S. G.	Pte
Dunn	J. 124848	Dvr	Eary	G. R.	Cpl	Edwards	S. T.	Dvr
			Eastham	F. C.	Sjt	Edwards	T.	Dvr
Dunn	R. B.	Dvr	Eastman	E. J.	Pte	Edwards	W. A.	Dvr
Dunn	R. W.	Pte	Eastwood	H.	Dvr	Edwards	W. E. J.	Pte
Dunn	S. M.	Dvr	Eastwood	R. F.	Dvr	Edwards	W. H.	Pte
Dunn	T.	Dvr	Eastwood	W.	Dvr	Edwards	W. J.	Dvr
Dunn	W. F.	Dvr	Eatock	G. B.	Dvr	Edwards	W. L.	Dvr
Dunne	J. T.	S/Sjt	Eaton	A.	Cpl	Eggie	W. J.	Dvr
Dunnigan	C.	Dvr	Eaves	W. H.	Dvr	Egginton	A. E.	Dvr
Dunning	L. T.	Dvr	Eccles	A. W.	Dvr	Egle	C.	Cpl
Dunning	T. N.	L/Cpl	Eccles	T.	Dvr	Eglin	E. B.	Pte
Dunningham	R. H.	Lt	Eccles	T. H.	Dvr	Eivers	D.	Dvr
Dunster	T. H.	Dvr	Ecott	J. B.	Pte	Element	S. E.	Dvr
Dunthorne	G. H. R.	L/Cpl	Eddershaw	E. R.	L/Cpl	Elford	S. W.	Capt
Dupvy	T. P.	Dvr	Eddington	B. H.	Dvr	Ellacott	J. E.	Dvr
Durack	L. C.	Dvr	Eddy	T. H.	Dvr	Ellams	L. J.	Dvr
Durbridge	J. A.	Dvr	Ede	R. J.	Dvr	Ellicott	S. F.	WO I
Durkin	J. E.	Lt	Eden	C.	Pte	Elliot	A.	Dvr
Durkin	T.	Dvr	Eden	C. B.	Capt	Elliott	A. J.	Dvr
Durrant	C. A. H.	Dvr	Edgar	R.	Dvr	Elliott	C. E.	Dvr
Durrant	D. P.	Cpl	Edgell	W. A.	Dvr	Elliott	E. W.	Pte
Durrant	J. W.	Dvr	Edgerley	C. B.	Lt	Elliott	F. J.	Dvr
Durrant	W. A.	Dvr	Edginton	F. A.	Dvr	Elliott	G. A.	Cpl
Durward	L. C.	Dvr	Edmonds	E. V.	Dvr	Elliott	G. A.	Dvr
Duthie	J.	Dvr	Edmonds	G. G.	Dvr	Elliott	H. E. A.	Dvr
Dutton	A.	Dvr	Edmondson	F.	Dvr	Elliott	J. B.	Lt
Dutton	N.	Dvr	Edmonston	A. W.	Dvr	Elliott	J. C.	Pte
Duvall	C. E.	L/Cpl	Edmunds	A.	Pte	Elliott	J. D.	Dvr

ROLL OF HONOUR

Elliott	R.	Dvr	Erskine	A.	L/Cpl	Evans	W.	Dvr
Elliott	W.	Dvr	Erwin	T. H.	Dvr	Evans	W. D.	Dvr
Elliott	W. H.	Pte	Esp	W. F.	Cpl	Evans	W. E.	Capt
Ellis	A. A. B.	Capt	Essen	G.	Dvr	Evans	W. F.	Dvr
Ellis	A. D.	Cpl	Etheridge	H. G.	Dvr	Evans	W. H.	Dvr
Ellis	A. E.	Pte	Etherington	J.	Dvr	Evans	W. R.	Lt
Ellis	A. F.	Pte	Etherington	T.	Pte	Eveleigh	O. F.	Dvr
Ellis	C.	Dvr	Eustace	A. N.	Dvr	Evenden	F. C.	Dvr
Ellis	C. D.	Sjt	Eustace	C. H.	Dvr	Evens	G. W.	Dvr
Ellis	D. E.	Dvr	Eustace	F. S.	Dvr	Everingham	J. E.	Dvr
Ellis	D. G.	L/Cpl	Evans	A.	Dvr	Everitt	R. C.	Dvr
Ellis	E. L.	Dvr	Evans	A. E.	Dvr	Everitt	S. F.	Pte
Ellis	F.	Dvr	Evans	A. H. R.	Dvr	Everton	J. T.	Dvr
Ellis	F. F.	Dvr	Evans	A. J.	Dvr	Ewart	A. J.	Dvr
Ellis	G. A. T.	Pte	Evans	A. J.	Pte	Ewers	G. E.	Pte
Ellis	J. C.	Pte	Evans	C. E.	Pte	Eyre	A. G.	L/Cpl
Ellis	J. R.	Dvr	Evans	C. S.	Dvr	Ezekiel	I. C.	Cpl
Ellis	P.	Dvr	Evans	D.	Dvr			
Ellis	R.	Dvr	Evans	D. C.	Dvr			
Ellis	R.	Pte	Evans	D. E.	Pte	Fahie	C. T.	Pte
Ellis	T.	Dvr	Evans	D. H.	WO II	Fahy	J. W.	Dvr
Ellis	V.	Sjt	Evans	E.	Dvr	Fail	W.	Dvr
Ellis	W.	Cpl	Evans	E. L.	Pte	Faint	J. W.	Dvr
Ellis	W.	Dvr	Evans	E. L.	L/Cpl	Fairbrother	W.	Dvr
Ellis	W. T.	Dvr	Evans	E. W.	Dvr	Fairclough	F.	Dvr
Ellison	M.	2/Lt	Evans	E. W. N.	Dvr	Fairhurst	G.	Dvr
Ellison	W. H.	Dvr	Evans	F.	Dvr	Fairhurst	H.	Dvr
Elmer	P. W.	Dvr	Evans	F. H.	Dvr	Fairless	G.	Dvr
Elms	P. F.	Dvr	Evans	G.	Dvr	Fairley	J. W.	Cpl
Elphick	K. A.	Dvr		204332		Fairman	G. H.	Cpl
Elsby	G.	Dvr	Evans	G.	Dvr	Fairs	H. P.	S/Sjt
Elson	J. D.	Pte		155797		Fairweather	R.	Dvr
Elson	P.	Cpl	Evans	G. L. T.	Dvr	Falconbridge, A. L.		Pte
Elston	J. H.	Dvr	Evans	H. A.	Dvr	Falconer	A. J.	Cpl
Elston	K. H. G.	Dvr	Evans	H. T.	Dvr	Falla	R. E.	Dvr
Elsworth	F. E.	L/Cpl	Evans	H. W.	Dvr	Fallon	W.	Dvr
Elvidge	W.	Dvr	Evans	I.	Dvr	Fallows	H. P.	Dvr
Elwis	R. W.	Dvr	Evans	J.	Dvr	Farley	C.	Dvr
Emblin	H.	Capt		264640		Farley	A. R. C.	Dvr
Emery	S. E. O.	Cpl	Evans	J.	Dvr	Farley	W. H.	Capt
Emmerick	C. A.	Dvr		10665876		Farley	W. J.	Dvr
Emmett	R. C.	Dvr	Evans	J. E.	Dvr	Farlow	C. J.	Capt
Emms	C. J.	S/Sjt	Evans	J. I.	Pte	Farman	H. E.	Dvr
Emslie	B. B.	Pte	Evans	J. R.	Pte	Farmer	J.	Sjt
Emus	L. A.	Dvr	Evans	L.	Pte	Farnell	R.	Dvr
Enderby	N.	Dvr	Evans	L. C.	L/Cpl	Farnsworth	E.	Dvr
England	B. F.	Dvr	Evans	P.	Pte	Farquharson, D.		Dvr
England	G.	Dvr	Evans	R.	Dvr	Farr	H.	Dvr
England	H.	Pte		161400		Farr	J. V.	Sjt
England	J. E.	Dvr	Evans	R.	Dvr	Farrah	A. A.	Dvr
England	W. H.	Dvr		175282		Farrant	J. D.	Dvr
English	F. D.	Dvr	Evans	R. C.	Sjt	Farrant	R. A.	Dvr
English	F. T.	Dvr	Evans	R. M.	Sjt	Farrant	R. V.	Dvr
Ennis	G.	Maj	Evans	R. S. R.	Dvr	Farrell	D.	Pte
Entwistle	E.	Dvr	Evans	S. P.	Dvr	Farrell	F.	Pte
Erdal	O. W.	Capt	Evans	T.	Dvr	Farrell	J. J.	Pte
Erickson	E.W.T.J.	Pte	Evans	T.	L/Cpl	Farrell	R.	Sjt
Erlam	S.	Dvr	Evans	T. D.	Pte	Farrer	H. E.	Dvr

ROLL OF HONOUR

Farrow	A. A.	Cpl	Fielden	R. J.	Pte	Fletcher	J.	Pte
Farrow	F.	Dvr	Fielder	R. E.	Pte	Fletcher	J. E.	Dvr
Farrow	F. S.	Dvr	Fielding	J.	Dvr	Fletcher	R.	Dvr
Farrow	G.	Dvr	Fieldstead	A. L.	Dvr	Fletcher	S. R. G.	Dvr
Farrow	V. C. H.	Capt	Fifield	L. E. W.	Dvr	Flett	J. O.	Dvr
Fathers	R. A.	Dvr	Figgett	F. J.	Dvr	Flint	J. H. T.	Cpl
Fatkin	H.	Dvr	Filler	L. J. O.	Dvr	Flint	N.	Dvr
Faulknall	G. A.	Dvr	Finch	J.	Pte	Flitney	D.	Dvr
Faulkner	F. H.	Dvr	Finch	W. F.	L/Cpl	Flitney	R. W. A.	Lt
Faulkner	F. T.	Pte	Findlay	J.	Dvr	Flood	H. K.	Dvr
Fawcett	F. F.	Capt	Findlay	R.	Cpl	Flower	C. J.	Dvr
Fawn	H.	Cpl	Fine	E.	Dvr	Flowers	B. J.	Pte
Fealey	L.	Pte	Finlay	A. J.	Dvr	Flowers	C. J. J.	Dvr
Fearnley	H.	Dvr	Finlay	W. J.	Capt	Floyd	J. F.	Dvr
Fearon	V.	L/Cpl	Finn	E.	Pte	Floyd	S.	Pte
Feather	G.	S/Sjt	Finn	W.	Dvr	Flynn	D.	Pte
Feathers	J. N.	Capt	Finn	W. J.	Dvr	Flynn	G.	Pte
Featherstone,	J. K. P.	Sjt	Finney	A.	Pte	Focken	F. J. W.	Capt
Featon	F.	Pte	Finney	J. H.	2/Lt	Foghill	A. H.	2/Lt
Feehally	J. T.	Maj	Finnis	R. D.	Cpl	Fogwill	G. A.	Sjt
Feest	H. C.	Dvr	Finny	D. M. M.C.	Capt	Foice	R. W. J.	Pte
Feint	R. F.	Cpl				Foley	F.	L/Cpl
Fell	A. W.	Lt	Firkins	H.	Dvr	Foote	E.	Dvr
Fell	V. J.	Dvr	Firth	A.	Dvr	Foote	F. E.	Sjt
Fellows	A. H.	Dvr	Firth	C. A.	Dvr	Footitt	G.	Dvr
Felton	B. C. W.	Pte	Firth	E.	L/Cpl	Forbes	G.	Dvr
Felton	E. E.	Cpl	Firth	H.	Dvr	Forbes	J.	Dvr
Fenn	A. G.	Pte	Firth	J.	L/Cpl	Force	J. W.	Capt
Fenn	H. J.	Dvr	Firth	J. W.	Dvr	Forcer	R.	Dvr
Fenner	S. A. J.	Dvr	Fish	T.	Dvr	Ford	A.	Dvr
Fenton	A. A.	Sjt	Fish	W. J.	Pte	Ford	A. E.	Capt
Fenton	J.	Dvr	Fisher	I. C.	Dvr	Ford	A. T. B.	Capt
Fenwick	A. H.	Dvr	Fisher	J. H.	Dvr	Ford	C. J.	L/Cpl
Fenwick	R. 10694831	Dvr	Fisher	J. T.	Dvr	Ford	C. O.	Pte
			Fisher	L.	Sjt	Ford	D. C.	Dvr
Fenwick	R. 172434	Dvr	Fitch	E. C.	L/Sjt	Ford	E. W. A.	Capt
			Fitch	H.	Cpl	Ford	G. T.	Dvr
Ferguson	D.	Dvr	Fitch	R. O.	Pte	Ford	H.	Dvr
Ferguson	P. F.	Dvr	Fitches	L. C.	Dvr	Ford	J. E.	Dvr
Ferguson	R. S.	Dvr	Fitton	H.	Dvr	Ford	V. E.	Cpl
Ferguson	W. E.	Pte	Fitzgerald	E.	Dvr	Forehead	R. C.	Dvr
Fernando	K. S. D.	Dvr	Fitzgerald	J.	Pte	Foreman	W.	Sjt
Fernau	R. L.	Capt	Fitzgibbon	A. G.	Dvr	Forest	I.	Dvr
Fernie	E. A.	Dvr	Fitzpatrick	L.	L/Cpl	Forrest	T.	Cpl
Ferrari	D.	Dvr	Flatt	S. A.	Pte	Forrester	A.	Sjt
Ferrett	W.	WO II	Flavell	G.	Dvr	Forrester	E.	Dvr
Ferrey	C. V. M.C.	Lt-Col	Flaxman	P. T.	Dvr	Forster	A.	Dvr
			Fleet	H. T.	Dvr	Forster	F. G.	L/Cpl
Ferrol	D. M.	Dvr	Fleisher	S.	Pte	Forster	W. T.	L/Cpl
Ffrench	D. F.	Capt	Fleming	G.	Dvr	Forsyth	R.	Dvr
Fidler	B. E.	Dvr	Fleming	H. A.	Pte	Forsyth	T. C.	Pte
Field	A. G.	Dvr	Fleming	J.	Cpl	Foster	C. S.	Sjt
Field	A. J.	Pte	Fleming	J. F. C.	Dvr	Foster	F. G.	Dvr
Field	D. H. P.	Dvr	Fleming	W.	L/Cpl	Foster	G.	Dvr
Field	F. A.	Pte	Fletcher	B. A.	Dvr	Foster	G. M.	Dvr
Field	J. H.	Pte	Fletcher	E.	Pte	Foster	J.	Dvr
Field	M. J.	Dvr	Fletcher	E. G.	Lt	Foster	J.	Pte
Fielden	H.	Pte	Fletcher	H.	Dvr	Foster	J. J.	Dvr

ROLL OF HONOUR

Foster	J. R.	Cpl	French	J.	L/Cpl	Galliford	J. E.	L/Cpl
Foster	W.	Cpl	French	J.	Dvr	Galsworthy	L. T.	Dvr
Foulds	W. H.	S/Sjt	French	T.	Dvr	Galton	W. J.	Pte
Fountain	S. W.	Dvr	French	W. G.	S/Sjt	Gambling	J. B.	Dvr
Fourie	N.	Lt	Freschini	A. W.	L/Cpl	Game	J.A.W.L.	Pte
Fowkes	H.	Dvr	Friend	J. E.	Lt	Gammie	D. A. H.	Pte
Fowlds	J. W.	Dvr	Frith	H.	Dvr	Gammons	E. G.	Dvr
Fowler	A. W.	Dvr	Frith	R. H. L.	Sjt	Gane	R.	Dvr
Fowler	E.	Dvr	Froggat	H.	L/Cpl	Gannon	J.	Dvr
Fowler	G. A.	Cpl	Frost	A.	Dvr		10672381	
Fowler	R. A.	Dvr	Frost	A. E.	Cadet	Gannon	J.	Dvr
Fowler	W.	Pte	Frost	E. F.	Dvr		14527676	
Fox	A. R.	Pte	Frost	F. D.	Dvr	Gannon	J. E.	Dvr
Fox	C. H.	Dvr	Frost	J. L.	Pte	Gannon	R. W.	Cpl
Fox	G.	Dvr	Frost	K. J.	L/Cpl	Gara	M.	Dvr
Fox	H.	L/Cpl	Frost	L. R.	Cpl	Garbett	A. L.	Sjt
Fox	J. A.	Dvr	Frost	P. B.	Pte	Garcia	A.	Dvr
	209732		Frost	R. F.	Pte	Gardiner	G.	Capt
Fox	J.	Dvr	Frost	T. W.	Pte	Gardiner	J. H.	Dvr
	14576535		Fry	C. F.	Dvr	Gardiner	K. L.	Sjt
Fox	J. F.	Pte	Fry	E. G. I.	Dvr	Gardiner	S. W.	Cpl
Fox	R. E.	L/Cpl	Fry	G. W.	Dvr	Gardner	H.	Pte
Fox	S. A. F.	Dvr	Fry	J. G.	L/Cpl	Gardner	J.	Pte
Foxall	J.	Lt	Fryer	A.	Dvr	Gardner	L. G.	Dvr
Foxon	T. G. V.	L/Cpl	Fryer	D. G.	Dvr	Garey	J.	Dvr
Foy	J.	Dvr	Fryer	R. A.	Dvr	Garmant	G. F.	Cpl
Fracis	E. P.	Capt	Fulcher	E. A.	Dvr	Garner	A.	Dvr
Fradley	W.	Dvr	Fulcher	F. S.	Dvr	Garner	E.	Dvr
Frampton	A.	Cpl	Fulford	G. A. T.	Dvr	Garner	J.	Dvr
Frampton	N. E. B.	Pte	Fuller	A. H. W.	L/Cpl	Garner	J. L.	Dvr
France	F. J.	Dvr	Fuller	J.	Pte	Garner	S.	Pte
Francis	C. W.	Dvr	Fuller	J. E. K.	L/Sjt	Garnett	E. A.	Dvr
Francis	D. E.	Capt	Fuller	R. A.	Dvr	Garnett	W. A.	Sjt
Francis	J. J.	Cpl	Fullerton	J. F.	Dvr	Garnhan	H. F.	Sjt
Francis	L.	Dvr	Fullick	H.	L/Cpl	Garrad	P. H.	Dvr
Francis	R. T.	Cpl	Furness	E.	Dvr	Garrett	A. H.	Dvr
Frankland	W.	Pte	Furnival	H.	Cpl	Garrett	A. H.	Sjt
Franklin	J. F.	L/Cpl	Furnivall	J. P.	Sjt	Garrett	L. E.	Pte
Franklin	P.	Dvr	Fyfe	J.	Dvr	Garrett	R.	Dvr
Franklin	R. J.	Dvr	Fyfe	N. H.	Dvr	Garthwaite	P.	Dvr
Franks	W. R.	Dvr				Gartland	P. J.	Dvr
Fraser	F.	Dvr				Garton	M. F. G.	Dvr
Fraser	R.	Dvr	Gadney	R. W.	Dvr	Garton	R.	Pte
Fraser	R. B.	Pte	Gadsden	A.	Dvr	Gascoyne	T. H.	Dvr
Frater	R. J.	Dvr	Gaines	J. C.	Capt	Gaskell	W. S.	Dvr
Frearson	A. S.	Pte	Gainsford	G. J.	Dvr	Gaskin	W. E.	Dvr
Free	D. G.	Pte	Gaisgory	D. L.	Lt	Gaskins	A.	Dvr
Freear	W.	Dvr	Galbraith	A.	Dvr	Gass	R. A.	Dvr
Freegard	H. B.	Dvr	Gale	A. P.	Capt	Gates	C. E.	Dvr
Freeman	A. W.	Dvr	Gale	D.	Dvr	Gates	M.	Dvr
Freeman	D. L.	Dvr	Gale	J.	Dvr	Gates	S.	Dvr
Freeman	E. G.	Dvr	Gale	R. P.	L/Cpl	Gaul	E. T.	WO II
Freeman	H.	Dvr	Gale	S. A.	Dvr	Gaunt	D.	Pte
Freeman	H. M.	L/Sjt	Gallacher	P.	Dvr	Gaw	H.	L/Cpl
Freeman	P. J.	Dvr	Gallagher	E.	Dvr	Gawthorpe	L.	L/Cpl
Freeston	T. S.	L/Cpl	Gallagher	J.	L/Cpl	Gawthorpe	S.	Sjt
French	G.	Pte	Gallagher	N.	Dvr	Gay	K. A.	Dvr
French	H. G.	L/Cpl	Gallifent	T. E. M.	Sjt	Gazeley	F. L.	Cpl

ROLL OF HONOUR

Geary	R. J.	Pte	Gilbert	J. F.	Sjt	Godfrey	A. R.	Dvr
Geary	W. H.	Pte	Gilbert	P.	L/Cpl	Godfrey	C. L.	Dvr
Geddes	A. J.	Pte	Gilbert	R. E.	Sjt	Godley	E.	Dvr
Geddes	I. D.	Cpl	Gilbert	R. P.	Dvr	Godwin	C.	Pte
Gee	S. A.	Dvr	Gilchrist	J. B.	Pte	Goff	K. W. G.	Dvr
Gee	T.	Dvr	Giles	B. J.	Dvr	Goff	W. E.	Dvr
Geere	K. J.	Dvr	Giles	R.	Cpl	Gold	A.	Dvr
Geissler	R. H.	Pte	Giles	R. A.	Dvr	Goldberg	J.	Pte
Gelder	D.	Dvr	Giles	W.	Dvr	Goldberg	S.	Pte
Gellatly	L. B.	Dvr	Gilfillan	W. C.	Dvr	Goldberg	S.	Dvr
Gemmell	J. D.	Dvr	Gilhooley	A.	Dvr	Golding	C. J.	Dvr
Gemmell	T. M.	WO I	Gill	A. C.	S/Sjt	Golding	E. W.	Dvr
Gent	J.	Dvr	Gill	H. W.	Maj	Golding	H. T.	Dvr
George	A. C. W.	Maj	Gill	H. W. F.	L/Cpl	Golding	R. H.	Dvr
	M.C.		Gill	J. A. G.	L/Cpl	Goldson	V. C.	Dvr
George	A. T.	Dvr	Gill	J. F. H.	WO I	Goldstraw	J. H.	Pte
George	J. F.	Dvr	Gill	R. H.	Pte	Goldsworthy	E. F.	Sjt
George	J. J.	Dvr	Gill	R. J. B.	Cpl	Goldsworthy	K. K.	Dvr
George	W. A.	Dvr	Gill	R. T. W.	Dvr	Goldthorpe	J. H.	Cpl
George	W. D.	Dvr	Gillanders	S.	Cpl	Gomersall	C.	Dvr
Geraghty	C.	Dvr	Gillard	H. W. J.	Dvr	Gompertz	A. G.	Pte
Geraghty	J. O.	Capt	Gillard	N. J.	Cpl	Gompertz, St.G.A.R.		Lt
Gerrard	T. C.	Cpl	Gillatt	G. D.	Lt	Gooch	A. W.	Dvr
Gerrish	T. J.	Dvr	Gillespie	R. J.	Dvr	Gooch	D. G.	Lt
Gethin	E.	Pte	Gillespie	W.	Dvr	Good	E. W.	Dvr
Gibbard	S. C.	Dvr		167772		Goodall	D.	Dvr
Gibbins	J. E.	Dvr	Gillespie	W.	Dvr	Goodall	E. L.	Cpl
Gibbons	B. T.	Dvr		190022		Goodall	H.	Dvr
Gibbons	W. C.	WO II	Gilley	G. W.	L/Cpl	Goodbrand	H. J.	L/Cpl
Gibbons	W. J.	Dvr	Gillham	R. R.	Pte	Goodchild	G. R.	Sjt
Gibbs	A. G.	Cpl	Gillings	B.	Cpl	Goodchild	H. R.	Dvr
Gibbs	C. H.	Dvr	Gillings	C.	Dvr	Goode	J. A.	Dvr
Gibbs	G. A.	Dvr	Gillings	F. C.	Sjt	Gooding	E. E.	Dvr
Gibbs	H. H.	Dvr	Gillon	T.	Dvr	Goodison	J. H.	Dvr
Gibbs	S.	Dvr	Gillson	G.	Dvr	Goodfield	E. G.	Dvr
Gibbs	S. E.	Dvr	Gilmore	E. P. F.	Dvr	Goodhill	J. R.	Dvr
Giblin	W.	L/Cpl	Gilmore	T.	Dvr	Goodlad	J. W.	Dvr
Gibson	A. S.	Dvr	Gilmour, M. R. McG.		Dvr	Goodman	H.	Dvr
Gibson	E.	Dvr	Gilroy	T.	Dvr	Goodman	J. E.	Dvr
Gibson	G.	Dvr	Gilson	L. S.	Dvr	Goodman	R.	Dvr
	146961		Girvan	N.	Pte	Goodman	S. C.	WO II
Gibson	G.	Dvr	Gladwell	L. J. H.	Dvr	Goodrum	F. R.	Dvr
	14710540		Glaister	G.	L/Cpl	Goodrum	S.	Dvr
Gibson	J.	Sjt	Glayzer	E. D.	Lt	Goodsell	S. E.	Cpl
Gibson	J. C.	Cpl	Gleadhall	J. G.	Dvr	Goodway	C. E.	Sjt
Gibson	J. L.	Lt	Gledhill	L.	Dvr	Goodwin	A. H.	Dvr
Gibson	J. W.	Pte	Glen	T. G.	Cpl	Goodwin	A. W.	Dvr
Gibson	N.	Pte	Glennon	A. E.	Dvr	Goodwin	C. G.	Cpl
Gibson	S.	Dvr	Glover	A. E.	Dvr	Goodwin	F.	Dvr
Gibson	W.	Dvr	Glover	L. A.	Dvr	Goodwin	F. C.	Capt
Gidney	R. K.	Dvr	Glover	T. W.	Dvr	Goodwin	F. S.	Dvr
Gifford	B. J.	Lt	Goad	M. J. J.	Cpl	Goodwin	J. H.	Dvr
Gilbert	A. G.	Capt	Goby	G. H.	Pte	Goodwin	R.	Dvr
	D.C.M.		Goddard	A. E.	Capt	Gora	M.	Dvr
Gilbert	B.	Dvr	Goddard	F.	Dvr	Gordon	J.	Pte
Gilbert	C. H.	Dvr	Goddard	H. L.	Dvr	Gordon	J. G.	Pte
Gilbert	D. W.	Pte	Goddard	J. R.	Pte	Gordon	R.	Dvr
Gilbert	J. F.	Dvr	Goddard	M. F.	Dvr	Gordon	R. L.	Dvr

ROLL OF HONOUR

Gordon	T.	Dvr	Grant	J.	Dvr	Greenfield	A. H.	Dvr
Gordon	W. G.	Dvr		249830		Greenfield	S. A.	Pte
Gorman	R.	Pte	Grant	J.	Dvr	Greenhalgh	A.	Dvr
Gorman	T.	Cpl		121363		Greenhalgh	R. D.	Sjt
Gormley	E.	Dvr	Grant	J.	Pte	Greenman	L. V. J.	Dvr
Gorrie	J.	Pte	Grant	R.	WO II	Greenslade	S. E.	Dvr
Gorton	E.	Cpl	Grant	R.	Dvr	Greenslade	W. G.	Dvr
Gorton	H.	Dvr		14317487		Greenstock	R. L.	Dvr
Gosbee	G.	Dvr	Grant	R.	Dvr	Greenup	J. B.	Pte
Gosby	L. T. G.	Dvr		257763		Greenwood	A. H.	Dvr
Gosheril	J. B.	Dvr	Grant	R. W. G.	Dvr	Greenwood	A. S.	Dvr
Gosling	W. C.	L/Cpl	Grant	W. E. H.	Dvr	Greenwood	H.	Sjt
Goss	E. C.	Dvr	Grantham	A.	Dvr	Greenwood	H.	Dvr
Goss	L.	Pte	Grassing	S. J.	L/Cpl		14837773	
Goudie	C.	Dvr	Grattage	H.	Dvr	Greenwood	H.	Dvr
Goudy	H. P.	Cpl	Graves	G.	Sjt		328731	
Gough	J.	Cpl	Graves	H. E.	Pte	Greer	G. C.	L/Cpl
Gough	T.	Cpl	Graves	J. H.	Dvr	Gregg	F.	Dvr
Gould	A. D.	Dvr	Gravil	J. H.	Dvr	Gregory	E.	Dvr
Gould	J. D.	Lt	Gray	G.	L/Cpl	Gregory	H.	Dvr
Gould	R.	Dvr	Gray	G. A.	Cpl	Gregory	J.	Dvr
Gouldbourne, G. A.		Dvr	Gray	J.	Cpl	Gregory	W. H.	Dvr
Goulden	B.	Dvr	Gray	J. O.	Dvr	Greig	S. V.	Maj
Goulder	W.	Dvr	Gray	J. S.	Dvr	Greig	W. W.	Pte
Goulding	D.	Dvr	Gray	R.	Cpl	Grey	G.	Dvr
Gout	R. L.	Cpl	Gray	T.	Pte	Grey	W. P.	Sjt
Gover	B.	Dvr	Gray	W. P.	Cpl	Gribb	G. A.	Dvr
Gower	R. T.	Dvr	Grayer	W. R.	Sjt	Grice	A.	Dvr
Gowrie	C. M.	Dvr	Greatbatch	W. H.	Dvr	Grice	A.	Sjt
Goyder	F. W.	Dvr	Greatorex	G.	Dvr	Grice	A. J.	Pte
Grace	C. F.	Dvr	Greatorex	R.	Dvr	Grice	D. H.	Dvr
Grace	C. H.	Dvr	Greedy	P. C.	Dvr	Grice	J.	Pte
Grace	C. J.	Dvr	Green	A.	Dvr	Grice	L. C.	Dvr
Grace	J.	L/Cpl	Green	A. C.	S/Sjt	Grierson	W. F.	Dvr
Grace	M.	Dvr	Green	A. E.	Dvr	Grieve	A.	Dvr
Grace	W. D.	Dvr	Green	B.	L/Cpl	Grieve	P.	L/Cpl
Grady	T.	Dvr	Green	B.	Dvr	Griffen	V. T. G.	Cpl
Graham	A.	Dvr	Green	C. B.	Dvr	Griffin	C. F. A.	Dvr
Graham	A. B.	Dvr	Green	C. D. M.	Cpl	Griffin	F. S.	Cpl
Graham	A. B.	S/Sjt	Green	C. F. W.	L/Cpl	Griffin	J.	Dvr
Graham	A. T.	Pte	Green	C. L.	Pte	Griffin	J. P.	Sjt
Graham	E. E.	L/Cpl	Green	D.	Dvr	Griffin	J. R. J.	Dvr
Graham	H. G.	Pte	Green	D. J.	Dvr	Griffin	L.	L/Cpl
Graham	J. M.	Dvr	Green	E. A.	Dvr	Griffin	T.	Dvr
Graham	J. W.	Pte	Green	F. C.	Dvr	Griffiths	A.	2/Lt
Graham	S.	Dvr	Green	F. H.	Dvr	Griffiths	A.	Dvr
Graham	T.	L/Cpl	Green	G.	Cpl	Griffiths	C. J.	Cpl
Graham	W.	Pte	Green	G. E.	Dvr	Griffiths	E.	Pte
Graham	W.	Dvr	Green	H. D.	Dvr	Griffiths	F. C.	Dvr
Graham	W. H.	Sjt	Green	H. G.	CQMS	Griffiths	F. J.	Pte
Grainger	C.W.A.A.	Pte	Green	J.	Pte	Griffiths	G.	Dvr
Granelli	M. C.	Dvr	Green	P. H.	Dvr	Griffiths	G. M.	Dvr
Grant	A. G.	Sjt	Green	R.	Maj	Griffiths	H.	Pte
Grant	C. C.	Dvr	Green	S. G.	Dvr		147483	
Grant	C. M.	Dvr	Green	S. J.	Dvr	Griffiths	H.	Pte
Grant	F.	Pte	Green	W.	Dvr		166237	
Grant	I.	Dvr	Greenall	A. E.	Pte			
Grant	J.	Cpl	Greenburgh	R.	Dvr	Griffiths	J.	Pte

ROLL OF HONOUR

Griffiths	J. E. 90858	Pte	Gwynn	W. K.	Dvr	Hall	W. D.	Dvr
Griffiths	J. E. 80638	Pte	Gyford	G. D.	Sjt	Hallam	J.	Dvr
Griffiths	J. L.	Pte	Hack	L.	Dvr	Hallam	R.	Dvr
Griffiths	R.	Dvr	Hackett	B.	Dvr	Hallan	J.	Pte
Griffiths	S.	Cpl	Hackett	J.	Dvr	Hallas	J.	Pte
Griffiths	S. J.	Dvr	Hackett	H. P.	Dvr	Hallas	P.	Pte
Griffiths	S. M. O.B.E.	Lt-Col	Hackett	H. R.	Dvr	Hallett	N.	L/Cpl
			Hackett	R. V.	L/Cpl	Halliday	H. W.	Cpl
			Haddock	F. W.	L/Cpl	Hallums	A. K.	Dvr
Griffiths	W. E.	Dvr	Hadley	A. R.	Pte	Halpin	G. E.	Capt
Grimes	J. W.	Dvr	Hadley	F.	Dvr	Halsey	A. W.	Dvr
Grimley	J. L.	L/Cpl	Hadley	J. T.	Dvr	Halsey	G. A. C.	Sjt
Grimshaw	J. W.	Dvr	Hadley	M.	L/Cpl	Halstead	H.	Dvr
Grimshaw	M.	Dvr	Hadwin	T.	Dvr	Ham	W. H. G.	Dvr
Grindall	E.	Pte	Hagger	S. C. B.	Sjt	Hamber	N. L.	Cpl
Grinnall	F. H.	WO II	Haggerty	A.	Dvr	Hambleton	A. G.	Dvr
Grisley	E. G.	Dvr	Haig	J.	Pte	Hambly	L. O.	Pte
Gronfein	H.	Dvr	Haig	J.	Sjt	Hamer	R.	Pte
Gronow	K.	Sjt	Haig	T. D.	Lt	Hames	J. G.	Dvr
Groom	G. K.	Dvr	Haigh	D.	Dvr	Hamill	H. B.	Dvr
Groombridge, G. W.		Dvr	Haigh	D. S.	Capt	Hamilton	A.	Cpl
Groonbridge, A. J.		S/Sjt	Haigh	F.	Dvr	Hamilton	B. R.	Capt
Grose	J. H.	Dvr	Haines	C.	Dvr	Hamilton	F. J.	Dvr
Grout	E. G.	Dvr	Haines	G. F. M.	Capt	Hamilton	F. W.	Dvr
Grout	F. W.	Dvr	Haines	J. R.	Cpl	Hamilton	G.	Pte
Groutage	H.	Cpl	Haines	W. F.	L/Cpl	Hamilton	G. H. A.	Pte
Grove	G. E. G.	Lt	Hainsworth	H.	Dvr	Hamilton	G. M.	2/Lt
Grove	N. W.	Dvr	Haldane	C. S.	Cpl	Hamilton	H.	Dvr
Grover	A. H.	Dvr	Halder	L. A.	L/Cpl	Hamilton	J.	Dvr
Grover	W. G.	S/Sjt	Hale	H.	Pte	Hamlett	C.	Dvr
Groves	F.	Sjt	Hale	P. J.	Dvr	Hamlin	E. C. H.	Dvr
Groves	J. W.	Pte	Hales	J. H.	WO II	Hammer	K. M. A.	Lt
Growden	W. W. E.	Dvr	Hales	T. H.	Dvr	Hammersley, H.		Sjt
Grundy	S.	Pte	Haley	R.	Cpl	Hammond	A. J.	Dvr
Grundy	T.	Dvr	Halifax	F. H. T.	Dvr	Hammond	F. L.	Dvr
Guard	C. E.	S/Sjt	Hall	A. 194766	Dvr	Hammond	G. V.	Pte
Gudgeon	M. W.	Pte	Hall	A. 127181	Dvr	Hammond	J. S.	Dvr
Guile	F. A.	Dvr				Hammond	L. C.	Dvr
Guiver	E. J.	Dvr	Hall	A. C.	Cpl	Hamnet	D. G.	Dvr
Gully	H. L.	Dvr	Hall	A. E.	Cpl	Hamp	R. H.	Dvr
Gummerson A. R.		Dvr	Hall	B. W.	Dvr	Hampson	W.	Dvr
Gunn	A. F. D.	Dvr	Hall	C. P.	Dvr	Hampton	W. J.	Dvr
Gunn	C. M.	Pte	Hall	E. L.	Dvr	Hance	F. A.	Dvr
Gunn	G. T.	Dvr	Hall	F. G.	Sjt	Hancock	G. J.	Dvr
Gunn	H. G.	Dvr	Hall	F. H.	Cpl	Hancock	K.	Dvr
Gunn	J.	Dvr	Hall	G.	L/Cpl	Hancock	S. B.	Dvr
Gunningham, W. J.		L/Sjt	Hall	G. E.	Cpl	Hancock	T. V. R.	Pte
Gunns	H.	Pte	Hall	H. A.	WO I	Hancox	D. A. E.	Cpl
Gurman	L. E.	Dvr	Hall	J.	S/Sjt	Hancox	J. H.	Cpl
Gurney	R.	Dvr	Hall	J.	Dvr	Hancox	R. W.	L/Cpl
Guthrie	F. C.	Dvr	Hall	J. L.	Lt	Hancox	W.	Pte
Guy	W.	Sjt	Hall	J. L.	Sjt	Handel	B.	Dvr
Guyll	G. C.	Dvr	Hall	J. W.	Dvr	Handy	F. Y.	Dvr
Guyte	W. C.	Dvr	Hall	L. G.	Dvr	Handyside	R.	Cpl
Gwilliam	R. G.	Dvr	Hall	P. W.	L/Cpl	Hankey	L. R.	Dvr
			Hall	S. G.	Dvr	Hankinson	J.	Pte
			Hall	V. B. R.	Dvr	Hanmore	W. J.	Dvr

ROLL OF HONOUR

Hann	A. A. C.	L/Cpl	Harris	J.	Dvr	Hartley	C. G.	Pte
Hann	G. G.	Sjt		285749		Hartley	T. L.	Dvr
Hanna	A. L.	Maj	Harris	J.	Dvr	Hartry	H. F.	Lt
	M.B.E.			14898142		Hartshord	A. D.	Dvr
Hannaford	S. J.	Dvr	Harris	J.	L/Cpl	Harvey	C. A.	Dvr
Hannah	F.	Dvr	Harris	J. J. J.	Dvr	Harvey	C. H.	Dvr
Hannon	M. T.	WO II	Harris	J. R.	Dvr	Harvey	E. J.	Dvr
Hansen	L. F.	Pte	Harris	N. C.	Dvr	Harvey	F.	Dvr
Hansley	J. W. C.	Dvr	Harris	P.	Dvr	Harvey	G.	Dvr
Hanson	J. W.	Sjt	Harris	R. E.	L/Cpl	Harvey	J.	Sjt
Hanson	J. W.	Dvr	Harris	R. H.	Dvr	Harvey	L. F.	Pte
Hanson	R. J.	Dvr	Harris	R. L.	Sjt	Harvey	P. N.	Maj
Hardacre	J.	Dvr	Harris	S. L.	Dvr	Harvey	P. W.	Pte
Hardcastle	J. E.	Dvr	Harris	T. J.	Pte	Harvey	R. H.	Dvr
Hardicker	J. A.	Capt	Harris	V. G.	Cpl	Harvey	R. J.	Pte
Hardie	A.	Dvr	Harris	W. D.	Pte	Harvey	R. M.	Lt
Hardie	T. S.	Lt	Harris	W. H.	Sjt	Harvie	G. R.	Dvr
Harding	C. A.	Cpl	Harrison	A.	Dvr	Harvie	S. O.	Cpl
Harding	J. R.	Cpl	Harrison	A. J.	Dvr	Harwood	L. A.	Dvr
Hardwick	J. H. G.	Dvr	Harrison	A. R.	Dvr	Harwood	R.	Dvr
Hardy	A. J.	Cpl	Harrison	C.	Dvr	Harwood	S. G.	Dvr
Hardy	D. R.	Dvr		72904		Haseldine	A. V.	Dvr
Hardy	J.	Pte	Harrison	C.	Dvr	Haselton	J. C.	Dvr
Hardy	P. G.	Cpl		191429		Haskell	T. E.	Dvr
Hare	J.	L/Cpl	Harrison	C. J.	Dvr	Haslam	F.	Cpl
Harfield	A. I.	L/Cpl	Harrison	E.	Dvr	Haslam	J. F.	Dvr
Hargrave	W. R.	Dvr	Harrison	E. B.	Dvr	Haslam	W. P.	Dvr
Harker	J.	Dvr	Harrison	F.	WO II	Hasler	R. G.	Sjt
Harland	W. G.	Pte	Harrison	F.	Dvr	Hastie	P. S.	Pte
Harland	W. H.	2/Lt		73865		Hastings	J. E. G.	S/Sjt
Harley	J.	Dvr	Harrison	F.	Dvr	Hastings	W. A.	Cpl
Harley	L. J.	Dvr		244863		Hatch	G.	Pte
Harlow	G.	Sjt	Harrison	G.	Capt	Hatch	W. W.	Dvr
Harman	A.	Dvr	Harrison	G. A.	Dvr	Hatcher	R. J.	L/Cpl
Harmsworth, S. A.		Pte	Harrison	G. B.	Cpl	Hatcliffe	H.	L/Cpl
Harner	E. L.	Dvr	Harrison	H.	Dvr	Hatfield	A. E.	2/Lt
Harniess	C.	Dvr	Harrison	H. R. A.	Dvr	Hathaway	S. C. G.	Dvr
Harper	C. H.	Dvr	Harrison	J.	Dvr	Hatton	D.	Dvr
Harper	F. L.	Pte	Harrison	J.	Pte	Hatton	H.	Dvr
Harper	I. R.	Dvr		236293		Hatwell	S. M.	S/Sjt
Harper	J.	Dvr	Harrison	J.	Pte	Haughey	J. J.	Pte
Harper	L. S.	Dvr		122026		Hawdin	H.	Cpl
Harrell	C. W.	Dvr	Harrison	R.	Dvr	Hawes	T. A.	L/Cpl
Harries	E.	Sjt		10702594		Hawker	C. G.	Sjt
Harrigan	M.	L/Cpl	Harrison	R.	Dvr	Hawkes	A. B.	Sjt
Harrington	R. E. F.	L/Cpl		14431941		Hawkes	L.	Dvr
Harris	A. E.	Pte	Harrison	S.	Pte	Hawkes	V. K.	Cpl
Harris	A. W.	WO II	Harrison	S. S.	Dvr	Hawkes	W. T. H.	Cpl
Harris	C. W.	Dvr	Harrison	V.	Dvr	Hawkins	E. F. W.	L/Cpl
Harris	E. W. C.	Dvr	Harrison	W.	Dvr	Hawkins	F. G.	Dvr
Harris	F.	L/Cpl	Harrison	W. A.	L/Cpl	Hawkins	G. W.	Dvr
Harris	F. E.	Dvr	Harron	R.	Dvr	Hawkins	J. A.	Sjt
Harris	F. J.	Pte	Harsley	G. D.	Dvr	Hawkins	W. A.	Dvr
Harris	G. E.	Pte	Hart	C. H. G.	S/Sjt	Hawkridge	C.	Dvr
Harris	G. S.	Dvr	Hart	P. E.	Dvr	Hawkridge	J.	Dvr
Harris	G. W.	Cpl	Hart	T. W.	Pte	Hawksworth, H.		Dvr
Harris	H.	Pte	Hart	W.	Dvr	Hawksworth, R.D.M.		Dvr
Harris	H. C.	Capt	Hart	W. F.	Pte	Hawley	J. D.	Lt

ROLL OF HONOUR

Haworth	H. H.	Dvr	Hedley	A.	Dvr	Herriots	F. G.	Dvr
Haxell	C. D.	Dvr	Hedley	F.	Cpl	Herson	C. H. A.	Dvr
Hay	A.	Dvr	Heeley	J.	Pte	Heseltine	F. O.	Sjt
Hay	A. W. D.	Pte	Hefferman	O. C.	Cpl	Hesketh	H.	Cpl
Hay	C.	Dvr	Heinink	A. F.	Pte	Hesketh	H.	Dvr
Hay	D. G.	Dvr	Hellens	M. H.	L/Cpl	Heslop	T. W.	L/Cpl
Hay	G. A.	Dvr	Hember	L. E.	Pte	Hesmond	W. R.	Dvr
Hay	G. A.	L/Cpl	Hemingway	G.	Dvr	Hesp	S. S.	Sjt
Hay	W.	L/Cpl	Hemming	B.	Dvr	Hester	A. H.	Pte
Hayden	F. R.	Dvr	Hemmingway, E.		Cpl	Hewer	C.	Dvr
Hayden	J. E.	Dvr	Hemstock	C.	Dvr	Hewitson	M. Y.	Capt
Haydock	A.	Dvr	Hemsworth	A. E. G.	Dvr	Hewitt	A.	Dvr
Haydock	W.	Dvr	Henders	W. A.	Dvr	Hewitt	L. J.	Cpl
Haydon	A. W.	Dvr	Henderson	A.	Dvr	Hewitt	S. C.	Dvr
Hayes	C. J.	Dvr	Henderson	A. S. H.	Dvr	Hewlett	G. A.	Dvr
Hayes	H. S.	Dvr	Henderson	D.	S/Sjt	Hewson	J.	WO I
Hayes	J. G.	2/Lt	Henderson	J. T.	Dvr	Hewson	J. E.	Dvr
Hayes	S.	Pte	Henderson	P.	Sjt	Heyes	H.	L/Cpl
Hayes	W.	Cpl	Henderson	R. J.	Dvr	Heyward	R. S.	Dvr
Hayman	J. W.	L/Cpl	Henderson	S.	WO I	Heywood	E. H.	Dvr
Haynel	R. V.	Sjt	Henderson	W.	Cpl	Heywood	J. W.	Dvr
Haynes	E. A.	Pte	Henderson	W.	Pte	Hibberd	G. O.	Pte
Haynes	W.	Pte		7606226		Hibbert	W. R. G.	Dvr
Haynes	W.	Dvr	Henderson	W.	Pte	Hibbs	E. P.	2/Lt
Hayton	R. W.	Dvr		2828898		Hibbs	W. J. F.	Dvr
Hayward	J. N.	Dvr	Hendrie	J.	Cpl	Hick	A. B.	Dvr
Hayward	R.	Cpl	Hendry	E. J.	Pte	Hickey	M.	Dvr
Haywood	H.	Dvr	Hendry	W.	Dvr	Hickey	R. L.	Pte
Hazell	C. J.	Pte	Hennessy	M. P.	Dvr	Hicklin	J. C.	Pte
Hazell	L. C.	Dvr	Hennessy	W.	Pte	Hickling	A. G.	Dvr
Head	C. G.	Dvr	Hennessy	W. E.	L/Cpl	Hickling	J. W.	Pte
Headland	F.	Pte	Hennessy	W. J.	Dvr	Hickman	C.	Pte
Headland	G. F.	L/Cpl	Henniker	L. J.	WO II	Hicks	F. G. A.	Lt
Headrige	G.	Dvr	Henry	J. C.	Dvr	Hicks	G.	L/Cpl
Heald	A.	Dvr	Henshall	A. N.	Dvr	Hicks	G. A.	Dvr
Healey	T. E.	Dvr	Henshall	J.	Pte	Hickson	J.	Dvr
Healey	W.	Sjt	Henshall	J. H.	Dvr	Higgins	A. J.	Sjt
Healy	P.	Dvr	Henshall	P.	S/Sjt	Higgins	E. E. E.	Dvr
Heard	E. W.	Dvr	Henson	R.	Dvr	Higgins	H.	Dvr
Hearn	H.	Dvr	Henson	R. S.	L/Cpl	Higgs	C. H.	Dvr
Hearn	S. J.	Pte	Henworth	J.	Sjt	Higgs	T. H.	Dvr
Heath	J.	Pte	Hepburn	R. P. C.	Maj	High	G.	Dvr
Heath	J.	L/Cpl	Hepher	L. S.	Dvr	Higham	F.	Dvr
Heath	L. A.	Pte	Hepton	A. R.	Dvr	Hignett	J.	L/Cpl
Heathcote	G. H. M.B.E.	Capt	Hepworth	E.	Dvr	Higson	F.	Dvr
			Herat	W. D. O.	Pte	Hilbert	P.	Dvr
Heathcote	R. G.	Dvr	Herbert	D.	Dvr	Hilder	J. F.	Pte
Heaton	F.	Dvr	Herbert	D. A.	Dvr	Hilditch	H. H.	Dvr
Heaton	H.	Sjt	Herbert	S. J.	Dvr	Hill	A.	Dvr
Heaton	R.	WO II	Herbert	T. J.	Capt		10674098	
Heaton	W.	L/Cpl	Herbert	V. A.	L/Cpl	Hill	A.	Dvr
Heaton	W. T.	Dvr	Herd	A. O.	Dvr		257221	
Hebberd	R. F. G.	Dvr	Herity	F.	Sjt	Hill	A. W. R.	Dvr
Hebden	J. W.	Cpl	Heron	P.	Dvr	Hill	D. K.	Dvr
Hebson	H.	Dvr	Heron	R.	Dvr	Hill	D. W.	Dvr
Heckford	E. V.	Dvr	Herrett	H.	Dvr	Hill	E. W.	Dvr
Hedges	H. G.	Dvr	Herring	J. L.	Pte	Hill	F.	Pte
Hedgington	A. V.	Cpl	Herring	R. H.	Sjt	Hill	F. A.	Dvr

ROLL OF HONOUR

Hill	F. H.	Dvr	Hobson	S.	Dvr	Holland	W. A.	Cpl
Hill	F. W.	Dvr	Hobson	V.	Dvr	Holley	A. J.	Pte
Hill	G. E. J.	Pte	Hockley	A. D.	Dvr	Hollingsworth, H. H.		Dvr
Hill	H. W.	Dvr	Hockridge	A. H.	Dvr	Hollins	G. F. A.	Dvr
Hill	J. 269231	Dvr	Hoddy	J. T. W.	L/Cpl	Hollins	P. L. F.	2/Lt
			Hodge	E. C.	Dvr	Hollingshead, H.		Dvr
Hill	J. 245242	Dvr	Hodge	F.	Dvr	Hollis	S. F.	Dvr
			Hodge	J. S.	Pte	Hollister	L. M.	Dvr
Hill	J. A.	Pte	Hodge	W. R. W.	Pte	Hollow	G. S.	Dvr
Hill	N. C. A.	Dvr	Hodgekinson, W. B.		Pte	Holloway	A. L. G.	Dvr
Hill	R.	Pte	Hodges	C. H.	Pte	Holloway	R. W.	Maj
Hill	R.	Dvr	Hodges	G. C. R.	Dvr		M.B.E.	
Hill	R. A.	Pte	Hodges	G. J.	L/Cpl	Holloway	V. L.	Sjt
Hill	R. A.	Dvr	Hodges	J. A.	Dvr	Holloway	W.	Sjt
Hill	R. S.	L/Cpl	Hodgkins	W.	Cpl	Holloway	W. V.	Dvr
Hill	T.	Dvr	Hodgskinson, R.		Dvr	Holman	E. R.	Dvr
Hill	W.	Pte	Hodgkisson	J.	Pte	Holman	J. D.	Dvr
Hill	W. E.	Dvr	Hodgson	A.	Dvr	Holmes	B. T.	Dvr
Hill	W. G.	Sjt	Hodgson	F.	2/Lt	Holmes	E. J.	Pte
Hillestron	J. A.	Dvr	Hodgson	G. C.	Pte	Holmes	G. B.	Cpl
Hillier	A. J.	WO II	Hodgson	H.	Dvr	Holmes	G. H.	Pte
Hillier	H. H.	Sjt	Hodgson	H. L.	WO I	Holmes	I. M. B.	Pte
Hillier	J.	Dvr	Hodgson	R.	Dvr	Holmes	J. A.	Dvr
Hillier	S.	Pte	Hodgson	S. R.	Cpl	Holmes	J. L.	Dvr
Hillman	A. J.	Dvr	Hodgson	T. A.	Dvr	Holmes	L.	Dvr
Hills	C. E.	Maj	Hodgson	W. E.	L/Cpl	Holmes	L. N.	Dvr
Hills	W. H. F.	S/Sjt	Hodgson	W. J. W.	2/Lt	Holmes	P. J.	Dvr
Hilton	J. T.	Dvr	Hoffman	C.	L/Cpl	Holmes	R. W.	Pte
Hilton	K.	L/Cpl	Hogbin	A. C.	Pte	Holmwood	W. E.	Dvr
Hinchcliffe	J. W.	Pte	Hogg	A. D.	Pte	Holohan	W.	Cpl
Hincks	M. T.	Capt	Hogg	G. D.	Dvr	Holroyd	D. A.	Cpl
Hincksman	M.	Dvr	Hoggard	H. E.	Pte	Holroyd	P.	Dvr
Hind	J. A.	Dvr	Hoggart	S.	Pte	Holroyd	R. C.	Dvr
Hinde	V.	Pte	Hoggett	J. A.	Cpl	Holt	C. A.	Dvr
Hindley	C.	Dvr	Hojan	J. A.	Pte	Holt	D.	L/Cpl
Hindley	C. J. C.	Lt	Holborow	F.	Cpl	Holt	H. A.	Pte
Hindmarsh	H.	Dvr	Holcroft	J. H.	Sjt	Holt	W. E.	Dvr
Hinds	J. F.	Dvr	Holcroft	T. A.	Dvr	Holtby	T. H.	Pte
Hinds	R.	Sjt	Holden	A.	Dvr	Holton	F. R. D.	L/Cpl
Hinds	W. T.	Sjt	Holden	I.	Dvr	Holton	R.	Pte
Hine	L. A.	L/Cpl	Holden	J.	Dvr	Holyoake	H. J.	Dvr
Hine	V. J.	Dvr	Holder	F. W.	Sjt	Homden	V. L. G.	Dvr
Hines	P. J.	L/Sjt	Holderness	R.	Pte	Home	J. L. F.	L/Cpl
Hingley	V.	Dvr	Holding	T.	Dvr	Honey	M. V.	Dvr
Hingston	F. W.	Dvr	Holdroyd	H.	Dvr	Honey	T. S.	CQMS
Hiorns	H.	Dvr	Holdstock	F.	Dvr	Honeysett	A. C.	Dvr
Hirst	E.	Cpl	Holdsworth	F. C.	Dvr	Hood	F. C.	Pte
Hirst	J.	L/Cpl	Holdsworth	H.	Dvr	Hood	G.	Dvr
Hiscock	L. E.	Dvr	Hole	J. E.	Dvr	Hook	H. W.	Pte
Hislop	A. McD.	Dvr	Hole	W. L.	L/Cpl	Hook	W.	Dvr
Hitchman	H. W.	Cpl	Holford	H. A. V.	Pte	Hooker	A. J.	Pte
Hitt	F.	Dvr	Holford	L.	Dvr	Hooker	D.	Dvr
Hives	J. H.	Dvr	Holgate	J.	Dvr	Hookway	R.	Dvr
Hoare	B. P.	Sjt	Hollamby	V. G.	Cpl	Hooley	E.	Pte
Hobbs	D.	Dvr	Holland	A.	Pte	Hooper	F. A. R.	S/Sjt
Hobcraft	W. E. W.	Lt	Holland	G. W.	L/Sjt	Hooper	R. G.	Dvr
Hobson	C. M.	Dvr	Holland	J.	Cpl	Hooper	W. R.	Pte
Hobson	J. R. W.	2/Lt	Holland	L.	Dvr	Hooton	G.	Dvr

ROLL OF HONOUR

Hope	A.	Dvr	Howarth	V.	L/Cpl	Hughes	W. A.	S/Sjt
Hope	A. A. C.	Dvr	Howarth	W.	Dvr	Hughes	W. S.	Pte
Hope	B.	Cpl	Howdle	M. J.	Dvr	Hugo	W. H.	Dvr
Hope	C. J.	Dvr	Howe	A. E.	L/Cpl	Hull	A. R. K.	Cpl
Hopkins	F. G.	Pte	Howe	G.	Pte	Hull	J. H.	Dvr
Hopkins	G. W.	Cpl	Howe	J. Mc E.	Dvr	Hull	P.	Dvr
Hopley	G. B. B.	Cpl	Howe	K. A.	Dvr	Hull	S. V.	Dvr
Hopper	G. R.	Dvr	Howell	A. L.	Pte	Hullyer	E. H.	Dvr
Hopson	E. H. E.	Dvr	Howell	B. A.	S/Sjt	Hulme	H.	Dvr
Hopson	H. J.	Pte	Howell	C.	L/Cpl	Hulme	J.	Dvr
Horden	E. A. C.	Dvr	Howell	C. C. H.	Sjt	Hulse	G. H.	Dvr
Horlock	F. F.	Dvr	Howell	C. F.	Dvr	Humber	T. H.	Cpl
Horlock	H. H.	Dvr	Howell	R.	Dvr	Hume	A.	Dvr
Hornby	F. W.	Dvr	Howells	M. E.	Dvr	Hume	A. F. W.	Dvr
Horne	J. F.	L/Cpl	Howes	C. S.	L/Cpl	Hume	J. E.	Cpl
Horne	L. E.	Capt	Howes	H. W. E.	Pte	Hume	L. R.	Pte
Horrigan	T.	Sjt	Howitt	R.	Dvr	Hume	R. H.	Dvr
Horsfall	J. W.	Dvr	Howlett	A. F.	Dvr	Humfrey	A. E.	Dvr
Horsfall	T. H.	Dvr	Hoy	G. D.	Dvr	Humphrey	A. W.	Sjt
Horsley	D. V.	Dvr	Hoyle	A.	Dvr	Humphrey	F. L.	Pte
Horswell	R. F.	Dvr	Hoyle	H.	Pte	Humphrey	J. H.	L/Cpl
Horton	F.	Cpl	Hubball	R.	Dvr	Humphrey	T. A.	Dvr
Horton	F. G.	Dvr	Hubbard	J. W.	Dvr	Humphreys	G. D.	Pte
Horton	H.	Dvr	Hubble	A. E.	Dvr	Humphreys	J.	Sjt
Hosegood	B. S.	Dvr	Huddart	A. H.	Capt	Humphries	A.	Dvr
Hosie	R. J.	Dvr		M.B.E.		Humphries	R. J.	Dvr
Hosking	G. A.	Sjt	Huddleston	D. W.	S/Sjt	Humphries	W. F. J.	Dvr
Hothersall	R. L.	2/Lt	Hudson	A.	L/Cpl	Hunnings	E.	Pte
Hough	M.	L/Cpl	Hudson	H.	Dvr	Hunt	A. J.	Cpl
Hough	R.	Dvr	Hudson	J.	L/Cpl	Hunt	F. W.	L/Cpl
Hougham	W. A.	Dvr	Hudson	J.	Dvr	Hunt	H. H.	Dvr
Houghton	H.	L/Cpl	Hudson	R. E.	Dvr	Hunt	J.	Dvr
Houghton	S. S.	Dvr	Hudspith	J.	Dvr	Hunt	J. D.	Dvr
Hoult	H.	Pte	Huff	E.	Pte	Hunt	J. S.	Sjt
Houltby	J. W.	Dvr	Huggins	S. A.	Dvr	Hunt	K. L.	Dvr
Hounslow	S. A.	Dvr	Hughes	A.	Dvr	Hunt	L. V.	Pte
Hounslow	S. G.	Pte	Hughes	A.	Cpl	Hunt	N. A.	Dvr
House	J. T.	Dvr	Hughes	A. E.	Dvr	Hunt	P. N.	Dvr
House	W.	Cpl	Hughes	C. L. R.	WO II	Hunt	R. C.	Dvr
Housego	S. C.	Dvr	Hughes	E.	Dvr	Hunt	S. G.	Dvr
Housley	L.	Dvr	Hughes	E. H.	Dvr	Hunt	S. J.	Dvr
Houston	R.	Dvr	Hughes	E. L.	Pte	Hunt	V. A.	WO II
How	A. G.	Cpl	Hughes	G. F.	Pte	Hunt	W.	Dvr
Howard	D.	Dvr	Hughes	H. T.	Dvr	Hunt	W. H.	Cpl
Howard	D. A.	Sjt	Hughes	I. W.	Dvr	Hunter	A.	Dvr
Howard	E. H.	Dvr	Hughes	J.	Cpl		4277422	
Howard	F. W. A.	Pte		156628		Hunter	A.	Dvr
Howard	J.	Cpl	Hughes	J.	Cpl		251083	
Howard	J. A.	Dvr		6140001		Hunter	A.	Dvr
Howard	J. H.	Cpl	Hughes	J.	Dvr		14758992	
Howard	R.	Pte	Hughes	J.	Pte	Hunter, A. C. McC.		Dvr
Howard	T. J.	Dvr	Hughes	J. O.	Pte	Hunter	A. E.	Dvr
Howard	W.	L/Cpl	Hughes	J. V.	Dvr	Hunter	B.	Dvr
Howard	W.	Dvr	Hughes	L. E.	Dvr	Hunter	E. A. J.	Maj
Howard	W. S.	Pte	Hughes	N. E.	2/Lt	Hunter	G. H.	Dvr
Howard	W. S.	Dvr	Hughes	R. R.	Dvr	Hunter	W.	Pte
Howarth	E.	Dvr	Hughes	T.	Pte	Hunter	W. L. R.	Dvr
Howarth	G. H.	Sjt	Hughes	W. A.	Sjt	Hurley	H. S.	Dvr

ROLL OF HONOUR

Hurley	R.	Pte	Inman	C. H.	Sjt	Jagger	M.	Dvr
Hurll	W. H. E.	Dvr	Innes	J.	Dvr	Jakes	D.	Dvr
Hurn	A. C.	Cpl	Insley	J. E.	Dvr	Jakeways	T. A.	Dvr
Hurren	E. G. J.	Cpl	Inward	H. J.	Pte	James	A.	Dvr
Hurry	T. E.	Dvr	Iredale	H. E.	Pte	James	A. A.	Cpl
Hurst	A. G.	L/Cpl	Ireland	L. F.	WO II	James	A. E.	L/Cpl
Hurst	E. C.	Dvr	Ireland	R. B.	Dvr	James	C.	Dvr
Hurst	W.	Dvr	Ireland	T.	Dvr		62946	
Husband	T.	Dvr	Ireson	L. A.	Dvr	James	C.	Dvr
Hustler	H.	Dvr	Ironside	H. C.	Pte		213387	
Huston	V. H.	Cpl	Irvine	J.	Cpl	James	C. D. R.	Pte
Hutchinson	A. E.	Dvr	Irvine	N. C.	Pte	James	C. E.	Pte
Hutchinson	F.	Dvr	Irving	A. M.	Lt	James	C. R.	L/Cpl
Hutchinson	H.	Dvr	Irwin	H.	Dvr	James	D. W.	Pte
Hutchinson	J.	Dvr	Irwin	I. K. K.	L/Cpl	James	E.	Pte
Hutchinson	J. C.	Pte	Isaac	R.	Dvr	James	E. H. L.	Capt
Hutchison	G.	Sjt	Isaacson	R. W.	Dvr	James	E. W.	Dvr
Huth	F. L.	Capt	Isger	R. F.	Pte	James	F. A.	Pte
Huthinson	W. G.	Dvr	Isky	B.	Dvr	James	F. P.	Dvr
Huttenbach	H. D.	Pte	Ison	R. G.	Dvr	James	G. C.	L/Cpl
Hutton	D. T.	Cadet	Israel	W.	Lt	James	H.	Dvr
Huxley	J.	Pte	Ives	F. J.	Dvr	James	J. H.	Dvr
Huxley	J.	L/Cpl	Ives	G.	Dvr	James	J. S.	Dvr
Huxley	W. H.	Dvr	Ives	L. R.	Dvr		170516	
Huzzey	N. E.	Dvr	Ivey	H. J.	S/Sjt	James	J. S.	Dvr
Hyde	A.	Pte					168212	
Hyde	D. J.	L/Cpl				James	K. H.	Dvr
Hyde	H.	Sjt	Jack	A. McG.	L/Cpl	James	L. E.	Dvr
Hyde	J.	Dvr	Jack	D. H.	Capt	James	L. W.	Cpl
Hyde	W.	Dvr	Jackson	A.	Dvr	James	M. P.	Dvr
Hyder	S.	Dvr	Jackson	A.	Pte	James	N.	Cpl
Hylton	C. W.	Dvr	Jackson	A. G.	L/Cpl	James	T. H.	Dvr
Hylton	R. F. L.	Dvr	Jackson	C.	Sjt	James	W.	Dvr
Hynd	W.	Dvr	Jackson	D. R.	L/Cpl	James	W. L.	L/Cpl
Hynds	P.	Dvr	Jackson	E. H.	Pte	James	W. T.	Capt
Hynes	A. J.	Dvr	Jackson	E. W.	Dvr		M.C.	
Hynes	W.	Dvr	Jackson	F.	Dvr	Jamieson	B. F.	Sjt
Hyslop	J. C.	Pte	Jackson	F. G.	Dvr	Jamieson	J. S.	Dvr
Hyslop	J. D.	Dvr	Jackson	F. S.	Pte	Jamieson	W.	Pte
			Jackson	F. W.	Cpl	Jamison	T. J.	Pte
			Jackson	G. H.	Pte	Jardine	E. B.	2/Lt
Ibberson	F.	L/Cpl	Jackson	G. R.	Dvr	Jardine	K. I.	Pte
Ibbotson	F.	L/Cpl	Jackson	H.	Dvr	Jardine	W.	Dvr
Iggleden	P. F.	WO I	Jackson	H. E.	Dvr	Jardine	W. A.	Dvr
Iles	E. R.	Dvr	Jackson	H. V.	Capt	Jarman	H. G.	Pte
Imrie	P.	Dvr	Jackson	J.	Sjt	Jarratt	G.	Dvr
Ince	C.	Dvr	Jackson	R.	Dvr	Jarrett	H. M.	Dvr
Ince	G. W.	Dvr	Jackson	S. F.	Dvr	Jarrott	R. G.	Pte
Ince	H. W.	Dvr	Jackson	S. F.	S/Sjt	Jarvie	J.	Dvr
Inch	K. F.	2/Lt	Jackson	T.	Dvr	Jarvis	F. C.	Dvr
Inchley	G. F.	Sjt	Jackson	W. H. G.	Dvr	Jarvis	F. W.	Pte
Ingarfield	A. H.	Dvr	Jacobs	E.	Dvr	Jarvis	J.	Pte
Ingham	F.	Sjt	Jacobs	H. R.	Dvr	Jarvis	L. H.	Dvr
Inglefield	W. H.	Cpl	Jacobs	R.	Sjt	Jarvis	W. E.	Pte
Inglis	R.	Dvr	Jacobs	W. A.	L/Cpl	Jary	C.	Dvr
Ingman	A. F.	Dvr	Jacobson	H.	Dvr	Jayes	G. C.	Dvr
Ingram	A. F. J.	Dvr	Jacques	A.	Dvr	Jeakins	R.	Dvr
Inkson	D.	Pte	Jacques	G.	Sjt	Jeeves	V. W.	Dvr

ROLL OF HONOUR

Surname	Initials	Rank	Surname	Initials	Rank	Surname	Initials	Rank
Jefferies	W.	Pte	Johnson	C.	Pte	Jones	A. S.	Dvr
Jefferies	W.	Dvr		234235		Jones	B.	Sjt
Jefferson	H.	Cpl	Johnson	C. W.	Dvr	Jones	C. H.	Pte
Jefferson	L. H.	Maj	Johnson	E.	Dvr	Jones	D. J.	Dvr
Jeffrey	J.	Cpl		190178		Jones	D. J. G.	Dvr
Jeffrey	J. B.	Sjt	Johnson	E.	Dvr	Jones	D. L.	Dvr
Jeffrey	J. G.	2/Lt		72237		Jones	D. M.	Sjt
Jeffrey	T. H. C.	Dvr	Johnson	E. G.	Cpl	Jones	D. O.	S/Sjt
Jeffries	R. S.	Cpl	Johnson	E. G.	Sjt	Jones	D. R.	Pte
Jenkins	A. H.	Dvr	Johnson	E. L.	Dvr	Jones	D. R.	Dvr
Jenkins	A. N.	Maj	Johnson	F. L.	Pte	Jones	D. R. L.	Dvr
Jenkins	A. W. S.	Dvr	Johnson	G. W.	L/Cpl	Jones	E.	Cpl
Jenkins	D. G.	Dvr	Johnson	H.	Sjt	Jones	E.	Dvr
Jenkins	E.	Dvr	Johnson	H. J.	Capt		123436	
Jenkins	J. H.	Pte	Johnson	J.	Pte	Jones	E.	Dvr
Jenkins	J.	Dvr	Johnson	J. A.	Sjt		193705	
Jenkins	J. R.	Cpl	Johnson	L. E.	Dvr	Jones	E. B.	Dvr
Jenkins	J. R.	Pte	Jonnson	N. W.	Dvr	Jones	E. D. C.	Cpl
Jenkins	R.	Dvr	Johnson	P. H.	L/Cpl	Jones	E. R.	Pte
Jenkins	R. E.	Dvr	Johnson	R.	Dvr	Jones	E. W.	Cpl
Jenkins	R. J.	Pte	Johnson	S.	Dvr	Jones	E. W. P.	Dvr
Jenkins	T. W.	Dvr	Johnson	S.	Cpl	Jones	F.	Dvr
Jenkins	W. R.	WO II	Johnson	S. C.	Dvr	Jones	F. W.	Sjt
Jenkinson	A. V.	Pte	Johnson	T.	Dvr	Jones	G.	Dvr
Jenkinson	F.	Dvr	Johnson	W. E.	Pte	Jones	G. B.	Pte
Jenkinson	W.	Cpl	Johnson	W. F.	Cpl	Jones	G. C.	Dvr
Jenner	H. J.	Pte	Johnson	W. H.	Pte	Jones	G. E.	Dvr
Jenner	L. R. F.	Dvr	Johnston	A.	Sjt	Jones	G. F.	L/Cpl
Jenner	R.	Dvr	Johnston	A.	Pte	Jones	G. H. B.	Dvr
Jennings	A. A. H.	Dvr	Johnston	J.	Pte	Jones	G. S.	Pte
Jennings	E.	Pte	Johnston	J. F.	Dvr	Jones	H.	Cpl
Jennings	J. G.	Dvr	Johnston	P.	Dvr	Jones	H. G.	Dvr
Jennings	S.	Dvr	Johnston	R. W.	Dvr	Jones	H. J.	Dvr
Jennings	T. P.	Dvr	Johnston	W. E.	L/Cpl	Jones	H. L.	Pte
Jenvey	A. G.	Dvr	Johnstone	D.	Cpl	Jones	H. O.	Sjt
Jepson	F.	Dvr	Johnstone	G. F.	Dvr	Jones	J.	Dvr
Jepson	S. E.	L/Cpl	Johnstone	J.	Dvr	Jones	J. E.	Pte
Jerrome	N. J.	Dvr	Johnstone	J. D. H.	Dvr	Jones	J. H.	Cpl
Jessett	W.	Sjt	Johnstone	J. R.	Pte	Jones	J. H.	Dvr
Jessiman	J.	Pte	Johnstone	T. Mc.C.	Dvr	Jones	J. L.	Dvr
Jessop	T.	Dvr	Johnstone	W. J.	Dvr		272716	
Jestico	S. W.	Sjt	Jolliffe	F. H.	Dvr	Jones	J. L.	Dvr
Jewitt	L. G.	Dvr	Jolly	A. W.	Dvr		66284	
Joachim	K. C.	Pte	Jonas	R. W.	Capt	Jones	J. L.	Pte
Jobling	C. W.	Dvr	Jones	A.	Dvr	Jones	L.	Pte
Jocelyn	H. J.	Dvr		174516		Jones	L.	L/Cpl
Joesbury	W. F.	Dvr	Jones	A.	Dvr	Jones	L.	Dvr
Johns	E.	Dvr		228571		Jones	L. A.	Lt-Col
Johns	M. L.	2/Lt	Jones	A.	Dvr		M.B.E.	
Johns	T. A.	Dvr		1826104		Jones	L. C.	Sjt
Johnson	A.	Dvr	Jones	A.	Cpl	Jones	L. D.	Dvr
Johnson	A. W.	Dvr	Jones	A. D.	Sjt	Jones	L. E. H.	Pte
Johnson	A.	L/Cpl	Jones	A. H.	Dvr	Jones	L. T.	L/Cpl
Johnson	A. E.	Pte		218967		Jones	L. W.	Dvr
Johnson	A. W. H.	Dvr	Jones	A. H.	Dvr	Jones	N.	Dvr
Johnson	C.	Pte		10667169		Jones	P.	Dvr
	157223		Jones	A. H.	Dvr	Jones	P. T.	Dvr
Johnson	C.	Dvr		10695576		Jones	R.	Pte

ROLL OF HONOUR

Jones	R.	Dvr	Keating	J. J.	Dvr	Kennan	L. W.	Maj
Jones	R. B.	Dvr	Keatley	C. W. R.	Pte		M.B.E.	
Jones	R. G.	Dvr	Keaveney	T. A.	Pte	Kennard	F. L.	Dvr
Jones	R. H.	S/Sjt	Keefe	G.	Cpl	Kennard	H. G.	WO II
Jones	R. J.	Dvr	Keegan	J.	Dvr	Kennard	W. D. W.	Dvr
Jones	R. O.	L/Cpl	Keegan	J. R.	Dvr	Kennedy	J. C.	Pte
Jones	S.	Dvr	Keel	R. J.	Dvr	Kennedy	J. R.	Dvr
Jones	S. A.	Cpl	Keeley	R. A.	Dvr	Kennedy	P.	Dvr
Jones	S. C.	Sjt	Keeley	W. J.	Dvr	Kennell	J. J.	Dvr
Jones	S. J.	Cpl	Keeling	A. J.	Dvr	Kenny	W.	Dvr
Jones	T.	Pte	Keeling	W. W.	L/Cpl	Keohone	W. B.	Pte
Jones	T. A.	L/Cpl	Keen	F.	Dvr	Kent	C. H.	Dvr
Jones	T. E.	Dvr	Keen	H.	Cpl	Kent	R. H.	Dvr
Jones	T. H.	Dvr	Keen	J. A.	Dvr	Kenton	J. W. C.	Cpl
Jones	T. O.	Dvr	Keen	R. A.	Dvr	Kenyon	E. A.	Cpl
Jones	T. W.	Dvr	Keenan	F. P.	Cpl	Kerfoot	L.	Dvr
Jones	W. E.	Dvr	Keeping	W. J. S.	Dvr	Kernaghan	J.	Dvr
Jones	W. G.	Cpl	Kefford	L. W. J.	Dvr	Kerr	F.	Dvr
Jones	W. H.	Cpl	Keggen	H. S.	Capt	Kerr	J.	Pte
Jones	W. R.	Dvr	Keggie	W. B.	Dvr	Kerr	J.	L/Cpl
Joplin	J. H.	Capt	Keilly	W. L.	Pte	Kerr	J. G.	Dvr
Jordan	J. T. T.	Pte	Kelgy	F.	Pte	Kerr	R. McL.	Dvr
Jordan	J. W. C.	Capt	Kelleher	T.	Dvr	Kerry	J. C.	Cpl
Jordan	W.	Pte	Kelleway	A. W.	Dvr	Kershaw	E.	Dvr
Joseph	T. H.	Dvr	Kelley	F. W.	Pte	Kershaw	E.	Pte
Jowett	J.	Pte	Ketley	A.	Dvr	Ketley	W. S.	Dvr
Jowitt	R. H.	Dvr	Kelly	A. 224071	Dvr	Kett	O. J.	Cpl
Joy	F. W.	Dvr	Kelly	A. 247632	Dvr	Kettle	S. R.	Sjt
Joyce	A. E.	L/Sjt				Keys	A. J.	Sjt
Joyner	J.	Dvr	Kelly	D. 179685	Dvr	Keywood	C. J.	Dvr
Juckes	R.	Dvr				Kibble	E.	Pte
Judd	E. R. F.	Dvr	Kelly	D. 126697	Dvr	Kidd	J.	Cpl
Judd	F. A.	Dvr				Kidd	L. G.	Dvr
Judd	J. L.	Cpl				Kidd	N. P.	L/Cpl
Judd	S. R.	Dvr	Kelly	D. 72293	Dvr	Kidd	S.	Dvr
Jung	G. L.	Pte				Kidney	T.	Dvr
Jury	E. F.	Dvr	Kelly	H.	Dvr	Killerby	T.	Sjt
			Kelly	J. J.	Dvr	Kilner	C. E.	Dvr
			Kelly	J. M.	Dvr	Kilpatrick	R. K.	Dvr
Kahn	R. J.	Dvr	Kelly	J. W.	Dvr	Kilpatrick	W.	L/Cpl
Kane	J. F.	Pte	Kelly	M. F.	Pte	Kilty	S.	Dvr
Karran	R. A.	Capt	Kelly	T.	L/Cpl	Kilvington	N. W.	Cpl
Karsten	P. W.	Dvr	Kelly	T. H.	Dvr	Kimberley	E.	Cpl
Katz	H. L.	Dvr	Kelsall	G.	Dvr	Kimche	C.	Pte
Kaufman	H.	Dvr	Kelvey	D.	Dvr	Kimpton	G. H.	Dvr
Kavanagh	D. T.	Capt	Kember	W. B.	Dvr	Kincey	L. C.	Dvr
Kay	D. L.	L/Cpl	Kemp	B. J.	Pte	King	A. A.	Dvr
Kay	J.	Dvr	Kemp	C.	Dvr	King	A. W. S.	Dvr
Kay	T. H.	Dvr	Kemp	J. A.	Dvr	King	C. C.	Dvr
Kaye	A. E.	Dvr	Kemp	P. W.	Dvr	King	H. C.	Dvr
Kaye	N.	Dvr	Kemp	W. J.	Dvr	King	H. J.	Cpl
Keam	S. G.	L/Cpl	Kempsford	H. J.	Pte	King	J.	Dvr
Kearney	H.	Pte	Kempster	B. B.	Dvr	King	J. F.	Sjt
Kearney	H. W.	Dvr	Kendall	A.	Pte	King	K. G.	L/Cpl
Kearney	J. J.	Dvr	Kendall	J. J.	Dvr	King	P. C.	Pte
Kearney	J. N.	Pte	Kendrew	J.	Dvr	King	P. E. T.	Dvr
Kearsey	H. J.	Dvr	Kendrick	J. E.	Lt	King	R. L.	Pte
Keast	F. J.	Pte	Kendrick	P.	Dvr	King	S. J.	Dvr

ROLL OF HONOUR

King	T. A.	Pte	Knight	W. C.	Dvr	Lancelott	G.	Dvr
King	T. J. A.	Cpl	Knightly	D. H. J.	Dvr	Land	W.	Sjt
King	V. J.	Dvr	Knighton	C.	Dvr	Lane	F. A.	Dvr
King	W. L.	Sjt	Knott	A. S.	Dvr	Lane	F. J.	Dvr
Kingscote	E. M.	Cpl	Knott	J.	Pte	Lane	H.	Dvr
Kingsford	E. C.	Cpl	Knowles	C. D.	Dvr	Lane	J. R.	Maj
Kingsland	F. W.	Cpl	Knowles	K.	Dvr		M.B.E.	
Kingsland	S.	Dvr	Kohring	G. L.	L/Cpl	Lane	N. E.	Dvr
Kingsley	A. J.	Dvr	Koll	O. A.	L/Cpl	Lane	T. H.	Pte
Kingsley	L.	Sjt	Korniloff	E. M.	Cpl	Lane	T. J.	Dvr
Kingwell	W. R.	L/Cpl	Kortright	M.	Maj	Lane	W. G.	Pte
Kinniburgh	J.	Dvr	Korzun	V. J.	Dvr	Lang	A.	Dvr
Kinsey	J.	Pte	Kreuder	F. G. A.	Pte	Langdon	I. H. J.	Dvr
Kinsey	J. R.	Dvr	Kuss	W. J.	Dvr	Langford	A. R.	Dvr
Kipling	P. N.	Cpl	Kyle	A.	Dvr	Langford	G.	Dvr
Kirby	A. T.	L/Cpl	Kyle	A. M.	Dvr	Langford	W. A.	2/Lt
Kirby	E.	Dvr				Langford	W. T.	Dvr
Kirby	L.	Dvr				Langley	C. G. E.	Dvr
Kirby	M. J.	Dvr	Lacey	F.	Dvr	Langley	F. A. P.	CQMS
Kirby	R.	Pte	Lacey	H.	Dvr	Langley	H.	L/Cpl
Kirby	R.	Dvr	Lacey	J. A.	Pte	Langley	J.	Dvr
Kirby	R. F.	Pte	Lacey	J. W.	Pte		270670	
Kirdwood	J.	Pte	Lacey	R. F.	Dvr	Langley	J.	Dvr
Kirk	J. W.	Dvr	Lacey	S.	Dvr		3782097	
Kirkby	R.	Dvr	Lacy	H. M.	Sjt	Langley	T. H.	Dvr
Kirkby	T. W.	Dvr	Ladden	J. J.	Dvr	Langridge	A. C.	Cpl
Kirkbride	W.	Dvr	Lafferty	L.	Dvr	Langridge	H. F.	Dvr
Kirkdale	A.	Dvr	Laidler	H.	Dvr	Laniff	C.	Sjt
Kirkham	J. W.	Dvr	Laidlaw	D. McB.	Dvr	Lanoe	E. P.	Lt
Kirkham	W. M.	Lt	Laidlaw	J. K. B.	Dvr	Lansbury	E. R.	Dvr
Kirkland	K.	Dvr	Laidman	W. R.	Dvr	Lansdell	E.	Dvr
Kirkwood	A.	Dvr	Lain	A.	Dvr	Lansdell	E.	Pte
Kirkwood	J.	Dvr	Laing	F.	Dvr	Lansley	C.	Cpl
Kirkwood	J. B.	Dvr	Laird	R.	Sjt	Lapish	J. W.	Dvr
Kirton	F. J.	Dvr	Lake	E. G.	Dvr	Lapthorn	F. W.	L/Cpl
Kissock	A. W.	Cpl	Lake	J. R.	L/Cpl	Lardner	A. L. G.	Cpl
Kitch	W. H.	Dvr	Lake	R. S.	Dvr	Large	A. R.	Pte
Kitchingman,	J.	Dvr	Lakin	J. F.	Dvr	Large	E. H.	Dvr
Kloss	R. L.	2/Lt	Lamb	A. J. R.	Maj	Large	H. W.	Dvr
Knaggs	R.	Dvr		D.S.O.		Large	W. N.	Dvr
Knapp	F.	Dvr	Lamb	F. C.	Sjt	La Riviere	A. L.	Pte
Knapp	F. J. R.	Dvr	Lamb	H. A.	Pte	Larkam	J. E.	Pte
Knee	F. W.	Dvr	Lambert	A. C.	L/Cpl	Larkin	A.	Pte
Knee	J. W.	Dvr	Lambert	E. H.	Dvr	Larkins	A.	Dvr
Kneight	A. E. D.	L/Cpl	Lambert	F.	Dvr	Larter	H.	Dvr
Knevett	V. G. H.	Pte	Lambert	F. N.	Dvr	Lascelles	H. V.	Dvr
Knight	A.	Pte	Lambert	J. A.	Pte	Lassman	M.	Dvr
Knight	A. S.	Dvr	Lambert	V. H.	Pte	Later	T.	Dvr
Knight	C. W.	Pte	Lambert	W. G.	Cpl	Latham	E. J.	Dvr
Knight	E. J.	Dvr	Lamble	D. J.	Dvr	Latham	T.	Dvr
Knight	E. J.	WO II	Lambourne	L.	Dvr	Latimer	H. J.	Capt
Knight	G. A.	Dvr	Lambton	J.	Dvr	Latimer	W. S.	Dvr
Knight	G. S.	L/Cpl	Lamont	A.	Capt	Latus	B.	Dvr
Knight	H. J. M.	Dvr	Lamprey	C. S. L.	Dvr	Lauder	T.	Dvr
Knight	J.	Pte	Lancaster	A.	Lt	Laughton	E. A. J.	Dvr
Knight	J. A.	Sjt	Lancaster	A. W.	Dvr	Launder	R. G.	L/Cpl
Knight	R. C.	Dvr	Lancaster	W.	Dvr	Laundy	R.	Dvr
Knight	R. J. C.	Pte	Lancaster	W.	Cpl	Laverick	J. T.	Dvr

ROLL OF HONOUR

Laverick	R.	Sjt	Lee	H. J.	WO II	Lewis	D. H.	Dvr
Lavers	R. W. L.	Dvr	Lee	J.	Dvr	Lewis	D. W.	Dvr
Law	A.	Dvr	Lee	L. C. R.	Dvr	Lewis	G. S.	Dvr
Law	A. S.	Sjt	Lee	L. L.	Pte	Lewis	G. W.	Dvr
Law	F. G.	Dvr	Lee	R.	Dvr	Lewis	H.	Cpl
Law	F. H.	Dvr	Lee	R. W.	Pte	Lewis	H.	Pte
Law	S.	L/Cpl	Lee	V.	Dvr	Lewis	H. J.	Dvr
Lawes	T. C.	Dvr	Lee	W.	Dvr	Lewis	J.	Sjt
Lawman	C. S.	Pte	Leech	J. F.	Dvr	Lewis	J. C.	Dvr
Lawrence	A. E.	Dvr	Leek	J.	Pte	Lewis	J. H.	Dvr
Lawrence	B. J.	Dvr	Leema	H. B. D.	Dvr	Lewis	N. H.	Dvr
Lawrence	F. W.	Dvr	Leeming	F.	Pte	Lewis	R. A.	Dvr
Lawrence	W. H.	Dvr	Lees	F. A.	Dvr	Lewis	R. S.	Dvr
Lawry	W.	Dvr	Lees	H.	Dvr	Lewis	T. A.	Pte
Lawson	F.	Dvr	Lees	J.	Dvr	Lewis	T. H.	Dvr
Lawson	H.	Dvr	Lees	J. R.	Dvr	Lewis	W. G.	Pte
Lawson	J. E.	Sjt	Lees	O. K.	Dvr	Lewis	W. J.	Dvr
Lawson	J. W.	Pte	Lees	R. F.	Lt	Lewis	W. T.	Dvr
Lawson	P. S.	Dvr	Lefever	A. N.	Cpl	Lewis	W. T.	Pte
Lawson	R. O. L.	Dvr	Leftwich	B. S. W.	L/Cpl	Lidgett	F.	Pte
Lawson	T.	Dvr	Legg	G.	Dvr	Lightbown	F.	Pte
Lawson	T. P.	Pte	Legg	G. C.	Dvr	Lightfoot	G.	L/Cpl
Lawton	S.	S/Sjt	Leggat	N. A.	Cpl	Lightwood	C. W.	Dvr
Lay	R. C.	Dvr	Legood	F. C.	Pte	Lilley	K. H.	Dvr
Layfield	A.	Dvr	Legood	J. C.	Sjt	Lilley	L. G.	Dvr
Layfield	A. I.	L/Cpl	Legood	S. F. E.	Pte	Linacre	J. H.	Dvr
Layhe	F.	Cpl	Leigh	A. H.	Sjt	Lincoln	A. L.	Dvr
Laytham	J.	Pte	Leighton	T. W.	Maj	Lincoln	H. J.	Cpl
Layton	G. H.	Cpl	Leighton	W.	Pte	Lincoln	R.	Dvr
Layzell	S. C.	Pte	Leishman	A.	Pte	Lindley	R.	Dvr
Le Bihan	E.	L/Cpl	Leland	F. J.	Lt-Col	Lindsay	N. C.	Dvr
Le Court	S.	Dvr	Lello	G. W.	Dvr	Lindsey	A. G.	Dvr
Le Feyre	B. N.	Cpl	Lennard	H. E. D.	Dvr	Line	P. D.	Dvr
Le Mesurier	B. G.	Capt	Lennie	C.	Pte	Lines	H.	Dvr
Le Moignan	A. H. J.	L/Cpl	Lenton	D. J.	Dvr	Linford	E.	L/Cpl
Leach	E.	Cpl	Lenton	R.	WO II	Linford	R. W.	Dvr
Leach	F.	Dvr	Leonard	H. B. H.	Cpl	Ling	L. E.	Dvr
Leach	F. J. V.	Dvr	Leonard	H. R.	Dvr	Ling	R. G.	Dvr
Leach	J. H.	Dvr	Leonard	J. D.	Sjt	Ling	W. A.	Dvr
Leadbetter	H. F.	L/Cpl	Leslie	R.	Dvr	Lingard	F.	Cpl
Leadley	A. V.	L/Cpl	Lester	A.	WO II	Linger	E. J.	Dvr
Leah	H. F.	L/Cpl	Lesueur	C. G.	Pte	Linklater	G.	Pte
Leak	R. F.	Dvr	Letchford	S. W.	Dvr	Linley	A. R.	Cpl
Leamey	J.	Pte	Letherbarrow,	E.	Dvr	Linley	R.	Dvr
Leamon	R. J.	Cpl	Lever	V.	Dvr	Linsell	A. C.	Dvr
Leamy	L.	Dvr	Levey	S. A.	Sjt	Lipman	R. B.	2/Lt
Lear	P.	Dvr	Levittee	R. E.	Pte	Lisle	G. H.	Dvr
Learmonth	A.	Dvr	Levitton	H. L.	L/Cpl	Lister	D.	Pte
Leary	A.	Dvr	Levy	I.	Dvr	Lister	E. L.	Dvr
Leaver	W. G.	Dvr	Levy	J.	Dvr	Lister	J.	Cpl
Leclercq	C. P.	Pte	Lewery	W. J.	Pte	Lister	N. W.	Dvr
Ledbury	B. A.	Dvr	Lewin	F. W. G.	Capt	Lister	P. R.	Lt
Ledgard	A.	Dvr	Lewis	A. J.	Dvr	Lister	R.	Dvr
Ledger	A. E.	L/Sjt	Lewis	C. H. B.	Pte	Litchfield	G. W.	Dvr
Ledger	G.	Dvr	Lewis	C. S.	Cpl	Little	C.	Dvr
Lee	A. J.	Dvr	Lewis	C. S.	Dvr	Little	D.	Dvr
Lee	A. J.	Sjt	Lewis	D.	Dvr	Little	J.	Pte
Lee	H. G.	Dvr	Lewis	D. G.	S/Sjt	Little	L.	Dvr

ROLL OF HONOUR

Little	L. R.	Cpl	Lord	A.	Dvr	Lynn	V.	Dvr
Little	R.	Pte	Lord	E.	Dvr	Lynock	T.	Pte
Little	T. J. W.	Cpl	Lord	P.	Pte	Lyons	F. R.	Sjt
Littleford	K.	Pte	Lord	R.	Pte	Lyth	R. A.	Pte
Littlejohns	S. B.	Dvr	Loudwill	T.	Pte			
Littlewood	H.	Cpl	Loughran	L. A.	Dvr			
Littlewood	L. R.	Pte	Loughridge	J.	Dvr	Mabbutt	M. C.	Dvr
Livingston	C. G.	Cpl	Louth	H. D.	Dvr	Macaskill	N. D.	Dvr
Lizius	G.	Dvr	Lovatt	H.	Dvr	Macdonald	G.	Dvr
Lloyd	A. A.	Pte	Love	A.	Lt	Macdonald	H.	Cpl
Lloyd	A. D.	Lt	Love	A. G.	Dvr	Macdonald	J.	Dvr
Lloyd	C. R.	Pte	Love	J. F.	Cpl	Macdonald	W. J.	Dvr
Lloyd	H.	Sjt	Loveday	W. H.	Pte	Macdonnell	T. E.	Sjt
Lloyd	H. C.	WO II	Lovegrove	L.	Dvr	Machin	A. J.	Dvr
Lloyd	J. D.	Cpl	Lovegrove	P. E.	Sjt	Machin	W. L.	Sjt
Lloyd	J. L.	Dvr	Lovekin	K. E.	Dvr	Mackay	J. J. B.	S/Sjt
Lloyd	J. R.	Dvr	Lovell	A. D.	Dvr	Mackay	M. B.	Pte
Lloyd	T. W.	Cpl	Lovell	C. C.	Dvr	Mackenzie	B.	Capt
Lloyd	W.	Dvr	Lovell	D.	Pte	Mackenzie	D.	Cpl
Lloyd	W. T.	Dvr	Lovell	E. S.	Cpl	Mackenzie	J. B.	Cpl
Loades	H. E.	Sjt	Lowe	C. F.	Dvr	Mackenzie	J. H.	Cpl
Loates	S. J.	L/Cpl	Lowe	F.	Dvr	Mackenzie	J. R.	Dvr
Lobley	W.	Dvr	Lowe	J.	Dvr	Mackenzie	R.	Pte
Loch	G. A.	Capt	Lowe	J. G.	Dvr	Mackenzie	W. A. B.	Dvr
Lock	H. J.	Dvr	Lowe	L. S.	Cpl	Mackie	W.	Dvr
Lock	J. G. S.	Sjt	Lowe	T.	Dvr	Mackinnon	R. A.	Sjt
Locke	C. R.	WO I	Lowe	T.	Pte	Macklen	F. T.	Dvr
Lockett	B. L.	Dvr	Lowe	W.	Dvr	Maclarty	J. W. J.	Dvr
Lockwood	C.	Sjt	Lowes	G. R.	Dvr	Maclean	R. N.	Lt
Lockwood	G. H.	Dvr	Lown	H. J.	Sjt	Maclellan	H. B.	2/Lt
Lockwood	W.	L/Cpl	Lowrey	A.	L/Cpl	Macleod	D. G.	Dvr
Lockyer	F. H.	Dvr	Lowry	D. C.	Cpl	MacLeod	N.	Dvr
Lody	A.	L/Cpl	Lowry	P. J. J.	Dvr	Macmaster	A.	L/Cpl
Lofthouse	W.	Dvr	Lowther	J. C.	Dvr	Macmillan	J. G.	Sjt
Logan	D.	Pte	Lowther	R.	Dvr	Macneill	I.	Dvr
Logan	J. B.	Pte	Loxam	W.	Pte	Macphee	A.	Pte
Logan	W. G.	Sjt	Loxton	E. L.	Capt	Macready	D. G.	Dvr
Lomas	D. H.	Dvr	Luchini	F.	Dvr	Madden	H.	Dvr
Lomas	F.	Dvr	Lucy	R. A. A.	Dvr	Maddison	J.	Dvr
Lomas	G. T.	Dvr	Ludlow	L. J.	L/Cpl	Maddock	D. G.	Sjt
Lomas	K.	Dvr	Lukes	C. J.	Pte	Maddocks	H. S.	Dvr
Lomas	T. G.	Dvr	Lummis	L. F.	Dvr	Maddox	F.	Dvr
London	H. W.	Dvr	Lunn	J.	Dvr	Maggs	D. J.	L/Cpl
London	J. W.	Dvr	Lunn	J. W.	Dvr	Maguire	V.	Dvr
Loney	H. G.	Capt	Lunn	T.	Dvr	Maguire	W.	Sjt
Long	J.	Dvr	Lupton	D. C. W.	Cpl	Mahaffey	G.	Dvr
Long	L.	Dvr	Luscott	P.	Dvr	Mahon	J.	Cpl
Longden	A.	Dvr	Lusted	E.	Dvr	Mahon	T.	Dvr
Longden	H. J.	Dvr	Lutton	W. J.	Pte	Maidment	E. F.	L/Cpl
Longden	W. S.	2/Lt	Lutz	F.	Dvr	Maidment	H. A.	Cpl
Longfield	S. J.	Dvr	Luxford	E. A.	Lt	Mailey	J.	Dvr
Longhurst	G. M.	Dvr	Luxton	W. G.	Dvr	Maillard	E. S.	Pte
Longley	G. W.	Dvr	Lyall	A.	Dvr	Mainprice	D. J.	2/Lt
Longman	J. R.	Dvr	Lynam	T. L.	Dvr	Major	H.	Cpl
Longmuir	A.	Dvr	Lynch	G. H.	WO II	Major	W. J. C.	Dvr
Longshaw	C. J.	Pte	Lynch	J.	Dvr	Makinson	J.	Dvr
Longstaff	T. G.	Dvr	Lynch	W. F.	Dvr	Malcher	H. F.	Sjt
Look	R. J.	Sjt	Lynn	J. J.	Cpl	Malcolm	A.	Cpl

ROLL OF HONOUR

Malcolm	S.	Dvr	Marsh	G.	Pte	Massé	J. M. H.	2/Lt
Malcolm	W.	Cpl	Marsh	H.	Pte	Massey	J.	Dvr
Malin	F.	Dvr	Marsh	J. E.	Dvr	Massey	L. A.	Dvr
Mallam	A. J.	Pte	Marsh	J. F.	Sjt	Massey	L. G.	Dvr
Mallinson	A.	Dvr	Marshall	A. G.	Cpl	Massie	C.	Pte
Mallinson	H.	Dvr	Marshall	A. H.	Dvr	Mastaglio	A.	Dvr
Mallinson	W. J.	Sjt	Marshall	E.	Sjt	Masters	G. C.	Cpl
Malloy	R.	Dvr	Marshall	F. R.	Pte	Masters	K. C.	Capt
Malone	T.	Pte	Marshall	G.	Dvr	Masters	W. K.	Dvr
Maloney	C.	Pte	Marshall	G. E.	WO I	Matchett	W.	Dvr
Maloney	W. T.	Dvr	Marshall	H.	WO II	Mather	C.	Dvr
Malpas	G.	L/Cpl	Marshall	H. W.	Pte	Mather	J.	Dvr
Manhood	D. F.	Pte	Marshall	J. H.	Dvr	Mather	W.	Dvr
Manktelow	R. J.	Pte	Marshall	L. J.	Dvr	Matheson	D. B.	Pte
Manley	J.	Cpl	Marshall	S.	Dvr	Matheson	M. S.	Dvr
Manlond	W.	Dvr	Marshall	W.	Sjt	Mathews	L.	Pte
Mann	C. F.	L/Cpl	Marshall	W.	Dvr	Mathews	W. H.	Dvr
Mann	H. C.	S/Sjt	Marshall	W.	Pte	Mathieson	W.	Dvr
Mann	J.	Dvr	Marshall	W. I. H.	Capt	Mattear	T.	Pte
Mann	K.	Dvr	Marshall	W. K.	Dvr	Matthew	G. W.	Dvr
Mann	L. A.	Pte	Marston	J.	Dvr	Matthews	A.	Dvr
Manners	R. C. S.	Lt	Martin	A. E.	Dvr		209529	
Manning	E. G.	Cpl	Martin	A. F.	Dvr	Matthews	A.	Dvr
Manning	E. S.	Pte	Martin	A. J.	Pte		263590	
Manning	F. E.	Cpl	Martin	F. R. N.	Sjt	Matthews	B. W.	Dvr
Manning	G.	Dvr	Martin	G.	Dvr	Matthews	C.	Lt
Manning	L. B.	Dvr	Martin	G. F.	Dvr	Matthews	D. C. J.	Sjt
Mansbridge	G.	Dvr	Martin	J. A.	Pte	Matthews	D. S.	Cpl
Mansell	H.	Pte	Martin	J. K.	Pte	Matthews	D. V.	Dvr
Mansfield	A.	Lt	Martin	L.	Sjt	Matthews	E.	Dvr
Manson	R. P.	Pte	Martin	L. C.	Dvr	Matthews	E. R.	Dvr
Mantell	T. W.	Dvr	Martin	L. S.	Cpl	Matthews	F.	Dvr
Mantle	E. H.	Dvr	Martin	R. E.	Dvr	Matthews	F. E.	Pte
Mapplebeck	J.	Dvr	Martin	R. G.	L/Cpl	Matthews	G. A.	L/Cpl
Mapplebeck	W. A.	Dvr	Martin	R. W.	Cpl	Matthews	H.	Dvr
Maquire	C.	Pte	Martin	S. J.	Dvr	Matthews	M. C. F.	Dvr
Marcham	H. J. G.	Pte	Martin	S. R.	Dvr	Matthews	R.	Dvr
Marchant	J. E.	Pte	Martin	W.	Dvr	Matthews	S. G.	Cpl
Mardell	K. G.	Dvr	Martin	W. A.	Pte	Matthews	S. R.	Dvr
Margary	M. B.	Capt	Martin	W. F.	Dvr	Matthews	W. H.	Dvr
Margerrison	J.	Dvr	Martin	W. F.	Lt	Mattimore	H.	Dvr
Marjoram	A. W.	Dvr		M.M.		Matty	A. W. C.	Dvr
Markham	A.	Cpl	Martin	W. J.	Dvr	Maunders	O. P.	Dvr
Markham, G. B. McF.		Cpl	Martindale	F.	Dvr	Maurer	A. H.	Dvr
Markham	H. G.	Dvr	Martindale	J. T.	Dvr	Maw	G. L.	Dvr
Markin	H. J.	Dvr	Martins	E. W. J.	Dvr	Mawer	C.	Dvr
Marklew	J. R.	Pte	Martins	G. A.	Dvr	Mawson	H. A.	Cpl
Marks	C. S.	Dvr	Marvell	R.	Pte	Maxey	A.	Dvr
Marks	H. J.	Sjt	Marvin	C. R.	S/Sjt	Maxwell	R. D.	Dvr
Marlow	W.	Dvr	Mashford	H. W.	Dvr	Maxwell	R. F.	Cpl
Marney	T.	Dvr	Maskell	F.	Pte	Maxwell	W.	Dvr
Marren	M. J.	Sjt	Maskell	J. F.	Dvr	May	A. H.	Pte
Marriott	G. W.	Pte	Maslen	E. J.	Pte	May	F. V.	L/Cpl
Marriott	H. P.	Cpl	Mason	D.	Dvr	May	L. W. J.	Dvr
Marriott	W.	Dvr	Mason	J.	Dvr	May	P. A.	Pte
Marsden	H. H.	Cpl	Mason	J. C.	Dvr	Mayer	A. G.	Sjt
Marsden	T. C.	Dvr	Mason	J. L.	Dvr	Mayes	A. E.	Dvr
Marsh	C. S.	L/Cpl	Mason	S. H.	Dvr	Mayhew	E. R. W.	Dvr

ROLL OF HONOUR

Maynard	A.	L/Cpl	McDonald	J.	L/Cpl	McLaren	T. C.	Cpl
Maynard	L. J.	Dvr	McDonald	W.	Sjt	McLauchlan	E.	S/Sjt
McAllister	A.	Dvr	McDonough	A. E.	WO II	McLauchlan	S. A. D.	Maj
McAllister	A. L.	Dvr	McDougall	D.	Dvr	McLaughlin	A.	Dvr
McAndrew	H.	Dvr	McDougall	H.	Pte	McLaughlin	A.	L/Cpl
McAngus	W. W. S.	Capt	McEwen	J.	Dvr	McLaughlin	F.	Dvr
McAuliffe	W.	Dvr	McEwen	P.	Maj	McLaughlin	J.	Dvr
McAuslane	P.	Dvr	McFadden	T.	Pte	McLaughlin	R. D.	L/Cpl
McAvoy	W.	Dvr	McFadyen	F. J.	Pte	McLean	A. W.	Sjt
McCabe	A. J.	Dvr	McGairl	W. J.	Dvr	McLean	H. B.	Sjt
McCabe	B.	Dvr	McGee	B.	Dvr	McLean	H. R.	Pte
McCabe	F. J.	Dvr	McGee	F.	Pte	McLean	L. H.	Cpl
McCallum	R.	Dvr	McGee	M.	Dvr	McLean	P.	Pte
McCann	G.	Pte	McGeorge	J. S.	Dvr	McLean	R.	Dvr
McCann	G. T.	Dvr	McGeown	F.	Dvr		2760455	
McCance	J.	Dvr	McGhee	T.	Dvr	McLean	R.	Dvr
McCarthy	A.	Dvr	McGillveray, A. M.		Dvr		10687987	
McCarthy	C. E.	Dvr	McGinlay	J.	Dvr	McLean	W. D.	Dvr
McCarthy	G. D.	Dvr	McGlone	T.	Dvr	McLeish	D. J.	Dvr
McCarthy	J. H.	Pte	McGonigle	J.	Dvr	McLellan	J. M.	Dvr
McCarthy	M.	Dvr	McGovern	P.	Dvr	McLeod	C.	Pte
McCarthy	W. J.	L/Cpl	McGowan	A.	Dvr	McLeod	J. C.	Pte
McCartney	W.	Dvr	McGrath	J.	L/Cpl	McLeod	J. Mc.L.	Sjt
McCaughey	C.	Dvr	McGrath	R. C.	Dvr	McLeod	P.	Dvr
McClary	G. W.	Lt	McGregor	R. S.	Pte	McLeod	W. U.	Lt
McClive	T. G.	WO I	McGuffie	J. S.	Cpl	McLoughlin	J. E.	Dvr
McClusky	A.	Dvr	McGurk	B. D.	Cpl	McLuckie	W. S.	Pte
McCole	A. A.	Dvr	McHardy	F.	Dvr	McMahon	F.	Pte
McConnell	A. K.	Dvr	McIntosh	A.	Dvr	McMahon	M. O.	Dvr
McConnell	F.	L/Cpl	McIntosh	A. S.	Dvr	McManiman, S. B.		Dvr
McConnell	J.	Dvr	McIntosh	H. A.	Dvr	McManus	D.	Dvr
McConnell	K. C. J.	Dvr	McIntosh	K.	Maj	McMenemy	P.	Pte
McConnell	W. I.	Capt	McIntosh	W.	Dvr	McMillan	D.	Pte
McConvey	A. J.	Dvr	McIntyre	A.	Dvr	McMillan	P.	Pte
McCormack	H.	Dvr	McIntyre	B.	Pte	McMurray	C.	Pte
McCormack	W. H.	Pte	McIntyre	J.	Dvr	McMurray	T. A.	Pte
McCourt	A. S.	Dvr	McKay	H.	Dvr	McMyler	J.	Dvr
McCoy	J.	Dvr	McKay	R.	Sjt	McNab	J.	Dvr
McCoy	M.	Dvr	McKay	R. M.	Sjt	McNair	W. A. T.	Cpl
McCoy	P. J.	Dvr	McKay	W.	Dvr	McNally	P.	Dvr
McCracken	C. R.	Cpl	McKean	T. C.	Dvr	McNamara	T. E.	Sjt
McCraw	R. W.	Dvr	McKechnie	D.	Pte	McNee	J. W.	Cpl
McCrory	E. E.	Sjt	McKee	J. E.	Dvr	McNeil	D. N.	Pte
McCrossen	W. J.	L/Cpl	McKee	N. S.	Pte	McNeil	J.	Dvr
McCulloch	C. H.	L/Cpl	McKegg	F.	Cpl	McNeill	A.	Dvr
McCulloch	R.	Dvr	McKenna	J.	2/Lt	McNeill	D. F.	Pte
McCullough	J.	Dvr	McKenna	J.	L/Cpl	McNeish	A. F. T.	Dvr
McCurrach	J. H.	Dvr	McKenna	J.	Dvr	McNeish	J.	Dvr
McDermott	C. J.	Dvr	McKenzie	H. D.	L/Cpl	McNiven	A.	Dvr
McDine	S.	Dvr	McKenzie	J.	Dvr	McNulty	J.	Dvr
McDonagh	T. C. G.	Dvr	McKeown	B. A.	Dvr	McPhee	A.	Dvr
McDonald	C. L.	Dvr	McKeown	F.	Dvr	McPherson	J.	Dvr
McDonald	C. S.	Dvr	McKeown	P. J.	Sjt	McQuade	C.	Pte
McDonald	D.	Dvr	McKie	J. A.	Cpl	McQuade	E.	Dvr
McDonald	G.	Dvr	McKillop	A. H.	Cpl	McQueen	D. G.	Dvr
McDonald	H.	Dvr	McKinnon	J. G.	Dvr	McRae	J.	Dvr
McDonald	H. L.	Dvr	McLachlan	R.	L/Cpl	McShee	A.	Dvr
McDonald	J.	Pte	McLaren	J.	Dvr	McStravick	W. J.	Dvr

ROLL OF HONOUR

McVay	R.	Dvr	Midgley	W.	Pte	Milton	J.	Dvr
McVean	W.	L/Cpl	Mileham	F. E.	Dvr	Minall	H.	Cpl
McVeigh	E. H.	Dvr	Miles	G.	Dvr	Mingay	A. C. J.	Sjt
McVie	G.	Pte	Miles	H. B.	Dvr	Minns	S. W.	Dvr
McWha	G.	L/Cpl	Mill	R. F.	Dvr	Minton	J.	Dvr
McWilliam	F. O.	Dvr	Millard	D. C.	Dvr	Mirams	E. E.	Cpl
Meacham	W. E.	Dvr	Millard	E. J.	Sjt	Miskell	M.	Pte
Mead	C. J.	Dvr	Millard	T. H.	Dvr	Mison	F. W.	Dvr
Meadows	R. L.	Dvr	Miller	C.	WO II	Missen	L. E.	Dvr
Meads	J.	Sjt	Miller	C. R.	Dvr	Mitchell	C. E.	Cpl
Mearns	R. B.	Sjt	Miller	D.	Dvr	Mitchell	D. R.	Pte
Mears	A. E.	Dvr		4608463		Mitchell	F. H.	Dvr
Meddle	J. T.	Pte	Miller	D.	Dvr	Mitchell	H. N.	Pte
Meechan	J.	Dvr		79807		Mitchell	L. J.	Dvr
	44256		Miller	D. J.	Pte	Mitchell	R.	Cadet
Meechan	J.	Dvr	Miller	E.	Dvr	Mitchell	R. H.	Dvr
	84381		Miller	F. G.	Dvr	Mitchell	R. T.	Dvr
Meehan	J.	Pte	Miller	F. R.	Pte	Mitchell	S.	Dvr
Meek	D. W.	2/Lt	Miller	G.	Pte	Mitchell	S.	Lt
Meese	H. J.	Dvr	Miller	H.	Dvr	Mitchell	W. G.	Dvr
Megson	G. R.	Dvr	Miller	J.	WO I	Mitchell	W. G.	L/Cpl
Meikle	G. K.	Dvr	Miller	J. E.	Pte	Mitchell	W. J.	S/Sjt
Meldrum	B. R.	Cpl	Miller	J. R.	Cpl	Mitten	D. R.	Dvr
Melia	T.	Pte	Miller	L.	Dvr	Mitton	R. B.	Dvr
Mellars	E. G.	Pte	Miller	R.	WO II	Mizon	E. A.	Dvr
Mellentin	L.	Sjt	Miller	R. D.	Dvr	Moar	J. W.	Dvr
Melling	C. P.	Pte	Miller	S. L.	Dvr	Moate	E.	Dvr
Mellis	A.	S/Sjt	Miller	W. D.	Pte	Mobbs	L. P.	Pte
Mellor	R.	Pte	Miller	W. J.	Cpl	Mock	S.	Pte
Melton	F. J.	Dvr	Millgate	G. A.	Dvr	Mockford	S. G.	Dvr
Melville	A. J. A.	Dvr	Millikin	L.	Dvr	Moffat	J. B.	L/Cpl
Melville	J. N.	Dvr	Millington	B.	Cpl	Moffat	J. R.	Pte
Menach	W. A.	Dvr	Millington	L. H.	Sjt	Moffat	L. M.	L/Cpl
Mendham	A. J.	L/Cpl	Mills	A.	Dvr	Moffat	M. R.	Dvr
Mentiplay	A.	Cpl	Mills	A. L.	Dvr	Moffat	T. H.	Pte
Menzies	D. M.	L/Cpl	Mills	E.	Cpl	Moffat	W. G. B.	Pte
Menzies	G.	S/Sjt	Mills	F.	Dvr	Moffat	S. A.	Dvr
Menzies	P.	Dvr	Mills	J.	Dvr	Moffett	G. T.	Dvr
Mercer	H. S.	Dvr		250967		Moffitt	F. G.	Dvr
Mercer	J. B.	Dvr	Mills	J.	Dvr	Mogg	B. H.	Dvr
Merricks	A. W.	Dvr		169536		Mogg	J.	L/Cpl
Merrifield	G. V.	S/Sjt	Mills	J.	Dvr	Moir	C.	Sjt
Merrin	W.	Cpl		132714		Molloy	J.	Dvr
Merrington	H.	Dvr	Mills	J. C.	L/Cpl	Molyneux	J.	Dvr
Merritt	E. H.	L/Cpl	Mills	J. K. C.	Pte	Monaghan	S.	Dvr
Merry	J. F.	L/Cpl	Mills	P. W.	Cpl	Money	H. V.	Pte
Metcalf	A.	Cpl	Mills	W. H.	Dvr	Monk	G. J.	Sjt
Metcalfe	J.	S/Sjt	Millward	H. J.	Cpl	Monk	W. F. C.	Pte
Metcalfe	L. H.	Dvr	Millward	J. A.	Dvr	Monkhouse	A. S.	Dvr
Metcalfe	R. W.	Dvr	Millward	M.	Dvr	Montefiore	L.	Capt
Meteyard	S. A.	Capt	Milne	L.	Cpl	Montieth	E.	Pte
Meyrick	F. G.	Dvr	Milne	W.	Sjt	Moody	K. H.	Pte
	M.M.		Milner	G.	Dvr	Moody	S. R.	Dvr
Meyrick	J.	Dvr	Milner	H.	L/Cpl	Moody	W.	Dvr
Michie	A. G.	Dvr	Milner	L. J.	Pte	Mooney, A. J. McC.		Dvr
Mickle-			Milroy	J.	Dvr	Moorcock	F. J.	Pte
wright	L. L.	L/Cpl	Milsom	S. F.	Dvr	Moore	A.	Dvr
Middleton	J. H.	Dvr	Milton	H. A.	Cpl		286098	

ROLL OF HONOUR

Moore	A. 194814	Dvr	Morris	F. F.	Dvr	Mowitt	A. A.	Dvr
			Morris	H.	Pte	Moy	P. G.	Dvr
Moore	A. S.	Dvr	Morris	H. J.	Dvr	Moyes	J. D. H.	Dvr
Moore	A. W.	Dvr	Morris	H. J.	Pte	Moyle	R.	Cpl
Moore	C. A. 185874	Dvr	Morris	H. K.	Cpl	Moyles	H. A. C.	Dvr
			Morris	H. K.	Dvr	Moyse	R. G.	Cpl
Moore	C. A. 126755	Dvr	Morris	H. V.	Dvr	Moyses	T.	Pte
			Morris	I.	L/Cpl	Muckle	H. H.	Dvr
Moore	C. H.	Pte	Morris	J.	Dvr	Muggeridge	A. J.	Sjt
Moore	C. H.	Dvr	Morris	J. H.	Dvr	Muir	A. R.	Lt
Moore	D.	Dvr	Morris	J. S.	Dvr	Muir	E. J.	Sjt
Moore	G. A.	Dvr	Morris	L. G.	WO II	Muir	E. T.	Dvr
Moore	H. 788851	Dvr	Morris	S.	Capt	Muir	M.	Dvr
			Morris	S. V.	Dvr	Muir	R.	Dvr
Moore	H. 51396	Dvr	Morris	T.	Pte	Muir	T. S.	Dvr
			Morris	T. I.	Dvr	Mulcany	T.	L/Cpl
Moore	J.	Dvr	Morris	T.	Cpl	Muldowney	N. J.	Dvr
Moore	J. F.	Dvr	Morris	T. H.	Dvr	Mulford	P.	Dvr
Moore	L.	Cpl	Morris	V.	Dvr	Mulholland	D.	Dvr
Moore	L. G.	Dvr	Morris	W.	Pte	Mull	M.	Dvr
Moore	R. H.	Pte	Morris	W.	Dvr	Mullen	A.	Dvr
Moore	R. W.	Pte	Morris	W. T.	Cpl	Mullen	S. J.	Sjt
Moore	S. E.	Pte	Morrish	E. D.	Pte	Mullineaux	R.	Sjt
Moore	W. F.	Dvr	Morrison	D. C.	S/Sjt	Mulliner	A. R.	Dvr
Moore	W. J.	Lt	Morrison	H. M. A.	L/Cpl	Mullinger	F. J.	Pte
Moreton	L. G.	Dvr	Morrison	J.	Pte	Mullins	D. G.	Dvr
Morgan	C. G. M.C.	Lt	Morrison	J. McI.	Pte	Mullins	J.	S/Sjt
			Morritt	G. E.	Dvr	Mullins	L.	Dvr
Morgan	D. J.	Pte	Morrow	S.	Dvr	Mullins	M.	Pte
Morgan	E.	Dvr	Morse	W. E.	Maj	Mundy	E. G.	Dvr
Morgan	E. G.	Capt	Mortimer	M. R. S.	Sjt	Munford	G. T.	Dvr
Morgan	E. R.	Dvr	Mortimer	W. S.	2/Lt	Munn	R. W.	Dvr
Morgan	F. C.	Dvr	Morton	A. S.	Pte	Munnerley	C.	Pte
Morgan	F. H.	Dvr	Morton	E. J.	L/Cpl	Munro	A.	Cpl
Morgan	G.	Dvr	Morton	H.	Dvr	Munro	G.	Pte
Morgan	H. F. J.	L/Sjt	Morton	J.	Pte	Munro	J. R.	Dvr
Morgan	O.	Dvr	Morton	R.	Dvr	Munro	W.	Dvr
Morgan	T. J.	Sjt	Moscardini	F. D.	Dvr	Munslow	G. L.	Dvr
Morgan	V.	L/Cpl	Moscrop	G. T.	Dvr	Munt	W. J.	Dvr
Morgan	W. A.	Dvr	Mosedale	H. C.	S/Sjt	Murby	H. S.	Sjt
Morgan	W.	Dvr	Moseley	B.	Dvr	Murch	W. R.	L/Cpl
Morgan	W.	Cpl	Moseley	E. H.	Dvr	Murfitt	A.	Dvr
Morgan	W. G.	L/Cpl	Mosley	J.	Dvr	Murfitt	G. A.	Dvr
Morgan	W. K.	Dvr	Moss	A.	WO I	Murkin	A. R.	Dvr
Morgan	W. S. C.	Pte	Moss	C. J.	Dvr	Murphy	A.	Pte
Morley	G.	Dvr	Moss	G.	Dvr	Murphy	A.	Dvr
Morley	R. G.	Dvr	Moss	G. L.	L/Cpl	Murphy	E.	Cpl
Morr	I. R.	Dvr	Moss	W.	Dvr	Murphy	E. T.	Pte
Morrell	E. J.	L/Cpl	Moss	W. S.	Pte	Murphy	H.	Pte
Morris	A. D.	Pte	Mossman	T. H.	L/Cpl	Murphy	J.	Dvr
Morris	A. L.	Pte	Mottershead, H.		Dvr	Murphy	J. M.	Sjt
Morris	B.	Dvr	Mottrain	L.	Dvr	Murphy	O.	Pte
Morris	D. J.	Cpl	Moughtin	P.	Dvr	Murphy	O.	Dvr
Morris	D. P.	Cpl	Moul	A.	Dvr	Murphy	P. J.	Lt
Morris	E. H.	Pte	Mould	W. A.	L/Cpl	Murphy	P. J.	Dvr
Morris	E. J. R.	Dvr	Mountain	D.	Dvr	Murray	A.	Pte
Morris	E. W.	Dvr	Mousley	J.	Cpl	Murray	A. E.	Dvr
Morris	F.	Capt	Mowatt	H.	Dvr	Murray	C.	Cpl

ROLL OF HONOUR

Murray	J. 10701803	Dvr	New	T.	Pte	Noblett	C.	S/Sjt
			Newall	F. N.	Sjt	Nock	A. L.	S/Sjt
Murray	J. 141393	Dvr	Newbold	G. W.	Dvr	Nodes	H. F.	Dvr
			Newbold	J.	Sjt	Nokes	W. G. J.	Sjt
Murray	J.	Pte	Newbon	C.	Pte	Nolan	E.	Dvr
Murray	N. M.	Pte	Newby	C.	Pte	Nolan	J. E.	Dvr
Murray	R. 192084	Dvr	Newham	H. M.	Lt	Nolan	W.	Cpl
			Newman	E.	Dvr	Noone	J.	Dvr
Murray	R. 190035	Dvr	Newman	E. D.	Cpl	Norfolk	M. B.	Pte
			Newman	E. J. W.	L/Cpl	Norfolk	W. T. H.	Dvr
Murray	T.	Cpl	Newman	G. S.	Dvr	Norgaard	C. C.	2/Lt
Murrell	J.	L/Cpl	Newman	J. T.	Dvr	Norkett	W. E.	Capt
Murrum	H.	Dvr	Newnham	G. S.	Dvr	Norman	C. E.	Dvr
Muscat	J.	L/Cpl	Newth	R. C.	Dvr	Norman	C. H.	Dvr
Musk	H.F.S.S.	Dvr	Newton	F.	Dvr	Norman	H.	Dvr
Mutch	J. W.	Sjt	Newton	G.	Dvr	Normoyle	D.	WO II
Mutlow	J. E.	Dvr	Newton	P. M.	Dvr	Norrington	T. W.	Cpl
Mutum	E. C.	Dvr	Newton	S.	Dvr	Norris	A.	Dvr
Myers	A. W.	Cpl	Newton	W. C.	Dvr	Norris	E. V. A.	Pte
Myhill	E. B.	Dvr	Neylon	J.	Dvr	Norris	F.	Dvr
Myson	E. R.	Dvr	Niblett	E. H.	2/Lt	Norris	G. W.	Dvr
			Nicall	G. H.	Cpl	Norris	L. G.	Dvr
			Nichol	A.	Pte	Norris	R.	Pte
Nash	B.	Dvr	Nicholas	J. L.	Pte	North	C. E.	Dvr
Nash	C.	Dvr	Nicholls	A. L.	Dvr	North	J. A. C.	Dvr
Nash	H. B.	L/Cpl	Nicholls	D. A.	Dvr	North	J. W.	Dvr
Nash	W.	Dvr	Nicholls	J. H.	Dvr	Northan	E. T. R.	Dvr
Nash	W. C.	L/Cpl	Nicholls	J. W.	Pte	Northrop	W.	Pte
Nash	W. D.	Cpl	Nicholls	S. W.	Capt	Norton	G. C.	Dvr
Naughton	A. C.	Dvr	Nicholls	W. W.	Dvr	Norton	H. J.	Cpl
Naylor	D. E.	Dvr	Nichols	F. P. R.	Lt-Col	Norton	N.	Dvr
Naylor	I.	Dvr		M.C.		Notson	E. H.	Capt
Naylor	R. S.	Cpl	Nichols	G. F.	Pte	Nottage	G. L.	Dvr
Neal	C. S.	Pte	Nicholson	A.	Dvr	Novis	J.	Cpl
Neal	F. H.	Dvr	Nicholson	A. A.	Dvr	Noy	R.	Dvr
Neal	G. H.	Dvr	Nicholson	A. J.	L/Cpl	Nuir	R.	Dvr
Neal	M. A.	Dvr	Nicholson	B.	Dvr	Nunn	D. C.	Capt
Neale	G.	Dvr	Nicholson	C. W.	Dvr	Nunn	J. B.	Dvr
Neary	H. T. J.	Dvr	Nicholson	R. W. C.	Sjt	Nunn	J. G.	Dvr
Neary	J.	Pte	Nicholson	W. H.	Cpl	Nunn	K.	Dvr
Neave	C.	Pte	Nickson	A.	Pte	Nutley	A. E. S.	L/Cpl
Neaves	E. J.	Pte	Nicol	W. J. M.	Pte	Nutman	J. H.	L/Cpl
Needham	C. R.	Dvr	Nicol	W. M.	Dvr	Nutt	J. L.	Sjt
Needham	E. R.	Sjt	Nicoll	P.	Cpl	Nutt	W.	Dvr
Needham	R. F. C.	Dvr	Nightingale	A. C.	Dvr	Nuttall	A.	Dvr
Needham	T.	Dvr	Nightingale	H.	Dvr	Nutter	C.	Dvr
Neighbour	H. W.	Dvr	Nimmo	R. A.	Cpl	Nutton	A. E.	Dvr
Neillis	J.	Dvr	Nisbet	A. R.	Cpl	Nuttycombe, G. P.		Dvr
Neilson	J. F. C.	Cpl	Nisbet	T.	Pte	Nye	G. A.	Pte
Nelson	A.	Dvr	Nish	J. P.	Dvr	Nyland	J. P.	Dvr
Nelson	D. E.	WO II	Niven	J. G.	Lt			
Nelson	H.	Dvr	Nixon	A. S.	Dvr			
Nelson	R.	Pte	Nixon	C.	Dvr	Oakes	L. B.	Capt
Nelson	T. H.	Dvr	Nixon	P.	Pte	Oakford	A. R.	Sjt
Nesbitt	L.	Dvr	Nixon	P. E.	Cpl	Oakland	L.	Pte
Nesham	A. H.	Dvr	Noble	C. M. D.	Dvr	Oakley	E. C.	Cpl
Neville	J. H. G.	Cpl	Noble	E.	Dvr	Oakley	E. T.	Dvr
Neville	L. W.	Dvr	Noble	H.	Dvr	Oakley	M. C.	L/Cpl

ROLL OF HONOUR

Oakley	R. C.	Pte	O'Neil	R.	Sjt	Page	A. M.	Pte
O'Beirne	M.	Pte	O'Neill	J. Y.	Pte	Page	A. W.	L/Cpl
Oborn	C.	Dvr	Onions	L.	Dvr	Page	C. H.	Dvr
O'Brien	A. J. C.	WO I	Oram	A. W.	Dvr	Page	E.	Dvr
O'Brien	D.	Cpl	Orange	C.	Cpl	Page	E. S.	Dvr
O'Brien	J.	Dvr	Orchard	H. J. D.	L/Cpl	Page	E. W.	Capt
O'Brien	J. D. P.	Pte	Orchard	J.	L/Cpl	Page	G. A.	Dvr
O'Brien	J. J. P.	Dvr	Organ	K. M.	Cpl	Page	H. J.	Dvr
O'Brien	T.	Dvr	Orr	R.	L/Cpl	Page	R. S.	Lt
O'Brien	W.	Pte	Orrell	S. A.	Pte	Page	S. T.	Dvr
O'Brien	W. J.	Sjt	Orris	P. W.	Pte	Page	V.	Dvr
O'Callaghan	H. T.	Pte	Orton	A.	Cpl	Page	W. A.	Dvr
Ochiltree	H. J. F.	Pte	Orton	H.	Dvr	Paget	D. V.	Dvr
O'Connor	A. E.	Dvr	Orton	J. W.	Dvr	Pagett	D. J.	L/Cpl
O'Connor	H.	Pte	Orton	N.	Dvr	Paice	S. O.	Sjt
O'Connor	J. D.	L/Cpl	Osborn	R. A.	Pte	Paine	B.	WO II
O'Connor, R.W.A.G.		Cpl	Osborne	D.	Dvr	Painter	A. H.	Capt
Oddie	G. E.	Dvr	Osborne	E. W.	Dvr	Palfrey	W. T.	Dvr
Oddy	H.	Dvr	Osborne	H.	Dvr	Palfreyman	J.	Dvr
Oddy	T.	Pte	Osborne	J.	Dvr	Palin	E. R.	Cpl
O'Donnell	E.	Pte	Osborne	T. D.	Dvr	Pallant	H. A.	Dvr
O'Donnell	J.	Dvr	Osman	S. E. B.	Sjt	Palmer	A. F.	L/Cpl
O'Dun	J.	Dvr	Ostick	J.	Dvr	Palmer	E. C.	Cpl
O'Dwyer	T. H.	Cpl	O'Sullivan	W. A.	Dvr	Palmer	E. C.	Dvr
Officer	C. G. R.	L/Cpl	Ottery	C. F. D.	Dvr	Palmer	E. H.	Dvr
Offord	S. G. J.	Dvr	Ovenden	C. R.	Dvr	Palmer	H.	Dvr
Ogden	C. E.	Dvr	Ovenden	W. C.	Pte	Palmer	T. H.	Pte
Ogden	R. K.	Dvr	Overall	C. P.	Dvr	Palmer	W. H.	Dvr
Ogden	W.	Cpl	Overfield	A. E.	Dvr		10663460	
Ogg	B. M.	Dvr	Overington	L. P. J.	Dvr	Palmer	W. H.	Dvr
Ogilvie	D.	Sjt	Overton	C.	WO II		273179	
Oglesby	R.	Dvr	Overton	C. R.	Dvr	Pannenter	D. J.	Dvr
Old	C. M.	Dvr	Owen	G. D.	Dvr	Paramore	L.	Pte
Old	T.	Dvr	Owen	F. E.	Sjt	Paramour	A. D.	WO I
Oldershaw	W.	Cpl	Owen	G.	Dvr	Pardoe	W.	Dvr
Oldfield	H.	Dvr	Owen	G.	Pte	Pardy	A.	Cpl
Oldroyd	A. E.	Dvr	Owen	H.	Dvr	Paris	W. N.	Sjt
Oldroyd	V. D.	L/Cpl	Owen	J. W.	Cpl	Park	I.	Dvr
Olds	R. A. E.	Dvr	Owen	R.	Dvr	Park	J.	Cpl
O'Leary	M.	Cpl	Owen	T. E.	Pte	Park	R.	Dvr
O'Leary	P.	Sjt	Owen	W. E.	Pte	Park	W. D.	Cpl
Olive	F. W.	Dvr	Owens	R.	Dvr	Parke	H. K.	Dvr
Oliver	G. R.	Pte	Owens	R. W.	Pte	Parker	A.	Dvr
Oliver	J.	Sjt	Owers	R.	Dvr	Parker	A. E.	Dvr
Oliver	M. F.	Dvr	Oxenbridge	A. F.	Dvr	Parker	A. L.	Pte
Oliver	R.	Dvr	Oxford	F.	Dvr	Parker	A. M.	Sjt
Oliver	R. D.	Pte	Oxlede	E. G.	Dvr	Parker	B. C.	Pte
Oliver	R. W.	L/Cpl	Oxley	F. A. J.	Pte	Parker	C.	Dvr
Oliver	S. G.	2/Lt	Oxnard	W. J. A.	Cpl	Parker	E. A.	Cpl
Oliver	W. A.	Sjt				Parker	E. T.	L/Cpl
Oller	L. V. J.	Dvr				Parker	F. W.	Dvr
Olley	G. P.	Dvr	Pack	C. J.	Dvr	Parker	J.	Dvr
Olley	R. E.	Dvr	Packer	A. J.	Dvr	Parker	J. F.	Pte
Olliver	S. G.	Dvr	Packer	E. G.	Cpl	Parker	L. J.	L/Cpl
O'Loughlin	A.	Dvr	Packham	R. B.	Dvr	Parker	R.	Sjt
O'Loughnane, B. T.		Dvr	Paddon	H. B.	Pte	Parker	R.	Dvr
Olsson	A. O.	Dvr	Padfield	L. J.	Dvr	Parker	T. L.	Pte
O'Neil	M.	Dvr	Padmore	L.	Dvr	Parker	W. H.	L/Cpl

ROLL OF HONOUR

Parker	W. J.	Dvr	Paton	G. B.	Pte	Pearson	W.	Dvr
Parker	W. R.	Pte	Patrick	H.	L/Cpl		146541	
Parkes	A.	Pte	Patrick	P.	Dvr	Peart	B. H.	Cpl
Parkes	E.	Dvr	Patrick	W.	WO II	Peart	R.	Dvr
Parkes	T.	Dvr	Patrick	W. P.	Pte	Peat	R. W.	Dvr
Parkin	W.	Dvr	Patterson	E.	Dvr	Peatfield	R. J.	Lt
Parkinson	A. J.	Dvr	Patterson	G. L.	Cpl	Peck	J. E.	Dvr
Parkinson	F.	Sjt	Pattinson	J. S.	Dvr	Peck	L. W.	L/Cpl
	110883		Paul	E. W.	Pte	Pedrozzollic	C. H.	Pte
Parkinson	F.	Sjt	Paul	G. V.	WO II	Peek	L.	Dvr
	178082		Paulley	E. J. V.	Pte	Peel	L.	Dvr
Parkinson	W.	Dvr	Paulson	H. C.	Dvr	Peer	R. F.	Pte
Parks	D.	Dvr	Pavey	F. A.	L/Cpl	Peggie	W. B.	Dvr
Parmenter	W. R.	Cpl	Pawley	L. H.	Dvr	Pegler	H. F.	Pte
Parnell	W. J.	Dvr	Pawsey	A.	Dvr	Pellier	R.	Dvr
Parnley	T.	Cpl	Paxton	D. F. H.	Sjt	Pelling	G. L. J.	Dvr
Parr	N. C.	Lt	Payne	A. J.	Dvr	Pelly	E. G.	2/Lt
Parr	W.	L/Cpl	Payne	A. J.	Cpl		D.S.O., M.C.	
Parrott	J. W.	Cpl	Payne	E. J.	Dvr	Pemberton	J. J.	Dvr
Parrott	L. J.	L/Cpl	Payne	F. H.	Dvr	Pemberton	J. K.	L/Cpl
Parrott	W. H.	Sjt	Payne	F. L.	Dvr	Pender	H. C.	Dvr
Parry	A. C.	Dvr	Payne	J. E.	Pte	Pender	J.	Dvr
Parry	C. A.	Pte	Payne	J. W.	Pte	Pendleton	D. L.	Dvr
Parry	G.	CQMS	Payne	J. W.	L/Cpl	Penfold	A. P.	Dvr
Parry	J. A.	Dvr	Payne	L. H.	Dvr	Penfold	E.	Cpl
Parry	N.	Pte	Payne	S. E.	Sjt	Penhaligon	T. E. J.	Maj
Parry	R.	Sjt	Payne	T. W.	Dvr	Penman	W.	Pte
Parry	R. T.	Dvr	Payne	W. F.	Sjt	Penna	P.	Pte
Parry	W. G.	Dvr	Peacey	J. B. S.	Lt	Pennington	A.	Dvr
Parsley	E. H.	Dvr	Peacock	L.	Dvr	Penniston	A.	Dvr
Parsons	A. J.	Dvr	Pearce	B. P.	Pte	Penny	G. A.	Dvr
Parsons	C.	Dvr	Pearce	C.	Dvr	Penny	G. E. W.	L/Cpl
Parsons	E. C. O.	Dvr		91608		Penrice	J. D.	Dvr
Parsons	E. T.	Sjt	Pearce	C.	Dvr	Penrose	G.	Dvr
Parsons	G. E.	Dvr		1040786		Penska	E. G.	Dvr
Parsons	G. R. W.	Pte	Pearce	C. H.	Dvr	Penston	W. V.	Dvr
Parsons	H.	Dvr	Pearce	E.	Dvr	Pentecost	F. C.	Dvr
Parsons	H. J.	Dvr	Pearce	E. G.	Dvr	Penty	H. T.	L/Cpl
Parsons	L. C.	Dvr	Pearce	G. S.	Cpl	Penzer	W. A.	Pte
Parsons	R.	Dvr	Pearce	G. W.	Dvr	Pepper	S.	Dvr
Parsons	R. E. W.	Cpl	Pearce	H. H.	Pte	Perera	P. A. T.	Dvr
Parsons	V. R.	Pte	Pearce	L. A.	Dvr	Perera	S. O. L.	Pte
Parsons	W. J.	Dvr	Pearcey	R.	Dvr	Perkes	R.	Cpl
Partner	W. G.	Cpl	Pearl	G. D.	L/Cpl	Perkins	A. C.	Capt
Partridge	A.	Cpl	Pearl	J. H.	Dvr	Perkins	E.	WO II
Partridge	J. H.	Pte	Pearman	E. W.	Dvr	Perkins	F. C.	Pte
Pascoe	F.	Dvr	Pears	N. A.	Lt	Perkins	H. J.	Dvr
Passey	C. F.	Dvr	Pearse	R. W.	Pte	Perkins	S. J.	Dvr
Passmore	A. V.	Dvr	Pearson	A.	Dvr	Perks	J. A.	Dvr
Passmore	E. T.	Dvr	Pearson	E.	2/Lt	Perks	L. M.	Sjt
Passmore	O. G.	Pte	Pearson	G. W.	Dvr	Perrett	G. A.	Pte
Patchesa	B. R.	Dvr	Pearson	J.	Dvr	Perring	R. S. H.	L/Cpl
Pater	D. A.	Pte	Pearson	J. A.	Cpl	Perris	G. A.	Capt
Paterson	A.	Dvr	Pearson	J. H.	Pte	Perrot	J. H. R.	Cpl
Paterson	F.	WO II	Pearson	O. O.	Dvr	Perry	A. S.	Dvr
Paterson	J.	Pte	Pearson	T.	Sjt	Perry	A. W.	L/Cpl
Pates	R. C.	Pte	Pearson	W.	Dvr	Perry	C.	Dvr
Paton	C. G.	Pte		99168		Perry	C. D.	Dvr

ROLL OF HONOUR

Perry	G. J.	Dvr	Pierpoint	M.	Dvr	Pollard	A.	Cpl
Perry	R. J.	Dvr	Piggott	C. F.	Dvr	Pollard	A. D.	L/Sjt
Perry	S. W.	Dvr	Piggott	V. E.	Dvr	Pollard	E. J.	Dvr
Perry	W. A.	Dvr	Pike	J. H.	Sjt	Pollard	S.	Cpl
Perry	W. F.	Dvr	Pilgrim	E. E.	Sjt	Pollock	J.	Dvr
Perryman	A. H.	Pte	Pilgrim	G.	Dvr	Pollock	S. K.	Cpl
Person	E. H.	Maj	Pilliner	C. E.	Dvr	Pollock	W.	Cpl
Pescodd	A. W. J.	Cpl	Pilling	E.	Dvr	Pollok	R. A.	Lt
Peter	J. L.	Pte	Pilling	J.	Capt	Pomeroy	C. H.	Dvr
Peter	J. R.	2/Lt	Pilson	J.	L/Cpl	Pomfrey	R. W.	Cpl
Peters	A. J.	Dvr	Pimlott	W. N.	Cpl	Ponter	J. R.	Dvr
Peters	D. H.	Dvr	Pincham	J.	Pte	Poole	D. E.	Pte
Peters	H. J.	Dvr	Pinchbeck	K. W.	Dvr	Poole	J.	Dvr
Peters	R.	Dvr	Pinder	E. J.	Capt	Poole	T. F. A.	Capt
Peters	W. E.	Dvr	Pinfold	F.	Pte	Poole	W. R. B.	Dvr
Petit	R.	Dvr	Pinfold	R.	Pte	Pooles	F. A.	Dvr
Pettigrew	A.	Cpl	Pink	G. F.	Dvr	Pooley	C. H.	Dvr
Petty	J. E.	Pte	Pinnell	F. J.	Pte	Pope	F. G.	Dvr
Phelps	A. H.	Dvr	Pipe	F. V.	Dvr	Pope	M. T.	Pte
Philips	R. H.	Sjt	Pipe	R. E.	2/Lt	Porritt	W.	Dvr
Philipson	T.	L/Cpl	Piper	C. H.	Dvr	Porter	H. A.	Cpl
Phillippo	R. P.	Dvr	Piper	I.	Cpl	Porter	J. R. H.	Pte
Phillips	C.	Pte	Piper	J. T.	Dvr	Porter	W. S.	Pte
Phillips	D.	Dvr	Piper	T. W.	Pte	Portway	P.	Capt
Phillips	D. D.	Dvr	Piper	W. P.	Pte	Post	R. J.	Cpl
Phillips	D. T.	Dvr	Pirie	A. C.	Dvr	Postings	S. O.	Dvr
Phillips	I.	Dvr	Pitchford	B.	Dvr	Potter	D. F.	Capt
Phillips	I. R.	Dvr	Pitman	M. G.	Dvr	Potter	E. C.	Pte
Phillips	J. A.	Pte	Pitson	E. H.	Dvr	Potter	E. L.	Cpl
Phillips	J. B.	Dvr	Pitt	A. W.	Dvr	Potter	F.	Dvr
Phillips	J. H.	Cpl	Pitt	F. S.	Cpl	Potter	G. E.	L/Sjt
Phillips	J. R.	L/Cpl	Pitt	P. T. W.	Sjt	Potter	L.	Dvr
Phillips	J. W.	Dvr	Pitt	T. F.	Cpl	Potter	R. F.	Pte
Phillips	T.	Dvr	Pittard	T. E.	Dvr	Potter	R.S.C.F.	Sjt
Phillips	T. A.	Cpl	Pitts	J. A.	Sjt	Potter	T. C.	Pte
Phillips	W.	L/Cpl	Place	G. F.	Pte	Potter	W. D.	Dvr
Phillips	W. C.	Dvr	Plackitt	F. A.	Dvr	Potts	G. M.	Dvr
Phillips	W. R. J.	Pte	Plaister	R. J.	Dvr	Potts	J. M.	Cpl
Philpots	J. H.	WO I	Plant	L.	L/Cpl	Potts	T. W.	Dvr
Phipps	T. W.	Sjt	Plant	L.	Pte	Potty	F. W.	Cpl
Pichard	J. E.	Pte	Plater	J. E.	Dvr	Pougher	I.	Dvr
Pickard	F.	Dvr	Platt	E.	Dvr	Poulter	F.	WO II
Pickard	A. J.	Dvr	Platt	W.	Lt	Poulter	H. C.	Capt
Pickering	A.	Dvr	Platt	W. W.	Dvr	Poulter	V. A.	Pte
Pickering	C. E.	L/Cpl	Playle	S. J.	Dvr	Poulton	E. G.	Pte
Pickering	F.	Dvr	Plews	J.	Dvr	Poulton	J. H.	Pte
Pickering	J. W.	Cpl	Plimmer	E. S.	Pte	Powell	A. E.	L/Cpl
Pickering	R.	Dvr	Plows	L. C.	Pte	Powell	A. J.	Pte
Pickersgill	C. N.	Dvr	Plows	W.	Sjt	Powell	G. R.	Cpl
Pickersgill	R.	Cpl	Plume	L. G.	Dvr	Powell	J.	Pte
Pickett	F.	Pte	Plumley	H. H.	S/Sjt	Powell	J.	Cpl
Pickett	T. O.	Pte	Plummer	H. I.	Pte	Powell	L. J.	WO II
Pickford	H. F.	Dvr	Plummer	H. J.	Dvr	Powell	R. W. G.	Dvr
Pickup	J. H.	Dvr	Plummer	H. R.	Dvr	Powell	R. W.	Dvr
Pidcock	G. A.	L/Cpl	Plunkett	J.	WO II	Powell	T. W.	Dvr
Piddington	W.	Dvr	Pocock	E. A. S.	Dvr	Powell	W. H.	Dvr
Pierce	A. R.	2/Lt	Poland	R. V.	WO II	Powell	W. J.	Dvr
Pierce	H. A.	Dvr	Polkinghorn	J.	Dvr	Power	J.	Pte

ROLL OF HONOUR

Power	P. J.	Cpl	Proctor	L.	Dvr	Rampley	F. G.	Dvr
Power	T.	Dvr	Proctor	T.	Dvr	Ramsay	J. P. M.	Cpl
Pownall	J.	Dvr	Proops	L. J.	Cpl	Ramsay	W. A.	Pte
Poynter	A. E. E.	Sjt	Prosser	E. F.	Dvr	Ramsden	A.	Dvr
Poynter	G.	Cpl	Prosser	J. T.	Dvr	Ramsden	T.	Dvr
Pragnell	R. F.	Dvr	Prout	D. G.	Dvr	Ramsey	G. M. S.	Dvr
Prague	N. A.	L/Cpl	Prowse	A. H.	Sjt	Ramsey	G. P.	Dvr
Prain	W.	Maj	Pryke	W. A.	Dvr	Randall	E. F. H.	Capt
Prater	V. G.	Pte	Pryor	S.	Dvr	Randall	W. G.	Dvr
Pratt	A. F. J.	Pte	Puddick, W. C. W. H.		Dvr	Randell	A. C.	Dvr
Pratt	B. P.	Dvr	Puddicombe	F. J.	WO II	Randle	W.	Dvr
Pratt	G. H.	Dvr	Pugh	W.	Dvr	Randles	W.	Dvr
Pratt	G. W.	Pte	Pullen	A. E.	Pte	Rands	A. E.	L/Cpl
Pratt	W. E.	Cpl	Pullen	J. F.	L/Cpl	Rands	J. H.	Sjt
Prattey	A.	Dvr	Pullen	R.	Dvr	Rands	W.	Dvr
Preece	A. J.	Dvr	Pulling	W. G.	Dvr	Rankin	H. A.	Sjt
Preece	H. W.	Dvr	Pullinger	E. E.	L/Cpl	Rankin	R.	Pte
Preece	J. D.	Pte	Purcell	P.	Pte	Rankin	T. J.	Sjt
Prentice	J.	Dvr	Purcell	W. J. E.	Dvr	Rankin	W.	Sjt
Prentice	N.	Dvr	Purdie	R. A.	Maj	Ransome	G. H.	L/Cpl
Presgrave	F.	Dvr	Purdon	T. McC.	Dvr	Rastrick	H.	Cpl
Preston, H. de G. W.		Dvr	Purdue	W.	Pte	Ratcliff	A. E.	Pte
Preston	T. G.	Dvr	Purdy	A.	Dvr	Ratcliffe	A.	Cpl
Preston	W. R.	Dvr	Purkis	H.	Dvr	Ratcliffe	G.	Dvr
Prestwich	J. G.	Maj	Purnell	A. E.	Dvr	Ratcliffe	L. F.	Dvr
Prestwood	T. J.	Pte	Pursey	C. H.	Cpl	Ratcliffe	S.	Pte
Pretty	W.	Dvr	Putnan	G. E.	Dvr	Ratcliffe	T. W.	Dvr
Prew	G. W.	Dvr	Puxty	E. F. E.	Dvr	Rathbone	G. W.	Dvr
Price	C. F. J.	Dvr	Pye	J. A.	Dvr	Rattigan	E.	Dvr
Price	C. J.	Dvr	Pynches	C. H.	WO II	Rattray	R. C.	Dvr
Price	C. W.	Sjt	Pyne	J.	Dvr	Raven	R. W.	Dvr
Price	D. E.	Cpl	Pyper	J. R.	Lt	Rawley	F. J.	Dvr
Price	F. J.	Cpl		M.C., Bar		Rawlings	H. R.	Pte
Price	G. W.	Dvr				Rawlinson	H.	Pte
Price	J. A.	Dvr				Rawlinson	H.	Dvr
Price	J. D.	Dvr	Quarrington, A. F.		Dvr	Rawlinson	J.	Sjt
Price	J. W.	Pte	Quick	I. L.	Dvr	Rawlinson	R. D.	Pte
Price	M.	Dvr	Quinn	F. J.	Dvr	Rawlinson	W.	Pte
Price	P. W.	Cpl	Quinn	R. W.	Dvr	Rawlinson	W. R.	Dvr
Price	R.	Dvr	Quirk	S.	S/Sjt	Rawson	F.	Dvr
Price	T. G.	Pte				Rawson	F. L.	Dvr
Price	W.	Dvr				Rawson	G.	Dvr
Prickett	A. G.	Sjt				Rawsthorn	J. W.	Dvr
Priest	A. L.	Dvr	Rabaidtti	L.	Dvr	Ray	G. Y.	Pte
Priest	F. H.	Maj	Raby	J. R.	L/Cpl	Ray	J. S.	Pte
Priest	H. G.	Dvr	Rachkind	S.	Dvr	Raymant	A. F.	Pte
Priest	S. J.	Dvr	Rackett	R.	Dvr	Rayne	A.	Dvr
Priestley	J. E.	Dvr	Rackham	C.	Cpl	Rayner	F.	Dvr
Prince	H.	Sjt	Radbourne	H. O.	Maj	Rayner	R. J.	Dvr
Printer	S. F.	Pte	Radcliffe	T. N.	Dvr	Rayner	S. V.	Dvr
Prior	S. G. L.	Lt	Rae	D.	Dvr	Reacord	R. L.	Pte
Pritchard	R.	Dvr	Rainbow	R. F.	Dvr	Read	C. B.	Cpl
Pritt	I.	Dvr	Rainey	R. L.	Dvr	Read	D. F.	Dvr
Probert	R. H.	Dvr	Rash	L. S. E.	Dvr	Read	E. A. W.	L/Cpl
Probert	W. G.	S/Sjt	Ralph	A. J.	Lt	Read	E. E.	Cpl
Procter	F.	Dvr	Ralph	G. A.	Dvr	Read, G. E. H. C.		Dvr
Proctor	A.	Dvr	Ramage	A. J.	S/Sjt	Read	H. W.	Dvr
Proctor	E.	Dvr	Ramell	J. L.	Dvr	Read	N. A.	Pte

ROLL OF HONOUR

Read	R. A.	Dvr	Reid	R.	Cpl	Richardson	A.	Dvr
Read	S. F.	Dvr	Reid	R. T.	Cpl		253318	
Read	T. W.	Pte	Reid	T.	Dvr	Richardson	A.	Pte
Read	W. H.	Dvr	Reid	W.	Pte	Richardson	A. C.	Dvr
Reade	E. E.	Dvr	Reidman	A. L.	Dvr	Richardson	A. T.	Pte
Reader	F. W.	Dvr	Reilly	J.	Sjt	Richardson	A. W.	Dvr
Readman	L.	Dvr	Remblance	H. E.	Dvr	Richardson	C. K.	Pte
Reaney	A. E.	Dvr	Rendell	A. W. H.	Cpl	Richardson	C. S.	Pte
Reardon	G.	L/Cpl	Renner	W. M.	Pte	Richardson	C. W. N.	2/Lt
Reaside	T.	Dvr	Rennick	R. R. K.	Lt	Richardson	D.	Cpl
Reay	F.S.K.C.	Dvr	Rennie	J.	Dvr	Richardson	D. W.	Pte
Redbond	R. L. C.	Dvr	Rennie	W. C.	WO II	Richardson	E. J.	L/Sjt
Reddall	A. L.	Pte	Revill	L. C.	Dvr	Richardson	G. A.	Dvr
Reddy	J. F.	Dvr	Rexstrew	F.	L/Cpl	Richardson	G. C.	Dvr
Redman	G. A.	Pte	Reynolds	A. C.	Dvr	Richardson	G. W.	Dvr
Redman	R. A.	Dvr	Reynolds	A. J.	Dvr	Richardson	J.	Pte
Redmayne	H.	Dvr	Reynolds	D. J. G.	Dvr	Richardson	L.	L/Cpl
Redmond	P.	Dvr	Reynolds	E.	Cpl	Richardson	R.	Dvr
Redrup	G. T.	Sjt	Reynolds	E. L.	Dvr	Richardson	R. E.	Cpl
Reed	A.	Dvr	Reynolds	F. M.	Dvr	Richardson	R. T. C.	Pte
Reed	A. J.	Pte	Reynolds	G. J.	Dvr	Richardson	W.	Dvr
Reed	C. C.	Dvr	Reynolds	J.	Pte	Richardson	W. G. C.	Dvr
Reed	G.	Cpl	Reynolds	J. W.	Dvr	Richardson	W. J.	Cpl
Reed	H. H.	Cpl	Reynolds	L. V.	Cpl	Riches	B. V.	Dvr
Reed	H. L.	Cpl	Reynolds	M. H.	Dvr	Riches	R. C.	Dvr
Reed	J.	L/Cpl	Reynolds	R.	Dvr	Richmond	A.	WO II
Reed	J. W.	Dvr	Reynolds	W.	Dvr	Richmond	A. M.	Dvr
Reed	M. J.	Pte	Reynolds	W. C.	Pte	Richmond	J. J. R.	Dvr
Reed	R. J.	Dvr	Reynolds	W. H.	Dvr	Rickaby	J. F.	Dvr
Reed	W.	Dvr	Rheeston	D. W.	Dvr	Rickerby	J.	Sjt
Reede	M. L.	Pte	Rhodes	G. H.	Cpl	Rickerby	T.	Dvr
Rees	A. T.	Dvr	Rhodes	J. E.	Pte	Ricketts	G. A.	Cpl
Rees	D. J.	Pte	Rhodes	O. P.	Capt	Ricketts	J.	Dvr
Rees	D. V.	Dvr	Rice	C. A.	Dvr	Ricketts	W. R.	Dvr
Rees	E. T.	Dvr	Rice	J. H.	Dvr	Riddell	A. S.	Cpl
Rees	F. C.	Dvr	Rice	T. G.	Dvr	Riddell	J.	Cpl
Rees	F. W.	Dvr	Richards	A.	Dvr	Riddle	F.	Pte
Rees	G. C.	L/Cpl	Richards	C.	Dvr	Riddle	P. A.	Dvr
Rees	J.	Dvr	Richards	E. C.	Sjt	Riddle	R. H.	L/Cpl
Rees	J. R.	Dvr	Richards	F.	Pte	Riddles	F. G.	Pte
Rees	L. J.	Dvr	Richards	F. A.	Pte	Ridehough	L.	Dvr
Rees	T. E. C.	Cpl	Richards	G.	Dvr	Rideout	A.	Pte
Rees	W. R.	Dvr	Richards	H.	Dvr	Rider	V. J.	Dvr
Reeves	G. E.	Capt	Richards	J. C.	Pte	Ridge	C. S.	Dvr
Reeves	J. P.	Dvr	Richards	J. H.	Dvr	Ridge	F.	Cpl
Reeves	T.	Dvr	Richards	L. G. N.	Dvr	Ridge	K. G.	Dvr
Reeves	W. G.	WO I	Richards	P. W.	WO I	Ridge	R. M. A.	L/Cpl
	D.C.M.		Richards	R.	Dvr	Ridgway	A. E.	Dvr
Reeves	W. J.	Dvr	Richards	R. A.	Dvr	Ridgway	E. J.	Dvr
Reid	A. D.	Capt	Richards	R. J.	Dvr	Ridgway	T. E.	Dvr
Reid	A. M.	Sjt	Richards	T. E.	L/Cpl	Ridley	A. H.	Cpl
Reid	F. W.	Pte	Richards	T. W.	Cpl	Ridley	A. S.	Dvr
Reid	H. C.	Dvr	Richards	W. C.	Dvr	Ridley	F. P.	Dvr
Reid	H. H.	Dvr	Richards	W. H.	Dvr	Ridley	N. A.	Dvr
Reid	J.	Cpl	Richards	W. J.	Dvr	Ridley	T.	Dvr
Reid	J. C.	Dvr	Richards	W. T.	Dvr	Ridsdale	L. F.	Cpl
Reid	J. P.	Pte	Richardson	A.	Dvr	Rigby	H.	Lt
Reid	N.	Dvr		113844		Rigby	L.	Dvr

ROLL OF HONOUR

Rigby	P.	Pte	Roberts	R. M.	L/Cpl	Roche	K. J.	Capt	
Rigelsford	J.	Cpl	Roberts	P. S.	Cpl		*M.C.*		
Rigg	R. T.	Dvr	Roberts	R.	Dvr	Rochfort	J.	Pte	
Rigg	W. E.	Dvr	Roberts	R. B. P.	Dvr	Rodger	W. J.	Pte	
Riggall	S. H.	Pte	Roberts	R. C.	Sjt	Rodgers	G. B.	Dvr	
Rigler	A. J.	Dvr	Roberts	R. E.	Dvr	Rodgers	R.	L/Cpl	
Rigler	W. J.	Pte	Roberts	R. F.	Pte	Rodgers	T.	Dvr	
Riglin	J.	Dvr	Roberts	R. G.	Dvr	Rodgers	T. H.	L/Cpl	
Riley	A. D.	Dvr	Roberts	R. H.	Dvr	Roe	D. E.	Dvr	
Riley	R.	Dvr	Roberts	R. R.	Cpl	Roe	D. H. M.	Dvr	
Riley	W.	Dvr	Roberts	T.	Sjt	Roe	H. W.	Dvr	
Rilstone	R.	Pte	Roberts	W.	Dvr	Roe	W.	Pte	
Rimmer	C.	Dvr	Roberts	W.	Pte	Roffey	T. J.	Dvr	
Rimmer	F.	Sjt	Roberts	W. F.	Dvr	Roger	R. A.	Dvr	
Rimmer	J.	Dvr	Roberts	W. J.	Sjt	Rogers	A. F.	L/Cpl	
Rimmington, H.		Dvr	Robertson	C. J.	L/Sjt	Rogers	B. S.	Capt	
Ripo	F.	Dvr	Robertson	G.	L/Cpl	Rogers	D. R.	Pte	
Rippon	J. H.	Dvr	Robertson	G. A.	Dvr	Rogers	E.	Dvr	
Ritchie	G.	Dvr	Robertson	G. S.	Pte	Rogers	E. J.	Dvr	
Ritchie	G.	Pte	Robertson	G. W.	Pte	Rogers	F. T.	Pte	
Ritchie	J. H.	Dvr	Robertson	J.	Pte	Rogers	G. F.	Pte	
Ritchie	V.	Dvr	Robertson	L.	Pte	Rogers	G. F. J.	Pte	
Ritson	D. H.	Pte	Robertson	L. H.	Dvr	Rogers	R.	Dvr	
Roach	C. J.	Dvr	Robertson	W.	Dvr	Rogers	V. H.	Cpl	
Roach	M.	Dvr	Robertson	W. H.	Dvr	Rogerson	H. A.	Dvr	
Robathan	P. S.	Dvr	Robinson	A.	Dvr	Rogerson	J.	Dvr	
Robb	J.	Dvr	Robinson	A.	S/Sjt	Roginson	F.	Sjt	
Robb	T. J.	Dvr	Robinson	A. E.	Pte	Rolfe	P. E. P.	Pte	
Robbins	C. A.	Pte	Robinson	B.	Dvr	Rolinson	W. E.	Dvr	
Roberton	R. D.	Pte	Robinson	C. H.	Dvr	Rolls	E.	Dvr	
Roberts	A. C.	L/Cpl	Robinson	D.	Cpl	Rolls	V. E.	L/Cpl	
Roberts	A. E.	Capt	Robinson	D. M.	Cpl	Rome	R. A.	Dvr	
	M.B.E.		Robinson	E. W.	Cpl	Roome	C. W. G.	Pte	
Roberts	A. E.	L/Cpl	Robinson	G.	Dvr	Rooney	P.	Dvr	
Roberts	A. F.	Dvr	Robinson	G. C.	Cpl	Root	H. A.	Cpl	
Roberts	A. N.	Dvr	Robinson	H.	Dvr	Roscoe	E.	L/Cpl	
Roberts	C.	Pte		257996		Rose	H. W.	Dvr	
Roberts	D.	Dvr	Robinson	H.	Dvr	Rose	J.	Cpl	
Roberts	D. J.	Pte		13010827		Rose	J.	Dvr	
Roberts	D. R.	Cpl	Robinson	H.	Sjt	Rose	J. J.	Dvr	
Roberts	E.	Cpl	Robinson	J.	Dvr	Rose	J. W.	Dvr	
Roberts	E.	L/Cpl	Robinson	J. E.	Cpl	Ross	A. D.	Dvr	
Roberts	E. H.	Dvr	Robinson	J. F.	Lt	Ross	C.	Pte	
Roberts	E. J.	L/Cpl	Robinson	J. L.	Dvr	Ross	C. A. H.	WO I	
Roberts	E. V. C.	L/Cpl	Robinson	J. R.	Dvr	Ross	N.	Dvr	
Roberts	F.	Dvr	Robinson	J. W.	Dvr	Ross	R.	Dvr	
Roberts	G.	Dvr	Robinson	L. A.	Pte	Ross	W. C.	Dvr	
Roberts	I.	Pte	Robinson	R. G. H.	Dvr	Ross	W. J.	Dvr	
Roberts	J.	Pte	Robinson	R. L.	Dvr	Rossiter	T. P.	L/Cpl	
Roberts	J.	Dvr	Robinson	R. V.	Cpl	Rostron	L.	Dvr	
Roberts	J. E.	Dvr	Robinson	T.	Dvr	Rothero	C. W.	S/Sjt	
Roberts	J. H.	Sjt	Robinson	T.	Pte	Rothwell	E.	Cpl	
Roberts	J. N.	Cpl	Robinson	T. B.	Dvr	Rothwell	F.	Cpl	
Roberts	J. T.	Dvr	Robson	A. R.	Dvr	Rough	A.	Dvr	
Roberts	L.	Dvr	Robson	J.	Pte	Roughley	D. W.	Dvr	
Roberts	M.	Dvr	Robson	R. S.	Dvr	Round	J.	Dvr	
Roberts	O.	Dvr	Roccia	A.	Dvr	Rourke	P.	Dvr	
Roberts	O. M.	Dvr				Rouse	P. J.	Dvr	

ROLL OF HONOUR

Rouse	S.	Dvr	Rutter	E.	Dvr	Saunders	R. N.	L/Cpl
Routh	A.	Dvr	Ruxton	G.	Dvr	Saunders	T. R.	Dvr
Rowland	J.	Sjt	Ryan	J.	Dvr	Sauntry	J. W.	Pte
Rowlands	F. L.	Dvr	Ryan	J. A.	Dvr	Savage	A. A.	Dvr
Rowlands	J. M. C.	Lt	Ryan	J. T.	Dvr	Savill	F. W.	Dvr
Rowlands	T. S.	Sjt	Ryan	L.	Dvr	Saville	J.	Dvr
Rowlandson	A. J.	Pte	Ryan	R. W.	Dvr	Savory	M.	Cpl
Rowbotham	A.	Dvr	Ryan	W. J.	Dvr	Saword	E. G.	S/Sjt
Rowbotham	W.	Dvr	Rymer	L. A. G.	Dvr	Sawyer	F.	Cpl
Rowe	H. E.	Sjt				Saxon	V. D. J.	Maj
Rowe	J.	Dvr				Saxton	E.	Dvr
Rowe	N.	Dvr	Sabine	L. G.	Dvr	Saxton	G. H.	Dvr
Rowe	N. P.	Pte	Sabourn	J.	Dvr	Saynor	D. C.	Dvr
Rowe	P. L.	Dvr	Saddington	R. E.	Dvr	Scaife	R. V.	L/Cpl
Rowell	C. G.	S/Sjt	Sadler	E. G. M.	Pte	Scales	G. A.	Pte
Rowles	A. W.	Cpl	Sadler	E. H.	Sjt	Scarborough	B. L.	Dvr
Rowley	A. E.	Dvr	Sadler	E. J.	Dvr	Scarbrow	A. G.	L/Cpl
Rowley	E. A.	WO II	Sadler	T. F.	Dvr	Scarce	W. R. H.	Pte
Rowley	H.	Dvr	Sadler	W. T.	Pte	Scarlett	R.	Cpl
Rowney	W. D.	Cpl	Saggers	A. C.	Dvr	Schafer	R. J.	Pte
Rowse	F. A.	Pte	Sails	K. A.	L/Cpl	Schalitz	I.	Pte
Rowson	W. H.	Pte	Sainsbury	A.	Cpl	Schevernels	E. V.	Dvr
Roxburgh	W. T.	Dvr	Sainsbury	M. W. G.	Dvr	Schofield	J.	Dvr
Roylance	L. J.	Dvr	Saint	A. B.	Dvr	Schofield	L. A.	Dvr
Royle	A. E. M.	L/Cpl	Sakne	J. T.	Dvr	Scholes	A.	Dvr
Royle	T.	Pte	Salisbury	A.	Dvr	Scholes	J. H.	Dvr
Ruben	A.	Dvr	Salloway	R. A.	Pte	Scholes	W.	Dvr
Ruck	A. E.	Dvr	Salmons	G.	Dvr	Schoolar	A.	Cpl
Ruddick	M.	Dvr	Salt	E.	Dvr	Schwartz	D. H.	Dvr
Ruddy	A.	Pte	Salt	L.	Dvr	Schwenk	G. H.	Cpl
Rudland	F.	Pte	Salthouse	A.	Dvr	Scobie	W.	Dvr
Rugg	L. J.	S/Sjt	Salvona	J. G.	Dvr	Scoble	F. J.	Dvr
Ruiz	J. E. V.	Dvr	Sampson	E. R.	Pte	Scofield	G. F. S.	Dvr
Rumsey	G. R. J.	WO II	Sampson	F. J. J.	Dvr	Scotcher	S.	Dvr
Rundle	L. G.	Pte	Sams	H.	Dvr	Scotland	J. H.	Sjt
Runnalls	H. A.	Dvr	Samson	M.	Pte	Scott	A. C.	Dvr
Rush	H.	Dvr	Samuels	P. W.	Sjt	Scott	A. M.	Dvr
Rush	J. F.	Dvr	Sanbidge	J. B.	Dvr	Scott	B.	Dvr
Rushbrooke	A. R.	Dvr	Sanders	E. T.	L/Cpl	Scott	C.	WO II
Rushton	A. 68969	Dvr	Sanders	R. G.	Dvr	Scott	C. E.	Dvr
			Sanderson	D.	Dvr	Scott	C. G.	Dvr
Rushton	A. 274574	Dvr	Sanderson	J.	Cpl	Scott	C. H.	Cpl
			Sanderson	L.	Pte	Scott	E. C.	Pte
Rushton	E.	Dvr	Sanderson	R.	Dvr	Scott	E. F.	Cpl
Russell	A. E.	Dvr	Sanderson	R.	Sjt	Scott	E. W.	Pte
Russell	F. J.	Sjt	Sanderson	T. E.	Sjt	Scott	F.	Dvr
Russell	G. E.	Cpl	Sanderson	W.	Dvr	Scott	H.	Dvr
Russell	H. G.	Dvr	Sanderson	W. S.	L/Cpl		192297	
Russell	J.	Dvr	Sands	J.	L/Cpl	Scott	H.	Dvr
Russell	J. B.	Pte	Sands	R.	Dvr		14649050	
Russell	J. W.	WO I	Sang	W. C.	Dvr	Scott	H. G.	Pte
Russell	P.	Dvr	Sangster	G. F.	Dvr	Scott, J. W. McL.		Dvr
Russell	R. G.	Dvr	Sansom	A. H.	Pte	Scott	J. A.	Pte
Russell	T. E.	Pte	Sansom	E. D.	Pte	Scott	J. H.	Dvr
Ruston	N.	WO I	Saunders	C. J.	Sjt	Scott	L. G.	Dvr
Ruth	L. J.	S/Sjt	Saunders	E.	Dvr	Scott	P. W.	Dvr
Rutherford	W.	Dvr	Saunders	F. D.	Dvr	Scott	R.	Pte
Rutland	H. J.	Dvr	Saunders	P. J.	2/Lt	Scott	R. G.	Dvr

ROLL OF HONOUR

Scott	R. J.	Lt	Sharp	W. J.	Pte	Sherlock	J. H.	Pte
Scott	W. 4976174	Dvr	Sharp	W. R.	Cpl	Sherrington	L.	Pte
			Sharpe	L. V.	Pte	Sherwood	G.	Cpl
Scott	W. 10677113	Dvr	Sharpe	L. W.	Sjt		B.E.M.	
			Sharpe	R.	L/Cpl	Sherwood	P. B.	2/Lt
Scott	W. G.	Dvr	Sharpington, F.		Dvr	Shevlin	P.	Pte
Scott	W. T.	Dvr	Sharples	J.	Dvr	Shiel	S.	Dvr
Scovell	K. T.	Dvr	Sharples	V. H.	Dvr	Shilson	J. H.	Dvr
Scrace	G. W.	Sjt	Sharrock	J.	Dvr	Shiner	T. E.	Pte
Scrase	W. H.	Cpl	Shaw	A.	Dvr	Shipgood	S. T.	Dvr
Screeton	C. A.	Dvr	Shaw	C.	Dvr	Shipman	T. N.	Dvr
Screeton	L. E.	Dvr	Shaw	F.	L/Cpl	Shippen	H.	Dvr
Scrimshire	R.	L/Cpl	Shaw	J.	Dvr	Shipton	N. A.	Dvr
Scrivener	C. H.	Dvr		14786177		Shobrook	G. R.	Capt
Scroggie	G.	Dvr	Shaw	J.	Dvr	Shone	A. J.	Dvr
Scrutton	L. M.	Capt		140920		Shopland	C. V. J.	Dvr
Seagrave	R. M.	Pte	Shaw	L.	Dvr	Shore	J.	Dvr
Seal	F. W.	Dvr	Shaw	R.	Dvr	Shore	R.	Dvr
Sealey	D. L.	Cpl	Shaw	R. G.	Dvr	Short	A. E.	Dvr
Seaman	E. E.	Dvr	Sheahan	L. E.	Dvr	Short	A. F.	Dvr
Searle	D. H. I.	2/Lt	Shearer	J.	Dvr	Short	H.	Dvr
Sears	L. C.	Dvr	Shearer	J. B.	Pte	Short	H. J.	Dvr
Sears	R. J.	L/Cpl	Shearman	E. R. A.	Dvr	Short	J.	Pte
Seaton	E. L.	Dvr	Shearman	P. M.	Capt	Short	J. H.	Dvr
Seaton	J. N.	Dvr	Shears	R. C.	Pte	Shotter	R. W. J.	L/Cpl
Seddon	A.	Pte	Sheath	G. A.	Dvr	Shovlin	T.	Dvr
Seddon	G.	Pte	Sheather	W. E.	Cpl	Shrubb	H. G.	L/Cpl
Seddon	I.	Dvr	Sheavills	W.	Dvr	Shrubsole	E.	Dvr
Sedgley	S. E.	Dvr	Shedden	W. S.	Pte	Shuttleworth, F.		Pte
Sedman	T. F.	Sjt	Sheehy	E.	Dvr	Shuttleworth, J.		Sjt
Selby	R.	Dvr	Shell	F. S.	Pte	Sibley	F.	Sjt
Self	R. E.	Dvr	Shell	J. R.	Dvr	Sibley	F. T.	L/Cpl
Sell	W. L.	Cpl	Shelley	A. P. T.	Lt	Sice	A. G. E.	Cpl
Sellings	P. G.	Dvr	Shelley	J.	Dvr	Siddle	W.	Cpl
Sells	J. F.	Dvr	Shelley	S. W.	L/Cpl	Siddons	F.	Cpl
Sells	V. G.	Dvr	Shellswell	W. A.	L/Cpl	Sidebotham	S.	Dvr
Semple	J. C.	Dvr	Shelmerdine	C.	Cpl	Sidey	T.	WO I
Senior	J. R.	Maj	Shelton	A. C.	Dvr	Siggers	W. C.	Dvr
Senior	R.	Dvr	Shelton	A. F.	Maj	Siggins	S. E.	Dvr
Senter	C. F.	Dvr	Shenstone	E. W.	Pte	Sighe	G.	L/Cpl
Sergeant	J.	Cpl	Shepherd	A.	Pte	Silverstein	W.	Dvr
Servant	D.	Dvr	Shepherd	A.	Dvr	Silvert	P.	Lt
Setti	A.	Dvr	Shepherd	C. H.	S/Sjt	Silvester	J. A.	Cpl
Sewell	E.	Dvr	Shepherd	E.	Dvr	Simcox	W. H.	Dvr
Sewell	J. J.	L/Cpl	Shepherd	E. J.	Dvr	Simes	L. N.	Dvr
Sexton	A. J.	Dvr	Shepherd	F.	Dvr	Simmonds	E.	Pte
Sexton	F. G.	Dvr		14735681		Simmonds	J.	L/Cpl
Shakeshaft	F.	Dvr	Shepherd	F.	Dvr	Simmonds	K. H.	Dvr
Shalders	S. S.	Pte		164253		Simmons	A.	Dvr
Shannon	C. J.	Dvr	Shepherd	J.	Dvr	Simmons	D. S.	Dvr
Shannon	J. H.	Dvr	Shepherd	J. W.	Pte	Simmons	G. R. B.	Capt
Shannon	W.	Pte	Shepherd	W. B.	2/Lt	Simmons	H. D.	Dvr
Shapero	H.	Sjt	Shepherd	W. H.	L/Cpl	Simmons	H. L.	Lt
Sharp	H. W.	Sjt	Shepherdson, R.		Dvr	Simmons	V. H.	WO II
Sharp	S.	Dvr	Sheppard	C. T. D.	Cpl	Simon	J. F.	Dvr
Sharp	S. D. J.	L/Cpl	Sheppard	J. A.	Pte	Simonds	E. R.	Dvr
Sharp	S. G.	Pte	Sheppard	W. A.	Cpl	Simpkins	E. V.	Dvr
Sharp	W. H.	Pte	Shepperd	J. E.	Cpl	Simpkins	M. F.	Cpl

ROLL OF HONOUR

Simpson	A. G.	Dvr	Sleet	G. P.	Dvr	Smith	F. G.	Dvr
Simpson	A.	Dvr	Sleigh	J.	Dvr		10684001	
Simpson	A. E.	Cpl	Sloman	B.	Dvr	Smith	F. G.	Dvr
Simpson	F. W. R.	L/Cpl	Small	C.	Dvr		141665	
Simpson	G. G.	Dvr	Small	F.	Sjt	Smith	F. H.	Dvr
Simpson	H.	Dvr	Small	J. N.	Sjt	Smith	F. J.	L/Cpl
Simpson	H. D. L.	Dvr	Small	K. C.	L/Cpl	Smith	F. L.	Capt
Simpson	J. A.	Cpl	Smalbridge	E. C.	Pte	Smith	F. W.	S/Sjt
Simpson	J. I.	Dvr	Smallman	H. N.	Pte	Smith	F. W.	L/Cpl
Simpson	M.	Dvr	Smallwood	G.	Dvr	Smith	G.	Dvr
Simpson	R.	Lt	Smart	W.	S/Sjt		10688521	
Simpson	R. S.	Dvr	Smeaton	W.	Dvr	Smith	G.	Dvr
Simpson	S. J.	Dvr	Smedley	A. E.	Pte		14255614	
Simpson	W. B.	Dvr	Smedley	W. R.	Dvr	Smith	G.	L/Sjt
Simpson	W. E.	Pte	Smeeton	J.	Dvr	Smith	G. S.	Dvr
Sims	E. A.	Dvr	Smewin	J. G. T.	Dvr	Smith	G. W.	Sjt
Sims	F. P.	Dvr	Smirthwaite	J. L.	Dvr	Smith	H.	Dvr
Sims	H. P.	Cpl	Smith	A.	Pte		124118	
Sims	I. G.	Dvr	Smith	A.	Dvr	Smith	H.	Dvr
Sims	W. H.	Dvr	Smith	A.	L/Cpl		137029	
Sinclair	D. H.	Dvr	Smith	A. E.	L/Cpl	Smith	H.	Dvr
Sinclair	G. C.	Cpl	Smith	A. E.	Dvr		79962	
Sinclair	H.	Pte	Smith	A. E. V.	Dvr	Smith	H.	L/Cpl
Sinclair	I. W.	Cpl	Smith	A. F.	Dvr		3608635	
Sinclair	R.	Pte	Smith	A. G.	Dvr	Smith	H.	L/Cpl
Sinclair	W. G.	Dvr	Smith	A. H.	Cpl		222339	
Sinclair	W. R.	Dvr	Smith	A. L.	Dvr	Smith	H. E.	Cpl
Singer	J. B.	Pte	Smith	A. P. W.	Pte	Smith	H. H.	Dvr
Singer	R. J.	Dvr	Smith	B. B.	L/Cpl	Smith	H. J.	Dvr
Singleton	A.	Dvr	Smith	B. F.	Cpl	Smith	H. W. V.	Sjt
Singleton	G.	Dvr	Smith	B. J.	Cpl	Smith	J. McB.	Dvr
Sisson	D. P.	Dvr	Smith	B. J.	Dvr	Smith	J.	Dvr
Sisson	R. G.	Dvr	Smith	C.	Dvr		1023774	
Skardon	J. J.	Dvr	Smith	C.	Pte	Smith	J.	Dvr
Skelton	J. W.	Pte	Smith	C. F.	Cpl		189211	
Skene	J. A. F.	Dvr	Smith	C. I.	Pte	Smith	J.	Pte
Skerratt	A.	Dvr	Smith	D.	Dvr		157718	
Skerritt	A. H.	Sjt	Smith	D.	Sjt	Smith	J.	Pte
Skerritt	W.	Pte	Smith	D. A.	Sjt		292182	
Skidmore	P.	Dvr	Smith	D. C.	Dvr	Smith	J. A.	Cpl
Skilbeck	W. E.	Dvr		99285		Smith	J. C.	Pte
Skingsley	A. J.	Pte	Smith	D. C.	Dvr	Smith	J. E.	Dvr
Skingsley	F. J. L.	Pte		14770781		Smith	J. E.	Cpl
Skinner	H. J.	Sjt	Smith	D. J.	Dvr	Smith	J. J.	Pte
Skinner	J. W.	Dvr	Smith	D. J.	L/Cpl	Smith	J. L.	Dvr
Skinner	N. W. G.	Capt	Smith	E.	Cpl	Smith	J. P.	Cpl
Skinner	W. J.	Dvr	Smith	E. C.	Pte	Smith	J. R.	Dvr
Sklair	A.	Dvr	Smith	E. C. H.	Dvr		149217	
Slade	F.	Dvr	Smith	E. R.	Pte	Smith	J. R.	Dvr
Slade	R. E.	Dvr	Smith	E. R.	Dvr		192466	
Sladen	A.	Dvr	Smith	E. S.	Dvr	Smith	J. S.	Dvr
Slater	B. C.	Dvr	Smith	E. W.	Pte	Smith	J. W.	Pte
Slater	E. A.	Dvr	Smith	F.	Dvr	Smith	L. A. F.	Pte
Slater	G. J.	Dvr		14420582		Smith	L. E.	Cpl
Slater	H.	Dvr	Smith	F.	Dvr	Smith	L. J.	Maj
Slay	S. L.	Dvr		221542		Smith	L. L.	Capt
Slaymark	J. E.	Pte				Smith	L. L.	Dvr
Slee	R. F.	Dvr	Smith	F. D.	L/Cpl	Smith	L. S.	Dvr

ROLL OF HONOUR

Smith	M.	Dvr	Snell	C. L.	Dvr	Spiers	P. J.	Pte
Smith	N.	Dvr	Snell	H. G.	Dvr	Spiller	E. G.	Dvr
Smith	N.	S/Sjt	Snelling	R. J.	WO I	Spillman	B. T.	Pte
Smith	N. A.	Dvr	Snodgrass	J.	Sjt	Spooner	F. P.	Pte
Smith	P. H.	Sjt	Snook	H. S.	Sjt	Spooner	W. A.	L/Cpl
Smith	R.	Dvr	Snooks	F. A.	Dvr	Sprackling	E. A.	L/Cpl
64021			Snooks	F. T.	Cpl	Spragg	E.	Pte
Smith	R.	Dvr	Snowden	E. J.	Dvr	Sprague	N. A.	L/Cpl
293032			Soanes	R. L.	Dvr	Sprake	R. F.	Dvr
Smith	R.	Cpl	Soanes	V. R.	Pte	Spratt	W.	Sjt
Smith	R.	Pte	Somerfield	L.	Dvr	Springall	J. H.	Dvr
Smith	R. A. F.	WO II	Somerset	A. F.	Maj	Sproat	E.	Dvr
Smith	R. C. E.	Pte	Sommers	J. J.	Sjt	Sproson	J.	Dvr
Smith	R. D.	Sjt	Soper	M. P.	Capt	Squibb	R.	Dvr
Smith	R. D.	Dvr	Soper	R. A.	Dvr	Squire	A. S.	L/Cpl
Smith	R. R.	WO II	Sorrell	J. F.	Dvr	Stacey	G. C.	L/Cpl
Smith	R. T.	Dvr	Sorton	J. E.	Sjt	Stacey	G. W.	Cpl
Smith	R. W.	Cpl	Soutar	J. W.	Dvr	Stacey	R. H.	L/Cpl
Smith	S.	Pte	Southall	C.	Dvr	Stacey	R. W.	Pte
Smith	S.	Dvr	Southam	A. P.	Sjt	Staff	G. J.	Dvr
Smith	S. H.	Dvr	Southcott	G.	Cpl	Stafford	F.	Cpl
Smith	S. S.	Pte	Sowrey	R. V.	Dvr	Stafford	J.	Pte
Smith	T.	Sjt	Spackman	A.	Dvr	Stagg	D. G.	S/Sjt
Smith	T.	Dvr	Spare	W.	Dvr	Stait	J. R.	Dvr
Smith	T.	Cpl	Spark	R. L.	L/Cpl	Staley	J.	L/Cpl
Smith	T. L.	L/Cpl	Sparkes	P. R.	Pte	Stalker	D.	Dvr
Smith	T. L.	Dvr	Sparks	C. F.	Dvr	Stammers	A.	Dvr
Smith	T. R.	Dvr	Sparks	F. C.	Dvr	Stamp	E. R.	Lt
Smith	T. W.	Dvr	Sparks	L.	Dvr	Stamp	R. O.	Dvr
Smith	V.	Pte	Sparrow	C. E.	Cpl	Stamp	S.	Cpl
Smith	V.	Dvr	Sparrow	F. S.	Sjt	Stancer	J. J.	WO II
Smith	V. E.	Dvr	Speak	T.	Dvr	Standidge	H.	Dvr
Smith	V. J.	Dvr	Spear	G. T.	Cpl	Stanford	W. F.	Dvr
Smith	W.	Dvr	Spearing	C. J.	Pte	Staniforth	A.	Cpl
90293			Spearing	H. C.	Dvr	Staniland	A.	Dvr
Smith	W.	Dvr	Speed	S.	Dvr	Stanley	A. J. C.	Pte
268967			Speight	E.	Dvr	Stanley	C.	Pte
Smith	W. D.	Dvr	Speight	W.	Sjt	Stanley	P. J.	Dvr
Smith	W. H.	Sjt	Speir	R.	Dvr	Stanley	R. T.	Dvr
33640			Spelman	W. J.	Pte	Stanley	W. R.	Pte
Smith	W. H.	Sjt	Spellman	W.	Dvr	Stannard	A.	Cpl
98336			Spence	A.	Dvr	Stannard	P. F.	Maj
Smith	W. J.	Pte	Spence	S. J.	Pte	Stansbie	L. J.	Dvr
Smith	W. R.	Dvr	Spence	W. W.	Dvr	Stant	E. W.	Dvr
126837			Spencely	A. R.	Dvr	Stanton	E.	L/Cpl
Smith	W. R.	Dvr	Spencer	E. F.	Dvr	Stanton	J. C.	Lt
4397938			Spencer	F. N.	Dvr	Stapleton	G.	Dvr
Smithe, A. L. St. C.		Capt	Spencer	H. T.	Dvr	Stapley	F. J.	Dvr
Smithson	M. S.	Capt	Spencer	L. M.	Pte	Stark	J. J.	L/Cpl
Smithson	R. J.	WO I	Spencer	R.	Dvr	Starling	H. E.	Lt
Smoker	L. C.	Dvr	Spencer	S. E.	Dvr	Starsmeare	B. H.	Lt
Smurthwaite, W. T.		Dvr	Spencer	S. G.	Dvr	Statham	G. E.	Dvr
Smyth	D.	Dvr	Spencer	W.	Dvr	Statham	H.	Dvr
Smyth	G. P.	Capt	Spendlow	W. G.	Pte	Staunton	J. F.	Cpl
Smythe	W.	Dvr	Spicer	R. K.	Pte	Stead	C. F.	Sjt
Snailham	H. G.	Dvr	Spicer	W. J.	Dvr	Stead	F. K.	Dvr
Snaith	J. T.	Dvr	Spiers	C. R.	Capt	Stead	G.	Cpl
Snashall	S. E.	Dvr	Spiers	D. K. B.	Dvr	Steadman	L. W.	Dvr

ROLL OF HONOUR

Steed	R. A.	Cpl	Stewart	G.	Sjt	Stott	J.	Sjt
Steel	D.	Dvr	Stewart	H.	Pte	Strachan	A. D.	Dvr
Steel	J.	Pte	Stewart	J. K.	L/Cpl	Strachan	V. A.	Pte
Steel	W. T.	Lt	Stewart	J. D. F.	Dvr	Straffon	A. R. T.	Cpl
Steele	C. H.	Dvr	Stewart	J. H.	Dvr	Strahan	P. K.	Dvr
Steele	J.	Dvr	Stewart	J. M.	Dvr	Stratfield	T. H.	Dvr
	195480		Stewart	R. G.	Capt	Stratford	G. W.	Dvr
Steele	J.	Dvr	Stewart	T. J.	Pte	Streek	F. C.	S/Sjt
	263454		Stewart	W.	Pte	Street	H. R. C.	Sjt
Steels	R. T.	Pte	Stiles	J. A.	Pte	Street	J. C.	Dvr
Steggles	A. J.	L/Cpl	Stilgoe	A. C.	Cpl	Street	P. A.	Dvr
Stenhouse	R.	Dvr	Still	G. H. T.	Pte	Street	R. H.	Dvr
Stent	D. H.	Pte	Still	J. W.	Dvr	Street	W.	Dvr
Stent	R. R.	Dvr	Still	R. H.	Cpl	Streete	D.	Dvr
Stephens	A. J.	Lt	Stilling	W. G.	Dvr	Streeton	A. J.	Dvr
Stephens	E. J.	Capt	Stinchcombe, H. G.		Dvr	Stretton	C.	Dvr
Stephens	H.	Pte	Stirk	F.	Pte	Stringer	J.	Dvr
Stephens	J. H.	Dvr	Stitt	J. T.	Pte	Stringer	J.	Cpl
Stephens	J. H.	Pte	Stock	A.	Dvr	Stringer	L. G.	Dvr
Stephens	L. P.	Pte	Stock	F. R. G.	Dvr	Strong	A. H.	Dvr
Stephenson	C. F.	Dvr	Stock	S. G.	Dvr	Stroughair	L.	L/Cpl
Stephenson	E. H.	Dvr	Stoddart	H.	Dvr	Stuart	D.	Dvr
Stephenson	G.	Dvr	Stokes	A. E.	Dvr	Stuart	H.	Dvr
Stephenson	J.	Cpl	Stokes	D. A.	Capt	Stubbs	J.	Dvr
Stephenson	W.	Dvr	Stokes	E.	Pte	Stubbs	J. J.	Dvr
Stevens	C. H.	Dvr	Stokes	J. A.	L/Sjt	Stubbs	P.	Cpl
Stevens	C. W.	Dvr	Stokes	T. N.	Dvr	Stubbs	R. P.	Dvr
Stevens	D. H.	Dvr	Stolerman	J. D.	Dvr	Stubbs	S.	Dvr
Stevens	H.	Dvr	Stone	E.	Dvr	Stubbs	W. S.	L/Cpl
Stevens	K.	WO II	Stone	G.	Dvr	Stump	L.	Dvr
Stevens	R.	Cpl		14212893		Sturman	W. F.	Dvr
Stevens	R.	L/Cpl	Stone	G.	Dvr	Sturt	W. H.	Pte
Stevens	R.	Dvr		182998		Styles	C. E.	Dvr
Stevens	R. M.	Dvr	Stone	G. C.	Dvr	Styles	G. C.	Dvr
Stevens	W. C.	Dvr	Stone	G. V.	Pte	Styring	H.	Dvr
Stevens	W. H.	Dvr	Stone	J. H.	Cpl	Such	J. W.	Pte
Stevenson	J.	Sjt	Stone	L.	Dvr	Sugden	C. J.	Pte
Stevenson	J. I.	Pte		67992		Sullivan	G. W.	Dvr
Stevenson	J. R.	L/Cpl	Stone	L.	Dvr	Summers	H. G.	Dvr
Stevenson	K. M.	Pte		151359		Summers	T.	Dvr
Stevenson	L. D.	Dvr	Stone	T. E.	Dvr	Summersgill, C. B.		Pte
Stevenson	O. M.	Dvr	Stone	W.	L/Cpl	Sumner	J.	Dvr
Stevenson	R. G.	Sjt	Stoneley	J.	Dvr	Sunderland	N. L.	Dvr
Steward	E. G.	Dvr	Stoner	A. C.	Dvr	Surr	A.	Dvr
Steward	F. C.	Dvr	Stoner	F. G.	Dvr	Sussex	A.	Cpl
Stewart	A.	Dvr	Stonham	D. H.	Lt	Sutch	S. J.	Dvr
Stewart	A. M.	Dvr	Stoodley	C.	Pte	Sutcliffe	H.	Dvr
Stewart	A. H.	Dvr	Storer	E. R.	Dvr		171674	
Stewart	A. E.	L/Cpl	Storer	H.	Pte	Sutcliffe	H.	Dvr
Stewart	A. R.	Capt	Storer	J.	Dvr		141486	
Stewart	C.	L/Cpl	Storer	J. A.	Cpl	Sutcliffe	C. N.	Sjt
Stewart	C.	Dvr	Storey	D. C.	Sjt	Sutherland	A.	Pte
Stewart	D.	Dvr	Storey	T.	Cpl	Sutherland	D. J.	S/Sjt
	2879783		Storr	F. H.	Dvr	Sutherland	W. M.	Dvr
Stewart	D.	Dvr	Storrar	D.	Dvr	Suttie	W. R. D.	Dvr
	2761895		Stoten	A. E.	Dvr	Sutton	A.	Dvr
Stewart	F.	Dvr	Stott	A.	Dvr	Sutton	C. R.	Dvr
Stewart	F. A. D.	WO I	Stott	J.	Pte	Sutton	C. T.	Pte

ROLL OF HONOUR

Sutton	E. J.	L/Cpl	Tamlyn	G. S.	Dvr	Taylor	J.	Dvr
Sutton	L. M.	Dvr	Tann	A. W.	Pte		127577	
Sutton	S. J.	Dvr	Tannahill	A.	Dvr	Taylor	J.	Dvr
Swaffer	R.	Dvr	Tanner	T.	Dvr		238515	
Swain	F. L.	Cpl	Taplin	J. H.	Dvr	Taylor	J.	Dvr
Swain	G. K.	Pte	Tapp	A. J.	Pte		1538535	
Swain	J.	Dvr	Tarplee	F. E.	Dvr	Taylor	J. A.	Dvr
Swain	J. W.	Dvr	Tarrant	J. H.	Dvr	Taylor	J. D.	Dvr
Swain	T. G.	Dvr	Tarrant	T.	Dvr	Taylor	J. E. B.	Cpl
Swaine	A. L.	Dvr	Tate	J. A.	2/Lt	Taylor	J. R.	Dvr
Swalwell	T.	Pte	Tate	J. H.	L/Cpl		14353909	
Swalwell	T.	Sjt	Tate	R. M.	Dvr	Taylor	J. R.	Dvr
Swan	J.	Cpl	Tatlock	H.	Dvr		4276902	
Swancot	A.	Dvr	Taulbut	J. L.	Dvr	Taylor	J. S.	Pte
Swann	J.	Pte	Taverner	E. J.	Cpl	Taylor	J. S.	L/Cpl
Swann	W.	Pte	Taverner	T. J.	Dvr	Taylor	J. W.	Pte
Swann	W. E.	Capt	Tawse	H.	Dvr	Taylor	K. W.	Lt
Sweeney	J.	Dvr	Tawton	A.	L/Cpl	Taylor	L.	Dvr
Sweeny	R. R.	Sjt	Taylor	A.	Pte	Taylor	M. D.	Dvr
Sweetman	H.	Dvr	Taylor	A.	Dvr	Taylor	R.	L/Cpl
Swenson	V. K.	Dvr		99997		Taylor	R.	Dvr
Swepson	G. E.	Cpl	Taylor	A.	Dvr		292345	
Swift	D. R.	Pte		10675473		Taylor	R.	Dvr
Swift	F. S. P.	Dvr	Taylor	A.	Dvr		254047	
Swinburne	H.	Dvr		14620812		Taylor	R. B.	L/Cpl
Swinglehurst, J. H.		Pte	Taylor	A.	Dvr	Taylor	R. G.	Sjt
Swinhoe	T. W.	Pte		4627614		Taylor	R. G.	WO I
Swinn	R. G.	Pte	Taylor	A. H.	Pte	Taylor	R. J.	Dvr
Switzer	G. W.	Pte	Taylor	A. J.	Dvr	Taylor	S. J.	Dvr
Syford	S.	Dvr	Taylor	A. W.	Cpl	Taylor	S. T.	Pte
Sykes	A.	Dvr	Taylor	B.	Dvr	Taylor	T. C.	Dvr
Sykes	A. A.	Cpl		1736948		Taylor	T. R.	Dvr
Sykes	C.	Dvr	Taylor	B.	Dvr	Taylor	T. S.	Dvr
Sykes	E. A.	Cpl		240411		Taylor	V.	Pte
Sykes	H.	Cpl	Taylor	C. R.	Dvr	Taylor	W.	Dvr
Sykes	R. G.	Pte	Taylor	C. T.	Dvr		232517	
Sykes	R. S.	Maj	Taylor	D.	Pte	Taylor	W.	Dvr
Sym	S. W.	Cpl	Taylor	D.	Sjt		179069	
Symes	V. J.	Dvr	Taylor	E. F. G.	Dvr	Taylor	W. E.	Cpl
Symonds	D. J. C.	L/Cpl	Taylor	F.	Dvr	Taylor	W. G.	L/Cpl
Sympson	J. P.	2/Lt		14506917		Taylor	W. J.	Dvr
Symthe	E. A.	Capt	Taylor	F.	Dvr	Taylor	W. J. N.	Sjt
Syndercombe, R. R.		L/Cpl		74067		Taylow	W.	Cpl
Syrett	G. T.	Pte	Taylor	F.	Dvr	Teal	G.	Cpl
				4619240		Teal	R. H.	Pte
			Taylor	G. E.	Dvr	Teale	J. C.	Dvr
			Taylor	G. F.	2/Lt	Tear	G. T.	Dvr
Taiano	R.	Dvr	Taylor	G. M.	Dvr	Tearrell	F. K. G.	Sjt
Tailby	C. T.	Pte	Taylor	G. P.	Maj	Teasdale	D.	Pte
Tainsh	W. K. M.	Cpl	Taylor	H.	Dvr	Teasdale	F. E.	Pte
Tait	A.	Sjt		137004		Tebbutt	D. H.	Dvr
Tait	J. G.	Sjt	Taylor	H.	Dvr	Telford	F.	Dvr
Tait	J. Y. R.	Dvr		288399		Telford	J. S.	Dvr
Tait	T. B.	Dvr	Taylor	H.	L/Cpl	Temple	T. T.	Pte
Tait	W. D.	Pte	Taylor	H.	WO I	Templeman	A. G.	Dvr
Taite	F. A.	Dvr	Taylor	H. G.	Dvr	Templeton	M.	Dvr
Talbot	D.	Dvr	Taylor	H. P.	2/Lt	Tennet	D. H.	Dvr
Talbot	T.	Dvr	Taylor	J.	Pte	Terrill	J.	Dvr

ROLL OF HONOUR

Tolson	J. C.	Pte	Trewick	R. R.	Cpl	Turner	W. J. S.	Dvr
Toman	W. G.	Dvr	Tricker	R. J.	Dvr	Turnham	F.	Dvr
Tomkinson	A.	Sjt	Trifitt	J. C.	Lt	Turnock	S. O.	Dvr
Tomkinson	R.	Dvr	Trigg	A. J.	Pte	Turpin	J. R. S.	Pte
Tomlin	W.	Dvr	Trigg	D. H. A.	Dvr	Turrell	J. H.	Dvr
Tomlinson	C.	Dvr	Trigg	W. P.	Pte	Turvey	H. A.	Dvr
Tomlinson	C. G.	WO II	Trilsbach	F.	Lt	Tutt	L. H.	Sjt
Tomlinson	C. V.	Dvr	Trinder	S. H.	Dvr	Tuttle	A. G.	Cpl
Tomlinson	J.	Dvr	Tritton	A. L.	Cpl	Twaite	J.	Pte
	13009997		Trollope	G.	Dvr	Tweddle	G. S.	Sjt
Tomlinson	J.	Dvr	Troop	C.	Dvr	Tweedale	H. E. A.	Lt
	272029		Trotman	A. P. S.	Sjt	Tweedale	H. J.	Dvr
Tompkins	A.	Dvr	Trott	A. E.	Dvr	Twiddy	J. L.	Cpl
Tompkins	F.	Dvr	Troughton	G.	Dvr	Twine	T. G.	Pte
Tompkins	R. B.	L/Cpl	Trubshaw	G. M.	Dvr	Tyas	R.	Pte
Tompkins	W. J.	Dvr	True	P. E.	Dvr	Tyler	P. A.	Cpl
Toms	D.	Cpl	Tuck	G. M.	Sjt	Tyrell	L. C. E.	Pte
Toms	E. V.	Pte	Tucker	C. E.	L/Cpl	Tyrer	P. F.	L/Cpl
Toms	F. W.	Sjt	Tucker	C. J. L.	Cpl	Tyrrell	A.	Dvr
Tonge	A. W.	Dvr	Tucker	H. B.	Capt	Tyson	D. F.	Dvr
Tonkin	G.	Pte	Tucker	J. E.	Dvr	Tyson	H.	Cpl
Tonks	R.	Dvr	Tuckett	J.	L/Sjt			
Toohey	M.	Pte	Tuke	S. J. M.	Maj			
Tooke	W. C.	L/Cpl		O.B.E.		Ulyatt	D. S.	L/Cpl
Toole	J.	Dvr	Tunbridge	J. F.	Dvr	Umney	A. C.	Dvr
Toon	H. W.	Pte	Tunnah	G. W.	Pte	Umpleby	A.	Dvr
Toon	W. J. A.	L/Cpl	Tunstall	L.	Dvr	Umpleby	C.	Dvr
Tooth	G.	WO I	Tunstead	G. E.	Dvr	Uncle	F.	Dvr
Topham	J. H.	Sjt	Turk	R. I.	L/Cpl	Underhill	W. J. R.	WO II
Topp	D. J.	Pte	Turnbull	A.	Dvr	Underwood	A. T.	Pte
Tossell	J. C.	Cpl	Turnbull	G. N.	Dvr	Unstead	W. P.	Dvr
Tovell	R.	Dvr	Turner	A. G.	Dvr	Unsted	E.	Dvr
Towell	J. S.	Dvr	Turner	A. J.	Dvr	Unsworth	W.	Dvr
Towers	A.	Dvr	Turner	A. P.	Dvr	Unwin	G. V.	Capt
Towler	P. N.	Pte	Turner	A. W.	Dvr	Upson	R. M.	Dvr
Townell	E.	Capt	Turner	E.	Pte	Upton	D.	Dvr
Townley	A. E.	Pte	Turner	E. A.	Pte	Upton	H. J.	Dvr
Townsend	D.	L/Cpl	Turner	F. M.	Pte	Upton	J.	Dvr
Townsend	E. C.	Dvr	Turner	G. H.	Pte	Upton	J. L.	Dvr
Townsend	F. A.	Sjt	Turner	G. H.	Cpl	Upton	W. M. B.	Dvr
Townsend	J. A.	Dvr	Turner	G. W.	Dvr	Ure	J. W.	Sjt
Townsend	T. H.	Dvr	Turner	H.	Dvr	Uren	G. T.	Maj
Townsend	W.	Dvr	Turner	H.	S/Sjt	Urquhart	J.	Dvr
Tracey	J.	Pte	Turner	H. E.	Dvr	Urquhart	R.	Dvr
Tracey	T.	Dvr	Turner	J.	Pte	Usher	H.	Dvr
Trainer	G.	Dvr	Turner	J. E.	Pte	Uttley	W.	Dvr
Tralaw	W. C.	Dvr	Turner	J. H.	Dvr			
Tranter	S. J.	Pte	Turner	J. M. T.	Dvr			
Travers	A. E.	Sjt	Turner	L.	Dvr	Vail	J.	L/Cpl
Travers	E. D.	Cpl	Turner	M. H.	Dvr	Vale	S. W.	Pte
Travers	N.	Pte	Turner	R.	Dvr	Valentine	K. L.	Dvr
Traviss	H.	L/Cpl	Turner	R. J.	Dvr	Valentine	R. J.	Pte
Tregaskis	W. J.	Dvr	Turner	R. T.	Dvr	Valle	E. J.	Sjt
Tregoning	J. T.	Capt	Turner	W.	Dvr	Vallely	F.	Dvr
Treherne	T. G.	L/Cpl	Turner	W. E.	Dvr	Valler	W. J.	Dvr
Treloar	A. R.	Cpl	Turner	W. F.	Dvr	Vandersteen	A. A.	L/Cpl
Tremelling	W. A.	Dvr	Turner	W. H.	WO II	Vanham	R. C.	Pte
Trewern	E. C.	WO II	Turner	W. J.	Dvr	Vaningen	G.	Dvr

ROLL OF HONOUR

Terry	E. G.	L/Cpl	Thompson	A. H.	S/Sjt	Thorp	H. H. B.	Pte
Terry	H. P.	Dvr	Thompson	C.	Dvr	Thorpe	A.	Dvr
Tesseyman	A.	Dvr	Thompson	C.	Sjt		157214	
Tetlow	J. H.	Dvr	Thompson	C. M.	S/Sjt	Thorpe	A.	Dvr
Tevendale	W.	Dvr	Thompson	C. S.	Dvr		183119	
Tew	J. A.	Dvr	Thompson	D. L.	Dvr	Thorpe	A. R.	Cpl
Thacker	A. B.	Dvr	Thompson	E. W.	Dvr	Thorpe	C.	Cpl
Thacker	W. A.	Dvr	Thompson	F.	Dvr	Thorpe	F.	L/Cpl
Thatcher	A. J.	Dvr	Thompson	F. J.	Pte	Thorpe	G. H.	Pte
Thatcher	C. A.	Cpl	Thompson	G.	Dvr	Thorpe	H. J.	Cpl
Thatcher	L. J.	Cpl	Thompson	H.	Dvr	Thorpe	J.	Cpl
Theaker	F.	Dvr	Thompson	H.	Cpl	Thorpe	J. W.	Dvr
Thick	R. C.	Dvr	Thompson	H. F.	Cpl	Thouless	J.	Dvr
Thirkell	J. E.	S/Sjt	Thompson	H. W.	Pte	Threipland	R. D.	Cpl
Thomas	A. A.	Dvr	Thompson	J.	Pte	Threlfall	S. P.	Dvr
Thomas	B.	Cpl	Thompson	J.	Dvr	Throckmorton, R. F.		Pte
Thomas	C. E.	Sjt		3783018		Throup	J. C.	Dvr
Thomas	C. J. E.	Pte	Thompson	J.	Dvr	Thurles	J. A. B.	Dvr
Thomas	C. R.	Capt		166250		Thurlow	H. W.	Cpl
Thomas	D. E.	Lt	Thompson	J.	Dvr	Thurlow	W. W.	Dvr
Thomas	E.	Dvr		7908792		Thurston	A. E.	Sjt
Thomas	E. A.	Dvr	Thompson	J. F.	Dvr	Thwaites	L.	Pte
Thomas	E. G. C.	Dvr	Thompson	J. G.	Dvr	Thwaites	R. E.	Dvr
Thomas	F. H.	Pte	Thompson	J. H.	Dvr	Tibbles	W. J.	Dvr
Thomas	G. H.	Dvr	Thompson	J. J. C.	Pte	Ticehurst	L. St. J.	Sjt
Thomas	G. T. W.	L/Cpl	Thompson	J. M.	Dvr	Tidball	R.	Cpl
Thomas	H.	Cpl	Thompson	J. W.	WO I	Tidd	J. E.	Sjt
Thomas	H. W.	Dvr	Thompson	L.	Dvr	Tideswell	F.	Dvr
Thomas	I. A. G.	Cpl	Thompson	N.	Pte	Tideswell	G.	Dvr
Thomas	J. A.	S/Sjt	Thompson	N. P.	Pte	Tidy	V. H.	Dvr
Thomas	J. E.	Dvr	Thompson	P. E.	Lt	Tierney	J.	Dvr
Thomas	K.	Dvr	Thompson	P. J.	L/Cpl	Tierney	J. A.	Dvr
Thomas	L.	Pte	Thompson	R.	L/Cpl	Till	A. E.	Dvr
Thomas	N. E.	Dvr	Thompson	R.	Dvr	Till	W. H.	Pte
Thomas	O.	Sjt		10687592		Tillekeratne	D. W.	Dvr
Thomas	R. C.	Pte	Thompson	R.	Dvr	Tillett	C. H.	Dvr
Thomas	R. J.	Dvr		1073608		Tilson	J.	Pte
Thomas	R. J.	Cpl	Thompson	T. N.	Pte	Tilt	J. L.	Dvr
Thomas	T. E.	Dvr	Thompson	W.	Pte	Timbs	W. H.	L/Cpl
Thomas	T. L.	Cpl	Thompson	W.	Dvr	Timmington, A.		Dvr
Thomas	T. S.	Cpl	Thompson	W. G.	Pte	Timmins	H. W.	Pte
Thomas	T. W.	Dvr	Thompson	W. H.	Dvr	Timms	F. A.	Sjt
Thomas	W.	Dvr	Thomson	H. W.	Dvr	Timperley	A.	Dvr
Thomas	W. E.	Cpl	Thomson	J.	Dvr	Tindall	G. E.	Dvr
Thomas	W. E.	Dvr	Thomson	J.	S/Sjt	Tinsley	J. L.	Dvr
Thomas	W. H.	S/Sjt	Thomson	J. C.	Dvr	Tinsley	R. L.	Dvr
Thomas	W. J.	Dvr	Thomson	R.	Dvr	Tinsley	R. M.	Dvr
	5678245		Thomson	S.	Cpl	Tinsley	W.	Pte
Thomas	W. J.	Dvr	Thomson	W. R.	Dvr	Tinson	S. S. C.	Cpl
	4207181		Thorley	A. J.	Pte	Tipper	W. F.	Pte
Thomas	W. T.	Pte	Thorley	J. H.	Dvr	Tipton	R.	Dvr
Thomond	F.	Pte	Thorley	J. W.	Pte	Titcombe	R. E.	Cpl
Thompsett	A. C.	Pte	Thornhill	C.	Dvr	Tite	D. F.	Dvr
Thompson	A.	Dvr	Thornton	A.	Dvr	Todd	A. E.	Pte
	224388			215772		Todd	R.	Dvr
Thompson	A.	Dvr	Thornton	A.	Dvr	Todd	W. H.	Dvr
	1755535			10687121		Toghill	H. G.	Pte
Thompson	A.	Cpl	Thorold	J. H.	Dvr	Tolan	B.	Pte

ROLL OF HONOUR

Vanner	A. W.	Pte	Wade	C. H.	Dvr	Walker	R. L. A.	Dvr
Vanner	J. E.	Dvr	Wade	G.	L/Cpl	Walker	S. D.	L/Cpl
Varaillon	J. L.	Dvr	Wade	G. F.	Pte	Walker	W.	L/Cpl
Varian	F.	Dvr	Wade	T.	Dvr	Walker	W. G.	Dvr
Varley	H.	Dvr	Wadey	R. M. H.	Pte	Walker	W. L.	Dvr
Varney	C.	Dvr	Wadey	R. V.	L/Cpl	Wall	D.	Sjt
Varney	F.	Pte	Wadsworth	A.	Pte	Wall	T. J. H.	WO I
Varney	S.	Dvr	Wagg	C. L.	Dvr	Wall	W. A.	Dvr
Vasey	D.	Dvr	Waghorn	A. W.	Dvr	Wallace	C.	Dvr
Vass	A. J.	Pte	Waghorn	T. E.	Dvr	Wallace	G.	Dvr
Vass	W.	Cpl	Wagstaff	E. B.	Cpl	Wallace	J. A.	Dvr
Vaughan	A.	Dvr	Wagstaff	F. C.	Sjt	Wallace	J. M.	WO I
Vaughan	D. E.	Cpl	Wagstaff	J. E.	Dvr	Wallace	W.	Dvr
Vaughan	E. R. G.	Sjt	Wainwright	A.	Pte	Waller	C.	Pte
Vaughan	I.	Dvr	Wainwright	H.	Dvr	Waller	G. H.	2/Lt
Vaughan	J. M.	Cpl	Wait	H. W.	Dvr	Waller	T.	Dvr
Vaughan	W. H. T.	Dvr	Waite	E. R.	Dvr	Walley	C.	Dvr
Vayro	E.	Dvr	Waite	F. W.	Dvr	Walley	J.	Sjt
Vecqueray	J.	Cpl	Waite	G. E.	Dvr	Wallington	W. F.	Cpl
Veevers	T.	Cpl	Waitt	A.	Pte	Wallis	C.	L/Cpl
Venables	E. K.	Dvr	Wake	J. W.	Dvr	Wallis	E. N.	Dvr
Verdon	J.	Dvr	Wakefield	W. S.	Dvr	Wallis	G.	Pte
Vereker	W. M.	Dvr	Wakeford	B.	2/Lt	Wallwin	J. L.	Pte
Verity	R.	Dvr	Wakeman	H. C.	Pte	Wallwork	J.	Dvr
Vernon	G. H.	Pte	Wakeman	H. W. J.	Dvr	Walsh	H.	Pte
Vernon	W.	Dvr	Walch	L. J.	Lt-Col	Walsh	J.	Dvr
Viard	A. P. B.	Dvr		O.B.E.		Walsh	J.	Sjt
Vickary	R. J.	Dvr	Walden	F. C.	Cpl	Walsh	P.	Dvr
Vickers	A.	Dvr	Walford	J. W.	Dvr	Walsh	S. C.	Dvr
Vickers	J. H.	Cpl	Walk	F. C.	Pte	Walshaw	L.	Dvr
Vickers	N.	Dvr	Walker	A.	Pte	Walshaw	L. R.	L/Cpl
Vickers	W. E.	Dvr	Walker	A.	Dvr	Walter	A.	Sjt
Vickery	W. J.	Dvr	Walker	A. J.	Dvr	Walters	A.	Dvr
Vidler	A. E.	Dvr	Walker	A. V.	L/Cpl	Walters	A.	Cpl
Vidler	C.	Dvr	Walker	B.	L/Cpl	Walters	C. T.	Dvr
Vidler	C. E.	Sjt	Walker	C.	Cpl	Walters	S.	Pte
Vigar	A.	Dvr	Walker	C.	Dvr	Walters	T.	Pte
Vince	G. J.	Dvr	Walker	C. W.	Sjt	Walton	B.	Dvr
Vince	S. J. T.D.	Maj	Walker	D. J.	Cpl	Walton	C.	Dvr
			Walker	D. R. B.	Dvr	Walton	D.	Dvr
Vincent	C. R. O.	Pte	Walker	E.	Cpl	Walton	F.	Dvr
Vincent	L. J.	Dvr	Walker	E.	Pte	Walton	G.	Cpl
Vine	G. H. T.	Pte	Walker	H.	Dvr		3761548	
Vine	S.	Cpl	Walker	H.	Pte	Walton	G.	Cpl
Viner	W. B.	Pte	Walker	J.	Dvr		57210	
Viney	P.	Dvr		240081		Walton	G.	Dvr
Vipond	H.	Dvr	Walker	J.	Dvr	Walton	I. M.	Dvr
Vizor	F. H.	Pte		166571		Walton	J.	Dvr
Vyner	J. P.	Dvr	Walker	J. E.	Cpl	Walton	J.	Cpl
			Walker	J. McC.	Sjt	Walton	W. F. C.	Dvr
			Walker	L.	Dvr	Wann	W.	Pte
Wacker	F. J.	Dvr		83335		Waple	R. E.	Dvr
Wadd	J. E.	Cpl	Walker	L.	Dvr	Warboy	A.	Dvr
Waddell	D. F.	Dvr		244531		Warbrick	J.	Cpl
Waddell	J. P.	Pte	Walker	M. P.	Sjt	Warburton	J.	L/Cpl
Waddington	J. R.	Pte	Walker	N.	Pte	Warburton	J.	Pte
Wade	A. C.	Dvr	Walker	P.	Dvr	Ward	A. W.	Cpl
Wade	B.	Cpl	Walker	R.	Dvr	Ward	E.	Dvr

707

ROLL OF HONOUR

Ward	E. G.	Pte	Watson	J.	Cadet	Weaver	G. H.	Dvr
Ward	F. C.	Dvr	Watson	J.	L/Cpl	Weaver	S. O.	Dvr
Ward	G.	Dvr	Watson	J.	Dvr	Weavers	H. C.	Cpl
Ward	J. J.	Dvr		7046761		Webb	A. C.	Pte
Ward	L. A.	Dvr	Watson	J.	Dvr	Webb	A. G. W.	Dvr
Ward	O. J.	Dvr		5054580		Webb	C. G.	Dvr
Ward	P.	Dvr	Watson	J.	Dvr	Webb	E. T.	Dvr
Ward	P.	Pte		10678348		Webb	F. H.	WO II
Ward	R. E.	Dvr	Watson	J.	Capt	Webb	G. H.	Dvr
Ward	R. F.	Lt		M.C.		Webb	H.	Dvr
Ward	R. W.	Dvr	Watson	J. G.	Cpl	Webb	H. A. F.	Dvr
Ward	S.	Dvr	Watson	J. H.	Dvr	Webb	H. E.	Dvr
Ward	W.	Lt	Watson	J. J.	L/Cpl	Webb	H. G.	Cpl
Ward	W. T.	Cpl	Watson	J. L.	Lt-Col	Webb	J. H.	L/Cpl
Wardle	J.	Cpl	Watson	K. D.	Dvr	Webb	K. J.	Dvr
Wardle	N. R.	Dvr	Watson	R.	Dvr	Webb	L. C.	Dvr
Wardleworth, T.		Dvr	Watson	T.	Dvr	Webb	S.	Dvr
Wareham	T. A.	Dvr	Watson	T.	Pte	Webb	S. C.	Pte
Waring	J.	L/Cpl	Watson	T. M.	Pte	Webb	T. B.	Pte
Warner	R. C.	Sjt	Watson	W.	Maj	Webb	W. H.	Cpl
Warr	W. R.	Pte	Watson	W.	Dvr	Webber	C. W.	Pte
Warren	F. J.	L/Cpl		103182		Webber	F. H.	Dvr
Warren	G. J.	Capt	Watson	W.	Dvr	Webber	J.	Dvr
Warren	J. C. A.	Sjt		4865235		Webber	J. T.	L/Cp
Warren	J. H.	Pte	Watson	W.	L/Cpl	Webber	S. S. J.	Dvr
Warrington	J.	Dvr	Watson	W. A.	Dvr	Webster	C. J.	L/Cpl
Warwick	A. C.	Pte		110439		Webster	F.	Dvr
Washington	W. S.	Dvr	Watson	W. A.	Dvr		14668790	
Waters	A. L.	Pte		272033		Webster	F.	Dvr
Waters	J. F.	Dvr	Watson	W. H.	Dvr		239772	
Waters	J. K. M.	Cpl	Watt	A.	Cpl	Webster	F. A.	Pte
Waters	L.	Dvr	Watt	D. P.	Dvr	Webster	S. G.	Sjt
Waters	R. F.	Dvr	Watt	G.	Dvr	Webster	W.	Capt
Waterworth	G.	Dvr	Watt	J.	Dvr	Webster	W. B. L.	Capt
Watkins	A. E.	Dvr	Watt	J.	Pte	Wedge	A. J.	Pte
Watkins	A. T.	Dvr	Watt	J. D.	Cpl	Weekes	S.	Dvr
Watkins	E. C.	Pte	Watt	J. M.	Dvr	Weeks	A. H.	Dvr
Watkins	G. H.	Pte	Watt	W. H.	Pte	Weeks	F. E.	Dvr
Watkins	I.	Dvr	Wattam	C.	Pte	Weeks	H. J.	Pte
Watkins	J.	Dvr	Watters	G.	Dvr	Weeks	H. W.	Cpl
Watkins	J. F.	Sjt	Watton	J. T.	Cpl	Weeks	R. G.	Dvr
Watkinson	S.	Pte	Watts	A. E.	Dvr	Weir	H. P.	Dvr
Watkinson	T.	Dvr	Watts	A. L.	Dvr	Weir	J.	L/Cpl
Watkinson	W. R.	Dvr	Watts	E. S. G.	Sjt	Weir	W. E.	Dvr
Watling	G. V.	Dvr	Watts	G.	Cpl	Welch	A. J.	Dvr
Watney	R.	Capt	Watts	G. C.	Cpl	Welch	E. G.	Pte
Watson	A. H.	L/Cpl	Watts	H. A.	Dvr	Welch	M. C.	Dvr
Watson	A. T.	Cpl	Watts	H. K.	2/Lt	Welch	W. C.	Dvr
Watson	C.	Cpl	Watts	J. N.	Dvr	Weldon	E.	Dvr
Watson	D. G.	Dvr	Waylen	T. A.	Dvr	Welfare	W.	WO I
Watson	E. J.	Pte	Weale	R.	Dvr		M.B.E.	
Watson	F. A.	Dvr	Weall	E. J.	Pte	Welham	B.	Dvr
Watson	G.	Dvr	Weare	F. J.	Dvr	Welham	E. H.	Dvr
Watson	G. W.	L/Cpl	Wearn	J. F.	L/Cpl	Welham	R. T. C.	Dvr
Watson	H. C.	Dvr	Weatherall	F.	Dvr	Welham	W. F.	Dvr
Watson	H. G.	Dvr	Weatherhead, S.		Sjt	Wellings	J.	Dvr
Watson	H. McD.	Dvr	Weatherhill	A. A.	Pte	Wellings	T. E.	L/Cpl
Watson	J.	S/Sjt	Weaver	F. L.	Dvr	Wellington	A.	L/Cpl

ROLL OF HONOUR

Wellington	G. T.	Capt	Wheeler	G.	Dvr	White	K. V.	Cpl
Wells	C. H.	Pte	Wheeler	H. J.	Dvr	White	P. G.	WO II
Wells	E. C.	Dvr	Wheeler	S. J.	Dvr	White	S.	Sjt
Wells	J.	Dvr	Wheeler	V.	Lt	White	T. W.	L/Cpl
Wells	J.	Sjt	Wheeler	W. F.	Dvr	White	W. G.	Dvr
Wells	J. H.	Dvr	Wheelwright, H.		Lt	White	W. L.	Pte
Wells	L. C.	Dvr		D.C.M.		White	W. R.	Dvr
Wells	R. C.	Cpl	Whelan	P.	Cpl	Whitehead	A. H.	Pte
Wells	S. A.	Cpl	Whetton	C. F.	L/Cpl	Whitehead	J.	2/Lt
Wellstead	L. J.	L/Cpl	Whewell	A. J.	Dvr	Whitehead	W.	Dvr
Wellsted	W.	Dvr	Whewell	F. W.	Pte	Whitehouse	H. H.	WO II
Welton	R. A.	Dvr	Whiberley	C.	Dvr	Whitehouse	J.	Dvr
Wensley	E. G.	WO II	Whinham	J. T.	L/Cpl	Whitehouse	P. A.	Dvr
Went	A. De Q.	Dvr	Whipp	T. A. D.	Dvr	Whiteley	E.	Pte
Went	J. R.	Dvr	Whipp	W. F.	Dvr	Whiteley	J. R.	Dvr
Werner	S. A. D.	Dvr	Whiskin	T. E.	Dvr	Whiteley	R.	Dvr
Wesson	F. W.	L/Cpl	Whitaker	G. F.	Dvr	Whitelock	P. D.	Cpl
West	A. M.	Capt	Whitaker	H.	Dvr	Whitelock	R. H.	Dvr
West	C. J.	Dvr	Whitby	W. R.	Dvr	Whiterod	J. A. R.	Sjt
West	G. W. 222623	Dvr	White	A.	Dvr	Whiteside	C. E.	Lt
			White	A. A.	Dvr	Whitfield	A. R.	Dvr
West	G. W. 115244	Dvr	White	A. F.	L/Sjt	Whitford	A.	Dvr
			White	B. E.	Maj	Whitham	G.	Dvr
West	H. N.	L/Sjt	White	C.	Dvr	Whiting	H. T.	Pte
West	J. 206777	Dvr	White	C. 14215627	Dvr	Whiting	R. H. J.	Dvr
			White			Whitley	J. D.	Pte
West	J. 44054	Dvr	White	C. 6711572		Whitley	W. T.	Dvr
			White	C. E.	Dvr	Whitlock	C. E. M.B.E.	Capt
West	J. W.	Dvr	White	C. G.	Dvr			
West	R. F.	Dvr	White	C. H.	Pte	Whitmore	R. A.	Dvr
West	W. L.	Cpl	White	D. H.	Pte	Whittaker	A.	Dvr
Westburgh	H. A.	Dvr	White	E. G.	Pte	Whittaker	C. B.	Sjt
Western	R.	Pte	White	F. J.	Dvr	Whittaker	F. A.	Pte
Western	W. H.	Lt-Col	White	G.	Dvr	Whittaker	P.	Dvr
Westhead	B. L.	Pte	White	G. A.	Dvr	Whittaker	S.	Dvr
Westlake	E. G.	Dvr	White	G. A.	Cpl	Whittall	A.	Dvr
Westley	C. H.	Dvr	White	G. E.	L/Cpl	Whittet	H. G.	Cpl
Westley	S. P.	Cpl	White	G. E. 200937		Whittick	J.	L/Cpl
Weston	E.	L/Cpl	White	G. E. 63914	L/Cpl	Whittingham, H.		Dvr
Weston	G. L.	Dvr				Whittle	A.	Dvr
Weston	L.	Capt	White	G. W.	Lt	Whittle	C.	Pte
Weston	R. G.	S/Sjt	White	H.	Pte	Whittle	E. H.	Pte
Weston	R. T.	Cpl	White	H.	Dvr	Whittle	G. E.	Dvr
Weston	W. F.	Dvr	White	H. L.	Dvr	Whittle	J. F.	Dvr
Westren	S. T. D.	Pte	White	H. M.	Pte	Whittle-		
Westwood	D. A.	Dvr	White	H. M.	Dvr	stone	R. A.	Dvr
Westwood	T.	Pte	White	H. W.	Dvr	Wholey	P.	Sjt
Wetherell	R. R.	Pte	White	J.	Dvr	Whyborn	R. S.	Dvr
Weymouth	C. P.	L/Cpl	White	J. 73038	Dvr	Whybrow	A. W.	WO I
Whaley	L. C.	Dvr	White	J. 4448890		Whybrow	G. W.	Dvr
Wharton	G. N.	Cpl				Whyte	A.	Dvr
Whatley	F. N.	Dvr	White	J. A.	Cpl	Whyte	G. R.	Dvr
Wheatcroft	A. L.	L/Cpl	White	J. C.	Dvr	Whyte	K. J.	Pte
Wheatley	A. C. W.	WO I	White	J. G. S.	Dvr	Whyte	W. G.	Pte
Wheatley	R. W.	Dvr	White	J. T. S.	Maj	Wickins	H.	Pte
Wheatman	A. M.	Dvr	White	K.	Dvr	Widdowson	G. E. R.	Dvr
Wheeldon	B. R.	L/Cpl	White	K. C. R.	Dvr	Widdowson	W.	WO I
Wheeler	C.	Pte	White	K. D.	Sjt	Wiehe	G. A.	Dvr

ROLL OF HONOUR

Name	Initials	Rank	Name	Initials	Rank	Name	Initials	Rank
Wigan	C. F. H.	Capt	Williams	F. M.	L/Sjt	Williscroft	A. E.	Dvr
Wiggham	J. S.	Pte	Williams	G. H.	WO II	Willmott	A. H.	Pte
Wiggins	A.	Dvr	Williams	G. R.	Dvr	Willoughby	R. A.	L/Cpl
Wiggins	A.	Cpl		247912		Wills	A. H.	L/Cpl
Wiggs	A. L.	Pte	Williams	G. R.	Dvr	Wills	J.	Sjt
Wightman	J. P.	Dvr		5445264		Wills	S.	Dvr
Wigington	H. W.	Dvr	Williams	H.	Pte	Willsher	A. G. P.	Cpl
Wigley	H. R.	Pte	Williams	H. D.	2/Lt	Willson	G. G.	Dvr
Wigmore	H. E.	Dvr	Williams	H. J. C.	WO I	Wilmore	A. H.	WO II
Wignall	W. R.	Dvr	Williams	H. T.	Dvr	Wilmore	F.	Dvr
Wilbraham	D.	Cpl	Williams	J.	Pte	Wilmot	C.	Pte
Wilcock	F.	Cpl	Williams	J.	Dvr	Wilmot	V. W.	Cpl
Wild	F. P.	Dvr		82319		Wilshere	R. A.	Dvr
Wild	L. H.	Maj	Williams	J.	Dvr	Wilshin	R. D.	WO II
Wild	S.	Dvr		273970		Wilson	A.	Dvr
Wilde	A. G.	Pte	Williams	J. A.	L/Cpl		60635	
Wilden	D. E.	Dvr	Williams	J. C.	L/Cpl	Wilson	A.	Dvr
Wilding	F. L.	L/Cpl	Williams	J. C.	Dvr		2752433	
Wiles	D. B.	Dvr	Williams	J. D.	Lt	Wilson	A.	Dvr
Wilkes	F. T.	Dvr	Williams	J. F.	Dvr		89306	
Wilkes	L. T. J.	Pte	Williams	J. G.	Dvr	Wilson	A. G.	Dvr
Wilkie	J.	Cpl	Williams	J. H.	Pte	Wilson	A. R.	S/Sjt
Wilkins	C. T.	Dvr	Williams	J. H.	Dvr	Wilson	C.	Dvr
Wilkins	J. T.	L/Cpl	Williams	J. R. H.	WO II		127112	
Wilkins	R. J.	Dvr	Williams	K. D.	Cpl	Wilson	C.	Dvr
Wilkins	S. J. W.	Dvr	Williams	L.	Dvr		10632532	
Wilkins	W. R.	Cpl	Williams	L. I.	Dvr	Wilson	D.	Pte
Wilkinson	A.	Dvr	Williams	L. R.	Sjt	Wilson	E.	Dvr
Wilkinson	A. G.	Dvr	Williams	M. B.	Dvr	Wilson	E. J.	Pte
Wilkinson	C.	Pte	Williams	N. L.	Dvr	Wilson	E. L.	Capt
Wilkinson	C. D.	Dvr	Williams	O.	Dvr	Wilson	E. S.	Dvr
Wilkinson	H. A.	Dvr	Williams	P.	Dvr	Wilson	G.	L/Cpl
Wilkinson	J. A.	Dvr	Williams	R.	Cpl	Wilson	G.	Dvr
Wilkinson	N. J.	Pte		3855042		Wilson	G. H.	Dvr
Wilkinson	S. R.	Capt	Williams	R.	Cpl	Wilson	G. S.	Dvr
Wilkinson	T. C.	Cpl		113516		Wilson	J.	Dvr
Wilks	A.	Dvr	Williams	R.	Pte		65827	
Wilks	A. J.	Capt	Williams	R. B.	Pte	Wilson	J.	Dvr
Wilks	H. A.	Dvr	Williams	R. P.	Dvr		10689708	
Willcock	A. E.	Pte	Williams	S. A.	Dvr	Wilson	J.	Pte
Willcox	J. H.	S/Sjt	Williams	S. J.	L/Cpl	Wilson	J. A.	S/Sjt
Willer	A. A.	Pte	Williams	T. H.	Dvr	Wilson	J. H.	Dvr
Willgoose	G. H.	Cpl	Williams	W.	Dvr	Wilson	J. S.	Cpl
Williams	A. G. O.	L/Cpl	Williams	W.	Pte	Wilson	J. S.	Pte
Williams	A. H.	Dvr	Williams	W.	Sjt	Wilson	J. W.	Dvr
Williams	A. W.	Pte	Williams	W. G.	Dvr	Wilson	L.	Dvr
Williams	B. C.	Pte	Williams	W. J.	Dvr	Wilson	L. C.	Sjt
Williams	C. E.	Dvr	Williams	W. J. F.	Dvr	Wilson	M.	Dvr
Williams	C. S.	Dvr	Williams	W. R.	Maj	Wilson	N. J.	Pte
Williams	D.	Dvr		M.B.E.		Wilson	N. E. T.	Lt
	14702060		Williamson	T.	Dvr	Wilson	R. H.	Dvr
Williams	D.	Dvr	Willis	C. T.	Dvr	Wilson	S.	Pte
	14664656		Willis	E.	L/Cpl	Wilson	S.	Dvr
Williams	D. C.	Cpl	Willis	E. A.	Dvr	Wilson	S. A.	Sjt
Williams	D. J.	Pte	Willis	H. J.	Pte	Wilson	S. P.	Dvr
Williams	D. T.	Lt	Willis	H. V.	Pte	Wilson	T.	Dvr
Williams	E. J.	Dvr	Willis	J.	WO I	Wilson	T. W.	Cpl
Williams	E. R.	Pte	Willis	V.	L/Cpl	Wilson	W. B.	Sjt

ROLL OF HONOUR

Wilson	W. R.	Dvr	Wood	R. G.	Cpl	Workman	J. E.	L/Cpl
Windsor	H. B.	Capt	Wood	R. L.	Capt	Wormald	C.	Sjt
Winfield	H. A. E.	Dvr	Wood	T. M. J.	Dvr	Worrall	J. H.	Pte
Wingrad	K.	Cpl	Wood	V. M.	L/Cpl	Worrallo	A.	Pte
Winn	W.	Dvr	Wood	W. E.	Dvr	Worsfold	J. W.	Pte
Winnan	D. F.	Dvr	Wood	W. H.	Pte	Worsfold	H.	Dvr
Winning	W.	Dvr	Wood	W. T.	Dvr	Worsley	L.	Cpl
Winser	T. E.	Cpl	Wood	W. W.	Dvr	Worthington, J.		Pte
Winslade	A. W. J.	Dvr		203821		Wragg	D. G.	Dvr
Winstanley	C.	Dvr	Wood	W. W.	Dvr	Wragg	H.	Dvr
Winter	C.	Cpl		286312		Wraith	N.	Cpl
Winter	C. D. J.	Sjt	Woodacre	J. A.	Dvr	Wrapson	A. H.	Sjt
Winter	D.	Dvr	Woodall	J. E.	Pte	Wren	C. E.	Cpl
Winter	E. G.	Cpl	Woodberry	J.	Pte	Wren	C. H.	Pte
Winter	E. H.	Dvr	Woodbine	G.	Dvr	Wren	S. J.	Pte
Winter	J.	Dvr	Woodcock	A. H.	Dvr		168761	
Winter	R. A.	L/Cpl	Woodcock	C.	Dvr	Wren	S. J.	Pte
Winter	T.	Dvr	Woodcock	G.	Dvr		169758	
Winterbourne, N.		Pte	Woodcock	R.	Dvr	Wrigglesworth, R.		Dvr
Winterflood	H. G.	Dvr	Woodfin	K. T.	Cpl	Wright	A.	Dvr
Winterton	H. G.	Capt	Woodford	G. A.	Dvr		14762720	
Winterton	R. H.	S/Sjt	Woodford	J.	Dvr	Wright	A.	Dvr
Winters	F. R.	Dvr	Woodgate	A. G.	Sjt		112879	
Winton	J. H.	Dvr	Woodgate	R. J.	Dvr	Wright	A.	Dvr
Wire	R. E.	Dvr	Woodhead	C.	Dvr		142395	
Wisdon	A. J. E.	Sjt	Woodhouse	C. B.	Dvr	Wright	A. C.	S/Sjt
Wise	R. L.	Cpl	Woodhouse	E.	Dvr	Wright	A. H.	Pte
Withers	F. G.	Dvr	Wooding	W. W.	Dvr	Wright	A. R. G.	Pte
Withers	H.	Dvr	Woodington	S. E.	WO I	Wright	B. S.	Sjt
Withers	J. H.	L/Cpl	Woodland	J. E.	Dvr	Wright	C.	Dvr
Withey	H.	Dvr	Woodman	E. C.	Dvr		272043	
Withycombe, R. E.		Dvr	Woodman	H. J.	Pte	Wright	C.	Dvr
Witty	R.	Dvr	Woodrow	A.	Cpl		259505	
Wolfe	W. W.	Dvr	Woodrow	C. A.	Cpl	Wright	C. R.	L/Cpl
Woling	K.	Dvr	Woods	C.	Cpl	Wright	D.	Pte
Wolstenholme, J. M.		Maj	Woods	C. A.	Pte	Wright	D.	Dvr
Wonderling	A.	Dvr	Woods	C. W.	Dvr	Wright	F. K.	Capt
Wood	A.	Dvr	Woods	D. E.	Dvr	Wright	G.	Dvr
Wood	C. T.	Cpl	Woods	R. A.	L/Cpl	Wright	G.	Pte
Wood	E. P.	Cpl	Woodward	D.	Pte	Wright	G. C.	Pte
Wood	E. P.	Dvr	Woodward	G.	Dvr	Wright	G. E. G.	L/Cpl
Wood	F.	Pte	Woodward	H.	Dvr	Wright	G. H.	Dvr
Wood	F. H.	Cpl	Woodward	J.	Cpl	Wright	G. T.	WO II
Wood	G.	Dvr	Woodward	J. L.	Dvr	Wright	H.	Cpl
Wood	G. A.	Dvr	Wooldridge	J. B.	Dvr	Wright	H.	Dvr
Wood	H.	WO II	Woolf	J.	L/Cpl	Wright	J.	L/Cpl
Wood	H.	Dvr	Woolfenden	N. B.	Pte		16219	
Wood	H.	Pte	Woolfson	J.	Dvr	Wright	J.	L/Cpl
Wood	H. A. V.	Dvr	Woollard	A. L.	Dvr		156802	
Wood	H. E.	Dvr	Woollard	S.	Cpl	Wright	J.	Dvr
Wood	H. G.	Dvr	Woollen	B. T.	Dvr		231495	
Wood	H. W.	Pte	Woolley	R. S.	Dvr	Wright	J.	Dvr
Wood	J.	Capt	Woolmore	C. W.	Dvr		134825	
Wood	J. E.	Dvr	Woolnough	A. S.	Pte	Wright	J.	Dvr
Wood	J. S. W.	Dvr	Woon	L. T.	Dvr		83896	
Wood	J. T.	Dvr	Wootten	E. T.	Dvr	Wright	J. D.	Dvr
Wood	L. M.	Dvr	Worbey	F. P.	Dvr	Wright	J. H.	Dvr
Wood	N.	Dvr	Wordley	F. H.	L/Cpl	Wright	J. W.	Dvr

ROLL OF HONOUR

Wright	L. A. N.	Lt-Col	Wytch	C. R.	S/Sjt	Young	D. R.	Dvr
Wright	L. H. D.	Dvr				Young	E. F.	Dvr
Wright	R.	Dvr				Young	E. F. G.	S/Sjt
	1572252		Yardy	E. V.	Dvr	Young	F. C.	Dvr
Wright	R.	Dvr	Yarnold	G.	Cpl	Young	G.	Pte
	10679664		Yates	A.	Cpl	Young	G. W.	Dvr
Wright	T. E.	Dvr	Yates	G. E.	Dvr	Young	J.	Dvr
Wright	W.	Dvr	Yates	G. F.	Cpl	Young	J. H.	Dvr
Wright	W. C.	L/Cpl	Yates	L. J.	Cpl	Young	O. J. R.	Pte
Wright	W. H.	Capt	Yaxley	V. W.	Dvr	Young	P. H. H.	L/Cpl
Wrightson	F.	Dvr	Yeadon	W. K.	Sjt	Young	R.	Pte
Wurr	R. G.	Pte	Yeo	F. G. W.	Dvr	Young	R.	Dvr
Wyatt	A. M.	Pte	York	J. E.	Dvr	Young	S.	WO II
Wyatt	C. W.	Dvr	Yospur	S.	Dvr	Young	S. C.	Dvr
Wyche	W.	Dvr	Young	A.	Pte	Young	T. E.	Sjt
Wylie	D. G.	Pte		6344381		Young	W. J.	WO II
Wylie	J.	Pte	Young	A.	Pte	Youngs	A. C.	Dvr
Wymer	C. C.	Dvr		238931				
Wymer	W. D.	Dvr	Young	C. A. C.	L/Cpl			
Wynne	W. H.	Dvr	Young	C. J. W.	Sjt	Zapp	V. I.	Sjt

GENERAL INDEX

Acts of Gallantry, Some (for full list of awards see page xix), 64, 74, 75, 76, 78, 79, 84, 128, 135-137, 139, 140, 142, 143, 145, 148, 149, 154, 158, 166, 167, 168, 199, 229, 230, 236, 239, 260, 261, 270, 271, 272, 285, 293, 295, 304, 348, 355, 374, 375, 376, 378, 385, 386, 387, 390, 394, 423, 568, 584, 605, 618, 641
Aden, 408, 483
Airborne R.A.S.C. (*see also* Divisions), 261, 374, 375, 386, 387, 394, 629-633, Ch. XIV
Air Despatch, 284, 285, 345, 346, 350, 351, 370, 386, 387, 388, Ch. XIII
Alamein, El, 114, 143-6, 149, 152, 153
Algerians, serving with R.A.S.C., 544
Algiers, Landing at, 222-4, 226, 227
Ambulance Drivers, 64, 75, 78, 140, 148, 239, 260, 285, 379, 619-23
Amphibious Transport, 159, 252-5, 258, 260, 272, 275, 276, 281, 282, 340, 353-5, 369, 377, 385, 447, 598-612
Andalsnes, Landing at, 96
Animal Transport, Camel, 172; Donkey, 157; Horse, 3, 7, 8, 11, 12, 19, 20, 22, 113, 212, 392, 435; Pack, 30, 58, 173, 202, 221, 224, 255, 256, 266, 270, 339, Ch. XV
Anti-Aircraft Command, 13, 15, 37, 381, 413, 420, 434, 439, 452, 481
Anzio, Landing at, 272, 273, 274
Arab Legion, 196
Arabia, 207
Arabs serving with R.A.S.C., 113, 208, 264
Arakan, 345, 347, 348
Archangel, 406, 448
Arctic, The, 406, 448, 473
Armies (British), First, Ch. VI; Second, Ch. X; Eighth, Chs. IV, VII, 237, 241, 246-8, 590; Tenth, 102, 201; Twelfth, 358; Fourteenth, 346, 356, 359
Armies (Canadian), First, 380, 381
Armies (French), First, 60, 62, 65; Second, 60; Seventh, 60, 61, 62; Ninth, 60, 61, 62; Tenth, 82
Armies (U.S.A.), Third, 380; Fifth, 257, 260, 262, 267, 268, 271, 272, 276, 278; Seventh, 252, 253; Ninth, 381
Army Catering Corps, 40, 371, 498
Army Groups, 11th, 359; 15th, 257, 258, 280; 18th, 237, 242; 21st, Ch. X, 487
Arnhem, Battle of, 380, 386, 387, 517, 518, 531, 532, 533, 611
Ascension Island, 407

Athens, 161, 287-97
Australian Army Service Corps, 130, 160, 166, 308, 317, 318, 333, 336, 522
Auxiliary Territorial Service (A.T.S.), 18, 412, 422, 423, 448, 450
Azores, the, 407, 506

Bakeries and Bread Supply, 57, 72, 94, 130, 148, 215, 220, 233, 240, 255, 261, 263, 283, 291, 294, 313, 315, 380, 458
Band, R.A.S.C., 7
Barrack Department, 3, 400, 501-7
Basutos, serving with R.A.S.C., 264
Beauman Force, 81, 85, 87
Belgian Army, 60, 172
Belgians serving with R.A.S.C., 392
Bermuda, 15, 407, 589
Board of Trade, 36, 52, 425, 457, 459
Bridging and Bridge Companies, 271, 272, 278, 385, 613, 617, 618
Burma, Operations in, Ch. IX, 520, 521, 522, 580, 581
Burma Army Service Corps, 341

Canadian Army Service Corps, Royal (*see also* Armies, Corps and Divisions), 396
Car Companies and Car Drivers, 64, 145, 293, 340, 376, 388
Cassino, Battle of, 267, 272, 274, 551
Ceylon, 360-6
Ceylon Army Service Corps and Ceylonese serving with R.A.S.C., 113, 264, 361, 364, 365, 574
Chanak, 5, 21
Chief Inspector of M.T. *See* Vehicles, Inspection of.
Chindwin, 342, 345, 352
Chinese, serving with R.A.S.C., 299, 333
Chinese (Perak), M.T. Companies, 307, 317, 321
Clerks, R.A.S.C., 3, 229, 396, 397, 503, 641
Cocos and Keeling Islands, 365, 408
Corps (British), I, 48, 375; II, 48; III, 59, 288; IV, 95, 340, 342, 344, 345, 348, 350, 352, 358; V, 223, 235, 238, 242, 243, 246, 247, 257, 262, 268, 272; VIII, 379, 391, 395, 397, 537, 538, 540, 615, 616; IX, 223, 242, 243, 246, 247; X, 145, 147-9, 257, 261, 267, 268, 270-3; XII, 384, 391, 395, 616; XIII, 130, 132, 133, 136, 137, 138, 146-9, 252, 257, 260-2, 268, 620, 621, 622; XXX, 132, 133, 135-8, 147-9, 252, 375, 376, 380, 382,

Corps (British), XXX—*cont.*
395, 531, 533, 603, 611, 615, 616, 620, 621
Corps (Indian), III, 319, 324, 330, 331; XV, 341, 358; XXXIII, 350, 351, 355, 357
Corps (Australian), 160, 164
Corps (Canadian), I, 280, 391, 392, 611; II, 385, 391, 602
Corps (New Zealand), 273
Corps (French), III, 83; IX, 82; XIX, 235, 238, 242, 243
Corps (Polish), 274
Corps (United States), II, 228, 235, 238, 242, 243, 245-7, 267, 268, 271, 273; VI, 267, 273, 274, 277; XVIII (Airborne), 390, 540
Corsica, 286, 570
Crete, Operations in, 167-9
Cypriots, serving with R.A.S.C., 59, 113, 122, 127, 128, 264, 546, 549, 552
Czechoslovakia, 15

DIVISIONS (BRITISH), **1st,** 6, 11, 48, 61, 70, 193, 223, 247, 250, 257, 273, 276, 280; **1st** Cavalry, 193, 197, 649; **1st** Armoured, 78, 80, 81, 83, 138, 140, 141, 142; **1st** Airborne, 253, 254, 261, 386, 387, 509, 518, 525, 527, 528, 530, 604; **2nd,** 11, 48, 61, 70, 73, 351, 352, 356; **2nd** Armoured, 128, 129, 130; **3rd,** 11, 48, 61, 62, 70, 72, 375, 379; **4th,** 11, 48, 61, 223, 237, 247, 291, 292, 294, 296, 623; **5th,** 6, 11, 59, 66, 70, 77, 201-253, 256, 258, 262, 268, 270, 272, 273-6, 280, 392, 548, 620; **6th,** *see also* **70th,** 197; **6th** Armoured, 223, 226, 238, 242, 247, 284, 595, 644; **6th** Airborne, 374, 375, 390, 394, 509, 534, 537, 539; **7th** Armoured, 113, 123, 127, 128, 133, 134, 135, 136, 138, 141, 142, 149, 154, 247, 257, 261, 267, 375, 379, 616; **10th** Armoured, 139; **11th** Armoured, 537; **12th,** 59, 65, 66; **15th,** 537, 615, 616; **18th,** 324, 325, 326, 329, 336; **23rd,** 59, 65, 66; **42nd,** 59, 66, 70, 72; **43rd,** 604, 617; **44th,** 59, 66, 70, 146; **46th,** 59, 65, 66, 223, 235, 246, 247, 257, 260, 267, 268, 272, 280, 288, 545, 548, 644; **48th,** 59, 61, 70; **49th,** 90, 236, 406; **50th,** 59, 66, 70, 141, 254, 256, 375, 376; **51st,** 59, 78, 80, 81, 82, 146, 147, 154, 155, 254, 256, 617; **52nd,** 83; **53rd,** 616; **54th,** 592, 597; **55th,** 430; **56th,** 257, 260, 261, 267, 268, 273, 285, 548; **70th** (*see also* 6th Division), 131, 136, 345, 346; **78th,** 223, 224, 225, 226, 229, 247, 253, 254, 257, 262, 268, 273, 545, 552; Guards Armoured, 389, 604, 617; Mobile (Egypt) (*see also* 7th Armoured), 46, 118, 121; R. Marine, 188, 189, 192, 528

Divisions (Indian), **4th,** 122, 127, 128, 129, 139, 140, 141, 157, 171, 173, 175, 275, 287, 555, 558; **5th,** 170, 171, 173, 173; **8th,** 257, 268; **9th,** 311, 319, 320; **10th,** 197; **11th,** 311, 319, 320, 321, 322, 329; **17th,** 341, 348, 356, 358; **19th,** 353, 386; **20th,** 351; **23rd,** 350; **34th,** 362
Divisions (Australian), **6th,** 113, 128, 129, 160, 164; **8th,** 311, 324; 9th, 128, 129, 130, 136, 146, 148
Divisions (Canadian), **1st,** 252, 256, 258, 268; **3rd,** 376
Division (New Zealand), **2nd,** 136, 141, 149, 154, 160, 165, 257, 268, 273, 552
Divisions (South African), **1st,** 133; **2nd,** 144; **6th,** 622
Division (East African), **11th,** 177, 350, 352
Divisions (West African), **81st,** 351, 352, 404; **82nd,** 351, 352, 404
Divisions (U.S.A.), **1st** Armoured, 236, 273; **3rd,** 254, 272; 9th, 236; 34th, 222, 223, 236, 242, 245-7, 278; 45th, 273; **82nd** Airborne, 387, 518, 528, 531, 534 **101st** Airborne, 387, 531, 534, 604
Division (Brazilian), 278
Dodecanese, operations in, 205-7, 573
Dukws. *See* Amphibious Transport.
Dunkirk, 29, 48, 71, 75, 77, 78, 420, 433, 438
Dutch serving with R.A.S.C., 392

EAST AFRICAN ARMY SERVICE CORPS, 113, 177, 178, 180, 182, 190, 350, 352, 586, 587
Eritrea, 170-6
Ethiopia, 6, 15, 175, 186-8

FALKLAND ISLANDS, 407, 456, 506
Faroe Islands, 406, 456, 568
Finland, 89
First Aid Nursing Yeomanry (F.A.N.Y.), 18, 433
Food, Ministry of, 36, 38, 413, 414, 417, 452, 453, 459, 461, 463, 466, 467-9
Food supplies. *See under* Supplies.
Forage, supply of, 106, 240, 283
French Forces, 158, 172, 197, 199, 222, 226-8, 545, 645; Forces of the Interior, 515; Service de l'Intendance, 55 (*see also* Armies)
Fuel and Power, Ministry of, 486, 505

GAMBIA, THE, 401, 403, 586
Gazala, 141, 142
Gibraltar, 14, 45, 218-21, 225, 227, 238, 455
Gold Coast, The, 402
Greece, Operations in, 160-7, 287-297, 571

Greek Army, 5, 161, 164, 167, 264, 291, 292, 294

HABBANIYA, 193, 196, 197
Health, Ministry of, 463
Home Forces G.H.Q., 413, 414, 421
Home Guard, 414, 415, 421, 422, 565
Hong Kong, Operations in, 298-304; maintenance of, 14, 455, 582
Hook of Holland, Operations at, 63
Horse Transport. *See* Animal Transport.

ICELAND, 406, 505, 567
India, 4, 5, 20, 29, 32, 338, 339, 346, 347, 359, 360, 362, 363, 457, 483, 519, 619
Indian Army Service Corps, Royal (*see also* Corps and Divisions), 5, 29, 30, 58, 122, 127, 144, 173, 174, 192, 201-6, 298, 308, 318, 335, 339-41, 344, 346, 347, 349, 359, 360, 500, 510, 519-22, 543, 549, 552, 647
Infantry, R.A.S.C. in role of, 237, 325, 386, 398, 418, 451
Iraq, Operations in, 192-7, 200-5
Irrawaddy, crossing of, 354, 355
Italian Army, 5, 264, 560
Italians serving with R.A.S.C., 264, 544, 549, 560, 561
Italy, Operations in, Ch. VI, 548-562

JAMAICA, 407
Jamaicans serving with R.A.S.C., 538
Java, 582, 647

KASSERINE, Battle of, 239, 242, 594, 643
Kenya, 177, 183, 187
Keren, Battle of, 171-173, 175
Kohima, 342, 348, 350

LABOUR, MINISTRY OF, 443, 499
Long Range Desert Group, 241
Long Range Penetration Group, 345, 510
Lybia, iv, 6, 28

MADAGASCAR, OPERATIONS IN, 178, 188-92
Malaya, Operations in, Ch. VIII, 647
Malays serving with R.A.S.C., 307, 310, 316, 317, 321-3, 331, 332
Malay States, Federated, Volunteer Force, 307, 311, 321, 323
Malta Army Service Corps and Maltese serving with R.A.S.C., 113, 127, 128, 211, 217, 583
Malta, G.C., 14, 45, 107, 108, 113, 210-17, 252, 583, 584
Manpower, 3, 8, 16, 17, 103, 104, 211, 224, 264, 316, 403, 418, 421, 422, 425, 433, 450, 477, 490-501
Mareth Line, 154, 156-159
Mauritians serving with R.A.S.C., 113, 264

Mauritius, 407
M.T. Maintenance Organization, Base and L. of C. Units, 19, 20, 23, 25, 27, 29, 58, 86, 115, 116, 181, 182, 211, 317, 323, 403, 423, 427, 432; Company Workshops, 139, 155, 171, 179, 180, 186, 199, 211, 227, 231, 303, 403; Transfer of responsibility for, 115, 116, 224, 404, 423, 424, 433, 443-6
Mersa Matruh, 117, 118, 122, 124, 125, 130-2, 138, 148
Mixed M.T. Companies, 422
Mobilization Centres, 104, 264, 417, 421, 494, 495, 620
Motor Coach Companies, 412, 418, 439
Motor Cyclists, 64, 75, 236, 624
'Mulberrys', 378, 576
Munich Crisis, Effects of, 2, 13, 15, 16, 27, 28, 36, 117, 426
Murmansk, 406

NARVIK, 89, 90, 93
Navy, Army and Air Force Institutes, 32, 37, 73, 371, 412, 413, 416, 453, 462, 464-7, 469
New Guinea, A.A.S.C. in, 522
New Zealand Army Service Corps (*see also* Divisions), 122, 152, 160, 166
Nigeria, 402, 404, 405
Normandy, Landing in, 371, 375, 376
Norway, Operations in, Ch. III, 436, 471

OFFICER CADET TRAINING UNIT (R.A.S.C.), 224, 421, 493, 494
Old Comrades Association, R.A.S.C., 7

PACK TRANSPORT. *See* Animal Transport.
Palestine, 6, 13, 17, 193, 197
Palestinians serving with R.A.S.C., 113, 208, 264
Persia, 201-5, 620
Petroleum, Bulk Storage, Development of, 235, 241, 266, 328, 478, 482, 487; Bulk Storage, Rehabilitation of, 112, 233, 234, 242, 263, 266, 633-7; Creation of Separate Supply, Organization, 47, 59, 477, 478, 489; Destruction of stocks, 85, 323, 331, 332, 390, 480, 481; Fire-fighting, 638; Oil Board, 42, 43; Oil Industry, 43, 45, 46, 233, 477, 479; Petroleum Board, 444, 488, 489; Pipelines, 112, 244, 266, 389, 390, 489; 'Pluto', 390, 489; Sources of, 485, 486; Supply and Distribution Systems, 43, 44, 45, 46, 59, 101, 110, 111, 181, 213, 214, 234, 243, 318, 346, 389, 403, 477, 481-485, 487, 488
Polish Army Service Corps, 136, 204, 205
'Popski's Private Army', R.A.S.C. with, 285
'Porter' transport, 349, 351, 352

RATION SCALES, SERVICE, 34, 35, 55, 72, 107, 108, 199, 213, 216, 219, 308, 335, 351, 353, 362, 453, 464-8; for Other Nations, 105, 199, 264, 483, 645
Rationing (National), effect on rations, the Services, 37, 459-69
Rations, Arctic, 473; Composite, 97, 108, 232, 255, 295, 369, 469, 470, 474, 475; Home Guard, 471; Jungle Pacific, 475, 476; 24-hour and Mess-tin, 472
Rhine, The Battle for, 381, 390, 391
Royal Air Force, Co-operation with, 193, 198, 284, 351, 370, 374, 387, 388, 394, 499, 500, 511, 523, 532, 648; Supply to the, 39, 43, 45, 55, 112, 152, 161, 169, 196, 219, 227, 231, 244, 407, 483
Royal Army Ordnance Corps, 23, 25, 26, 115, 116, 167, 404, 424, 443-445, 509, 512, 513, 515, 619
R.A.S.C. Fleet, 30, 78, 207, 221, 265, 300, 302, 319, 335, 355, 360, 378, 405, 406, 435, 499, Ch. XVI, 647
Royal Electrical and Mechanical Engineers, 25, 26, 115, 116, 404, 424, 443-45, 500, 590, 619
Royal Navy, Naval Operations, 96, 98, 166, 189, 320, 365; Co-operation with, 39, 105, 214, 217, 261, 300, 302, 362, 378, 423, 456, 499, 584
Russia, Aid to, 200-7, 448, 506

SAAR TERRITORY, 5, 6, 56
St. Helena, 407
Salerno, Landing at, 260, 262
Sardinia, 283, 570
Shanghai, 5, 8, 298
Sheep (live), Supply of, 107, 283, 314, 362, 647
Sicily, operations in, 249-56, 546, 570
Sidi Barrani, 125, 127, 128, 138
Sierra Leone, 401, 402, 436, 585, 586
Singapore, 14, 305, 307, 310, 313, 315, 316, 324, 326-34, 647
Singapore Volunteer Corps, 307
Somaliland, British, 15, 187; Italian, 15, 186
South Africa, 'Q' Services, 144; Cape Coloured Corps, 113, 171, 178
Special Air Services, 511, 515, 523
Spitzbergen, 406, 566
Sudan Defence Force, 113, 114, 169, 170, 176
Supply, Ministry of, 23, 25, 26, 428-32, 439, 447, 479, 506
Supplies (Food), Exploitation of Local Resources, 70, 71, 73, 106, 174, 216, 219, 233, 240, 282, 283, 307, 455, 456; Sources of, 35, 36, 313, 409-10, 452-6
Supply Organization, 37, 52, 56, 57, 67, 68, 93, 94, 104, 105, 161, 173, 180, 186, 196, 198, 202, 213, 214, 219, 228, 232, 240, 243, 248, 250, 263, 265, 278, 282, 290, 292, 299, 307, 308, 312, 315, 320, 330, 376, 388, 402, 417; Supply Depots, Base, 57, 79, 84, 105, 232, 294, 388, 406; Supply Depots (D.I.Ds.), 76, 86, 105, 165, 168, 202, 206, 225, 228, 232, 243, 255, 260, 291, 292, 330, 351, 362, 376, 377, 388, 389, 639-45; Supply Depots, Field, 127, 128, 130, 131
Supply Reserve Depots, 38, 425, 456, 457
Syria, Operations in, 192, 197-9, 648-51

TANK TRANSPORTERS, 114, 138, 145, 156, 208, 238, 239, 245, 246, 340, 356, 357, 385, 393, 590-2, 592-8
Ten-ton M.T. Companies, 114, 117, 120, 130, 131, 134, 145, 161, 208, 230
Tientsin, 298
Tipper Companies, 58, 227, 239, 271, 392, 395, 396, 612-19
Tobruk, 108, 113, 128, 130, 136, 137, 141, 144, 148, 149
Trans-Jordan Frontier Force, 199
Transport, Ministry of, 415, 419, 439, 565
Transport, R.A.S.C., Reorganisation of, 422, 441, 442; Shortage of, 57, 112, 172, 180, 182, 227, 230, 238, 265, 315, 316, 381, 403
Tripoli, 108, 112, 113, 114, 128, 129, 154, 155, 159
Troop Carrying, 12, 60, 67, 127, 137, 143, 144, 179, 229, 242, 245, 415, 430, 513
Tunis, 155, 222, 223, 226, 228, 247, 248

UNITED STATES OF AMERICA, American Field Service, 285; Arrival of forces in United Kingdom ('Bolero'), 424, 425; Equipment and supplies from, 30, 44, 114, 159, 203, 229, 415, 430, 448, 456, 485, 486, 506; Gasoline Organisation, 234, 241, 242. (*See also* Armies, Corps and Divisions)

VEHICLES, DESIGN OF, 22, 23, 24, 27, 427, 430, 431, 448; Inspection of, 20, 25, 155, 436; Provision and Supply of, 24, 27, 28, 50, 54, 58, 114, 211, 316, 427-32, 439

W.D. FLEET. *See* R.A.S.C. Fleet.
Water Supply and Water Tank Companies, 77, 114, 123-7, 129, 132-3, 183, 213, 239, 365, 433, 579
Water Transport. *See* R.A.S.C. Fleet.
West Africa, 401
West African Army Service Corps, 113, 181, 351, 352, 401-6
Western Desert Force, 127, 131
West Indies, 15, 407, 581, 588
Workshops (M.T.). *See* M.T. Maintenance Organisation.

YUGOSLAVIA, 284, 571

INDEX OF NAMES

The ranks and titles shown do not take account of changes since the end of the Second World War

ABERCROMBIE, PTE. R. H., 79
Ackrill, Sgt. G. H., 139
Adderley, Lieut.-Colonel R. B., 544
Alexander, Field-Marshal The Hon. Sir Harold, 156, 237, 247, 257, 258, 274, 280, 282, 291
Ali Ben Ali, Cpl., 558
Allen, Colonel W. J., 491
Anders, General, 204
Anderson, Lieutenant-General Sir Hastings, 9
Anderson, Lieutenant-General Sir Kenneth, 223
Andrews-Levinge, Lieut.-Colonel K. T., 303
Appleton, Lieut.-Colonel G. R., 475
Archibald, Brigadier G. K., 52, 60, 495
Arden, Brigadier P. A., 359, 370
Arkwright, Major-General, 288, 296
Arnott, Major T., 561
Askew, Dvr. V., 64
Atkinson, 2nd Lieutenant J. G. P., 168
Atwill, Colonel R. C., 491
Auchinleck, General Sir Claude, 95

BAILLIE, LIEUTENANT C., 76
Baker, Dvr. F. A. J., 272
Baldry, Dvr. R., 78
Ballard, Captain, 633
Band, Captain V. H., 293
Barratt, Dvr. A., 199
Bavin, Colonel A. J., 407
Beeston, Major W., 628
Bennett, Brigadier C. V., 182
Berridge, Lieut.-Colonel C. T., 544
Beuttler, Brigadier V. O., 68
Beveridge, Sir William, 443
Birdwood, Field-Marshal Lord, 338
Bland, Lieutenant F. J., 374
Blunt, Brigadier G. C. G., 60
Bond, Brigadier D. H., 47
Bott, Dvr. C. F. V., 260
Bowden, Colonel C. E., 494
Bowyer, L/Cpl. G., 229
Boyd, Captain J., 626, 627
Boyd Orr, Sir John, 463
Brander, Major-General M. S., 14, 25, 430, 494
Broach, Lieutenant, 230
Brodie, Major H., 504
Browne, Brigadier C. E., 102, 491, 494

Buckle, Brigadier D. H. V., 396
Buhayar, Pte. E. S., 167
Buller, General Sir Redvers, 1
Burrows, Dvr. E. G., 285
Burrows, Dvr. N., 75
Burt, Sgt., 376
Burton, Sir Geoffrey, 430
Butler, L/Cpl. R., 236
Byford, Colonel R. A., 40

CAHILL, DVR. A. D., 285
Cahill, Brigadier M. J., 290
Cameron, Colonel D. C., 8, 30
Campbell, Lieutenant, 630
Carey, S.S.M., 337
Carter, Major-General Sir Evan, 4
Carter, Dvr. J. W. E., 293
Carton de Wiart, Lieutenant-General Sir Adrian, 90
Cathcart, Professor E. P., 463
Caudwell, Dvr. E., 260
Chamberlain, Rt. Hon. Neville, 38
Cheyne, Brigadier D. G., 623
Childs, Major E. W., 352
Chilton, Dvr., 605
Chrystal, Brigadier C. I., 653
Chubb, Mr. H. Emory, 568
Churchill, Rt. Hon. Winston, 28, 155, 272, 295, 377, 432, 439, 578, 601
Clark, General Mark, 226, 257, 258, 276, 280
Clark, Mr. W. R., 564
Clark, Captain H. D., 355
Clarke, Sgt. J., 84
Clarke, Lieutenant-General J. G. W., 197, 649
Clarke, L/Cpl. J. P. L., 145
Clegg, Dvr. J. H., 337
Clifford, Brigadier G. H., 136
Clover, Brigadier F. S., 132
Coates, Dvr. J. S., 423
Collings, Major-General W. d' A., 132, 367, 399
Collins, Brigadier A. F. St. C., 76
Cooke, Brigadier R. T., 396
Copland, Cpl., 556
Craig-McFeely, Colonel W. N., 491
Crane, Major C. P. R., 394, 631
Cranmer-Byng, Captain J. L., 386
Crawford, Captain J. M., 136
Crawford, Major-General J. S., 25, 430

Creighton, Dvr. L. P., 148
Crofton-Atkins, Major-General Sir Alban, 4
Crompton, Dvr. S., 158
Crump, Brigadier F. H., 152, 158
Cubley, Captain H. E., 633
Cunningham, General Sir Alan, 188
Custance, Lieut.-Colonel C. E., 495
Cuthbertson, Major J. R., 375

DARLAN, ADMIRAL, 227
Dashwood, Captain L., 609
Davey, Able Seaman R. E., 568
Davies, Major-General G. F., 4
Davis, Brigadier C. E., 328, 362, 364
Day, Lieutenant, 598
De Neuville, Lieutenant, 618
Dentz, General, 199, 652
Dewar, Major A. J., 302, 304
Dickens, Cpl. L. W., 272
Divers, Brigadier S. T., 141, 258
Doenitz, Admiral, 391
Drummond, Sir Jack, 463
Dudgeon, Lieut.-Colonel J. Hume, 270, 544, 549
Duff Cooper, Mr., 34
Dugdale, Captain J. F., 139
Duncan, Dvr. G., 145
Dunkley, Mr. A. W., 444
Dunlop, Lieut.-Colonel R. A. E., 190
Durrant, Cpl. J., 84

EASSIE, BRIGADIER W. J. F., 367
Edge, Dvr. J., 624
Eglon, Cpl. E., 355
Eisenhower, General 222, 228, 229, 235, 236, 257, 258, 368, 377, 601
Elliot, Colonel R. H., 494
Elson, Mr. E. W., 584
Evans, Dvr. A. I., 423
Evans, Dvr. R., 524

FAIRCHILD, L/CPL. J. H., 64
Farquharson-Roberts, Colonel M. F., 364, 494
Ferguson, Dvr. G., 606
Ferrey, Captain C. V., 76
Fitzherbert, Major-General E. H., 14, 451, 492
Fleming, Lieut.-Colonel R., 544
Forward, Major A., 76
Francis, Dvr. S., 158
Fraser, Sir William, 43
Freyberg, General, 158
Fry, L/Cpl. L., 618
Fuller, Colonel N., 46

GALE, LIEUTENANT-GENERAL SIR HUMFREY, 14, 222, 368, 396, 420
Gallagher, Brigadier H. N., 491
Galloway, Cpl. D., 285

Gardiner, Colonel H. A. C., 210
Gardner, Cpl., 618
Geddes, Lieut.-Colonel H. H. E., 166
George VI, His Majesty King, 54, 377
Gibb, Major-General Sir Evan, 9, 10, 11
Gillespie, Brigadier J. K., 169, 237
Gilman, Brigadier H. J., 149, 258
Gilmour, Major R., 139
Goldney, Major-General C. le B., 68, 102, 455
Goode, Colonel E. R., 169
Goodfellow, Brigadier H. C., 445
Gort, Field-Marshal Lord, 65
Gould Marks, Captain L. A. F., 78
Govan, Dvr. J. C. W., 76
Green, Lieutenant S. A., 641
Greenberg, Dvr. J., 337
Grierson, Major W. C., 136
Gurnham, Dvr. E. O., 423

HACKER, BRIGADIER E. S., 497
Hall, Lieut.-Colonel D. R., 156
Hall, Dvr. J., 355
Hall, Dvr. W. H., 64
Harris, Cpl., 618
Hartley, Dvr. T. S., 148
Hawtin, Lieut.-Colonel J. H., 190
Hazleton, Major-General P. O., 4
Hedges, Brigadier K. M. F., 429
Henderson, Lieutenant P. J. W., 140
Hesber, Captain J. B., 390
Higgins, Pte. J. F., 337
Hills, Colonel R. W. W., 435, 543
Hillman, Captain A., 134
Hinde, Brigadier H. M., 92, 224, 232, 237, 257, 494
Hinton, Cpl., 618
Hobson, Dvr. H., 293
Holden, Mr., 302
Holleron, L/Sgt. E., 142
Hore-Belisha, Rt. Hon. Leslie, 7
Hornsby, Major M. J. B., 377
Horrocks, General Sir Brian, 149, 607
Houghton, Dvr. G., 158
Howell, Lieutenant M. H., 303
Hudson, Dvr. V. F. G., 140
Hughes, Sgt. R. F., 385
Hughes, Dvr. W. J., 236
Humphreys, Brigadier L. G., 68
Hunter, Captain I. G., 348
Hurman, Major, 599
Hutchinson, Cpl. W., 387

JACKSON, SGT., 571
Jefferies, Lieut.-Colonel T. H., 526, 528
Jenkins, Brigadier A. de B., 75, 76, 370
Jenson, Major H. M. J., 337
Johnson, Cpl. C. E., 337
Johnson, Captain J. E., 260
Johnstone, Pte. W., 78

INDEX OF NAMES

Jones, C.S.M. A., 78
Jones, Sgt. C. H., 642
Jones, Major Knill, 628
Jones, Pte. P., 641
Joseph, Colonel A. K., 46
Jury, Dr. G. H., 272

KAVANAGH, CAPT. D. T., 532
Kaye, Dvr. H., 423
Keast, Mechanist Sergeant-Major, 303
Keddie, Cpl. A. M. W., 423
Keir, Dvr. A., 272
Kelsall, Colonel H. A., 132
Kemal, Mustafa, 5
Kent, Captain J. C., 136
Kerr, Major-General H. R., 95, 368, 409, 494
Knightly, Cpl. L. T. C., 394

LANGDON, MAJOR C. B., 75
Lawton, Dvr. A. A., 236
Le Clerc, General, 158
Lee, Dvr. J. G., 64
Leese, Lieutenant-General Sir Oliver, 355
Leese, Dvr. R., 260
Leese, Sgt. W. J. C., 641
Leggatt, Captain R. G., 33, 39
Leith, Captain, 600, 605
Lewenhaupt, Captain, 631
Lilley, Dvr. L., 75
Linden, Captain B. W. M., 376
Lines, L/Cpl. S. B., 355
Long, Mr. C., 584
Luff, Brigadier C. M. C., 347, 351
Lymer, Brigadier, R. W., 396
Lynch, Cpl. J., 385

MACHLIN, DVR. G. W., 148
Mackay, Major A. S., 295
Mackesy, Major-General P. T., 90, 95
Mackie, Colonel J. C., 25, 437
Mackintosh, A. M., 47
Macleod, Major-General C. W., 10, 14
Mann, Cpl. G. P., 271
Mann, Lieutenant W. M., 74
Mansfield, Lieutenant J. K., 74
Marland, Sgt. L., 230
Marsh, Major, 337
Matthews, Brigadier A. E., 645
Medlicott, 2nd Lieutenant J. C., 84
Meese, L/Cpl. A. A., 355
Merrivale, Cpl., 75
Milford, Major P., 624, 626
Millea, Dvr. R., 260
Mitchell, Reverend L., 627
Mitchell, Lieutenant W. S., 337
Moisson, Captain E. F., 337
Molyneux, Major E. V., 135
Montgomery, Field-Marshal Sir Bernard, 154, 235, 254, 257, 367, 368, 374, 391, 601
Morris, Colonel J. H., 36
Moulton, Dvr., 625
Mountbatten, Admiral Lord, 347
Murphy, Dvr. P., 236

NEWTON, MAJOR K., 159
Niblett, Colonel H., 21
Nichol, Captain W. M., 145
Niven, Lieutenant J., 561

O'BRIEN, DVR. J., 355
O'Connor, Captain T., 154
O'Connor, General Sir Richard, 501
Ord, Dvr. A., 78
Orford, Cpl. E., 270

PACKE, LIEUT.-COLONEL M. ST. J., 528
Paget, General Sir Bernard, 90
Paragreen, Dvr. V. E. T., 145
Patton, General, 389
Per Sanveg, Mr., 92
Phile, Lieutenant G. C. G., 375
Pick, Mr. Frank, 498
Pinder, Colonel E. C., 494
Philips, Sgt. B., 229
Pitcher, Dvr. D. V., 272
Platt, General Sir William, 177
Platten, L/Cpl. C. H., 140
Popperwell, Cpl. K., 378, 577
Powell, Lieut.-Colonel W., 297
Pownall, General Sir Henry, 362
Prickett, Dvr. W., 293
Priest, Dvr. J. W., 64

RAFF, COLONEL, 642
Raymond, Colonel H. P., 210
Rea, Major J. W., 142
Reckitt, Brigadier J. T., 364
Richards, Colonel C. W., 328
Richardson, Major-General T. W., 33, 495
Riddell, Major Duncan, 142
Ridge, Dvr. C. S., 423
Ridgeway, General Matthew, 528
Rimmer, L/Cpl. G. L., 139, 140
Rivett Carnac, Vice Admiral, 577
Roberts, Lieutenant (716 Coy.), 630, 632
Roberts, 2nd Lieutenant R. C., 639, 641
Roberts, Dvr. R., 239
Roberts, Captain W. H. B., 137
Rochberg, L/Cpl. S., 166
Rommel, General, 129, 147, 148, 157, 237
Rossall, Lieut.-Colonel G. E. C., 337
Rowcroft, Major-General E. Bertram, 25, 445, 492
Rowe, C.S.M., 239
Ruff, Major F. G., 398
Rushby, Cpl. R. E., 74

Salmon, Sir Isidore, 40
Sankey, Dvr. J. E. S., 76
Sanson, Dvr. A. N., 75
Saunders O'Mahoney, Colonel C. C., 25
Savage, Major, 644
Scobie, Lieutenant-General Sir Ronald, 287
Seed, Cpl. J. O., 140
Sharp, Major C., 629
Sharpe, Cpl. G. H., 270
Shaw, Dvr. A. G., 137
Shaw, Dvr. K. E., 260
Shearsby, Dvr. F., 261
Shepherd, Dvr. E., 64
Sinclair, Sir Robert, 444
Skinner, Sgt., 599
Smith, Sgt. A. E., 577
Smith, Major-General C. M., 118
Smith, Cpl. L., 618
Smith, Dvr. 'Yorky', 629
Snowden Smith, Major-General R. T., 14, 33, 38, 437, 494
Sonnino, L/Cpl. W., 128
Spafford, Brigadier P. L., 491
Sparshatt, Mr. G., 569
Spears, Captain, 159
Sproston, Cpl. C. B., 387
Starhem, Captain, 97
Stern, Dvr. A., 239
Sturges, Major-General Sir Robert, 188
Sutherland-Waite, Captain S., 630
Sykes, Major R. S., 337

Tams, Sgt. W. J., 376
Tapp, Colonel H. A., 495
Tebutt, Dvr. W. G., 148
Tipper, Dvr. B. A., 148
Tomlinson, Dvr. J., 148
Tope, Major-General W. S., 25
Treleavan, Lieutenant, 639
Tresidder, Lieutenant, 304
Tudor, Brigadier C. L. St. J., 54, 82
Turff, Captain, 631

Turner, Captain C. C., 302

Unwin, Colonel E. S., 494
Urquhart, Major-General, 531

Valentine, Lieutenant P. W., 166
Varney, Cpl. J. A., 605
Venning, General Sir Walter, 564

Walker, Dvr. T., 140
Wallsworth, Dvr. B., 64
Ward, Major-General Dudley, 292
Warren, Colonel W. R. V., 95
Waters, Dvr., 602
Watson, Lieut.-Colonel J. A., 149
Watts Allen, Colonel E., 441
Wavell, Field-Marshal Lord, 192
Weeks, Lieutenant-General Sir Ronald, 444
Whatsize, Dvr. J., 143
White, Brigadier E. S., 237
Whittal, Sgt., 631
Whittaker, L/Cpl., 387
Whitty, Major-General H. M., 258
Wicks, Captain R. S., 74
Wier, S.S.M., 337
Williams, Brigadier C. J., 96
Willshire, Dvr. R., 239
Wilson, Field-Marshal Sir Henry Maitland, 201, 258
Wilson, Sgt., 374
Wingate, Major-General Orde, 345, 510
Witchell, Lieutenant G. C. H., 75
Witt, Brigadier T. E., 491
Woodason, Dvr. H., 261
Woolnough, Dvr., 625, 627
Wragby, L/Cpl. A. S., 199
Wright, Colonel H. M., 502

Yeabsley, Sgt. R. J., 378, 577

Zoumberis, L/Cpl. J., 128

www.ingramcontent.com/pod-product-compliance
Lightning Source LLC
Chambersburg PA
CBHW060406300426
44111CB00018B/2842